ISBN 978-1-5282-0714-0
PIBN 10914061

CALIFORNIA
HIGHWAYS AND PUBLIC WORKS

California Highways
and Public Works

Official Journal of the Division of Highways,
Department of Public Works, State of California

KENNETH C. ADAMS, Editor

HELEN HALSTED, Assistant Editor

MERRITT R. NICKERSON, Chief Photographer

Vol. 35   January-February   Nos. 1-2

*Public Works Building
Twelfth and N Streets
Sacramento*

CONTENTS

Published in the interest of highway development in California. Editors of newspapers and others are privileged to use matter contained herein. Cuts will be gladly loaned upon request.

Address communications to

CALIFORNIA HIGHWAYS AND PUBLIC WORKS
P. O. Box 1499
Sacramento, California

Storm Damage

By GEORGE F. HELLESOE
Maintenance Engineer, Division of
Highways

*Repair of Highways Will
Cost Millions of Dollars*

Sets New Record

AN INTENSE, tropical type storm enveloped the northern and central portion of the state during the week prior to the Christmas holidays. Most of the major drainage systems as far south as the Tule River in Tulare County were deluged by abnormal amounts of rain, resulting in an unprecedented runoff and causing damage to the state highway system, as presently estimated, at over $11,000,000.

In addition, damage to county roads has been estimated at approximately $19,500,000 and to city streets at some $700,000, for an over-all total of public road damage in excess of $31,000,000. Approximately $4,500,000 is required for emergency repairs—making it possible to reopen roads to traffic—while the balance is the estimated cost of rebuilding the damaged facilities for permanent use.

Practically all major north-south highways in the area were at one time or another closed by flooding, requiring the detouring of through traffic via circuitous routes which in some cases were later also engulfed by the spreading flood water. All transcontinental routes over the Sierra-Nevada Range, as well as major east-west laterals through the Coast Range north of San Francisco, were blocked for a time by slides, high water, washouts or bridge damage.

As the immediate functions of maintenance personnel under such conditions are the preservation of the highway structure wherever possible, the marking of dangerous locations or the barricading of impassable sections of road, and the establishment of detours, around-the-clock operation by all available personnel of the Maintenance Department assisted by representatives of the Bridge Department

By FRANK B. DURKEE
Director of Public Works

On behalf of Governor Goodwin J. Knight and myself, I desire to express our appreciation for the unselfish devotion to duty displayed by the engineers and personnel of the divisions of the Department of Public Works during the December and January floods.

Many of these employees worked around the clock during the critical period foregoing their Christmas and New Year's holidays. The tasks confronting State Highway Districts I, II, III, IV, V, and VI, were stupendous. Major efforts were required for emergency repairs to damaged roads to permit resumption of traffic.

Special commendation is due the maintenance personnel of the Division of Highways and engineers of the Division of Water Resources who labored ceaselessly during this period. The latter division worked with U. S. Army Engineers, the State Reclamation Board, military personnel from Camp Beale, and volunteer crews to save levees on the Sacramento, Feather, Yuba, San Joaquin rivers, and their tributaries, and to rescue persons trapped in the flood waters.

A word of appreciation is due the Communications Section and also photographers of the department who were out day and night compiling a pictorial record of the unprecedented floods.

To all who helped we extend our thanks and commendation.

and the Engineering and Supply sections were required for many days to carry out this responsibility.

At times the only direct means of communication between the field forces and their headquarters or between the districts and Sacramento was by means of the division's radio system.

Rainfall amounts for the storm which began at many points in Northern California on December 16th were exceptional at many locations. The Weather Bureau reports that at Hoberg's in the Coast Range south of Clear Lake 19 inches of rain fell in two days—December 19th and 20th. An equal amount was reported for a five-day period at Brush Creek in the Feather River basin. Camptonville on the Yuba River received more than 13 inches of rain on December 22d and 23d. Snow melted by warm rain which fell in some areas of the Sierras to above the 7,000-foot level added to the volume of flood waters which cascaded from the canyons.

As flood waters began to recede and the magnitude of the damage became apparent, outside equipment and labor were rapidly recruited from the construction and logging industries and other sources. Working under authority of the Declaration of Emergency declared by Governor Knight, heavy earth-moving equipment of every description was concentrated on the task of restoring travel on the highway network. A number of emergency contracts were let for the construction of temporary bridges where major bridge damage was sustained. At one location a Bailey type bridge was used to temporarily replace a lost bridge span.

Repair of road damage and the opening of transcontinental routes across the Sierras to unrestricted traffic was further hampered early in January by exceptionally heavy snowfall and blizzard conditions which closed the Donner Summit and Echo Summit roads for short periods.

The rapidity with which severely damaged roads were made passable to traffic serves to indicate the preserverance, resourcefulness and stamina of the personnel of the division who are now faced with the gigantic task of restoration of the highway system following one of the most severe storms in the history of the state.

District I—$2,950,850
By RUDOLPH BERGROTH
District Office Engineer

December 21, 1955, will long be remembered in a great portion of California and especially in Northern California. Unprecedented rainfall in the watersheds of all rivers and streams rapidly filled streams bankfull and, before the day passed into history, it was obvious that flood stages would be recorded; and, in most areas subject to floods and damage by high water, a major disaster was in the making.

The date to Humboldt County has double significance. The ironical coincidence is that December 21, 1955, was the anniversary of the 1954 earthquake that rocked the Humboldt Bay area, causing considerable damage and leaving Humboldt County with an uninhabited courthouse and the City of Eureka likewise without its city hall. It is further odd that the immediate Eureka area during the flood period received no considered abnormal rainfall—the amount being far less than surrounding areas and other stations throughout Northern California.

Floods Over Wide Area

In Northwestern California, however, the 1955 flood has shunted the earthquake with its seemingly disastrous damage into the background. The destructive flood and high water were prevalent over a wide area, affecting numerous communities and facilities and, at this writing, no firm estimate of the dollar value of the damage is yet available, but it is conceded by all that it will total many millions of dollars.

District I of the Division of Highways, with headquarters in Eureka, includes the Counties of Mendocino, Lake, Humboldt, Del Norte, and portions of Trinity and Siskiyou. The district contains 14 state highway routes totaling 853.61 miles of rural state highways.

To those familiar with California and its varied weather conditions, it will be noted that this district contains those counties well known for heavy rainfall.

Long History of Damage

The district's highway system has always been plagued by slides, slipouts, washouts, etc., as brought about by heavy rains. Hardly a highway project is designed in the district without considerable study entering into it involving drainage structures with adequate openings, embankment stabilization, flattening or benching cut slopes, placing horizontal drains, embankment protection along streams, and other features necessary to counteract the ravages of heavy rainfall with its resultant water-soaked earth and bankfull streams. Old-timers will recall the first constructed highways in the district that did not contain these modern design features to provide a stable, closure-free highway during winter months, and slides and slipouts were an accepted winter maintenance problem.

Along Route 1 (US 101, Redwood Highway) in years gone by, it was a foregone conclusion that road closures would probably occur at Lanes Flat, Bridges Creek Slide, Red Mountain Bluffs, Blue Slide, Hartsooks Slide, Garberville Bluffs, Redway Bluffs, Shively Bluffs, Greenlaw Bluffs, and other locations remembered by "old-timers." As old sections of highway were reconstructed or superseded, utilizing features to eliminate slides, slipouts, and washouts; and old slides became stabilized by the constant removal of material over the years, or corrective measures were applied, road closures during the winter became less common.

Stories and reminiscings of the trials and tribulations in keeping roads open in the old days, and the high waters of 1915 and 1937 were cast into the background by the Christmas week flood of 1955.

Every route in the district sustained damage ranging from comparatively inconsequential damage to destruction of catastrophic proportions. When the full details are summed up it will, in all probability, show that the District I highways suffered the most extensive and serious damage of the 11 highway districts in the State of California. Further, it will undoubtedly prove to be the most extensive and widespread damage ever sustained by portions of the California State Highway System at one time.

The major streams, which were generally in high-water stages in the early part of the week, and the increasing rainfall in all the major watersheds soon resulted in record-breaking gauge heights and discharges, and the devastating high water and inundation of contiguous areas. The highways utilizing the water level grades of the various streams to traverse the rugged terrain of the district were extremely vulnerable to damage. First reports of approximate high-water elevations at various locations were discounted and charged up to hysteria; however, a number proved to be essentially correct.

Astounding Discharges

Estimated discharges of some of the major streams during full flood conditions are rather astounding. The South Fork Eel River, near Miranda, was discharging 136,000 cfs., which is approximately twice as much as ever recorded. The Eel River at Scotia was discharging 470,000 cfs., establishing a record high. The Van Duzen River at Dinsmore recorded 21,500 cfs.; the Mad River at Forest Glen 33,000 cfs., and approximately one-half mile upstream from the US 299 crossing, 80,000 cfs. Redwood Creek at Orick 45,000 cfs., and the Klamath near Somes Bar was recording 180,000 cfs., and near Klamath Glen 400,000 cfs. The Smith River near the US 199 crossing recorded approximately 170,000 cfs. Rainfall such as that in Branscomb area of Mendocino County —which totaled 31.82 inches in 10 days prior to December 26th—accounts for these discharges.

The streams, having generally crooked courses, rugged beds and

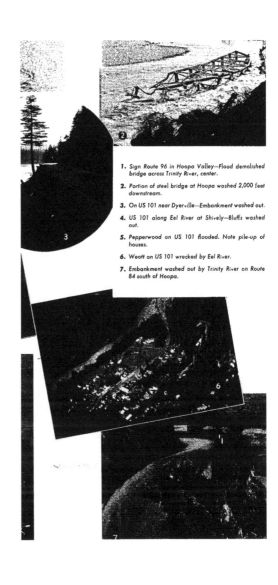

1. Sign Route 96 in Hoopa Valley—Flood demolished bridge across Trinity River, center.

2. Portion of steel bridge at Hoopa washed 2,000 feet downstream.

3. On US 101 near Dyerville—Embankment washed out.

4. US 101 along Eel River at Shively—Bluffs washed out.

5. Pepperwood on US 101 flooded. Note pile-up of houses.

6. Weott on US 101 wrecked by Eel River.

7. Embankment washed out by Trinity River on Route 84 south of Hoopa.

shore lines, turbulence and eddies, together with high velocities, had an extremely damaging effect on the highway facilities subjected to inundation. To add to the damage caused by parallel creeks and rivers, cross streams and normally small watercourses became small raging torrents overtaxing the capacities of drainage structures, with resultant flooding and washouts of roadbeds.

First Closure

The first closure in the district on Wednesday, December 21st, will probably never be known, but the first indication of trouble came from the southern portion of the district. The streams flowing southerly, with watersheds in the area receiving intense and continued rainfall, had comparatively short distances to travel to the lowlands subject to flooding. Possibly Route 16, the Hopland-Lakeport highway, was the first closure when it was closed at 5.30 p.m. on December 21st, due to high water in the Russian River. As rivers and streams continued to rise, reports came over the district's radio communication system and into the district office that evening in rapid sequence from all parts of the district, and the seriousness of the situation was made obvious.

By morning of December 22d, all routes were closed and any detailed information was impossible to obtain since telephone communications were out throughout the area and many portions of the highway system were inaccessible, with waters still rising to the crests in the lower basins of the streams. The reports received revealed that all the various damages causing road closures were present: slides, washouts, settlements, bridges and approaches damaged, and, although it was not realized at that time, even houses floating onto the traveled way at several locations impeded access into flooded areas when water receded.

In Southern Mendocino and Lake Counties, although road closures occurred by flooding the highway in these areas, the damage incurred was inconsequential in the over-all district picture, and all highways were opened as soon as waters receded.

On Route 15 (Sign Route 20), approaches at the easterly end of the North Fork of Cache Creek bridge were partially washed out and slope paving damaged.

On Route 70, Ukiah-Talmage Road, the high water of Russian River caused considerable pavement damage.

On Route 48 (Sign Route 128) some washouts occurred due to scour by high water in the Navarro River.

Mendocino Not Hard Hit

At Anderson Creek and Dry Creek, cross streams changed channels at crossings, but not to any irreparable or serious extent, and, in general, the highways under the Boonville maintenance territory jurisdiction were open to all traffic upon recession of high water. Route 56 (Sign Route 1), on the Mendocino Coast, gave no serious trouble.

On Route 1 (US 101) the first serious damage occurred at Longvale, where approaches to the bridge across Long Valley Creek Crossing No. 1 were washed out. As soon as waters receded approaches were restored. From this point to Laytonville, actual damage was relative nominal, generally consisting of some washouts, eroded shoulders, and minor slides.

The sector of Route 1 (US 101) from Laytonville to Scotia, a distance of approximately 105 miles, will, it is hoped, retain the record for all time as incurring the most extensive and serious damage ever inflicted upon such a length of state highway during a single storm. Within this section, the concentration of damage occurred between Leggett and South Scotia Bridge, a distance of approximately 68 miles. In this 68 miles, US 101 parallels the South Fork of Eel River at generally nominal elevations above stream-bed, and previously recorded high waters, and joins the main Eel River at Dyerville.

Slides and Slipouts

Damage to this section was of all descriptions: major and minor slipouts and slides, culvert blockage, undermined pavement, and washed out shoulders at discouraging intervals. The only major structure damage was the settlement of the box abutment at

the northerly end of the Smith Point Bridge, south of Benbow.

It should be noted that some of the "old-time" trouble spots previously mentioned herein again came into questionable prominence and persisted in giving trouble at this time. Slides at Greenlaw and Shively Bluffs continue to necessitate attention. The old Blue Slide washout south of Benbow was reactivated to a serious degree and is one of the major problems in restoration efforts.

The communities of Myers Flat, Weott, and Pepperwood were almost completely inundated, and receding waters left silt on the highway traveled way to depths of over two feet. Pioneering an emergency road through the Pepperwood area was further impeded by buildings that had floated onto the traveled way. Motel cottages, overturned and practically completely demolished, had floated onto the traveled way when waters receded. As they were, to a great extent, intact and single-lane traffic was able to shoofly around them, arrangements were made by the Division of Highways with professional house movers for the removal of these houses from the highway right of way in a repairable condition.

From South Scotia Bridge to Fortuna, where roadway grades are below this particular high water elevation, damage consisted mainly of erosive action on the generally low embankments and shoulders, and debris and drift on the highway.

Damage North of Arcata

From Fortuna to Arcata, the highway remained normal. Beyond Arcata, at what is known as Arcata Bottoms and where the Mad River traverses the flatlands at the northerly extremity, the damage to highway facilities by the overflow of Mad River was of major consequence. The approach spans and approaches to the Turner Draw Bridge were washed out and approaches to smaller structures across

eott where high waters were to awning height.

epperwood inundated by Eel River.

gn Route 1 between Fernbridge and Ferndale—
ater flowed over many square miles.

ign Route 1 between Ferndale and Fernbridge—
mbankments destroyed by Eel River.

ign Route 1 near Ferndale—Box culvert washed out.

S 299 along Trinity River west of Del Loma—Ma-
onry wall, left, topped by high waters.

S 101 at Dyerville on south fork Eel River. Note
arge slides blocking highway on left.

overflow channels known as Moore Draw and Boyd Draw were washed out. At the major structure in the area, the bridge across Mad River, four spans of the timber approach at the north end of the structure were completely demolished.

From Arcata to Orick, Route 1 suffered what is considered negligible damage in this instance. At Orick, Redwood Creek overflowed its banks and damaged levees constructed after the Redwood Creek flood of 1953, and Orick was again flooded. Highway damage was not consequential.

Major Catastrophe

As we go into Del Norte County, the major catastrophe of the area occurred at the Town of Klamath, where almost complete destruction of the town resulted from the overflow of the Klamath River. The northerly approach to the Douglas Memorial Bridge, carrying US 101 across the Klamath River, was washed out.

From Klamath to Crescent City and on to the Oregon line, Routes 1 and 71 (US 101) suffered no extraordinary damage.

Although the Smith River registered record high water, Route 1 (US 199), from Crescent City to Grants Pass, Oregon, which follows the Smith River Canyon, the general damage consisted of no extraordinary slides and some washouts, but not of particularly serious nature. Route 81, North Bank Road connecting US 101 and US 199, did suffer some washout damage.

Mad River Bridge

On Route 20 (US 299) partial washout of approach fills of the Mad River Bridge occurred. On a series of forest highway projects under construction between Berry Summit and Willow Creek by the U. S. Bureau of Public Roads, major slides, slipouts, and washouts were prevalent, which made road opening a difficult process.

From Willow Creek to the district boundary, where the highway follows the Trinity River, dropping to "water grade" at Cedar Flat, washouts, slipouts, and slides were prevalent.

The Cedar Flat Maintenance Station, formerly located on a small flat area between the highway and Trinity River, is a complete loss—not a sign of the foreman's cottage or truck shed with gas tank remains—and the former site is completely washed away. The Cedar Flat Bridge was in jeopardy for a period of time as the raging waters topped the deck of the bridge and threatened to demolish the structure. The easterly approach embankment, however, finally was penetrated by the river and pressure on the structure was relieved.

Hoopa Bridge Destroyed

Route 84, Sign Route from Willow Creek to Weitchpec, suffered major damage by slides, slipouts, and washouts, including complete loss of the steel truss bridge, together with center pier, that afforded crossing of the Trinity River at Hoopa. The main span of this steel structure was rolled downstream and finally came to rest approximately 2,000 feet from the bridge site.

Other serious damage in this area was incurred by Route 46, Martins Ferry to Weitchpec, and up the Klamath River through Orleans, on to the district boundary. Within these limits, the approaches to Bluff Creek Bridge were washed out, with Bluff Creek breaking a new channel at the location.

Route 56 (Sign Route 1) in Humboldt County, from Fernbridge to Ferndale, presented extensive damage when flood waters from the Eel River receded. The concrete bent approach at the south end of Fernbridge Bridge across the Eel River was seriously damaged. Bridge approaches were washed out at other structures and a large box culvert at Arlynda Corners was completely destroyed. Intervening roadway had shoulders completely washed out and pavement undermined for a distance of as much as six feet.

Van Duzen River

High waters in the Van Duzen River and Yager Creek resulted in damage and road closures on Route 35 (Sign Route 36). A pier on the Yager Creek Bridge at Carlotta was apparently undermined and jarred loose by heavy drift, necessitating closing of the bridge.

Cooperation of the Northwestern Pacific Railroad resulted in an agreement between the Division of Highways and the railroad to temporarily plank the parallel railroad bridge so that light traffic could make the Yager Creek crossing.

Farther east, on Route 35, in the Grizzly Creek area, major washouts and slides seriously hampered road opening. Beyond Bridgeville no extraordinary damage was inflicted on Route 35.

Pioneering 'trails'' into stricken areas to bring in assistance and emergency vehicles was the first order of business by the maintenance crews. This also allowed some appraisal of the damage and immediately instigated restoration activities.

Extra Forces Employed

Field offices immediately hired privately owned equipment and additional manpower to supplement regular state maintenance equipment and personnel in an endeavor to open roads as soon as possible. Additional state forces were brought in from areas suffering lesser damage to the Laytonville-Scotia area where, as previously mentioned, the most lengthy section of highway was damaged severely.

Within this area, during the height of efforts to open the road, there were engaged in the work approximately 150 pieces of equipment of various kinds and in excess of 200 men. This was the greatest concentration of men and equipment ever assembled on a sector of state highway. Equipment belonging to approximately 70 different companies and individuals comprised this assemblage of equipment.

At this writing, full-scale restoration activities are still underway and many sections of highway are still in no condition to handle traffic in a normal manner. Men of the Bridge Department are in the district handling, in their usual able manner, the necessary bridge work.

Damage Almost $3,000,000

At this time it is estimated that the dollar value of the damage to District

I state highways will approximate $2,950,850. The greater portion of the damage occurred in Humboldt County, where it is expected that $1,901,850 will have to be expended to restore highway facilities. The least amount of damage occurred in Lake County, where it is estimated to amount to approximately $20,000.

It must be mentioned that companions to the state highways in land transportation facilities within the district; namely, the county roads and the Northwestern Pacific Railroad, also suffered severe and extensive damage.

Of the counties comprising the district, Humboldt's county roads incurred the greater portion of road damage. As an indication of the magnitude of the Humboldt County Road System damage, surveys of the situation have revealed that some 38 bridges have been damaged or completely lost, with indications that approximately 19 are completely out or will require complete replacement.

The Division of Highways is rendering Humboldt County emergency assistance at this time by arranging the financing and emergency contracting for the restoration of county roads and bridges on a priority basis to open roads into various areas to re-establish land transportation to communities.

The Northwestern Pacific Railroad has a major restoration job to contend with, including replacement of sidehill trestle along the precipitous Scotia Bluffs, along the Eel River just downstream from Scotia.

Story Incomplete

This would be only a very small part of a complete saga of the 1955 California flood, or even of the complete story of the floods within the area covered by this brief. All of the story will probably never be put together. Stories of destruction, tragedy, and despair, and probably humor as well, would have to be tracked down. We know there are innumerable factual stories of friend helping friend, neighbor helping neighbor, and stranger helping stranger, and stories of cooperation and extreme endeavor on the part of individuals, agencies,

and others throughout the area during the length of the emergency.

We have heard of stories wherein strangers, going in opposite directions and anxious to get to homes not too distant, were confronted with a washout who then and there traded pickups to continue in their desired direction, after making arrangements to return each others vehicles at a later date.

We also heard a story of a large bobcat seen hanging onto a log being carried down a swollen stream. He was snarling, but desperately hanging on. Possibly humorous, knowing that cats dislike water, but certainly a tragedy to the bobcat.

As for the Redwood Highway and other routes, they will be back in normal service and the vacationists and tourists from all parts of the Country will be traversing them in increasing numbers. They will marvel at beautiful vistas of placid, shimmering streams, snap pictures of these vistas unaware that these streams could show up the futility of man against the natural elements. They will look with askance and doubt at the "native" as he shows them where the water was in his house during Christmas week, 1955.

District II–$2,586,145

By J. W. TRASK
District Engineer

The one predictable feature of California weather is that it is unpredictable. This was amply demonstrated in the Redding district this fall and early winter.

Normally, beginning in September, there are some fall rains. These continue intermittently, with some snow in the higher altitudes, until about mid-December. Then storms of greater intensity and duration occur and the snow blanket is built up in the mountains.

This year there were no fall rains. About the middle of November, a heavy snow fell over most of the district. This was followed by more or less continued intermittent storms that put rain in the valleys and snow in the highlands. Even this was at variance with the normal pattern. It was much heavier in the Trinity, Feather and Klamath watersheds than in the Pitt and Sacramento areas which usually have the heaviest snow cover.

Highway entirely destroyed at Chipps Creek on Feather River

Rain Creates Emergency

About the twentieth of December, the temperature rose and a warm rain began falling all over the district up to above the 5,000-foot level. The rain itself put down as much as five inches in 24 hours in some places. Coupled with the water from the melting snow, streams rose everywhere. Immediately messages began to pour into the Redding District Office from the Klamath River area in Siskiyou County, the Feather River area in Plumas County, and all along the Trinity River in Trinity County. The district radio went on almost a 24-hour shift. The district began lining up equipment which could be used as soon as more definite information about damages was available. Equipment, supplies, and personnel were dispatched and shifted to meet the emergencies as they materialized.

The pattern of the storm was developed by the twenty-fourth of December. Bridges were damaged and sections of highway washed out in all three of the watersheds.

As soon as it was possible to do so, a crew of engineers visited the damaged areas. They estimated costs of emergency repairs to put the highways in operation and also amounts which will be required for restoration. Work began immediately on those of an emergency nature, and at the time this article goes to press will be largely accomplished.

SISKIYOU COUNTY

The major damage sustained was located in Scott Valley on Route 82, and along the Klamath River on Route 46.

On the highway between Etna and Fort Jones, the Scott River destroyed the bridge near Fort Jones. The bridge over Kidder Creek was also washed out. Patterson Creek bridge had the approaches damaged.

Along the Klamath River, the section between Walker and the junction of Route 3 received only nominal damage consisting of small slides and shoulder erosion.

The section between Walker and Seiad contains the bridge over the mouth of Scott River which was destroyed in its entirety. Washouts and erosion damages were also heavy.

Between Seiad and Happy Camp, damage was confined to slides and slipouts, with some damage to approaches to the Seiad Creek bridge.

Similar damage was sustained between Swillup Creek, the district boundary, and Happy Camp. However, due to the highway being narrower and not constructed to present standards, the cost of emergency repairs will represent almost half the total amount for full restoration.

Between Yreka and Weed, damage was sustained at Parks and Greenhorn Creeks.

TRINITY COUNTY

The Trinity River first strikes the highway near Vitzthum's and roughly parallels the location for about two miles until it reaches Douglas City where it is crossed by a bridge which takes the highway to Weaverville.

A section of heavy concrete riprap bank protection and the highway itself were washed out near Vitzthum's. About 170 feet of the Douglas City bridge over the Trinity was lost.

To catalog the highway damage along the Trinity River below Junction City would be a long recital of bank erosion and complete washouts. The approach of Canyon Creek bridge at Junction City was swept out. Damage was sustained at many other structures.

The road from Douglas City to Peanut received some scour. This was heavy near Redding's Creek.

SHASTA COUNTY

Route 3 in this county was protected from major damages by Shasta Dam. The only damage on this route was a slide near Antler in the Sacramento Canyon. Minor damages from erosion were suffered on Mount Lassen-Mount Shasta highway, south of the intersection with the road to Alturas. A mud slide occurred on Route 29 west of Platina.

TEHAMA COUNTY

Like Shasta County, Tehama received protection from Shasta Dam on the main routes. The highway west to Hayfork received minor damage by erosion. Route 47, the cutoff between Chico and Chester, had very minor damages. On the road to Susanville, damage was minor but rather widely spread. It consisted of shoulder scour, debris on the roadway, and some pavement restoration.

Slides and erosion east of Arch Rock Tunnel on US 40 Alternate, Butte County

UPPER—Temporary detour under construction on Trinity River two miles from Douglas City.
LOWER—Typical damage along Trinity River.

MODOC COUNTY

Only damage sustained by this county was a culvert washout on the road between Alturas and the Nevada state line.

LASSEN COUNTY

The Susan River flooded the highway in the vicinity of Litchfield on the road to Alturas and east of Susanville. Damages were minor. Largest item was requirement for placing riprap at Secret Valley Creek.

Very small damage occurred between Susanville and Doyle.

Beyond Doyle, Long Valley Creek washed out the highway where it crosses the Quincy-Reno route, and again where it crosses the Susanville-Reno connection. Culverts were overloaded at both places.

From Susanville to Reno, damage was relatively light. Major costs were in connection with one structure over Long Valley Creek which was wrecked and one which was damaged.

The southern end of Lassen County takes in a portion of the Quincy-Reno highway. A structure over Long Valley Creek was wrecked there.

PLUMAS COUNTY

There is no point in trying to list the damage to the Feather River Highway. Beginning just beyond Jarbo Gap, the amount of water was simply more than the channel could carry.

Highway slopes were washed out, the road undermined, and in some cases flooded and torn out in its entirety. Slides of huge boulders were dumped in the canyon completely obliterating the highway. One of these was estimated to contain 100,000 cubic yards.

At another place, a cut through "onion skin" rock broke loose. This is a stratified material sloping toward the highway. It is difficult to be certain just how much material will come in at this location.

At Bardee Creek, near Pulga, a slipout removed the entire roadway section to the extent of about 75,000 cubic yards.

The route from Blairsden to Sierra county line received some scour and damage to the bridge over the south fork of the Feather River; otherwise damage was minor.

The route from Lake Almanor to the Feather River was severely damaged in three places where it parallels Indian Creek. Scour at other locations was extensive.

TOTAL FLOOD DAMAGE IN DISTRICT II

	Repairs	
County	Emergency	Restoration
Siskiyou	$113,565	$503,835
Trinity	151,910	1,068,810
Shasta	16,060	7,150
Tehama	8,770	20,955
Modoc	1,760	2,100
Lassen	23,650	71,555
Plumas	260,945	335,080
	$576,660	$2,009,485

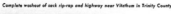

Complete washout of sack rip-rap and highway near Vitzthum in Trinity County

District III–$925,000

By A. M. NASH
District Engineer

Rains in the latter part of November and the first of December had already saturated the soil in the mountains and valleys of Northern California so that the unprecedented heavy warm rains beginning December 18, 1955, did not disappear into the earth but caused a heavy run-off in all the mountain streams and rivers.

Damage to state highways in the district amounted to approximately $925,000.

Rain at elevations up to 10,000 feet rapidly melted the snow pack which was about six feet deep at Yuba Pass, Donner, and Echo Summit.

On December 21st at 8 p.m. word was received from District II that US 40 Alternate was closed in the Feather River Canyon, and from then on there was very little sleep obtained among the highway personnel in District III.

On December 22d information began coming in from the different territories of road closures due to flooding and washouts along the Yuba, Feather and American Rivers.

Considerable sections of road were washed out above Downieville on Sign Route 49, the Yuba Pass Highway. Sections of the road were washed out on US 50. There were serious fill slipouts on Sign Route 20 and US 40. There were also flooded sections of road on US 40 and US 50.

US 40 Alternate Closed

US 40 Alternate north of Marysville was closed between Marysville and Oroville by an overflowing of the Feather River flood crest into Simmerly Slough near Marysville, and from inundation of a considerable section of this road which lies on low ground adjacent to the Feather River between Union School and Oroville.

The Yuba River, in common with all other Sierra streams in this district, was rising rapidly, and in view of the unprecedented high flood stages reported from the upstream reaches, the Marysville Levee Commission alerted the District III highway authorities to the possible necessity of closing US 99E at the D Street Bridge so that a low gap in the levee at this point

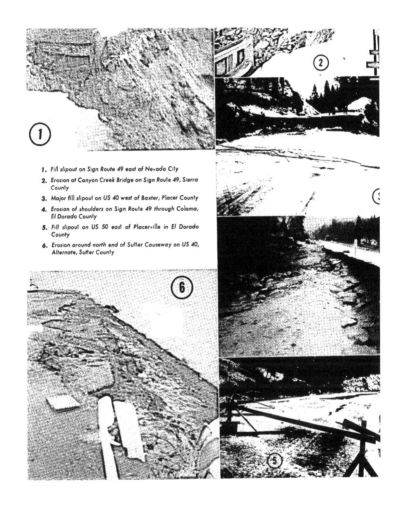

1. Fill slipout on Sign Route 49 east of Nevada City
2. Erosion at Canyon Creek Bridge on Sign Route 49, Sierra County
3. Major fill slipout on US 40 west of Baxter, Placer County
4. Erosion of shoulders on Sign Route 49 through Coloma, El Dorado County
5. Fill slipout on US 50 east of Placerville in El Dorado County
6. Erosion around north end of Sutter Causeway on US 40, Alternate, Sutter County

could be closed. At 4 p.m. December 22d the bridge was closed to traffic to effect the placement of planks and sand bags, since the roadway forms about a four-foot depth gap in the levee at the bridge ends.

Our crews were working removing drift from the D Street Bridge throughout the afternoon and all through the night of Thursday, December 22d, and other men under the authority of the Levee Commission were strengthening the levees at the approach.

Marysville Evacuated

On Friday, December 23, 1955, the river stages began approaching record heights in the Marysville area, and soon after noon Marysville was ordered to be evacuated by 4 p.m. The only vehicle escape route by that time was over the 10th Street Bridge to Yuba City.

About midnight, Friday night, the west levee on the Feather River south of Yuba City broke and flooded a major portion of Yuba City and thousands of acres to the south—completely closing US 40 Alternate between Marysville and the Sutter Bypass.

After flood waters had subsided, work was immediately started on emergency restoration of the closed highways to permit one-way traffic on the sections that were closed by slides, slipouts and washouts.

All truck traffic was prohibited over US 40, and because of the condition of the road where there was a slipout at Steep Hollow, only trucks of an emergency nature were permitted to detour via State Sign Routes 49 and 20 between Auburn and Emigrant Gap. This detour was caused by a major slipout of a fill one-quarter mile east of Baxter.

Crews were sent out consisting of representatives of the district, Headquarters Office, and the Bureau of Public Roads to make an estimate of the storm damage including emergency restoration, complete restoration and/or improvements on all state highways. Similarly, road damage survey teams comprised of district, Bureau of Public Roads, Bridge Department representatives, and the county road commissioners were sent out to estimate the emergency repair and restoration costs on city streets and county roads.

Work of Restoration

Work at present is going on restoring roads to two-way traffic throughout District III by day labor forces, by emergency contract, and by the use of rented equipment.

Continuous storms throughout the first of January, including heavy snow storms at times, have hampered the work considerably since it is necessary to stop repair work in many locations and go about the business of snow removal.

On US 99, south of Sacramento, the highways were in danger for a considerable time from the rising waters in the Cosumnes River and its overflow channels. However, when the height of the water reached the top of the stringers of the bridges over the Cosumnes overflow, a levee upstream broke and spread water over the lowlands of the area, relieved the condition, and saved the bridge from washing out.

The height of water in the Yolo Bypass was such that it was necessary to sandbag the approaches on the west end of the Yolo Causeway on US 40 west of Sacramento to prevent water from covering the highway in that area.

The "River Road" between Woodland and Sacramento was closed by waters from the Fremont Weir flowing into the Yolo Bypass and will, undoubtedly, remain closed for some time because of the continuing high stage of the Sacramento River.

The flooding of Yuba City and southern Sutter County was a major disaster in which many lives were lost, livestock killed by the thousands, and millions of dollars' damage done to property. One hundred and ten Division of Highways employees suffered damage ranging from minor flooding of garages to complete loss of houses and belongings. Fortunately, no division personnel or their families lost their lives, although there were narrow escapes.

The work of rehabilitating homes took employees, their families and friends up to two weeks away from work while co-workers carried on with the problem of opening and restoring highways. Permanent repairs to homes, of course, will be continuing into the summer and fall.

The Marysville-Yuba City area will long remember the "Christmas" flood of 1955!

District IV–$750,000

By D. C. RYMAN
District Maintenance Engineer

District IV, which comprises the nine Bay area counties of Sonoma, Marin, Napa, Contra Costa, Alameda, San Francisco, San Mateo, Santa Clara and Santa Cruz, was lashed by several hard gales and rainstorms from December 18th to 25th causing approximately three-quarters of a million dollars damage to the state highways.

Major arterial highways such as the Eastshore Freeway, Bayshore Freeway and US 101 south of Morgan Hill were flooded and closed during the height of the storm. Several other routes were closed by flooding, slides, slipouts, washouts, fallen trees, plugged culverts and one bridge failure. Nearly 500 men and 300 pieces of state-owned and rented equipment worked tirelessly around the clock to open the highways and restore safe public travel. All highways were opened to traffic on January 11, 1956, but there are many one-way sections which will require several months to restore to their original width.

First Storm December 18th-19th

The first heavy storm struck on December 18th and continued throughout December 19th. The Russian River in Sonoma County overflowed its banks east of Geyserville and adjacent to Guerneville where it reached a record flood stage of 47.8 feet and all highways in the area were closed until December 20th when the river receded.

The new highway in Napa County from Capell Valley to the uncompleted Monticello Dam on Putah Creek was damaged by slides and slipouts but remained open to one-way traffic. State Sign Route 1 on the coast south of San Francisco was closed due to hundreds of tons of mud sloughing from the bluffs above the highway.

Six-hundred-foot washout on Route 107 in Alameda County

Long washout on Sign Route 9 west of Saratoga in Santa Clara County

Slipout on Sign Route 5 south of La Honda in San Mateo County

Rock slide west of Junction 56, Route 6 on Sign Route 128, Napa County

Large slide which blocked highway from Waterman Gap to Big Basin State Park, Santa Cruz County

Small washout only one of many on Niles Canyon Highway, Alameda County

Slipout for full length of roadway, Sign Route 128, Napa County

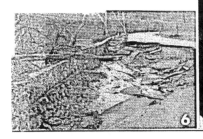

Second Storm December 22d-23d

The second and most severe rains started early December 22d and continued through December 23d, raising the total rainfall for the storm to 10 inches in the immediate Bay area and a high of 30 inches in the Santa Cruz Mountains and Guerneville area.

North Bay Area

The Russian River again flooded, reaching the highest stage recorded with a flow of 90,000 second-feet. Portions of the communities of Geyserville, Healdsburg, Sebastopol and Guerneville were inundated and the highways were closed until December 27th. In Napa County, the Putah Creek flowed over the uncompleted Monticello Dam with a record flow of 90,000 second-feet and the new highway was shut tight with slides and slipouts. It required continuous work until January 6, 1956, to remove several thousand yards of slide material and to construct a detour to open the highway to one-way traffic. State Sign Route 128 between Rutherford and Monticello was also closed from slides and washouts until January 6th.

Santa Cruz Area

A large portion of the City of Santa Cruz business district was flooded to a depth of six feet by the high flow of the San Lorenzo River December 22d-24th, during which a record flow of 35,000 second-feet was reached. Two piers of a new bridge under construction were washed out.

State Sign Route 9 from Santa Cruz to Felton and the two highways leading into Big Basin State Park were closed by large slides and slipouts which destroyed many large redwood trees. The park area was isolated until December 26th.

Saratoga Creek went on a rampage washing out the entire highway for several hundred feet west of the town of Saratoga. Severe erosion along the creek, washouts, and slides damaged the entire route from Saratoga to Saratoga Gap.

The Los Gatos-Santa Cruz Highway, State Sign Route 17, was threatened by slides and plugged culverts several times. Recently placed concrete channel lining on the Los Gatos Creek which is under construction

was partially ripped out. The new Lexington Dam on Los Gatos Creek was completely filled and water

flowed over the spillway at the rate of 25,000 second-feet.

Gilroy-Watsonville Area

The Uvas, Llagas and Carnedero Creeks overflowed, closing all highways in the Gilroy area. US 101 was closed from Morgan Hill south to the county line. State Sign Route 52 was flooded at the Hollister Junction and the Hecker Pass portion west of Gilroy had slides, washouts, and a pier of the Uvas Creek bridge was undermined, dropping two spans of the deck. Slides also occurred at Pacheco Pass east of Gilroy.

These flood waters continued their ravaging damage throughout the Pajaro River channel, which caused erosion along Route 67, the Chittenden Pass Road, and flooded the Watsonville area December 24th and 25th.

East Bay Area

The Eastshore Freeway was closed on December 23d due to the overflow of San Lorenzo Creek. The Jackson Street Underpass on Route 105 in Hayward was flooded. The main arterial between Oakland and Walnut Creek State Sign Route 24 was kept open only by continuous work "around the clock" by both the Maintenance Department and a contractor. A heavy deluge of mud washed into the Broadway Tunnel ventilating equipment room.

Alameda Creek washed out several sections of the Niles Canyon Highway Route 107 between Niles and

Flooded Visalia Airport Interchange, Tulare County

Sunol. A protection wall 600 feet in length collapsed when topped by the creek. These flood waters continued downstream and flooded the Niles-Centerville-Alvarado area, closing State Sign Route 17. Damage in the Pittsburg and Livermore areas was light.

Bayshore-Alviso Area

The stream channels beginning with the San Francisquito Creek on the north to the Guadalupe River on the south overflowed, flooding several subdivisions, the Bayshore Highway, the Agnew Underpass, and isolating the town of Alviso. Highways leading to Alviso were closed until December 30th due to the combination of the flood waters and high tides.

District V—$312,000
By L. E. ELDER
District Maintenance Engineer

On December 22, 1955, one of the heaviest holiday season storms recorded in recent years struck the Central Coast Counties of San Benito, Monterey, San Luis Obispo and Santa Barbara. Heavy rains continued throughout the Christmas week end with a final tapering off during the night of December 28th.

According to records compiled by the Salinas *Californian*, the Salinas Valley area, as of December 28th, had received a season's total rainfall totaling the fourth highest season's total in an 83-year record of rainfall. The rains during December have made it the fifth wettest December since 1872. Rainfall figures for the rest of the

UPPER—Flooded section of US 99 through Chowchilla, Madera County.
LOWER—US 99 flooded south of Chowchilla.

Central Coast Counties appear to indicate a record rainfall of about the same magnitude as that experienced in the Salinas Valley.

Heavy Rainfall

Many places throughout the four counties experienced exceptionally heavy rainfall during the second and

Pumping equipment set up in Chowchilla

third day of the storm, in a few instances, attaining almost cloudburst proportions with the resultant run-off carrying debris and drift across the highways and causing extensive damage to existing highway facilities.

As an example, 8.45 inches of rain was recorded at the Big Sur Maintenance Station for the 24-hour period beginning at 8 a.m. on December 23d, and 6.45 inches at Willow Springs, 3.14 inches at Hollister, 2.77 inches at Seaside and 2.64 inches at Paso Robles all for the same period. During the following 24-hour period on December 24th, all areas except Buellton and Santa Barbara received rainfalls varying from 1.55 inches to 4.02 inches with Priest Valley receiving 3.42 inches, Atascadero 3.36 inches, Big Sur 3.75 inches, Willow Springs 3.35 and San Luis Obispo 4.02 inches. On December 25th, the storm reached its peak in the Santa Barbara area with a rainfall of 2.90 inches being recorded at Lompoc, 6.33 inches at San Marcos,

2.94 inches at Buellton and 1.96 at Santa Barbara.

Main Roads Kept Open

In spite of the severity of the storm, District maintenance personnel, by working around the clock, managed to keep all the main line roads open for the heavy volume of holiday traffic. Only three main routes experienced closures. Route 117 was closed between Salinas and Monterey on December 24th for a period of 21 hours due to flooding at the Salinas River crossing west of Salinas. Sign Route 150 over San Marcos Pass was closed to all but local traffic for a period of about 10 days due to storm damaged embankments on a portion of the route now under construction.

Sign Route 1, between San Simeon and Carmel was closed early on December 23d. Historically, the highway between San Simeon and Carmel has always been considered a road highly susceptible to extensive damage during heavy storm periods due to slides, washouts and flooding by the numerous creeks and canyons throughout the area. The December storm proved to be no exception. Extensive damage was experienced to the existing bridges across San Carpojo Creek, White Creek and Mill Creek. Approximately 60,000 cubic yards of embankment will be required to replace a portion of the roadway at a point about 10 miles south of Big Sur where flash floods washed out the entire roadbed. Numerous minor and several major slides have completely blocked a 50-mile stretch of this road between San Carpojo Creek and the Big Sur River. However, several months will be required to complete repairs to damaged structures and to restore the existing traveled way to its original condition prior to the storm.

It has been estimated that it will cost about $312,000 to repair the damaged structures and restore the roadbed to its original condition.

UPPER—Storm damage to roadway 10 miles south of Big Sur River at Redwood Canyon on Sign Route 1. LOWER—Damage to sacked concrete riprap at downstreams side of Jungle Inn Bridge across San Benito River 20 miles south of Hollister on Route 119, San Benito County.

District VI—$1,400,000

By T. M. WHITLEY
Assistant District Maintenance Engineer

The storm that struck Northern California during the Christmas holidays was first seriously felt in District VI on December 23d. During that day and through the ensuing week several sections of state highway were flooded by high water, numerous washouts occurred, and several bridges were damaged, some seriously. The total amount of damage to state highways in the district is estimated at approximately $1,400,000.

Perhaps the most serious loss occurred in the Kings River Canyon on Sign Route 180. In the vicinity of Boulder Creek, where the highway and the Kings River jointly occupy a steep, narrow canyon, approximately 4,000 feet of road was completely washed out. Because this particular stretch is impassable, an on-the-spot inspection of the flood damage has not been made. However, aerial observation and reports by employees of the

LEFT—Damage to roadway fill at east end of San Benito River Bridge, 0.9 mile west of Hollister, Route 22.
RIGHT—Damage at same section.

View of downstream side of San Carpojo Creek Bridge 22 miles north of Cambria on
Sign Route 1, San Luis Obispo County

national park indicate that there may be approximately seven or eight other washouts of a serious nature.

Three Rivers Damage

The next most seriously damaged sections are on Sign Route 198 in the vicinity of Three Rivers. Immediately east of the bridge across the south fork of the Keweah River approximately 1,600 feet of road was lost and the Kaweah River, straightening its course, overtopped the highway and occupied an area approximately 1,000 feet south of the previous location of the route. Other washouts occurred in Pumpkin Hollow, approximately six miles east of Three Rivers, and at the gateway to Sequoia National Park, the easterly approach to the bridge across the Kaweah was destroyed.

Fortunately, the damage on Sign Route 180 occurred beyond the point where that highway had previously been closed by snow through Kings Canyon National Park and no one has been inconvenienced to date by the loss of that section of the state highway. On Sign Route 180 it was necessary to restore service as soon as possible to the community of Three Rivers, to other residents along the highway easterly and for the employees of Sequoia National Park, whose headquarters are at Ash Mountain. This was done by using as a detour the former state highway around the large washout at the South Fork of the Kaweah and by immediate emergency repairs to other sections. Use of the former state highway as a detour required shoring up and redecking a county bridge, which had partially failed.

Visalia Interchange Flooded

US 99, the principal artery of traffic through the district, was not seriously damaged although it was necessary to detour traffic from portions of it over various other routes for the better part of the week December 25th to 31st, inclusive. Portions of the interchange of US 99 and Sign Route 198 near the Visaiia Airport were flooded when Mill Creek broke across the nearby airport and entered depressed areas of the interchange. With the failure of the pumps, it was necessary to dewater the underpass with whatever pumping equipment could be obtained.

Heavy flooding occurred in the vicinity of Chowchilla due to high water in Ash and Berenda Sloughs. Although no serious damage occurred to the highway itself, the flooded condition necessitated a long, tedious job of pumping the water into the Chowchilla River. This work required about one week's steady pumping, during which time it was necessary to detour US 99 traffic to other state highways to the west.

Visalia Hard Hit

Although damage to state highways in the community was negligible, the City of Visalia was hard hit when a diversion weir at McKays Point at the junction of the St. Johns and

UPPER—View of upstream side of El Capitan Creek showing debris at inlet end of structure. El Capitan Creek is located 16.5 miles north of Santa Barbara on US 101. LOWER—View of upstream side of San Carpojo Creek Bridge 22 miles north of Cambria on Sign Route 1, San Luis Obispo County.

Kaweah Rivers near Lemon Cove, carried way, permitting discharge of both streams through the bed of the Kaweah and flooding Visalia. This water eventually found an outlet to the southwest through Mill Creek, Packwood Creek and Cameron Creek. As previously stated, it was excess water in Mill Creek which flooded the Visalia Airport Interchange. High water in Packwood and Cameron

Creeks resulted in minor damage to state highways.

Loss of the diversion weir and resultant heavy flow in the Kaweah River, which carried tremendous amounts of debris, resulted in the deposition of approximately 2½ feet of silt and debris on State Sign Route 65 for about one-half mile each side of the Keweah River bridge. One of the concrete piles under the bridge

Flood damage vicinity El Portal—Excavating for footings for detour bridge to be constructed right of Station 198. Note rock foundation.

Flood damage vicinity El Portal—Inlet end of culvert plugged by tree Station 198.

Flood damage vicinity El Portal. Looking easterly over damaged 8' x 8' concrete box Station 198. Also shows temporary walkway constructed over tree blocking culvert.

was broken and knocked out of line. This, together with loss of the approaches, required closure of this section.

On State Route 131, one of the piers of the bridge across the Kaweah was undermined. The pier dropped approximately eight inches and this portion of the bridge was displaced downstream about two inches. Repairs to the pier are now under way and it is anticipated that the bridge will be restored to service in the near future.

District X–$1,275,000

Flood damage to streets and highways in District X during the recent disaster was gratifyingly small, considering the large volume of precipitation and runoff. The estimated total damage to state highways was $1,000,000 for restoration. In addition, it was estimated that the sum of $275,000 would be required to restore county roads and city streets to preflood condition.

The greatest damage to state highways occurred on Route 18 in Mariposa County, the "All-Year" Highway to Yosemite, when the Merced River and its tributaries, Pigeon Creek and Crane Creek, overflowed their banks, destroying the entire roadbed in several locations. The total estimated damage for restoration of this route is $550,000.

In Alpine County, the high water in the East and West Forks of the Carson River occasioned damage to Routes 23 and 24 in several locations, amounting to an estimated $260,000 for restoration.

Of the nine counties comprising District X, Stanislaus County apparently suffered the greatest damage to roads and bridges in the amount of $175,000 estimated for restoration. Damage to bridges constituted the greater portion of this loss.

C. M. (Max) Gilliss
Permanent Deputy

Assistant Deputy Director of Public Works C. M. (Max) Gilliss has been given a permanent appointment as deputy director by Director of Public Works Frank B. Durkee. He has been acting as deputy director since last September. He passed a civil service examination for his new job.

Gilliss assumed the duties of special representative of the Department of Public Works on December 1, 1952. In August, 1953, he was named assistant deputy director.

Flood damage vicinity El Portal—Excavating for footings for detour bridge upstream on Pigeon Creek.

Flood damage vicinity El Portal—Looking westerly from box culvert, showing pathway to temporary pedestrian bridge. Express parked on detour approach to Pigeon Creek temporary bridge.

Flood damage vicinity El Portal—Looking easterly over concrete box at Pigeon Creek.

FLOODS DO PROPERTY DAMAGE ESTIMATED AT $200,000,000

By R. R. REYNOLDS, Senior Hydraulic Engineer, and C. G. WOLFE,
Associate Hydraulic Engineer, Division of Water Resources

December, 1955, will be remembered in California as a record-breaking month whenever rainfall or floods are discussed. Heavy warm rains originating far out in the Pacific swept across Northern California during the five days just preceding Christmas. Another storm of major intensity occurred on December 26th and 27th. Together, these two storms produced sufficient rainfall to make the month one of the wettest, if not the wettest, Decembers since 1867. Heaviest rains were concentrated along the north coast, in the hills north of Santa Cruz, in the area south of Clear Lake, in the mountains above Shasta Dam, and in the Sierra Nevada watersheds of the Yuba and Bear Rivers. Over 30 inches of rain in less than 10 days were recorded at stations in these areas.

Frequent light rains followed, and during January 13th, 14th and 15th, 1956, another major storm brought new danger and renewed anxiety to the flood areas. Fortunately, no widespread flooding resulted from this storm. However, the prolonged wet period left tremendous amounts of water in the river channels, basins, and by-passes of Northern and Central California. The rate of drainage of this water from the Sacramento Valley will be very slow and cannot be accelerated, since it is controlled by the natural slope of the valley.

Tragic Results of Storms

Result of this intensive rain was spectacular and tragic. Peak flows on at least 18 major streams in the State exceeded previous flows. During December the Klamath River reached a peak of 400,000 cubic feet per second, which was about one-third greater than the previous recorded maximum flood on that stream. Likewise, the Russian River more than doubled its previous peak flow with a discharge of 47,000 cubic feet per second. Major floods in California were recorded on

TOP—Folsom Dam and Reservoir on December 24, 1955 (Corps of Engineers Photo).

BOTTOM—Town of Klamath with Klamath River at flood stage.

coastal streams from Nacimiento River on the south to the Klamath River on the north, and in Sierra streams from Kern River to the Sacramento River.

Damage Runs Into Many Millions

In the Sacramento Valley, Shasta and Folsom Dams effectively controlled the high flows of the upper Sacramento and American Rivers, while uncontrolled flows originating in the Feather River Basin caused damages in the order of $65,000,000 within the flood plain of the Feather River between Yuba City and Verona. Friant Dam on the San Joaquin River and Pine Flat Dam on the Kings River effectively controlled the flows from the upper watersheds of these streams.

Streams causing severe flood damage were the Klamath, Eel, Van Duzen, Russian, Mad, Napa, San Lorenzo, Nacimiento, Tule, Kaweah, lower San Joaquin, Tuolumne, Stanislaus, Calaveras, Mokelumne, Cosumnes, Bear, Yuba, and Feather Rivers, and Petaluma, San Lorenzo, and Alameda Creeks.

Damage from these floods was staggering. Roads and bridges were washed out, homes flooded, valuable farm lands inundated, livestock drowned, and communications disrupted. At least 62 persons lost their lives. Total damage from the flood has not been fully determined, but present estimates indicate it may be as high as $200,000,000.

Yuba City Bears Brunt

Hardest hit were Yuba City together with 100,000 acres of Sutter County's Peach Bowl, which were flooded as a result of a disastrous break in the levee on the west bank of the Feather River in the early morning hours of December 24th.

Early in the emergency, State Engineer Harvey O. Banks put the entire staff of the Division of Water Resources into the battle with the high waters.

The office of the flood control function of the division was fully staffed on a 24-hour basis, beginning at midnight December 21st. Hydrologic data and information regarding the high flows occurring on streams through-

TOP—Break in Feather River levee at Nicolaus. BOTTOM—Break in Feather River levee south of Yuba City, Sutter County.

out Northern and Central California were collected by means of the division's radio stream gage network, constant telephone contact with various federal agencies and division personnel in the field, and communications with

Aerial view of City of Marysville at critical stage of flood on December 23, 1955 (Sacramento Bee photo)

numerous independent agencies and private individuals. These data were compiled by the staff to document the flood for future design studies, and, in addition, were made available to the general public and intertested agencies. By use of these data, it was possible during to flood period to forecast and give warnings on peak stages some 48 hours in advance of their occurrence.

Water Resources Division Efficient

The Division of Water Resources dispatched equipment, supplies, and manpower, and supervised flood-fighting activities along the levee below Nicolaus, where a major break eventually occurred on December 23d. Subsequent flood-fighting activi-

ties by the division along the Natomas Cross Canal successfully averted the inundation of many thousand acres of rich agricultural lands, residences, and public utilities in Reclamation District 1000 just north of Sacramento. In addition, division personnel constantly patrolled over 200 miles of levee, made necessary repairs to weakened levee sections, and kept the Sacramento office informed of flood problems in the critical areas. Technical supervision by division personnel was furnished to many public districts during the flood period.

The levee on the left bank of the Feather River near Verona was breached December 24th by division forces to relieve the water pressure caused by the Nicolaus break. The

right bank levee of the Feather River opposite Nicolaus was breached Christmas day to drain the water from the area inundated by the break below Yuba City. Gates of the Sacramento Weir were opened to maintain the level of the Sacramento River below critical flood stage.

In addition, the division during the flood emergency secured and operated numerous pieces of heavy equipment, and dispatched to the critical areas many truckloads of burlap bags, canvas, tools, and other supplies necessary for the flood fighting. During the emergency period, about 900 men were employed in flood fighting.

During the flood emergency, valuable assistance, material, and equip-

22

Crews work to save north levee of Natomas Cross Canal. (US Air Force photo)

ment was furnished to the Division of Water Resources by the Division of Forestry, the California Highway Patrol, the Office of Civil Defense, the Department of Employment, Mather and McClellan Air Force Bases, the Sacramento Signal Depot, and the Arden-Carmichael School District.

COUNTIES GET INCREASED NATIONAL FOREST RECEIPTS

A check for $2,994,976.12 has been sent to the State Treasurer as California's share in the cash revenues from the national forests, according to a statement by Chas. A. Connaughton, Regional Forester of the United States Forest Service.

This payment represents 25 percent of the gross receipts from the sales of timber, grazing fees, and other land uses of the national forests in California, for the year ended June 30th.

As provided by law, the State apportions the money received to the counties having national forest land within their boundaries. Thirty-nine of the State's 58 counties will thus receive funds for local school and road expenditures. The amount received by each county is proportional to the national forest acreage in the county.

Mr. Connaughton says that this year's receipts to the counties represent an 18 percent increase over last year.

FOR GOOD HIGHWAYS

LANCASTER

GENTLEMEN: For the past year I have been receiving your magazine. I have enjoyed every bit of it and I appreciate very much all of the good work you are doing.

I look forward each month to receiving the magazine. I have been a resident of California for over 40 years, and have owned a car since 1916, and I can see a wonderful change and improvements that have been made. I am 100 percent for good highways.

Yours truly,

Z. R. OXFORD
1655 E. Lancaster Blvd.

JACKSONVILLE

The town of Jacksonville, California, is named after Colonel Alden Jackson who settled there in the autumn of 1849.

THANK YOU

SANTA MONICA

DEAR MR. ADAMS AND HELEN HALSTED: I have received this magazine for some seven years. I have kept past copies for reference to past events in the highway system. I look forward for each new issue to arrive. The layout and photography are well done. Mr. Nickerson is to be congratulated along with you two.

Yours truly,

RICHARD BERK
1134 23d Street

FROM LOS ANGELES

LOS ANGELES

DEAR MR. ADAMS: I have been receiving and enjoying your interesting and educational journal for several years and wish right now to express my appreciation for the privilege of continuing to receive it.

Yours respectfully,

A. J. BORDEN
1616½ W. 12th Street

and Public Works

Carquinez Project

Revenue Bonds Sold and Major Contracts Awarded

By LEONARD C. HOLLISTER, Projects Engineer—Carquinez

On JUNE 15, 1955, Governor Goodwin J. Knight signed Senate Bill 1450 authorizing the Department of Public Works to 'lay out, acquire and construct" two new bridges across Carquinez Strait. One bridge was to be located adjacent to the existing Carquinez Bridge and the other to be located about six miles upstream, between Benicia and Martinez. The bill also authorized the California Toll Bridge Authority to issue revenue bonds and to reimpose tolls upon the existing Carquinez Bridge for the purpose of financing the construction of the two new bridges and their approaches.

Senate Bill 1450 was passed by the 1955 Session of the California State Legislature under the sponsorship of Senators Luther E. Gibson and George Miller, Jr., and Assemblymen Donald D. Doyle, Samuel R. Geddes and S. C. Masterson.

On June 16, 1955, Frank B. Durkee, Director of Public Works, assigned the work contemplated under this legislation to George T. McCoy, State Highway Engineer. Exactly four months later four major contracts were advertised for bids involving a large portion of the construction work in connection with the new parallel Carquinez Bridge and its Contra Costa County approach.

Revenue Bonds Sold

On December 13, 1955, the California Toll Bridge Authority sold $46,000,000 worth of Series A Bonds in accordance with the Resolution dated October 4, 1955, authorizing Carquinez Strait Bridges Toll Bridge Revenue Bonds. The interest rate called for is 3¾ percent payable semi-annually. Later, as plans progress, an additional issue of Series B Bonds can be sold for financing work on the Benicia-Martinez Bridge and the remaining freeway work through Vallejo.

Because these first four contracts were large and involved types of construction work not frequently encountered in the usual highway contracts, prospective bidders were given a full six weeks' time to study the projects and make up their bids.

The first four contracts to be advertised and awarded include the following work: (1) Two and nine-tenths miles of freeway work in Contra Costa County extending from just north of the city limits of Hercules to the beginning of the bridge approach at Crockett; (2) The deep pier foundation work for the main bridge across Carquinez Strait; (3) The superstructure work, including the fabrication and erection of large steel double cantilever truss spans of the main bridge; and (4) The construction of the south approach and connecting interchange ramp spans through Crockett.

Contra Costa County Freeway Approach

The freeway project from Hercules to Crockett is exceptional not only because of the amount of money in-

Map showing the relation of the Carquinez Bridge and the Benicia-Martinez Bridge to the general San Francisco Bay area. ——▶

This map shows how approximately 12½ miles of US 40 between Richmond and the Carquinez Bridge will be relocated and constructed to full freeway standards by mid-1958 when the parallel Carquinez Bridge is expected to be completed. This section of US 40 now runs on congested San Pablo Avenue and takes a tortuous route through several communities of northern Contra Costa County. One contract is now under way and five others have been awarded. Now under construction and scheduled for completion in September, 1956, is a six-lane divided freeway between slightly south of Potrero Avenue in Richmond and south of Hilltop Drive, east of San Pablo, at a contract cost of $5,107,922.

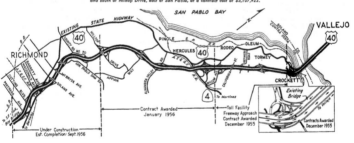

volved but because it includes the largest cut ever undertaken by the Division of Highways. The project includes 11,200,000 cubic yards of excavation and involves 455,000,000 station yards of overhaul.

Eight and one-half million cubic yards of this total excavation are to be taken from the big hill at the top of Crockett which has often been referred to as the "Big Cut." The depth at the largest section of this cut varies from 245 feet at the centerline of roadway to 350 feet at the high point to the side. The width at the top is 1,370 feet (about four average city blocks), and the total length is 3,000 feet.

Huge Excavation Job

To complete this 11,200,000 cubic yards of excavation on schedule the contractor must plan to excavate, haul and place about 30,000 cubic yards of excavation each working day. This is at a faster rate than called for in any of the contracts so far let by the Division of Highways.

It will be interesting to watch the contractor move in with his many pieces of heavy earth-moving equipment. The clockwork efficiency of his organization and equipment will pay big dividends for as can be seen a reduction in cost of as little as one cent a cubic yard will net a total saving to him of $112,000. The contractor's bid price for this roadway excavation was 25.6 cents per cubic yard.

Because of the size of this cut, preliminary studies included consideration of a tunnel. Geological conditions and economy of construction however, indicated considerable advantage to the open cut.

The "Big Cut"

To maintain structural stability the "Big Cut" will have two-to-one side slopes and horizontal benches 30 feet wide placed each 60 feet of depth. In addition, immediately following the excavation from top down to the first 30-foot wide bench, horizontal drains will be placed to drain underground water away and keep the sides of the cut dry, reducing the possibility of slides to a minimum. The drains will extend back into the sides of the cut for a distance of approximately 150

feet. This process of benching and draining will continue as excavation progresses from the top of cut on down to the final grade of the roadway. It is estimated that 20,000 lineal feet of these drains will be required.

Ten bids were received on this freeway job and Ferry Bros., John M. Ferry, Peter L. Ferry, L. A. and R. S. Crow, a joint venture of Glendale, California, contractors were the low bidders at $7,098,690.20.

Substructure Contract

The construction of the foundations for the main bridge across Carquinez Strait just 200 feet upstream from the existing bridge will require special skills and equipment for the deep water piers not often encountered in the usual highway contract.

The most spectacular operation in the construction of these foundations will be the sinking of large concrete caissons to bed rock approximately 135 feet below the surface of the water.

The lower portion of these piers, which measure 53 feet wide by 102 feet 6 inches long (about the size of a good city lot), will be precast at some location not far from the site of the bridge, launched into the waters of the bay and floated to the bridge site. At the bottom of these precast caissons will be a heavy fabricated steel cutting edge made from thick steel plates.

Positioning of Caissons

After being carefully positioned by heavy anchorages and guide towers,

additional sections will be added and the caissons will be lowered through the water and overburden to bedrock. The caissons will be lowered through the mud, sand and gravel by excavating material out from the bottom through 18 precast wells built into the caissons. In addition to excavation through these wells, provision will be made so that powerful streams of water can jet up from the sides of the cutting edges at the bottom if found necessary. These jets can cut away material from the sides and will reduce friction as the huge mass of concrete is gradually lowered to its final position on bedrock at the bottom.

During this sinking operation, which will take several months, great care must be exercised to keep the caisson from tipping or lowering too fast on one side or one corner. If it should get out of vertical then it must be righted by a carefully planned sequence of excavation and jetting.

Over half of the work in the foundation contract lies in these three caisson piers which will cost a little more than $1,000,000 each. Other work will include the construction of two shore piers and one water pier 50 feet wide by 113 feet long founded on 260 steel bearing piles driven to bedrock.

As can be seen in the picture of the bridge, the center tower will have an extensive pier protection or fender system which will be founded on large steel pipe piles 24 inches in diam-

1370 ft.

350 ft.

Architectural sketch of the "Big Cut" which helps to give one the feeling of immensity that will be gained on driving through

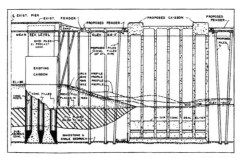

This sketch shows a section of the foundation work at the center tower of the bridge. To the right the section of the large concrete caisson is shown at its final resting place on bedrock at the bottom. To the left can be seen a half section of the existing caisson. The new and the old will be connected with one big fender protection system supported on the 24-inch-in-diameter 150-foot-long concrete-filled steel cylinder piles.

eter and 150 feet long, driven to bedrock and then filled with concrete. On top of these pipe piles will be placed large reinforced concrete girders and slabs surrounding the center tower and offering protection against navigation.

Five bids were received on the work involved in this contract. Mason and Hanger, Silas Mason Co., Inc. and F. S. Rolandi, Jr., Inc., a joint venture, were the low bidders at $5,454,694.16.

Superstructure Contract

The fabrication and erection of the superstructure of the main bridge across Carquinez Strait will also require special skills and equipment not usually encountered in normal highway construction.

There will be approximately 14,000 tons of steel to be erected 146 feet above the waters of Carquinez Strait. Because of the height, the depth and current of the water, and navigation requirements, most of this steel will be erected by cantilevering out from the piers to avoid the use of falsework. Each of the main spans of the double cantilever construction will be 1,100 feet long, with two side spans each 500 feet long and a central tower 150 feet in width.

The design of the new parallel bridge will be similar in span length and shape to the existing bridge but otherwise the two designs will be quite different because the new design will have a wider roadway and will incorporate several recent developments in modern bridge design.

Four Lanes of Traffic

The new structure will provide for four lanes of traffic on a 52-foot clear roadway supported by two trusses 60 feet apart. This will call for much heavier construction than the existing structure, which is 42 feet center to center of trusses and provides for only three lanes of traffic.

The new design features which make use of recent developments in bridge construction are: (1) the use of high strength bolts instead of rivets for field connections at the truss joints; (2) fabrication of the heavy truss members and floor beams by use of welding rather than riveting; and, (3) the use of a new high strength weldable steel nearly three times as strong as the ordinary structural steel used in bridge construction.

Bolted field connections were chosen in preference to rivets because the designers believe that field bolts will do their work with more assurance than the field driven rivets. In addition they feel that there is a good possibility that field bolts will show

economy over field rivets on truss connections of this magnitude. These bolts are ⅞ inch, 1 inch and 1¼ inch in diameter. The smaller bolts are used for secondary bracing member connections, the 1-inch bolts are used in the main truss joints, and the large size bolts are used for the exceptionally heavy center tower joints. One average truss joint will require approximately 600 of these 1-inch bolts. The whole job will require 570,000 pounds of bolts or six freight car loads.

Welded Fabrication of Trusses

Welded fabrication of truss members is relatively new, and the great advances that welding has made in the past few years indicate that considerable economy can be realized by fabricating the heavy truss members by this method. It reduces the number of parts to be fastened together and simplifies and speeds up both design room time and shop work. As an example there are 29,440,000 pounds of steel to be fabricated and the low bid for this steel was $8,091,776 which is an average of 27.49 cents per pound. If through simplified shop work the fabricating costs can be reduced by as much as one-half cent per pound, it will result in a saving of $147,000 for the superstructure contract.

Three types of steel were used in the design of these trusses, they were: (1) structural steel known as A7, (2) a somewhat higher strength low alloy steel known as A242, and (3) a recently developed extra high strength steel with good weldable qualities known as T1.

High Strength Steel

The use of this new extra high strength steel T1 capable of resisting 90,000 pounds per square inch when placed under tension, indicated a saving of approximately $800,000 according to design computations. This large saving in cost was made in spite of the fact that the base price for the new steel was approximately 5.7 cents per pound more than regular structural steel.

This extra high strength steel was used in only the very heavily stressed members of the trusses. Because the heavily stressed members require such large sections of steel they become

DIVISION OF HIGHWAYS   BRIDGE DEPARTMENT

Architectural sketch of the Crockett Interchange structure showing the approaches to the new and old bridge and the on and off ramps for use of traffic originating in the Crockett area

very stiff and when bent to conform to the large deflection of the 1,100 foot truss span, high internal bending stresses are set up. The vertical deflection of the trusses due to the dead weight of these long spans will be as much as 27 inches. The smaller these individual members are the less resistance they offer to the trusses conforming to this 27-inch deflection and therefore the smaller will be their stress due to bending. As an example the weight of one of these heavily stressed members would be 748 pounds per foot when designed of low alloy steel and only 400 pounds per foot when designed of this extra high strength steel. The high strength steels therefore made it possible to reduce the size of these heavily stressed members an appreciable amount and resulted in a considerable savings in the final cost.

Four bids were received on this project, which is the largest contract let to date by the Division of Highways. The low bidder was the United States Steel Corporation who submitted a bid of $9,489,126. This is the same firm that fabricated and erected the steel superstructure for the existing Carquinez Bridge and the San Francisco-Oakland Bay Bridge.

Crockett Interchange Structure

The south end of the main bridge structure will connect to a series of approach girder spans and ramp connections known as the Crockett Interchange Structure.

Traffic headed south from Sacramento and wishing to turn off at Crockett will use the existing bridge and the existing approach spans as an off ramp.

Traffic heading north from San Francisco and wishing to turn off at Crockett will be provided with a ramp taking off from the end of the "Big Cut" and swinging down under the approach spans and entering Crockett near the present intersection of Pomona Street and the existing highway. Crockett traffic headed for San Francisco will take off at this same intersection by use of a southbound on ramp. Crockett traffic headed toward Sacramento will take off from Pomona Street near Seventh Avenue and turn

north by use of an on ramp. All of these connections will provide this area an easy access to the freeway and when completed will, figuratively speaking, place Crockett and vicinity at the front door to the San Francisco Bay area.

48 Girder Spans

The plans for this interchange structure call for the construction of approximately 48 girder spans ranging in length from 120 feet to 180 feet. These girder spans will require the fabrication of 4,250 tons of structural steel and the placing of 25,000 cubic yards of concrete.

In addition to this structural work there will be considerable grading and paving for the relocation of city streets. Approximately 300,000 square feet of new pavement will be placed in Crockett.

Architectural sketch showing how the Toll Plaza will appear on the Vallejo end approaching the bridge

Unfortunately the construction work in this area will make it necessary for more than 70 families living in the Crockett vicinity to find new dwellings. As is often the case with improvements that benefit all of the people, a few are sometimes temporarily inconvenienced.

Because of the sudden nature and rapid development of this Carquinez Bridge project since the last session of the State Legislature, families whose property is required for the construction of the interchange and the relocation of the city streets, have not had sufficient time to adequately provide for new homes. In order to relieve this situation, the State has provided that families may remain in their dwellings if necessary until July 1, 1956. In any event the relocation of this many families in a very small community like Crockett does involve hardships. The people of Crockett have faced this situation courageously and in a spirit of cooperation. We are sure that all who will benefit from this project appreciate this spirit of cooperation.

Eleven bids were received on the work involved in the construction of this interchange structure and local road improvements. Peter Kiewit Sons Company was the low bidder at $4,661,462.

Future Contracts

In addition to these four contracts to be financed by Series A bonds there remains to be let a contract for the work from the north end of the bridge to a point about 0.2 miles north of the existing Vallejo Wye. This contract will include the construction of the Toll Plaza and Administration Building, and the widening of the Vallejo Wye. In order to adequately handle traffic with a minimum of delay it is planned to have 16 on-side toll booths for the initial construction with provision for four additional booths as traffic increases. This work is scheduled for advertisement in May of 1956.

A small mechanical and electrical contract is also to be advertised early in the spring of 1956. This work will provide for electrical power for beacon and navigation lights, and supply compressed air for maintenance operations of the two bridges.

Contractors and resident engineers gathered at the site of parallel Carquinez Bridge to discuss start of project.

TOP ROW, LEFT TO RIGHT: Russell G. Cone, Vice President, Mason and Hanger, and Project Manager for the substructure contract of the Main Bridge with Mason and Hanger, Silas Mason Co., Inc., and F. S. Rolandi, Jr., Inc.; E. E. McKeen, Erecting Manager for the steel work on the superstructure of the Main Bridge with United States Steel Corporation; F. S. Rolandi, Jr., Contractor on the substructure contract with Mason and Hanger, Silas Mason Co., Inc., and F. S. Rolandi, Jr., Inc., joint venture; Homer Olsen, Job Superintendent on the Crockett Interchange structure with Peter Kiewit Sons' Co.; L. G. "Bud" Waigand, Job Sponsor on the Crockett Interchange Structure with Peter Kiewit Sons' Co.; R. C. "Dick" Philbert, Superintendent of earth moving operations on the "big cut" job with Ferry Bros., John M. Ferry, Peter L. Ferry and Sons, and L. A. and R. S. Crow; Robert Hoyt, Superintendent of excavation on the Crockett interchange structure with Peter Kiewit Sons' Co.; J. L. "Jim" Ferry, Contractor on the freeway contract including the "big cut" with Ferry Bros., John M. Ferry, Peter L. Ferry and Sons and L. A. and R. S. Crow, a joint venture; P. R. "Pat" Ferry, Contractor on the freeway contract including the "big cut"; Albert Lindquist, Superintendent bridge construction on the freeway contract.

LOWER ROW, LEFT TO RIGHT: Oscar Johnson, Senior Bridge Engineer, representative of the Division of Highways on the substructure and superstructure contracts for the Main Bridge and the Crockett Interchange contract; Wallace H. Ames, Associate Bridge Engineer, assistant resident engineer on the three-bridge structure contracts; Francis Donaldson, Vice President, Mason and Hanger Co. here from his New York office to look over the job on the foundation work for the Main Bridge; V. O. Smith, Senior Highway Engineer, representative of the Division of Highways on two large freeway contracts to the south of the bridge, one of which includes the contract for the "big cut" job; C. P. Sweet, Resident Engineer on the freeway contract including the "big cut."

Following the completion of the new bridge late in 1958 all traffic on the existing bridge will be stopped and routed temporarily over the new structure. This will be necessary in order to make the connections between the old bridge and the new approaches and ramps in Crockett. In addition the curbs on the old structure will be rebuilt and the roadway resurfaced to provide for 34 feet 4 inches between curbs, making the structure safer for the three lanes of traffic than is now provided by the 30-foot roadway width.

Completion in 1958

This work will be timed for advertisement in the summer of 1957 so that the contractor will have ample time to get his materials purchased and structural steel fabricated and be ready to start construction immediately after opening the new bridge to traffic. This will reduce to a minimum the period that traffic in both directions will be required to use the four lanes of the new bridge. Upon completion of this contract all southbound traffic will be switched back to the old bridge and

... Continued on page 66

Magazine Street Interchange on US 40 in Vallejo Area

By ROY M. CHALMERS, Project Design Engineer, District X

Independent of the Carquinez Toll Bridge Project but a future integral part of it in operation, an interchange at Magazine Street in Vallejo is now under construction as the first step toward conversion of US Highway 40 in and near Vallejo to full freeway standards.

A contract was awarded on December 5, 1955, for the construction of the interchange and an overcrossing at Magazine Street, a frontage road west of the existing highway between Sequoia and Alhambra Streets, and the realignment of the intersection at Magazine Street east of the existing highway.

The work is scheduled for completion in the summer of 1956, so that it will be of benefit to through and local traffic for two years before the scheduled operation of the over-all Carquinez Toll Bridge Project.

Traffic Volumes High

Since US 40 is the main highway between Sacramento and the San Francisco Bay area, traffic volumes are currently high and are expected to increase materially in the future. The construction of this overcrossing and interchange at Magazine Street will eliminate one of the undesirable connections at grade existing along this route. Traffic moving through this

Historic bid opening. First day of four successive days of bidding on four Carquinez Bridge projects. LEFT TO RIGHT: Morby Swanson, Richard H. Wilson, Assistant State Highway Engineer; Frank Palermo of Wilson's staff; State Highway Engineer Geo. T. McCoy.

intersection is presently delayed by traffic-actuated signals made necessary by the large volume of cross traffic. The 1954 average daily traffic count indicates that there are approximately 1,000 cars a day crossing the highway at this point and 20,000 cars a day traveling along the main highway. In addition, there are approximately 1,400 cars a day making left turns.

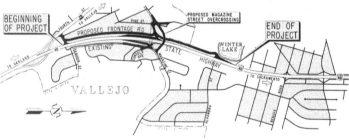

These large volumes of conflicting traffic movements are the principal contributing cause of a high accident frequency.

The construction of this overcrossing and accompanying interchange should markedly reduce these accidents in the future, when the traffic signals are removed and uninterrupted flow is permitted.

Frontage Road

The urban type frontage road planned for west of the highway, and terminating opposite Alhambra Street on this project, will ultimately be connected with a proposed frontage road from the north to become a part of the over-all development through Vallejo. This frontage road is to be constructed with two 12-foot lanes with an 8-foot paved shoulder on the outside and a barrier curb next to the outer separation between the freeway.

The existing east connection of Magazine Street will be improved by constructing a standard deceleration lane which in turn requires realigning the present frontage road east of the highway. A portion of the existing acceleration lane will be retained for use until the highway is widened to a six-lane freeway.

The approaches to the overcrossing have been designed with two 12-foot traveling lanes, and paved 5-foot shoulders, bordered with metal guard rail.

A considerable volume of pedestrian traffic across the freeway at this location is anticipated due to the rapidly growing urban development. Pedestrian crossings at grade are presently controlled by traffic signals. Provision will be made for pedestrians to use the overcrossing by construction of a sidewalk on the structure and a walk outside the guard rail on the approaches.

All features of these improvements have been positioned to accommodate the development of this highway into a divided six-lane freeway.

Vallejo, like many other California towns, has been growing rapidly in the past few years. One of the major present and future development areas lies east and southeast of the Magazine Street intersection. The elimination of this grade crossing will prove to be a

RETIREMENTS FROM SERVICE

Hans P. Williamson

A testimonial banquet and party at the Richmond Golf Club on the evening of December 16, 1955, attended by many friends and colleagues, honored the retirement of Hans P. Williamson, Senior Engineer of the Division of San Francisco Bay Toll Crossings.

Williamson was born on November 29, 1885, near Ludington, Michigan, and was educated in the Michigan public schools. In 1916 he graduated from the University of Michigan,

HANS P. WILLIAMSON

receiving a bachelor of civil engineering degree. His first work after graduation was with Babcock & Wilcox and Carnegie Steel Company in Ohio and Pennsylvania, respectively, where he was employed in the design of plant buildings and maintenance engineering.

In 1920 Williamson went to Portland, Oregon, where he was married to Helen A. Cowles who had preceded him in the westward migration from Michigan. He worked in Portland for consulting engineers on building and industrial plant design and on steel fabricators.

The Williamsons moved to California in the spring of 1922, and after short engineering engagements with private concerns in Northern California, Williamson entered his first State service in the Division of Highways, Bridge Department, Sacramento, in November, 1923. For approximately two and one-half years he worked on design of steel and concrete spans for many of California's

valuable asset to the city by permitting uninterrupted transportation between the metropolitan section west of the main highway and one of its rapidly growing residential areas east of the freeway.

early highway bridges. He resigned this position in July, 1926, to return to Oakland to join the Pacific Coast Engineering Company.

In June of 1933 Williamson rejoined the state service in the Design Department of the San Francisco-Oakland Bay Bridge. Except for a short period of transfer to the Division of Architecture in 1938, Williamson remained with the San Francisco-Oakland Bay Bridge project until December, 1940.

In the following year Williamson returned to the Bridge Department of the Division of Highways in Sacramento, working on designs for many modern bridges in the state highway system until April, 1949, when he was transferred to the Division of San Francisco Bay Toll Crossings.

Since coming to Bay Toll Crossings and until his retirement on November 30, 1955, Williamson has been senior engineer (SFBTC) in direct charge of groups engaged in all aspects of superstructure design, including those for the proposed parallel crossing for the San Francisco-Oakland Bay Bridge and for the Richmond-San Rafael Bridge which is to be opened to traffic in October, 1956.

The Williamsons plan to travel to Michigan during 1956 but will return to their home at 3589 Fruitvale Avenue in Oakland. A son, Stanley C. Williamson, who is a teacher for the San Pablo School District, resides with them.

NO TRAFFIC PROBLEM

In 1895 there were only four passenger cars registered in the United States.

FIRST RACE

The first automobile race in America was held in Chicago on Thanksgiving Day, 1895.

LAKE ALMANOR

Lake Almanor, one of California's largest artificial lakes, is 45 miles in length.

Southern Crossing

By NORMAN C. RAAB
Projects Engineer

THE DIVISION of San Francisco Bay Toll Crossings, of the Department of Public Works, presented its report on the feasibility of financing and constructing a Southern Crossing of San Francisco Bay to the California Toll Bridge Authority at its meeting in Sacramento on December 13, 1955. An appropriation for the preparation of this report was authorized by the Legislature in the 1953 session.

The proposed Southern Crossing of San Francisco Bay will have its westerly terminus in the vicinity of Third and Army Streets in San Francisco, and its easterly terminus on Bay Farm Island in the City of Alameda.

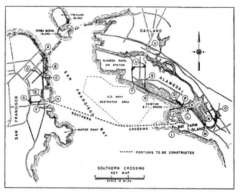

CONSTRUCTION BASED ON 25 CENT TOLL

Freeway connections from the bridge termini are to be made to the Bayshore and Eastshore Freeways on both sides of the Bay.

The Toll Bridge Authority has filed the report with the State Legislature for consideration of suggested amendments to the statutes pertaining to the approach system on both sides of the Bay, and for further policy determination. It is anticipated that the report will be before the Legislature at a special session in March of this year.

Numerous engineering, economic, and other factual matters relating to the construction of the Southern Crossing have been presented and discussed in the preceding parts of this report. The following conclusions can be made:

1. Although many difficult and unusual problems will be encountered, the entire project is feasible from an engineering and construction standpoint.

2. Contract plans and specifications for the largest single unit, the underwater crossing of the transbay section, will be completed and bids could be received by the early part of 1956. This procedure will indicate, prior to the sale of bonds, whether construc-

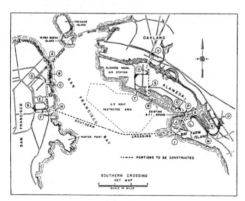

CONSTRUCTION BASED ON 30 CENT TOLL

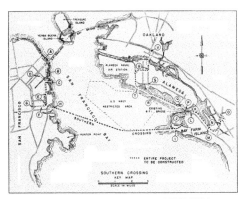

SOUTHERN CROSSING
KEY MAP

SCALE IN MILES

CONSTRUCTION BASED ON 35 CENT TOLL

tion costs are within financing limits.

3. Contingent upon receiving favorable bids on the underwater crossing work and the sale of revenue bonds, construction of the transbay crossing could start in the latter part of 1956.

4. It is estimated that the transbay crossing could be opened to traffic in 4½ years after the start of construction; the entire project including approaches could be completed in 5½ years.

5. The project as described by the statutes and reported on herein could be financed with an automobile toll of 35 cents on the Southern Crossing and a toll increase to 35 cents on the Bay Bridge at the time the Southern

Crossing is opened to traffic; however, this report does not take into consideration approach revisions as described and outlined in the *Assembly Journal* for March 23, 1955.

6. The entire project except the overwater crossing, with minimum approaches to street level, is adaptable to stage construction.

7. The accompanying Table IX-1 shows estimated length of the project that could be built together with the amounts of revenue bonds that could be redeemed by tolls obtained from users of the Bay Bridge and the Southern Crossing and put into effect at the time the latter is opened to traffic.

R. L. Bishop New State Highway Commissioner

After 12 years of devoted service as a member of the California Highway Commission, F. Walter Sandelin of Ukiah tendered his resignation to Governor Knight in December. On

R. L. BISHOP

January 13th the Governor appointed Robert L. Bishop, auto dealer of Santa Rosa, to succeed him. Bishop was named for a four-year term. His appointment is subject to confirmation by the State Senate.

In a letter to Governor Knight, Sandelin said, 'Serving as a member of the commission has been an esteemed privilege and an honor. I am grateful to have had the opportunity of participating in the California highway building program."

Sandelin was first appointed by Governor Earl Warren in 1943 and reappointed in 1944, 1948, and 1952.

The new commissioner was born in Springfield, Missouri, in 1897.

He is a member of the Santa Rosa City Board of Public Utilities and the citizens' advisory committee for the

... Continued on page 45

TABLE IX-1

Auto toll (cents)	Bond issue ($1,000)	Repayment (years)	Project, miles			Total
			West Bay	Trans Bay	East Bay	
25.............	180,000	27	1.5	7.5	2.5	11.5
30.............	225,000	30	4.0	7.5	6.5	18.0
35.............	250,000	30	5.5	7.5	11.5	24.5

By T. W. RODGERS, Senior Bridge Engineer

Bridges on state highways in Northern and Central California were struck a severe blow by the warm snow-melting storm of Christmas week 1955, which turned normally controllable streams into raging torrents. Five structures, three being classified as major bridges, were completely destroyed and 17 others were damaged to the extent that their use by vehicular traffic stopped. Countless others will require major to minor repairs but their use, for the time being, has not been restricted. An early estimate indicates that about $2,000,000 will be required to return the destroyed and damaged structures to permanent standards; in addition, approximately a quarter of a million dollars has been spent to close the missing gaps on an emergency basis so that traffic service could be restored as soon as possible.

More Work to Be Done

In addition to the losses known at this time, subsiding waters in rivers and creeks are expected to reveal serious weakening of bridge pier foundations. Fortunately this weakening halted in time to keep spans from collapsing but the defects must be repaired before future high flows can complete the job of destruction. Cost of this work quite easily could reach a quarter of a million dollars due to large number of structures possibly affected.

Bridges under construction on routes not yet open to public travel also suffered flood damage estimated at this writing to amount to approximately $100,000. Falsework was weakened and will have to be rebuilt. In some cases the progress of contractor's work had not reached the superstructure, thus leaving piers and abutments in less favorable position to withstand fast currents than if all members had been completed so as to tie them together.

Dangerous Debris Drift

While high water is often considered responsible for destruction of bridges, this menace alone will quite often leave a structure virtually unscathed. Actually, the real villians are the accompanying threats, drift and scour. They pack the lethal punch, producing tremendous forces and excessive currents, that will send the stoutest of man-made works to oblivion. The story of the Christmas storm as it affected bridges again illustrates this fact. The urgency of drift removal explains the presence of state highway crews and equipment on bridges during the period of high flow.

Although the drift problem is usually associated with Northern California counties, where the natural litter of the forests and the residue of logging operations along streams creates an annual headache for highway maintenance forces, it also occurs in Central California. There the same trouble occurs from the local habit of dumping prunings, parts of fruit trees and other rubbish in normal dry creek beds. The huge mound of such debris which packed the channel entrance to the Saratoga Creek bridge and contributed to the lengthy overflow of the Bayshore Highway (US 101 Bypass) north of Santa Clara is a good example.

Although the cases of bridges submerged were well scattered throughout Northern and Central California, the most sizable damages and greatest monetary losses were concentrated in Humboldt, Siskiyou and Trinity Counties. The partial account that follows describes some of the most serious damage as well as other experiences of interest.

HUMBOLDT COUNTY

The major bridge over the Trinity River at Hoopa on State Sign Route 96 was the most serious loss of the storm due to its size and the isolating of towns to the north. The unprecedented flow, after rising above deck level, literally floated the smaller steel truss span out of sight, dumped the 225-foot main span into the channel, and toppled concrete piers. Crossing this large river immediately with a temporary structure was a difficult problem.

Farther north on this route between Orleans and Weitchpec all trestle spans and an abutment of the Bluff Creek bridge were washed away, completing the isolation of the latter community. Fortunately the main steel truss span was left intact so that returning the bridge to service will be made easier.

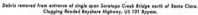

Debris removed from entrance of single span Saratoga Creek Bridge north of Santa Clara. Clogging flooded Bayshore Highway, US 101 Bypass.

34

North of Arcata on US 101 four timber trestle spans adjoining the main spans were carried away from the swollen Mad River and several nearby trestles were damaged sufficiently to interrupt traffic.

South of Eureka on State Highway Route 56 the big Eel River bridge at Fernbridge suffered the loss of the westerly concrete span and several connecting spans settled precariously.

Railroad Bridge Used

At Carlotta on State Sign Route 36 the undermining and partial toppling of a pier of the Yager Creek bridge left the continuous steel beam spans suspended in midair, closing the bridge to traffic. Although a project after the January, 1953, flood had deepened pier foundations, the massive collection of drift this time was too much to resist. Had not the Northwestern Pacific Railroad Company made its parallel bridge available for motor traffic, towns to the east would have been cut off for some time from the coastal area.

Several miles north of Garberville and just west of US 101 the joint county-state park bridge over the South Fork of Eel River in Whitmore

Grove State Park was weakened by high water and the battering of drift against truss members in the 300-foot main span. Until repaired, traffic was restricted to light cars only.

SISKIYOU COUNTY

Near Hamburg on State Sign Route 96 the two large steel truss spans of the Scott River bridge were carried away and the main pier destroyed, isolating Happy Camp and other Klamath River towns until a detour could be provided.

Another Scott River bridge, this one at Fort Jones on State Highway Route 82, was completely washed away although of modern concrete design. The center pier of the two-span bridge at nearby Kidder Creek dropped several feet due to undermining, seriously damaging it. The major forest fires in Siskiyou County late last summer, which permit quick concentrated runoffs from denuded hills and mountains, are believed mainly responsible for these losses.

On US 299 at Douglas City the concrete pier columns of the westerly spans of the Trinity River bridge were broken by the brutal pounding of giant logs and trees carried by the

extremely high water. These three concrete end spans after this loss of support collapsed completely. Traffic was restored to this main west-east Northern California route by the emergency installation of Army type Bailey bridge units that provided a one-lane temporary span so located to permit construction of permanent spans beneath later.

Further west on US 299, high water rose to deck level at the Trinity River bridge at Cedar Flat. Hard pressed maintenance men, foreseeing the danger, bulldozed away the top of the adjacent road fills, making more room for the raging river and relieving the pressure on the bridge. Even so, lower truss members suffered considerable damage. Their action undoubtedly saved the structure from the same fate experienced down-river at Hoopa.

PLUMAS COUNTY

Just south of Blairsden on State Sign Route 89 the recently completed bridge over the Middle Fork of the Feather River carried traffic without interruption while the former steel truss span several miles upstream which formerly served this route was closed due to high water. An accompanying shift in the main channel flow undermined a main pier of the old bridge, causing several feet of settlement. Supports under approach spans were swept away.

Several miles further south on Route 89 the oblique flow of meandering Sulphur Creek caused the undermining of all three bridge piers but the toughness of this continuous concrete slab design preserved it so that after peak flow subsided, light traffic was allowed to use the structure.

LASSEN COUNTY

In the southeast corner of Lassen County Long Valley Creek burst its banks, harassing travelers who had chosen to use US 395 along California's eastern boundary to escape the closures on the other trans-Sierra highways. The bridge four miles south of Doyle was completely lost, causing the blocking of US 395. A detour 60 miles west over US 40 Alternate crossed another Long Valley Creek bridge. A partial washout here re-

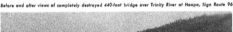

Before and after views of completely destroyed 440-foot bridge over Trinity River at Hoopa, Sign Route 96

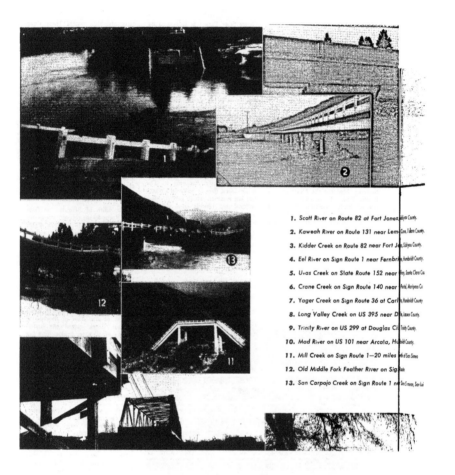

1. Scott River on Route 82 at Fort Jones, Siskiyou County.

2. Kaweah River on Route 131 near Lemon Cove, Tulare County.

3. Kidder Creek on Route 82 near Fort Jones, Siskiyou County.

4. Eel River on Sign Route 1 near Fernbridge, Humboldt County.

5. Uvas Creek on State Route 152 near Gilroy, Santa Clara Co.

6. Crane Creek on Sign Route 140 near Portal, Mariposa Co.

7. Yager Creek on Sign Route 36 at Carlotta, Humboldt County

8. Long Valley Creek on US 395 near Doyle, Lassen County.

9. Trinity River on US 299 at Douglas City, Trinity County.

10. Mad River on US 101 near Arcata, Humboldt County.

11. Mill Creek on Sign Route 1—20 miles north of San Simeon

12. Old Middle Fork Feather River on Sign Route

13. San Carpojo Creek on Sign Route 1 near San Simeon, San Luis

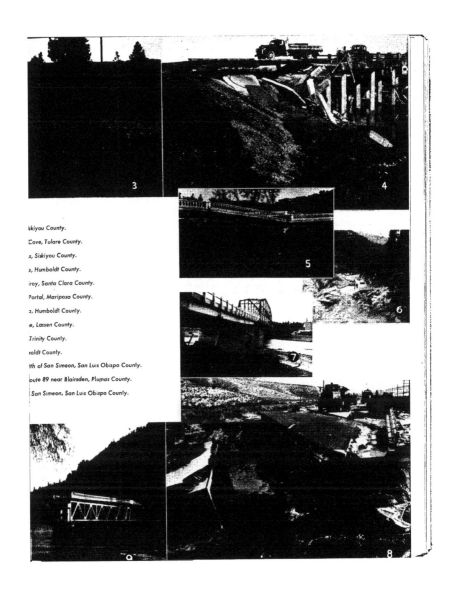

stricted traffic to one lane and for a
time threatened to cut this last remaining trans-Sierra link.

SUTTER AND YUBA COUNTIES

State highway bridges in this area,
the scene of the costly and tragic
Feather River levee break which inundated Yuba City, remained intact and
escaped serious injury although river
levels were exceedingly high. The veteran concrete structure on US 99E
over the Yuba River at Marysville,
known locally as the D Street bridge,
was overtopped and abandoned for a
time as the river rose upward to tops
of the main dikes. It was reopened to
traffic after the water had receded, no
serious structural defects being apparent.

North of Marysville on US 40 Alternate the timber trestle over Simmerly Slough was under 10 feet of
water, the bridge deck being almost
that distance below the nearby levee
top. This relatively quiet backwater
of the Feather River did not disturb
the buoyant structure however, and it
was returned to service as soon as
minor road damage on this route could
be repaired.

Before and after views of demolished 200-foot Scott River Bridge near Hamburg, Sign Route 96

Chipps Creek Bridge on US 40 Alternate near Belden buried in silt and rock carried by rampant stream.
insert shows digging out operation.

A few miles east of Yuba County in
Sierra County the North Fork Yuba
River ran rough shod over the three
steel truss spans on historic Highway
49. During the height of the storm
they were submerged under several
feet of fast water and pounded by
giant timber. Miraculously the structure escaped destruction. Although
damaged, its capacity was not impaired sufficiently to prevent its use
afterwards.

SANTA CLARA COUNTY

Uvas Creek rose to deck level on
the bridge west of Gilroy on Hecker
Pass Road, State Sign Route 152,
causing the undermining and partial
collapse of two concrete spans after
a large tree lodged against a pier.

Heavy rainfall forced many streams
over their banks and the Madrone
Underpass and Agnew Underpass on
US 101 and US 101 Alternate filled
like giant bathtubs when this overland
sweep of water become more than
pumps could handle.

MARIPOSA COUNTY

Up State Sign Route 140, the Yosemite All-year Highway, road damages along the Merced River were
heavy and a number of bridges were
left standing alone like ghosts by
washed gaps in road approaches. Only
the all-concrete Crane Creek bridge

Emergency Bailey Bridge being pushed across gap in Trinity River Bridge at Douglas City, US 299

near El Portal was impassable with one abutment projecting into midair over a gaping cavity caused by stream erosion.

TULARE COUNTY

The Kaweah River, cresting at record heights, hammered successively at seven state highway structures down the rocky canyons of the Sierra and over the San Joaquin Valley, carrying the debris of decades. Near the entrance to Sequoia National Park on State Sign Route 198 the river was reported over the three concrete arch spans at Pumpkin Hollow, tearing away road approaches.

North of Lemon Cove the overflow onto lowlands kept water from over-topping the bridge on State Highway Route 131 but drift and scour never-theless caused the settlement of one pier. North of Exeter on State Sign Route 65, the river running several feet over the deck, formed a dam of debris that forced the water through the road approaches beyond the ends of the bridge. Only one concrete piling was broken on the structure, however.

MONTEREY AND SAN LUIS OBISPO COUNTIES

The only major bridge damage in this area was along scenic State Sign Route 1 which follows the California coast line. Near San Simeon fast cur-

rents in San Carpojo Creek under-mined a concrete pier under the main truss span and it settled several feet. Two other timber spans sagged when their underpinnings were carried away.

Large logs battered vital truss members of Trinity River structure at Cedar Flat, US 299. Bridge saved by diverting flow through gap bulldozed in road fill.

Ten miles north the log span which is located on the slide at White Creek and is accustomed to movement during heavy precipitation slid down the hill several feet at one end. At Mill Creek, 10 miles further north, both abutments of this three-span steel structure slid down the precipitous mountain side, leaving end span beams hanging pre-cariously from the remaining piers.

While lack of space prevents telling of the emergency and other measures taken by various units of the Division of Highways to protect, restore and repair bridges, it must be said that the job was pushed through hectic, some-times seemingly endless, days with an inspiring team spirit by all that helped make the task easier.

READER PLEASED

CLOSE FOLLOWING

Rear-end collisions are one of the most common traffic accidents and yet they're so easy to avoid. All you have to do is allow enough room between your car and the vehicle ahead. What's "enough room"? One car length for each 10 miles per hour of your speed is a fairly safe margin at speeds up to 50. Above that allow a little more.

WHEELS WERE INCLUDED

Back in 1906, fenders for automo-biles were sold as extra equipment, notes the California State Automobile Association.

STANDING TIMBER

Oregon has more standing timber than any other state in the Union.

TURBO-JETS BURN FUEL FAST

A medium-power turbo-jet aircraft engine burns its own weight in petro-leum fuel every 20 minutes.

Traffic Bar

Durable Installation Is Developed
In Materials and Research Laboratory

By *HERBERT A. ROONEY, Associate Chemical Testing Engineer* and
JAMES A. CECHETINI, Assistant Physical Testing Engineer

THE PROJECT described in this article was in response to a request from Headquarters Maintenance that the

On January 21, 1955, an experimental installation was made at the Fulton Avenue and U. S. 40 intersec-

tion east of Sacramento as shown in *Photograph No. 1.* Twelve of the longitudinal and transverse bars at the

Materials and Research Department develop a durable adhesive for cementing concrete traffic bars in place. The object was to eliminate the steel dowels heretofore used in fastening concrete bars to a road surface.

Dowels remaining on a highway become a traffic hazard when a bar is knocked loose or shattered by impact. The asphalt emulsion type adhesive currently used with one type of traffic bar does not maintain its bond to a road surface when the bars are subjected to frequent impact. An epoxy-thiokol adhesive developed in the laboratory under the direction of E. D. Botts, Senior Chemical Testing Engineer, was used for bonding experimental concrete traffic bars to the concrete road surface on this project.

UPPER—Experimental traffic bars immediately after installation. LOWER—Traffic bars cemented with asphalt emulsion after two to three months.

Experimental bars after 11 months

east end of the dividing strip between the westbound and left turn lanes were removed and replaced by concrete bars made in the department and cemented in place with the epoxy-thiokol adhesive. The layer of asphalt emulsion remaining on the road surface after taking up the old traffic bars was removed and clean concrete exposed by the use of a concrete abrasion machine.

The epoxy-thiokol adhesive used in this installation has exceptional bonding power to clean portland cement or asphaltic concrete surfaces. For this reason it was deemed sufficient to apply the adhesive only to a zone one inch wide around the perimeter at the bottom of the bar. The location was ideal for the test in that the traffic bars dividing the two traffic lanes were hit frequently by trucks and many bars of the previous installation had been moved or broken.

Composition of Experimental Bars

The experimental concrete bars, designed by L. P. Kovanda and J. A. Cechetini of the Concrete Section, have the same cross section dimensions as illustrated in the 1949 Maintenance Manual, page 393, except they are recessed on the bottom to reduce weight and are cast in sections one foot long to reduce the difficulties in handling and in application to irregular road surfaces. The facing or outer portion of the bars to a depth of three-eighths of an inch is composed of white portland cement, titanium dioxide white pigment and glass spheres as an aggregate. The inner portion of the bars is composed of ordinary portland cement mortar. With this composition the bars are inherently reflective and do not require periodic painting and beading of the surface as any wear exposes new beads.

Results of Test

Prior to this test installation, it was necessary to replace several of the bars which were cemented with asphalt emulsion every few months. The bars had either worked loose or were shattered by traffic, as shown in *Photograph No. 2.* Despite the constant impact of trucks in the past year, none of the experimental concrete bars cemented with epoxy-thiokol adhesive has worked loose. The bars have shown excellent resistance to the severe abrasion and impact to which they have been subjected. *Photograph No. 3* shows the condition of the experimental installation after approximately 11 months. *Photograph No. 4* is a closer view of part of the installation after 11 months.

Conclusion

Although this project was confined to a portland cement road surface, preliminary laboratory test data and results obtained from actual road tests in cementing traffic buttons to an asphalt plant-mixed surface indicate similar satisfactory results should be obtained by using the epoxy-thiokol adhesive for the installation of these concrete traffic bars on plant-mix highways. The epoxy-thiokol adhesive is more expensive than asphalt emulsion, but considering the fact that less of the former is used and a more permanent job obtained, the comparative over-all costs would appear to favor the type of installation described, especially in areas where traffic bars are subject to impact by traffic.

Experimental bars after 11 months, closeup

Public Hearings

Highway Commission Seeks Full Information on Freeway Routings

By FRANK B. DURKEE, Director of Public Works

WITH MORE than 10 percent of the motor vehicles in the entire Nation registered in California, this State has for years had a tremendous problem of providing adequate highways. The continued rapid increase in population and traffic during and since World War II has made the development of modern freeways along the principal state highway routes a matter of extreme urgency for the safety and welfare of our people.

Fortunately, California has had during this critical period the advantage of forward-looking legislation on which to base the steady expansion of its freeway network in accordance with sound long-range planning.

From the standpoint of future development, one of the gravest responsibilities delegated by the Legislature to any state agency is that of route adoption—the spelling out of highway locations between termini or control points established by Legislature when it designates a route as a state highway. Determination of routings, particularly freeway routings, is the keystone of the highway program in this State.

Commission Responsibility

Recognizing that state highway routings are matters of state-wide effect and interest, the Legislature has vested full authority for route determination in the California Highway Commission. The commission is by law a seven-man body which "shall represent the State at large * * *." (Sec. 70.2, Streets and Highways Code.)

Throughout the years the commission has sought to discharge most conscientiously the responsibility for route determination on the basis of the greatest good to the greatest number.

At the same time, the Highway Commission takes full cognizance of the needs and desires of the individual

Typical of the meetings called by the Division of Highways for public information and discussion of tentative freeway routing proposals is this session in the Mendocino County Courthouse in Ukiah on January 17, 1956. It was the second such meeting in the case of a proposed freeway route for US 101 in the vicinity of Ukiah, called by District Engineer A. S. Hart of District I. Hart is using a large aerial mosaic of the Ukiah area in his presentation.

communities, large and small, which the freeways must traverse. It is the commission's firmly established policy, originally stated in 1948 in a resolution which has since been revised and expanded, to give every possible consideration to local interest consistent with the solution of the over-all traffic problem.

Full Public Information

The commission's policy calls for full public information concerning the various alternative routings studied by the Division of Highways, public meetings at which the engineering and economic data can be explained and questioned, and, if desired or considered necessary by the local governmental authorities, a public hearing by the commission. As a part of this procedure, the commission may and some-

times does schedule public hearings on its own initiative.

Only after full opportunity has been provided for the presentation of all facts and arguments does the commission take final action to adopt a route and declare it a freeway.

The next major step before construction can begin involves a *freeway agreement* between the State and the city or county (or both) concerned. This freeway agreement spells out the necessary adjustments of local streets and roads as a result of the proposed freeway.

Section 100.2 of the Streets and Highways Code makes a freeway agreement mandatory before any local street or road can be closed by the State. The State may, legally, proceed with freeway construction without an agreement, as long as separation struc-

for greater local traffic safety and relief of local congestion. The adoption of a freeway location also establishes the pattern and often provides the opportunity for sound, long-range planning of the community, for urban renewal, and other developments.

The engineers of the Division of Highways have had the full benefit of the thinking of engineers and planners of the respective cities and counties in solving freeway location problems in the public interest. This cooperative approach is undoubtedly another factor in California's nationally recognized leadership in freeway development, which has grown out of our sound structure of laws governing route determination and freeway agreements, supplemented by a Highway Commission policy of full consideration for local as well as statewide needs.

TEACHER USES MAGAZINE

THE UNIVERSITY OF NEW MEXICO
Albuquerque, New Mexico

California Highways and Public Works

GENTLEMEN: I would like to thank you for continuing to send me *California Highways and Public Works*. I have found this magazine to be of great value to me as a teacher and an excellent source of material for my classes in Highway Engineering. The articles on the effect of freeways on the economy of surrounding areas are of special interest.

Very truly yours,

MARVIN CLARK MAY
Associate Professor

RACING WASTES GAS

Don't race your engine while waiting for the light to turn green, advises the National Automobile Club. Let the other fellow get away first if he wants to, and waste his gas!

OLDEST FORMATIONS

The Alabama Hills, located to the west of Lone Pine in Inyo County, are reported by the National Automobile Club to be among the oldest geological formations on this continent.

UPPER—Shows the front portion of the Chico State College auditorium on January 20, 1956. On the stage at the right of the picture are four members of the California Highway Commission, conducting the public hearing; at the two tables at the left are engineers of the Division of Highways, who used the maps in the background to explain their recommended and possible alternatives for a freeway location for US 99E in the Chico area. The speaker, standing in the first row with back to camera, is Mayor Theodore Meriam of Chico. LOWER—Shows the same auditorium on July 14, 1955, at a public meeting called by District Engineer A. M. Nash of District III to explain the results of freeway routing studies in the Chico area. The speaker in foreground is Dr. H. Thurston Hatch, Chico superintendent of schools. (Lower photo courtesy of Chico Enterprise-Record.)

tures are provided for every local road or street intersection; but in practice, this has never been seriously considered. Negotiations leading to freeway agreements have occasionally extended over a period of years.

Experience in many parts of California has shown properly located freeways to be beneficial to the local community as well as to traffic. The improved service thus provided to large volumes of vehicles also makes

and Public Works

JOE BEAVER vs. STATE OF CALIFORNIA

By H. CLYDE AMESBURY, District Traffic Engineer

Down on the South Fork of the Feather River they're a feudin'. It isn't a shootin' war but both parties are mighty determined.

The parties to the dispute are a small furry denizen named Joe Beaver and Cecil Koenig, the maintenance superintendent of the Division of Highways at Quincy.

To provide a little background for the argument, the following items are supplied:

Joe and his family lived in a small stream just south of Blairsden. This past year, the division awarded a contract to reroute the highway and crossed Joe's stream. The plans called for a fill which the contractor proceeded to place. This met with Joe's wholehearted approval; a dam was being constructed and a very substantial one just where he wanted it. However, he was horrified to note they left a hole in it containing a pipe 36 inches in diameter and it didn't hold water. With the best intentions in the world and in a spirit of helpfulness, he proceeded to plug the hole.

Joe Cost State Money

During the course of construction, the contractor spent about $300 unplugging the pipe. Joe knew very well you couldn't have a dam with a hole in it! He busily plugged away and hoped the contractor would see the light.

Finally, the contractor completed his work and with the pipe all clean had it accepted by the State. Then in a few days before the maintenance department took over, Joe plugged the pipe tight.

Now appears Cecil Koenig; he was horrified to find a pipe plugged on his new job. He sent a crew to clean it out. They worked from 8 until 3 o'clock and had it about completed. That night Joe assembled his family and next morning when the crew returned the pipe was plugged again. Looked like Joe won this round.

Then Cecil tore out the plug and built a contrivance of steel posts and

Creosote bucket still on fence. Joe had the water about two feet over the pipe.

Pictures of beaverproof barrier

mesh to keep Joe away from the upper end of the culvert. Cecil claimed he won that round.

Joe examined and investigated this addition to the landscape for about a week until he was certain it wasn't some kind of a trap to catch an unsuspecting and helpful beaver. Then he tunneled under the wire and plugged the pipe. That round he won.

What Next?

Cecil looked over the situation, cleaned out the culvert, spotted where Joe came under the wire, and hung a bucket of creosote with a small hole in the bottom where the liquid dripped out over the location. Joe apparently got some of this on his fur. Maybe he got some in his eyes. If there had been a referee he would have screamed "low blow" and "foul." He definitely had an odor such as no beaver ever had before and was probably ostracized by his family. Cecil claimed that round.

Joe waited about 10 days. The weather turned cold. The creosote stopped dripping and Joe and family happily restored the dam by plugging the culvert. Joe claimed the round.

Cecil then came out and unplugged the pipe and drove a series of steel stakes just below the mesh and close enough together so Joe couldn't get through. Cecil is claiming this round and tentatively claiming the contest.

As for Joe, he doesn't concede anything.

BISHOP MADE COMMISSIONER

Continued from page 33 . . .

Los Guilucos School for Girls. In addition he is a member of the Redwood Empire Association and chairman of the Industrial Committee of the North Coast Council of the State Chamber of Commerce.

Bishop is past president of the Santa Rosa Chamber of Commerce and the Santa Rosa Rotary Club. He was the first general chairman of the Santa Rosa United Crusade. Recently he became a member of the neighbors flood committee, which was organized to help flood victims in Northern California.

Harding Retiring, Telford Moves Up to Assistant State Highway Engineer

Paul O. Harding, Assistant State Highway Engineer in charge of state highway development and operation in Los Angeles, Orange, and Ventura Counties for the past six years, is retiring after 27 years of outstanding service with the California Division of Highways.

Appointment of Edward T. Telford to succeed Harding was announced by State Highway Engineer G. T. McCoy.

Harding has been closely identified with the world-famous metropolitan freeway network in the Los Angeles area since August, 1947, when he became a district engineer under S. V. Cortelyou. He succeeded Cortelyou as Assistant State Highway Engineer when the latter retired in October, 1949.

Freeways and expressways in the three counties comprising District VII of the Division of Highways now include 182 miles of completed projects and 45 additional miles under construction, costing a total of $414,000,-000 for construction and rights of way. For the 1956-57 Fiscal Year alone, the construction and right of way budget for District VII totals about $86,000,000, covering additional projects planned and designed under Harding's supervision.

Harding was born in Garden City, Kansas, in 1893. From 1912 to 1915 he worked on location surveys in Oregon, after which he began his studies at the University of Nebraska. These studies were interrupted by service in World War I as a first lieutenant in the 27th Field Artillery, but were completed in 1922 when he received his B.S. degree in civil engineering.

Moving to California in 1923, Harding first worked for municipal and private engineering organizations. In 1929 he joined the Division of Highways as an inspector and instrumentman in District IV at San Francisco.

In 1931 he became assistant to the district construction engineer, and in 1933 he was placed in charge of the location and design of the approaches to the San Francisco-Oakland Bay Bridge, later supervising construction

of these approaches. In 1937 he was promoted to Assistant District Engineer of District IV.

In 1942 Harding was appointed District Engineer of District X, with headquarters at Stockton, where he remained for five years, until his transfer to District VII.

Harding is a member of the American Society of Civil Engineers and an honorary member of the American Right of Way Association. He was one of the founders of the California State Employees Association and was its second president, in 1932.

His responsibility for the planning and construction of the vast freeway network in the Los Angeles metropolitan area has made him a participant in many civic and governmental activities relating to the development of that region during the past eight years.

Telford will be promoted from the position of district engineer in charge of planning, a post he has held for the past three years. Telford's former duties are being assumed by District Engineer George Langsner, who has been in charge of operations for District VII. District VII includes Los Angeles, Orange and Ventura Counties.

To fill Langsner's position, McCoy announced the appointment of Lyman R. Gillis, presently Assistant District Engineer in District IV, with headquarters in San Francisco.

Harding who has spent 27 years in the state highway organization, the last six years in charge of District VII, is handing over to Telford the responsibility for a program involving more than $100,000,000 a year in expenditures, including $86,000,000 budgeted for the 1956-57 Fiscal Year for construction purposes, including rights of way. Freeways and expressways in District VII amount to 182 miles completed and 45 miles under construction, costing a total of $414,-000,000. Most of the work under the accelerated highway construction program has been accomplished during Harding's tenure in the district.

. . . Continued on page 67

Los Banos

*City Finds a Solution for
Its Grave Parking Problem*

By HARRY J. WEBB, District X

WHEN THE owners of commercial establishments catering to highway traffic ask that parking on the highway be prohibited, we think this is news.

This unusual situation developed on State Sign Route 152, Pacheco Pass Highway, through the southern portion of Los Banos a little over a year ago. At that time, the property owners along Pacheco Boulevard petitioned the city officials of Los Banos to enact the necessary ordinance for prohibiting all parking on the highway within the corporate limits.

The property owners and the city officials recognized the fact that the 58-foot city street section would not be adequate for four lanes of traffic without such action. Unless the free flow of traffic were assured, it was felt that public demand would result in an ultimate re-route around the town.

Off-street Parking

Pacheco Boulevard does not traverse the main business district and, as mentioned above, the majority of business establishments depend upon the motorist for revenue. The merchants have met this problem by providing off-street parking on practically a 100 percent basis.

A resurvey one year later found Pacheco Boulevard free of congestion with adequate capacity to handle the rapidly increasing traffic on Route 152.

The editor of the *Los Banos Enterprise*, F. A. Merrick, who is vitally interested in highway matters, particularly those affecting the community, is of the opinion that both the traveling public and the property owners are pleased with the results. Property values have remained firm and business has improved. Many local residents now patronize the establishments since congestion has been reduced and off-street parking provided.

UPPER—Medical Center parking. LOWER—Off-street parking at Restaurant.

No Accidents

Chief of Police R. H. McSwain states that the elimination of parking, especially truck parking, has improved visibility and safety. Since the ordinance was enacted, he said, there have been no reported accidents on Pacheco Boulevard.

Enforcement of the ordinance has presented little difficulty inasmuch as

UPPER—No parking signs Pacheco Blvd. LOWER—City owned parking lot.

motorists generally prefer to park off the highway.

The city clerk, Michael Dambrosio, is enthusiastic about public reaction. Residents are pleased with the improved conditions and the attractiveness of Pacheco Boulevard. The city council of Los Banos is cognizant of the advantages of off-street parking and has provided public parking lots with no charge to the motorist.

Certainly, the City of Los Banos has lived up to its reputation as a progressive community and should be commended for its action in furthering progress.

WEARINESS AND WORRY

Two enemies of safe driving are weariness and worry. Weariness slows down reaction time and worry affects concentration. You can't always stop worrying when you get behind the wheel of your car, says the California State Automobile Association, but you can take a rest if you're weary. Give yourself a break, don't drive when you're tired.

D. H. McMillan

D. H. McMillan, Senior Structural Designer for the State Division of Architecture, was honored by fellow employees at a farewell dinner December 15th in Sacramento. He retired December 28, 1955, after more than 39 years of state service.

McMillan was born and reared on his father's stock farm in the hills of Yuba County where he also attended grammar school. Following graduation from the Sacramento High School, he worked for a time with his father. In June 1914, he quit the farm to work for the State as a messenger clerk with the Division of Architecture.

D. H. McMILLAN

In a short time he was promoted to senior clerk and remained in that position until he resigned in 1919 to work for the 12th Naval District in San Francisco. As a junior draftsman in the Bureau of Construction and Repair, he worked on plans of U. S. Navy destroyers and submarines.

A year later McMillan returned to the Division of Architecture as a mechanical draftsman, inspecting steel shipments fabricated by the Palm Iron Works for the construction of the California State Building in San Francisco's Civic Center. By 1931 he had been promoted to associate structural engineering draftsman preparing drawings of schools, gymnasiums, hospitals, and other state facilities.

During World War II he worked for a short time with the U. S. Engineers and for Ellison & King, a structural engineering firm in San Francisco. At Ellison & King he detailed the plans of 26 concrete ships for the U. S. Maritime Commission.

In December 1943, he returned to Sacramento and the Division of Architecture.

McMillan plans to return to the Yuba County hill country of his childhood where with his wife, Jeanette, he expects to pursue his first and only avocation, livestock ranching.

Cost Index

*Rises During Fourth Quarter of
1955 Highway Construction*

By RICHARD H. WILSON, Assistant State Highway Engineer,
H. C. McCARTY, Office Engineer, and
JOHN D. GALLAGHER, Assistant Office Engineer

THE CALIFORNIA Highway Construction Cost Index stood at 212.6
(1940 = 100) for the fourth quarter
of 1955, a rise of 1.9 percent over the
208.6 for the third quarter, and 12.3
percent over the first quarter of 1955.

For the entire calendar year of 1955
the Index stood at 203.8. This is an
over-all increase of 5.3 percent over
the 193.5 for the calendar year of
1954.

The computations for the fourth
quarter Index were made excluding
three large contracts awarded for construction of the new parallel bridge
across the Carquinez Strait at Crockett.
The total amount of these three contracts is nearly $20,000,000 and the
concentration of this amount of money
and the large quantities of steel
(12,880,000 pounds of structural steel,
10,740,000 pounds of high strength
low-alloy structural steel and 5,820,000
pounds of high strength T-1 structural
steel) were such that their inclusion
would have unbalanced the entire
Index for the quarter. While the
poundage of high strength steel was
much less than would have been required had the bridge been built entirely of ordinary structural steel, the
cost per pound for the high strength
steel was much higher than for
straight structural steel. An unusually
large structure such as the Carquinez
Strait Bridge is not comparable from
the cost standpoint to the normal
highway project, even in this day of
six, eight and ten million dollar freeway jobs.

However, as a matter of interest
and comparison a separate computation of the Cost Index was made including the Carquinez Bridge. The
result of including these bridge quantities and prices brought the Index to
228.8, which is approximately 7 per-

cent higher than the normal Index
without the three Carquinez Bridge
contracts.

Even though the rise in the California Highway Construction Cost
Index during the fourth quarter of
1955 was only 1.9 percent it antici-

pates a continuation of the rise begun
in the second quarter of 1955.

The accompanying tabulation shows
the California Highway Construction
Cost Index by years from 1940
through 1953 and by quarters for
1954 and 1955.

STATE OF CALIFORNIA
DEPARTMENT OF PUBLIC WORKS
DIVISION OF HIGHWAYS

PRICE INDEX
CONSTRUCTION COSTS

1940 = 100

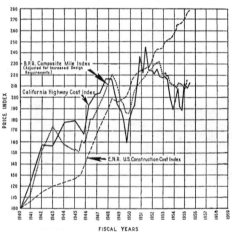

FISCAL YEARS
(JULY 1 TO JUNE 30)

Year	Cost index
1940	100.0
1941	125.0
1942	157.5
1943	156.4
1944	177.8
1945	179.5
1946	179.7
1947	203.3
1948	216.6
1949	190.7
1950 (1st Quarter 1950—160.6)	176.7
1951 (4th Quarter 1951—245.4)	210.8
1952	224.5
1953	216.2
1954 (1st Quarter)	199.4
1954 (2d Quarter)	189.0
1954 (3d Quarter)	207.8
1954 (4th Quarter)	192.2
1955 (1st Quarter)	189.3
1955 (2d Quarter)	212.4
1955 (3d Quarter)	208.6
1955 (4th Quarter)	212.6

Projects awarded during the quarter included seven freeway jobs with large quantities and corresponding lower unit costs (the southerly approach to the Carquinez Bridge alone involves over 11,000,000 cubic yards of roadway excavation). In the face of the effect of these large projects in lowering unit prices the over-all result was a rise of nearly 2 percent.

As stated above it is the opinion of this department that this rise, small as it is, adds to the rise for the year as a whole and is an indication of further increases in the months ahead.

Another straw in the wind indicating increases in highway construction costs is the drop in the average number of bidders during 1955 as shown in the tabulation further on in this report.

Inspection of the average unit prices bid during the fourth quarter of 1955 for the eight items upon which the California Index is based (see accompanying tabulations) shows an increase in five items and a decrease in three. Roadway excavation dropped about 10 percent from 41 cents per cubic yard to 37 cents. This drop may be laid almost entirely to the 25.6 cents price on the 11,200,000 cubic yards of excavation on the Hercules to Crockett approach to the Carquinez Bridge. Untreated rock base was down from $2.33 to $2; this, however, is merely back to where it was in the second quarter of 1955. The average price of $2.33 for rock during the third quarter was undoubtedly the direct result of the rock plants strike in Southern California during the summer. The only other decrease was

a drop of $1.70 per ton in the price of asphalt concrete, but the total quantity of this item is so small as to have little effect on the Index.

Plant-mixed surfacing rose from $5.43 per ton to $5.52 per ton; portland cement concrete pavement was up from $13.46 to $15.05 per cubic yard; structural concrete rose from $49.64 to $52.72 per cubic yard; bar reinforcing steel rose from $0.093 to $0.099 per pound; and structural steel was up from $0.132 to $0.144 per pound.

In the computations made for the Index including the three Carquinez Bridge contracts the unit prices were more or less the same with the exception of bar reinforcing steel, which was up to an average of $0.103 per pound; and for structural steel including the large quantities of high strength low-alloy and T-1 steels which go into the bridge the average unit price was $0.223 per pound.

It is believed that a steady upward trend in highway construction costs is now established. The increases in labor and rising material costs have had their effect and competing bidders are no longer able to devise methods of cutting prices and trimming profits. The people of California have benefited during the past year by the efforts of the construction industry in creating devices to keep highway construction costs relatively stable in a period when general prices were rising; it is an excellent example of the benefits to the public of the contract system based upon competitive bidding.

The accompanying chart, showing the California Highway Construction Cost Index, the *Engineering News-Record* Construction Cost Index and the United States Bureau of Public Roads Composite Mile Index compares the three, all reduced to the 1940 = 100 base. The *Engineering News-Record* Index, based upon materials and labor prices, comprises all types of construction and is nation-wide in scope. During the fourth quarter of 1955 this Index continued the steady rise begun in 1950 and reached 278.3 which was 0.76 percent higher than in the third quarter.

... Continued on page 67

CALIFORNIA DIVISION OF HIGHWAYS AVERAGE CONTRACT PRICES

	Roadway excavation, per cu. yd.	Crusher run base, per ton	Plant mix surfacing, per ton	Asphalt concrete pavement, per ton	PCC pavement, per cu. yd.	PCC structures, per cu. yd.	Bar reinforcing steel, per lb.	Structural steel, per lb.
1940	$0.22	$1.54	$2.19	$2.97	$7.68	$18.33	$0.040	$0.063
1941	0.26	2.31	2.84	3.18	7.54	23.31	0.053	0.107
1942	0.35	2.81	4.02	4.16	9.62	29.48	0.073	0.103
1943	0.42	2.26	3.71	4.76	11.48	31.76	0.059	0.080
1944	0.50	2.45	4.10	4.50	10.46	31.99	0.054	0.132
1945	0.51	2.42	4.20	4.88	10.90	37.20	0.059	0.102
1946	0.41	2.45	4.00	4.68	9.48	37.38	0.060	0.099
1947	0.46	2.42	4.32	5.38	12.38	48.44	0.080	0.138
1948	0.55	2.43	4.30	5.38	13.04	49.86	0.092	0.126
1949	0.49	2.67	4.67	4.64	12.28	48.67	0.096	0.117
1950	0.40	2.25	4.26	3.75	11.11	43.45	0.079	0.094
1951	0.49	2.62	4.34	5.00	12.21	47.22	0.102	0.159
1952	0.56	2.99	5.00	4.38	13.42	48.08	0.098	0.150
1953	0.51	2.14*	5.31	4.58	12.74	50.59	0.093	0.133
1st Quarter 1954	0.45	2.28	4.23	4.78	14.89	47.52	0.092	0.126
2d Quarter 1954	0.38	2.09	4.39	5.18	14.28	47.12	0.093	0.114
3d Quarter 1954	0.43	1.85	4.68	7.00	12.63	49.59	0.095	0.162
4th Quarter 1954	0.35	1.78	4.83	....	13.13	46.06	0.094	0.135
1st Quarter 1955	0.39	1.69	4.55	....	13.44	40.66	0.095	0.140
2d Quarter 1955	0.42	1.99	5.39	....	14.46	51.36	0.098	0.136
3d Quarter 1955	0.41	2.33	5.43	5.70	13.46	49.64	0.093	0.132
4th Quarter 1955	0.37	2.00	5.52	4.00	15.05	52.72	0.099	0.144

* Untreated rock base substituted for crusher run base at this point.

County Project

Butte Completes Oroville By-pass To Relieve Traffic Construction

By E. H. WYMAN, Associate Highway Engineer, and
MARSHALL JONES, Butte County Director of Public Works

OPENING CEREMONIES for FAS Route 1169 in Butte County held October 31, 1955, marked completion of the project which has been under construction intermittently since 1947. The route was first proposed by former Supervisor Scott Lawton and Oroville City Councilman Bernard Richter in 1946 as a truck route to relieve congestion on Montgomery Street, US 40A, through Oroville.

As lumber is one of the main industries of the Oroville area, Montgomery Street, first laid out in early 1850 and little changed in width since that time, was literally alive with huge logging and lumber trucks. A steep grade at the east end of the street added to the traffic problem. The project was endorsed wholeheartedly by local residents after a lumber truck with faulty brakes ran wild through the business area causing considerable property damage.

Right of Way Donated

Right of way for a major portion of the route was donated, largely through the efforts of Mr. Richter, and the first portion of the project started. This consisted of the grading of various sections lying between connecting city streets and county roads both by small contract and county forces. The base and light surfacing were placed by county forces on various portions as funds were available. The route was not open to through traffic due to the necessity of constructing three underpasses and taking care of drainage on Dry Creek which the route follows for approximately one-half mile.

During 1950, through the efforts of Supervisor Dan Pellicciotti and the Oroville Chamber of Commerce, the road was established as an FAS route, and the first project, the construction of three underpasses and a new channel

for Dry Creek, was started under the direction of Bert Paxton, former road commissioner for Butte County. Con-

struction of this portion of the project was completed in 1953 by C. K. Moseman Construction Company of Bel-

Beginning of FAS Route 1169 looking easterly from junction of FAS Route 1169 with US 40 Alt. and Oroville-Richvale highway. End of FAS 1169 at its intersection with US 40 Alt. in the extreme upper left corner.

50

Looking easterly. Connection with US 40 Alt. at top of picture. Southern Pacific Railroad and Western Pacific Railroad underpasses in foreground. Lincoln Street, Meyers Street and Olive Highway intersections in center.

mont. This proved to be an extremely difficult operation due to the work lying in the bottom of Dry Creek and progressing through a winter which saw the heaviest rainfall in this area since 1890.

Upon completion of the structures, county forces graded and surfaced the roadway including additional base and light surfacing from the intersection at State Highway Routes 87 and 21A through to Oroville-Quincy county road (old state highway to Quincy

via Bucks Lake). This left approximately 0.7 of a mile to be constructed to open the route to state highway Route 21 east of Oroville. This project, FAS 1169(2), started in August, 1954, was completed in June, 1955. The project just completed, FAS 1169(3), covered the regrading of approximately one-quarter mile of an existing city street, the placing of additional base on approximately three-quarters of a mile and the placing of three inches of surfacing from

Route 87 south of Oroville to the old Oroville-Quincy highway. The last project was financed with state, federal, county and city funds.

Traffic Signals Planned

This route is now beginning to carry a large percentage of both through and local traffic. It is anticipated that a considerably larger volume will be carried upon completion of traffic signals at Myers Street intersection, one of the busiest in the county, where traffic, particularly trucks, have difficulty crossing. The City of Oroville is now in the process of preparing plans for the signals.

The county day-labor and contract projects were completed at an approximate cost of $150,000. The three FAS projects were constructed at a cost of $429,000. The approximate total cost of the complete route was $579,000. Marshall Jones, Butte County Director of Public Works, under whose direction the last two projects were completed, has reported a great deal of satisfactory comment has been received from both local and outside highway users since the completion of this route.

Looking westerly along FAS 1169 on the left and US 40 Alt. diverging to the right, which intersect again in background near the Feather River Bridge south of Oroville. Bridge at right center is on S. H. Route 87 to Chico.

GLAD YOU LIKE IT

VALLEJO

DEAR MR. ADAMS: I wish to take this opportunity to congratulate you and your very capable staff for the splendid job you are doing in compiling the information relative to the highways and their progress in this State and disseminating it to the public. I have learned many things about this great State of ours from the *California Highways and Public Works* and would miss it very much if it were discontinued.

Sincerely yours,
ROBERT T. MONAGAN, SR.
1401 Rice Street

Whitton Succeeds General Merrill As A. A. S. H. O. Head

Less than two days after his election as President of the American Association of State Highway Officials, Major General Frank Dow Merrill, Commissioner of Public

FRANK D. MERRILL   REX M. WHITTON

Works in New Hampshire, died in Fernandina Beach, Florida, at the age of 52.

In accordance with the association's constitution, the new president for 1956 is Rex M. Whitton, Chief Engineer of the Missouri State Highway Department, who had been elected first vice president at the same New Orleans convention of A. A. S. H. O. at which General Merrill was chosen president to succeed G. T. McCoy, State Highway Engineer of California.

General Merrill's election to the presidency of A. A. S. H. O. climaxed the second of his two distinguished careers. He was graduted from the U. S. Military Academy in 1929 and from the Massachusetts Institute of Technology in 1932. He advanced through military ranks to brigadier general in 1943 and major general in 1944, when he was commander of United States forces in the India-Burma theater. Later he was chief of staff of the U. S. 10th Army.

During his far eastern service in World War II the bold and successful exploits of his troops earned them the nickname of "Merrill's Marauders."

Retired in 1947 for disability incurred in World War II, he was

A.A.S.H.O. POLICY STATEMENT ON FEDERAL LEGISLATION — 1956

The American Association of State Highway Officials urges the Congress to enact an expanded and adequate highway program early during the second session of the 84th Congress and to make funds authorized thereunder available for apportionment to the several states by July of 1956.

Further delay in taking action will cause additional critical traffic congestion and accidents, as well as create indecision at all levels of government in highway planning and construction and thereby materially retard the economy of the United States.

Any federal-aid program authorized by the Congress should be administered by the Bureau of Public Roads and constructed by the state highway departments—a working relationship

appointed New Hampshire Commissioner of Highways in 1949 by Govcruor Sherman Adams. He had been active in A. A. S. H. O. since that time, serving as a regional vice president in 1952 and as first vice president in 1955. During the past few years he had been closely identified with the planned A. A. S. H. O. Road Test Project soon to get under way in Illinois.

The new A. A. S. H. O. president, Rex Whitton, has been on the staff of the State Highway Department of Missouri since 1920, shortly after his graduation from the University of Missouri.

His first work was with a survey party, and he advanced through nearly every phase of highway engineering work, including 15 years as engineer of maintenance, to become the department's Chief Engineer in 1951.

Whitton has long been active in A. A. S. H. O., and has been chairman of its committee on maintenance and equipment. During the past year he served on the legislative committee, testifying before congressional committees on proposed Federal highway legislation.

that has proved so successful over the past years.

Federal Aid Increase Needed

An enlarged adequate highway program should indicate the intent of the Congress to construct the 40,000 mile Interstate System in not more than 15 years and to provide a progressive increase in the federal-aid to the secondary, urban, and primary systems. The initial authorization should be for a period of five years.

The matching of funds for the construction of the interstate system should be on a 90 percent federal and 10 percent state basis, with the matching on the other systems as now provided under existing legislation.

A 20 percent transfer provision should be allowed between secondary, urban, and primary allocations to make the highway program flexible enough to meet the most pressing needs of the individual states.

Funds for the construction of the interstate system should be initially apportioned on a basis of need as indicated by the Section 13 Study as reported by the Bureau of Public Roads, and as indicated by future successive needs estimates; such successive estimates to be made first in 1957 and in five-year intervals thereafter. The apportionment to the other systems should be on the present basis.

Moving of Utilities

The subjects of reimbursing for the moving of utilities from public highway rights of way, of labor relations and requirements, and of vehicle sizes and weights should not be included in federal statute but should be matters to be determined at the state level.

It is recommended that the Congress give consideration to the dedication of more of the general fund to road construction in view of the federal responsibility in the national defense system of highways.

. . . Continued on page 67

District VII

By PAUL O. HARDING
Assistant State Highway Engineer

Appraisal of Work During Past Five Years

Freeways Report

Four years ago I prepared a story for *California Highways and Public Works* on the role of the State Division of Highways in the development of a freeway system for the Los Angeles metropolitan area. Each year since then I have prepared a progress report, attempting to summarize what had been accomplished during the previous year. Since this present writeup is the fifth of the series it will perhaps be of interest to consider the accomplishments of the past five years.

Consideration of what has happened freeway-wise in District VII on the basis of the past five-year period is suggested because of the report just released by the California Taxpayers Association regarding population growth in this State. The figures made public by this association indicate that California's population has increased since the 1950 census, 27.2 percent—almost 3,000,000 persons additional—so that the population of California is now approximately 13,465,000. In Los Angeles County their records show a 31.8 percent increase since 1950 with the estimated population now 5,473,000. The California Taxpayers Association states that the greatest increase during the past five years in any one county has occurred in Orange county where the gain in population is 101.1 percent, with the estimated total now being 434,800.

Increase in Population

This tremendous increase in population within the area of District VII, which comprises the three counties of Los Angeles, Orange and Ventura, has brought to pass a corresponding increase in vehicular traffic on our highways. Mr. G. T. McCoy, State Highway Engineer, has just made public release of the 1955 state-wide

PAUL O. HARDING

traffic count figures. As Mr. McCoy says, on a state-wide basis the traffic volumes during the year 1955 have increased 8.79 percent. The rate of increase in traffic on the freeways in this district has considerably exceeded this figure. The increase in average daily traffic on the freeways of this area, comparing the traffic today with traffic one year ago, and also five years ago is shown by the following:

	1955	1954	1950
Hollywood (4-level westerly)	180,000	168,000	64,000
Pasadena (Elysian Park)	112,000	110,000	56,000
Santa Ana (Soto Street)	113,000	90,000	25,000
San Bernardino (Soto Street)	88,000	80,000	25,000
Harbor (4-level southerly)	160,000	125,000	—
Colorado (at Linda Vista)	27,000	30,000	—
Long Beach (Pacific Coast Highway)	31,000	10,000	—
Using 4-level interchange	250,000	200,000	—

From the above tabulation it will be recalled that five years ago there were only disconnected portions of the four major freeways in the Los Angeles area that were then open to public traffic and that these sections at that time had not come into full use.

Freeways Completed

The lengths of full freeways in District VII that were completed during 1955 are the following:

Santa Ana Freeway—
From First Street, Santa Ana, to Browning Boulevard .... 2.4 miles
Golden State Freeway—
From Sepulveda Boulevard to north city limits of Los Angeles .... 3.0 miles
Colorado Freeway—
From Avenue 64 to Eagle Rock Boulevard .... 0.8 mile
Foothill Freeway—
From Hampton Road to Montana Street in Flintridge area .... 1.8 miles

Total .... 8.0 miles

I find in reviewing my four previous articles that each one contains some reference to current and past legislative enactments that affected financing of highway and freeway construction. Therefore, it will perhaps be in order at this time to summarize briefly state highway financing.

Highway Financing

State highway construction was first started in California in 1912 from a bond issue of $18,000,000 passed by the people in 1910. A second bond issue of $15,000,000 was voted by the people at an election in 1916. Again in 1919 a $40,000,000 bond issue was voted. Then the 1923 Legislature passed an enactment creating a 2-cents-per-gallon gasoline tax. This was the start of the pay-as-you-go financing. In 1928 this tax was increased to 3 cents per gallon, with 1 cent going to counties and 2 cents reserved for maintenance and improvement of the state highway system.

In recognition of city problems, by legislative authority, Statutes of 1931, a policy of cooperation in construction was inaugurated for those portions of the highway routings within the cities, and in 1932 several miles within cities were improved by state and local cooperation. In further recognition of this problem Chapter 767, Statutes of 1933, provided that the Department of Public Works would annually expend from the state highway fund an amount equal to the net proceeds of one-fourth of 1 cent per gallon tax of motor vehicle fuel upon state highway routes within incorporated municipalities. Still further recognition of this problem was given by the Legislature in 1935 which provided an additional one-fourth cent of the gasoline tax for maintenance, rights of way, construction or improvement on streets of major importance within the cities, off the state highway system.

Gas Tax Increase

Both the 1933 one-fourth cent and 1935 one-fourth cent were taken from the state highway 2 cents of gas tax, thus reducing the expenditures upon the state rural system to 1½ cents. Coincident with the legislation reallocating these gas tax funds, the Legislature in 1933 and 1935 added some 6,800 miles of rural county roads to the state system, which, with the extended routes through the cities, resulted in a total state highway system of approximately 14,000 miles.

The Collier-Burns Highway Act of 1947 increased the gas tax to 4½ cents per gallon and supplemented this by other motor vehicle fees, which, however, were more than offset by a 2-cents-per-gallon allocation to cities and counties for roads and streets not on the highway system. The 1953 Legislature increased the state gasoline tax to 6 cents per gallon, also increasing supplemental taxes in proportion, but made this increase effective for only two years, after which both the gas tax and supplemental fees were to be decreased to the 5¼-cent equivalent. The 1955 Legislature passed enactments to prevent the ½-cent-

What Does It Mean?

Over the length and breadth of California wherever the far-flung work of the Division of Highways, Department of Public Works, is in operation, this insignia will be found on automobiles, trucks, tractors, buildings, and other places too numerous to mention.

This familiar insignia attracts the casual attention of the public and the more or less added interest of the thousands of employees associated in the division, but the query of this article is directed to the meaning of the Latin phrase on the inner circle of the emblem: "Robur directum scientia est via fortunae."

Ask any number of officials or employees of the department what the sentence means and a negative answer is the reply. Here is the answer: "Labor directed by science is the way to fortune."

per-gallon decrease and make the 6-cents-per-gallon state gasoline tax and supplemental fees in continuing effect.

Right-of-Way Problem

In the metropolitan Los Angeles area those freeways of the system providing the greatest traffic service are, naturally, those which lie through the most densely settled areas where the right-of-way problem is extremely acute, and may entail expenditures of more than 50 percent of the total cost of the project. Planning for such freeways must be on the basis of providing sufficient right-of-way funds to permit construction for traffic relief at the earliest possible date. The advance purchase of rights of way while properties are still unimproved has become recognized as the most effective planning and cost control in the

protection of future freeways. By following this procedure, very considerable savings to the State have been effected, particularly where major highway improvements are involved such as freeways located on new alignment which require extensive widths of right of way through potential subdivision areas.

Legislation was adopted by the State Legislature in 1952 whereby the sum of $10,000,000 was provided in a special fund known as the "Highway Right-of-Way Acquisition Fund," for the express purpose of acquiring rights of way on which development was imminent. This fund was later changed to a revolving fund and increased by $20,000,000, making a total of $30,000,000 available on a statewide basis.

Summary of Savings

A brief summary of the advance acquisition of rights of way and the estimated savings realized in District VII, which has been accomplished to date through this fund, is as follows:

Fiscal year ending	No. parcels acquired	Am't paid from Hwy. Acq. Fund	Estimated savings
6-30-53	28	$269,400	$1,614,000
6-30-54	363	3,873,550	27,111,000
6-30-55	522	5,092,544	42,000,000
Total	913	$9,235,494	$70,725,000

In addition to the above, the California Highway Commission has authorized the acquisition of other properties amounting to $14,000,000 with an anticipated additional saving of $90,000,000. Acquisition is progressing rapidly on these other properties.

In this five-year period, 1950-55, the record of accomplishment reveals 11,629 parcels of land acquired at a total cost of $137,466,464. Right-of-way clearance work has increased correspondingly, a total of 4,435 houses having been sold and removed from the right of way by the House Sales Section for a total return to the State of $7,706,716. Tabulation showing this record year-by-year follows:

Fiscal year ending	No. of parcels acquired	Total cost	No. of houses sold	Am't received house sales
6-30-51	1,733	$16,538,846	599	$1,200,347
6-30-52	1,415	15,244,133	343	·746,747
6-30-53	1,616	19,051,707	334	699,568
6-30-54	3,390	40,971,476	1,508	2,252,396
6-30-55	3,475	45,660,302	1,651	2,807,658
Total	11,629	$137,466,464	4,435	$7,706,716

In connection with this sale and removal of houses from the right of way, it is of interest to note that notwithstanding the fact that certain areas of land acquired for rights of way are removed from the tax rolls, over 90 percent of the buildings which are sold and removed in the clearance of right of way are relocated to other locations and replaced on the tax rolls, rehabilitated and modernized in the relocation process to add years to their useful life. In this manner, what might appear to be a loss of taxable property assessed by the county is more than offset. Past experience has proven that the appreciated value of properties abutting freeways, particularly in industrial areas due to improved accessibility, creates increased assessed values to such an extent that freeway right-of-way acquisition does not reduce the value of taxable property but decidedly increases it.

Another very important activity of the District Right-of-Way Department is the rental of buildings on lands acquired and held for future freeway construction. In such cases, all state-owned properties suitable for renting are rented or leased under rental agreement containing adequate cancellation clauses until shortly before highway construction commences. A record of the income derived from the rentals of these properties is as follows:

Fiscal year ending	Units	Yearly earnings
6-30-51	332	$180,680
6-30-52	587	304,532
6-30-53	1,090	418,290
6-30-54	1,305	597,731
6-30-55	1,742	888,252

The Division of Highways is forced to be in the rental business in order to keep houses occupied until the time arrives that the right of way has to be cleared for construction. This is the only effective way of preventing van-

STATE OF CALIFORNIA
DEPARTMENT OF PUBLIC WORKS
DIVISION OF HIGHWAYS

DISTRICT VII
FREEWAYS

Legend

COMPLETED OR UNDER CONSTRUCTION
BUDGETED
UNDER FREEWAY RESOLUTION

JANUARY 1, 1956

Scale in Miles

dalism and keep a neighborhood from becoming rundown and deteriorated. While the rents received total substantial sums, the other considerations are of even greater importance.

Work of Legal Staff

As we have noted above, while every effort is made to secure rights of way by amicable negotiation with property owners, in some instances it is necessary for the State to resort to eminent domain proceedings and start condemnation of private properties. The number of parcels carried through condemnation is only about 2 percent of the total number acquired, the other 98 percent being consummated by negotiation and mutual agreement. The condemnation of rights of way for District VII and the other south-

ern counties is carried out by the legal department. During the five-year period 1950 to 1955 the district staff has carried out 248 condemnation suits for rights of way, totaling $4,101,495.

Before right-of-way agents start negotiations with property owners for areas that are needed for rights of way for freeways and other state highways the fair market value of each parcel is determined. The appraisal of property is conducted in a detailed, comprehensive manner not only ascertaining all of the salient features of each particular piece of property but also making an extensive search of the records to determine the sale price of comparable or similar properties in that particular neighborhood. It is in this painstaking and careful manner, with the review

and approval of the Sacramento headquarters office, that the fair market value of each parcel is determined.

Condemnation Policy

If the right-of-way agents, after opening negotiations with property owners, are unable to reach a satisfactory settlement with them, it is then necessary for the State to resort to condemnation proceedings. Were it not for the right of eminent domain, highway improvements would bog down and many times be impossible to carry out. The right of eminent domain is an important right of the people and its exercise is very necessary in order that state highway projects and freeway projects go forward, otherwise one recalcitrant property owner could hold up a project indefi-

STATUS OF DISTRICT VII FREEWAY PROJECTS—JANUARY 1, 1956

	Total miles	Completed projects		Under contract		Right of way costs	Total costs to date
		Miles	Constr. costs	Miles	Constr. est.		
Pasadena Freeway 4-Level Structure to Glenarm St., Pasadena	8.2	8.2	$10,434,200			$1,009,100	$11,443,300
Hollywood Freeway Spring St. via Cahuenga Pass to Junction Golden State Freeway near Wentworth St.	16.8	10.0	28,949,200		172,500	28,360,000	57,481,700
Santa Ana Freeway Spring St. (Los Angeles) to Junction of San Diego Freeway near El Toro	42.8	32.4	39,165,000	2.6	4,983,600	16,480,000	60,628,600
San Bernardino Freeway Santa Ana Freeway near Los Angeles River to San Bernardino County Line in Claremont.	30.7	15.7	19,007,500	15.0	15,537,700	16,015,000	50,560,200
Harbor Freeway 4-Level Structure to San Pedro	22.4	3.9	11,221,800	8.4	18,556,500	48,600,000	78,378,300
Long Beach Freeway Pacific Coast Highway in Long Beach to Huntington Dr. in South Pasadena	21.5	7.9	10,891,100	4.8	8,671,200	18,435,000	37,997,300
Golden State Freeway Junction of Olympic and Santa Ana Freeway near Soto St. to Kern County Line	72.7	47.2	18,646,600	2.4	5,102,700	24,640,000	48,389,300
Ventura Freeway Vineland Ave. to S. County Line Ventura and N. County Line Ventura to Santa Barbara County Line	65.7	39.1	12,484,100		53,000	11,148,000	23,685,100
San Diego Freeway Golden State Freeway near San Fernando Reservoir to San Diego County Line	93.7		310,300	1.2	2,256,300	15,335,000	17,901,600
Colorado Freeway Eagle Vista Dr. in Eagle Rock to Holly St. in Pasadena	2.2	2.2	6,139,200			2,295,000	8,434,200
Foothill Freeway Hampton Rd. to Montana St. in Flintridge	2.0	2.0	2,107,200			624,000	2,731,200
Glendale Freeway Los Angeles River to Ave. 36, near Eagle Rock Blvd.	1.6					3,005,000	3,005,000
Artesia Freeway Normandie Ave. to Santa Fe Ave. and Palo Verde Ave. to Santa Ana Canyon Freeway.	21.7	1.9	1,010,900	6.2	2,877,600	2,140,000	6,028,500
Santa Ana Canyon Freeway Newport Beach to Riverside County Line	27.4	12.7	2,990,600			1,258,000	4,248,600
Ojai Freeway West Main St. in Ventura to 0.4 mi. north of Foster Park	5.7			4.1	2,100,000	1,000,000	3,100,000
Other Freeways Covered by Resolution of Adoption by Highway Commission	127.7					3,075,000	3,075,000
Total	565.8	182.2	$160,357,700	44.7	$60,311,100	$193,419,100	$414,087,900

nitely. When a condemnation suit is instituted, the issue is not to determine if the property shall be taken but only to determine how much shall the State pay for it. The necessity for the legal taking of private property by condemnation is authorized by the California Highway Commission in the passing of resolutions to that effect.

Bridge Department Accomplishments

One of the most important elements in freeway design and construction are the grade separation bridges. Without bridges to carry cross traffic, pedestrians, vehicles and railroad trains, either over or under freeway traffic, we would have no freeways as we know them today.

Following is a summary of completed and going contracts in District VII listed under the fiscal year in which budgeted:

Fiscal year	Number of structures	Value
1950-51	68 bridges	$11,500,000
1951-52	47 bridges	7,000,000
1952-53	34 bridges	5,500,000
1953-54	117 bridges	19,900,000
1954-55	76 bridges	11,900,000
	342 bridges	$55,800,000

Accompanying this story is a tabulation, Status of District VII Projects, January, 1956. This tabulation shows in convenient form the total miles of state highway over which the California Highway Commission has adopted freeway resolutions. With this authority given by the commission, the Division of Highways is authorized to proceed with development of freeway plans, right-of-way acquisition and construction. The first six freeways on this list within the limits of Los Angeles County have all been developed as full freeways. This means that all access rights of abutting property have been acquired and that grade separation bridges and subways have been built to carry all cross arterials either under or over the freeways.

Other freeways listed in this tabulation, planned for ultimate full freeways, have for the most part as a first stage been developed as expressways with access rights controlled and with central dividing strips to separate opposing traffic but without grade separation structures. In the case of those freeways so developed as expressways where cross streets intersect at grade, this stage of design usually has the intersections channelized and signalized. In the case of the Santa Ana Freeway in Orange County some sections have already been constructed as full freeways while other sections presently on expressway basis are being rapidly converted to the full freeway status.

In order to determine the progress that has been made in the last five years in the District VII freeways, reference is made to the status as of January 1, 1951. As of that time the total length of state highways covered by freeway resolutions totaled 290.9 miles as compared with the total today of 565.8 miles. Completed freeway and expressway projects in 1950 totaled 65.1 miles whereas the total January 1, 1956, is 182.3 miles.

The full force and effect of the Collier-Burns Highway Act in 1947 and subsequent legislation on freeways for District VII, is shown by comparing the total costs to date on January 1, 1951, of $136,346,200 with the January 1, 1956, total of $414,087,900.

Pasadena Freeway

When the first six-mile unit of completed construction on the portion of this freeway from Avenue 26 in Los Angeles to Glenarm Street in Pasadena, then called "Arroyo Seco Freeway," was dedicated and opened to public traffic on December 30, 1940, it was acclaimed as the West's first freeway. Subsequently, extensions were made to this section of completed freeway to extend it southerly through Elysian Park to a connection with the Hollywood Freeway at the four-level structure.

The last unit of construction, one-half mile in length in the City of Los Angeles between College Street and the Hollywood Freeway, was completed and opened to traffic on September 22, 1953. This was the most important event on the Pasadena Freeway that occurred during the past five-year period. On that date for the first time all levels of the unique traffic interchange structure, comprising four levels with connecting roadways to take care of all necessary traffic movements, was put into full operation. The Elysian Park section of the Pasadena Freeway in the four-level traffic interchange structure is 250,000 vehicles per day.

Harbor Freeway

The Harbor Freeway extends 22.4 miles from junction with the Hollywood Freeway in the four-level traffic interchange structure southerly to Battery Street in the San Pedro district of the Los Angeles Harbor.

From the standpoint of construction this is a new freeway since five years ago nothing had been completed and opened to traffic. Some construction on grade separation bridges was in progress at that time near the northerly end. Five years ago the record shows that $10,500,000 had been expended for rights of way and $3,000,000 on contracts to get construction under way. As of today the total expenditures on the Harbor Freeway total $78,378,000. Two and nine-tenths miles of the Harbor Freeway have been completed between the Hollywood Freeway and 23d Street in Los Angeles. According to 1955 traffic counts this section of freeway is now carrying a total of 160,000 vehicles per day.

Four contracts are now in progress on the Harbor Freeway covering 8.4 miles and costing $17,332,500. All the construction is scheduled for completion by spring of 1957.

Right-of-way acquisition is being carried on and nearly all the parcels have been acquired necessary to complete this freeway.

Long Beach Freeway

The Long Beach Freeway is also one of the newer freeway developments. The start of construction was heralded by groundbreaking ceremony at the southerly terminus of this freeway at Pacific Coast Highway, State Highway Route 60, in the City of Long Beach, on June 27, 1951, less than five years ago. Since that time there has been steady progress of construction on this important freeway in the East Los Angeles metropolitan area.

Looking east along recently completed Colorado Freeway. Eagle Rock, center left. Pasadena, center background.

In addition to this nearly completed contract there are in progress three other construction contracts providing for an additional 3.8 miles of freeway construction for which the total of the construction allotments is approximately $5,400,000. For continuing construction on the Long Beach Freeway the 1956-57 Fiscal Year budget carries an item of $4,915,000.

Hollywood Freeway

It is of interest to note that all construction units of the original 10-mile length of Hollywood Freeway from Vineland Avenue in the San Fernando Valley to Spring Street in the Los Angeles Civic Center, were completed and opened to public traffic during the past five-year period.

The first useable section of the Hollywood Freeway to be opened to public traffic was the three-mile section between Grand Avenue and Silver Lake Boulevard. This was opened to public traffic on December 27, 1950, with final completion and acceptance of the construction contracts being made on February 13 and 16, 1951.

The final construction contract to complete this 10-mile unit of the Hollywood Freeway was completed

The total length of the Long Beach Freeway from Pacific Coast Highway (Route 60) in Long Beach to Huntington Drive in East Los Angeles approaching the City of Alhambra is 21.5 miles. As of the present time, 7.9 miles of the Long Beach Freeway have been completed from Pacific Coast Highway northerly to the crossing with Atlantic Boulevard east of the City of Compton. Also completed in the East Los Angeles area during 1954 are two railroad grade separation bridges to carry the Long Beach Freeway over the Santa Fe Railroad freight yards and the Union Pacific Railroad freight yards. Both of these structures are about one-fourth mile long and the construction cost of these two is $2,660,000.

On July 22, 1954, a contract was awarded for one mile of freeway construction and eight bridges between Sheila Street and Verona Street where junction is made with the Santa Ana Freeway. The contract allotment for this construction is $2,692,000. The work is over 85 percent completed. It is anticipated that this contract will be completed in March, 1956.

Looking north along Harbor Freeway from above Washington Boulevard in Los Angeles

LEFT—Looking southerly along Harbor Freeway from Fourth Street in Los Angeles five years ago, when construction on Statler Hotel and Harbor Freeway were progressing simultaneously. RIGHT—Same location from air showing late afternoon full traffic load as of present.

Looking southeast along Santa Ana Freeway showing construction in progress now nearing completion on Long Beach Freeway. New construction provides traffic interchange between the two freeways.

and accepted by Director of Public Works Frank B. Durkee on August 5, 1954.

On basis of 1955 traffic counts, the average daily vehicular traffic on the Hollywood Freeway westerly of the four-level structure, is 180,000 vehicles per day. There have been individual counts that have exceeded this.

The Hollywood Freeway Extension joins the main Hollywood Freeway near the intersection with Lankershim Boulevard and extends northerly 6.8 miles to the proposed Golden State Freeway near Wentworth Avenue.

District VII right-of-way forces are concentrating on acquiring rights of way for the Hollywood Freeway northerly extension for the 1.1-mile unit extending from Lankershim Boulevard to Moorpark Street where early construction is scheduled. On January 12, 1956, bids were opened for construction of two bridges on this section of freeway; one across the Los Angeles River, and the other at Vineland Avenue. This project, for which the contractor, Oberg Construction Corporation, submitted the low bid of $910,694, is to be financed from items in the 1955-56 construction budget of $1,100,000.

There is an item in the 1956-57 Fiscal Year budget in the amount of $2,350,000 for carrying out the additional structures and freeway construction necessary to comple this 1.1 miles of freeway. The construction schedule calls for advertising this important contract early this summer.

Santa Ana Freeway

California Highways and Public Works issue of September-October, 1955, carried a detailed illustrated story about the Santa Ana Freeway by W. L. Fahey, District Engineer, who retired from state service on December 1, 1955.

The progress of right-of-way acquisition and construction on this freeway during the past five years has been very extensive. Five years ago only 12.3 miles were completed and open to traffic, whereas today, a total of 32.4 miles are completed, at a total cost of $61,000,000. 1955 traffic counts indicate that near Soto Street in the City of Los Angeles, the average daily traffic is 113,00 vehicles per day.

San Bernardino Freeway

The total length of the San Bernardino Freeway, formerly called "Ramona Freeway," between the junction with the Santa Ana Freeway at the Aliso Street bridge over the Los Angeles River to the San Bernardino county line, is 30.8 miles. The San Bernardino Freeway is now completed outbound from the junction with the Santa Ana Freeway in Los Angeles easterly to Rosemead Boulevard east of Alhambra, a distance of 9.3 miles. An additional 6.3 miles through the cities of Pomona and Claremont, from San Dimas Avenue to the San Ber-

LEFT—Looking east along Hollywood Freeway toward Los Angeles Civic Center as it looked five years ago, with traffic moving on top level only of four-level structure. RIGHT—Looking easterly along Hollywood Freeway toward Civic Center with heavy traffic on four-level interchange structure.

nardino county line, was opened to public traffic December 1, 1954. On this same date 7.2 miles of completed construction adjoining in District VIII, extending through Upland and Ontario to Archibald Avenue in San Bernardino County, was also opened to traffic.

Four contracts are now in progress on the San Bernardino Freeway, ex-tending for 15.3 miles. These construction allotments total $16,466,500. When these four construction contracts are completed late next summer, the entire length of the San Bernar-dino Freeway in Los Angeles County from the Los Angeles River at Aliso Street junction with the Santa Ana Freeway to the San Bernardino County line will be completed. This indicates

the extent of the accomplishments that have been carried out during the past five years.

Five years ago there were only six miles of the San Bernardino Freeway that were completed and opened to traffic. This was the most westerly section extending from the Los An-geles River bridge to Helen Drive in the City Terrace area just easterly of

LEFT—Looking east along Hollywood Freeway, showing late afternoon traffic near four-level structure as of five years ago. RIGHT—Same location showing late afternoon traffic as of now. This is a typical condition that produces an average daily traffic count of 180,000 vehicles.

and Public Works

the Los Angeles city limits. The total expenditures to date on the San Bernardino Freeway for the 30.8 miles, including moneys spent and obligated for rights of way and construction, is approximately $50,000,000. The traffic on the completed portions of the San Bernardino Freeway has been steadily increasing. The average daily traffic in 1950 was 25,000 vehicles per day whereas recent counts taken at Soto Street show 88,000 vehicles per day. This tremendous increase in traffic is to a considerable extent due to the unprecedented building program in the areas passed through. As one example of this, information has come to us that the City of West Covina in 1950 had a population of 2,667 whereas recently the estimated population is 28,631.

Looking northeasterly, showing completed San Bernardino Freeway over Garfield Avenue

Ventura Freeway

The Ventura Freeway extends from the Hollywood Freeway near Vineland Avenue in the San Fernando Valley to the Santa Barbara county line, a distance of 65.1 miles. Of this mileage, 39.1 miles have been completed at a construction cost of $12,484,000 to four-lane divided highway or expressway standards. This completed construction is all westerly of the west city limits of Los Angeles at Calabasas. Seventy-five percent of this construction was carried out during the past five years.

The California Highway Commission on May 18, 1955, adopted a freeway routing to carry the Coast Highway (U. S. Highway 101) through the City of Ventura. Plans are now in progress so that construction can go forward whenever financing can be arranged for this entire 5.5 miles through the City of Ventura.

Within the City of Los Angeles, the Highway Commission has adopted freeway resolutions covering 16 miles of the Ventura Freeway from the westerly city limits of Los Angeles near Calabasas to the existing terminus of the Hollywood Freeway. District right-of-way forces are now actively engaged in acquiring rights of way throughout the entire length of the Ventura Freeway in Los Angeles from Hollywood Freeway Extension to Calabasas at the west city limits. Much right of way has already been cleared from Sepulveda Boulevard westerly and a construction contract for two bridges is now under way. One of these bridges is to carry the Ventura Freeway over Topanga Canyon Road and the other is to carry the freeway over existing Ventura Boulevard. Funds in the amount of $6,270,000 for completion of the construction within this area for 3.8 miles between Kelvin Avenue and Calabasas and for 2.6 miles from Sepulveda Boulevard to Encino Avenue are included in the 1956-57 Fiscal Year budget.

San Diego Freeway

Much has been accomplished on the San Diego Freeway, formerly called "Sepulveda Freeway," within the last five-year period. The right-of-way expenditures to date of January 1, 1956, total almost $18,000,000.

The first unit of construction on this freeway was for structures between Waterford Street and Casiano Road, and bids were opened on August 26, 1954. This construction includes the large grade separation bridge to carry Sunset Boulevard over San Diego Freeway and three other smaller bridges. This bridge construction is expected to be completed by the time this story is published.

Looking east along San Bernardino Freeway, showing construction progress through City of El Monte

Present construction of the freeway proper on this portion of the San Diego Freeway between Waterford Street and Casiano Road is 40 percent completed, and will be finished next fall.

The section immediately to the south between Waterford Street and Ohio Street was let to contract in January. The low bid was $2,465,402.50. Upon the completion of this contract, scheduled for early in 1958, 3.3 miles of freeway in the West Los Angeles area will be available to the traveling public. In the San Fernando Valley the construction of a bridge structure to carry the San Diego Freeway over Ventura Boulevard is now under way. Funds in the amount of $4,565,000 for the construction of the traffic interchange layout between the San Diego and the Ventura Freeways have been budgeted in the 1956-57 fiscal year, and this work will be combined with the construction of the Ventura Freeway between Sepulveda Boulevard and Encino Avenue, and advertised later this year.

The Newer Freeways

The remaining freeways on the accompanying tabulation are newer freeways as compared with those higher on the list, and all might be called products of the past five years because five years ago construction had not been started on them. All that had been accomplished five years ago were route adoptions by the California Highway Commission, allocation of funds for right-of-way acquisition and preparation of designs and plans for construction.

The Colorado Freeway, extending from Eagle Vista Drive in Eagle Rock to Holly Street in Pasadena, being entirely complete with the new Pasadena Pioneer's Bridge over the Arroyo Seco, is of vital importance to the people of Pasadena and this area. The last unit of construction on the Colorado Freeway from Eagle Vista Drive to Avenue 64 was completed July 28, 1955.

The portion of the Foothill Freeway from Hampton Road to Montana Street in the Flintridge area, 1.8 miles in length, was reported in detail in the September-October, 1955, issue of *California Highways and Public*

Works. This important project, completed October 28, 1955, was also welcomed by the people of Pasadena, Flintridge and Altadena because it corrected an exasperating traffic congestion at Devil's Gate Dam.

Golden State Freeway

During the past five years, the portion of the Golden State Freeway, U. S. Highway 99, locally known as the "Ridge Route" between Tunnel Station and the Kern county line, 45.2 miles in District VII, has been converted to a four-lane expressway. The total cost of this reconstruction, completed February, 1953, was $13,-

Looking east along Ventura Freeway through Camarillo

500,000. Southerly from Tunnel Station for 27.5 miles the Golden State Freeway is to be carried out to full freeway standards to its southerly terminus at junction with the Santa Ana Freeway. Of this portion the northerly three miles from Tunnel Station southerly to Sepulveda Boulevard was completed at a cost of $3,200,000 on August 25, 1955.

On the Golden State Freeway two very important contracts have been started that affect the Griffith Park area. The first of these was awarded on August 15, 1955, carrying an allotment of $748,000, provides for the construction of two grade separation bridges at Los Feliz Boulevard in the City of Los Angeles. The anticipated date of completion is in the summer of 1956. The second contract, awarded October 3, 1955, called for grading and paving 4.2 miles of the Golden State Freeway in the Cities of Los Angeles, Glendale, and Burbank, extending from 0.9 mile south of the Los Angeles River in the City of Los Angeles to Ash Avenue in the City of Burbank. Included in this construction are six bridges and three pedestrian undercrossings.

Continuing Construction

For continuing construction on the Golden State Freeway within the City of Los Angeles there are two construction items in the 1956-57 Fiscal Year budget that provide for building 2.7 miles of this freeway southerly from near the Rodger Young Village to Glendale Boulevard for which the budgeted funds total $4,890,000. It is expected that this unit of construction will be advertised this spring. Combining this sum with the allowance set up for acquisition for rights of way on the Golden State Freeway the funds available in the 1956-57 Fiscal Year budget total $17,890,000.

Right-of-way activities are under way for acquiring all rights-of-way needed for the Golden State Freeway in the City of Los Angeles between Glendale Boulevard and junction with the Santa Ana Freeway. Right-of-way funds for the complete acquisition of right of way for project to be constructed in East Los Angeles between Sixth Street near the Santa Ana Free-

Looking southerly along Golden State Freeway, showing grade separation between Golden State Freeway and Southern Pacific Railroad, center left, and traffic interchange connection with Sepulveda Boulevard-San Fernando Road and Foothill Boulevard. San Fernando Reservoirs in background.

way and Mission Street northerly of the San Bernardino Freeway are included in the 1955-56 Fiscal Year right-of-way budget, and efforts are being made to concentrate on clearing this right of way. Completion of the Golden State Freeway through the City of Los Angeles, connecting it with the Santa Ana Freeway, the San Bernardino Freeway and the Pasadena Freeway, is of vital importance in clearing up traffic congestion on present freeways serving the Los Angeles Civic Center and business district.

Glendale Freeway

On the Glendale Freeway for the 1.6-mile section between the Los Angeles River and Avenue 36 near Eagle Rock Boulevard, plans are now completed and construction funds are included in the 1956-57 Fiscal Year budget in the amount of $3,270,000. This includes grade separation over Taylor Yard tracks of the Southern Pacific Railroad. Advertising of this contract is expected later this year. The 1.5-mile section of this freeway from the Los Angeles River extending it southerly to Glendale Boulevard

was adopted by the Highway Commission on December 14, 1955.

The Artesia Freeway which is a part of State Highway Route 175 extends from Coast Highway Route 60 in Redondo Beach to a junction with the Santa Ana Canyon Freeway in Orange County near Olive. Of this total length of 34 miles, 21.7 miles have been adopted by the California Highway Commission as freeway routing. These two sections of freeway in Los Angeles County extend from Normandie Avenue to Santa Fe Avenue, and in Orange County from Palo Verde Avenue to the Santa Ana Canyon Freeway. On these freeway sections during the past five years, 1.9 miles between Normandie Avenue and Main Street were completed at a cost of $1,000,000. We have under construction at the present time between Central Avenue and Santa Fe Avenue a unit 2.2 miles in length, having a construction allotment of $1,700,000, which will be completed this spring. In Orange County a section four miles long extending from Cypress Avenue to the Santa Ana Canyon Freeway, having a construction allotment of

$1,200,000, that is also scheduled for completion this spring. Plans are in progress for the remaining portions of this important east-west freeway.

The Santa Ana Canyon Freeway for which total expenditures now are $4,248,000, including the improvement of Route 43 through Costa Mesa in Orange County, is largely a development of the last five-year period.

The Ojai Freeway in Ventura County is one of the most recent freeway developments. Construction to freeway standards from West Main Street in the City of Ventura northerly for 4.1 miles is now under construction, with completion date set for midsummer of 1956.

Other Freeways

In addition to the above described freeways, the California Highway Commission has adopted freeway routings during the past five years for 127.7 miles of additional freeways upon which as yet no construction has been started.

Limitation of space prevents detailed description of these very important freeway projects that are so badly needed in this area. Designing of these freeways is being pushed as fast as other commitments will permit, and good use of advance right-of-way funds is being made whenever critical situations arise where action must be taken now to protect future rights of way from impending private developments which if permitted to go forward would cause great increase in future costs of rights of way. However, there are some of these freeways of such great importance they should be briefly mentioned.

The Riverside Freeway was adopted by the Californuia Highway Commission on November 18, 1954. This freeway resolution covered 10.9 miles extending from junction with the Golden Gate Freeway, State Highway Route 4, in Griffith Park westerly to Sepulveda Boulevard, State Route 158, which included the last remaining section of Ventura Freeway that had not previously been adopted as a freeway.

San Gabriel River Freeway

The California Highway Commission adopted the route for the San Gabriel River Freeway on December 15, 1954. This freeway extends from the junction with the Garden Grove Freeway near Long Beach to a junction with the San Bernardino Freeway near El Monte, a distance of 23 miles. Design is now under way in order to acquire vacant property subject to industrial and residential development under the advance right-of-way acquisition program.

The portion of the Pomona Freeway between Potrero Grande Drive and the junction of Route 19, a length of 18 miles, was adopted by the Highway Commission on April 2, 1954. Notwithstanding the intense subdivision activity in the Puente area, right-of-way needs for the freeway have been established ahead of the numerous subdivisions, and acquisition of vacant property is under way.

On June 21, 1955, the Highway Commission declared that portion of existing Route 23 (US 6) between Route 4 (US 99) and Solamint, a distance of seven miles, to be a freeway. The commission has announced their intention to hold a public hearing on February 9, 1956, for a proposed freeway route between Vincent Y and junction of Route 59, a distance of 19.6 miles. The latter section passes through the Palmdale-Lancaster area where there is considerable activity in new industry and subdivisions.

The California Highway Commission adopted the route for the Olympic Freeway between La Cienega Boulevard and the Santa Ana Freeway on May 21, 1954. Funds for right-of-way acquisition are available between the Harbor Freeway and the Santa Ana Freeway, and design studies are now in progress. Due to the heavy industrial development in the area between Harbor Freeway and the Santa Ana Freeway it has proven economically feasible to design and construct a continuous viaduct so as to hold to a minimum the cost of rights of way required for this freeway and secure other advantages.

Outlook for the Future

There is good reason to believe that the next five years will see fully as much if not more freeway development in this area than has been ob-tained during the past five-year period because great advantage will be had of previously made right-of-way purchases. Also, it may be anticipated that with increasing vehicle registration, increasing moneys will become available. It is, however, obvious that this area is not getting the freeways which it needs quickly enough to meet the expanding requirements of growing population. The present hope is that Congress may this year pass legislation increasing federal aid, particularly for use on interstate highway routes. This would be a substantial help but when population growth is as explosive as is now being experienced in this area, it would appear that still other additional funds must be provided if the people are to have all the freeways and other highway facilities that are so badly needed.

As has been stressed in this and previous articles, close cooperation among all governmental and civic organizations is the basic key to success in providing a tangible freeway system which must represent the greatest good to the greatest number of people in this great State of ours.

CARQUINEZ PROJECT

Continued from page 29 . . .

northbound traffic will continue to use the new four-lane structure.

This project along with the freeway work into Richmond, Berkeley and Oakland are scheduled for completion late in 1958. At this time the last remaining traffic bottleneck will have been broken between the two great areas of the San Francisco Bay and the Sacramento Valley.

Plans are underway for the remaining work contemplated by the legislation such as the freeway through Vallejo and the Benicia-Martinez Bridge and approaches. This work is tentatively scheduled for advertisement in the latter part of 1956.

DEATH VALLEY

Death Valley is approximately 140 miles long and covers 2,981 square miles, reports the California State Automobile Association.

COST INDEX

Continued from page 49 . . .

During the third quarter the U. S. Bureau of Public Roads Composite Mile Index rose 3.1 percent reaching 215.1. This Index is based on actual highway contract prices, as is the California Index, but on a nation-wide scale. It will be noted that the trends of this Index follow those of the California Index. Figures for the Composite Mile Index during the fourth quarter of 1955 are not available at this writing.

In view of the highway construction cost trends, as indicated by the Index, it is our belief that 1956 will see an accelerating upward spiral in bid prices.

NUMBER AND SIZE OF PROJECTS, TOTAL BID VALUES AND AVERAGE NUMBER OF BIDDERS

(July 1, 1955, to December 31, 1955)

Project volume	Up to $50,000	$50,000 to $100,000	$100,000 to $250,000	$250,000 to $500,000	$500,000 to $1,000,000	Over $1,000,000	All Projects
Road Projects							
No. of Projects	143	50	39	13	5	2	252
Total value*	$3,875,906	$3,768,003	$6,917,693	$4,853,857	$3,828,132	$2,612,921	$24,356,317
Ave. No. Bidders:	6.0	4.7	6.3	5.5	7.0	9.0	4.7
Structure Projects							
No. of Projects	21	7	4	2	3	4	41
Total Value*	$329,294	$462,596	$531,699	$845,215	$1,792,939	$19,049,288	$23,011,031
Ave. No. Bidders:	4.4	8.0	4.5	5.5	9.2	5.5	5.5
Combination Projects							
No. of Projects						4	17	21
Total Value*					$3,403,122	$61,890,662	$64,993,784
Ave. No. Bidders:					9.0	7.2	7.6
Summary							
No. of Projects	164	57	43	15	12	23	314
Total Value*	$3,905,100	$4,230,604	$7,449,392	$5,699,072	$8,723,193	$83,252,971	$113,360,132
Ave. No. Bidders:	6.1	5.1	6.1	5.5	8.3	7.0	5.0

* Bid items only.

Total Average Bidders by Months by Calendar Years

	Jan.	Feb.	Mar.	Apr.	May	June	July	Aug.	Sept.	Oct.	Nov.	Dec.	Avg. yr.
1955	5.5	5.8	6.7	5.5	5.0	4.4	4.9	4.3	4.4	5.4	6.2	5.4	5.3
1954	7.5	6.4	6.8	6.9	5.7	6.3	6.7	6.0	6.6	7.9	7.0	6.4	6.9

A. A. S. H. O. STATEMENT

Continued from page 53 . . .

Such additional revenues as may be needed in the judgment of Congress for financing an enlarged highway program could be obtained by using one or more of the following, and it is suggested that the Congress explore these possibilities:

(a) A reasonable increase in the present federal motor fuel tax.

(b) A reasonable tax or an increase in tax on items not now taxed by the states but that will serve as a measure of highway use.

(c) The reasonable use of short term credit financing with due consideration to its effect upon the national debt limitation.

GOOD GUIDE

HUNTINGTON PARK

California Highways and Public Works

DEAR SIRS: We have enjoyed your magazine very much and when we take trips through the State we use it as a guide to find the best routes to travel. This past summer we covered a great deal of the country in Northern California and plan to go more places this coming year so we do not want to miss a single copy of your journal for the next year or so, as we save each copy and loan them to our friends too.

Thanking you so much,

MR. AND MRS. O. H. WILLIAMS
3123 Walnut Street

HARDING RETIRING

Continued from page 45 . . .

Telford's duties during the past three years have included supervision not only of the planning phase of metropolitan freeway projects but also of the traffic engineering and design functions of the district.

The new Assistant State Highway Engineer is a native of Santa Barbara. After service in World War I in the infantry, he worked successively on highway surveys, railroad location and mining operations. He joined the staff of the Division of Highways in 1927 as a civil engineer in the Fresno district, and in succeeding years served in district offices in Bishop, and Eureka, and at Sacramento headquarters. He was a resident engineer on construction projects in the Los Angeles area from 1932 to 1936.

In 1950 Telford was appointed Engineer of Design for the Division of Highways, and subsequently Traffic Engineer. It was the latter position which he left to become District Engineer in District VII in February, 1953.

Telford also served in World War II, much of the time in North Africa and the India-Burma Theater.

District Engineer Langsner, in transferring from operations to planning, is returning to a field in which he has specialized for the past several years. He has been on the staff of District VII since his graduation from California Institute of Technology in 1931, and from 1949 to 1955 was responsible for the design of many of the metropolitan freeways in the Los Angeles area. Last year he was promoted to the post of district engineer to succeed W. L. Fahey upon the latter's retirement.

Gillis, the new district engineer—operations, has been on the Division of Highways staff since his graduation from the University of California in 1938. He has served in various capacities in District IV since 1941, except for military service with the Navy Civil Engineers Corps in World War II and the Korean conflict. Last year he was appointed assistant district engineer in charge of construction for District IV, which includes nine counties in the San Francisco Bay area.

NOVEMBER, 1955

Alpine County—FAS 960—On Diamond Valley Road, between State Highway Route 23 near Woodfords and Springmeyer Ranch, 4.5 miles. Construct graded roadbed and surface with road-mixed surfacing on imported base material. Contract awarded to Lee Const. Co., San Leandro, $78,606.

Calaveras County—Sign Route 4—At Avery, 0.2 mile. Construct cement treated base and surface with plant-mixed surfacing. drainage correction. Contract awarded to Rice Brother's, Inc., Lodi, $26,851.80.

Calaveras and Tuolumne Counties—Portions between 3.8 miles south of Angels Camp and 1.6 miles south of Stanislaus River, 2.7 miles. Grade and surface with road-mixed surfacing on untreated base. Contract awarded to H. Earl Parker Inc., Marysville, $244,119.70.

Fresno County — FAS 1230 — Across Fresno Slough By-pass at James Road. Two reinforced concrete slab bridges to be constructed and 24-inch reinforced concrete pipe culvert. Contract awarded to Thomas Construction Company, Fresno, $59,-908.89.

Imperial County—State Route 201—Near Alamorio, between Route 187 and 0.5 mile north, 0.5 mile. Grade and surface with road-mixed surfacing on untreated base. Contract awarded to N. L. Basich, South San Gabriel, $57,739.50.

Kern County—State Route 139—Between Rio Bravo School and Jackson Avenue (portions), 0.3 mile. Construct road-mixed surfacing, furnish and install corrugated metal pipe and pipe-arch culverts. Contract awarded to Irv. Guinn, Contractor, Bakersfield, $5,083.50.

Kern and Inyo Counties—At various locations. Producing and stockpiling sand. Contract awarded to John M. Ferry, Glendale, $14,925.

Los Angeles County—US 99—In Los Angeles between Edward Avenue and Delay Drive, 0.2 mile. Widen the existing roadbed by grading, placing plant-mixed surfacing on untreated base and on existing portland cement concrete, apply seal coat and construct concrete curbs and sidewalks. Contract awarded to Jesse S. Smith, Glendale, $24,869.50.

Los Angeles County—US 99—In San Fernando, on San Fernando Road between Fox Street and Hubbard Avenue, 1.1 miles. Heating, mixing and relaying the existing surfacing and then surfacing with plant-mixed surfacing. Contract awarded to G. J. Payne Co., Los Angeles, $12,316.28.

Los Angeles County—On US 6, 99, SR 134, in Los Angeles, Glendale and Burbank, between 0.9 mile south of Los Angeles River and Ash Avenue, 2.4 miles. Construct graded roadbeds and surface with portland cement concrete pavement and plant-mixed surfacing on cement treated base, seven undercrossings, one overcrossing, one bridge and separation completion of which provides an eight-lane divided freeway with frontage roads and connections. Contract awarded to Vinnell Co., Inc. & Vinnell Constructors, Alhambra, $4,040,782.

Los Angeles County—On Foothill Boulevard at San Dimas Avenue, 0.2 mile. Constructing a graded roadbed and surfacing with plant-mixed surfacing on untreated base, construct drainage facilities. Contract awarded to Ralph J. Laird, La Verne, $20,110.75.

Los Angeles County—In the City of San Fernando, on Maclay Avenue at Fourth Street, Fifth Street, Glenoaks Boulevard and Seventh Street. Traffic signal systems and highway lighting at four locations. Contract awarded to Galland Electric Co., South Gate, $14,576.76.

Los Angeles County—Between three miles and 3.6 miles north of Pacific Coast Highway, on Topanga Canyon Road, 0.6 mile. Construct a graded roadbed and place plant-mixed surfacing on untreated base, completion of which provides a roadway on new alignment, eliminating many curves. Contract awarded to Lowe & Watson, San Bernardino, $202,178.95.

Los Angeles County—Between Melrose Avenue and Linda Vista Avenue Off-ramp on Colorado Freeway. Roadside development. Contract awarded to K. E. C. Co., Artesia, $61,573.66.

Los Angeles County—In Hawthorne, at the intersections of Hawthorne Boulevard with 138th Street, with 135th Street and with 132d Street. Traffic signal systems to be furnished and installed or modified. Contract awarded to Sherwin Electric Service, Los Angeles, $9,576.

Los Angeles County—On US 66, 101, at the Santa Ana Freeway-Lakewood Boulevard Interchange. Construct drainage facilities on divided freeway. Contract awarded to Angeles Construction Co., Downey, $3,602.

Los Angeles County—In the vicinity of Long Beach and Lakewood, at the intersections of Carson Street with Palo Verde Avenue and with Los Coyotes Diagonal-Studebaker Road. Furnish and install traffic signal and highway lighting systems. Contract awarded to Fishback & Moore, Inc., Los Angeles, $34,466.

Madera County—Sign Route 145—On Madera Avenue between Cottonwood Creek and 0.5 mile north, 0.5 mile. Furnish and place imported borrow, two corrugated metal pipe arches and plant-mixed surfacing. Contract awarded to Stewart & Nuss Inc., Fresno, $10,063.

Riverside County—At Keen Camp Maintenance Station. Constructing a cottage and a pump house (with pump and pressure tank), furnishing and installing a water supply system, sewer system and discharge line to be constructed. Contract awarded to Loren B. Smith, Covina, $20,982.50.

Riverside County—At various locations across Perris Valley Storm Drain and San Jacinto River, on Nuevo Road and Martin Street between about two and seven miles northeasterly of Perris. Four reinforced concrete slab bridges. Contract awarded to C. B. Tuttle, Los Alamitos, $98,134.40.

San Bernardino County—In San Bernardino, at District VIII office and laboratory buildings. Intercommunication system to be furnished and installed. Contract awarded to Fairfax Radio Electric Co., Los Angeles, $3,955.

San Bernardino County—On US 91, 466—Between two miles east of Yermo and 10 miles east of Baker, 0.3 mile. Place plant-mixed surfacing on existing bridges and approaches. Contract awarded to G. W. Ellis Construction Co., North Hollywood, $10,500.

San Bernardino County—In the City of San Bernardino, at Highland Avenue and Mt. Vernon Avenue, 0.5 mile. Grade and surface with plant-mixed surfacing and approaches, girder bridge, signals, lighting and illuminated signs. Contract awarded to R. M. Price Co., Altadena, $784,876.05.

San Diego County—US 80—Between 0.2 mile east of Maryland Avenue and 0.2 mile east of Baltimore Drive, near La Mesa, 0.8 mile. Grading and paving with plant-mixed surfacing on untreated base and imported subbase and constructing frontage roads, ramps and connections, and a steel girder overcrossing. Contract awarded to V. R. Dennis Const. Co., Hillcrest Sta., $410,913.

San Diego County—US 395—At the intersection with Sign Route 76, 0.3 mile. Grade and channelize an intersection, surface traffic lanes with plant-mixed surfacing on untreated base. Contract awarded to E. L. Yeager Co., Riverside, $19,073.10.

San Diego County—US 395—In San Diego, between Fulton Street and Aero Drive, 2.0 miles. Constructing a graded roadbed for a frontage road and surfacing with plant-mixed surfacing, a rein-forced concrete box girder bridge undercrossing and a welded steel plate girder bridge overcrossing with reinforced concrete deck. Contract awarded to Griffith Co., Los Angeles, $668,472.

San Diego County—Sign Route 76—In the City of Oceanside, between Santa Barbara Street and Mesa Drive, 0.8 mile. Grade and surface with plant-mixed surfacing on untreated base, widen to four-lane divided highway. Contract awarded to R. E. Hazard Const. Co., San Diego, $93,599.

San Diego County—Sign Route 94—Between College Avenue and Campo Road, 2.5 miles. Grading and paving with portland cement concrete on cement treated base, for constructing a six-lane divided freeway together with the necessary ramps and interchange lanes and street connections, four undercrossings, two overcrossings, one underpass and one separation. Contract awarded to Guy F. Atkinson, Long Beach, $2,863,722.50.

Stanislaus County—Sign Route 132—Across San Joaquin River, about 13 miles west of Modesto. Repair an existing bridge. Contract awarded to C. C. Gildersleeve, Grass Valley, $2,888.88.

Tulare County—Sign Route 134—Between 0.3 mile east of Ash Avenue and Route 132 near Tulare. Storm sewer system and electrically operated drainage pumping plant to be constructed. Contract awarded to W. M. Lyles Co., Avenal, $35,538.76.

DECEMBER, 1955

Alameda County—Eastshore Freeway—At Centerville Elementary School and at Irvington Elementary School. Flashing beacon systems to be furnished and installed. Contract awarded to Manning and Whitaker, San Francisco, $2,389.96.

Alameda County—State Routes 228 and 105—Between plant-mixed surfacing, constructing cement treated base, median curbs and island surfacing and repairing failed areas, 1.5 miles. Contract awarded to Clements Const. Co., Centerville, $39,050.50.

Calaveras County—FAS 1150—Between 1.0 mile and 3.3 miles northeast of Altaville, 2.3 miles. Constructing a graded roadbed, placing imported subbase material and untreated base and surfacing with road-mixed surfacing, drainage structures to be furnished and installed. Contract awarded to Beerman & Jones, Sonora, $131,912.40.

Colusa County—Sign Route 20—Between South-ern Pacific Railroad in Williams and 5 miles east. Construct new fence and drainage facilities. Contract awarded to E. H. Thomas Co., Sacramento, $33,430.75.

Fresno County—Sign Route 180—Between 0.5 mile south of Mendota and 0.3 mile east of Panoche Road. 0.6 mile, constructing a graded roadway and surfacing with road-mixed surfacing on imported borrow. Contract awarded to Paul E. Woof, Fresno, $20,964.80.

Fresno County—Sign Route 145—Between Kerman and 2.1 miles north (portions), constructing a graded roadbed and surfacing with plant-mixed surfacing, 0.4 mile. Contract awarded to C. E. Ruberts & Son, Coalinga, $9,012.50.

Fresno County—FAS 1231—On Belmont Avenue, between Clovis Avenue and Academy Avenue, construct a graded roadbed placing imported base material, constructing a cement treated base and surfacing with plant-mixed surfacing, a reinforced concrete girder bridge to be constructed, 8.0 miles. Contract awarded to Baun Const. Co., Inc., Fresno, $323,255.30.

Humboldt County—US 101—At Rohnerville Road. Reinforced concrete pipe culvert to be installed. Contract awarded to Mercer Fraser Co., Inc. and Mercer Fraser Gas Co., Inc., Eureka, $9,247.75.

Imperial County—FAS 649—Between State Highway Route 12 and New River near El Centro. Constructing a graded roadbed, surfacing with plant-mixed surfacing on imported base material and applying fog seal coat. 5.6 miles. Contract awarded to Basich Bros. Const. Co. & N. L. Basich, South San Gabriel, $259,903.95.

Imperial County—US 80—Between Alamo River and 0.1 mile east of Holtville. Constructing a graded roadbed, placing imported subbase material and surfacing with plant-mixed surfacing on cement treated base and existing pavement, clearing and grubbing to be performed, a special reinforced concrete drop inlet and concrete curbs, sidewalks and driveways to be constructed, right of way monuments and raised traffic bars, completion of which will provide a four-lane divided highway, 1.3 miles. Contract awarded to N. L. Basich, South San Gabriel, $157,547.00.

Kings County—Sign Route 41—Through Pyramid Hills, about 15 miles southwest of Kettleman City, constructing a two-lane highway by grading, placing plant-mixed surfacing on cement treated imported subbase material and constructing plant-mixed surfacing dikes, and roadway to be finished. 2.0 miles. Contract awarded to Valley Paving & Const. Co., Inc., Pismo Beach, $150,390.50.

Kings and Fresno Counties—FAS 623 and 945—On 6th Avenue, between Fargo Avenue and Excelsior Avenue; and on Excelsior Avenue between 19th Avenue and Kings River. Constructing a graded roadbed and surfacing with plant-mixed surfacing on cement treated base, clearing and grubbing to be performed and the roadway to be finished, 5.7 miles. Contract awarded to Granite Const. Co., Watsonville, $160,420.00.

Lake County—ILAK-1044—On Butts Canyon Road between Napa County line and 1.8 miles northwesterly. Grading a two-lane roadbed, placing untreated base, applying penetration treatment and drainage facilities, 1.8 miles. Contract awarded to Lange Bros. & Hastings, Lakeport, $98,629.05.

Los Angeles County—In the city of Los Angeles, San Diego Freeway at Ventura Boulevard. Construct embankments, widening existing streets and placing plant-mixed surfacing on untreated base, construct undercrossing, channelization, curbs, sidewalks, drainage facilities, sewers, highway lighting and signal system for freeway, 0.1 mile. Contract awarded to Oberg Bros. Const. Co., Inglewood, $460,861.50.

Los Angeles County—State Route 166—Between Orange Grove Avenue and Vernon Avenue, install a watering system and a chain link fence. Contract awarded to D & M Sprinkler Co., Long Beach, $2,971.65.

Los Angeles County—State Route 166—Between Camfield Avenue and Pioneer Boulevard, roadside areas to be developed and planted, 7.5 miles. Contract awarded to K E C Company, Artesia, $30,-990.92.

Los Angeles County—State Route 167—Between 0.3 mile south of Southern Avenue and Atlantic Boulevard. Construct graded roadbeds and surface with portland cement concrete pavement on cement treated subgrade and plant-mixed surfacing on untreated base and cement treated base and install highway lighting and directional sign system, and construct eight structures and three pumping plants, completion of which provides a new six-lane divided freeway with bridges at: Florence Avenue Overcrossing, Gage Avenue Overcrossing, East Walker Underpass, Standard Oil Co. Pipe Line Overcrossing, Slauson Avenue Overcrossing, Retaining Wall No. 180, Chell Depot Overhead, Chell Depot Storm Drain, and Florence Avenue Overcrossing Pumping Plant, Gage Avenue Overcrossing Pump Plant and Slauson Avenue Overcrossing, 3.4 miles. Contract awarded to Ukropina, Polich, Steve Kral & John R. Ukropina, San Gabriel, $3,188,422.10.

Los Angeles County—State Route 178—In the City of Long Beach over Route 178 at Long Beach City College. Construct a combination welded plate girder and concrete slab bridge, sidewalks and chain fence to be constructed and a highway lighting system to be furnished and installed, providing a pedestrian overcrossing. Contract awarded to N. M. Saliba Co., Gardena, $52,527.00.

Los Angeles County—FAS 852—On Valley Boulevard, between Ferrero Lane and 0.1 mile east of

Turnbull Canyon Road. Construct a graded roadbed and surfacing with asphalt concrete on untreated base, constructing a steel beam bridge with reinforced concrete deck, drainage facilities and roadway to be finished, 1.9 miles. Contract awarded to Clifford C. Bong & Co., Arcadia, $686,-047.30.

Madera County—Sign Route 152—At Berenda Slough, about 3.3 miles west of Califa, reinforced concrete bridge to be constructed and approaches to be graded and surfaced with plant-mixed surfacing on untreated base, 0.6 mile. Contract awarded to R. E. Hertel, Sacramento, $181,409.70.

Marin County—State Route 1—Between 2.0 miles north of Dolan's Corner and 2.5 miles south of Tomales, at various locations. Culverts to be reconstructed and underdrain to be constructed. Contract awarded to Ghilotti Bros., Inc., San Rafael, $15,812.80.

Monterey County—State Route 118—At Blanco-Cooper Road, 3.2 miles northwest of Salinas construct a graded roadbed, place imported subbase material and untreated base, surfacing with plant-mixed surfacing and applying seal coats, 0.4 mile. Contract awarded to Valley Paving & Const. Co., Inc., Pismo Beach, $36,212.00.

Monterey County—FAS 660—On Los Laureles Grade Road, between 0.7 mile north of Carmel Valley Road and Summit, constructing a graded roadbed by grading and placing selected material on a portion of the roadbed, 2.3 miles. Contract awarded to Jess H. Harrison, San Ardo, $167,-104.00.

Orange County—US 101—Between Browning Avenue and Fourth Street. Furnishing and placing plant-mixed surfacing, preparing planting areas and planting, 2.1 miles. Contract awarded to K E C Company, Artesia, $23,401.72.

Orange County—US 101 Alternate—At the intersection of Coast Highway with Los Patos Avenue, approximately one-half mile southeasterly from Sunset Beach. Constructing channelization, furnishing and installing a three-phase full traffic-actuated signal system and highway lighting, 0.3 mile. Contract awarded to Cox Bros. Const. Co., Stanton, $38,276.95.

Orange County—FAS 826—On Katella Avenue, between Stanton Avenue and Santa Ana Freeway. Constructing a graded roadbed and placing plant-mixed surfacing on untreated base, drainage facilities to be furnished and installed, 5.1 miles. Contract awarded to Sully-Miller Contracting Co., Long Beach, $316,471.90.

Riverside County—FAS 734—On 56th Avenue between Monroe Street and Coachella Valley Storm Drain at Thermal. Grading and surfacing with plant-mixed surfacing on imported base material, 3.5 miles. Contract awarded to Baun Const. Co., Inc., Fresno, $197,396.20.

San Benito County—FAS 669—On Fairview Road and Shore Road, between Fallon Road and Bolsa Road, construct graded roadbed, place impotted subbase material and untreated base, apply penetration treatment and seal coat, 7.5 miles. Contract awarded to Valley Paving & Const. Co., Inc., Pismo Beach, $140,014.00.

San Diego County—At various locations. Sealing pavement joints, 21.2 miles. Contract awarded to James M. Pope, Downey, $58,498.75.

San Joaquin County—In Manteca, on Main Street at Yosemite Street. Traffic signal system to be furnished and installed. Contract awarded to Collins Electrical Co., Inc., Stockton, $11,277.00.

San Mateo County—Bayshore Freeway—Between 1.5 miles south of San Francisco County line and 0.4 mile north of Butler Road Overcrossing. Construct graded roadbeds and railroad embankments, a welded steel girder bridge with reinforced concrete deck slab and a reinforced concrete box girder bridge, for six-lane divided highway on new alignment, 3.5 miles. Contract awarded to Guy F. Atkinson Co., South San Francisco, $2,039,702.00.

Santa Clara County—US 101—About 6 miles north of Morgan Hill, at Encinal Elementary School. Install a flashing beacon system. Contract awarded to Progress Electric, Palo Alto, $1,897.00.

Santa Clara County—Sign Route 17—At the intersection with Trimble Road, at north city limit of Milpitas. Install a span-wire mounted flash-

ing beacon system and highway lighting. Contract awarded to Ets-Hokin and Galvan, Oakland, $1,888.00.

Santa Clara County—State Route 17—At intersections of San Jose-Los Gatos Road with Union Avenue and with Campbell Avenue, in and near Campbell. Install traffic signal and highway lighting and construct channelization. Contract awarded to Leo F. Piazza Paving Co., San Jose, $70,449.00.

Santa Clara County—Sign Route 17—Between Sign Route 17 and Santa Clara Street. Constructing graded roadbeds, paving with portland cement concrete on cement treated subgrade, placing plant-mixed surfacing on existing pavement, frontage roads, ramps and connecting roads and surfacing with plant-mixed surfacing on cement treated base, three bridges, one overcrossing and one underpass, 1.6 miles. Contract awarded to Leo F. Piazza Paving Co., San Jose, $1,535,052.80.

Santa Clara County—FAS 996—On Santa Clara-Los Gatos Road, between Vasona Junction and Shelburne Way. Constructing a graded roadbed and surfacing with plant-mixed surfacing on untreated base, reinforced concrete drainage structures to be constructed, 10.0 miles. Contract awarded to Edward Keeble, San Jose, $218,393.90.

Shasta County—US 99—II-SHA-3-C—Between Crespos and Vollmers. Grading and surfacing with plant-mixed surfacing on cement treated base and untreated base, completion of which will provide a four-lane divided highway, 2.0 miles. Contract awarded to Guy F. Atkinson Co., South San Francisco, $1,294,763.70.

Out of the Mail Bag

SHARES MAGAZINE
South Pasadena

Mr. K. C. Adams, *Editor*

Dear Mr. Adams: I am very happy to know that I will continue to receive *California Highways and Public Works* magazine.

You perhaps might be interested in knowing that this magazine is forwarded to four different offices, all of which are very interested and get a great amount of pleasure from the reading of this magazine.

I expect to increase this recirculation to at least six offices within the near future.

Again thanking you for your courtesies, I am

Yours very truly,

G. B. Foster
701 Brent Ave.

CONGRATULATIONS
PACIFIC ROAD BUILDER AND
ENGINEERING REVIEW

Mr. Kenneth C. Adams, *Editor*

Dear Ken: Congratulations on another fine magazine—the November-December issue of *California Highways and Public Works*. Every article is closely read by me as part of my constant search to uncover a new development in highway construction. I now find that I am personally acquainted with more and more of your staff of resident engineer writers and this increases my interest in the articles.

Belated season's greeting to you and your staff.

Yours very truly,

Harold Shaw, *Editor*
Pacific Road Builder and
Engineering Review

FROM T. V. A.
TENNESSEE VALLEY AUTHORITY
Chattanooga, Tennessee

Mr. Kenneth C. Adams, *Editor*

Dear Mr. Adams: I have received two copies of your magazine which I have certainly enjoyed. Though I am a sanitary engineer in the field of water supply and sewage treatment, my first love was highway construction, having worked summers during high school and college days in Mississippi when that state's construction progress was just getting underway.

You are doing a good job in presenting the problems of financing, design, right-of-way acquisition, and construction. The people of California should be proud of their active and progressive highway department.

Sincerely yours,

William Ward Filgo
Public Health Engineer

FROM PENNSYLVANIA
Pittsburgh, Pa.

Dear Mr. Adams: Thanks very much for enabling me to receive copies of your wonderful magazine.

I want you to know I have thoroughly enjoyed the past issues I have received.

You will understand this by reason of the fact that I am employed as a construction inspector (highways) and of course have had considerable experience along these lines.

I can see you have a wonderful highway construction program on out there and it's certainly interesting to see what is going on out in your wonderful state.

Respectfully,

Charles E. Pfeil

FROM ALBION COLLEGE
ALBION COLLEGE
Albion, Michigan

Mr. K. C. Adams, *Editor*

I would like to say "thank you" and to let you know that I appreciate receiving your magazine.

The issues are made available to our engineering students on the combined plan. Those interested in civil engineering receive stimulus and knowledge from the issues. In many cases they can see where the fundamentals of mathematics and physics are used. Which helps.

Many of us wish that our state highway department had the fine public relations which yours seems to have.

Yours truly,

Edmund E. Ingalls
Professor Mathematics
In charge of students on the
Combined Plan in Engineering

KEEP BACK COPIES
Felton

Mr. K. C. Adams, *Editor*

Dear Mr. Adams: We cannot express our sincere appreciation enough for this wonderful educational and enlightening magazine.

The well written articles and illustrations, the detailed costs of construction, causes us to read your magazine from cover to cover.

We have all copies sent us for years and very often refer back to old copies, and note the profound advancement in our highway building. We wish to thank you again.

Sincerely,

Mr. and Mrs. J. F. Schutte
614 Highway 9 South

INDEX TO CALIFORNIA HIGHWAYS AND PUBLIC WORKS

JANUARY TO DECEMBER, 1955

INDEX OF AUTHORS

INTERESTED IN HIGHWAYS

LOS ANGELES 36

MR. K. C. ADAMS, *Editor*

GENTLEMEN: I greatly appreciate being on your mailing list and assure you that I am interested in the development of our wonderful highways.

I always look forward to receiving my copy of *California Highways and Public Works*. It is most interesting and educational from cover to cover.

Yours very truly,

JOHN H. DIELMAN
256 S. Orange Drive

DEPARTMENT OF PUBLIC WORKS
SACRAMENTO, CALIFORNIA

CALIFORNIA
STATE HIGHWAY SYSTEM

ALIFORNIA
VAYS AND PUBLIC WORKS

California Highways
and Public Works

Official Journal of the Division of Highways,
Department of Public Works, State of California

KENNETH C. ADAMS, Editor

HELEN HALSTED, Assistant Editor

MERRITT R. NICKERSON, Chief Photographer

Vol. 35   March-April   Nos. 3-4

Public Works Building
Twelfth and N Streets
Sacramento

CONTENTS

Published in the interest of highway development in California. Editors of newspapers and others are privileged to use matter contained herein. Cuts will be gladly loaned upon request.

Address communications to

CALIFORNIA HIGHWAYS AND PUBLIC WORKS
P. O. Box 1499
Sacramento, California

Freeways In District IV

By B. W. BOOKER
Assistant State Highway Engineer

*Bay Area Network Is
More Readily Evident*

THE CHRONICLING of the development of the Bay area freeway system has followed the varied pattern of its construction. From the time of the opening of the first freeway section in 1947, as each small segment took form, articles appeared in various publications describing the planning and procedures which brought that section into being.

Although sometimes not apparent, these disconnected segments were part of an over-all plan. One might well have asked why the plan was not progressive in the sense of creating a continuous freeway, each completed segment extending the initial unit toward its ultimate destination. The answer is that priority of construction units have followed a logical pattern predicated on elimination of the worst deficiencies as quickly as possible within financial limitation. It was necessary to fit the construction program accordingly, and hence the disjointed aspects of the early stages.

Not until 1953, when various major projects were completed in the immediate metropolitan areas, did the plan unfold to a point wherein it was possible to treat the completed portions as an integrated development. Each year thereafter, it has been an interesting and pleasant task to record in this journal the progress of the preceding year, and to outline the program of current and future construction.

Complete System

In discussing the growth of the area's modern highways, one becomes conscious that the word "freeway" occurs with sometimes monotonous regularity. Actually, the goal is not merely to build this type of facility. The objective is to create a complete

B. W. BOOKER

system of all types of highways capable of moving people and goods rapidly, safely and conveniently between concentrations of population, at the same time affording similar service to dispersions along the routes. Since the main artery of such a system is the freeway, the name has become synonymous with modern highway development.

It would be difficult to imagine a modern public work upon which more people depend than that of motor transport and the roads upon which it operates. Affecting our daily programs and our manner of living as it does, it is to be expected that conflict of interests will arise in its construction and in its operation, and it follows that from such conflict will arise criticism. In the foreground of this criticism is the allegation that

freeways are obsolete immediately after completion.

Logically, the fact that freeways are traveled to their maximum capacity is the reverse of obsolescence. It is conclusive proof that the freeway has accomplished its purpose. The advantages offered have drawn traffic from congested streets and roadways, the force of the attraction being limited only by the capacity of the facility. Pausing for a moment to reflect upon the rise of traffic volume since 1947, when the first section was opened, we can readily contemplate the complete strangulation of the area if the present freeways disappeared, and the system was returned to its pattern of that date.

Problem of Future

Obviously, the routes presently being constructed will not meet the needs of the future. It is equally obvious that we should not attempt to construct the ultimate development at this time. To do so would seriously delay initial correction of the numerous severe deficiencies throughout our highway system. Current construction does provide for additional lanes to be built when needed, and in one case, that of the Eastshore Freeway south of High Street, we are now constructing the additional lanes provided for in the original design.

However, the useful number of lanes which can be expected to operate efficiently is limited and studies are being made of new routes for area traffic distribution. Complicating such studies is the unusual geography of the area. Separated by the waters of the bay, the two great centers of population on the easterly and westerly sides must be served by virtually two systems, the integration of the sys-

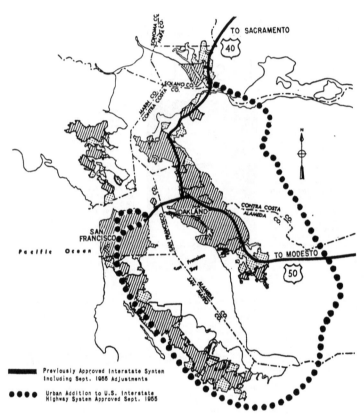

TO SACRAMENTO

40

TO MODESTO

50

SAN FRANCISCO

OAKLAND

Pacific Ocean

██████ Previously Approved Interstate System
Including Sept. 1955 Adjustments

●●●● Urban Addition to U.S. Interstate
Highway System Approved Sept. 1955

tems being dependent upon crossings available. The cost and complexity of transbay facilities understandably limits their construction, thus creating restrictive controls in planning a balanced network.

New Major Routes

The year 1955 witnessed a significant step toward the creation of new major routes in District IV. As approved by Commissioner C. D. Curtiss of the U. S. Bureau of Public

Roads, the National System of Interstate Highways was adjusted and augmented in the amount of 135 miles in the Bay area. These highways are eligible for substantial allocations of Federal Interstate System funds under the terms of legislation now being considered by the Congress.

Much of the routing added was already established as a part of the State Highway System and planning for the future development of these as freeways is generally well advanced.

Portions of the future freeway system in San Francisco are included in the addition but studies of the general location of these routes are not complete to date.

A major part of the addition is a 115-mile circumferential route around the San Francisco Bay area. This route begins at the south city limits of San Francisco and runs southeasterly, west and roughly parallel to US 101 (El Camino Real) then swings easterly in the vicinity of San Jose, veering northerly through central Alameda County and the San Ramon Valley in Contra Costa County to the Martinez-Benicia area, finally connecting with US 40 in Vallejo.

From San Francisco to San Jose, the proposed route would constitute a new highway not presently in the State Highway System. From a connection with Sign Route 17 west of San Jose, it follows the general location of State Sign Routes 17 and 21 as far as Benicia. A substantial portion of the East Bay route is in the planning stage, in design, or is currently under construction. The general location of the new route is shown on the accompanying map. It is apparent thereon that it will supplement the services of the present Bayshore Freeway on the San Mateo Peninsula as well as El Camino Real and the various local arterials accommodating both the through and many of the local traffic desires. Likewise, on the East Bay side, it will supplement the Eastshore Freeway and the transcontinental US 40, serving through traffic and the expanding local traffic of central Alameda and Contra Costa Counties along the way.

Sixty-three Construction Projects

As of March 1, 1956, District IV had a total of 63 construction projects under way. Twenty-seven of these involved development of the freeway network.

Seventy-one miles of new freeway construction were included in the

work under progress. Budgeted and not yet started are another 27 miles of freeway improvement. After completion of the 1956-57 Fiscal Year construction program, a total of 250 miles of freeway will be in service in this district.

The district is currently operating under a program of $61,647,000 for construction and right of way in the 1955-56 Fiscal Year and $59,172,000 in the 1956-57 Fiscal Year. In addition, contracts under way as part of the Carquinez toll facility project amount currently to $28,834,000, of which $20,877,000 represents work located in District IV.

Status of District IV freeways is indicated on the accompanying map. Development of this network of modern arterials of safe, convenient and rapid transportation is becoming more and more apparent as the fruits of previous years of planning and endeavor are rapidly being transformed from blueprints to realities, commensurate with the availability of funds for highway construction.

Highlights of Progress

Highlights of the progress of these transformations during the past 12 months together with mention of projects financed but not yet under construction are indicated in the following excerpts from activities on our various freeway routes.

BAYSHORE (JAMES LICK FREEWAY AND SKYWAY)

Several additional units of this freeway were placed into service during the past 12 months.

Except for a short portion southerly of Third Street which will be completed in conjunction with the "open water" fill relocation now under way south of the city limits, all of Route 68 within the city has now been completed as a full freeway.

Traffic now traverses this six- and eight-lane Skyway from Third Street near the south city limits directly to the San Francisco-Oakland Bay Bridge.

Skyway service is also provided via a portion of the Central Freeway along 13th Street from the Division Street Interchange toward the Golden

Gate Bridge. It presently terminates at South Van Ness Avenue and Mission Street.

The completed Skyway has already been a boon to both intracity and intercity traffic. With the completion of the part of the Embarcadero Freeway from the Bay Bridge to the Broadway Tunnel, portions of which are now financed or under way, effective distribution of Skyway traffic within the downtown San Francisco area will be accomplished.

More and more use of the Skyway is being made for mass transit through the scheduling of busses destined for areas as far from downtown as Lake Merced.

Some 110,000 vehicles traverse the Skyway daily. All of these users are afforded a scenic, awe-inspiring panoramic view of the San Francisco skyline previously unseen by the multitudes of vehicle users who traveled the low level congested city streets.

The unit between Hester Avenue and Alemany Boulevard was started in June, 1953, and completed in September, 1955. Contractor on this $2,400,000 project was Charles L. Harney, Inc. This project is the southernmost part of the completed freeway in San Francisco and has practically eliminated the severe congestion at the Third Street intersection as well as along the old Bayshore Boulevard during peak hours. This will be further improved in the future when traffic will be routed over the Third Street Interchange and across the open water fill project to the south. This will be effected upon completion of the latter project presently contemplated for mid-year 1957.

The $3,900,000 unit from Eighth Street to Fourth Street which was started in October, 1953, was completed in July, 1955. This was also constructed by Charles L. Harney, Inc., and is 0.7 mile long.

The project from Fifth Street to Third Street was constructed by Eaton and Smith at a cost of $900,000. This was started in May, 1954, and completed in July, 1955. It connects the Skyway with the San Francisco-Oakland Bay Bridge and also will serve as a part of the connection to

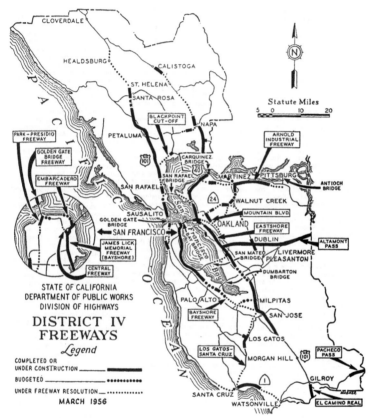

CLOVERDALE

HEALDSBURG

CALISTOGA

ST. HELENA

SANTA ROSA

BLACKPOINT CUT-OFF

NAPA

Statute Miles
5   0   10   20

PARK – PRESIDIO FREEWAY

PETALUMA

ARNOLD INDUSTRIAL FREEWAY

GOLDEN GATE BRIDGE FREEWAY

CARQUINEZ BRIDGE

EMBARCADERO FREEWAY

SAN RAFAEL BRIDGE

MARTINEZ   PITTSBURG

ANTIOCH BRIDGE

SAN RAFAEL

WALNUT CREEK

24

SAUSALITO

MOUNTAIN BLVD.

GOLDEN GATE BRIDGE

OAKLAND

EASTSHORE FREEWAY

SAN FRANCISCO

DUBLIN

ALTAMONT PASS

JAMES LICK MEMORIAL FREEWAY (BAYSHORE)

SAN MATEO BRIDGE   LIVERMORE PLEASANTON

CENTRAL FREEWAY

DUMBARTON BRIDGE

STATE OF CALIFORNIA
DEPARTMENT OF PUBLIC WORKS
DIVISION OF HIGHWAYS

PALO ALTO

MILPITAS

BAYSHORE FREEWAY

SAN JOSE

DISTRICT IV
FREEWAYS
Legend

LOS GATOS

COMPLETED OR
UNDER CONSTRUCTION _____ ▅▅▅▅

LOS GATOS– SANTA CRUZ

MORGAN HILL

PACHECO PASS

BUDGETED _____ ●●●●●●●●

GILROY

UNDER FREEWAY RESOLUTION___ ●●●●●●●●●●●

SANTA CRUZ

MARCH 1956

WATSONVILLE

EL CAMINO REAL

the Embarcadero Freeway, construction of which is now under way.

CENTRAL FREEWAY

The first portion of the Central Freeway was placed in service during

the past year with the completion of three projects by Charles L. Harney, Inc. This freeway is also on an elevated structure and is a part of the Skyway.

The unit along 13th Street from the Division Street Interchange to South Van Ness Avenue and Mission Street provided Central Freeway service to and from the south. It was started in

July, 1952, and completed in March, 1955. It consisted of two contracts, one for the substructure and footings, the other for the superstructure. The unit connecting the Central Freeway with the Skyway and Bay Bridge was started in June, 1952, completed in April, 1955. All three projects amounted to one mile in length and cost $5,000,000.

Plans are nearing completion for the continuance of this freeway from South Van Ness Avenue to Turk Street, a distance of approximately 1.1 miles. Right-of-way acquisition is now under way. This future unit, like the rest of the Skyway, will be elevated viaduct, but will be a two-level facility. Three southbound lanes will be elevated over the three northbound lanes and all will be elevated over the existing city street system, with most streets remaining open.

EMBARCADERO FREEWAY

Construction of the first project on this multilane elevated freeway was started in May, 1955, and is now in progress. This work is being performed by MacDonald, Young and Nelson, and Morrison, Knudsen Co., Inc., at our estimated cost of $5,600,-000. It is 0.9 mile long and will provide a connection between the Skyway and Mission Street at Main and Beale Streets. The Oakland bound movement and the extension of the freeway to Howard Street is estimated at $2,000,000 and is now under way under a contract with C. L. Harney, Inc. Plans for the continuance of this freeway past the Ferry Building to Broadway are virtually complete and it is expected that a contract will be advertised in May of this year. This will complete the total of 1.5 miles between the Bayshore, Bay Bridge and Broadway. It is planned to eventually extend this freeway to a connection with the Central and Golden Gate Freeways near Lombard Street. Studies are in the early stages at present and the location for this future development has not been determined.

SOUTHERN FREEWAY

With virtual completion of the Bayshore (James Lick) Freeway in

James Lick (Bayshore) Freeway in San Francisco toward Bay Bridge; Seventh and Eighth Street ramps in lower center; Fourth and Fifth Street ramps in center

San Francisco, and as the most needed units of the Embarcadero and Central Freeways are now in design and construction stages, planning has been directed to other near future segments of the much needed integrated San Francisco system.

To this end, preliminary reconnaissance studies have been completed covering the Southern Freeway which begins at the south city limits near Junipero Serra Boulevard and traverses generally on relocation along the Southern Pacific Railroad roadbed and Alemany Boulevard to the Alemany Interchange on the Bayshore

Freeway. This location has been presented to the public in a recent meeting held for informational purposes. The Highway Commission held a public hearing on the proposed location on April 6, 1956, in San Francisco.

The City of San Francisco is well advanced with their plans for the extension of the Southern Freeway from the Bayshore-Alemany Interchange to a junction with the proposed Southern Crossing and Embarcadero Freeway in the vicinity of Third and Army Streets.

RIGHT—First stage of Embarcadero Freeway construction; Bay Bridge approaches left.
LEFT—Embarcadero Freeway construction showing connection to Main and Beale Streets.

GOLDEN GATE FREEWAY

Included in the 1956-57 Freeway Construction Program is the amount of $3,900,000 for the revision of the interchange between the Golden Gate and Park Presidio Freeways at the south approach to the Golden Gate Bridge. This 1.3-mile project will add two more lanes to the Golden Gate Freeway between the Park Presidio Freeway and the Marina approach resulting in a total of eight lanes as well

LEFT—Construction scene on Bayshore Freeway, looking south from Third and Bayshore Interchange in San Francisco toward Sierra Point. RIGHT—Open water fill for Bayshore Freeway across Candlestick Cove. Grading operations at Sierra Point in foreground.

as revising the ramp connections accordingly. This project should be under construction by the end of this year.

BAYSHORE FREEWAY, SAN MATEO COUNTY

The over water fill section between the completed freeway at Third Street in San Francisco southerly to Candlestick Point and across the open water of an arm of San Francisco Bay to Sierra Point and connecting with the completed freeway near Butler Road, in South San Francisco is the only portion of the freeway remaining to be completed between the Bay Bridge and just north of Redwood City. With the exception of this remaining link, construction of which is now under way, the entire 25 miles can now be traveled on a full six-lane freeway to Alemany Interchange and on eight lanes to the bridge.

When completed in 1957, this project will afford six lanes of full freeway with provisions for eight lanes in the future. The present six-lane highway will continue to serve adjacent property and as an entrance into the city.

A saving of as much as 20 minutes of travel time in one direction will be realized by the great number of commuters who twice daily traverse this route.

On the north end of this unit, construction was performed by Edward Keeble. The contract was for grading and structures between Third Street and Candlestick Point. This $700,000 project is 0.7 mile long, and was completed in October, 1955. Paving will be done upon completion of the remaining portion of the grading and structures of the over water fill unit.

Over Water Project

From Candlestick Point southerly, work was previously completed on two contracts for filling experimental sections of embankment, displacing the highly fluid bay mud which reaches a maximum depth of 70 feet. The first job extended 0.3 mile southerly from Candlestick Point. It was performed by Edward Keeble and amounted to $160,000. The second experimental fill, 0.4 mile long, was not contiguous to the first one. It was performed far-

ther south in the Bay where the mud depth was greater. This job was done by Guy F. Atkinson and cost $860,-000. The fill closing the gap between the two experimental fills was started in April, 1955, and completed in February, 1956. John Delphia performed this 0.8-mile job at a cost of $400,000.

Continued progress has been made by the Guy F. Atkinson Co. over the remaining portion of the grading and structures in this unit of the freeway. This work is comprised of two contracts, one of which was completed in October, 1955. Construction totals $3,800,000.

The last project in this unit, the paving of this 3.6-mile link in continuous freeway is included in the 1956-57 Fiscal Year construction program and will be advertised for bids this summer.

BAYSHORE FREEWAY, SAN MATEO TO SANTA CLARA COUNTY LINE

After this next year's construction progress is completed, the entire Bayshore Freeway in San Mateo County will have been completed. In June, 1955, the Piombo Construction Co. completed the initial six-lane future eight-lane freeway between 16th Avenue in San Mateo and Bransten Road near the San Carlos-Redwood City limits. This project was started in July, 1953, and cost $4,100,000. It eliminated many serious points of

Bayshore Freeway, showing completed portion at Holly Street in San Carlos, northerly to San Mateo

traffic conflict and provides interchange for local traffic distribution at 19th Avenue in San Mateo, East Hillsdale Boulevard further south, Ralston Avenue in Belmont, and Holly Street in San Carlos.

The remaining eight miles of freeway from Bransten Road to south of the Santa Clara County line is composed of four projects. Three of these amount to $7,000,000 and are included in the 1956-57 construction program. Construction will commence about July of this year. The other project, the Willow Road Interchange, is nearing completion at a cost of approximately $850,000. L. C. Smith Company is contractor on this proj-

ect which started in May, 1955. It is now in use by traffic and eliminates the most congested intersection on the Bayshore Highway.

SKYLINE BOULEVARD, SAN MATEO-SAN FRANCISCO COUNTIES

In December, 1954, a 2.3-mile portion of expressway on Skyline Boulevard between Edgemar Road and Alemany Boulevard was placed in service. Plans have been completed for the future relocation for Sign Route 1 as an expressway from Edgemar on the coast to connect with the Skyline Boulevard expressway at Edgemar Road. Actual construction is dependent on availability of funds.

In July, 1955, continuation of the expressway northerly of Alemany Boulevard 1.3 miles to the south city limits of San Francisco was started under a contract awarded to Charles L. Harney, Inc. This project cost approximately $350,000. Concurrently, also under construction by Charles L. Carney for the City of San Francisco has been the 1.0-mile portion north of the city limits to Lake Merced Boulevard, also as an expressway and costing $350,000. Both projects were opened to traffic on March 15, 1956.

These Skyline Boulevard projects provide another major connection to and within San Francisco from the rapidly developing residential areas in

Willow Road Interchange on Bayshore Freeway, looking north

8

US 50 Interchange at Foothill Boulevard. Route 228 connection to Eastshore Freeway in background.

San Mateo County along the skyline and coastal routes.

EASTSHORE FREEWAY, ALAMEDA COUNTY

The two remaining unconstructed projects of the Eastshore Freeway between San Jose and Oakland are now contracted or financed. When these projects are completed, a total length of 38 miles of continuous freeway will be in service.

The nine-mile unit from Warm Springs to Beard Road north of Centerville is included in the 1956-57 Fiscal Year construction program. It is expected that this $6,000,000 initial four-lane, future six-lane freeway will be advertised in May, 1956, with construction starting in June.

The 5.8-mile portion from Beard Road northerly to Jackson Street in Hayward is being constructed by Gordon H. Ball and Ball & Simpson at a cost of $4,600,000. This is also

an initial four-lane, future six-lane freeway. Besides interchanges at each end of this project local traffic distribution will be provided by interchanges at Alvarado-Niles Road, Whipple and Alquire Roads, and Tennyson Road.

Work has now started on the addition of two lanes to the existing four-lane portion of the Eastshore Freeway between Route 228 and High Street in Oakland. Work on this $2,000,000 project is being done by Fredrickson & Watson Construction Co. As is generally done in freeway design, provision was made in the original plans for the addition of the two lanes in the center median width. Provision was also made in the original structures for the present expansion and very little loss of original construction is involved. The funds which would have been required for the two lanes at the time of original

construction were more effectively used for extending the freeway further south from Lewelling Boulevard to Jackson Street which resulted in considerably earlier traffic service to the area.

The two additional Eastshore Freeway lanes are now required in conjunction with the completion of the connection from the Eastshore Freeway at US 50 and Foothill Boulevard near Hayward which will add more traffic to the already heavily traveled existing four-lane freeway. This $2,900,000 project is 2.9 miles long and is expected to be completed in early summer of this year. The work is being performed by Ball & Simpson, Erickson, Phillips and Weisberg. It is to be a four-lane freeway.

EASTSHORE FREEWAY, OAKLAND

The only portion of the Eastshore Freeway in Oakland remaining to be

financed is the 0.9-mile unit from
Fallon Street to Market Street.

In September, 1954, Fredrickson &
Watson Construction Company, and
M & K Corporation started constructing the unit from Market Street
between Fifth and Sixth Streets to
Eleventh and Cypress Streets. This
elevated, eight-lane freeway was completed in October, 1955, and cost $1,-
700,000 for the 0.8 mile.

The remaining 1.4 miles from the
foregoing project to the distribution
structure is now under construction
in the two separate contracts with
Grove, Shepherd, Wilson & Kruge of
California at an estimated total cost
of $8,700,000. This section will be an
eight-lane double-deck viaduct with
opposing traffic carried on different
levels.

The $4,500,000 contract expanding
the distribution structure at the east
approaches to the Bay Bridge was
completed in October, 1955. This
project expanded the original structure which had been carrying a volume of 120,000 vehicles per day. The

Dublin Interchange looking north; showing two-lane freeway recently constructed with provision for future four lanes northerly to Contra Costa county line

*LEFT—Mountain Boulevard. Freeway under construction; LaSalle Avenue Overcrossnig in center; Park Boulevard Interchange ahead. Existing street to left to be uti-
lized as frontage road. RIGHT—Mountain Boulevard Freeway, completed portion to Moraga-Thornhill Intersection in foreground; construction from Moraga-Thornhill to Park Boulevard in background.*

LEFT—East 14th Street Interchange, looking toward Eastshore Freeway. Through planning, development of area provided for freeway prior to construction. RIGHT—Eastshore Freeway, University Avenue north.

expanded facility will now effectively handle double the present traffic without congestion. Cross weaving of traffic necessitated on the original structure has been eliminated. The entire facility is a five-level one which provides three levels of highway movements on top of two levels of railroads which are also separated.

North of the distribution structure along the shore line of Berkeley and Albany to El Cerrito Overhead the eight-lane freeway is rapidly nearing completion. In 1954 it was completed from the distribution structure to northerly of Ashby Avenue.

From Ashby Avenue to El Cerrito Overhead, Peter Kiewit Sons Company, who had constructed the unit to the south, continued the freeway improvement. This project cost $4,-800,000 and was completed in September, 1955.

The foregoing project did not include paving and structures for the 1.6 miles between University Avenue

and El Cerrito Overhead. Stolte, Inc., and Gallagher & Burk, Inc., are contractors for this remaining $2,250,000 job which started in January, 1955, and which is expected to be completed in July, 1956.

US 40

The entire 12.5 miles from Jefferson Avenue in Richmond to the new bridge across the Carquinez Straits at Crockett are now under construction. The improvement will be an initial six-lane freeway with provision for future eight lanes north of Richmond. A separate and new bridge is to be constructed across the Carquinez Straits east of the existing bridge. This bridge will provide for four lanes of northbound traffic. The existing bridge will be maintained and used for southbound lanes.

Northerly of the city limits of Hercules near the Arnold Industrial Freeway intersection, the improvement is being financed by special toll bridge

bonds. Southerly of that point, the project is financed from regular state highway user funds.

From Jefferson Avenue in Richmond to County Road 24 north of Rollingwood, Fredrickson & Watson Construction Company and M & K Corporation are the contractors. Construction began in November, 1954, and it is expected that this 4.8-mile project will be completed in the fall of 1956 at a cost of $5,400,000.

The toll financed projects in this district including the bridge, a portion of which is in District X, are as follows:

Contracts Under Way Description	Estimated construction cost
N. of H. C. L., Hercules to Crockett Road, 2.9 miles .... Contractors—Ferry Bros., John M. Ferry, Peter L. Ferry, L. A. and R. S. Crow	$7,829,000
Crockett Interchange and approach ramps... Contractors—Peter Kiewit Sons Company	5,090,000
Carquinez Bridge substructure............ Contractors—Mason & Hanger, Silas Mason Co., Inc. and F. S. Rolandi, Jr.	5,942,000
Carquinez Bridge superstructure .... Contractors—United States Steel Corp.	9,973,000

UPPER—Completed portion of Eastshore Freeway from Market to 10th. Remaining portion from 10th to Distribution Structure shown left to right in center of photograph. LOWER—Eastshore Freeway northerly; Jones Avenue in foreground; Hegenberger Road beyond.

McCammon-Wunderlich Contracting Co. are the contractors for a $7,-400,000 project from south of County Road 24 to the toll bridge projects north of Arnold Industrial Freeway. This unit is 4.9 miles in length.

An outstanding feature of the south approaches to the bridge is an earth cut to be made just south of Crockett. This cut will be 245 feet deep on center line. Approximately 8,500,000 yards will be removed. It is the largest cut ever undertaken by the California Division of Highways. Details of the project were covered in Mr. Hollister's article in the January-February issue of *California Highways and Public Works.*

Interchanges providing local traffic service along the route north of County Road 24 will be at County Road 24 (Hilltop Drive), Appian Way (Maloney Road), Alhambra Valley Road (Pinole Valley Road), Arnold Industrial Freeway, Willow Road, future county road (near Tormey), Crockett.

US 50, FOOTHILL BLVD., AND MacARTHUR FREEWAYS

In 1954, a 1.5-mile portion of this four-lane future six-lane freeway bypassing Castro Valley was completed. To the west, the 2.9-mile freeway connection to the Eastshore Freeway is under construction. That project was discussed hereinbefore in conjunction with the Eastshore Freeway.

East of Castro Valley, a $4,600,000 project is now under construction. This job begins west of Center Street in Hayward and ends at the completed freeway 2.3 miles west of Dublin. Peter Kiewit Sons Company is the contractor on this project which started in October, 1955. When this unit is completed a continuous freeway or expressway will be in service for the 51 miles between Tracy and Oakland via US 50 and the Eastshore Freeway.

From Castro Valley north, another freeway will eventually be constructed through Oakland to the distribution structure at the east approach to the Bay Bridge. To this end, planning and design are now under way, and a location for the MacArthur Freeway along MacArthur Boulevard between the distribution structure and Park Boulevard, approximately 3.5 miles, has been adopted by the California Highway Commission. Acquisition of rights of way has already commenced.

This additional freeway will serve US 50 and adjacent local traffic, much of which now uses the Eastshore Freeway as an entrance into and through Oakland. It will also effectively serve the future heavy residential developments contemplated through the areas served by this route.

MOUNTAIN BOULEVARD

This improvement in the City of Oakland when completed will provide 9.3 miles of full freeway from Sign

Route 24 near Lake Temescal following the general route of Mountain Boulevard to a connection with Foothill Boulevard (US 50) near San Leandro.

Joint Highway District No. 26 was dissolved in July, 1954, but the County of Alameda and City of Oakland have agreed to continue to finance a total of $300,000 per year matching a like contribution by the State toward the continued improvement of this freeway through the Oakland hills.

Two projects were placed under way on this route during the past year. These supplement the previously completed portion which extends from north of Broadway Terrace to south of the Moraga Thornhill intersection, a distance of 2.3 miles.

One of the projects is being constructed by Charles L. Harney. It covers the 1.3 miles between Thornhill Drive and Ascot Drive. Cost is estimated at $1,250,000. Completion is expected in mid-summer of this year. Included in the project are the La Salle Street Overcrossing and the Park Boulevard Interchange. Provision is made in the latter design for the connection of the Shepherd Canyon Freeway into Moraga which will junction with Mountain Boulevard Freeway at this point in the future.

The other project amounting to approximately $130,000 was the Lincoln Avenue separation which was constructed by Stolte, Inc., and Gallagher & Burk, Inc., and completed in December, 1955.

Continuation of this facility to the south is contemplated as rapidly as development. Material progress has been made toward alleviating this condition.

OAKLAND-WALNUT CREEK-MONUMENT

Accelerated development through the northern half of Contra Costa County is continuing. In the past, congestion along the highways servicing the areas had been rapidly approaching a condition which could seriously affect the continuance of this rate of development. Material progress has been made toward alleviating this condition.

In March, 1955, a 1.2-mile section of initial six-lane future eight-lane freeway consisting principally of the Orinda Interchange was completed by Frederickson & Watson Construction Company at a cost of $1,500,000.

Route 69 Freeway through Richmond; Macdonald Interchange lower center and San Pablo Avenue Interchange in center

Further east a 2.8-mile Lafayette By-pass project was started in September, 1955. It will result in a full freeway by-passing the town to the north and allows the existing highway to remain as a high standard uncongested local arterial servicing the needs of the rapidly growing Lafayette community. Work is being performed by Gordon F. Ball. Construction will cost $3,300,000.

Also under construction is the Pleasant Hill Road Interchange at the east end of the Lafayette By-pass. This project, like the Orinda Interchange, will afford effective relief to a seriously congested intersection. Contractor on this $1,300,000 job is Stolte, Inc., and Gallagher & Burk, Inc. Completion is expected in mid-summer, 1956.

From the Pleasant Hill Road Interchange to the vicinity of the north city limits of Walnut Creek, plans are nearing completion and right-of-way acquisitions are under way. This future unit will by-pass Walnut Creek to the west.

Northerly of Walnut Creek from Oakland Boulevard to 0.3 mile north of Monument a $2,900,000 unit of the

TOP—Distribution Structure from Bay Bridge toll plaza east. LOWER—Distribution Structure in Oakland looking east; three levels of highway structure over two levels of railroad.

14

freeway is also under contract to Stolte, Inc., and Gallagher & Burk, Inc. This unit is a part of the recent addition to the Interstate Highway System. Work started in October, 1955, and is 25 percent complete. Completion of this unit will afford relief to the 27,000 vehicle drivers and their passengers now using the existing two-lane highway daily.

MONUMENT-MARTINEZ-BENICIA BRIDGE

Preliminary studies have been completed for the southern approaches to the Martinez-Benicia Bridge. Construction of this freeway as a toll facility, the financing of which is in conjunction with the Carquinez Toll Bridge project now under way, was authorized by the Legislature in 1952.

The legislation sanctioned a toll facility from Arnold Industrial Freeway south of Martinez to a connection with State Highway Route 74 in Benicia. South of Arnold Industrial Freeway, the proposed facility will be financed from regular state highway funds.

Public hearings by the commission were not deemed necessary by Contra Costa County and the City of Martinez. The Highway Commission has announced that in its March meeting, adoption of the route as proposed between Route 75 north of Monument to the Solano county line, a distance of 7.5 miles, will be considered. The proposed improvement is a part of the recent additions to the Interstate Highway System which is further indication of the importance of this additional major north-south regional and interstate arterial.

WALNUT CREEK-DUBLIN

In 1955, the California Highway Commission adopted a route for the extension of the Central Contra Costa Freeway System from Walnut Creek to south of Danville. This four-lane future six-lane full freeway will be on relocation through the hillsides east of San Ramon Creek and outside of the beautiful Orchard Valley. Design and right-of-way acquisition have been in progress during the past year.

Further south, 2.2 miles of initial two lanes of a future six-lane freeway

were constructed between the Contra Costa-Alameda county line to south of US 50 at Dublin. This project was under contract to Fredrickson & Watson Construction Co. It cost $550,000 and was completed in November, 1955. Included in the contract was a full interchange with US 50 south of Dublin which eliminated a serious atgrade intersection between these two important routes.

All of this route is included in the recent additions to the Interstate Highway System.

DUBLIN-MISSION SAN JOSE

Other activity on this interstate highway route occurred in January, 1955, when the California Highway Commission adopted a route for the future development of a four-lane freeway between Mission San Jose and Sunol. Location will be along the general location of the existing highway with substantial reductions in grade over Mission Pass. Design studies are presently under way.

LOS GATOS-SANTA CRUZ

Congestion relief to areas outside of the immediate metropolitan sphere is also underway in the Los Gatos area. Here, a 2.1-mile freeway is being constructed on a bypass of this critically congested city and when completed, the freeway will remove the large volumes of through traffic from the local street system thereby leaving the latter for the orderly functioning of local activities.

Completed in November, 1955, was a $370,000 contract for a bridge at Main Street on this unit of the freeway. The work was by Carl N. Swensen Company.

Under way is the major contract amounting to approximately $1,300,000 for the 2.1 miles between the sidehill viaduct south of the city, to Saratoga Avenue at the northern extremities. This work is being done by L. C. Smith Company. Included in this project is a relocation of Los Gatos Creek for a distance of 6,000 feet requiring a concrete line channel for the entire length and a double 18-foot x 15-foot x 450-foot concrete box culvert. Here the freeway passes

over the channel and under the Main Street Bridge. The storms of the past winter resulted in an approximately $150,000 damage to the contractor's work on this drainage revision which was under way at that time. This project is expected to be completed in midsummer.

To start soon is a connection from the freeway easterly to a junction with San Jose Avenue at Charles Street. Part of this work will be financed by the City of Los Gatos as a cooperative project.

Acquisition of rights of way over the remaining portion of the Sign Route 17 Freeway to San Jose and beyond to a connection with the Bayshore Freeway is accelerating so that this freeway development can continue as rapidly as funds become available.

In Santa Cruz, a new freeway entrance into the city is being provided from existing Sign Route 17 at the north city limits to Mission Street. This project will provide a much needed facility for traffic distribution in the Santa Cruz area and is a part of the eventual freeway from San Jose to Santa Cruz. This project will cost $1,100,000 and the contractor is the Granite Construction Company. It is expected that the job will be completed in midsummer, 1956.

US 101 BYPASS, SAN JOSE AREA

A project which will improve the existing three-lane facility to an initial four-lane future six-lane full freeway from the present junction of US 101 Bypass and Sign Route 17 to Santa Clara Street is now in progress. This project is 1.6 miles in length, and will cost $1,800,000. The contract is being performed by Lew Jones and Leo F. Piazza and will eliminate the last of the three-lane width north of San Jose on this heavily traveled route.

OTHER MAJOR PROJECTS IN SAN JOSE AREA

South of San Jose, on US 101 from Ford Road to Llagas Creek the remaining three-lane sections on this route are being eliminated by the construction of a four-lane divided conventional highway over this 12.7-mile

Northerly at new Richardson Bay Bridge under construction

length. The contractor is Carl N. Swensen Co., Inc., and construction will approximate $550,000. This project is now open to traffic.

On Sign Route 9 between Lawrence Station Road east of Bayshore Freeway and 0.2 mile east of the San Jose-Alviso Road, a bypass of the town of Alviso which will be the initial construction of two lanes of a future freeway on new alignment and above flood and tide water level is financed and expected to be under contract in August, 1956. This project will approximate $1,000,000 construction cost.

On Sign Route 9 from 0.5 mile south of McClellan Road to Route 2 the existing, narrow two-lane facility with little or no shoulders is to be widened and shoulders added as interim relief prior to the future freeway development from El Camino Real to Los Gatos. An amount of $320,000 is allocated for this 3.9-mile improvement, and construction is expected to start in April, 1956.

US 101—GOLDEN GATE BRIDGE TO SANTA ROSA

Continued progress is being made toward the near future realization of a completed freeway between the Golden Gate Bridge and Santa Rosa.

The improvement of the Waldo approach to the western end of the Golden Gate Bridge to six-lane freeway standards was dedicated and opened to traffic on March 20, 1956.

Work on this four-mile facility between the bridge and Manzanita has been accomplished in two contracts.

The Guy F. Atkinson Company completed a $4,500,000 contract in April, 1955. This was the major project and covered grading, construction

of a twin bore and various separation structures. The second contract now practically completed and amounting to $1,300,000 for completing the drainage, paving and lighting over the project and lining the existing tunnel was done by the A. G. Raisch Company. The Golden Gate Bridge and Highway District contributed $5,000,000 to the total financing.

From Manzanita northerly 5.8 miles to the Greenbrae intersection, full freeway construction is either under way or advertised and several bad intersections are being eliminated.

A new $3,200,000 six-lane structure is being constructed across Richardson Bay by Duncanson-Harrelson Co. and Pacific Bridge Co. Completion is estimated for early 1957. The existing bridge will be removed.

Immediately northerly of the Richardson Bay Bridge job a 2.4-mile contract will extend the freeway to 0.3 mile north of Alto and eliminate the serious condition at the Alto intersection by providing a clover-leaf interchange. This project amounts to $1,300,000 and is being done by Dan Caputo Company and Dan Caputo and Edward Keeble. Efforts are directed toward the completion of this project by the end of this year.

From the foregoing project to 0.6 mile north of the Greenbrae intersection, a distance of 3.2 miles, another project continuing the freeway is expected to be under contract in June, 1956. The sum of $2,900,000 has been allocated for the work which will provide a full freeway to north of Corte Madera Creek, eliminate a serious intersection at Tamalpais Drive and connect with the stage construction of the portion of the Greenbrae Interchange now underway. Most of the grading for the future extension to California Park Overhead will also be done.

Greenbrae Interchange

The Greenbrae Interchange project, amounting to $950,000, is being constructed by Carl N. Swenson Company. It is expected to be completed at the end of this year. This project will eliminate the southbound intersection conflict existing at the present intersection but another con-

16

tract for the completion of the interchange will be required.

Included in the 1956-57 Fiscal Year construction program is the replacement of the existing bridge across the Northwestern Pacific Railroad at Forbes Overhead north of San Rafael. The existing bridge is nearing the end of its structural life. The new bridge and approaches which will cost approximately $500,000 for 0.8 mile is expected to be under contract in midsummer of 1956.

In Sonoma County, as a part of the freeway extension bypassing the congested Petaluma business district, two sets of twin structures were completed in April, 1955. This work cost $900,-000 and involved structures across the navigable channel of Petaluma Creek and also across the Northwestern Pacific Railroad. The work was done by Erickson, Phillips and Weisberg.

The remaining work covering the entire freeway development from one mile south of Petaluma Creek to three miles north of Cotati at Wilfred Crossing, a distance of 13.5 miles, consists of two contracts, both of which are being performed by Parish Bros., Inc., and Carl N. Swenson, Inc. Total construction cost for both contracts amounts to $6,000,000. The southernmost contract, including the bypass of Petaluma, is expected to be completed in September, 1956, and the remaining work by the end of the year.

Early continuation of the freeway construction northerly to Santa Rosa is assured with the inclusion of that five-mile project in the approved 1956-57 Fiscal Year construction program in the amount of $2,900,000. Construction is expected to be under way early this summer.

US 101—SAN RAFAEL-RICHMOND BRIDGE

A contract covering the development of a two-mile portion of the western approach to the San Rafael Bridge is expected to be under way in May of this year. An item of $900,-000 has been included in the 1956-57 Fiscal Year construction program for the work which will provide a four-lane freeway westerly from the bridge to Sir Francis Drake Boulevard. One deck of the bridge will be open to traffic by October of this year and this project is timed to provide an adequate approach upon completion of the four-lane bridge. It is expected to be completed in midsummer, 1957. Limits of the project extend nearly to US 101, but this is primarily for the incorporation of earthwork encountered in the initial job into the future extension of the freeway from Sir Francis Drake Boulevard to US 101 at the San Quentin Wye. Present work will include an interchange at Sir Francis Drake Boulevard.

NAPA AREA

A 2.7-mile section of freeway on Sign Route 37 in Napa County was

LEFT—Looking north along Waldo approach to Golden Gate Bridge. Sausalito Interchange in foreground. Note eXtensive grading required. RIGHT—Looking south along Waldo approach to Golden Gate Bridge. New tunnel eXit on left. Spencer Avenue Overcrossing in foreground. Note viaduct construction to avoid eXtensive fills just north of tunnel. Photograph shows two-way traffic on new lanes. Upon completion new lanes will serve northbound traffic and eXisting roadway on right will carry southbound.

completed in November, 1955. This project extends easterly from a point two miles east of the Sonoma-Napa county line. Arthur B. Siri, Inc., was the contractor on this $450,000 project which constructed the initial two lanes of a future four-lane freeway with right of way and access control initially provided.

Acquisition of rights of way is now under way for the future development of the St. Helena Highway as a freeway from Union Station at the north end of the Napa Bypass to Rutherford. Construction, however, has not been financed.

The initial two lanes of a future four-lane freeway are under construction between four miles north of St. Helena to Calistoga, a distance of 3.7 miles. This project is under contract to Huntington Brothers and will cost approximately $550,000. Completion of the work is expected by the end of this year. This is another instance of the stage construction of a future freeway and at the same time correcting today's deficiencies with a minimum expenditure of today's funds, thus enabling the correction of other deficiencies in the area earlier than could otherwise have been financed.

CONCLUSION

Perhaps the greatest motivating force in the demand for improvement of highways has been the consciousness of the users themselves that needs were outgrowing the facilities available. One has but to become involved in slow-moving or conflicting traffic patterns to resolve there and then that something must be done. In any one given situation all motorists on the highway are involved and all suffer the consequence of inadequacy. This broad effect results in united and cumulative demand for relief.

Of as great, or even greater consequence is the matter of safety. In contrast with the effect of a traffic tie-up, damage to life and property involved in an accident is restricted to individuals or small groups. Our minds seem to have a defensive shield against catastrophes which occur about us daily, and we persist in our refusal to project ourselves into the field of accident liability. Only through the efforts of safety councils, traffic engineers and forward-looking newspapers and journals has the subject of safety been kept in the foreground of public conscience.

Fortunately, safety, convenience and expeditious movement are not incompatible. These three elements are served alike in fundamental freeway features. Elimination of grade crossings, reduction

of side friction due to multiple access, high standards of grade and alignment, wide traffic lanes and improved signing, have, among numerous other features, produced facilities which encourage safe and convenient travel at maintained speeds over long distances.

As can readily be appreciated, the reduction of minor accidents usually attending vehicles traveling in the same direction, is not as impressive as the reduction of accidents involving fatalities. It is with the latter type that we are overwhelmingly concerned. The quoting of statistics is ordinarily unproductive, however, the comparison of 2.15 fatal accidents per hundred million miles of travel on freeways, against 8.38 like accidents for the same distance on ordinary rural roads, is more articulate than any descriptive phrase.

As we work toward the creation of an adequate network, we are fully aware that freeways alone are not a complete solution to the traffic problems, particularly with respect to the movement of commute traffic in peak hours in the urban areas. However, we believe that they are the heart of any transportation pattern augmented as it may be. With this firm conviction in mind we will continue to develop the system, confident that each year will bring added safety, pleasure, utility and convenience to public travel in the area.

STATUS OF DISTRICT IV FREEWAY PROJECTS
March, 1956

	Total miles	Completed projects		Under contract		Budgeted		Right of way expended and budgeted
		Miles	Const. cost	Miles	Const. cost	Miles	Const. cost	
Bayshore and James Lick Freeway; Bay Bridge to Ford Road south of San Jose.	56.6	27.5	$35,043,000	5.3	$5,515,000	7.4	$5,740,000	$32,472,000
Central Freeway; James Lick Freeway to Turk Street	1.8	1.0	4,973,000					5,300,000
Embarcadero Freeway; Bay Bridge to Broadway	1.8			1.3	7,701,000	1.1	5,300,000	10,344,000
Golden Gate Freeway; Lyon Street to Route 56	1.1					1.1	3,900,000	
Park Presidio Freeway; Golden Gate Bridge to Fulton Street	2.1	1.3	1,439,000					$50,000
US 101; Golden Gate Bridge to Lytton	66.6	24.3	*12,441,000	20.0	*12,790,000	8.3	6,038,000	7,666,000
Black Point Cutoff; Ignacio to Sears Point	7.3	0.8	1,090,000					280,000
Route 69; Route 1 to Richmond-San Rafael Bridge	3.4					2.1	900,000	483,000
Napa Area and Solano county line to Calistoga (portions)	37.9	14.3	3,235,000	3.7	555,000			1,619,000
US 40; El Cerrito Overhead to Carquinez Bridge	13.6		391,000	11.7	†41,708,000			8,566,000
Arnold Industrial Freeway; Hercules to Bridgehead Avenue	22.0	14.7	4,672,000		40,000			1,196,000
Monument-Martinez—to Solano county line	7.4							
Oakland to Arnold Industrial Freeway near Ohmer	19.8	3.1	1,929,000	6.7	7,446,000			9,530,000
Mountain Blvd.; Tunnel Road near Lake Temescal to San Leandro	9.3	1.1	11,408,000	1.3	11,617,000	1.0	2950,000	11,125,000
Eastshore Freeway; Richmond-San Rafael Bridge to Bayshore at San Jose	52.7	26.5	25,709,000	0.3	17,557,000	9.0	5,755,000	21,435,000
Altamont Pass; San Lorenzo to San Joaquin county line	33.6	26.3	6,983,000	7.3	7,465,000			6,230,000
Route 107; Route 8 to Walnut Creek (portions)	10.1	2.1	850,000					789,000
Pacheco Pass; 1 mile east of Bell's Station to Merced county line	8.3	3.2	1,286,000					12,000
El Camino Real; Ford Road south of San Jose to San Benito county line (portions)	5.8	5.5	935,000					846,000
Four miles south of Davenport to Watsonville	21.0	7.7	2,740,000	1.3	1,068,000			3,846,000
San Jose to Santa Cruz (portions)	19.9	1.3	1,339,000	2.0	1,736,000	0.4	$40,000	6,367,000
Route 113; Bayshore to Eastshore Freeway	8.0					2.1	610,000	99,000
Skyline Boulevard; Edgemar Road to Lake Merced Boulevard in San Francisco. (Note: Major part of 1.0 mile in San Francisco financed by city—approximately $285,000 constr.)	3.9	3.9	1,325,000					764,000
Totals	419.7	167.4	$119,375,000	69.5	$105,158,000	33.4	$32,463,000	$114,679,000

* Includes total of $5,000,000 by Golden Gate Bridge and Highway District.
† $28,834,000 Toll Bridge Funds in this amount.
‡ Includes City of Oakland and Alameda County contributions.

Waldo Project

Golden Gate Bridge Freeway Is Opened

WITH ALL branches of the armed services participating, the Redwood Empire Association staged a spectacular dedication of the new Golden Gate Bridge Freeway celebrating the opening on March 20 of the additional westerly freeway tunnel just to the north of the Golden Gate Bridge.

Many dignitaries from the Redwood Empire counties, federal and state officials, headed by Lieutenant Governor Harold J. Powers, Director of Public Works Frank B. Durkee, George T. McCoy, State Highway Engineer, B. W. Booker, Assistant State Highway Engineer, Secretary of State Frank M. Jordan and Chelso Maghetti, Secretary of the Highway Commission, participated in the dedication. Bands from the 6th Army with headquarters at San Francisco, and the Hamilton Air Force provided stirring music for the occasion. Jet bombers from the 349th Fighter Bomber Wing broke the barrier in the air above the tunnels while a 49-ton army tank crashed through the barrier on the ground to the accompaniment of salutes from a battery of army cannon.

Vice President Dan E. London of the Golden Gate Bridge and Highway District acted as master of ceremonies, assisted by Committee Chairmen Thomas P. Ludcke and Ted Huggins. Among the speakers were Powers, Durkee, McCoy, Highway Commissioners James A. Guthrie, San Bernardino; H. Stephen Chase, San Francisco; Robert E. McClure, Santa Monica, and Robert L. Bishop, Santa Rosa, former Highway Commissioner Walter Sandelin, Ukiah; Reed W. Robinson, President of the Redwood Empire Association, George P. Anderson, President, and James Adam, General Manager, of the Golden Gate Bridge. Sydney Kesser represented Mayor George J. Christopher of San Francisco.

LT. GOV. HAROLD J. POWERS

At the conclusion of the celebration an auto caravan took officials and guests to Bermuda Palms in San Rafael for luncheon. State officials and highway commissioners went on to Santa Rosa where Commissioner Bishop was guest of honor at a civic dinner sponsored by the Chamber of Commerce. Bishop is the newest member of the highway commission, recently appointed by Governor Knight.

The very successful celebration was organized by Clyde Edmondson, general manager of the Redwood Empire Association and his staff.

Financing of the new unit of the Empire's $400,000,000 system of all-year highways is being done largely by the Golden Gate Bridge and Highway District, which is participating to the extent of $5,000,000. The remaining $750,000 is from the State Highway Fund.

Some 2,000,000 cubic yards of earth were used for fills on the freeway. Engineers of the State Division of Highways estimate that it would require 300 trains, each with 100 cars, to transport that quantity of dirt.

Huge Fills

Earth for the fills was obtained from excavations of the widened freeway, the borings of the new tunnel and from the sizable mound that remained at the north end of the Golden Gate Bridge after the original approach was built. Earth and rock from the mound was also used, after a special treatment, as a new base for the reconditioned original approach.

The A. G. Raisch Co., San Rafael, which had a $1,320,000 contract for relining the new tunnel, reconditioning the old tunnel and the final paving of the new and old approaches, subcontracted the tiling work to the Mills and Hinz Tile Co., San Francisco, and the Rigney Tile Co., Oakland.

Some 120,000 square feet of clincher-back tile was used in fully tiling the new 1,000-foot tunnel and partially tiling the original tunnel. Tile for the job was made by Gladding McBean and Co., San Francisco, the only firm on the Pacific Coast to make this type of tile.

Tiling of Tunnel

The subcontractors employed 21 tile setters and 21 helpers on the tunnel jobs which required three and a half months to complete and which cost $150,000.

The tile setters worked from an especially-built scaffold on wheels which permitted them easy access to all points of the tunnel arches. Tiling on the old tunnel extends upward four and a half feet. Above this tiling is a network of pipes designed to take care of leakage. A strip of tiling 17 inches wide extends along the two strings of tunnel lights in the old tunnel to permit an easy tie-in if it is decided to complete the tiling at some future date.

Traffic No Longer Impeded

With the completion of the project, traffic over what was known as Waldo Grade no longer will be impeded

greatly by slow-moving vehicles. Engineers of the State Division of Highways say that the six-lane freeway will assure a much smoother flow of traffic up the grade and will, additionally, increase the safety factor for motorists.

The new tunnel, which cost $1,-750,000 and which has been handling two-way traffic pending reconditioning of the old tunnel and approach, will accept only northbound traffic with the reopening of the old tunnel. However, the full capacity of traffic flow will not be immediately utilized, for the pavement in the easterly tunnel will be resurfaced lane by lane.

The original four-lane approach, which handled two-way traffic and which now is converted into a three-lane artery for southbound traffic, was opened in 1937. The original approach was built at a cost of $1,226,-

UPPER—Aerial view of twin tunnels looking northerly, showing Golden Gate Bridge Freeway as it emerges from north portal. LOWER—Army tank crashes through barrier, signalizing freeway opening on March 20.

130, exclusive of the old tunnel which cost an additional $630,346.

The old and new approaches which now combine to form the Golden Gate Freeway have a total cost of more than $8,000,000. Thus the four miles of highways, including the twin tunnels, cost an average of $2,000,000 per mile to build. The freeway extends from the northern end of Golden Gate Bridge to a point a short distance beyond the bottom of the Waldo Grade.

Two Viaducts Built

The greatest fill on the new freeway was made near the crest of the grade, where 500,000 cubic yards of earth were dumped to provide a foundation for the widened highway. As the fill was built upward, it was tamped repeatedly with sheeps-foot rollers to settle the earth. A 50-ton roller was used to pack solid the top few feet of the fill to make a firm base for the highway.

Another substantial chunk of earth, about 242,000 cubic yards, was needed for the fill in the canyon where the Fort Cronkhite tunnel was extended 108 feet in order that the added footage might be built up to accommodate the widened highway at this point.

Just to the north of the tunnel, it was necessary to construct two viaducts over which the northbound lanes of the freeway pass. Engineers pointed out the terrain at this point was too steep for a fill.

As a safety measure, the north and southbound traffic lanes have a median dividing strip extending from the northern end of the Golden Gate Bridge to the bottom of Waldo Grade. The strip ranges in width from 6 to 16 feet and is six inches high at the curb. Additionally, there are guard rails, made of metal plate, at points of potential danger.

Work on the most vital traffic link with the Redwood Empire—the $35,-000,000 Golden Gate Bridge—began about 23 years ago, on January 4, 1933. The bridge was opened to pedestrian traffic on May 27, 1937, and a day later to vehicular traffic.

Employees Receive Twenty-five-year Awards

Employees of the Division of Highways who became eligible for 25-year awards during December, 1955, and January-February, 1956, are:

Name	Total service Yrs.	Mos.	Days		Name	Total service Yrs.	Mos.	Days
ELIGIBLE ON December 31, 1955					**ELIGIBLE ON January 31, 1956**			
District III					**District VII**			
Stout, William C.	25	0	28		Wakefield, Allen N.	25	0	3
District IV					**District VIII**			
Dake, Fred	25	0	15		Denny, Earl C.	25	0	6
District VII					Lloyd, John J.	25	0	7
Harris, Paul M.	25	0	16		**District X**			
District IX					Barber, Tom	25	0	23
Holt, Herman	25	0	9		Malatesta, Louis J.	25	0	16
Central Office					**District XI**			
Baumgart, Walter M.	25	0	21		Ellis, Jack A.	25	0	28
Kerri, Gurne R.	25	0	9		**Central Office**			
Shop 8					Balfour, Frank C.	25	0	00
Young, Homer	25	0	30					
Headquarters Shop					**ELIGIBLE ON February 29, 1956**			
Hamlin, Harold H., Sr.	25	0	29		**District I**			
Department of Public Works					Snook, Earl V.	25	0	14
Division of Contracts & R/W					**District IV**			
Vance, Mable A.	25	0	22		Levier, Gilbert W.	25	0	21
					Morrill, Paul M.	25	0	23
ELIGIBLE ON January 31, 1956					**District VI**			
District I					Miller, Scott	25	0	15
Paul, Bertus Leroy	25	0	16		Steinman, John J.	25	0	13
District IV					**District VII**			
Davis, Dewitt D.	25	0	21		Verges, Reymond August	25	0	28
Greene, Clifton F.	25	0	20		Welsh, Joseph F.	25	0	6
District V					**District X**			
Leisett, Theodore	25	0	9		Daniels, James B.	25	0	4
					District XI			
					Elliott, James B.	25	0	15

The six-lane bridge, now meshing with the six-lane freeway, was designed to accommodate more than 283,000 automobiles for a 24-hour day, and an estimated 70,000,000 automobiles and 6,000,000 trucks annually.

In 1936, vehicular traffic between San Francisco and Marin County was 1,654,741; these vehicles were transported by ferryboat. In 1947, some 10 years after the Golden Gate Bridge was in operation, vehicular traffic had climbed to 7,816,147. In 1955, the vehicular count was 13,952,329.

An all-time high in Golden Gate Bridge traffic is anticipated in 1956 as the population of the Redwood Empire continues to mount and the influx of tourists increases. The growth of traffic over the bridge is reflected in the figures for January when 1,036,-594 vehicles crossed the span, an increase of 72,630 over the same month in 1955.

KIND WORDS FROM MRS. HYATT

3634 Brockway Court
Sacramento 18, California

DEAR MR. ADAMS:

Your January-February, 1956, copy of Public Works magazine is a priceless document — wonderful reporting of a terrible tragedy. You and your assistants can be congratulated, as can the State of California, for the heroic work done by the Public Works men.

Sincerely,
DELTA GARST HYATT
(Mrs. Edward Hyatt)

During the 1954-55 Fiscal Year 20 grade crossings on state highways were closed or abandoned by changes in highway alignment, construction of grade separations or abandonment of railroad tracks, and three new grade crossings were opened, making a total of 832 such crossings on state highways on June 30, 1955.

Exit Bottleneck

New Highway Through Badlands
In Riverside County Completed

By K. B. STONE, Resident Engineer

THE RECONSTRUCTION and widening of U. S. Highway 60, Riverside County's "Main Street," was brought one step nearer to completion with the formal opening of the 5.2-mile highway through what is locally known as the "Moreno Badlands." Dedication ceremonies at the junction of U. S. Highway 60 and State Sign Route 79 on February 16, 1956, officially opened

the newly completed section to public travel. Amid hills whitened by an overnight snowfall of two inches, Lieutenant Governor Harold J. Powers cut the unique ribbon, made up of a chain of Riverside County's principal agricultural produce. Assemblyman Lee M. Backstrand of Riverside acted as master of ceremonies. The combined bands from Banning

and Beaumont High Schools interspersed the speeches with excellent musical numbers.

Queen Scheherazade of the Riverside County Fair and National Date Festival did not brave the snow or wintry blasts, which made Lieutenant Governor Powers feel right at home, but sent two of her camels to lead the cavalcade, after the dedication cere-

UPPER LEFT—On left, upper and lower, are shown photos of road through the Badlands. On right, upper and lower, are views of the new highway taken at the same location.

monies, to the opening of the Date Festival at Indio. Roy F. King, President of the Indio Chamber of Commerce, acted as toastmaster for the dignitaries at a luncheon given in their honor.

Jack Rabbit Trail

The first road through the Badlands was a wagon road, built back in 1895-96, which naturally snaked back and forth through the rough terrain. In 1913, the people of Riverside County, aware that their future commercial and agricultural progress was highly dependent on good roads, set up the Riverside County Highway Commission, with W. B. Clancy as president and George M. Pearson, then county surveyor, as engineer for the commission. A. C. Fulmor succeeded Mr. Pearson as county surveyor, and was one of the originators of the present route.

One of the routes selected for construction was a road from Moreno to Beaumont, which became known as the "Jack Rabbit Trail." The road was constructed in 1915-16, and for years served as an important link between the county seat and the fast-developing desert and agricultural district to the east. In 1923-24, the Jackrabbit Trail was paved and immediately experienced a large increase in traffic.

New Route Located

In 1931, this road became part of the state highway by legislative act. Because of the narrowness of the trail and its many sharp curves, it soon became apparent to the State that the road could not handle the fast-increasing traffic and the larger and heavier trucks. Immediate steps were taken by the State Highway Commission to alleviate the rapidly increasing traffic congestion. In 1934-36, construction of the present U. S. Highway 60 from Box Springs Grade to Beaumont on an entirely new location and alignment was started and completed. With the later completon of improvements to U. S. Highway 60 from the Los Angeles County line to Riverside, and by freeway improvements east of Beaumont on U. S. Highways 60, 70 and 99 (See *U. S. Progress by J. Dekema, Public Works, July and August, 1954*), additional traffic was

These are the Badlands through which, upper, new highway runs and lower, looking easterly toward summit on old road, showing hazardous passing movement around slow-moving truck. The first road through the Badlands was built in 1895-96 in rugged terrain.

diverted to this road, and a serious bottleneck developed through the Badlands and on to the junction of U. S. Highway 60 with U. S. Highways 70 and 99 at Beaumont. This congestion was further aggravated by truck traffic, often resulting in long lines of slow-moving cars.

Partial Access Control

By 1953, plans were practically completed for the construction of 5.2 miles of four-lane highway with partial control of access through the Badlands. By this time the truck and bus traffic had grown to 13 percent. The accident rate had risen to 4.0 accidents per motor vehicle mile.

. . . Continued on page 52

UPPER—Camels leading the cavalcade of the Beaumont and Banning High School bands, and the parade of cars. Taken at the junction of US 60 and Sign Route 79. LOWER—Lt. Gov. Powers cutting the unique ribbon at the dedication. Left to right: Carl M. Davis, President, Riverside County Board of Trade; Senator Nelson S. Dilworth, Hemet; Lt. Gov. Powers; William Jones, Chairman Riverside County Board of Supervisors; Assemblyman Lee M. Backstrand, Riverside.

Santa Claus

Popular Roadside Business
Successful on Frontage Road

By JOHN F. KELLY, Headquarters Right of Way Agent

A UNIQUE name, attractive merchandising displays, good business management and a location along a main highway route are the principal factors contributing to the success of a group of roadside businesses known as Santa Claus, along U. S. Highway 101 in Southern California near Santa Barbara.

Along every major highway the traveling public has a choice of innumerable roadside businesses. Unfortunately, some of these businesses turn out to be a bad choice for the motorist. In these cases, poor management leaves the merchants with only the unsuspecting public who stop by once. Merchandising based upon the theory—where there is traffic, there is business—cannot expect to succeed.

Luckily for the traveling public, all roadside merchants are not happy highwaymen who feel they are going to get a certain amount of business just because they are located alongside a major highway. The successful roadside merchants realize that good business is not based upon chance, but upon sound business principles, regardless of where it is located. Santa Claus is an example of a group of roadside businesses that has attained success by treating the highway motorist as a customer who is wanted rather than one to be exploited.

Success Story

The business growth along U. S. Highway 101 at Santa Claus is a typical American success story, and like all success stories, it didn't just happen.

Santa Claus began in 1948 when Mr. Pat McKeon acquired an orange juice stand along the coast highway near Carpinteria. At that time there were several other roadside businesses in the immediate area, but none of them had made any special effort to attract the highway motorist. Recognizing the value of advertising in

An active and prosperous looking commercial area today, might have been referred to as a marginal roadside development a few years ago. Fence in left of photo separates frontage road from through traffic lanes of eXpressway.

building up a business, Mr. McKeon named his juice stand Santa Claus. The name implies good will, and has been used as the theme for developing good public relations with the highway motorist. Customers turning off the highway are welcomed by a friendly voice on a loud speaker, and out-of-state travelers are given a special greeting referring to their home state. Customers leaving Santa Claus are wished a Merry Christmas and asked to return. All highway travelers feel good about a friendly welcome, particularly when they are some distance from home. They will remember this place and tell their friends to stop at Santa Claus. This is the best type of advertising any merchant can get. Of course advertising is just one phase of good merchandising. Courtesy, service, and good merchandise at a fair price are essential before advertising can be effective. Santa Claus

businesses have all these essentials for success, and the result has in effect been Christmas throughout the year for the owners.

Good business management made it possible for the orange juice stand to be enlarged into a confectionery and date shop in 1950; a western and novelty shop was built in 1951; a pottery shop added in 1953, and a cafe known as "Santa's Kitchen" was built in 1954. This cafe has done so well that the owner plans to enlarge the building in the near future, in order to accommodate an additional 100 customers.

Santa Claus Area

Although the name Santa Claus applies only to the businesses owned by Mr. McKeon, the name is now used to identify all of the roadside businesses in the immediate area.

Santa Claus is contained within a half-mile strip of land along the southerly side of U. S. Highway 101, eight miles southeast of Santa Barbara and one mile west of Carpinteria. The Southern Pacific Railroad main line tracks southerly of the highway limit the highway frontage in this area to a maximum depth of 150 feet.

From the standpoint of driving distances between major cities or tourist attractions, the Santa Claus area is not a location that would be considered a logical site for the development of a commercial area catering to the highway motorist. Nearby Santa Barbara is the natural stopping place for all travelers in this section of the State. This world-famous city offers so many attractions to the motorist, it seems almost inconceivable that a group of roadside businesses, entirely dependent upon highway patronage for their livelihood, could succeed in the face of such odds. Despite the competition, original ideas and sound business principles have made it possible for the Santa Claus retail outlets to attract so many motorists that one of their biggest problems today is providing adequate parking facilities for their highway customers.

Highway Changed

Highway frontage at Santa Claus had direct access into a three-lane conventional highway until the average daily traffic on U. S. Highway 101 made it necessary for the State Division of Highways, during 1953-1954, to convert this substandard highway into a four-lane divided expressway. The curve in the alignment of the former highway made it possible to retain that portion of the highway in front of the roadside busi-

nesses at Santa Claus as a frontage road. Entrances were created at each end of the business area, approximately 1,500 feet apart, opening into a grade crossing of the expressway. A 36-inch chain link fence separates the old and the new highway to restrict access from the expressway to the frontage road.

Before the present highway revision became necessary, Santa Claus had become a popular stopping place for motorists. During the construction of the new highway the roadside merchants were greatly concerned about their future. Granted, this area would continue to have its unique name, the merchandising displays would remain as attractive, and management would be unchanged; but would a location on a frontage road, behind a fence with restricted access from the through traffic lanes, destroy the highway location that formerly had been considered so important to the success of these businesses catering entirely to the traveling public?

Retail Business Gains

A comparison of the year before and the year after completion of the new highway facility in December, 1954, reveals that businesses at Santa Claus which formerly had direct access into the conventional highway have made very substantial gains in gross sales after being placed on the frontage road. The source of authentic information for making this comparison has been from the reports made by each retail outlet to the State Board of Equalization for the purpose of paying state sales tax.

Those retail outlets which had not been in existence prior to the opening of the frontage road at Santa Claus were not included in the before-and-after comparison, although the records revealed they were doing exceptionally well considering the short time the businesses had been in operation.

Frontage Road Favorable

Acceptance of the frontage road as a suitable location for a retail business catering to the needs of the highway motorist is apparent at Santa Claus. Three major brand service stations have been constructed on this frontage road during the past year. The success of the existing Santa Claus business enterprises undoubtedly influenced these companies to build in this particular area. However, the popularity of Santa Claus could not attract enough customers if a frontage road were detrimental in serving the highway trade.

The group of retail outlets at Santa Claus provide services needed by the highway motorist. Retail developments on this frontage road is an example of the one-stop service which will undoubtedly become the type of roadside merchandising the motorist will find in California as the freeway mileage increases. . . .

Roadside Merchant's Letter

The letter by Mr. McKeon, the man who put this group of roadside businesses "on the map," expresses the feeling of a merchant who developed a successful business enterprise along the side of a conventional highway, and then experienced managing those

. . . Continued on page 51

Diagram shows roadside businesses on frontage road at Santa Claus. Shaded lines indicate new eXpressway.

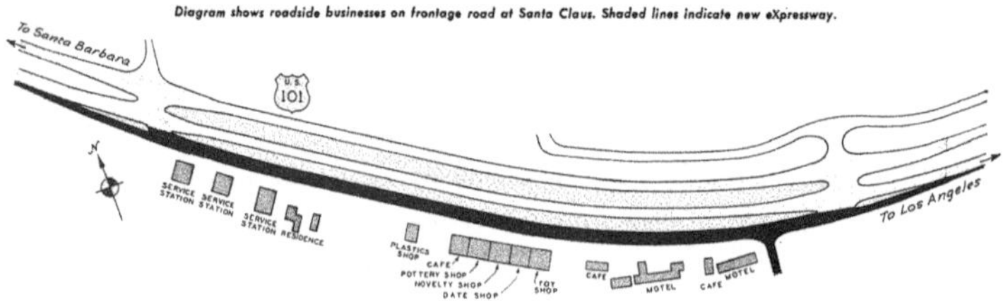

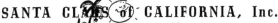

SANTA CLAUS of CALIFORNIA, Inc.

PAT McKEON
PRESIDENT

JUNE McKEON
VICE-PRESIDENT

SANTA CLAUS • CALIFORNIA
P. O. BOX 488 • CARPINTERIA January 16, 1956

John F. Kelly
Headquarters Right of Way Agent
Division of Highways
Sacramento, California

Dear Sir:

The new highway has been completed in front of my businesses now
for a little more than a year. In this time I have been able to
make comparisons before and after. So as not to keep you in sus-
pense, I will state now that everything has been most favorable.

As my business grew, and especially the last year on the old road,
it became very apparent to me that the new highway with its turnoffs would definitely be to my advantage. My parking problem was
becoming both difficult and dangerous. If you can imagine a car
moving along at approximately 45 miles an hour with other cars
following close behind on a curve having to suddenly pull off of
a three lane highway and into a 10 foot parking space, you can
understand what I mean by dangerous. I estimate that I lost 20%
new business, and was not able to accommodate 10% of my already
established business because of this road condition.

The summer of '55 was the first season on the new frontage road.
My fears and anxious moments were over. Not only was my parking
problem solved, but my parking area was considerably enlarged.
Customers were able to safely turn in and leisurely find a parking
space. I found that they would have a tendency to stay longer, which
meant added business for me. My records show a 50% increase over
the previous year.

Three major oil companies have now built new stations along this
strip. Property values took a sharp incline. Business prospects
for the entire area brightened. All in all, the new highway was
definitely a turning point in our success. The future is laid out
for us. We can plan expansion without that fearful question "What
if the highway - - - - - - - - ?

In closing I would like to commend you on your field personnel engaged in this construction work. They were without exception most
cooperative in every way - most helpful under all circumstances.

Very sincerely yours,
SANTA CLAUS OF CALIFORNIA, INC.

Pat McKeon

PM/j

DATE SHOP
GOURMET SHOP

GIFTS from CALIFORNIA

BASKET SHOP
WESTERN SHOP

California Bridges

Construction Costs Moved Upward During 1955

By W. J. YUSAVAGE, Assistant Research Technician, Bridge Department

THE THREE-YEAR decline in bridge item bid prices from the peak level of the third quarter of 1951 was reversed during the last three quarters of 1955. The cost level as of the end of the fourth quarter of 1955 is 8 percent higher than the average level of costs during the calendar year 1954 and 10 percent lower than the high average level of costs recorded during the calendar year 1951.

A general upswing in the trend of costs began in the second quarter of 1955 when the cost index value jumped to a reading of 237 from a reading of 217. The third and fourth quarters confirmed the rising trend with readings of 228 and 237 respectively. The level of costs for successive periods is presented graphically in the accompanying chart which summarizes the course of California bridge construction costs since 1933.

Value and Volume of Bridge Construction

Table I is a tabulation of statistics relating to the value and volume of the California Bridge Department construction program. The current value is shown in column VI where the figures represent the current dollar value of low bids for the various periods since 1934. Columns IV and V give the value and volume of bridge construction in the form of indexes, utilizing the value of base period 1939-1940 as the reference point of 100.

The index of value is computed by relating the value of any quarter to the average quarterly value ($5.1 + 5.2 million/8 = $1,287,500) of the eight quarters of 1939-1940. Thus the value index for the fourth quarter of 1954 is $7,600,000/$1,287,500 or 590.

The volume of bridge construction is defined as the relative physical quantity of bridge construction put in place during a given period. It is an inverse function of the cost index since a higher level of costs reduces the relative value of money and so

This article is the fourth of an annual series dealing with California Bridge Construction Costs. The most recent article appeared in the March-April, 1955, issue.

For total California highway construction costs the reader is referred to a series of articles entitled, "Cost Index" by R. H. Wilson, H. C. McCarty, and J. D. Gallagher. These articles appear regularly in California Highways and Public Works.

reduces the relative volume of construction while a lower level of costs increases the relative value of money and thus increases the relative volume of construction.

The index of volume is computed in exactly the same way as is the index of value after each of the quarterly dollar values have been modified by the cost index values of the respective quarters. Thus the volume index for the fourth quarter of 1954 is $7,600,000/213 (cost index) = $3,568,000. This new value is then related to the average quarterly value of the eight base quarter values of 1939-1940, as, $3,568,000/$1,287,500 or 227. The 227 indicates that the actual physical bridge construction activity during the fourth quarter of 1954 was 277 percent greater than that which occurred during 1940.

The value and volume indexes show the marked increase in bridge construction which has accompanied the augmentation of state highway budgets during recent years. As a result of legislation which substantially increased highway user tax revenues during 1953 and the consequent continued development of full freeways with their requisite separation structures, expenditures during the past year for bridge construction rose to nearly $48,000,000 or to approximately 900 percent of the average annual rate of expenditure during the base period 1939-1940.

The indexes do not include the revenue bond expenditures for the construction of the Carquinez Bridge and approaches' since the character of the financing the construction and also the character of the design of the Carquinez Bridge are different from the usual character of California bridge construction. Inclusion of the Carquinez statistics would have the effect of raising the cost index to a value of 248 or to about 5 percent greater than the 237 reading for the fourth quarter of 1955. Also, adding the contract cost of $19,500,000, the approximate bid value of the bridge and approaches, to the dollar value of low bids would raise the normal budget figure from a total of $48,000,000 to $67,500,000.

General Trends

Average unit prices for the various items of construction as compiled for each quarter show a general upward trend during the last three quarters of 1955. Average bid prices for all major construction items, viz., concrete (structures), reinforcing steel, furnishing steel and concrete piling, and structure excavation are all up approximately 10 percent over the average bid prices of the first quarter of 1955.

This upward trend in construction costs began in the second quarter of 1955 when most of the contracts for another round of wage increases were negotiated. The increase in costs to the State may therefore be assumed to be the result of the economic adjustment the contractor organizations have made in response to the rising costs of labor and materials.

Outlook

The present upward trend of construction costs is currently in a period of transition. Construction costs for the various items vary from quarter to quarter with the high and low values showing a wider than normal variation. The condition implies a situation of adjustment wherein some of the contractor organizations precede others in making adjustments to a new cost situation. It is therefore presumed that the level of costs will stabilize at a somewhat higher level than the present one of 237. The new level may fall within an index range of 240-245 or at a level which is 12 percent greater than the average level of costs during the calendar year 1954.

The present indications are that construction activity for the United States will be slightly higher in 1956 than the record breaking 57 billion dollars of construction put in place during 1955. In this connection there are predictions that a record year of 60 billion dollars will be realized in 1956.

In view of this, the year 1956 may well be another year of wage increases and also of comparatively reduced competition, a combination of circumstances which may possibly add another 5 percent to the present level of bridge construction costs.

NEW TRAFFIC TEXTBOOK

A textbook on traffic engineering by three Yale faculty members is dedicated to one of the co-authors. The book, "Traffic Engineering," is dedicated to the late Theodore M. Matson, Director of the Bureau of Highway Traffic at Yale until his death. The manuscript for the textbook, first ever written on the subject of traffic engineering, was completed just before Mr. Matson's death last year.

The two other authors of the book, published by the McGraw-Hill Company, are Fred W. Hurd, now Director of Yale's Bureau of Highway Traffic, and Wilbur B. Smith, Research Associate in Transportation at Yale.

A total of $23,614,271 was expended by the Division of Highways for maintenance work, including operation and repair of the Martinez-Benicia Ferry System, during the 1954-55 Fiscal Year.

TABLE I

INDEXES RELATING TO CALIFORNIA BRIDGE CONSTRUCTION AND PERIODIC DOLLAR VALUES OF LOW BIDS ON CALIFORNIA BRIDGE CONSTRUCTION

I Year	II Quarter	III Index of the cost of California bridge construction (1939-1940—100)	IV Index of the value of California bridge construction (1939-1940—100)	V Index of the volume of California bridge construction (1939-1940—100)	VI Dollar value of low bids on California bridge construction (in millions of dollars)
1934		94	60*	64*	3.1
1935		88	138*	157*	7.1
1936		98	72*	73*	3.7
1937		114	60*	53*	3.1
1938		99	78*	79*	4.0
1939		101	99*	98*	5.1
1940		99	101*	102*	5.2
1941		122	78*	64*	4.0
1942		158	80*	50*	4.1
1943		165	16*	9*	.8
1944		153	29*	19*	1.5
1945		167	109*	65*	5.6
1946	1st	156	342	219	4.4
1946	2d	190	295	155	3.8
1946	3d	182* 224	247* 148	133* 66	12.7 1.9
1946	4th	217	202	93	2.6
1947	1st	224	280	125	3.6
1947	2d	216	629	291	8.1
1947	3d	215* 219	443* 450	202* 206	22.8 5.8
1947	4th	223	412	185	5.3
1948	1st	220	233	106	3.0
1948	2d	225	365	162	4.7
1948	3d	229* 238	307* 381	134* 160	15.8 4.9
1948	4th	231	249	108	3.2
1949	1st	207	186	90	2.4
1949	2d	210	342	163	4.4
1949	3d	201* 191	233* 194	117* 102	12.0 2.5
1949	4th	187	210	112	2.7
1950	1st	177	124	70	1.6
1950	2d	195	357	183	4.6
1950	3d	202* 212	262* 171	129* 81	13.5 2.2
1950	4th	235	396	182	5.1
1951	1st	243	528	217	6.8
1951	2d	250	948	379	12.2
1951	3d	248* 256	617* 598	247* 234	31.8 7.7
1951	4th	253	396	157	5.1
1952	1st	239	396	166	5.1
1952	2d	236	1,017	431	13.1
1952	3d	235* 239	561* 652	237* 273	28.9 8.4
1952	4th	223	179	80	2.3
1953	1st	243	140	58	1.8
1953	2d	224	707	315	9.1
1953	3d	229* 231	522* 893	227* 387	26.9 11.5
1953	4th	235	350	149	4.5
1954	1st	221	691	313	8.9
1954	2d	217	1,196	551	15.4
1954	3d	219* 220	870* 1,002	399* 455	44.8 12.9
1954	4th	213	590	277	7.6
1955	1st	217	1,039	477	13.3
1955	2d	237	500	211	6.4
1955	3d	228* 228	930* 1,047	408* 461	47.9 13.4
1955	4th	237	1.148	484	14.7

* Average annual information.

The division opened bids on 638 projects during 1954-55.

1,197 division employees had 25 or more years of service on June 30.

Freeway Interchange
Intricate Three-level Structure Progresses

ON JULY 19, 1954, the Attorney General approved a $2,477,821.40 contract for the construction of a section of the Long Beach Freeway extending from the present northerly terminus near Olympic Boulevard, thence south across the Santa Ana Freeway to the Atchison, Topeka and Santa Fe Railway yard, known as Hobart Yard in East Los Angeles, a distance of 1.04 miles. Work was started on July 12, 1954, slightly more than three years after groundbreaking ceremonies at the southerly terminus of the Long Beach Freeway. Other contracts are now under way and still others are contemplated in the near future that will permit unrestricted travel from Long Beach to the Santa Ana Freeway.

The Long Beach Freeway will connect the U. S. Naval installations at Long Beach and Terminal Island with the industrial area in Los Angeles and vicinity. This freeway was first suggested as early as 1921, but it was not until some 20 years later that the formal proposal was made by the Los Angeles Regional Planning Commission. Various proposals for the location were presented including location within the Los Angeles River Channel and locating opposing roadways on opposite banks of the river as well as locating the entire freeway adjacent to one bank of the river.

Adopted Route

The adopted route will parallel the Los Angeles River, first on one side and crossing to the opposite side in South Gate, from Long Beach to the Cheli Air Force Depot south of Santa Fe yards. From this point the freeway leaves the river to continue north and join with the Santa Ana Freeway. Included in this project are 1.04 miles of freeway grading and paving, ramps and eight major structures.

The intricate Santa Ana Freeway-Long Beach Freeway interchange is made up of five structures and constitutes a three-level separation. Even

UPPER—Looking westerly at Long Beach-Santa Ana Interchange. LOWER—Looking northerly showing in center interchange structures that will provide for traffic movement between the Santa Ana Freeway and the Long Beach Freeway. Completed structure to left will carry southbound Long Beach Freeway traffic and one to right will carry northbound.

the names of the structure give some indication of the complications, with such names as Route 167 EBd & NBd Interchange / Route 166 Separation. The three levels are made up of the Santa Ana Freeway at the bottom level, and the ramps passing over the Santa Ana Freeway and under the Long Beach Freeway at the middle level. These multilevel interchanges are common to interchanges between major freeways where rights of way are restricted. In other words, where horizontal expansion is restricted, the vertical dimension must be expanded.

Five Structures

The five structures of the interchange are of the box girder type and are complicated in design because all are on curves, changing gradients, superelevations up to 12 percent, some with reversing superelevations and some with reverse curves. These factors, in addition to the restricted vertical clearances, complicated construction of the falsework and form work.

Falsework for the spans across the Santa Ana Freeway required a clear span of 40 feet 0 inches and maintenance of the minimum legal vertical clearance of 13 feet 6 inches. The contractor used 24-inch WF 110-pound steel I beams which were placed normal to the Santa Ana Freeway lanes and supported the superstructures which crossed at various skews. Since all of the interchange structures cross the Santa Ana Freeway at various skews, some very severe, and since it was necessary to place the falsework normal to the freeway to reduce the span length, the problem of correcting for deflection of the steel falsework beams developed.

Concentrated loads of the box girder diaphragms and girder stems, combined with the uniform load of the bottom slab, occurred at different locations on each of the steel beams. Deflections were calculated separately for each different loading, and adjustments were made by wedging the joist and stringers as required. Complexity of form work and danger of working adjacent to heavy traffic were not the only problems confronting the contractor. Practically all of the interchange structures are supported on concrete piles and the contractor chose the option of cast in drilled hole piles. The material was firm and drilling was satisfactorily done with a rotary bucket drill and an auger drill with very little caving. These drilled holes were 16 inches in diameter and the presence of many small children passing through and playing in the construction area caused the contractor to adopt a policy of filling all holes with concrete immediately, or otherwise protecting the children from falling in the holes and causing another "Kathy Fiscus" case.

Considerable care was taken to warn traffic of the restricted vertical and horizontal clearances. Reflectorized signs were placed on the Santa Ana Freeway as much as a mile in advance of

UPPER—Looking along westbound lanes of Santa Ana Freeway. Northbound separation in foreground. Eastbound-northbound interchange under construction. Southbound separation in background. LOWER—Looking southeasterly along Santa Ana Freeway showing southbound separation bridge for Long Beach Freeway in foreground. Westbound separation bridge in right center background and eastbound-northbound interchange left center.

construction to warn truckers with high loads to turn off at Olympic Boulevard. Floodlighted signs were placed on existing overhead structures warning of restricted clearances ahead. Lighted signs were placed on the falsework stating, "Impaired Clearance 13'6"."

Despite these precautions overheight loads were another cause of construction problems. During most of the job it was necessary to have steel falsework beams across the Santa Ana Freeway lanes which restricted the vertical clearance. From the start, overheight loads struck the beams.

The contractor welded 3-inch x 3-inch angle struts to the first four beams on the approach side in order to protect the falsework and prevent individual beams from being knocked down onto the freeway. This steel frame was sufficiently rigid to withstand all subsequent shocks. Some overhanging loads sideswiped the falsework posts, but this was held to a minimum by constructing concrete crash walls to support the posts.

The contractor on this project was Ukropina, Polich, Kral & Ukropina. J. M. Curran acted as resident engineer for the Division of Highways.

By GEO. T. McCOY, State Highway Engineer

In the past 10 years, California has quadrupled its highway construction program and now stands ready to turn out plans, specifications and miles of modern highway at an even faster rate if the funds are made available—all in the face of a nation-wide shortage of more than 4,000 highway engineers.

How, despite that handicap, has the State been able to complete 1,000 miles of multilane divided highway in 10 years, with another 300 now under construction and another 200 miles to be advertised for bids this year?

The answer is a combination of modern management and technical methods. Developed and applied more intensively in recent years under the spur of a vastly increased highway construction program, these methods are effecting huge savings in three precious commodities—time, money and professional manpower.

New Techniques

The new techniques and devices range from greater use of subprofessional aids and technicians to aerial photographs from which location maps and even grading plans can be quickly produced; from new, simplified technical manuals to the latest electronic computing machines which calculate earthwork quantities and solve complex geometric problems in a fraction of the time formerly needed.

The eventual full use of these and other known methods will double engineering output. In particular, the application of photogrammetry and automation techniques, in combination, is regarded as the greatest advance in the science of highway engineering in many years.

At the same time, the highway contractors have more than kept pace, with streamlined operations of their own. Ever-larger earth-moving machines change the face of a landscape in a matter of days; moving assembly lines or "paving trains" can already place up to three-quarters of a mile of 12-foot concrete lane, eight inches thick, in one eight-hour day; batching plants serve up just the right mixture of rock, sand and asphalt at the touch of a button. Single contracts run as high as $6,000,000 or even more.

Competition Keen

And competition is as keen as ever, assuring the motorist the most highway for his tax dollar. On a recent typical freeway job, there were nine bidders, with a difference of only $154,000 between the lowest bid of $1,975,000 and the fifth lowest.

California's transportation growing pains, always severe, became acutely critical after World War II, and are still intense. From less than 3,000,000 motor vehicles in 1940, the State's traffic load rose to more than 6,000,000 by 1955 and is now approaching 7,000,000.

Highway construction, financed on a depression-born basis before World War II, came to a standstill during the war. The financing picture improved in 1947 with the Collier-Burns Act, and again in 1953 when the continued growth of traffic made still faster highway construction a matter of life and death to Californians—in the literal as well as the economic sense.

Noticeable progress is being made. California is now spending about $250,000,000 a year for highway construction purposes — admittedly not enough to provide the safe and adequate highways the State desperately needs, but enough to keep the situation from getting worse—and could effectively spend more. Where are the engineers to plan and build these modern trafficways, including many complex metropolitan freeways?

Shortage of Engineers

Far too few are coming out of the engineering colleges. The various state highway departments say that they need 4,000 more engineers right now. But the entire Nation's class of 1954 in civil engineering numbered less than 3,600; probably no more than 700 of them went into highway engineering and a third of these did not stay there long—quite understandable in the light of the higher salary and other inducements offered them in other fields.

Since there were not enough engineers to be had, the California Division of Highways, like other such agencies, stepped up its quest for ways to make more efficient use of what engineers it had and could get. Hand in hand with this effort, the constant struggle to stretch the highway tax dollar a little further, particularly in the face of rising costs, was intensified.

The battle continues without letup. It has not been won, but major gains have been made on several fronts and new victories are in prospect.

Photogrammetry Saves Time

There are six principal fields in which ways have been found to get highways planned and built in California with a saving in time, money and engineering manpower:

1. *Photogrammetry*, or measurements using aerial photographs, is already saving the time and effort of an estimated 200 engineers a year. In one section of California, two ground survey crews plus an aerial mapping contractor produced 75 miles of preliminary surveys that would otherwise have required seven additional ground crews for the field work alone. Remarkably accurate maps can be plotted and drawn from aerial pictures, permitting even the drawing of detailed design plans.

The Division of Highways estimates the cost of obtaining data by ground survey methods at an average of $3,500 a mile for a strip of terrain 400 feet wide. By aerial photography, it averages $1,000 a mile for a strip 1,200 feet wide.

2. "*Automation*," or, more accurately, the use of electronic computing equipment to make and check engineering calculations which are time-consuming, tedious and costly when done manually by engineers in the drafting room. Tabulating machines have long been useful and economical in computing and analyzing traffic statistics, cost data and other figures, but now they have also been put to work on two types of calculations used directly in highway design.

One type is the calculation of traverses, or survey lines. The engineer in the drafting room instead of laboriously figuring and then checking the unknown bearings, distances or areas for a parcel of land, now sends in the available data to the Headquarters Office in Sacramento. There the material is punched onto cards, fed into the machines, and the solutions mailed back. To complete 1,000 to 3,000 traverse courses daily in this fashion takes 12 to 24 hours of key punch and tabulating machine operation time, on the part of technicians and operators. It would take five to seven times as long for the same work to be done by engineers using manual methods.

In addition to saving on engineers, the machine process saves an estimated $2,000 a month in money—it costs five cents per course by machine, against 13 cents per course by conventional methods, not including checking.

Machine Computations

Another and newer machine process computes the cubic yardage of earth to be moved for highway cuts and fills. Using field notes, the terrain data are punched onto cards, fed into the machine and the geometric solutions come out. A number of steps in the conventional design process, such as plotting of roadway cross-sections, are eliminated by this method. Various alternate locations for the highway can be quickly compared as to size and cost of earthwork involved, and the cheapest practical location readily selected. On one 10-mile divided highway project through roll-

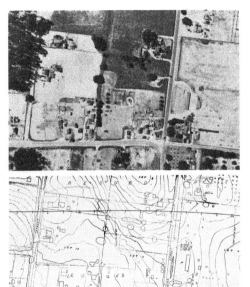

PHOTOGRAMMETRY—Above, a portion of an aerial vertical photograph taken along US 101 in southern San Luis Obispo County. Below, a corresponding portion of the detailed map which was plotted and drawn directly from the aerial photograph. The dark line running across the map near the top is the center line of the proposed four-lane eXpressway which will be under construction this spring. Modern photogrammetric methods drastically reduce the need for detailed ground surveys, thus saving many engineering man-hours for the Division of Highways in getting construction of modern highways under way.

ing terrain, machine computation of earthwork quantities saved the time of four engineers for one month.

3. *Management and Organization* techniques are being used liberally to conserve engineering time and manpower. The statistician, the delineator (female as well as male), the research technician, the junior executive, the construction inspector—the abilities of

these and other workers are being effectively utilized throughout the highway organization.

4. *Efficiency* is being further emphasized in routing procedure not yet adaptable to machine operation. Improved surveying instruments, calculators, and other equipment; simplified drafting and reproduction

. . . Continued on page 52

Colorado River

New Bridge Across Mighty Stream Nears Completion

By N. G. HALLIN, Senior Bridge Engineer

THE EARLY entrances to California proved to be very hazardous, what with the high mountains, wide deserts and large rivers to cross. Much of California's history lies in the routes of entrance to the State and not the least of these is the entrance at Yuma, Arizona. The first barrier to the westward traveler is the crossing of the mighty Colorado River.

A notable crossing of the river occurred in 1774 when on February 9th, Juan Bautista de Anza led a group of 32 people including 20 soldiers across the Colorado River bound for Monterey, California. The successful crossing was made a short distance upstream from the juncture with the Gila River and is reported to be the first made by soldiers of the King of Spain and was celebrated by the firing of a salute of musketry. However, the crossing could not have been made without incident had not Anza negotiated successfully with the Yuma Indians prior to entering their territory and attempting the crossing. Anza sought out the Indian chief and was hospitably received. Gifts consisting of tobacco, beads and toys were distributed among the Indians and in return the Indian chief offered to have his strongest braves assist in the crossings of the Colorado River.

In the year 1775 Anza led another party of 240 people across the Southwest bound for San Francisco. This crossing of the Colorado River was made upstream from the previous one because the latter crossing was found to be impassable.

First Ferry at Yuma

Local tradition has it that the first ferry at Yuma was a raft built in Michigan and drawn across the continent on a prairie schooner and floated down the Colorado River to Yuma. A considerable portion of the '49ers took the route through Yuma and crossed the Colorado River by

Existing Yuma Bridge on right and railroad bridge on left

ferry. In the fall and spring of 1850-51 the ferry carried 60,000 people at $2 a head. In 1858 the Butterfield Stage started operations on the route through Yuma and crossed the river on a ferry at a charge of $5 for a four-horse team. The famous California Column ferried itself across the river at Yuma in 1866. During this period there were two ferries in operation, one operated by the Yuma Indians and one by Don Diego Jaeger. Service was interrupted from time to time due to Indian attacks and this was one reason for establishing an Army fort at Yuma.

Freight and transportation to and from Yuma and vicinity was provided to a considerable extent by boat and included a trip from Yuma to the mouth of the Colorado River by steamboat thence by sea-going vessel to San Francisco. Construction of La-

guna Dam in 1909 stopped freighting up the river; however, the Colorado River is still classified as a navigable river and as such is under the jurisdiction of the Corps of Engineers, United States Army.

Railroad Builds Bridge

The first structure built across the river in this vicinity was the Southern Pacific Railway bridge constructed in 1878. There was no provision made for wagons and the ferries continued to operate until 1915 when the present highway bridge was designed and constructed by the U. S. Department of Interior, Office of Indian Affairs. This bridge is located about 1,500 feet upstream from the original railroad bridge and spans the river from the rocky hill on the Arizona side, which once housed the notorious territorial prison, now a museum, to a

34

New Yuma Bridge across Colorado River nearing completion

similar rocky point on the California side upon which stands a Catholic Mission to the Indians.

The bridge consists of a 336-foot steel curved chord subdivided panel through Pratt truss span and a 105-foot steel warren deck truss span on spread footings. It provides an 18-foot roadway with two five-foot sidewalks.

In 1916 the road across the Sand Hills area west of Yuma was improved in order to connect to the bridge across the Colorado. This improvement consisted of the wooden plank road, parts of which may still be seen along the present road, and was the first attempt to cross the area with a road. After considerable study of the movement of the sand dunes the present facility was constructed in 1926.

Present Span Inadequate

The present railroad bridge was constructed parallel to and immediately upstream from the highway bridge in 1922. The existing highway bridge was redecked in 1943 and it was necessary to close the structure for periods up to an hour while work was being performed. In order to reduce the delay and also to remove some heavy loads from the structure while it was being redecked, the Army constructed a pontoon bridge across the river immediately downstream from the existing bridge.

With the ever-increasing size and number of vehicles the present highway structure has become inadequate and by modern standards is lacking because of the narrow width, poor alignment, steep approach grades, and restricted sight distances. To correct

these deficiencies the States of California and Arizona are jointly engaged in constructing a new highway crossing of the Colorado.

Design of Structure

Many of the problems involved in the design and construction of the new crossing have been lessened by the regulation of flow in the river by Hoover Dam, Davis Dam, Parker Dam, Headgate Rock and to a small extent by Imperial and Laguna Dams. Highest water on record is at elevation 137 on January 22, 1916, which is the apparent maximum since 1867. In spite of the regulation of flow, the under side of steel for the new struc-

tuce is set at elevation 150. The structure will provide two 28-foot roadways, divided by a 6-foot dividing strip, and one 5-foot sidewalk. The structure consists of five spans of riveted plate girders supporting a reinforced concrete deck and supported on solid reinforced concrete piers on steel pile foundations. The spans vary from 155 feet to 180 feet and total 837 feet from paving notch to paving notch.

Joint Venture

Many of the precrossing arrangements required of the pioneers and explorers were also required of the two states before a successful crossing

... Continued on page 57

UPPER—Highway approach from existing bridge to new Yuma span.
LOWER—Approach bridge to new Yuma structure.

Freeway Development of US 99-

First Unit of Lodi to Sacramento Freeway

By JAMES E. WILSON, Project Design Engineer, District X

ANOTHER SECTION of California's Valley Highway, US 99, was brought to full freeway status recently by the completion of a project between Lodi and Sacramento. Local interests have long advocated relief from this traffic bottleneck, and this project marks the beginning of a series of improvements which will make this portion of US 99 one of the most modern in the State. The 3.45-mile project, just completed by M. J. B. Construction Company and Lord and Bishop of Stockton, is the first of several projects to be completed on this section. The limits are from Jahant Road in San Joaquin County to 0.5 mile north of the San Joaquin-Sacramento County line.

Coincident with the policy of the Division of Highways to make US 99 a full freeway, this project provides interchanges at Collier and Liberty Roads with full traffic movements at each. Approximately 18,700 feet of frontage roads are provided to serve residences and small businesses.

Geometric and Structural Features

The new northbound lanes were constructed to provide a 40-foot width of median. This allows for an ultimate development into a six-lane freeway with 16-foot median width. The existing traveled way, composed of 22 feet of pavement, placed in 1938, was widened and resurfaced with plant-mixed surfacing and is now being utilized as the southbound lanes. All travel lanes are 12 feet in width.

The new lanes are constructed of an eight-inch uniform thickness of portland cement concrete on four inches of cement-treated subgrade. A 12-inch layer of imported subbase material completes the structural section, giving a total depth of 24 inches. The native soil consisted of highly expansive material for which special treatment was necessary. The two feet of material directly below the structural section was removed and relaid with a moisture content in excess of optimum. Shoulders to the right and left of the driver are graded to a width of 10 feet and 5 feet, respectively.

Median shoulders consist of a two-foot plant-mixed surfacing border and three feet of untreated base. Outside shoulders are surfaced with plant-mixed surfacing on untreated base for a width of eight feet.

Widening and reconstructing the existing traveled way involved trenching out on the median side a width of $4\frac{1}{2}$ feet and the placing of eight inches of Class "A" cement-treated base. Shoulder failures accompanied by high maintenance costs necessitated the reconstruction of the outside shoulder, which was removed and replaced with 10 inches of untreated base. The concrete pavement was then subsealed with asphalt to correct a pumping condition. A contact blanket of two-inch minimum thickness of Class "A" plant-mixed surface was placed on the old portland cement concrete pavement as a wearing course, and the shoulders were surfaced in the same manner as the newly constructed lanes.

Structures

Welded steel girder bridges were used for the Collier and Liberty Road overcrossing structures. Spans are supported by reinforced concrete bents and abutments. The

... Continued on page 38

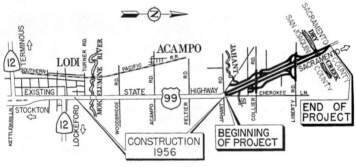

0 in Two Counties Moves Ahead

Progress of Freeway in Sacramento County

By P. C. SHERIDAN, Assistant District Engineer, District III

A 5.1-MILE SECTION of US 99-50 between 0.5 mile south of Elk Grove Road and 1.8 miles south of Florin Road is now under contract and is scheduled for completion about August of 1956. The Granite Construction Company is the contractor. Also under contract is the highway lighting for the project with Luppen and Hawley Company.

The existing highway, which is now a 20-foot concrete pavement, will be widened and resurfaced to effect a 24-foot traveled way for the future southbound lanes. The northbound lanes will be new construction of 24-foot portland cement concrete pavement. Frontage roads are being constructed the full length of the project on both sides. The freeway lanes are separated by a 46-foot median to provide for future development to six lanes.

Grade separations and interchanges are being constructed at the Elk Grove Road and Sheldon Road intersections. Two bridges are being widened and five new bridges constructed.

The normal right of way width is 234 feet to accommodate the frontage roads being constructed on both sides.

Second Unit Nearly Ready

Plans, specifications and estimates are ready for a second unit in Sacramento County which should be advertised within the very near future. This is a 7.1-mile unit and extends from near the San Joaquin County line to 1.6 miles south of the Cosumnes River. Like the unit now under construction, it will utilize the existing highway, widened and resurfaced, as the southbound lanes and a new 24-foot concrete pavement for the northbound lanes. There are about 8.25 miles of frontage roads, and like the first unit,

the normal right of way width is 234 feet where frontage roads are to be constructed, and provision is made in the 46-foot median for future development to six lanes.

The structures include an underpass at the lone branch of the Southern Pacific Railroad and grade separations and interchanges at C Street, Simmerhorn Road, Amador Avenue, State Route 34 Junction, and Arno Road. Four bridges are to be widened for the southbound lanes and parallel new bridges constructed for the northbound lanes.

Third Unit Is Budget Item

The preparation of plans is nearing completion for a 5.9-mile unit with advertising tentatively scheduled in November of this year. This unit will extend from 1.8 miles south of Cosumnes River to 0.5 mile south of Elk Grove Road. Again, the four freeway lanes will be developed similar to those on the two projects discussed above. There will be approximately 6.3 miles of frontage roads on a normal right-of-way width of 246 feet where frontage roads are to be developed.

The structures include an overhead for the northbound lanes at the Southern Pacific Railroad at McConnell, using the existing underpass for southbound lanes. Overcrossings and interchanges are planned at Dillard Road and Grant Line Road. The existing bridge at Badger Creek will be widened for the southbound lanes and a parallel new structure constructed for the northbound lanes, and a new structure for both sets of lanes are to be constructed at Cosumnes River and the Cosumnes River Overflows.

South Sacramento Freeway

Plans are in the design stage for the last section, which will extend the 7.2 miles between 1.8 miles south of Florin Road and U Street in Sacramento. The complexity of this section is such that it will probably be constructed in several units. However, rights of way have been in the

... Continued on page 38

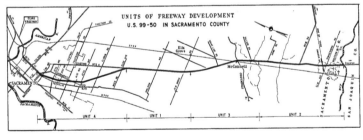

UNITS OF FREEWAY DEVELOPMENT
U.S. 99-50 IN SACRAMENTO COUNTY

FIRST UNIT

Continued from page 36 . . .

deck of reinforced concrete provides 26-foot width clear roadway and a single sidewalk five feet in width.

North and south channels of Dry Creek were spanned by reinforced concrete slabs 171 feet and 825 feet in length. These slabs were supported by concrete pile bents 22 feet on centers. A minimum width of traveled way of 31 feet 10 inches was provided without concrete wheel guards. Railing consists of corrugated metal beam railing.

Several smaller drainage structures were constructed, including a 12-foot by 10-inch concrete box culvert at Jabant Slough and a double six-foot by five-inch concrete box culvert near Liberty Road.

Drainage

Except for the sections near the beginning and the end of the project, the area is generally flat valley country devoted to grazing. This made drainage somewhat of a problem since there were few natural cross channels and less than the minimum ground slope for good surface flow. The traveled ways were generally elevated above natural ground and ditch grades were as flat as 0.1 percent. Profile grades of all new construction were rolled in a manner that maintained a minimum grade of 0.12 percent.

Right of Way

In 1938, a 120-foot right of way was acquired to accommodate a four-lane highway having a 22-inch median. Under stage construction the two southbound lanes were constructed, the northbound lanes to be constructed when needed. At that time 16 parcels were acquired at a total cost of $22,000. In 1948, the Weber Act, "a provision that improvements adjacent to highways should be kept back in case of future widening," was invoked by the San Joaquin County Board of Supervisors covering 10 feet on the west and 30 feet on the east side of the existing right of way.

Extensive changes in design standards with development to an ultimate six-lane full freeway necessitated purchase of additional rights of way in

Aerial view of the new section of freeway on US 50-99 between Jahant Road and 0.5 mile north of the Sacramento County line, looking north. Collier Road Overcrossing is shown in center of picture, Liberty Road Overcrossing in background. County line is along Dry Creek, where row of trees grows beyond Liberty Road Overcrossing.

1953-54. Where no frontage roads were constructed, a minimum width of 160 feet was necessary. Where frontage roads were constructed on both sides, a minimum of 220 feet was needed. Seventy-nine parcels were purchased at this time at a total cost of $470,000.

The work, costing approximately $1,052,000, was under the direction of Harold Atherstone, Resident Engineer for the Division of Highways.

Another project will bridge the gap between Lodi and the project just discussed. This will complete the four-lane development between Stockton and the northerly limits of District X.

SACRAMENTO COUNTY

Continued from page 37 . . .

process of acquisition for several years and it may be expected that financing may be accomplished within the next

several years. This section is on new alignment and initially four lanes will be constructed south of Florin Road with provision for an ultimate six lanes, and six lanes will be constructed from Florin Road into Sacramento with provision for ultimate eight lanes.

There will only be about two miles of frontage roads because traffic can be routed over the existing road and street networks.

South of Florin Road the normal right of way width is 160 feet to accommodate the ultimate six lanes and north of Florin Road is 190 feet to accommodate the ultimate eight lanes.

Structures include bridges across Beacon Creek, Dome Creek, Florin Creek, and Morrison Creek and overcrossing structures at the intersection with the old highway on the south end, Mack Road, Florin Road, 47th

. . . Continued on page 52

38

House Moving

It Has Become Big Business
For Right of Way Division

By WARREN K. BRANSCUM, Right of Way Agent

ONE THOUGHT that flashes through the mind of everyone who drives for the first time on a freeway in metropolitan Los Angeles, is, "where did the houses go to allow for the construction of the highway?"

The answer to this question at the present time is anywhere within a 100-mile radius of Los Angeles, from Bakersfield to San Bernardino.

At the close of World War II the Los Angeles area was faced with the greatest housing shortage in its history. The Division of Highways was confronted with a double problem, that of accelerating a lagging highway construction program without aggra-

vating the housing crises. In the years immediately following World War II, the purchaser of a house to be moved was required to continue renting the house to its present tenants for a period of six months and to provide temporary housing while the building was being moved. At that time it was further required that no house could be moved more than four miles from its original location.

Since housing is no longer an acute problem in the Los Angeles area, buyers of improvements have been freed of these restrictions. Even though there is an abundance of single-family tract houses available for purchase in

the suburbs, the market for houses to be relocated remains strong. Only a small percentage of houses in the path of freeway construction are not relocated and again utilized as homes. This small percentage consists of substandard houses that cannot be economically renovated to meet the present building code. The clearance of improvements from the right of way area is not only a big job, but it is also BIG BUSINESS.

House Buying Industry

Virtually a new industry has been developed in the area by this policy of selling houses to be removed. In the

View of Harbor Freeway looking southerly from Santa Barbara Avenue, showing the right of way area under construction clear of all improvements

past 10 years there have come on the business horizon men who are skilled in analyzing which buildings can economically be relocated, t h e house buyer. These men have investigated the building codes and requirements of the many incorporated cities in the Los Angeles area as well as the requirements of the surrounding counties. They buy for cash at state auctions and sell the homes delivered to the lot of the final purchaser on credit. No bank or finance company will issue a long term real estate loan on improvements until the house is permanently affixed to the land, that is, the foundation put in, and all utilities connected. The house buyer finances the move and extends credit for a one-year period until the ultimate purchaser can get a real estate loan through normal loan agencies. The Division of Highways usually allows approximately ninety (90) days for improvements to be cleared from the right of way area. If the buyers have not sold their houses by this final clearance date, these houses are moved to storage lots and prospective customers can visit from 15 to 20 houses at each of these "used house lots."

House Moving Industry

House moving is not a new industry in the area. However, it has undergone a tremendous expansion program since the close of World War II. Of the 23 recognized house movers in the area, six firms have come into existence in the last 10 years. Old established firms are now moving three and four times as many houses as were moved prior to the accelerated highway program. So far in 1955, the house moving industry has averaged moving 17 houses a night, five nights a week. In a year's time this will amount to 4,420 houses. This constitutes the housing for 22,000 people. That means each year in the Los Angeles area sufficient housing is relocated to house a city the size of Ventura. Sixty percent of all buildings being so relocated come from public works projects of which the freeway program is the major contributing operation.

Technological developments in the house moving industry have resulted in a greater efficiency. With the en-

A 16-unit apartment house was cut into five units to facilitate moving. This is a view of one of such units.

trance into the house moving business of the hydraulic house jack, the use of pneumatic-tired dollies and powerful prime mover trucks, the industry has undergone a change equal to the industrial revolution in business.

Moving Is Cheaper

In fact, a house mover, hiring the same number of men as he hired in the late twenties, can move three to four times as many houses as he did then. This has resulted in keeping moving costs to a minimum. A five-room house can now be moved for approximately the same cost that it could be moved in 1930, in spite of the inflation that has taken place in the past 25 years. The distance that a house can be economically m o v e d has been greatly extended. With present equipment a five-room house can move down the street at a rate of speed as much as 20 to 25 miles per hour. A house can now be moved from the

central Los Angeles area to an outlying suburb in a matter of four hours while in the late thirties, this move ordinarily took approximately two days. Recently several houses have gone to San Bernardino, a distance of 62 miles, and some houses have been moved as far as Bakersfield, which is 119 miles. Ten years ago, such moves would not have been even considered.

Techniques Advanced

House m o v i n g techniques and know-how have also advanced greatly in the past decade. One technique that has been developed is the cutting of sprawling California style improvements into sections. These sections are then moved separately and the structure is reassembled on the new site. This technique has been used extensively on 2- and 3-story multiple unit apartment buildings and California ranch-style houses. The structures are reassembled so skillfully that it is im-

. . . Continued on page 69

By GEORGE M. WEBB, Traffic Engineer

Prepared for presentation at a meeting of the Advisory Committee on Freeway Traffic Control of the Assembly Interim Committee on Transportation and Commerce, at Los Angeles.

Accident reports furnish an important part of the basic information for the budgeting, planning, and design of highways. Accident studies point out the critical locations on the highway system, and analysis of the accidents provides the best clue to the proper corrective measures. Effective planning is based on the traffic volumes and accident rates, and progressive design is based on the effectiveness of highway features and designs, as shown by the accident experience.

California's full freeways are, and have continually been, the safest system of highways in the world. The 1954 fatality rate on California's full freeways was 27 percent and 29 percent lower than the comparable rates for the New York Thruway and the New Jersey Turnpike, respectively, the closest competitors. In California, freeway accident rates are approximately one-half and fatality rates less than one-fourth of those for conventional highways.

California Pioneered

California pioneered the full freeway with the opening of the Arroyo Seco Parkway, now the Pasadena Freeway, in 1940. The Division of Highways has continuously studied freeway accidents and operation to provide the basis for improved design. Designs are not static, but freeway design is a proven safe design and changes must be approached with caution and supported by sound factual data.

Copies of all accident reports made by the California Highway Patrol are received by both the Headquarters Traffic Department of the Division of Highways and the appropriate Highway District. In addition, accident reports, as made out by the city police departments for urban freeways, are obtained from the city by the district

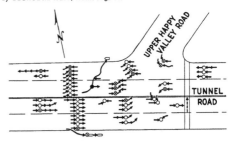

Before
(SEPT. 26, 1950 TO SEPT. 26, 1952)

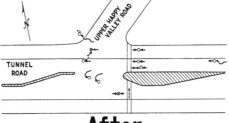

After
(SEPT. 26, 1952 TO SEPT. 26, 1954)

Simplified collision diagrams for State Sign Route 24 (Tunnel Road) in Contra Costa County at intersection with Upper Happy Valley Road for two years before and two years after channelization project. Follow-up study for the next two years showed that the improvement was successful in drastically reducing accidents. In studying such problem locations, accident reports are summarized for ready analysis on "detail cards," illustrated below.

offices and copies are forwarded to Headquarters Traffic Department. All accidents occurring on rural state highways and urban freeways are located to the point on the highway system at which they occurred. Within the districts and at headquarters, the accidents are spotted on sec-

IT-CC-75-A
Upper Happy Valley
Rd Intersection

			L	DAYLIGHT		R	RARELY		P	PANEL OR PICKUP
			D	DARK		F	FREQUENTLY		T	TRUCK
			DA	DARK W/LIGHTS		PED	PEDESTRIAN		TT	TRUCK & TRAILER
			NS	NOT STATED		C	CAR-		M	MOTORCYCLE
			N	NEVER		B	BUS			

ACC. NO.	DATE	TIME	USE	SEVERITY F	NF	PDO	1	2	USE	DESCRIPTION
1	9 16 49	1725	L			✓			F N	c²ea, det. bres, hit c²ea in rear, noexplanation, road under const.
2	9 14 49	1755	L		2				NS F	c²va, excessive speed, applied brees to avoid hitting v² making left turn, crossed double line hitting c²ea headon, road under const.
3	10 15 49	1540	L			✓			R F	c²ea stopped, attempting left turn, c²,³ea on stopped, c²hit in rear by c²ea at excessive speed
4	10 20 49	1650	L		3				NS F	c²ea swung over double line, hitting c²wa headon
5	11 6 49	1745	D			✓			F F	c²ea stopped for traffic, resulting in a 4-car rear end (raining)
6	11 6 49	1717	D			1			R NS	c²ea stopped in E-1, resulting in a 3-car rear end (raining)
7	11 6 49	1717	D			✓			R PL	c²ea in E-2 came upon previous acc., broadsided into N-2, hit c²va headon sideswipe (raining)
8	11 8 49	1125	D			✓			F F	c²ea in E-2 hit in rear as he stopped for v² making left turn, by c²ea, both at excessive speed
9	11 27 49	0830	D		5				F R	c²va making left turn out of U.H.V. road, hit by c²va (HBD&RI)
10	1 29 50	1440	L		1				F F	c²ea made improper left turn in front of c²va
11	2 20 50	0730	L			✓			R PL	c²ea stopped for traffic ahead, hit in rear by c/ea, 4-car rear end, caused by excessive speed
12	2 2 60	1515	L		2				F R	c²ea stopped for traffic ahead, 4-car rear end
13	4 16 50	1852	L			✓			N F	
14	4 28 50	1200	L			✓			F F	c²ea making left turn hit c²va starting up from parked position
15	4 29 50	1930	D			✓			F F	c²ea, exceeding safe speed, hit c²ea who stopped for traffic

tion profiles or section index cards which, in either case, represent a log of the highway showing the position of intersections, structures, city limits, and other identifying features. Developing concentrations of accidents at any one point can be readily noted. Such locations are studied and the accident pattern analyzed to determine corrective measures.

Accident Reports Coded

After the accident reports have been located, the accidents occurring on the rural state highway system are coded for punching on IBM cards. With traffic data also coded for punching, the accidents and the traffic factors are combined mechanically to develop accident rates and injury accident rates for each section or shorter segment on the State Highway System. In addition, many standard and special tabulations are obtainable from the punched data, including rates by each type of road as broken down by: (a) number of lanes; (b) degree of access control; and (c) type of divi-

sion, if any. The punched data are also available as an aid in many special studies undertaken by the traffic department.

The Accident Analysis Section of the Traffic Department studies points of accident concentration and all points involving recommendations by the Highway Patrol. Accidents are plotted and analyzed to determine the accident pattern and the appropriate corrective measures. After correction has been made, the location is still watched to determine the effectiveness of the correction. Occasionally, it may be necessary to make further improvements to control the accidents at a specific location. These before and after studies, which are continually being made at points of highway improvement, generally provide a sound basis to determine the effectiveness of any specific type of corrective measure.

Accident Analysis

Accident analysis is a specialized phase of traffic engineering. It requires not only an engineering background,

but also considerable training in the specific field as well as in analytical and statistical methods. Engineering judgment, developed to a high degree by experience in this field, is essential in determining the proper corrective measures. The apparently obvious answer, as often proposed by untrained observers, is often far from the correct solution to an accident problem.

Major Reports

A substantial portion of the work of the Accident Analysis Section involves studies to determine the effectiveness of specific design features. Some of these studies result in major reports which receive national distribution. The majority of the reports, however, are not developed to such a formal stage but are effective for the use of the Division of Highways in answering specific questions of design or effectiveness of highway features.

Among major reports issued by this department was the report "Median Study, 1952." This study was based on more than 12,000 accidents occurring over a period of two years on some 500 miles of four-lane divided or undivided rural highways. The formal report was presented before the Highway Research Board in 1953 and was republished by that agency. It has received national acclaim as the most comprehensive and complete study of median dividers ever attempted.

Record of Medians

Basically, this study shows that for rural highways and the range of traffic volumes encountered on such roads, medians *without* physical barriers have a substantially better safety record than barrier-type medians, even though the barrier is located in the center of a wide earth median. Briefly, the studies show that a positive divider is twice as safe as a traversable median in preventing approach-type accidents (head-on and head-on sideswipe), but for each such approach-type accident eliminated, there will be five additional single car accidents reported, primarily involving the barrier. In the over-all accident picture, medians with a physical barrier show approximately 10 percent more persons killed or injured than do traversable-type medians.

The "Median Study" did show, however, that barrier-type medians showed to better advantage as traffic volumes increased, and indications were that such medians might prove of advantage at traffic volumes in excess of those available in the report.

Pasadena Freeway

Although the Pasadena Freeway, the earliest freeway design, has what is now considered a substandard width of median, it does carry large volumes of traffic and the existing four-foot low curbed median offers little resistance to crossing. However, over some lengths of this freeway, the existing curb has been backed up by a high barrier curb or guard rail installed in the median. The rate of accidents involving the median is 31 percent higher for lengths with barrier-type median than for lengths with low curbed median, as shown by a study covering seven years of operation.

On the other hand, approach-type accidents are extremely rare on this freeway. This is due primarily to the fact that the majority of median crossings occur in peak hours and the highly directional flow results in very light traffic movements on the opposing lanes. Vehicles are forced across this narrow median but only rarely is one involved in an approach-type accident.

Guard Rail Installation

In spite of the fact that the Division of Highways has never experienced a reduced accident rate by the installation of a physical barrier within an existing median, a serious record of

Freeway design improves with eXperience, but basic safety features built into some of the earlier full freeways are still paying dividends in terms of saving life and limb. The North Sacramento Freeway, in operation since 1948, has an eXcellent record. Its seven-year accident rate (all types) is 1.56 per million vehicle miles and its fatality rate 1.84 per hundred million vehicle miles.

Accident records on rural eXpressways show that medians without physical barriers make for greater over-all safety. This recently completed section of US 99 north of Redding was designed with a wide traversable dividing strip.

crossed-median accidents has given cause to install back-to-back guard rail on a two-mile section of the San Bernardino Freeway. Bids for this improvement were opened November 25, 1955. The alignment and width of median on this section of freeway is no longer adequate according to present-day standards for high volume metropolitan freeways. This location has a better chance than any other location on the State Highway System of showing an improvement in traffic safety by the installation of a positive barrier.

Another major report issued by the department was a report on "Intersection Accidents on Divided Highways." This report was presented at the 1953 meeting of the Highway Research Board and reprinted in a bulletin issued by the board. It primarily sets forth the relation between accidents and entering traffic volumes at divided highway intersections and provides a basis for determining the accident savings that could be achieved

by separation of any specific intersection.

Signalized Intersections

A recent report, "The Relation Between Accidents and Traffic Volumes at Signalized Intersections" was presented at the 1955 annual meeting of the Institute of Traffic Engineers. As the title implies, this report provides a basis on which future accidents may be estimated if an intersection is signalized, which information is of prime importance in considering the signalization of an existing intersection.

Other Accident Studies

Among the many traffic studies undertaken by the department that did not result in a published report are the following:

"Urban Expressways" report. This report was for technical use and was circulated only within the Division of Highways. It pointed out that expressways with intersections at grade were not a satisfactory installation from the

accident standpoint in urban areas. Safety achieved by the elimination of private access and the installation of a divider was offset by the excessive number of accidents at the intersections due to the wider intersections and the generally higher speeds of through traffic. This report had great impact on design policy in that it resulted in the establishment of a standard of full freeways with intersections separated for major highways in built-up areas.

Other reports for use in design were a study of the relation of sight distance to accident rates on two-lane highways and a study relating shoulder width to accidents, also on two-lane highways.

The study "Guard Rail at Bridge Ends," made for design information, was later published in the *California Highways and Public Works* and *Western Construction* magazines.

Other informal departmental reports covered, from the accident standpoint, the effect of increasing

44

Analysis of accident reports showed clearly that in urban areas expressways with intersections at grade need to be replaced as soon as financially possible by full freeways with intersections separated by structures. UPPER—The Rosecrans-Firestone Intersection on the Santa Ana Freeway near Norwalk in 1952. LOWER—Aerial view of the same location completed to full freeway standards in 1955.

curve radius and the installation of stated (advisory) speed signs on curve accidents.

Proper Spacing on Off-ramps

A study of proper spacing of on- and off-ramps in freeway design was published in the September-October, 1955, issue of the *California Highways and Public Works* magazine under the title "Freeway Ramps—Proper Spacing Important in Preventing Accidents."

A two-year sample of accidents on the heaviest traveled portions of the Hollywood and Pasadena Freeways was very carefully analyzed from all angles in a search for the basic factors responsible for accidents on high-volume freeways. No formal report has been issued but data available in this study have been useful to the department. General findings include a factor that was previously known—that accidents rise sharply when a road is carrying traffic volumes in excess of the practical design capacity. Another item disclosed by this study was the high percentage of accidents involving on- and off-ramps and the fact that off-ramp accidents were three times as frequent as on-ramp ac-

cidents on high-volume freeways. This information was utilized in the ramp study mentioned above. The

third item disclosed by this study was the fact that in spite of the low traffic volumes, the 2 to 3 a.m. accident peak

This picture (taken before installation of the guard rail) of evening rush hour traffic last summer on the San Bernardino Freeway near downtown Los Angeles indicates why back-to-back guard rail has just been installed in an effort to reduce crossed-median accidents on this section built in 1948. Subsequent sections of this and other heavily traveled metropolitan freeways provide a wider median, straighter alignment, adequate shoulders and other improved elements of safe design.

cisco areas, as well as the composite rate of these three locations.

Driver Responsibility

The extremely high percentage of accidents in which a driver failure or a driver condition was involved points out a tremendous field for traffic accident reduction. The performance of drivers and drivers' attitudes are things beyond the scope of the engineer's activities. It would seem that the high percentage of accidents which involve driver behavior or attitudes should be classed as a social problem. This approach to the prevention of traffic accidents opens up a field of great possibilities in accident reduction and points out the best line of endeavor for safety-minded citizens, citizens' groups, organizations, service clubs, and others who desire to do something constructive to improve traffic safety. The Division of Highways is eager to cooperate with all such efforts, and will continue to place its engineering knowledge and experience at the disposal of any group making an all-out attack on the traffic safety problem.

Influence on Planning

The accident and injury accident rates on highway sections are an important consideration in the planning and budgeting for future highway improvements. In addition, locations of accident concentration, the solution of which requires a major construction project, rate high in the competition for highway funds. The importance of accident rates in planning is emphasized in departmental instructions covering the preparation of planning programs. The accident rate for each project is studied in the selection of projects for inclusion in the planning program. Special consideration is given to those sections having a high or abnormal accident rate.

Influence on Design

The influence of accident studies on design has been rather thoroughly covered in the listing of various formal and informal reports, virtually all of which are aimed at the checking of existing designs and the improvement of design standards. No change in design standards is undertaken without

was as high as that during the morning peak hour and almost as high as that during the evening peak hour. The high percentage of "had been drinking" accidents occurring in these early morning hours definitely ties the accident peak to the closing of the bars at 2 a.m.

Although not directly related to design, the coding of accident information allows us to easily isolate reported causes of accidents. In the study of freeways, it might be interesting to know that 95 percent of reported causes involve driver violations or condition. Vehicle conditions, roadway causes, and miscellaneous causes combined to a total of only 5 percent. The table below shows a breakdown of accident causes for a one-year sample of freeway accidents in the Los Angeles, San Diego and San Fran-

	Los Angeles		San Diego		San Francisco		Composite	
	No.	%	No.	%	No.	%	No.	%
Violations of rules of the road	428	69	95	75	31	45	554	68
Improper speed	35	6	4	3	5	7	44	5
Had been drinking	100	16	19	15	20	29	139	17
Other driver conditions	29	4.5	7	6	6	9	42	5
Miscellaneous (including condition of vehicle, road, etc.)	29	4.5	1	1	7	10	37	5
Totals	621		126		69		816	

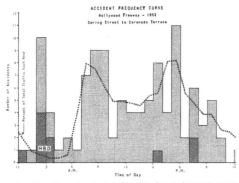

ACCIDENT FREQUENCY CURVE
Hollywood Freeway - 1953
Spring Street to Coronado Terrace

Accident analysis sometimes reveals a pattern beyond the possibility of correction by engineering measures. As this chart shows, accidents on the close-in section of the Hollywood Freeway are about as numerous in the 2 a.m.-3 a.m. period as in the morning and evening rush hours although traffic volume is much lower. The shaded portion of the vertical bars indicate the number of accidnets in which police reports noted "had been drinking."

referring to such accident information as is available to indicate the influence that such change will have on the safety picture.

From the standpoint of public benefit, there is no doubt that engineering use is the most important use of accident reports. Both the location for improvement and the type of corrective measure, as well as the basis for improved design standards, are obtained from analysis of accident reports. The cumulative effect of corrections at locations where accidents are happening and the expanding mileage of freeways and expressways are at present providing great improvement in safety on state highways.

It follows that the best use of the highway dollar for greatest public benefit is to build freeways based on tested and tried designs specifically developed to move large volumes of traffic expeditiously and with the maximum safety.

The world's heaviest-traveled highway—the close-in section of the Hollywood Freeway carries an estimated 180,000 vehicles per day, far in eXcess of its practical design capacity. Yet in 1954 it had one of the best safety records in history for a major trafficway—only 0.8 fatalities per hundred million vehicle miles of travel.

SIGN LIGHTING FIXTURE DEVELOPMENT IN DISTRICT IV

By VERNON H. WAIGHT, Associate Electrical Enginer, and
JOHN R. BRASS, Associate Highway Electrical Engineer

The ever-increasing number of miles of California highways built to freeway standards has brought into focus the need for adequate signing. Essentially, signs serve to guide drivers, especially those unfamiliar with the particular stretch of highway, in order that they might make the proper choice of direction at an interchange. When placed in advance of the interchange, signs serve to segregate traffic into proper lanes before reaching the point of divergence.[1, 2]

Need for Sign Lighting

Considering the above mentioned points, the necessity for adequate visibility of signs at night becomes apparent; clearly a sign without means for such visibility would be less useful at night than an automobile without headlights.

Originally all signs were small and low-mounted, and night visibility was provided by utilizing reflectorized messages activated by vehicular headlights. The increasing speed of freeway traffic has demanded larger signs,[2] signs which in turn have required greater mounting heights, in order that they might be located in narrow gores or above the roadway.[3] These larger signs are mounted on posts and bridges at heights of 15 to 17 feet. Some means should be provided for illuminating large overhead-mounted signs.

Early Sign Lighting Installations

The earliest single-post mounted directional signs in District IV were placed along the Bayshore Freeway between Colma Creek and Burlingame. The sign panels had black letters on a white background. Illumination was provided by incandescent lamps in porcelain enamel sign reflectors mounted along the top of the sign panel. This type of fixture and mounting resulted in lighting that was characterized by a bright reflected image of each fixture on the sign panel, an effect which resulted in poor night legibility of the signs.

In 1948 there was brought to our attention a fluorescent fixture of the showcase type, designed primarily for interior use. The unit was installed, top-mounted, as a replacement of the incandescent units on a sign at the Broadway-San Mateo Interchange on the Bayshore Freeway. Although in retrospect this fixture appears embryonic as compared to the latest fixture, it resulted in a much improved lighting job and in addition, clearly indicated the superiority of a line type light source for panel lighting.

Some time later a southern California manufacturer introduced a top-mounting sign lighting fixture with a trough-shaped reflector.

Principles of Good Sign Lighting

Fundamental principles[4] which should be observed to insure an efficiently and effectively illuminated sign are:

1. Provide uniform brightness of sign message. (Uniform illumination may not provide uniform brightness due to reflections.)

2. Make the brightness of sign panel sufficient so that it will stand out in contrast with its immediate surroundings.

3. Permit neither direct nor reflected glare.

4. Make the lighting equipment inconspicuous and so located that it will not interfere with the view of the message.

Comparison of Fluorescent and Incandescent Lighting

Before continuing any general discussion of fluorescent sign lighting fixtures, it is desirable to consider the reasons for selecting the fluorescent tube source over conventional incandescent sources.

1. The continuous line source, provided by fluorescent lamps, furnishes inherently superior uniformity of illumination horizontally across the sign panel.

2. Fluorescent lamps provide better uniformity of illumination from top to bottom of the sign panel. Illumination from a small light source decreases inversely as the square of the distance from the source. However, illumination from a line (fluorescent) source decreases inversely only as the distance from the source.

3. Considering top-mounted fixtures, the lower brightness of the fluorescent lamps causes less reflected glare on the sign panel from the source being "mirrored" in the sign panel.

4. The uniformity of illumination is less affected by burnout of one fluorescent lamp due to the overlapping light from other lamps.

5. Fluorescent lamps provide at least twice the lamp life.

6. Fluorescent lamps, including ballast losses, consume approximately one-half the power for equal light output.

Faults of Top-mounted Fixtures

One of the most disturbing effects from conventional methods of lighting porcelain signs from above, is that the light source is "mirrored" in the semiglossy surface of the sign into the drivers' eyes, especially on rainy nights. This effect causes black portions of the sign to appear very nearly as bright as the white portions, which reduces legibility, and accounts for the often heard remark that too much light is directed on the signs. Actually the measured illumination level on these signs is not high, and the same or much higher level produced by bottom-mounted fixtures is quite comfortable and produces excellent visibility. (See Figures 1 and 2.)

Due to the fact that any improvement in light control in bracket-arm, top-mounted fixtures will intensify the reflected image, any work done in this direction does not appear promising.

Top-mounted fixtures adjacent to the face of the sign (not on arms), produce glaring reflections only near the top of the sign. This glare has less

effect on visibility of the sign than the glare from bracket-arm, top-mounted fixtures, but is nevertheless undesirable.

During daylight hours top-mounted fixtures produce shadows on the sign panels which reduce legibility.

Advantages of Bottom-mounted Fixtures

The first bottom-mounted fluorescent fixtures were proposed and installed only to fill in the low light level at the bottom of signs over four feet high. These fixtures had little or no light control, they cut off light at the bottom of the sign and they were otherwise unsatisfactory in durability of reflector and in certain mechanical details. Because bottom-mounted fixtures do not have the faults of top-mounted fixtures mentioned above, a new design was proposed and a plan was drawn up for a fixture which would have sufficiently good light distribution to satisfactorily light, from the bottom, any sign size up to seven feet high.

In some localities, with severe dust and soot conditions, it would appear that only top-mounted fixtures would operate satisfactorily. However, a well designed bottom-mounted fixture will initially direct a much higher percentage of total lamp lumens on the sign than conventional top-mounted fixtures, thereby compensating for a possible poorer maintenance factor. It should also be pointed out that only the top glass in a properly designed bottom-mounted fixture will have the large deposits of dust and soot, and in addition to being easily cleaned, it is self-cleaning to some extent. Open top-mounted fixtures are not only difficult to clean, but in addition are not self-cleaning.

Features of New Design

The functional requirements of the new design were as follows:

1. The brightness of the sign panel should be as nearly uniform as possible.

Due to the greater distance of the top of the sign from the source and the unfavorable angle of the surface at the top with the light "beam," the light intensity toward the center of the top row of letters should be about three times the light intensity toward the bottom of the sign.

This figure is based on positioning the source of light one-half the sign panel height out from the bottom of the panel. Placing the fixture in closer to the bottom of the sign requires greater relative light intensity toward the top of the sign which is difficult to obtain. Placing this fixture further out reduces the relative intensity required toward the top of the sign but requires excessively long support arms. Since fixtures without any light control ability had been previously placed about one-half the sign height from the bottom of the sign, it was assumed that with a considerable degree of light control excellent uniformity could be obtained at this distance.

Light Output Factor

2. Most of the light output should be directed on the sign panel. Previous bottom-mounted fixtures had considerable light output vertically upward but relatively little output on the sign, due to the lack of control from the ineffectual bent metal reflector and the diffuse white enamel reflecting surface.

3. The reflectors should be housed in a corrosion-resistant, raintight and dust-tight enclosure with a sealed transparent window.

4. The housing should be designed to facilitate access for cleaning, removal of reflectors and lamp replacement. It was suggested by one manufacturer that it would be preferable not to hinge the glass window, as in previous designs, but to have the window fixed and provide one access door at the back of the fixture away from the sign. This position provides easy access to the lamps and reflectors and reduces the possibility of glass breakage. The reflectors (see *Figure 3*) may be easily wiped clean of dust and dirt and do not trap dirt at any point.

5. The fixture should be made up of lamp length units, which could be assembled to fit any length sign. (See *Table I*.) This standardization of sizes would reduce manufacturing costs, since fixture fabricators could concentrate on making two or three different size units. In addition, the shipping problems would be simplified. Previously the fixtures were made in one piece to fit each sign panel, the length

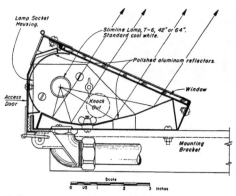

Lamp Socket Housing.

Slimline Lamp, T-6, 42" or 64". Standard cool white.

Polished aluminum reflectors.

Window

Access Door

Knock Out

Mounting Bracket

Scale
0   1/2   1   2   3   Inches

Fig. 3. Cross-section of bottom-mounted sign lighting fixture showing control of light "rays".

of which varied widely. Thirty-eight-foot-long boxes would have been required for some recent sign fixtures.

Special Reflector Required

The problem of obtaining light intensity toward the top of the sign equal to approximately three times the light intensity toward the bottom of the sign, without wasting light in any direction, was solved by the use of a polished metal reflector with a cross-section made up of a combination of a cylinder and parabola (*see Figures 3 and 4*). No other shape of reflector known to the writers will outperform the "paracyl" in these respects. A full parabolic reflector shape wastes much direct light toward the sky. Surfaces other than polished metal "mirror" surfaces, such as white porcelain or white enamel, do not provide any great amount of light control but act for the most past as secondary diffuse sources, emitting light in all directions.

The material used as the reflector consists of an aluminum sheet with a layer of special, high purity aluminum on one side. This layer presents a reflecting surface that is very smooth

and specular but at the same time, by its very nature, is subject to both abrasion and corrosion. To protect this surface, the reflector sheet is subjected to an electrochemical process, consisting primarily of surface preparation of the metal, brightening, formation of aluminum oxide and sealing of the surface. The final result is a clear, smooth, hard, continuous coating of aluminum oxide, nonporous and resistant to abrasion and corro-

sion. The reflecting surface, with proper maintenance and use, should remain at or very near its original condition indefinitely.

Selection of Proper Fluorescent Lamps

The lamps used, 42-inch long and 64-inch long T-6 (¾-inch bulb diameter) Standard Cool White, were selected for the following reasons:

1. The small diameter of these lamps provides good light control. Theoretically the best control would be secured by using a thin line source. Larger tubes such as the 1½-inch T-12 when operated at 425 milliamperes, provide only about 15 percent more lumens per foot than a T-6 operated at 300 milliamperes; and the poorer light control will offset the higher light output.

2. The 42-inch and 64-inch lamp lengths provide sufficient flexibility to meet any of the standard sign sizes as may be seen in *Table 1*. This cannot be said of 72-inch and 96-inch lengths.

3. Before the cool white lamp was selected, both daylight and warm white were tried in sign fixtures, the latter primarily because of its high efficiency rating. From an appearance standpoint neither was satisfactory, the daylight appearing too harsh, and the warm white, although it possessed the highest lumen rating, unexpectedly appearing dim. The cool white displayed neither of these bad effects and accordingly was adopted.

Illumination Levels

Field measurements of existing fluorescent sign lighting installations

TABLE I

SIGN LIGHTING FIXTURE ARRANGEMENTS AND ELECTRICAL DATA

Length of sign	Number and nominal size of fixture units	Lighting fixture bracket spacing	Total watts and series — multiple* transformer rating for various sign heights		
Feet-inches	Inches	Inches	40"	60"	90"
10' (120)	1-43, 1-65 (108)	11.5, 20, 40.5, 31	65 (100)	90 (150)	123 (150)
12' (144)	2-65 (130)	17, 31, 48, 31	70 (100)	99 (150)	133 (200)
14' (168)	2-43, 1-65 (151)	11.5, 20, 37, 31, 37, 20	86.5 (100)	124 (150)	166 (200)
16' (192)	1-43, 3-65 (173)	17, 31, 38, 20, 38, 31	96.5 (150)	137 (200)	184.5 (300)
18' (216)	3-65 (195)	17, 31, 44.5, 31, 44.5, 31	106.5 (150)	152 (200)	202 (300)
20' (240)	2-43, 2-65 (216)	11.5, 20, 36.5, 31, 42, 31, 36.5, 20 ...	120 (150)	170 (200)	230 (300)
22' (264)	4-65 (260)	17.5, 31, 25, 31, 35, 31, 35, 31 ...	140 (200)	198 (300)	266 (350)
24' (288)	2-43, 3-65 (281)	12, 20, 30, 31, 35.5, 31, 35.5, 31, 30, 20	156.5 (200)	223 (300)	299 (350)
26' (312)	1-43, 4-65 (303)	17.5, 31, 36, 31, 30.5, 20, 30.5, 31, 36, 31	166.5 (300)	236 (300)	317.5 (500)
28' (336)	5-65 (325)	16.5, 31, 37, 31, 37, 31, 37, 31, 31	176.5 (300)	251 (350)	335 (500)
30' (360)	2-43, 4-65 (346)	11, 20, 31.5, 31, 37, 31, 31, 37, 31, 31.5, 20 ...	190 (300)	269 (350)	363 (500)

120 ma, 200 ma, and 300 ma ballasts are used respectively for 40", 60" and 90" sign heights. The same 2-lamp ballast is used for 1-42" and 1-64" lamp as for 2-64" lamps.
* Where sign lighting is fed from a series circuit, the series-multiple transformer rating (in VA) to be used is indicated in parenthesis.

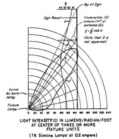

LIGHT INTENSITY(I) IN LUMENS/RADIAN/FOOT
AT CENTER OF THREE OR MORE
FIXTURE UNITS
(T6 Slimline Lamps at 0.2 ampere)

Fig. 4. Curve showing light distribution from typical sign fixture installation.

of the older type, taken by District IV in 1951, indicated an average illumination level of 8 to 20 foot-candles and a vertical maximum to minimum ratio of 5 to 1, up to 40 to 1.

Present average levels of illumination using the new fixture are in the range of 25 to 35 foot-candles with a vertical maximum to minimum ratio of 2 to 1 or less.

Approximately the same level of illumination is maintained on various size sign panels by using the following rule: "Fixtures for sign panels 40, 60 and 90 inches high shall use 120, 200 and 300 milliampere ballasts respectively." Light output per foot of lamp length is approximately 300, 430 and 520 lumens per foot for 120, 200 and 300 milliampere ballasts respectively. Therefore, the light level on 90-inch signs will be approximately 23 percent less than on 40-inch signs, using the inverse relationship previously mentioned.

Ideally the light level on each sign should be determined for optimum contrast with the surrounding lighting conditions. This is an involved subject which would require considerable investigation and may lead to much higher light levels than are presently used in bright surrounds.

New Fixture Installed

The first bottom-mounted fixtures, as described above, were installed on two post-mounted signs on the Rich-ardson Avenue off-ramp of the Golden Gate Bridge approaches. These fixtures were placed in service in August, 1952, and are still providing very satisfactory illumination. All sign lighting installed in District IV since August, 1952, has been of the new type, and these installations are providing excellent sign illumination. Since August, 1952, the design of this type of fixture has been improved in minor ways. No further changes are contemplated for the future, since standardization on the design indicated in the plan, as developed by District IV, will ultimately result in reduced cost of the units. Further refinements are certainly conceivable and will be incorporated as such improvements are developed and their value recognized.

SUMMARY

From observation of many existing sign lighting installations of different types and study of the factors involved, the following points become evident:

1. Top-mounted incandescent lighting of directional signs produces objectionable glare, in the form of reflected images of the fixture in the sign panel, and provides poor uniformity of brightness.

2. Top-mounted fluorescent lighting of directional signs produces less objectionable glare, in the form of reflected fixture images, than incandescent lighting, and provides fair uniformity of brightness.

3. Bottom-mounted fluorescent lighting does not produce glaring reflections of the fixtures. Therefore improvement in light control and intensities with this type of fixture will result in improved visibility of the sign.

Recent Innovations

The most recent improvement on the bottom-mounted sign lighting fixture has been the introduction of a light shield. The shield was devised to eliminate light seen when the sign is approached from the rear. By using 16 gauge metal for this shield and splicing it together between fixtures, it serves the additional functions of lining up the fixtures and practictally elimi-

SANTA CLAUS

Continued from page 26 . . .

businesses on a frontage road with restricted access into the through traffic lanes of the highway.

This roadside merchant's letter has revealed the principal conclusions to be made in analyzing the effect of placing the roadside businesses at Santa Claus on a frontage road.

1. Safe parking and accessibility for the motorists patronizing roadside businesses are factors inherent in the frontage road that do not exist on the heavily traveled thoroughfare.

2. Spectacular increases in gross sales among existing businesses, and the volume of business performed by new retail outlets, indicates the monetary effect of the frontage road at Santa Claus upon retail business.

3. The modernization of existing improvements and the sizeable investments made on new retail outlets are visible evidence of the enhanced property value along the Santa Claus frontage road.

4. The frontage road has provided a stability in highway design which has given confidence to the property owners that improvements can be made with assurance and that the traffic flow for which the new highway was designed will persist for the life of the facility.

A total of 592 state highway construction contracts were awarded during the 1954-55 Fiscal Year. These contracts had a value of $263,770,000, including construction engineering and right-of-way acquisition, and covered improvement to 2,203 miles of highway and 352 bridge and grade separation structures.

nating the strain on the ends of the fixtures where the connecting conduit attaches.

REFERENCES

1. *California Highways and Public Works,* Jan.-Feb., 1951, pp. 6 ff.
2. *California Highways and Public Works,* Mar.-Apr., 1951, pp. 53, 54.
3. *Planning Manual,* Part 8, Index 8-504.4.
4. *I.E.S. Lighting Handbook,* Second Edition, pp. 11-19.

EXIT BOTTLENECK

Continued from page 24...

The area traversed by the road is composed of low hills having very steep slopes and supporting a light cover of foothill vegetation. The formation is of a sedimentary origin with heavy stratifications, some of which approach the vertical. At about Station 70, the road crosses the San Jacinto Fault. Many of the clay strata have, through heavy pressure, become very dense and hard.

The contract for the construction was awarded to Matich Brothers and Matich Brothers Paving Company of Colton on January 27, 1955, with work starting February 21, 1955, and proceeding without interruption to its completion, except for a 10-day delay because of strike conditions. During construction, traffic was carried through the first mile, which was in comparatively open country, without interruption. At the junction with State Sign Route 79, it was routed over this road to its junction with the Old Jack Rabbit Trail, thence over it until it connected with U. S. Highway 60, about a mile beyond the end of the proposed project. To accomplish this, it was necessary, under agreement with Riverside County, to repair and widen the trail. Under this arrangement, and in view of the heavy traffic, the inconvenience to travel was slight, and very few accidents were reported. Closing the project to travel shortened the construction period by four months.

Extensive Excavation

The heavy and modern equipment used by the contractor was able to handle all material without recourse to blasting. While some of the cuts were 150 feet in depth with corresponding fills, the contractor experienced no difficulty in their construction. Roadway excavation involved the removal of 595,000 cubic yards, with an overhaul of 6,000,000 station yards. The 187-foot cut at the summit involved 95,000 cubic yards of excavation alone. The project developed an excess of roadway excavation on the westerly end which was used to construct embankment for the future

freeway extension beyond. One hundred twenty-three thousand tons of imported base material were brought in, with an average haul of 4.9 miles. Seven thousand three hundred sixty barrels of cement were used to stabilize the top eight inches of the imported base subgrade. Thirty-one thousand tons of mineral aggregate used in the asphalt paving operations were obtained from the contractor's commercial plant in Redlands.

Because of the rough terrain, many drainage structures were required. On the westerly end of the job, in order to minimize inconvenience to traffic, the reinforced concrete box culverts were precast in 10-foot sections and swung into place with a crane. Corrugated metal pipe ranged in size from eight-inch side drains to double 72-inch cross drains. In all, there were approximately 110 structures involved, some of which required stone riprap.

J. N. Matich of Matich Brothers acted as general superintendent for the contractor. The State was represented by H. C. Prentice, District Construction Engineer, and K. B. Stone, Resident Engineer.

SACRAMENTO COUNTY

Continued from page 38...

Avenue, 41st Avenue, Sacramento Boulevard, Fruitridge Road, 21st Avenue, 12th Avenue, Fifth Avenue, Second Avenue, and a viaduct at Broadway, which will also separate the California Traction Company tracks on X Street. In addition, pedestrian overcrossings are planned at 34th Avenue, 27th Avenue and Eighth Avenue.

This unit in part is within the "built-up" area of Sacramento and will tie in with the 29th-30th Street one-way couplet which connects on the northerly end with the Elvas Freeway, US 99E to the north, which was completed in May last year.

The final unit to complete US 99 in Sacramento County to connect the South Sacramento and Elvas Freeways will be the north-south crosstown freeway located between 29th and 30th Streets which with the east-west crosstown freeway is now in the advanced planning stage.

ENGINEER SHORTAGE

Continued from page 33...

techniques; and shorter, more concise engineering reports are all saving engineering time and manpower.

5. *Manuals* governing and guiding the work of each department are in use throughout the division. These manuals are recognized as being among the most complete and up to date in the Nation. With these guides, less experienced engineers can perform more difficult types of work and newly recruited engineers can be rapidly trained.

6. *Communications* by two-way radio and teletype, for some time a valuable time-saving tool in highway administration and maintenance, is becoming an engineer-saving factor in the field. Radio has been used in establishing and checking triangulation for bridges across large bodies of water; members of survey parties relay positions and data by walkie-talkie; and the use of two-way radio in automobiles to conserve the time of resident engineers and assistants on large construction jobs is being explored.

Ideas and Devices of Future

These are some of the present ideas and devices to combat the engineer shortage. In the near future are, of course, further improved techniques: bigger and better electronic data processing machines; teletyping of figures and computations instead of mailing them; and expansion of photogrammetry into more and more detailed highway planning.

When the Legislature enacted the present level of highway user taxes in June, 1953, the Highway Commission and the Division of Highways translated more than $87,000,000 in added revenues into construction projects and right-of-way allocations without a moment's delay. This was because the plans were ready, or nearly ready, in advance. By using all modern methods available to combat the engineer shortage, and developing new ones, the Division of Highways is still able to keep its planning far enough ahead to handle additional construction if and when it is assigned.

Road Restoration

District I Performs Big Job in Flood Areas

By RUDOLPH BERGROTH, District Office Engineer

THE SEQUEL to the story of the high water, floods and resultant damage to highways in District I during the 1955 Christmas week floods is the account of restoring the many miles of severely damaged highway facilities: first to the ability to carry emergency traffic, and then to normal traffic.

When December 22, 1955, dawned, radio communication between the district office, field offices, and mobile units was almost continuous reporting on road closures and such conditions as could be determined. As the data was compiled, it was evident that the district was confronted with an unprecedented situation as to the extent of road closures and damage to highways, coupled with the extreme necessity of providing access into the flooded areas, towns, and communities as soon as possible.

Damage Inestimable

The South Fork of the Eel River, the main Eel River, and the Klamath River, as well as other streams in the district generally, did not crest until late in the day of December 22 and many portions of the highway routes were inaccessible so that the real extent of the damage to highway facilities was yet unknown as December 22 terminated with the definite promise of further damage as waters receded.

On December 23, as more detailed reports were received from the field and flood waters were receding, it was revealed that all the state highway routes in the district, with few exceptions, were closed to through traffic by reason of damaged or destroyed bridges, slides, slipouts, washouts, silt and debris on traveled ways, pavement damage, fallen trees, and even buildings that had been floated and deposited on the roadway. The only excepted routes were those in Lake County and southern Mendocino County where damage was compara-

tively minor and traffic was able to proceed as soon as flood waters receded.

Areas Isolated

The Eureka-Humboldt Bay area and the towns and communities throughout the district were isolated in varying degrees. Roads and highways were impassable, telephone facilities were destroyed, and the Northwestern Pacific Railroad was out of service for an indefinite period. Radio and aircraft were the only remaining means of communication with the rest of the State and these facilities were taxed to their capacity. Before access to the outside was re-established, the Humboldt County Airport at McKinleyville experienced the greatest activity in its history as a commercial airport as aircraft of all descriptions endeavored to serve the normal and emergency passenger and freight needs of the area.

It was readily realized that US 101, the main line in the district south from Eureka, was closed for some indefinite period. North of Eureka, two locations damaged by other than high water caused closures. In the Mad River area just north of Arcata, washed out approaches to overflow channel structures and the completely demolished north approach span of the Mad River Bridge closed US 101; however, a detour route over a narrow county road was available. The real closure preventing access to the outside was the washed-out north approach embankment to the Douglas Memorial Bridge spanning the Klamath River. The balance of US 101 to Crescent City was open and US 199 to Grants Pass and US 99 presented only some comparatively small slides which were cleared without undue difficulty.

High Priority

It became imperative to provide access from the Eureka-Humboldt Bay area to the rest of the State and, ac-

cordingly, the replacement of the washed-out embankment approach to the Douglas Memorial Bridge received high priority in the first roadway restoration activities. Construction equipment was rushed from Eureka to the south end of the bridge, other equipment was mobilized at the north end, and work started on replacing the embankment as soon as high water receded to such an extent that replacement material would not be washed away. During the late afternoon of December 25, US 101 and US 199 were opened to emergency traffic from Eureka to Grants Pass with restrictions on load limit on that portion of the route in our neighboring State of Oregon where the storm also resulted in damage to highways.

The other closed highways in the district were receiving immediate attention, with no priority set on any particular sector as opening of all routes was of vital importance and openings were only dependent upon the magnitude of the road closure elements and the extent of the problems involved in the road restoration activities.

During the height of the flood, US 101 was closed to through traffic from Little Lake Valley, just north of Willits, to just north of Alton. As these limits of closure were to a great extent the result of flooding of the highway, with no peak of serious consequence, the recession of flood waters reduced the limits from near Cummings to South Scotia Bridge, a distance of approximately 92 miles.

Access Imperative

This record-breaking length of severely damaged and closed main line state highway involved numerous communities and peoples, and a number of flooded towns and areas. It was therefore imperative that some semblance of a road be provided as soon as possible. The imperativeness was accentuated by the need of relief agencies to gain access to the flooded areas of Myers, Weott, Pepperwood, and other places in the South Fork of the Eel River Canyon.

The first stage in road restoration was to provide a "pioneer" or emergency road to all areas sufficient to accommodate emergency vehicles, and also to gain access to the various severely damaged locations and appraise the extent of the damage to immediately formulate plans for full-scale roadway restoration at the earliest possible moment.

The pioneer road work was immediately undertaken by state forces and equipment, supplemented by extra personnel hired on the spot and privately owned equipment as available in the damaged areas.

It was interesting to note that the intense and widespread development of the logging and lumber industries since World War II throughout the area comprising District I was of considerable benefit during the emergency. The utilization by the industry of similar equipment, such as tractor-dozers, graders, loaders and dump trucks as used in highway construction and maintenance, and the wide dispersal of such equipment proved to be an important factor in the road opening work. Equipment was made available to the Division of Highways without hesitancy and was generally in close proximity to the damaged sections of highways throughout the district. The equipment, ranging from chain saws to the largest tractor-dozers and loaders, together with operators, rendered valuable assistance in the opening of roads.

Repairs Rushed

The pioneering started and progressed in both directions from many locations between points of closure and wherever equipment was available, together with Division of Highways personnel, to instigate the work and provide supervision. Field forces were authorized to procure additional personnel and equipment as necessary. As flood waters receded, advancement north from Willits was not too difficult. A washed-out approach to a small bridge spanning Long Valley

Flood damage repair work to the Smith Point Bridge across South Fork Eel River on US 101, six miles south of Garberville. Note damaged north approach span.

Creek at Longvale was the only serious situation, but the comparatively small embankment was soon replaced and the route was opened to restricted traffic as far north as Leggett during the afternoon of December 24. In the north, receding waters permitted opening of the highway to normal traffic as far south as Scotia after removing debris and drift from the traveled way. South of Scotia in the Pepperwood area, which had been completely inundated, opening the road presented a little more difficult problem. Buildings had been floated onto the highway and a two-foot depth of silt prevented passage of any type of vehicle other than a high-powered grader. Some small cottages almost completely demolished were bulldozed off the traveled way and graders pioneered a one-way track through the silt and around larger houses almost intact but reposing on the roadway.

Emergency Traffic Moved

In the evening of December 24 the pioneer road had penetrated as far south as Weott, another community that suffered complete inundation of

its main level. Work had also been progressing northerly from Cummings, both ways from Garberville, and southerly from the Weott area. By December 27, the route had been traversed for its entire length and emergency traffic was negotiating the badly damaged 100-mile section.

The pioneer road then permitted transport of heavier and more proper equipment into the most troublesome areas to supplement that already in use. Such equipment as four 1½-cubic-yard shovels, together with other incidental equipment, was brought in to work on the several most troublesome areas of damage and to widen and strengthen the existing facility in order to permit passage of all traffic.

By December 30, the work in the South Fork Eel River Canyon had restored US 101 to a condition where two-axle trucks were permitted to travel the Cummings-Scotia sector. On January 5, the section was open to all traffic.

Indescribable Damage

The damage confronting the crews was of every description imaginable:

54

washouts, slipouts, undermined pavements, settlements, slides, debris on roadway ranging from saw logs to brush and down trees, and plugged culverts. Fortunately, with the exception of the Smith Point Bridge spanning the South Fork Eel River approximately six miles south of Garberville, no major structure damage occurred within this severely damaged portion of US 101. At the Smith Point Bridge, settlement of the northerly approach span occurred and finally the driving of steel "H" piles into the unstable foundation area had to be resorted to as a means of supporting that end of the structure.

Personnel, regular and emergency; equipment, both state-owned and private, were concentrated within the 100-mile limits in unprecedented numbers.

The magnitude of the work and equipment and personnel being used was beyond the scope of the normal Maintenance Department supervisory personnel to properly direct, and engineers were separated from their regular duties and assigned to the restoration work to assist in the supervision.

Ten Areas on US 101

As the restoration work progressed, and general cleanup and repair of damage was done, locations of major slides, settlements, slipouts and washouts failed to respond to immediate road opening treatment. In general, there were 10 areas on US 101 between Cummings and Scotia that constituted major problems and, in many locations, it was obvious that retreats into hillsides would have to be resorted to in order to establish a stable roadway with sufficient width to accommodate normal traffic.

At this stage, contracts were made with contracting firms with proper and adequate road building equipment and experience. Tractors with steel tracks and other equipment of the logging and lumbering industry, as used in pioneering the road restoration and proper for the use intended, was improper for more detailed highway work. Organized contracting firms with experienced supervisory and other personnel finally rendered extraordinary service.

Rains Continued

The restoration activities were hampered by rains, ranging from intermittent to heavy lengthy downpours. River bars, as a source of material for backfill of slipouts, washouts, settlements, and as a surfacing material, were inundated by recurring high water in streams, delaying many phases of the work. Slides, settlements, and slipouts already supersaturated were made continually active by further rains, closing the road for intervals and necessitating additional work.

During the period December 29 to January 5, wherein first emergency traffic was permitted and then light general traffic and finally two-axle trucks, road blocks and convoys were utilized to screen and conduct traffic through this lengthy damaged portion of US 101 and where the extreme activity was taking place to restore the highway to normal traffic. As work progressed and road conditions improved, traffic volumes increased and lengthy convoys had to be abandoned as undesirably long shutdowns occurred at the various locations of activity in order to permit passage of the convoys. Traffic was finally allowed to proceed on their own, but subject to delays at various points. The traveling public can be commended for their forbearance in accepting such delays with little or no complaint.

The continuing rains made necessary major activity well into February, and slides and settlements were aggravated causing isolated short closures. US 101 north of Eureka, which was virtually trouble free, had heavy rains on January 14 and 15 that resulted in partial washout by the again swollen Klamath River of the north approach to the Douglas Memorial Bridge, closing the road until the forenoon of January 16. Heavier than normal rain on February 19 to 23 caused further damage and road closures on US 101 and other routes, and concern to district personnel with the picture of the Christmas week catastrophe still very vivid in the minds of all.

Other Routes Affected

It is possibly noted that the account of the US 101 situation has been dwelt

on for some length. It is not the intent to minimize the closures and road openings or restoration activities on the other routes in the district, where, at various locations, conditions and difficulties encountered were of the same description as on US 101. During the period of major activity on US 101 to the south of Eureka crews of both state and contracting firms were carrying on similar activity at various separated locations on US 101 to the north as well as all the other routes that suffered damage.

The major restoration project on US 101 north of Eureka was the replacement of the northerly timber approach spans of the Mad River Bridge and replacement of washed-out approaches to the overflow channel structures just southerly of Mad River.

State Sign Route 1 in Humboldt County, between Ferndale and Fernbridge, on US 101, a distance of approximately four miles, incurred extensive and severe damage to roadway and structures. The west-end approach spans of the Fernbridge Bridge across the Eel River were severely damaged and were replaced by embankment. Complete washout of embankment approaches to bridges across overflow channels and washed-out embankments and undermined pavement had to be replaced. At Arlynda Corners a large concrete box culvert was completely demolished, and the chasm was bridged by a timber bent trestle.

Washouts Damage US 299

US 299 suffered considerable damage, especially from Berry Summit easterly. On the portion between Berry Summit and Willow Creek, where two contracts were under way by the U. S. Bureau of Public Roads, slides, slipouts, and washouts were prevalent and these, together with the rugged terrain, caused considerable difficulties in opening and maintaining a roadway of sorts. From Willow Creek easterly and especially from Cedar Flat easterly, where US 299 follows the Trinity River, high water did considerable damage in the form of washouts. Opening the road to one-way traffic was not unduly difficult, but activities to restore a full two-lane roadway were considerable.

State Sign Route 36 received its share of damage, including a serious washout in the Grizzly Creek area which hindered opening road to through traffic at least to Bridgeville, the comparatively sizable community of the area. On this route also, near Carlotta, the bridge spanning Yager Creek was in jeopardy when one of the piers was undermined and partially tipped, leaving continuous steel beam spans without support. Through the fine cooperation of the Northwestern Pacific Railroad, their adjacent railroad bridge was made available and it was planked, enabling the passage of light traffic during the period the highway bridge was under repair.

Hoopa Bridge Lost

On the Willow Creek-Weitchpec highway, in addition to closures by slides and washouts, the complete destruction of the 440-foot bridge spanning the Trinity River delayed opening the Willow Creek-Orleans-Yreka route to through traffic. It was necessary to construct a low level, temporary, pile bent bridge downstream from the destroyed bridge, which construction was delayed by further high water in the Trinity River. The temporary structure was open to all traffic on February 7; its use, however, was shortened as heavy rains of February 20 and 21 caused further high water in the Trinity River and 216 feet of the temporary structure was washed out. Arrangements for repair were made immediately by the Bridge Department and work proceeded without hindrance and the structure was again opened to traffic on March 9.

At Bluff Creek, on State Sign Route 96 between Weitchpec and Orleans, the approach span to the bridge spanning that stream was completely washed out. A temporary log bridge was rushed to completion and opened to traffic on January 11. The south half of this temporary structure was again washed out by high water in the creek on January 15. Repairs were again undertaken and, on January 25, traffic was allowed to cross the new temporary structure.

US 101 near Piercy, Mendocino County; removing slide after Christmas week storm and floods

Tremendous Job

A few statistics might be in order to indicate the magnitude of the road opening and restoration work that was carried on. During the period December 19, 1955, to January 31, 1956, 416 pieces of privately owned equipment were engaged by means of service agreements to participate in the work throughout the district. In addition to this equipment, there was the state-owned equipment and contractors' equipment that was working on restoration projects covered by emergency, cost-plus contracts. Construction equipment of all descriptions was represented, ranging from the smallest one-man chain saw to large track-laying power shovels. Emergency help was hired throughout the district by the field offices to supplement the regular state forces and these totaled 177 men in the laborer and equipment operator classifications. The bulk of this help, 124 men, was used in the Garberville territory.

As previously stated, when pioneer roads were put through and as restoration work progressed it became obvious that organized construction firms with adequate and proper personnel and equipment could better handle various phases of the work under contract. Change in procedure from equipment rental basis to contractual procedure resulted in additional capable personnel and supervisory employees, such as superintendents and foremen, to the end that over-all efficiency was increased. At this writing, 31 emergency contracts were entered into to perform the restoration of roadway and bridges. These contracts covered work of all kinds, bridge building and repair, culvert rehabilitation and new installations, removing major slides, backfilling settlements and washouts, and even placing new pavement in the Ferndale and Arcata areas during a break in the weather.

Supervisory Work Divided

The highway facilities within the Garberville maintenance territory suffered the greatest and most widespread damage, including the lengthy closure on US 101 and the severely damaged State Sign Route 1 between Ferndale and Fernbridge. The restoration work being of such magnitude, it was necessary to divide the supervisory work. E. J. "Al" Smart, highway superintendent at Garberville,

56

handled the state crews and directed work of rented equipment. H. W. "Hod" Benedict, of the district's engineering staff, served as resident engineer on the many emergency contracts. These men were ably assisted in the field and office by many other maintenance personnel and engineers too numerous to list.

Highway Superintendent J. A. Brown, of the Eureka territory, had his territory extended to include the Ferndale-Fernbridge route and he was assisted at this location and at other locations within his territory by a number of the engineers.

Crescent City Area

The Ukiah territory Highway Superintendent, C. H. Sackett; R. W. Sorin, Superintendent at Boonville, and H. L. Nelson, at Crescent City, territories in which highway damage was not as severe as in other areas, nevertheless had more than the ordinary winter maintenance problems to cope with.

In addition to the engineering help, the Garberville maintenance forces were supplemented by five state foremen and seven equipment operators. These men were temporarily transferred from areas where highway damage was not overly severe.

The Bridge Department assigned numerous personnel to operate under the supervision of "Al" Lernhart, Alton Kay, and W. Langenbach, to help in the district to assess bridge and other structure damage to determine and supervise necessary restoration and repair measures.

Contractors Cooperate

The local and other contractors deserve high commendation for their splendid cooperation in assisting in review of damage, organizing repair crews, and rendering over-all exceedingly fine cooperation in making available their equipment, dispatching it to trouble areas, and in performance of work on the emergency contract basis.

The over-all direction of the work at district level was by Alan S. Hart, District Engineer, assisted by C. P. Sweet, Assistant District Engineer,

Operations, and C. G. Ure, District Maintenance Engineer.

It is realized that many details of damage, restoration measures, problems encountered and equipment utilized, are missing; details that would prove to be of interest to engineers, construction men, and others. A full account, including all details, would be a book.

In retrospect and with all due respect for the losses suffered by all, lessons learned by bitter experience, features of highway design were proved and disproved, and we can therefore derive some measure of consolation from the not soon to be forgotten experience.

COLORADO RIVER

Continued from page 35 . . .

could be attempted. The new alignment swings to the south just west of Winterhaven, California, and crosses the river on tangent to line up with Fourth Avenue in Yuma, which becomes US 80 to the east. This alignment crosses Indian property about 3,000 feet downstream from the existing highway crossing and it was necessary to negotiate with the Quechan Indian Reservation tribal council for the required right of way. These arrangements differ only in degree from those made by Captain de Anza and actually consumed considerably more time. Application was made jointly by California and Arizona to the Corps of Engineers, U. S. Army, for a permit to construct the bridge.

Some local objections were voiced in regard to the alignment of the new road, but most of the objections were satisfied when it was decided to leave the existing structure in place to serve the Indian school on the north side of the river and the Bard agricultural area on the California side. This also provides an auxiliary crossing in case of emergency.

Completion This Spring

While most of the concrete aggregate is obtained in the vicinity of the structure, the structural steel was fabricated in Gary, Indiana, and hauled across the continent by rail to the site. This could be compared to the first

Mrs. Mabel A. Vance

After 25 years of state service, Mrs. Mabel A. Vance of the Division of Contracts and Rights of Way of the Department of Public Works retired on January 27, 1956. On that date she was tendered a luncheon at the Elks Club in Sacramento by fellow workers and former associates.

At her luncheon her boss, Robert E. Reed, Chief Counsel of the Public Works Department, handed her two photographs that puzzled her no end. They were pictures of a 21-inch television set. Mrs. Vance couldn't figure out the significance of the photos until Reed explained to her that the television set was in her own living room. Reed then told how Harry L. Fenton of his staff gained entrance to Mrs. Vance's apartment after she left for work Friday morning, had the set moved in, and took photographs of it. He naturally had to rearrange the furniture somewhat, so she did not recognize her own living room.

The set was a gift to Mrs. Vance from her friends who attended the luncheon.

---

ferry raft which was constructed in Michigan as previously noted.

The contract for the new bridge is financed by Arizona Federal Aid funds, State of Arizona funds, California Federal Aid funds and State of California funds. Fred J. Early, Jr., Co., Inc., of San Francisco holds the contract for the amount of $1,236,-765. California has recently completed a contract for its approach in the amount of $386,886 by Silberberger Constructors and J. B. Stringfellow of Riverside, California, and Arizona has an approach contract under way by Heuser and Garrett of Phoenix for the amount of $302,675.

The design for the new structure was done by the Bridge Department of the California Division of Highways and construction is being handled by the same agency with A. K. Gilbert, one of California's veteran engineers, as the resident engineer. Completion of the new crossing and approaches is scheduled for spring, 1956.

Traffic Safety Committee to Intensify Work

The solution of the traffic accident problem is a joint responsibility involving both public officials and the general public — GOVERNOR KNIGHT.

In recognition of the responsibility incumbent on the public officials in California, Governor Knight has requested his Traffic Safety Committee to intensify its efforts to coordinate and render more effective the combined forces of all state agencies in the fight against traffic accidents.

The Governor's Traffic Safety Committee was first organized in 1946 pursuant to a recommendation of the President's Highway Safety Conference, which called for joint public and official action. The California group was the first one formed; but up to this year, it has not conducted a full-time program. It has been a coordinating agency; and now the coordination of official action is linked with an extensive program embracing all phases of traffic accident prevention.

The objectives of the committee are:

1. Reduction of traffic accidents, deaths and injuries on California streets and highways.
2. Safe and efficient movement of traffic in every section of the State.
3. An adequate system of highways, designed, constructed and maintained to meet the challenge of California's constantly increasing traffic.
4. A California Highway Patrol sufficiently large to provide protection for all sections of the State, with adequate equipment and facilities in keeping with modern enforcement demands.
5. A court system with sufficient number of judges and prosecutors, together wtih staff and facilities, to provide uniformly high standards in the hearing and adjudication of traffic cases.
6. Highest standards in school safety education programs, designed to prepare our youth to safely cope with the dangers of today's traffic.
7. Personnel and equipment to provide for driver licensing and regulating

Governor Knight's traffic safety committee in session. Left to right: Theodore H. Jenner, Departmental Secretary to Governor Knight; Director of Public Works Frank B. Durkee; Bernard R. Caldwell, Commissioner, California Highway Patrol; Ernest B. Webb, Director of Industrial Relations; Paul Mason, Director of Motor Vehicles; Peter E. Mitchell, President, Public Utilities Commission; Heman Stark, Director of Youth Authority; W. A. Huggins, Highway Patrol. Seated: Roy E. Simpson, Superintendent of Public Instruction; Governor Goodwin J. Knight; Director of Finance John M. Peirce.

procedures which will make certain that only those who are competent and properly prepared are permitted to drive.

8. Full provision for coordination of State's official traffic safety program with organized nonofficial activities, emphasizing development of public understanding of and support for official efforts.

9. Proper recognition, encouragement and support of traffic safety programs of citizen support groups and others interested in safety.

The administration of the committee's program is the responsibility of W. A. Huggins, executive secretary, and his staff. Mr. Huggins has served with the committee since its formation in 1946.

The committee has sponsored and directed six state-wide meetings of the Governor's Traffic Safety Conference. A recent three-day annual conference called together recognized experts in the traffic-safety field, leaders of industry and government, and interested laymen, all sharing a sincere desire to reduce the tragic traffic tolls. Robert Mitchell, president of the Consolidated Rock Company of Los Angeles, was general chairman of the 1955 conference.

This conference is typical of the many activities participated in or sponsored by the Governor's Traffic Safety Committee, and to pinpoint the problems, has these divisions: commercial vehicle, driver licensing, education, engineering, enforcement, public information, and teen-age division.

In addition, 19 regional safety clinics were held and numerous local safety activities sponsored or supported. The Governor's Traffic Safety Committee, through its staff, has aided in the organization of local safety councils, participated in school and college safety programs, and has had a prominent part in many commercial vehicle fleet safety programs.

All national safety programs have been given support; and this year, the committee is co-sponsor of a regional traffic court conference being held at the University of Southern California. Other sponsors are the American Bar Association and the Traffic Institute of Northwestern University.

. . . Continued on page 60

58

Some Job

Official Records Salvaged From Flood-swept Maintenance Shop

By J. C. TIBBITTS, Chief Clerk, Equipment Department

THE EQUIPMENT DEPARTMENT's Shop 3 and office in Yuba City, at the confluence of the Feather and Yuba Rivers, were practically wiped out in the December disastrous floods. After the waters receded the water line on the office wall was a little over nine feet above the floor.

The entire front of the office had been glass. Both of these large windows were broken out. A few Christmas decorations above the nine-foot mark fluttered forlornly. Two wooden desks and their contents, including typewriters, were missing. A few days later they were located in nearby vacant lots among other debris. One other wooden desk was perched crazily on top of some filing cabinets; all other desks, chairs, tables, counters, etc., were misplaced wherever the surging current had pushed them.

On December 27, 1955, we took a crew from Headquarters Shop, Sacramento, to salvage what was possible of the Shop 3 records and papers. The water had come back in a little during the previous night and there were 12 inches of "thick" water on the floor. Much important current work that had been in desk trays or in binders was floating or submerged in this water.

With the back of a truck inside the office the loading started. The floating and submerged material was picked up first; we picked up anything we saw or tripped over.

Next, all desks were opened and all paper work removed. All wooden desks had to be forced open. Unused stationery and forms were left wherever stored except for press-numbered bills, receipts, and revolving fund checks.

Next, all filing drawers were loaded. Some cases had to be loaded with two or three drawers in them as the drawers would not open because of swollen papers. It was impossible to

Yuba City on Christmas Eve. Shop 3 is in circle in left background. Thirty cars are in adjoining parking lot.

sort the material at this point as a thick layer of silt on, in, and over everything called for a thorough wash job first.

Finally all the miscellaneous records were loaded. These included a safe ledger, a Cardineer wheel, Kardex cabinets, etc.

Back in Sacramento these records next went through our wash rack. The mud and silt were washed off the surface of each binder, bundle, file drawer, Kardex tray, and the records in special equipment.

Now it was possible to "roughly" sort the material into records we wanted (and had space and time to save), and a discard pile. The records discarded were probably three to one, compared to those saved. The swollen material had to be pried out of many of the file drawers with bars. Every paper and every record could have

been salvaged in fair shape had there been the need, the space, and the time.

From this point on it was a matter of spreading, drying, turning, picking up and resorting the material. For drying, a large section of one of the large shop buildings was cleared and heat left on night and day. Folders of material were spread open over all the floor of this area. One of the paint stalls, with its forced heat and heat lamps was pressed into service. The use of two large ovens in an adjoining laboratory building was a lifesaver in drying all records on ledger card stock and other hard-to-dry materials.

After the dried material had all been picked up, it had to be sorted and put in filing order. It had been impossible to keep the folders in much semblance of order. New folders were prepared, the material was re-

. . . Continued on page 60

New Army Reserve Program Attracts State Employees

State employees are discovering unprecedented financial and career benefits for entire families under the new Army Reserve program.

A recent survey of personnel in the 311th Logistical Command, headquarters Los Angeles, largest headquarters reserve unit in the Nation, reveals that over 22 percent of the organization are state, federal, county and city employees.

This percentage of a single reserve organization receives career training and full pay and promotion benefits, adding to the family income while serving the country in the highest tradition of the citizen-soldier. Further, the retirement feature, if put in terms of a private insurance benefit, could not be purchased by the individual for less than $35,000 to $45,000. Still more advantages accruing to countless state employees include various military schools available throughout the year with personnel receiving full pay and allowances for attendance in addition to state pay which is authorized for military leave.

The 311th is a high echelon headquarters organization which conducts primarily civilian-type training throughout the entire year including summer camp and under leaders who rank among the top professional, industrial, educational, financial and civil service leaders in the Southern California community.

UPPER—CDR F. T. Pritchard, CEC, USN, Officer in Charge of the U. S. Naval School, Civil Engineer Corps Officers (CECOS) at the Naval Construction Battalion Center, Port Hueneme, welcoming a group from the engineering staff of the California Division of Highways, Sacramento, to the school. They graduated February 20, 1956. The group included, left to right: LCDR Richard N. Doolittle, CEC, USNR; CDR Claude H. Darby, CEC, USNR; Capt. Charles M. Herd, CEC, USNR; LCDR Edwin Jensen, CEC, USNR, and CDR Pritchard. LOWER—Division of Highways employees in Active Army Reserve: Warrant Officer Herman Behrens, left, points out a new training area designated for young reservists of the 311th Logistical Command, to Major Andrew Lynn.

TRAFFIC SAFETY COMMITTEE
Continued from page 58 . . .

California has won outstanding national honors in these related traffic safety fields:

First place—
Traffic engineering ....Last 5 years
First place—
Enforcement ....Last 5 years
First place—
Driver licensing ....Last 3 years
First place—
Public information ....Last 4 years

California has won the honor award in school safety education, and a plaque from the National Association of Surety and Casualty Companies for high school driver education.

Through the programs sponsored, supported, or participated in by the Governor's Traffic Safety Committee, it is hoped that California will be made safer by making traffic safety everybody's business.

SOME JOB
Continued from page 59 . . .
moved from the old folder, shaken down in an Electro-Jogger, and placed in the new folder.

Everything saved is legible, even though it may be dirty and rumpled.

Some of the important records saved were: job files, recent correspondence, all personnel records, stock cards, control and subsidiary ledgers, recent accounting records and claim schedules, recent purchase orders, property records, survey reports, and loss reports.

There were some 66 units of equipment which were submerged in the muddy waters. These were transported to Sacramento Headquarters Shop, where they have been thoroughly inspected and those worth salvaging placed in the process of reclaiming, the others surveyed and preparations made for their disposal.

Reflection Cracks

Wire Mesh Reinforcement In Bituminous Resurfacing

By ERNEST ZUBE,* Supervising Materials and Research Engineer

INTRODUCTION

The problem of what to do about reflection cracks occurring in bituminous resurfacing blankets placed over old portland cement concrete pavements has been a subject of much concern and paving engineers have long been seeking a satisfactory solution. These cracks not only present an unsightly appearance, but often develop subsequent spalling which presents a difficult maintenance problem. The cracks may appear at any time from a month up to a few years after construction, depending upon the condition of the underlying concrete pavement. Vertical movement of the slabs, commonly referred to as rocking slabs, is the most common cause. Other contributing factors are the type and volume of traffic, particularly heavy truck traffic, the thickness of the new blanket and probably to a lesser degree, at least in California, the temperature differential of the seasons. *Figure 1* shows typical reflection cracking of a thin bituminous blanket placed over old concrete pavement on one of our main roads. This picture bears out the fact that reflection cracking is not entirely due to horizontal movements caused by temperature changes in the underlying concrete, as evidenced by the absence of cracking in the lighter-traveled passing lane. In this case it is obviously caused by vertical movements of the slabs under heavy traffic.

Number of Methods Used

A number of methods have been used in an attempt to prevent or at least retard reflection cracking. Subsealing or mud jacking of the old concrete pavement slabs prior to blanketing has been tried and although this process greatly reduced the amount or intensity of cracking, it has not completely eliminated the trouble.

* Paper presented at the 35th annual meeting of the Highway Research Board, Washington, D. C.

Typical Reflection Cracking. Both lanes resurfaced June, 1954, with 1-in. thick bituminous mix. Note absence of cracks in passing lane at left. Cracks began to appear after one month. US 40 near Fairfield.

In many cases, particularly when the old concrete pavement is badly faulted or broken and structurally inadequate to carry the traffic loads, a blanket of granular material 4 inches to 8 inches in thickness is placed and covered with 3 inches to 4 inches of new surfacing. However, existing curbs and gutters or structures and the additional cost of raising shoulders very often do not permit such a substantial increase in thickness.

In other instances, the thickness of the new asphaltic surfacing has been increased in an attempt to eliminate or minimize this cracking. Even the so-called open graded mixes of the macadam type possessing somewhat more flexibility than dense mixes have been tried but still have not completely solved the problem.

Varying Degree of Success

From the varying degree of success obtained by any of the above-mentioned methods it appears that prevention of the vertical movement of slabs caused by the passage of heavy trucks is the most important step towards eliminating or delaying the appearance of reflection cracks. In recent years it has been the standard practice of the California Division of Highways to subseal with asphalt before blanketing any concrete pavements showing signs of movement or pumping of the slabs.

It is of interest to note that bituminous blankets placed on many miles of old broken concrete pavements which were built in the early twenties without expansion or contraction joints (but which during the years of service have developed random cracks) are usually free from reflection cracking. This is also true of the pavements covered with the granular cushion courses.

One of the more recent and promising proposals for eliminating or diminishing the number of reflection cracks is the use of some type of wire mesh reinforcing laid directly on the concrete slab or placed between the leveling and surfacing courses of the bituminous blanket. Although the first attempt to use such material was apparently made in Michigan in 1937, it was not until after the last world war that the use of some form of wire mesh became more widespread. In 1946 the State of Texas placed two projects involving the use of so-called wire fabric and reports from Texas engineers indicate that this method apparently reduced crack formation. Since that date numerous experimental installations of welded wire fabric have been placed in various states and reports in general indicate favorable results in crack suppression.

Types of Wire Mesh

Another form of wire mesh is expanded metal sheets of small diamond size mesh which are used to cover

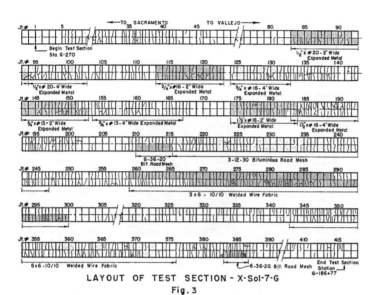

LAYOUT OF TEST SECTION - X-Sol-7-G

Fig. 3

Fig. 3—Layout of test section. Fig. 4—Comparative sizes of the various types of metal used.

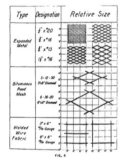

Type	Designation	Relative Size
Expanded Metal	½″x²20	
	¾″x²16	
	¾″x²13	
	1½″x²16	
Bituminous Road Mesh	3-12-30 3″x8″ Diamond	
	6-36-20 6″x12″ Diamond	
Welded Wire Fabric	3″x 6″ ⁹⁄₁₀ Gauge	
	6″x 6″ ⁹⁄₁₀ Gauge	

FIG. 4

only the individual joints and cracks in the existing concrete pavement. This method of treatment was developed in England, where a number of test sections were placed in 1951. Reports received in 1953 indicate that this application shows a definite promise of delaying or materially reducing the amount of cracking.

It might be well to outline briefly the types of wire mesh that have been used in the various trial installations both in the United States and England.

The two primary types of wire mesh are known as expanded metal mesh and welded wire fabric. The expanded metal mesh is produced by feeding stock sheets into a machine which cuts and expands the solid sheet into a diamond-shaped mesh. The diamonds vary in size from one-fourth by 1 inch to 6 by 12 inches and the gauge of metal can also be varied. The sheets with the smaller-sized diamonds are usually cut into 4- by 8-foot size and are used in building construction for open partitions, door panels, shelving, etc. The larger-sized diamond mesh is used for reinforcement in concrete construction work and may be secured in sheets as large as 12 by 16 feet. The small diamond mesh sheets are normally produced with the long dimension of the diamond parallel to the long axis of the sheet, whereas the large diamond mesh is produced with the long dimension of the diamond at right angles to the long dimension of the sheet. Welded wire fabric is produced by spot weld-

Fig. 2—Condition of old concrete pavement random cracks.
EXPANDED METAL. Fig. 5—Stud driver used in fastening sheets to P.C.C. pavement. Fig. 6—Two-foot wide sheet fastened along leading edge. Paver approaches from left. Fig. 7—Two-foot wide sheet placed over random crack. Fig. 8—Typical eXpanded metal test section just prior to paving. Short section of longitudinal joint covered.
BITUMINOUS ROAD MESH. Fig. 9—Test section with 3- by 8-in. diamond mesh. New centerline will be at inner edge of wire. On left, sheets cover four feet of cement treated base. Fig. 10—Lapping of sheets. Wires are tied with hog rings about every fifth diamond. Fig. 11—Sleds used to hold down road mesh and welded wire fabric.

ing wires to form rectangles. These sheets may have openings of 3 by 6 inches or 6 by 6 inches or any other dimension desired by the consumer. The gauge of the wire may also be varied, and rolls containing up to 300 feet are available. However, the majority of the installations have been laid with sheets 11 feet 6 inches wide by 8 feet long.

The California Division of Highways has constructed three experimental projects in which various types of metal reinforcement were used. Two of the projects, one in District V and one in District VI, were of a somewhat minor magnitude and involved the use of welded wire fabric only.

These two projects are described rather briefly in the paper presented before the Highway Research Board in January, 1956, and will not be included here.

This article will describe the major installation which was placed in District X and involved the placing of eight different types of metal reinforcing.

US 40, SOLANO COUNTY

The test section is located near the town of Vallejo on US 40, the main arterial between Sacramento and San Francisco, a four-lane heavily traveled highway. The average daily traffic count is about 20,000 vehicles with about 15 percent of heavy truck traffic.

This installation was completed in June, 1954. It is a rather complete test section in that all of the recommended types of wire mesh were placed under similar construction conditions and in areas where the existing pavement was of the same general nature in respect to amount and severity of cracking. The test sections involved the travel and passing lanes of the westbound travel way only.

The existing 20-foot wide concrete pavement, constructed in 1935, had been mud jacked and later subsealed with asphalt and some bituminous patches had been placed by the Maintenance Department in past years.

As the old pavement showed signs of vertical movement, the contract provided for subsealing the existing slabs again with hot asphalt. Before re-

surfacing, the traveled way was widened with cement-treated base to provide a standard 24-foot cross-section with full paved shoulders. This widening resulted in a two-foot shift of center line. The resurfacing consisted of three inches of plant-mixed surfacing, one-half inch maximum size aggregate, placed in two layers and topped with one inch of open-graded mix, one-half inch maximum aggregate. The grading of the bituminous mix conformed to the specifications shown below:

	Percent Passing	
Sieve Size	Dense Graded	Open Graded
½ in.	95–100	100
⅜ in.	75–90	90–100
No. 4	50–70	35–50
No. 8	35–50	15–32
No. 16	. . .	0–15
No. 30	15–30	. . .
No. 200	4–7	0–3

A careful crack survey of the existing portland cement concrete pavement was made and the location of the various test sections laid out. Alternate control sections without reinforcement but showing similar cracking were provided so as to permit ready comparison with each test section. Figure 2 is typical of the condition of the old concrete pavement and Figure 3 shows the general layout of the test sections.

The following forms of wire mesh were used in the test sections:

Type	Mesh Size
Expanded metal	½ in. by No. 20
	¾ in. by No. 16
	¾ in. by No. 13
	1½ in. by No. 16
Bituminous Road Mesh	3-12-30 (3- by 8-in. diamonds)
	6-36-20 (6- by 12-in. diamonds)
Welded Wire Fabric	3- by 6-in.–10/10 gauge
	6- by 6-in.–10/10 gauge

Figure 4 illustrates the comparative sizes of the various types of metal used.

Expanded Metal

The expanded metal was delivered to the job site in 2-foot and 4-foot-wide strips by 8 feet long. As the expanded metal is rather expensive the two- and four-foot-wide sheets were being tried in order to determine the most economical size which would prevent crack formation. The 8-foot

long sheets were satisfactory for the passing lane as 8 feet of old concrete pavement remained due to a shift of the center line. For the 12-foot-wide travel lane some sheets where cut in half and an 8-foot and 4-foot long sheet used, allowing an overlap of about three inches. All joints such as expansion and contraction joints and random cracks of the slabs were covered with the metal. Short sections of the longitudinal joints between the old concrete and new cement-treated base were also covered with 2-foot and 4-foot-wide sections of the metal. (See Figure 8.)

The variation in the random crack patterns, encountered mainly in the travel lane, required a great deal of fitting and cutting of the sheets. In a number of cases, a random crack could not be entirely covered with a 2- by 8-foot sheet and required the use of 4- by 8-foot sheets.

The sheets were securely fastened to the old pavement by means of a standard stud driver, see Figure 5. In this operation a stamping disc, two inches in diameter was laid on the metal mesh, taking care to center the disc in the center of the diamond. The operator, after loading the gun with the correct stud and cartridge, placed the gun over the disc and fired the charge. The stud penetrated the disc and concrete, and pulled the mesh into tight contact with the pavement. After a few trials it was decided that a stud having an over-all length of 1-15/32 inches was best suited. A heavy charge cartridge No. 832 was used in order to obtain the required penetration. Satisfactory anchorage was obtained in the cement-treated base by using a stud having an over-all length of 2-31/32 inches and a light No. 232 powder charge.

The one-half inch by No. 20, two-foot-wide sheets were placed first to determine proper stud spacing. The eight-foot-long sheet was fastened at both the leading and trailing edges with about five studs and also at a number of spots on either side of the joint.

On passage of the paver over the sheets it was noted that a definite vertical bow appeared in the sheet immediately after the paver treads moved onto the leading edge. It was not possible to determine if the sheet returned to its original shape after the paver moved past. There were no indications of distress caused from failure of the studs to hold the wire in place, as far as longitudinal movement was concerned.

Transverse Cracking

Immediately after the first roller pass, transverse cracking appeared in the mix over the expanded metal sheets. This cracking became more severe on the final roller pass, although the metal was tight against the pavement as determined from the protruding edge of the sheet. On a number of sheets a very definite bump was present, mainly at the leading edge. Generally cracks appeared over both the leading and trailing edges and in a number of cases there also were three or four transverse cracks spaced about five inches apart. However, the next morning after approximately 15 hours of traffic most of the cracks had healed, although the leading and trailing edge cracks were still noticeable.

It was then decided to fasten the sheets only at the leading edge and to determine the least number of studs necessary to hold the sheet in place. Various numbers of studs were used including the absolute minimum for an eight-foot-long sheet, one at each corner and one in the center of the leading edge, see Figure 6. This proved to be satisfactory and resulted in a considerable saving as each stud in place costs about 25 cents.

Stud-driving Operations

Stud-driving operations proved quite successful in the passing lane, with very few failures due to shattering or excessive penetration. Some difficulties were encountered in the travel lane where the concrete appeared to exhibit marked variations in degree of hardness. In numerous instances the stud would penetrate only one-half of its normal distance, or would bend and shatter the concrete, or the charge would drive the stud completely through the disc necessitating the driving of additional studs.

There was no difficulty in the paving operations in any of the expanded metal sections. None of the sheets, including those fastened at the leading edge with only three studs, were torn

loose by either truck or paver movement. It was noted that some longitudinal movement on a large number of sheets occurred under the traction stresses of the paver. This movement was in the same direction as the forward movement of the paver and was about ¼ inch to 1 inch for the ¾-inch diamonds and 1 inch to 1½ inches for the 1½-inch diamonds. This movement undoubtedly was caused by the forward shifting of the entire sheet, until the studs which were fired in the center of the diamond encountered the edge of the metal.

The rather severe cracking following rolling as noticed in the beginning, where both leading and trailing edges were fastened, was not noted where only the leading edge was fastened. Paving and rolling operations were normal and very little cracking, following rolling, was noted.

The best size of diamond, from the construction viewpoint, appears to be either the three-fourths by No. 16 or the three-fourths by No. 13. The lighter stocks were harder to handle and more difficult to fasten securely. The three-fourths by No. 13 in both 2-foot and 4-foot-wide sheets was easiest to lay and showed the least movement under paver traction forces. However, the 1½ by No. 16 can be laid and if it retards the cracking as efficiently as the three-fourths by No. 13 then the lighter metal would be the most advantageous from an initial cost standpoint.

Bituminous Road Mesh

The bituminous road mesh was delivered to the job in sheets measuring 11 feet 6 inches in width and 8 feet in length. The sheets (3- by 8-inch diamond) were laid along the median strip at various locations in the 600-foot test section and placed continuously on the pavement as needed. Due to widening of the pavement, as mentioned before, the wire mesh extended four feet over the cement-treated base in the passing lane. Only 20 sheets of the large 6- by 12-inch diamond mesh were laid.

The leading edge of the first sheet was securely fastened to the pavement through the use of the stud driver, at about one-foot intervals. All succeeding sheets were lapped one diamond,

taking care that the sheets in place always overlapped the sheet being laid. The next operation was the fastening of the individual sheets to each other. This was done by two men, each equipped with a supply of medium-sized hog rings and a hog ring clipper. About four to five rings were used at each lap, the wires being tied along the length of the diamond. The first diamond on each edge of the sheet was always fastened as well as two or three diamonds in between. The hog rings, when crimped into lock position, do not rigidly clamp the wires together and the rings could be freely moved in a longitudinal direction. Vertical movement, however, is restricted to a large extent. The 3-12-30 mesh laid very flat against the pavement and there was very little curl or raised areas along the entire 600-foot section.

Sleds Used

In order to pave over the large sheets it was necessary to provide sleds which forced the sheet to remain flat during movement of the paver. These sleds were fastened to the front of the paving machine and dragged over the sheets just in front of the auger feed. Figure 11 shows the sleds just before being attached to the paver. A total of five sleds were used, each nine feet long. The sleds used on the outside of the Barber-Greene tracks consisted of regular 60-pound railroad rails. The three sleds placed between the tracks were especially constructed from heavy bar stock to a total height of two inches in order to fit under the paving machine.

No particular difficulty was encountered with paving over the bituminous road mesh, except on a curve when due to the uneven traction of the paving machine a slight shifting of the mesh occurred and in one instance some of the wire for a distance of about 30 feet lifted suddenly out of the leveling course and had to be removed. After proper coordination of the truck driver and paving machine operator no further trouble was encountered. Occasional transverse cracks formed almost at once following the paver and in some cases after the first roller pass. Most of these cracks appeared at the laps of the sheets but were ironed out in the final rolling. However, the few that remained on opening the level course to traffic, had healed after overnight traffic. Some of the leveling course mixture was removed, after the rolling, in order to determine the location of the wire. The mesh in all cases was within one-fourth inch of the concrete pavement.

Welded Wire Fabric

This material was delivered to the job in sheets measuring 11 feet 6 inches wide and 8 feet long. Laying operations were the same as previously described for the bituminous road mesh. The fabric was laid so that for the 3- by 6-inch mesh the 3-inch spaced wires were transverse to the direction of travel and the longitudinal wires were uppermost. The first sheet was securely fastened to the pavement at about one-foot intervals. Each sheet was overlapped six inches and tied on the longitudinal wires only with hog rings. These sheets, having a one-inch projection of wire, seemed easier to lap than the bituminous road mesh

and had less tendency to catch. Generally, the wire laid quite flat, although in some areas the sheets were raised from three inches to four inches, due to warping of the wire, above the pavement prior to paving operations. While laying this first section of welded wire fabric it was believed that the movement of the wire ahead of the paver would begin to accumulate enough forward longitudinal movement to cause buckling of the sheets. Therefore, as an experiment, it was decided to secure the leading edge of a sheet about every 150 feet. The overlapping sheet at this point was left free. The idea here was to take up all longitudinal forward movement of the previously laid sheets at this free joint. Close observations during paving operations did not disclose any marked movement of the sheets and any such small movement as occurred was taken up at the individual laps. We, therefore, concluded that this precaution would not be necessary in any future operations.

There were no difficulties in laying the mix over the section and the sleds appeared to iron down the mesh in an excellent manner. Cracking of the mix was very similar to that encountered with the bituminous road mesh. There were occasional transverse cracks, mainly at the laps, which appeared immediately after the mix was laid. Most of these tended to iron out after the final roller pass and the remaining ones had healed after overnight traffic. Removal of the mix in numerous locations along the 600-foot section indicated that the fabric was about one-half inch to three-fourths inch above the concrete pavement. The surface course was placed without any difficulties and no cracks of any kind were noticed.

Crack Survey

Three detailed surveys have been made of the job since its completion in June, 1954. The first, in January, 1955, revealed a few fine short transverse cracks in the nonreinforced control sections and none in any of the

BITUMINOUS ROAD MESH. *Fig. 12—Close-up of paving operations. Note sled attachment on left. Fig. 13—Position of mesh after placing leveling course.* **WELDED WIRE FABRIC.** *Fig. 14—Fastening leading edge of first sheet. Fig. 15—Laying 3- by 6-in. wire fabric. Left edge covers 4 ft. of cement treated base.*

TABLE 1

Cost Analysis for Wire Installations on Contract 55-10TC2, 8-Del.y-6

Type of Metal		Expanded Metal		Expanded Metal		Expanded Metal		Expanded Metal		Bituminous Road Mesh		Welded Wire Fabric	
Size		1/2"x#20	1/2"x#20	3/4"x#16	3/4"x#16	3/4"x#13	3/4"x#13	1-1/2"x#16	1-1/2"x#16	3-12-30	6-36-20*	3"x6"	6"x6"
Width or Width and Length		2'	4'	2'	4'	2'	4'	2'	4'	11'-6"x8'	11'-6"x8'	11'-6"x8'	11'-6"x8'
Materials Costs													
Metal Sheets	$	128	256	143	286	203	406	115	230	860	489	665	478
Delivery and Unloading	$	26	26	26	26	26	26	26	26	52	52	52	52
Studs	$	46	46	46	46	46	46	46	46	3	3	3	3
Cartridges	$	24	24	24	24	24	24	24	24	2	2	2	2
Discs	$	6	6	6	6	6	6	6	6	(Included in cost of cartridges)			
Tie Supplies (Hog rings)	$	-	-	-	-	-	-	-	-	3	3	3	3
Sled Installation on Paver	$	-	-	-	-	-	-	-	-	40	40	40	40
Total Material Costs	$	230	358	345	388	305	508	217	332	960	589	765	578
Labor Costs		24	24	24	24	24	24	24	24	79	79	79	79
Grand Total	$	254	382	259	412	329	532	241	356	1039	668	844	657
Total Sq. Yds of Pvt. in Section		444	444	444	444	444	444	444	444	1701	1701	1701	1701
Cost/Sq.Yd of Pvt. Surface	$	0.57	0.86	0.61	0.93	0.74	1.20	0.54	0.80	0.61	0.39	0.49	0.38

*Only 30 sheets of 6-36-20 Bituminous Road Mesh were laid. The noted cost figures are theoretical values for laying an area equivalent to the 3-12-30 Bituminous Road Mesh and welded wire fabric sections

TABLE 2

Cost Per Sq. Yd. of Various Types of Wire Mesh

Type	Designation	Width of Expanded Metal	Case I Joints only* — Cost prorated per 180 sq.ft. of pavement Assumed that concrete is 12' wide with 15' joint spacing: Metal Cost	Installation Cost (4 Studs per 12' Sheet	Cost Per Slab 15' long x 12' wide	Cost/sq.yd. of mesh	Case II Joints plus one Transverse Crack Per Slab* — Cost prorated per 180 sq. ft. of pavement Assumed that concrete is 12' wide with 15' joints and 1 transverse crack per slab: Metal Cost	Installation Cost (4 Studs Per 12' Sheet	Cost Per Slab 15' long x 12' wide	Total Cost/ sq. yd. of mesh
Expanded Metal	1/2"x#20	2'	3.66	1.52	5.18	0.26	7.32	3.04	10.36	0.52
		4'	7.32	1.52	8.84	0.44	14.64	3.04	17.68	0.88
Expanded Metal	3/4"x#16	2'	4.09	1.52	5.61	0.28	8.18	3.04	11.22	0.56
		4'	8.18	1.52	9.70	0.49	16.36	3.04	19.40	0.98
Expanded Metal	3/4"x#13	2'	5.79	1.52	7.31	0.36	11.58	3.04	14.62	0.72
		4'	11.58	1.52	13.10	0.65	23.16	3.04	26.20	1.30
Expanded Metal	1-1/2"x#16	2'	3.29	1.52	4.81	0.24	6.58	3.04	9.62	0.48
		4'	6.58	1.52	8.10	0.40	13.16	3.04	16.20	0.80
Bituminous Road Mesh	3-12-30 (3"x8" diamonds)		10.23	1.97	12.20	0.61	10.23	1.97	12.20	0.61
Bituminous Road Mesh	6-36-20 (6"x12" diamonds)		5.77	1.97	7.74	0.39	5.77	1.97	7.74	0.39
Welded Wire Fabric	3x6-10/10		7.91	1.97	9.88	0.49	7.91	1.97	9.88	0.49
Welded Wire Fabric	6x6-10/10		5.69	1.97	7.66	0.38	5.69	1.97	7.66	0.38

*Coverage applies to eXpanded metal only

wire mesh sections. The second survey in May, 1955, after 11 months of traffic, did not show any material change and no crack over six feet long. The latest survey, made in December, 1955, revealed slightly more transverse cracking in the control sections, two cracks extending over the entire width of 20 feet of the old pavement. No transverse cracks of any kind were visible in the wire mesh sections. Therefore, as of this date no conclusions can be drawn except that so far there is no difference in the relative abilities of the various types of wire mesh to prevent or retard reflection cracking.

At this later survey, however, considerable longitudinal edge cracking was noticed in both the travel lane and passing lane. This cracking extended along the joint between the old concrete pavement and the newly laid widening strip of cement-treated base. As none of the longitudinal edge along the travel lane was covered with wire mesh this cracking is irrelevant as far as the wire mesh is concerned. However, in the passing lane which is underlain only with eight feet of old portland cement concrete due to a shifting of center line, the eight-foot-long expanded metal sheets placed over the joints were laid to the edge of the old pavement only. The bituminous wire mesh and welded wire fabric, however, extended the full width of the new pavement and covered four feet of the new cement-treated base. It was noted that no longitudinal cracking occurred over the joining edge which was covered with the bituminous road mesh or welded wire fabric. The total length of the project is 8,320 feet. Of this distance, 6,540 feet or 78.6 percent consisted of the nonreinforced edge and 1,780 feet or 21.4 percent is covered with metal. Approximately 1,200 feet comprising 18.3 percent of the nonreinforced edge section has developed longitudinal cracking. It appears that up to this time the bituminous road mesh and welded wire fabric has definitely prevented longitudinal cracking.

Cost Analysis

It is difficult to present an accurate cost analysis where a number of relatively short test sections are involved. The installation of the various types of wire mesh was not part of the original contract and was performed under "extra work" and, therefore, no bid prices are available. However, an attempt has been made to present a cost comparison based on our observations during construction and cost figures supplied by the resident engineer. Labor costs, transportation and unloading costs and the price paid for construction and installation of the sleds all tend to reflect somewhat

Table 3

Cost Per Mile of Various Types of Wire Mesh for Specific Condition of Existing Concrete Pavement

Type	Designation	Width of Expanded Metal	Original Concrete Condition (12' Lane with 15' Joint Spacing): Jts. Only No Cracks Cost/Mile for 24' Pvt. Width	Jts. + 1 Transverse Crack Per Slab. Cost/Mile for 24' Pvt. Width
Expanded Metal	1/2" x #20	2'	$ 3,660	$ 7,320
		4'	6,196	12,392
Expanded Metal	3/4" x #16	2'	3,942	7,884
		4'	6,900	13,800
Expanded Metal	3/4" x #13	2'	5,068	10,136
		4'	9,152	18,304
Expanded Metal	1-1/2" x #16	2'	3,380	6,760
		4'	5,632	11,264
Bituminous Road Mesh	3-12-30 (3"x8" Diamonds)	-	6,588	6,588
Bituminous Road Mesh	6-36-20 (6"x12" Diamonds)	-	5,492	5,492
Welded Wire Fabric	3"x6"-10/10	-	6,900	6,900
Welded Wire Fabric	6"x6"-10/10	-	5,350	5,350

Cost/Mile of 1" of added thickness of P.M.S. for 24' Pavement = $ 3,878
Cost/Mile of 1½" of added thickness of P.M.S. for 24' Pavement = 5,817
Cost/Mile of 2" of added thickness of P.M.S. for 24' Pavement = 7,756
(Based on average cost price of $5.19 per ton in place)

higher prices due to the short test sections. The final analysis is based on the cost of mesh per square yard of pavement. This method was selected as the only way that a true cost comparison could be made between the small diamond sheets which covered the individual joints and cracks only, and the wire mesh which covered the entire pavement.

Three tables showing analyses for different conditions are presented. *Table 1* shows the actual cost of the metal reinforcing on this job calculated on the basis of square yards of pavement covered. The 6- by 6-inch welded wire fabric appears the least expensive with the large diamond bituminous road mesh only slightly higher in cost. As the handling and installation of these two types of metals are similar, the final cost depends primarily upon the original price of the metal. The cost of the expanded metal per square yard of the pavement is noticeably higher and is greatly influenced by the number of random cracks and the cost of fastening.

A direct cost comparison between the small diamond expanded metal sheets and the mesh which covers the entire pavement is difficult to make. On a pavement exhibiting little random cracking and where only the expansion and contraction joints would be covered, the cost of the expanded metal would be greatly reduced. A relative comparison may be obtained by assuming various conditions of the concrete pavement as shown in *Table 2*. In Case I the joints only are to be covered whereas Case II assumes the coverage of at least one random crack per 15-foot slab. The cost figures are based on the actual installation costs as shown in *Table 1*. The first assumed condition indicates that the two-foot-wide expanded metal sheets are less expensive than mesh which covers the entire slab. In the second assumed condition where one additional crack per slab is to be covered, the cost of the expanded metal is exactly doubled and exceeds the cost of the bituminous road mesh and welded wire fabric. The cost of the four-foot-wide sheets, of course, is considerably higher. As badly cracked concrete pavements very often have

more than one random crack per slab it would appear from this analysis that the cost of covering these cracks with expanded metal sheets of either two-foot or four-foot widths would be prohibitive. On the other hand, the cost of the other two types of wire mesh which cover the entire pavement remains the same regardless of the number of random cracks.

In *Table 3* a cost comparison, for the same specific conditions of the pavement as shown in *Table 2*, has been calculated in terms of cost per mile for a 24-foot width of pavement. For further comparison the cost of adding an increasing thickness of plant-mixed surfacing is included at the bottom of the table. The cost of plant-mixed surfacing is based on average bid prices current in California. Roughly, the cost of either the large diamond bituminous road mesh or the 6- by 6-inch welded wire fabric is equal to the cost of 1½-inch thickness of plant-mixed surfacing.

As stated, the cost comparisons presented are approximate only. There is little doubt that large-scale installations of any of the wire mesh types described, together with experience gained by contractors, should show an appreciable reduction in cost.

SUMMARY AND CONCLUSIONS

The various types of wire mesh used and described in this report can be laid and paved over by conventional construction equipment without undue difficulty. The plain expanded metal placed over joints and cracks only, required no modification of equipment. The bituminous road mesh and welded wire fabric required some type of hold-down device in order to press the wire flat against the old pavement and prevent the tracks of the paving machine from catching in the mesh. On pavements that are badly cracked or extensively patched it would appear that the use of wire mesh which covers the entire pavement would be more feasible and economical than the use of individual sheets placed locally over the joints and cracks only. Care should be taken in transporting and handling these sheets. The flatter the sheets, the less difficulty will be encountered with springiness and resulting cracking of

the mix after placing. Any twisted or kinked sheets should be discarded. When paving on curves the paving machine operator should carefully control the traction of the paver so as to avoid shifting of the wire mesh.

The cost analysis indicates that the welded wire fabric is the least expensive of the various types of metal used. The large diamond bituminous road mesh can be considered competitive with the welded wire fabric and the two-foot-wide sheets of the expanded metal when placed over expansion or contraction joints only. The cost of the continuous wire reinforcement is equal to about 1½ inches thickness of bituminous surfacing.

A few transverse cracks have appeared in the control sections but none in the wire-reinforced sections. At this date there is insufficient evidence to form an opinion regarding the effectiveness of the various types of wire mesh used in preventing or retarding reflection cracking. There is, however, definite evidence that the wire reinforcement has prevented the formation of longitudinal cracks.

Although these experimental sections should eventually provide some very definite data regarding the beneficial effects, if any, of the various types of wire reinforcement to prevent or retard reflection cracking, it would appear that in any future installations thought should be given to incorporating one or two other variations such as: Vary the thickness of surfacing from perhaps two inches to four inches in the reinforced sections, and in certain control sections increase the thickness of the bituminous mix so that the price per square yard of the nonreinforced portion is equivalent to that of the wire reinforced section. There is evidence that an increase in thickness of bituminous surfacing may not entirely prevent reflection cracking but the magnitude or severity of such cracking may be greatly delayed and reduced. This is demonstrated to some extent by the pavement represented by *Figure 1* where a one-inch blanket began to show reflection cracking after 30 days when compared to the District X job where the four inches of bituminous surfacing in the control sections has

... Continued on page 71

HOUSE MOVING

Continued from page 40 . . .

possible to find the cut lines after the operation is completed.

The various municipal and county agencies require that a building being relocated on a lot to be renovated and redecorated so as to make the building consistent with the majority of the houses in the neighborhood. A house moved in must be as good or better than any house within a 1,000-foot radius of the new site. This requirement applies both to the exterior and interior of the improvement. The electrical wiring and plumbing systems are inspected and are required to meet current standards. The renovating of these improvements to meet such requirements add years of safe and useful life to the older houses that are moved.

Moving Problems

The movement of the houses within a metropolitan area is not without its problems. The housing crises has been replaced with the world's greatest traffic headache. To facilitate movement of houses without the snarling of traffic, all house moving must be done between the hours of midnight and 6 a.m. Traffic during these hours is relatively light, however, there is a small percentage of drivers during these hours who may become confused upon sighting a house rolling down the street. There have been accidents at the rate of one per week in which drivers have collided with houses being moved. One such driver had lodged his car underneath a house in the process of movement. When the policeman questioned him as to what had caused the accident, his reply was, "I have driven this same street for the last 10 years and I never saw that house before."

Problem of Overpasses

Another problem is the construction of overpasses in the freeway program. The normal overhead clearance of such overpasses is about 15 feet. However, the usual minimum height of a one-story house in transit is approximately 22 feet. With each grade separation, good routes are becoming more and more difficult to find for movement of improvements from the central Los Angeles area. Overhead wires also present a problem within the metropolitan area. It is necessary for various utility company employees to be available to raise wires in order to allow houses to pass. In some instances the cost of moving wires is greater than the cost of moving the house.

There is no house moving authority established in the State of California to enforce safety regulations on the house mover. Therefore, to advance the moving industry, the reputable house movers have joined together in an association known as the House Moving Contractors Association and they police their own industry. Any improvement more than 36 feet in width must have a permit of feasible movability issued by a committee of three representatives of the association in addition to the necessary transportation permit issued for use of city streets, county roads or state highways. The association, through its efforts, has done much to make the house moving industry safe and prosperous.

Today, house moving in the Los Angeles area amounts to about $7,000,000 annually. Add to this the resale price of the houses, together with labor costs of carpenters, plumbers and workers necessary to renovate the homes, the relocation of improvements in the Los Angeles area will amount to a sum in excess of $15,000,000 annually. This is Big Business.

Sales Section

In 1946, as the postwar highway program was being accelerated and freeway construction was again started in earnest, it became apparent that there was need for a section within the Division of Highways to handle the sale of improvements and the clearance of right of way, together with the renting of houses that had been purchased but were not immediately needed for construction. No one at that time could foretell that the clearance program would reach the immensity of its present operation.

It normally takes from one year to eighteen months to buy sufficient right of way to award a construction contract. Rather than remove the houses immediately, after purchase, it has been the policy of the Division of Highways to allow the improvements to remain in place until such time as the property is needed for construction. Instead of allowing the houses to remain vacant, the rental section has been successful at renting them at the current rental rates. The Los Angeles office has approximately 1,750 such houses now being rented. This house pool is in a constant state of flux because of the acquisition and sales program. Approximately 40 to 60 prop-

LEFT—A 16-unit apartment house in the process of being reassembled at its new location. RIGHT—Sixteen-unit apartment house fully reassembled at the new location. These units were so expertly finished it is now impossible to find the cuts that were necessary to move the building. This building was originally located in Sherman Oaks and was relocated in El Segundo.

LEFT—Frame residence prior to relocation. RIGHT—Same residence after relocation. This residence was completely renovated and is now an attractive stucco house.

erties are added weekly by purchase and subtracted weekly by sales from this group.

Timing in Sales

Timing in house sales is of the essence. If the improvement is sold long before the property would be needed for construction, the State is deprived of rents that it would have collected. Furthermore, if less than 90 days is allowed to the purchaser for clearance, the house brings a lower return on the market. Notwithstanding these facts, the right of way must be cleared and be available to the contractor upon the awarding of the construction contract. Timing is related to the price that an improvement will bring on the market in another way. If too many houses are sold in a short period of time, the market becomes flooded and the sale prices are lower. By the same token, if sales are too slow to stimulate interest in the area, the market tends to become stale and stagnant and the sale price of the improvement is lower.

All salable improvements are sold at public auction on the premises. The buyer is required to "put up" a $1,000 faithful performance bond for the removal of improvements in a manner acceptable to the State by the removal date specified at time of sale. It is the further responsibility of the purchaser to determine whether or not the buildings are m o v a b l e as well as whether or not they will be permitted to move into a certain locale or neighborhood. In addition, the buyer must obtain moving permits from each political subdivision through which the improvement is to pass.

Last year the House Sales Section in the Los Angeles district sold 2,250 units for a total return to the State of $2,073,000. In addition to this it collected $888,000 in rents. This money is added to the Gas Tax Fund for freeway construction. This is BIG BUSINESS.

Vandalism

One problem that grew with the accelerated program was vandalism. This problem is twofold. First, the vacant h o u s e s awaiting sale are plagued by youthful vandals. This problem first started with the unquenchable desire of youth to heave a rock through a plate glass window. The second phase of this problem is the professional vandal. Several individuals saw an opportunity to pick up side money by scavengering state-owned houses.

Vandalism in these two forms became so extensive that it could no longer be ignored regardless of the fact that most houses were redecorated inside and out during the relocation process. The various municipalities were sympathetic with the State's problem of vandalism but did not feel justified in hiring additional police to guard state property. The various areas in which these properties are located were so widespread that a system of night watchmen or foot patrolmen was impracticable. To cope with this ever-growing menace the House Sales Section was authorized to hire three state policemen as motorized units to rove the various areas. These patrolmen vary their hours and routes so that no one will be able to predict their time and place or know when to expect them. The results of

this program have been heartening. In the first six months of 1955, 69 convictions of theft were obtained through the courts, and professional vandalism has almost been completely eliminated.

Parents Held Responsible

The abolishment of youthful vandalism has not been quite so successful because of the difficulty of prosecuting minors. However, on September 2, 1955, legislation became effective governing the prosecution of juvenile offenders. Under this new law, the parent is held responsible for the acts of vandalism by the child. Upon apprehension, the parents of each child are required to reimburse the State for the damage done. Although the parents do not publicize the apprehension and the effect thereof, you may be sure that the child's playmates and friends receive full details of this together with details of other punishments administered by the parent. So effective has been this law that the waning of youthful vandalism is already apparent.

Results

Los Angeles like most other cities had not experienced growth by large subdivisions and housing projects, with a house on every lot, until the early 1940's. As a result, there were a number of vacant lots in the older sections of the city. To build a new house in such a section would result in an over-improvement. With the program of relocation of improvements for freeway construction, most of these lots have now been utilized for the relocation of houses that are consistent with other homes in those neighbor-

USED HOUSE LOTS—Many lots in the Los Angeles area display as many as 25 to 30 homes that are for sale to be moved onto lots of prospective buyers

A public auction of an apartment house in North Hollywood conducted by state personnel

hoods at a price that is economically feasible.

The Los Angeles area has never known the tenement housing that has plagued most large cities. This does not mean that this city does not have any slums or substandard housing areas. For the most part, the slum areas consist of one-story slums crowded closely together. The freeways passing through these older sections of the city have done much to eliminate many of these one-story slums. These substandard houses are frequently on the fringe of industrial areas.

For years these industrial areas have creeped like an amoeba, constantly overflowing its boundaries, as a result of individual requests for zone variances and zone changes. This problem has continued to exist despite the tireless efforts of the various planning commissions to draw a permanent boundary to separate residential and industrial zones. The freeway frequently forms a good dividing strip or buffer zone making a permanent boundary to separate these two zones. The remaining old homes on the industrial side of the freeway are immediately gobbled up for industrial development. The owners of residential improvements on the other side of the freeway have a new sense of security and are no longer reluctant to spend money on needed repairs and rehabilitation of the properties.

Once again Yankee ingenuity is due commendation. Not only has this farsighted program netted a substantial monetary return to state coffers for highway construction; but through the wholehearted cooperation of private enterprise and the public works program the public has received a double dividend. A house that is good before it is moved is good after it is moved. An older house is rejuvenated and modernized in the relocation process

REFLECTION CRACKS

Continued from page 68 . . .

shown practically no reflection cracking so far. Traffic is similar in both cases. Another variation might be to place, prior to resurfacing, a cushion course of granular material varying perhaps in thickness from four inches to six inches over the old pavement and compare the cost and effectiveness with the wire-reinforced sections. One other alternative might be to add rubber in various proportions to the

to add years of useful life. Many dwellings on the verge of discharge from service without honor have been recalled by relocation to do another "hitch" of honorable service as a home in one of the fastest growing population centers in the world. This is Good Business.

bituminous mixture as a possible method of reducing reflection cracking.

ACKNOWLEDGMENTS

The work described herein was performed under the general direction of Mr. F. N. Hveem, Materials and Research Engineer, California Division of Highways. Excellent cooperation was extended by the Resident Engineer, Mr. L. E. Daniel of District X.

The writer wishes to especially acknowledge the efforts of Mr. John Skog who took care of most of the detailed work and assisted the Resident Engineer during the placing of the test sections.

Assignments
Transfers Affect Three Districts

THREE District Engineer assignments for the California Division of Highways, effective March 1st, were announced by State Highway Engineer G. T. McCoy:

A. M. Nash, District Engineer of District III, with headquarters at Marysville, was transferred to District V, with headquarters at San Luis Obispo.

A. M. NASH

J. W. Trask, District Engineer of District II, Redding, was transferred to District III, Marysville.

H. S. Miles, Assistant District Engineer in District IV, San Francisco, was promoted to District Engineer of District II, Redding.

When Nash assumed responsibility for District V, Acting District Engineer, L. L. Funk, returned to his previous assignment as Assistant District Engineer—Planning. District V includes the counties of Santa Barbara, San Luis Obispo, Monterey and San Benito.

J. W. TRASK

Nash had been District Engineer at Marysville, a district which includes 11 Sacramento Valley and mountain counties, since 1952. His earlier service included two periods as District Engineer of District I, Eureka, and one three-year assignment as Engineer of Design for the Division of Highways, at headquarters office in Sacramento.

He has been an employee of the Division of Highways since 1920, following aviation service in World War I. A native of Elk City, Kansas, Nash studied at the University of Washington. He has served on important national committees of highway officials concerned with highway design and administration.

Trask had been on the staff of District II, which includes seven north central and northeastern counties, since 1943. He became district engineer in 1950. A native of Lincoln, Kansas, he has been with the Division of Highways since coming to California in 1928, serving first with the Bridge Department and later on various assignments, including that of resident engineer on the Newcastle Tunnel on US 40 in 1931.

Trask is a graduate of Utah State College and served in World War I with the Army Corps of Engineers.

Miles, the new District Engineer of District II, joined the Division of Highways in 1931 upon graduation from the University of California, and

H. S. MILES

has been engaged in various engineering and administrative assignments in the San Francisco Bay area district ever since. He was District Maintenance Engineer of District IV from 1947 to 1950, and since 1950 has been Assistant District Enigneer—Administration.

Miles was born in Elmira, New York, but came to California as a child and attended public schools in San Francisco. He has long been active in civic affairs in his home community of Millbrae, San Mateo County. Miles is married and has a 10-year-old daughter.

GOODWIN J. KNIGHT
Governor of California

CALIFORNIA HIGHWAY COMMISSION
FRANK B. DURKEE . . Director of Public Works and Chairman
H. STEPHEN CHASE . . . . . San Francisco
JAMES A. GUTHRIE . . . . San Bernardino
ROBERT E. McCLURE . . . . Santa Monica
ROBERT L. BISHOP . . . . . . Santa Rosa
FRED W. SPEERS . . . . Escondido
CHESTER H. WARLOW, Vice Chairman . Fresno
C. A. MAGHETTI, Secretary . . . . . . Davis
T. FRED BAGSHAW . . . . . . Assistant Director
A. H. HENDERSON . . . . . . Deputy Director
C. M. "MAX" GILLISS . . . . . Deputy Director

DIVISION OF HIGHWAYS
GEO. T. McCOY
State Highway Engineer, Chief of Division
J. W. VICKREY . . . Deputy State Highway Engineer
CHAS. E. WAITE . . Deputy State Highway Engineer
EARL WITHYCOMBE . . Assistant State Highway Engineer
F. W. PANHORST . . . Assistant State Highway Engineer
J. C. WOMACK . . . . Assistant State Highway Engineer
R. H. WILSON . . . . Assistant State Highway Engineer
F. N. HVEEM . . . Materials and Research Engineer
GEORGE F. HELLESOE . . . . Maintenance Engineer
J. C. YOUNG . . . . Engineer of Design
G. M. WEBB . . . . Traffic Engineer
MILTON HARRIS . . . . . . Construction Engineer
H. B. LA FORGE . Engineer of Federal Secondary Roads
C. E. BOVEY . Engineer of City and Cooperative Projects
EARL E. SORENSON . . . . . . Equipment Engineer
H. C. McCARTY . . . . Office Engineer
J. A. LEGARRA . . . . Planning Engineer
J. P. MURPHY . . . . Principal Highway Engineer
F. M. REYNOLDS . . . Principal Highway Engineer
E. J. SALDINE . . . . Principal Highway Engineer
A. L. ELLIOTT . . . . Bridge Engineer—Planning
I. O. JAHLSTROM . . Bridge Engineer—Operations
J. E. McMAHON . . Bridge Engineer—Southern Area
L. C. HOLLISTER . . Projects Engineer—Carquinez
E. R. HIGGINS . . . . Comptroller

Right of Way Department
FRANK C. BALFOUR . . . Chief Right of Way Agent
E. F. WAGNER . . . Deputy Chief Right of Way Agent
GEORGE S. PINGRY . . . . . . Assistant Chief
R. S. J. PIANEZZI . . . . Assistant Chief
E. M. MacDONALD . . . . Assistant Chief

District IV
B. W. BOOKER . . Assistant State Highway Engineer

District VII
E. T. TELFORD . . Assistant State Highway Engineer

District Engineers
ALAN S. HART . . . . District I, Eureka
H. S. MILES . . . . District II, Redding
J. W. TRASK . . . . District III, Marysville
J. P. SINCLAIR . . . . . District IV, San Francisco
L. A. WEYMOUTH . . . . . District IV, San Francisco
A. M. NASH . . . . . District V, San Luis Obispo
W. L. WELCH . . . . District VI, Fresno
GEORGE LANGSNER . . . . District VII, Los Angeles
LYMAN R. GILLIS . . . . District VII, Los Angeles
C. V. KANE . . . . . District VIII, San Bernardino
F. E. BAXTER . . . . District IX, Bishop
JOHN G. MEYER . . . . . . District X, Stockton
J. DEKEMA . . . . District XI, San Diego
HOWARD C. WOOD . . . . Bridge Engineer
State-owned Toll Bridges

DEPARTMENT OF
PUBLIC WORKS
SACRAMENTO, CALIFORNIA

DIVISION OF CONTRACTS AND RIGHTS OF WAY

Legal
ROBERT E. REED . . . . . . Chief Counsel
GEORGE C. HADLEY . . . . . Assistant Chief
HOLLOWAY JONES . . . . . . Assistant Chief
HARRY L. FENTON . . . . . . Assistant Chief

DIVISION OF SAN FRANCISCO BAY TOLL CROSSINGS
NORMAN C. RAAB . . . . Chief of Division
BEN BALALA . . . . . Principal Bridge Engineer

DIVISION OF WATER RESOURCES
HARVEY O. BANKS, State Engineer, Chief of Division
WILLIAM L. BERRY . . . Assistant State Engineer
Water Resources Investig.tions, Central Valley
Project, Irrigation Districts
W. G. SCHULZ . . . . Assistant State Engineer,
Sacramento River Flood Control Project, Su-
pervision of Safety of Dams, Sacramento-San
Joaquin Water Supervision
L. C. JOPSON . . . . Assistant State Engineer,
Water Rights and Water Quality Investigations
MAX BOOKMAN
Principal Hydraulic Engineer, Los Angeles Office
HENRY HOLSINGER . . . . . Principal Attorney
T. R. MERRYWEATHER . . . Administrative Officer

DIVISION OF ARCHITECTURE
ANSON BOYD . . . State Architect, Chief of Division
HUBERT S. HUNTER . . . Deputy Chief of Division
ROBERT W. FORMHALS
Administrative Assistant to State Architect

Administrative and Fiscal Service
EARL W. HAMPTON
Assistant State Architect, Administrative
HENRY R. CROWLE . . . . . . Fiscal Assistant
THOMAS MERET . . . Construction Budgets Architect
WADE O. HALSTEAD
Principal Estimator of Building Construction
STANTON WILLARD . . Principal Architect, Standards

Design and Planning Service
P. T. POAGE
Assistant State Architect, Design and Planning
ROBERT M. LANDRUM . Chief Architectural Coordinator
ARTHUR F. DUDMAN . Principal Architect, Sacramento
JAMES A. GILLEM . . Principal Architect, Los Angeles
CHARLES PETERSON
Principal Structural Engineer, Los Angeles
CARL A. HENDERLONG
Principal Mechanical and Electrical Engineer
CLIFFORD L. IVERSON . Chief Architectural Draftsman
GUSTAV B. VEHN . . Supervising Specifications Writer
JOHN S. MOORE . . . Supervisor of Special Projects

Construction Service
CHARLES M. HERD . . . Chief Construction Engineer
CHARLES H. BOCKMAN
Assistant to Chief Construction Engineer

AREA CONSTRUCTION SUPERVISORS
THOMAS M. CURRAN . . . . . . Area I, Oakland
J. WILLIAM COOK . . . . . Area II, Sacramento
CLARENCE T. TROOP . . . . Area III, Los Angeles

AREA STRUCTURAL ENGINEERS
SCHOOLHOUSE SECTION
MANLEY W. SAHLBERG . . . Area I, San Francisco
M. A. EWING . . . . Area II, Sacramento
ERNST MAAG . . . . . . Area III, Los Angeles

printed in CALIFORNIA STATE PRINTING OFFICE ⬭1528⬭ 31700 2-56 41,500

World famous San Francisco-Oakland Bay Bridge
in color. Aerial photo by Merritt R. Nickerson, Chief,
Photographic Section, Department of Public Works

ORNIA
D PUBLIC WORKS

California Highways
and Public Works

Official Journal of the Division of Highways,
Department of Public Works, State of California

KENNETH C. ADAMS, Editor
HELEN HALSTED, Assistant Editor
MERRITT R. NICKERSON, Chief Photographer

Vol. 35   May-June   Nos. 5-6

Public Works Building
Twelfth and N Streets
Sacramento

CONTENTS

Published in the interest of highway development in California. Editors of newspapers and others are privileged to
use matter contained herein. Cuts will be gladly loaned
upon request.

Address communications to
CALIFORNIA HIGHWAYS AND PUBLIC WORKS
P. O. Box 1499
Sacramento, California

Directions
for the
Traveler

Signposts
Directions for the Traveler Are Hundreds of Years Old

By GEORGE M. WEBB, Traffic Engineer

For HUNDREDS of years, signposts have guided the traveler on his way, whether a pilgrim traveling on foot or a motorist on an eight-lane freeway.

Ancient traffic signs are described in the 1954-55 winter issue of *Road International*. One relic of the past, nearly 300 years old, is located in England upon the Cotswolds at the intersection of the roads to Gloucester and Worcester. This is believed to be the oldest signpost in Britain. It is carefully preserved by the British highway authorities. Four iron arms point the ways to Worcester, to Oxford, to Warwick, and to Gloucester.

When a traveler wanted to know how far it was to any one of these towns, he consulted the side of the appropriate arm. It is known as the Cross-Hands.

Old milestones are also found in Britain which give distances and directional information to the traveler. The distances are given to towns with only the first letter of the place name. Some of the old milestones carried only the number. The traveler was expected to know where the roads led.

Pioneer Signs on US 50

Travelers along modern US 50 between Placerville and Lake Tahoe can still glimpse some of the stone mileposts on which have been engraved the distance easterly from Placerville. In Central Illinois, rural road markers of a generation ago consist of a map cast in iron, with the location of the particular marker indicated by a star. Thus, by careful and leisurely inspection, the traveler could determine his location and his route.

These signs of bygone days would be of little value with present-day speeds and traffic volumes. Today, traffic signs are recognized as an integral part of a modern highway—essential to its operation and to the

This marker on US 50 in El Dorado County shows the distance to Placerville

safe, orderly, and smooth flow of traffic.

The Division of Highways continually studies and improves signing techniques to keep pace with the ever-increasing traffic demands and to provide California motorists with superior signing service. Signposting has changed throughout the years along with other highway features, but its purpose to guide the traveler remains the same as in olden times.

Auto Increased Travel

When the automobile came into popular use, people traveled farther and faster than ever before. Longer trips over new roads were commonplace, and there were more people using strange roads far from their homes. This increased travel, particularly travel for long distances, created a strong demand for legible signs. As highways and automobiles improved, speeds increased and so did the need for adequate highway signs that could be read from a moving car.

Types of Signs and Uniformity

There are three general types of traffic signs in use today:

1. *Warning* signs to caution drivers of the need for added alertness or reduction in speed;

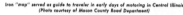

Iron "map" served as guide to traveler in early days of motoring in Central Illinois
(Photo courtesy of Macon County Road Department)

2. *Regulatory* signs to inform motorists of regulations governing movement;

3. *Guide* signs for guidance and directional information.

Obviously, traffic signs of all types should follow uniform standards and be placed in accordance with uniform practice so they will have the same meaning and require the same action on the part of motorists wherever encountered. State-wide uniformity on county roads, city streets, and state highways minimizes drivers' confusion and contributes materially to the safe, orderly, and expeditious movement of traffic.

National uniformity is likewise important. California follows the general standards of the Manual on Uniform Traffic Control Devices for Streets and Highways approved by the American Association of State Highway Officials, Institute of Traffic Engineers, and the National Committee on Uniform Traffic Laws and Ordinances. State-wide uniformity on county roads and city streets, as well as state highways, is encouraged by membership and active participation in the deliberations of the California Sign Committee, the Engineering Division of the Governor's Traffic Safety Conference, and other professional groups.

General Rules for Use of Signs

Signs are essential where special regulations apply, where unusual conditions are not self-evident, and to furnish directional information. They should be used wherever there is a real need but not profusely. Too many signs detract from the effectiveness of those necessary for safety and guidance.

Well-known rules of the road or general provisions of the Vehicle Code are not generally required on traffic signs. Drivers are expected to know the rules for safe operation of their vehicles, and a multiplicity of needless signs with long messages would be distracting and serve no useful purpose.

Guide Signs

Except for the foregoing general comments, this discussion is limited to guide signs. The function of guide

UPPER—Diamond-shaped yellow sign indicates a warning; reflectorized arrow specifically warns of curve to right ahead. LOWER—Speed limit signs are most familiar examples of regulatory type sign.

signs, as the name implies, is to guide motorists along routes and to destinations of their choice, to inform motorists of intersecting routes, to direct to cities or towns, and, to a lesser extent, to furnish information and to identify locations not readily apparent.

The modern highway with adequate visibility and easy curvature to accommodate all normal driving speeds reduces the need for warning and regulatory signs. However, the increased width and higher speeds, and the necessity for making decisions far

Directional information is purpose of guide signs

in advance of turnoffs or intersections greatly increases the importance of the guide signs. This is particularly true on full freeways. Practically no warning signs are needed on freeways except on ramps and connections at interchanges.

Like the early day traveler, the motorist on present-day conventional highways takes advantage of familiar scenes, landmarks, buildings, and geographical features for information as to his whereabouts and the location of intersections and points where choice of direction is made; but the full freeways, with wider rights of way and no businesses or buildings of any kind fronting directly on the highway, present a sameness which may make identification of location difficult. This further brings out the need for guide signs of adequate legibility placed a considerable distance in advance of turnoffs.

It has been frequently said that directional signs were needed only for the infrequent user or the complete stranger on a highway. This is not true on the modern highway with access completely controlled and no intersections at grade. Even frequent users need signs to identify locations and turnoffs.

State-wide Problem

The extensive highway improvement program now under way in many cases removes traffic from congested business streets. This traffic is diverted to the newly constructed routes, generally freeways, which bypass the main business district. This makes the subject of adequate directional signing of great interest to many communities and areas throughout the State. The state-wide scope of the problem requires that it be treated on a uniform state-wide basis.

The state-wide signing practice of the Division of Highways has evolved through the years in meeting changing conditions, increased traffic, and the growth of communities along the expanding network of state highways.

California Sign Committee

Current state highway signing practice, while it is the responsibility of the Division of Highways, was not developed alone by this division. Much of it stems from the studies and consultations of the California Sign Committee which was organized to promote orderly, safe, and consistent signing throughout the State. Members of the Sign Committee are the State Division of Highways; California State Automobile Association; Automobile Club of Southern California; California Supervisors Association; League of California Cities; and Institute of Transportation and Traffic Engineering of the University of California. The individuals who represent these organiza-

tions on the committee are directly concerned with highway signing.

All matters pertaining to type, size, color, positioning, and use of signs are agreed upon after considerable study by this committee, and the several members observe these agreements very closely. Although this organization is advisory only, it has been very effective in securing uniformity on California roads, streets, and highways. Informal meetings of this committee are held as needed, generally several times a year.

Basic Principles and Standard Practice

Certain principles must be followed if signing is to achieve the best results in guidance and safety. One such principle is that the number of place names which can be used effectively on a single sign is distinctly limited. Except under very unusual conditions, the number should not exceed three. Drivers of vehicles moving at present-day speeds are unable to read a long list of place names and directional arrows. Neither can they stop or slow down without hazard to traffic.

A study by the Institute of Transportation and Traffic Engineering of the University of California indicated that the number of drivers' errors in reading signs increases sharply if the number of names on a sign exceeds three. This study also indicated that a dividing line between destinations in opposite directions is of great benefit in reducing drivers' errors in reading signs. As a result, it has now become standard practice of the Division of Highways to use the dividing line be-

This sign once guided travelers in Southern California, but would obviously be impossible to read and digest from a vehicle driving on a modern highway at normal speed

tween destinations on new standard directional signs or replacements.

Reassurance Signs

To reassure motorists that they are on the right road and to tell them how far it is to points along the route, reassurance guide signs are placed facing outbound traffic at the outskirts of cities or towns and just beyond principal highway junctions. These signs generally show (1) the next town, (2) the next county seat, road junction, or important city, and (3) the end of the route. All of the towns named are on the route being traveled. Where the road divides, locations in each direction may be shown, and cities designated as the termini may be alternated on the bottom line of successive signs. Distances are shown to the nearest mile for each destination.

This reassurance sign does not need to be very prominent because it does not call for immediate action by the driver; but it must still be easy to read from a moving vehicle. The standards for this sign on freeways and major highways have recently been improved from plain five-inch letters to reflectorized six-inch letters. This makes for easy reading both day and night at highway speeds.

On high-standard roads, in particular, signs must be both located and proportioned so that motorists may recognize the messages, comprehend the meaning, make decisions, and direct their vehicles into the proper lane without a reduction in speed.

Tip to Freeway Motorists

When driving a freeway for the first time, a motorist should always consult a map to find out which exit will lead to his destination. A single exit in a metropolitan area generally leads to many city streets and destinations. Only the name of the street to which the ramp connects and one place name or route number can be shown on the sign; so the motorist must know the name of the exit where he wants to turn off. In other words, a driver must know in advance where he wants to go if he expects to get there without confusion or mistakes.

The main purpose of highway guide signs is to tell the motorist how to reach his destination by the shortest

Newer guide signs include divider between destinations in different directions

and most efficient route. Any message on a sign which would tend to influence the motorist's decision or to encourage him to turn off the highway at a particular road or area is not within the scope of proper highway signing.

State and US Markers

On any route, there are nearly always a great number of possible destinations and connecting highways, and it has been found impracticable to place signs along highways or at turn-offs naming all possibilities. As a state-wide practice, it has been found necessary to restrict the naming of locations on a given route to those actually on the route, and, in conformance with findings of the Institute of Transportation and Traffic Engineering, to limit to three the number of destinations on a single sign under all but the most exceptional conditions.

Obviously, it would be impossible to place a sufficient number of signs on the highways to enable a motorist, without knowledge of the general direction or local geography, to find his way merely by looking for place names on traffic signs.

Consequently, as a matter of primary guidance, considerable use is made of state and US highway route markers. Under present-day conditions in California, a motorist unfamiliar with a geographical area needs the assistance of a road map, and road maps are readily available. We believe that most motorists rely upon such assistance and that the route markers in use provide generally adequate directional information.

US Numbered Routes

The importance of a nation-wide system of numbered highways was recognized in the early 20's, and the American Association of State Highway Officials (AASHO) requested the Secretary of Agriculture, under whose offices the Bureau of Public Roads at that time operated, to name a committee for the purpose of formulating a plan or system of numbered highways. The association was asked by the Secretary of Agriculture to develop such a system. This system was developed and officially adopted in 1926. The American Association of State Highway Officials is made up of the 48 State Highway Departments and the Highway Departments of Puerto Rico, Hawaii, and the District of Columbia, and the US Bureau of Public Roads.

The selection of US sign routes and the assignment of numbers is a function of the Executive Committee of AASHO. Over the years, this committee has developed a set of policies

New type reassurance signs are larger and reflectorized for easy nighttime as well as daytime reading

for the purpose of facilitating travel on the main interstate lines over the shortest routes and best roads.

AASHO Policies

In accordance with these policies, it has been the practice of the Division of Highways to request that the best route from a traffic service standpoint be designated as the basic US route. Therefore, when a highway is reconstructed to higher standards on new alignment, either through or

around a city or community, this new routing is signed as the basic numbered route.

Included in the established policies of AASHO is the provision that "No additional road shall be added to the US numbered road system, and no existing US road shall be extended except where there is a definite showing of an adequately improved highway carrying an established and necessary line of interstate traffic not otherwise provided for by existing US routes

6

and for which traffic adequate service cannot be provided by state route numbers.

"Extension of present US numbered routes may be made only when the proposed extension is in the general direction of the present route.

"Proposed extensions shall not be made when, to do so, it is necessary to duplicate US routes already established, unless the duplication is for a short distance and the routes then diverge, ending in different terminal points."

There is obvious need for these well-established policies because designation of inadequate routes not providing the best traffic service would discredit the entire system of US numbered routes. Also, extensive or unwarranted use of alternate or business routes would result in confusion and lack of confidence in numbered routes on the part of motorists.

For the sake of uniformity, US sign route policies are also followed in the establishment of California state sign routes insofar as they apply.

The route numbers are used extensively by the makers of road maps. Businesses that cater to the traveler use route numbers to tie in the location of their businesses in their advertising.

Business Districts and Business Routes

With the extension of the freeway system with no businesses fronting directly on the highway, it becomes more and more important to designate to motorists where services normally required by the traveler may be found. On directional signs, this is accomplished by designations such as *central district*, *business district*, *downtown*, or *civic center*, and sometimes the name of a district or area within a city.

It is frequently found desirable to designate a "business" route on a section of former state highway which is relinquished when the community which it serves is bypassed by a new freeway. Proposed business routes must be submitted for approval to AASHO. These business routes are principally within the corporate limits of a city and provide the traveling public with the opportunity to travel through the business section.

UPPER—New type shields to indicate US and state-numbered routes are larger than before. LOWER—Motorists desiring to enter the business district are clearly notified which direction to take.

Business Route

In cases of this type where a business route would be of benefit to the motorist, and local authorities are in accord and agree to place and maintain the necessary signs, it is the division's practice to recommend approval to AASHO. When a business route is approved, all directional signs on the state highway directing to the business route are installed and maintained by the Division of Highways. The remaining signs on the business route are installed and maintained by the city or county.

The use of the business route is a convenient and logical way to direct a stranger so that he can easily find his way to the business section, transact his business, and then proceed to find his way back to the main highway by following the route shields.

The Division of Highways recognizes that the business centers of bypassed communities and along old routes provide needed services to the highway user, and every effort is made to give recognition to these business districts in a manner consistent with the principle of providing the best possible signing for all highway users.

Either overhead illuminated or reflectorized signs are installed where practicable at the connections with the road leading to the business district and the main highway. In addition, where there are other connections from the freeway to the business district, supplementary signing is also provided.

Frontage Roads and Roadside Business

When the construction of a new freeway separates developed property from the existing local road or street system and leaves no suitable connection to the freeway, it is frequently necessary to provide access to the property by construction of a local service road parallel to the freeway. This type of road is designated as a frontage road. In the case of new construction, they are parallel to the freeway. Often the old highway, or portions of the old highway, roughly parallel to the new freeway, will serve as a frontage road. Frontage roads have proven to be advantageous locations for businesses, especially those which provide necessary services for motorists.

The problem of providing adequate directional signs to roadside businesses on frontage roads or on old roads bypassed by construction of freeways developed about 1949. Signs with various wordings were considered, such as *roadside services, roadside business, roadside business area, roadside motels,* etc.

Roadside Business

A sign reading *roadside services* was considered satisfactory for locations where the business on the frontage road consisted of service stations, garages, etc., but would not convey the correct message for sleeping accommodations, restaurants, or roadside stands or other types of business. A sign reading *roadside motels* seemed to be too restricted for many locations. For example, sleeping accommodations might be had in hotels, inns, resorts, tourist cabins, or cottages. A broader term seemed necessary. The word *accommodations* was seriously considered but it was decided it was too long to place on a sign. A sign reading *roadside business* includes all types of services and accommodations and is consistent with our present signing practice of placing *business* signs with route markers to indicate business routes not on the main highway and providing direction to business districts.

Approaching a turnoff from a major rural freeway, the motorist is notified repeatedly of route to follow to by-pass or enter city

In 1951, signing to motel areas was discussed at a conference of the Motor Hotel Association of California. The practice of placing a reflectorized *frontage road* sign in advance of the intersection and a plain sign reading *roadside business* near the intersection was agreed upon.

One of the important factors in the development and use of the sign reading *roadside business* was that the use of a uniform standard sign to designate these businesses would soon cause it to become known by the public. Motorists, when they recognized such a sign, would know that roadside services were available.

A survey was made by the Division of Highways Right of Way Department on the effect of bypassing roadside business. Operators of motels, restaurants, etc., were contacted and appeared satisfied with the wording of the signs, but expressed concern regarding their placement and visibility. As a result of this survey, the signs are now being placed farther in advance of the intersection and the *roadside business* signs are reflectorized for night visibility.

As a further aid to motorists seeking roadside businesses, the *roadside business* signs are placed in the median as well as on the right shoulder on multi-lane divided highways, where the median is of sufficient width to accommodate the signs. One of the most important factors in the statewide use of uniform standard signs reading *roadside business* is that their continued and consistent use will further increase their effectiveness.

Metropolitan Freeway Signing

It is a long step from the first roads and streets used by automobiles to the present-day six- and eight-lane freeways in the large metropolitan areas. Likewise, it is a long step from the early signing to that which is now required on these freeways which carry a tremendous traffic load.

It is a fact that the signing cannot be separated from the freeway because it is an integral part of it. Adequate signing is essential to completeness and satisfactory operation of the modern freeway. The high volumes carried by this type of facility greatly increase the signing requirements.

For example, volumes which preclude changing lanes at will on the approach to an exit make it necessary to provide much greater advance notice of the turnoff. There was a time when 50 feet in advance of an intersection was adequate. Later, the distance increased progressively to several hundred feet, to one-quarter mile, to one-half mile, and now one mile is considered a desirable distance for the first indication of a turnoff from a

These signs for the information of motorists fall into the same category as the signs on the opposite page

metropolitan freeway. This desirable distance is not always obtainable, due to limitations on design and the need for frequent connections to provide

proper traffic service in highly developed areas.

Positive indications of the lane to use for different exits are very necessary. Drivers also need to know the approximate distance to the off-ramp they expect to use.

New System of Signing

After careful study of this problem by traffic engineers of the Division of Highways, a new system of signing has been devised for metropolitan freeways. The main features of this system of signing are:

1. In order to inform drivers of their general location and the distance to the exit which they are seeking, signs will be placed indicating the next three exits and the distance thereto in miles and tenths. A typical sign of this type is shown in *Figure 1.* These signs will be located as soon as practicable after passing an exit and, of course, would list the next three exits. As soon as an exit was passed, its name would be dropped from the top line and the second line would move up to the top position. A new exit name and distance would then be added on the bottom. The names for the exits would be street names, road names, route numbers, or any other name which best fits local conditions. These signs will be frequent reminders to motorists so that they will be prepared to turn off when they reach the exit that will take them to their destination.

Overhead Illuminated Signs

2. Overhead illuminated signs will be placed at exits in the gore; that is, in the triangular area between the turnoff and the main freeway lanes. These signs will carry the name of the off-ramp, positioned directly over the off-ramp with a vertical arrow pointing downward to the approximate center of the ramp. The other side of the sign will normally be over the outside freeway lane, and will carry the name of the next exit ahead, with an arrow pointing downward to the approximate center of the outside lane. This will give motorists the greatest possible advance notice of the proper lane to use for an exit without overlapping the preceding turnoff. *Figure 2.*

3. At intermediate locations between exits, sign bridges may be erected to carry the name of the next exit and other directional information

UPPER—"*Frontage Road*" sign is motorist's first indication of roadside business area ahead. LOWER— "*Roadside Business*" sign notifies traveler of where he may leave freeway to obtain desired services.

for the guidance of motorists. With this system of signing, the names of all major exits will be indicated generally three times on overhead illuminated signs. *Figure 3.* It is a well-known facts that drivers, through inattention or distraction, frequently pass even a prominently-placed sign without comprehending it. The repetition of the exit names and lane indications should reduce this problem to the minimum. *Figure 4.*

Highway designs, including signing, are continually being improved. It is not economical or practical to go back and revise all previous designs and installations whenever a new and better way of signing is developed. Consequently, the new signing described herein is, for the most part, only on the drawing boards, and will be seen

only on new projects and at locations where the need is most urgent for this improved type of signing.

California has taken the lead in developing overhead illuminated freeway signs and rates high nationally in the field of traffic control. Uniformity, so vitally necessary for effective signing, is obtained by an up-to-date looseleaf manual setting forth uniform standards and policies for signs and other traffic control devices used on state highways. Uniformity and adequacy of signing on California county roads and city streets is, with a few exceptions, very good, largely through the activities of the California Sign Committee.

The driver must not be left out of the picture. The best signs in the world are no positive assurance that

10

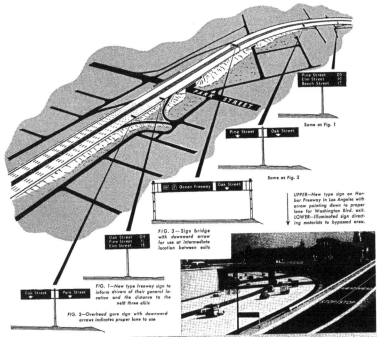

Pine Street 0½
Elm Street 1½
Beech Street 1½

Same as Fig. 1

Pine Street   Oak Street

Same as Fig. 2

[60] [2] Ocean Freeway   Oak Street

FIG. 3—Sign bridge with downward arrow for use at intermediate location between exits

Oak Street 0½
Pine Street 1½
Elm Street   1½

Oak Street   Park Street

FIG. 1—New type freeway sign to inform drivers of their general location and the distance to the next three exits

FIG. 2—Overhead gore sign with downward arrows indicates proper lane to use

UPPER—New type sign on Harbor Freeway in Los Angeles with arrow pointing down to proper lane for Washington Blvd. exit. LOWER—Illuminated sign directing motorists to bypassed area.

a few drivers won't make mistakes or take a wrong turn occasionally. Drivers must take their share of the responsibility. They should study a map when using a highway or a metropolitan freeway for the first time so they will know what routes to follow and where to turn off to reach their destination, and above all be alert and courteous, and follow the rules of the road at all times. Careful, competent driving, combined with safe highways and adequate traffic signs, will surely contribute substantially to smooth, orderly traffic flow.

First Highway Tunnel

Don Francisco Sánchez
Bored It in 1800's

By E. D. DREW, Associate Engineer Geologist, Materials and Research Department

WHAT is probably the oldest highway tunnel in California is located near Sign Route 1 about six miles south of San Francisco at Mussel Rock, just a few hundred feet from where the famous San Andreas Fault meets the ocean.

The writer first noticed the tunnel several years ago while engaged in a geological survey of the area. At first it appeared to be one of the natural arches or sea caves frequently seen along the coast. Upon closer examination at low tide, chisel and pick marks were found on the walls of the tunnel. There is also evidence of a crude cut and grade just beyond the north end of the tunnel.

By glancing at a topographic map or air photo it will be seen that an almost unbroken beach strand extends from Laguna Salada to a point near the Cliff House in San Francisco. The point of interruption is at Mussel Rock where for a short distance the beach is blocked by a high rock cliff.

History of Tunnel

In order to obtain some history of the tunnel, inquires were made of old-timers who were all in accord that the tunnel had been built many years ago by one of the California dons, probably Don Francisco Sánchez.

Don Francisco Sánchez, one of the early Californians, was at one time the hacendado of the Rancho San Pedro, consisting of 8,926.46 acres granted to him on January 26, 1839. It was from Montara Mountain, later a part of Rancho San Pedro, on October 28, 1769, that Sergeant José Ortega, under command of Gaspar de Portolá, first caught a glimpse of the northern coast and San Francisco Bay. Portolá at this time overlooked the significance of the discovery and recorded, "I saw nothing." Fr. Crespi, the spiritual guardian of the party, reported in his diary, "It is a very large and fine harbor. All his majesty's and Europe's navies could be sheltered here."

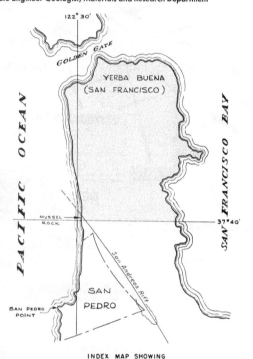

INDEX MAP SHOWING
LOCATION OF MUSSEL ROCK,
RANCHO SAN PEDRO AND YERBA BUENA.

The rancho is mentioned as early as March, 1793, when a Captain Brown of H. M. Navy stopped for a short

Four views of ancient tunnel and cut through Mussel Rock below Sign Route 1 in San Mateo County

visit, anchoring at nearby San Pedro Point. According to legend, the original Sánchez home was constructed in 1817. The material used was obtained from a wrecked Spanish ship driven on to the beach at San Pedro Point. Several very old anchors can be seen today at the point.

In their book, "The Spanish and Mexican Adobe and Other Buildings in the Nine San Francisco Bay Counties 1776 to About 1850," G. W. Hendry and J. N. Bowman say:

"The Sánchez Adobe Dwelling stands on the north side of San Pedro Creek and on the south side of the road about one mile east from the new

coast highway; it is in the lower San Pedro Valley.

"It is not marked on the diseño of 1839 but is found on several surveys of the '50's and '60's, and labeled 'Francisco Sánchez Old Adobe.' Sánchez had earlier, in 1834, applied for a grant in this area but had been denied a grant in this area but had been denied by Indians; before this grant was finally made he had occupied the land. His brother José de la Cruz Sánchez testified in the land case that he had a house on the land about 1837 or 1838 and was living in it before the date of the grant; General Vallejo testified to the same facts; but no statement was

made as to the building material. At this time and in this place it may be inferred that it was of adobe and nothing has been found to indicate that this early adobe was not the one that is now standing. There is a local legend that a house was built there late in the preceding century and that it had been reconstructed in 1817 and that the present dwelling was erected in 1842; but nothing of a documentary nature has been found as to these stories.

"It is possible that he built a palizada house about 1837 and an adobe soon after the grant in 1839, but no evidence has been found as to that fact.

. . . Continued on page 52

Fourth Street Project

*Traffic Barrier in
Los Angeles Removed*

By LYALL A. PARDEE, City Engineer, City of Los Angeles

Upon the completion of the Fourth Street open cut and elevated extensions to the Harbor Freeway project on May 1, 1956, the City of Los Angeles gained a sorely needed traffic artery through the Bunker Hill area which has been a barrier to the downtown business district of the City of Los Angeles for many years.

Celebrating the completion of this important cooperative project a ribbon-cutting ceremony was held starting at 10 a.m. on May 1 under the sponsorship of the Los Angeles City Downtown Business Men's Association. The colorful ceremony was culminated in a trial run being made over the new highway by soapbox derby contestants. The principal address of the day was made by Mayor Poulson of the City of Los Angeles who, in the course of his remarks, said, "This is an example of teamwork by many groups and individuals, including the members of the city council, the staffs of the Bureau of Engineering and the Traffic Department, and the businessmen of the downtown area."

Bunker Hill Area

Roughly, the area between Temple Street on the north, Fifth Street on the south, Hill Street on the east and Flower Street on the west constitutes what is known as the Bunker Hill area, a steep hill just west of most of the downtown Los Angeles business district and Civic Center area. The only access through the hill, traffic wise, was via the Second and Third Street Tunnels or via First Street which crossed the hill on ascending and descending grades of over 11 percent. The Third Street Tunnel, however, is only a narrow two-lane tunnel and in handling two-way traffic has been the cause of tremendous traffic congestion for all vehicles going either to or from the business district.

One-way Streets

One of the prime factors in the Fourth Street project was to alleviate

E. T. Telford, Assistant State Highway Engineer

this congested traffic situation in the Third Street Tunnel. With the opening of the Fourth Street project, Fourth Street has been made a one-way street eastbound from Boylston Street to the juncture with Fourth Place, about 1,000 feet east of Alameda Street. At the same time, Third Street has been designated a one-way street westbound between Alameda Street and Boylston Street, thus improving the one-way traffic flow in Third Street at least 50 percent through the narrow tunnel and adding Fourth Street as an entirely new eastbound through traffic artery.

In order to accomplish the opening of Fourth Street as a through traffic artery it was necessary to acquire and improve a new street easterly from Third Street at Boylston Street to Beaudry Avenue at Fourth Street. Two roadways were constructed from Beaudry Avenue easterly, the southerly roadway replacing the existing Fourth Street as a local street between Beaudry Avenue and Figueroa Street.

The northerly roadway was constructed to receive the off ramps from both the northbound and southbound roadways of the Harbor Freeway and to connect these ramps as well as Fourth Street with the present Fourth Street project about 425 feet west of Figueroa Street. All of this work was built with the Harbor Freeway.

Passes Through Bunker Hill

The present Fourth Street project as now completed extends easterly from the work described above. It begins with a viaduct approximately 687 feet in length spanning Figueroa Street and Flower Street on a 1 percent ascending grade. The viaduct terminates at the bluff about 100 feet east of Flower Street where the roadway then passes into an open cut passing through Bunker Hill. This cut rises easterly on a 4.5 percent grade and makes transition by means of a long vertical curve to an 8 percent descending grade which meets the existing elevation of Olive Street and Fourth Street. The through roadway just described provides a four-lane roadway 44 feet wide across the viaduct and through the cut to Grand Avenue. At this point the roadway is widened one lane on the south side to permit the efficient handling of the large number of automobiles desiring to make right turns at Olive Street.

Between Olive Street and Hill Street the existing roadway, 40 feet wide, was widened to 49 feet, which is as much as it was possible to obtain within the present street right of way. Due to large buildings adjoining Fourth Street in this block, the cost of widening would have been prohibitive. This will also make available an additional lane for right turning traffic at Hill Street which is the terminus of this project. To provide for proper access between the portions of Bunker Hill north and south of the cut, bridges were constructed at Grand Avenue and at Hope Street.

Looking easterly from intersection of Fourth Street and Beaudry Avenue, showing in background downtown Los Angeles business area and in foreground, right, one-way ramp over Harbor Freeway leading to Figueroa Street; in foreground, left, the roadway for eastbound Fourth Street traffic over Harbor Freeway, Figueroa Street, and Flower Street.

Total Cost $3,348,700

The total cost of the Fourth Street open cut project was approximately $3,377,200. Broken down, this amount included $266,000 for engineering, $126,000 for right-of-way costs in connection with acquisition and condemnation, $1,575,000 for acquisition, actual right of way and property damage and $1,410,200 for construction.

Because this open cut project divided the Bunker area into two parts and removed an existing surface street in Fourth Street between Hope and Olive Streets, one of the requirements of this improvement was to give the people living in this area a new inlet and outlet to the downtown district. This was provided by a new 30-foot street with a 24-foot roadway called

Third Place which was located 110 feet north of the center line of the new Fourth Street between Hope Street and Grand Avenue. Third Place will then proceed easterly to Olive Street on a curving alignment, to avoid an existing five-floor concrete garage building located at the northwest corner of Fourth Street and Olive Street. The work easterly of

This indeX map indicates the manner in which Third Street and Fourth Street have been put into operation as a pair of one-way streets by the Los Angeles City Traffic Department of which Lloyd M. Braff is General Manager

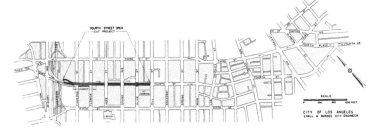

UPPER—Grading operations in progress. Timber bridge shown was erected as traffic detour for Hope Street. CENTER—Grading operation under way across Grand Avenue. Traffic was detoured to east on timber bridge not shown in photograph. LOWER—Shown in foreground are details of falsework for Hope Street Bridge on Fourth Street. Harbor Freeway in background.

These three photographs were taken at same location as shown on opposite page after completion of project construction. (Note stairways for pedestrians to left of bridge carrying Grand Avenue over Fourth Street.)

and Public Works

Grand Avenue will be included in a separate city contract.

Unique Feature

Another unique feature of the design also had to do with this same garage building. This garage had an entrance on Fourth Street about 140 feet west of Olive Street, but the new grade of Fourth Street, due to the open cut, lowered the street level in front of this entrance about 12 to 14 feet thus making impractical the maintenance of this entrance. In order to give the garage the same facilities as it had prior to the construction of this project, a new entrance was designed to join the west side of the building at the third floor level from the new Third Place· east of Grand Avenue. This work was a part of the present contract.

Another design feature was the provision of parking lanes on either side of Fourth Street between Grand Avenue and Hope Street and between Hope Street and the viaduct. By means of reverse curves in the curb alignment, the roadway was widened 10 feet on each side to allow for emergency parking. Between Olive Street and Grand Avenue, the south side of Fourth Street was widened 11 feet to allow for an extra lane with a traffic island provided west of the intersection of Olive Street to permit cars to turn into Olive Street without hindering the through traffic on Fourth Street.

Grand Avenue Bridge

Another unusual design feature of this project, to take care of a future plan for reducing the grade on Grand Avenue was in the construction of the Grand Avenue Bridge over the Fourth Street open cut project. Grand Avenue between Fourth and Fifth Streets is now on a steep grade varying up to 19 percent. The city plans to reduce this to a short 16 percent grade at Fifth Street and then further reducing to a 9.32 percent grade for about three-fourths of the distance to Fourth Street. The bridge as designed provided hinges at both ends so that it could be lowered to meet the proposed change in grade. However, before it was constructed, funds were allocated assuring the lowering of Grand Avenue to the proposed final grade, and the bridge was therefore constructed to this grade. It was connected by means of a temporary roadway to the existing grade, necessitating a dip in the traveled surface of Grand Avenue until the new improvements are built.

Inasmuch as both Grand Avenue and Hope Street are now main arteries for traffic from the Hollywood Freeway to the downtown area and access to the hill, they could not be closed during construction of the open cut project. It was therefore necessary to build a detour on each street with temporary timber bridges to permit traffic to use them and at the same time to provide access by the contractor for excavating the open cut area in Fourth Street.

History

Although this project is now completed after nearly two years of construction, there were many problems involved in the original planning which started some 20 years ago. It had been periodically considered since then but was actively revived in 1949

Perspective sketch looking northeasterly showing how the recently completed Fourth Street open-cut construction in the City of Los Angeles and existing Third Street are tied into the Harbor Freeway by connecting ramp interchange roadways and now operate as one-way streets, Third Street for westbound traffic and Fourth Street for eastbound traffic.

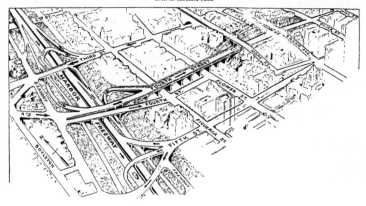

with the construction of the Harbor Freeway, with the additional suggestion of constructing a viaduct approach at the westerly end to separate grades with Figueroa and Flower Streets.

The original idea was to tunnel under Bunker Hill with various schemes ranging between the location of the easterly terminus at either Hill Street or Olive Street and with various connecting grades. In fact there were in all eight different schemes, each investigated for practicability and cost.

It was first proposed to build a full tunnel, by normal tunneling methods with direct connection to Hill Street. After a public hearing, the Los Angeles City Council, on March 7, 1951, decided upon a combined tunnel with viaduct extension with an easterly terminus at Olive Street. However, preliminary estimates of cost of building tunnels or open cuts of different lengths and grades, ranged anywhere from $2,612,400 to $3,956,500 and these studies were eventually set aside in favor of an open cut through the Bunker Hill area with a maximum 8 percent grade west of Olive Street. This was known as Scheme No. 8 and was the one finally adopted.

Different Plans Studied

The city engineer was instructed on November 20, 1952, to prepare the necessary plans and specifications for the construction of the Fourth Street project on the basis of an open cut with sloped banks.

This again brought a demurrer from the property owners along Fourth Street and on Bunker Hill who hired a private engineer to represent them and who requested the city council that further consideration be given to Scheme No. 3 which was an open cut with straight alignment and retaining walls but on a grade differing from that of Scheme No. 8. This again delayed final action by the city council until a comparative study could be made of the two schemes. To adopt Scheme No. 3 as presented by the property owners would have necessitated a signed waiver of damages by all the property owners fronting on the south side of Fourth Street.

Auto caravan lines up following ceremonies dedicating the Fourth Street project

The owners were given 15 days to sign these waivers with at least 80 percent of the affected property owners waiving any damage claims in order for the council to adopt Scheme No. 3. When the necessary 80 percent were not received, the council reverted to its previous stand of adopting Scheme No. 8. Final authority to proceed with the plans was obtained on July 29, 1953.

Three Agencies Share Cost

Financing of this project was shared among three agencies; the City and County of Los Angeles and the California State Division of Highways. The State financed the construction of the viaduct located on the west end of the project at a cost of approximately $650,000. The balance of the project including the cost of the surveys and plans, right of way acquisition, and construction of the open cut section was financed jointly from the gas tax funds of the City and County of Los Angeles.

The project was designed by the Street and Freeway Design Division

of the city engineer's office and was constructed under state contract by Webb and White, contractors of Los Angeles.

The writer is now city engineer, succeeding Lloyd Aldrich who was city engineer at the time the project was designed. Merrill Butler is engineer of design and Hugo H. Winter, now assistant engineer of design, was in charge of the Street and Freeway Design Division during the time preliminary studies and investigations and contract plans were prepared. Hazen A. Wright, head of the Structural Design Division, supervised the design and planning of the viaduct. Charles D. Weinstock of the Street and Freeway Design Division supervised much of the design and planning of the project from its early planning stages.

Construction

The following paragraphs record some of the major construction details.

Bids for this project were open June 24, 1954, and a contract was awarded on June 30, 1954. Actual work was started on July 19, 1954.

(A) The State awarded a contract covering the construction of Fourth Street between the Harbor Freeway and Hill Street to Webb & White, contractors, for the sum of $1,135,000. The contract time was 375 working days with a penalty of $100 per day for overrun of time. Original completion date was January 23, 1956, but because of right of way, strike delays, and weather delays, the original completion date was extended about 90 days.

(B) This contract involved building three bridges and making a heavy roadway cut through Bunker Hill. The three bridges were:

1. Reinforced concrete box girder viaduct over Flower Street and Figueroa Street and extending from the Harbor Freeway to the west side of Bunker Hill.
2. A reinforced concrete bridge over Fourth Street at Hope Street.
3. A steel girder bridge with concrete deck over Fourth Street at Grand Avenue.

A maximum 35-foot-deep roadway cut was made through Bunker Hill between Flower and Olive Streets.

The work included in this contract extended from Harbor Freeway easterly by means of a viaduct and a cut through Bunker Hill to Hill Street, a distance of 2,445 feet, or 0.463 mile.

Fourth Street Viaduct

(C) The Fourth Street Viaduct over Flower Street and Figueroa Street is 687 feet long and provides for a 43-foot roadway. It also provides for considerably more than the required minimum vertical clearances above the streets crossing underneath. At Flower Street a spiral concrete stairway leads up to the roadway elevation of the viaduct. It is supported by two abutments and eight intermediate reinforced concrete rectangular piers. The piers are supported by six caissons approximately 25 feet deep with 3-foot diameter shafts and the abutments belled out 6 to 9 feet in diameter. These caissons were a special problem to the contractor due to gas seeping into shafts from the ground and endangering the workmen. The caissons carried the pier loads down onto the underlying blue shale.

Due to the extreme height of the viaduct over the city streets, very heavy falsework was required to sup-

Ribbon cutting ceremonies. Left to right: John Anson Ford, Supervisor, Third District, Los Angeles County; Richard P. Magpiong, Boys' Week Acting County Supervisor, County of Los Angeles; Norris Poulson, Mayor, City of Los Angeles; Bruce Gardner, Boys' Week Acting Mayor, City of Los Angeles; Edward R. Valentine, Chairman, Downtown Development Committee of Downtown Business Men's Association of Los Angeles; Robert E. McClure, State Highway Commissioner. The soap box derby drivers are Jim Burwell, Wayne Ford, and Lynn Erickson.

port the deck forms during the placing of the concrete. The falsework consisted mainly of wood pile bents which supported wood and steel stringers, wood joints and plywood forms.

Heavy Roadway Cut

(D) A heavy roadway cut was required for that portion of Fourth Street through Bunker Hill. It had a 35-foot maximum depth and required 135,000 cubic yards of roadway excavation.

(E) The paving of Fourth Street consisted chiefly of four 11-foot portland cement concrete lanes on Fourth Street with asphalt concrete approaches at the Harbor Freeway. The bridges at both Hope Street and Grand Avenue were topped with asphalt pavement to match the adjacent city streets.

(F) Work between Hill Street and Olive Street involved changes to two buildings whose basements extended under the sidewalk area. Paving was made difficult in this area due to the numerous manholes and utilities in the street. Inconveniences were caused to the occupants of the buildings adjacent during wet weather because of

the street being torn up and paving being delayed due to the gravel suppliers strike.

(G) Among the 87 pay items included in the contract for this project there were 8,000 cubic yards of structure concrete 135,000 cubic yards of roadway excavation, 250,000 pounds of structural steel, 1,552,000 pounds of reinforcing steel, 2,000 cubic yards of portland cement concrete pavement, and 4,300 tons of asphalt concrete paving.

(H) As previously stated, this project was designed by the City of Los Angeles. The contract supervision was assigned to the State Division of Highways and administered by the Bridge Department. District VII engineering personnel supervised all roadway items.

Representing the State were Oscar A. Johnson, resident engineer, succeeded by Warren B. James, resident engineer for the Bridge Department. H. E. Belford was senior supervising engineer for District VII, with J. Smith and W. Hashimoto as district representatives. James S. White, co-partner in Webb & White, directed the work for the construction company with Ken Murray acting as superintendent.

20

Silver Strand

Major Project Is Nearing Completion in San Diego

By C. WIGGINTON, Assistant Highway Engineer

WHEN BIDS were opened June 23, 1955, for reconstruction of a portion of State Sign Route 75 on Coronado's Silver Strand, it marked the addition of a new chapter to the history of California's romantic past and fabulous future. The Silver Strand, a narrow stretch of sandy beach about seven miles in length, besides providing San Diego with a fine harbor by separating San Diego Bay and the Pacific Ocean, is also the means of saving Coronado and North Island from being an island.

Transportationwise, the Strand has served practically every mode of travel available to man from the pedestrian to the motor car; from the railroad to amphibious vehicles, and one may even see an occasional airplane on its way to North Island by truck. Usually, one thinks only of Coronado as a vacation pleasureland and yet ironically, this home of fun and sun is one of the Nation's greatest bastions of air and naval defense. Its beautiful palms shelter alike the stately mansions of the elderly retired, the defense workers' modest homes, and the residences of navy recruit and grizzled admiral.

Work Started in July, 1955

On July 20, 1955, the Daley Corporation of San Diego, successful bidder for the project with its quotation of $768,038, began operations. The job extends from R. H. Dana Place in Coronado to Coronado Heights near Palm City, a total length of 7.8 miles, with J. R. Cropper assigned as Resident Engineer representing the State Division of Highways. Construction was planned so that most of the original 22 feet of concrete pavement could be used for the northbound lanes. When completed, four 12-foot lanes of divided highway will be available to serve traffic.

Southern end of Strand on Palm Avenue prior to construction. Divided highway in background marks completed portion of first unit.

Inasmuch as the northern end of the Strand is the site of the U. S. Naval Amphibious Base, the contract provides for rearrangement of its buildings and utilities as necessary. The Division of Beaches and Parks of the State of California maintains extensive areas on both sides of the Strand for public use, and construction includes a bridge and three pedestrian undercrossings to serve the beach facilities. A frontage road opposite the Coronado City Hall is also included among the provisions.

Problems for Engineer

Every construction project invariably presents problems challenging engineer and contractor alike, and this job followed the usual pattern. Of great concern was the Strand's most attractive feature, an overabundance of sand, and sand does not provide the best surface for vehicle operation, especially for heavily loaded construction equipment. In the Fort Emory cut there was sufficient select material available to cover about five miles of noncohesive beach sand. The

LEFT—View northerly toward Coronado. New lanes for southbound traffic under construction on left. Existing concrete pavement on right provides two lanes of travel for northbound traffic. Note new frontage road on right serving bay development area. RIGHT—Northerly end of Strand before construction.

contractor, at his option, elected to spread this material as far as the increased cost of haul would permit. There was then left about two miles of plain beach sand with no cover over which to operate. It was decided to bring up the moisture of the beach sand to 20 percent and place cement-treated base directly upon the sand. To everyone's satisfaction, it was found that equipment could get into and out of the zone of operations without seriously rutting the grade. The small ruts which did develop were knocked down with hand labor and the area rewatered. This method proved satisfactory throughout the job. Occasional pockets of dredged sand were encountered containing sea shells which made an excellent base. Unfortunately, these materials were rather sparse in occurrence.

Old Traffic Artery

Historical research revealed that the Strand has proven a traffic artery as far back as one can trace. Prior to 1918, the pedestrian or the equestrian depended upon following a road of sorts over earth and sand which had in essence "jes' growed"! About 1918, a concrete pavement was placed as part of the improvement from the

south city limits of Chula Vista to Coronado. Material for the construction was hauled from the Otay River in wagons pulled by mules.

In the early forties, Fort Emory's growing military demands occassioned a relocation in order to serve the needs of national defense, resulting in an improvement of this route, by this time State Sign Route 75, from Ninth Street in Palm City to the north end of Fort Emory. In 1944-1945, a succeeding project extended the improvement from Fort Emory to the City of Coronado. When the Montgomery Freeway was constructed to the International Border, a three-level structure was built connecting the Montgomery Freeway (US 101) to State Sign Route 75 on Palm Avenue. Palm Avenue was very restricted and in need of improvement structurally; and as the business development was growing almost beyond expectations, considerable amounts of traffic were generated along Palm Avenue.

In 1954, a contract was let improving State Sign Route 75 from its connection to the Montgomery Freeway at the three-level structure through the developed business section along Palm Avenue and to the

beginning of this present improvement. With the completion of the latest project, during July of this year, Route 75 will be a four-lane divided highway over its entire length.

History of Coronado Area

Historically, the area of Coronado and North Island abounds in fact and fiction. Originally, North Island was truly an island, in character as well as name. Reclamation of the narrow passageway between Coronado and North Island has resulted in their forming one land mass with no separation other than a military fence. San Diego's first distinguished visitor, Juan Rodriguez Cabrillo of Portugal, who arrived September 28, 1542, was either unimpressed with the possibilities Coronado presented or else he was a very unobservant type of an explorer. He had a few kind words to say about San Diego in general; but as far as the island was concerned, praise was conspicuous by its absence. July 1, 1769, Father Junipero Serra and party arrived in town after shanks-maring it from Loreto in distant Baja California from whence they had departed March 9, 1769. Here again we find no mention of Coronado, occasioned no doubt by a

22

lack of interest in anything resembling sand after what the party had been through during their weary footsore trek.

Once Grazing Land

The first official notice of the island was taken by Don Pedro Carrillo in 1846, who petitioned Governor Pio Pico to grant him 4,185 acres of sagebrush and sand-covered island in order to graze cattle. May 15, 1846, said petition was granted by Pio Pico, naming the island the Peninsula of San Diego and noting that these 4,185 acres would provide two grazing sites, and adding that for what it was worth, Carrillo, his children, and his children's children could have it throughout eternity.

Eternity for Carrillo lasted for one year when he sold the parcel to Bezar Simmons for $1,000 and figured he'd made a right smart financial move. Simmons in turn sold the holding to Archibald Peachey and William Aspinwall for $10,000, who held it until 1886 and disposed of it for $110,000 to the Coronado Beach Company, the original developers of modern Coronado.

E. S. Babcock, head of the firm, decided that this potential paradise only suffered one major drawback; nobody knew anything about it. He decided to publicize the place, and after a whirlwind nationwide campaign, he began a public auction of subdivided lots on November 13, 1886. More than 6,000 people came from all over the United States, including San Diego, to buy a piece of California's golden pleasure land. It may be somewhat of a surprise to learn that even then real estate was at a premium. The first lot went to Major Levy Chase for $1,600, and history notes that the good major was offered $2,000 for his lot 'ere the sun set that same evening.

Famous Hotel Built

Even though the development hit the peak of the land boom of the eighties, Babcock and his group decided that Coronado must have substance in order to assure its future. Accordingly, plans were laid to provide a hotel sufficient to attract the easterners. Upon seven and one-half

acres Hotel del Coronado came to life boasting 750 rooms, 11,000 square feet of ballroom and theater, and a dining room capable of seating 1,000 people.

During the late 1880's and 1890's Coronado enjoyed great popularity as a resort area, and National City and the surrounding territory became thriving industrial and business centers.

Railroads Begin Operating

Two railroads operated out of San Diego to the south, serving both National City and Coronado. One traveled to the International Border, carrying vast numbers of people commuting to their work. National City was something of a railroad center. However, following the recession and removal of heavy railroad traffic, many of the houses, including a number owned by the railroad, were moved away. It was not unusual to see a parade of lighters crossing the bay, each with a house on board.

The second railroad traveled from San Diego, around the Silver Strand, to Coronado. Each of these railroads carried from 10 to 15 coaches on a run and operated on an hourly schedule.

Transportation was also available on a steamer from National City to San Diego and thence across the bay to Roseville. This was a popular and gala trip with music and gaiety at a high pitch.

Tent City

By the turn of the Twentieth Century, a rather curious development was under way. Clustered to the south of the hotel was an extensive collection of cottages (using the term loosely). These cottages, in the main, were sided with tent cloth and thatched with palm fronds. The settlement soon grew to a point that it was named "Tent City." This became a mecca for the vacationer. The furnishings were rather crude, boasting cast-off beds from the hotel, wavy mirrors, and running water in the town square from whence the vacationer ran to his cottage, pail in hand. But withal, possessing the appeal of a California type "Mediterranean villa." Truly, life was wonderful! With the relocation of the highway during the early forties, it was decided that Tent City must go. Amid many cries of the faithful, road construction began and many of the cottages were moved to Palm City and Coronado Heights, with a few

State Sign Route 75 joins US 101 at three-level structure in Palm City. Left center marks beginning of completed first unit of Route 75.

sand until barracks, hangars, etc., could be built. The greatest amount of construction was accomplished just before and during World War I, and many of the old hangars, offices, and the old Army hospital are still in use by the Navy.

Ferry to Coronado

In those difficult early days the only access to North Island was by small ferry from a wharf located between Broadway and Market Streets in San Diego. A landing dock was constructed on the island. In later years a fill and bridge was placed across the Spanish Bight, connecting North Island to Coronado and providing access for vehicles to the island.

During the years from 1913 to 1938, the Army continued to operate an airfield and supply depot known as Rockwell Field, often called "The Cradle of Army Aviation." In the meantime, the Navy had been given

UPPER—Looking south on Silver Strand during construction. Temporary detours provide passage as pedestrian underpasses are built. Silver Strand State Park on right and left. LOWER—North end of Silver Strand at Coronado on Sign Route 74. New construction on ocean side will provide a four-lane divided highway.

. . . Continued on page 59

destined as forest cabins in the back country. So ended a frivolous rollicking era dedicated to fun and sun with the war years lying ahead.

Army Moves In

As the military value of North Island became more and more apparent, the Army and the Navy began casting envious and covetous eyes upon this area. In 1893, game hunters on the island were mildly disturbed by construction activities for the Zuninga Shoal Jetty; and the opening of the Twentieth Century found 38½ acres reserved for the military. The years rolled by until in 1913, North Island became the site of the first base of the infant Army Air Corps. The First Aero Squadron, which was the beginning of the Army Air Corps, had been organized as the Aviation Section of the Signal Corps in Augusta, Georgia; moved on to Texas City, Texas, and was assigned to duty at North Island early in 1913. From this small beginning of 78 men, 16 officers and 8 aeroplanes, grew the great Army Air Corps. The men were billeted in tents on the

Redwood Freeway

Fifty Miles of Highway Planned

By GEORGE LEATHERWOOD, District Advance Planning Engineer

THE COMPLETION of the Redwood Highway study US 101 in Southern Humboldt County for 50 miles through the heart of the Redwood Empire as a single project on a full freeway basis places this accomplishment at the top for projects of such length and magnitude undertaken by the State of California Division of Highways.

The present traveled way through the world-famous Humboldt Redwood State Parks is Northwestern California's only highway artery. All north and south motor vehicle traffic must, of necessity, pass through these groves. In the redwood flats the trees stand scarcely more than 12 feet from the centerline, and the road itself is composed of short tangents and small radius curves. It is truly a scenic highway, but as a modern transportation facility is completely obsolete.

These redwood flats were acquired by the State Division of Beaches and Parks through the joint efforts of individuals, conservation-minded groups, and the State of California at a time before any essential modernization of the original 1914 road was undertaken.

Study Started in 1953

The existing state highway traversing this section has gone through the same economic evolution as other highways throughout California. First came a trail for foot and horseback travel. Then came its widening and relocation to accommodate wheeled vehicles. Then came powered transportation of faster speeds that again demanded improvement and relocation. The efficiency, speed, and volume of these latter vehicles have increased on a steadily rising curve with the result that the type and location necessary to provide a suitable facility outstripped the State's means of financing such a project.

On August 20, 1953, notwithstanding the financial problems involved for a project of this magnitude, a study

UPPER—Looking northerly down South Fork of Eel River, Phillipsville and Redwood Highway at right of picture. Typical of the terrain to be traversed by the Redwood Freeway. LOWER—Existing Redwood Highway just north of Garberville is benched into Garberville Bluffs along South Fork of Eel River. New location of proposed Redwood Freeway will supersede this portion of Redwood Highway.

was started between the Mendocino county line and Jordan Creek, a distance of approximately 50 miles via the existing highway.

In instigating this project, the district proceeded with an extensive preliminary exploration study through the media of aerial photographs and U. S. Quadrangle sheets followed by aerial reconnaissance and field investigations. Upon completion of this first phase and satisfied that the area had been thoroughly explored, it then became possible to outline the area required for reconnaissance type aerial survey at a scale of 1"-400' and 20' contours.

Aerial Survey Made

On October 30, 1953, the district requested an aerial survey of the area needed which covered 30,000 acres, which survey was delivered and accepted on November 12, 1954.

With these relatively detailed maps to work with the task of developing the numerous possible locations progressed smoothly. Trial lines and profiles were developed and studied. When satisfied that the placement was firm to the extent these maps would permit, they were transferred to vellum transparencies and the cut, fills, bridges, interchange ramps and other planimetric features that would aid in visualizing the proposal were added.

Individual natural controls were not unlike similar physical features encountered elsewhere; however, their abundance, combined with high standards of design, provided a constant engineering challenge.

The redwood trees bordering the river and extending into the canyons and up the hillsides were given a great deal of publicity as being the prime physical control for any new location due to their majestic size and tranquil beauty that bring visitors from all parts of the North American Continent and other parts of the world. Actually, these trees were only one of numerous controls.

River Economic Barrier

In addition to the trees, there was the rugged, meandering South Fork of the Eel River Canyon with the river acting as an economic barrier. The configuration of the terrain forming the spurs, ridges, and side canyons coupled with the unstable formation common to this region were by far the more formidable controlling factors.

Last, but most important to consider, is the highway user who foots the bill for projects of this nature. Within reasonable financial limits, modern highways are located to do the most good for the greatest number on both a local and regional basis. Each vehicle, regardless of type, weight, class, where it came from, and where it is going, becomes a factor in the final determination of what can be done to provide the greatest return to the highway user in terms of comfort, safety, and money invested.

Although right of way is not a factor in the sense of physical control, it

UPPER—Redwood Highway passes through Richardson Grove State Park, a popular recreational area. Through traffic, vacation traffic, and pedestrian movements are in conflict on this now obsolete main line highway. CENTER—Redwood Highway south of Garberville. Note the heavy commercial traffic utilizing the route, resulting in long queues of traffic. BOTTOM—Redwood Highway at Holbrook Grove. This is a typical portion of the Redwood Highway to be superseded by the proposed Redwood Freeway.

does have an important bearing in the over-all picture. Property lying in the path of the various studies was carefully considered. In most instances it is a matter of pure economics; however, there are times when aesthetics enter into the problem. How can the value of say a grove of 5,000-year-old trees, 10 feet to 20 feet in diameter and 300 feet high, be evaluated; or, other natural phenomena? Surely not by board feet, cubic feet or other media of measurement.

Concurrently with the projection, estimates of cost were prepared for each line. These estimates included clearing, earthwork quantities, cost of stabilization, drainage, bridges, base material, surfacing, right of way and numerous incidental items that make up the final estimate.

Traffic Volume and Type

As the work progressed, geological studies were made in the broad sense for estimating the approximate amount to be set up for stabilization of excavation slopes and embankment foundations.

For the purpose of determining what volume and type of traffic would use the various alternate locations, a traffic origin and destination survey was made in which interview field stations were established. Vehicles of all types were stopped and their drivers questioned regarding the origin and destination of their trip and whether they preferred a highway passing through or around the redwood groves.

From this information, it then became possible to prognosticate the type and volume of traffic that would make use of each line over a 20-year period. Truck traffic was given special attention due to its importance to the economic welfare of the State as a whole and to the fact that it is the basic prime mover for outgoing forest products and incoming goods and commodities manufactured elsewhere. For these reasons, grades were carefully analyzed regarding their effect on truck operational cost and became one of the factors governing the final selection of routes.

Study Is Submitted

This information was then reduced to time and distance via each line and combination of lines that made up a routing and finally to cost of travel in dollars. Knowing the cost of travel via the present facility, it then became a simple matter to compare each alternate to this latter, relative to cost of construction to determine which line would do the most good for the highway users on a local and regional basis.

Finally, on September 27, 1955, the study closed on its second important phase with the submission of the project report for headquarters review and deliberations.

On November 30, 1956, a preliminary headquarters review was held in Sacramento with full scale projection maps, profiles, translite aerial film exhibits showing the dedicated redwood groves and traffic flow diagrams.

On Thursday, January 19, 1956, the Beaches and Parks and Highways Commissions held a joint review in Sacramento, using the same exhibits as in the preliminary review. The presentation described lengths, rise and fall, estimates of cost, unusual features, effect to state parks and the value to highway users.

Public Hearings Held

Both commissions approved the proposal in principal reserving their final action until they could review the broad aspects of the study.

On January 25, 1956, G. T. McCoy, State Highway Engineer, approved the location as recommended.

On February 8, 1956, a public hearing was held in Garberville at the Garberville Theater. Approximately 350 people attended; some from as far south as San Francisco and as far north as Crescent City. The same exhibit maps and presentation as in the Sacramento hearings were used.

Upon completion of the presentation, the audience was invited to express its views regarding this proposal. Notwithstanding the tremendous impact an improvement such as described would have at a local level, there was not a single dissenting voice. However, there were numerous representatives from civic organizations who expressed their satisfaction and concurrence in the proposed routing.

Supervisors and Highway Commission Act

On the Monday following this hearing, the Humboldt County Board of Supervisors passed a resolution favoring the recommended route and waiving a formal commission hearing.

On March 21, 1956, the California State Highway Commission at its regular meeting adopted the proposed routing thus officially clearing the way for surveys, design and construction.

So far, this article has described the highlights of important events that have transpired between the dates August 20, 1953, and March 21, 1956. Without going into a great amount of detail, the proposed location can best be described as a line generally following either on the east or west side of the South Fork of the Eel River from Mendocino County line to Dyerville, the confluence of the South Fork and Eel River a distance of 33.4 miles via the recommended line versus 40.4 miles via the existing highway. From Dyerville it follows the westerly slopes of the Eel River to Jordan Creek, a distance of 9.5 miles via the recommended line versus 9.6 miles via the existing highway for a total length of 42.9 miles and 50.0 miles, respectively, or a savings of 7.1 miles.

Design of Freeway

It is planned as a full freeway on a standard 60-foot, four-lane divided section without access to the abutting properties except through planned frontage roads and interchanges.

The existing road will be preserved for local, tourist and recreational traffic as well as serving as a frontage road for a good portion of its total length. By removing heavy hauling equipment and fast through traffic, its value to the public will be considerably enhanced and a pleasure to drive when time is no longer a factor.

The savings in length of travel more or less indicates that large reductions were made by taking advantage of the shorter distance across loops in the meandering river.

In general, the recommended line is slightly higher than the existing with a total rise and fall of close to 5,600 feet versus 4,600 feet in the existing facility over its total length. However,

the weighted grade which is the sum
of the vertical ordinates divided by
its length is only 3.55 percent for the
first 14 miles and less than 2 percent
for the next 36 miles. Perhaps the
most outstanding feature of the proposed improvement to the highway
user is the reduction and elimination
of the number of substandard curves.
The recommended line contains 143
curves of minimum 50 miles per hour
and 3,800 degrees total curvature;
whereas, the existing road contains an
assortment of compound, broken back
and reversing curves totaling 10,000
degrees of curvature, with safe speeds
reduced to as low as 20 miles per
hour.

River Crossings

The South Fork of the Eel River
will be crossed six times with major
structures. In most instances, these
bridges are planned to serve a twofold purpose of crossing the river and
also act as a separation structure over
the existing highway.

When this section is constructed
and placed in service, highway users
from wherever they originate will be
able to pass through this area and enjoy maximum safety, physical comfort and convenience. Commercial
traffic will have tangible proof of savings in operational cost. Through traffic will be free from dangerous cross
movements and long slow-moving
traffic queues. Commuting traffic will
have safe ingress and egress through
conveniently located interchanges.
Tourists will be able to view changing
scenery and close inspection of groves
or places they wish to visit by making
use of these interchange facilities.
Communities will benefit by the removal of impatient through traffic,
thus making their streets safer and
more inviting to the bona fide customer.

Study Took Two and One-half Years

Of incidental interest is the amount
of time and effort that went into this
study. It may be noted in the text that
it was a matter of 2½ years from its
inception to approval by the Highway
Commission. However, it was a matter of less than 11 months from delivery of the aerial survey maps to sub-

... Continued on page 37

TOP—Redwood Highway crosses the South Fork of the Eel River at Dyerville. This bridge will continue to
serve as part of traffic interchange system on new freeway. CENTER—The Blair-Lonsdale State Park on the
Redwood Highway in Humboldt County, typical of the large redwood groves which were a major factor in
determining new highway location. BOTTOM—Richardson Grove State Park in southern Humboldt County,
with existing Redwood Highway passing through the large, stately trees.

US 40

*Four-laning Progresses—New
Ben Ali-Roseville Freeway Dedicated*

By HELEN HALSTED, Assistant Editor

THE 13-MILE Ben Ali-Roseville Freeway was officially opened to traffic Tuesday morning, April 24th, when Lieutenant Governor Harold J. Powers, representing Governor Goodwin J. Knight, applied a torch to the "golden" chain across the freeway, signalizing completion of the $5,500,-000 project.

Governor Knight was officiating at two dedications in Santa Clara County on that day, one a ribbon cutting at the opening of the section of US 101 between Ford Road and Madrone, the other at the formal dedication of the Lexington Dam near Los Gatos.

Helicopters, band music, the presentation of colors, invocation and speeches were features of the ceremonies at the Spruce Avenue overcrossing about half way between Roseville and Ben Ali. Sponsored by the Roseville Area Chamber of Commerce, the Greater North Area Chamber of Commerce, and the Greater Sacramento Chamber of Commerce, the event was attended by 500 representatives of gratified civic organizations, officials, and citizens from surrounding communities. The armed forces were well represented at the road opening. Major General Roy L. Green, USA, Commander of the 49th Infantry Division, and Colonel Johnnie R. Dyer, Commander of McClellan AFB, dropped in for the ceremonies by helicopter.

Senator Johnson Master of Ceremonies

Music was provided by the Roseville Joint Union High School Band and a color guard of the California Cadet Corps of San Juan Union High School presented the colors. The invocation was by the Rev. Floyd Brown, pastor of the First Baptist Church of Roseville. State Senator Harold T. Johnson of Placer County was master of ceremonies and he introduced a host of state and local officials.

State Highway Engineer George T. McCoy at microphone. CENTER—Selden Menefee, President Greater North Area Chamber of Commerce. LEFT—State Senator Harold T. Johnson.

Speakers at the ceremonies included Senator Earl Desmond, State Highway Engineer George T. McCoy, Director of Public Works Frank B. Durkee, and Lieutenant Governor Powers, and others.

Freeway Law Constitutional

Durkee pointed out that litigation over the relocation of US 40 (State Route 3) between Ben Ali and Roseville established two things: one, that the freeway law is constitutional; and two, the right of the California Highway Commission to relocate any part of the State Highway System. The so-called bond act roads are in no different category with respect to their location than other highways in the system.

Governor Powers in a brief but forceful speech said that since the Legislature took cognizance in 1947 of the need for more highway financing, $1,650,000,000 had been spent for highways—more than had been spent in all the 37 years previously.

McCoy's remarks were as follows:

"Today you are celebrating, with appropriate ceremonies, the completion of an important 13-mile section of the State Highway System. It is also an important part of the National System of Interstate Highways.

Long Range Planning

"California is currently spending some $250,000,000 per year on state highway construction (including rights of way). Mile by mile, and in accordance with carefully worked out long-range planning, we are obtaining a highway system adequate to meet our needs—but it will take a long time, under the present financing program, to do the job.

"Experience has taught us that the only permanent solution to the problem of building traffic capacity and safety into highways is to make them freeways. The Federal Government has recognized this fact, also, and requires the states to plan all interstate system highways on a freeway basis. Like other truly worthwhile things, freeways tend to be expensive.

"As you have undoubtedly seen in the newspapers, the Congress is now considering legislation which, if enacted, will nearly double our highway construction program in California. The bulk of the increased federal funds would be concentrated on the interstate system. This would mean faster improvement of US 40 and other interstate routes in California, and at the same time would release more of our state funds for use on other highways.

"Freeway design improves with experience. Each new freeway that we build incorporates some improvements over those which were built earlier, and this project is no exception.

"Speaking for the engineers and the other workers of the State Division of Highways, we pledge our continued full-scale efforts toward providing the people of California with a system of freeways and other modern highways of which they can be proud. We shall continue to build these highways as rapidly as available funds permit."

Durkee's talk included the following information regarding U. S. Highway 40:

US 40 Progress

1. The length of US 40 from San Francisco to the Nevada line is 211 miles on the traveled way.

2. Not including the Ben Ali-Roseville section, 100 miles have been completed to four-lane standards. Opening of the Ben Ali-Roseville Freeway will increase this by 13.5 miles.

3. Fourteen projects are under way (including work at Carquinez and the Ben Ali-Roseville Freeway) covering a total of 31.6 miles at an approximate total cost of $54,000,000 (see list).

4. Freeway declarations now cover 159 miles of US 40 between San Francisco and the Nevada line. (A tentative routing for 16 miles between Donner Lake and Floriston was discussed at a public meeting in Truckee April 7th.)

5. Projects budgeted but not yet advertised for bid cover 21 miles and will cost a total of approximately $11,364,000.

(a) One mile east of Newcastle to Elm Avenue in Auburn, 3.1 miles, grading and paving for freeway, total estimated cost $1,646,000.

(b) Heather Glen to Colfax, 6.1 miles, expressway, total estimated cost $3,250,000.

(c) Colfax to near Magra, 6.5 miles, expressway, total estimated cost $3,868,000.

(d) Near Floriston to Nevada line, 5.3 miles, expressway, total estimated cost $2,600,000.

Projects Under Construction on US 40

1. Toll Plaza and Port of Oakland Overcrossing revise facilities, $2,635,000 (Bay Bridge funds).

2. South of University to El Cerrito Overhead, eight-lane freeway, 1.9 miles, $2,230,000.

3. 0.2 mile south of Jefferson to south of County Road 24, freeway, 4.8 miles, $5,461,000.

UPPER—Lieutenant Governor Harold J. Powers applies torch to "golden" chain. LOWER—Auto caravans head for Sacramento and Roseville following dedication ceremony.

4. South of Hilltop Drive to north of Hercules, freeway, 4.9 miles, $7,413,000.

5. North of Hercules to Crockett Road, freeway, 2.9 miles, $7,829,000 (toll bridge funds).

6. Carquinez Bridge substructure, $5,942,000 (toll bridge funds).

7. Carquinez Bridge superstructure, $9,973,000 (toll bridge funds).

8. Crockett Interchange, freeway and bridge approaches, $5,090,000 (toll bridge funds).

9. Between Vallejo Wye and Alhambra Street, 0.9, grade surface and structures, $474,000.

10. Ben Ali to 0.5 mile east of Roseville, freeway, 13.5 miles, $5,400,000.

11. One mile east of Newcastle to Elm Street in Auburn, structures for freeway, $391,000.

12. West Auburn Underpass, $505,000.

13. One mile west of Applegate to Heather Glen, expressway, 2.7 miles, $644,000.

14. Colfax to Yuba Gap, truck turnouts, $100,000.

New Directional Signs

The Ben Ali-Roseville Freeway is not only a typical modern freeway in its design and construction, but it may also be a model for highways of

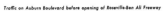

Upper and lower case letters are used in directional signs on the new Ben Ali-Roseville Freeway. The signs were installed on a test basis in an attempt to improve readability. Heretofore only overhead illuminated signs were of this type, the others all capital letters.

BEN ALI-ROSEVILLE FREEWAY

Length—13.5 miles from Ben Ali to 0.5 mile east of Roseville

Approximate cost (including right of way)—$5,500,000

Work began July 17, 1953

Major contracts:

1. Between 1 mile south and 0.5 mile east of Roseville—grading 3.5 miles and construction of six bridges; awarded June 10, 1953—cost $1,389,237; Ukropina, Pollock, Kral and Ukropina, Contractor.

2. Between Ben Ali and Placer County line—construct seven bridges and approaches; awarded August 6, 1953—cost $659,976; Ukropina, Pollock, Kral and Ukropina, Contractor.

3. Between Ben Ali and one mile south of Roseville, grading 10.3 miles and surfacing frontage roads and overcrossing roads; awarded December 7, 1954, cost $812,000; A. Teichert & Son, Inc., Contractor.

4. Between Ben Ali and 0.5 mile east of Roseville—plant-mixed surfacing on cement treated base, 13.1 miles; awarded December 17, 1954—cost $1,691,-807; Baldwin Contracting Co., Inc., Contractor.

the future as far as directional signs are concerned.

The Division of Highways has installed certain directional signs on the Ben Ali-Roseville Freeway on a test basis in an attempt to improve readability and better serve the motoring public. If they prove successful, some of the sign types may become standard and take their places on the highways throughout the State.

The principal difference which an observing motorist will note is the use of small letters after initial capitals (upper and lower case) in the directional signs. Heretofore only overhead illuminated signs were of this type. Others were all capital letters. Most newspapers have long since adopted the upper and lower case

style in their headlines for better readability.

One of the most interesting developments will be noted at night at the east-bound Fulton Avenue turnoff. There black light (ultra violet) will be used to illuminate fluorescent material on 18-inch and 12-inch letters reading "Fulton Avenue" and a directional arrow pointing to the right. The sign is 18 feet long and 40 inches wide and is placed 17 feet above the ground.

First Application

This is the first application in highway signing in California of the black light principle which makes the letters of a sign glow and stand out while the background remains invisible. Such signs have been used in commer-

cial advertising where permanence is not the important factor that it is in highway signing.

Weathering rapidly reduced the effectiveness of the fluorescent material on such signs previously tested for highway use. Now a method of putting a porcelainized, glass-like finish over the letters has been developed which preserves the fluorescence.

On the conventional reflective signs, colored backgrounds are being tested as possible replacement for the standard black. Green reflective sheeting is used for directional signs and blue for *no turn* signs.

Against the green reflectorized background two types of lettering are being tested—metal cut-out letters fitted with reflector buttons and cut-out letters made of reflective sheeting.

Traffic on Auburn Boulevard before opening of Roseville-Ben Ali Freeway

Sacramento Canyon

Interesting Background of New State Highway

By H. CLYDE AMESBURY, District Traffic Engineer

WE who now live here in Shasta County accept the route through the Sacramento Canyon as being the main thoroughfare to the north, but there is every reason to believe that this is only true since the relatively short era of modern transportation.

Prior to the coming of the white men, it is probable that the canyon route was little used. It was too tough. Such north and south travel as there was detoured around it. It is significant that the first white man to reach Shasta County, which occurred in 1829, came from the north but did not come through the canyon.

Jedediah Smith first came to the San Gabriel Mission, near what is now Los Angeles, in 1828. He had 18 men and 300 horses and mules. He was not welcomed by the Spaniards and was forced to leave. He went back to Salt Lake City, but next year he started out again. This time he came down the Columbia River, turned south at Walla Walla and arrived in the vicinity of Sacramento by following the American River. This he named the Wild River because the Indians who had never seen a white man, fled wildly at his approach.

From the Sacramento area, he turned north along the east bank of the Sacramento, crossed some place in the vicinity of Red Bluff and came into Shasta County. The expedition there turned west into Trinity County and the vicinity of Burnt Ranch.

At this time there was considerable mystery as to whence the Sacramento River came. One old map showed it as draining from the Great Salt Lake.

Coming of Trappers and Traders

Trappers and traders followed the footsteps of the Smith expedition to reach the Sacramento Valley, but they did not come through the canyon. They mostly came from Oregon down the lower Klamath Lake area,

DEVELOPMENT OF TRAVELED WAYS FROM THE SACRAMENTO VALLEY TO YREKA 1825-1956

thence southwest to the Pit River and Cow Creek to the valley.

Oddly enough, the first activity that might be considered as an effort to use the canyon route was the attempt to move a herd of cattle from California to Oregon. This occurred in 1837 and was an endeavor by Ewing Young.

He came to California in 1830 and soon after went to Oregon. He became acquainted with, and indignant at the Hudson Bay Company because they would not let the settlers buy any cattle. The company owned 28 head and they wouldn't sell any.

Young formed the Willamette Cattle Company with a capital of $3,000. He was president, and a Mr. Edwards was treasurer. He then came down to California to buy cattle and take them back to Oregon.

Deal in Cattle

As a first step, he went to Santa Cruz and bought 40 head of horses. Then he went to see Governor Alvarado at Monterey to arrange for buying cattle. At first he met with a blank refusal. After lengthy negotiations, he finally got an order on the San Francisco Mission to sell him 30 bulls and 170 cows. He was then to be allowed to buy enough additional to bring his herd up to 700 head. He was to pay the Spanish Governor for the 500 head even though the cattle belonged to the Mission.

When he presented his order to the Mission Padres they did not wish to dispose of any cows and deliberately misread the order to mean that they were to supply 170 bulls and 30 cows. This meant more trips to Monterey and Santa Cruz. Finally, he got this straightened out.

The Missions were required to gather the cattle, but when Young went to get them, he found some of them had been starved and beaten to bring them under submission to the extent that they could not travel. Again Young engaged in a hassle and finally got these animals replaced. Finally, he was ready. Don't forget that Young originally had only $3,000. With this, he had purchased 40 horses, 700 head of cattle, bought necessary supplies and had enough to hire men to help take the herd to Oregon. The price of beef was not as high then in California as it is now.

Fording a River

The crew and herd started out. At the first river they encountered, the San Jose, the herd absolutely refused to cross. Crossing rivers wasn't in their contract. The drivers then built a raft, lassoed a few calves and ferried them across. The theory was that the cows would follow. It didn't work. Finally they had to build a holding corral on the opposite bank, lassoed

Typical highway construction in Sacramento Canyon about 1928. Dotted line shows road before relocation.

a few head at a time, and dragged them across the river with the raft. It took 30 days to get the herd across this stream.

On August 14, 1837, they crossed the Sacramento River near Red Bluff. Shortly thereafter, he passed through Poverty Flat, now the site of Redding, and started up the canyon.

Picture, if you can, the trials facing this undertaking. In the first place, these cattle were only a shade less wild than deer. Prior to the start of the drive, they had never been handled and were continually trying to break away and escape. Some did break away in this upper valley and formed the nucleus of the wild cattle that were here when the settlers came later. Cow Creek got its name from these same wild cattle. Then in August, the Sacramento Canyon is blazing hot. The hills are baked hard and dry. We have no record that there was even a trail. Cattle feed must have been scarce.

Tough Trip

Soon after entering the canyon, Edwards recorded in his diary that, "Over the different steeps, thru compact masses of Chameese and Manzanita, in and out of the successive craggy canyons, they urged and forced the stubborn cattle."

The drivers want to quit but had no place to go if they did.

Later Edwards wrote, "Lofty mountains exchanged for deep and difficult canyons. On every hand Alps rise above Alps and mingle with the clouds. A repulsive mountain rises before us."

Finally, they reached Chasty Valley. Spelled C-H-A-S-T-Y. They lost 170 head of cattle on the way, but had traded some horses for cattle and actually came through with 724 head.

From here on the trip to Oregon was relatively easy. As to profits, one stockholder said he would trade his for a drink of water, so it couldn't have been a very successful venture.

Later several other mounted parties came down the canyon.

Gold Discoveries

Gold discoveries in 1849 greatly increased travel and while the first north and south stage travel went west from Shasta to French Gulch, thence north into Scott Valley and Yreka, settlements south of that place in the vicinity of Mount Shasta and Weed, made demands for a route through the canyon.

At this time, Shasta 'The Queen City" was the metropolis of Northern California. In fact, with Sacramento and San Francisco, it shared the honor of being one of the three largest towns in the State. Los Angeles was only a Mexican pueblo.

In 1849, a combination stage and mule train schedule was put in operation by way of Buckeye, Pit River, Dog Creek and Soda Springs. Passengers traversed the first 17 miles from

Shasta to Pit River by coach, then they traveled 40 miles to Soda Springs by mule back where they again took the stage for the final 49 miles to Yreka.

The mule trains generally consisted of 30 to 40 mules with packers. Each passenger was allowed 40 pounds of baggage and a canteen of water. The advertisements of the day dwelt heavily on that fact that everything was done for the passenger's comfort.

The First Road

Between 1850 and 1871, highways were in the making. They were mostly ungraded and unsurfaced. One stage going the 40 miles from Red Bluff to Shasta spent 2½ days traveling the last 11 miles. Comment on the record: "We were visited by a storm."

We do not know too much about the building of a road through the canyon. Doubtless, it was accomplished by working from both ends and consisted of first knocking off points and clearing so that wagons could get through. Doubtless bridges were built over tributary streams only to be washed out and built again. It it also highly probable that after the road was first opened, there were considerable periods when soil and flood conditions closed it to all but pack train travel.

First Highway Bond Issue

In 1902, the Legislature extended the powers of the Legislature so that a State Highway System could be designated and in 1909 a bond issue of $18,000,000 was voted to build such a system. In 1911, a highway commission was organized and seven district offices established. This commission was assigned Room 118 in the State Capitol. T. A. Bedford was the first district engineer of the Redding district.

The minutes of the meetings of this first highway commission are of interest to us now. They owned considerable stock; horses for survey wagons, saddle horses and animals for general use in hauling light passenger vehicles. Quite a lot of time was devoted to securing a suitable brand. Finally, they decided on a device which represented two letter C's placed backwards to each other and some distance apart. A bar connected them to represent a C, an H, and a C.

In other meetings, some considerable time was devoted to securing a car for the use of the commission. The choice simmered down to either a 28-horsepower Franklin or a 32-horsepower Cadillac.

This commission made a good start; many present highway policies were conceived by this same body and are still being followed.

On February 8, 1912, the commission voted to have the highway engineer make a reconnaissance of US 99 in Division II, between Redding and Dunsmuir.

Construction Begun

Apparently, this report was prepared in piecemeal. In covering the 13-mile section from Mullin's Ranch to La Moine, Bedford reports, "Practically all the through traffic between the Sacramento Valley and Oregon passes over this section when the road is in good condition, but a large portion has been diverted over other roads of late on account of the miserable condition of the county road. The width of the traveled way will average about eight feet." A little further on he says, "The existing road has rather crooked alignment with some curves as sharp as a 20-foot radius. The grades are fairly light with

the exception of the grade in and out of Dog Creek near Delta and the grade from the saddle into La Moine. These grades run as high as 15 percent in places."

On the section between Castle Crags and Dunsmuir, Bedford says, "There is considerable local travel for this part of the country, over this section. * * * The width of the traveled way is 12 to 16 feet." Later, he says, "Grades are up to 12½ percent."

Altogether, we get the picture of a narrow, crooked, unsurfaced road that was never very good at best and impassable in portions of the year.

Four-lane divided highway near south end of Sacramento Canyon, 12 miles north of Redding

The Highway Commission began construction of the road through the canyon in 1912.

New Highway Needed

It proceeded partly by day labor, but generally by contracts. These cover the period from 1914 to about 1930. The total expenditures in this period amounted to about four and one-half million dollars. When you consider that in order to bring this figure in line with present day dollar value, it would be necessary to multiply it by about three; then compare this 13½ with today's 17 million dollar estimate for the canyon construction. It appears that the State will get a lot more for its money today than it did then. The existing road was located, in no small degree, in such a way as to get through the country the most economically. The new highway, besides being over twice as wide, will be built to a location which provides certain necessary sight distance and grades.

F. W. Haselwood came to Redding as district engineer in 1932. He replaced H. S. Comley who told him that he was free of one worry. The road up the Sacramento Canyon was built and would need no more attention. In accordance with the traffic requirements at that time, it was. The phenomenal increase in population and traffic in our State has now rendered it obsolete. It cannot take care of present day traffic and unless replaced will be a serious bottleneck within a few years.

Even the section from Bass Hill to Antler that was constructed to clear the reservoir created by Shasta Dam, is not up to present day standards. However, it is likely to serve for quite a few years because other sections of the highway are much more in need of attention.

First Contract in 1952

In 1952, the first contract looking toward the reconstruction of the Sacramento Canyon was let. This was for four miles of divided highway north of Dunsmuir. This was followed in 1953 by a contract for a new bridge over the Sacramento River in Dunsmuir. This was the only part of the canyon project that could

Reconstructed highway around Shasta Lake. Pit River Bridge in background. Terrain across the lake is typical of that over which Edwards drove his cattle.

be built without a complete study of the entire canyon relocation.

Accordingly, the entire canyon from the new bridge south clear down to the north end of the relocation around Shasta Lake was photographed by aerial survey. A contour map was then prepared. From this a tentative location was made. This was then placed on the ground and checked. This probably saved two years of time. After this was accomplished, it was possible to pick out any individual section, prepare plans and let a contract for construction with the assurance that the work done would finally fit into the completed whole.

Last year, the Division of Highways completed the relocating and constructing of the 12-mile section of highway between Redding and Shasta Lake. This was accomplished by an expenditure of about $2,700,000.

Three Contracts Under Way

Beyond the portion of highway that was relocated around Shasta Lake, three contracts are under way that represent an expenditure of an additional $4,500,000. This covers the construction of a new bridge over Dog Creek and 6.5 miles of highway. All of these should be completed in 1956 or early in 1957.

The surveys are completed and plans are under way for the balance of the 19 miles that remain between the north end of the current contracts and the Sacramento River Bridge in Dunsmuir.

A real start is being made on the Sacramento Canyon reconstruction. We do not know how long it will be before the entire canyon will be completed. It depends on several factors, the most important is when the Highway Commission can make funds available.

However, when it is all completed and you can safely drive from Redding to Dunsmuir at a sustained speed of 55 miles per hour, try and remember Ewing Young. Think about him trying to herd those wild cattle over

. . . Continued on page 72

SUSANVILLE-ALTURAS ROAD IN LASSEN AND MODOC GETS IMPROVEMENT

By H. C. HOLUM, Assistant Highway Engineer

When the State took the road between Johnstonville and Alturas into the State Highway System in 1933, it got a road that had never been located as a highway; it was merely established through usage.

While the entire section was deficient, the worst portion was between Secret Valley and Ravendale in Lassen County. The road ran into and out of gulches, around the points of hills and dodged lava outcrops. Cuts and fills were limited to about two feet in depth. It advanced by indirection. As a route for exploring the area, it was ideal. As a route for getting through the area, it left much

to be desired. Sometimes the road ascended a short steep pitch with a short radius curve on top. These added a certain sporting hazzard to night driving, because after ascending the rise and the vehicle's headlights were still pointing above the horizon, the driver had to make a rather abrupt turn without full benefit of his lights!

Outside of adding light surfacing and patching the same, very little had been done to this section in the following years. There were several reasons. First, due to the volcanic character of the country, any grading would involve drilling and shooting

lava. It would be expensive. Second, anything accomplished would be for temporary relief and would not fit into the final plan and location. Third, highways in other locations carrying much heavier traffic had to have priority due to congestion and a high accident rate.

Survey Made in 1946

The district made a survey in 1946 over the entire section. After the Collier-Burns Act became a law in 1947, plans were completed for a 3-mile portion located between 6.5 and 9.5 miles north of Secret Valley, using these plans, the Bureau of

This photo is typical of the old Susanville-Alturas road

This photograph shows a typical section of the completed new highway

REDWOOD FREEWAY
Continued from page 28 . . .

Public Roads awarded a contract to Harms Bros. for its construction. This was completed in 1951 at a cost of $307,000.

In 1952 a section was constructed 2.08 miles in length, extending south from the bureau project, by A. Teichert & Sons, Inc. The resident engineer was Ellis Engle. It was completed in 1953 at a cost of $333,214.

In the fall of 1953, Harms Bros. received a contract from the Division of Highways to construct the balance of the southern portion. This was 4.7 miles long and extended from Secret Valley to the completed highway at the north end. It was completed at a cost of $547,392. R. J. Felton was resident engineer.

In the fall of 1954, Harms Bros. was awarded a contract on the northerly and last section. This project covered 7.3 miles and extended from the north end of the bureau project to Ravendale. It was completed in October, 1955, at a cost of $563,780. The writer was resident engineer.

Savings in Time

All of the foregoing projects totaling 17 miles consist of an all-paved 32-foot section providing two 12-foot lanes with 4-foot shoulders.

Approximately 26 miles north of Ravendale, between the communities of Madeline and Likely, another contract was awarded to Harms Bros. in October, 1955, at a low bid of $301,898, to grade and pave a 3.5-mile section in the north end of Lassen County. The project extends between Sagehen Summit and Dry Creek. The existing road is very narrow and crooked, with short steep grades. The project is being constructed on entirely new alignment and will be completed by fall. This project will also be a 32-foot all-paved section with 4-foot shoulders.

The improvements, completed and under way, will provide a considerable savings in time and distance to the traveling public. At the same time, in comparison with traveling over the old "tortuous trail," the route can be traveled with driving comfort and a relief from accident hazards.

mission of the completed study to headquarters.

The 43 miles submitted and adopted was the result of over 200 miles of detailed investigations at an engineering cost of close to $40,000 including the aerial survey.

The successful conclusion of a project of this magnitude that involves a great number of people, communities, towns, industries, and interorganizational divisions within State and local governments indicates the smoothworking policies that dictate and guide such projects through the intricacies of complex physical, personal, and theoretical problems involved in such an undertaking.

The endorsement of the recommended line by the Division of Beaches and Parks, which is responsible for the preservation of the dedicated groves and recreational areas, was the result of close liaison and mutual understanding of problems that demanded the utmost in cooperation by both organizations.

In conclusion, credit should be given to the generous volume of intelligent publicity accorded this study by newspapers, radio, and television. Following official news releases that the study had been completed, these organizations went all out to present the facts through their particular medium. In one instance, a team of four television specialists was dispatched to attend the Sacramento hearing which they recorded pictorially and by sound.

These recordings and pictures were later released through a series of television broadcasts in their entirety. The value of this publicity paid off by the prompt acceptance of the recommended routing by a well-informed public.

During the 1954-55 Fiscal Year the total number of contractors prequalified to bid on the various types of state highway construction increased from 691 to 780. The combined bidding capacity of these 780 prequalified contractors is estimated to be $1,472,-000,000.

California Highways and Public Works is indebted to William F. Kilcline, Manager of the News Bureau of the California State Automobile Association, for the following clarification of the histories of US 40, US 50, and Sign Route 24, popularly known as the River Road between Sacramento and Oakland:

Since the uncertainty about the routing of the Lincoln Highway also involves the routing of the Victory Highway, it will be necessary to go into some detail to clear up the matter. This is especially true when an analysis of the available information shows there are three sources for the misunderstandings on the locations of these famous highways.

The first uncertainty or misunderstanding arises from the fact that in the East and in the Midwest, the Lincoln Highway runs north of the Victory Highway and follows U. S. Highway 30 through Philadelphia, Chicago and Omaha. At Salt Lake City, the Lincoln and Victory Highways merge and continue as one route through the Great Salt Lake Desert to Wendover, Utah, where the Lincoln Highway (following U. S. Highway 50) strikes southward and becomes the southern route into northern California and the Victory Highway, following U. S. Highway 40, continues westward and becomes the northern route into California. This merging and crossover of the two cross-country highways in the Utah-Nevada area is not always clearly understood by many people. (Before the completion of the highway across the Great Salt Lake Desert, it should be remembered, too, that the Lincoln Highway turned southward to Main Forks, on the southern tip of the Great Salt Lake, then took a southwesterly course through Tooele, Granite Mountain and Ibapah, Utah, to Shellbourne, Nevada, then south to Ely, Nevada.)

The second uncertainty arises from the fact that the Lincoln Highway was the first cross-country route to be promoted and developed, but the Victory Highway, though the second cross-country route to be promoted

and developed, was the first to be completed as a through route. This was a situation to keep any political pot boiling. Naturally, before the Victory Highway was promoted and its construction began in earnest, every city and town wanted to be situated on the Lincoln Highway, particularly in California. Thus in this State, the highway over Donner Summit (US 40) and the highway over Echo Summit (US 50) were originally designated alternate Lincoln Highway routes.

But with the promotion and development of the northern trans-Sierra route (U.S. 40) as the Victory Highway, it was generally agreed that the southern trans-Sierra route (U.S. 50) would thereafter enjoy the sole right to be designated the Lincoln Highway route in California.

Of course, interested parties on the northern route continued for a time to cling to the advantage of keeping a double name for their highway. In other words, they accepted the Victory Highway designation but, at the same time, clung to the Lincoln Highway designation, too. There would have been a definite clarification of this matter, no doubt, had not the federal highway numbering system come into existence at about this time.

With the advent of the federal numbering system for highways, highway officials, and motoring public were less concerned about maintaining the correct use of names for highways than they were concerned about federal and state numeral designations. Besides, it helped them to maintain a certain air of neutrality in local fights over appropriations and the use of these names. Signboards, markers, plaques carrying highway names consequently declined, the use of highway names disappeared, and the use of highway names consequently declined, especially since the "promoting organizations" began to go out of existence. A new generation of tourists arose who preferred to follow numbered

routes because of their mathematic-like accuracy and, gradually, the Lincoln and Victory Highway, what with changes, realignments and other developments, suffered accordingly in the matter of the public's knowledge of their exact routing.

To increase the confusion, upon the completion of the Yolo Bypass, the present U. S. Highway 40 was designated as an alternate Lincoln Highway route.

Original Lincoln Highway

The original Lincoln Highway turned south from the State Capitol to Stockton and then east through Livermore to Oakland and San Francisco. The new routing then gave two designated Lincoln Highways from Sacramento to the Bay area, US 50 and US 40. This latter route is properly a part of the Victory Highway, since this highway follows US 40 from the Eastern Seaboard all the way cross country through Baltimore, Columbus, St. Louis, Denver, Salt Lake City, and Reno to Oakland and San Francisco. It also should be pointed out that the Lincoln and Victory Highway Associations, in their efforts to obtain funds, made several reroutings which involved the "River Road" (State Highway 24) between Sacramento and Oakland. In other words, there was a short time in which US 50, US 40 and State Highway 24 were a three-way choice for Lincoln Highway travelers and US 40 and State Highway 24 were a two-way choice for Victory Highway travelers between that State Capitol and the Bay area. Thus the Lincoln and Victory Highway, upon approaching their Pacific Coast termini overlapped again, as they did through the Great Salt Lake Desert in western Utah.

This is a general picture of the situation and perhaps the explanations of the uncertainties that have arisen do not fit every specific case regarding the Lincoln and Victory Highway routings; nevertheless, they do show the over-all pattern of the misunderstandings and their causes.

Tulare Bypass

Community Made Successful Adjustment to Highway Change

By JOHN F. KELLY, Headquarters Right of Way Agent

DECEMBER, 1953, was an important date to the citizens of Tulare, and to the thousands of motorists using U. S. Highway 99, the popular Valley Route between Los Angeles and San Francisco. This date marked the completion of a 7.9-mile freeway between Tulare Airport and Tagus in Tulare County.

To the highway motorists this new freeway meant that another vital link had been added in bringing a desired goal into reality; a continuous four-lane divided roadway connecting Southern and Northern California.

To the citizens of Tulare the new freeway meant that several thousand vehicles driving through the center of their town each day would be diverted to a new highway bypassing their community. In the opinion of many people this new highway alignment, so far away from the central section of the town, might result in economic ruin to retail business in Tulare, and therefore might seriously damage the general economy of the community.

Tulare is about an hour's drive from Bakersfield or Fresno, and approximately midway between Los Angeles and San Francisco, on U. S. Highway 99. Like all other towns along a main traffic arterial, the highway route became one of the first commercial areas in the community. As the town grew, nearly every type of business enterprise located along the highway, creating a ribbon-type business area extending for a distance of nearly five miles, with the center of this ribbon development near the junction of the highway extending east and west to Lindsay and Corcoran. As often happens during the growth of communities, the center of business areas shifts to new locations. During Tulare's growth the main business area shifted to K Street, parallel with the former highway route.

Aerial view showing freeway bypass of Tulare. Old highway can be identified by row of trees across upper right portion of photo. Interchange in center of picture shows Lindsay highway left of freeway and Tulare street on the right. This street extends west to intersection with old highway in vicinity of central business district, right of photo.

Highway Change

The present highway change also follows an almost predictable pattern in the normal development of most of California's cities. Although to Tulare's citizens this removal of through traffic presented an immediate cause of unrest because of anticipated property depreciations, experience in similar situations has indicated a more satisfying and beneficial effect than is normally expected.

Although it has always been our policy to accept willingly the responsibility for analyzing the over-all eco-nomic climate of a community that has had its traffic and travel habits changed by freeway construction, experience has not simplified the problem of evaluating the changing effect but rather has accentuated the need of being fully cognizant of, and completing a thorough analysis of the major contributing factors of the economic growth of the area.

As a general concept it can be stated that every improvement, whether it be water supply, drainage, or highways that performs a service to the public at a lower unit cost than the facility it replaces, represents a capital gain to the community and, therefore, an economic benefit.

In the case of freeway development, every construction is thoroughly justified by reason of the transportation savings to the individual motorist. These savings represent added purchasing power in additional transportation or other fields for every resident who utilizes the facility, and, therefore, the dispersion of these savings is a measure of general economic gain. However, the problem of freeway influence, although involving these general benefits, must be demonstrated for maximum clarity not by general benefits enjoyed by the community, but rather by the special measurable benefits on individual properties either through their increase in value or the improvement or diminution of their business attraction potential.

In individual instances this matter of highway influence may have a marked effect, sometimes factually, but unfortunately many times psychologically; however, to measure this effect by factual information requires that the major contributing factors to economic growth be first analyzed and properly evaluated.

In spite of the exaggerated importance often given to the highway effect individually on these properties, it is a relatively small percentage of the influence exercised by these broader fields.

Community Income

In the case of the City of Tulare, as is true in every economic study, it was apparent that before measuring this highway influence it would be necessary to determine the fluctuation or stability in the fields representing the City of Tulare's major source of income. The trend in this basic income stream affects every businessman and every property owner in the community to an extent far in excess of the revisions of its transportation system. It is axiomatic that the fluctuation in this income stream is the factor that will determine to the greatest extent the economic status of the community.

The transportation system, and in Tulare that means the highway system, can increase or reduce the income stream in some specific location for those businesses primarily catering to the highway traffic. However, from past experience it has been proven that this effect is generally temporary in nature, and is subject to almost immediate stabilization by the readjustment of the traveling habits of the public, and the merchant's adaptability to accept and to capitalize on these traveling habits.

Again, and I think it is worthy to repeat, that such changes created by a diversion of traffic are temporary in nature, and are small percentagewise in the relationship to the entire community economy, and in the final analysis will recuperate so that in the broad concept the community will derive not only the calculated saving to the individual motorist, but the additional benefits inherent in an improved transportation facility.

In a study of the City of Tulare it was apparent that the area's basic income stream depended upon its agricultural production; therefore, in the following analysis specific consideration is given to this field.

Secondary effects which also loom large in the economic picture, such as relative population growth both in the county and in the city, and the relative employment factor, have also been given thorough analysis. The property sales and building activity are also major fields of activity that tie very closely to the rise and fall of the basic income stream.

This is particularly true in the industrial development where new industrial growth or expansions of existing plants are noticeably allied to the agricultural field.

It is not until these major fields have been studied and properly evaluated that it is possible to apply the additional effect of traffic and traveler behavior pattern to those properties and businesses catering to highway travel so that the contributions of the highway changes can be measured.

Agriculture

Our analysis of Tulare's income stream indicated that the majority of farm income around Tulare relies upon cotton and dairying, whereas agriculture in other sections of the county is more diversified.

Tulare is referred to as the center of the cotton belt in the county, and this crop has been one of the biggest sources of cash income to farmers in this area. Acreage planted to cotton is under the jurisdiction of the Federal Government, and during the past four years the acreage allotted for the production of cotton has been reduced approximately 50 percent. The acreage taken out of cotton has been planted to substitute crops; however, the income from these other crops is substantially smaller than the cash return from cotton.

This reduction of cotton acreage in the Tulare area has had a marked effect upon the purchasing power among the farmers, and in turn directly influences the economic welfare of Tulare.

Individual cotton farmers in the Visalia and Porterville areas were also hurt by the reduction in acreage allotted to cotton production; however, the diversification of agriculture around these communities has provided other revenues to help offset the reduced cotton income so that the economic status of those communities was not as seriously influenced by the decrease in revenue from one particular crop.

The dairy industry at Tulare is generally considered to be second to cotton in importance as a source of revenue from agriculture. The income from dairying has decreased in recent years because of several adverse factors, such as the growing competition from other producers selling to their chief metropolitan market, and an increasing trend in reducing dairy operations in favor of other types of agriculture utilizing irrigation water.

Gradual changes by individual farmers, from dairying into other fields of agriculture, is very likely being done because of necessity or the opportunity to achieve higher incomes. Even if individual incomes improve, and Tulare benefits financially, dairying as a key industry supporting the general economy has been diminishing, and, in so doing, the many business enterprises closely associated with this specific phase of agriculture have been affected.

There has been a marked effect upon the number of agricultural workers in the Tulare area because of the reduced cotton allotment, crop changes, and the reduction in dairying. In addition, the mechanization of the cotton industry has further reduced man-power requirements. Because of these changes, Tulare County has suffered a decrease of approximately 4,000 farm laborers.

At present there are 34 principal crops in the county, each requiring more than 500 seasonal workers, the greatest demand for workers being in the eastern portion of the county commonly referred to as the "thermo belt."

In the Tulare area, cotton is the principal field crop requiring farm laborers. The use of cotton picking machines has become so popular in this area that approximately 65 percent of the cotton grown during the past three years has been picked by machine.

This decreasing employment was so pronounced that it became necessary for the farm labor office at Tulare to close in November, 1953. The State Department of Employment now is able to serve the Tulare area adequately with mobile units.

This sharp reduction in the number of migratory workers at Tulare could not help but have an influence on business receipts, particularly noticeable among certain types of retail outlets. The loss of hundreds of customers who made purchases in the business district during five to six months of every year can, and do, seriously affect the gross receipts of many businesses.

Population

The 1955 estimated population of California areas and counties revealed the population of Tulare County was 2.9 percent lower than in 1950. During this same five years the population throughout the State increased 23.1 percent.

In May, 1955, a special census was conducted in the City of Tulare, and the report shows a 6.49 percent population increase within the city limits since 1950. A special census made in 1954 and 1955 in the larger cities of Tulare County revealed population

Looking north on K Street, Tulare's "main street," parallel with old highway route

increases since 1950 similar to the gain made in Tulare. The annexation of areas which had been outside the city limits in 1950, and the normal increases of births over deaths have accounted for a portion of the population increases in the cities. With allowance for these increases which do not comprise new migration into the communities, Tulare and other cities have not suffered the population decline that occurred in the over-all total for the county. The reduction in the employment of approximately 4,000 farm laborers during recent years is reflected in the county population figures rather than in the cities. Nearly all of the farm laborers reside in areas outside the city limit boundaries.

The population loss in the rural areas of the county will definitely influence business conditions, and indirectly affect the economic conditions of the cities who are dependent upon the purchasing power produced by agriculture in the surrounding areas.

Traffic

In the selection of possible routes for any highway relocation, traffic studies are made to determine the destinations of all vehicles driving through a community. Prior to the construction of the freeway bypass of Tulare, traffic studies revealed that 60 percent of the traffic entering the city passed through without stopping. In other words, 60 percent of U. S.

Highway 99 traffic indicated a preference for a bypass of the town wherever it was located.

The average daily traffic count in 1955 revealed that 78 percent of the highway traffic bypassed the south entrance into the town. A certain percentage of these vehicles entered the city at the five interchanges on the freeway between the north and south entrances. The traffic counts clearly reveal that the freeway in its present location is performing the traffic service for which it was designed by removing from Tulare's streets only the highway motorists who have no intention of stopping in the community.

Consequently, the decrease in the number of through highway travelers in front of the ribbon-type business development extending along the old highway in Tulare has improved the safety and parking conditions for the local customers patronizing these retail outlets. The improvement in this area for local shopping is fairly well proven by the fact that these retail outlets which cater to the needs of the people living in the Tulare area showed the greatest increase of any business sector in Tulare after the rerouting of through traffic to the freeway.

Retail Business

The largest available source of factual information used in this study was in relation to retail business. This data consists of sales tax reports of the businesses in the City of Tulare, as well as those businesses located outside city limit boundaries serving the city and suburban areas. This statistical information provides a thoroughly reliable indication of the economic trend in the community.

The basis of this retail business portion of the study has been a comparison of the two years *before* and *after* the completion of the Tulare freeway bypass in December, 1953. To determine whether the gains or losses of retail business in Tulare follow the trend normally expected during a given period of time, a comparison was made with all retail outlets in Tulare County.

To ascertain if the removal of through highway traffic from the center of Tulare has had a direct effect upon those businesses in the community most likely to benefit from the patronage of highway motorists, gross sales of service stations, and eating and drinking places, have been tabulated separately.

The gains and losses of the retail businesses in Tulare, as compared with Tulare County before and after the freeway opened, are illustrated in the chart on page 43. The service stations represent 13.5 percent of the total number of retail outlets in the community, and the eating and drinking places account for 18 percent of the total. Sixty-five percent of the retail businesses in the community are the "all other" group, the businesses that depend entirely upon local patronage for their livelihood.

Service Stations

A tabulation of the total sales of all service stations in Tulare revealed that gross sales during the two years after the completion of the freeway bypass decreased 9.54 percent as compared to the two years prior to that date. During the same period of time gross sales of all service stations throughout Tulare County declined 4.37 percent.

With full consideration given to all factors contributing to the sales activity of service stations, a portion, but not all, of the loss suffered by stations in the City of Tulare in excess of the losses of stations throughout the county, represents the volume of business lost from motorists using the by-

pass during the two years it has been open.

In considering the loss and gain of any business catering primarily to through highway traffic, it is necessary to resort to the fundamental changes that occur in any transportation revision; for example, if any revision of traffic flow was made in a conventional manner there would be a tendency first by all business catering to the traveling public, and then by any business which might have a portion of its income from the traveling public, to seek new locations adjacent to the new facility.

One of the greatest advantages of freeway construction with its control of access is that it restricts the use of the land adjacent to the new facility to such an extent that general businesses will find it more advantageous to continue operations in their existing locations than to attempt to re-establish in the vicinity of the interchange structures to the new facility. However, in the case of service stations, it is only natural that they should reappraise their merchandising policies in relationship to location, and if their policy and the bulk of their business is derived from the highway, to attempt to locate at strategic locations that would guarantee the greatest potential patronage.

If those businesses making this decision were able to ascertain the most suitable location, and to start operations at the time the freeway was open, an immediate shift of the location of gross sales would take effect, and in the over-all totals the community would retain its income stream. However, a period of readjustment is necessary. This period of readjustment all occurs during the study period after the opening of the freeway. Therefore, it follows that the total sales during the period of adjustment will be less than the expectancy for the area, and will increase as stations make the necessary adjustment.

In this study it is possible to trace this reaction to some degree. You will note separate tabulations on the service stations located along the superseded highway, and in various sectors of Tulare. It is possible, using this tabulation, to determine the effect of rerouting traffic within specified areas.

The actual analysis of the entire service station picture cannot be made until the readjustment has been completed.

Eating and Drinking Places

In addition to service stations, the retail outlets in Tulare selling food with nonalcoholic drinks, beer and wine or liquor, have been segregated from the remainder of all other types of business in the community because they are most likely to benefit from the presence of highway motorists, and by the same token could be damaged to the same degree by the loss of highway traffic. A review of the gross sales of all eating and drinking places in Tulare, as compared with the same class of retail outlets throughout the county, reveals that business activity was virtually the same. During the two years following the completion of the freeway bypass, gross receipts among this class of businesses in Tulare decreased 12.01 percent. During the same period the eating and drinking places throughout the county decreased 12.07 percent in gross sales.

This comparison indicates that loss of gross sales among eating and drinking places in Tulare was not the direct result of removing through highway traffic from the central portion of the city. Tulare was the only city in the county subjected to a major highway change during the time this comparison was made; therefore, it is apparent that other factors influencing business conditions in this area were primarily responsible for the loss to eating and drinking places.

A separate tabulation has been made to determine whether business receipts of eating and drinking places within specific sectors of the city may have been influenced to a larger degree than others by the rerouting of highway traffic around the city.

All Other Business

The segregation of service stations and the eating and drinking places leaves the remainder of business enterprises in the community in a category which we are referring to as the "all other" group. These are the businesses which derive very little, if any, benefit from the highway traveler. In fact, the congestion caused by through highway traffic along business streets has been found in previous economic studies to have been extremely detrimental to this group of retail outlets. They are the businesses which usually reflect the greatest benefits directly following the removal of highway congestion.

In Tulare the majority of retail outlets in the community are represented in the all other group. They have shown a gain of 8.0 percent in gross sales during the two years following the freeway bypass as compared with the two years prior to that date. The same class of retail outlets elsewhere in the county increased only 2.51 percent during the same period of time.

In view of other factors influencing the economic status of Tulare during the four years covered by this study, it is apparent that the removal of highway traffic was not damaging to the majority of retail business in the community. Following the pattern of analysis of the traffic-catering businesses, a separate tabulation of gross sales within specific business sectors in Tulare was developed to trace, if possible, the business shift resulting to the majority of retail outlets in Tulare following the construction of the freeway bypass.

Total Business Gains

The total gross sales in Tulare were 5.36 percent greater during the two years after the freeway opened as compared with the two years before. A tabulation of total volume of retail sales in Tulare County for the same period shows an increase of 1.29 percent. This reveals that the City of Tulare enjoyed a 4.07 percent increase over and above that of the county, or over and above that required to attain equal status with the normal trend in business conditions in this general area.

The damage caused to the general business conditions in the community by the losses among some businesses which had previously catered to highway traffic when it was routed through the city, was more than offset by the gains made by the majority of retail outlets after the freeway opened. It is noteworthy that these gains were made during a period when the general source of community in-

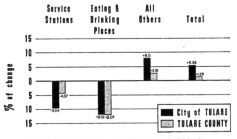

RETAIL BUSINESS COMPARISON

Based on total sales volume two years before and after opening Tulare Freeway By-Pass (December 1953)

Illustration of gross sales increase or decrease in Tulare as compared with Tulare County during the same period

come was subjected to several adverse conditions.

Business Sectors

In addition to comparing total retail business in the community with the county, the accompanying tabulation has been made to trace the degree of influence upon retail business within specific areas attributable to the re-routing of highway traffic away from the center of the city. The basis for comparison in these sectors has been the same as throughout the community, that is, two years before and after the completion of the freeway bypass.

As a further check on business conditions within specific areas in the city, a segregation has been made between those retail outlets most likely to be directly affected by the highway, and the businesses which do not benefit from highway customers.

The map of Tulare and accompanying tabulation show the location of the business sectors, and the gains or losses of retail business in those specific areas.

Area A

The Lindsay highway extending east from the freeway is the newest and fastest-growing business area in

the community. Although the retail businesses along this conventional highway are outside the city limits, they are patronized by residents in the city and in the suburban areas.

Every type of retail outlet in this sector has enjoyed substantial gains in gross sales since the freeway opened. The smallest increase in gross business receipts was made by the service stations. These stations were too far from the old highway route to have suffered any loss because of traffic re-routing in the city. Traffic on the Lindsay highway in front of the retail outlets in Area A increased 16.37 percent from 1953 to 1955. With traffic conditions favorable to service station business, the assumption would be that business gains should have been as high as the increase in gross sales by other classes of retail outlets. Apparently local influence and not through highway traffic is responsible for the difference in the volume of gross sales.

Area B

Inyo Street, extending west from the old highway route in a perpendicular direction, is also the highway between Tulare and Corcoran. Motorists using Highway 99 when it was

. . . Continued on page 65

We found the road signs in New Zealand very adequate, much more so than we had expected. The most familiar and interesting signs to us were the following: A speed restriction sign is a circular disc with a red circle around the outside and with black figures on a central white background. Of these signs, 19 out of 20 show the figure 30. There are a few cases in which additional street restriction is imposed, such as 15 miles per hour or 10 miles per hour and a similar sign is used there. The sign doesn't have any statement as to "miles per hour" or "speed limit," just the figures. The motorist is supposed to know what it means. When you come to the end of the speed restriction zone, instead of a sign with which you are familiar which would say "End 30 Mile Zone," there is only a circular disc about the same size as the other but with a black diagonal bar on a white background. This is called the "De-restriction" sign. And wherever there is a speed restriction sign, somewhere further along you will find the "De-restriction" sign. Strange to say, we found a good many De-restriction signs which didn't seem to be in any way associated with restriction signs.

ROSS DEWDNEY

Parking Limit Signs

Parking limit signs or no parking signs have a lemon yellow background with black letters. "No parking" has the letters "N P" on this sign; parking limit signs have a large P and underneath, the number of minutes permitted.

We discovered that New Zealand does not use the curb marking signs with which we are familiar, but these no parking signs and parking restriction signs are much larger and more clearly marked than our own.

Recently returned from an extended visit in New Zealand where he studied driver licensing procedure and traffic laws, Ross Dewdney, Driver Improvement Analyst of the California Department of Motor Vehicles, has included in his report some interesting observations on highway signs and road markings used "Down Under," which may be of interest to readers of *California Highways and Public Works*. Following are excerpts from Mr. Dewdney's report.—Editor.

In connection with parking, we discovered that they require much greater clearance from intersection corners and from pedestrian crosswalks than they do from fire plugs.

Stop signs are much more infrequent than they are in California. A great many streets which we would mark as through highways and protect with stop signs are not so protected over there. However, they do have a good many stop signs which are similar in shape to our own, not quite so large, colored a lemon yellow instead of red, with black letters.

All the large cities have a few signal lights, with similar light patterns to ours, but we had expected a good many more than we found.

Caution Signs Frequent

Caution signs of various sorts are very frequently used and are quite adequate. Of course, to one familiar with California signs one is slightly amused at the wording used. What we call curves are always "bends," and such signs as "sharp bends" or "caution—deceptive bends," are quite frequent. We also discovered that a slippery road was apt to be called "greasy."

New Zealand is very proud of its school patrol system in which the honor of being on the school patrol is determined on a merit system. We discovered that the boys or girls, as

the case may be, who are on the school patrol, regard their position very seriously. They are given a stop sign on a pole similar to the school patrols in this Country. We found, however, that the orders of the school patrol are much more vigorously enforced, and we learned that persons who violated the orders of the school patrol were really apt to get a rough going over by the magistrate.

Crosswalks Well Marked

As mentioned above, not every sidewalk extension is an authorized pedestrian crosswalk. The crosswalks, however, were well marked. The usual marking was a series of vertical bars, the bars being perhaps six feet long and approximately two feet apart going across from one curb to the other. We found these crosswalks very easy to see and found that pedestrians in these crosswalks were usually treated with utmost courtesy. Woe to the pedestrian, however, who tries to cross anywhere else. The car driver has the right of way and really knows it. With this exception, we discovered that New Zealand drivers are, as a whole, much more courteous and considerate of others than our California ones. We noticed that they were especially careful and courteous out on the open road when they would come to a band of sheep or cattle. Such occurrences are very, very many and very frequent, since New Zealand is primarily a livestock country, with emphasis on sheep and on cattle. Even on the important through highways a person would have to stop or slow down to a crawl a dozen times a day because of the bands of livestock going one way or the other.

Directional Signs

Directional and mileage signs are very frequent and well marked. As you came to a crossroad you would see anything from one to eight or nine of these signs in both directions on the crosswalk, one sign for each of the major points to which the road would lead. The signs are painted yellow with black letters and are maintained by the Automobile Association, and they do a very good job. The signs usually contain the mileages which we found to be quite reliable. In one or two places we found that instead of a series of single signs, several places were listed on a single sign. This was especially true in Christchurch and one or two other places.

In the North Island, most of the many narrow bridges have a sign at *one end* which reads, "Narrow Bridge, please give way." At the other end of the same bridge the sign would simply read "Narrow Bridge." The idea is that a person traveling in one direction would give the right of way to the person traveling in the other. We learned that this was purely a matter of courtesy, that there was no law requiring it. The signs were so distributed that signs on half of the narrow bridges would give the right of way in one direction and the other half in the other direction. In the South Island, however, there were no such signs. Apparently in this and a good many other respects, the usual procedures and rules varied from one island to another.

Speaking of Bridges

Speaking of bridges, we found that New Zealand has a great many old one-way bridges, becoming rather decrepit and dilapidated and about ready to cave in. All of them were marked by signs limiting the size of trucks which might pass over them. We discovered, however, that the country is replacing these by modern bridges just as rapidly as they can. Being a country with much rainfall and many rivers and streams, of course, the bridges are numerous and they can't all be replaced at once. In the South Island there are many long bridges. Some of these have been replaced by good structures, a few have not. One of the most interesting of the "have nots" was a monstrosity said to be about 4/5 of a mile in length with rails fastened to the timbers of the bridge and extending the entire length thereof. A person with an Austin or certain other very

small cars had sufficient room on each side of the tracks to fit between the outside track and the bridge railing. Persons with normal vehicles, however, had to drive with their right-hand wheels on the inner side of the rails. Considering the fact that all New Zealand railroads are narrower than standard gauge, this brings vehicles in reasonably close contact as they pass one another! We have been wondering ever since what happens when a train starts to cross the bridge at one end and the 3/5 of a mile at the other end is occupied by vehicles!

Road Conditions

The travel folders usually grade the New Zealand roads in three different types: (1) "sealed roads"; (2) "metal roads"; (3) just plain roads.

The better roads are called sealed roads because the customary type of pavement used is a surface in which gravel or other aggregates are tar sealed. This forms a very good surface and one of considerable endurance. There are a few miles of concrete pavement, some of bitumin, all of which are included in this general category of sealed roads. By comparison, I would say that most of these sealed roads are fully as good as our better country roads and some of our state highways. New Zealand does have a few miles of four-lane divided highways. These are called motor ways. Some 20 miles of good motor ways are found in a stretch just north of Wellington on the coast route, not quite equivalent to our freeways because of numerous intersections. Then there are two stretches of approximately seven miles each, in the Auckland area, of good freeway. This freeway is just being opened at the present time.

Metal Roads

The second classification of roads, called "metal road," is something of a puzzle. The word "metal" seems to designate either large gravel or crushed rock. The metal roads we found are apt to be very dusty, rather treacherous because of loose rock or gravel, and tend to be quite "washboardy." What puzzled us was that that road maps and even the guide

published by the Automobile Association show no distinction, practically speaking, between these metal roads and good tar sealed roads. The Automobile Association puts out an instructive and interesting booklet, usually quite reliable, describing in some detail each stretch of road that you will be traveling over and lists the approximate speed which you can expect to make over that stretch of road.

For good roads, they use the figures "ATS" meaning, "average touring speed." We found that in most stretches metal roads were designated as "ATS" just the same as the good sealed roads. Perhaps this is due to the fact that the average New Zealander seems to drive just as fast on the metal roads as he does on the sealed road; perhaps he finds that the faster he drives the more he avoids the bumps! To us, however, some of these metal roads were rather disappointing. There is much work being done on these roads, many of them being gradually transformed to sealed roads. In other words, it should not be many years before New Zealand will have an extensive network of excellent roads.

Not So Good

During the construction process, however, we found some of the going rather unpleasant because it seems they expect you in most cases to drive over the road during construction time. In many cases the base of the road seems to be rocks about the size of your fist or larger. Needless to say, traveling over a two-mile stretch of such roadway was a bit painful. We also discovered that during these road construction processes there was a noticeable lack of flagmen and other guides to direct the traveling public as to which way to go and how to get there. At one stretch we came suddenly upon a tar sealing in process. We didn't want to go through the stretch of gooey tar and there were no guides to tell us what to do. We did remember, however, that a quarter of a mile down the road there had been a fellow leaning on his shovel whose duty was perhaps to guide us but who had failed to do so. So we had to back up a quarter of a mile and then take a detour to the side. This lack of guides or flagmen was not universal and in some places we found them very courteous and very helpful.

The "just plain roads" include dirt roads and roads in which a few rocks had been placed to fill up the holes and which scrapers had gone over once in a while. Usually before you get on to these you have some sort of description as to what you may encounter and actually we didn't find many of them too bad—or at least we expected what we came to. In general we decided that it was the best policy not to get too far off the beaten tracks.

"Guinea Pig Highway"

One of the most interesting experiments being carried on at present in New Zealand is on a 100-mile stretch of highway between Wellington and a town with the unpronounceable name, "Packakariki." Driving south one comes to a most interesting sign: "You Are on the Guinea Pig Highway." Then follows in rather rapid succession numerous signs, many new and different, each aimed at securing public reaction and performance—studied to determine their effect on the driver. In addition, according to published news releases, it is intended on this road, "to righten and correlate control," and "to test new methods of catching the erring motorist."

At strategic points along this route there are located radio equipped "traffic stations" from which long stretches in each direction are visible. These stations are in constant contact with patrol cars. Microwave speed detectors and polaroid cameras are used to detect violators.

One interesting signs says "yellow bars show spacing for 40 m.p.h.," and we see a series of horizontal bars across the traffic lane to show how far apart cars should be for 40 m.p.h. We also noted use, in places, of the solid-broken line combination so familiar in California.

Out of the 5,252 bridges on the State Highway System, only 16 are posted for reduced loads and 63 for restricted speed.

PHOTOGRAMMETRY PROGRAM EXPANDED

Another step toward getting highway projects ready for contract more rapidly under California's stepped-up highway construction effort has been announced by the State Division of Highways.

L. L. FUNK

State Highway Engineer G. T. McCoy said that a new unit has been set up to expand and improve the division's state-wide photogrammetry program, which makes use of modern aerial photographic techniques to reduce the need for time-consuming ground surveys in highway location and design.

Under the general direction of Principal Highway Engineer F. M. Reynolds, the new unit will be headed by L. L. Funk, who has been Assistant District Engineer—Planning of District V in San Luis Obispo for the past six years. Funk will be assisted in his new assignment by R. H. Fulton, Senior Highway Engineer.

Both Funk and Fulton have been closely associated with the development of the division's photogrammetry program.

Nation-wide Recognition

Funk's work in using and adapting photogrammetric techniques in the production of highway plans in District V, which includes Monterey, San Benito, San Luis Obispo and Santa

RALPH LEJONHUD

Barbara Counties, has won nation-wide recognition for him and the California Division of Highways.

Funk's position in the San Luis Obispo district will be filled by Ralph Lejonhud, at present Planning Engineer for District XI in San Diego. A graduate of the University of California at Berkeley, Lejonhud has been with the division since 1941.

Photogrammetry Important

The division's new photogrammetry unit, which Funk will head, will not only be responsible for developing a state-wide photogrammetric program but will also carry on research to improve the quality and usefulness of photogrammetric processes and equipment as well as disseminate to all the districts the latest information in the photogrammetric field.

. . . Continued on page 48

46

ORIGINAL HIGHWAY COMMISSION HAD PROBLEMS TOO

By A. D. GRIFFIN, Assistant District Engineer, District VII

Back in 1911 and 1912 the first California Highway Commission, appointed by Governor Hiram Johnson, was confronted with problems similar to those now faced by Governor Goodwin J. Knight's highway commissioners, but, of course, not of such magnitudinal proportions. At least at this late date it so seems to Newell D. Darlington, former member and later chairman of the original highway commission, who retired from state service on January 8, 1923.

On a recent visit to Los Angeles Director of Public Works Frank B. Durkee, chairman of the present commission, paid a visit to Mr. Darlington and the two reminisced about old times. Darlington and Charles D. Blaney of Saratoga and Burton A. Towne of Lodi, were appointed commissioners by Governor Johnson on August 8, 1911.

Darlington said that the present state highway commissioners are faced with substantially the same kind of decisions to make that the original commissioners had, and that then, as now, many times they were forced to establish locations for new state highways that made them "anything but popular with the local people." Durkee told Darlington that he considered the original state highway commissioners had done a wonderful job in laying foundations for the State Highway System, and that the achievements of today would not have been possible had it not been for their capable leadership and wisdom in getting the system off to such a good start.

First Commission Meeting

The first meeting of the old Highway Commission was held in Sacramento on August 9, 1911, and Ben Blow in his book 'California Highways," published in 1920, quotes Governor Johnson as addressing his new commission as follows: "Gentlemen, you face a tough job. You are expected to build for 18 million dol-

Newell D. Darlington (left), member of original Highway Commission, and Director of Public Works Frank B. Durkee reminisce in Mr. Darlington's home

lars a highway system that the best engineers of the Country have estimated will cost from 35 to 50 million dollars."

Quoting still further from this book, Mr. Blow said: "In justice to the gentlemen named, it may be said that the magnitude of the job did not terrify them in the least. They were all men of affairs. Each had made good in his own particular line of effort, and as a committee they took up, with Mr. Towne as chairman under the statutory compensation of $3,600 a year each, what was then probably the biggest road building job of modern times."

Darlington was born in January, 1874, reared in Pennsylvania, and graduated with degree in civil engineering from Lafayette College in

the City of Easton, Pennsylvania, in 1895. He came to California shortly thereafter. He first entered public service in 1909 when he was appointed by Mayor George Alexander of the City of Los Angeles as a member of the City Public Utilities Commission. Later he was appointed by Mayor Alexander as a commissioner on the City Board of Public Works, from which position he resigned June 30, 1911, to accept appointment to state service by Governor Johnson.

Exchange of Reminiscences

It might be said in passing that Director Durkee in point of service is not to be classed as a newcomer himself. He started his state service in November, 1923, when he became editor of *California Highways and*

Public Works. After being admitted to the Bar, he joined the legal staff of the department and later was appointed Deputy Director of Public Works, and on August 3, 1951, Governor Earl Warren appointed him Director of Public Works upon the occasion of Charles H. Purcell's retirement. Durkee is also chairman of the California Highway Commission, so he now holds the same position formerly held by Darlington.

As early as 1919, Durkee had contact with the original Highway Commission as this excerpt from commission minutes on February 26, 1919, attests:

11 a.m. A delegation consisting of Mr. Durkee and Dr. Copeland, representing the Chico Chamber of Commerce, appeared and urged the commission to begin early construction of that section of the state highway between Nelson and Biggs.
Chairman Darlington explained that the commission was not in a position to make any promise on account of the shortage of funds but stated that the commission would take the matter under advisement and improve or complete said road as soon as funds were made available.

Durkee and Darlington enjoyed very much their discussion of old times and old friends. Darlington has a well stocked library and is an avid and enthusiastic reader. He keeps abreast of the times and maintains a keen interest in current state highway affairs. On his desk, among copies of current periodicals, were recent issues of *California Highways and Public Works*.

Darlington said that he found the complexity of the modern freeways the State is now building, somewhat overwhelming when he compared them with the highways on which he had responsibility in the old days. He said that the rapid growth of the State and the tremendous increase in population and number of automobiles had far exceeded his most optimistic expectations.

Darlington's home is on the palisades along the west bank of the San Gabriel River near the Whittier Narrows Dam, and when the future Pomona Freeway (State Highway Route 172) is constructed, he will be able to carry out personal inspection of part of the construction right from his home.

Young Engineers on Job in District VII

Photographed after their promotions in Highway District VII, which includes Los Angeles, Orange, and Ventura Counties, are Lyman R. Gillis, left, Assistant District Engineer, who was transferred from District IV, San Francisco, and George Langsner, who was elevated to the position of district engineer in charge of planning, to succeed Edward T. Telford, who took the post of Paul O. Harding, Assistant State Highway Engineer, when Harding retired last January.

PHOTOGRAMMETRY

Continued from page 46 . . .

In the light of a growing nationwide shortage of trained engineers and the strong possibility of a still further accelerated California highway construction program as a result of legislation now being considered by Congress, time- and manpower-saving techniques such as photogrammetry are assuming ever greater importance.

According to McCoy, photogrammetry and the use of electronic machines to compute engineering calculations are the two most promising techniques yet developed to aid highway engineers who now find themselves faced with the biggest expansion program of highway construction in history.

The Right of Way Department of the Division of Highways concluded 9,444 transactions during 1954-55.

New Highway Teletype System Is Installed

A new state-wide private line highway teletype system for the Division of Highways is being installed to replace the present teletype system used by the division, State Highway Engineer George T. McCoy announced. Installation started on May 21. It is anticipated the new teletype system will correct present operating problems as well as greatly increase the efficiency of the system.

The new system is known as a Teletypewriter Automatic Dispatch System (TADS) and transmits automatically by tape at 60 words per minute. The teletype operator merely prepares a message in tape form, places the tape in the teletype transmitter, and the machine does the rest.

Transmitters Automatic

Transmitters are automatically started in any predetermined sequence, eliminating the need for continuous watching by the operator for an opportunity to seize the line. Several transmissions can be made from one continuous tape so that the tape may contain messages to several different points, and the equipment will automatically route them to the proper destinations. The teletypes are started and stopped and stations selected by the transmission of single letters inserted on the tape. Contention between stations is entirely eliminated, and the system operates with a maximum of speed and the minimum of attention on the part of the operator.

The system will be comprised of a north and south circuit as is presently used. Typing reperforators in Sacramento administration will automatically make tape for cross transmissions between circuits. In addition, Sacramento Communications will have automatic reperforating interceptors on each circuit. Should any tape be accidentally misdirected, the message will be automatically intercepted on a tape, thus preventing a message from becoming lost. The tape will then be directed to the proper station.

In Memoriam

ROGER T. BALLOCH

Roger Thurston Balloch, 56, an employee of District X, died April 7, 1956, in the Oakland Veterans Administration Hospital. He served as a blueprinter from March 17, 1952, until his death.

He was a veteran of World War II in which he served as a captain in Army Intelligence. An active member in the Masonic Lodge, Mr. Balloch was president of the Sojourners in Stockton. He was a member of the Maj. Gen. Henry Knox Blue Lodge of Masons in Boston, the only military Blue Lodge; a member of the Stockton Body of Scottish Rite Masons, the Ben Ali Temple of Shriners, the Sons of the American Revolution, the Military Order of the World War, past commander of the Disabled American Veterans, and the Society of the Cincinnati. Membership in the latter organization requires that an ancestor must have served either with George Washington or Lafayette.

Masonic funeral services were held in Stockton April 11, 1956. Burial was in New Bedford, Mass.

In Memoriam

WILLIAM BRUCE PIPER

William Bruce Piper, Resident Engineer with the Bridge Department of the Division of Highways, died in Santa Ana on April 11, 1956.

Bruce was born in Prescott, Arizona, on August 5, 1888. After graduating from Stanford University he obtained his early experience in highway building with the Highway Department of the State of Arizona. He joined the Division of Highways of the State of California in 1928.

His work with the Bridge Department was as resident engineer on major bridge structures throughout the State.

Bruce made friends wherever he went, and will be remembered for his kindness, his pleasant manner and his willingness to be of assistance to all with whom he associated.

GRIFFITH COMPANY WINS TOPPER FOR BEST 1955 DISTRICT VII CONTRACT

With Charles E. Waite, Deputy State Highway Engineer, making the presentation Friday evening, May 18, 1956, the contracting firm of Griffith Company, Los Angeles, was the recipient of the "Topper" trophy for having completed the No. 1 state highway contract in District VII during 1955. Joe Porcher, representing the company, accepted the award from Waite. The winning contract was a section of the Golden State Freeway between Sepulveda Boulevard and the north city limits of Los Angeles which replaces the most southerly three-mile section of the Ridge Route just north of the town of San Fernando.

E. T. Telford, Assistant State Highway Engineer, District VII, making presentation of "Topper" trophy to Robert H. Butler, State Resident Engineer

A similar trophy was presented by Edward T. Telford, Assistant State Highway Engineer, to Robert H. Butler, who was state resident engineer in charge of construction on the project. Butler recently resigned from state service to join the contracting firm of Weardco Construction Co. of Montebello. Milton Harris, State Construction Engineer, presented certificates of merit to Hal McGregor and Bill McCray, the superintendents on the job for the Griffith Company and to state engineers who participated in the construction.

Scene of the award presentation was the Fifth Annual "Bonneroo," a stag banquet sponsored by the District VII

Construction Department of the California Division of Highways and staged this year at the Rodger Young Auditorium in Los Angeles. The annual affairs, this being the fifth of its kind, are primarily held for the purpose of honoring contractors and resident engineers who completed the 10 best state highway contracts in District VII, comprising Ventura, Los Angeles, and Orange Counties, during the preceding calendar year.

The winners for 1955, announced at the Bonneroo, were:

No. 1—Golden State Freeway, Los Angeles Co.—Sepulveda Blvd. to north city limits of Los Angeles—Griffith Co., Contractors; R. H. Butler, Resident Engineer.

No. 2—Highway 101, Ventura Co.—Central Avenue to Santa Clara River near El Rio — Frederickson-Watson, Contractors; B. A. Gentry, Resident Engineer.

No. 3—Santa Ana Freeway, Orange Co.—Browning Avenue to First Street near Tustin—Winston Bros., Contractors; J. L. Needham, Resident Engineer.

No. 4—Highway 101, Ventura Co.—Punta Gorda to Santa Barbara County line—McCammon-Wunderlich, Contractors; G. E. Dickey, Resident Engineer.

No. 5—Ventura Road, Ventura Co.—Lord Creek to Town of Fillmore—R. R. Hensler, Contractor—Hugh Whitnall, Resident Engineer.

No. 6—Artesia Avenue, Los Angeles Co.—Normandie Avenue to Main Street—Sheets Construction Co., Contractor; L. W. Sixt, Resident Engineer.

No. 7—Foothill Freeway, Los Angeles Co.—Hampton Road to Montana Street, connecting La Canada to Pasadena across Devil's Gate Dam—Peterson & Baker and Dragline Rentals Co., Contractors; C. J. Verner, Resident Engineer.

No. 8—Hawthorne Blvd., Los Angeles Co.—Pacific Coast Highway to 174th Street—M. S. Mecham and Sons, Contractors; L. W. Sixt, Resident Engineer.

No. 9—Hueneme Road, Ventura Co.—Wood Road to Laguna Road—Frederickson-Watson Construction Co., Contractors; W. K. Loban, Resident Engineer.

No. 10—Palos Verdes Dr., Los Angeles Co.—City limits of Palos Verdes to Narcissa Drive—Tomei Construction Co., Contractor; F. N. Owens, Resident Engineer.

The contracts are rated primarily on the basis of workmanship and ex-

... Continued on page 52

Cost Index

Highway Construction Prices Up During First Quarter of 1956

By RICHARD H. WILSON, Assistant State Highway Engineer,
H. C. McCARTY, Office Engineer, and
JOHN D. GALLAGHER, Assistant Office Engineer

DURING the first quarter of 1956 state highway construction costs were up 16.0 percent over the first quarter of 1955 and were up 10.1 percent over the first quarter of 1954. The Index stands at 219.5 (1940 = 100) for the first quarter of 1956 which is 3.2 percent higher than the fourth quarter of 1955 which preceded it.

The Index for the first quarter of 1956 shows an increase of 7.7 percent over the Index for the year 1955.

At the fourth quarter of 1955, a separate Index was prepared to include bid prices and quantities for the three contracts for constructing a new parallel bridge across Carquinez Strait. The resulting Index of 228.8 was approximately 7 percent higher than the normal Index without the Carquinez Bridge contracts and it exceeds the present Index figure by 4.2 percent. Reasons for excluding Carquinez Bridge contracts from the normal Index were based on the extremely large quantities of special steels included in design of the bridge that are not comparable in price to those found in normal highway construction.

It was our opinion last year that the sag in the Index was temporary. At that time, it was believed that construction costs would reverse to an upward direction resulting from increased labor costs. This opinion is substantiated again in this quarter and it is believed that, with many labor contracts in various fields coming up for renegotiation, a further rise will be observed in the second quarter of this year.

The California Highway Construction Cost Index prepared since 1940 is shown on the accompanying tabulation.

Competition among contractors is evidenced by the average bidders per project as shown on the accompanying table of "Number and Size of Contracts." The average number of contractors per contract, while below the average for 1954, is slightly above the average for 1955.

The table showing average unit prices bid during the first quarter of 1956 for the eight items upon which the California Index is based (see accompanying tabulation) shows an increase in five items and a decrease in three. Roadway excavation rose about 8 percent from 37 cents to 40 cents. In the previous quarter the drop was attributed to extremely large quantities and low unit price for freeway construction on US 40 between Hercules and Crockett, on the south approach to the new Carquinez Bridge. The unit price for this quarter still

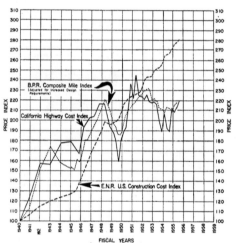

**PRICE INDEX
CONSTRUCTION COSTS**

1940 = 100

FISCAL YEARS
(JULY 1 TO JUNE 30)

NUMBER AND SIZE OF PROJECTS, TOTAL BID VALUES AND
AVERAGE NUMBER OF BIDDERS

(January 1, 1956, to March 31, 1956)

Project Volume	Up to $50,000	$50,000 to $100,000	$100,000 to $250,000	$250,000 to $500,000	$500,000 to $1,000,000	Over $1,000,000	All Projects
Road Projects							
No. of projects	40	5	12	6	6	1	70
Total value	$558,686	$333,360	$2,305,314	$2,205,171	$4,413,001	$1,477,870	$11,195,382
Ave. No. bidders	4.5	5.0	5.8	7.7	5.0	5.0	5.1
Structure Projects							
No. of Projects	9	2	2	3	1	1	18
Total value*	$195,322	$116,742	$286,379	$1,296,358	$910,694	$1,880,383	$4,664,679
Ave. No. bidders	3.3	8.5	4.5	7.7	9.0	4.0	6.1
Combination Projects							
No. of projects						7	7
Total value*						$18,173,661	$18,173,661
Ave. No. bidders						6.4	6.4
Summary							
No. of projects	49	7	14	9	7	9	95
Total value*	$754,008	$449,962	$2,491,693	$3,504,529	$5,323,695	$21,510,814	$34,033,632
Ave. No. bidders	4.6	6.0	5.6	7.7	5.6	6.0	5.4

* Bid Items only.

Total Average Bidders by Months

	January	February	March	Average for first quarter
1956	5.9	5.1	5.1	5.4
1955	8.5	5.8	5.7	6.9

AVERAGE CONTRACT PRICES

	Roadway excavation, per cu. yd.	Crusher run base, per ton	Plant mix surfacing, per ton	Asphalt concrete pavement, per ton	PCC pavement, per cu. yd.	PCC structures, per cu. yd.	Bar reinforced steel, per lb.	Structural steel, per lb.
1940	$0.32	$1.54	$3.19	$2.97	$7.66	$18.33	$0.040	$0.083
1941	0.36	2.31	3.84	3.18	7.54	23.31	0.053	0.107
1942	0.35	2.81	4.02	4.16	9.63	29.45	0.073	0.105
1943	0.43	2.36	3.71	4.76	11.48	31.76	0.089	0.080
1944	0.30	2.45	4.10	4.80	10.46	31.99	0.064	0.132
1945	0.51	2.43	4.20	4.88	10.90	37.20	0.069	0.102
1946	0.41	2.45	4.00	4.68	9.48	37.28	0.060	0.099
1947	0.46	2.62	4.33	5.38	12.36	48.44	0.080	0.136
1948	0.55	2.63	4.30	5.38	13.04	49.86	0.092	0.136
1949	0.49	2.67	4.67	4.64	13.28	48.67	0.096	0.117
1950	0.40	2.25	4.26	3.75	11.11	43.45	0.079	0.094
1951	0.49	2.62	4.34	5.00	13.21	47.22	0.102	0.159
1952	0.56	2.99	5.00	4.38	13.62	45.08	0.093	0.150
1953	0.51	2.14*	5.31	4.88	13.74	50.89	0.093	0.133
1st Quarter 1954	0.46	2.28	4.23	4.75	14.89	47.63	0.092	0.126
2nd Quarter 1954	0.38	2.09	4.39	5.18	14.35	47.13	0.093	0.114
3rd Quarter 1954	0.43	1.85	4.68	7.00	13.63	49.39	0.095	0.162
4th Quarter 1954	0.35	1.76	4.63	...	13.13	46.06	0.094	0.138
1st Quarter 1955	0.39	1.69	6.65	...	13.44	60.66	0.095	0.140
2nd Quarter 1955	0.42	1.99	5.39	...	14.46	51.36	0.098	0.136
3rd Quarter 1955	0.41	2.33	5.43	5.70	13.46	49.64	0.093	0.133
4th Quarter 1955	0.37	2.00	5.52	4.00	13.05	52.72	0.099	0.144
1st Quarter 1956	0.40	2.08	5.40	6.50	14.05	52.51	0.105	0.166

* Untreated rock base substituted for crusher run base at this point.

is one cent below that for the third quarter of 1955. Untreated rock base increased from $2 to $2.08. This 4 percent increase probably reflects additional labor costs resulting from the settlement of the extended labor dispute in rock plants in the southern part of the State during the latter part of 1955. Asphalt concrete pavement made a 62 percent jump from $4 to $6.50 per ton. This advance is primarily due to the low quantity of this type pavement used during the period.

Bar reinforcing steel and structural steel rose from $0.099 to $0.105 and from $0.144 to $0.166 per pound respectively. Of the eight items used for Index purposes, structural steel prices had the greatest effect in the upward trend. This is undoubtedly due to the increasingly short supply and delayed deliveries of steel, reflecting the heavy demand for repair of flood damage in the northeastern states.

Plant mixed surfacing dropped from $5.52 to $5.40 per ton and it is now below the price for the third quarter of 1955. Portland cement concrete pavement dropped $1 to a price of $14.05 per cubic yard. Structural concrete decreased slightly from $52.72 to $52.51 per cubic yard.

The accompanying graph showing the California Highway Construction Cost Index, the *Engineering News-Record* Construction Cost Index and the United State Bureau of Public Roads Composite Mile Index compares the three, all of which are reduced to 1940 = 100 base.

The *Engineering News-Record* Index shows a steady rise since 1949. Slight leveling offs have occurred since, but at no time has a downward course been evident. During the first quarter, this Index rose 0.9 percent over the fourth quarter of 1955 to 280.8 Index points.

The Bureau of Public Roads Composite Mile Index has, in most instances, approximated the pattern of California's Index. First quarter figures for the bureau's Index are not available at this time. Should past behavior be a criterion, it is reasonable to assume that the Composite Mile Index will also continue in an upward direction. During the fourth quarter of 1955, this Index increased 1.3 percent from 215.1 to 217.9, a rise of 2.8 points. The fourth quarter rise was slightly less than California's 1.9 percent increase in the same period.

ERNIE SMITH TROPHY IS ESTABLISHED

Commemorating the first civilian flight across the Pacific, which originated in Oakland, by Major Ernie Smith and Emory Bronte, a perpetual trophy has been instituted by Trans World Airlines for award to the 80th Detachment of the Air Force ROTC at San Francisco State College.

To be known as the "Smith-Bronte Award," the trophy was presented by Major Ernie Smith, now a TWA sales account executive, to the cadet with the "greatest leadership potential in aviation," during presentation ceremonies following full-scale parade maneuvers at the school's football stadium on Tuesday, May 15th. He is Edmund X. Loughran, 21, of 3763 20th Street, San Francisco.

Smith and Emory Bronte, now a Honolulu businessman, made the historic flight on July 14, 1927, in a high-winged monoplane which crash-landed in a group of Kawae trees on the Island of Molkai when it ran out of gas.

During Fiscal Year 1954-55 the Division of Highways spent approximately $280,000 for the installation and maintenance of signs on state highways.

Maintenance work, including painting, washing and post straightening was performed on 117,000 state highway signs during the 1954-55 Fiscal Year.

FIRST HIGHWAY TUNNEL

Continued from page 13 . . .

No doubt the legend refers to the Mission Dolores house * * *. Until further evidence is forthcoming it may be assumed that the present house or the basic part of it was erected about 1837."

Don Francisco was the unwitting leader of a punitive revolt against the new American Government. The fiasco, called the "Battle of Santa Clara," resulted in the wounding of two Americans and the death of one of the Californian's horses.

Turning to other pursuits, Don Francisco probably recognized the possibility of a smooth-traveled way to the pueblo of San Francisco. With an abundance of cheap labor available, he undertook the construction of a tunnel through Mussel Rock. Whether or not this is the way it happened, the fact remains that here is a man-made tunnel, and old records show that the beaches were used as a travel route. It is easy to imagine the don and his caballeros, probably accompanied by their senoritas garbed in colorful and picturesque costumes, heading along the beach at low tide to attend a fiesta in San Francisco.

Francisco Sanchez was a son of Jose Antonio Sanchez of Buriburi. He was born at San Jose about 1807; for a short time he was a San Francisco Presidio soldier and the remainder of his days were spent in the Bay area.

GRIFFITH COMPANY

Continued from page 49 . . .

cellence on the various major items of work and smoothness of the finished pavement. Job complexity, safety, and diligence of contract prosecution are also factors which are considered in judging the 10 best projects.

Attending the affair were 700 contractors, material suppliers, and state highway personnel. Among the guests were C. M. Gilliss, Deputy Director of Public Works, California; C. E. Waite, Deputy State Highway Engineer; R. H. Wilson, Assistant State Highway Engineer, Sacramento; E. T. Telford, Assistant State Highway Engineer, District VII; Milton Harris, State Construction Engineer, Sacramento; L. R. Gillis, District Engineer, Operations; George Langsner, District Engineer, Planning; W. F. Maxwell, President, Associated General Contractors; S. R. Kennedy, Los Angeles County Road Commissioner; A. S. Koch, Orange County Road Commissioner; Dan Penkoff, Galion Iron Works.

INCREASE IN NUMBER OF VEHICLES ENTERING CALIFORNIA

A total of 36,455 motor vehicles entered California during October of this year, 12,624 more than entered during October, 1954.

Highway Superintendent A. E. Cooper and Highway Foreman H. E. Grosser (in mouth of tunnel) pose for picture in Mussel Rock

MOBILE OFFICE TRAILERS DESIGNED BY STATE

By EARL E. SORENSON, Equipment Engineer

The acute housing shortage which developed during the early and middle forties was partially solved by the Equipment Department through supply house trailers to engineering personnel on isolated jobs. These trailers were furnished for housekeeping, with heating and cooking facilities, running water, bedroom and dining furniture, closets and storage areas.

The shortage of field office space was provided for by purchasing unequipped house trailers consisting of the basic trailer unit, provided with only heating facilities. Crude office furniture was improvised in the field. Some 200 of these office and house trailers were purchased.

Concurrently with the easing, in the early fifties, of the shortage in living quarters the need for field offices increased, and was cared for by conversion of the house trailers to office use by the removal of all housekeeping facilities.

New Design Suggestions

Serving the purpose, after a fashion, they were never too satisfactory. They were not sufficiently well constructed for the rough usage to which they were subjected on construction jobs, nor were they properly insulated against the wide range of climate in various parts of the State. Heating and cooling were both difficult owing to the restricted dimensions.

They have supplied, and are still filling, a very urgent need. They also demonstrated the need for units specifically designed for the purpose.

The Equipment Department therefore contacted the various using agencies to obtain data on their requirements, prior to the design and construction of a prototype.

A state-wide request for design suggestions brought out the following desirable features:

A floor space of from 200 to 300 square feet, and division into two separate rooms, permitting the resident engineer a private office, the maximum

UPPER—Interior view of drafting room. LOWER—Looking through file room into resident engineer's office.

width legally allowed, a high ceiling for better air conditioning, complete insulation for heat and cold, air conditioning equipment, and office furniture to be provided by using standard desks, drafting tables, map racks, lockers and storage facilities.

In other words, they were to provide facilities as nearly like that of a standard office as possible.

Shops Build Serviceable Unit

It was not practical to incorporate sanitary facilities, this because of limited space and the difficulty of maintaining them in satisfactory operating condition. It was also found that offices were usually parked where these facilities were already available or could be installed separately by the contractor as part of the construction job.

With the above general requirements in mind, the Equipment Department designed a unit approximately 34 feet in length, with a ceiling height approaching eight feet, and of maximum allowable width.

Incidentally, the recently enacted statutes, which exclude the clearance lights, door handles, etc., from the eight-foot maximum allowable width, will permit an additional four inches

UPPER—Left-hand exterior entrance to trailer. LOWER—Resident engineer's office.

of width which, although seemingly small, is very important in a unit of this kind.

The trailer is constructed almost entirely of steel, using two-inch square, high tension steel, tubular members for the floor and ceiling joists, and also for wall studding.

The outside covering is of body sheet steel, the inside finish Masonite, with trim of chrome. The floor, walls and ceiling are all insulated with a full two inches of spun glass.

Heavy duty electric wiring is incorporated which will handle a maximum load.

Fluorescent fixtures are provided over all desks and drafting tables, with numerous electrical outlets for the various appliances used in a modern office.

A forced-draft heater is installed in one end and connected to a plenum running the entire length of the trailer, with numerous adjustable outlets for controlling the circulation. Liquid petroleum is provided for heating fuel.

Provisions are made at the other end of the plenum for the installation of a compressor-type cooling unit. Valves or dampers are provided to regulate and control the flow of hot or cold air, whichever is desired.

Permanently installed jacks and blocking pads are provided at the corners of the trailer body to facilitate leveling and blocking when parked.

Based on past experience with mass-produced trailers, sturdy and well-designed units of this kind should have a useful life of an estimated 20 years, with only nominal costs for maintenance.

While the initial cost of the unit is high, it will be offset by the anticipated long life. Its use in lieu of temporary buildings, now quite commonly provided as a contract item, should result in a considerable saving over a long period of time.

The pilot model has been completed and is now on a state-wide tour, visiting all districts, where it will be on display for those interested. The tour is being supervised by Construction Department personnel who will, in this manner, not only acquaint the districts with the new unit but also obtain their reaction and, no doubt, valuable suggestions.

DRIVES LAST RIVET

At 2.30 p.m. on May 10, Jim Austin, steelworker for Peter Kiewit Sons' Co., and Judson Pacific-Murphy Corp., contractors for steel construction on the Richmond-San Rafael Bridge, had the honor of driving the last rivet on the huge span. Austin lost a leg during construction of the bridge. The same crew that drove the first rivet on the structure was on hand for the driving of the last one.

L. R. McNeely

On February 17, 1956, a retirement party was held for L. R. McNeely, better known as "Doc," in San Bernardino. Farewell gifts included a wrist watch and a matched set of luggage. He retired from the State Division of Highways on February 29, 1956, after completing 35 years of continuous service.

At the time of his retirement, "Doc" was Assistant District Engineer—Operations for District VIII. He had held this position since January, 1951.

McNeely commenced work in District VII in 1920, his first job being that of chainman with a survey party. During this period of time "Doc" covered the territory which now consists of Districts VII, VIII, and XI. At one time during this period, only one survey party was employed.

He was graduated from the University of Missouri in 1912 with a B.S. degree in agriculture. From February, 1913, to June, 1915, he was employed at the agricultural experiment station of the New Mexico Agricultural College, Las Cruces, New Mexico, performing irrigation tests of alfalfa crops. He subsequently worked as a rodman and chainman with the Los Angeles County Flood Control and Southern California Edison Company until 1920.

McNeely has encountered all types of highway construction, and at the time of his promotion to Senior Highway Engineer in 1945 he was made District VIII Maintenance Engineer. In 1947 he was promoted to Supervising Highway Engineer in the district and placed in charge of administration and maintenance. "Doc" has been a registered civil engineer since 1931.

McNeely saw service in the American Expeditionary Force in France from March, 1918, to May, 1919.

"Doc" plans to maintain his home in Southern California, but has not formulated any definite plans as to how he will spend his well-earned retirement time.

Director Durkee Adds Analyst To His Staff

Frank B. Durkee, Director of Public Works, has announced the addition to his staff of John H. Stanford of Sacramento, Supervising Administrative Analyst. Stanford will make studies and provide consulting services for the director and the divisions of the department on organization and management problems. Recent administrative surveys of the department initiated by the Senate Committee on Public Works and the Joint Legislative Budget Committee recommended the establishment of this kind of position. The appointment became effective on May 21st, and was made from a civil service list following a nation-wide examination.

Stanford is a graduate of the University of California, receiving his master degree in public administration from Syracuse University. During the war he served in the U. S. Air Force in various grades from private to captain. For the past 10 years, Stanford has been employed by the State of California. For three years he was administrative officer of the Department of Insurance in San Francisco. For seven years he held positions of increasing responsibility in the management analysis section of the Department of Finance. He is the President of the Sacramento Chapter of the American Society for Public Administration.

By June 30, 1955, contracts covering a total of 6,785 center-line miles of state highway construction had been placed under way during the eight years following passage of the Collier-Burns Highway Act in 1947.

The sum of $1,675,158 was expended by the Division of Highways for snow removal and sanding icy pavement during the Fiscal Year 1954-55.

Fire hazard and noxious weed control on state highways cost $419,000, and $1,167,470 was expended for erosion control and care of trees during the Fiscal Year 1954-55.

Out of the Mail Bag

NICE LETTER

California Highways and Public Works

GENTLEMEN: The writer is an old lady who has always been very active in getting about the state, but for the past two years has been confined to a wheel chair. I wish to say I find the *California Highways* magazine just as interesting from a wheel chair as I did from the steering wheel of my car. Never a copy comes that I do not tear it apart and send pages in letters to less fortunate friends who must still live in the east and other less desireable places—some in foreign lands.

Very truly,

MRS. M. E. ROSS

THANK YOU

KEYSTONE AUTOMOBILE CLUB
Philadelphia 2, Pennsylvania

MR. K. C. ADAMS, *Editor*

I would not want to miss your magazine. It is one of the best and most informative documents I receive. Congratulations to you and your entire organization on this publication.

Cordially yours,

WM. C. CANNING
Engineering Director

HIGHWAY DIRECTORY

SAN DIEGO 17

California Highways and Public Works

I wish to take this opportunity to thank you for a very interesting and informative magazine. It has many times settled discussions as to new roadways, freeways, etc.

Thank you again.

WILLIAM K. WORKS

THAT THEY WILL DO, COLONEL

SAN DIEGO 15, CALIFORNIA

MR. KENNETH C. ADAMS, *Editor*

DEAR MR. ADAMS: The reports of the district engineers and the illustrations depicting the terrible and devastating flood disasters which recently occurred throughout the State as published in the January issue of *California Highways and Public Works* are most revealing and edifying.

The illustrations give a clearer understanding of the damage that the flood waters caused than could be conveyed by any other media. There is one consolation left us in this sad affair; no matter how severe the damage, our highway engineers, bridge engineers and employees are capable of restoring the road beds and bridges to safe and standard conditions.

With best wishes,

Sincerely yours,

GEORGE RUHLEN
Colonel, U. S. Army, Retd.

INTERESTED IN HIGHWAYS

YOSHIMURA NURSERY
Gardena, California

K. C. ADAMS, *Editor*

DEAR SIR: As a former employee of the Division of Highways in Fresno, I'm still very interested in the work you are doing in improving the highways and freeways of this State. And since our trucks use them quite a bit, it's very interesting to read about the future plans of your department.

May I thank you very much for your kindness in sending the magazine to me.

Yours truly,

JOHN FUJITA

A VETERAN WRITES

Yountville, California

KENNETH C. ADAMS, *Editor*

I am so pleased to get your highway magazine. We eat it up here. I have been down five months. Just beginning to get a bit strong again. They tell me I sure was sick, but they take good care of us and are so kind to us. So, if you have a spare line in your beautiful magazine to give the doctors and nurses a boost, I ask you, from the bottom of my heart, please do so. I will be a very happy friend. I feel a bit better now.

Again thanking you for all of us shut-ins. I am as always,

Sincerely,

JOSEPH KISBER
Veterans Home

FROM OHIO

THE UNION METAL MANUFACTURING CO.
Canton 5, Ohio

MR. K. C. ADAMS, *Editor*

DEAR MR. ADAMS: For a number of years I have been enjoying reading this fine publication which is so well illustrated and has such excellent format and interesting articles. After reading the magazine I circulate it among a number of our officials and sales people here.

Fortunately, I count among my good friends many of the officials of the California Highway Department and that makes the magazine even more interesting. You and your staff are to be congratulated on producing such a fine, attractive publication.

Very truly yours,

W. A. PORTERFIELD
Vice President in Charge of Sales Promotion

GENEROUS OFFER

SOUTHWESTERN PORTLAND CEMENT COMPANY
Los Angeles 14, California

Thomas E. Rich, *Right-of-Way
Agent
Division of Highways, District VIII
San Bernardino, California*

Dear Mr. Rich: Mr. Halstead forwarded me your right-of-way map 426584, which shows crossing of certain lands near Victorville owned by this company, together with report from you as to the area needed and offering a price for what seems to be a total of 4.85 acres.

We are glad to comply with your request for right-of-way contract and the terms of your proposal number 7242 are satisfactory, except in the following particulars:

Paragraph 2, item A, suggests the sum of $1,204 in consideration of grant deed No. 7242, and lists the stipulations and exceptions. Realizing the very great need for this improvement, the benefit which will accrue at Victorville and environs in which so many of our employees live, and through which our commerce now moves, we should like to amend the terms to provide that you pay the grantor the sum of $1 for the property instead of $1,204.

While the sum is not large, it will indicate to you the encouragement of the project and our belief that it will be of great value to our State and the local community as well.

If agreeable to you and you will redraw the papers, we will be glad to execute them and place them in your hands promptly.

Very truly yours,

G. E. Warren
President

APPRECIATE MAGAZINE

Dear Sirs: I can not tell you how much we appreciate the California Highways and Public Works magazine. We have lived here in Pasadena since 1923 so you can realize the changes we see in our highways, and the magazine helps us to know the work the State is doing all around us. Our freeways are wonderful down here.

Sincerely,

Mr. and Mrs. Chas. Howard

ENJOYABLE READING

Yuba City

Gentlemen: May we take this opportunity to thank you for your very fine publication *Highways and Public Works*. We read and enjoy thoroughly every issue.

Each issue covers so completely any changes in our highways and we are thus able to know new routes in advance, saving "wear and tear" mentally in driving. We are also made aware of the tremendous amounts of work involved to keep our highways and our public buildings in good shape in every way.

Thank you for the wonderful issues of your magazine.

Yours truly,

Mrs. O. A. Nichols

FROM SISTER STATE

OREGON STATE HIGHWAY DEPARTMENT
Salem, Oregon

California Highways and Public Works

Gentlemen: I would like to express my appreciation for your publication and to assure you that I find it very valuable in my work. Since our states are so close together, our problems have much similarity, and I find your studies of maintenance problems very thorough and applicable to our problems.

Respectfully,

F. W. Farrar
District Maintenance Supt.

WHAT'S COOKING?

La Mesa, California

Editor Adams

Dear Sir: You can be sure that *California Highways* is appreciated and thoroughly read. It is passed along to other engineers and finally finds a resting place in the library of a local junior high school. It gives the retired engineer an insight into what is going on in highway development. Its reading relieves the feeling of being the lower half of a double boiler "all steamed up but not knowing what's cooking."

Sincerely,

L. L. Mills

FROM LOS ANGELES

COUNTY OF LOS ANGELES
DEPARTMENT OF PARKS AND RECREATION
DESCANSO GARDENS
La Canada, California

K. C. Adams, *Editor*

Dear Mr. Adams: I for years have been going to write you to express my appreciation for your wonderful magazine.

In my work in Los Angeles County I find *California Highways* one of the most valuable magazines from an educational standpoint—to say nothing of the interesting facts which you publish. I have a file of them that I am referring to constantly.

William L. Newman
Director of Public Relations

WE THANK YOU

MISSOURI STATE HIGHWAY COMMISSION
Jefferson City, Missouri

Dear Sirs: I wish to take this opportunity to express sincere appreciation for the privilege of being included on your list to receive your splendid publication.

Those responsible for the makeup of this publication deserve commendation for the instructive and human interest items supplemented by excellent photography.

Yours very truly,

J. J. Corbett
Engineer of Construction

WE AGREE WITH YOU

Chicago, Illinois

Gentlemen:

Thank you for your past issues of your magazine which I have found very instructive and entertaining.

I have had occasion to use your 'Freeways in Southern California" and I can say that they are wonderful and safe for all drivers who use them.

As a civil engineer engaged in construction work, it was a treat to see your highways, after reading about them in your magazine. Your highway organization is hard to beat, and I want to congratulate them on the wonderful work they are doing.

Capt. E. W. Falanders, C. E.

Tough Job

Santa Ana Freeway Widening Carried Out Under Heavy Traffic Conditions

By DON FRISCHER, Resident Engineer

UNDER THE WATCHFUL eyes of passing motorists, the ultimate construction of the Santa Ana Freeway on the 2.3-mile section between Camulos Street and Olympic Boulevard in the East Los Angeles area was completed.

The work on this contract, which started January 6th of this year, involved widening an existing six-lane freeway to eight lanes by replacing the existing 34-foot median strip with two 12-foot portland cement concrete pavement lanes, curbs and gutters, plant-mixed surfacing, and an almost continuous 6,600-foot metal plate guard rail mounted both in a median retaining wall and on the ground. In addition, 53 catch basins were constructed and existing storm drains extended.

To provide working space in this particularly cramped area, the existing pavement in both directions was restriped as three 11-foot lanes, and double stripes were placed three feet from the inside edges. Between the hours of 9 a.m. and 3 p.m. the contractor was allowed to barricade the inside lanes in each direction for his own use.

Despite the heavy traffic (80,000 vehicles per day) which flowed past the construction operations within inches of the workmen and equipment, an excellent safety record was achieved by the contractor. Unfortunately there were some minor collisions, usually involving what the newspapers referred to as "mechanized sidewalk superintendents." None of these accidents resulted directly from the construction operations but occurred because drivers got to watching construction activities instead of keeping their eyes on the road.

Several deviations from the usual construction procedures were allowed by the contract special provisions, particularly in paving. The paving mixer was operated on the newly con-

On left, paving construction operations; on right, typical of conditions before construction

structed cement treated subgrade. In this manner the contractor was able to work normal eight-hour shifts. To achieve early strength in the pavement, calcium chloride was added in amounts up to 1½ percent by weight of cement. Not only was the contractor allowed sooner than usual use of the newly placed traffic lanes by virtue of early strength, but the addition of the calcium chloride served to prevent the random cracks so frequently found in new pavement.

Despite cramped working area and heavy traffic the contract was completed well within the specified 90 working days. The cost of construction amounted to slightly over $500,-000. Ray Mason was superintendent for the Contractor Webb and White. The contract was under the general

supervision of Frank B. Cressy, district construction engineer, and Basil N. Frykland, field supervisor.

Stage Construction

Some 15 years ago when the first designs on the Santa Ana Freeway were being prepared, limited funds for construction made it necessary that plans be prepared on the basis of stage construction to take care of immediate traffic needs. Following this principle much of the first construction on the Santa Ana Freeway provided pavement lanes less in number than the contemplated ultimate future requirement. The right of way, however, was obtained sufficient in width for the ultimate construction. Then through the agricultural areas of Orange County the first designing and original construction was carried out on the basis of providing an expressway or divided highway facility rather than building a full freeway. Thus, in Orange County we have had many signalized intersections at grade with cross traffic arterials where we did not erect the bridges that would have been necessary to provide full freeway operation. By following these methods millions of dollars were saved, for the time being, at least, so that many more miles of divided highways and stage-construction freeways were constructed and put to traffic use that would otherwise not have been built.

Population Growth

The growth of population both in Los Angeles County and in Orange County has well been described as "explosive" in nature. This has had its reflection in increased volumes of traffic using the freeway facilities. Latest traffic counts on the Santa Ana Freeway in the City of Los Angeles near Soto Street indicate that the average daily traffic is now 113,000 vehicles. The time has now come that divided-highway sections of the Santa Ana Freeway should be reconstructed to full freeway status. Two such construction contracts are now in progress in Orange County to convert sections of expressway to full freeway status from Santa Ana, through Anaheim and Buena Park to the Orange-Los Angeles County line. These contracts will be completed in 1957. In Los Angeles County between Norwalk and Buena Park four bridge structures at cross highways were completed September 27, 1955, that converted some four miles of expressway to full freeway status.

Just recently completed is this 2.3-mile section in the East Los Angeles area that provides for widening the existing six-lane freeway to eight lanes. Other contracts of this same character will have to be carried out from time to time as the pressing traffic need develops for additional traffic lanes on freeways. There are many miles of freeways in this district where right of way has been obtained of sufficient width that necessary future widening can be carried out, when the time comes, with a minimum interference to traffic and without the neces-

This photo shows extent of widening operations

sity of getting additional rights of way. This procedure is really good business because in this manner it is possible for the State initially to build longer mileage minimum-width freeways and divided highways to serve existing traffic rather than build shorter lengths of full freeways to ultimate standards.

First Freeway Widening

The widening of the Santa Ana Freeway between Camulos Street and Olympic Boulevard to provide eight lanes is logically the first freeway lane widening to be undertaken in this district because of the current construc-

tion contracts on the Long Beach Freeway easterly of Olympic Boulevard and plans for early construction on the Olympic Freeway and the Golden State Freeway westerly of Camulos Street. This section of the Santa Ana Freeway between Camulos Street and Olympic Boulevard will be in effect a connecting traffic arterial between these three other freeways, and eight-lane width is well justified.

When the traffic needs so warrant, other reconstruction contracts of a similar nature will have to be carried out from time to time on our freeways.

SILVER STRAND

Continued from page 24 . . .

permission to occupy part of the island; and with the development of the Navy and retrenchment of the Army, it was finally decided to turn the entire island over to the Navy; and Rockwell Field closed its doors in 1938.

The Navy early established a small facility on the island and began enlarging its holdings. As the location offered such a strategic position for repair and refitting of naval vessels, its importance grew in stature until

in 1935, North Island became the largest Naval Air Station in the United States. Today, North Island is one of the Navy's prime operating centers.

Strange it is that State Sign Route 75, one of the shortest, if not the shortest, route in the State Highway System should serve such a potent place in our network of fine roads. We feel certain that were the venerable Cabrillo to return to this scene of his first discovery, he would offer his abject apologies for dismissing the sand-covered islands so lightly.

JANUARY, 1956

Alameda County—Eastshore Freeway— Between Beard Road and Jackson Street. Construct graded roadbeds, pave with portland cement concrete on cement treated sub-grade and with plant-miXed surfacing on cement treated base and construct 11 bridges and one pumping plant, completion of which will provide a new four-lane divided freeway together with frontage roads, ramps and connections at: Hesperian Boulevard Overcrossing (north); Patterson Slough; Alameda Creek (frontage road); Alameda Creek; Alvarado Overcrossing; Whipple Overflow; Whipple Road Undercrossing; Alquire Road Overhead; Ward Creek; Tennyson Road Overcrossing; Route 105/69 Separation; Route 105/69 Separation Pumping Plant, 5.8 miles. Contract awarded to Gordon H. Ball & Ball & Simpson, Berkeley, $4,326,890.70.

Alameda County—State Route 105—Across San Francisco Bay, between San Mateo and Hayward. Repair portions of reinforced concrete spans of bridge. Contract awarded to Johnson Western Constructors, San Pedro, $444,555.

Contra Costa County—Sign Route 4—On Railroad Avenue at Oak Street. Construct drainage facilities and place untreated base and plant-miXed surfacing. Contract awarded to "L" & "Y" Const. Co., Oakland, $3,225.70.

Contra Costa and Solano Counties—At Martinez-Benicia Ferry Slips and Wharves. Construct a ferry boat. Contract awarded to Pacific Coast Engineering Co., Alameda, $616,500.

El Dorado County—US 50—Placerville to 29 miles easterly (emergency contract). Remove slides and restore drainage. Contract awarded to Joe Vicini, Placerville, $30,000.

Humboldt County—US 101—At north end of North Scotia Bridge (Emergency Contract). Repair embankment and placing riprap. Contract awarded to Humboldt Constructors, Eureka, $15,000.

Humboldt County—US 101, US 299, and State Route 85—Reconstruct roadway embankments and bridge approaches (emergency contract). Contract awarded to Arthur B. Siri, Inc., Santa Rosa, $11,000.

Humboldt County—Sign Route 36—At three locations in the vicinity of mile 3.50 (emergency contract). Reconstruct roadway. Contract awarded to Humboldt Const. Inc., Eureka, $30,000.

Humboldt County—Sign Route 96—Across Trinity River. Construct a bridge (emergency contract). Contract awarded to Ben C. Gerwick, Inc., San Francisco, $60,000.

Humboldt County—County Road—Across South Fork of Eel River at Maple Hill (emergency contract). Construct timber bridge. Contract awarded to W. S. Selvage, Eureka, $40,000.

Humboldt County—County Road—Across South Fork Eel River to Redway (emergency contract). Repairing bridge. Contract awarded to Judson Pacific-Murphy Corp., Oakland, $50,000.

Inyo County—US 395—Between Birchim Canyon and Whiskey Canyon. Construct a graded roadbed and place plant-miXed surfacing on untreated base and apply seal coats, completion of which will provide a two-lane highway on new alignment with four-lane passing locations, 11.8 miles. Contract awarded to R. A. Westbrook, Inc. and Morrison-Knudsen Co., Inc., Los Angeles, $1,318,157.75

Kern County—US 99—Between California Avenue and 17th Street, on Union Avenue. Widen the existing roadway and place plant-miXed surfacing over untreated base and eXisting pavement and construct a steel girder bridge, completion of which will provide a six-lane divided highway together with a Union Avenue Underpass, 0.3 mile. Contract awarded to Griffith Co., Los Angeles, $384,352.90.

Kern County—State Route 141—On Oak Street at Brundage Lane, Chester Lane, 18th Street and 19th Street. Install traffic signal systems and highway lighting and construct channelization. Contract awarded to Griffith Company, Los Angeles, $41,699.

Kern County—FAS 887—Between Columbus Street and Main Canal, on Manor Street near Bakersfield. Construct a graded roadbed and surface with plant-miXed surfacing on a cement treated base and construct a reinforced concrete bridge at Panorama Drive Overcrossing, 0.4 mile. Contract awarded to Earl Brown, Beverly Hills, $184,942.

Los Angeles County—US 101—Between Los Angeles River and 0.2 mile west of Vineland Avenue. Construct an embankment, grade and pave Vineland Avenue with asphalt concrete and grade and pave a detour, and construct two bridges, the Los Angeles River Bridge and Vineland Avenue Undercrossing, to provide for a future freeway. Contract awarded to Oberg Const. Co., Inglewood, $910,694.

Los Angeles County—At the intersections of Verdugo Road with Acacia Avenue, Maple Street, Colorado Street, Broadway, Wilson Avenue, Chevy Chase Drive, LeXington Drive, Monterey Road, and Glenoaks Boulevard and Canada Boulevard with Colina Drive. Modify traffic signal systems and highway lighting and construct channelization. Contract awarded to Fischbach and Moore, Inc., Los Angeles, $36,835.

Los Angeles County—San Diego Freeway—Between Ohio Avenue and Waterford Street. Construct roadbeds, pave with portland cement concrete pavement on cement treated subgrade, surface with plant-miXed surfacing on cement treated base, untreated base and concrete base and construct seven bridges, a pedestrian undercrossing, retaining walls and a pedestrian undercrossing to be eXtended, completion of which will provide a new eight-lane divided freeway together with bridges, the Bonsall Avenue Undercrossing, Bonsall Avenue Pedestrian Undercrossing, Pepper Avenue Undercrossing, Wilshire Boulevard Undercrossing, Sepulveda Boulevard Undercrossing Wilshire Off-Ramp South, Sepulveda Boulevard Undercrossing Wilshire On-Ramp South, Sepulveda Boulevard Undercrossing Wilshire Off-Ramp North, Sepulveda Boulevard Undercrossing Wilshire On-Ramp North, San Vicente Boulevard Pedestrian Undercrossing (altered) and retaining walls, 1.1 miles. Contract awarded to Thompson Const. Co., Inglewood, $2,465,402.50.

Marin County—Sign Route 1—Between 1.1 miles and 4.4 miles north of Stinson Beach. Construct a graded roadbed and surface with plant-miXed surfacing on untreated base. 0.3 mile. Contract awarded to Brown-Ely Co., Contractors, Box 474, Corte Madera. $26,793.

Mariposa County—Sign Route 140—Between 4.2 miles and 0.1 mile west of Mariposa. Construct a graded roadbed, place plant-miXed surfacing on untreated base and eXisting surfacing. Contract awarded to Basun Const. Co., Inc., Fresno, $234,702.30.

Mendocino and Humboldt Counties—US 101—Piercy to Ohman Creek. Reconstruct slipouts, washouts and slides (emergency contract). Contract awarded to Arthur B. Siri, Inc., Santa Rosa, $75,000.

Mendocino and Lake Counties—Sign Route 20—Between 0.2 mile east of North Fork of Cold Creek and Laurel Dell. Construct a graded roadbed, place imported subbase material and untreated base, surface with plant-miXed surfacing on cement treated base material, surface with plant-miXed surfacing and apply seal coats, 3.2 miles. Contract awarded to Stecker & Scott, Sun Valley, $228,344.50.

Monterey County—US 101 and Sign Route 156—At Prunedale Junction, about seven miles north of Salinas. Construct an acceleration lane with plant-miXed surfacing on untreated base. Contract awarded to William Radtke and Son, Gilroy, $7,495.60.

Monterey County—Sign Route 1—At Soledad Drive, at the south city limit of Monterey. Grade, place plant-miXed surfacing on untreated base and construct portland cement concrete curbs and gutters, completion of which will provide channelization. Contract awarded to Buttler and Fox Contractors, Salinas, $3,709.50.

Napa County—Sign Route 29—Between four miles north of St. Helena and Calistoga, 3.8 miles. Construct a graded roadbed, place plant-miXed surfacing on cement treated base, existing pavement and selected material and apply seal coats, part of which is on new alignment, for two lanes of ultimate four-lane divided highway. Contract awarded to Huntington Bros., Napa, $481,849.40.

Orange County—US 101 Alt—At the entrance to El MorriO Elementary School. Install flashing beacon system. Contract awarded to Ed. Seymour, Long Beach, $2,795.

Orange County—State Route 175—Between Placentia Avenue and Carbon Canyon Creek, on Orangethorpe Avenue. Surface with plant-miXed surfacing and adjust manholes to grade, 1.8 miles. Contract awarded to Sully-Miller Contracting Co., Orange, $7,313.20.

Orange County—Between Wright Street and Euclid Avenue, on Garden Grove Boulevard. Install semi-traffic actuated signal systems and highway lighting and roadway improvements. Contract awarded to Ed. Seymour, Long Beach. $37,137.50.

Placer County—US 40—Between 1.6 miles east of Newcastle and 0.1 mile east of Nevada Street. Construct graded roadbeds and ramps and two concrete slab bridges and one welded steel bridge at Hallbom Road Undercrossing, Auburn Ravine Undercrossing and Nevada Street. Overcrossing to provide for a future four-lane divided freeway. Contract awarded to Thomas Const. Co., Fresno, $369,953.70.

Placer County—US 40—At Crystal Springs Slipout, 0.3 mile west of BaXters. Construct a bridge (emergency contract). Contract awarded to Pacific Bridge Co., Contractor, San Francisco, $40,000.

Plumas County—Sign Route 89—Across Sulphur Creek. Repairing a bridge and approaches (emergency contract). Contract awarded to R. E. Hertel, Sacramento, $20,000.

Riverside County—US 70-99—About three miles north of Palm Springs, at Indian Avenue. Construct graded roadbeds and place plant-miXed surfacing on imported base material and eXisting pavement and construct a welded plate girder bridge, completion of which will provide a new traffic interchange, 0.5 mile. Contract awarded to O. B. Pierson, Inc., Los Alamitos, $192,603.35.

San Francisco County—Bayshore Freeway—Between Army Street and Seventeenth Street. Pave roadside areas with plant-miXed surfacing, construct a maintenance building and prepare and plant areas, 1.1 miles. Contract awarded to Stephen L. Vistica & Son, San Mateo. $82,875.70.

San Francisco County—Bayshore Freeway—Between Alemany Boulevard and Army Street. Prepare and plant roadside areas, 1.0 mile. Contract awarded to Associated Engineers, Inc., Palo Alto, $45,370.95.

San Luis Obispo County—Sign Route 1—Between Morro Bay and Cambria, at four locations. Install corrugated metal pipe culverts, place untreated base and plant-miXed surfacing and construct portland cement concrete drainage structures. Contract awarded to R. McCray, Santa Maria, $4,404.25.

San Luis Obispo County—FAS 684—Between 4.8 miles and 5.5 miles west of Paso Robles. Construct a graded roadbed and road approaches, 0.7 mile. Contract awarded to Los Gatos Construction Co., Los Gatos, $40,576.

San Mateo County—Sign Route 1—At the intersection with Manor Drive, in Edgemar. Install

60   *California Highways*

a two-phase full traffic-actuated signal system with highway lighting and advance warning flashing beacons, place plant-miXed surfacing on untreated base and on eXisting pavement. Contract awarded to Hall Sloat Electric Co., Inc., Oakland, $19,884.

Santa Barbara County—US 101—Between 0.7 mile and 1.3 miles west of Carpinteria. Construct corrugated metal pipe culverts at five locations and eXtend an existing corrugated metal pipe arch culvert. Contract awarded to Hurst Concrete Products, Santa Barbara, $2,335.

Santa Clara County—Sign Route 17—0.2 mile south of Moorpark Avenue and Stevens Creek Road, near San Jose. Construct embankment of imported borrow material, 0.6 mile. Contract awarded to Los Gatos Const. Co., Los Gatos, $31,855.

Solano County—State Route 208—About 0.7 mile northwest of Vallejo at Napa River. Repair fenders of bridge. Contract awarded to Healy Tibbitts Const. Co., San Francisco, $2,230.

Sonoma County—US 101—On West Street at First Street. Install traffic signal system. Contract awarded to Karl F. Stolting, Santa Rosa, $9,446.

Trinity County—US 299—At Douglas City Bridge. Supplemental Bent (emergency contract). Contract awarded to Fredrickson & Watson Const. Co., Oakland, $8,000.

Tulare County—State Route 131—Across Kaweah River, about 18 miles east of Visalia. Bridge repair (emergency contract). Contract awarded to Intrusion-Prefakt, Inc., Cleveland, $8,000.

Tulare County—Sign Route 63—At Cottonwood Creek and at Cottonwood Creek Overflow, about 8.5 miles north of Visalia. Construct metal beam bridge railing on two bridges and metal plate guard railing on approaches. Contract awarded to Seaboard Const. & Diving, Richmond, $5,085.

Ventura County—Sign Route 23—About four miles southeast of Moorpark. Install a corrugated metal pipe culvert. Contract awarded to Taylor & Hoover, La Canada, $1,680.99.

Ventura County—FAS 1164—Across Santa Clara River, on Ventura-Hueneme Coast Line Road. Constructing a reinforced concrete bridge. Contract awarded to C. B. Tuttle, Los Alamitos, $574,714.

Yuba County—US 99E—Between 0.2 mile south of Seventh Avenue in Olivehurst and Yuba River Bridge at Marysville Grade, place plant-miXed surfacing on cement treated base and on untreated base, remodel a portion of an existing bridge and install highway lighting systems, completion of which will provide a new four-lane divided highway together with necessary ramps, speed change lanes, frontage roads and road connections, 3.7 miles. Contract awarded to Baldwin Contracting Co., Inc. and H. Earl Parker, Inc., Marysville, $930,580.39.

FEBRUARY, 1956

Butte and Plumas Counties—US 40 Alt.—Jarbo Gap to Indian Creek. Remove slides, restore drainage facilities and remove debris (emergency contract). Contract awarded to Richter Brothers, Oroville, $150,000.

Contra Costa County—US 40—About two miles north of San Pablo, at Tara Hills Drive. Install a flashing beacon system and highway lighting. Contract awarded to Manning & Whitaker. Division of Coopman Electric Co., San Francisco, $1,979.

Contra Costa and Solano Counties—Sign Route 21—At Martinez and near Benicia. Repair the existing ferry slips. Contract awarded to Healy Tibbitts Construction Co., San Francisco, $154,556.

Del Norte County—US 101—At Station 138+. Erosion protection (emergency contract). Contract awarded to Mercer Fraser Co, Inc, Eureka, $1,700.

Fresno County—US 99—Between Cherry Avenue and Princeton Avenue, portions. Construct graded roadbeds, place concrete pavement on cement-treated subgrade, place plant-miXed surfacing on untreated base, construct six reinforced concrete bridges and three pumping plants, completion of which will provide a four- and six-lane divided freeway together with overcrossings, grade separations and pumping plants at: Ventura Street Overcrossing; Ventura Street Overcrossing Pumping Plant; Kern Street Overcrossing; Tulare Street Overcrossing; Tulare Street Overcrossing Pumping Plant; Fresno Street Separation; Tuolumne Street Overcrossing; Stanislaus Street Overcrossing and at Stanislaus Street Overcrossing Pumping Plant. 1.2 miles. Contract awarded to C. K. Moseman, Redwood City, $1,568,300.50.

Fresno County—Sign Route 41—Between Shields Avenue in Fresno and 0.3 mile north of Shaw Avenue. Construct a graded roadbed and place plant-mixed surfacing on cement-treated base and eXisting pavement, modify traffic signal and highway lighting systems, completion of which will provide a new six-lane divided highway. 2.3 miles. Contract awarded to Richards-Underdown Company, Fresno, $318,361.

Humboldt County—US 101—Between Eel River Lodge and Greenlaw Bluff. Repair washouts, slipouts and remove slides (emergency contract). Contract awarded to Mercer Fraser Co., Inc., Eureka, $105,000.

Humboldt County—US 101—Near Pepperwood. Remove flood-deposited houses and debris from highway (emergency contract). Contract awarded to A. C. Johnson & Sons, Eureka, $10,000.

Humboldt County—US 101—About two miles north of Arcata, at Turner Draw. Construct graded roadbeds for approaches and a detour, place plant-miXed surfacing on untreated base over imported subbase material and construct a reinforced concrete bridge across Turner Draw. 0.1 mile. Contract awarded to Mercer Fraser Co. and Mercer Fraser Gas Co., Inc., Eureka, $50,448.98.

Humboldt County—US 101—At Mad River Bridge. Construct embankment protection (emergency contract). Contract awarded to Tom Hull, Gas Co., Inc., Eureka, $50,448.98.

Humboldt County—US 101—At Mad River Bridge, Boyd Draw and Moore Draw Bridges. Reconstruct portions of approaches and bridges (emergency contract). Contract awarded to Tom Hull, Eureka, $35,000.

Humboldt County—US 299—At Mad River Bridge. Repair approaches (emergency contract). Contract awarded Mercer Fraser Co., Inc., Eureka, $2,500.

Humboldt County—US 299—Willow Creek to Hoopa Bridge across the Trinity River. Remove slides and reconstruct drainage facilities and roadway (emergency contract). Contract awarded to J. Ira McNutt, Springfield, Oregon, $40,000.

Humboldt County—Sign Route 36—At Yager Creek Bridge. Repair bridge (emergency contract). Contract awarded to Mercer Fraser Co., Inc., Eureka, $8,000.

Humboldt County—Sign Route 96—Across two channels of Bluff Creek. Construct two log bridges and approaches (emergency contract). Contract awarded to J. J. Tracey, Eureka, $10,000.

Humboldt County—Sign Route 1—At Arlynda Corners. Construct timber pile bridge (emergency contract). Contract awarded to Mercer Fraser Co., Inc., Eureka, $25,000.

Humboldt County—Sign Route 1—Between Fernbridge and Ferndale. Reconstruct washouts, embankments, pavement and culverts (emergency contract). Contract awarded to Mercer Fraser Co., Inc., Eureka, $90,000.

Humboldt County—Sign Route 1—Between Route 1 and Arlynda Corners. Place plant-miXed surfacing (emergency contract). Contract awarded to Arthur B. Siri, Inc., Santa Rosa, $12,850.

Humboldt County—Sign Route 96—Across Trinity River at Hoopa. Construct approaches to temporary bridge (emergency contract). Contract awarded to J. Ira McNutt Construction Co., Springfield, Oregon, $10,500.

Humboldt County—On Howe Creek Road, Price Creek Road and Blue Slide Road. Remove slides, repair washouts and place rock surfacing (emergency contract). Contract awarded to J. L. Conner, Jr., Eureka, $15,000.

Humboldt County—On Weymouth Bluff Road, Howe Creek Road, Price Creek Road and Blue Slide Road. Repair and replace bridges (emergency contract). Contract awarded to J. J. Tracey, Eureka, $18,000.

Humboldt County—Across North Fork of Bear River at Ambrosines. Log bridge (emergency contract). Contract awarded to W. S. Selvage, Eureka, $10,000.

Humboldt County—On Burrell Road, Conklin Creek Road, Cooke Road and at Mill Creek. Remove slides, repair washouts, place rock surfacing and construct log bridge (emergency contract). Contract awarded to Ted May, Eureka, $12,000.

Humboldt County—State Park Boundary to Fruitland on Dyerville Loop Road. Remove slides and restore roadway (emergency contract). Contract awarded to John Burman and Sons, Eureka, $12,000.

Humboldt County—At Mad River at Giacomini Ranch. Reconstruct pile bents (emergency contract). Contract awarded to Mercer Fraser Co., Inc., Eureka, $4,000.

Humboldt County—In Eureka. Construct alterations and improvements at shop building. Contract awarded to Singleton Company, Eureka, $4,250.

Humboldt County—Across Mattole River at Gardners. Repair bridge and approaches (emergency contract). Contract awarded to E. J. Armstrong & Son, Inc., Eureka, $16,000.

Humboldt County—Across Bear River at Lowerys and across Bonanza Creek Bridge on Upper Bear River. Repair bridges and approaches (emergency contract). Contract awarded to Tom Hull, Eureka, $3,000.

Humboldt County—The Lighthouse Bridge, across Mattole River, at Petrolia. Repair bridge and approaches (emergency contract). Contract awarded to E. J. Armstrong & Son, Eureka, $15,000.

Humboldt County—Across Larabee Creek at Larabee. Repair bridge (emergency contract). Contract award to J. J. Tracey, Eureka, $10,000.

Humboldt County—Between Bald Hills Road and the vicinity of Weitchpec. Remove slides, surface and construct a bridge (emergency contract). Contract awarded to J. L. Conner, Jr., Eureka, $10,000.

Los Angeles County—US 66—ApproXimately 2.5 miles east of Monrovia, on Huntington Drive at Fish Canyon Road-Crownhaven Drive. Constructing channelization and furnishing and installing a traffic-actuated signal system and highway lighting. Contract awarded to Osborn Company, Pasadena, $44,287.15.

Los Angeles County—Sign Route 71—On Bellevue-Arroyo Avenue at Holt Avenue, at Pomona city limit. Modify traffic signal system. Contract awarded to Galland Electric Co., Inc., South Gate, $4,394.

Los Angeles County—Between Montebello and Whittier, at intersection of Rosemead Boulevard with Manzanar Avenue-Havenwood Drive. Install a traffic-actuated signal system and highway lighting. Contract awarded to C. D. Draucker, Inc., Los Angeles, $13,827.

Mendocino County—US 101—Between Station 386 and Station 391. Repair washouts and place riprap (emergency contract). Contract awarded to Lange Brothers & Hastings, Lakeport, $20,000.

Mendocino County—US 101—At Station 151. Construct roadway around timber crib (emergency contract). Contract awarded to Arthur B. Siri, Inc., Santa Rosa, $5,000.

Mendocino and Humboldt Counties—At various locations. Remove slides and debris and reconstruct roadway (emergency contract). Contract awarded to Humboldt Constructors, Inc., Eureka, $30,000.

Mendocino and Humboldt Counties—Between Rattlesnake Summit and Scotia. Repair and replace culverts (emergency contract). Contract awarded to Harold Hastings, Lakeport, $10,000.

Mendocino and Humboldt Counties—Between Jitney Gulch and one-half mile north of Myers Flat. Repair slides and washouts (emergency contract). Contract awarded to John Burman and Sons, Eureka, $20,000.

Mendocino County—Sign Routes 128 and 1—At Elk Creek and others locations and at Big River. Repair washouts (emergency contract). Contract awarded to Granite Construction Co., Watsonville, $20,000.

Mendocino County—Sign Route 1—Across Brush Creek, near Manchester. Construct a reinforced concrete bridge and grade and surface with road-miXed surfacing the approaches. 0.3 mile. Contract awarded to Thomas Construction Co., Fresno, $131,722.65.

Modoc County—US 299—Between eight miles north of Adin and Pit River Bridge. Place plant-mixed surfacing on the eXisting pavement and on untreated base. 9.2 miles. Contract awarded to Baldwin Contracting Co., Inc., Marysville, $210,218.44.

Riverside County—MAFB Access Road—Between Avenue "C" and Graham Street. Construct a graded roadbed, place imported borrow, imported base material, cement-treated base and plant-miXed surfacing and construct two bridges, completion of which will provide a grade separation and overhead, at March Field Road Overcrossing and at March Field Off-ramp Overcrossing. 1.9 miles. Contract awarded to E. L. Yeager Co., Riverside, $462,940.90.

Riverside County—US 60-70-99—Between 0.8 mile north of Indio Overhead and Indio Grade. Place plant-miXed surfacing on cement-treated base and on existing pavement and construct two bridges, completion of which will provide a four-lane divided highway with bridges at Coachella Storm Drain and Indio Overhead. 2.7 miles. Contract awarded to Altfillisch Construction Co. and Love & Watson, Downey, $488,031.60.

San Bernardino County—US 70-99—Across South Channel Warm Creek, about 0.8 mile south of San Bernardino. Repair the existing bridge. Contract awarded to Louis J. Strona, Pomona, $6,930.75.

San Bernardino County—US 66—At the Amboy Maintenance Station. Construct a cottage and install utilities. Contract awarded to Cal. Const. Co., San Bernardino, $13,400.

San Diego County—US 395—Between Richmond Street and Fulton Street. Paint metal plate guard railing. 3.3 miles. Contract awarded to Geo. C. Punton, San Diego, $2,467.50.

San Diego County—Sign Route 94—Between Wabash Freeway in San Diego and 0.6 mile east of Euclid Avenue. 2.4 miles. Grade and pave with portland cement concrete pavement on cement-treated subgrade, place plant-miXed surfacing on cement-treated base and imported base material, construct one wended structural steel and three reinforced concrete bridges, completion of which will provide a new six-lane divided freeway together with ramps, interchange lanes and street connections at Las Chollas Creek-Home Avenue On-ramp Bridge, at Home Avenue Off-ramp Overcrossing, at 47th Street Overcrossing, and at Euclid Avenue Overcrossing, all on new alignment. 2.4 miles. Contract awarded to Guy F. Atkinson Co., South San Francisco, $2,062,928.70.

San Diego County—FAS 732—Between Brockton Street and Magnolia Avenue in El Cajon. Construct a graded roadbed, place imported subbase material and plant-miXed surfacing on imported base material and on eXisting surface and apply seal coats, completion of which will provide a four-lane divided highway together with road connections, approaches and crossroads. 2.0 miles. Contract awarded to Ralph B. Slaughter, Julian, $352,452.

San Francisco City and County—Between 10th Street and Fourth Street, adjacent to Bayshore Freeway. Construct chain link fence. Contract awarded to United States Steel Corp., Amer. Steel & Wire Div., Cyclone Fence Dept., Oakland, $18,711.

San Joaquin County—US 99—Between 0.3 mile north of Lathrop Road and 0.4 mile north of Turner Station. Construct graded roadbeds, pave with portland cement concrete on cement-treated base, surface with plant-miXed surfacing on untreated base and on eXisting pavement and construct a steel bridge, completion of which will provide a four-lane divided highway together with frontage roads and ramps, including the Turner Station Overhead. 2.5 miles. Contract awarded to A. Teichert & Son, Inc., Sacramento, $914,045.70.

San Joaquin County—US 99—Between Lodi and 0.5 mile north of Jahant Road. Construct a graded roadbed and surface with portland cement concrete on cement-treated subgrade and plant-mixed surfacing on untreated base and construct five bridges and one pumping plant, completion of which will provide a four-lane divided freeway together with bridges at: Mokelumne River; Woodbridge Road Overcrossing; Acampo Road Overcrossing; Peltier Road Overcrossing; Jahant Road Overcrossing; and a pumping plant at Acampo Road Overcrossing. 4.8 miles. Contract awarded to M. J. B. Cons'r. Co. and Lord & Bishop, Inc., Stockton, $1,975,959.20.

San Mateo County—US 101—At Carmelita Avenue and at Chapin Avenue, on El Camino Real. Install traffic signals. Contract awarded to R. Flatland, San Francisco, $6,000.

San Mateo County—At Burlingame Maintenance Station. Reconstruct electrical systems. Contract awarded to Coopman Electric Co., San Francisco, $1,358.

Santa Barbara County—US 101—Between El Capitan Creek and 0.6 mile west of Arroyo Hondo, about 23 miles west of Santa Barbara. Clean and paint the eXisting guard railing and install metal plate guard railing, guide posts, and culvert markers. 7.6 miles. Contract awarded to L. J. Grey & Sons, Balboa, $20,177.80.

Santa Clara County—US 101—On El Camino Real at El Monte Avenue. Install a traffic signal system. Contract awarded to Progress Electric, Palo Alto, $8,896.

Santa Clara County—State Route 42—At the intersection of Santa Cruz Avenue with Saratoga Avenue. Install a two-phase pre-timed traffic signal system. Contract awarded to L. H. Leonardi Electric Construction Co., San Rafael, $2,999.

Shasta County—US 299—Between 0.7 mile east of the west city limit and Southern Pacific Railroad Overhead. Construct a graded roadbed, place imported subbase material and place plant-miXed surfacing on cement-treated base and untreated base. 1.5 miles. Contract awarded to Fredrickson & Watson Const. Co., Oakland, $185,330.55.

Trinity and Humboldt Counties—Sign Route 36—Between Bridgeville and Forest Glen. Repair culverts and remove slides (emergency contract). Contract awarded to Lennon Brothers, Inc., Fortuna, $21,000.

Trinity County—US 299—Cedar Flat to District II line. Restore roadway (emergency contract). Contract awarded to Arthur B. Siri, Inc., Santa Rosa, $40,000.

Tulare County—Sign Route 65—At Tule River Bridge at Porterville. Construct pier protection (emergency contract). Contract awarded to Thomas Construction Co., Fresno, $6,618.

Tulare County—FAS 1212—Between Grevilla Street 0.5 mile south of Porterville and Porterville State Hospital. Construct a graded roadbed and surface with plant-miXed surfacing on imported base material. 2.0 miles. Contract awarded to L. B. Wells Construction Co., Visalia, $83,867.

MARCH, 1956

Contra Costa County—Between Esmond Avenue and McBryde Avenue, on San Pablo Avenue. Grade and pave parking lanes with portland cement concrete on untreated base and construct curbs. Contract awarded to O. C. Jones & Sons, Berkeley, $11,577.50.

Humboldt County—US 101—Between 0.6 mile north of Plaza Avenue in Arcata and 1.0 mile south of Mad River, and on US 299 between US 101 and Mad River, grade and surface, to provide a 4-lane divided freeway and eXpressway together with frontage roads, 2.9 miles. Contract awarded to Mercer Fraser Co., Inc. & Mercer Fraser Gas Co., Inc., Eureka, $629,224.48.

Imperial County—State Route 187—Across Alamo River, about three miles east and seven miles north of Brawley redeck and widen two bridges. Contract awarded to R. E. Staite & Roy C. Ek, San Diego, $23,691.75

Kern County—US 466—At Mt. Vernon Avenue, about 0.5 mile east of Bakersfield. Install flashing beacon and highway lighting system and construct channelization. Contract awarded to Dicco, Inc., Bakersfield, $13,930.

Kern County—US 399—Between Sunset Railroad and 1.4 miles north of Taft. Grade roadbed and place plant-miXed surfacing on cement treated base, and install a highway lighting system, completion of which will provide renewed eXisting highway and four-lane divided highway on new alignment, 2.4 miles. Contract awarded to PhoeniX Const. Co., Inc., Bakersfield, $241,327.30.

Los Angeles County—US 101—Between 0.4 mile west of Washington Boulevard and the Orange County line. Widen the existing roadbed and place plant-miXed surfacing on untreated base and eXisting pavement and construct an eXtension to the Whittier underpass, completion of which will provide a seventy-six foot street, 4.8 miles. Contract awarded to J. E. Haddock, Ltd., Pasadena, $1,477,869.90.

Los Angeles County—US 66—Between 0.1 mile west and 0.2 mile east of Fifth Street, near Azusa on Alosta Avenue. Widen the eXisting roadway with plant-miXed surfacing on untreated base and apply seal coats, 0.3 mile. Contract awarded to J. E. Haddock Ltd., Pasadena, $15,783.30.

Los Angeles County—US 6—Between Lancaster and Kern County line, at seven locations. Replace corrugated metal pipe culverts. Contract awarded to Ed Waters, Van Nuys, $6,693.20.

Los Angeles County—US 66—Between Princeton Road and 0.2 mile southeast of Colorado Boulevard, 0.4 mile. Grade, place imported subbase material and untreated base, surface with plant-miXed surfacing and apply seal coat, completion of which will provide a four-lane divided highway. Contract awarded to Osborn Co., Pasadena, $43,017.55.

Los Angeles County—US 66—Between Colorado Boulevard and Melrose Avenue. Pave with plant-mixed surfacing, install watering system and prepare and plant with trees and shrubs, 1.0 mile. Contract awarded to Moulder Bros., Glendale, $52,753.01.

Los Angeles and Orange Counties—Between Coyote Creek and Ball Road, on the Santa Ana Freeway, 6.5 miles. Grade, pave with portland cement concrete on cement treated subgrade, place plant-miXed surfacing on untreated base, and construct 16 bridges and two pumping plants, completion of which will provide a six-lane divided highway together with frontage roads, interchange roads, speed change lanes and connections to eXisting streets. Bridges at Artesia Avenue undercrossing; Western Avenue overcrossing; Route 171/174 separation; Stanton Avenue overcrossing; Stanton Avenue on-ramp overcrossing; Fullerton Creek; Brookhurst Avenue Overhead; Brookhurst Avenue overcrossing; La Palma Avenue overcrossing; Euclid Avenue overcrossing; Euclid Avenue off-ramp overhead; Lincoln Avenue overcrossing; Broadway overcrossing; Anaheim underpass; Santa Ana Street overcrossing; and Ball Road overcrossing. Pump plants at Route 171/174 separation and at Lincoln Avenue. Contract awarded to J. E. Haddock Ltd. and R. M. Price Co., Pasadena, $5,929,776.30.

Los Angeles County—Between Narcissa Drive and Crenshaw Boulevard, on Palos Verdes Drive south. Grade and surface with plant-miXed surfacing on untreated base and imported base material, completion of which will provide a four-lane divided highway, 1.1 miles. Contract awarded to Westway EXcavating Co., Los Angeles, $212,-582.85.

Marin County—US 101—Alto intersection. Drainage correction. Contract awarded to Ghilotti Brothers, Inc., San Rafael, $6,945.

Marin County—FAS 608—Between Lagunitas School and 3.2 miles west of FairfaX. Construct a graded roadbed and place selected material, 2.6 miles. Contract awarded to John Delphia, Patterson, $270,106.

Mendocino County—US 101—About 39 miles north of Willits, at Rattlesnake Creek. Construct an unlined tunnel for a channel change. Contract awarded to Mercer Fraser Co., Inc. & Mercer Fraser Gas Co., Inc., Eureka, $38,590.00.

Mendocino County—US 101—Between Low Gap Road—Brush Street, and 0.2 mile north of Ford road. Construct a graded roadbed and surface with plant-miXed surfacing on cement treated base, 0.7 mile. Contract awarded to Arthur B. Siri, Inc., Santa Rosa, $133,058.50.

Mendocino County—Sign Route 128—Between Coon Creek and Ornbaun Creek, about four miles southeast of Boonville. Construct a graded roadbed, place imported subbase material, place plant-miXed surfacing on cement treated base and on untreated base and apply seal coat, 0.8 mile. Contract awarded to Granite Const. Co., Watsonville, $152,-103.00.

Monterey County—At the intersection of SR 1 with Ocean Avenue, Near Carmel. Install traffic signal system and highway lighting and construct channelization. Contract awarded to Granite Const. Co., Watsonville, $14,016.50.

Orange County—US Alt. 101—Across San Juan Creek overflow, about 3 miles northwest of San Clements. Repair a timber trestle bridge. Contract awarded to Macco Corporation, Paramount, $5,828.

Orange County—At intersection of Ocean Avenue with Main Street, in Huntington Beach, and at intersections of Newport Boulevard with Via Lido and of Pacific Coast Highway with Seaward Road and with Morning Canyon Road, in Newport Beach. Furnish, install and modify traffic signal systems and highway lighting systems and construct channelization. Contract awarded to Ed. Seymour, Long Beach, $54,727.

Riverside County—SR 18—Between 0.4 mile south of 14th Street and 0.3 mile north of Russell Street. Construct two graded roadbeds, place imported base material; construct cement treated subgrade and Portland cement concrete pavement; place plant-miXed surfacing over imported base material, cement treated base and eXisting pavement; construct six bridges and a pumping plant, completion of which will provide a new section of four-lane divided highway with bridges at: 14th Street overcrossing, Eighth Street separation, Seventh Street undercrossing, Third Street undercrossing, Riverside Junction underpass, Spruce Street overcrossing and pump plant at Riverside Junction underpass, 2.2 miles. Contract awarded to Griffith Co., Los Angeles, $1,885,484.60.

Riverside County—SR 74—Between 9.5 miles east of Hemet and 1.1 miles west of Mountain Center. Grade the eXisting roadbed, place plant-mixed surfacing and apply seal coats, 7.3 miles. Contract awarded to Matich Constructors, Colton, $118,476.

San Bernardino County—US 70, 99—At Milliken Avenue and at Holt Boulevard connection, near Ontario. Grade a deceleration lane and surface with plant-miXed surfacing and construct metal plate guard railing. Contract awarded to Ralph J. Laird, La Verne, $3,823.10.

San Bernardino County—At Alabama Street, on Colton Avenue, near Redlands, and at Marshall Boulevard, on E Street in San Bernardino. Install traffic signal systems and construct concrete curb median widening. Contract awarded to Paul R. Gardner, Ontario, $26,740.

San Bernardino County—US 91—Between 0.3 mile south and 0.3 mile north of Cable Creek, about 4 miles north of San Bernardino. Grade the eXisting shoulders, surface the existing roadway and shoulders with plant-miXed surfacing, 0.6 mile. Contract awarded to Vernon Paving Co., Fontana, $4,062.

San Bernardino County—SR 2 and State Route 188—Across west fork Mojave River about 9 miles and 11 miles north of Crestline. Construct graded roadbeds for detours, construct bridge approaches and reconstruct two steel girder bridges at west fork Mojave River at two locations. Contract awarded to Hubbs Equipment Co., Colton, $38,280.

San Diego County—On south Harbor Drive at Sampson, Beardsley and Sigsbee Streets. Grade and surface left turn lanes with plant-miXed surfacing on untreated base, 0.5 mile. Contract awarded to M. H. Golden Const. Co., San Diego, $7,515.20.

San Diego County—SR 94—Between 0.5 mile east of Euclid Avenue and 0.3 mile east of College Avenue. Install Highway lighting and illuminated sign systems. Contract awarded to Hall Slout Electric Co., Inc., Oakland, $36,105.

San Francisco County—State Route 224 (Embarcadero Freeway)—Between San Francisco-Oakland Bay Bridge at Fremont Street and Howard Street. Construct portions of a multilane multilevel separation of reinforced concrete box girder spans supported by reinforced concrete bents and construct contour graded areas and replace portions of city streets with plant-miXed surfacing on portland cement concrete base, 0.9 mile. Contract awarded to Chas. L. Harney, Inc., San Francisco, $1,859,- 283.40.

San Francisco County—Between 15th and 16th, San Bruno and Vermont Streets, at the San Francisco maintenance station. Install three metal buildings, construct concrete curbs and pave portions of the yard areas with plant-miXed surfacing on untreated base. Contract awarded to Box Const. Co., Berkeley, $28,830.

San Luis Obispo County—FAS 1208—Between 0.5 mile and 4.1 miles west of Templeton. Grade, place imported subbase and imported base materials, place plant-miXed surfacing and apply seal coat, 3.6 miles. Contract awarded to Madonna Construction Co., San Luis Obispo, $111,625.

San Mateo County—US Bypass 101—Between Millbrae Avenue in Millbrae and 0.4 mile north of Broadway in Burlingame. Prepare and plant roadside areas, 0.4 mile. Contract awarded to Stephen L. Vistica & Son, San Carlos, $1,656.

Santa Clara County—SR 9—Between 0.4 mile south of McClellan Road and US 101. Widen and surface with plant-miXed surfacing on cement treated base and over the eXisting pavement, install one traffic signal system with highway lighting and modify two existing traffic signal systems with highway lighting, 4.0 miles. Contract awarded to L. C. Smith Co., San Mateo, $316,279.80.

Sonoma County—US 101—Across Mark West Creek, four miles north of Santa Rosa. Construct a reinforced concrete bridge and construct graded approaches and surface with plant-miXed surfacing on untreated base. Contract awarded to Bridges Const. Co., San Jose, $66,292.90.

Sonoma County—At the Schellville maintenance station. Construct a metal building. Contract awarded to Stevenson Pacific, Redwood City, $3,- 343.

Yolo County—Between Johnston and Pendergast Streets on Main and East Streets, and between Johnston and East Streets on Oak Avenue. Install traffic signal system and highway lighting and construct drainage facilities. Contract awarded to A. Teichert & Son, Inc., Sacramento, $35,223.50.

Yolo County—At the Division of Highways Nursery about 10 miles west of Sacramento, near Davis, repair and improve a lath house. Contract awarded to A. Teichert & Son, Inc., Sacramento, $2,260.50.

APRIL, 1956

Del Norte County—US 101—Across Panther Creek, about two miles north of Klamath. Construct a detour of imported borrow, surface with plant-miXed surfacing; grade and surface the approaches with untreated base material and plant-miXed surfacing, and construct a reinforced concrete bridge, 0.2 mile. Contract awarded to Osborne Bowie Eng. Contrs., Crescent City, $71,907.

Del Norte County—US 101—Between 0.4 mile and 0.8 mile north of Wilson Creek, about 13 miles south of Crescent City. Grade and surface with plant-miXed surfacing on cement treated base and construct a reinforced concrete bridge, completion of which will provide a four-lane highway, part of which is on new alignment eliminating a bad curve, 1.1 miles. Awarded to Natt McDougall Co., Portland, Oregon, $552,100.21.

Humboldt County—US 101—Between 0.2 mile south of Elk River and south city limit of Eureka. Widen the eXisting two-lane approaches and surface with plant-miXed surfacing on cement treated base and construct a precast concrete bridge, completion of which will provide a four-lane divided facility, 1.5 miles. Awarded to Mercer, Fraser Gas Co., Inc., and Mercer, Fraser Co., Inc., Eureka, $249,141.26.

Humboldt County—US 299—Across Trinity River at Hoopa. Grade bridge approaches and surface with road-miXed surfacing on untreated base and construct a welded plate girder bridge, 0.4 mile. Awarded to Peter Kiewit Sons' Co., Medford, Oregon, $710,276.50.

Imperial County—US 80—At Pack Ditch, about 11.3 miles west of Winterhaven. Construct a triple reinforced concrete box culvert and place plant-miXed surfacing on untreated base. Awarded to R. E. Staite-Roy C. Ek, San Diego, $25,004.15.

Kern County—US 466—Between Keck's Corner and 0.3 mile easterly, about 44 miles west of Wasco. Construct a graded roadbed and place plant-miXed surfacing on cement treated base, and construct a reinforced concrete box culvert with headwalls and end walls, 0.3 mile. Awarded to Rand Const. Co., Bakersfield, $25,467.50.

Kern County—US 466—Between 2.3 and 4.6 miles east of Lost Hills. Construct bridge approaches and detours, place imported borrow and cement treated base, surface with plant-miXed surfacing and construct three bridges and a box culvert, at Goose Lake Canal Bridge, bridge across Main Drain Canal, West Side Canal Culvert and bridge across Main Flood Canal, 0.4 mile. Awarded to Thomas Const. Co., Fresno, $134,385.

Kern County—Sign Route 33—Between Eighth Street and Lincoln Avenue, on Kern Street. Grade the shoulder areas and surface with plant-miXed surfacing. Awarded to PhoeniX Const. Co., Inc., Bakersfield, $2,176.50.

Lake County—Sign Route 29—Across Thompson Creek, about two miles south of Lakeport. Construct a reinforced concrete bridge and grade approaches and surface with plant-miXed surfacing on untreated base, 0.1 mile. Awarded to Robert R. Murdoch, Lafayette, $40,958.

Los Angeles County—At Hillcrest Blvd., on La Brea Ave. Install traffic signal system and highway lighting. Awarded to Westates Electrical Constr. Co., Los Angeles, $6,600.

Los Angeles County—Long Beach Freeway—Between 0.4 mile south of Imperial Highway in Lynwood and Dozier Street. Grade and pave with portland cement concrete pavement on cement treated base and construct four reinforced concrete and one rivered plate girder bridges and two reinforced concrete pumping plants, completion of which will provide a new six-lane divided freeway together with interchanges and off and on ramps; bridges at Salt Lake Avenue Overhead, Garfield

Avenue Undercrossing, Route 174/167 Separation, Southgate Underpass, Clara Street Overcrossing, and Pumping Plants at Southgate Underpass and at Clara Street Overcrossing, 3.8 miles. Awarded to Webb & White and W. J. Disteli, Los Angeles, $4,174,204.

Madera County—US 99 and Sign Route 152—Between Califa and Merced County Line. Construct graded roadbeds, place imported subbase material, pave with portland cement concrete on cement treated subgrade and plant-miXed surfacing on cement treated base and untreated base, and construct seven bridges, two pumping plants, and modify an eXisting pumping plant, completion of which will provide freeway, together with frontage roads, ramps and interchanges, bridges at: Route 32/4 separation; Califa Overhead; Road 24-E Overcrossing; Berenda Slough Bridge; Road 26-E Overcrossing; Ash Slough Bridge; and Le Grand Ave. Overcrossing, all on new alignment, and four-lane divided, 7.0 miles. Awarded to Fredericksen & Kasler, Sacramento, $2,285,809.35.

Marin County—Sign Route 37—Across Novato Creek, about 9.5 miles north of San Rafael. Repair a reinforced concrete bridge. Awarded to C. C. Gildersleeve, Grass Valley, $8,152.

Marin County—Sign Route 1—Across Arroyo San Geronimo, about 0.2 mile south of Point Reyes Station. Clean and paint bridge. Awarded to R. W. Reade and Co., Berkeley, $1,940.

Monterey County—Sign Route 1—About 55 miles south of Monterey, at Limekiln Creek. Construct a reinforced concrete bridge and construct graded approaches and pave with plant-miXed surfacing on cement treated base. Awarded to James B. Allen and Lee Arnold, Inc., San Carlos, $361,980.

Nevada County—Sign Route 20—Between 0.4 mile west of Casey's Corner and Rough and Ready, about five miles west of Grass valley. Place road-miXed surfacing on untreated base and redeck and widen a steel stringer and a timber stringer bridge, 2.1 miles. Awarded to M. J. Ruddy & Son, Modesto, $72,176.35.

Orange County—At Commonwealth Ave. and at Artesia Ave., on Grand Ave. Modify the eXisting and install new traffic signal systems and highway lighting. Awarded to Sherwin Electric Service, Los Angeles, $9,396.

Orange County—Across Brea Canyon Creek, on bridge. Construct a pedestrian walk. Awarded to E. S. and N. S. Johnson, Fullerton, $2,793.

Riverside County—Sign Route 111—Between Ramon Road and Indian Trail. Widen the eXisting roadway and bridge by grading and surfacing with plant-miXed surfacing, completion of which will provide a four-lane roadway, and widened bridge across Tahquitz Creek, 1.3 miles. Awarded to E. L. Yeager Co., Riverside, $136,476.50.

San Francisco City and County—On Bayshore Freeway—Between Third St. and Alemany Blvd. Pave areas with plant-miXed surfacing, construct a maintenance building, install a watering system, install a plant box, prepare and plant trees and shrubs, 1.2 miles. Awarded to Stephen L. Vistica & Son, San Mateo, $62,066.30.

San Francisco City and County—Golden Gate Bridge Approach—Between the Toll Plaza and Sign Route 1. Contract new concrete bases for a monument and drinking fountain, construct plant-miXed surfacing pavement widening on concrete base, and prepare and plant areas. Awarded to Watkin & Sibbald, San Anselmo, $22,794.10.

San Luis Obispo County—US 101—Between Hourihan Grade and Russell Turn, about 3.6 miles to 10.1 miles north of Santa Maria Grade. Pave with portland cement concrete on cement treated subgrade, place plant-miXed surfacing on cement treated base and concrete pavement and construct three reinforced concrete bridges, completion of which will provide a four-lane divided highway with bridges at Robbing Street Overcrossing, Nipomo Creek Frontage Road Bridge and at Nipomo Creek, all on new alignment, 7.1 miles. Awarded to Madonna Const. Co., San Luis Obispo, $1,777,164.

San Luis Obispo County—US 101—Between Arroyo Grande Creek, near Oceano. Grade a two-lane roadway, place plant-miXed surfacing on untreated base and construct a reinforced concrete bridge, 0.4 mile. Awarded to Madonna Const. Co., San Luis Obispo, $79,827.

Santa Cruz County—State Route 42—About 2.6 miles northerly of Governor's Camp, in Big Basin State Park. Construct a graded roadbed and embankment and place plant-miXed surfacing on untreated base, 0.3 mile. Awarded to Granite Const. Co., Watsonville, $16,875.

Siskiyou County—Sign Route 96—Across Swillup Creek, about 20 miles south of Happy Camp. Construct a reinforced concrete bridge. Contract awarded to Rett Company, West Sacramento, $34,678.50.

Trinity County—US 299—Between Court Street in Weaverville and 1.8 miles east. Construct a graded roadbed, place imported subbase material, untreated base and cement treated base and surface with plant-mixed surfacing, 1.8 miles. Awarded to Mercben, Fraser Co., Inc., and Mercer, Fraser Gas Co., Inc., Eureka, $183,306.

Trinity County—US 299—On US 299, Trinity River at Douglas City (emergency contract). Assemble Baily Bridge and remove debris. Awarded to United States Plywood Corp., $2,150.

Tulare County—US 99—Across freeway, about 120 feet north of the intersection of County Road 128 and Avenue 80. Construct a reinforced concrete bridge, install lighting system, and place imported borrow and plant-miXed surfacing for the approaches, completion of which will provide a new pedestrian overcrossing. Awarded to Thomas Const. Co., Fresno, $58,180.

Ventura County—State Route 9—Near Saticoy on Los Angeles Ave. about 0.5 mile north of Santa Clara Ave. Grade and surface with plant-miXed surfacing on untreated base and construct reinforced concrete culverts, and apply seal coats, 0.3 mile. Awarded to Paul V. Pollock, Ventura, $23,168.40.

Ventura County—State Route 9—Across the Santa Clara River, near Saticoy. Remove and reconstruct a portion of bridge, and remove and reconstruct curbs and railings of bridge across Santa Clara River. Awarded to W. F. MaXwell Co., Los Angeles, $605,441.50.

Yuba County—At the State Highway District Office and Laboratory Building in Marysville. Prepare and plant ground areas. Awarded to R. B. Gregory, Berkeley, $1,800.31.

Employees Receive Twenty-five-year Awards

Employees of the Division of Highways who became eligible for 25-year awards on March 31, and April 30, 1956, are:

Name	Total service			Name	Total service		
	Yrs.	Mos.	Days		Yrs.	Mos.	Days
ELIGIBLE ON March 31, 1956				**ELIGIBLE ON April 30, 1956—Continued**			
District I				**District I—Continued**			
Parker, Elmon L.	25	0	13	Robson, James Daniel	25	0	6
District III				Smart, Elwin J.	25	0	6
Engrahm, Alvin E.	25	0	7	**District II**			
District IV				Davis, Edward E.	25	0	12
Miles, Herbert S.	25	0	23	**District IV**			
Norris, Robert Johnston	25	0	4	Loeffler, Paul A.	25	0	26
DISTRICT VII				Milner, Donald C.	25	0	17
Bray, Otis	25	0	20	**District V**			
Dene, Sylver P.	25	0	27	Beuttler, Louis James	25	0	2
Tibbet, Edward P.	25	0	16	**District VI**			
District VIII				Stumbaugh, Wayne S.	25	0	00
Smith, Neil L.	25	0	17	**District VII**			
District X				Decker, Ralph E.	25	0	21
Pleau, Henry L.	25	0	16	Madden, Russell J.	25	0	18
DISTRICT XI				**District VIII**			
Jorgensen, J. Frank	25	0	15	Barrett, W. V. (Bill)	25	0	00
Bridge Dept.				**District X**			
Greene, George A.	25	0	28	Black, Darrell J.	25	u	14
Verner, Carl J.	25	0	24	**Bridge Dept.**			
Headquarters Shop				Ivy, Raymond J.	25	0	27
Keleher, James J.	25	0	18	Maury, Harris K.	25	0	21
ELIGIBLE ON April 30, 1956				Turpen, Loretta	25	0	9
District I				**Headquarters Shop**			
Burgess, Bernard J.	25	0	11	Revelino, James B.	25	0	16
Leger, Leslie L.	25	0	3	Schang, Robert M.	25	0	14

THE MONARCHS

Visit Monterey, Pacific Grove, or Carpinteria and you're almost sure to hear about the butterflies. In this case, points out the National Automobile Club, the butterflies will be the giant monarchs, their reddish-brown wings veined with black. And you'll hear about them because of their most unusual semiannual migratory flight that takes them over the hundreds of miles from Alaska to California.

There are migratory flights and migratory flights but that of the monarchs is most unusual for they fly only one way and then die; their progeny fly back to the starting point in Alaska.

Cycle Occurs Each Year

Let us look at the cycle as it occurs each year. In the late summer, monarchs from the meadowlands of Alaska start to congregate in large groups and move down the coast. As they go, they are joined by other monarchs along the way and soon great masses of them are winging their way southward. Down along Washington and Oregon they go, and into California. In Central California they wing out across Monterey Bay and then begin to take to the trees at Monterey, Pacific Grove, and farther south at Carpinteria. On the same Monterey pines and live oaks on which they have been swarming for the years, they settle down, each hanging to the end of a pine needle, leaves folded, dormant. For four long months they nap there, and then, with the coming of spring, they awaken.

In the early spring they breed and die. Their progeny flutter about the hills and valleys, feeding on the milkweed, gaining strength for the long journey back to the North. And then, one day, these butterflies born in Monterey begin to move out in little groups, begin to move up the coast, Northward they go, feeding lightly on plant nectar as they go, and coming at last to the meadowlands that their parents had left the late summer before. There they will breed and die and their progeny will come down to Monterey.

So strange is this flight that each year the arrival of the monarchs is celebrated by a butterfly pageant in Pacific Grove and police of the area are not slow to arrest anyone found disturbing or destroying the butterflies during their long winter sleep.

A total of 10,530,725 toll-paying interurban train and bus passengers crossed the San Francisco-Oakland Bay Bridge during the Fiscal Year 1954-55. A new high record of 31,728,722 vehicles crossed the bridge during the same period.

TULARE BYPASS

Continued from page 43 . . .

routed through the city did not drive by the retail outlets on Inyo Street, and it is extremely doubtful if these businesses derived any benefit from this source.

Eating and drinking places were the only business group in this area that enjoyed an increase in gross sales during the two years after the freeway opened. As all business in this area showed a decline and the only type of business showing an increase was the type catering to highway travel, it is reasonable to assume the losses suffered by the other businesses were not caused by diverting U. S. Highway 99 traffic to the freeway bypass.

Area C

All retail outlets along the entire 7.9-mile length of the old highway route, bypassed by the freeway, were included in this business sector. These retail outlets, because of their location, would be most directly affected by the freeway bypass.

The service stations on the old highway suffered the heaviest loss of gross sales in this sector. As compared with service stations in other sectors of Tulare it is apparent that a portion of the loss is directly attributable to the rerouting of the highway traffic to the new freeway.

Eating and drinking places on the old highway route suffered a loss in gross sales amounting to 8.51 percent. This decrease was not as great as the losses suffered by the same group of businesses located in some other sectors of the city. However, there were eating and drinking places in business sectors in the community which enjoyed an increase in gross sales during the two years following completion of the freeway. We can assume that this type of business on the old highway route was affected to a certain degree by the change in highway routing; however, in view of the loss in some of the other sectors which were not affected by highway traffic, it would be wrong to attribute the entire loss to the highway change.

The highest business increase made by any group of retail outlets at any location in Tulare were the retail businesses along the old highway route

catering to the needs of the local buyers.

Area D

K Street, the "main street" of Tulare, is one block east of the old highway route. Although traffic on the highway through the city was routed on a parallel street, the close proximity of the main business street undoubtedly attracted some travelers.

The sale of merchandise in a large majority of the retail outlets on this street is influenced by local purchasing power, and does not appeal to a stranger driving through the town.

The relatively high losses in gross sales among service stations and the eating and drinking places represented a relatively small volume of the business performed on K Street, as evidenced by the fact that their losses did not substantially change the loss shown by the majority of business as a part of the total business activity on the street.

In comparing the majority of businesses, identified as the all other group, on K Street with the same class of retail outlets on the two parallel streets shown on the accompanying chart as Sectors C and F, business catering to local buyers in those areas enjoyed high increases in gross sales following the rerouting of through traffic to the freeway. It is noteworthy that the highest gain was made in Sector C, the old highway route.

Area E

Tulare, Kern, King, and Inyo Streets, extending in a perpendicular direction east of the old highway route, suffered a loss in total business volume amounting to 2.72 percent during the comparative period of time in this study.

Any benefit these businesses would derive from highway motorists using the old highway would only be from those travelers who desired to stop and shop in the Tulare business district. The fact that the freeway bypass percentage of traffic shows that in general only those motorists who had no intention of stopping in Tulare are using the bypass, indicates that the rerouting of highway traffic to the freeway bypass should have little, if any, influence on gross busi-

ness receipts among these retail outlets.

Area F

L Street is parallel and two blocks east of the old highway route. The service stations and the eating and drinking places on L Street decreased in gross sales during the two years after the freeway bypass opened; however, they represented such a small percentage of the total business volume on this street that their losses had very little effect on the gains made by the other business on this street.

Area G

Single retail outlets located outside the specific business sectors at various locations throughout the community have been tabulated into a miscellaneous group. None of these businesses are in locations where they were directly affected by motorists using the old highway route.

Area H

The retail outlets located on approach roads adjacent to the new freeway have opened for business subsequent to the date the freeway bypass was completed. It is not possible to show any comparison of these businesses because there were none in operation while highway traffic was routed on the old highway.

Property Sales

A review of real estate sales from January, 1951, to July, 1955, along the principal streets in Tulare indicate there has been a slight increase in sale prices. The investigation of sales covered these specific areas: (1) the entire 7.9-mile length of the old highway route which had been bypassed by the freeway; (2) K Street, Tulare's "main street"; (3) Tulare Street, principal business street perpendicular to old highway and K Street; and (4) Lindsay Highway.

The greatest number of real estate transfers taking place within a specific commercial area in Tulare was along K Street, and the fewest transfers were found on the Lindsay Highway. This was at first surprising because this area is perhaps the most active section from the standpoint of new commercial building activity. How-

and Public Works

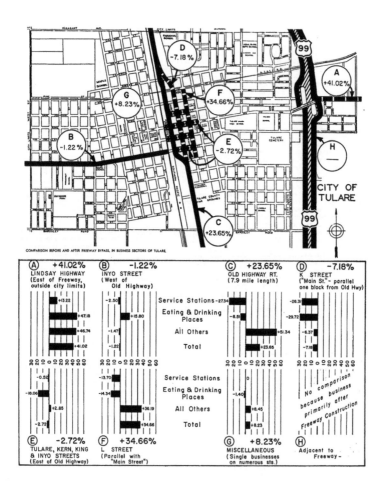

COMPARISON BEFORE AND AFTER FREEWAY BYPASS, IN BUSINESS SECTORS OF TULARE.

ever, an investigation revealed that the majority of construction was taking place on leased sites. This certainly is indicative of the property owners' confidence in the growth potentials of this area.

The sales of unimproved properties along the old highway route indicated a slight increase in the cases where comparisons could be made.

In general, the price trend in Tulare has been increasing; however, the real estate market has not been extremely active. The lack of a sufficient number of transfers of unimproved properties where accurate comparisons could be made precludes the opportunity to set forth a distinct pattern showing the exact degree of price change which has taken place before and after the rerouting of highway traffic around Tulare.

Building Activity

A comparison has been made of the total building activity before and after the completion of the Tulare freeway bypass in December, 1953. In order to determine whether the growth in Tulare has followed the normal expectancy for building activity in this portion of the San Joaquin Valley area, a comparison has been made with other cities of comparable size located in this vicinity.

The following percentages show the gains and losses in building activity during the two years after the completion of the freeway at Tulare as compared with the previous two years.

Tulare	+ 38.55%
Porterville	+ 24.64%
Visalia	+128.03%
Hanford	− 13.35%
Delano	+ 90.04%

A review of the cities with increased building activity during the past two years shows that Tulare has kept pace with the other cities, with the exception of Visalia. Every city enjoys the benefit of municipally or government-financed construction which adds substantially to the building activity during a particular year; however, the three million dollar county courthouse in Visalia has greatly exceeded any single expenditure in the other cities, and for this reason Visalia does not present a true comparison with the other cities having normal building growth.

Assessed Value of Real Estate

The increase in assessed valuation of real estate in the City of Tulare has been slightly slower than in some of the other cities in this general area. A comparison of the change does not indicate any appreciable difference in growth or property valuation.

The changes in assessed valuation of cities in the San Joaquin Valley area during the two years following the completion of the freeway bypass in Tulare as compared with the two years prior to that date are listed below:

Tulare	+ 8.82%
Porterville	+10.94%
Visalia	+15.95%
Hanford	+ 0.90%
Delano	+14.16%

Conclusion

In summarizing this study, the basic problem is to analyze a minor influence during a major economic change. The highway rerouting in Tulare occurred at a time when the community was subjected to changes in the principal sources of income affecting the entire economy.

In making the final analysis to differentiate between the economic reaction to the change in income stream within the local area, and the change in income stream resulting from a traffic pattern, this study has shown that:

(1) The majority of retail outlets in the community dependent upon local buying power, and particularly those on the old highway route, have enjoyed gains substantially higher than the county average during the two years after completion of the freeway bypass.

(2) The retail outlets most likely to benefit from highway traffic routed through the city have decreased in gross sales; however, only a portion of their losses are attributable to the rerouting of through traffic to the freeway. These businesses represent a relatively small share of total business activity and their losses have not seri-

ously affected the community gain.

(3) Property sales, building activity, and other reliable indicators of growth and development in the community have shown a steady upward trend.

In view of the many adjustments the community was required to cope with, Tulare has succeeded in the face of what appeared to be overwhelming odds to surpass the normal economic trend in the general vicinity since December, 1953, the completion date of the freeway bypass.

The new freeway gives Tulare a modern highway facility to aid in developing a strong, self-reliant economy not influenced by the unpredictable buying habits of the traveling public.

Sources of Factual Data

State Board of Equalization
State Department of Finance
State Department of Employment, Tulare County Office
Security Title Insurance Co., Tulare County Branch
Tulare County Assessor, Recorder
Tulare County Farm Advisor
Tulare County Annual Agricultural Crop Reports, Agricultural Extension Service
King County Farm Advisor
City Clerk, Assessor, Tax Collector, and Building Inspector of Tulare, Visalia, Porterville, Hanford, and Delano

LIKES MAGAZINE

OXHEY, WATFORD
HERTS, ENGLAND

The Editor

DEAR SIR: You have been sending me copies of *California Highways and Public Works* since 1947 and I should like once again to thank you for this courtesy. Your magazine has been greatly appreciated, not only by me, but by all professional staff who have served under me since 1947. During this period I have been employed on engineering works in several parts of the world and *California Highways and Public Works* (which is forwarded to me from my home address) has always been eagerly awaited by senior and junior staff members alike.

I look forward to receiving it in the future and assure you that it will be given the widest circulation wherever I may be.

Yours sincerely,

W. J. COZENS

Another Freeway

Contra Costa County Bond Issue Project

By W. C. DALTON, Assistant Director of Public Works, Contra Costa County

IN RECENT years, new highways have been completed in Contra Costa County with such frequency as to become commonplace. However, the Ygnacio Valley Road extension drew exceptional public interest, as evidenced by the number of inquiries as to when it would be opened to traffic.

This project had almost reached completion in December of last year, well ahead of schedule, when the heavy rains halted work. From the end of the heavy storm period until April 12, 1956, when traffic was routed over the new road, the intense public interest in this project was a revelation to the county board of supervisors, as well as to the engineers of the county public works department. As a result, an extra effort was made by everyone concerned with the project to open it to traffic as early as possible.

Benefit to Commuters

The interest in this new highway link stems from the improvement in service in will render to commuters between the Pittsburg-Antioch industrial area and the central county residential valleys, and to travelers between the eastern and western county areas, as well as commercial interests using and serving the project area. As a contrast to the sudden excitement in the final months of construction, this route has been under study at various times since 1928 when J. H. Obermuller (retired), Assistant Engineer Surveys and Plans, of the Division of Highways, included it as part of a "reconaissance survey between Oakland and Stockton"—a survey jointly sponsored by Alameda, Contra Costa, and San Joaquin Counties. In 1950, George Berry, Assistant Road Commissioner of Contra Costa supervised a study of the new link, and it is worth noting that very substantial agreement exists between both earlier surveys and the final construction.

The Ygnacio Valley Road extension connects the intersection of

Special acknowledgment is due Contra Costa County for the constructive vision that has made such limited access expressways a reality.

G. T. McCOY
State Highway Engineer

Ygnacio Valley Road and Oak Grove Road over new alignment with the intersection of Kirker Pass Road and Clayton Road, a distance of 4.1 miles. The westerly end of Ygnacio Valley Road extension is located about three miles northeast of the center of Walnut Creek and the easterly end four miles southeast of the heart of Concord. The road passes through the property of the Cowell Portland Cement Company (now inoperative). Its highest elevation is 455 feet where it traverses Lime Ridge from which there are many vantage points that present broad and expansive views of both Ygnacio and Clayton Valleys.

Included in Bond Program

With the earlier surveys and studies of this route and the knowledge of development and traffic patterns in the area which indicated its importance, the public works department (formerly the road commissioner's office) recommended its inclusion in the bond program and the Tudor Engineering Company of San Francisco agreed with the department's findings. Accordingly, in the Tudor Report of March, 1952, to the board of supervisors, it was recommended that the extension be included in the road bond program. It was given the designation of Project H(2).

Also considered necessary for development, service, and safety reasons along this Walnut Creek-to-Pittsburg route were: Bond Project H(1) which provides for reconstruction of the existing Ygnacio Valley Road from Walnut Creek to Oak Grove Road;

the addition of a slow traffic lane on the steep grades of Kirker Pass Road (Bond Project L(1)); and the reconstruction of approximately two miles of the existing Kirker Pass (Bond Project L(2)).

Bond Issue Approved

Following the approval of the $10,-250,000 road bond issue by the voters at the June 3, 1952, election, aerial photographs and topographic maps were prepared of the area to be traversed, and Norman T. Riffe, Civil Engineer of Martinez, was retained to prepare construction plans. Concurrent with the design work, action was taken to have the proposed highway included in the federal-aid secondary road net in Contra Costa County.

A total of 21 bids were received (by the Division of Highways on January 5, 1955), the lowest being $547,527.95 by Transocean Engineering Corporation of Hayward, which was awarded the contract.

The contractor started work on February 15, 1955, with 260 working days allowed for completion. The winter weather conditions and additional time granted because of extra work would have extended the contract completion date into July. The contract was accepted by the State Director of Public Works on April 20, 1956, well ahead of the legal deadline.

Design of Highway

The typical geometrical section provides two 12-foot-wide traffic lanes with eight-foot-wide paved shoulders on each side. On the summit grades four 12-foot lanes with shoulders are provided for passing of slow-moving vehicles. Curvature of the highway is to modern standards, and maximum grades are approximately 6 percent.

Structurally, the highway was built for an anticipated increase in car and truck traffic. Nominally up to 14½ inches thickness of subbase material,

A view of the recently completed Ygnacio Valley Road Extension constructed by Contra Costa County as a limited access eXpressway under the Federal Aid Secondary Highway Program and the County Road Bond Issue Program

a 6-inch thickness of untreated base material and a 2½-inch thickness of plant-mix surfacing were used.

Some of the major items of work were: 590,000 cubic yards of roadway excavation, 7.7 miles of fence, 2,800 lineal feet of culvert pipes, 50,000 tons of base rock, and 17,000 tons of plant-mix surfacing.

Sufficient right of way has been acquired to provide for future widening of the roadway to four lanes. Much of the work on this project was performed with provisions for future widening.

Control of Access

Because of the increase in highway safety and service standards and the phenomenal growth of the area, the actual construction of the road exceeds the recommendations of the Tudor report. The most significant improvements beyond the report are:

A. Acquisition of four-lane right of way instead of two-lane.

B. Provisions for future four lanes by partial construction of a four-lane section, widening of structures, and design of future roadway including a median.

C. Increased structural strength and fully improved shoulders.

D. Provision for future creek and channel developments by the flood control district.

E. Control of Access. This is one of the most important features of this project. Much of this project area is valuable subdivision and commercial property and without access limitations severe restrictions on capacity and safety could be expected within a few years. Adequate traffic service to the area by feeder and secondary roads is being incorporated in the county master plan.

Contra Costa County's federal-aid secondary highway projects have also been milestones in the progress of the $10,250,000 county road bond issue starting with the improvement of the Byron Highway as reported in the November-December, 1953, issue of this magazine. These FAS projects are constructed under a cooperative program involving the county, the State

Division of Highways and the U. S. Bureau of Public Roads.

Comprehensive Program

Of the 18 major routes or projects selected for improvement under the bond issue program, work has started on 13 as of April, 1956. A total of 40 contracts are contemplated to complete all work on the road bond program and of these, 27 contracts are under way or have been completed. Before the end of the fiscal year, three additional major contracts will be awarded. Total completion of the entire road bond issue program is expected late in 1957. Contract work complete totals $5,314,000, and the total value committed to date is $7,466,000.

This county has been able to convert sections of four primary county roads to limited access freeways during the bond issue program. Portions of the San Pablo Dam Road between Orinda and the dam, all of the Cum-

. . . Continued on page 72

Desert Highway

Mojave-Barstow Route Improvement Completed

By ROBERT M. KELLY, Resident Engineer

ANOTHER PORTION of US 466 has recently been completed to modern two-lane standards. Situated in the Mojave Desert, between Mojave and Boron on the Mojave-Barstow road, the improvement consisted of eight miles of full grading, 12 miles of widening and the channelization of two intersections, a total distance of 21.7 miles. The total cost of the project was $571,711.48, one of the largest single contracts ever awarded in District IX, which has headquarters in Bishop, and is under the direction of District Engineer F. E. Baxter.

The history of the formation of this road is typical of all desert roads. Where one wagon passed, another followed in the same tracks until a trail was formed. The County of Kern did some maintenance work to make the road passable until the route was adopted into the State Highway System in 1919. The dirt road continued until 1930 when the state maintenance forces applied a penetration oil treatment. The first contract was let in 1938 when a portion of this road was regraded and surfaced with road-mixed surfacing. The remainder was improved by contracts in 1947.

Air Force Base

In recent years the development of this desert area has increased tremendously with the establishment of Edwards Air Force Base at Muroc, midway between Mojave and Boron. The climatic conditions and the wide expanse of the Mojave Desert make this area ideal for the experimental type of aircraft operating from this base. Many of the aircraft corporations are establishing major facilities in this area. World speed and altitude records have been made by aircraft operating from these bases. A very colorful sight in the crystal clear desert atmosphere are the many patterns of jet trails across the sky with the

UPPER—Section of Mojave-Barstow highway before improvement. LOWER—Newly completed section of desert highway.

snow-capped San Bernardino and Sierra Mountains as a backdrop.

The Pacific Coast Borax Company at Boron has started an extensive remodeling program at their site just north of Boron. The old underground mining system is being replaced by an open pit which will vary in depth from 250 to 400 feet. Included in the development will be new buildings for processing the raw material. This is one of the largest deposits of borax in the Country and its uses in every-

day affairs have increased to a total of more than 50 which include: water-softener, cleanser, grease-solvent, deodorant, preservative and shampoo.

Industrial Growth

Adding to the industrial growth of this area is the recently completed cement plant just west of the town of Mojave. This plant is of the latest modern design with an elaborate dust collection system designed to prevent any harmful smog condition from arising.

70

With all of the new activities in the vicinity the colorful town of Mojave has grown considerably from the water stop it was in the early days of the railroad. In addition to being the junction point between the Southern Pacific and Santa Fe Railroads, it is at the cross point of U. S. Highways 6 and 466. With heavy snows occurring on U. S. Routes 40 and 50, US 466 is the route used for eastbound traffic from Central and Northern California. Agriculture and other developments in western Arizona have increased the truck traffic to 15 percent.

The area traversed is typically desert mesa at the foot of a low mountain range. The sparse vegetation consists of sagebrush, greasewood, and a spotting of Joshua trees.

Project Completed in April

The contract for the construction was awarded to Harms Brothers, a construction firm of Sacramento. Work was started on September 14, 1955, and completed on April 18, 1956. Although the road was constructed during the winter months the weather was with the contractor and the contract was completed with no unusual delays or shutdowns. The traffic was carried through the construction with little inconvenience and delay although the contractor had several operations in progress at all times.

To further expedite the traffic through the construction, the contractor resorted to watering the imported borrow in the borrow pits. A rain-maker system with water supplied by nearby wells was used. Test holes were made to determine the time of wetting to give the proper uniform moisture content. This method speeded up the road operation, eliminated the dust nuisance and the delays to traffic were held to a minimum. Major quantities involved in the contract consisted of 255,000 tons imported borrow, 46,000 tons base material, and 46,000 tons of plant-mixed surfacing. The contractor produced the aggregate with a primary and a secondary crusher with a 5,000-pound Madsen batch plant completing the mixing operation.

Desert Washes

Several desert washes cross the highway at various locations. Normally

Desert scene showing section of new highway between Mojave and Boron

these are dry but cloudbursts are not uncommon in this desert country resulting in capacity flows. Four dip sections were constructed at strategic locations to take care of these situations. For the normal runoff, four 24-inch reinforced concrete pipes were installed at the center of the 750-foot-long dip. As the name implies, the profile of the roadway is dipped in a depressed vertical curve with the pavement sloped to the outlet side. The slopes are paved with plant-mixed surfacing from the edge of pavement to a point eight feet below the natural surface of the ground acting as a cutoff wall to prevent undermining the roadbed. During heavy runoffs the water, by the roadway design, is diverted to these dip sections where the roadway has been constructed to withstand the onslaught. Many more smaller culverts were constructed, including a storm drain system in the Town of Mojave.

J. Shelden and T. Kelley acted as general superintendent and project superintendent, respectively, for the contractor. The State was represented by J. R. Jarvis, District Construction Engineer, and the author.

Canada Officials Study Highways In California

Four officials of the Ministry of Highways of the Province of Ontario, headed by Hon. James N. Allan, Minister of Highways, were in Sacramento in April to study California's freeway program.

The Canadian province is just launching a large-scale program of controlled access highways. Allen said many of Ontario's problems of route selection and right of way acquisition are similar to those which have been faced and solved in California.

"We have read a good deal about the progress on your highways," he added, "and we want to see just how California plans, manages and finances these freeways and expressways. In Ontario, our King's Highways, as they are called, do not go through the cities but the provincial government does participate in the financing of the connecting links through the cities."

Accompanying Allan were: M. A. Elson, Deputy Minister of Highways; W. J. Fulton, Director of Planning and Design; and C. A. Robbins, Director of Services.

The Canadian group conferred with Director of Public Works Frank B. Durkee and State Highway Engineer G. T. McCoy before entering into three days of conferences with members of the Division of Highways staff. Most of their attention was devoted to the planning and right of way phases of the California highway program.

MAGAZINE IS HELPFUL

UNITED STATES
DEPARTMENT OF THE INTERIOR
Geological Survey

SAN FRANCISCO 11, CALIFORNIA

MR. KENNETH C. ADAMS, *Editor*

DEAR MR. ADAMS: When I received your March-April, 1956, edition I could not resist the temptation to write to you at once to compliment you on the stunning cover.

CANADA LIKES OUR FREEWAYS

ONTARIO
Department of Highways

TORONTO 2, ONTARIO

*California Highways and
Public Works*

GENTLEMEN: I have had the good fortune to receive *California Highways and Public Works* for the past few years. The articles dealing with the many phases of highway engineering have always been most informative and interesting.

The wonderful aerial views of California's freeways certainly point out the rapid modernization of your highway system with the views of the Hollywood-Santa Ana Freeway particularly fascinating.

Again, many thanks.

Sincerely,

TOM MAHONY
Supervisor, Accident Records and Administration
Traffic Engineering, Province of Ontario

SACRAMENTO CANYON

Continued from page 35 . . .

the steep, blazing, trackless, sun-baked hillsides in this same canyon in August, 1837.

Try to figure what Young and his chronicler Edwards would say if they could step into a modern car and make the canyon trip in about an hour in comfort; the same one that required about a month of hardship to negotiate.

*Acknowledgment made to "Shasta County"
by Rosena A. Giles*

Your journal has proved most helpful to us in keeping abreast of projects in the State which is one of our major duties here. It also helps us to foresee a demand for topographic quadrangles and order our sales stock of these maps to meet the expected demand. I am therefore most grateful for having a place on your mailing list.

Sincerely yours,

JEAN V. MOLLESKOG
Inquiries Specialist

GENERAL PRENTISS TAKES OVER AS EXECUTIVE VICE PRES. OF ARBA

Maj. Gen. Louis W. Prentiss (USA Ret.) has assumed his duties as Executive Vice President of the American Road Builders' Association.

General Prentiss, who succeeded General Eugene Reybolds (USA Ret.) as ARBA's executive head, has a background of over 35 years of distinguished military service. He is 56 years of age and a native of the District of Columbia. He is a graduate engineer of the Colorado School of Mines and entered the Army as a second lieutenant, field artillery, in 1921. After regular Army service he transferred to the corps of engineers in 1929 and has held increasingly important posts in the corps. The general became best known, perhaps, after his appointment by President Truman, in December, 1952, as Engineer-Commissioner of the District of Columbia. He served during 1953 and 1954 in that capacity and was a popular administrative figure in Washington, D. C. He was promoted to major general by President Eisenhower in 1954. In December of that year he took over command of the Engineer Center at Ft. Belvoir, Va., and served in that post until his Army retirement this week.

ANOTHER FREEWAY

Continued from page 69 . . .

mings Skyway between the Franklin Canyon Summit of State Highway 4 and the Crockett Highway, two sections of the Pleasant Hill Road between Martinez and Lafayette and the Ygnacio Valley Road extension are all limited access highways. One other project, the Loveridge Road interchange, is within and adjacent to the state freeway area. All of these freeway designs provide sufficient right of way for future expansion as traffic increases.

The resident engineer for the Ygnacio Valley Road extension was Robert S. Latchaw and Harold Hudson was project manager for Transocean Engineering Company. Contra Costa County Public Works Director is Victor W. Sauer.

GOODWIN J. KNIGHT
Governor of California

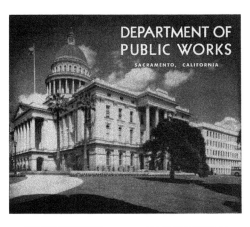

DEPARTMENT OF PUBLIC WORKS
SACRAMENTO, CALIFORNIA

CALIFORNIA HIGHWAY COMMISSION

FRANK B. DURKEE . Director of Public Works
and Chairman
H. STEPHEN CHASE . . . . . San Francisco
JAMES A. GUTHRIE . . . . San Bernardino
ROBERT E. McCLURE . . . . Santa Monica
ROBERT L. BISHOP . . . . . . Santa Rosa
FRED W. SPEERS . . . . Escondido
CHESTER H. WARLOW, Vice Chairman . Fresno
C. A. MAGHETTI, Secretary . . . . Davis
T. FRED BAGSHAW . . . . . . Assistant Director
A. H. HENDERSON . . . . Deputy Director
C. M. "MAX" GILLISS . . . . . . Deputy Director

DIVISION OF HIGHWAYS

GEO. T. McCOY
State Highway Engineer, Chief of Division
J. W. VICKREY . . . Deputy State Highway Engineer
CHAS. E. WAITE . . . Deputy State Highway Engineer
EARL WITHYCOMBE . Assistant State Highway Engineer
F. W. PANHORST . . Assistant State Highway Engineer
J. C. WOMACK . . . Assistant State Highway Engineer
R. H. WILSON . . . Assistant State Highway Engineer
F. N. HVEEM . . . Materials and Research Engineer
GEORGE F. HELLESOE . . . . Maintenance Engineer
J. C. YOUNG . . . . Engineer of Design
G. M. WEBB . . . . Traffic Engineer
MILTON HARRIS . . . . . . Construction Engineer
H. B. LA FORGE . Engineer of Federal Secondary Roads
C. E. BOVEY . Engineer of City and Cooperative Projects
EARL E. SORENSON . . . . . . Equipment Engineer
H. C. McCARTY . . . . Office Engineer
J. A. LEGARRA . . . . Planning Engineer
J. P. MURPHY . . . . Principal Highway Engineer
F. M. REYNOLDS . . . . Principal Highway Engineer
E. J. SALDINE . . . . Principal Highway Engineer
A. L. ELLIOTT . . . Bridge Engineer—Planning
I. O. JAHLSTROM . . . Bridge Engineer—Operations
J. E. McMAHON . . Bridge Engineer—Southern Area
L. C. HOLLISTER . . . Projects Engineer—Carquinez
E. R. HIGGINS . . . . Comptroller

Right of Way Department

FRANK C. BALFOUR . . . Chief Right of Way Agent
E. F. WAGNER . . Deputy Chief Right of Way Agent
GEORGE S. PINGRY . . . . Assistant Chief
R. S. J. PIANEZZI . . . . Assistant Chief
E. M. MacDONALD . . . . Assistant Chief

District IV

B. W. BOOKER . . . Assistant State Highway Engineer

District VII

E. T. TELFORD . . . Assistant State Highway Engineer

District Engineers

ALAN S. HART . . . . District I, Eureka
H. S. MILES . . . . District II, Redding
J. W. TRASK . . . . District III, Marysville
J. P. SINCLAIR . . . . . District IV, San Francisco
L. A. WEYMOUTH . . . . District IV, San Francisco
A. M. NASH . . . . . . District V, San Luis Obispo
W. L. WELCH . . . . District VI, Fresno
GEORGE LANGSNER . . . . District VII, Los Angeles
LYMAN R. GILLIS . . . . . District VII, Los Angeles
C. V. KANE . . . . . . District VIII, San Bernardino
F. E. BAXTER . . . . District IX, Bishop
JOHN G. MEYER . . . . District X, Stockton
J. DEKEMA . . . . District XI, San Diego
HOWARD C. WOOD . . . . Bridge Engineer
State-owned Toll Bridges

DIVISION OF CONTRACTS AND RIGHTS OF WAY

Legal

ROBERT E. REED . . . . Chief Counsel
GEORGE C. HADLEY . . . . Assistant Chief
HOLLOWAY JONES . . . . Assistant Chief
HARRY S. FENTON . . . . Assistant Chief

DIVISION OF SAN FRANCISCO BAY TOLL CROSSINGS

NORMAN C. RAAB . . . . . Chief of Division
BEN BALALA . . . . . Principal Bridge Engineer

DIVISION OF WATER RESOURCES

HARVEY O. BANKS, State Engineer, Chief of Division
WILLIAM L. BERRY . . . Assistant State Engineer
Water Resources Investigations, Central Valley
Project, Irrigation Districts
W. G. SCHULZ . . . . Assistant State Engineer,
Sacramento River Flood Control Project, Su-
pervision of Safety of Dams, Sacramento-San
Joaquin Water Supervision
L. C. JOPSON . . . . . Assistant State Engineer,
Water Rights and Water Quality Investigations
MAX BOOKMAN
Principal Hydraulic Engineer, Los Angeles Office
HENRY HOLSINGER . . . . . . Principal Attorney
T. R. MERRYWEATHER . . . Administrative Officer

DIVISION OF ARCHITECTURE

ANSON BOYD . . . State Architect, Chief of Division
HUBERT S. HUNTER . . . . Deputy Chief of Division
ROBERT W. FORMHALS
Administrative Assistant to State Architect

Administrative and Fiscal Service

EARL W. HAMPTON
Assistant State Architect, Administrative
HENRY R. CROWLE . . . . Fiscal Assistant
THOMAS MERET . . . Construction Budgets Architect
WADE O. HALSTEAD
Principal Estimator of Building Construction
STANTON WILLARD . . Principal Architect, Standards

Design and Planning Service

P. T. POAGE
Assistant State Architect, Design and Planning
ROBERT M. LANDRUM . Chief Architectural Coordinator
ARTHUR F. DUDMAN . Principal Architect, Sacramento
JAMES A. GILLEM . . Principal Architect, Los Angeles
CHARLES PETERSON
Principal Structural Engineer, Los Angeles
CARL A. HENDERLONG
Principal Mechanical and Electrical Engineer
CLIFFORD L. IVERSON . Chief Architectural Draftsman
GUSTAV B. VEHN . . Supervising Specifications Writer
JOHN S. MOORE . . . Supervisor of Special Projects

Construction Service

CHARLES M. HERD . . . Chief Construction Engineer
CHARLES H. BOCKMAN
Assistant to Chief Construction Engineer

AREA CONSTRUCTION SUPERVISORS

THOMAS M. CURRAN . . . . . . Area I, Oakland
J. WILLIAM COOK . . . . . Area II, Sacramento
CLARENCE T. TROOP . . . . Area III, Los Angeles

AREA STRUCTURAL ENGINEERS
SCHOOLHOUSE SECTION

MANLEY W. SAHLBERG . . . Area I, San Francisco
M. A. EWING . . . . . . Area II, Sacramento
ERNST MAAG . . . . . . Area III, Los Angeles

Fields in bloom near Hollister, San Benito County, on Route 22, looking westerly toward San Juan Bautista. Photo by M. R. Nickerson, Chief, Photographic Section, Department of Public Works.

California Highways
and Public Works

Official Journal of the Division of Highways,
Department of Public Works, State of California

KENNETH C. ADAMS, Editor

HELEN HALSTED, Assistant Editor

MERRITT R. NICKERSON, Chief Photographer

Vol. 35   July-August   Nos. 7-8

Public Works Building
Twelfth and N Streets
Sacramento

CONTENTS

Published in the interest of highway development in California. Editors of newspapers and others are privileged to
use matter contained herein. Cuts will be gladly loaned
upon request.

Address communications to

CALIFORNIA HIGHWAYS AND PUBLIC WORKS
P. O. Box 1499
Sacramento, California

Record Span

By NORMAN C. RAAB,
Projects Engineer

Richmond-San Rafael Bridge
About Ready for Traffic

New Crossing

THE RICHMOND-SAN RAFAEL Bridge, one of the largest construction projects in the San Francisco Bay area, is to be opened to highway traffic on September 1, 1956. This structure, although it does not lay claims for any outstanding features, can, however, be classified as one of the world's largest bridges as shown on the accompanying chart.

Dedication Plans

Elaborate plans for the opening of the Richmond-San Rafael Bridge are being developed by the Department of Public Works and the citizens of Marin and Contra Costa Counties.

On Friday, August 31st, at 11 a.m., official dedication of the bridge will take place at the toll plaza. Governor Knight will deliver the dedicatory address and will unveil a bronze tablet containing an historical record of the project.

Following the dedication ceremony, the structure and buildings will be open for public inspection until 6 p.m. No automobile traffic will be allowed on the bridge during this inspection period.

At 12.01 a.m., Saturday, September 1st, the first vehicle will pass through the toll lanes and the bridge will be opened for business.

Plans are being completed for civic participation and celebration as a part of the opening ceremonies.

On July 10th, the California Toll Bridge Authority adopted the following toll schedule for the bridge:

No.	Classification	Toll
1	Automobile, motorcycle, tricar, light delivery automobile, ambulance, hearse, housecar, noncommercial truck, station wagon, and taxi	$0.75
2	Commutation book (for Class 1 vehicles except light delivery automobile and noncommercial truck) *	18.75
3	Class 1 vehicle drawing a 1-axle trailer	1.25
4	Class 1 vehicle drawing a 2-axle trailer	1.50
5	Truck, 2-axle	1.25
6	Truck,† 3-axle	1.75
7	Truck, 4-axle	2.50
8	Truck, 5-axle	3.00
9	Truck, 6-axle	3.50
10	Truck, 7-axle	4.00
11	Bus, 2-axle	1.50
12	Bus, 3-axle	1.75
13	Vehicles not otherwise specified	5.00

* Book to contain 50 one-way tickets each good for a single passage at any time during the two consecutive calendar months, or fractional part thereof, for which sold.

† A truck shall include a truck-tractor, or any combination of truck, truck-tractor and trailer or semitrailer.

Preliminary work was started July 1, 1950, under an appropriation by the State Legislature in the amount of $200,000 for an engineering report as to the feasibility to finance and construct a vehicular crossing connecting Contra Costa and Marin Counties. A favorable report on the project prompted the 1951 Session of the Legislature to appropriate an additional $750,000 to be used for further studies and the preparation of plans and specifications for the major contracts. The project, in general, consists of a four-mile overwater crossing with a short piece of highway approach in Marin County and a somewhat longer approach in Contra Costa County.

Two Important Events

In December of 1952, two important events took place to bring the project closer to a reality:

1. The California Toll Bridge Authority authorized the sale of not to exceed $72,000,000 of Richmond-San Rafael Bridge toll bridge revenue bonds; however, it was stipulated that the initial issue of Series A bonds should not exceed $62,000,000.

2. Bids were opened on the two major contracts for the construction of the substructure and the superstructure work; and the low bids were found to be, in each case, below the engineer's estimates. In February of 1953, revenue bonds in the amount of $62,000,000 were sold, and the two major contracts were awarded. The following month work was started on the scheduled 3½-year construction period.

Bond Issue Money

The money obtained from the bond issue for the completion of the upper deck for highway traffic was distributed as follows:

Construction fund	$50,000,000
Current interest fund	10,000,000
Construction reserve fund	2,000,000
Total	$62,000,000

The construction fund of $50,000,000 was further budgeted as follows:

Construction contracts	$45,000,000
Right of way	1,600,000
Salaries and wages	2,000,000
Equipment	100,000
Operating expenses	1,500,000
Insurance	600,000
Appropriation repayments	800,000
Interest on unexpended funds	−1,600,000
Total	$50,000,000

The interest on the $62,000,000 bond issue is payable from the current interest fund of $10,000,000 during the 3½-year construction period and for six months thereafter. Any money remaining is to go into the bridge reserve fund.

The construction reserve fund of $2,000,000 could be used in the event the $50,000,000 was insufficient to complete the construction and open

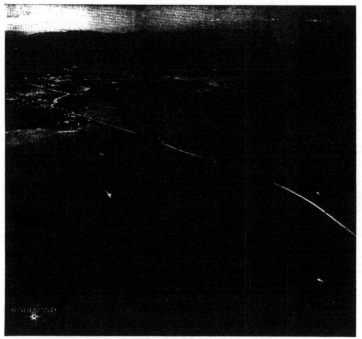

This aerial view of the Richmond-San Rafael Bridge is looking toward the City of Richmond on the Contra Costa County shore

the bridge to traffic in the allotted time. This $2,000,000, along with any surplus in the construction fund, is to be placed in the reserve fund within six months after the bridge is in operation. There is to be accumulated and remain in the bridge reserve fund the sum of $5,500,000 during the period in which bonds are outstanding.

The work performed under the construction fund was divided into 15 different contracts in order to allow similar work to be performed by one contractor and so as to complete certain phases of the project prior to the work of others. Construction could not interfere with Richmond-San Rafael Ferry traffic or the operations of local industries.

The contracts under the construction fund were as follows:

Contract No.	Title	Amount
1003	Substructure	$14,700,000
1004D	Superstructure	24,400,000
1005	Mole fill	280,000
1006	Paving	460,000
1007	Trestle approach	190,000
1008	Richmond approach	870,000
1009	San Rafael approach	210,000
1010	Buildings and toll plaza	360,000
1011	Electrical work	1,100,000
1012	Toll collection equipment	480,000
1015	Separation structures	650,000
1018	Traffic stripes and signs	20,000
1019	Girder spans	830,000
1020	Pier backfill	220,000
1022	Maintenance facilities	260,000
	Total	$45,000,000

Governor Knight Interested

On October 26, 1954, Governor Goodwin J. Knight issued a statement that it would be advantageous to the State and to the motoring public if

2

This aerial view of the new northbay crossing is looking toward San Rafael on the Marin County shore

the construction of the lower deck of the bridge were not delayed.

It was estimated that additional funds of $6,000,000 would be required to provide for an ultimate six lanes of traffic. The estimated traffic figures were reviewed; and it was the opinion of the department's consultants on traffic, financing, and revenue that this additional liability could be repaid from the bridge revenue.

The State Legislature, by Chapter 159, Statutes of 1955, authorized a loan

from the State School Land Fund. These funds became available for expenditure as of September 7, 1955.

Five Contracts

Five contracts were prepared for the completion of the project, and at present the following contracts have been awarded:

Contract No.	Title	Amount
1014	Highway lighting	$260,000
1017	San Quentin approach	2,920,000
1018A	Traffic stripes and signs	20,000
1021	Lower deck paving	1,140,000

When this work is completed, the structure will then provide two 36-foot roadways; three 12-foot lanes of traffic on the upper deck to San Rafael and the same provision on the lower deck to Richmond.

The quantities of materials used in the construction are here listed for phases I and II. The latter is for the completion of the lower level of the bridge for an ultimate six lanes of traffic.

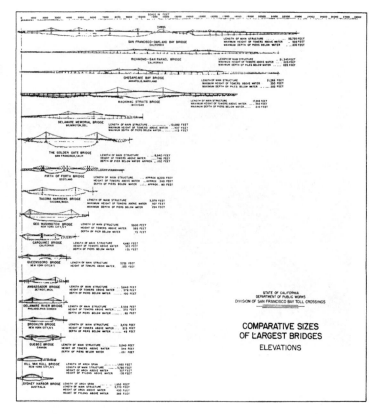

COMPARATIVE SIZES
OF LARGEST BRIDGES

ELEVATIONS

STATE OF CALIFORNIA
DEPARTMENT OF PUBLIC WORKS
DIVISION OF SAN FRANCISCO BAY TOLL CROSSINGS

STRUCTURAL MATERIAL					PILING				MISCELLANEOUS			
	Standard concrete	Light-weight concrete	Rein-forcing steel	Struc-tural steel		Concrete	Timber	Steel		2½" Pipe	Cable	Timber	Paint
	c. y.	c. y.	ton	ton		l. f.	l. f.	l. f.		l. f.	l. f.	M. B. M.	gallons
Phase I	101,270	16,560	6,010	50,000	Phase I	000	201,000	558,170	Phase I	45,400	251,900	1,100	65,000
Phase II	11,110	23,140	2,990	3,000	Phase II	53,000	000	7,930	Phase II	13,500	64,600	000	000
Totals	112,380	39,700	9,000	53,000	Totals	53,000	201,000	566,100	Totals	58,900	316,500	1,100	65,000

. . . Continued on page 22

Freeway Traffic Flow

By GEORGE M. WEBB, Traffic Engineer, and
KARL MOSKOWITZ, Assistant Traffic Engineer

THE INCREASE in California population (3½ million in 10 years) and vehicle registration (also 3½ million in 10 years) has been reflected in a tremendous increase in traffic volumes throughout the State and particularly in the metropolitan areas of Los Angeles and San Francisco.

To accommodate this traffic, an increasing program of freeway construction is being carried on by the California Division of Highways and more is being planned. Because of the large sums of money expended on this program, a constant re-evaluation of design standards is essential to assure that the greatest possible traffic service is provided for each dollar.

Opinions based on casual observations of traffic movements are not sufficiently reliable for the important decisions required in the design of these projects. To gain factual information for the designer, numerous counts of traffic flow on freeways have been made since the first ones were opened to traffic. The most recent of these counts was a carefully planned study begun in the San Francisco and Los Angeles areas in 1955. An analysis of these data, together with tentative conclusions, is presented in 'Freeway Capacity Study of 1955," published by the California Division of Highways.

Because of the increasing evidence of public interest in this subject, this article will point up some of the facts contained in the report, which runs to 41 typewritten pages and 61 graphs and figures. The full report is available on request.

The field work basically consisted of counting and classifying traffic by type of vehicle in five-minute intervals and in each lane; measuring and recording speeds, and keeping a descriptive record of the type of operation, i.e., free-flowing, smooth but crowded, or congested. Motion pic-

At a four-level traffic interchange which can carry up to 20,000 vehicles per hour, a demand of 23,000 vehicles per hour has the same result

tures were also made for the purpose of illustrating, better than words can, the type of flow experienced at various volume levels and as affected by design features. These films are primarily for training and instruction of division personnel.

FINDINGS OF STUDY

Some of the facts found out in the study are:

1. The highest one-way volume observed during one hour was 8,082 ve-

hicles southbound on the five-lane weaving section of the Harbor Freeway immediately south of the four-level interchange in Los Angeles. Some other high hourly volumes were as follows (all figures are one-way traffic in the direction of heavier flow):

Four Lanes One Way (Eight-lane Freeways)

Hollywood Freeway westbound from four-level interchange	7,793
Hollywood Freeway westbound at Vermont	7,548
Hollywood Freeway westbound at Mulholland	6,419
Bayshore Freeway southbound at 22d St.	6,002

UPPER—Congestion is relative. At an intersection of two-lane highways with a capacity of 1,600 vehicles per hour, 1,800 vehicles per hour produced congestion.
LOWER—At an intersection of three-lane, one-way city streets, capacity 2,000 vehicles per hour, an additional 100 vehicles per hour produced congestion.

Three Lanes One Way (Six-lane Freeways)
Hollywood Freeway eastbound at Highland.. 6,630
Pasadena Freeway northbound at Ave. 35.. 5,268
Eastshore Freeway northbound at 19th St..... 4,270

Two Lanes One Way (Four-lane Freeways)
Santa Ana Freeway westbound at Florence . 3,962
Eastshore Freeway southbound at Hegen-
berger 3,020

2. Freeways in large metropolitan areas (1,000,000 and more persons) carry an hourly volume up to 25 percent higher than hourly volumes on freeways in less populated areas (under 500,000) with no greater momentary degree of congestion. This is because of the sharp peak demand which lasts less than an hour in smaller metropolitan areas. In the large metropolitan areas, the peak flow which causes this particular degree of congestion will last much longer.

3. As most regular users of freeways must have noted, freeway traffic at high volumes is not evenly divided by lane. The shoulder lane (except at ramps) never carries nearly as much traffic as the other lanes, even with no trucks. For this reason, a three-lane roadway (one-way) will carry a somewhat greater average volume per lane than a two-lane roadway.

4. A three-lane roadway (one-way) was observed to be capable of carrying more traffic per lane than a two-lane one-way section by comparing the two sections at ideal operating conditions. There is no four-lane one-way roadway available for observation which has as ideal a combination of geometrics and demand as this three-lane section, but it is believed that under the same conditions a four-lane roadway will in turn average more traffic per lane than a three-lane section. The highest volume observed on a four-lane roadway was 7,793 in an hour (westbound on the Hollywood Freeway immediately west of the four-level interchange).

Undesirable Congestion

5. Undesirable congestion is usually experienced when traffic volumes increase to the point where operating speeds are reduced to 35 miles per hour. At this speed, traffic is practically bumper to bumper; there are very few normal gaps available for lane-changing, and there is noticeable

UPPER—Even slight upgrades significantly reduce capacity when truck volumes are appreciable. Note uneven distribution of traffic by lanes. LOWER—Another view of the four-level structure showing normal midday operation.

driving tension even for short rides. Also, at this speed stoppages can occur quickly even from a single driver's faulty maneuver or hesitation. And finally, when congestion reduces speeds to 35 miles per hour it means that the lanes nearest the median are carrying 2,000 vehicles or more per hour. Expressed another way, this gives an interval between vehicles of only 1.8 seconds.

It is believed that volumes which result in an average freeway speed of 45 miles per hour should be considered the practical capacity of the freeway. At an average speed of 45 miles per hour the traffic in the shoulder lane will average about 40 miles

per hour and traffic in the median lane will average near 50 miles per hour.

6. Upgrades as small as 2 percent significantly reduce capacity when truck volumes are appreciable. On downgrades of significant length, average volumes of 2,000 vehicles per lane per hour can be carried with no congestion.

7. The comfortable operating volume for one direction of an eight-lane freeway (based on a 45-mile-per-hour minimum average speed) at an average location with undulating grade lines in a large urban area with 200 to 250 trucks and busses per hour is about 5,500 vehicles per hour, distributed as follows:

	v.p.h.
Lane 1 (next to shoulder)	800
Lane 2	1,100
Lane 3	1,800
Lane 4 (next to median)	1,800
	5,500

The foregoing indicates that for a typical urban four-lane roadway (one-way) and about 3 percent trucks (up to 200 per hour) a round figure of 1,500 vehicles per lane per hour may be considered the practical capacity for eight-lane freeways. Four-lane freeways with an equivalent percentage of trucks have a considerably lower average capacity per lane because of the inefficient use of the outside lane.

8. Determination of maximum volume which can enter a freeway at one point is more dependent upon the sum of the ramp volume and the adjacent lane volume than it is upon the length of the merging area (acceleration lane and taper).

APPLICATION OF TRAFFIC STUDIES TO DESIGN

When the Pasadena Freeway was designed more than 15 years ago, it was a pioneer in its field. There were practically no similar facilities in existence anywhere upon which predictions could be made as to operating characteristics or volume. But shortly after it was built, traffic counts and

observations were made on it and, as the years went by, similar counts were made on other facilities which were gradually coming into existence in other parts of the United States.

The results of these various counts were made available to the engineering profession through technical journals such as the magazine "Public Roads" and the "Proceedings" of the Highway Research Board of the National Research Council, and these formed the basis for design of later freeways.

Finally, in 1949, the Highway Capacity Committee of the Highway Research Board (which had the active cooperation of the California Division of Highways, and on which the division has been and is represented) thought that enough data had been collected to produce a manual called the "Highway Capacity Manual." Later counts, including the study mentioned at the beginning of this article, have confirmed with remarkable agreement the findings published in the Highway Research Board Manual.

Evolution in Design

By comparing the Pasadena Freeway with the Harbor and Hollywood Freeways, the evolution in freeway design which has taken place as a result of traffic studies is obvious.

A few of the more important changes are listed here:

1. Metropolitan freeways are now designed for eight lanes instead of six.
2. Inlet ramps are provided with acceleration lanes.
3. Easier curves have been provided, primarily to decrease accidents in the off-peak hours rather than to increase speeds.
4. Lane widths have been increased from 10 or 11 feet to 12 feet.
5. The taper lengths at merging areas have been increased.
6. "Escape hatches"—i.e. merging lanes beyond the exit noses at points where the freeway drops a lane, are provided.
7. The median separation has been widened to 22 feet and an emergency refuge area provided on the inside as well as the outside. This change is just now being noted in actual constructed freeways; it was on the drawing boards some time ago.
8. Signs have been made much larger, more legible, and positioning has improved. Signs have now been designed which will provide greater advance notice for drivers to move to proper lanes well in advance of freeway exits.

Another view of merging traffic from left-hand entry

UPPER—Harbor Freeway in Los Angeles. Everyone starts home at once. LOWER—Hollywood Freeway in Los Angeles, Highway Avenue on-ramp. Note merging movement from left, with contrasting pavement in merging area.

Freeway operation under peak-load conditions is extremely sensitive. Hasty, ill-advised changes in design or traffic control devices could be very detrimental to the safe, orderly movement of traffic. Furthermore, changes and additions are costly. For these reasons, the Division of High-ways must proceed carefully and then only after thorough study. A very large initial and continuing operating expense could be incurred by plac-

Merging traffic from left-hand entry, as it looks to the driver

ing electrical control devices in, or "gadgeteering" existing freeways. The benefits, in terms of reduced congestion, are doubtful; the only certain result of such a program would be to divert funds from construction of additional needed freeways.

· It must be clear that even freeways have a capacity; that is to say, a limit to the volume they will carry. By its very definition, capacity is the volume of traffic that can be handled without congestion. If the demand exceeds the capacity, there will be congestion. This is just as sure as the fact that if you pour a gallon of water in a one-half gallon container, it will overflow.

At the present stage of development, there are several places on metropolitan freeways in California where the demand exceeds the capacity for about an hour every day in each direction.

There is one point in Los Angeles where more than 23,000 vehicles pass through the intersection of two freeways in one hour every weekday evening. Nine thousand of them make either right or left turns. This is a fantastic volume of traffic to go through

a single intersection in one hour. As long as the demand remains less than 20,000 cars an hour, traffic keeps flowing smoothly. This facility has tremendous capacity without backlogging, but whenever *that* capacity is exceeded somebody has to wait.

1. *Additional Traffic Lanes.* The first and most obvious cure for congestion is to provide more traffic lanes. This can be accomplished either by adding lanes to the existing freeways or by construction of additional freeways in different locations.

When existing freeways are eight lanes already, or when they feed into eight-lane freeways, the better way of bringing demand and capacity into balance is to build additional freeways which lie closer to the desired travel lines of many of the present freeway users. To illustrate this, consider the case cited above where the demand is 23,000 vehicles per hour. More than a quarter-million trips a day go through this point; this amounts to one of every eight cars in the entire Los Angeles area (or one in every 16 cars twice a day). It is certain that this many people do not go through this one point because they have busi-

ness right there; they do it because, so far, it is the best way to get where they want to go. When there are shorter or straighter or quicker ways, they will use them instead. Increasing the capacity of a freeway beyond eight lanes would postpone the day when additional freeways become available. It would also put a concentrated strain on the city street feeders that would be very difficult to overcome.

2. *Modifications in the design* of existing freeways are made whenever it is found practicable to do so and when it is believed that they will help. Examples of this are to be found where exit lanes have been widened at the connections with city streets to prevent backing into the freeway and where off-ramp locations have been redesigned. In some instances, additional pavement delineation by means of asphalt (for the purpose of warning traffic that a lane is to be dropped) or diagonal arrows have been used to better inform motorists what channels they should follow.

3. *Improved Signing.* Although California freeways from the beginning have had larger signs and more advance signing than any other state highways and as much as any modern roads anywhere, the problem of ade-

quate signing is continually being reviewed and changes are bieng made to meet the challenge of freeways carrying far more than the designed capacity. Specifically new signs have now been designed to tell drivers sooner what lane to use for the next exit and to give distances to succeeding exits. (Latest signing practices were described and illustrated in the May-June, 1956, issue of *California Highways and Public Works*.)

4. *Traffic Control.* The importance of adequate traffic control for the purpose of keeping traffic moving and taking action with regard to stoppages occasioned either by disabled vehicles or collisions must be recognized.

The removal of disabled vehicles from the traveled way is extremely important when traffic flow is at saturation volumes. One lane blocked for 10 minutes under such conditions will cause a stoppage which backs up and does not totally dissipate for 90 minutes. By that time, of course, although the traffic on the freeway is all moving again, the tail end of the jam has

moved back to include the on-ramps and even the downtown streets. As many as 10,000 cars can feel the effects of such a stoppage. This is essentially an enforcement problem.

Speed Limits. The capacity of a freeway lane is about three times that of a lane in a city street. The ratio depends on the amount of control imposed on the city street traffic and the time intervals between vehicles. During long intervals, or "gaps," the traffic flow is zero. Intersections, signals, and other controls create these gaps. In order to make full use of all freeway lanes, traffic must be allowed to fill up the gaps between vehicles. This means that variable speeds are necessary, and lane changing is essential. Imposition of controls which would freeze speeds or prohibit lane changing (provided that they could be enforced) would be certain to reduce capacity and increase delay.

It has been found that when hourly volumes are such as to permit comfortable driving on a freeway, i.e. 1,500 vehicles per lane, the *average*

speed for all lanes is 45 miles per hour. More than half of the cars are going faster than that, and half of the cars in the median lane are going more than 50 miles per hour. When speeds are reduced to where the faster cars are going only 45 miles per hour, congestion has set in. When volumes reach the point where traffic is slowed down to 35 miles per hour, it is virtually impossible to "speed," and cars are so close together that driving becomes tense.

Imposing a low speed limit other than the basic speed law now in the statutes, which requires reasonable, prudent speed, could have only these effects: it would make law violators out of a high percentage of the off-peak drivers; it would create "lane-block" barricades of three- or four-abreast drivers proceeding at a frozen speed; and it would cause a large number of drivers to be watching their rear-view mirrors at times when they should be watching the car ahead. A speed limit during periods of congestion would, of course, be mean-

Hollywood Freeway, with traffic from the Pasadena Freeway merging. This is what a peak-hour flow of 7,800 vehicles per hour in one direction looks like.

ingless because nobody is going more
than 40 miles per hour anyway.

MECHANICAL DEVICES

Many ideas have been advanced for
elaborate control measures, including
electrical and mechanical devices, almost all of which cost very large sums
of money, both for initial installation
and for continuing operation. In most
instances, the effects of such devices
have not been adequately studied or
considered.

For example, suggestions have been
made that electric signs to be actuated
by various means be installed for the
purpose of advance warning of stalls
and wrecks on freeways. Some of the
technical problems to consider before
adopting such signs are these:

1. In multiple collisions, the vehicles involved are following *immediately* behind
the first car which gets in trouble. There
is no place where warning devices could
be installed, and no particular instant at
which they should be activated, to warn
cars that the fellow 100 yards ahead is
about to have a collision.

2. For the purpose of warning the more
distant traffic of congestion ahead, it would
be necessary to rely on motorists at the
scene to find the proper button and push
it. Generally, no one (unless personally involved) even gets out of his car at the
scene of an accident.

3. A very elaborate electrical detecting
device might possibly be invented, which
would automatically illuminate signals to the
rear when traffic slowed down beyond a
certain point, say 25 miles per hour. (It
would not be possible, of course, for presently available electrical devices to tell the
difference between stopped traffic and no
traffic at all. Either condition would indicate the same to a detector in the pavement.) The design would have to be such
that no false alarms would be turned in,
or it would soon be worthless. A system
which would accomplish the desired results
has not been devised to date. Additionally,
even simple lane control signals at periodic
intervals would cost several hundred thousand dollars per mile, including the complicated electrical circuits, structures to support the lights, and so on.

A few people have suggested traffic
signals on freeways. It does not take
much imagination to visualize the
chaos that would result from such a
measure. Enough unfortunate experience has been had with traffic signals
on relatively low-volume expressways
to state categorically that the number
of collisions at each signal during a

At saturation volumes, even minor collisions will cause a back-up of traffic, which will take several
minutes to dissipate.

year would be enormous. And, of
course, the congestion resulting from
stoppage, and the effect it would have
on capacity, are obvious.

TELEVISION

An eastern city is considering the
installation of television on several
miles of freeway for the purpose of
keeping traffic under surveillance at
all times from a central location. Representatives of the Division of Highways have discussed this installation
with officials of the city and manufacturers of equipment.

In considering television, one must
not lose sight of the fact that this
provides only a method of seeing what
traffic is doing and does nothing directly to reduce accidents or congestion. Television could indirectly provide means for rapid dispatching of
emergency vehicles and in this way
reduce delay due to wrecked or
stalled vehicles. At the present time,
it is the thinking of Division of Highways engineers that the cost of such
an installation on California metropolitan freeways would exceed the benefits obtainable from it. In other words,
the sum of money required for the
initial installation (several hundred
thousand dollars) and subsequent operation (several hundred thousand

dollars per year) of a television system would provide greater benefit to
highway users if spent to provide additional freeways.

SUMMARY

1. Very high volumes of traffic are
being carried on metropolitan freeways in California.

2. When the volume exceeds the
capacity, delay results.

3. Many improvements in design
have been made as a result of research
and experience.

4. Solutions to congestion lie primarily in providing more travel lanes,
mostly on new alignments which are
closer to desired travel lines. In addition to this primary solution, modifications are being made in design and
directional signing is being improved.

5. Extreme caution is required in
the contemplation of restrictive control devices on freeways. The fundamental difference between freeways
and ordinary streets is the lack of restrictive control devices. The result
of this removal of controls is safer
operation, higher speeds, and greater
capacity.

6. In spite of the congestion, the
existing freeways are, to date, the safest, quickest ways available for motor
vehicles to get from one point to
another.

Informative Study

Report on Open Graded Plant-mixed Surfacing

By W. C. CARROLL, Assistant Engineer, Construction

THE FOLLOWING report is a discussion of facts about open graded plant-mixed surfacing, which have been established by the experiences of highway construction personnel in the field. Because the use of a thin top course of O. G. PMS has been restricted to a certain few areas of the State, the number of field engineers experienced in this type of bituminous pavement mixture is necessarily limited. Therefore, the principal aim of this exposition is to present all available information about this material to other interested field engineers.

To start with, the material should be defined. Generally speaking, open graded PMS is a bituminous mixture in which the grading of the mineral aggregate is deliberately left open so that the voids of the coarse aggregate are unfilled by finer aggregates. A relatively higher asphalt content provides thicker asphalt films which bind the mixture together when maximum mineral aggregate surface contact is made.

In order to give greater meaning to this definition the following discussion of the specifications for mineral aggregate and bituminous binder is presented.

MINERAL AGGREGATE

Open graded PMS is covered in Article (e) of Chapter II under Section 20, entitled "Plant-Mixed Surfacing" in the Standard Specifications. Mineral aggregate (which must be either broken stone or gravel or natural material having essentially the same qualities of angularity or surface irregularities and roughness as broken stone), shall be tough, durable, sound and free from vegetable and other deleterious substances. This is much the same as the requirement for the dense graded mineral aggregates.

The combined mineral aggregate when tested shall conform to the following requirements:

Comparison of Mineral Aggregate Grading Requirements

Sieve sizes	Percentage passing sieves				
	Type A PMS ½" max.	Type B PMS ½" max.	Type B PMS ⅜" max.	Type C PMS ½" max.	Open graded PMS
¾"	100	100		100	
½"	95-100	95-100	100	95-100	100
⅜"	75-90	80-95	95-100	80-95	90-100
No. 4	50-70	55-75	65-85	57-78	30-50
No. 8	35-50	38-55	47-65		15-32
No. 16					0-15
No. 30	15-30	18-32	25-39	21-34	
No. 200	4-7	4-8	5-12	4-9	0-3

Loss in Wet Shot Rattler Test	37% max.
Loss in Los Angeles Rattler Test (after 500 revolutions)	40% max.
Film Stripping	25% max.
Swell (test to be made on material passing No. 4 sieve)	0.030" max.

The film stripping test is only made on mineral aggregates proposed for use in O. G. PMS and is a very important test. Borderline material in respect to this test specification should not be used.

Of the various mineral aggregate requirements, those for grading show the major difference. To illustrate this difference, let us compare open graded with dense graded mineral aggregate grading specifications.

From the table above, the decrease in the amount of material between the No. 4 and No. 200 sieves is clearly indicated; the voids are unfilled, resulting in exactly what the name implies, an open graded mixture.

At the hot plant the mineral aggregate for open graded PMS is separated into two sizes which are stored in separate bins. One bin contains that portion of the material retained on a No. 4 sieve, the other contains the remainder of the material which passes a No. 4 sieve. There are no other additional requirements at the central mixing plant.

In some areas of the State excessive quantities of fines in the mineral aggregate stockpiled for use in open graded PMS necessitate the changing of screens on the plant.

Experience indicates that excessive fines will cause bleeding if the asphalt content has not been correctly computed for the specified open graded PMS mineral aggregate grading. Further, if the mineral aggregate is graded on the fine side of the grading specifications and the asphalt content is set too high, bleeding may result.

BITUMINOUS BINDER

The specifications for the bituminous binder to be used in open graded PMS are the same as those used in dense graded PMS. The amount of bituminous binder added to the mineral aggregate is between 3½ percent and 5 percent, by weight of the dry mineral aggregate.

On page 6 under Test Method No. Calif. 303-A in the Materials and Research Department Laboratory Manual of California Standard Test Procedures, it is stated that the formula used to determine the bitumen ratio for open graded mixes is 1.5 Kc + 2.5. It is further stated that no correction need be applied for viscosity. The

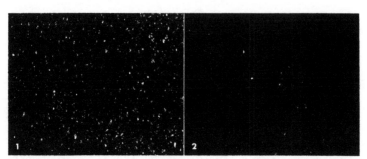

PHOTO No. 1. Close-up view of open graded PMS showing typical surface texture. PHOTO No. 2. Close-up view of dense graded PMS showing typical surface texture.

bitumen ratio computed from the above formula would be the same whether liquid asphalt SC-6 or paving asphalt, grades 150-200 or 85-100 was used.

It should be noted that open graded PMS appears over-oiled and has a very uniform surface texture. See photos No. 1 and No. 2. It is not necessary to apply a fog seal to a newly placed open graded PMS.

It seems logical to follow up our discussion of the mineral aggregate and bituminous binder requirements with a discourse on the various problems most frequently encountered in the manufacture and placement of open graded PMS.

HEATING AND TEMPERATURE CONTROL

Particular care should be taken during the manufacture of open graded PMS material to avoid overheating or 'burning" the mixture. If borderline weather conditions exist, it is recommended that the paving of open graded PMS be halted rather than risking overheating of the mixture for the sake of handling and placement. Overheating very often accounts for raveling due to fact that the asphalt film thickness on the aggregate has been reduced below that which is required to maintain what cohesion binds the material together. Generally, it is recommended that the mineral aggregate be heated to not over 275 degrees F.

In connection with this problem of heating open graded PMS at the plant and reducing the loss of temperature of the mixture from the plant to the street, it has been found that the dump truck beds can be effectively heated before first loaded with open graded PMS in the mornings by using hot aggregate from the plant bins. All loads delivered during the day should be covered.

Any cold lumps of open graded PMS should be removed from the receiving hopper of the paver. If not removed, these lumps will cause dragging of the screed unit and probable failure by raveling.

UNDERLYING SURFACE CONDITIONS AND TREATMENT

It is very important that the surface upon which the open graded PMS is to be placed shall be clean, dry and tacked with a fog spray of asphaltic emulsion.

Experience indicates a fog spray of emulsion used as a tack coat is justified where open graded PMS is being placed on top of a dense graded PMS. The rate of application of the fog spray tack coat will generally vary from 0.05 to 0.10 gallon per square yard depending upon the surface conditions. A dusty surface on the dense graded PMS combined with the rapid cooling of the open graded PMS aids slippage failures.

All delays in handling and placing open graded PMS should be eliminated, the material should be placed as soon as it is received on the job site.

FEATHER EDGING

Because the open graded PMS is intended to be used as a wearing surface over the dense graded PMS structural section, feather edging of the open graded wearing surface at the edges in order to eliminate the sudden dropoff is necessitated. Open graded mixes have also been successfully feathered at the edge of PCC gutters.

It should be noted that several of the districts call for tapers at the outside edges of the open graded PMS blanket. These tapers, which vary from 4 inches to 1 foot in width are made using the hand rake or a diagonal strike-off plate extension fitted to the paving machine screed. This strike-off plate scalps off most of the ½-inch and ⅜-inch rock, leaving the fines along the tapered edge. This screed-attached, taper strike-off has one advantage of leaving the edge looking more uniformly aligned. However, in time, under traffic, the edge usually becomes slightly ravelled and appears much the same as the hand-raked tapered-edge. It is recognized that satisfactory rolling of a taper is something desired but seldom obtained. This sometimes incomplete and uneven compaction of the tapered

14

edge accounts for the ravelling due to lack of "set" of the mixture. Also, spotty tacking at the edges of the pavement to be paved over with an open graded PMS blanket will promote ravelling of the tapered edges.

It has been suggested that fine mixes be used to construct the tapered edges on the open graded PMS wearing surface blanket. This is not recommended if water will be trapped in the open graded PMS.

THICKNESS REQUIREMENTS

Open graded plant-mixed surfacing is usually placed as a blanket 0.05 to 0.10 foot in thickness. Although a ½-inch thickness has been specified in the past, it is more common to find thicknesses from ¾ to 1¼ inches. Some of the districts have changed the grading requirements for open graded PMS mineral aggregate to require 100 percent passing the ⅜-inch sieve. This change allows the spread of a slightly thinner blanket and makes feather edging easier. Since the placing of a thinner blanket is thought to provide a smoother surface, it is suggested that the thickness be that minimum which will just prevent dragging of the screed unit on the paver.

Further discussion of the minimum thickness of the open graded PMS blanket as affected or controlled by the maximum sized aggregate and degree of irregularity of the surface of the underlying pavement is necessary to establish another fact about this type of material which has been learned by practical experience.

The coarse aggregate in the open graded PMS material must be interlocked as much as possible. If the material is allowed to drag between the screed and a high point in an irregular underlying surface the coarser mineral aggregate will be spread out or "opened up," resulting in little or no surface contact among the various rocks. (This discussion deliberately avoids introduction of cohesion or stability values because of insufficient test data being available at this time.) A dragged section of the open graded PMS material will soon ravel away, since the thicker asphalt films are ineffective as a binder because of the

PHOTO No. 3. Here rakers are forming the one-foot taper section on the left and trimming the longitudinal joint on the right. PHOTO No. 4. Shows what a routine operation the paving of open graded PMS is. PHOTO No. 5. The breakdown roller doesn't have to delay getting onto fresh mat.

decreased interlocking and surface contact of the aggregate.

RECOMMENDATION

Therefore, it is recommended that the on-the-street thickness of the blanket be governed by the degree of irregularity of the underlying surface and the maximum size of aggregate. If a section of pavement does show signs of dragging immediately behind the paver, it has proven wise to blade off this faulty section and immediately replace it with a thicker and tighter knit mat. It follows that the more uniformly true the underlying dense graded PMS material has been paved, the closer the average thickness of the open graded PMS material will approach that shown on the typical section.

It is important that the major high points in the underlying surface be observed ahead of the paver, using a string line to determine approximate screed settings, and that these locations be marked outside the width of the working area. However, this suggestion does not intend to advocate "over-control" of the screed adjustments.

FINISHING AND ROLLING

Because of its grading and relatively high asphalt content, open graded PMS used as a wearing surface is easily placed with any of the self-propelled mechanical spreading and finishing machines in use today.

Although the open graded PMS tends to cool much faster than dense graded PMS, no unusual rolling problems are incurred. However, it should be emphasized that care must be taken to avoid over-rolling open graded PMS. In most cases only one breakdown pass and/or one finish pass with the rollers are required. Excessive rolling will cause slippage failures. *Do not over-roll!*

PRODUCTION

Aside from local problems in providing sufficient quantities of properly graded mineral aggregates, open graded PMS is no detriment to plant production. (Note photos No. 3, 4 and 5.)

No unusual segregation problems have been encountered during the

PHOTOS Nos. 6, 7, and 8. These photos all illustrate the following advantages of an open-graded PMS blanket: TOP—surface dry condition during a rain. CENTER—Better delineation of E. P.'s. LOWER—Improved visibility of center stripe during a rain.

manufacturing or paving operations. When relatively thin blankets are to be paved, normal plant and street production has been maintained by using two pavers in tandem. No additional spreading and compacting costs are introduced.

ADVANTAGES

Now that we know about the mineral aggregate and bituminous binder requirements, and have been advised of problems we might encounter during the manufacture and placement phases of our dealings with open graded PMS, we will undoubtedly wonder why we are using this material; what advantages does this type of bituminous paving mixture have?

One of the important advantages of the open graded PMS wearing surface is its improvement of the riding quality of the pavement surface. The table below, which was compiled from records of roughometer reports made on various bituminous paving jobs throughout the State, clearly indicates this point of advantage.

It should be emphasized that this smoothness has two effects: (1), easier riding surface and, (2) reduction of impact loading, one of the principal factors which reduces the life of pavements. In addition, road noises caused by the vehicle tires operating on a rough surface are greatly reduced by this smoothness.

There are different theories which attempt to explain why the thin open graded PMS wearing course so effectively improves the riding smoothness of the bituminous pavement. (It has also been used to improve the smoothness of PCC pavements on bridges and in tunnels.)

One of these is based on the idea that any additional thin blanket course, whether dense or open graded, will remove a certain amount of roughness built into the course immediately below. This belief was definitely proven on a recent paving job in one of our southern districts where the 3-inch dense graded PMS was placed in three 1-inch courses. The roughometer index for this particular job was 6, which places this method of bituminous pavement construction in competition with that of adding an open graded wearing surface to a 3-inch

Roughness Index (Inches per Mile)

	Ben-Ali to Roseville Freeway	Waldo Grade on U.S. Hwy. 101 bet. San Rafael & Golden Gate Bridge	U.S. Hwy. 50 Clarksville to Shingle Springs	Porterville Bypass	SSR #20 nr. Clear Lake
Dense graded PMS leveling course..........	13	No R.I. obtained	No R.I. obtained	14	16"
Dense graded PMS surface course..........	8	12	14 8	9	8"
Open graded PMS surface course (thin blanket-0.04' to 0.08' in thickness)........	4	5	7 5	5	4"

dense graded PMS pavement which has been constructed in two lifts. However, as can be seen from the table above, the open graded PMS still has a lower roughness index.

Leveling Action

In addition to the above theory there is the hypothesis ("something assumed for the purpose of argument") that all of the excess asphalt and most of the fine aggregate actually tends to flow within the lower section of the open graded blanket around and below the lower portions of the coarse mineral aggregate; this "leveling" action by the more plastic elements of the mix fills depressions while the more stable ⅜-inch material above this plastic section is kneaded (by the rollers and vehicular traffic) until a relatively smooth surface results.

It should be mentioned that at the present time it is not feasible to test open graded PMS mixes for cohesion and stability. Further, our design criteria do not recognize open graded PMS as a part of the structural section. It is considered as being a type of seal coat. However, it is strongly felt that future laboratory studies of open graded mixes will change this classification.

Another important advantage of the open graded PMS used as a wearing surface is its relatively dry surface during wet weather. The well known fog spray which whips up from the wet pavement and

throws back onto the windshield of the following vehicle and so on, ad infinitum, is greatly reduced.

(See Photos Nos. 6, 7 and 8 which illustrate the surface dry conditions during a rain, delineation of edges of pavement and improved visibility of the center stripe during a rain.)

At one time open graded mixes were heralded for their attributes which provide a good nonskid surface. However, more recent tests do not entirely support this idea.

The following information was excerpted from a 'Report on Trends of Skid Resistance Tests of Three Highways Pavement Surfaces' which was prepared by Ralph A. Moyer, Research Engineer, and Gale Ahlborn, Graduate Research Engineer, Institute of Transportation and Traffic Engineering, University of California.

OBJECT OF TESTS

'These results of skid resistance tests have been collected to show the history and trends of three types of pavement surfaces. The tests on these surfaces are not as complete and frequent as should be for a complete analysis, but the results do show some indications of the effect of age, season and traffic.

"The test results referred to are lengthy and difficult to incorporate in this report. However, the basic findings are as follows: Open graded PMS is generally smoother than other types of pavement but does not have as high a coefficient of friction. Gener-

and Public Works

17

ally, however, the friction values for a dense graded PMS with rounded gravel aggregate and a high percentage of fines, are lower than open graded PMS, especially in tests made using the smooth tread tires.

"The lowest friction values were obtained on a section of open graded PMS which was completed and opened to traffic on the same day. It is thought that the asphalt films covering the aggregate particle were slightly more oily when these surfaces were first opened to traffic than several weeks later and that this oiliness contributed to the lower friction values which were obtained near the end of the construction period."

Another Advantage

Still another advantage of open graded PMS is derived from the fact that the uniform surface texture of the open graded PMS wearing course clearly delineates the traveled way from the shoulder areas thus providing a well-marked and easily followed lane for vehicles in all kinds of weather. With the exception of rare instances when there might be snow on the surface, traffic stripes are always visible, rain or shine. (The photos Nos. 9 through 18, inclusive, illustrate how open graded PMS wearing surfaces surpass seal coats for delineation purposes.)

One minor advantage of open graded PMS which is worthy of comment results from the flexibility of this material. The very nature of the grading of the mineral aggregate and relatively high asphalt content used in the open grade PMS wearing surface minimize reflection cracking from underlying pavements. Since it is more nearly a flexible pavement course it "gives" or heals over failure cracks which occur in the dense graded PMS pavement underneath.

As in any discussion of a subject of this kind, there are exceptions to the above statements. However, in the majority of these exceptions the failure cracks in the underlying pavement were excessively wide and most probably should have been filled with a fine mix, asphaltic joint filler material, or slurry seal before the open graded blanket was placed. It follows that open graded PMS should

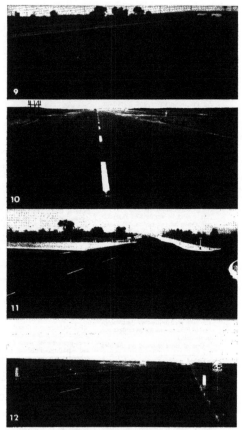

PHOTO No. 9. View of O. G. PMS blanket showing delineation characteristics—chip seal to be placed on shoulders. (No taper.) PHOTO No. 10. Question: Where are the E. P.'s? There they are! PHOTO No. 11. Here's what the O. G. looks like when carried through an intersection. PHOTO No. 12. Again the effective delineation of the open-graded PMS is clearly illustrated.

not be placed on a yielding base because the continuous flexure will definitely cause complete failure.

LIMITATIONS

As is true of all construction materials, there are limitations of usage which must be recognized and reckoned with when the use of open graded PMS is being considered. The next few paragraphs are devoted to acknowledging the known instances where open graded PMS should not be used.

In the northern districts where seasonal ice and snow conditions require the use of chains by vehicular traffic, it has been considered impracticable to use open graded PMS blankets. The expansive force of the ice exerted against the coarse aggregate combined with the cutting force of the tire chains erodes the coarse aggregate out of the mat. Also, the treads and blades of seasonal road clearing equipment damage the open graded PMS much more than they do the dense graded PMS.

However, there is one case in a northern district where this material was used on a road which is blanketed with as much as a foot of snow for short duration during the winter. In the two years that this open graded PMS blanket has been down there have been only slight failures—less than would normally be expected with dense graded PMS. Further, since there is less chance for ice to form on the open graded PMS surface, sanding operations were cut in half after the open graded PMS blanket was placed. *(Photos 19 through 21, inclusive, show the winding and steep graded mountain road on which the above-mentioned open graded PMS was placed.)*

Wearing Surface

In connection with our discussion of limitations of usage, there are a few examples of unsuccessful usage of open graded PMS as a wearing surface which should be mentioned to emphasize the need for proper utilization of open graded mixes as surface courses.

Among these is the case in a southern district where the structural section specified one inch of open graded PMS on top of two inches of dense

PHOTO No. 13. Another illustration of delineation characteristic of O. G. PMS. PHOTO No. 14. A section of Highway US 101 south of Klamath at the Freshwater Lagoon where recent floods inundated this section. Still in good condtion. PHOTO No. 15. Delineation characteristic of O. G. PMS shown again. This pavement is one of the best in the State for smoothness and appearance.

graded PMS and road mixed shoulders constructed flush with the edge of pavement grades on the open graded surface. It follows that water shedding off the 2 percent slope within the one inch of open graded top course was trapped at the down slope edges and under existing heavy traffic conditions stripping of the asphalt from the aggregate was promoted during wet weather until ravelling occurred at these outside edges. This was a clear case of misuse of the open graded PMS wearing surface.

Another case involved the use of a half-inch blanket course of open graded PMS and dirt shoulders. In wet weather the water shedding through the open graded PMS saturated the dirt shoulders making their use very hazardous. Damage to the edges of pavement resulted from loss of base support due to base saturation. This certainly would have occurred regardless of the type of pavement. However, the open graded PMS blanket provides such a surface dry appearance that the unwary driver was deceived into thinking that the surface of the shoulder was merely damp and would support his car.

There are other cases where open graded PMS was misused in much the same way. It is important that the nature of the material be recognized and provisions made to accommodate the surface drainage water in a practical manner. *(Inspection of the photos Nos. 9 through 18, inclusive, showing the various typical road sections with open graded mix as a wearing surface will illustrate this statement.)*

We have discussed the material, its manufacture and placement problems, its advantages and its restriction of use, as well as examples of misuse. Since we are trying to recognize all of the problems which arise from the use of open graded PMS, it is necessary that maintenance problems be discussed.

MAINTENANCE

In all fairness it must be admitted that open graded PMS is not easily patched. In fact, it is usually patched

with an SC-4 dense mix which promotes its own growth by trapping water in the open graded PMS on its up-slope side. It has been suggested that a hood and fire pot could be used to insure dry surface conditions in the area to be patched and that the open graded PMS could be hand mixed and placed at the patch area by maintenance crews trained in the technique of constructing open graded PMS mixes. The fear of promoting bleeding by the uncontrolled build-up of asphalt in the area to be patched provides the main argument against this method. This fear would be well founded if the mix were on the fine side of specified grading.

It has also been suggested that a small portable bituminous mixer capable of producing adequate and uniform open graded PMS material at the site of the failed area could be used successfully. This method has yet to be tried.

The maintenance engineer of one of our southern districts reports that a sizable stockpile of open graded PMS material using SC-4 has been manufactured and successfully used to patch failed areas. This is the first encouraging report of an attempt to improve patching methods where open graded PMS is involved.

COST

After all of the preceding discussions, we finally come to the subject of cost. Those readers who are familiar with the item bid prices for different types of seal coats, and for dense as well as open graded PMS will undoubtedly be familiar with the comparative costs in their respective districts.

Discussions of the comparison of costs of the chip seal and open graded PMS blankets often conclude that the open graded PMS blanket is too expensive to justify its additional cost. However, in the light of the many advantages noted above and considering the cost comparisons which follow, it is not thought that this is a fair conclusion.

The following is a comparison which has been made using the total of bid prices for the items of screenings (seal coat), and mineral aggregate (open graded PMS) and paving asphalt and asphaltic emulsion for contracts in 1954.

Total quantities were divided into total costs to arrive at average prices.

Next it was assumed that 5 percent of the total cost of open graded PMS is in the asphalt—and that one-third of the total cost of the chip seal coat is due to the asphaltic emulsion. These assumptions are based on figures extracted from *Contract Cost Data, 1954, Construction Department*. The following figures were removed from the same source:

Code 64, Paving Asphalt (PMS)
   90,500 tons at $22.0972
   (call $22.10) $1,999,392.02

Code 73, Mineral Aggregate
(open graded PMS)
   50,840 tons at $4.5735
   (call $4.57) $232,515.25

Code 60, Asphaltic Emulsion
(seal coat)
   10,503 tons at $33.9099
   (call $33.91) $356,155.93

Code 68, Screenings, Seal Coat
   150,826 tons at $6.0472
   (call $6.05) $912,074.56

1. Cost of open graded PMS:
  Pav. Asph: 5% × $22.10 = $1.11
  Min. Agg: 95% × 4.57 = 4.34

   Average cost of open ——
   graded PMS per ton.... $5.45

2. Cost of seal cost (using screenings):
  Asphaltic Emuls (seal coat):
  $\frac{2}{27}$ × $33.91 = $2.52
  Screenings (seal coat)
  $\frac{25}{27}$ × $6.05 = $5.60

          $8.12 per ton

Again from the tonnage basis it can be seen that the open graded is cheaper than the chip seal.

It might be well to convert these figures to area comparison in order to remain impartial.

---

* Based on .25 gal./S. Y. (or approx. 2 lbs.) of emuls. and 25 lbs. of screenings/S. Y.

PHOTO No. 16. Showing delineation effect of O. G. PMS, also treatment of intersection areas as regards placement of O. G. PMS. PHOTO No. 17. Showing delineation effect of O. G. PMS on Highway US 101 north of Crescent City. PHOTO No. 18. Another photo showing delineation effects of O. G. PMS blanket on US 101 north of Eureka. PHOTOS Nos. 19, 20, and 21. Illustrations of the usage of open-graded PMS blankets on mountain roads where moderate winter weather conditions are experienced. Improved delineation is apparent.

1. Cost of open graded PMS:
   Average cost = $5.45 per ton using 6 lbs. per square foot of one-half inch thickness, the area covered by a ton is 320 sq. ft. or approximately 35.5 sq. yd.
   Unit cost = $0.15/ sq. yd.

2. Cost of chip seal:
   Average cost = $8.12 per ton using 27 lbs. of material (includes both asphalt and screenings) per square yard, the area covered by a ton is 74 sq. yd.
   Unit cost = $0.11/ sq. yd.

Another report on a cost comparison between the chip seals and dense graded PMS blankets in which the loss of rock screenings which have been paid for was taken into account has been prepared by Mr. Berndt Nelson, Assistant Construction Engineer,

Headquarters Construction Department, at the time he was Construction Engineer of District VIII:

"In this area PMS averages approximately $5 per ton in place. This includes the cost of the mineral aggregate and the paving asphalt which are bid at the same unit cost although as separate items. The average cost of Class 'C' medium seal coat is $5.50 per ton for rock screenings and $38 per ton for asphalt.

"If we compare these two ways of rebuilding an existing surface on the basis of a square yard covered, we will arrive at the following cost analysis:

"(1) Cl. 'C' Med. Sl. Ct.
Asph. 0.25 gal./s.y. at $38/ton or $0.15833/gal. .... $0.0396/s.y.
Screen 0.20 lbs./s.y. at $5.50 ton or $0.00275/lb. .... .0550/s.y.

Total .... $0.0946/s.y.
Call .... $0.095 /s.y.
"(2) PMS Blanket:
PMS (½" thickness) 6.25 lbs./s.f. × 9 s.f./s.y. × $0.0025/lb. = $0.14/s.y.

"The comparison so far is based on the assumption that full benefit is obtained from the 20 pounds of screenings placed, which is decidedly not the case. Tests have been taken on the seal coat jobs placed this last season to determine the amount of screenings which stuck on to the pavement. The average is 13.3 pounds on the good jobs, indicating a waste of one-third of the screenings, even when only 20 pounds were originally placed. Therefore, no benefit was obtained from one-third of the screenings, although paid for; the cost of the quantity which did stick has been increased by this wasted amount.

"A comparison of the amount of material actually providing a wearing surface on the road will show the following results:

"(1) Screenings and asphalt per sq. yd. .... 13.3 lbs. screenings
1.0 lb. asphalt

Total .... 14.3 lbs./s.y. at $0.095/s.y.
Cost .... $0.0067/lb.
"(2) Dense graded PMS blanket .... 56.3 lbs./s.y. at $0.14/s.y.
Cost .... $0.0025/lb.

"Summarized, the Class 'C' medium seal coat in terms of quantity of material obtained cost 2.68 times as much as PMS material."

There are many cities throughout the State which are using the open graded PMS as a resurfacing material. One of these, Palo Alto, has kept good cost data records for the period of the last four years. After talking to Mr. I. T. Johnson, Public Works Superintendent of that city, the following information was obtained.

The average cost of resurfacing city streets with open graded PMS during the last four years is $0.21 per square yard. The double course chip seal using mixing-type of asphaltic emulsion cost $0.23 per square yard. From his records it is apparent that a chip seal of durability equivalent to that of the open graded PMS blanket is not any cheaper than the latter. Mr. Johnson further noted that the city has made a practice of sealing the open graded PMS in the gutters which cuts down considerably on raveling failures in the gutters during the rainy season.

Intangibles enter into this discussion of cost comparison between the chip seal and open graded PMS. Certainly the intended purpose of the seal as well as appearance or deliberate effect desired must enter into the de-

cision. However, it is hoped that the above-noted cost data will put the cost of open graded PMS material into a better perspective.

RECOMMENDATIONS

It is deemed necessary to clarify the recommendation for more widespread utilization of open graded mixes for thin wearing surface blankets. The open graded PMS wearing surface should be placed on top of dense graded PMS travel way pavements and paved shoulders with full recognition of its water shedding characteristic. It should not be used where water can be trapped within the open graded PMS. Open graded PMS should not be used to correct any deficiencies in the underlying base material or dense graded PMS.

CONCLUSION

In conclusion it is opined that a more state-wide utilization of open graded PMS wearing surfaces will provide many more miles of smoother riding and safer bituminous pavements and reduce maintenance costs. Any questions arising from reading the information set forth in this report should be addressed to the author at Construction Headquarters Office.

RECORD SPAN

Continued from page 4 . . .

In the performance of the work under this project due credit is here given to the many persons engaged in the tasks of obtaining the various materials, the fabrication of these materials into bridge members, and the placing and erection of these members into the structure. Their accomplishments should be recognized by the multitudes this bridge will serve in the Bay area.

COMMENDATION

6777 California Avenue
Long Beach 5, California

Division of Highways
Stanton Division

Gentlemen: I wish to take this opportunity to commend your department, and to express my thanks to two of your employees in particular, Mr. Hazard and Mr. Allen, for the courteous and helpful service which was rendered to my sister and me when our car stalled in some deep water on Artesia Boulevard.

We were sitting there, at a complete loss, wondering what to do, while numerous cars were passing us by without a single offer of help, when Mr. Hazard and Mr. Allen came along. Not only did they push our car clear of the water and traffic, for which we were deeply grateful, but then they stopped and went to a considerable amount of trouble to get the car started again and this was no small matter since it had been so completely flooded by the backwash from passing cars. After getting us out of a difficult predicament and saving us a lot of trouble and expense, it was with a great deal of reluctance that they gave us their names.

As native Californians, it makes us very proud to know, from first hand experience, of the very fine public services performed by the Division of Highways.

Yours sincerely,
Mrs. Dorise L. Claesson

Topanga Canyon

Major Reconstruction Project on
Sign Route 27 Is Completed

By K. D. LEWIS, Resident Engineer, and
ROBERT W. AKIN, Assistant Resident Engineer

TOPANGA CANYON BOULEVARD, State
Sign Route 27, extends from US
101-A, Pacific Coast Highway near
Malibu, to US 101, Ventura Boule-
vard at Woodland Hills, thence across
the west end of the San Fernando
Valley to intersect with State Sign
Route 118 at Chatsworth. Topanga
Canyon Boulevard was taken into the
State Highway System in 1933. From
Pacific Coast Highway to Ventura
Boulevard it traverses the Santa Mon-
ica Mountains.

On October 14, 1955, a contract to
grade and pave Topanga Canyon Boulevard from 3.0 mile to 3.6 mile north
of Pacific Coast Highway with three
inches of plant mix surfacing over
four inches of untreated rock base,
along with drainage facilities, was
awarded to Lowe and Watson, engineering contractors of San Bernardino. The contract allotment was
$220,000. The contract time was 100
working days.

The completion of this project has
brought Topanga Canyon Boulevard

to a uniform standard of alignment
and width for the entire length from
Pacific Coast Highway to the San Fernando Valley. By improving sharp
curves and providing ample roadway
width and sight distances it is sincerely hoped that the accident rate
will be lowered materially.

Recreational Route

With the warm summer months the
exodus of people from the San Fernando Valley to the beaches is under
way and they will now find a safer
and faster route between valley and
ocean.

Topanga Canyon Boulevard has
long served as a traffic link between
the communities in the West San Fer-
nado Valley and the recreational areas
along the ocean beaches. Before the
advent of World War II this area was
considered a secluded retreat way off
in the Santa Monica Mountains. Many
retired people and members of the
Hollywood movie colony built homes
along or on top of the canyon walls.

These photographs show construction work on Topanga Canyon Boulevard reconstruction project

At the rim of the canyon Richard Dix, the one-time movie star, built a home with views that cover the full 360 degrees of the horizon. The panorama extends from Thousand Oaks in the northwest, out over the San Fernando Valley and the Sierra Madre Mountains to the north, the Santa Monica Mountains to the east, Long Beach, Palos Verde, Santa Monica to the south, and back up the coast to Point Dume in the west. Catalina Island and Channel Islands on a clear day seem to be just offshore.

After World War II others came and built homes along the canyon floor and along the walls. These people wanted quiet and seclusion for their homes yet they could not be too far away because they needed to earn the daily bread in the aircraft plants and other business enterprises in the San Fernando Valley or in the Santa Monica and Culver City areas. At present there are over 6,500 people living in this once isolated relatively uninhabited spot. There is a modern grammar school, stores, restaurants, a weekly newspaper and a United States Post Office flourishing in the canyon. New homes are being constructed continually and some day this once quiet canyon will doubtless be as thickly populated as similar canyons closer to Santa Monica and Hollywood.

Traffic Volume Increasing

As the San Fernando Valley has increased in poulation the traffic on Topanga Canyon Boulevard has also increased proportionally. Many daily users of this important state highway live in the valley and commute to their jobs in Santa Monica and other points along the coast. In addition to the large increase in weekday traffic, the week-end traffic has increased even more. The present average daily traffic is 4,600 vehicles per day with a peak of 710 per hour in the area that has been reconstructed.

The records of traffic accidents in the project area show that the majority of the accidents involved single vehicles which apparently went out of control and ran off the roadway or struck roadside barriers. This was principally due to the sharp curves, having central angles of almost 180

degrees and the very narrow roadway. The existing traveled way seemed to hang to the near vertical cliffs above the creek bed nearly 200 feet below.

The existing grades on the project averaged 6 percent and the curving alignment might be described as serpentine. To effect a better alignment it was necessary to increase the grade on the first half of the project to 6.6 percent, while it was reduced to 2.6 percent on the remainder. The sight distances were also increased and the roadbed designed with maximum superelevation where possible.

Excavation Details

The major item in the contract was 80,765 cubic yards of roadway excavation. Due to the necessity of removing overhanging material on cut slopes and the fact that the roadway excavation did not swell as predicted, this quantity was increased to 98,873 cubic yards at the completion of the contract. The grading was carried out with four (4) crawler-type tractors and scrapers during the day shift and with a 2½-cubic-yard capacity shovel and three rear dump trucks on the night shift. A pioneer road was constructed along the top of the cuts. The Southern California Edison Company and the General Telephone Company placed a shoo-fly line around the project along this road. From this road the bulldozers started to bring down the sliver cuts. At times there was barely room to maneuver the equipment between the new and the existing cut slopes. The bulldozers would overcast the material to the existing roadway where the scrapers would pick it up and carry it to the embankment site. The new cut slopes rose as high as 150 feet above the roadbed, and the fill slopes extended very nearly the same distance below.

It was originally estimated that 60 percent of the total excavation would need to be done with powder. After starting the operation, however, it was found that practically all the excavation could be done with a heavy tractor cat equipped with a ripper. It was found that the rock was cracked and fissured to such an extent that in only one instance was powder needed to carry out excavation completely. This occurred in a through cut where

a dome of extremely hard sandstone was encountered. When the overhang was brought down the first holes were loaded with powder at approximately 0.3 pounds per cubic yard of material to be shot. This shot proved very ineffective. The quick-acting high percentage powder used lost most of its force in the cracks and fissures and only about 5 percent of the expected material came down. By changing to slower-acting bag powder, and a 20 percent to 40 percent stick-type with a slightly heavier loading, the results were more favorable. The quick acting powder was later used in the sandstone dome. Because of the fissures and cracks in the rock only about 20 percent of the total excavation needed to be shot.

Drainage Construction Problems

The drainage facilities for the project consisted of three large diameter reinforced concrete culverts to drain the canyons, the largest being 72 inches in diameter, and four small diameter culverts and six down drains to clear the roadway. An interesting problem arose when it came time to lay the 72-inch pipe as it was to be placed on a 32.5 percent grade and the site was inaccessible to a crane. The problem was solved, however, by the use of a nine-ton capacity fork lift. Extensions were constructed for the forks with a raised tip to prevent slipping. The extensions were then padded to lessen the possibility of cracking a section of pipe. Due to restricted storage facilities the pipe was stored near the end of the job; the fork lift would travel to the storage yard, pick up one of the eight-ton sections, and return to the culvert location. When the fork lift was in position at the top of the trench a heavy tractor cat with bulldozer was then attached to the rear of the lift by use of a short cable. This cable was attached to the back of the dozer blade, running under it to the trailer hitch on the lift. As both pieces of equipment proceeded down the trench the heavy tractor and bulldozer acted both as counterbalance and brake for the fork lift. Once the section of pipe was placed the joint was closed by using the tips of the extensions to apply pressure on the pipe at the same time adjusting the invert to the established line. This method of closing the joints proved highly satisfactory as it not only closed the joints to a maximum degree but, by having the previous section of pipe set true, the remaining sections followed with a minimum amount of adjustment needed to effect a good alignment.

Culvert Test Installation

One may wonder at the large sizes of these culverts but it must be remembered that this is a mountainous area with very steep terrain and a relatively large water shed above each culvert. Whereas the total yearly rainfall may not run much over 20 inches a single storm may bring as much as five inches, and the intensity may run over one inch per hour. Due to this high runoff rate and the large quantity of accompanying abrasive material and debris, the single 54-inch culvert near Station 66 was selected by the District VII drainage department as a test installation for a new process asphaltic lined corrugated metal pipe manufactured by a local company. A 16-foot length of the asphalt-lined metal pipe was installed at the outlet end of the 54-inch reinforced concrete pipe. In this way identical conditions of flow will provide direct comparison between the two types of pipe. By placing the test section at the outlet, should failure occur, very little expense would be entailed to remove and replace the experimental section.

No Detours Available

The major problem confronting the contractors Lowe and Watson at the beginning of the contract was the handling of public traffic. Due to the terrain no detours around the project could be established and the road could not be closed entirely. According to the special provisions the contractor was required to provide a minimum 20-foot width of traveled way during the hours of 6 to 9 a.m. and 4 to 8 p.m. on weekdays and full time on weekends and holidays. In effect, this cut the working time of the day shift to 6½ hours for which the men had to be paid eight hours. Preparing a roadbed for traffic caused some operations to be cut down by at least another hour. Only earthwork was

UPPER—Looking southerly along completed reconstruction on Topanga Canyon Boulevard showing old superseded roadway in background. LOWER—Looking northerly along section of completed reconstruction on Topanga Canyon Boulevard.

performed at night, and time for the night shift was also reduced by the time it took to cover the rough grade and to blade it smooth for use of public traffic. During each period of opening during weekdays the traffic would nearly reach the maximum peak as described above. "Notice to the Public" signs were placed at the entrances of each road leading into the canyon. These signs stated the hours during which the road would be open to traffic. However, human nature being what it is, several cars each day would drive merrily by them to suffer disappointment by being turned back at

the barricades. Most of these motorists were very cooperative.

In spite of the bad storms which caused so much damage throughout California this winter, the contractor lost only 13 days due to inclement weather. During three periods of bad weather it was necessary to close the road to all traffic because of slippery grade as well as the danger of falling rocks and slides. Closures of this type are nothing new to the users of Topanga Canyon Boulevard, as even before construction slides occurred that would close the road for several days at a time following heavy storms.

Colton Underpass

Is Answer to the Problem of Delays at Railroad Crossing

By W. H. CRAWFORD, Senior Highway Engineer

Opening of the Eighth Street Underpass project in Colton is the answer to the long-standing problem of traffic delays at the Southern Pacific Railroad crossing in Colton on US 395-91 and State Sign Route 18. The project, having a total cost of about $1,000,000, is in the heart of the City of Colton, in San Bernardino County. The project begins at L Street and ends at existing Route US 99, also known locally as I Street.

Dedicate Underpass

Councilman Woodrow Miller presided over the dedicatory ceremonies, which were jointly sponsored by the City of Colton and the Colton Chamber of Commerce. A plaque was presented to Charles K. Dooley, publisher of the local newspaper, *The Courier*, in appreciation of the work by him and his committee, appointed by the city council, in obtaining the railroad underpass.

The ceremonies, witnessed by a large attendance of interested persons, were climaxed when State Senator James E. Cunningham cut a silk ribbon stretched across the roadway and State Highway Commissioner James A. Guthrie delivered the dedicatory address as the official representative of Governor Goodwin J. Knight.

Special Recognition

Many officials from the surrounding area, the Southern Pacific Railway, and the State Division of Highways, were on hand for the important occasion. Following a greeting by Harold Gridder, President of the Chamber of Commerce, they were introduced.

Among them were: State Senator James E. Cunningham; State Highway Commissioner James A. Guthrie; S. Wesley Break, Chairman of County Board of Supervisors; Supervisor Paul J. Young; Raymond H.

State Senator James E. Cunningham, left, cuts ribbon formally opening the project to public use. He is assisted in this pleasant task by Highway Commissioner James A. Guthrie, center, and Charles K. Dooley, Chairman of Underpass Committee.

Gregory, Mayor of San Bernardino; Assemblymen Jack A. Beaver, 72d District, and Eugene Nesbit, 73d District.

E. E. Duque, President of the California Portland Cement Company, and Vice Presidents L. E. Bancroft, Archie D. McCall, and Richard A. Grant; H. Brand Atwood, Assistant Public Relations Manager of the Southern Pacific, and T. A. Purcell, Assistant Superintendent of the Yuma Division of Southern Pacific.

Also present was Allen R. Craigmiles, veteran employee of the Southern Pacific, who was the towerman who had operated the traffic-control gates at the Eighth Street grade crossing for the past 45 years.

From the Division of Highways were: Clyde V. Kane, District Engi-

neer, District VIII; Assistant District Engineer-Operations, E. G. Bower; District Construction Engineer, H. C. Prentice; and District Right of Way Agent, Ray E. O'Bier.

Dedicatory Talks

Representatives of the agencies which participated in the financing of the underpass project spoke briefly. They were: Mayor Alva Duke for Colton; Supervisor Paul J. Young for the county; District Engineer Clyde V. Kane for the Division of Highways; and W. E. Eastman, Superintendent of the Yuma Division of the Southern Pacific Company.

During the time the public was assembling for the program, a concert of favorite selections was given by the Colton Union High School Band.

Eliminates Bottleneck

Construction of the Eighth Street Underpass is an important step in the relief of traffic congestion in urban areas on US 395-91 and State Sign Route 18. Both routes in Colton follow the alignment of Eighth Street to its intersection with existing Route US 70-99 near the center of Colton. US 70-99 is presently being constructed to full freeway standards on new alignment one block south of its present location. This new location of US 70-99 will be a portion of the San Bernardino Freeway, which has its origin in Los Angeles. The freeway is adjacent on the north to the Southern Pacific Company's right of way for its main line and four other existing tracks leading to the Colton Yards.

The grade crossing at the Southern Pacific tracks, which was eliminated by this project, has been a bottleneck to vehicular traffic dating back to horse and buggy days. An article appearing in the Colton newspaper, dated October, 1891, states: "The people of the city, and particularly of South Colton, are subjected to a great inconvenience by the trains blockading the crossings at the Southern Pacific Depot."

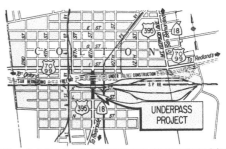

Vicinity map showing the location of the Colton Underpass and the relationship to other state highways in the area

Heavy Train Movements

Heavy train movements on the main line and switching operations on the other tracks made it necessary to install traffic-control gates in 1911. These gates, which were in continuous use for 45 years, were, in the last years of their service, lowered as much as 100 times daily and were down for about 4 hours out of every 24.

The present average daily traffic on Eighth Street at the underpassing is estimated at 18,000 vehicles, with a peak hour volume of 1,500. The peak hour occurs daily, Monday through Friday, and the traffic flow is approximately equal in each direction.

The project, which begins at L Street, follows the alignment of Eighth Street for approximately one-

LEFT—*Before construction. Looking southerly along Eighth Street, showing a typical traffic jam at the Southern Pacific Railroad crossing. RIGHT—After construction. View looking southerly along Eighth Street at junction with US 99.*

fourth mile to I Street, passing under, in turn, the Southern Pacific Railway and the San Bernardino Freeway.

In general, the work consisted of the construction of three bridges, a graded roadbed, construction of cement-treated base, placing plant-mixed surfacing on the newly constructed base, and the construction of a graded detour with imported base material and plant-mixed surfacing. The three bridges are designated "Eighth Street Underpass," "J Street Off-ramp Undercrossing," and "Eighth Street Undercrossing."

The Eighth Street Underpass is a steel girder and concrete slab deck bridge 60 feet 6 inches long, consisting of one span supported on reinforced concrete abutments to carry the railroad tracks over Eighth Street. The bridge provides a clear width of 124 feet and a clear roadway width of 44 feet and two sidewalks each five feet in width for Eighth Street.

Undercrossings

The J Street Off-ramp Undercrossing is a reinforced concrete box girder bridge, 58 feet 8 inches long, consisting of one span supported on reinforced concrete abutments. The bridge provides a roadway width of 22 feet and two safety curbs for the off-ramp, and a clear roadway of 44 feet and two sidewalks, each five feet wide, for Eighth Street.

The Eighth Street Undercrossing is a reinforced concrete box girder bridge 60 feet long, consisting of one span supported on reinforced concrete abutments, to carry the San Bernardino Freeway over Eighth Street. The bridge provides for the freeway, two roadways each 46 feet in clear width, a median strip eight feet wide, and two safety curbs; and for Eighth Street, a clear roadway width of 44 feet and two sidewalks each five feet wide.

Reinforced concrete retaining walls were constructed joining the bridge abutments in a manner to form one continuous structure. Stairways were constructed on each side of Eighth Street near the north right of way line of the Southern Pacific Company, to provide pedestrian access to the railroad property and yards.

Continuous street lighting was provided for the entire length of the pro-

Looking northerly along Eighth Street, showing in turn the Eighth Street Underpass, the J Street Off-ramp undercrossing, and the Eighth Street Undercrossing. Note completed embankment for the San Bernardino Freeway shown in right background.

ject. A drainage pumping plant was also installed to remove runoff that will accumulate in the depressed portion.

The Problem of Railroad Tracks

The problem of constructing the underpass beneath the railroad tracks without disrupting the railroad's use of its facilities was accomplished by first constructing two shoofly trestles through construction to carry three tracks and routing railroad traffic thereon. This made it possible to construct approximately two-thirds of the underpass deck. Traffic was then routed over the permanent structure on temporary alignment until trestles were removed and last sections of the deck were placed. When the deck was completed in all respects, the original five tracks were returned to final location. The clear width of 124 feet between railings will provide space for future tracks to the north and to the south of existing tracks.

All of the track work and restoration of the railway tracks and ballast and removal of shoofly trestles and tracks was performed by the Southern Pacific Company's forces.

Agitation for the Eighth Street Underpass project was started in 1941, when a delegation from local organizations of Colton, San Bernardino, and vicinity met with the California Highway Commission and requested construction of a grade separation struc-

ture on Eighth Street at Southern Pacific Company's tracks. In 1944, the Colton Underpass Committee was appointed by the City of Colton and, headed by Charles K. Dooley, continued work on the project. In 1952, the advanced stage of development of plans for conversion of US 99 to full freeway standards made it both necessary and desirable to add to the original project the two undercrossing structures previously mentioned, to effect complete separation of the proposed freeway.

Work on the project was started January 14, 1955, bringing to a close 14 years of effort by its local sponsors for its construction.

This was a cooperative project financed jointly by the Southern Pacific Company, the County of San Bernardino, the City of Colton and the State of California.

The R. M. Price Company was the contractor, with R. M. Harris, Superintendent. Don Alden was the Resident Engineer for the State Bridge Department, and the District VIII Representative was B. D. Gilbert.

In Oklahoma City, Attorney Clarence P. Green told police a 10,000-pound bulldozer belonging to one of his clients had been "stolen or innocently misappropriated, depending upon your view of mankind."

Delano Bypass

Freeway Eliminates Bottleneck On US 99 in Kern County

By O. R. ADAMS, Resident Engineer

AT 11.30 A.M. on June 22, 1956, the Delano Bypass Freeway extending from one mile south of the Delano Underpass to one-half mile north of County Line Road, a length of four miles, on US 99 in Kern County was opened to traffic and another bottleneck had been eliminated.

Immediately traffic on the old highway through Delano was reduced to a comfortable volume and, being of a local nature, assumed a leisurely pace. Use of the Delano Underpass, a hazardous spot on the old highway at the south side of the city, has been eliminated except for use by local traffic. Moreover, units of the city police and fire departments can now move across the city with a freedom not previously enjoyed. On the other hand, through traffic on the freeway

is able to traverse the city without reducing speed. Thus one more step is completed in the Division of Highway's plan to make US 99 a freeway from the Mexican border to the Oregon line.

Freeway Agreement in 1952

Negotiations with the City of Delano were completed and a freeway agreement signed in October, 1952, requiring the construction of an interchange at Airport Avenue, the south limits of Delano. Concrete paving at the Delano end of the construction project under way in 1952 between McFarland and Delano was terminated somewhat farther south than was originally planned for that contract, to permit construction of the interchange at the Airport Road

without the necessity for removal of any concrete pavement. In December of 1952, a freeway agreement for this proposed location was also completed with the County of Kern. Purchase of right of way and access rights was started soon thereafter. The contract for doing the construction work was approved December 16, 1954, with a contract time of 380 working days and an allotment of funds slightly in excess of $2,000,000. The contract will be completed in about 365 working days at a cost of $1,981,000, exclusive of engineering and right of way.

Traffic volumes on US 99 have increased steadily for many years until at present very few highways of such length in the Nation are as heavily traveled. On the old highway all of this traffic was confined to a two-lane

Normal traffic through Delano before bypass improvement

roadway which passed through the City of Delano, where speeds were necessarily restricted to 25 miles per hour. Traffic at intersecting streets each block through the city added to the congestion. Both the through traffic and the local cross traffic interfered with and delayed each other. Business properties of varying size and nature lined the highway. A few blocks to the west existed probably the least prosperous section of the city and in some cases the least desirable. Economics demanded that, if an adequate modern facility be provided, relocation was necessary.

New Alignment

The freeway, therefore, is on new alignment which, at the southerly end and through Delano, passes about one-quarter mile west of the former US 99 then veers northeasterly across the Southern Pacific Railroad tracks and the old highway on an overhead structure then northerly to the end of the project north of County Line Road.

UPPER—North Delano Overhead Crossing. In right background Southern Pacific Railroad and old US 99, looking northerly. LOWER—South end of project. Temporary crossing in foreground. View is looking southerly. Old south entrance to Delano in left center.

30

UPPER—Airport Road Overcrossing. View is looking southerly. LOWER—Cecil Avenue Overcrossing. This photo of freeway is looking southerly.

This project is the southerly one of three adjacent contracts all of which will be completed by early fall and which will provide an additional 18-mile section built to full freeway standards. Moreover, the divided highway aspect will be continuous from Los Angeles to a point a short distance north of Plaza (Visalia Interchange). This should be a welcome feature to tourists and truckers alike.

Freeway Features

General features of this contract are that two lanes of concrete pavement are provided in each direction, these being separated by a median width of 46 feet. If necessary, in the future, an additional 12-foot lane in each direction can be constructed within the median, yet retaining a 22-foot median width. On the median side the present pavement is bordered with two feet of plant-mixed surfacing and three feet of cement-treated base forming an all-weather shoulder. The outside shoulder has an eight-foot width of plant-mixed surfacing and an additional two feet of soil. Through cut sections the plant-mixed surfacing is extended beyond the eight feet to provide a paved gutter.

Twenty Ramps

Twenty ramps at various locations through the project provide for on and off movements of traffic. A frontage road and two connection roads are further service features. The frontage road serves local business; the first connection road is new construction of one block of city street to provide adjacent parallel streets to the freeway through town; and the second is a relocation of a street moved to maintain minimum standards for freeway ramps.

There are six grade separation structures, five of which are reinforced concrete box girder type construction with open type abutments. At these structures the freeway is in a depressed section passing beneath the transverse traffic movements. The sixth structure, a plate girder type with reinforced concrete deck, is really two similar but separate parallel structures which carry the new freeway over the Southern Pacific Railroad and the old highway.

Construction Details

The contractor lost no time in getting started with the construction of this balanced earthwork project. Excavation of County Line Road depressed section at the north end of the job and structure work at this location were started almost simultaneously on December 13, 1954. Four 20-cubic-yard scrapers completed the earthwork on the project by early June, 1955. Much of the time this equipment worked two shifts a day and on many days moved as much as 15,000 cubic yards of material. The earthwork operation was always directed at building the only major fill on the project to a high enough elevation to permit the start of work on the abutments for the North Delano Overhead structure.

A second objective was to provide a working place for the other structures at Airport Road, Fourth Avenue, Eleventh Avenue and Cecil Avenue as soon as possible. The footings for abutments and bents on all structures were set on cast-in-place piles. Thus, the first work at each structure location was the drilling of pile holes, placing the reinforcing steel cage and pouring the concrete for the pile. At several of the structure locations the abutments were nearly complete before the excavation of the depressed section for the freeway was started.

Parallel Structures

By the first part of May, 1955, when the plate girders for the North Delano Overhead structure arrived at a railroad siding in Delano, the contractor was ready to begin placing them. Each of the parallel structures at this location has six spans with three girders being required on each span. A single span in each structure crossed over the Southern Pacific Railroad and the placing of girders had to be coordinated with train movements. Another span of each structure had to be placed over the old highway and its traffic.

Placing of Girders

The individual plate girders are about 110 feet long, 6 feet high and weigh nearly 18 tons. Because of the weight and bulk, one girder at a time was trucked from the railroad siding to the structure site. With a 30-ton truck crane, the girders were picked off the truck, turned about 90 degrees while being raised some 25 feet, then positioned and made secure. Placement of the first girder over the highway took 13 minutes, during which time the traffic was stopped as a safety precaution. Placing of each of the other five girders spanning the highway required a traffic stoppage of 10 minutes or less. Even the traffic that was inconvenienced by having to stop seemed not to be dissatisfied at being delayed by such a well-organized operation.

Other structures were started well before this and were completed, except for minor details by midsummer of 1955, at which time the tempo of work tapered off to a conservative pace, and during most of the next few months placing of curbs, cement-treating the base for ramps and placing the plant-mixed surfacing on them were the major items under construction. In January, 1956, concrete paving operations were started, and since this project and the one adjacent to it on the north were being undertaken by the same contractor, the paving operation moved from one project to the other in paving each lane. Daily production in this item was often above 4,700 lineal feet of concrete pavement 12 feet wide.

Some 48 mercury vapor type luminaires light the location of on and off ramps including many of the reflectorized permanent signs nearby. A large illuminated sign at the south end of the project with the words "Tulare" and "Delano" and the appropriate directional arrows is a guide for the northbound traffic. At the north end a similar illuminated sign reading "Bakersfield" and "Delano" serves the southbound vehicles.

Division of Highways Bridge Department representatives on the project were Mr. Loren L. Krueger, Mr. Walter J. Bedel, and Mr. Jack D. Norberg, in turn. The contractor was Gordon H. Ball and San Ramon Valley Land Company.

Traffic Markings

Pasadena Experiment on Colorado Street a Success

By DOUGLAS C. MACKENZIE, City Engineer of Pasadena

THIS ARTICLE describes a unique application of traffic engineering to improve and expedite the safe movement of a very heavy volume of traffic on a primary business street through the heart of a city.

The street is Colorado Street in the City of Pasadena. It is the main business street in Pasadena, U. S. Highway 66, and California State Highway Routes 161 and 9.

Colorado Street has a right of way width of 100 feet and a traveled roadway width of 70 feet curb to curb.

It connects directly with the Colorado Freeway at the new Pioneers Bridge over the Arroyo Seco and extends easterly across Pasadena and into the fast growing business district in

DOUGLAS C. MacKENZIE

Los Angeles County area to the east of Pasadena.

It is the main east-west truck route through Pasadena, carries local, intercity and transcontinental bus lines and a traffic volume in excess of 20,000 vehicles in a 12-hour period, 7 a.m. to 7 p.m., on an average day. There are heavy turning movements at many of the major street intersections.

All major intersections are signalized. The traffic signals are operated on a fixed time progression in both directions on Colorado Street.

Description of the Problem

As the 70-foot street width curb to curb is too narrow to accommodate three traffic lanes in each direction

Traffic control markings on Colorado Street in Pasadena. Photographs by Pasadena Police Department.

with a parking lane on each side of the street for many years it has been marked with a double center and two 13½-foot-width traffic lanes in each direction and an eight-foot parking lane on each side.

"Far corner" bus loading zones have been standard practice in Pasadena since prior to 1950. All bus loading zones on Colorado Street are "far corner" zones.

Traffic flow was continually interrupted at intersections by vehicles desiring to turn left or right, particularly in the lanes next to the center of the street by vehicles turning left; however, many times vehicles desiring to turn right were held up by heavy pedestrian traffic at the intersection and during these times blocked the movement of traffic in the traffic lane next to the parking lane so that vehicles in both traffic lanes would be delayed through an entire cycle of the traffic signals.

Description of How Street Was Remarked

All the traffic lane lines, except the parking lane lines were removed.

The street was remarked, as shown in the accompanying photographs, with a 10-foot width center island with "left turn" lanes, using double lane lines and pavement lettering reading "Left Turn Only." The length of the left turn lane pockets at the various intersections were tailored to accommodate the number of vehicles normally desiring to turn left during a traffic signal timing cycle as determined by traffic counts at all intersections—some are designed to accommodate three or four vehicles and some six, eight, ten or more vehicles.

Parking on the near corner was prohibited for approximately four car lengths to provide a "right turn" lane and pavement lettering was installed reading "Right Turn Only."

Traffic stripes were marked to provide two 11-foot-width traffic lanes in each direction.

The photographs on page 33 were taken in the morning when the traffic was very light so the markings can be more easily seen. The black vehicle in the photograph is in the left turn lane, the light colored vehicles are in the two eastbound traffic lanes, other vehicles are standing in the parking lane and the right turn lane is unoccupied.

Tournament of Roses Parade on New Year's Day, 1955. Photo by Pasadena Star News.

Raised Bars Not Used

Attention is directed to the fact that this traffic control design has been accomplished entirely by painted pavement striping, lettering and curb painting. Because Colorado Street is the route of the annual New Year's Day Tournament of Roses Parade it is not feasible to use raised islands, bars or other raised markers in the street.

The remarking on Colorado Street from Arroyo Parkway to Mentor Avenue, a distance of 11 blocks, approximately one mile, was done in March, 1954, after approval had been granted by the California Division of Highways.

After the revised traffic control marking had been in operation for two and a half months during which time its effect on the movement of traffic was critically observed and studied it was agreed by the California Division of Highways, the Board of Directors of the City of Pasadena, the Police Department and the Engineering Department that it had very materially improved the safe and expeditious movement of traffic on this portion of Colorado Street,

... Continued on page 36

34

State's Loss

*George F. Hellesoe Retires
As Maintenance Engineer*

Gᴇᴏʀɢᴇ ꜰ. ʜᴇʟʟᴇꜱᴏᴇ, Maintenance Engineer for the Division of Highways, retired on July 6th after nearly 31 years in state service.

Hellesoe's successor is Frank E. Baxter, formerly District Engineer of District IX with headquarters at Bishop.

E. R. Foley, a staff engineer in the division headquarters at Sacramento, was promoted to Baxter's post as head of the district office at Bishop.

Testimonial Dinner

About 350 friends and associates of Hellesoe gathered in the Empire Room of the Hotel Senator on June 28th at a testimonial dinner. Some twenty former associates who preceded George in retirement were present to welcome him into their ranks.

Assistant State Highway Engineer Earl Withycombe acted as master of ceremonies. The honored guest and Mrs. Hellesoe were accompanied at the speakers' table by Director of Public Works and Mrs. Frank B. Durkee, District Engineer and Mrs. Alan S. Hart, George's successor, Frank E. Baxter and Mrs. Baxter, and Assistant Maintenance Engineer Nelson R. Bangert and his wife.

Director Durkee and Hart were the principal speakers, and the latter took George Hellesoe to task for the December, 1955, floods which disrupted the economy of the Redwood Empire. After the presentation by Bangert of a check representing contributions from a host of George's friends as a down payment on a station wagon for his projected tours, George handled the rebuttal to the lasting enjoyment of all present. In addition to the station wagon fund, George was presented with a beautifully bound book containing the signatures of about 3,000 employees of the department and other friends.

Hellesoe was appointed division maintenance engineer in 1949. Since then he has been directly responsible

GEORGE F. HELLESOE

for keeping the 14,000 miles of highway in the State Highway System in repair and open to traffic and for directing the expansion and intensification of the division's maintenance program necessitated by the tremendous increase in traffic during and since World War II. Under Hellesoe the present state-wide two-way FM radio setup between maintenance forces in the field and the Sacramento and district headquarters was developed to facilitate maintenance and other division operations.

Born at Jolon, Monterey County, Hellesoe began his engineering career in 1910 and for the next seven years was engaged in railroad construction, location, valuation and maintenance work which took him all over the western United States, Mexico and Alaska.

He first came to work for the Division of Highways in 1918 and stayed

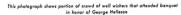

This photograph shows portion of crowd of well wishers that attended banquet in honor of George Hellesoe

been eliminated to the extent that traffic may proceed in the two traffic lanes in each direction in accordance with the coordinated traffic signal timing system in effect on the street.

Course for Traffic Engineers Planned

Designed for traffic engineers concerned with research, planning and signalization in cities over 300,000 population, counties, and states, and for instructors of traffic engineering, a two-week course on Simulation and Theory of Traffic Flow has been planned for next fall on the Los Angeles campus of the University of California.

Planned by the U. C. L. A. Institute of Transportation and Traffic Engineering and the Engineering Division of University of Extension, the course will be held September 10th to 21st, these dates having been selected to permit traffic engineers from distant points to attend the course on their way to the annual Institute of Traffic Engineers meeting in San Francisco the following week.

Instructional staff for the course will be composed of members of the U. C. L. A. ITTE staff, authorities from other universities and research agencies, and practicing traffic engineers. A detailed syllabus is being prepared as a text during the course and as a reference book after it is completed.

Persons interested in the course may obtain advance registration forms by addressing requests to the Institute of Transportation and Traffic Engineering, University of California, Los Angeles 24, California.

PLAN HIGHWAY SAFETY GROUP

Public Works Superintendent Ben E. Nutter will attempt to form a "Citizens for Highway Safety,' group in Hawaii. Mr. Nutter quoted statistics to show that such organizations on the mainland had helped to reduce traffic deaths considerably.

FRANK E. BAXTER

E. R. FOLEY

until 1920, with time out for military service.

From 1920 to 1927 he was with the U. S. Bureau of Public Roads, after which he returned to District III of the Division of Highways as locating engineer. The headquarters of District III at that time were in Sacramento.

He subsequently served as Maintenance Engineer of District I at Eureka, Construction Engineer of District II at Redding, and Maintenance Engineer of District IV in San Francisco. In 1946 he returned to District I as district engineer, a position he held until his appointment three years later as maintenance engineer for the entire division.

Baxter was born and raised in Los Angeles. An engineering graduate of the University of California at Berkeley, he came to work for the Division of Highways in 1930. The first 21 years of his career were spent in District VI at Fresno where he served as materials engineer, office engineer, and finally as maintenance engineer. In 1951, he was promoted to assistant district engineer in charge of operations of District II at Redding, where he served until his appointment in 1954 to District Engineer of District IX at Bishop.

Foley, also a native Californian, was born and raised in Nevada City. He

came to work for the Division of Highways shortly after his graduation in engineering from the University of California at Berkeley in 1932. From 1935 to 1950 he was assigned to the Bridge Department, first as resident engineer and later as assistant construction engineer. From 1942 to 1946 he served with the U. S. Navy and was in the South Pacific with the 46th Seabee Battalion. Since 1951 he has been in charge of the road inventory section of the division's highway planning survey.

TRAFFIC MARKINGS
Continued from page 34 . . .

authorization was given to extend the revised traffic control marking to the remainder of East Colorado Street.

In Operation Two Years

So in June, 1954, the marking was installed from Mentor Avenue to the east city limits, a distance of 31 blocks —approximately two and a half miles.

This traffic control marking has been in operation for two years. It has proven even more successful than was contemplated in improving the movement of traffic. Compliance with the painted markings by the motoring public has been very excellent and turning movement interference has

San Bernardino Freeway

By LYMAN R. GILLIS, District Engineer

THE YEAR 1956 is a most significant one in the history of the San Bernardino Freeway in Los Angeles County. During this year four construction contracts, covering a continuous length of 15.3 miles from Rosemead Boulevard nine miles east of Los Angeles, through the cities of El Monte, West Covina, and extending to Pomona, will be completed. These four contracts with allotments totaling $15,423,000 were started during the year 1954, and progressed simultaneously to completion.

On September 22, 1954, Governor Goodwin J. Knight officiated at the groundbreaking ceremonies that were conducted under the auspices of the El Monte Chamber of Commerce which started off the Peter Kiewit Sons' Company contract through that city. As this is written the estimated date for completion of this 3.9-mile unit of the San Bernardino Freeway from Rosemead Boulevard through the City of El Monte to the San Gabriel River, for which the con-

LYMAN R. GILLIS

struction allotment is $6,400,000, is July 20, 1956.

Magazine Articles

Three stories have been published in *California Highways and Public*

Works about this freeway in the issues of September-October, 1951; January-February 1952, and in March-April, 1953.

Old Ramona Freeway

It should be noted that these three stories referred to this freeway as the "Ramona Freeway." This was the local name that at that time was used to describe the part of this freeway in Los Angeles County. It took this name from the fact that a comparatively short length of the routing of this freeway followed along an existing street in Alhambra and Monterey Park that was called Ramona Boulevard. The name 'San Bernardino Freeway" is a most logical one indicating the easterly terminus.

State Highway Route 26, that has now become the San Bernardino Freeway, was taken into the State Highway System by action of the State

LEFT—Looking easterly along completed San Bernardino Freeway through Alhambra and Monterey Park, showing Rosemead Boulevard (the beginning of newly constructed freeway) in the extreme background. RIGHT—Looking easterly from and of present construction operations showing completed San Bernardino Freeway approaching City of Pomona. Los Angeles County Fairgrounds shown background right.

LEFT—Air view of 450-acre exposition park, home of Los Angeles County Fair in Pomona. The view gives a good idea of the space set aside for auto parking. RIGHT—Looking easterly along main promenade of the Los Angeles County Fair showing one of the familiar sightseeing trains in foreground, and the grandstand in background.

Legislature in 1931. The State Division of Highways has since then undertaken a continuous program of construction that by the end of this year (1956) will provide a six-lane full freeway 30 miles long extending from Los Angeles to Pomona.

Famous Pomona Fair

The City of Pomona is the home of the Los Angeles County Fair which, starting in 1922 from small be-

ginnings, is held annually the latter half of September. It might be said that the Los Angeles County Fair and the San Bernardino Freeway have grown up together; both enterprises started from small beginnings, and both have now attained full maturity. From an idea to an annual exposition of national and even international acclaim within a comparatively few years, the Los Angeles County Fair serves as a gigantic display wherein the agricultural, industrial and cul-

tural accomplishments of the Pacific Southwest are set forth dramatically in a panorama of infinite variety and appeal.

Fair Properties Total $20,000,000

Highway development and the amazing increase in the use of the automobile provides an interesting chapter in the story of the county fair. At first parking was no problem. The comparatively few cars found ample space in the plot around the entrance.

Looking northeast toward routes 158/26 separation structure on Rosemead Boulevard

Looking easterly from Barranca Street Overcrossing under construction

This convenient situation did not continue for long. As attendance increased from a constantly widening area it brought a corresponding increase in the number of cars and the space set aside soon became inadequate. The management was quick to envision the future and meet the challenge.

Huge Parking Area

Thus it was that almost from the beginning, adequate parking had its place in the master plan of the fair. As more land was acquired for increased facilities, provision for the automobile was an important part in those facilities, until today some 260 acres are given over to surfaced parking areas capable of accommodating around 35,000 vehicles. Last fall 271,-921 cars were parked. In the previous year there were 293,997. The peak single day in 1955 had 34,222 cars, and on the top day in 1954 there were

34,272 cars. The above figures do not include busses and other vehicles, nor does it take into account the large number of cars parked along approaching city streets and on private property.

Approach to the fairgrounds was greatly facilitated in 1949 with the opening of four-lane Ganesha Boulevard as a shortcut from the then Holt-Garvey highway, now the San Bernardino Freeway, to a main entrance gate where an underpass and overpass insures a steady traffic flow. There are now gates on all four sides of the grounds allowing convenient entrance from north, south, east and west.

Freeway Benefits Fair

It is considered that the San Bernardino Freeway is the main traffic artery to the fairgrounds and it is estimated that 70 percent of the people attending the annual county fair,

of which there have been over 1,000,-000 during each of the 1954 and 1955 seasons, come and leave by way of the San Bernardino Freeway.

Contract Completed in June

The contract for four miles of the San Bernardino Freeway carried out by Griffith Company, from the San Gabriel River to Puente Avenue at the west city limits of West Covina, was fully completed and opened to traffic on June 4, 1956. The completed grade separations on this section have eliminated signalized intersections at grade and have already greatly increased ease of traffic flow. Also the scheduled completion in July of this year of the four miles of freeway through the City of El Monte area from Rosemead Boulevard to the San Gabriel River, for which the contractor is Peter Kiewit Sons' Company, will also tremendously improve traffic flow conditions by the elimina-

UPPER—Looking westerly from eastern end of paving construction. LOWER—Looking westerly showing grading between Pomona and West Covina.

tion of many other busy signalized intersections.

Where construction is in progress from the west city limits of West Covina to Ganesha Boulevard under the two Winston Brothers contracts, conditions of traffic flow will be much improved during the coming Los An-geles County Fair season than they are at the present time. The presently existing signalized intersections at grade at Orange Avenue and at Irwin-dale Avenue will have been eliminated by the grade separation bridges now under construction, leaving only two or three signalized intersections at grade to slow up traffic for the entire 30-mile length of the San Bernardino Freeway between Los Angeles and Pomona.

Fifty-three Bridge Structures

The four current construction con-tracts on the San Bernardino Freeway include all phases of highway and bridge construction. On this 15 miles of freeway there are 53 major bridge structures, many of which have been completed, with others still under construction.

I am indebted to James E. McMahon, Principal Bridge Engineer for the southern area of the State, and his Construction Assistant, George L. Laird, for the detailed information that they have furnished me relative to outstanding features of bridge construction on these four major contracts on the San Bernardino Freeway. The bridge construction is being reported in grouping the work into two units.

UNIT 1—ROSEMEAD BOULEVARD TO
SAN GABRIEL RIVER

The bridge work included in this unit consists of 14 reinforced concrete box girder bridges, for reinforced concrete cored slab bridges, two reinforced concrete tee beam bridges, seven structural steel bridges, five reinforced concrete tunnel structures, six reinforced concrete cantilever retaining walls and a reinforced concrete pump house.

For these 39 major structures the principle items involved are 35,700 cubic yards Class A portland cement concrete, 1,368,000 pounds structural steel, 140,844 linear feet concrete piling, 5,778,000 pounds reinforcing steel

and 24,000 cubic yards structure excavation. The total bridge items aggregate a contract cost of $2,987,-258.82.

One of the major items was the driving or drilling of the piles. The contractor decided to design and develop a unique method of drilling and pouring the piles. The specifications required that approximately one-third of the piles be driven to specified tip elevation and this was done by Raymond Concrete Pile Company as subcontractor. The contractor decided to drill the balance of the piles, approximately 3,000. The contractor felt that he could afford to experiment a bit and attempt to build a drill rig of his

Looking southwest on Rosemead Boulevard, showing interchange and frontage road at routes 77/26 separation. San Bernardino Freeway running from left to right of photo.

Looking easterly from River Grade Road Undercrossing

own. At first he attempted to stabilize the subsoil by injecting a solution of sodium bicarbonate and sodium silicate into the ground at three-foot centers around pile locations. The next day, using 16-inch auger the contractor attempted to drill the holes. As the soil was gravelly, the stabilizing did not take effect as planned and the holes had a tendency to cave. The contractor then decided to develop a pressure rig.

Pile Pouring

This consisted of an auger made of a five-inch ID pipe for the shaft. The auger was drilled to the correct depth, concrete was placed into a two-cubic-yard pot which was hoisted up the leads and dumped into another two-cubic-yard pot on top of the drill. The concrete was then allowed to enter the shaft and as it came out the drill head at the bottom, the auger

MAP A. Peter Kiewit & Sons' Co. contract, eXtending from Rosemead Boulevard through El Monte to the San Gabriel River

Length of Project 20,927.70 feet -3.96 miles

was slowly pulled out. Thus the pile was poured in much the same way as tremie concrete is poured. When the hole had been filled to within 10 feet of the ground surface, the auger was removed, cleaned off, and then put back into the hole to clean the top two feet of concrete. The steel cage was then inserted and the remainder of the pile poured. Several load tests were made on piles poured in this manner and all tests proved satisfactory.

All bridge work on this unit was completed well ahead of schedule by the Peter Kiewit Company. Mr. Ward White was the project superintendent for the contractor. H. R. Lendecke was the bridge representative for the Division of Highways.

UNIT 2—FROM THE SAN GABRIEL RIVER TO POMONA

The structures included in this unit comprising three separate contracts consist of 13 undercrossing structures, one railroad overhead, six stream crossing bridges, two pedestrian overcrossings and six pump houses at a total contract cost of $2,260,000.

All of the major structures are of reinforced concrete which required the placing of approximately 29,000 cubic yards of concrete, 5,233,000 pounds reinforcing steel and 78,000 cubic yards of structure excavation and backfill. The six pump houses were constructed at undercrossings that could not be drained economically by gravity lines. The pumps

provide a combined pumping capacity of 10,750 gallons per minute.

Prestressing was of special interest and was used for various reasons in the design of these structures. The Freyssinet System of post-tensioning was used in the construction of the Bess Avenue Pedestrian Overcrossing to reduce the dead load and permit the precasting of the two main spans in the median and the erection over the traveled way with only a short interruption of traffic. Seven cables, each containing 18 wires were cast in each span and later stressed to produce a force of 570,000 pounds in each span.

Prestressing Bridges

The two frontage road bridges over Big Dalton Wash were also prestressed using the Freyssinet System to permit the lowering of the profile grade three feet on the frontage roads without reducing the channel opening under the bridges. Ninety-six cables, each containing 18 wires were cast in the bottom slab and girders of each span and were later posttensioned with hydraulic jacks to produce a force of 6,898,000 pounds in each span.

The Roebling System of prestressing, using seven one-inch galvanized wire strands stressed to 52,500 pounds per strand, will be used to posttension four of the girders of the existing bridge over Walnut Creek Channel. The portion of the existing structure to be prestressed was de-

signed for lighter loads and was constructed over 20 years ago. This stressing operation will bolster the old structure to present day standards and so permit it to carry the eastbound freeway lanes. This strengthening operation resulted in a large saving to the State in that the existing structure could be utilized in place of having to be demolished and then replaced.

The bridge structures included in this first contract of this unit were constructed by the Griffith Company under the direct supervision of H. L. McGreggor and R. MacCracken. The structures in the second and third contracts were built by the Winston Bros. Co. under the supervision of H. McCutcheon. The Bridge Department was represented in the field by W. A. McIntyre and T. M. Field.

Details of Road Work

Much interest besides the bridge construction has developed on the four major construction contracts that make up this 15 miles of freeway construction. Detailed information regarding the road work has been furnished me by Basil M. Frykland and James D. Hetherington who have had continuing responsibilities in connection with the construction of the San Bernardino Freeway for many years past. Hetherington was field office engineer and has been in close touch with all phases of construction. He held this position until about one year ago when he was promoted to the

MAP B. Griffith Co. contract, extending from the San Gabriel River to west city limits of West Covina

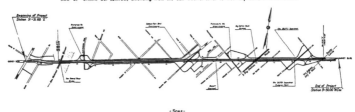

- SCALE -

Length of Project= 17,627.88 feet = 3.34 miles

position of resident engineer and given supervision of other construction projects in this vicinity.

Forty Miles of Freeway

Completion of this section of the freeway, together with the already completed units from the interchange in downtown Los Angeles to Rosemead Boulevard west of El Monte and from San Dimas Avenue westerly of the City of Pomona, through Pomona and Claremont in Los Angeles County and the Ontario-Upland areas of San Bernardino County, will provide the motorist with over 40 miles of full freeway from Metropolitan Los Angeles well into San Bernardino County. No longer will the traveling public be delayed by cross traffic at signalized intersections nor slowed by restrictive speed zones through local developments.

The four construction contracts between Rosemead Boulevard and San Dimas Avenue constitute one of the greatest projects ever undertaken in California on a single freeway at one time. Total construction allotments alone are in excess of $15,000,000.

Other Contracts

From Rosemead Boulevard easterly the contracts are as follows:

Peter Kiewit Sons' Company has the four-mile section from Rosemead Boulevard (Route 168) through the City of El Monte to the San Gabriel River that was awarded September 13, 1954, and approved September 28, 1954. The contract allotment of $6,391,600 made this the largest single highway contract awarded by the State of California up to that time.

Griffith Company had the 3.3-mile section from Durfee Avenue (easterly of the San Gabriel River) to 0.5 mile east of Puente Avenue near the west city limits of West Covina that was awarded June 30, 1954, and approved July 28, 1954. The contract allotment for this section was $3,549,900. This contract was completed and accepted by Director of Public Works Frank B. Durkee on June 11, 1956.

Winston Bros. Company has the 4.2-mile section from 0.3 mile east of Puente Avenue near the west city limits of West Covina to 0.3 mile east of Citrus Avenue that was awarded November 12, 1954, and approved December 10, 1954. The contract allotment for this section is $3,048,200, and completion is scheduled for January, 1957.

Winston Bros. Company also has the 5.2-mile section from 0.3 mile east of Citrus Avenue in West Covina to Ganesha Boulevard near the west city limits of Pomona that was awarded February 25, 1955, and approved March 16, 1955. The contract allotment is $2,432,900 and completion is scheduled for December, 1956.

Numerous Structures

The magnitude and complexity of the Peter Kiewit Sons' Company contract may be visualized when it is considered that this single contract called for the construction of 29 major structures—26 bridges, two tunnel sections and one pedestrian undercrossing—and required over two million yards of roadway embankment. Fill material was required for approximately three miles of the contract, from the Rio Hondo River to the San Gabriel River, to raise the roadbed above the surrounding terrain permitting the freeway to cross over the waterways and existing traffic arteries. The fill was constructed generally with a base width of 260 feet and 132 feet crest width. Fill material was obtained from a number of sources—the excavation of the Hill Street Tunnel in the Los Angeles Civic Center, Arcadia Wash and Eaton Wash flood control projects, Monterey Park borrow pit, Whittier Narrows County recreational area and Consolidated Rock Products Company's Durbin pit.

Six-lane Divided Roadway

Besides the construction of the above-mentioned structures and placing of fill material, this contract included paving with portland cement concrete the six-lane divided roadway and the construction of frontage roads on both sides of the freeway for a

MAP C. Winston Bros. contract, extending from west city limits of West Covina to Citrus Avenue

Length of Project 22,100 feet - 4.18 miles

distance of about three miles, together with numerous on- and off-ramps from the freeway to surface streets.

Peter Kiewit Sons' Company was represented by Thomas H. Paul, District Manager; Ward W. White, Project Superintendent; Brad F. Lockwood and R. L. Davis, Project Engineers.

Resident Engineer for the State of California was B. N. Frykland until his advancement February, 1956, to construction department supervisor. His successor as resident engineer was C. J. McCullough. James E. Martin and W. D. Knutsen served as principal assistants and R. Lendecke was State Bridge Department representative.

Traffic Through Construction

While not as complex as the Peter Kiewit Sons' Company contract the Griffith Company contract was complicated by the stage construction necessary to provide for passage through the construction area of the large volume of public traffic using this route. From the San Gabriel River to the existing freeway west of Pomona, the new freeway construction follows the alignment of existing Garvey Avenue (State Route 26). The Griffith Company contract called for the construction of the eastbound freeway lanes including bridges as first stage construction while traffic was maintained on Garvey Avenue. Traffic was also permitted to cross the construction area at all major cross streets. Upon completion of this first stage operation,

traffic was diverted from the existing highway to the three new eastbound lanes, which were striped, utilizing the paved shoulder as a portion of one lane, for four lanes of traffic. The westbound freeway portion was then constructed over the old pavement with the most northerly lane of existing pavement being salvaged as a portion of frontage road to serve local business.

Like the Kiewit contract the Griffith Company contract called for raising the freeway grade above the surrounding low area. However, the fills are generally only a few feet above the existing grade except where the freeway crosses over the Pacific Electric Railway Company line. Fills in this area are over 25 feet above the existing ground line. In all, over 900,-000 cubic yards of fill material was required. All material was hauled from Consolidated Rock Company's Durbin pit located approximately 1½ miles north of the project.

West Covina Construction

J. F. Porcher, General Construction Superintendent for the Griffith Company, headed the supervisory personnel for the contract with H. G. McGregor as construction superintendent. McGregor was promoted in 1956 and was succeeded by A. A. Kinnamon who completed the contract as construction superintendent.

For the State, B. N. Frykland and C. J. McCullough were also resident engineers on this project. The principal assistant was K. M. Johnson. W.

A. McIntyre represented the State Bridge Department until his promotion and transfer when he was replaced by T. M. Field.

Winston Bros. Company, with two contracts having a combined mileage of 9.4 miles of San Bernardino Freeway work between Puente Avenue, near the west city limits of West Covina and Ganesha Boulevard near the west city limits of Pomona, has a total of 13 bridges to erect, 10 of them under the first contract through the City of West Covina.

The first Winston Bros. Company contract from 0.5 mile east of Puente Avenue to 0.3 mile east of Citrus Avenue in the City of West Covina is generally similar to the Griffith Company contract. This contract calls for the construction of a six-lane divided freeway with grade separations at major intersections. Two stages of construction are required to provide for traffic through the construction area. At the time of writing, stage one construction has been completed and traffic diverted to the completed freeway portion. Completed to date are the eastbound lanes from Puente Avenue to Orange-Pacific Streets and the westbound lanes to the vicinity of Holt Avenue on the second contract.

Second Stage of Project

Winston Bros. are, as much as possible, working their two contracts as one project. A portion of the completed westbound section mentioned above extended into the second contract.

MAP D. Winston Bros. contract, extending from Citrus Avenue to Ganesha Boulevard

Length of Project 27,690.02 feet = 5.21 miles

At the present time Winston Bros. are constructing the bridges for the second stage and are reconstructing the salvaged portions of Garvey Avenue as a frontage road for local traffic. Unlike the Kiewit and Griffith Company contracts, all fill material to raise the freeway above the surrounding ground surface is being obtained from the cuts for underpass construction within the contract.

Construction under the second Winston Bros. contract must be carried out in three stages. First stage construction required the building of frontage roads and the construction of detours to permit construction of the Holt Avenue and Via Verde undercrossings. This work has been completed. Second stage construction, which is now in progress, calls for completion of bridge structures and paving of portions of freeway to permit diversion of traffic from Garvey Avenue. Completion of the second stage work will permit construction of the remainder of the freeway. Since most of this project is through the Kellogg Hills section, earthwork involves high cuts and fills to widen the present roadbed. Approximately 1,000,000 cubic yards of material must be moved with 39,000,000 station yards of overhaul. Excavation operations are complicated by the fact that a large portion of the material must be hauled across dense public traffic.

Unlike the three contracts to the west, which call for imported subbase and base materials, all subbase and base materials are being obtained from cut within this project. To improve the quality of materials used as base for the concrete pavement and plant mix surfaced ramps and frontage roads, all base materials are being cement treated.

Kellogg Hills Section

Of particular interest on the Kellogg Hills section of freeway was the requirement for jacking a total of 2,000 feet of various size drain pipe under the existing roadway. This was necessary at numerous locations where traffic could not be interrupted to permit trenching. For further information on this phase of work the reader is referred to the story by Resident Engineer R. M.

UPPER—Typical undercrossing, Sunset-Irwindale Undercrossing. CENTER—Prestressing operation at Big Dalton Wash. LOWER—Erecting precast superstructure at Bess Avenue.

Innis in the September-October 1955 issue of *California Highways and Public Works.*

Supervisory personnel for Winston Bros. on the two contracts are Hugh S. Thompson, project manager, and Ted Little, general superintendent.

B. N. Frykland was also resident engineer on the first Winston project with C. S. McCullough, present resident engineer. Norman C. Brinkmeyer is principal assistant. The State Bridge Department was represented by W. A. McIntyre, with T. M. Field presently in this position.

Resident engineer for the second Winston contract is R. M. Innis, with Harry Frazier as principal assistant. T. M. Field is State Bridge Department representative.

I am indebted to C. V. Kane, District Engineer, and C. G. Beer of District VIII for the information that follows regarding the San Bernardino Freeway developments in that district.

In District VIII

The present easterly terminus of the full freeway portion of the San Bernardino Freeway is at Archibald Avenue where grade separation and interchange ramps are in operation. The full freeway from the Los Angeles County Line to Archibald Avenue has a length of 7.15 miles. East of Archibald Avenue the expressway has grade intersections at Turner Avenue and Milliken Avenue.

Grade separation structure and interchange ramps have been constructed and in operation at Etiwanda Avenue since October 1955. Between Etiwanda Avenue and the City of Colton, there are a number of grade intersections. There is also a grade separated full interchange at Cedar Avenue.

At the present time, full freeway is under construction through the City of Colton beginning at Rancho Avenue on the west and extending eastward to the US 99-395 interchange, and from this point northerly to Mill Street in the City of San Bernardino.

The portion under construction consists of two contracts. Estimated completion date on the portion from Rancho Avenue to Warm Creek is November 1, 1956. The contractor on

this portion is W. F. Maxwell. The estimated completion date on the portion from Warm Creek to Mill Street is February, 1958. The contractor on this portion is Charles McCloskey and Crowell and Larson.

Plans are in preparation for full interchanges to replace all of the existing grade intersections between Archibald Avenue and Colton, but no definite construction schedule has been determined as yet.

Importance of Freeway

The importance of the San Bernardino Freeway in the development of the freeway system in District VII is not always fully appreciated. It is a portion of one of the main east-west traffic arterials on the U. S. system of interstate highways. The 30-mile section between Los Angeles and Pomona has the unique distinction of carrying three U. S. Highways designated by the Nos. 60, 70 and 99. This fact, alone, indicates the vital importance of the San Bernardino Freeway in the federal system of highways. It is the main connection between the Los Angeles metropolitan area and Imperial Valley, directly serving agricultural areas and industry. It is extensively used by recreational traffic between the metropolitan area and the many scenic and resort centers in the mountains and desert areas of Riverside, San Bernardino and Imperial Counties.

Within Los Angeles County, the San Bernardino Freeway is the major east-west arterial through the San Gabriel Valley, directly connecting the rapidly expanding cities of Los Angeles, Alhambra, Monterey Park, El Monte, and West Covina with Pomona and Claremont. In addition to many important city streets and county roads, seven state highway routes (2, 4, 62, 77, 167, 168 and 170) are intersected and at all these locations grade separations and interchange ramp connections with the freeway are provided. The freeway also serves a number of communities not directly traversed, such as Pasadena, San Gabriel, Temple City, Arcadia, Monrovia, Baldwin Park, Puente, Covina and Glendora. Although the development of the San Gabriel Valley is predominantly residential,

Cleaning drill rig auger

there is a corresponding expansion of local business areas and there is also considerable development of new industrial areas.

Cost Is $50,000,000

In round numbers this 30.7 miles of the San Bernardino Freeway in District VII, from the westerly terminus from the junction of Santa Ana Freeway to the Los Angeles-San Bernardino County line, has cost a total of $50,000,000.

The traffic service which this freeway is providing is indicated by traffic counts. Five years ago there were only six miles of the San Bernardino Freeway that were completed and opened to traffic. This was the most westerly section extending from the Los Angeles River bridge to Helen Drive in the City Terrace area just easterly of the Los Angeles City limits. The traffic on the then completed portions of the San Bernardino Freeway has been steadily increasing. The average daily traffic in 1950 was 25,000 vehicles per day whereas recent counts taken at Soto Street show 88,000 vehicles per day. This tremendous increase in traffic is to a considerable extent due to the unprecedented building program in the areas passed through.

This explosive growth in the San Gabriel Valley area may be attributed in no small measure to the development of the San Bernardino Freeway and the fact that the area is thus brought closer, measured in travel time, to the Los Angeles metropolitan area.

Bidders Pulled Out of a Hat

When an organization of contractors goes about letting a contract for itself, the method will vary considerably, although not entirely, from the detailed procedure followed by the Department of Public Works in dealing with the same contractors. Competitive sealed bids are submitted—but not everybody gets a chance to bid.

The Associated General Contractors of America, Southern California Chapter, is about to put up a new chapter building. Which of the chapter members should get the job?

As described in the chapter's news bulletin, the procedure first called for asking how many of the member firms were interested. There were 22 responses.

The building committee then listed the name of each interested firm on a separate piece of paper and placed all these names in a hat (the news bulletin does not say whose).

Chapter President Walter F. Maxwell then drew six names, and these firms constituted the official bidders' list. Plans were sent to each of the six lucky ones, and at a designated time the bids are to be opened in the presence of the bidders.

"Although this procedure may seem contrary to custom and practice within the construction industry," the news bulletin states, "we feel certain of your understanding of the Building Committee's problem in this connection, and that under the circumstances the committee is to be complimented for its fair and unbiased treatment in the handling of a situation which inevitably arises when a general contractors' trade association decides to build a new home for itself."

UPPER—Erecting steel at East El Monte structure. LOWER—Drilling pile holes at El Monte structure.

HORN AND "HORSE SENSE"

Many a motorist depends a great deal more on his horn than on his "horse sense" to get him by in traffic.

The National Automobile Club points out that you've probably seen the type. Somehow or other he seems to feel that if he blows that horn loud enough and long enough and often enough, all will go well. When he finds himself caught in traffic that is a little congested, he just starts to blow his horn. Whenever anyone interrupts his line of travel in the slightest, he leans on that button. Whenever he's approaching an intersection, he makes no slow down in his speed, makes no allowances for the cars that might be coming in the other direction, but just blasts the horn and then crashes on through.

Don't drive so. It's always much better to use that horn sparingly and to use your brakes, your steering wheel, and your accelerator more skillfully and more judiciously. Don't depend on your horn. Depend on your "horse sense" to get you by in traffic.

Cost Index

*Rises Reported During
Second Quarter of 1956*

By RICHARD H. WILSON, Assistant State Highway Engineer; H. C. McCARTY, Office Engineer;
L. B. REYNOLDS, Assistant Office Engineer

DURING the second quarter of 1956, state highway construction costs were up 16.6 percent over the first quarter of 1956 and were up 20.4 percent over the second quarter of 1955. The Index stands at 255.9 (1940 = 100) for this period which is 66.9 Index points above a low established in the second quarter of 1954. The first quarter of 1956 was 3.2 percent above the fourth quarter of 1955.

At the end of the fourth quarter of 1955, a separate Index was computed to include bid prices for construction under the Toll Bridge Act of the new parallel bridge and approaches across Carquinez Strait. The reasons for excluding the Carquinez Bridge contracts from the normal Index were based on the extremely large quantities of special steels and extremely large excavation yardage included in the design of the project that are not comparable in price to those found in normal highway construction. The combined Index for the fourth quarter of 1955 was 228.8, as opposed to 212.6 for the normal highway Index, and was at an all-time high. The present normal highway Index now exceeds the combined Index (normal plus the Carquinez contracts) by 11.8 percent in the second quarter of 1956.

Opinion has been expressed in several preceding Cost Index releases that construction costs would continue in an upward direction and that any sags which might occur would be temporary. These predictions have held up as a review of the graph will show.

Several labor contracts directly affecting the construction industry have recently been consummated, resulting in increased labor rates and fringe benefits. At the same time material prices have risen and such increases can be partially attributed to increased labor costs in the various in-

dustries. Labor rates affecting the crafts where contracts have not yet been renewed can be expected to follow in an upward direction.

The present labor situation in the steel industry is now having its effect in the construction field through cur-

tailment of steel deliveries to contracts now under way. The uncertainty in future deliveries will affect prices on construction projects which have been advertised for bids and also will affect prices on projects which will be advertised for bids in the future.

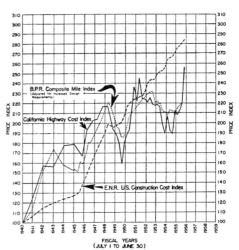

STATE OF CALIFORNIA
DEPARTMENT OF PUBLIC WORKS
DIVISION OF HIGHWAYS

**PRICE   INDEX
CONSTRUCTION   COSTS**
1940 = 100

Material suppliers are no longer offering long-term firm prices on their commodities which will have its effect on many of the larger contracts that require several years for their completion.

For some indefinite reason, competition among contractors is on the decline. In the first quarter of 1956, the Division of Highways had a normal average of 5.4 bidders on each project, but during the second quarter of this year the average dropped to 3.8 bidders per contract. In previous quarters when a lag occurred in the average number of bidders, the final average for the period was bolstered by a few particularly inviting projects. This situation has not occurred during the second quarter. Bids have recently been received on several attractive projects in the "back yards" of many firms in the industry where considerable competition could be expected, but which did not materialize with the result that the average number of bidders per contract remains low.

Some effect on bidder competition may be due to the large volume of private work in subdivision construction and work of similar nature that has attracted some of the contractors who previously have been bidding on highway projects. These private projects provide an 'in and out' operation which do not require tying up a large amount of equipment and material over a long period.

It is possible that many contractors have not shown interest in current highway work in anticipation of the forthcoming federal highway program. If this federal program has been a deterrent to bidder competition, it can be expected that an increase in the average number of bidders will occur as actual construction under the federal program will of necessity be slow in getting under way. The greater part of the federal funds applies to the interstate system, and the backlog of plans and right of way commitments on this system have not been built up to immediately absorb any considerable increase in actual construction projects over the present expanded state program. Federal regulations and standards for the interstate system have not yet been issued

NUMBER AND SIZE OF PROJECTS, TOTAL BID VALUES AND AVERAGE NUMBER OF BIDDERS

(January 1, 1956, to June 30, 1956)

Project volume	Up to $50,000	$50,000 to $100,000	$100,000 to $250,000	$250,000 to $500,000	$500,000 to $1,000,000	Over $1,000,000	All projects
Road Projects							
No. of projects...	130	29	43	17	15	1	235
Total value*.....	$1,799,298	$2,241,296	$7,251,659	$5,935,043	$11,466,782	$1,477,871	$30,201,949
Ave. No. bidders.	2.7	4.3	4.4	5.5	4.3	5.0	4.1
Structure Projects							
No. of projects...	35	6	8	7	5	1	62
Total value*.....	$585,746	$390,139	$1,105,961	$2,866,290	$3,679,497	$1,559,284	$10,586,917
Ave. No. bidders.	4.3	4.8	4.9	6.0	7.2	4.0	4.8
Combination Projects							
No. of projects...	--------	--------	--------	--------	1	18	19
Total value*.....	--------	--------	--------	--------	$995,554	$44,317,184	$45,212,738
Ave. No. bidders.	--------	--------	--------	--------	5.0	5.4	5.4
Summary							
No. of projects...	155	35	51	24	21	20	306
Total value*.....	$2,468,044	$2,631,435	$8,357,620	$8,801,333	$16,141,833	$47,654,339	$86,101,604
Ave. No. bidders.	3.8	4.4	4.5	5.6	5.0	5.3	4.3

* Bid items only.

Total Average Bidders by Months

	Jan.	Feb.	Mar.	Apr.	May	June	Avg. for six months
1956	5.9	5.1	5.1	4.1	4.7	3.3	4.3
1955	5.5	5.3	6.7	5.6	5.0	4.4	5.3

NUMBER AND SIZE OF PROJECTS, TOTAL BID VALUES AND AVERAGE NUMBER OF BIDDERS

(July 1, 1955, to June 30, 1956)

Project volume	Up to $50,000	$50,000 to $100,000	$100,000 to $250,000	$250,000 to $500,000	$500,000 to $1,000,000	Over $1,000,000	All projects
Road Projects							
No. of projects...	262	79	82	30	20	3	477
Total value*.....	$4,275,104	$6,009,304	$14,199,282	$10,788,900	$14,994,914	$4,090,792	$54,458,266
Ave. No. bidders.	2.9	4.6	5.2	5.5	5.0	7.7	4.4
Structure Projects							
No. of projects...	56	13	12	9	8	5	103
Total value*.....	$1,015,040	$852,735	$1,637,660	$3,711,505	$5,472,436	$20,508,872	$33,397,948
Ave. No. bidders.	4.3	6.5	4.6	5.9	5.0	5.2	5.6
Combination Projects							
No. of projects...	--------	--------	--------	--------	5	35	40
Total value*.....	--------	--------	--------	--------	$4,397,676	$105,907,846	$110,305,522
Ave. No. bidders.	--------	--------	--------	--------	5.2	6.3	6.0
Summary							
No. of projects...	319	92	94	39	33	43	620
Total value*.....	$5,390,144	$6,862,039	$15,836,912	$14,500,405	$24,865,026	$130,907,210	$198,361,736
Ave. No. bidders.	3.9	4.9	5.2	5.6	5.2	6.3	4.7

* Bid items only.

Total Average Bidders by Months

	July	Aug.	Sept.	Oct.	Nov.	Dec.	Jan.	Feb.	Mar.	Apr.	May	June	Avg. year
1955-56	4.9	4.3	4.4	5.4	6.2	5.4	5.9	5.1	5.1	4.1	4.7	3.3	4.7
1954-55	6.7	5.0	6.5	7.3	7.0	6.4	5.5	5.3	6.7	5.6	5.0	4.4	6.1

THE CALIFORNIA HIGHWAY CONSTRUCTION COST INDEX

Year	Cost Index
1940	100.0
1941	125.0
1942	157.5
1943	156.4
1944	177.8
1945	179.5
1946	179.7
1947	203.3
1948	216.6
1949	190.7
1950 (1st Quarter 1950—160.6)	176.7
1951 (4th Quarter 1951—245.4)	210.8
1952	224.5
1953	216.2
1954 (1st Quarter)	199.4
1954 (2d Quarter)	189.0
1954 (3d Quarter)	207.8
1954 (4th Quarter)	192.2
1955 (1st Quarter)	189.3
1955 (2d Quarter)	212.4
1955 (3d Quarter)	208.6
1955 (4th Quarter)	212.6
1956 (1st Quarter)	219.5
1956 (2d Quarter)	255.9

by the federal authorities, and a further delay to actual construction projects must be expected due to the necessity of heavy right of way expenditures in the first few years to clear the way for future construction of interstate projects.

Six items of the eight used in computing the Construction Cost Index have shown a rise during this quarter. Some of these increases can be partially attributed to the large volume of emergency repair projects resulting from storm damage during last winter which involves very difficult work and which have been put under contract in this quarter. Roadway excavation, Class A portland cement concrete (structures) and structural steel, the items which have the most effect on the Index rise are in this category. Roadway excavation stood at $0.51 while in the previous quarter it was at $0.40. Structure concrete is at $57.13, an increase of $4.62 per cubic yard, and structural steel jumped from $0.166 to $0.219 per pound.

The graph on page 49 showing the California Construction Cost Index, the *Engineering News-Record* Construction Cost Index and the United States Bureau of Public Roads Composite Mile Index compares the three, all of which are reduced to

1940 = 100 base. The latter two indexes are based on nation-wide figures.

The *Engineering News-Record* Cost Index continues in an upward direction this quarter which is practically a continuation of its first quarter rate of increase. It is up 3.5 points or 1.25 percent over the first quarter of 1956.

The rate of rise in the Bureau of Public Roads Composite Mile Index for the first quarter of 1955 conforms

closely to the previous quarter. It continues to approximate the pattern of the California Index. Figures for the second quarter are not available at this time, but past behavior of the Composite Mile Index leads us to believe that second quarter computations will show a continued climb. During the first quarter the Bureau of Public Roads Index stood at 220.0, which was up 0.96 percent over the previous period.

AVERAGE CONTRACT PRICES

	Roadway excavation, per cu. yd.	Crusher run base, per ton	Plant mix surfacing, per ton	Asphalt concrete pavement, per ton	PCC pavement, per cu. yd.	PCC structures, per cu. yd.	Bar reinforced steel, per lb.	Structural steel, per lb.
1940	$0.22	$1.54	$2.19	$2.97	$7.68	$18.33	$0.060	$0.083
1941	0.26	2.21	2.84	3.18	7.54	23.31	0.063	0.107
1942	0.35	2.81	4.02	4.16	9.62	29.48	0.073	0.103
1943	0.42	2.36	3.71	4.76	11.48	31.76	0.069	0.060
1944	0.50	2.45	4.10	4.60	10.46	31.99	0.064	0.132
1945	0.51	2.42	4.20	4.88	10.90	37.20	0.059	0.102
1946	0.41	2.45	4.00	4.68	9.48	37.28	0.060	0.099
1947	0.46	2.43	4.32	5.35	12.38	48.44	0.080	0.138
1948	0.55	2.43	4.30	5.38	13.04	49.86	0.092	0.126
1949	0.49	2.67	4.07	4.64	12.28	48.67	0.096	0.117
1950	0.40	2.25	4.26	3.75	11.11	43.45	0.079	0.094
1951	0.49	2.62	4.34	5.90	12.91	47.23	0.102	0.189
1952	0.56	2.99	5.00	4.89	13.42	48.06	0.098	0.150
1953	0.51	2.14*	5.31	4.58	13.74	50.59	0.093	0.133
1st Quarter 1954	0.45	2.35	4.23	4.75	14.89	47.82	0.092	0.126
2d Quarter 1954	0.38	2.09	4.29	5.18	14.28	47.12	0.093	0.114
3d Quarter 1954	0.43	1.85	4.68	7.00	13.63	49.59	0.095	0.162
4th Quarter 1954	0.35	1.78	4.63	...	13.13	46.08	0.094	0.135
1st Quarter 1955	0.39	1.69	4.55	...	13.44	40.66	0.095	0.140
2d Quarter 1955	0.43	1.99	5.39	...	14.46	51.36	0.096	0.136
3d Quarter 1955	0.41	2.33	5.43	5.70	13.46	49.64	0.092	0.132
4th Quarter 1955	0.37	2.00	5.52	4.00	13.05	53.72	0.099	0.144
2d Quarter 1956	0.40	2.08	6.40	6.50	14.05	52.51	0.106	0.165
3d Quarter 1956	0.51	2.06	6.27	...	14.64	57.13	0.113	0.219

* Untreated rock base substituted for crusher run base at this point.

ORINDA CROSSROAD

THE ORINDA ASSOCIATION

P. O. Box 97, Orinda, California

DEAR MR. DURKEE: The Board of Directors of the Orinda Association wish to thank you as head of the Department of Public Works, and Mr. B. W. Booker of Division Four of the Division of Highways, for the beautiful landscaping of the Orinda Crossroads.

The plantings are now attractively green. The oleanders are starting to bloom, giving color greatly adding to the effect.

We are deeply appreciative of these thoughtful efforts for beautification. We know that the more this type of planting is done to alleviate the scars of road building, the more interest people will take in helping to further such work, and the ultimate results of such interest should be a program that

will turn our roads and freeways into parkways.

Most sincerely,

MRS. RITCHIE R. WARD

LIKES OUR HIGHWAYS

DEAR MR. ADAMS: I've driven on an average of 100 miles per day for the past 40 days, over the finest system of roads and highways, anywhere. Quite a number of times I've driven to the East Coast by various routes, as well as Canada and there is *nothing—anywhere*—to compare to even our secondary state highways. Your work must be particularly gratifying when you can keep many persons informed as to the work that is being done as well as projects for the future.

Thank you very much.

Sincerely,

HUGH BROWN

El Monte

Governor Knight Opens New Section of Freeway in South

By C. A. MAGHETTI, Secretary, State Highway Commission

NEGOTIATIONS which began as far back as 10 years between the California Highway Commission and the City of El Monte came to a successful conclusion Monday, July 16, 1956, when Governor Goodwin J. Knight snipped the ribbon which opened up four more miles of highway through El Monte on the San Bernardino Freeway.

Over 300 persons joined in the eventful occasion which was preceded by a luncheon in the Civic Auditorium hosted by the Rotary Club of that city.

Presented for introduction were many of El Monte's leading citizens. Included in the group were Charles Gallagher, President of the Rotary Club; Arden Danesson, President of the Chamber of Commerce; William Allen, Mayor; City Councilmen Dale Ingram, Lester Dagley, R. L. Johnson, and Sidney Cading; Fred King, City Administrator; Telpher Wright, former assistant to the city council.

Former city officials present who were in office at the beginning of negotiations were: Ex-Mayor R. C. Miller; Councilmen Cecil Cady and Chester Langan.

Representing the state office were: Highway Commissioners James Guthrie of San Bernardino, and Fred Speers of Escondido, C. A. Maghetti, Highway Commission Secretary, and C. Max Gilliss, Deputy Director of Public Works.

Supervisor Herbert Legg represented the County of Los Angeles.

From the district highway office: Lyman R. Gillis, District Engineer; Frank B. Cressy, Assistant District Engineer; W. D. Sedgwick, Assistant District Engineer; A. D. Griffin, Assistant District Engineer; L. S. Van Voorhis, Assistant District Engineer (Design); L. M. Wade, Senior Highway Engineer (Design); Basil Frykland, District Construction Engineer

Governor Knight officiates at El Monte Freeway dedication. Left to right: Governor; C. M. Gilliss, Deputy Director of Public Works; Highway Commissioner Fred W. Speers, Assemblyman L. M. Backstrand, Highway Commissioner James A. Guthrie.

(Field); C. J. McCullough, Resident Engineer; Wally Knudson, Assistant Resident Engineer; and James Martin, Senior Highway Engineer.

From the Bridge Department of the Division of Highways: James McMahon, Principal Bridge Engineer; George Laird, Bridge Construction Engineer; and Bob Lendecke, Bridge Representative.

In his speech, Governor Knight complimented the work of the Highway Commission, the Department of Public Works, Division of Highways, and the El Monte City Council for the joint efforts which made the freeway possible. He referred to the time, September 22, 1954, when he made a special trip from Sacramento to officiate at the ground-breaking ceremonies.

He continued in part:

"We are dedicating today a splendid four-mile section of the San Bernardino Freeway through El Monte, on which traffic will flow within a few days. This freeway section, which extends from Rosemead Boulevard to the San Gabriel River, is typical of the freeways California is building today.

"But impressive as it is, this freeway is only a part of the picture in this area, for the year 1956 is a most significant one in the history of the San Bernardino Freeway in Los Angeles County.

"During this year four construction contracts, covering a continuous length of a little over 15 miles from Rosemead Boulevard nine miles east of Los Angeles, through the Cities of El Monte, West Covina, and extending to Pomona, will be completed at a cost of nearly fifteen and a half million dollars. Of this amount, nearly $6,400,000 was expended on the El Monte project.

"Completion of the four projects in this area, together with already completed sections, will provide the motorist with over 40 miles of full freeway from metropolitan Los Angeles well into San Bernardino County.

"No longer will the traveling public be delayed by cross traffic at signalized intersections nor slowed by restrictive speed zones through local developments.

"The entire freeway program in Southern California will be stepped up under increased federal aid for highways under legislation just signed by the President.

'During the past 10-year period, the amounts budgeted or spent for highway construction purposes have reached the impressive total of more than $1,640,000,000."

NEW YORK LETTER

STATE OF NEW YORK
DEPARTMENT OF PUBLIC WORKS
Albany 1, N. Y.

GENTLEMEN: I wish to express my appreciation of your *California Highways and Public Works* magazine and certainly wish to continue on your mailing list.

Two Ladies About To Cut a Ribbon

Mrs. Anthony Nizetich, President of San Pedro Chamber of Commerce, Women's Division (left), and Mrs. Jean Hagler, President of the Wilmington Chamber of Commerce, Women's Division (right), cooperated in cutting ribbon on June 4, 1956, upon the opening of the westerly traffic lanes to southbound traffic on the Harbor Freeway between Pacific Coast Highway in Wilmington and Battery Street in San Pedro. At this ceremony Harold Coulthurst, Chairman of Transportation and Traffic Division of the Wilmington Chamber of Commerce was master of ceremonies. Among the speakers were Vincent Thomas, Assemblyman for the 68th District; Jack Yount, Vice President for Vinnell Constructors of Alhambra, representing the contractors; and Edward T. Telford, Assistant State Highway Engineer in charge of District VII. The easterly lanes of this 2.8 miles section of freeway were opened to northbound traffic on June 19, 1956.

I have been a close reader of your excellent magazine since about 1950 and your articles on Rights of Way have been of great interest to me in my capacity of Chief Appraiser in New York State, especially on our "Thruway" and subsequent similar construction now in the planning stage.

I compliment you highly on your excellent composition and photographic material. I read your magazine from cover to cover.

Please extend my regards to Messrs. Frank Balfour, George Pingry, E. M. McDonald, and R. S. V. Pianezzi of your Rights of Way Department who were so kind and cooperative on my last visit to Sacramento back in 1950.

Very sincerely yours,

JAMES R. BARNARD

Associate Land and Claims Adjuster

MAGAZINE FAN

San Francisco, July 2, 1956

MR. FRANK B. DURKEE
Director of Public Works

DEAR FRANK: Thanks for the magazine, *California Highways and Public Works*. It is a very fine magazine, which gives a huge amount of information about our State. The pictures tell a wonderful story about engineering and how things are done.

Several of my friends have used it to get important facts that they were interested in. It is also wonderful for students who are interested in mechanical work and development. It would be a good magazine to have in every school library.

Sincerely,

CHAS. A. LEININGER

New Money
Effect of Federal Highway Bill on State of California

THE ESTIMATED $367,500,000 in federal aid for highways which California is scheduled to receive during the next three years under the legislation just passed by Congress will mean many additional miles of modern highways throughout the State, it was announced by State Director of Public Works Frank B. Durkee.

State highway design and survey crews and right of way appraisers have been working overtime for several months to prepare projects for the construction stage.

The initial effect of the increased funds will be felt largely in additional allocations by the California Highway Commission for rights of way, Durkee indicated. He pointed out that this was the case in 1953, when highway revenues were sharply augmented by increased California highway user taxes. The result has been an increase in multilane divided highways of 450 miles in three years.

Full Speed Ahead

"Acquisition of rights of way now will clear the way for construction to proceed full speed ahead in succeeding years, when the really substantial federal contributions provided in the bill begin to come in," he explained. "The 1956-57 program, with an additional $63,700,000 in federal highway aid for California, is only a prelude to the following 12 years when we hope to complete the entire 2,172 miles of the interstate system in this State to freeway standards."

Although the bulk of the additional federal funds for California is earmarked for freeway development on the interstate system routes, the effect will be to speed up improvement on all types of state highways. Applying the federal money to the interstate system highways will release large amounts of state funds for other routes, in accordance with long-established state policy of meeting the most urgent needs in all areas as available funds permit.

Planning Will Pay Off

"For the second time in three years," Durkee said, "the flexible long-range planning program of the Division of Highways and the advance route adoption policies of the Highway Commission are about to pay off for the people of California in the form of better highways without waste of time and effort."

Instead of the approximately $40,-000,000 per year in federal aid for state highways which California has been receiving since 1954, which is being increased to about $104,000,000 for 1956-57, the federal highway allocation for California state highways is expected to amount to about $135,-000,000 in 1957-58 and to $152,000,000 in 1958-59.

Beginning in 1959-60, California's share of federal funds for the interstate system will be even larger, under the terms of the new legislation.

Interstate System

For the first three years of the augmented program, the apportionments to the states are being based on the traditional factors of area, population, and mileage of certain postal routes. For the following 10 years, however, the federal legislation provides for apportionments to be made on the basis of the needs of the interstate system. In California, because of great distances, heavy urbanization, difficult terrain and the State's particular dependence on highways for transportation in both urban and rural areas,

the need for modernization of these important routes is especially urgent.

In addition to state highways, additional federal funds are provided in the new legislation for improvement of important county roads on the federal aid secondary system. These are often referred to as "farm to market" or "feeder" roads.

The federal aid secondary allocation for 1956-57 for California is increased from the previous $7,500,000 to $8,800,000 and will be stepped up $200,000 and $300,000 a year respectively in the two succeeding years. Under California law, 87½ percent of these funds are made available to the counties for road construction, to be matched by county or state funds, or both. The matching basis is 58 percent federal and 42 percent county-state.

The new legislation also provides increased funds for state highways on the federal aid primary and urban systems. These must also be matched by the State on a 58-42 basis.

Apportionments to State

On the interstate system, however, the Federal Government is supplying 90 percent of the funds, with the State paying only 10 percent. This is because the Congress has recognized the rapid modernization of the 40,000-mile interstate highway network as a primary responsibility of the Federal Government.

Apportionments to California under the new legislation are as follows:

Year	Interstate system	Primary system	Urban highways	Secondary (feeder roads)	Total
1956-57		(In millions of dollars)			
Previous basis	(9.8)	(14.5)	(15.4)	(7.5)	(47.2)
New legislation	57.0	2.6	2.8	1.3	63.7
Total 1956-57	66.8	17.1	18.2	8.8	110.9
1957-58	96.9	17.7	19.0	9.0	142.6
1958-59	114.1	18.2	19.6	9.3	161.2
Three-year totals of added funds	268.0	38.5	41.4	19.6	367.5

54

Border Span
New Crossing of the Colorado River Dedicated

By C. WIGGINTON, District Administrative Assistant

OFFICIALS of Arizona and California hailed completion of the new bridge spanning the Colorado River at Yuma when some 5,000 area residents attended the ribbon-cutting ceremony marking the official opening of the bridge to traffic. Governor Ernest McFarland of Arizona and California Director of Public Works F. B. Durkee, representing Governor Goodwin J. Knight, wielded king-sized scissors which severed the ribbon at the center of the bridge and were the principal speakers for the occasion.

Other notable speakers included Yuma Mayor Hugh Faulds; Hugh Osborne, Chairman, Imperial County Board of Supervisors; Arizona Highway Commissioner William Copple; and District Manager of the Southern California State Chamber of Commerce Clark Galloway. Imperial County governmental representatives included: Supervisor Earl Cavanah, Assemblyman J. Ward Casey, El Centro Mayor J. P. Morgan, and Councilman George Bucklin of El Centro. The California Division of Highways numbered among its representatives California Highway Commissioner Fred W. Speers, Commission Secretary C. A. Maghetti, and Assistant State Highway Engineer F. W. Panhorst.

Arizona State Senator Harold Giss served as master of ceremonies, presenting many personalities and colorful events. National Defense was represented by a National Guard drill team and the Yuma Air Base furnished a flight of jet aircraft. Music for the occasion was supplied by the Yuma Indian Band and the Yuma Elementary School Band.

Dedication ceremonies were held at the new Arizona Inspection Station on the Arizona side of the bridge. Relocation of the bridge has resulted in new inspection stations for both Arizona and California as well as new

UPPER—New Colorado River Bridge. LOWER—Governor McFarland of Arizona and Director of Public Works Durkee shake hands at dedication ceremony.

approaches to the bridge on either side.

On the California side, from Winterhaven to the Colorado River, a distance of 0.8 mile, it was necessary to provide new alignment of US 80 to meet the new bridge. On February 16, 1955, Silberberger Constructors, Inc., and J. B. Stringfellow Co. of Riverside began construction of a four-lane divided highway with channelization provided as necessary. K. L. E. Greenleaf was appointed resident engineer for the State Division of Highways in charge of the California approach to the Colorado crossing. A welded plate-girder bridge 212 feet in length with reinforced concrete deck was built across the California Wasteway Canal, providing two 26-foot-wide roadways. Four spans are supported on concrete-pile bents with concrete-pile foundations and concrete abutments at either end. This contract was completed December 16, 1955, at a construction cost of $382,600 and was opened to traffic when the Colorado River Bridge was dedicated.

BURLEIGH DOWNEY RETIRES

Burleigh R. Downey, Maintenance Engineer of the Michigan State Highway Department, retired July 8th after 50 years of distinguished service in the engineering profession, 26 years of which have been with the Highway Department. Downey will remain active as a part-time engineering consultant. With Mrs. Downey, he will make an extended European trip during which time he will lecture before highway engineers of several countries and also visit his daughter and family, Capt. and Mrs. E. A. Rajala, and their son, Karl, in Athens, Greece. Captain Rajala is assistant U. S. military attache in the Greek capital.

New Expressway

Orange County Dedicates
Limited Access Highway

A FESTOON made of supersize oranges strung on a rope was cut instead of the traditional ribbon when city, county, and state officials participated in the recent opening of the first link of the Houston Expressway, on Sign Route 14, in Orange County, a four-mile limited access highway running from Cypress Avenue east to Santa Ana Canyon Road.

The ceremonies were held at the Anaheim side of Placentia Avenue near the west end of the $1,154,900 project.

Gordon H. Wood, President of the Placentia Chamber of Commerce, cut the rope of oranges held by other officials. The Valencia High School band, of Placentia, provided music for the highway opening. A convoy of cars then formed and led by Captain Herbert Null of the California Highway Patrol, carried the participants over the new route. Then followed a luncheon in the Orangewood Ranch Cafe on Orangethorpe Avenue.

Among officials attending were Edward T. Telford, Assistant State Highway Engineer; L. R. Gillis, District Engineer; F. B. Cressy, Supervising Highway Engineer; and A. D. Griffin, Assistant District Engineer, all of the State Division of Highways; Leon T. Gillilan, Mayor of Placentia, and Charles A. Pearson, Mayor of Anaheim, and Orange County Road Superintendent Al S. Koch.

Beyond Cypress Avenue the new Houston Expressway link provides a new route for Orangethorpe Avenue, eliminating two grade crossings of the Santa Fe Railway, one a mile east of Placentia and the Yorba crossing, where Orangethorpe Avenue turns toward the Santa Ana Canyon Highway.

The new road underpasses the railroad and has a double bridge over the Santa Ana River and a bridge over westbound traffic on the Santa Ana Canyon Parkway. It merges into eastbound traffic without a stop.

Freeway ceremony opening the first portion of the Houston Street Freeway from Cypress Avenue east four miles to Santa Ana Canyon Highway. Left to right are Al Koch, Orange County Road Superintendent; Edward Telford, Assistant State Highway Engineer; L. R. Gillis, District Engineer; Gordon H. Wood, President of the Placentia Chamber of Commerce, cutting the ribbon; Leon T. Gillilan, Mayor of Placentia; and Charles Pearson, Mayor of Anaheim. In background are members of the Valencia High School band.

Pioneer Spirit

Exemplified Following Disastrous Floods in Northern Counties

By A. F. KAY, Associate Bridge Engineer

THE FRONTIER spirit of the Old West always seems ready to revive and turn into a tangible asset when disaster strikes western communities. The full story of the disastrous floods throughout Northern California this past winter would include hundreds of stirring examples of courage and ingenuity by residents of hard-pressed localities.

Particularly in our north coastal counties, last December's floods left many small communities completely cut off from any access to the main roads. Although transportation facilities were quickly restored on major highways, outside help was unable to reach many isolated settlements and the job of restoring roads and bridges was left mainly to the local citizens, who had to solve their problems by use of materials, equipment and tools locally available. With native ingenuity they quickly restored and replaced many of the damaged bridges to a usable condition.

Use Material at Hand

For the most part, these people depend on logging and lumbering operations for their livelihood. They are loggers and logging equipment operators, skilled in handling all the tools and equipment necessary in cutting and hauling logs and timber. With ordinary construction material unavailable and all bridges and roads out so nothing could be hauled from the outside, the only way temporary bridges could be built and the roads opened quickly was to use the only source of material left—the logs and timber from the local forests.

It would take a book to tell all about the work of restoring the washed out and damaged roads and bridges. A few examples will illustrate the willingness exhibited by everyone to help and get the work done.

UPPER—Debris left at site of old Bull Creek Bridge. LOWER—Constructing temporary bridge of redwood logs.

Bridges Repaired

To replace the washed out Larabee Creek Bridge, the Pacific Lumber Company of Scotia cut special timbers, trucked them to South Fork, loaded them on a work train of the North Western Pacific Railroad and persuaded the railroad to deliver them to the job site as the train went by.

This area was doubly isolated by bridges being washed out across Eel River and Larabee Creek.

Five 60-foot logs were used to span the Eel River at Maple Hills. Trucking these logs down US Highway 101 was out of the question. A logger from the Salmon Creek area offered to get them for W. S. "Buster" Selvage, who was building the bridge, by the time the pile bents were ready. The logger made good on his promise.

To help in getting washed out portions of the Eel River Bridge at Fernbridge repaired, the Hanson Pacific Lumber Company of Fortuna gathered up a crew and cut much needed 12 by 12-inch by 40-foot timbers for the job while their mill was still partially under water.

For the Slater Creek Trestle on the Blue Side Road which isolated the Howe Creek and Price Creek areas, a 50-foot pile was needed. This was obtained over night and hauled to the site by the Foster Drayage Company.

Two Log Bridges Built

The washout of half the Bluff Creek Bridge isolated the towns of Orleans and Weitchpec along the Klamath River. Construction of a standard timber bridge would have taken weeks. Two 50-foot log bridges were built and the road opened in nine days. The distance to the job from Eureka by way of Willow Creek, Hoopa and Weitchpec was 85 miles. With the bridge over the Trinity River at Hoopa washed out, Contractor J. J. Tracey had to get to the job site via Crescent City and Grants Pass, Oregon, and down the Klamath River, a distance of 315 miles. After getting word in Eureka to proceed, Contractor Tracey was on the job the next day with a three-quarter-ton pick-up truck and a bedroll. A local catskinner knew where there were two tractors, but they were 12 miles up in the mountains and under three feet of snow. The contractor said, "not so fine, but get them anyway." A local forest ranger located suitable logs but, again, these were in a remote area five miles from the job site and along a narrow and little used road. With a "never say die" attitude, the contractor and the local loggers were able to build two bridges within nine days and open the road to traffic.

This spirit of cooperation and teamwork by the loggers, the contractors, the lumber mills, the truckers, the rail-

TOP—Maple Hill Bridge over South Fork of Eel River. NEXT—Temporary Bear River Bridge. NEXT—Temporary Home Creek Bridge. BOTTOM—Reconstructed Price Creek Bridge.

UPPER—Showing flood-damaged Larrabee Creek Bridge. LOWER—Repair work on bridge under way.

Marc C. Fosgate

Marc C. Fosgate, Assistant District District Engineer, Operations, for District X of the Division of Highways, retired July 6th after 35 years of state service.

For the past 19 years Fosgate has been a resident of Stockton, having reported to District X in 1937 as district construction engineer. When the Division of Highways was reorganized in 1947 and he was required to handle the expanded highway pro-

MARC C. FOSGATE

roads, and all who lived and worked in these areas made it possible to accomplish what seemed like an impossible task. The will and the spirit of the western pioneer is not gone. It is still with us ready to meet any emergency or challenge.

CONSTRUCTION EMPLOYMENT HITS ALL-TIME HIGH IN MAY

More workers were employed in the construction industry in May than ever before in the history of California, according to Ernest B. Webb, State Director of Industrial Relations.

Construction contractors employed 295,600 workers in May. This was 27,300, or 10 percent, more than in May a year ago.

FROM KANSAS CITY

CITY PLAN COMMISSION
Kansas City, Missouri

K. C. ADAMS, *Editor*

DEAR MR. ADAMS: We have found your publication *California Highways and Public Works* to be of great interest and value to us here in Kansas City as we move forward on our own highway construction program. We very much appreciate the continuation of our name on your mailing list.

Sincerely yours,

PHILIP E. GEISSAL
Chief Planning Engineer

gram, Fosgate was promoted to assistant district engineer in charge of operations. In this assignment he has been in charge of the district construction program averaging approximately $10,000,000 a year in road building projects. He has also been responsible for the maintenance of about 1,400 miles of state highways in Alpine, Amador, Calaveras, Mariposa, Merced, Sacramento, San Joaquin. Solano, Stanislaus, and Tuolumne Counties. He also supervised the construction engineering on federal aid secondary county highway projects in these counties.

Prior to working in District X he was district maintenance engineer in

... Continued on page 65

Nojoqui Expressway
Bad Section of US 101 Finally Is Eliminated

By A. M. NASH, District Engineer

THE HISTORIC route followed by US 101 through the rugged Santa Ynez Mountains between Gaviota and the Santa Ynez River at Buellton, Santa Barbara County, long considered one of the worst sections between the Mexican border and San Francisco, because of its steep grades and reversing curves, has become an 11-mile stretch of continuous four-lane divided expressway. Completion of the 4.1 miles between 1.0 mile north of Nojoqui Summit and 0.5 mile south of the Santa Ynez River marked the final step in eliminating this bad section of old highway.

This latest portion to be completed and the subject of this article begins at the foot of Nojoqui grade, northerly terminus of the four-lane divided expressway constructed over Nojoqui Summit in 1951. From here the new lanes follow narrow, winding Nojoqui Creek gorge northward on alignment and grade designed for travel at 60 miles per hour. Minimum curve radius on the new lanes is 1,223 feet compared with 750 feet on the old highway. Just south of the Santa Ynez River the new lanes transition into the older two-lane highway which is on tangent alignment until joining the Buellton Expressway.

Difficult Terrain Obstacles

Seldom have more difficult terrain obstacles been encountered in the design and construction of an expressway than those presented by Nojoqui Creek gorge. This is perhaps best illustrated by the following data. Within a two-mile stretch nine individual bridge structures, averaging 196 feet in length, were constructed over Nojoqui Creek. The creek channel was realigned at five different locations which involved the removal of over 210,000 cubic yards of ditch and channel excavation. Also, in the same area, in a three-quarter mile stretch, over 660,000 cubic yards of

UPPER—Looking north on new eXpressway, with Buellton in background.
LOWER—View looking south on eXpressway.

roadway excavation was removed in making two cuts.

The special provisions required that public traffic be allowed to pass through the construction area unobstructed and with the least possible delay at all times. This was accomplished despite the severe restrictions of the narrow gorge.

Storm Damage

An unusually severe rainstorm which started on December 23, 1955,

and continued intermittently over the next few days caused Nojoqui Creek to rise to flood stage. Considerable erosion took place along the banks of one of the channel changes and for a time the stability of a newly constructed bridge abutment was threatened. Heavy stone riprap was placed along the banks of the creek, in the vicinity of the threatened bridge, to prevent further destructive erosion.

Channel Change vs. Bridge Alternatives

During the course of the design of this project, it was first proposed to construct a channel change on the left between Stations 180 and 190 and thus eliminate the need for constructing four new bridges. Cost comparison studies, however, indicated that a channel change alternative would develop approximately 500,000 cubic yards of excess material that could only be disposed of outside the right of way. This, along with other considerations, pointed to higher costs and therefore effectively ruled out the channel change in favor of building the bridges.

The plan finally adopted involved removal of 882,000 cubic yards of roadway excavation with 17,260,000 station yards of overhaul. An excess of 140,000 cubic yards of roadway excavation was developed and utilized to construct embankment for future lanes ahead and, also, to widen embankments on this project.

Structural and Geometric Features

A uniform 46-foot width of median has been provided throughout the project with the exception of the portion between Stations 172 and 223 where the median is 22 feet in width. Ultimate development to a six-lane freeway may be accomplished in the future by widening on the outside where the median is narrow and on the inside where the wider median has been provided.

The southbound lanes are surfaced throughout the length of the project with portland cement concrete. The northbound lanes are surfaced with plant-mixed surfacing where it was possible to use the existing highway as a base for second stage construction. Otherwise, the northbound lanes are also surfaced with portland cement concrete.

Structures

Reinforced concrete T-girder bridges were used for each of the nine new bridge structures. Spans are supported by reinforced concrete piers and abutments. The deck slabs of reinforced concrete provide clear roadway widths of 28 feet in addition to two safety curbs, each 1 foot 9 inches wide. An exception to the latter is

This view is looking south and shows overpass in center

the private road approach bridge on the left at Station 166 which provides a 12-foot width of roadway and two curbs, each 1 foot wide.

Many smaller drainage structures were constructed, the majority of which were extensions of existing facilities. Included among these were four existing 8 feet x 8 feet reinforced concrete boxes which were extended in one case with a similar structure, in another with 96-inch reinforced concrete pipe and in the other two instances with 90-inch and 72-inch corrugated metal pipes respectively.

Construction to Buellton Scheduled

Construction of the additional 0.8 mile of expressway required to connect onto the existing four-lane di-

vided highway through Buellton is tentatively scheduled to begin in 1958. This project will involve construction of two additional bridges to carry new southbound lanes across the Santa Ynez River and Nojoqui Creek.

Construction of the project just completed between 1.0 mile north of Nojoqui Summit and 0.5 mile south of Santa Ynez River, including construction of the bridges, was performed under one contract which was awarded to joint venturers, B. J. Ukropina, T. P. Polich, Steve Kral, John R. Ukropina and Madonna Construction Company of San Luis Obispo on September 15, 1954. Work began on the day the contract was awarded and was completed at a cost of $1,905,126.

This view is looking north on expressway

and Public Works

Out of the Mail Bag

LETTER TO THE GOVERNOR

INGLEWOOD CHAMBER OF COMMERCE
Inglewood, California

June 4, 1956

HON. GOODWIN J. KNIGHT
State of California
State Capitol, Sacramento,
California

MY DEAR GOVERNOR: I had occasion to make an automobile trip on Highway 99 between the San Francisco Bay area and Los Angeles. I do not travel the roads too often because I usually take a plane to save time—so my last automobile trip on the same route was something over a year ago.

May I take this occasion to congratulate you and your State Highway Commission for the rapid improvements that are being made in the highways of our State. It is becoming a pleasure to drive on 99, since almost the entire route is now a divided highway.

I would compliment, too, the marvelous engineering for freeways within the Bay area and the Los Angeles metropolitan area. It continues to amaze me that, with all the obstacles and complexities confronting the Highway Department people any freeways are constructed at all.

I think the Highway Commission is doing a fine job in trying to be fair with everyone . . . very frequently under trying circumstances.

Just taking a few minutes out to toss some bouquets your way. With kindest personal wishes.

Sincerely and respectfully,

RUBEN NEUHARTH
Secretary-Manager

MAGAZINE USED IN SCHOOL

OFFICE OF THE SUPERINTENDENT OF SCHOOLS
Riverside County

K. C. ADAMS, *Editor*

DEAR MR. ADAMS: It occurred to me that you might be interested in knowing how this magazine helps us in school work. My wife teaches "Modern California" in the fourth grade. In addition to being helpful in teaching children about a tangible service of our State Government *California Highways* is valuable in teaching the study of maps since aerial photographs of known areas make map reading meaningful. The magazines are saved and loaned to teachers with whom I work in the country.

You are performing a valuable service to the people of the State of California and we do appreciate it.

Sincerely yours,

RAY W. JOHNSON
Superintendent of Schools

BOOST FOR DEPARTMENT

MARSH & McLENNAN
San Francisco

MR. KENNETH C. ADAMS, *Editor*

DEAR MR. ADAMS: May I add one other to the many letters of congratulation which you have received on your interesting and valuable magazine.

I feel that the people of this State should have great pride in the remarkably fine job done by the Department of Public Works, and it is therefore most fitting that the loyal and able people who make up the department should have their efforts chronicled in your splendid publication.

Sincerely,

THERON L. PRENTISS
Vice President

MANY THANKS

ROCKLAND, MAINE

MR. KENNETH C. ADAMS, *Editor*

DEAR MR. ADAMS: As an employee of the Maine State Highway Department, I have an opportunity from time to time to see your fine magazine at the office. It is a grand magazine—in my opinion, the best in its field.

I find it particularly interesting as I lived in California for many years prior to settling here in Maine. Each time I see a new issue of California Highways and Public Works, I marvel at the changes that have taken place in your highway system since my departure from the coast 10 years ago.

Very truly yours,

GUY NICHOLAS

READ IN MILWAUKEE

MR. KENNETH C. ADAMS, *Editor*

DEAR SIR: You perhaps might be interested to know that my copy of *California Highways and Public Works* goes with me when attending meetings and citizen discussion groups.

New divided highways are under construction near and around Milwaukee and we are gleaning lots of valuable information from your fine magazine.

It is read from cover to cover and is found to be very educational.

Sincerely yours,

MR. AND MRS. CLARENCE
SCHUMACHER
Milwaukee 12, Wis.

California Highways and Public Works

SIRS: We have been receiving your publication for several years and as we finish reading it we send it on to various public offices of officials here in Oklahoma, hoping the information may have good influence on future road building and planning. It goes to small towns along routes we have traveled where the old main streets connect with the equally old highways.

We hope your publications have helped the towns west of Oklahoma City to accept the bypassing of their townships when 66 will be widened in the future.

Every year, usually in February, we are *home* for a vacation to visit our folks in Berkeley, Alameda, and Oakland. We ski up on US 40 where we first tried it in 1938-39-40. The wonderful new highway from Oakland to beyond Sacramento keeps us *always* going home for our fun! We have skied in Colorado, Utah, Idaho, Washington and Oregon. None have California's facilities, beautiful roads or *maintenance.*

With Oklahoma's present "Turner Turnpike" in use, and plans for another in the immediate future, we have reason to be proud of our *home* state and the great network of multi-lane highways free of any tolls! From actually driving on the Turner Turnpike we know your new highways have better surfacing and a better margin of safety.

The constant rising cost of owning and driving a car has gradually limited our touring habits to the point where we will not use a turnpike or toll road if a good alternate is available. To us, a toll road is a private road, closed to the average tourist traveling on a limited budget. It also can mean deliberate pressure on cars to use the toll road by neglecting repairs on the alternate. This is not our American way, and we hope the solution to better highways can be solved as you are doing with good planning and free roads.

Thank you sincerely,

MRS. JAMES O. SAVAGE

MAGAZINE USED AS HANDBOOK

CONTRACTORS STATE LICENSE BOARD
San Francisco

California Highways and Public Works

GENTLEMEN: For several years your magazine has come bringing current practice in highway and bridge construction, the result of laboratory research and tests on materials used in heavy construction, comparative cost data and modus operandi using recently accepted techniques and practices.

When a man has a desk job in an industry as active and changing as the heavy construction industry he is hard put to keep abreast of what is going on "in the field." Your magazine, supplemented by an occasional field trip, keeps me sufficiently close to the head of the parade to, at least, hear the music; if not see the band.

Your magazine stimulates my imagination, keeps me abreast of current techniques and practices in the field and is of greater value to me than many of the expensive "handbooks" in the preparation of examination material for such contractors' examinations as general engineering contractor; cement and concrete contractor; excavating, grading, trenching, paving, surfacing contractor and other classifications of contractor directly, or indirectly, operating in the heavy construction industry.

Very truly yours,

HARRY W. ABRAHAMS,
Examiner, Grade 2,
Contractors' State License Board

THAT IS PURPOSE OF MAGAZINE

TIBURON, CALIFORNIA

MR. K. C. ADAMS, *Editor*

DEAR SIR: At this time I wish to thank you and state that I appreciate receiving *California Highways and Public Works.*

It not only is a very instructive and interesting magazine but has been a great help in disseminating information about just where our gas tax money is being spent.

Sincerely,

WALTER C. THIERBACH

PRAISE FROM OVERSEAS

COUNTY BOROUGH OF TYNEMOUTH
Borough Surveyor's Office

NORTH SHIELDS, ENGLAND

KENNETH C. ADAMS, *Editor*

DEAR SIR: For some time now I have been privileged to receive, regularly, copies of the official journal of the Division of Highways, Department of Public Works, State of California. I peruse them with great interest, and pass them to members of my engineering staff and subsequently they go to the county engineer and surveyor of Durham County Council—one of the largest highway authorities in England.

Yours sincerely,

DONAL M. O'HERLIHY

OUTSTANDING PUBLICATION

PORTLAND CEMENT ASSOCIATION
Memphis 3, Tennessee

California Highways and Public Works

GENTLEMEN: *California Highways and Public Works* magazine is an outstanding publication and the copies I have seen will certainly help us in our promotion of better development of highways in Tennessee and Arkansas. The September-October issue, a copy of which I saw briefly, contained some very interesting and, I believe, useful articles on freeway construction in your fine State that should interest people in this section of the Country.

Yours very truly,

JOHN L. FEAGIN
District Engineer

ANOTHER COMPLIMENT

LOS ANGELES 42

K. C. ADAMS, *Editor*

DEAR SIR: I want to take this opportunity to thank you for including me on your mailing list and to express my sincere appreciation for the fine magazine and its entertaining and informative articles.

Extending my best wishes to you and thanking you again for your courtesy, I am

Yours truly,

IRVING ANGEL

A. K. Gilbert

A. K. Gilbert, associate bridge engineer with the Division of Highways Bridge Department, retired on July 1, 1956, after a 27-year career with the State.

A dinner was held in honor of Mr. Gilbert on June 6th at Swally's Key Club in Los Angeles. At the time of retirement, Gil was resident engineer on the construction of the Colorado River Bridge at Yuma.

Gilbert received his engineering education at the University of Utah where he studied mining engineering. He obtained his early experience with the Anaconda Copper Company of Butte, Montana, and later with the Utah Copper Company at Bingham, Utah.

After coming to California he worked for five years with the Pacific Gas and Electric Company before joining the Division of Highways in 1929. His work with the bridge department has been as resident engineer on many of the major bridge structures throughout the State. His wide knowledge of bridge construction and his pleasant, straightforward manner have won for him the friendship and respect of his associates.

All of Gil's friends wish him many happy years of retirement. He plans to devote part of his time to travel and prospecting.

This Letter Is Self-explanatory

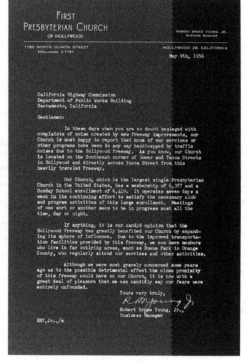

ARRESTS FOR SPEEDING

The California Highway Patrol made 83,530 arrests for speeding in the first four months of 1956.

SUDDEN STOPS

If you make sudden stops or turns in traffic without giving any warning, you're in for trouble.

Frank Escobedo Is Deputy Director Of Public Works

Frank B. Durkee, Director of Public Works, has announced the promotion of Frank J. Escobedo from Per-

FRANK J. ESCOBEDO

sonnel Officer to Assistant Deputy Director. He will assist the director and deputy directors on departmental administrative matters.

Escobedo is a graduate of the University of California at Berkeley, where he also completed graduate study in the Bureau of Public Administration. During his 14 years of state service, his work has been concerned primarily with personnel administration. He was a personnel officer in another state agency for five years prior to his coming to the Department of Public Works, where he has worked in a similar capacity since September, 1954. For 2½ years preceding that date, he was the personnel director for the City of Philadelphia.

Escobedo succeeds C. M. "Max" Gilliss who was appointed deputy director last January.

PUBLIC WORKS SECRETARY OF BRAZIL VISITS HERE

On a tour of the West, Euclides Triches, State Secretary of Public Works, State of Rio Grande do Sul, Brazil, called upon Director of Public Works Frank B. Durkee. His official duties in his native country are similar to those of Durkee. He is a participant in the foreign leader program of the International Educational Exchange Service of the U. S. Department of State.

Triches is particularly interested in highways, irrigation in land waterways, water problems, and public works construction. He spent some time with officials of the Division of Water Resources. He expressed great interest in California's water problems.

FOSGATE

Continued from page 59 . . .

District II with headquarters in Redding, and resident engineer in District IV at San Francisco.

Previous to his state service Fosgate worked at railroad and irrigation engineering and spent considerable time on railroad location and construction in Alaska. His tales of experiences in Alaska are many.

Fosgate was born in Paso Robles and attended grade and high school in Gilroy and State College in San Jose. His family consists of wife, Ina Mae; son, Marc Otis of Stockton, and daughter, Susan Anne, presently attending San Jose State College. He also has two grandchildren.

Marc's hobbies are cribbage, golf, hunting, fishing, and farming. He has a 30-acre ranch in Fiddletown, Amador County, an important element in his retirement plans.

Fosgate has been active in the affairs of the California State Employees' Association and served a term as president of the highway chapter in Redding. A Master Mason, he is a member of Masonic Lodge No. 57 of Santa Rosa.

Upon retirement, Marc and his wife plan to make an automobile trip to the Northwest and upon return, keep busy with his farming at Fiddletown and town living in Stockton.

UPPER—Director of Public Works Frank B. Durkee shows Mr. Triches an artist's drawing of parallel Carquinez Bridge. LOWER—Assistant State Engineer W. G. Schulz explains State Water Plan to Mr. Triches.

LETTER TO DIRECTOR

CONNECTICUT GENERAL LIFE INSURANCE CO.

Hartford, Connecticut

June 8, 1956

DEAR MR. DURKEE: We greatly appreciate your kindness in sending the material regarding your State's ambitious highway program. Several of us have been reading the material and have found many ideas which we believe will be extremely valuable not only in our commission's report but also in helping Connecticut to formulate a comprehensive long-range program.

In reading your material, we are increasingly impressed by the job California has done and the example which you have set for other states to follow.

With our sincere thanks.

Very truly yours,

JAMES H. TORREY
Secretary

Highway Work Was Hard in 1913

On August 7, 1912, Percy A. Towne, Chairman of Governor Hiram Johnson's original highway commission, turned the first spadeful of earth signalizing the start of actual construction work on California's State Highway System in San Mateo County.

Ransome-Crummey Co., San Francisco, was the contractor on this first highway contract. Edward E. Snider, 99 Wood Lane, Fairfax, California, was superintendent for the contracting firm and Leon Clark was resident engineer for the State. Mr. Snider

Director of Public Works of Boys State Appointed

Newly appointed Director of Public Works James W. Ellis of Calipatria called at the Department of Public Works in Sacramento on June 21st to pay his respects.

Jim, 17, was appointed to his post by

JAMES W. ELLIS

Governor Richard Hammes, San Diego, of the Boys' State, which held its annual encampment on the State Fairgrounds, concluding its sessions on June 21st.

Jim is the son of Mr. and Mrs. Gordon W. Ellis of Calipatria. His father is a highway foreman at Calipatria and is past president of the Imperial Chapter of California State Employees' Association.

The young Director of Public Works was recently elected President of the Calipatria High School student body. He passed a civil service test for engineering aid and went to work for the Division of Highways for the summer vacation on June 25th.

Estimated motor vehicle travel on the rural state highway system for 1954, based on the usual state-wide traffic counts, was 16.1 billion vehicle-miles, an increase of 1.4 percent over 1953.

---

found these old pictures in his photograph album, taken in March, 1913, at Uncle Tom's Cabin, a famous landmark in San Mateo County. They show a roller and truck used in those early days. Clark is in the driver's seat of the truck and Mr. Snider is standing by the roller.

"I think this truck is the first one used to haul asphalt on a state highway," Mr. Snider writes, "we had to wind it up by hand. It held six dumps or 54 cubic feet."

ACCIDENTAL DAMAGES TO STATE FACILITIES

By W. D. SEDGWICK, Assistant District Engineer, Maintenance

When thinking or reading about accidents on our highways, we usually have in mind loss of life, injuries or damages to the vehicles. Little thought is given to the damage done to the highway or its facilities.

In State Highway District VII, which includes only Los Angeles, Orange and Ventura Counties, during the year between March 1, 1955, and March 1, 1956, 1,300 loss reports were processed involving a total of $133,-577. Of this amount, $91,557 was collected from the parties causing the damage and $42,020 was expended from the gasoline tax funds and charged to maintenance, because the cost was not recoverable. If policing agencies do not have report covering the accident, which caused the damage, there is little chance of recovery.

There are many repairs due to vehicle accidents which are too minor to collect the cost of as it would cost more to collect than the cost of the repairs. These total an appreciable addition to the above figures.

Damage to Signs

In this district where the state highways probably handle the heaviest traffic in the world, the traffic signals are very important and must be kept in operation. The items involved in the 300 loss reports handled by our signal crews included repairs to 114 signal poles, 154 signal heads, 5 controllers, 57 street light poles, 41 luminaires and 19 flashes, for a total cost of $58,876.

The warning, regulatory, and guide signs come in for their share of damage from vehicles. Many of the signs are costly and 102 reports totalled $3,204 in repairs.

Almost the full time of a three-man crew is required to repair damaged fences on the freeways. The cost of these repairs amounted to $30,273.

Other items which are continually having to be repaired due to vehicle damage are guard rails, $18,054; bridge rails, $10,161; and sight posts and reflectors, $5,219.

Clearing Debris

In addition to repairing the damaged facilities, our forces are called out by the California Highway Patrol to sand and oil spilled on the pavement, clear the traveled way of bales of hay, boxes of tomatoes, broken glass, and many other types of debris due to vehicle accidents.

With the heavy traffic on the freeways in the City of Los Angeles which have been completed to date, there were 487 accident reports involving damage to state facilities which cost $28,868 for repairs in one year.

In consideration of the number of loss reports and costs of repairs during the past few years, the rapid increase during this last year is something to think about.

Cost During Five Years

The annual cost of repairs during the last five years is as follows:

1951-52	$43,454
1952-53	45,271
1953-54	54,820
1954-55	78,032
1955-56	133,577

(Period of this report)

During recent years more and more lighting standards, guide posts, traffic signals, signs and guard rails are being placed for the safety and convenience of motorists. Admittedly, there are more of these facilities that can be hit and damaged by cars out of control, but excessive speed is one of the major causes of these accidents. This does not necessarily mean exceeding the legal or posted speed limit. Too often the driver says, "I was only going 35-40 miles per hour when the car in front of me stopped, and I had to swerve to miss it, when I hit the fence, guard rail, or light or signal post." He was exceeding the safe speed limit for existing conditions.

Studies are continually being made to place the highway facilities in such positions that they will be effective but be less likely to be hit and therefore more economically maintained.

E. G. Van Leeuwen

E. G. Van Leeuwen, Associate Highway Engineer, District V, retired on July 6, 1956, after 37 years of state service.

"Van" was born in Minneapolis, Minnesota, on July 2, 1891. Two years later the family moved to San Francisco. An event of April, 1906, displaced them as far south as San Jose, where "Van's" high school education was completed. He then entered the University of Santa Clara and was graduated in 1915 with the first graduating class in civil engineering.

For four years he was employed by the City of San Jose, the County of Santa Clara and the United States Geological Survey. In 1919 he entered state service as a draftsman for the then Division V, San Luis Obispo. During the following 10 years he was promoted through various grades to associate highway engineer. He was transferred in 1929 to District I, Eureka, where he served as chief draftsman and as resident engineer. In 1937 he was transferred to District X, Stockton, and in 1941 returned to District V, San Luis Obispo. In 1950 he was appointed district safety supervisor, which office he held until his retirement.

"Van's" genuine interest in employee welfare caused him to serve the State Employees' Association in a number of local chapter offices and as regional director for two terms. In addition to these activities, he has been active in the California Society of Professional Engineers, the American Society of Safety Engineers, the Veterans of Safety, National Safety Council and Tau Beta Pi, national engineering honor society. He is also a member of various Masonic bodies in San Jose, San Luis Obispo and San Francisco.

He will continue to maintain his home in San Luis Obispo.

At the close of the 1954-55 Fiscal Year the Division of Highways was operating some 145 land radio stations and 650 mobile radio units throughout the State.

NEW RECORD

Sport fishermen and wild game hunters in the United States set a new record by purchasing 33,046,361 licenses during the fiscal year that ended June 30, 1955, according to the National Automobile Club. That was 392,162 more licenses than they purchased during the previous year.

CALIFORNIA PLACES SECOND

California sold 1,285,980 fishing licenses during the 1954-55 season to place second in the United States, reports the National Automobile Club. Minnesota placed first with 1,374,942 licenses sold.

State Fair

Will Start on August 29th For a 12-Day Run

THE "SPIRIT OF '56" State Fair and Exposition—themed in tribute to the energy and industry of modern Californians—will roar into life August 29th for a 12-day run. Most of the 800,000 visitors expected to share in the celebration will see one phase of the State's growth en route—the broad new miles of roadway in the vast State Highway System.

No one will go away dissatisfied either, because State Fair officials have rounded up a program that has something for everyone. There will be Hollywood star-studded night shows, thoroughbreds pounding around the track, band concerts and the aristocracy of the livestock world.

Fair directors have returned to the variety show format for evening performances, featuring three different shows, each with a four-night run. Talent already selected includes Eddie Fisher, Bob Crosby and Dennis Day.

Other top ranking evening events will include the nightly horse show, oldest continuous equestrian event in the West; and mammoth fireworks displays.

More Racing

There will be an additional day of racing. The exposition will open on a Wednesday, rather than on Thursday as in past years, allowing those who follow the ponies one extra day at the pari-mutuels.

The race meet, to be 10 days in length, will be held on all days except Sundays. There will be several stake races, featured by the classic Governor's Handicap on September 6th, carrying a purse of $20,000 added.

The exposition, a sure thing to wreck most records accumulated in its previous 101 years, will show products of the State in scores of buildings with emphasis on agriculture, horticulture, livestock, floriculture, mining and manufacturing.

As in past years, most of those attending the Fair will flock to the Counties Building and Hall of Flowers. There are few, if any, exhibit halls more sensational.

Roaring waterfalls, limpid lily ponds, outdoor gardens, huge simulated redwood trees, and more than 1,000,000 blooms, shrubs, potted plants, cut specimens, and trees form a breath-taking panorama of the floriculture world.

Much to See

The huge Counties Building is the delight of young and old. A symphony of light, color, and motion, it is filled with booths representing the counties of the State, their products, tourist attractions, natural resources, recreational facilities, and other advantages.

From the Counties Building visitors may fan out into a vast display of all the things shown at a fair. There will be sewing exhibits, canned and preserved foods, cooking demonstrations, wine tasting events, carnival attractions, hot dogs, exotic foreign dishes, hobby shows, more than 5,000 head of livestock, an art show, wildlife displays, rabbits, thousands of birds from pigeons to seldom seen 'show' chickens, and many, many other items.

There are 207 acres of buildings, spacious lawns, shaded areas with benches, food stands, first aid stations, restaurants, horse barns, paved streets and walks, flowers, checking stands, and almost countless other places and things.

There is a fire station, headquarters for police, a bank, telegraph office, and a post office. There are fountains with iced drinking water, air-conditioned buildings, and a candy store.

The exposition is, literally, a city within a city, providing every comfort for those who come to wonder.

Transportation from the heart of Sacramento is provided by express busses, and the Fairgrounds is within easy taxicab distance from any part of the city. Those with their own autos will find conveniently located parking lots adjoining the grounds.

Farewell

Division of Water Resources Leaves Public Works Department

By ROBIN R. REYNOLDS, Senior Hydraulic Engineer, Department of Water Resources

On JULY 5, 1956, one of the divisions of the Department of Public Works, the Division of Water Resources, became a part of the new Department of Water Resources, created by the Legislature.

To head up the new department, Governor Knight appointed Harvey O. Banks as director and Mercel J. Shelton of La Mesa as deputy director. Banks was formerly State Engineer and Chief of the Division of Water Resources. Shelton is from Southern California, where he was general manager and chief engineer of the La Mesa, Lemon Grove and Spring Valley Irrigation District in San Diego County.

Major Reorganization

The legislative act brought about a major reorganization of the State's water agencies. On July 4th, the Division of Water Resources, the State Engineer's Office, the State Water Resources Board, and the Water Project Authority were abolished. In their places, on July 5th, the Department of Water Resources, the State Water Board, and the State Water Rights Board came into existence. The new department succeeds to all the powers, duties, and responsibilities of the abolished agencies except the administration and adjudication of water rights, which have become the responsibility of the new Water Rights Board.

In addition, the new department succeeds to all the powers, duties, and responsibilities formerly vested in the Department of Finance with respect to state filings for unappropriated waters in furtherance of general and coordinated plans for water development. The State Reclamation Board is continued in existence within the department, but with its present duties, responsibilities, and personnel continued.

On July 5th, Governor Knight appointed Henry Holsinger of Sacra-

HARVEY O. BANKS

mento, W. P. Rowe of San Bernardino and John B. Evans of Oakland members of the newly created State Water Rights Board.

The board will rule on legal rights to use the State's water resources for development of hydroelectric power and water supplies for industrial, municipal and farming purposes.

The new State Water Board has the same membership as the former State Water Resources Board, but its purpose and duties are to confer with, advise, and make recommendations to the Director of Water Resources with respect to any matters and subjects under his jurisdiction.

The creation of the new department to administer state control and development of the very important and valuable water resources is not only a major reorganization of the executive branch of the State Government but is also a vital demonstration of the increasing state-wide interest and concern regarding water.

Water Resources Division Created in 1929

The Division of Water Resources was formed in 1929 by combining the Division of Water Rights and the Division of Engineering and Irrigation, which were divisions within the Department of Public Works. However, an interesting history lies back of the Division of Water Resources. This history traces the growth of water development and water law in California. It also shows the impact which droughts, floods, depressions, wars, and general social and economic progress have had on development of the executive branch of the State Government to define and meet state responsibility for needed and orderly water resources development.

When California was admitted to the Union in 1850, the Constitution of 1849 contained no provision with respect to water and its use. The first Legislature, however, adopted the common law of England as the rule for decision in the State. With regard to the field of water law, this action of the first Legislature was to come in conflict with local customs and usages of the miners and early farmers, causing litigation and uncertainty which resulted in the slow development of the State's present unique water law.

Office of State Engineer Dates Back

The first Legislature also recognized the need for a state engineering office, and the Surveyor General, a constitutional and elective official, was given responsibilities in some ways comparable with present responsibilities of the Department of Public Works. The actual Office of State Engineer was first created in 1878 and continued until 1889, when it was abolished. The office was not created again until 1907. The State Engineer during this early period, Wm. Ham Hall, investigated the State's water resources and recommended that the

70

waters of the great Central Valley be developed in a systematic manner. The surveys and studies made by Hall and data which he collected revealed certain basic problems which were to become important and were to influence future water development in the State. The major problem, the maldistribution of sources of water supply with regard to locations of water requirements, was noted by Hall and others who followed. Since Hall's time, water development planning in California has aimed for a solution to this basic problem. Future water projects must be constructed to solve this problem.

Pioneer Agencies

When the Office of State Engineer was abolished in 1889, the State Mineralogist was made ex officio State Engineer. This arrangement continued until 1893, when the Office of Commissioner of Public Works was created. The California State Debris Commission was created in the same year. In 1897 a Department of Highways and the Lake Tahoe Wagon Road Commission were formed.

An important change occurred in 1907, when the Department of Engineering Act was passed, and all the former duties of the Commissioner of Public Works, Department of Highways, Lake Tahoe Wagon Road Commission, and the Debris Commission were delegated to the Department of Engineering under the State Engineer. In addition, all engineering work of the San Francisco Harbor Commission, and the design and construction of buildings and works of all state hospitals, prisons, schools, and other institutions were made duties of the department. Authority was also given to the department to carry out flood control investigations and construction, to cooperate with the Federal Government and its agencies in making surveys and investigations, and to perform other engineering duties. At that time, practically all engineering activities of the State Government, except those remaining with the Surveyor General, were vested in the Department of Engineering.

Secretary of State Frank M. Jordan poses with new officials of the Department of Water Resources before swearing them in. LEFT TO RIGHT—Henry Holsinger, Chairman of newly created State Water Rights Board; Secretary Jordan; Director of Water Resources Banks; and Marcel J. Shelton, Deputy Director.

Water Matters Become Important

An expansion of state governmental activities began in about 1911 with the trend to set up new offices to administer special and definite duties. Many of the new offices were assigned responsibilities which had formerly been those of the State Engineer. As a result, water matters became an increasingly important part of the responsibilities of the State Engineer.

A new and independent water agency, the State Water Commission, was formed in 1914. The commission was responsible for the administration of procedures to appropriate water.

Following World War I, in 1921, there was a major reorganization of the State Government. The Department of Public Works was created at this time. The department consisted of the Divisions of Highway, Architecture, Land Settlement, Water Rights, and Engineering and Irrigation. The State Highway Engineer was ex officio director of the department. In 1923 the State Engineer was made Director of Public Works. In

1927 the department was again reorganized and an independent directorship was created. In 1929 the Divisions of Water Rights and Engineering and Irrigation were combined within the department to form the Division of Water Resources under the State Engineer as chief of the division.

Six State Engineers

Six persons have occupied the Office of State Engineer since the Department of Engineering was created in 1907. Nathaniel Ellery served as State Engineer from 1907 to 1911, W. F. McClure from 1911 to 1926, Paul Bailey from 1926 to 1927, Edward Hyatt from 1927 to 1950, and A. D. Edmonston from 1950 to 1955. Edmonston retired from state service on November 1, 1955, and Harvey O. Banks was appointed to the position, which he occupied until the position was abolished on July 4, 1956. He then became director of the new Department of Water Resources.

The new department will be responsible for all planning, construction, and administrative activities of the State pertaining to the development, regulation, and use of water resources. These activities include design and construction of the Feather River Project, operation and maintenance of flood control projects, water master service, supervision of state water filings, supervision of dams, surface and ground water and water quality measurements and investigations, water conditions forecasting and reporting, Sacramento-San Joaquin water supervision, land and water use surveys, state maps and surveys, geologic investigations, state-wide water development planning, ground water studies, delta and bay barrier studies, special cooperative investigations, major and local water development programs, waste water reclamation, water quality monitoring, Central Valley Project cooperation and studies, review of Federal reports, Sacramento River Trial Distribution activities, California district studies and investigations, and work for interstate compact commissions.

The Department of Water Resources is organized to include three divisions, the Division of Water Resources Planning under W. L. Berry; the Division of Water Resources Project Development under W. G. Schulz, and the Division of Administration under T. R. Merryweather. The Southern California District Office will be under the direction of Max Bookman. The law creating the new department provided that employees of the organizations abolished would be transferred automatically to the new department. In this manner many positions in the new department are being filled, although a number of vacancies exist in many classifications. Plans are being made to move most of the personnel of the department to new temporary quarters pending the availability of suitable quarters at some future date.

As one of its last acts the Water Project Authority adopted the following resolution proposed by Chairman Durkee:

WHEREAS, The State Legislature in 1953, by the Abshire-Kelly Salinity Control Barrier Act, Stats. 1953, Ch. 1104, directed the Water Project Authority to investigate and study the feasibility and economic value of construction by the

GOVERNOR AGREES WITH YOU

AMERICAN SOCIETY OF CIVIL ENGINEERS
New York

The Honorable Goodwin J. Knight
Governor of California
Sacramento, California

Dear Sir: Acting in behalf of the American Society of Civil Engineers in convention at Knoxville, its board of directors has voted unanimously to commend you for an outstanding act of public service to your great State of California.

We refer to your recent selection and appointment of Harvey O. Banks and Mercel J. Shelton to be director and deputy director, respectively, of the newly created Department of Water. These men are distinguished members of our profession and our society. We are as confident as you are that they will ably perform the professional and executive duties of these new offices which are so important to the economy of California, now that it is faced with the urgent necessity of fully developing its water resources and protecting large areas from devastation by flood.

Very truly yours,
E. R. Needles
President

State of a suitable barrier or barriers for salinity and flood control purposes, and for the purpose of affording a supply of fresh water for irrigation, domestic uses and related purposes; and

WHEREAS, On March 30, 1955, there was transmitted to the Legislature a "Report on Feasibility of Construction by the State of Barriers in the San Francisco Bay System"; and

WHEREAS, Said report contained the recommendations of the Department of Public Works, Division of Water Resources, and the recommendations of the board of consulting engineers; and

WHEREAS, Pursuant to the recommendations of the authority in said report the Legislature in 1955 passed the Abshire-Kelly Salinity Control Barrier Act, Stats. 1955, Ch. 1434, which made appropriations to the authority for the further investigation and study of the Junction Point Barrier and Chipps Island Barrier as described in said report, for the purpose of developing complete plans for accomplishing delivery of fresh water to

the San Francisco Bay area, including the counties of Solano, Sonoma, Napa, Marin, Contra Costa, Alameda, Santa Clara, San Benito and San Mateo, and the City and County of San Francisco; providing urgently needed flood protection to agricultural lands in the Sacramento-San Joaquin Delta; conducting subsurface exploration work in the delta and designing facilities appurtenant to the proposed cross-delta aqueduct, including the so-called Biemond plan; obtaining more complete information on the hydrology of the delta; and study-integration of the proposed project in the California Water Plan; and

WHEREAS, Such studies and investigations are now under way and it is contemplated that a report thereon will be furnished to the Legislature not later than March 30, 1957; now, therefore, be it

Resolved by the Water Project Authority, That: (1) it hereby expresses its belief in the great importance of said project to the State of California; and (2) that, by this resolution, it recommends that said Bay Barrier and related studies, including studies of the cross-delta aqueduct and water supplies for the bay area and nearby counties, be continued under the new Department of Water Resources to the end that all facts relative thereto, whether provided for by existing appropriations or requiring additional appropriations, be ascertained as expeditiously as possible and that, thereafter, consideration be given to the integration of said project with the California Water Plan; and be it further

Resolved, That the chairman be and he is hereby requested to transmit copies of this resolution to the Governor of California and to each House of the State Legislature.

WE HOPE TO

Covina

Mr. K. C. Adams, *Editor*

Dear Mr. Adams: I felt it was proper to write and congratulate all who have anything to do with the making up of your tremendously interesting publication, *California Highways and Public Works.* It is a grand piece of work and you should be proud of it. Keep up the present standard, by all means.

Appreciatively yours,
Ralph Barstow
2580 North Oregon Avenue

GOODWIN J. KNIGHT
Governor of California

DEPARTMENT OF
PUBLIC WORKS
SACRAMENTO, CALIFORNIA

CALIFORNIA HIGHWAY COMMISSION

FRANK B. DURKEE . . Director of Public Works
and Chairman
H. STEPHEN CHASE . . . . . San Francisco
JAMES A. GUTHRIE . . . . San Bernardino
ROBERT E. McCLURE . . . . Santa Monica
ROBERT L. BISHOP . . . . . Santa Rosa
FRED W. SPEERS . . . . . . Escondido
CHESTER H. WARLOW, Vice Chairman . Fresno
C. A. MAGHETTI, Secretary . . . . . . Davis
T. FRED BAGSHAW . . . . . . Assistant Director
A. H. HENDERSON . . . . . . Deputy Director
C. M. "MAX" GILLISS . . . . . Deputy Director

DIVISION OF HIGHWAYS

GEO. T. McCOY
State Highway Engineer, Chief of Division
J. W. VICKREY . . . Deputy State Highway Engineer
CHAS. E. WAITE . . Deputy State Highway Engineer
EARL WITHYCOMBE . Assistant State Highway Engineer
F. W. PANHORST . . Assistant State Highway Engineer
J. C. WOMACK . . . Assistant State Highway Engineer
R. H. WILSON . . . Assistant State Highway Engineer
F. N. HVEEM . . . Materials and Research Engineer
FRANK E. BAXTER . . . . . Maintenance Engineer
J. C. YOUNG . . . . Engineer of Design
G. M. WEBB . . . . Traffic Engineer
MILTON HARRIS . . . . . Construction Engineer
H. B. LA FORGE . Engineer of Federal Secondary Roads
C. E. BOVEY . Engineer of City and Cooperative Projects
EARL E. SORENSON . . . . . Equipment Engineer
H. C. McCARTY . . . . Office Engineer
J. A. LEGARRA . . . . . . Planning Engineer
J. P. MURPHY . . . . Principal Highway Engineer
F. M. REYNOLDS . . . . Principal Highway Engineer
E. J. SALDINE . . . . Principal Highway Engineer
A. L. ELLIOTT . . . . Bridge Engineer—Planning
I. O. JAHLSTROM . . . Bridge Engineer—Operations
J. E. McMAHON . . Bridge Engineer—Southern Area
L. C. HOLLISTER . . . Projects Engineer—Carquinez
E. R. HIGGINS . . . . Comptroller

Right of Way Department

FRANK C. BALFOUR . Chief Right of Way Agent
E. F. WAGNER . . . Deputy Chief Right of Way Agent
GEORGE S. PINGRY . . . . Assistant Chief
R. S. J. PIANEZZI . . . . Assistant Chief
E M. MacDONALD . . . . Assistant Chief

District IV

B W. BOOKER . . . Assistant State Highway Engineer

District VII

E. T. TELFORD . . . Assistant State Highway Engineer

District Engineers

ALAN S. HART . . . . District I, Eureka
H. S. MILES . . . . District II, Redding
J. W. TRASK . . . . . . District III, Marysville
J. P. SINCLAIR . . . . . District IV, San Francisco
L. A. WEYMOUTH . . . . District IV, San Francisco
A. M. NASH . . . . . District V, San Luis Obispo
W. L. WELCH . . . . District VI, Fresno
GEORGE LANGSNER . . . . District VII, Los Angeles
LYMAN R. GILLIS . . . . District VII, Los Angeles
C. V. KANE . . . . . District VIII, San Bernardino
E. R. FOLEY . . . . District IX, Bishop
JOHN G. MEYER . . . . . . District X, Stockton
J. DEKEMA . . . . District XI, San Diego
HOWARD C. WOOD . . . . . . Bridge Engineer
State-owned Toll Bridges

**DIVISION OF CONTRACTS AND
RIGHTS OF WAY**

Legal

ROBERT E. REED . . . . . . Chief Counsel
GEORGE C. HADLEY . . . . . . Assistant Chief
HOLLOWAY JONES . . . . . . Assistant Chief
HARRY S. FENTON . . . . . . Assistant Chief

**DIVISION OF SAN FRANCISCO BAY
TOLL CROSSINGS**

NORMAN C. RAAB . . . . Chief of Division
BEN BALALA . . . . Principal Bridge Engineer

DIVISION OF ARCHITECTURE

ANSON BOYD . State Architect, Chief of Division
HUBERT S. HUNTER . . . Deputy Chief of Division
ROBERT W. FORMHALS
Administrative Assistant to State Architect

Administrative and Fiscal Service

EARL W. HAMPTON
Assistant State Architect, Administrative
HENRY R. CROWLE . . . . . . Fiscal Assistant
THOMAS MERET . . . Construction Budgets Architect
WADE O. HALSTEAD
Principal Estimator of Building Construction
STANTON WILLARD . . Principal Architect, Standards

Design and Planning Service

P. T. POAGE
Assistant State Architect, Design and Planning
ROBERT M. LANDRUM . Chief Architectural Coordinator
ARTHUR F. DUDMAN . Principal Architect, Sacramento
JAMES A. GILLEM . . Principal Architect, Los Angeles
CHARLES PETERSON
Principal Structural Engineer, Los Angeles
CARL A. HENDERLONG
Principal Mechanical and Electrical Engineer
CLIFFORD L. IVERSON . Chief Architectural Draftsman
GUSTAV B. VEHN . . Supervising Specifications Writer
JOHN S. MOORE . . . Supervisor of Special Projects

Construction Service

CHARLES M. HERD . . . Chief Construction Engineer
CHARLES H. BOCKMAN
Assistant to Chief Construction Engineer

AREA CONSTRUCTION SUPERVISORS

THOMAS M. CURRAN . . . . . Area I, Oakland
J. WILLIAM COOK . . . . . Area II, Sacramento
CLARENCE T. TROOP . . . . Area III, Los Angeles

**AREA STRUCTURAL ENGINEERS
SCHOOLHOUSE SECTION**

MANLEY W. SAHLBERG . . . Area I, San Francisco
M. A. EWING . . . . . . Area II, Sacramento
ERNST MAAG . . . . . . Area III, Los Angeles

During the latter part of August and the early days of September last year a series of disastrous fires devastated over 300,000 acres of California's forests and watersheds. To the people living in the mountain communities, fire's destructive power was a very real thing for they observed land resources, property, and equipment going up in smoke. To most of the people in valley cities, and metropolitan areas it was just another of those disasters that unfortunately occur. In these areas there was no immediate effect on business or community life and probably the only tinge of concern felt by many was a passing hope that the fires were not affecting a favorite recreational area or would not last long enough to interrupt the hunting trip for later in September. This is a perfectly natural feeling for too few people see too little of the State's surface structure to fully appreciate the State's complete interdependence and the relationship of the populated centers and rural valley farm lands with the mountain resources that are often hundreds of miles away. Few people have the opportunity to look behind the scenes at the interplay of human and natural resources that together are building the great economy of California.

Because there is no direct or immediate effect on local business or community life when a forest fire in a remote part of the State burns, few people realize that fire continues to eat into the very strength of the State. Fire impairs the holding capacity of a watershed, exposes soil to erosion, wipes out today's, as well as tomorrow's timber supply and directly affects the economy of adjacent communities so dependent on timber and recreational resources for their livelihood.

The serious impact of the fire losses of last year on the State's basic resources and on local and regional economy explains the reason for considerable public interest in preventing a similar catastrophe this year and in future years. Preventing wild fires before they start is certainly the first line of defense. Every man, woman, and child in California has a role to play and can accept an individual responsibility by being careful with the use of fire and those things which start fires while at home, when on the highways, and during work or recreational trips to the wild land areas.

California Highways
and Public Works

Official Journal of the Division of Highways,
Department of Public Works, State of California

KENNETH C. ADAMS, *Editor*

HELEN HALSTED, *Assistant Editor*

MERRITT R. NICKERSON, *Chief Photographer*

Vol. 35   September-October   Nos. 9-10

*Public Works Building
Twelfth and N Streets
Sacramento*

CONTENTS

Published in the interest of highway development in California. Editors of newspapers and others are privileged to
use matter contained herein. Cuts will be gladly loaned
upon request.

Address communications to

CALIFORNIA HIGHWAYS AND PUBLIC WORKS
P. O. Box 1499
Sacramento, California

San Fernando Valley Freeways

By J. E. ECKHARDT and L. S. VAN VOORHIS
Assistant District Engineers, District VII

Excellent Progress Is Being Made

THE SAN FERNANDO Valley is a very important part of the City of Los Angeles lying between the Santa Monica Mountains, the Santa Susana Mountains, the San Gabriel Mountains, and the Verdugo Mountains. In the northerly part of the valley is the City of San Fernando occupying the unique position of being entirely surrounded by another city when the City of Los Angeles in the early twenties extended its limits to include the San Fernando Valley. The valley roughly comprises the same area as the old original "Rancho Mission de San Fernando" of early Spanish days.

Its history, past and present, is most interestingly set forth in the book entitled, "San Fernando Valley," by W. W. Robinson, published by the Title Insurance and Trust Company of Los Angeles, California, that is available to applicants free upon request. A collector of Californiana would do well to obtain this book for his library. From the foreword of this book by Stuart O'Melveny, President of T. I. and T. Company, is quoted the following:

Historical Past

"San Fernando Valley summarizes the story of the whole of California. Formerly there were Indian villages along the water courses of the valley. Antelope once raced its broad plains. Spanish explorers, beginning in 1769, crossed the valley. It had a mission period, then rancho days. Revolutionary armies marched its length. The valley had a gold rush, an era of pioneer settlement. Great sheep and wheat ranches gave way to small farms, fruit orchards, communities, large population areas, and industry."

There is in this book much valuable information about the Mission San Fernando Rey de Espana that was established September 8, 1797, by Fr. Juan Crespi. If even more detailed information is desired concerning the early days of the San Fernando Mission, reference can be made with profit to *California Highways and*

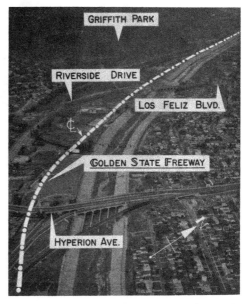

Public Works, issue of January-February, 1945.

Referring again to the T. I. & T. book, Mr. Robinson has considerable of interest to report about the historic trails and roads giving access to the San Fernando Valley, referring to them as "gateways." In the light of recent freeway developments in the valley what he has to say about two

of these gateways is of particular interest:

Gateways to Valley

"By Cahuenga Pass, once so narrow only horsemen could use it, now a broad multi-laned highway crowded with cars, the explorer of the 1950's could quickly leave the San Fernando Valley and be in Hollywood. He may prefer to extend his tour to Burbank, the city which today is usually described as being in the easterly end of San

Fernando Valley. It is at least a 'gateway' to the valley. Before the city existed its land was shown on old maps as the 'Puerto Suelo' —or gateway. Burbank has its own interesting story, for it was a part of the 4,000-acre Rancho Providencia, which—in the 1860's came into the hands of Dr. David Burbank (whence the name of the city), and also a part of the 36,000-acre Rancho San Rafael, whose first owner was Corporal José Maria Verdugo of the Spanish Army. Today Burbank, with its 80,000 people, largely fills the area of the 'gateway' of Spanish days, close pressed by the Verdugo Mountains to the north and the Santa Monicas to the south. Through it runs the old highway, the San Fernando Road, over which in the Spanish and Mexican periods ox-drawn carretas lumbered between the Pueblo of Los Angeles and the Mission of San Fernando. Burbank is a city of homes, parks, schools, churches, manufacturing plants, and is an aircraft and motion picture center. Lockheed Aircraft Corporation is here, so, too, the huge Warner Brothers Studio, the Walt Disney Studio, and the acreage used for outdoor 'shooting' by Columbia Pictures Corporation."

Cahuenga Pass

The Cahuenga Pass gateway, southerly of the Universal-International Studios called "Universal City," is now the location of the Hollywood Freeway with its 10 miles of completed construction into the Los Angeles Civic Center. The Burbank gateway is now the location for the Golden State Freeway, which is under construction. Another historic gateway into the valley via Sepulveda Canyon is the location for the San Diego Freeway. As the accompanying map shows, the San Diego Freeway will roughly parallel Sepulveda Boulevard, and the Ventura Freeway will be substantially along the general route of Ventura Boulevard, the old "Camino Real." The Golden State Freeway to the northwest leading over the Ridge Route to Bakersfield has a northerly branch, taking off just beyond the City of San Fernando, called the Sierra Highway that goes through Fremont Pass, another important "gateway."

Public Hearings Held

The evolution of the present freeway pattern in the San Fernando Valley from the old historic trails of the padres into modern freeways has been natural and logical as the mode of transportation has changed from oxcart to automobile. Even so the establishment of freeway routings by the

SEPULVEDA FLOOD CONTROL BASIN

DEVONSHIRE ST.

CHATSWORTH ST.

SAN DIEGO FREEWAY

SEPULVEDA BLVD.

California Highway Commission and the solving of engineering problems in connection therewith has not been an easy task. The engineers of the State Division of Highways have cooperated with the engineering staffs of the various cities in the valley in working out engineering details of planning and design so that the resulting freeways will provide the greatest traffic service for the lowest possible cost. The California Highway Commission has held many public hearings in establishing the freeway routes in the San Fernando Valley.

Typical of these public hearings was the one held July 14, 1954, regarding the Riverside-Ventura Freeway location and, in this instance, the commission published a report setting forth for the people of the San Fernando Valley the difficult problems which were being faced. Significant statements are quoted from the report as follows:

"The broad aspects of the problem are evidenced by the fact that the San Fernando

Valley is an area of some 200 square miles completely surrounded by physical barriers with only five major gateways susceptible of development to highway standards capable of serving dense vehicular traffic. These main gateways are Calabasas on the west, Weldon Canyon-Newhall on the north, Sepulveda Boulevard and Cahuenga Pass on the south, and the narrow valley of the Los Angeles River to the southeast.

Conclusions of Commission

"Among the conclusions reached by the commissioners, on the basis of the information and data submitted to the commission and upon independent on-the-ground investigation by the commission, are:

"1· An exterior examination of the homes along three lines under consideration indicates, generally speaking, that they balance out in quality though not in quantity. The majority of the homes on any one of the lines are beautiful properties with appropriate lawns and gardens with a value well above the average of California residences, but we cannot say that any finer properties will be taken on one line than on the others.

"2· Much has been said at the hearing and in the documents filed about giving consideration to the human values as well as to the engineering considerations. We acknowledge that we have given serious consideration to those values. In last analysis

2

we have to balance out 159 additional homes and 106 more residential units which Line I requires over Line III, and 270 more homes and 110 more residential units over Line IV, against objectionable features inherent in Lines III and IV. Places of residence can be moved. Admittedly, it takes time to develop gardens and to change residences into homes but a few years accomplishes these adjustments. A freeway located in the wrong place is an uncorrectable error and the whole community suffers irreparably and continuously over a great many years.

Sound Problems

"3. In speaking of the detriments on Lines III and IV, we are not thinking so much of the potential injuries directly to the sound recording companies except as these are reflected in the general economy of the community. Experience has taught that discontinuance of paychecks over extended periods results in community economic upsets and sometimes in family financial tragedies. These matters are essentially 'human values' and such wounds are not easily healed.

"4- From a community standpoint, the so-called 'disturbance' of the occupants of the homes not taken but left adjacent to the freeway will, in our opinion, more than be offset by the material reduction of identical kinds of disturbance to occupants of homes on city streets for there is certain to be far less start-stop traffic if Line I is constructed. Finally, from the same broad community standpoint, the material reduction of traffic volumes and traffic hazards on the city streets and avenues is a major community value in the favor of Line I. This clearly appears when we measure the over-all character of the traffic in the south portion of the San Fernando Valley. The far greater percentage of it is of local origin and very largely also for local destination."

Highway Commission Action

The above paragraphs are quoted because of their direct application to the problems of freeway location in the San Fernando Valley and also because the situation portrayed is typical of the thoughtful and detailed consideration which the members of the California Highway Commission give to these problems. As shown on the map accompanying this story, all of the freeways for the San Fernando Valley have been covered by the adoption of freeway resolutions by the California Highway Commission. After the commission has adopted freeway resolutions fixing the general location of the freeway route, the State Division of Highways can then start detailed designs, negotiate for the acquisition of rights of way, and proceed with construction contracts as funds can be provided therefor.

San Fernando Valley, an area where the population has more than doubled in the last 10 years (325,000 in 1946 to 790,000 in 1956), has developed growing pains such as few areas in Southern California have ever experienced. One of the most critical is the problem of transportation. With the Santa Monica Mountains separating the valley from industrial and business developments of other Los Angeles areas, and with the valley lying in the path of the only natural traffic routes leading from Los Angeles to the north, the inevitable result has been the development of very serious traffic problems. The completion of the Hollywood Freeway to Lankershim Boulevard and Vineland Avenue

at a cost of $55,000,000, while providing some traffic relief, has also been responsible to a degree for the rapid development that has occurred in the valley. This same statement could of course, be made regarding almost any undeveloped area through which a section of freeway is completed. However, it is particularly applicable to the San Fernando Valley.

Golden State Freeway

As shown on the accompanying map, present plans propose the development of the Golden State Freeway and the San Diego Freeway as additional routes connecting the valley with the Los Angeles metropolitan area. By providing the Olympic Free-

SAN FERNANDO VALLEY FREEWAYS

Legend

COMPLETED_____ ▬▬▬
UNDER CONSTRUCTION_____ ▬ ▬ ▬
OR BUDGETED
UNDER FREEWAY RESOLUTION____ooooo

SCALE

2   1   0   2   4
▬▬▬▬▬▬▬▬▬▬▬▬
MILES

Prepared By—F. O'Connor

way as an east-west route through the industrial area just south of the central business district of Los Angeles, further aid in the distribution of traffic will be provided. The Ventura-Riverside Freeway will provide for east-west movement through the valley, serve as a connecting link with the other freeways proposed and provide for traffic destined for the coastal area

to the north. On the Ventura Freeway westerly of Calabassas, at a cost of $14,000,000, all but 3.2 miles of the 37 miles to the City of Ventura, have been completed to freeway or expressway standards. The Golden State Freeway will provide the main route from the valley north over the Ridge Route to the San Joaquin and Sacramento Valleys.

Hollywood Freeway Extension

A major step in the rapidly developing freeway construction for the San Fernando Valley occurred when Director of Public Works, Frank B. Durkee, on August 16, 1956, awarded the contract to Griffith Company for construction of a 1.1-mile unit of the Hollywood Freeway Extension. This unit extends from Lankershim Boule-

4

vard to Moorpark Street and carries a construction allotment of $2,172,000. The contract plans provide for an eight-lane freeway section, with completion of construction scheduled for October, 1957.

Initial construction work on this freeway link started with the award of contract on January 20, 1956, to Oberg Brothers for the two bridges to carry this freeway over the Los Angeles River and over Vineland Avenue. This bridge construction contract has an allotment of $1,022,500 and is 35 percent completed, with the estimated date of completion being December, 1956. A part of the Oberg Brothers contract provides for the relocation of Tujunga Wash with a new drainage structure northerly of the existing crossing under Vineland Avenue. By building the channel in the new location it becomes possible to replace the existing Vineland Avenue bridge with roadway embankment.

This new freeway unit will provide better collection and distribution facilities for San Fernando Valley traffic utilizing the Hollywood Freeway because of the new interchange facilities provided at Vineland Avenue and the temporary ramps to be constructed connecting with Moorpark Street. These will be additional traffic facilities supplementing the on-and-off connections from the present westerly end of the Hollywood Freeway at Ventura Boulevard.

Ventura Freeway

The full potential of this one-mile unit of the Hollywood Freeway Extension, however, will not be realized until the interchange system with the Ventura Freeway is provided and the Ventura Freeway is fully completed westerly to Calabasas, the west city limits of Los Angeles. On this later portion of the Ventura Freeway, much has been accomplished with respect to the acquisition and clearing of necessary rights of way, and some bridge construction has already been started.

Construction is under way on two bridges to carry the new Ventura Freeway over Topanga Canyon Road and over existing Ventura Boulevard in the Woodland Hills area of the San Fernando Valley. This contract, also

with Oberg Brothers, is now 70 percent complete and carries a construction allotment of $703,700. The work is scheduled for completion November, 1956.

Two sections of the Ventura Freeway in the San Fernando Valley are covered by allocations in the 1956-57 Fiscal Year budget as adopted by the California Highway Commission last November. One of these units extends from Kelvin Avenue to Calabasas and will utilize the two bridges now under construction by Oberg Brothers. This section is 3.8 miles in length and carries a budget allotment of $3,600,000. The plans are completed, the right of way is clear for construction, and bids were opened on August 30, 1956. The low bidder was the Fredericksen & Kasler of Sacramento, and the low bid was $3,435,889.

Second Section of Freeway

The second section of the Ventura Freeway, 2.6 miles in length, extending from Sepulveda Boulevard to Encino Avenue, is to be combined as a single project with the section of the San Diego Freeway from a point near Valley Vista Boulevard to Burbank Boulevard, 1.8 miles in length, which will include the interchange between the Ventura and San Diego Freeways. An allotment of $7,535,000 for the combined project is carried in the 1956-57 Fiscal Year Budget. This 1.8-mile section of the San Diego Freeway will provide connections with the bridge to carry the San Diego Freeway over existing Ventura Boulevard now under construction by Oberg Brothers, contractors. This contract carries a construction allotment of $500,000 and is now 90 percent completed. The estimated date of completion is October, 1956. The plans for this 1.8-mile section of the San Diego Freeway in the San Fernando Valley are complete, and right of way acquisition is satisfactorily progressing so that it is expected that construction will be under way on the combined unit of the Ventura Freeway and San Diego Freeway early this fall.

This leaves two sections of the Ventura Freeway between the west city limits of Los Angeles and junction with the Hollywood Freeway Extension that require future financing be-

fore construction can proceed. One of these is from Encino Avenue to Kelvin Avenue in the Reseda area, 3.9 miles in length. The other section is from Sepulveda Boulevard to a connection with the Hollywood Freeway Extension through the Studio City area, 5.3 miles in length. Good progress is being made on right of way acquisition for these other sections. On these two units a construction schedule cannot be established at this time because the matter of financing will have to be worked out by the California Highway Commission in its consideration and determination of future state highway budgets.

Riverside Freeway

An easterly extension of the Ventura Freeway, known as the Riverside Freeway, will provide a connection with the Golden State Freeway. Plans are now being prepared on this 4.8-mile freeway. This is a vital link in the freeway system necessary to provide badly needed traffic service to the San Fernando Valley because, when the Riverside Freeway and the Golden State Freeway between Burbank and Boyle Heights in East Los Angeles are completed, an additional traffic arterial will then be available to supplement the existing Hollywood Freeway. This is the most practical and most expeditious way in which we can secure relief from the traffic congestion now existing on the Hollywood Freeway that, according to late traffic counts, is carrying a maximum load of 185,000 vehicles per day.

Completion of these first priority freeway units for the San Fernando Valley will provide an alternate route into or around the Los Angeles Civic Center and downtown area. These freeway units, when completed, will certainly do much to relieve the traffic overload now existing on the Hollywood Freeway between the San Fernando Valley and the Los Angeles Civic Center.

It is very desirable to have these particular sections of freeway completed, or nearly so, before further units of the Hollywood Freeway Extension are put under construction to bring it to its northerly terminus at a junction with the Golden State Freeway near Pacoima, otherwise the

and Public Works 5

RIVERSIDE DRIVE

N.B.C. STUDIO

OLIVE AVE.

ALAMEDA AVE.

RIVERSIDE FREEWAY

ST. JOSEPH'S HOSPITAL

N

traffic now using San Fernando Road and Riverside Drive would be diverted to the Hollywood Freeway Extension, and additional traffic would then be forced onto the already overcrowded Hollywood Freeway.

San Diego Freeway

Another freeway that should be mentioned that is of great interest to San Fernando Valley motorists, because its development and completion will greatly improve traffic conditions in the valley, is the San Diego Freeway. This freeway is 93.7 miles in length. It extends southerly from junction with the Golden State Freeway near the City of San Fernando

in close vicinity to existing Sepulveda Boulevard over the Santa Monica Mountains through the West Los Angeles area and along the easterly side of the Los Angeles International Airport. Then it swings easterly, passing to the south of the Long Beach Municipal Airport and then southeasterly into Orange County, to a junction with the Santa Ana Freeway at El Toro. Then it proceeds in close vicinity to existing U. S. Highway 101 through San Juan Capistrano and San Clemente to the Orange-San Diego county line.

The construction of the bridge to carry this freeway over Ventura Boulevard has already been described.

Other construction is now in progress in the West Los Angeles area. Work on the Sunset Boulevard Overcrossing and three other nearby bridges costing $723,000 was completed February of this year. In this same area, construction under two contracts with the Thompson Construction Company is now in progress to complete 2.3 miles of the San Diego Freeway between Ohio Avenue and Casiano Drive. The construction allotments total $4,000,000. The estimated date of completion is March, 1957. The construction includes seven reinforced concrete bridges and the extensive traffic interchange system at Wilshire Boulevard.

6

Over the entire length of this freeway at various locations, planning, designing, and right of way acquisition is in progress as well as the construction that has been described. In many locations, advance right of way acquisition funds, frequently called "Chapter 20 Money," have been utilized in the purchase of vacant lands to forestall construction of private improvements which, if allowed to proceed, would have made future right of way cost many times greater. On the San Diego Freeway, $5,000,-000 have been expended from Chapter 20 Money. The total expenditures to date for right of way acquisition and construction on this freeway is close to $28,000,000. The 1956-57 Fiscal Year budget contains an allotment for right-of-way acquisition on the San Diego Freeway of $2,740,000.

The San Diego Freeway is a traffic facility badly needed by the San Fernando Valley motorists, being valuable because it will take through traffic around the built-up and heavily congested Los Angeles business and industrial areas. When completed, a large portion of the through traffic now using the Hollywood and Santa Ana Freeways can to great advantage utilize the San Diego Freeway as a bypass route. It will be of further value when the future Olympic Freeway has been constructed for traffic destined for Los Angeles, because then another alternate route supplementing the Hollywood Freeway will be available.

Golden State Freeway

In District VII the Golden State Freeway is 72.7 miles in length, extending northwesterly from the junction with the Santa Ana Freeway in the Boyle Heights area of East Los Angeles, skirting Elysian Park, through Griffith Park, through sections of the Cities of Glendale and Burbank, through the San Fernando Valley in the general vicinity of San Fernando Road, and over the Ridge Route to the Los Angeles-Kern county line near Lebec. Forty-five miles of this freeway from the north city limits of Los Angeles to the Los Angeles-Kern county line have been completed at a cost of $12,000,000, as a four-lane divided expressway. In fact, this highway facility operates as a freeway because crossroads are infrequent and roadside development is sparse.

From the north city limits of Los Angeles for three miles southeasterly, therefrom, the Golden State Freeway has been developed as a full freeway providing connections on freeway standards to the north, with the Sierra Highway through Fremont Pass and connections to the east with Foothill Boulevard, and to the south with Sepulveda Boulevard and San Fernando Road. This three-mile section of freeway, that is sometimes called "The Tunnel Station Job," was constructed at a cost of $3,300,000 and

was opened to public traffic August, 1955.

There are three construction contracts now in progress on the Golden State Freeway in the Burbank-Glendale and Griffith Park area of Los Angeles. These three contracts are with the Vinnell Co., Inc., and Vinnell Constructors. The contracts provide full freeway construction for five miles between Glendale Boulevard in Los Angeles and Ash Street in Burbank. The total of the three construction allotments is $10,000,000. The work is scheduled for completion late 1957 or early 1958.

While much progress has been made in design and right-of-way acquisition on other units of the Golden State Freeway, a construction schedule for completion is not available at this time because this is dependent upon availability of construction funds as to be determined by the California Highway Commission in its consideration of future budgets.

Foothill Freeway

Of all the freeways that will ease traffic conditions in the San Fernando Valley, the least progress has been made on the Foothill Freeway.

As of this date there are two miles of the Foothill Freeway in the Flintridge-Altadena area in the vicinity of Devil's Gate Dam Reservoir, that have been covered by freeway resolution by the California Highway Commission, and completed. A special problem existed at this location due to

LEFT—Construction of bridge across Los Angeles River. RIGHT—This photo shows construction through Burbank.

intolerable traffic conditions where Foothill Boulevard was previously carried on a narrow two-lane roadway over the crest of Devil's Gate Dam. In correcting this situation it was necessary for the State Division of Highways to construct a short section of the Foothill Freeway to full freeway standards. This was completed and opened to traffic in October, 1955, at a total cost of $2,700,000.

Advance preliminary engineering studies are now in progress upon various sections of the Foothill Freeway in order to expedite its development, although no recommendations have been made to the California Highway Commission by the State Highway Engineer as to specific locations for the Foothill Freeway easterly and westerly from the completed section. It is to be expected that advance planning will now be expedited because the Foothill Freeway has been taken into the U. S. Interstate Highway System and is now eligible for participation in the new federal aid funds that have been created by the Federal Aid Highway Act of 1956.

In Interstate System

Other freeways in the San Fernando Valley that have been taken into the U. S. Interstate Highway System are the Golden State Freeway and the San Diego Freeway. It is to be expected that right-of-way acquisition and construction will be speeded up on all freeways in the San Fernando Valley area by reason of the additional funds made available to California under the Federal Aid Highway Act of 1956.

The California Highway Commission met in Sacramento during the latter part of the month and on August 25, 1956, announced the addition of $47,245,000 to the state highway right-of-way acquisition program, and $16,300,000 to the construction program for the 1956-57 Fiscal Year. Of these amounts, $2,000,000 was allocated by the commission for increase to the right-of-way acquisition program for the Golden State Freeway. In commenting upon this, Director of Public Works Durkee, chairman of the commission, said:

"Our planning is necessarily based on acquiring rights of way in an orderly manner ahead of construction. The necessary

speedup in acquisition of right of way, as reflected in this action by the commission, is very important in the early advancement to the construction stage of many projects. The right of way actions involve some major construction projects which may be included in the 1957-58 Fiscal Year budget, now under consideration by the commission for adoption within the next two months, or in succeeding fiscal years."

Freeways for the San Fernando Valley have created many complicated and difficult problems that have been solved, but many more still lie ahead which have not yet been settled. Successful solutions that have been worked out have been to a large extent because of the splendid cooperation which has been received from the city and county public officials and the engineering departments of the cities through which the freeways are located. We are sure subsequent agreements will be reached on other pending and future matters in a like manner, because there is every reason to believe that the same spirit of mutual cooperation will continue.

"THE BRETHREN OF THE ROAD"
GARDEN GROVE

Few of the countless thousands of automobile and truck drivers who pass over California's fine highways realize the time, money and thought it takes to design, build and maintain these smooth rivers of traffic.

The first ones to come along are the surveyors—those boys who plant stakes in odd spots and make the various measurements in three dimensions necessary to gain the required data, assisted by airplane photographs. The design boys next do their bit and turn out a roll of plans ready to start construction. The Right of Way boys meantime have secured title to the necessary property over which the highway will be built. Then come the construction men, who, along with the materials department and bridge men, direct the placing of foundation and wearing surface, most of which is done by experienced contractors.

Now the Maintenance Department takes over. These men are truly the "Brethren of the Road." No matter how severe the weather, rain, snow or drought, earthquakes, floods or fire, these determined men are constantly

Division Slates Opinion Survey Among Employees

What do Division of Highways employees think of their opportunities to work effectively, their training needs, their opportunities for advancement, their supervision and other aspects of their jobs?

In the near future the division is planning to conduct a state-wide employee opinion survey to find the answers to these and related questions. Purpose of the survey is to provide a sound basis on which to plan for increased efficiency and decreased employee turnover, particularly with respect to technical personnel.

The first step will be to obtain a frank, forthright expression of the individual employee's point of view. The employee opinion survey is a well-recognized method of providing this information in large-scale private industry and has been adapted to governmental agencies as well. It was tried on a pilot basis in one district of the Division of Highways, and produced worthwhile results.

Forms will be distributed to each employee. Questions will be asked about his views concerning his job. The form will not be signed, and will not be identified in any way with the individual employee who fills it out. Complete anonymity is of course essential to obtaining an objective picture.

When the results of the survey have been tabulated and analyzed, they will be published in *California Highways and Public Works*.

---

on the job, day and night, keeping the highways passable at all times. To them, probably as much as to any other group, we owe much more consideration than has been given at times in the past. Many of these men have been injured or killed in the performance of their duty. Whenever you see an orange-colored pickup, truck or piece of heavy equipment with a diamond ◇, bear in mind that they are trying to serve you 100 percent in spite of all difficulties. Give them your support.

W. V. BRADY

Eureka Slough Bridge
Precast and Prestressed Structure Unusual Job

By ALTON F. KAY, Associate Bridge Engineer

WITH THE completion July 24, 1956, of the Eureka Slough Bridge on US 101 the previously dedicated Michael J. Burns Memorial Freeway, a dream since 1944, was completed. An uninterrupted flow of traffic between the Cities of Arcata and Eureka in Humboldt County is now a reality. The structure was completed and opened to traffic on a well-planned schedule without undue activity as the local motorists, driving daily between these hub cities, were used to seeing between trips portions of bridges develop from out of space to form an integral part of the over-all structure.

Advantages

This is one of the advantages of precast and prestressed concrete. To be able to construct over 50 percent of the value of the structure at a central location where critical materials and skilled labor are abundant and transport it to an area having a deficiency of skilled labor and erect it with a minimum of personnel is a second advantage. Undoubtedly many motorists can remember the 2¼ years required to build the parallel bridge. This new structure was cast, erected and finished within the span of one year. Yes, indeed, speed is an even greater advantage, as this time included the fabrication of a second set of 105-foot girders to replace a set lost at sea during a sudden violent storm.

Design Detail

The structure, entirely of concrete, consists of ten 30-foot precast and prestressed spans on the west and 18 similar spans on the east of a central 105-foot span also precast and prestressed by the post-tensioning method.

The structure was founded on 26 precast and prestressed concrete pile bents, two composite steel and concrete abutments with two center concrete piers on untreated timber foundation piles.

The 20-inch x 20-inch square piles ranging in length from 45 to 105 feet were of a complete new design developed in the design section of the Bridge Department. The precast and pretensioned concrete piles were cored

LEFT—Air view of completed Eureka Slough Bridge with City of Eureka in the background. RIGHT—This is another aerial photo of new bridge.

and Public Works

9

with a 12-inch Sonovoid and the 18
⅜-inch wire strands were placed in a
14-inch circle around the hollow core,
then pretensioned to 200,000 pounds
per pile. These piles have many desired advantages, having an inherent
strong resistance to bending. Despite
their excessive length the piles were
picked up with a two-point pickup
with relative ease and without noticeable deflection or danger to the piles.
Pretension forces kept all transverse
cracks tightly closed, making the piles
more resistant to the corrosive actions
of salt water. Storage and transportation were effected with ease from the
contractor's precasting yard at Petaluma via 200-foot converted LSM's
down Petaluma Creek, San Pablo Bay
to the Golden Gate, up 300 miles of
notoriously rugged coast to Humboldt Bay and to the site at Eureka
Slough.

Precast Piles

At the precasting yard in Petaluma
the contractor, Ben C. Gerwick, Inc.,
cast these piles on two specially prepared heavily reinforced concrete
casting beds 300 and 500 feet long.
Pretensioning through the total length
of the bed was supplied in one operation thus allowing up to 500 linear
feet of piles to be cast in one opera-

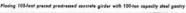

LEFT—Five hundred-foot precasting bed showing sequence of operation. RIGHT—Pile driver
picking up 105-foot precast prestressed concrete pile.

tion. A sequence of operations allowed
three rows of piles to be cast in each
bed without handling. Live steam
hoods were used for curing at a controlled temperature of 140 degrees for

approximately 40 hours during which
time the concrete in the piling developed compressive strength in excess
of 4,000 pounds per square inch. This
allowed releasing the jacks and storage
in the LSM.

At the site a 30- x 120-foot scow
driver was fitted with 100-foot steel
pendulum leads provided with a
moonbeam to drive the 3:12 batter
piles. The barge was a well-equipped
pile driver having a 60-h.p. steam
boiler with a three-drum engine. Two
additional three-drum deck engines
and three air tuggers provided lines
for maneuverability. A 10-ton block
of concrete plus a standby 15-ton
steam pile hammer were mounted on
a movable car placed transversely
across the stern of the driver to compensate for the 3:12 batter. A 10S
steam pile hammer supplying 32,500
foot pounds of energy completed the
driving setup. The majority of the
piles were driven to bearings, ranging from 45 to 60 tons but for test
purposes some piles were driven to
as much as 170 tons as computed by
the *Engineering News* formula with
only minor damage to the pile heads
and none to the remainder of the pile.

Placing 105-foot precast prestressed concrete girder with 100-ton capacity steel gantry

As the site is within the tidal flat of Humboldt Bay and driving was done from floating barges it was necessary to align the piles and bents from two directions simultaneously. This was further complicated in the King bents which consisted of six piles all battered 3:12 with the northerly or ebb tide pile battered transversely to the left. The southerly or flood tide pile battered transversely to the right. The remaining four intermediate piles were battered alternately easterly and westerly parallel to centerline. In order to properly locate the pile from two transits simultaneously it was necessary, using a tolerance of one inch, to take into account the fluctuation of the tide, the grade of the structure, the batter of the pile, and also the draft of the barge, with and without, the pile and hammer suspended.

This was accomplished by setting control points along the bent line produced to a point in the sidewalk of the old structure and a specially constructed survey platform in the previous King bent. A calibrated gauge was placed horizontally across the front gunwales of the scow. Each pile offset and batter distances were calculated as functions of the tide, batter, list, etc., and the scow positioned by reading these functions on the gauge with the two transits. This was a continuously changing operation as during certain stages of the tide the functions changed at a rate greater than the time allowed to spot the pile.

With the exception of the 105-foot precast and prestressed concrete girders the remaining 28 spans consisted of nine, 4-foot by 15-inch by 30-foot precast, pretensioned cored slab units each. Two hundred fifty-two of these units were also cast on the special precasting beds at an average rate of 15 per week. Again three-eighths-inch wire strands were used for pretensioning. A total of 35 strands were simultaneously pretensioned to 400,000 pounds per unit. The weight of each unit was 9.8 tons.

The deck units were barged to the site in groups of approximately 60

... Continued on page 43

UPPER—Precasting bed of the contractors' Petaluma Yard showing end of one pile and beginning of second pile. CENTER—Placing steam hoods on new piling. LOWER—Seagoing LSM with load of piling being brought into Eureka Slough.

New Span Open

Richmond-San Rafael Bridge
Approaches Being Built

By T. FRED BAGSHAW, Assistant Public Works Director

Governor and Mrs. Knight unveil bronze plaque placed on granite stone at Administration Building, Toll Plaza, of Richmond-San Rafael Bridge

THE RICHMOND-SAN RAFAEL Bridge was formally dedicated on August 31, 1956, and opened to traffic at 12.01 on the morning of September 1, 1956.

Dedication ceremonies, presided over by Frank B. Durkee, Director of Public Works, were high-lighted by the dedicatory address by Governor Goodwin J. Knight, which is reproduced in adjoining columns.

Band music was provided by the 561st Air Force Band of the California National Guard, Don Schary, Chief Warrant Officer, conducting.

An American Flag was presented by William B. Howe, President of the Richmond Allied War Veterans Council. Alfred P. Peracca, Grand President of the Native Sons of the Golden West, on behalf of Richmond Parlor No. 217 and Mt. Tamalpais Parlor No. 64 of San Rafael, made a presentation of the California Bear Flag. Both flags were accepted by Governor Knight on behalf of the State of California and were appropriately raised by a Color Guard from the Mt. Diablo Council, Boy Scouts of America.

Distinguished Guests

Following an invocation by Reverend Kenneth Coates of the Mira Vista Congregational Church and President Richmond Council of Churches, Director Durkee introduced those on the speaker's platform, including Mrs. Knight, United States Senator Thomas H. Kuchel, Congressman John F. Baldwin, George T. McCoy, State Highway Engineer, and Mrs. McCoy; Harry E. Crean, member California Toll Bridge Authority, and Mrs. Crean; Mr. and Mrs. Oliver Olson, representing the Richmond-San Rafael Ferry Company; State Highway Commissioners H. Stephen Chase and Robert L. Bishop, Fred Panhorst and Howard Wood, State Bridge Engineers, B. W. Booker, Assistant State

GOVERNOR TELLS OF DREAM COME TRUE

Dedicating the Richmond-San Rafael Bridge, Governor Goodwin J. Knight said:

The culmination of a dream, which this event represents for the people of Contract Costa and Marin Counties, and for the Bay area, has been realized through the cooperation of a large number of public agencies, working in harmony with the citizens and leaders of many communities.

The need for this magnificent bridge, linking the north coast agricultural, residential and recreational empire with the eastbay industrial centers, has long been recognized by civic leaders. It is interesting to recall that the impetus for this tremendous undertaking was generated by the people of the communities most directly affected, who expressed their needs and

... Continued on page 17

12

Highway Engineer, San Francisco; Mrs. Durkee, T. Fred Bagshaw, Assistant Director of Public Works, and Mrs. Bagshaw; Senator and Mrs. George Miller, Jr., Senator John F. McCarthy, Assemblyman and Mrs. S. C. Masterson, Assemblyman Richard H. McCollister, Contra Costa Supervisor Jack Cummings and Mrs. Cummings, Marin Supervisor Walter Castro, Mayor W. A. Cannon of Richmond and Mrs. Cannon, John McInnis, San Rafael City Councilman; John Inglis of Blyth Co., bond underwriters; Phil Murphy, representing contractors on the project, and Mrs. Murphy; Preston H. Kelsey, representing joint insurance brokers; Highway Patrol Commissioner Bernard R. Caldwell, Assemblyman Donald Doyle, City Manager of Oakland Wayne Thompson, and Robert Walsh.

Haggerty Speaks for Labor

George P. Anderson, President Golden Gate Bridge and Highway District, one of the speakers, said: "We bring from the Golden Gate Bridge and Highway District to you, Governor Knight, for your special interest in the project, to Director Durkee, to Engineer Raab, and to the artisans and workmen without whom the structure could not have been built, a word of warm congratulation

Nostalgic commuter watches disappearing Richmond-San Rafael Ferry on its last run following midnight opening to traffic of the new bridge

for an important work well done, and the completion of a vital link in our system of highways which will have a great and beneficial impact on this entire area.'

Speaking for organized labor, C. J. Haggerty, Secretary-Treasurer of the California State Federation of Labor, said: "The dedication of this great

structure marks another of the many milestones graphically portraying the splendid relationship which exists in this State between management and labor. This great structure has been erected without one moment's loss of time because of disputes between the labor organizations and the contractors involved. Cooperation has been

Dedication scenes. LEFT—Public Works Director Frank B. Durkee, Governor Knight, Mrs. Knight, T. Fred Bagshaw, Assistant Public Works Director. RIGHT—Miss Contra Costa, Barbara Jean Westbrook, Concord; Director Durkee, Governor Knight, Norman C. Raab, Projects Engineer, builder of bridge; Mrs. Knight, Miss Marin, Yvonne Barri, San Rafael.

carried to the highest degree in safety measures observed in the building of this bridge with its splendid results of only one fatality and one serious injury."

Engineer Raab Praises Cooperation

Norman C. Raab, engineer in charge of the project, pointed out that the work had progressed on schedule, saying: "This structure is not the creation of one man, or one group of men; it has resulted from the united efforts of the adjacent communities, the numerous industries, contractors and engineers, and the backing of the State administration. I would like at this time to thank all the personnel of the Division of San Francisco Bay Toll Crossings for their part in this undertaking. Their accomplishment, we believe, will be recognized by the multitudes this bridge will serve in the San Francisco Bay Area for many years to come."

A bronze plaque containing historic information on the project was unveiled by Mrs. Virginia Knight.

Father Daniel McAlister of St. Raphael's Parish, San Rafael, gave the dedication.

Anticipated Traffic

The bridge and its facilities were then thrown open for public inspection and an estimated 10,000 people took advantage of the opportunity to walk out on the bridge.

At the present time and for a period of another year, only the upper deck will be in operation. When approach facilities are completed on the Marin side, both decks will be in service, providing three 12-foot lanes on each deck. It is estimated that the first full year of operation will result in 4,000,-000 vehicle crossings, compared with 1,000,000 yearly carried by the ferries. The bridge can accommodate 20,000,-000 vehicles a year comfortably.

While it is too early to get a reliable indication of traffic volume, the early reports indicate that the basic estimates will prove to be justified.

Ferries Go Out of Service

Opening of the bridge signaled a time for celebration and four days of official ceremonies and fiesta were held. The end of an era of leisurely but time consuming transportation

CALIFORNIA TOLL BRIDGE AUTHORITY

GOVERNOR GOODWIN J. KNIGHT
Chairman, California Toll Bridge Authority

DIRECTOR OF FINANCE JOHN PEIRCE
Member of Authority

LT. GOV. HAROLD J. POWERS
Member of Authority

DIRECTOR OF PUBLIC WORKS FRANK B. DURKEE
Member and Secretary of Authority

HARRY E. CREAN
Member of Authority

across the bay by picturesque ferry boats was at hand. The ferry boats which had been operating for 41 years were now stilled but not without a note of sadness as many recalled restful trips across the water against the cool bay breezes.

New Era of Development

A new era of development and growth has been with us for some time and the supplanting of the ferries by the bridge and its extensive approaches was dictated by need for a direct and faster link between the

14

UPPER—Looking west at immediate approaches to Toll Plaza of Richmond-San Rafael Bridge on Contra Costa County side. LOWER—Map shows approach system on east side of span.

commercial, industrial, and residential centers of the East Bay and the North Coast's agricultural, residential, and recreational areas.

In their best year of service the ferries handled approximately 1,000,000 trips per year. In contrast, it is conservatively estimated that the new bridge will handle over 4,000,000 trips in 1956-57. The growth is further emphasized by estimates of 6,000,000 annual trips by the next decade and 8,000,000 by 1976.

Considerable work is being planned for the freeway approaches which are required to handle such volumes of traffic. Approach projects are now

under way by both the Division of Bay Toll Crossings and the Division of Highways. The latter organization is designing freeway connections to each end of the bridge work and these extend from the Eastshore Freeway, US 40, at Albany, in Alameda County, to US 101 just south of San Rafael, in Marin County. This represents a total distance of 13.5 miles including the bridge, all of which will be discussed hereinafter.

Division of Bay Toll Crossing Projects

Details pertaining to the bridge contracts were presented in the July-August edition of *California High-*

ways and Public Works in an article by Norman C. Raab, Projects Engineer.

In general, the bridge is 21,343 feet long (4.04 miles) and is second to the Bay Bridge by 1,377 feet as the longest high-level structure in the world.

Presently, only the top deck of the bridge is being used for two lanes of traffic (one lane in each direction). On completion of the lower deck and approaches, which is expected by midsummer of 1957, the top deck will serve the three eastbound lanes and on the lower deck will be the three westbound lanes.

The Division of Bay Toll Crossing projects include the immediate approaches to each end of the bridge. On the east end, the approach extends from Castro Street and includes a traffic interchange at Marine Street. It also includes an extensive grade separation structure at Scofield Avenue and traffic interchange westerly thereof which serves the piers and bay frontage.

Six-lane Freeway

This approach is 1.1 miles long and provides a six-lane freeway at an approximate cost of $3,200,000. Not included in the foregoing costs is the construction of the toll gates and administration buildings. The toll plaza provides eight toll collection gates on each side of two administration buildings. At present only half of the gates are in use and the remainder will be placed in service at the time of the opening of the lower deck.

At the west end of the bridge, the Bay toll crossing approach will provide six traffic lanes and extends to the easterly turnoff to San Quentin and includes a traffic interchange struc-

Toll collector awaits first automobile to cross Richmond-San Rafael Bridge. Driver is Tony Cortese, Richmond.

ture at this location. This project is 0.9 mile long and will cost approximately $3,600,000. The major portion of this approach involves two new concrete structures from the west end of the bridge. These will replace the existing timber trestle which has served as an approach to the ferries and will also replace the timber trestle con-

structed as a temporary connection to the upper deck. When the three-lane lower deck structure is completed, all traffic will be routed over it so that the existing and temporary timber trestles can be removed and the upper deck approach structure constructed.

The entire toll crossing endeavor consists of 20 contracts and the over-

Richmond-San Rafael Bridge looking west. Old ferry wharf right. Upper deck permanent approach under construction left.

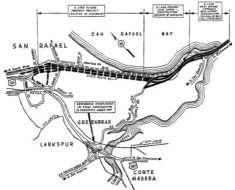

Map showing approach system on Marin County side of bridge

all costs, including right of way, will approximate $68,000,000.

Division of Highway Approaches

The Division of Highways has coordinated the improvement of its approaches to provide the proper traffic service during the several stages of bridge development. Under two contracts, in 1952 and 1954, at a cost of $340,000, the street system between Topeka Street and Marine Street was reconstructed to a six-lane divided city street as an interim improvement. These, together with the toll crossing approaches, have replaced winding city streets past the extensive Standard Oil Company refineries and on into Richmond.

An initial six-lane future eight-lane freeway is now under design between the Eastshore Freeway, US 40, in Albany, and the bridge approach at Marine Street. On February 17, 1955, the California Highway Commission adopted the routing for this future freeway connection. The southeasterly terminus is at the El Cerrito Overhead near Golden Gate Fields and the routing follows Hoffman Boulevard in Richmond to approximately 14th Street where it diagonals to approximately Virginia and Fourth Streets and along Virginia to Standard Avenue and Garrard Boulevard, thence along Standard Avenue to the bridge approach at Marine Street. This future freeway is approximately 6.4 miles long and when completed, construction and rights of way will cost about $13,500,000.

Construction on Marin Side

On the Marin side of the bridge the Division of Highways now has under construction a three-fourth-mile six-lane freeway to and including an interchange at Sir Francis Drake Boulevard, East. This project is the first phase in the construction of an eventual two-mile stretch of freeway between the bridge and US 101 near Tiburon Street in San Rafael. Construction cost will approximate $950,-000.

This project is scheduled for completion in the late spring of 1957 and in advance of the time that the lower deck of the bridge is opened to traffic. It will adequately care for traffic volumes expected at that time.

The project includes an approximately 700-foot-long overcrossing to carry westbound traffic off the bridge onto Sir Francis Drake Boulevard,

... Continued on page 57

GOVERNOR TELLS DREAM
Continued from page 12 . . .

their wishes through their local public officials.

The State of California exhibited sympathy and cooperation when a delegation appeared in Sacramento early in 1950 and presented a preliminary report which had been prepared and financed by the City of Richmond and the County of Marin. Your people had a vision, and after supporting your beliefs with sound engineering and economic arguments, your State Government found it feasible to approve the project and to carry it to a successful conclusion.

Necessary Legislation

An important early step was the passage of necessary legislation. On this phase of the development of this project, full credit must be accorded your Senatorial and Assembly representation in Sacramento, for all required legislation was advanced in an expeditious manner, although not always without difficult opposition. The important point was, however, that you were working together. You had resolved local differences and when the legislative conflict was most difficult, you were united, and most certainly effective. Too much credit cannot be given to Senator George Miller, Senator Jack McCarthy, Assemblyman Dick McCollister, Judge S. C. Masterson and Judge Tom Keating, and I would now like, on behalf of the California Toll Bridge Authority, to thank them for the outstanding legislative work they performed. Their efforts represent an important contribution to the building of this Richmond-San Rafael Bridge.

Raab Makes Record

Once the legislative problems were solved, the next step was the completion of plans, specifications, design and the engineering and administrative work required to get construction under way. The California Toll Bridge Authority assigned this responsibility to the State Department of Public Works and the project has been under the direct control and supervision of the Chief of the Division of San Francisco Bay Tolls Crossings, Mr. Norman C. Raab, whom you have met here today. I am pleased to report that Mr. Raab, and the technical people and other staff members of his division, have achieved an outstanding record in the task of advancing this project. The project has encountered a minimum of administrative problems. There have been no delays in the execution of the various contracts. All estimates have proven to have been sound, as evidenced by the fact that contractual bids have come well within the limits established.

Financed by Revenue Bonds

As in most matters, money is a very necessary ingredient in the accomplishment of a major undertaking. This one is no exception. This is a toll bridge facility and has been financed entirely by the sale of toll revenue bonds. Taxes are always a problem and a necessary evil, and we constantly try to keep them as low as possible and yet serve the people adequately. This structure, the cost of its building and the cost of operating and maintaining it, will not result in 1 cent of general tax obligation for the people of this area or of the State of California. It has been financed entirely through the sale of revenue bonds. This means that many individuals the world over have advanced the money, through the purchase of these bonds, and they are depending on the return of their money together with a normal rate of interest. The sale of $62,-000,000 in revenue bonds was completed through a syndicate headed by Mr. Charles Blyth of San Francisco. Mr. John Inglis is here representing the financial interests. I wish to thank him and his associates for the confidence you have shown in the future of the San Francisco Bay area, and its ultimate growth and destiny, by arranging the necessary financial support so that the bridge could be built.

Fifteen Contractors on Project

All state work is done on an open, competitive bid basis with private business and on this project 15 separate contractors have been involved, with contracts ranging from the smallest for $18,000 to the largest for $25,-000,000. The State's relationship with these firms has been most satisfactory. The success of their efforts is attested by the completion of this bridge in

record time. Mr. Phil Murphy, of the Judson Pacific Murphy-Kiewit organization is here to represent the contractors on this project. Mr. Murphy's firm had the largest single contract, representing about one-half the cost of the bridge. Through him, I want to congratulate all of the contracting firms for their work on this modern traffic facility.

This is the week end of the Labor Day holiday, and I am especially pleased to pay tribute to the workmen whose skill, courage, sweat and toil resulted in the creation of this masterpiece of construction. It is my understanding that not one day of work has been lost through labor disputes during the 3½-year construction period. The low rate of accidents to workmen is outstanding for a project of this magnitude. This speaks well for the care shown by the workmen themselves and for preventive efforts on the part of management.

Workmen Congratulated

It had been my hope that we could have assembled all of the workmen who had a part in building this bridge, in a seat of honor, so that proper credit and respect could be paid to each and every one of them. However, they number more than 2,000 skilled men, and no practical way could be devised to arrange their participation in that manner. I have, however, personally thanked each workman by card for his contribution to the project. Representing the workingman on the platform today is one of labor's most enlightened and effective leaders, my old friend, C. J. Haggerty, Secretary-Treasurer of the California State Federation of Labor. Neil, speaking for the people of California, I want to extend sincere thanks, congratulations, and best wishes to every man and woman who had a hand in the building of this bridge.

Not much need to be said about the value and the necessity of this over-water traffic link between two of the Bay area's finest and most populous sections.

It is here—a reality at last—for all to view in all of its splendor, and for all citizens to enjoy.

This tremendous structure is ample evidence of the manner in which

things are done efficiently, rapidly, and on a grand scale under our traditional American system of free and competitive enterprise.

On behalf of the people of the San Francisco Bay area, and on behalf of all of the people of the State of California, I am proud to dedicate this structure to the men and women whose vision conceived it, and to those whose hearts, hands and minds fashioned it.

VALUE OF LIMITED ACCESS FREEWAYS

Writing in the July issue of *American Highways*, John A. Volpe, Public Works Commissioner of Massachusetts, discusses at length the value of limited access expressways. He says:

"Raytheon Manufacturing Company, with plants in Waltham and Newton, has become the second largest employer in Massachusetts. There are 19,500 workers, and the annual pay roll is $75,000,000. In 1948 Raytheon had 600 workers, and the pay roll was only $250,000.

"Charles Francis Adams, Jr., Raytheon's president, attributes the company's growth in great part to the contribution Route 128 has made to the mobility of workers. 'Good roads and safe roads make their mobility possible,' he says.

"'Give a man or woman an automobile or membership in a car pool, and good highways to travel on, and distance becomes no barrier to accepting a job or seeking out a better one,' Adams declared. He pointed to an analysis of home communities of employees in Raytheon plants. It showed they came from 239 separate corporate communities in Massachusetts. In addition, 130 people came each day from New Hampshire, 40 from Maine, and 35 from Rhode Island."

FROM LOUISIANA

STATE OF LOUISIANA
DEPARTMENT OF HIGHWAYS

Mr. KENNETH C. ADAMS, *Editor*

DEAR MR. ADAMS: I have received your July-August issue of *California Highways and Public Works*. This publication is indeed most interesting and I want to thank you for placing my name on your list to receive same.

Yours very truly,

H. L. LEHMANN

Harbor Freeway

*Construction Progress
On Important Project*

By MAURICE E. CAMP and RAY A. COLLINS, Resident Engineers, District VII

FREEWAY CONSTRUCTION of considerable interest to the people of Los Angeles and vicinity was completed during 1956 or is now rapidly progressing toward completion on the Harbor Freeway. This freeway when completed will extend for 22.4 miles from its northerly terminus at the intersection with the Hollywood Freeway at the four-level traffic interchange structure near the Los Angeles Civic Center to its southerly terminus at Battery Street in the San Pedro area. As of today the total spent and obligated for rights of way and constructing on the Harbor Freeway stands at $84,000,000. At the northerly end of the completed 4.3-mile section the average daily traffic is now 175,000 vehicles.

With the football season now at hand it is of special interest to fans attending the Exposition Park Memorial Coliseum games that there are now four freeway traffic lanes available to southbound traffic with outlet ramps at Exposition Boulevard and at Santa Barbara Avenue that lead directly to the coliseum. To facilitate the northbound traffic movement at end-of-game time there are inlet ramps located at Santa Barbara Avenue, at Exposition Boulevard and at Hope Street. To accommodate the heavy pedestrian traffic occasioned by football fans parking on the easterly side of the freeway a 12-foot clear width pedestrian undercrossing has been put into service at 38th Street to take people under the freeway.

Bus Ramps Constructed

Bus ramps have been constructed under an agreement with the City of Los Angeles for north and southbound traffic on Jefferson Boulevard and southbound traffic at Santa Barbara Avenue. Another pedestrian undercrossing has been constructed at 40th Place for use with a bus ramp to be constructed on the adjacent con-

tract, for northbound traffic at Santa Barbara Avenue.

Immediately following the ribbon-cutting ceremony held on March 27, 1956, under the sponsorship of the Los Angeles Chamber of Commerce, a 1.4-mile section of eight-lane freeway and two lanes of a southbound distributor road from 37th Street to Santa Barbara Avenue were opened to traffic, extending the southerly temporary terminus of completed Harbor Freeway 4.3 miles from the four-level traffic interchange structure which distributes traffic to the Hollywood, Pasadena, Santa Ana and San Bernardino Freeways. Lieutenant Governor Harold J. Powers officiated at the ribbon cutting ceremony. With public traffic on the main freeway lanes it was then possible to complete the ramps at Flower Street and 23d Street where temporary widening had been provided to handle traffic at the temporary terminus of the freeway portion that had been opened to traffic after a previous contract was completed.

To speed up traffic movement temporary interchange ramp facilities, in addition to the normal inlet and outlet ramps at Santa Barbara Avenue, were constructed two lanes wide for distribution of traffic via the east and west frontage streets which were also constructed on this and the next contract southerly of Santa Barbara Avenue.

Freeway Contract

This contract for 1.4 miles freeway construction between 23d Street and Santa Barbara Avenue was awarded on April 1, 1954, to J. E. Haddock, Ltd., of Pasadena, California, with a contract allotment of $3,438,300. The major elements of this work in addition to the roadwork consisted of 10 retaining walls, one storm water pumping plant and three pedestrian undercrossings. Numerous storm drains and sanitary sewer lines were

relocated by the contractor, and gas, electric, water, and telephone facilities were relocated by the various public utility companies.

Due to a relatively dry winter season and to the fact that the natural soil excavated on this project was of a granular nature very little time was lost because of rain. The project was finished well ahead of the 400 working-day contract time, adjusted to include approved additional time allowances. This was made possible by the very cooperative efforts of the prime contractor who takes pride in doing a good job and making it available to the public as quickly as possible.

Heavy Excavation

The major portion of the fill material on this project came from roadway excavation on the freeway between 24th and 32d Streets and this material was placed between Grand Avenue, near 32d Street, and 39th Street. Borrow areas in the roadway excavation section of the next contract southerly of Santa Barbara Avenue, where the freeway is below existing ground level, supplied the remainder of the earth required to complete the portion between Grand Avenue and Santa Barbara Avenue. There were 542,649 cubic yards of roadway excavation and 13,883,989 station yards of overhaul involved in this contract.

All of the select material placed on this project in the backfill of bridge abutments, retaining walls and storm drain structure backfill, as well as to construct the structural section of the roadbed, was excavated in the vicinity of Adams and Flower Streets where the freeway section cut through an old streambed. During the excavation to a depth 30 feet below the normal street level for a storm drain pipeline north of Adams Boulevard, Assistant Resident Engineer Jack L. Nausler uncovered the remains of a prehistoric animal. The bones were so chalky and in such a state of general disintegration that it was impossible to remove and preserve them as a unit. It was found that the animal had one stubby horn about eight inches long and a very thick skull bone structure. There was a very unusual double row of teeth in a portion of the jawbone.

Structural Section of Roadbed

The material for the structural section of the roadbed was processed at the excavation site by removing oversized materials, including boulders which ran from 6 to 10 inches in diameter, crushing them in a jaw crusher and recombining the product with the fine material which bypassed the crusher. This material was conveyed by a continuous belt into seven-cubic-yard dump trucks which distributed it to the point of use on the grade.

In the roadway section which was within the select material excavation area the select material was left in place with a small working excess at the time of roadway excavation and later processed in place by scarifying and windrowing with a motor grader. This was followed by reduction to material within specification limits by the use of portable hammer-mill type crushers. The material was processed with the use of a rock buster pulled by a tractor at the start of this work. This machine did a good job of reducing the material but all of the material from the largest boulders down to the fine sand was passed through the hammers and more fines were produced than were needed. This equipment was replaced with a loader combined with a grizzly to separate the oversize material which was crushed with a hammer mill and recombined with the fines as discharged onto the roadbed.

Pavement Placed

After placing steel forms the upper four inches of this crushed select material was cement-treated with 3½ percent portland cement for use as subgrade under eight-inch class "B" portland cement concrete pavement and the upper six inches was mixed with 2 percent portland cement where used as base under four-inch type "A" plant-mixed bituminous paving.

Lt. Gov. Harold Powers clips ribbon to open new Harbor Freeway section. Shown are, from left, Supervisor Kenneth Hahn, Chamber of Commerce Vice President John C. McHose, Councilman Don Allen, Powers, Councilman Charles Navarro, Sixth Agricultural District Vice President Norman Lyon, Councilman Gordon Hahn, Police Chief William Parker, Highway Commissioner Robert McClure.—Los Angeles Examiner photo.

This cement treating process was carried out by bulk delivery of cement into the windrowed material, followed by mixing with a mixer through which the water was added, spreading with a land plane, rolling with a three-wheel steel roller, and finish rolling with a pneumatic-tired roller. The surface of this material was sealed with liquid asphalt MC-2 when completed. The pavement was placed with conventional equipment.

Cross-over galvanized steel water lines were placed in four-inch asbestos cement conduit under the roadway structural section prior to cement treatment to facilitate the future installation of watering systems for roadside planting in this area. Testing of completed waterline installations was done with nitrogen gas under pressure. In driving steel headed pins for the concrete paving forms the seemingly impossible happened. One long pin was driven clear through a 2½-inch pipe and casing.

Box Girder Bridges

In constructing the reinforced concrete box girder type bridges over city streets, timber false work was used to meet city requirements, but structures constructed over freeway cut sections were supported on aluminum tubing falsework for simplicity in handling, moving, and expediting the work.

On the Harbor Freeway contract between 23d Street and Santa Barbara Avenue as above described, Maurice E. Camp was resident engineer and the principal assistants were Chester Palmer and Robert Klesges. The Bridge Department representative was H. J. Scott. Mr. George Wiggers was general superintendent for contractor J. E. Haddock.

Contract Number 54-7VC75-F

In addition to the 1.4-mile section of eight-lane freeway between 23d Street and Santa Barbara Avenue that was opened to public traffic on March 27, 1956, a 2.8-mile length of the Harbor Freeway in the City of Los Angeles between Battery Street in San Pedro and Pacific Coast Highway in Wilmington was completed and put into full use for public traffic on June 19, 1956. Details of this construction were described by Resident Engineer F. E. Sturgeon in the July-August,

1955, issue of *California Highways and Public Works*. This contract was with the Vinnell Company, Inc. and Vinnell Constructors of Alhambra under a joint venture. The contract allotment was $3,395,800. The contractor was represented by Jack Yount, Vice President for Vinnell Constructors, and G. M. McAfee, project manager.

For general description and background information regarding the Harbor Freeway since its inception, about 20 years ago, reference can be made to the comprehensive story by W. L. Fahey, then District Engineer in District VII, who retired from state service a year ago, that was published in May-June, 1954, issue of *California Highways and Public Works*. Since Mr. Fahey's story was published two very important units of construction were put under contract on the Harbor Freeway.

Between Santa Barbara and Gage Avenues

Bids were opened March 17, 1955, for the section of the Harbor Freeway between Santa Barbara Avenue and Gage Avenue with J. E. Haddock, Ltd., of Pasadena, submitting the low bid of $4,484,517.10. Clearing

and grubbing operations began on April 11, 1955.

This 2.5-mile section of freeway and the 1.76-mile section following it are on a new alignment roughly midway between, and parallel to, the heavily traveled thoroughfares of Broadway and of Figueroa Street, which is existing State Highway Route 165. The major cross streets are Slauson, 54th and Vernon. The typical section provides for eight lanes of concrete pavement with 16-foot asphalt paved median for emergency parking. The same type of surfacing is also to be used on the shoulders, speed change lanes and ramps. Provision is being made for special bus loading ramps at Slauson Avenue and Santa Barbara Avenue. Frontage streets are being constructed on each side of the freeway except at the Slauson Avenue intersection area.

Bridges on Project

Bridges on this project consist of two undercrossings, the Slauson Avenue Overhead, eight overcrossings and five pedestrian undercrossings. In addition there is a pumping plant at 54th Street and numerous retaining walls throughout the job. The contractor

elected to use drilled piling to support the bridge foundations.

The pumping plant at 54th Street will have three pumps each capable of pumping 5,000 gallons per minute under a 37-foot head. There will also be a small auxilliary cleanup pump.

This section of the freeway is on a fill from the beginning at Gage Avenue until it passes over the Slauson Avenue Overhead, then it ducks below 54th Street and remains in a cut below ground surface until rising to pass over Santa Barbara Avenue to join the previously completed portion of the Harbor Freeway. Considerable rearrangement of public utilities was required in the cut section, particularly at Vernon Avenue where Los Angeles Transit Lines tracks were involved.

Storm Drain Facilities

Extensive storm drain facilities are required to maintain the existing flow pattern of storm waters westerly across the freeway to Figueroa Street. An 8.75-foot x 4.5-foot reinforced concrete siphon at 47th Place and a similar 11.5-foot x 4.5-foot siphon at 45th Street are being built, as well as 36-inch steel pipe storm drains in the

Construction on Harbor Freeway looking north from 79th Street

bridge decks of several of the city street overcrossings. Top of cut walls are being constructed throughout the below ground surface section to prevent overflow of surface run-off water into the freeway. These walls serve to channel overflow surface water across the bridges at the street overcrossings. In the fill section or the above ground surface section of the freeway 60-inch to 72-inch paved invert corrugated metal pipe are used to carry the storm water under the freeway. Surcharges were constructed and left in place for 45 days at the pipe locations to mitigate damage from later subsidence.

This job was 65 percent completed on September 1st and is approximately one month ahead of schedule. Concrete paving operations are scheduled to begin in December of this year and will be finished in three months. This should permit opening this freeway section to public traffic in April, 1957, with all work being completed about June 1, 1957.

George Wiggers is general superintendent for J. E. Haddock and Ray Collins is resident engineer, with Pat N. Scott as principal assistant. Homer Scott represents the State Bridge Department.

Southerly Section

The section of the Harbor Freeway from Santa Barbara to Gage Avenue is followed by another section extending southerly to 92d Street. The contractor on this section is Guy F. Atkinson Company. The job is 1.76 miles long and the amount of the contract allotment is $4,947,000. Work was commenced August 1, 1955, and was 65 percent completed on September 1, 1956. It is expected that this section will be opened to traffic in April, 1957, and all work will be completed in July, 1957.

The freeway is an eight-lane concrete roadway with a 16-foot median and is constructed entirely on an embankment approximately 20 feet high. There are seven bridges provided for cross-street undercrossings. The structures at Florence Avenue and at Manchester Avenue are welded steel girder bridges 107 feet long. At the five other locations, the bridges are rigid frame structures of the reinforced concrete box girder type varying from 64 feet to 86 feet in length. All bridges have concrete decks and all are carried on Raymond concrete piles. In addition there are seven concrete pedestrian undercrossings 8 feet x 8.5 feet varying from 163 feet to 249 feet long and two concrete pedestrian undercrossings in the Manchester Avenue area.

Twenty-five local city cross streets are brought into the frontage roads, which parallel the freeway the whole length of the job except in the Manchester Boulevard area. These frontage roads are curbed, surfaced with plant-mixed surfacing, have a width of 32 feet, and become an integral part of the city street system the one on the east being designated Grand Avenue and the one on the west being called Flower Street.

Full Cloverleaf

At Manchester Avenue there is a full cloverleaf interchange. At 70th and 77th Streets there are on and off ramps, the former serving Florence Avenue. From 88th Place to 90th Street, temporary on and off ramps will be constructed to connect with the frontage roads, to serve as temporary terminal ramps until the next southerly section of the freeway is opened to traffic. All ramps are surfaced with plant-mixed surfacing.

At two locations storm water drainage is carried under the freeway by 9-feet x 6-feet reinforced concrete boxes. At 84th Street a 10-foot x 11-foot reinforced concrete box was built under the freeway. The ends are now closed off by brick bulkheads but the structure will later form a part of a county flood control project. At another location a 66-inch corrugated metal pipe acts as a storage chamber to carry storm waters across the freeway. There are, of course, the usual large number of catch basins and storm drains.

The formation of the freeway embankment which constituted 1,050,000 cubic yards of imported borrow has presented an ever-changing problem. The material has come from over 20 different sources, many of these being excavations for large buildings in the vicinity. The sports arena site located in Exposition Park has supplied about 190,000 cubic yards. This is of unusual interest since the contractor paid the Los Angeles Coliseum Commission $23,500 for the privilege of ex-

LEFT—Harbor Freeway looking north from Flower Street. RIGHT—This is a view of Harbor Freeway looking north from Santa Barbara Avenue.

cavating and acquiring this material. It had been previously estimated by this commission that the excavation of the sports arena would cost them about $200,000. Each borrow pit has furnished a different class of dirt, the only common feature of which has been the satisfaction of the "R" value of 15.

Compaction

This nonuniformity would have required great skill in obtaining satisfactory compaction by the old sheepsfoot and air-port roller methods. However, on this job a comparatively new piece of equipment was used. This self-propelled roller with its four 69-inch wheels having tires formed by staggered rows of steel pads, presents an unusual appearance that makes one very skeptical as to its usefulness. However, traveling at five miles per hour in six passes it attains a 90 percent relative compaction. The weight of the roller is 16 tons and the compressions are 580 pounds per inch of face on both front and rear wheels. The speed of the roller enables it to cover large areas before the moisture content has diminished. The front wheels are 23 inches wide and the rear wheels are 31¼ inches wide. The engine is diesel and the horsepower 110.

Placing the bridge backfill has been an interesting operation since the manufacturers' agents demonstrated new and unusual equipment on this job. The vibrating rollers have been especially effective in securing 95 percent relative compaction in granular material. The model used was a self-propelled roller 28 inches wide and 22 inches in diameter which can be operated 3½ inches from a wall. It weighs about 800 pounds but, due to the internal eccentric construction, it delivers a centrifugal force blow of 1½ tons at the rate of 60 blows per second. This model roller has a roller 54 inches wide and 30 inches in diameter and weighs 3,200 pounds. This roller is towed by a tractor and can roll 5½ inches from a wall. It delivers a 5½ ton centrifugal blow at the rate of 75 blows per second. The efficiency of these rollers is due to their ability to produce a wide, deep pond of moving particles instead of the narrow pyramid produced by a static roller.

Construction on Harbor Freeway looking south from 49th Street

New Type Pneumatic Roller

A new type of pneumatic roller for compacting imported subbase material and cement treated subgrade was also used. The roller, with ballast, weighs 13 tons, it is self-propelled by a powerful diesel engine and it is the only type of pneumatic tired roller on which all drive wheels oscillate. There are five front wheels and four rear, or drive, wheels. This roller has produced splendid results.

The description of these rollers and their operation is described in detail above because they show a distinct advance in earthwork compaction, an operation that has rapidly become one of the most prominent and important topics of highway building discussion.

Another exceptional feature of this project is the forming for concrete work on the over-crossing bridges and the pedestrian undercrossings. The forms were designed by the contractor's San Francisco office and were fabricated on the job by Palmer Paulson, the contractor's bridge superintendent. These forms were very substantially made and so designed that they could be reused for duplicate structures without being dismantled. The forms were dragged into place on rollers by a crane. Deck forms for one-half of a vehicular bridge were moved into place for the other half in 1½ hours. Pedestrian undercrossing deck forms were moved ahead and set to grade in about an hour. In the latter operation the deck steel was placed at the same time as the wall steel and the deck forms then rolled under it. The methods of bridge construction and the appearance of the structures are of the highest quality.

Money Saved

Since paving operations on the J. E. Haddock contract and the Guy F. Atkinson contract will commence at about the same time, it was found possible to eliminate the construction of the temporary ramps on the Haddock contract. This not only saves the State many thousands of dollars, but of even more importance, it obviates the necessity for several complicated changes in temporary traffic routing which would have been necessary under the original plan. A mild rivalry has developed between the two adjoining contractors, each trying to finish his project first. It will be interesting to see the result.

John Skells is the project manager for Guy F. Atkinson. The contractor's bridge superintendent is Palmer

. . . Continued on page 42

and Public Works   23

By W. B. McINTOSH, County Road Commissioner, and
T. G. VAUGHT, Assistant Engineer

It was in February of 1924. A grim motorist was urging his Model T Ford up Hayden Hill in Lassen County, California. The snow had been flying and the ruts were soupy. The stroke of the pistons gradually slowed until the Model T was forced to yield to the abrupt grade.

When the pounding of the motor stopped the jingle of harness began. The desperate motorist looked up the grade and saw a man briskly driving his team toward the bogged-down Ford. He turned out to be a businessman. The tariff was $5 a pull without whisky and slightly lower with whisky, depending upon its quantity and quality.

After the Model T had been pulled over the summit, the rancher pocketed his fee, climbed into his wagon and

> This new county highway is a splendid example of what can be accomplished under the FAS Program with relatively small annual apportionments of federal, state, and county funds. It has been a privilege to have been associated with the county and the U. S. Bureau of Public Roads in this co-operative venture.
>
> G. T. McCOY
> State Highway Engineer

notched the wagon seat with his knife. The Model T was number 87 on the list of vehicles that had been towed over Hayden Hill.

Pioneer Route Was Trail

That was the Susanville-Bieber route of 1924. In those days it was a barely

passable trail winding from the county seat in Susanville to Big Valley and the northern part of the county. Today, what was once a trail has grown into Joint Highway No. 14, the longest continuous federal-aid secondary construction in the State of California. It is 67 miles of surfaced highway connecting the southern and northern halves of Lassen County and serving as an arterial for feeders from the central one-third of the county. The northbound traveler finds Joint Highway No. 14 a more direct route from U. S. Sign Route 395 to Adin, Canby, Klamath Falls and points farther north.

On August 26th the supervisors of Lassen County sponsored a dedication ceremony and barbecue to celebrate the completion of the final unit of

Section of recently completed Lassen County FAS Route the longest completed County Federal-aid Secondary Road in California

Joint Highway No. 14. State Senator
Stanley Arnold dedicated the highway to the public in an address given
at Colley Point, the site selected to
erect a monument and plaque commemorating the efforts of those responsible for building the route.

During the barbecue, which fol-
lowed the dedication ceremonies,
Peter Gerig, an original director of
Joint Highway District No. 14; H. S.
Miles, District Engineer for State
Highway District II; H. B. La Forge,
Engineer of Federal Secondary Roads;
O. H. Swaney, U. S. Bureau of Pub-
lic Roads; J. W. Trask, District En-
gineer for District III; Louis Ara-
mayo, District II Federal Secondary
Engineer, and supervisors and direc-
tors from both Modoc and Lassen
Counties made addresses commending
the spirit behind the construction of
Joint Highway No. 14.

Work Started in 1929

These festivities marked the end of
an endeavor which began in 1929. In
October of that year the supervisors
of Lassen and Modoc Counties appointed a board of directors for the
Lassen-Modoc Joint Highway District No. 14. Peter Gerig of Big Valley; F. W. Caldwell, of Modoc
County, and L. R. Cady, of Susanville,
were the original directors of the district. James A. Nutting was appointed
as attorney for the district and M. J.
Tilley was selected as the district
engineer.

These men had as their goal the
construction of a highway from Susanville, California to Malin, Oregon,
by way of Bieber in Lassen County
and Lookout in Modoc County. This
proposal met with the approval of C.
H. Purcell, then State Highway Engineer for the State of California, who
considered this route an essential link
in a highway east of the Sierras.

The first survey of this route was
conducted in 1928-29 by the California Highway Department, which, at
the request of the Lassen County
Board of Supervisors, was searching
for the most direct passage between
Susanville and Bieber. This survey
passed west of Hayden Hill. However, during the 26 years of this project many changes were made in the
original alignment and many more

were proposed. The major change
consisted of a new survey which
placed the highway in its present
alignment, leading from Susanville to
Adin in Modoc County. The reason
behind this change may be traced to
the construction of a highway between Canby, in Modoc County to
a point west of Malin, Oregon.

Many Agencies Cooperate

Grading began in 1930 over the
more mountainous section between
Willow Creek Valley and Eagle Lake.
Since that year there have been 16
individual agencies, both public and
private, which have contributed to the
building of the highway. The major-

ity of these agencies were private contractors. During the depression years
the C. C. C. and the W. P. A. made
notable progress. Working out of a
camp in Willow Canyon, members of
the C. C. C. partially graded approximately five miles of road between the
camp and Adin.

Hand laborers under the W. P. A.
were responsible for building Antelope Grade, two miles of the most
precipitous roadway in the entire
route. This grade was roughed out
in two seasons, during which time as
many as 132 men worked on the job.

Throughout the entire project Lassen County forces, under Thos. W.

... Continued on page 37

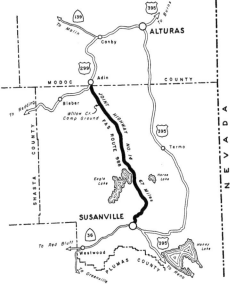

Lassen County recently completed this final section of the Susanville-Adin Highway, FAS Route 988, under the Federal-aid Secondary Highway Program. Construction was started in 1929 under jurisdiction of Joint Highway District No. 14.

Carquinez Bridge

Seven Million Pounds of Caisson Placed in Strait

By LEONARD C. HOLLISTER, Projects Engineer, Carquinez

ON MONDAY MORNING, July 16, 1956, at exactly 8.30 a.m., Contractors Mason and Hanger and F. S. Rolandi, Jr., jockeyed into position the 7,000,-000-pound bottom 39-foot section of the caisson for Pier No. 2 on the new parallel Carquinez Bridge project.

The hour of 8.30 in the morning was selected after considerable study of the tides and currents of the Carquinez Strait. At this time on this date there began an exceptionally long period of slack tide during which time the currents of both the ebb and flood tide of Carquinez Strait were at a minimum. This provided the contractor with a long period of slow moving currents in which to position the caisson and get it anchored to the 16 anchors which will hold the caisson rigidly in position during the sinking operations.

Huge Caisson

This reinforced concrete caisson will be 53 feet wide by 102 feet 6 inches long, the area of a moderately sized city lot large enough on which to build a six-room house, two-car garage, a patio, barbecue, flower garden and lawn. When completed the pier will be 149 feet high approximately the height of a 13- or 14-story office building. The caisson is divided into 18 open dredging wells each about 14 feet square. The contractor has been carefully planning the operations in connection with the sinking of these caissons for several months since the beginning of the contract which officially started on December 28, 1955.

The first operation in connection with the construction of one of these caissons was the fabrication and erection of the 400,000-pound structural steel cutting edges which were fabricated and erected at the Bethlehem Pacific Coast Steel Shipyards in San Francisco. These steel "cutting edges" are so called because they protect the bottom 13 feet of the reinforced con-

Erection of the 53-foot X 102-foot 6-inch caisson at the Bethlehem Pacific Coast Shipbuilding drydock. "False bottoms" for each of the 18 dredging wells can be seen, also the reinforcing trusses and 4-inch precast eXterior slab can be seen above the darker shaded steel cutting edge.

crete walls and partitions of the caisson. Their sharp edges at the bottom assist in cutting through the mud, sand and gravel during their downward path to bedrock at the bottom.

Steel Cutting Edges

These steel cutting edges were then assembled on one of the shipbuilding yards huge drydocks. After assembly of the steel cutting edges which are approximately 13 feet deep, the contractor added the bottom 30-foot section of the reinforced concrete caisson securely anchoring it to the steel cutting edges. The caisson was then rigged up and made ready for flotation by sealing of the 14-foot-square openings of each of the open dredging wells by the use of large dome-shaped timbers. These timber seals at the bottoms of the wells are called "false bottoms" because they are not a permanent part of the pier and because they are later removed after flotation is no longer necessary. After making the caisson seaworthy the drydock was then lowered into the water under the caisson and the caisson made to float. The caisson was then carefully examined for leaks and after determining it satisfactory was christened the *Arnold* after Arnold Hanger, president of Mason and Hanger. It was then floated to Vallejo where it was moored until the date for its positioning and the start of its journey to the bottom of Carquinez Strait where it will rest on bedrock 132 feet below the water level.

Not New, But Difficult

The work involved in constructing and sinking this caisson which will cost slightly more than $1,000,000 is not new in bridge construction history. For instance, deepwater caissons

One of the rounded corner sections of the 4-inch precast slabs being unloaded at the contractor's dock where it will be transported to the pier by a barge

Inside the caisson. Placing reinforcing steel and setting forms preparatory to the next 10-foot lift of concrete to be placed on the caisson.

were used in the construction of the San Francisco-Oakland Bay Bridge, the Golden Gate Bridge, the Tacoma Narrows Bridge and on many other large bridge projects throughout the United States. Regardless of this, the sinking of these caissons always involves a certain amount of risk and contractors are continually searching for safer and more economical methods of sinking them to bedrock at the bottom. The contractor for the foundation work on the Carquinez Bridge plans some new construction methods and sinking operations which have not been used on any previous deepwater caisson construction work.

One of these features is the use of 4-inch reinforced concrete precast slabs which will be used around the exterior surface of the whole caisson. These 4-inch slabs will become an integral part of the 3-foot-thick reinforced concrete outside walls. They will be supported by small steel trusses cantilevered up from the 3-foot-thick wall which has been placed at the bottom.

Precast Slabs

These precast slabs have several advantages: (1) They form a 4-inch watertight shell completely enclosing the caisson and because of their lighter weight as compared to the thicker walls temporarily increase the flotation qualities of the caisson. This is of considerable advantage in towing the caisson to the site and during the critical positioning and sinking operations. (2) It has a further advantage in that it acts as an outside form for the 3-foot caisson walls which are expensive to erect and requires valuable time during the sinking operations. (3) A third advantage is that there will be no formwork to remove from the outside and no finishing and patching to the exterior walls which will again save valuable time. The contractor hopes that these features will allow him to lower the caisson through the water and mud at the rate of 10 feet per day.

Sinking Caisson

The caisson will have approximately 90 feet of water through which to be lowered, at which point it will start

Concrete hoppers and traveling belts. Between concrete pours the concrete hoppers and frames are lifted from the caisson by large cranes and temporarily stored on a barge adjacent to the caisson.

LEFT—Contractors sectional model of the caisson showing the timber "false bottoms," the concrete hopper and traveling belt that delivers concrete to any place on the caisson. There are two hoppers for each caisson. RIGHT—Caisson model used by the contractor in studying method of attaching anchorage gear to caisson. There are four anchorage lines on each side of caisson which are attached to concrete anchors buried in the bed of the stream. These anchors hold the caisson in position against the strong Carquinez Strait currents.

on its path through about 42 feet of mud, sand, and gravel. Once the caisson is founded in the mud the usual method of sinking is to excavate the bottom from under the caisson with clamshell buckets through the 18 dredging wells provided for in the design. The contractor on this job plans an entirely different method of excavation. Instead of the clamshell bucket method of excavation the contractor plans to lower through the four center dredging wells powerful "Chicksan Intelli-Giant Jets." These jets can be operated at pressures from 30 to 300 pounds per square inch and their manufacturer claims that they can shoot a jet through 40 feet of water and cut clay at that distance. The plan then is to use these powerful jets to cut the bottom from under the caisson and pump the mud, sand, and gravel to the top where it will be discharged into barges and taken to the predetermined disposal area in the bay. These jets will be rigged up so that they can be lowered or raised to any position, can turn in any direction horizontally, and can be pointed up or down in any direction vertically. This method of excavation should

28

Foundation work in progress at the Carquinez Bridge. Caisson sinking is in progress at Pier No. 2 adjacent to far bank. Construction at each of the other piers is also under way. New piers for the Crockett Interchange can be seen at lower left.

greatly speed up excavation operations and allow the contractor to maintain his 10-foot-per-day schedule for lowering the caisson.

When the caisson reaches bedrock at the bottom the area underneath the caisson will be thoroughly cleaned of all loose materials and sediment, the timber false bottoms released, and the bottom 25 feet of the caisson's open dredging wells will then be filled with concrete. This will provide a foundation base 25 feet thick over the entire area of the pier.

For Completion in 1957

The remaining work will then consist of capping the pier with reinforced concrete and setting the huge anchor bolts for the commencement of erection of the steel towers for the superstructure of the bridge. The work on this pier is scheduled for completion May 1, 1957.

The total foundation contract for this project consists of an anchorage abutment set in the bluffs on the Solano side of the Carquinez Strait, three deepwater pier founded on 240 steel bearing piles, each capable of supporting a load of 28 tons, and an anchorage pier on the Crockett side 125 feet high. This contract was awarded to Mason and Hanger, Silas Mason Co., Inc., and F. S. Rolandi, Jr., for $5,-454,694.16. Oscar Johnson is Bridge Department representative for the three bridge construction contracts

and Reed Neff is the resident engineer on the foundation contract. This contract is part of the work authorized by the Legislature and the California Toll Bridge Authority for the construction of two new bridges across the Carquinez Strait. The work of these projects is under the jurisdiction of California Division of Highways, G. T. McCoy, State Highway Engineer.

VEHICLES ENTERING CALIFORNIA

A total of 579,354 vehicles entered California during July, 1956, an increase of 27,937 over the vehicles that entered during July, 1955. This total included 541,847 automobiles, 32,683 trucks, and 4,824 busses.

In Castro Valley

New Freeway Connects US 50
With Eastshore Freeway

By J. D. COLLINS, Resident Engineer

ON WEDNESDAY, August 22, 1956, District IV climaxed a first when a freeway connecting two previously completed freeways was opened to traffic. This freeway, known only as Ala-228-A, connects the Castro Valley Freeway, US 50, with the Eastshore Freeway, Highway Route 69, near San Lorenzo.

Opening day ceremonies were held at 11 a.m. on the main roadway, with a backdrop of structures comprising the Foothill Boulevard Interchange. Sponsorship of the ceremonies was by the Alameda County Highway Advisory Board Committee with Chairman Chester E. Stanley presiding. In attendance were C. A. Maghetti, Secretary of the California Highway Commission; B. W. Booker, Assistant State Highway Engineer of District IV, and many public officials of the State, County of Alameda, and the neighboring Cities of Hayward, Oakland, and San Leandro, and the Towns of San Lorenzo and Castro Valley.

Construction of the 2.932 miles of four-lane freeway was performed by Ball and Simpson, Erickson, Phillips and Weisberg, contractor. The contract was approved July 8, 1954, with a contract time of 360 working days and an allotment of funds of $2,899,-203.35. The final construction cost is $2,759,000 excluding right of way and construction engineering costs. Since widening of the previous highway facility was not feasible, complete new right of way was acquired to accommodate the new construction.

Eight Bridges in Project

Included in the project were eight bridges described as follows:

Castro Valley Boulevard Undercrossing. A reinforced concrete girder bridge about 319 feet long consisting of five spans, providing a clear roadway width of 28 feet between curbs.

Aerial photo showing Foothill Boulevard Interchange

Route 5 Northbound Interchange Separation. A reinforced concrete girder bridge about 312 feet long consisting of six spans and providing a minimum clear roadway width of 28 feet between curbs.

Route 5/228 Separation. A reinforced concrete box girder wye bridge with leg lengths of about 460 feet and 486 feet, each with seven spans. Each leg provides a clear roadway width of 28 feet between curbs.

Route 228/105 Separation. A reinforced concrete box girder bridge about 140 feet long consisting of two spans and providing a minimum roadway width the 80 feet between curbs.

Kent Avenue Overhead. A welded steel plate girder bridge over the Western Pacific Railroad about 409 feet long consisting of five spans and providing a roadway width of 68 feet between curbs.

Ashland Avenue Undercrossing. A reinforced concrete box girder bridge about 63 feet long consisting of one span and providing a roadway width of 80 feet between curbs.

Clark Avenue Overhead. A welded steel plate girder bridge over the Southern Pacific Railroad about 237 feet long consisting of three spans and providing a roadway width of 68 feet between curbs.

30

California Highways

Hesperian Boulevard Undercrossing. A reinforced concrete box girder bridge about 85 feet long consisting of one span and providing an average roadway width of 113 feet between curbs.

New Route Saves Time

Significant of the new route is the saving of time and the considerable safety increase to motorists and commercial vehicles. Prior to the opening, vehicles moving in a westerly direction toward Oakland or San Francisco, encountered in the relatively short distance, two full stop signs, three traffic signal systems, the two main line railroad crossings at grade, and during the school year traffic generated by the San Lorenzo High School which fronts on the route. A conservative estimate of time was ap-

. . . Continued on page 39

RIGHT—New structure on left and existing span on right

BELOW—Castro Valley Project ribbon cutting. LEFT TO RIGHT—Walter Luikn, director, California Real Estate Association; C. A. Maghetti, secretary, California Highway Commission; Mayor Raymond P. Kranelly of Alameda, W. A. Kinney, president, San Leandro Chamber of Commerce; Al Weymouth, District Engineer of the Division of Highways, San Francisco; Mayor Thomas O. Knick, San Leandro; Supervisor Chester E. Stanley, chairman, Alameda County Highway Advisory Committee; Supervisor Francis Dunn, Chairman Kent D. Pursel, Alameda County Board of Supervisors; Barney W. Booker, Assistant State Highway Engineer, San Francisco.

NEW RICHARDSON BAY BRIDGE OPENED

Northbound traffic began using the new $3,000,000 Richardson Bay Bridge on US 101 in Marin County on September 20th. Southbound traffic will continue using the old bridge until work on the southbound approach in the new span is completed.

The new bridge, which is a key link in the project of turning US 101 into a six-lane freeway, has two three-lane roads divided by a wide center strip. It has been constructed to allow for ready expansion to eight lanes.

When completed, the old four-lane bridge, which has been carrying an increasingly heavy load of traffic since it was built 25 years ago, will be torn down. Work on dismantling the span is to be completed early in January.

The job of building the 2,800-foot span began in September, 1954, with driving of steel piles through as much as 110 feet of mud and into the bay's rock floor.

Banning Freeway

Wintertime Bottleneck Finally Eliminated

By E. A. BANNISTER, Resident Engineer

WITH THE RECENT opening of the freeway through the City of Banning, one of the worst wintertime bottlenecks of traffic in Southern California has been eliminated. This freeway carries US 60-70-99 through San Gorgonio Pass. Because of the rapid development of the Coachella Valley and its popular winter desert resorts, as well as the steady increase of interstate travel, the former two-lane route through Banning had become a real problem to week-end drivers.

Because it is the lowest mountain pass entering the Los Angeles basin from the interior, San Gorgonio Pass had an early start as a major traffic route. In the year 1820, Captain Jose of the Cocomaricopa Indians of Arizona undertook to establish a one-man "messenger service" between the Colorado River and the mission at San Gabriel. The journey required from 15 to 20 days over a route known to have passed through Agua Caljente (Palm Springs) and the San Gorgonio Pass, at the eastern end of which now stands the City of Banning. About 1857, at least two freight companies attempted to operate freight lines through the pass to serve the growing mining industry of the desert country. However, it was not until 1865 when General Phineas Banning started to operate a stage line from Wilmington to Yuma that there was

Looking easterly showing freeway under construction through Banning

Plan and profile of state highway in Riverside County between 22d Street in Banning and 0.7 mile east of Banning

any regular travel through the pass. The one-rut trail of Captain Jose had advanced to the status of a two-rut wagon road, over which poured the early day pioneers seeking new homes in California.

First Auto Into Banning

In 1884, the townsite of Banning was surveyed, but it was nearly 30 years before it became an incorporated city. It is reported that in 1909 the first automobile reached Banning from Redlands after "nine hours of much labor and many repairs." With the rapid settlement of the Imperial and Coachella Valleys, it became apparent that the road through the pass would have to be improved to meet the increase in traffic. At a reported cost of $64,000, the road between Beaumont and Banning, about six miles, was surfaced.

A year later, work was started on a concrete-surfaced road from a little east of Banning to Yuma. This road was destined to become US Highway 99. The sum of $115,000 was appropriated for its construction. In 1922, the City of Banning paved Ramsey Street, its main east-and-west street and the one which, for many years, all the traffic through the pass would use. At the same time, the State High-

. . . Continued on page 46

Looking west along new freeway which parallels former state highway (Ramsey Street) through Banning. Interchange with east end of Ramsey Street in foreground.

Looking west showing former state highway (Ramsey Street) on right and completed freeway on left

EXAMPLES OF FILMSTRIP PHOTOS
AND NARRATION

TITLE SHOT

"Asphalt Plant Operation."

To keep the hot bins up there in the plant consistently filled he's got to regulate the flow down
here in the cold feed to provide enough—but not
too much—of each size. It takes some juggling at
first.

The accuracy of a pyrometer can be checked by
placing a hand thermometer in a shovel full of hot
aggregate and comparing the temperature of the
two instruments—the two should check within about
10 to 15 degrees.

If the sizes are not coming out right—and the cold
feed is operating O. K.—and the bins are operating O. K.—then you ought to check the timing of
the cycle to see that each bin is receiving and putting out the right amount.

After letting it set for 20 minutes we immediately
measure the height of the sand. The sand equivalent is determined by dividing the reading at the
top of the sand by the reading at the top of the
clay and multiplying by 100.

Training Aids

Construction Engineer, and Visual Specialist

essary to obtain full sequence pictures, especially of construction operations, picture taking cannot be accomplished within a short prescribed period.

Projected Still Pictures

A movie, of course, is the most advantageous way of showing certain highway activities but for some subjects there are equal or greater advantages in a series of projected still pictures with appropriate descriptive narration. Because of the limitations mentioned, the division has actually made little use of movies in the past. Undoubtedly movies will be employed in the future where the benefits warrant that medium.

Although the division has used filmstrips in the training program of the Right of Way Department, Bridge Department and Equipment Department, in the employee safety program and in several public information presentations, by far the greatest use to date has been in the Construction Department's training program.

Filmstrips have been produced or scheduled on five general subjects within the Construction Department's scope:

1. Concrete pavement construction;
2. Asphalt plant operations;
3. Plant-mix surfacing operations;
4. Earthwork operations;
5. Drainage structures.

First Three Units Completed

The first three units in this series have been completed and are being used. The Earthwork Operations filmstrip has just been completed and made available for showing to highway personnel. The one on Drainage Structures is now being processed into final form and should be available before the end of the year.

Although much of the information in these films was written and pictured for the new men, considerable information was covered in detail for

EXAMPLES OF FILMSTRIP PHOTOS
AND NARRATION

Up there on the profile cut A is hauled ahead to make up part of the embankment area. Below, on the mass diagram curve, when the curve is above the balance line it indicates hauling AHEAD; when the curve is below it indicates hauling BACK.

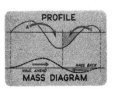

A settlement platform operates like a water-level gage. We pour water into the glass tube on the right until it levels off—then, by checking from time to time we can determine the amount and rate of settlement.

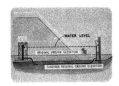

It's obvious that a contractor just can't run his equipment out over a swamp. He'll have to first place a layer of material across the area that's thick enough to support his equipment.

Cut slopes are designed at various angles depending on the stability of the natural ground and the economy of construction and maintenance.

This is type A soil stabilization. The obvious purpose of these wood grids is to hold the top soil in place. Their expense is justified where erosion might cause a serious maintenance problem in heavy metropolitan traffic.

the benefit of some of the more experienced personnel. Not only does the material serve as a refresher for the old hands, but it also covers new and improved methods or equipment that may be unfamiliar to personnel in some areas of the State.

In a broad sense the five functions covered by these training aids constitute the basic training requirements of the Construction Department. In any one of the five units there are numerous operations which could easily justify a complete filmstrip production by itself. Initially, at least, a broad coverage of the five functions serves the widest need.

Major Subjects Covered

As an example of the scope of these filmstrips, the major subjects covered by Earthwork Operations are: purpose, grading diary, working tools, right of way staking, clearing staking, centerline staking, slope staking, clearing and grubbing (heavy, medium and light), disposal of debris, cooperation with Forest Service, heavy grading, typical equipment, general soil types, materials report, mass diagram, excavation and slopes, stripping, selected material, benches, underdrains, all excavation, blasting, rough grading, traffic through the work, embankment preparation, recompacting, cross-drainage, drainage structures, concrete boxes, compaction, watering, subsidence, borrow pits, stabilization and erosion control.

Many technical reproduction problems had to be met and solved in the production of the filmstrips. The varying exposures and field conditions under which the pictures were taken required black and white "masking" of the original colored slides to obtain a master and prints within tolerable density limitations. Although the major portion of the photography was performed for some of the filmstrips by the regular photographic staff of the division, much of the 35 mm. color photography was done by other Headquarters Staff or district personnel. Reproduction of illustrative charts, diagrams and drawings is now accomplished by a direct process in the Headquarters Photographic Section, then assembled with the field pictures into the master filmstrip.

Earlier Film Strips Improved

In the earlier filmstrips the critical need for training aids made it necessary to work in a somewhat improvised manner, by utilizing available pictures, and writing the script around them. Later filmstrips have been developed in the more direct and comprehensive manner of starting with a complete script. This process has utilized to the maximum extent the services of the men with best knowledge of the subject to achieve full coverage of the field. For example, in "Earthwork Operations" the preliminary outline was prepared in conference with experienced engineers representing both the northern and southern districts. This insured coverage of different types of projects and variety of terrain and construction conditions.

Later, in the detailed writing of the script there were, of course, many instances where changes, additions and deletions became necessary. Also review of partly completed portions showed "gaps" or entirely new areas of information to be considered. These revisions were handled without difficulty during the course of production.

All photographic work, including the production of filmstrip copies, is now performed by division personnel but disc records from division tape transcriptions are obtained under contract.

Standard Equipment

A 35 mm. projector with filmstrip attachment and a record player with 33⅓ R. P. M. speed are standard equipment in all of the highway districts. Some additional units are available in Headquarters.

Most of the completed subjects consist of some 400 to 500 separate pictures, with two accompanying discs, recorded on both sides. Each record side has a 20 to 25 minute playing time.

Although it is difficult on the basis of relatively short experience to appraise the worth of these training aids there is ample evidence that they are extremely valuable. Like other training devices, their worth is increased by extended use. In the case of the construction films several districts not only show the films at central gatherings in district offices but actually take

these visual aids to the jobsites. There the films are viewed by the resident engineer's staff and sometimes by the contractor's supervisory personnel in advance of the project's reaching the particular stage covered by the filmstrip.

Knowledge of some elements can be gained only through actual working experience, but the speed with which the knowledge is gained can be increased materially by the use of these visual aids. The benefits of the construction films extend not only to construction personnel but to designers and people engaged in other functions. Men with primarily office experience, or with field experience some years ago, have been quick to realize the advantages to be gained from acquaintance with these films showing up-to-date processes and equipment.

DRIVERS' LICENSES

There were 6,721,409 drivers' licenses outstanding in California as of June 30, 1956, reports the National Automobile Club. Of this total, 6,309,372 were operators' licenses and 412,037 were chauffeurs' licenses.

AN INTERESTING HISTORICAL LETTER

The following interesting letter has been received by *California Highways and Public Works* from Frank M. Stanger, San Mateo County Historian and Executive Secretary of the San Mateo County Historical Association:

I am writing to add some historical data to the article by E. D. Drew titled "First Highway Tunnel," in your journal for May-June, 1956.

To see the ruined tunnel through Mussel Rock called "probably the oldest highway tunnel in California" is an interesting surprise. It may possibly qualify for this distinction, but it was not built by Francisco Sanchez, and there is some doubt whether the route for which it was planned can properly be called a highway.

First about Sanchez. As owner of Rancho San Pedro, he remained throughout his life a *ranchero* who had little interest in roads of the American type. His mode of travel was horseback and he died in 1862, aged 57 years, as a result of falling from a horse. His house still stands in San Pedro Valley, just back of the new town of Linda Mar and is now known as the Sanchez Adobe. It is county property and is open to the public as a historic monument under the management of the county recreation commission.

Sanchez' land grant of 8,926 acres dates officially from 1839, and it was his home from then until his death. But the present house was not completed until 1846. This is shown by his recorded testimony given in a case of land litigation in 1854. The pertinent passage is as follows:

"Q. Where do you live?
"A. On my ranch.
"Q. How long have you lived there?
"A. Since 1839; in the present dwelling house since 1846."

After Sanchez' death his estate passed through considerable litigation, as a result of which the rancho was divided among several owners. One of these turned out to be Richard M. Tobin who was also one of the founders of San Francisco's Hibernia Bank. Mr. Tobin was originally from Ireland; he had lived for some time in Chile and from there came to California in gold rush times. His portion of Rancho San Pedro lay along the coast and included the site of the later village of Pedro Valley. It was at this point that he built his ranch house, which soon doubled as a summer resort or vacation spot for the family.

For the Tobins to drive from San Francisco to "the ranch" entailed considerable hill climbing, and they naturally looked for an easier route. As Mr. Drew points out in his article, there is a straight stretch of beach from the Cliff House to Sharp Park, except for the single barrier, Mussel Rock. This beach at low tide would make a magnificent driveway for a smart team and buggy, with easy access and egress at either end—but for Mussel Rock. Hence it was Tobin who tried to break this barrier with a tunnel.

But the sea would have none of it. The local legend has it that the tunnel was no more than finished when the sea blocked it with sand and cave-ins. His daughter, Mrs. C. Tobin Clark, as a small girl remembers having her father's ruined project pointed out to her, and his grandson, Cyril Tobin, also remembers the family story about it. Neither of them, however, will venture to date the undertaking, but a good guess would be some time in the 1870s.

Does this make it the oldest tunnel? Perhaps Mr. Drew's Research Department will have the answer. As to the use of the word "highway," it would seem that Mr. Tobin's primary concern was a road to his own ranch, though doubtless he had no thought of monopolizing it, and he may have had in mind the development of the entire valley. If so, his beach route might have become a scenic highway. It might even have been the first highway with controlled traffic—controlled, that is, by the tides.

Sincerely,

F. M. STANGER
San Mateo County Historian

𝔍𝔫 𝔐𝔢𝔪𝔬𝔯𝔦𝔞𝔪

FRANCES SEVENS MARSH

Frances Sevens Marsh, Headquarters Traffic Department's oldest employee from the point of service, passed away suddenly on July 25, 1956.

As Frances Sevens she started work with Division of Highways as a file clerk in December of 1936. In June, 1939, she transferred to the Safety Department, the forerunner of the existing Traffic Department. At the time of her death she was a senior clerk supervising accident coding and traffic computations for the Traffic Department.

Frances Marsh exhibited extreme loyalty to her friends and fellow workers. Her warm consideration for others was outstanding and she was most friendly and helpful in the adjustment of new employees. These qualities will be sorely missed by her many friends in the Division of Highways.

EXAMINATIONS FOR ENGINEERS

The United States Civil Service Commission has announced examinations for highway engineer and bridge engineer positions paying $5,335 to $8,990 a year, for duty principally with the Bureau of Public Roads of the Department of Commerce.

Applicants must have had appropriate engineering education and experience. For positions paying up to $6,115 a year, education alone may be qualifying. Full information regarding the requirements may be obtained at many post offices throughout the Country, or from the U. S. Civil Service Commission, Washington 25, D. C.

Applications will be accepted by the Board of U. S. Civil Service Examiners, Bureau of Public Roads, Department of Commerce, Washington 25, D. C., until further notice.

COUNTY ROUTE COMPLETED

Continued from page 25 . . .

Ogilvie and Wm. D. McIntosh, have been instrumental in continuing both construction and maintenance.

A problem which repeatedly presented itself was the selection of each section of the route to be improved. This was especially so during the years of depression and limited funds. The scarcity of funds, coupled with pressure from competing projects, almost closed down Highway 14 two separate times. Yet, Joint Highway No. 14 remained to hold its ground as

a worthwhile project. Now that it is a surfaced thoroughfare its many advantages are obvious. It enables Big Valley residents to reach their county seat in both winter and summer; serves as a farm to market road; improves logging conveniences; facilitates the movement of livestock; encourages tourist travel, as well as provide freight and bus routes.

It is unlikely that the motorist whose Model T Ford was the 87th automobile to be unceremoniously dragged over Hayden Hill could have foreseen these advantages on that cold February day in 1924.

Retirements *from* Service

Retirement of George S. Pingry as Assistant Chief Right of Way Agent for the Division of Highways after 29 years of state service was announced by State Highway Engineer G. T. McCoy.

RUDOLF HESS

Pingry's duties in the supervision of all state highway right of way activities in Central and Northern California have been assumed by Headquarters Right of Way Agent Rudolf Hess, who becomes acting Assistant Chief Right of Way Agent. For the 1956-57 Fiscal Year the right of way budget for this area involves a scheduled expenditure of $46,730,000.

Pingry's headquarters have been in San Francisco, but McCoy said that for the present Hess will maintain offices in both Sacramento and San Francisco, spending part of his time in each location.

Pingry joined the Division of Highways in 1927 at its Fresno office, after spending eight years in real estate and right of way work following his graduation from the University of Wash-

ington. He later was District Right of Way Agent at San Diego, and moved to San Francisco in a similar capacity in 1945. He was promoted to Assistant Chief Right of Way Agent in 1947.

GEORGE S. PINGRY

His plans for "retirement" include property acquisition work on a contract basis for the City of Sacramento Redevelopment Agency.

Pingry has been a member and a chapter president of various professional societies in the right of way and appraisal field, and a regional director of the California State Employees Association. He is the recipient of a 25-year service award presented by the American Association of State Highway Officials. As a resident of Daly City, he has served on that city's recreation and planning commissions. He is also a member of the Commonwealth Club of California.

Hess, who is a graduate of San Francisco public schools and attended Healds Engineering College there, began work with the Division of High-

Forest N. Busby

After 35 years with the Division of Highways, Forest N. Busby retired in August, 1956. "Buzz" was born in Eugene, Oregon, on July 15, 1891. During his early years he lived in Elwood, Nebraska, and Clark-

FOREST N. BUSBY

stone, Washington, and worked as truck driver and farmer. After a year and a half as fireman in the Navy, "Buzz" took a testing job with the Materials and Research Department at its old location at the State Fair Grounds.

...Continued on page 39

ways in 1929 as a junior engineering aid in the Fresno office. In the following year he was transferred to the San Francisco district, where he worked in right of way engineering and right of way appraisal and acquisition for the next 17 years, except for two years as an inspector on highway construction.

In 1947 Hess was transferred to the Sacramento Headquarters Office of the Division of Highways, where he was placed in charge of developing the land economics studies which have become nationally famous in recent years as illustrating the beneficial effect on community business of properly located freeways. He also edited the division's right of way manual, the first of its kind in the Nation, and was responsible for in-service training of right of way personnel.

Hess is a member of the American Right of Way Association and the Society of Residential Appraisers. He is currently president of the local chapter of the S. R. A. His home is at 2781 Herbert Way, Sacramento.

Joseph M. Kane

Joseph M. Kane, Assistant Office Engineer of the Division of Highways Headquarters Office in Sacramento, retired on August 6th after 29 years with the State.

Kane has been responsible for the production of the division's "Standard Specifications" for more than a quarter of a century. These specifications, which set up the standards governing the execution of all highway construction work performed by or for the division, are nationally recognized. They have served as a model for other organizations and have been extensively used as a reference by other states and federal government agencies.

JOSEPH M. KANE

He has also supervised the preparation of individual job specifications on more than 2 billion dollars worth of highway construction since coming to work for the State.

Kane was born in Genoa, Nevada, attending public schools there and in Carson City. He studied engineering at the University of Santa Clara and later at the University of California, receiving his bachelor of science degree in 1918. He served as a second lieutenant in the U. S. Army during World War I.

Kane's first professional employment as an engineer was as a computer and draftsman with the Nevada Department of Highways in Carson City. He subsequently became chief testing engineer and then office engineer for the department.

He came to work for the California Division of Highways in 1927 and was soon placed in charge of preparing "Standard Specifications" and general specifications for highway contract work, a position which took on vital importance as the amount of highway construction increased.

Kane and his wife, Doris, reside at 905 45th Street in Sacramento. He is a member of the American Society of Civil Engineers and is past Commander of the American Legion, Department of Nevada.

Mary Hatton

Mary Hatton, Supervising Clerk, Department of Public Works, left State service on October 1 after 20 years.

Mary worked for the Department of Motor Vehicles, for the Department of Finance and for the past 15 years has been employed by the Department of Public Works. She started her Department of Public Works employment at Headquarters Shop in 1941 and then moved to Highway Planning and for the past five years has supervised the clerical staff in the director's office.

MARY HATTON

She is the daughter of the late Mary and George Korich. She was born in the small mining town of Ruth, Nevada, and attended grade and high schools in Sacramento. She is married to Thomas W. Hatton, Inspection Specialist, at McClellan Air Force Base.

She plans to devote her time to keeping house and gardening, one of her principal hobbies. She was tendered a farewell luncheon by fellow employees on September 19.

FOREST N. BUSBY

Continued from page 38 ...

From that beginning in July 18, 1921, he has worked continuously for the Materials and Research Department, moving with it in 1922 to its present location on Serra Way, Sacramento. "Buzz" has worked at a variety of laboratory tests, but during recent years his assignments have been entirely in the aggregate unit.

Busby's retirement is noted with a twinge of regret by the old-timers in the department. They feel the loss of another link with the modest beginnings of the department. They will miss his punctuality—it is said you could set your watch by "Buzz." They will also miss the aroma of good cigars as he was never without one and smoked them to the end.

It is probably a fact that Buzz has sieved more sand and fine aggregate than any other individual in the United States. He certainly merits the title of Mr. "Fine Grade."

CASTRO VALLEY

Continued from page 31 ...

proximately 20 minutes to travel the route as compared to a present time of approximately four minutes. Vehicles moving eastbound toward the San Joaquin Valley were more fortunate in that one less full stop was encountered; however, a 6 percent upgrade on Mattox Road more than compensated for this loss.

The Foothill Boulevard Interchange mentioned hereinbefore presented the greatest construction as well as design problem in that three state highways converge in this area and the work had to be performed without still allowing these important highways to provide their service. A series of detour systems were planned early in the construction stage, which when set into operation progressively during construction, handled the traffic with a great degree of safety.

In addition to the Foothill Boulevard Interchange, complete or partial interchanges were constructed at East 14th Street, State Highway Route 105, and Hesperian Boulevard.

Adjacent to the west end of the project, construction is nearing completion on the widening of the Eastshore Freeway from four lanes to six lanes from Washington Avenue to High Street in Oakland. Adjacent to the Castro Valley Freeway or to the east of Ala-228-A, construction is under way through Dublin Canyon. When this project, which is scheduled for completion next summer, is completed, a continuous freeway or expressway will be in service for the 51 miles between Oakland and Tracy via the Eastshore Freeway, Ala-228-A, and US 50.

PROGRESS REPORT ON U. S. 40 IMPROVEMENTS

By R. C. GROUT, Assistant Highway Engineer

GENERAL

More nation-wide attention has been focused on U. S. Highway 40 in the past few years than on any other major route. U. S. 40 has been brought to the attention of the general public through the many news items covering the need of an adequate trans-Sierra route and due to the many severe winter snow storms in the Donner Summit area.

The portion of U. S. Highway 40 in California traverses the full width of the State between San Francisco and the Nevada state line just west of Reno. This 210 miles of highway traverses every type of terrain that could be expected with a highway. The construction of this route to full freeway status involves all types of major design and construction problems starting in the metropolitan San Francisco Bay area, continuing easterly across the flat Sacramento Valley farm lands, and then climbing up and over the rugged Sierra Nevada Mountains. The planning and development of this route to a multilane full freeway between San Francisco and the Nevada state line is a tremendous project. Approximately 125 miles have already been constructed to

Existing US 40 between Floriston and Nevada state line which is to be widened to four lanes. Farad Powerhouse in left background on Truckee River.

multilane standards. The remaining 100 miles are either under construction or in various stages of planning and design.

PRESENT STATUS

Between San Francisco and West Sacramento the route has already been constructed to a four to eight-lane

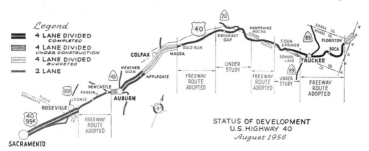

Legend
- 4 LANE DIVIDED *COMPLETED*
- 4 LANE DIVIDED *UNDER CONSTRUCTION*
- 4 LANE DIVIDED *BUDGETED*
- 2 LANE

STATUS OF DEVELOPMENT
U.S. HIGHWAY 40
August 1956

divided facility. Portions of this section have been constructed on an expressway basis. However, future plans
are to convert to full freeway standards. Through Sacramento studies are
progressing for a full metropolitan
type freeway. This involves a complete study of all traffic in and about
the City of Sacramento. Connections
will be made to U. S. Highway 50
which continues easterly through Sacramento and on to Lake Tahoe, and
also with U. S. Highway 99 which
enters the city from the south.

Roseville Freeway

From Sacramento to east of Roseville a full four-lane freeway is now

in operation. The section between
Roseville and Newcastle is well along
in the design stage, and, if financing
will permit, should be under construction within the next two years. Be-

tween Newcastle and Auburn a four-
lane expressway is under construction.
    Between Auburn and Heather Glen
a four-lane divided facility is now in
operation.

LEFT—Looking easterly from near Wise Powerhouse. Auburn on hills in background. RIGHT—Beginning of project about one mile east of Newcastle looking easterly.

The section between Heather Glen and Magra (six miles east of Colfax) and the section between Floriston and the Nevada state line are budgeted and should be under construction this fall.

The routes on the three sections, Magra to Blue Canyon Road; Hampshire Rocks to Soda Springs; and east end of Donner Lake to Floriston, have all been adopted and declared freeways by the California Highway Commission. At present they are in various stages of planning and design, and it is hoped that these sections can be constructed and opened for traffic prior to the 1960 Winter Olympic games to be held at Squaw Valley. The two remaining sections, Blue Canyon Road to Hampshire Rocks and Soda Springs to east end of Donner Lake, have been studied and will be presented to the Highway Commission for adoption within the next few months. With the route adoption of these two sections and the exception through Sacramento and the Yolo Causeway, the entire route of U. S. 40 in California will have been adopted and declared a freeway.

Looking easterly—Hallbom Road Undercrossing under construction

Considerable Progress Made

The speed with which this series of plans along the not-yet-modernized sections of U. S. 40 are translated into actual construction to provide a continuous stretch of divided highway extending from San Francisco to the Nevada state line depends upon the availability of funds.

Considerable progress has been made in bringing U. S. 40 up to modern standards. Financing of this enormous undertaking has not been easy. Progress was accelerated when the California State Legislature increased the highway user taxes in 1953. Undoubtedly many of the projects now under way, or budgeted on this route, would have had to wait several years if the additional revenues provided by 1953 legislation had not been available.

With the additional federal financing provided by Congress on interstate highways, the reality of U. S. 40 becoming a full freeway throughout California will be greatly accelerated. Continuous improvement of this route is one of the outstanding examples of the benefits of long range planning for the development of through routes

which are so important to a vast and growing state such as California and our mechanized nation that has come to depend so heavily on motor vehicle transportation.

HARBOR FREEWAY

Continued from page 23 ...

Paulson. The State Division of Highways is represented on the job by Ray A. Collins, resident engineer, and his principal assistant, Mitchell L. Gould. Homer Scott represents the Bridge Department, with Pete Hixson as his principal assistant.

On August 24th the California Highway Commission announced the addition of $47,245,000 to the state highway right of way acquisition program and $16,300,000 to the construction program for the 1956-57 Fiscal Year. In the construction program allocation, the commission set aside $6,000,000 to provide construction to extend the Harbor Freeway 2.8 miles southerly from 92d Street to 124th Street. This will provide for grading, paving, and the necessary structures

to build an eight-lane full freeway, complete in every detail.

The plans for this southerly extension of the Harbor Freeway have been completed. The necessary rights of way have substantially all been secured so that advertising the contract is anticipated very soon. Actual construction on this important link of the Harbor Freeway should be in progress before the end of 1956. The construction schedule will provide for completion during midyear 1958.

Taking into account the two construction contracts now in progress and the recently financed 2.8-mile unit, there remains of the 22.4 miles total only a nine-mile link of the Harbor Freeway to be done. Designs and preparation of plans for the remaining link of the Harbor Freeway are well along toward completion and the right of way acquisition program for this future construction is well advanced. Completion of the remaining link of the Harbor Freeway awaits allocation of construction funds by the California Highway Commission when future budgets are under consideration.

EUREKA SLOUGH

Continued from page 11...

and positioned with a 60-ton boom mounted on the pile driver. The LSM load of units were received about once a month and were unloaded and positioned in approximately one week. Grouting and transverse post tensioning using seven-eighths-inch strands post-tensioned to 59,000 pounds usually took the remainder of the time.

The main channel span consisted of seven precast and prestressed concrete girders 105 feet long. The initial set were cast using ten 1⅛-inch strands post-tensioned to a force of 865,000 pounds per girder. These girders with a net weight of 68 tons were also cast in the Petaluma yard and loaded onto one of the LSM's for the trip to Eureka. However, a sudden violent storm capsized the LSM off Cape Mendocino less than 20 miles from their destination and the total shipment was lost.

Fast Work

The contractor supplied a second set of girders which were post-tensioned using ten 1⅛-inch high-tensile steel rods. Although these girders were shipped on two flat barges and weighed 68 tons each the contractor positioned them in a matter of eight hours or approximately one hour and ten minutes per girder.

The lifting of the girders from the barge to their final position in the span

was accomplished by the use of a 108-foot steel gantry capable of lifting 100 tons and traveling transversely approximately 80 feet. Power for the gantry was supplied by a 250 h.p. diesel motor and a two-drum engine mounted on the gantry. Transverse movement was supplied by two air tuggers which positioned the girders within the tolerance required.

The Division of Highways Bridge Department may well be proud of this now well-known structure. It has been nationally publicized in an article in the American Society of Civil Engineers by John A. Roebling, Sons, of Trenton, New Jersey, and featured by Pacific Road Builder and Western Construction trade journal magazines.

The contractor was Ben C. Gerwick, Inc., of San Francisco, and Mercer Fraser Company of Eureka was subcontractor for the approaches.

This contract was under the administration of the Bridge Department of the Division of Highways, F. W. Panhorst, Assistant State Highway Engineer-Bridges; I. O. Jahlstrom, Operations Engineer. Roadwork included in the contract was under the supervision of District I, Division of Highways, A. S. Hart, District Engineer.

The writer was the Resident Engineer for the Bridge Department, assisted by Raymond E. Davis, Lowell C. Allen, and Ray Samuelson, Associate Bridge Engineers.

STRIPED BASS IN CALIFORNIA

Back in 1879, according to the National Automobile Club, there wasn't a striped bass to be had in California. At that time, however, some enterprising fellow scooped 132 little stripers from the Navesink River in New Jersey, put them into a tank and on a train, brought them out to California, and dropped them into the water just off Martinez. Three years later they dropped another 300 stripers into the Suisun Bay.

And then Mother Nature took over. A five-pound female bass may spawn as many as 250,000 eggs in one season, a 12-pounder may spawn 1,250,000 eggs, and it is estimated that a 75-pounder would probably spawn close to 10,000,000 eggs.

So well have the females been spawning down through the years that in 1948 California anglers took well over 1,500,000 striped bass from local waters and this hardly put a dent in the total number of stripers that lurk beneath the surface of the waters around our State. During June and July, when eggs are hatching, the total number of tiny fish in such bodies of water as Suisun Bay and the San Joaquin Delta must be almost astronomical.

H. W. Benedict, Highway Engineering Associate of District I, was in direct charge of the roadway portion of this contract.

Under the leadership of William A. Sparling, Secretary-Manager of the Oakland Chamber of Commerce, the Alameda County Highway Advisory Committee on August 21st, in Sacramento, presented to the California Highway Commission its recommendations for projects it desires included in the 1957-58 budget. The recommendations are:

WILLIAM A. SPARLING

Group A: Projects Upon Which Actual Construction, Including Programed Acquisition of Rights of Way shall be prosecuted in the Fiscal Year 1957-1958:

State Route 69—Eastshore Freeway

1. (Sign Route 17) Complete construction northwest of Fallon Street in the City of Oakland.

2. (US 40) Complete rights-of-way acquisition and initiate construction of the Eastshore Freeway in Albany to connect with the Alameda County-Contra Costa county line.

State Route 226

1. Estuary Crossing. Program rights-of-way acquisitions and initiate construction utilizing state highway funds, if legally possible, with the provision that such highway funds be returned to Alameda County highway allocations from toll bridge authority funds when authorized.

2. In Alameda. Program rights-of-way acquisition and initiate construction from northerly end of Bay Farm Island Bridge to Fernside Boulevard.

3. In Alameda. Reconstruct Central Avenue between Webster Street and Sherman Street.

4. In San Leandro. Reconstruct Davis Street between Southern Pacific Railroad and East 14th Street.

State Route 226 and 75—In Oakland

(Portion of Sign Route 24) Complete route adoption between Alameda-Contra Costa county line and Eastshore Freeway; continue planning and surveys and formulate a program for correction of spot deficiencies.

State Route 227—Mountain Boulevard Freeway

Increase program of state allocations and accelerate construction.

State Route 5—Foothill Boulevard and MacArthur Boulevard

1. (Sign Route 9) Expedite route studies, surveys and plans for Route 5-C from Hayward to Niles, together with correction of the three-lane portion from Sycamore Avenue to the unincorporated town of Decoto by addition of a fourth traffic lane.

2. (US 50) MacArthur Boulevard. Initiate construction of first unit in Oakland, accelerate route adoption and continue programed purchase of rights of way.

State Route 105—In Oakland, San Leandro, and Hayward

Initiate planned purchases of rights of way preparatory to early construction from Route 5 to Route 69 in the vicinity of Hayward on Jackson Street.

. . . Continued on page 54

Guests at luncheon at Sutter Club in Sacramento given by Alameda County delegation: STANDING, HEAD TABLE, LEFT TO RIGHT—Robert L. Bishop, H. Stephen Chase, California Highway Commission; Frank B. Durkee, Director of Public Works and Chairman of Commission; Chester E. Stanley, Chairman, Alameda County Highway Advisory Committee and Member, Alameda County Board of Supervisors; Chester H. Warlow, Highway Commissioner; Clifford E. Rishell, Mayor, City of Oakland; George T. McCoy, State Highway Engineer.
SEATED, ON THE LEFT, OUTSIDE ROW—C. A. Maghetti, Secretary, California Highway Commission; George Cook, Assistant Secretary; G. Homer Hamlin, Director of Public Works, San Leandro; Richard Wilkinson, Planning Director, City of Fremont; F. Robert Coop, City Manager, Fremont; Wesley McClure, City Manager, San Leandro; Thomas O. Knick, Mayor, San Leandro.
SEATED, ON THE LEFT, INSIDE ROW—Howard Sipe, Oakland Chamber of Commerce; W. A. Sparling, Secretary, Alameda County Highway Advisory Committee, General Manager, Oakland Chamber of Commerce; Wayne Thompson, City Manager, Oakland; C. Philip Nutzman General Manager, Alameda Chamber of Commerce; Stanley Whitney President, Alameda Chamber of Commerce; C. E. Bovey, State Engineer, City and Cooperative Projects; John A. Morin, Superintendent of Streets, City Engineer, Oakland.
SEATED, ON THE RIGHT, OUTSIDE ROW—H. B. LaForge, Engineer of Federal Secondary Roads; F. W. Panhorst, Assistant State Highway Engineer; Frank C. Balfour, Chief Right of Way Agent; R. H. Wilson, Assistant State Highway Engineer; John J. Amaral, Secretary, Pleasanton Chamber of Commerce; James W. Trimingham, Mayor, Pleasanton; Harry Bartell, Former Member and Chairman, Alameda County Board of Supervisors.
SEATED, ON THE RIGHT, INSIDE ROW—George Herron, Administrative Associate to Alameda County Surveyor; Jack Rees, Chairman, Highway Committee, Hayward Chamber of Commerce; Floyd Sparks, Hayward Daily Review; Edward Phillips, Director of Public Works, Hayward; Douglas Smith, City Manager, Hayward; Arthur C. Phillips, Mayor, Hayward.
In addition to those shown in the picture Carl Froerer, City Manager of Alameda, and Mrs. Irene Moresi, Member of the City Council of Alameda, attended the meeting.

MERIT AWARD BOARD WINNERS

Employees of the Department of Public Works receiving certificates of award and commendation during June and July, 1956, are:

Mrs. Eloise D. Carson, Sacramento, $100 and a certificate of award for suggestion recommending that in writing the specifications for highway contracts, the specification writers eliminate the longhand penciled copy of the proposal bid items as it duplicates the engineer's estimates. To be reviewed in one year.

Claude L. Horton, San Diego, certificate of commendation for suggestion recommending that a bucket-type auger for drilling postholes for installing signs.

William Chin, Highways, Bishop, $30 for suggestion for a method of calculation of earthwork quantities from contour maps.

Russell A. Flint, Highways, Oakland, for three suggestions: $25 for the modification and improvement of toll collection equipment key identification system; $150 for modifications and improvements of the toll collection equipment freight lanes recorder and ticket printing, charge or cash ticket and money separation; $25 for modification and improvement of toll collection equipment fare recorder button boxes.

Laurence E. Rundle, Highways, Santa Barbara, $15 for suggestion recommending the use of an electric drill in the lapping of blades on power lawn mowers, which reduces the expense of having such power lawn mowers sharpened.

Cherie Mae Carroll, Architecture, Sacramento, $10 for suggestion recommending a revision of the monthly report of contract performance and modification and of the cur-

rent reporting procedure in order to eliminate duplication of effort.

Phillip L. Brown, Architecture, Los Angeles, for suggestion recommending that the division include one set of white copies on architectural prints.

Milton C. Heaney and *James O. Darr,* Sacramento, $100 to be divided equally for suggestion recommending that a one-inch grid system and horizontal and vertical center lines be printed on the reverse side of standard drawing sheets used by the division.

Benjamin L. Potter, Arroyo Grande, $40 for suggestion recommending a simple checking device for pedestrian buttons and detector contact units; and $65 for suggestion in which he devised an economical method of reinstalling luminaire poles after they have been knocked down by traffic accidents. Reduces time to repair from three man-days to four hours.

Herbert M. McAllister, Carmichael, $100 for suggestion in which he developed a light gin pole with a block and tackle to be used for handling medium- and heavy-weight signs.

Charles G. Andert, San Diego, $10 for suggestion for a method of computing the hours that mercury vapor lamps have burned. This is a concise and compact table.

Pippo M. Scandurra, San Francisco, $150 for suggestion suggesting the use of "Contak" film on tracings, cloth or paper, in lieu of coloring each map individually.

Employees Receive Twenty-five-year Awards

Employees of the Division of Highways who became eligible for 25-year awards prior to May 31, and June 30, 1956, are:

Name	Total service Yrs.	Mos.	Days	Name	Total service Yrs.	Mos.	Days
District III				**District VII**			
Chidester, Arad B.	25	0	23	Greenwald, Herman V.	25	0	28
				Struble, Mildred	25	0	23
District IV							
Blair, Frank H.	25	0	26	**Central Office**			
Rasmussen, R. H.	25	0	18	Greule, Katherine	25	0	18
Webb, Wallace M.	25	0	11	McCarty, Henry C.	25	0	0
District V				**Shop 5**			
Parrish, Isaac R.	25	0	7	Larson, Philip A.	25	0	9

PARTS AND TIRES

More than 893,995 people are employed in motor vehicle parts and tire manufacture in the United States.

A man is getting along the road to wisdom when he begins to realize that his opinion is just an opinion. —*Supervision.*

Here's the Scope Of Gigantic New Highway Program

Here are some of the highlights of the economic impact of the new national highway program.

Expenditures this year are expected to reach 5.2 billion dollars, not including cost of rights-of-way. Within five years, the annual figure will reach 8 billion dollars.

Total expenditures over 13 years—possibly 100 billion dollars, including federal, state and local contributions.

Materials needed annually: cement, 113 million barrels, 68 percent above current requirements; concrete aggregates, nearly 663 million tons, an increase of about half; bituminous products, about 9.2 billion tons, a boost of 44 percent; steel, well over 3.6 million tons or 65 percent more than presently used; lumber, 680 million board feet, a 57 percent increase; timber piling, over 22 million linear feet, up 57 percent; concrete and clay pipe and tile up 50 percent and 63 percent respectively; oil products, an increase of 49 percent, explosives, up 52 percent.

Employment—By 1957, an increase of 130,000 persons employed full time in highway work will be needed beyond the 250,000 currently so employed. By 1960, another 160,000 men will be employed.

Equipment—Slightly less than 1 billion dollars worth of additional equipment will be needed to raise the present 5.2 billion dollars highway expenditure to 6 billion dollars. Another 1 billion dollars would be needed to reach an 8 billion dollars annual highway program. Further outlays in proportionate amounts will be required until the peak rate is reached, after which only replacement expenditures would be necessary—but these amounts alone would then total more than 1 billion dollars a year.—*Washington Report.*

DUCKS

California hunters bagged 3,289,000 ducks during the 1955 season. This bag was down 5.9 percent from 1954 largely because of the floods in the Sacramento Valley.

Completed construction, looking east toward San Gorgonio Avenue Overcrossing

BANNING FREEWAY

Continued from page 33 . . .

way Commission completed the job by paving sections at both ends of Ramsey Street. A concrete pavement 0.42 foot thick and 16 feet wide was laid down. This was later widened 4 feet, and in 1941, it was resurfaced. At the same time, another road was built to handle westbound traffic, and the transition from the dirt road to a divided highway had started.

Week-end Congestion

Because of the low-level passage through the mountains, all the traffic from both the east and west passing over Highways 60, 70, and 99 flowed through Banning on Ramsey Street. On week ends during the desert wild flower season and when special events occurred at Palm Springs, the traffic congestion on Ramsey Street became so great that it was necessary to route traffic on other city streets to relieve the bottleneck. Truck traffic had constantly increased until it totaled 21 percent of the daily vehicles in 1954.

With a view to relieving this congestion, plans were prepared to construct a four-lane divided freeway passing through Banning to the south of Ramsey Street between Livingston and Bryant Streets and paralleling the Southern Pacific Railroad right of way, its western terminus being between 22d and 23d Streets and the eastern terminus being about three-fourths of a mile outside the eastern city limits. The natural material found in this section varies from the sand, gravel, and boulders of the San Gorgonio debris cone at the east to an unconsolidated clay and silt in the western area. Total length of the freeway is 3.7 miles. The section between Stations 255+50 and 280+00 is depressed. The construction of five bridges was included in the plans, with on- and off-ramps at both ends and at Eighth Street and Hargrave Street.

Four Bridges

Four of the bridges, including the West Ramsey Street Overcrossing, Eighth Street Undercrossing, Hargrave

Undercrossing, and the East Ramsey Undercrossing, were built under a separate contract. Three of these bridges are of the box girder-type and one slab-type, with an average length of about 65 feet and vertical clearance of 15 feet. The contract for the construction of these bridges was awarded to J. A. Thompson & Son. Work started in the first part of November, 1954, and was completed January 14, 1956, at a cost of $262,383. J. A. Hoban was Resident Engineer for the State Bridge Department during the construction period.

Second Contract

The second contract, for the construction of the freeway and the San Gorgonio Street Overcrossing, was awarded to the Thompson Construction Company in the amount of $1,-103,171. Work under this contract was started the nineteenth of May, 1955, and completed in September of 1956. The four traveled lanes have a concrete surface eight inches thick, and each lane is 12 feet wide. The subgrade consists of four inches of ce-

46

ment-treated imported material laid on an imported base. Livingston and Bryant Streets were resurfaced and serve as frontage roads through the business district of Banning.

One of the major items of work was the clearing of the right of way. Ninety-four structures had to be removed or demolished. Thirty-eight of the structures were handled by separate right of way clearance contracts, and 56 were demolished by the freeway contractor in his clearing operations. These ranged in size from 80 to 25,000 square feet and were of frame, brick, concrete block, and corrugated iron construction and included huts, dwellings, motels, hotels, office buildings, warehouses, a laundry, and a large cannery building. Most of these buildings were in a substandard condition.

The major portion of the 298,000 cubic yards of roadway excavation was moved from the depressed section, with the balance being moved from contour gradings sections at the east and west interchange areas.

Borrow and Base Material

Imported borrow and base material in the amount of 338,000 tons were obtained from a pit site owned by the

City of Banning one mile south of the project. The material was removed from the pit in deep trenches in order that the city could use it for a garbage disposal site.

Numerous drainage structures were required, the largest being a 10- x 6-foot reinforced concrete box culvert 420 feet in length and requiring 3,100 cubic yards of structure excavation and backfill. One 6- x 3-foot box culvert was precast in five 10-foot sections and was placed under the existing traveled way at little inconvenience to traffic.

Considerable cold and windy weather was encountered during the placing of the 15,600 cubic yards of Class "B" concrete pavement. Due to the weather, the initial sawing of the 60-foot interval joints was delayed for as long as 24 hours. Very few cracks developed due to this delayed sawing.

Frontage roads, ramps, and the connections to the existing traveled way were paved with 26,000 tons of plant-mixed surfacing.

The right of way was fenced on each side of the freeway for the entire length of the project. Chain link fence 48 inches and 72 inches in height was placed on the portion within the city limits, and new property fence

was placed on the portion outside the city limits.

The south roadway was opened to eastbound traffic on May 21, 1956, and was followed by the opening of the north roadway on July 3, 1956. Motorists driving between the Los Angeles metropolitan area and Palm Springs and other desert resorts this winter should find traffic conditions greatly improved.

BUTTE COUNTY HAS BIG BUDGET

Current budget for road construction and maintenance in Butte County is $1,350,000.

On August 24, 1956, the county had completed under the F. A. S. program reconstruction of 5.8 miles of the Chico-Butte City Road at a cost of $205,000.

According to Marshall Jones, director of public works, the county proposes to initiate work this fall on reconstruction of about two miles of the Oroville-Quincy Road near Oroville, at an estimated cost of $225,000.

The new federal highway legislation will have virtually no effect on the county's operations, since it adds only $35,000, or about 2.5 percent to total county funds.

Before construction, looking east along Ramsey Street from Third Street, showing typical traffic conditions

By HERBERT A. ROONEY, Associate Chemical Testing Engineer, and
E. D. BOTTS, Senior Chemical Testing Engineer

In the May-June, 1955, and January-February, 1956, issues of this magazine the use of epoxy-thiokol adhesives for cementing traffic line center markers and raised traffic bars to highway surfaces was described. As a result of the encouraging results obtained with this adhesive from several experimental installations, the Materials and Research Laboratory initiated field and laboratory research projects to ascertain if this adhesive could be used for miscellaneous repairs on concrete bridges and highway surfaces. It was realized from cost considerations that the use of epoxy adhesives would be limited to repair projects and could hardly be considered as a primary construction material such as portland cement or asphaltic concrete.

In the laboratory several concrete beams 6 inches x 6 inches x 30 inches were broken in flexure using third point loading. After breaking, the two pieces of each beam were cemented together with an epoxy-thiokol adhesive and allowed to cure for seven days at temperatures not less than 70 degrees F. The cemented beams were again subjected to flexure, and the breaks occurred in sections of the beams other than the point at which the adhesive was applied. This dramatically illustrated that the adhesive bond was stronger than the concrete itself.

Success Achieved

In view of the success achieved in cementing old concrete surfaces together with the epoxy-thiokol adhesive, it was then decided to ascertain if this adhesive would effectively bond new concrete to old concrete. There has been no satisfactory commercial product of our knowledge which would do this without the bond between the new and old concrete being weak because of shrinkage. Each of several 6-inch x 6-inch x 30-inch concrete beams were broken in flexure. One end of each broken beam section

PHOTO 1

was coated with the adhesive and fresh concrete immediately cast against it. The reconstituted beams were approximately half old concrete and half new concrete made to the original dimensions. Some were cured in a saturated moist room and others in the open air under wet bats. In no case did there appear to be any shrinkage at the epoxy-thiokol bond between the old and new concrete sections of the reconstructed beams. The new concrete was a dry mix having a slump of 2 to 2½ inches. After curing from two to four weeks the beams were again subjected to flexure. All breaks occurred in the concrete, the adhesive joint between the old and new concrete sections remaining intact as shown in *Photograph No. 1.*

Tried on Yolo Causeway

The first field application of this adhesive in joining new to old concrete was tried on December 21, 1954, on the Yolo Causeway in Yolo County. There had been a number of failures of the concrete deck slab at the joints on the west portion of the bridge between the westerly abutment and bent 130. This portion of the bridge consists of a creosoted wooden pile trestle with timber stringers, reinforced concrete deck slab, and a one-inch asphaltic surfacing. It is believed failures of the concrete slab have occurred chiefly due to insufficient thickness of the slab to provide adequate coverage for the layers of reinforcing steel. A section of the concrete deck slab at the transverse joint left of bent 115, approximately 2 feet by 4 feet, was

PHOTO 2

removed. The adhesive was applied to the edges of the break in the slab immediately before fresh concrete was placed in the patch. The concrete was Class "A," hand mixed, containing about 1½ percent calcium chloride and using a high early strength cement. Weather conditions were adverse, with heavy fog and a temperature during the day of between 35 and 40 degrees F. On March 17, 1955, the asphalt surfacing over the patch was removed and the concrete patch examined. There was excellent bonding between the new and old con-

crete, and no signs of cracking or other failures were visible. *Photograph No. 2* illustrates this patch.

Similar satisfactory results were obtained in May, 1955, in cementing old concrete to old concrete and new concrete to old concrete in repairing the haunches, bents, and caps on the Marina Viaduct in San Francisco.

On US 99E

In May, 1955, the department was requested by District III to repair a section of abraded concrete highway surface on US 99E, eastbound lane

in Sacramento County, where severe raveling of the concrete surface had occurred over a distance of approximately 200 feet. The potholes or cavities ranged from a half inch to several inches in diameter and from one-quarter to about two inches deep. Most of these cavities occurred along a strip about one foot wide and parallel to the longitudinal joint of the concrete pavement. The cavities were cleaned free of oil and dirt by sandblasting. About six gallons of an epoxy-thiokol and sand mortar tinted to the color of the concrete surface was used. The mortar was poured into the cavities from a mixing pot and troweled to the level of the highway surface. Operations were started at 11 a.m. and completed by 12.45 p.m. The mortar had set sufficiently by 3.30 p.m. to bear traffic. The compressive strength of the mortar was about 9,000 pounds per square inch. the epoxy-thiokol adhesive mortar had excellent adhesion to the concrete even when applied in thin layers. At this date, July, 1956, all repaired spots are in excellent condition. This is a typical case where neither asphaltic concrete nor portland cement concrete could be successfully adapted to this type of repair work. *Photograph No. 3* illustrates this project.

Grouting of Steel Bolts

Laboratory tests performed in September, 1953, showed that the epoxy resin adhesive had excellent properties for the grouting of steel bolts in concrete. Five-eighths-inch diameter bolts were grouted into concrete monuments in two-inch diameter holes, eight inches deep. After proper curing of the adhesive, attempts were made to pull out the bolts by the application of a tension load. In all cases the bolts broke in tension at 14,000-pound load, the grout remaining intact.

While this material as used in the experiments noted above has been exceptionally successful, it should be emphasized that it is not a "cure-all" and must be handled with due consideration for its peculiarities. The adhesives used in the above projects were formulated in the laboratory to meet the conditions of the jobs concerned. Types of curing agents and

PHOTO 3

Road Commissioner, Southern Rhodesia, Studies Our Highways

J. H. Durr, Commissioner of Roads and Road Traffic of Southern Rhodesia, was the guest at the regular monthly meeting of the California Highway Commission in August.

J. H. DURR

Under the auspices of the United States Government, through the U. S. Bureau of Public Roads, Mr. Durr is in this country studying highway planning as related to the problems of Southern Rhodesia. Renewing acquaintance with American highway officials and highway practices made on a similar visit 17 years ago, Durr has been in the United States for the past two months, with particular attention to planning at the national level in Washington, D. C., and in the States of Louisiana, Texas, and Oklahoma. Durr has been especially interested in the basic concepts of access-controlled highway planning (freeways) in which California has had more experience and has made more progress than any other state.

Mr. Durr said: "I am very concerned that our highway planning in Southern Rhodesia, with present traffic problems far less critical than yours, proceed on a sound, long-range basis."

GOOD ROADS FOR MEXICO

MEXICO CITY—During the seventh annual assembly of the Mexican Roads Assn. it was revealed that in 1956, Mexico will spend 762 million pesos on highway development. That is about 63 million dollars in U. S. money and a sizable expenditure for Mexico.

A bright pupil looked thoughtfully at an examination question, which read: "State the number of tons of coal shipped out of the U. S. in any given year." Then his brow cleared and he wrote: "1492, none."

fillers were used in each formulation which were best suited to the project. The curing agents for the adhesive must be thoroughly mixed into the mixture immediately prior to use, and it is imperative that the surface to which the adhesive is applied be thoroughly cleaned of oil and dirt by wire brushing or sandblasting. When properly formulated and applied, this adhesive should find extensive adaptations to highway projects. It is equally and emphatically true that unless the adhesive is prepared, handled, and applied properly the results can be very unsatisfactory and expensive.

A total of 572,043 automobiles, trucks, and busses entered California during August of this year, according to the National Automobile Club. This figure represented an increase of 72,443 over the number of vehicles entering California in August, 1955.

ROPES TO CATCH SPEEDERS

Today they use radar to catch the speeders. In 1905, according to the National Automobile Club, they used ropes.

At that time, Delaware traffic police would disguise themselves as workmen, post themselves along the highway, and then swing heavy ropes across the highway to stop any motorist who was exceeding the speed limit of eight miles per hour.

HIGHWAY SIGNPOSTING

An early Oregon road sign project was the "Rainbow Highway," now called The Dalles-California Highway (US 97). According to the National Automobile Club, the road was designated by bands of colors, on fence posts, telephone poles, junipers and pines, marking the route from the Columbia River to Southern Oregon.

Change can be very disturbing—
particularly if it affects a roadside
business you have established, maintained and operated in the same location for many, many years. If the
change is due to a highway improvement project, the many problems involved with rearranging your business enterprise during the construction period can appear particularly
disheartening.

But at least one roadside merchant,
whose livelihood depends to a large
extent on automobile traffic past his
door, is attempting to capitalize on
just such a necessary readjustment.

He is Terry Curtola, owner of
Terry's Waffle Shop, located at the
intersection of U. S. Highway 40 and
Magazine Street in Vallejo, slightly
north of the Carquinez Bridge. Look
what's happening to Terry's!

Magazine Street Overcrossing

At this point US 40, a major interstate route, is the northern approach
to the Carquinez Bridge. Highway
traffic is presently delayed by traffic-
actuated signals made necessary by
the large volume of cross traffic at
Magazine Street and by many left
turn movements. These conflicting
movements are the principal cause of
a high accident frequency, which construction of an overcrossing and interchange at Magazine Street is designed
to eliminate.

Conversion of this section of US 40
to full freeway will eliminate the present direct highway entrance into the
well-established restaurant, since construction will necessitate taking in excess of 4,000 square feet of land across
the front.

Highway requirements will eliminate the private parking area adjacent
to the main entrance and will also take
a portion of the building. The loss of
777 square feet of selling space on the
main floor, plus a similar reduction of
storage area in the basement, will require considerable remodeling and rearrangement of the business operations within the remainder of the
building.

*Unobstructed view of Terrys as seen from frontage road beneath Magazine Street Overpass.
Off ramp for southbound traffic left of piers.*

The very thought of all the work
necessary to accomplish the realignment of the highway and the consequent reorganization of the business
might be enough to make any merchant pessimistic about the future.
But not Curtola. He has chosen to
"accentuate the positive."

Sidewalk Superintendents

Cognizant of the average American's abiding interest in "sidewalk su-
perintending," Curtola is making a
studied effort to turn this factor to
his own advantage. Customers at
Terry's are given a special invitation
to watch the changes that will take
place around the restaurant during
the construction period. They are enrolled in "Terry's Waffle Shop Chapter of the Sidewalk Superintendents
Society," are given an official membership card, and are told that they
will be mailed a map for their use
after completion of the new highway
facility.

The fact that many another business throughout the State has been relocated, and is now flourishing, due to
a frontage road is not unique in California freeway history. But Curtola's

optimistic attitude about the future,
exemplified by his enthusiasm to use
a major change as a means of advertising promotion, is refreshingly new
to everyone associated with highway
construction.

Curiosity Pays Off

Curtola has reasoned that public reaction to this unique form of business
advertising should be highly favorable. It has already created considerable
interest among his patrons who now
make it a point to return to Terry's
to note the progress of the work.
There are many roadside businesses
affected by the highway construction,
but Curtola has managed to focus the
attention of a large segment of the
motoring public on his particular enterprise.

Curtola believes that curiosity will
continue to pay off for him because
he feels it will induce many return
visits to his restaurant. And when the
freeway is completed, he expects to
reap dividends from his novel merchandising plan when customers return to "test" their maps, as well as
their recollection of the "old" Terry's
against the new.

Out of the Mail Bag

LETTER FROM PAKISTAN

c/o CENTRAL FISHERIES DEPT.

KARACHI 3, PAKISTAN

DEAR MR. ADAMS: I had the pleasure of visiting U. S. A. where I stayed for one year and received training in Fisheries Sciences at the School of Fisheries, University of Washington, Seattle. During my training period I had an opportunity of observing the fisheries establishments and processing plants throughout the coast line.

In San Diego I met Mr. R. A. Scot, Supervisor in Charge, Public Health (Fish Cannery) at No. 7 B Street, Pier Building. Mr. Scot was a very kind, sympathetic and very considerate man and went a long way to help me in my line. I cannot forget his kindness and am unable to repay him in any way. It was in his office that I came across a copy of the *California Highways and Public Works* which I borrowed to read. While going through the contents I found that this magazine carried a great deal of valuable, very useful, and very informative material.

I requested Mr. Scot to put me on your mailing list. Since then I have continuously received this useful publication.

Although by profession I am attached to fisheries science, yet I find your magazine to be a great value and an excellent source of material of great interest. After going through the pages I very often wish that I was an engineer by profession.

I would like to thank you for continuing to send me *California Highways and Public Works*, and wish you all achievements and success hereafter.

Very truly yours,

S. A. JALEEL

Assistant Director

(Socio-Economics)

YOU SHOULD KNOW

RAND McNALLY & COMPANY

Printers-Publishers

SAN FRANCISCO

MR. KENNETH C. ADAMS, *Editor*

DEAR MR. ADAMS: We at Rand McNally look forward to each issue of *California Highways and Public Works* with good reason.

First, we are able to keep posted on the multitude of changes and improvements to our California highway system. I venture to say that almost all important changes to our California road and street maps were first brought to our attention through studying your magazine.

Secondly, we find the many technical and historical articles very informative and interesting to read.

Thank you for the many years of wonderful issues we have already received.

Sincerely,

RAND McNALLY & COMPANY

JOHN F. STEWART

MAGAZINE GIVES PLEASURE

SURREY HILLS, E. 10

VICTORIA, AUSTRALIA

The Editor

DEAR MR. ADAMS: *California Highways and Public Works* still brings us much pleasure and knowledge. For many years we have watched it grow with your highways. My copy has a wide circulation and has made many friends for California.

We were very sorry for all who suffered in your floods. Here too, floods cause havoc, and we will watch your counter measures with great interest. Progress in California gives us courage for our own problems.

Thanking you for the privilege of receiving your magazine,

I am,

ARTHUR O. GYLES

APPRECIATIVE READER

GLENDALE

MR. K. C. ADAMS, *Editor*

DEAR SIR: I again want to thank you for your fine publication and want to take this opportunity to inform you that I look forward to its coming and would not want to miss a single copy of your magazine.

The illustrations in your magazine helps me to know what is going on and gives me a clearer and better understanding of the road and freeway progress the State is making from month to month.

Very truly yours,

GROVER KIHORNY

POPULAR READING

VERNER G. RICH, D.D.S.

Fullerton

Editor

California Highways and Public Works is one of the most popular items in my reception room. This surprised me, considering that I take several popular type magazines for my patients' enjoyment.

Yours truly,

V. RICH

WE WILL TRY

CARMEL

MR. KENNETH C. ADAMS, *Editor*

DEAR MR. ADAMS: Congratulations on the May-June issue. It is the best one yet. While I cannot believe you can do better, I hope you will.

Every issue has so much to offer the interested citizen.

Congratulations.

Sincerely yours,

WESLEY W. KERGAN

HIGHLY COMPLIMENTARY

DENVER, COLORADO

California Highways and Public Works

DEAR MR. ADAMS: Once again I have the opportunity to thank you, and the State of California, for a very wonderful magazine, which I have now enjoyed reading for many years.

To many of us residing outside the State of California, the entire State is a kind of Wonderland, but to those of us in the highway engineering field, California is even more of a wonderland because of its tremendous strides in its design and construction of highways. So many years ahead, in design and construction, of any other area in this country and abroad, the work of your Highway Department serves well as a text book for the younger engineers rising in the profession. California can well be proud of its highway and public works engineers.

I would like to take this opportunity to express further my admiration for the work you are doing with *California Highways and Public Works*. This is in relation to its internal effects on your departments. All too frequently, the engineers in any public group, especially in state highway departments, are deeply submerged and their names and faces, no matter how worthy, are seldom brought to the public's attention. In your magazine, it is my opinion, that you are doing an invaluable service to these men (and women) by giving them the rewards of public recognition through their contributed articles on the work they have accomplished. I note, too, that you do not confine your contributors only to the state forces, but that you accept articles from your city engineers, and others. This is a splendid idea. As a morale builder within the various forces in your own State, and discounting entirely any effects which may come from outside your borders, your magazine should be of inestimable value. While we all, ostensibly, work for money, there is no compensation quite so great as that of public recognition and inferred appreciation of work done, whether he be the highest, or

COOPERATION

THE PACIFIC TELEPHONE AND TELEGRAPH CO.
Santa Ana, California

EDWARD T. TELFORD
Assistant State Highway Engineer
Los Angeles

DEAR SIR: I think you will be interested to know that we telephone people do appreciate your help when emergencies occur on our highways. The following is a copy of note I received from one of my people who felt that the help of your people should not go unnoticed:

SANTA ANA, June 22, 1956

K. K. *Bathgate, District Construction Superintendent, Santa Ana:*

On behalf of the Pacific Telephone and Telegraph Company I would like to personally thank the California State Highway Maintenance Division, Brea, for the service rendered by their flagmen at the scene of an accident, which occurred about two-thirds of a mile north of Central Avenue on Brea Canyon Road at a double curve with restricted vision. Telephone and electric power service was interrupted by a truck that knocked over a 60-foot pole.

One of the contributing factors in enabling our maintenance crews to safely and quickly restore service was the excellent cooperation of the California highway maintenance flagmen. The location of the accident possessed unusual accident possibilities. To reduce the possibilities of any further accident, protective barricades and equipment as well as flagmen were provided. These precautions regarding safety were essential to the performance of a safe job.

We greatly appreciate the service rendered; it places emphasis on the importance of the jobs we do and the urgency of the services we render, and in the same breath it admonishes us that despite our haste and urgency, we take the time to make sure that we perform our work safely.

R. K. LETHIN
Supervising Construction Foreman

Let me add my personal thanks also. It is certainly gratifying to know that our people are working together as a team in serving the public.

Yours truly,

K. K. BATHGATE
District Construction Superintendent

the lowest, in any organization. Your magazine fills well this need.

Again thank you.

Yours very truly,
JAMES R. BENSON
Consulting Bituminous Engineer

LETTER IS APPRECIATED

DICKINSON & SON, REALTORS—INSURANCE
Los Angeles 57

MR. E. F. WAGNER
Assistant Chief Right of Way
Agent
Division of Highways, District VII
120 South Spring Street
Los Angeles 12, California

DEAR MR. WAGNER: I have just concluded the last of a series of transactions with the Division of Highways involving the acquisition by the State of some 9 or 10 separate pieces of property for the Long Beach Freeway right of way. Some of the negotiations were handled by Richard G. Rayburn and others by Jack M. Miller of your department and extended over the past two years.

I wish to take this opportunity to inform you of the friendly, courteous, patient yet efficient manner with which both of these gentlemen handled these transactions. I had many meetings with them, inasmuch as some of the properties were quite involved, and although in most instances I felt that I was not being paid a sufficient amount for the property, they were able to persuade me to accept their offer.

The Division of Highways is to be commended for having men of such high calibre in its employ.

With best personal regards, I remain

Very truly yours,

WILLIAM G. DICKINSON

YOURS FOR THE ASKING

State of Louisiana
DEPARTMENT OF HIGHWAYS
Baton Rouge 4, Louisiana

MR. KENNETH C. ADAMS, *Editor*

DEAR MR. ADAMS: I wish to thank you for copy of your May-June, 1956, issue of *California Highways and Public Works* which we recently requested. This publication certainly has a lot of very interesting as well as informative data. We are most grateful to you for this issue.

Yours very truly,

H. L. LEHMANN
Testing and Research Engineer

In Memoriam

GEORGE M. LEATHERWOOD

The sudden death of George M. Leatherwood, Senior Highway Engineer in charge of the Advance Planning Department, District I, on July 30, 1956, came as a severe shock to his many friends and associates.

George was born in Prescott, Arizona, August 9, 1904, and started his engineering career in 1922 with the Los Angeles County Road Department, serving with that organization until 1936.

In 1936 he started his career with the Division of Highways, State of California, as Resident Engineer on highway projects in District III in Marysville. From 1937 to 1942 George worked with the Location Department of District VII in Los Angeles, leaving there to serve as Civilian Assistant to the Chief Engineer, U. S. Corps of Engineers, U. S. Army, in Nicaragua, San Salvador, and Guatemala.

In 1943 he returned to District VII as Chief of Surveys, in which position he served until 1950 when he transferred to District V at San Luis Obispo where he served as Assistant Design Engineer.

In 1951 George moved to Eureka to become Locating Engineer for District I. He was later assigned to the position of Advance Planning Engineer where he was doing an exceptional job. Probably his major accomplishment was the outstanding work done in connection with the location of the proposed full freeway through the Southern Humboldt County Redwood Groves. The ideas which he developed in planning the location through the redwoods resolved a controversy of long standing, and this freeway, when built, will stand as a monument to George's engineering ability.

George was vitally interested in flying, having built and flown sailplanes in the early 1930's. He received his private pilot's license in 1933, which he kept valid until he left for Central America in 1943. He was a staunch believer in the use of aerial surveys and, ironically, the use of a helicopter for aerial reconnaissance of the primitive areas of northwestern California led to his untimely passing.

The helicopter in which George was a passenger crashed on US Highway 299 near the North Fork of the Mad River after the rotor blades were sheared off after striking a tree.

Mr. Leatherwood was a member of the American Association of Professional Engineers and of the American Congress of Surveying and Mapping.

He is survived by his wife, Sara, and a sister, Mrs. Lucille McNeely, of Glendale, to whom his many friends in the state service extend sincere sympathy.

In Memoriam

DENNIS J. KELLEHER

Dennis J. Kelleher, 48, an employee of the San Francisco-Oakland Bay Bridge, died May 18, 1956, in San Francisco. He served as a toll sergeant and, in earlier years, as a toll collector. He entered state service on November 2, 1936.

Denny was born in San Francisco and was a lifelong resident of that city. He was one of the initial employees of the San Francisco-Oakland Bay Bridge and was a member of the staff on the opening day of the bridge to traffic, November 12, 1936.

Denny possessed the ability to make friends and will be remembered for his pleasant manner, his never-failing kindness, and his willingness to be of assistance to all with whom he was associated. He is survived by his wife, Mabel, a son, Donald, and a daughter, Joan, to whom sincere sympathy is extended.

2. (Sign Route 21) From San Mateo County Boundary to junction with State Route 108. Route studies, with particular reference to Newark area.

State Route 108

1. (Sign Route 21) From State Route 5 near Mission San Jose to junction with State Route 107 near Sunol. Expedite surveys and design to take early advantage of federal highway funds as a part of the Interstate Highway System.

2. (Sign Route 21) From State Route 107 near Sunol to State Route 5 east of Livermore. Route determination and protection of rights of way with particular reference to Livermore.

State Route 206—In Berkeley

(Sign Route 24) Route studies.

State Route 233

1. Vicinity of High Street. Route studies, surveys and plans and protection of rights of way between Route 69 and Route 5.

2. Park Boulevard Extension. Surveys and plans and acquisition of rights of way from Route 227 to the Alameda County-Contra Costa County boundary line.

State Route 226 and 75—In Oakland, Alameda and San Leandro

Initiate programmed purchases of rights of way preparatory to early construction.

ALAMEDA PROJECTS

Continued from page 44 . . .

Group B: Projects Upon Which Expenditures Should Be Made for Planning, Surveys, Designs, Acquisitions and Protection of Rights of Way During the Fiscal Year 1957-1958

State Route 105—In Oakland, San Leandro, and Hayward

Surveys and plans for correction of spot deficiencies from State Route 233 southeasterly involving consideration of the rerouting of part of this route to make use of San Leandro Street and San Leandro Boulevard, and extend San Leandro Boulevard to connect with existing State Route 105 in the vicinity of 136th Avenue.

(Legislation for rerouting will be presented to the 1957 Session of the Legislature.)

State Route 5—MacArthur Boulevard and Foothill Boulevard

1. (US 50) Route studies, surveys and protection of rights of way for MacArthur Boulevard through Oakland and San Leandro on portion not budgeted for planned acquisition and construction.

2. (US 50) Expedite route studies, surveys, and protection of way southerly from San Leandro to connection with Route 228, and correct spot deficiencies.

3. (Sign Route 9) Expedite route studies, surveys and plans for Route 5-C from Decoto to vicinity of Warm Springs and correct spot deficiencies.

State Route 107 .

1. (Sign Route 21) From State Route 108 near Sunol to Contra Costa County boundary. Route studies to take early advantage of federal contributions if this route is adopted into the Interstate Highway System.

US 99

Only Few Bottlenecks Remain
Between Sacramento and Los Angeles

Sᴛᴀʀᴛ ᴏꜰ construction of seven miles of freeway on U. S. Highway 99 in the vicinity of Galt, south of Sacramento, signals the end of another of the few remaining bottlenecks on this highway between the Capital City and Los Angeles. The work is being done under a $2,784,349 contract awarded to A. Teichert & Son, Inc., of Sacramento.

This project is to be built as a full freeway, with no crossings at grade and no left turns. It is between 0.7 mile south of Galt and 1.6 miles south of the Cosumnes River. A total of $3,600,000 has been budgeted for its construction. It will provide four lanes, with provision for an ultimate six.

The contract calls for grading and paving for the northbound lane of the freeway and widening and surfacing the existing highway for the southbound traffic lanes. There will be 12 structures to provide four overcrossings, an underpass, a separation at the intersection of State Sign Route 104 and six bridges over various creeks and sloughs.

Four Overcrossings

The overcrossings are at C Street in Galt, Simmerhorn Road, Amador Avenue and Arno Road. Railroad tracks will be carried over the freeway at the Galt Underpass. About 8¼ miles of frontage roads will parallel the freeway, connecting to local roads and giving access to adjoining land and roadside business.

Two-lane traffic will be maintained on US 99 at all times during construction.

Another in the series of improvements which will make US 99 one of the most modern highways in the State was recently completed. This was the 3½-mile freeway between Jahant Road, north of Lodi, and a half mile north of the San Joaquin county line, at a construction cost of approximately $1,052,000.

U. S. Highway 99 has been or is being developed as a four-lane freeway throughout San Joaquin County with the exception of a short section through Lodi. The Stockton Bypass and an adjoining section between Stockton and Lodi, constructed several years ago, are expressways, with some crossings still at grade.

Full Freeway Completed

Full freeway construction has been completed from north of Ripon to Lathrop Road (Manteca Bypass), and from Turner Station to Kingsley Road, north of Manteca. Other full freeway sections now under construction will close three gaps in the four-laning of US 99 through San Joaquin County to the Sacramento county line. These three sections total 10.2 miles in length and will cost approximately $4,940,000 to construct.

The construction is from Lathrop Road north of Manteca to north of Turner Station; from Kingsley Road to Mariposa Road; and from just north of Jahant Road. A freeway routing has been adopted in the Lodi area, east of the present four-lane undivided highway, but construction funds have not yet been budgeted.

In Sacramento County, in addition to the section in the vicinity of Galt, 5.3 miles of US 50-99 between a half mile south of Elk Grove Road and 1.8 miles south of Florin Road is being converted from two lanes to a four-lane full freeway at a construction cost of approximately $1,629,000. This section is expected to be completed this fall.

320 Miles of Multilane Highway

The only section between Lodi and Sacramento which has not been widened to four lanes or which is not now under construction is between 1.8 miles south of the Cosumnes River to just south of Elk Grove Road, and $2,250,000 has been budgeted for that. This 5.9-mile section is sched-

uled to be under construction early next year.

To the south, almost all of the 320 miles of US 99 between Stockton and the San Fernando area of Los Angeles County have been completed or are under construction as multilane divided highway. The longest continuous section of divided multilane highway (except for two short undivided sections at railroad separations) is the 160-mile stretch from just north of the Visalia Airport Interchange in Tulare County to three miles south of Tunnel Station northwest of San Fernando.

Construction has started on the 4.5-mile Atwater Freeway in Merced County under a $2,528,993 contract.

The Fresno Freeway is still under construction, with one short section north of the city now in use and two contracts under way for the balance of the freeway.

A 14-mile freeway section in Tulare County from a half mile north of Pixley south on US 99 to the Kern county line has just been completed. The remaining seven miles of US 99 in Tulare County have now been put under construction as freeway. A four-lane freeway through the City of Delano, north of Bakersfield, was recently completed.

Association Has Pen Used by President to Sign Federal Aid Act

Through the courtesy of Sherman Adams, the assistant to the President, the pen used by President Eisenhower in signing the Federal Aid Act of 1956 was presented to A. E. Johnson, executive secretary of the American Association of State Highway Officials. The pen, properly framed, will be displayed at the general offices of the association.

By A. C. DILDINE, Senior Equipment Engineer

Design and preparation of specifications and the procurement of certain types of equipment are closely allied with the operational requirements of the various districts and departments of the State of California's Division of Highways. The Equipment Department of the Division of Highways works closely with all other departments in procuring the special types of equipment required to assist them in their work.

One of the problems encountered which requires a specialized item of equipment is a means for servicing overhead lights and signs used on the highways when built-in service facilities are not available on the lights or signs. To accomplish this work, it is necessary to place men and material within working distance of the signs. One method of accomplishing this is by using a hydraulically-operated tower platform mounted on a suitable truck that can carry the crew and all

supplies and materials they may want to the sign. Such units are in operation for this work.

Design of Tower Lift

The tower lifts used by the Division of Highways are mounted on four-ton trucks with the hydraulic rams fastened directly to the truck frame directly behind the cab. The bed of the truck is equipped with a special body to carry supplies, tools and materials for the crew.

The elevation of the tower is obtained hydraulically from a pump that is operated from a power takeoff on the chassis transmission.

Control of the tower is provided on the working platform with another set of controls mounted directly behind the cab of the truck. The tower may thus be controlled from either position. The platform may be revolved through a full 360-degree revolution by the operator, on the tower.

A telescoping ladder is provided to allow access to the platform at any height. Guard rails and toe boards are also provided for the safety of the workmen. It is impossible to over-extend the tower as the hydraulic rams are equipped with overflow holes to bypass the hydraulic fluid with no stress on the hydraulic system when maximum extension is reached. The tower may reach a platform height of 30 feet to allow a working height of 35 feet.

Mounted on Hydraulic Rams

The platform is mounted on the hydraulic rams through special heavy duty insulators that provide complete electrical insulation in any type of weather. The crews are thus protected from accidental electrical shock.

The Equipment Department has designed, built and installed special hydraulically operated outriggers to level the unit and provide maximum stabil-

Tower lift truck, showing the position of the hydraulic leveling arms. An arm is located on each side of the truck.

ity when the tower is used on super-elevated sections of the road surface. These outrigger type leveling devices make it possible to use the tower in any location and thus give the operating departments an even more versatile tool.

Maintenance work accomplished by the use of the towers must necessarily be done at times when traffic flow is the least. For that reason, the majority of the work is accomplished in the midmorning and midafternoon.

NEW SPAN

Continued from page 17 . . .

East, and has been designed to allow for possible future widening of that local facility. This county road will serve as the main approach to the bridge from southern Marin County. It traverses westerly of San Quentin Prison and connects with US 101 at the Greenbrae Interchange. It is a substandard two-lane road and will need improvement to modern standards to adequately care for the traffic desiring to use it as a connection to the bridge. Being a county facility, however, it is not eligible for financing from state highway funds.

Future Construction

The project also includes grading for a future four-lane freeway byond

With the use of equipment such as the hydraulic towers the American construction equipment industry is making notable contributions to the economical maintenance of highways. Modern highways which are such a vital part of our way of life, for transportation, communication, defense and recreation are always improving and a large part of this improvement is due to the development of modern tools such as the tower lift.

the initial project to the junction with US 101. This grading is in progress along both sides of the existing highway as far west as Simms Street on the south and Tiburon Street on the north. It is being done to make use of excess fill material resulting from the going freeway work and will also allow time for the material to settle before base and surfacing is applied in a future project. Plans for this continuation of the freeway are now nearly complete and when funds are available, the portion presently being graded will be converted to a full freeway, complete with frontage roads. A full traffic interchange will be located between Simms Street and Verdi Street.

The total freeway connection from the toll crossing approach to US 101

will approximate $3,000,000 in cost for construction and right of way.

The Division of Highways work is under the direction of Assistant State Highway Engineer B. W. Booker, who is in charge of the Bay area District IV activities with offices at 150 Oak Street in San Francisco.

Richmond-San Rafael Bridge Measurements

Total length (5½ miles)	29,045 ft.
Main structure length (4.04 miles)	21,343 ft.
Center to center of trusses	42 ft.
Width of roadway between curbs	36 ft.
Length of main span	1,070 ft.
Maximum height of towers above water	325 ft.
Maximum depth of piers below water	222 ft.
Vertical clearance above main channel	185 ft.
Vertical clearance above secondary channel	135 ft.
Horizontal clearance at navigation channels	1,000 ft.

Quantities of Materials

Structural steel	53,700 tons
Reinforcing steel	8,500 tons
Standard concrete	110,100 cu. yds.
Lightweight concrete	40,200 cu. yds.
Concrete piling	53,000 ft.
Timber piling	268,200 ft.
Steel piling	572,700 ft.
Electrical cable	318,300 ft.
Pipe (2½-inch)	55,800 ft.
Paint	65,000 gals.

Construction Fund	$50,000,000
Construction Reserve Fund	2,000,000
Interest during construction	10,000,000
Series A bonds	$62,000,000
Completion lower deck	6,000,000
Loan—School Land Fund	$68,000,000

LIKES OUR HIGHWAYS
ARCADIA, CALIFORNIA

Editor: We wish to commend you for the fine highways we saw; built, building and read about as planned in *California Highways and Public Works.* This summer we have traveled 2,400 miles from Southern California to the State of Oregon along Highway US 101. The work that has been done in two years is staggering. What lies ahead takes your breath away. The recent article on the planned freeway in the redwoods makes one glad they live in this great State of ours.

For us let it be said, we are glad to pay for what we are receiving in highways. No other state can match us. Keep up the good work and more power to you in these days of rough economic going.

Sincerely yours,
JAMES COGSWELL

and Public Works

CORRELATION OF GEOMETRIC DESIGN AND DIRECTIONAL SIGNING

EDITOR'S NOTE: The text of a paper on "Correlation of Geometric Design and Directional Signing" by George M. Webb, Traffic Engineer, California Division of Highways, is too long and too profusely illustrated to be reproduced in its entirety in *California Highways and Public Works.* The complete study has been made available in printed form, however, and copies may be obtained by writing to George M. Webb, Traffic Engineer, Division of Highways, P. O. Box 1499, Sacramento, California.

The problem of providing adequate directional information is a factor in highway planning which must be taken under consideration long before the highway reaches the construction stage. This is particularly important in the case of modern freeways, with their often complex interchanges in urban areas.

Among the points made in this study are:

The critical element with regard to signing is the stranger, even though he is but a small portion of the total traffic. If directional signing is adequate for the stranger, it will also be adequate for the local motorist.

Simplicity Watchword

Simplicity should be the watchword for those who design the highways. The highway engineer has come to the realization that, in addition to the advantages from a signing standpoint, a simpler and more practical interchange pays off in greater traffic interchange service and in reduced road-user operating costs.

The final and crucial test of an otherwise satisfactory design lies in the signing. If a traffic interchange layout does not lend itself to proper signing, it is not a good design.

The first step in developing a working relationship between the people who are doing the designing and the traffic people who are responsible for the signing is to bring about an understanding of common problems.

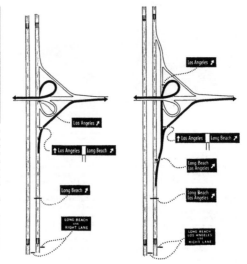

Diagram illustrates comparative signing problems for a four-quadrant cloverleaf with and without collector road. Note that in the figure at the left (without collector road) the name of the second off-ramp appears only once in advance of the turnoff. With collector road (figure at right) there are four advance notifications of the second turnoff, two preceding the collector road.

The signing problems of any project must be brought to the attention of the geometric designer when the project is in its earliest design stages. At that time consideration should be given the following items:

Factors to Consider

(1) Need for providing continuity of sign routes and freeways.

(2) Allowance for all 12 traffic movements, if at all possible, at interchanges where two sign routes intersect. A reasonable amount of circuity of travel is permissible for the minor movements if these movements can be properly signed so that

traffic flow from one route to the other is possible.

(3) The avoidance of "pulled-apart" interchanges because of the difficulty they create in directing traffic back on to the freeway. Simple and compact interchanges, even when the first cost is a little more, are preferable.

(4) Provision for adequate distance between ramps. This consists of 1,000-foot minimum between exits on the freeway and 600-foot minimum between a freeway exit gore and a collector road gore.

(5) Provision for adequate visibility for exit ramps and their signs.

58

(6) Allowance for adequate gore width on rural freeways where reflectorized signs are to be used.

(7) Avoidance of ramps for local traffic movements, within the interchange area when two freeways intersect, because of complicated design and signing.

(8) Provision for collector road, if feasible, when cloverleaf-type of interchange is used. (See accompanying chart.)

Sign Route Greatest Aid

Place names, sign routes, and street and freeway names are the principal means of directing traffic. Of these, the greatest aid to the really long-distance traveler is the sign route.

Experience has shown that today's vehicular speeds preclude the use of more than three names on a sign. As a matter of fact, on a freeway it is very desirable to limit this to one name and in no case more than two. The U. S. or State Route shield becomes the long distance traveler's handiest friend because it is readily recognizable even at high speeds. For example: when two freeways cross, the signing gets involved; "Junction US ₉₉" is a lot simpler to see and comprehend than "Junction San Bernardino Freeway."

Advance indication of turnoff points and repetition of that message so as to give the motorist ample warning are other important considerations in highway signing. This is extremely important on metropolitan freeways because of the large volumes and high speeds of traffic. Under these conditions, the motorist needs to know of an impending turnoff, particularly a branch connection, about one mile in advance so that he can move over to the proper lane preparatory to the actual turnoff.

The paper points out that simple and effective directional signing, after all, is merely a reflection of good planning and design because the signing, in the final analysis, is an integral part of the highway.

CONVERTIBLE HARDTOPS

Convertible hardtops may soon be available to car buyers, according to the National Automobile Club. At least two manufacturers are working with models that have retractable steel tops.

and Public Works

STATE HIGHWAY ENGINEER ANSWERS A LETTER

Mr. James B. Dofflemeyer
471 Mischele Drive
San Pablo 12, California

Dear Mr. Dofflemeyer: The copy of your letter of August 5, 1956, to Assemblyman Donald D. Doyle which you forwarded to this office contained a number of comments on California's state highways in comparison to those of other Western states—generally to the effect that other states have accomplished far more than California with less money.

You are correct in your statement that the California Highway Commission, and not the Congress of the United States, has direct jurisdiction over the expenditure of funds for state highway improvement in California. With reference to the two routes of which you are specifically critical, US 99 north of Shasta Lake and US 40 west of the Nevada state line, conversion of both routes to modern four-lane freeways is currently being pushed as rapidly as available funds permit, and in fact more rapidly than ever before in history. The current state highway budget as adopted by the Highway Commission contains items totalling nearly $11,000,000 for four-lane freeway construction on 18 miles of US 40 in the Colfax area and near the state line; while a number of freeway projects are now under construction on US 99 in the Sacramento River Canyon comparable to the already completed sections between Redding and Shasta Lake and the section just north of Dunsmuir.

Different Reactions

We receive quite a number of letters from Californians who have returned, like yourself, from motor trips through other states. Some of these letters are critical of some specific feature of our highways, but the great majority compare our highways favorably with those they have seen elsewhere. Individual experiences and conditions encountered on a trip will of course vary, which may account in part for the different reactions expressed by those who write.

Your suggestion that the members of the Highway Commission travel the highways of other states to learn how they are designed and constructed is one which has long ago been adopted in practice. Members of the commission, and of our engineering staff, do in fact make it a practice to observe highways from the planning and construction viewpoint whenever they travel outside the state. In addition, we keep abreast of developments elsewhere through active participation in the work of the American Association of State Highway Officials.

Lead in Freeway Development

From our contacts with officials and leading citizens of other states, we have gathered the impression that California is acknowledged throughout the Nation to be one of the leading states in freeway development. However, we are painfully aware of the serious traffic problems which you mention, and are constantly seeking ways to stretch the highway tax dollar farther in terms of permanent, safe, free-flowing highways.

Your letter reflects a thoughtful concern with our highway problems and an active interest in what is being done to solve them.

Very truly yours,
G. T. McCoy
State Highway Engineer

65 Million Vehicles On Road in 1956

The government forecasts a 4 percent increase in motor vehicle registration this year, which would put 65,275,000 passenger cars, trucks and busses on the roads.

At the same time, the Bureau of Public Roads said a projection showed the number of motor vehicles will reach 81,000,000 by 1965.

Borrow Site Headaches

By J. M. ASBILL, District Right of Way Agent, Appraisals; and
P. C. MORRIS, District Materials Engineer

UNTIL A FEW years ago, imported borrow presented a minor problem in highway construction. Cut and fill could usually be balanced out so as to cause a minimum of borrow or waste. Cross-country roads, as a rule, followed the general contour of the area traversed. What if there was a 7 or 8 percent grade? It just meant shifting a few more gears. There were a few railroad crossings with separation structures; otherwise, crossings were at grade. With the advent of the freeway, with its multiple lanes, its long radius curves, its minimum grades, and its large and complex separation structures and interchanges, the acquisition of imported borrow became a major problem.

Borrow Pits Become Important

In the day of the conventional highway, with its comparatively low standards, the contract specifications only stated, "so many tons of imported borrow," and it was up to the contractor to secure it from the most convenient local source at whatever price he could buy it for. Nothing really to it. Then, borrow came into its own as one of the major items of construction. In some instances, contractors went into an area and tied up all available borrow so that it wasn't possible for more than one or two firms to bid on a job.'

In order to prevent this possibility from developing to the extent that competitive bidding would in any way be curtailed, a procedure was established to provide that the Division of Highways by borrow agreement with owners of suitable material, secure the right to remove sufficient material from their property to construct the highway in the manner proposed. The procedure further provides that when a contract is advertised for bid, the special provisions will designate the location or locations where such material can be se-

Looking west along Santa Ana riverbed, showing borrow operations in foreground. Piers under construction for new southbound US 395 bridge west of existing South E Street Bridge.

cured, the manner of access and the price that the contractor will have to pay. It is not required that the contractor use the designated site, but it is available for his use.

A casual look at a topographic map of the area south of the City of San Bernardino would indicate that the

acquisition of imported borrow in that area would present a very small problem. This is the story of how misleading a casual look at anything can be.

Three-level Interchange

A construction project covering a portion of the San Bernardino Freeway was being prepared for advertising. The termini of the project were: "Between Warm Creek on Route 26 to South E Street, and Route 43 between Route 26 and Lytle Creek." Route 26 is a portion of U. S. Highway 99 and intersects U. S. Highway 395 at South E Street. A large above-ground three-level interchange is planned at the intersection of the two major routes. Construction of this interchange will require approximately 1,850,000 tons of imported borrow and 63,500 tons of base material.

By the end of October, 1955, all appraisals had been made, and a major portion of the right of way had been acquired, and all unacquired right of way was under order for possession, but no adequate source of borrow had been definitely located on which negotiations were possible, and there was insufficient time to institute eminent domain proceedings. True, we had been looking at sites since March, 1955, but so far, nothing had materialized. We had explored the possibility to the west, but that meant hauling through the City of Colton, and the cost of haul would have been prohibitive.

Lack of Sources

To the east, there are orange groves until you get to the City of Redlands. No possible source in that direction. To the north, the City of San Bernardino. There, the Santa Ana River meandered in a northeasterly direction almost at the point of intersection of US 99 and US 395. However, because of the large quantity of material required, it appeared that at least 20 separate ownerships would be involved. To the south, the topographic map showed many small hills of likely material with a minimum number of improvements. It looked good, but wasn't. Property owners in the ara just didn't want to sell. Either they believed the price offered was too low, or they were concerned with possible land defacement.

We found one site where sufficient material could be secured, and we signed up the owner on a borrow agreement; however, the county was able to grant a zoning variance which would have permitted the area to be utilized as a borrow site only on the basis of an indirect haul route.

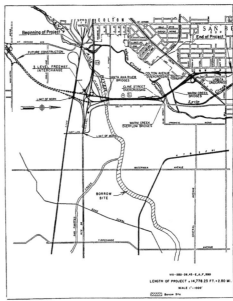

Map of project showing borrow site in lower center

VIII - 580 - 26, 43 - E, A ; F, 880
LENGTH OF PROJECT = 14,778.25 FT. = 2.80 MI.
SCALE 1" = 1000'
▨ Borrow Site

There were also several other reasons why the State did not look with favor on this pit; mainly, the fact that, even with a direct route, the haul was 3½ miles long. It would be necessary to haul over county roads, and it was also necessary to cross the main line of the Southern Pacific Railroad at grade.

Only One Choice

Looking over the situation, we were faced with "Hobson's Choice." It had to be the Santa Ana River or else. There was no other economical source.

The prerequisites of a good borrow site are as follows:

1. A short haul, for if the haul is too long, no matter how cheaply the material can be bought, it is still expensive material.

2. Insofar as possible, an unobstructed haul, that is, ability to haul material without using any county road or city street.

3. If possible, secure all material from one source.

4. Avoidance of grade crossings of railroads or highways.

5. Ability to remove material from the source by the use of heavy off-road earth-moving equipment. This ties in with No. 2 above.

6. Minimum land defacement.

and Public Works

61

7. Minimum number of owners with whom it is necessary to negotiate.

River Bed Ideal

Of course, there are other requisites; however, the seven given above are the most necessary to a good source of material. Except for the seventh, the Santa Ana River bed was ideal. Anyway, there appeared to be no other alternative, and the word was given by the district engineer to acquire this source.

The Santa Ana River drains an area of 2,480 square miles, of which 54 percent is rough mountains and 46 percent is alluvial fans and gently sloping valley floor. The total length of the river is about 100 miles, but continuous flow throughout its length is evident only during winter flood periods. Five great floods have been recorded in the basin since 1811. In 1938, the maximum peak discharge on the Santa Ana River at Riverside was estimated at 100,000 cubic feet per second.

San Jacinto Fault

The stream channel is generally well defined by low banks, and through the borrow area ranges in width from 100 to 600 feet. The average stream gradient in the area is about 30 feet per mile. A series of northwest-southeast faults cross the Santa Ana River Basin in the vicinity of the lower end of the borrow area. The San Jacinto fault forms what is known as the "Bunker Hill Dike," which acts as a barrier to ground-water flow near the freeway crossing of the river. Above the dike, the ground water is relatively close to the surface. (Midsummer borings in the streambed above the dike indicated water at about 10 to 12 feet.) Below the dike, the water sinks below the range of the test borings.

The geologic instability of the extensive mountain region at the head of the river, together with repeated forest fires, uncontrolled tributary mountain streams, and mountain road construction, has contributed to a high sedimentation rate, ranging from 1,400 to 9,800 cubic yards per square mile per year at and below the canyon mouths. Of the tributary streams, San Timoteo Creek (which discharges into the borrow area from the southeast)

Hauling borrow material from the Santa Ana River bed east of South E Street

is especially bad as a producer of flood waters and a large amount of sediment from the dry farmed areas through which it flows.

Rapid Sedimentation

In view of the rapid sedimentation, it is unlikely that the borrow area will remain as a depression for any great length of time. It is indeed possible that the contractor may never have to cut out to the upper end of the area if there are enough storms during the life of the contract to keep replenishing his excavated areas.

When the original maps were prepared, it appeared that in order to secure sufficient material from this source, it would be necessary to carry the excavation to a depth of from 4 feet to 20 feet, depending upon the depth that a clay formation underlying the surface sand in the riverbed was reached. The length of the borrow site was approximately three miles, that is, from 1,400 feet west of E Street to about 1,000 feet northerly of Tippecanoe Avenue. A total of 22 separate ownerships would be involved.

It may appear that undue emphasis is being placed on separate ownerships. But, in acquisitions of this type, the difficulties are not multiplied by the number of separate ownerships, but, more nearly, by the square of the number of property owners involved. If there is any doubt, just try to get 22 people to agree on any one subject.

Right of Way Acquisition

In a normal acquisition program for right of way, the owners know that the fair market value is being offered for the property required. They may quibble and haggle, but the fact is actually known. They are also, as a rule, cognizant of the fact that under the law of eminent domain, the State can take possession of the property and proceed with construction while awaiting for the courts to adjudicate the fair market value if an agreement cannot be reached.

This is not the case in the acquisition of a borrow site. It is true that borrow can be secured by eminent domain proceedings; however, an order for immediate possession cannot be taken. The delay in waiting for a condemnation trial makes acquisition by condemnation almost impossible unless material requirements are determined several years in advance. It is normally necessary to sell the owner on the idea that it is a "good deal" for him to sign the agreements.

Borrow Agreement

The agreement proposed to be secured is known as a "borrow" agreement and provides, in essence, that the owner has granted to the State, its contractor, or assigns, the right to enter upon the property of the grantor and remove therefrom material of the quality and quantity provided therein. As a rule, the consideration for this right is a nominal sum of $1; however, it is possible to pay up to $25 for the right, if required, and in case of large holdings, up to $10 per acre. The period covered is from six months (rarely) to two or more years (generally). The borrow agreement is for all practical purposes a form of option. If material is removed, payment for the material will be at the fair market rate; however, there is no guarantee that any material will ever actually be removed. That is entirely up to the contractor who is awarded the contract after competitive bidding. If he takes the material, so good. If he doesn't, the property owner only has an option agreement.

Experience has indicated that as time passes, more and more owners of borrow material are placing a different connotation on the word "borrow" than is meant or implied. Borrow, in engineering terms, simply means the taking from some other source material that cannot be produced by cut sections and is required for fill on any given project. To owners, however, it has the general connotation that would be given to

Large culvert under US 99 used by contractor's equipment to shorten haul and avoid interference with traffic

the word by a lender of money; only in this case we are asking to borrow their land. You are met with the same cool, fishy stare from the owner of borrow material that you could expect to receive from the banker from whom you asked for a loan of money without offering to put up any collateral except the possibility that it might, sometime, be repaid by somebody else.

All Owners Paid

In order to eliminate some of the objections that would be raised by the property owners, provision was made in the borrow agreements that if any material whatever was removed from any of the properties involved, all of the property owners would be paid. While the site would not be mandatory to the contractor, nevertheless, if he used the site, all owners would receive payment. This was necessary because, should even a small flood occur, the excavation on the lower portion would be filled in and the up-river owners, while supplying the material, would not actually have their property excavated. On the other hand, if heavy flow did not materialize, it would probably be essential to remove material from all the properties.

Regardless of the above difficulties, as negotiations were started on the project, there was no defeatism in the minds of the negotiating agents. Almost immediately, six borrow agreements were secured from private owners. Then, we hit a snag.

Utilities Involved

The Atchison, Topeka and Santa Fe Railway Company, under whose bridge it was necessary for the State

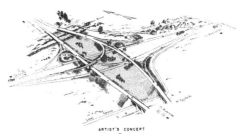

ARTIST'S CONCEPT
or
THREE LEVEL INTERCHANGE
HIGHWAYS 395 AND 99

and Public Works

63

LEFT—Scraper crossing scales used for weighing material from the river bed borrow area. RIGHT—Scrapers loading in borrow site west of South E Street. Use of river bed material avoided hauling on or across any streets or railroads.

to pass in order to secure required material, raised an objection that if the material was removed in the manner proposed, there was a possibility that in the case of a flood, the abutments of the bridge would be so weakened as to endanger the bridge.

So we drew some more maps which changed the method of taking material from underneath the bridge; however, in this connection, it was necessary to renegotiate four of the contracts that had previously been acquired.

We started again, and then we hit snag No. 2.

The plans indicated that there was a coaxial cable belonging to the Pacific Telephone and Telegraph Company crossing the river channel just westerly of the Tippecanoe Avenue Bridge. Further investigation brought out the fact that in order to continue this cable service, it would be necessary for the State to lower the cable. This particular cable provides for transmission of telephone and television service between Phoenix and Los Angeles. In conversation with representatives of the telephone company, it was brought out that the cost of lowering the cable would be approximately $120,000. For the amount of material involved, this cost was prohibitive; therefore, it was necessary to revise our plans again.

Negotiations Renewed

Plans were redrawn providing for widening of our zone of operations and shortening of the distance. We would not go only a short distance easterly of the Waterman Avenue Bridge, but on a much wider basis.

Negotiations were recommenced; and so the job progressed. An obstacle would appear; plans would be revised —negotiations were like a make-break electric current, now on, now off. With each change, the distance up the river was shortened, the area widened, and the depth of excavation generally reduced to assure a more even flow should the river flood.

By the middle of April, all necessary agreements had been assured with the exception of a parcel owned by the City of Riverside Water Department. This property was located westerly of the Waterman Avenue Bridge. Crossing the river channel is a 36-inch water line belonging to the city. The river crossing of the pipe is 550 lineal feet in length and is located approximately 12 feet below the river flow line.

Pipeline Protected

We would not shorten our distance any more; we had to have the material. The Riverside City Water Department naturally expected full protection of its vital pipeline. It was finally agreed that the State would

protect the line by driving sheet piling downstream from the pipeline across the entire river bed.

The end was in sight; we thought we had it made. Then it was brought to our attention that there might be a contingent liability to the city were a flood to occur and damage the property either above or below them due to the removal of material that would change the river grade. There were two courses open; either the State would assume a continuing liability or would purchase the property outright. After further negotiations, it was decided to buy the property, reserving to the City of Riverside Water Department an easement for its pipeline, and the right to reacquire the property after completion of the freeway construction.

On May 16, 1956, this project was certified by the district for construction. The securing of a borrow site had involved an engineering and acquisitions project that only a few years ago would have sufficed to secure right of way for three or four miles of conventional highway. Was it worth the effort? Here is the final box score:

A Summing Up

As mentioned in a preceding section, the only other available source within a reasonable haul distance was a gravel hill southeast of Loma Linda.

Negotiations were completed for this site on the basis of $0.05 per ton for the first 70,000 tons and $0.01 per ton for any additional material that might be removed up to 2,000,000 tons.

This site had a haul to the beginning of the job of approximately 3½ miles, of which three miles would have been over county roads. In addition, there would have been a crossing at grade of the main line tracks of the Southern Pacific Railroad.

The cost differential on material from this source was based on the possibility that imported base material only might be removed and the owner was unwilling to tie up his land on the chance that the contractor might only remove 70,000 tons at $0.01 per ton. Material from the Santa Ana River bed will not meet requirements for base, and it is possible that the contractor will secure his base material from a commercial source.

Based on imported borrow alone (1,850,000 tons), the total cost of material from either source is approximately the same. However, the cost of the material alone is not the big factor; the major factor is haul.

The average hauling distance is 3½ miles for the hillside site and one mile for the Santa Ana River site. Based on $0.05 per ton-mile, which is a conservative figure, the 2½ additional miles haul would have cost the State a total of $0.12½ cents per ton for each ton hauled. Multiplied by 1,850,-000 tons, the savings in haul alone will amount to $231,250 by using the river source. Added to this figure would be the cost of repairing damage done by heavy dump trucks to county roads and an undetermined amount for delays at the railroad grade crossing. It is also believed that a considerably more favorable bid was received by reason of the fact that the contractor could use heavy off-road earth-moving equipment without any restrictions.

Conservatively, the over-all saving to the State will equal $250,000. Regardless of the number of headaches that may have been caused in securing material from this source, you could still buy a whale of a lot of aspirin for a quarter of a million dollars.

TECHNIQUES OF MAKING LAND ECONOMIC STUDIES*

By GEORGE T. McCOY, State Highway Engineer

As a prelude to any discussion of the mechanics involved in developing California's land economic studies I believe it advisable to comment upon the policy underlying their preparation. This policy, based on the exigency of a rapidly expanding highway program, requires that all of our studies be designed to meet an immediate need which may, considered from an academic standpoint, place certain limitations on their scholastic importance.

The impact of access-controlled highways as a factor in land economics is almost unlimited. In our initial considerations to study this influence, we were aware of the advantages from a long-range viewpoint of exhaustive research as an aid to highway planning; however, as worth while as such an extended survey would be, immediate knowledge in this field of economic influence was, and still is, required as a means of substantiating today's decisions for highway requirements. Land economic facts are also required as background material for our land appraisers so that they can be in the best possible position to determine the appreciation or depreciation of lands remaining adjacent to these freeway developments. Under California's undeviating policy to pay every property owner every cent to which he is entitled for the portion of his land required for highway use, and the damages, if any, to the remainder of his land, such information is of paramount importance.

Another facet of the preliminary analysis of our economic study needs was the ruling out of any studies of highway bypasses or realignments that did not include the taking of access rights. In a dynamic economy such as California's, the increase in population and motor vehicle use is so rapid that changes in highway usage anticipated in a 20-year period have occurred in less than half that time.

It is, therefore, possible to observe the fallacy of bypasses without access controls with such clarity it is unnecessary to prepare formal studies to document this fact.

In limiting our studies to access-controlled highways, we have included, besides freeways which prohibit any openings from private property into the through lanes of traffic, partial control of access which we term "expressways" and which allow certain openings under special conditions. As a generalization on this facet, we have now come to the conclusion based on completed studies that the expressway, a compromise between the conventional highway and the freeway, economically falls into a compromise category as to ultimate benefits. It offers something better than the conventional highway as to retaining economic stability in existing areas, but, also, because of its compromise nature it does not offer the same protection as the full freeway. As a result of our observations, it is now our tendency to build less of the expressway highways and move from the conventional highway to the full freeway, avoiding this interim development.

After determining the type of highway facility to be studied, the next determination was the establishment of specific goals and the areas to come under study. First it was necessary to determine what effect, if any, freeway construction had on established areas. If an industrial area was bypassed by a freeway would it reduce or increase the demand for lands in the established industrial area. The same question could be posed as to established commercial and residential districts, whether the freeway with its interchange structures would create competitive areas capable of siphoning off a great bulk of the real property needs for these uses to the end that the effect would be detrimental to the established areas.

Secondly it was apparent that the studies should make a clear determina-

* This article appeared in the July, 1956, issue of *American Highways*, official publication of American Association of State Highway Officials of which Mr. McCoy is past president.

tion as to any change of land use on properties abutting or adjacent to the freeway brought about by its construction, or whether the development of the lands under the influence of the freeway would be a development that could not otherwise occur without a transportation facility of this type.

In summary our conclusions were:

1. Study all access-controlled bypasses or realignments.

2. Use the most practical methods of research so that the results of the studies could be put into immediate use.

3. Determine the economic effect on all *established areas*, be they industrial, commercial, or residential.

4. Determine the actual economic effect on lands *adjacent* to the freeway, both as to retained current use and change of land use.

To accomplish these goals within a reasonable time it was apparent at the outset that analysis would have to depend upon comparative methods. On this premise we concluded that the major fields of inquiry would involve the use of: (1) land sales; (2) sales tax returns, and (3) the personal interview. Although these methods can be considered empirical in nature, they have proved successful in meeting our immediate needs.

Land Sales

The principal source of factual data to conclusively show how the economic status of a given area can be influenced by the construction of a freeway bypass is the trend in land values revealed through property transfers. Considerable information in the field of real estate transfers is obtained through an investigation of all local government records, records of local title and abstract companies, and records of real estate offices. In addition to the applicable sales data, the investigation includes a review of rental rates, the trend in land uses and development, and the areas of new building activity.

The procedure used in making this type of study consists of *first*, determination of the limits of the area influenced by the access-controlled highway; *second*, the selection of a comparable area which has been and is currently subjected to the same eco-

nomic influences with the exception of the highway influence. This will provide the ideal situation because it affords the opportunity for direct comparison and thereby eliminats any doubt as to the trend established in the area of study. If an area cannot be found for comparison, the study must rely upon conclusive evidence of changing value within the area influenced by the access-controlled highway; *third*, consideration of the element of time. A direct comparison over the longest period of time possible before and after construction of the highway is desirable. However, the availability of factual sales data may limit the length of time covered by the study.

An economic study must be conclusive; therefore, the success in using land sales and development as a guide in determining the influence of a new freeway depends upon a sufficient number of sales in both the area under study and the area or areas determined to have comparability to reveal a definite trend in land valuation. In an area where the real estate market has been active, there is an opportunity to obtain remarkable success by the use of land sales. When this situation occurs, the established trend in land values and development in any one area will provide an indication of how the entire economy of a community is affected by an access-controlled highway, as well as providing a key to how other communities will be affected.

Sales Tax Returns

Unfortunately, real estate activity and land development is not very active in some communities. Rather than wait several years until there are an adequate number of property transfers, a technique should be used which will produce factual results from a different phase of the economy which changes more rapidly than the real estate market. A factual study based upon retail business can provide conclusive results within a relatively short period of time. Retail business in nearly every community is directly affected by the construction of a new access-controlled highway. A beneficial or adverse effect upon the business district will definitely influence

the economy of the entire community.

All retail outlets in California, except those which provide a service such as hotels, motels, dry cleaners, etc., are required to report their gross income to the State Board of Equalization for sales tax purposes. These reports are made quarterly and certified by the business operator as to their accuracy. The reports indicate the income of the individual retail outlet and like personal income reports to the Bureau of Internal Rvenue, are highly confidential. The Governor of California authorized the Division of Highways to inspect these gross income figures submitted by the retail outlets to the Board of Equalization because it would provide an accurate source of information to determine how the access-controlled highway affects retail business. In exercising this right, it was understood that confidential figures were being used and that the right to use these figures was limited to making economic studies. To protect the businessman and not reveal the gross income of any single retail outlet, any reference to this information is made through percentages on business as a group such as service stations, cafes, etc.

The procedure followed in making this type of study is to first determine which retail oulets are within the area of influence. In the rural communities, all of the retail outlets are likely to be in the study because the entire business districts of the smaller cities are usually built along the highway route and are directly affected by any change in the highway. Retail outlets to be studied in urban communities are generally those which have been located along the old highway route or in some other way are directly affected by a change in the highway alignment.

This type of study requires a direct comparison with an area which has followed the same general economic trend with respect to changes in sales activity, but which has not been subjected to the direct effect of a change in the traffic pattern. Retail business lends itself very well to making a comparison before and after the construction of a new highway. Retail business is subject to seasonal fluctuation; therefore, if the time period for the study covers a portion of a year, the same time period should be used in the before and after comparison for greatest accuracy.

A comparison of the grand total gross revenue before and after the highway improvements will be sufficient to show the gain or loss which has taken place in all retail business. In California, we segregate the businesses by type in order to also determine the effect of the highway change upon those businesses which cater to the highway motorist and are more likely to be seriously affected by a rerouting of traffic. Service stations, cafes, and bars are placed in this category and a special analysis of business sales is made for those specific retail outlets.

The sales tax method has been found to be extremely successful in providing a true indication of the economic impact of access-controlled highways because of these advantages which it affords:

1. This type of study is based on absolute facts.

2. A direct comparison can be made of business activity before and after the construction of the new highway.

3. All business in the community with the exception of the service type of retail outlet is included in the study, giving a wide scope to the study.

The study of the gross sales of an area will reveal the trend that can be anticipated in land values. Business activity will eventually be reflected in the rent which can be paid and the sale price of the property. If business areas retain their same volume of sales after the removal of through traffic, they will retain their same desirability. In all of our studies completed to date it has developed that not only have they retained their value, but, because of increased gross sales, they have been made more desirable and have increased in value.

The Personal Interview

The third technique we have used is the personal interview method. Although this method of obtaining information is one of the most popular devices used for making surveys, our experience has been that it is the least desirable from a factual standpoint. The principal reason for making land economic studies is to instill confidence and knowledge instead of opinions and conjecture which are bound to exist without knowledge of the true facts.

Several years ago when California realized the necessity of developing land economic studies, the personal interview technique was used because it was a popular method. It was our assumption that if reliable people were used for making the interviews, we would obtain good results. We engaged a nationally-known appraiser to proceed entirely independent of the Division of Highways with an investigation to determine by the opinion of roadside merchants in a specific area the effect of a new expressway which had diverted through traffic from the old highway route in front of those business establishments. A tabulation of all the information showed a wide variance of opinion on the effect of the access-controlled highway. The inconsistency of this type of report was exposed at a later date by a review of the sales tax returns of the same business operators who had been interviewed. As an example of the inaccuracy found from this opinion survey, one retail business claimed that they had suffered a 58 percent loss after the construction of the access-controlled highway. The gross revenue which they reported for sales tax purposes showed a 3 percent gain in business during that period of time. Another retail business claimed an average loss of 15 percent in business; however, their tax statements revealed a 48 percent gain. The opinions reported by several other business operators failed to coincide when a comparison was made with their tax statements submitted under sworn affidavits.

Having experienced the shortcomings of the interview method, we have relied principally on other techniques for making land economic studies. However, it is possible to make a factual study using the interview method. Recently we completed a state-wide study on the economic effect of ac-

cess-controlled highways upon the motel industry using the interview method. This method was used because it provided the only means of obtaining the information needed to make a study of this particular type of business. A check sheet was prepared to serve as a guide in obtaining the information from the motel owners. Gross receipts for the business were obtained from the motel owners' records and from their income tax statements. This was an exhaustive and time-consuming study because we were required to personally contact the owner as well as his predecessors in those cases where the current ownership was of a short duration. The motel owners were assured that their business receipts would be handled in a confidential manner. The participation on the part of the motel owners was voluntary and we were extremely successful in obtaining excellent cooperation.

The success in using the personal interview to obtain data for a factual study is dependent upon sales ability of the interviewer to convince the property owner that he can benefit from the knowledge obtained through a factual study; and that the accuracy of the study is his responsibility to provide absolute facts.

The disadvantage of using the personal interview for making an economic study greatly overshadows its advantages. This technique is costly because of the time required to develop factual data. The participation on the part of the property owner is strictly voluntary and the risk of not obtaining adequate facts is always prevalent.

The following is a typical outline used in the preparation of an economic study. At the risk of oversimplification, we feel that reasonable adherence to this type of outline will produce a factual and usable economic study:

A TYPICAL OUTLINE USED IN MAKING AN ECONOMIC STUDY

I. Purpose of Study

A. Determine effect of highway change upon:
1. Land values
2. Land development
   a. Residential
   b. Commercial
   c. Industrial
3. Business activity

II. Type of Highway Improvement

A. Freeway
  1. Bypass—new alignment
  2. Conversion of old alignment
  3. Frontage road

III. Highway Facts

A. Date new highway agreement (between state and local community)
B. Date right of way acquisition
C. Date construction started and completed
D. Design of new highway
E. Traffic, accidents, parking

IV. Area of Study

A. Property and business adjacent access-controlled highways
B. Property and business zone of influence
C. Property and business in comparable area

V. Basis of Study and Time Period

A. Comparison before and after highway construction
B. Direct comparison with comparable area

VI. Local Economic Influences

A. Population
B. Map of area
  1. Highway routes
  2. Growth trend in community
C. sources of income
  1. Local industry
    a. Highway influence
    a-1 Terminal or destination stop

VII. Documentary Evidence

A. Records and reports from governmental agencies and private business
  1. State. Board of Equalization
  2. State Department of Finance
  3. State Department of Employment
  4. County offices of Assessor, Recorder, Tax Collector, Clerk, Planning Commission
  5. City offices of Assessor, Tax Collector, Building Inspector, Planning Commission
  6. Agricultural Extension Service, Farm Bureau and Advisors
  7. Title and Abstract Co. records
  8. Oil companies—service station gallonage
  9. Chain store headquarters—reports of individual retail outlet gross business
  10. Property owners, real estate offices—property transfer data

VIII. Conclusion

A. The conclusion is an analysis of the detailed factual data presented in the report. This summary of basic issues should be concise.

I cannot recommend too highly the necessity of making these studies as a guide to engineering decisions and as an important step in building good public relations. It has been our experience that among the many benefits derived from the development of sound and factual land economic studies, those that are immediately apparent are:

1. The improved accuracy of property appraisals, particularly in the field of estimating the value of severance damages and the results from the restriction of access rights.

2. The availability of documented material on the freeway effects on property development.

3. A building of confidence in the public as to the thoroughness of the highway's land acquisition procedures.

4. The reduction in costly delay in constructing new freeways by the possibility of supplying information to the communities so that they may properly evaluate the economic impact.

A bibliography of economic studies published by the California Division of Highways:

"Tulare Bypass," May-June, 1956, California Highways and Public Works Magazine.
"Santa Claus," Mar.-Apr., 1956, California Highways and Public Works Magazine.
"Camarillo Study," Sept.-Oct., 1955, California Highways and Public Works Magazine; April, 1956, Traffic Engineering.
"Templeton Bypass," July-Aug., 1955, California Highways and Public Works Magazine.
"America's Highway Problems and Their Likely Effect on Real Estate Markets," October, 1954, The Appraisal Journal.
"Industry and Frontage Roads," July-Aug., 1954, California Highways and Public Works Magazine.
"Industry and Freeways," May-June, 1954, California Highways and Public Works Magazine.
"Motels and Freeways," Jan.-Feb., 1954, California Highways and Public Works Magazine; 1955, Roads International; 1955-1956, American Society of Appraisers—Appraisal and Valuation Manual.
"Four Years After," May-June, 1953, California Highways and Public Works Magazine.
"The One-Way Street," Mar.-April, 1953, California Highways and Public Works Magazine; May, 1953, Highway Research Board.
"Anderson Study," Jan.-Feb., 1953, California Highways and Public Works Magazine; May, 1953, Highway Research Board.
"Land Values Before and After Freeway Development," October, 1952, American City.
"Shell Beach Study," Nov.-Dec., 1951, California Highways and Public Works Magazine.
"Freeway Values," Sept.-Oct., 1951, California Highways and Public Works Magazine.
"Escondido Study," July-Oct., 1951, California Highways and Public Works Magazine.
"Temecula Study," July-Oct., 1951, California Highways and Public Works Magazine.
"By-Pass Effect," May-June, 1951, California Highways and Public Works Magazine.
"Factual Studies," Mar.-April, 1951, California Highways and Public Works Magazine.
"Westlake Community," Mar.-April, 1951, California Highways and Public Works Magazine.
"Business Benefited by Expressway," Mar.-Apr., 1951, California Highways and Public Works Magazine.
"Fairfield Study," Jan.-Feb., 1951, California Highways and Public Works Magazine.
"Auburn Study," May-June, 1950, California Highways and Public Works Magazine.
"Freeway Ups Business," Jan.-Feb., 1950, California Highways and Public Works Magazine.
"Boost for Freeways," Nov.-Dec., 1949, California Highways and Public Works Magazine.
"Service Town, U. S. A.," Sept.-Oct., 1949, California Highways and Public Works Magazine.
"Outer Highway," Jan.-Feb., 1949, California Highways and Public Works Magazine.
"Freeway Is Profitable to Vineyard Co.," Sept.-Oct., 1948, California Highways and Public Works Magazine.
"Effect of Freeway Development on Adjacent Land Values in California," Nov.-Dec., 1947; Jan.-Feb., 1948; Mar.-Apr., 1948; California Highways and Public Works Magazine.

El Monte Merchants Find Freeway Boon, Not Bane to Business

El Monte merchants are surprised, and pleased to note that completion of the San Bernardino Freeway appears to have helped rather than hindered their business.

Edward Scott, manager of the El Monte Chamber of Commerce, reported today that with few exceptions businessmen on Valley Boulevard are reporting increased sales, and also are jubilant over the best dollar days in the city's history, held recently.

Scott credits the fact that Valley Boulevard is no longer clogged with heavy trucks, allowing shoppers to get to the business section easily and at their leisure.

"Generally speaking," he said, "the businessmen of El Monte are much happier now than they were when the freeway was first planned and the State was trying to obtain rights of way."—*San Gabriel Valley Tribune.*

HOW TRUE!

K. C. ADAMS, *Editor*

DEAR SIR: Congratulations to you and your staff for the fine work you are doing in preparing such a comprehensive magazine, *California Highways and Public Works.* I am sure few realize the magnitude of the road building going on in California.

I came from Illinois six years ago and have never seen anything to compare to it back there. Everything in the West seems to have the pioneer spirit to do the impossible.

J. B. WISE, Los Angeles

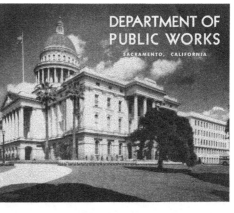

DEPARTMENT OF PUBLIC WORKS
SACRAMENTO, CALIFORNIA

P. O. BOX 1499
SACRAMENTO, CALIFORNIA

RETURN POSTAGE GUARANTEED

SEATTLE 4, WASHINGTON

R56

PAID
Sacramento, Cal.
Permit No. 152

From this section of Feather River Highway (US 40 Alternate) in Plumas County the motorist gets a splendid view of Spanish Peak in background and Feather River on left

NOVEMBER-DECEMBER
'56

California Highways
and Public Works

Official Journal of the Division of Highways,
Department of Public Works, State of California

Public Works Building
Twelfth and N Streets
Sacramento

KENNETH C. ADAMS, *Editor*

HELEN HALSTED, *Assistant Editor*

MERRITT R. NICKERSON, *Chief Photographer*

Vol. 35   November-December   Nos. 11-12

CONTENTS

COVER
*June Lake on Route 111
in Mono County receives
first blanket of winter
snow—Photo by Robert
Munow, Photographic Section,
Department of Public Works,
M. R. Nickerson, Chief*

Published in the interest of highway development in California. Editors of newspapers and others are privileged to use matter contained herein. Cuts will be gladly loaned upon request.

Address communications to

CALIFORNIA HIGHWAYS AND PUBLIC WORKS
P. O. Box 1499
Sacramento, California

Angeles Crest

Half Century Dream of Engineers Realized

By GEORGE LANGSNER,
District Engineer

Highway Opened

AFTER NEARLY a half century of co-operative effort and expenditures totaling some $10,000,000, the Angeles Crest Highway across the San Gabriel Mountains has been completed, and after dedication ceremonies on November 8, 1956, was opened to public use.

The Angeles Crest Highway, having its westerly terminus at the intersection of Haskell Avenue with Foothill Boulevard in La Canada, extends easterly for 55 miles to the Big Pines recreational area in the Angeles National Forest.

This new highway saves motorists between Los Angeles and Big Pines, 42 miles of travel when compared with the best route previously available. It makes the summer and winter recreational areas of the U. S. Forest Service much more accessible than formerly.

Great Cooperative Effort

The inception of the Angeles Crest Highway dates back some 50 years when the people of Southern California began to recognize the need for additional access to the recreational facilities in the Angeles National Forest. While many organizations and individuals had a part in taking the original steps toward consummation, special mention should be made of the important parts played by the Pasadena Board of Trade, the predecessor of the present Pasadena Chamber of Commerce; the U. S. Bureau of Public Roads, the National Forest Service, and by the Automobile Club of Southern California.

The first engineering work of record that was done on the Angeles Crest Highway was sponsored and financed by the Automobile Club of Southern California. In 1919, Henry W. Keller, as chairman of the Roads and Highways Committee of the Automobile Club of Southern Califor-

GEORGE LANGSNER

nia, authorized an expenditure of $2,200 for the engineering firm headed by J. B. Lippincott for a reconnaissance survey to be used as a basis for later location studies for the Angeles Crest Highway. Ernest E. East, in his capacity as Chief Engineer of the Automobile Club of Southern California, and Harold F. Holley, as Assistant Chief Engineer (recently retired), both made many reconnaissance trips with Lippincott and others dating back as far as 1919. These two engineers did much to keep alive public interest in the Angeles Crest Highway project until the State Division of Highways started the location surveys in 1928 and initiated construction in 1929. Thereafter, East and Holley maintained a lively interest in the project and made frequent trips over the project consulting with State High-

way and U. S. Public Roads representatives.

Taken Into State Highway System

The Angeles Crest Highway, as Legislative Route 61, was taken into the State Highway System in three parts. The westerly section from Foothill Boulevard in La Canada to the Mt. Wilson Road at Red Box Divide was brought into the State Highway System by the Bond Amendment of 1919. The middle section from the Mt. Wilson Road at Red Box to Pine Flats became a part of the State Highway System by Statutes of 1931. The easterly section from Pine Flats to the Los Angeles-San Bernardino county line was taken into the State Highway System by the Statutes of 1933.

Allocations of state highway funds for construction on the Angeles Crest Highway were first made in 1929 by the California Highway Commission. In subsequent budgets the commission provided funds for this project so that essential work could go forward.

Among the former members of the California Highway Commission having their homes in Southern California who have maintained, through the years they so faithfully served the people of California, a lively interest in furtherance of the Angeles Crest Highway, where Philip A. Stanton, Amerigo Bozzani, Harrison R. Baker, as well as present commissioners James A. Guthrie and Robert E. Mc-Clure.

Top-level Decisions

In carrying the Angeles Crest Highway project through to final completion there have been, from time to time, many top-level decisions that had to be made by the Sacramento staff. State Highway Engineer G. T. McCoy and Director of Public Works Frank B. Durkee are, and have always been, most enthusiastic in their support of action to advance the Angeles Crest Highway.

In order to assist in the prisoner rehabilitation program as provided by laws, the decision was made that as much as possible of the construction on the Angeles Crest Highway be done with prison labor working out of honor camps.

Many top-level conferences have been necessary between the Sacramento headquarters staff of the State Division of Highways and the State Department of Corrections. Between these two state departments a most cooperative spirit has always existed relative to the many difficult problems that have arisen in connection with the utilization of prison labor for state highway construction on the Angeles Crest Highway.

These Men Worked Hard

The first camp was first opened under the jurisdiction of the California State Prison at San Quentin where J. B. Holohan was then warden. Work continued under wardens Court Smith and Clinton P. Duffy. Throughout the period correctional officer H. A. Hinshaw was in charge of the camp. Working with him were correctional officers George Lessick, James Rodden, S. Knutson, W. Garrett, W. Ballard, L. McGinnis, H. Johnson, R. Doggett, H. E. Breakbill, Gus Opitz, A. L. Jewett, John Madigan, Bert Gothic, Frank Trip, James Ledden, John Butler, Lester Higgins, Ralph Shera, A. P. Lambdin.

Honor camps were closed shortly after the United States entered World War II and reopened in June, 1946, at the direction of Richard A. McGee, Director of Institutions. It was then a unit of the California Institution for Men at Chino, under Superintendent Kenyon J. Scudder, and continued under Superintendent F. R. Dickson. Chief camp supervisors during the period were George Winter, now field representative of the department; Malcolm Harris, now Deputy Director of the Department of Alcoholic Beverage Control; William Beckley and Johnnie Breen. Supervisor in charge of the opening of the camp was Harry Hoop. Subsequent supervisors were Beckley, now retired, Joe Hendrix,

Looking easterly along Angeles Crest Highway near Dawson's Saddle, showing attractive rock masonry retaining wall on left

Holly Weeks, Walter Slead, John Tisdale, now retired, Walter Stone, Charles Hamilton, and the late Paul Brockmeir.

Louis W. Baugh is presently in charge of the camps.

Federal and State Agencies Cooperate

The location and preliminary engineering on the Angeles Crest Highway, extending over a period of several years, was carried out by personnel of the U. S. Bureau of Public Roads and of the State Division of Highways. There was continual cooperation and harmonious liaison between these two groups of highway engineers. Generally speaking, the State took care of surveys for the westerly section between La Canada and Red Box, whereas, the U. S. Bureau of Public Roads handled the easterly section from Red Box to Big Pines.

In January, 1928, Assistant Engineer J. H. Obermuller, on the staff of Sacramento Headquarters Surveys and Plans Department, made a report to his chief, Fred J. Grumm, Engineer of Surveys and Plans, in which he outlined the preliminary reconnaissance survey of the Angeles Crest Highway

2

that he had made in company with Robert L. Thomas, Locating Engineer for District VII. (All three of these men have since retired from state service.) In his report, Obermuller makes these significant comments:

Obermuller Report

"The country from the mouth of the Arroyo Seco to Red Box was studied for determination of a routing on which final survey of the project should be started. The two routes surveyed in 1923 by preliminary lines by Frank Waller, U. S. Bureau of Public Roads, the one previously in 1919, by A. N. George for the State, the routing via the existing Edison Company Road, and the possibilities for alternative positions in location, were viewed in the field from the roads and trails and from advantageous peaks. No representative idea of routing can be secured in this brush-covered canyon except from such vantage points. The conclusions reached on that reconnaissance were that hand-level scout lines should be run over a considerable portion of

routings approximating the position of the high lines surveyed by Waller and George. This would furnish information regarding doubtful grade connections on advanced alignment standards and permit more reliable recommendation for preferable routing."

Purcell Starts Surveys

Shortly after Obermuller made his report to Grumm, State Highway Engineer Charles H. Purcell authorized Spencer V. Cortelyou, then district engineer of District VII, to start location surveys for the Angeles Crest Highway with Division of Highways forces. A start was made later in 1928 with a survey party of which W. H. Irish was chief. About the same time came a second survey party under Donald G. Evans, who recently retired from the position of Construction Engineer on the Sacramento headquarters staff. These two survey parties worked under the supervision of Robert L. Thomas, then Location Engineer for District VII (now retired). Henry Hawthorne was the

field office engineer on the job assisting "Bob" Thomas. These two survey parties were supplemented by additional survey party personnel during the years 1929 and 1930. Among the District VII engineering employees (in addition to those mentioned above) who made a very considerable contribution to the original location surveys on the Angeles Crest Highway, were: R. L. Adkins, C. T. Berry, E. F. Burge, W. P. Devine, C. Fox, C. C. French, A. L. Hawkins, B. E. Hooper, A. W. Hoy, R. M. Haverstick, Henry Hawthorne, V. B. Kolks, J. Q. McAndrew, B. F. Morris, A. E. Newton, L. F. Phillips, T. T. Peasnall, C. R. Smith, N. D. Soderblom, W. H. Suverkrubbe, and Harry H. Wildy.

Problem of Steep Slopes

The Angeles Crest Highway was designed and constructed to provide a 30-foot roadway with 200-foot radius curves as minimum standard for alignment and as maximum standard for rate of grade. Considering the rough mountainous country passed through these are considered as of sufficiently

Index map of Angeles Crest Highway

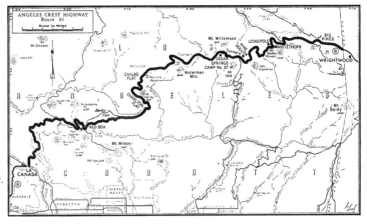

high standard. Actually, only a few 200-foot curves were put in at the start and later the minimum was established at 300 feet. Over two of the steep canyons it was found more economical to construct bridges than to build retaining walls to hold back roadway embankments, and in one instance of the location being along very steep side hill, a half bridge was constructed. In many other locations the slopes of the mountain sides were so steep that fill slopes would not catch and masonry retaining walls, reinforced concrete cribbing or metal bin-type cribbing had to be used.

Two Tunnels Built

The most spectacular construction on the Angeles Crest was the building of two tunnels and these were handled by Camp 37 forces from the present location at Cedar Springs. Near West Islip Saddle, the topography is very rugged and precipitous. Two steeply sloping ridges projecting out from the face of Mt. Williamson proved to be too steep for construction of even narrow pioneer roads. At this location, two tunnels had to be constructed. The first tunnel is 680 feet in length and the second tunnel is 470 feet in length. The two tunnels are separated by 87 feet of open-cut roadway. The tunnels were constructed to a section 32 feet wide x 21½ feet high, and the portals have been faced with very appropriate and picturesque rough stone masonry.

On the section of the Angeles Crest Highway between Cedar Springs and West Islip Saddle the excavation is for the most part through hard solid rock requiring that 80 percent of the excavation must be blasted.

The story of the Angeles Crest Highway is one of cooperative effort on the part of several organizations and of many people, women and children as well as men. The loyalty of the wives and children of State Division of Highways regular civil service employees working in Honor Camp 37, who gave up the conveniences and pleasures of urban life to live in small cottages adjoining the day labor camp, certainly was a big factor contributing toward the success of the project.

The children in camp of school age, numbering from 6 to 12, attended the

View of westerly portal of Tunnel No. 1 near Camp 37 Honor Camp on Angeles Crest Highway, with Tunnel No. 2 visible through Tunnel No. 1

"little red school house" right there in Camp 37, and were instructed in all elementary grades by competent teachers furnished by the Pasadena City School District. Bringing the school to the children saved the 74 miles of round trip travel that would have been incurred had the children been required to go to school in La Canada.

U. S. Forest Service Aid

The story of the Angeles Crest Highway is also a story of the Angeles National Forest which it traverses. Had it not been for the active interest of the U. S. Forest Service in leaving no stone unturned to get a high standard road constructed within the Angeles National Forest from La Canada to Big Pines, this project might have been much longer delayed in the building.

Great credit is due to William V. Mendenhall, the forest supervisor for the Angeles National Forest for his enthusiastic support in furtherance of the Angeles Crest Highway and his energetic drive for U. S. Forest Road Funds to be allocated for 16 miles of construction that was carried out by the U. S. Bureau of Public Roads. Mendenhall is most emphatic as to the great benefit that the Angeles Crest Highway has been to the Angeles National Forest. He unequivocably states that this new highway facility has im-

proved the management, the development and the forest fire fighting ability of his staff by 100 percent.

In 1933 there was a very destructive forest fire which denuded of vegetation the mountain sides and canyons above Montrose. At that time only a short section of the new Angeles Crest Highway was traversible. Mendenhall says that in his opinion the fact that forest service fire fighting equipment and personnel had the use of a portion of the Angeles Crest Highway to get back into the mountains and fight this fire, reduced to a very considerable extent the great damage caused by this fire. It will be recalled that early in 1934 the heavy rains falling on the burned-off areas of the Angeles National Forest caused, what has been referred to as the "Montrose Flood," that resulted in many persons losing their lives and millions of dollars of property damage. In Mendenhall's opinion, had it not been for the Angeles Crest Highway this catastrophe would have been much worse than it was.

Made National Forest

Bill Mendenhall well knows this area. He was born and reared in Pasadena. He became a forest ranger in the Angeles National Forest Lopez Canyon District, in 1911, and was stationed there for many years. For a

4

UPPER—Completed Angeles Crest Highway at entrance to Upper Chilao recreational area in the Angeles National Forest. LOWER—Looking easterly showing long embankment slopes where junction occurs between Crystal Lake Highway and Angeles Crest Highway. Completed Angeles Highway to left. Crystal Lake Road under construction, to right.

short time he served in the Santa Barbara National Forest, and then in 1929 was appointed forest supervisor for the Angeles National Forest. In this capacity he has watched the Angeles Crest Highway grow and develop since initial construction was first started.

The creation of Angeles National Forest dates back to congressional action in 1891, followed by official proclamation of President Benjamin Harrison in 1892. The area was first called "San Gabriel Timberland Reserve." Then in 1908 the name was changed to Angeles National Forest.

One of the points of interest on the Angeles Crest Highway is Newcomb's Ranch located just beyond Chilao Camp grounds about midway between La Canada and Big Pines. This ranch is 160 acres in extent, homesteaded in 1878 by Louis Newcomb. This is the only privately owned land on the Angeles Crest Highway within the forest boundary. Newcomb was one of the pioneers whose knowledge of the back country was officially recognized by his appointment in 1898 as one of the first forest rangers by the newly organized National Timberland Reserve.

Story of Forest

The Angeles National Forest consists of some 700,000 acres of mountains, canyons and forest lands. The people of this area have always been very appreciative of the recreational facilities offered by the U. S. Forest Service. W. W. Robinson, in his "The Story of the Angeles National Forest," as published in 1946 by the Title Insurance and Trust Company of Los Angeles, described the situation as follows:

"The people of the towns and valleys of Los Angeles County have always gone to the San Gabriel Mountains for recreation.

"Before the creation of the forest reserve, however, they got little farther than the ferny dells and the paddle pools at the mouths of canyons. With the building of trails and dirt roads under ranger supervision, the people began to learn more about the playground that lay beyond the western fringes.

"Today, paved highways and automobiles carry 'the people'—thousands of them—into the vast interior of the Angeles National Forest and make them acquainted with its endless miles of deep canyons, its sharp peaks, its chaparral-covered or pine-studded slopes and its rolling, timbered areas. They introduce them to a world of spectacular vistas, swiftly changing views, mountainsides smoking in mist or shimmering in the sun, valleys of dark shadow or hilltops tapestried in

6

green. During 1945, visitors to the forest numbered 1,310,000. The forest caters to the people. There is a supervisor of recreation on the forest supervisor's staff, and every ranger has 'recreational' activities second in importance only to fire prevention.

Camping Grounds

"Charlton Flats, with its stand of ponderosa pine, incense cedar and bigcone spruce, is, under forest supervision, a paradise for the Sunday picnicker. This place was once the goal of the sweating three-day hiker. Now it is the end of a quick drive from Los Angeles for father, mother and the children, who arrive spick and span with twice too much lunch. The ground is soft with pine needles and the air is fresh with pine scent.

"At Chilao, a little farther on, are camping grounds for those who like to go to sleep with the whisper of the pines in their ears. There are trailer units, too, as well as a corral for the horses of those who ride through on the old Sturtevant Trail from Sierra Madre. Chilao, when snow covered, has slopes that are good for safe and sane sledding.

"The same Angeles Crest Highway that introduces the people of Southern California to the beauties and pleasures of Charlton Flats, Chilao and other play areas, carries them on to Mt. Waterman and the joys of winter tobogganing and skiing. A chair lift takes the skier from the highway level at 7,000 feet to near the summit at 8,000 feet, giving him a thrilling view and a tug at the pit of his stomach. On the mountain top are a thousand acres of open, rolling slopes and two supplementary tow ropes. To this land of shining snow comes the parade of those wearing ski pants, windbreakers and many-hued shirts, the people who use strange words like 'slalom' and 'crouch' and 'telemark.'

Scope of Work Increased

"In due time this same highway will be extended to the Big Pines recreational area which is under the jurisdiction of the Valyermo Ranger Station. Big Pines is now reached from the desert side of the Angeles Forest by way of Mint Canyon, or by way

Mt. Waterman Ski Lift on Angeles Crest Highway

of Cajon Pass and Wrightwood. In winter it has been visited on Sundays by 20,000 people—devotees of skating, sledding and skiing. The ski tow on Table Mountain, overlooking the area, has a vertical rise of 500 feet. Skiers get a startling desert view from Table Mountain at Holiday Hill and Baden-Powell—black pines against blue-white. Blue Ridge, also of this area, has ski-heaven slopes."

Since Mr. Robinson wrote about the Angeles National Forest in 1946, the U. S. Forest Service has greatly increased the scope of its activities. As of 1955, Mendenhall reports that the number of yearly visitors has increased to 1,700,000. There are also now in use at Holiday Hill and Kratka Ridge, additional areas where winter visitors can enjoy the sport of skiing. Additional camp ground facilities along the Angeles Crest Highway are being provided. There will soon be in operation on the newly opened section between Cedar Springs and Blue Ridge, three additional picnic areas with tables and cooking facilities located at Pine Hollow, White Thorn, and Lodgepole.

Beautiful Country

In 1934, Spencer V. Cortelyou, then District Engineer and later Assistant State Highway Engineer, in charge of District VII until his retirement in 1949, in describing the Angeles Crest

Highway, wrote in *California Highways and Public Works:*

"As the ascent is made, a beautiful vista is unfolded. From certain prominent points a view can be had of Los Angeles, Pasadena, Glendale and many other cities and small towns in the flatter country below. On exceptionally clear days the ocean and Catalina Island can also be seen.

"Care was used in planning the construction of this road to avoid making high cut or fill slopes which could be seen from the valley. The beauty of the mountain slopes in the vicinity of Los Angeles (particularly north of Hollywood and Beverly Hills) has been destroyed in many cases by the construction of subdivision streets and roads making unsightly gashes in the forest cover. To avoid these long fill slopes at exposed places, the excess material was hauled farther into the mountains and deposited out of view to make parking places and picnic grounds.

Striking Scenic Views

"Wherever possible, in the construction of this highway, the scenic points have been graded so as to form areas where cars can park overlooking the valley below."

In addition to the scenes mentioned by Cortelyou, of the Los Angeles coastal plain, there are many striking views of the San Gabriel Mountains, Mohave Desert, and the distant Sierra Nevada Mountains as one crosses Cloudburst Summit at 7,000 feet, and Dawson Saddle nearly 8,000 feet in elevation.

The construction on the Angeles Crest Highway was handled as four separate and distinct operations which however often overlapped each other, both as to sections of the Angeles Crest Highway being worked on, and with respect to the time element. The first construction by regular state highway contracts was in 1929 and extended from La Canada four miles northerly. Then, two day labor camps, Camp D and Camp K, were established during 1930-33 as a relief measure to alleviate the unemployment situation, especially for transient homeless men in the City of Los Angeles and vicinity. This work consisted of grading pioneer roads, clearing and grubbing, and erosion control. Then in 1930 to 1934, state highway contracts completed the construction from La Canada to Red Box.

The next phase of construction was a group of eight contracts, from 1934 to 1950, carried out by the U. S. Bureau of Public Roads and financed from National Forest Highway Funds.

Pioneers of Angeles Crest project—1. L. A. McCandless (1928-1942); 2. H. L. Waste (1930-1945); 3. H. D. Johnson (1947-); 4. W. B. Stout (1929-); 5. H. L. Leventon (1928-1937); 6. A. N. Lund (1922-1931); 7. B. H. Henry (1930-1947); 8. R. C. McFarland (1930-); 9. G. D. Grant (1921-1925); 10. H. F. Caton (1947-); 11. Ed Rawson (1919-1947); 12. W. B. Albertson (1915-1947); 13. R. W. Brown (in foreground) (1918-1926)

These expenditures, according to Bureau of Public Roads records, totaled $1,308,381 and the construction work was on various sections of the Angeles Crest Highway between Red Box and Big Pines.

State and U. S. Funds

Simultaneously with this work being carried on by the U. S. Bureau of Public Roads, the State Division of Highways through day labor work orders financed from funds budgeted by the California Highway Commission extending over the years 1935 through 1956, excepting during the war years, carried out construction work utilizing honor camp labor. This was done in cooperation with the State Department of Corrections. The work conducted by Honor Camp 31, Honor Camp 35, and Honor Camp 37, completed all the remaining construction between Red Box and Big Pines that was not completed by the U. S. Bureau of Public Roads contracts.

During the years 1930 through 1956, the California Highway Commission has made 22 allocations of funds totaling $6,336,205 for day labor work on the Angeles Crest Highway.

The earlier camps, Camp "D" and Camp "K," were operated during the years 1930-33 on the section of the Angeles Crest Highway between La Canada and Red Box, and were largely for the purpose of providing worthwhile work to relieve the unemployment then existing in the Los Angeles area. The superintendent in charge of Camp "D" was A. N. George, and the resident engineer was M. L. Bauders. For Camp "K," C. C. Rossi was superintendent, William Axtman was his assistant, and M. L. Bauders was resident engineer.

Operations of Camps

Later the three honor camps previously referred to were established to utilize prison labor as supplied by the State Department of Corrections. Camp 31, located three miles east of Red Box, was put into operation in August of 1935 with Benjamin H. Henry as superintendent and M. L. Bauders as resident engineer. In 1937, this camp was moved to a new location near Newcomb's Ranch and called Camp 35. The location was

again changed in 1939 to Cedar Springs and was known as Camp 37. Honor Camp 37 remained in operation until it was closed down in September 1942 when the World War II situation became acute and shortages of critical material developed. Operations were resumed in June, 1946, the camp being reopened with William E. Melcher and Frank B. Cressy, who had just returned from a tour of duty with the U. S. Navy, in charge. Ben Henry resumed his old post as superintendent, taking over from Frank Cressy when the latter was promoted to the position of district construction engineer for District VII. In 1948, when Ben Henry accepted an assignment in the District VII office, Harry D. Johnson became superintendent of Camp 37, and has been continuously in charge up to the present time.

During the periods of day labor camp operation many engineers on the District VII staff had assignments as resident engineers on this work. Among these were: M. L. Bauders, Eugene Burge, W. J. Calvin, Ralph Chase, Ray De Groff, W. D. Eaton, G. E. Farnsworth, E. W. Fehsenfeld, K. M. Fenwick, J. M. Lackey, W. E. Melcher, F. A. Read, P. R. Reed, L. F. Phillips, and H. A. Wildy.

During the period of construction on the Angeles Crest Highway the work was successively under supervision of District VII Construction Engineers L. M. Ransom, A. N. George, F. B. Cressy, E. G. Bower, and Bruce A. Gentry. During the construction period, general supervision was the responsibility of District Engineers S. V. Cortelyou (later promoted to Assistant State Highway Engineer), P. O. Harding (later promoted to Assistant State Highway Engineer), M. E. Cessna, W. L. Fahey, George Langsner, and Lyman R. Gillis. General supervision is now exercised by Assistant State Highway Engineer Edward T. Telford, District VII.

Rehabilitation Program

During the year 1948 the *San Francisco News* reprinted a series of articles on California state prisons and the problems of organization and operation that faced the State Department of Corrections. In this reprint edition

the editor of the *San Francisco News* prefaced the issue as follows:

"What happens after sentence? Where does the prisoner go? What kind of treatment does he get? What kind of food does he eat? Where does he sleep? What work, if any, does he do? What interest have you, the taxpayer, 'the people of California,' in this prisoner? Do you care, for that matter, whether he comes back alive to the responsibilities of citizenship or with senses deadened to anything but crime?

"You should care, because he is an expensive 'guest' while in prison; and potentially an expensive ex-criminal, unregenerate and bent upon more expensive crimes upon release; or, having served his term in custody, is a new person, with a new outlook upon life, with new determination to become a useful member of society.

"It was to inquire into these alternatives, this cost of custody, confirmation in crime, or rehabilitation of the prisoners of the State, that Al Ostrow, reporter, and Herman C. Bryant, head photographer for *The News*, toured the prisons of California, examined every cell, every shop, every yard, every infirmary. They saw everything.

S. F. News Articles

"What they found is that California is conducting the most extensive and progressive experiment in reclaiming human beings, in straightening out distorted minds, in rehabilitating men and women to become useful citizens ever attempted in the history of penology.

"The story was told in a series of articles, with pictures, and is reprinted here. The story is entitled, 'Send 'Em Back Alive!' "

In his story Ostrow has considerable to say about State Highway Honor Camps. In discussing the operation and accomplishments of Camp 37 on the Angeles Crest Highway, he said:

"There was enough dynamite in the cache to rip open the seams of both Folsom and San Quentin prisons, and the men handling it were convicts.

"But Harry Johnson, the rugged State Highway Department Engineer in charge of the Angeles Crest road camp at Cedar Springs, was not apprehensive.

" 'We're too busy building a highway through mighty rough country to worry about such things,' he confided.

"The camp is 6,800 feet above sea level, amid the scenic splendor of Angeles National Forest, not far from the famous Mt. Wilson Observatory. This is the type of upland grandeur that inspired the inscription on the State Office Building in Sacramento: 'Bring me men to match my mountains.'

Few Escapes From Camps

"Freedom seems particularly precious in the wide open vistas of the Coast Range, where bald rocks tower boldly above the timber line and great trees sway gently in the embrace of pine-flavored breezes. A man with a number who has spent several years

and Public Works   9

These old photos show snow conditions at Angeles Crest Road Camp No. 37 in Los Angeles County. UPPER LEFT AND RIGHT—A 12-foot depth of snow is indicated by views of tank in center of each photograph. LEFT—Before heavy snowfall. RIGHT—After heavy snowfall with top of tank just Visible. CENTER LEFT—Free family quarters near Camp 37. CENTER RIGHT—Camp equipment shop. LOWER LEFT—Removing snow from road through camp. LOWER RIGHT—Clearing snow to office entrance.

behind prison bars might easily become intoxicated by the fresh atmosphere and decide to take a deep draught of liberty.

"It's easy to escape from Angeles Crest—but few men do. They have too much to lose by running away, and a lot to gain by staying.

"There are no armed guards and no guns at Angeles Crest. The custodial force consists of two officers whose job, aside from the nose counting, is about the same as that of policemen in any isolated construction camp. Their job is made easier—or perhaps harder—by the fact that intoxicating liquor and gambling are banned.

"The prisoners work side by side with 25 foremen employed by the Highway Department. They blast tunnels through the mountains, crush rocks, build culverts, pour concrete, clear underbrush, cut timber, and scale the crags to knock loose projections which might eventually fall and block the highway.

"The prisoners expect to stay only six months to two years each. All of them are that close to parole.

Careful Selection of Workers

"Carefully selected from the inmate population of the California Institution for Men at Chino, most are volunteers eager to get out of confinement and into the bodybuilding outdoors, as well as to save up some money before their release.

"The punishment for breaking the rules at Angeles Crest is immediate return to Chino. Men who violate the confidence of the classification committee which assigned them to the camp by running away lose their parole dates and face an additional penalty of a year to life at San Quentin or Folsom for escaping from a state prison.

"The road camps are part of the program of the State Department of Corrections designed to send men out of prison better prepared for normal social life than when the gates closed behind them; to 'send them back alive.'

"The number of men who can be sent to the camps is rigidly limited by security considerations. There wouldn't be much point in sending a lot of prisoners whose records indicate they would very likely attempt to escape from the camps as they are presently run. That would only make trouble for the camp officials, and also for the men—since statistics show that close to 99 percent of America's escaped convicts are recaptured."

Legislation in 1915

For many years while he was assistant construction engineer on the Sacramento headquarters staff, George A. Tilton, Jr. had the responsibility of general supervision over all honor camps operated by the State Department of Corrections and the State Division of Highways. Published shortly after his death, George Tilton's book, *Prison Road Camps*, based on a series of articles he had written in *Califor-* *nia Highways and Public Works*, fully covered the history and legislation behind this activity as well as detailing the accomplishments.

The employment of prison labor for the construction of state highways in California was first advocated in a bill introduced in the 1915 Legislature by Assemblyman B. B. Meek of Butte County, who later held the office of Director of Public Works from 1927 to 1931. This bill was enacted into law and became the basis for establishment during that year of honor camps in various locations throughout the State. As honor camp operations employing prisoners on highway work proceeded, the need for changes in the law was recognized, and the original legislation was modified by statutes of 1923, 1935, 1941 and 1947. The law now provides that inmates shall be paid a daily wage of $3.50, from which are deducted necessary expenses. The law also provides that nonconvict personnel be assigned to supervisory positions and to all jobs requiring skilled labor, such as shovel operators and truck drivers. Prisoners are not automatically assigned to highway work in the honor camps; they must first make a voluntary request and meet certain minimum requirements to become eligible. There are far more applicants for service in the honor camps than there are jobs to be filled. As George Tilton expressed it:

Eligibles Eager to Work

"There is probably no greater pleasurable anticipation in the gamut of human emotions than the prospect of departing prison environment after years of close confinement. Having once reached the eligible list, the inmate eagerly awaits the time he is to be sent to a camp. Immediately prior to prison departure, he is interviewed personally by a prison official and told that he is being placed on his honor to obey all camp rules, and that he is expected to work at any tasks assigned to him.

"Upon arrival in camp, new inmates are promptly assigned to comfortable quarters and acquainted with camp routine and rules by the senior camp supervisor responsible for their custody. The day following arrival in camp, the prisoner comes in active contact with state highway personnel for the first time, and the relative freedom of an outdoor life."

Honor Camp 37, with respect to responsibility for the inmates, is under the jurisdiction of the Superintendent of the California Institute for Men near Chino, that is operated by the State Department of Corrections. One of the main duties of the honor camp superintendent is to maintain close contact and harmonious cooperative relations with the camp supervisors and correctional officers of the State Department of Corrections. The operations of Honor Camp No. 37 on the Angeles Crest Highway work have proven over the years that the productiveness of inmate labor is comparable to that of free labor.

Withycombe Report

Assistant State Highway Engineer Earl Withycombe, in submitting his annual progress report on honor camp projects as of June 30, 1956, comments as follows:

"The Department of Corrections is responsible for inmate welfare in the camps. The Department of Public Works pays to the Department of Corrections $3.50 per inmate day on a day's worked basis. The Department of Corrections in turn feeds, clothes and pays the inmate $15 per month on a six-day week basis, or $18 per month on a seven-day week basis.

"During the last fiscal year all major grading operations were completed on the final 16 miles of the Angeles Crest Highway, Road VII-LA-61-C,D between the camp and Blue Ridge, 2.1 miles westerly of Big Pines.

"Activities during the spring of 1956 were concentrated on the cleanup of minor slides and sloughs into the gutter which was performed with rented equipment. The power shovel was utilized in removing a major slide which had occurred during the winter and completing some rock excavation.

"Fine grading operations were completed and selected material was placed on the roadbed for bituminous surfacing operations to be performed by contract during the summer.

"Unusually good weather conditions also permitted continuation of grading operations on the Crystal Lake Road, VII-LA-62-B for 1.2 miles southerly from the intersection with Route 61 at Islip Saddle. This section requires extensive drilling and blasting operations as the location is generally in rock formation.

"A total of 452,658 cubic yards of excavation were moved this year at an average cost of $1.09 per cubic yard. To date a total of 4,179,929 cubic yards have been moved at an average cost of $0.76 per cubic yard.

"The inmate quota of this camp is 100 men, but population varies during the year depending on the weather. The average inmate population was 79 for the year, the lower figures during the winter months pulling down the average. This spring the district requested an increase to 114 men because of favorable working conditions.

"During the year H. D. Johnson was superintendent, W. E. Wescott, Sr., was field office assistant and E. F. Burge was resident engineer."

Erosion Control

Meldon L. Bauders, now District VII City and County Cooperative Projects Engineer, was resident engineer at various times on Angeles Crest Highway construction between 1929 and 1939. During this period, one of the chief problems was erosion control. Mel Bauders states that during the Angeles Crest construction Charles J. Kraebel, senior silviculturist for the U. S. Department of Agriculture, Forest Service, spent considerable time on the job, to the end that adequate erosion control features could be worked out during construction, explaining the whys and wherefores of erosion control, and personally put on practical demonstrations to show how the work should be done, even to seeding of slopes. In 1935 Kraebel's handbook was published, entitled *Erosion Control on Mountain Roads*. In this book many references are made to the Angeles Crest Highway, and Kraebel's grasp of his subject is well shown by the following excerpts:

"The rapid increase of motor traffic into the mountainous parts of California during recent years has compelled the building of many new high-standard roads and the reconstruction of old roads along modern lines. Much of this traffic is pleasure bent, and the new roads are devoted largely to the opening of recreational areas, particularly in the national forests and national parks. That these roads often disfigure the very charms they are intended to reveal is one of the unfortunate results of the high standards on which they are built and the rugged topography which they necessarily traverse. Another result, even more serious from the economic viewpoint, is the long train of damages from erosion beyond the rights of way for which the new roads are almost invariably though by no means unavoidably responsible.

Battle With Nature

"No sooner is a new road constructed than the forces of nature are at work to destroy it. Water and wind, cold and heat, and the constant pull of gravity, all combine to break up the road surface, tear down the fills, and round off the squared edges of shoulder berms and back slopes—in short, to eradicate the entire road and cause the area occupied by it to revert to the wild state. On newly improved roads the wear by traffic is unimportant compared with the work of these natural forces, and of these forces the most powerful by far is water.

UPPER—Looking easterly along Angeles Crest Highway approaching Big Pines recreational area, showing side of road development for motorists who wish to park off the highway. LOWER—Completed Angeles Crest Highway with centerline marking for traffic striping at Blue Ridge Summit, three miles westerly of Big Pines recreational area.

"The direct cause of all this damage is, of course, the movement of enormous quantities of soil and rock which are loosened during construction and started on a suddenly accelerated descent to the sea. In most sections of California a great part of this displaced material finds its way almost immediately into stream channels, reservoirs, water-spreading grounds, and irrigation works. The damage to water supplies created by such deposits has in some localities reached serious proportions. Recreational values are similarly hard hit, in the extermination of fish in pools filled by the eroded silt and sand, in the destruction of camp grounds, in the despoliation of streamside beauty by mud and boulder flows, and in damage to roads and bridges."

Erosion Work Important

H. Dana Bowers, supervising Landscape Architect for the State Division of Highways, and Kraebel conferred innumerable times in working out the erosion control features to incorporate in the Angeles Crest Highway construction work, to the end that damage from storm water flow would be kept to a minimum. Regarding this feature of the Angeles Crest Highway construction, Dana Bowers has this to say:

"Erosion control methods have been considerably simplified and perfected since the 'early' days of 1935. At that time we were just becoming erosion conscious, a consciousness that was accelerated by the ever-increasing soil losses occurring on higher cut slopes resulting from the demand for improved alignment and grades.

"For many years erosion control was a period of trial and error, and almost any-

body's idea was given a trial. In retrospect it is now somewhat amusing to review the many approaches to the problem. Practically everything was done in an effort to protect the raw slope surfaces, except the single natural method—the use of grass. Barriers of every kind and description, from steel to fish netting, were employed, all of which required hand labor to install. In those days hand labor was plentiful and cheap, but as the depression eased off and good times and high prices arrived, it became the popular thought of the day to avail ourselves of more economical methods.

"Consequently, because of economics, plus observation and analysis of the various erosion control methods that had been installed, we finally arrived at the present method we are using which involves the use of straw, cereal grain and other seeds, fertilizer, and for compaction a modified type

of sheep's foot roller. We call this method our Type "C" stabilization. We also found that compaction of the slope surface into which straw had been incorporated was of paramount importance. Water more slowly penetrates a hard surface, therefore reducing saturation and slump. The straw imbedded into the surface serves the same purpose as the grass root mat that would form as the season progressed. In short, we are now merely imitating, on a speeded up schedule, nature's age-old method that can be observed on every hillside, but it took us years to see it!"

Many passing references have been made in this story to the U. S. Bureau of Public Roads and the part its personnel played in bringing to consum-

mation the completed Angeles Crest Highway. As shown on the accompanying tabulation, the U. S. Bureau of Public Roads carried out eight separate construction contracts, building 16 miles of the Angeles Crest Highway at a cost of approximately $1,-300,000.

The location engineering for the Angeles Crest Highway between Red Box and Big Pines was carried out by H. A. Alderton and Henry A. Garber, location engineers for the U. S. Bureau of Public Roads. H. A. Alderton is now Principal Highway Engineer in the U. S. Bureau of Public Roads District Office in Sacramento.

The operations by the U. S. Bureau of Public Roads were under the general direction of the Division Engineer in San Francisco, Charles C. Morris, until 1946. Since 1946 and to date, the operations have been under the general direction of the District Engineer in Sacramento, E. C. Brown.

Los Angeles County has a big stake in the Angeles Crest Highway. Until a few years ago, the Los Angeles County Department of Parks and Recreation operated the Big Pines County Park at the easterly end of the Angeles Crest Highway. This area has now been returned to the jurisdiction of the U. S. Forest Service as a part of its recreational activities in the Angeles National Forest.

In Mt. Wilson Area

In 1934 the U. S. Bureau of Public Roads with some $500,000 of U. S. Forest Road money completed a contract for five miles of scenic highway connecting Mt. Wilson with the Angeles Crest Highway at Red Box. This was a very important highway because it gave the people of California easy access by automobile, via the already completed portion of Angeles Crest Highway to Red Box, to the hotel and Carnegie Institute Observatories on top of Mt. Wilson. It superseded an old single-lane steep and curving wagon road on the south slope of Mt. Wilson, known as "The Toll Road." During later years the top of Mt. Wilson has taken on an industrial aspect due to the installation of television transmission towers atop the mountain. Had there not been the Angeles Crest Highway and the Los

Angeles County maintained road from Red Box to Mt. Wilson, the problems of making and maintaining these television transmitting installations might have proven insurmountable.

Another important project developed by the Los Angeles County Road Department is the Angeles Forest Highway northerly to Vincent that connects with the Angeles Crest Highway at Clear Water Canyon about four miles from La Canada. This has proven to be a very important additional highway facility for motorists traveling between the Palmdale area of Antelope Valley and the Pasadena-Los Angeles area.

New Recreation Areas

In the April 9, 1956, issue of the *Los Angeles Mirror-News*, Staff Writer Charles Ridgway, in describing construction work on the Angeles Crest Highway, in part writes as follows:

"No wide freeway this—just a two-lane rock-littered trail not quite ready for a coat of asphalt. But when the State Highway Commission recently appropriated a final $180,000 for paving this most rugged of mountain roads, the realization of a 30-year dream was in sight. The highway will open vast new recreation areas. Exciting ski slopes will bring Wrightwood and Big Pines Park 27 miles closer to Los Angeles and provide a new outlet to the desert.

"Resident Engineer Eugene Burge can remember back to 1928 when he helped survey for the beginning of Angeles Crest Highway at La Canada. During the 1930's the road construction wound its way past Lookout Mountain, through Red Box Gap around Mt. Wilson, across Barley Flat to Mt. Waterman and Kratka Ridge. Except for a turnoff over Angeles Forest Highway to Palmdale, it was a 40-mile road to nowhere.

"It was in 1946 before engineers returned to open a construction camp at Cedar Springs and begin picking away at those last 16 miles. With them came 'trusties' from Chino Prison, men who thought they had it tough for a few years until they came up against the mountains.

"'Just put a man on a jackhammer for about a week if you want to see the meanness leave him,' advises one supervisor. Through the years the prisoners—50 to 100 at a time—have scraped away at the rocks under the supervision of 30 Division of Highway employees. Almost without exception, the Chino men have come away better citizens because of their experience.

Camp Has Own School

"And the men who watch over them wouldn't trade their job for any other.

About 35 families of supervisors and other 'free' workers live in a separate camp about a mile from the prisoners' barracks. The camp's one-room school has eight students. Camp Superintendent Harry Johnson has been on the job since it started in 1946. Johnson is eligible for retirement but is waiting until the job is finished. Why does it take so long? Take a look back over what has already been done. There are two tunnels through Mt. Williamson totaling more than 1,000 feet in length. There's a huge cut across the face of sheer cliffs near Islip Saddle. It's only one of many as the road winds up to a summit of nearly 8,000 feet at Mt. Baden-Powell.

"'At first,' explains Frank Cressy, superintendent of construction for Division of Highways District VII, 'it's almost all hard work. When the path is wide enough, bulldozers move in to help, but every yard of the way has to be blasted with dynamite. You begin at the top, blow the rocks loose, then roll the debris down into the canyon 400 or 500 feet below. The camp uses nearly 1,000 pounds of dynamite every day.'

"Cressy this week conducted a tour over the road for L. R. Gillis, new district engineer for construction in Los Angeles, Orange and Ventura Counties. Even for Gillis, it was hard to believe the huge rock piles leaning against the mountain sides were man-made. It looks like dangerous work and it is. Workers must constantly watch for rocks tumbling from above. Bulldozers crawl along the edge tipping dangerously as they push still more dirt and rocks into the canyons. And there is a sense of pioneering adventure, breaking through a wilderness to bring it within reach of civilization."

As fast as sections of the Angeles Crest Highway have been completed and the traveled way oil-treated, these sections were opened to public traffic, and from that time forth became the responsibility of the District Maintenance Department.

Maintenance Department

The first section that was opened was 2½ miles, extending from La Canada into the Angeles National Forest. This occurred in the latter part of 1931 when I. S. Voorhees was the district maintenance engineer. Subsequently, other units as completed were turned over to the Maintenance Department, until 38 miles were in use, taking traffic as far as Cedar Springs. Succeeding Voorhees as maintenance engineer was W. L. Fahey, who was promoted to district engineer in 1950 and who retired from state service November, 1955. W. D. Sedgwick succeeded Fahey as assistant district engineer, and maintenance work on

14

UPPER LEFT—Looking northeasterly along Angeles Crest Highway at Cloudburst Summit, entering the Mt. Waterman winter sports area. UPPER RIGHT—View looking westerly from Cloudburst Summit, elevation 7,000 feet, showing Angeles Crest Highway winding through the forest. CENTER—View from location 10 miles northeasterly of La Canada showing the Angeles Crest Highway along the side of the mountains approaching Red Box, background right. Road to Switzer's Camp showing in foreground. LOWER LEFT—View of completed Angeles Crest Highway six miles northeast from La Canada at the 3,000-foot elevation. LOWER RIGHT—Angeles Crest Highway where it enters south boundary of Angeles National Forest. Note crib wall supporting roadbed, center left.

UPPER—Ribbon cutting by Director of Public Works Frank B. Durkee. **Left to right:** Roger Jessup, Supervisor, Los Angeles County; Victor Jory, Master of Ceremonies; Fred Dickson, Superintendent, California Institute for Men, Chino; Durkee; G. T. McCoy, State Highway Engineer; Harrison R. Baker, former member of California Highway Commission; S. Wesley Break, Chairman, Board of Supervisors, San Bernardino County; Elmer Wilson, Chairman, Convention and Tourist Committee, Pasadena Chamber of Commerce; John Anson Ford, Supervisor, Los Angeles County. LOWER—Honor Camp 37 cottages for State Division of Highways employees. The building at left is the schoolhouse operated by the Pasadena City School District.

the Angeles Crest Highway is now part of his responsibilities.

The maintenance crews who presently maintain the road from the junction of Foothill Boulevard in La Canada to its temporary terminus at Cedar Springs, work out of the La Crescenta and Chilao Maintenance Stations.

During the summer months of May to September, the maintenance of the roadway is of a general nature typical of many mountain roads. The traveled way surfacing is patched where necessary to maintain a smooth, hazard-free surface. The shoulders and ditches are graded and kept clean of slough and other debris. Guard rails, sight posts and culvert markers are painted, restenciled and replaced as necessary.

A large part of the Angeles Crest Highway is constructed along steep side hills and through ridges where slopes are acted upon by wind, rain and snow. To keep the road safe during heavy rains, maintenance trucks equipped with rock plows patrol the Angeles Crest Highway constantly. Frequently between storms crews gather up slide material with skip loaders, and trucks haul it to disposal areas. Unlike many other locations in the State, slide material and rocks cannot be bladed or dumped in any convenient gully or canyon. Every effort must be exercised to avoid unsightly spoil banks, and slide material must be hauled to specifically designated locations where the disposal will not be unsightly.

For many winters the Angeles Crest Highway has been kept open from La Canada to Cedar Springs. This is the nearest snow country for winter sports in the Los Angeles area. One of the big problems without ready solution is traffic control during snow removal operations. Several times in the past, the number of vehicles attempting to reach winter sports resorts has been so great that the snow plows could not operate and motorists

at the resorts could not leave. On some of these occasions it became necessary to close the highway temporarily to incoming traffic until the roadway could be cleared.

CONSTRUCTION CONTRACTS CARRIED OUT BY STATE

Description	Date	Contractor	Total cost	Resident engineer
La Canada to 2½ mi. north—grading	8-14-29	H. W. Rohl Co.	$270,063	A. N. George
Bridge across La Canada Canyon	12- 9-29	Whipple Eng. Co.	35,167	R. W. Van Sfan
2½ mi. north La Canada to 4 mi. north—grading	1-27-30	T. M. Morgan Paving Co.	309,712	A. N. George
La Canada to 2½ mi. north—oiling	12- 1-30	Chas. A. Ladeveze	6,366	A. N. George
4 mi. north La Canada to Colby C. —grading	4-15-31	T. M. Morgan Paving Co.	452,747	M. L. Bauders
Bridge across Fern Canyon	8-13-31	Houghton and Anderson	31,470	R. W. Van Sfan
At La Canada—oiling	10- 6-31	Square Oil Co.	2,248	A. I. Bird
Between Colby and Mt. Wilson road—grading	9-20-33	Jahn and Bressi Const. Co.	357,122	C. P. Montgomery
Between Cedar Springs and Blue Ridge—oiling	7-12-56	E. C. Young	135,219	F. W. Luchsinger
			$1,600,114	

CONSTRUCTION CONTRACTS BY U. S. BUREAU OF PUBLIC ROADS

Location	Cost	Type of work	Dates	Res. Engr.
Red Box to 1.367 miles east	$131,359	Grading and drainage	1-27-37 7- 3-37	E. E. Hopson
4.272 miles to 9.243 miles east of Red Box	300,463	Grading and drainage	9-12-35 7- 3-37	H. Booth
9.243 miles to 12.5 miles east of Red Box	142,700	Grading and drainage	5-17-37 10-11-37	E. E. Hopson
18.96 miles to 21.02 miles east of Red Box	133,861	Grading and drainage	5- 1-39 12- 8-39	B. H. McCain
21.02 miles to 22.75 miles east of Red Box	142,841	Grading and drainage	9- 8-39 8-22-40	B. H. McCain
Red Box to 12½ miles east	36,346	Road mix surfacing	6-15-39 10-17-39	B. H. McCain
9.15 miles to 10.72 miles east of Islip Saddle	145,716	Grading and drainage	5-14-34 7-12-35	Roy Schmidt
13.79 miles to 15.90 miles east of Islip Saddle	275,095	Grading, drainage and road mix surfacing	1950	C. F. Slorm
	$1,308,381			

The California Highway Patrol renders splendid cooperation, assigning extra men and patrol cars to the area on weekends when the snow sport travel is the heaviest.

· DRIVER ALERTNESS

Motorists should be aware that the most frequent type of accidents on freeways are rear-end and sideswipe collisions, warns the California State Automobile Association.

The AAA motorists' organization points out that freeways could be made even safer than they are if the number of rear-end and same-direction accidents on these controlled access traffic ways could be reduced.

Alertness by drivers can do much toward accomplishing this reduction.

Freeway drivers, therefore, should be particularly heedful of sudden changes in speed, following too close, passing, lane-changing, and cutting in.

and Public Works

17

During the calendar year of 1955 there was a total of 65 fatal accidents, resulting in 81 fatalities, on the 208.22 miles of operating full freeways. Based on 3,061,722,000 vehicle miles of operation, the 1955 fatality rate, full freeway, rural and urban, was 2.65 fatalities per 100 million vehicle miles. This represents a sharp increase from the very favorable rate of 1.92 fatalities per 100 million vehicle miles experienced in 1954.

(The over-all fatality rate for rural state highways in California in 1955 was 8.36 per 100 million vehicle miles.)

Chart No. I shows the fatality rates on California full freeways, by years, 1941 through 1955. It may be noted that, although this graph centers about the area representing rates of 2.0 to 2.5, there has been considerable fluctuation in the rate for the individual years. In this respect it may be noted that the 2.65 is not the highest rate of record, nor is the 1954 rate of 1.92 the lowest rate. A study of cyclic fluctuation in this graph indicates a reasonable chance for the rate to again drop in the future.

Expanding Fatalities

The year 1955 was a year of expanding fatalities nationwide. Since March of 1955, each month has shown an increase over the numbers killed for the corresponding month of the prior year on a national basis. It may well be noted that the two major facilities which most closely approached California freeways' fatality rate for 1954 experienced substantial increase in 1955. The fatality rate on the New York State Throughway increased from 2.44 in 1954 to 2.83 in 1955, and the New Jersey Turnpike increased from 2.47 in 1954 to 2.76 in 1955. In spite of the substantial increase in the California rates, it is noted that California's 1955 freeway fatality rate is again lower than these two comparable type eastern facilities.

CALIFORNIA FREEWAYS
Fatality Rates by Years 1941 through 1955

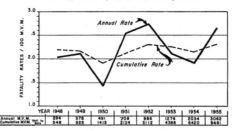

In addition to the nationwide upswing, there is another important factor involved in California's increased rate. This factor is the expanding mileage of rural full freeways. Whereas, prior records represented primarily urban freeways, the 1955 record is based on 109 miles of rural as compared to 99 miles of urban freeways. The effects of higher speed on rural freeways and their inclusion in mileage subjected to a higher percentage of long-distance travel, resulted in a fatality rate (rural only) of 3.13 fatalities per 100 million vehicle miles as compared to a rate of 2.41 for the urban portion of the system. The building of rural freeways, which is currently progressing at a faster rate than the construction of urban freeways, is expected to exert an increasing upward influence on the basic composite fatality rate.

Details of 1955 Freeway Fatal Accidents

Table I, showing basic data on 1955 freeway fatalities, is significant primarily in the fact that 12 of the 65 fatal accidents were pedestrian accidents involving 13 of the 81 persons killed. This percentage is unduly high considering freeways are fenced and posted for "Motor Vehicles Only." It also represents an extreme increase from 1954 when there were only two pedestrian fatalities on full freeways. In 11 of these accidents causing 11 deaths the pedestrians were on the freeway in violation of the law. Keeping hitchhikers and other pedestrians off the full freeways is an enforcement problem. The increase in number of pedestrian fatalities in 1955 is responsible for a substantial part of the increase in the fatality rate over 1954.

Lighting

Table I also shows light conditions under which freeway fatal accidents occurred in 1955. It may be noted that only 28 percent of the fatal accidents occurred during daylight hours with 72 percent occurring during the hours of darkness. Pedestrian accidents were similarly distributed with 75 percent of pedestrian accidents occurring during darkness. The period from 11 p.m. to 3 a.m., which involved only 5 percent of the vehicle miles, accounted for 34 percent of the fatal accidents on freeways.

18

TABLE I

BASIC DATA ON 1955 STATE-WIDE RURAL AND URBAN FULL FREEWAY FATALITIES

Item	
Number of fatal accidents	65
Persons killed	81
Persons injured in fatal accidents	61
Number of pedestrian accidents	12
Pedestrians killed	13
Total million vehicle miles	3,061.722
Fatalities/100 MVM	2.65

Item	No.	Percent of total
LIGHTING		
Daylight	18	28
Darkness	47	72
No artificial lighting	18	28
From 11 p.m. to 3 a.m.	22	34
Pedestrian accidents:		
Daylight	3	25
Darkness	9	75
No artificial lighting	6	50
WEATHER		
Cloudy or clear	60	92
Raining (1 foggy)	5	8
ELEMENT TYPES		
Single car accidents	40	62
Two or more car accidents	25	38
VEHICLE CONDITION		
No defects	52	80
Defects	2	3
Unknown	11	17
ROADWAY FEATURES		
Curved road	21	32
43 percent of single car accidents are on curved sections		
17 percent of two or more car accidents are on curved sections		
Straight road	43	66
Unclassified	1	2
Level grade	46	71
Up-grade	5	8
Down-grade	8	12
Unknown	7	11

Table I shows that 62 percent of the accidents involved a single car, as compared to 38 percent two or more car accidents. Vehicle condition is not an important factor as is specifically noted on only 3 percent of the fatal accidents.

Roadway Features

Under roadway features, also shown in Table I, the majority of accidents as expected occurred on straight road

---

TABLE II

TABULATION OF 1955 FREEWAY FATAL ACCIDENTS BY TYPE AND SEVERITY

Items studied	Approaching		Overtaking		Single vehicle		Total vehicles	
	No.	Percent of total	No.	Percent of total	No.	Percent of total	No.	Percent of all accidents
Accidents	9	14	16	24	40	62	65	100
Persons killed	18	22	20	25	43	53	81	100
Persons killed/accidents	2.0	...	1.25	...	1.1	...	1.2	...
Persons injured	28	46	19	31	21	34	61	100
Persons injured/accidents	3.11	...	1.2	...	0.5	...	0.9	...
Pedestrians killed	0	0	4	31	9	69	13	100

TABLE III

DRIVER CONDITION AND VIOLATIONS INVOLVED IN 1955 FREEWAY FATALITIES

Items studied	Approaching		Overtaking		Single vehicle		Total vehicles	
	No.	Percent of type	No.	Percent of type	No.	Percent of type	No.	Percent of all accidents
Driver condition								
H. B. D.	3	33	2	11	10	38	15	23
Normal	3	33	6	33	9	23	17	26
Sleepy	0	0	2	11	5	13	7	11
Unknown *	3	33	7	39	16	40	24	37
Epileptic	0	0	1	6	0	0	1	2
Causes								
Speed	4	40	4	22	22	55	30	46
Following too closely	0	0	3	17	0	0	3	5
Turning	0	0	4	22	2	5	6	9
Parking	0	0	1	67	0	0	1	2
Changing lanes	6	60	4	22	1	3	10	8

* Eleven additional accidents could reasonably be also H. B. D. due to statements of witnesses, time of accident and facts surrounding the accident.

(66 percent) and level grade (71 percent). More significant perhaps is that 32 percent of all fatal accidents and 43 percent of the single car fatal accidents occurred on curves. These percentages of fatal accidents on the relatively small percentage of curve alignment on California freeways should well refute the argument of those who advocate deliberate curvature to reduce monotony.

Fatalities by Type of Accident

Table II shows a breakdown of accidents and fatalities by basic accident types. It may again be seen that single vehicles accounted for 62 percent of the fatal accidents but only 53 percent of the number killed. Overtaking accidents accounted for 24 percent of the fatal accidents and 25 percent of the persons killed. Head-on type accidents, as might be expected, had by far the highest severity with 14 percent of the accidents involving 22 percent of the fatalities and 46 percent of the persons injured in fatal accidents. Although the percentage of

head-on fatalities shows a drop from 1954 when more than one-third of freeway fatalities were due to head-on collisions, the 18 persons killed in such type accidents leaves no room for complacency.

Traffic density on California's highest traffic freeways makes it probable that a crossed median accident will be a head-on and probably fatal. Median guard rails on the heavy volume freeways could probably have prevented the majority of these cross median head-ons. In this respect, it would also have prevented a deliberate attempt to U-turn across the median of the San Bernardino Freeway in the Pomona area which resulted in the death of three young people. This accident is not classed as a head-on since they were run down by a truck in the near inside lane before completing their maneuver.

Driver Condition

Table III shows driver condition and basic causes by type of accident. It may be noted that had-been-drinking drivers were involved in 23 percent of the fatal accidents. Drinking was most significant in the single vehicle and head-on type accidents involving 38 percent and 33 percent of such accidents respectively. Sleepy and asleep drivers involved 11 percent of fatal accidents. More significant was the fact that driver condition was checked as "unknown" or not stated on 37 percent of the accident reports. Of the 24 accidents in which driver condition was not stated by the reporting officer, 11 accidents could probably be classed as involving drinking drivers due to the statements of witnesses and facts surrounding the accident.

Chart No. 2 sets forth graphically the relation between driver condition and hours of occurrence of 1955 fatal accidents on California's freeways. The high rate of fatal accidents during the lightest traffic period between 1 a.m. and 3 a.m. is again apparent together with the high percentage of drinking and fall-asleep accidents during the early morning hours. This chart again graphically points out incomplete information with the large areas of unknown or not stated.

Violations

Table III also notes violations by type of accident. Speed is the primary cause of freeway fatalities involving 46 percent of the fatal accidents, with 55 percent of the single vehicle accidents and 40 percent of the head-ons being primarily due to the excessive speed. Speed does not appear as the major factor in total highway accidents and ranks third as a causative violation on total freeway accidents; but for the restrictive class of freeway fatal accidents, a high percentage of which occur in light traffic hours, speed is by far the major violation involved.

Improper turning is involved in 9 percent of the total accidents and 22 percent of the overtaking type accidents. Improper lane changes are involved in only 8 percent of the accidents but are a basic cause of the vehicle going out of control and cross-

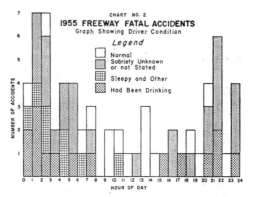

CHART NO. 2

1955 FREEWAY FATAL ACCIDENTS
Graph Showing Driver Condition

Legend

☐ Normal
▦ Sobriety Unknown or not Stated
▤ Sleepy and Other
▨ Had Been Drinking

ing the median as shown in 60 percent of the head-on accidents.

CONCLUSIONS

1. Past experience would indicate that the fatality rate on full freeways may well experience a drop in the next year or two, but the expanding of rural freeways at a faster rate than urban will exert a continuing upward influence on freeway fatality rates.

2. Serious violations are the primary cause of the following two fatal accident categories which contribute very substantially to the freeway fatality rate.

a. Pedestrian fatalities which involve pedestrians illegally on full freeways.

b. The high percentage of fatal accidents in the lowest traffic night and early morning hours in which drinking and excessive speed are the predominate causative factors.

3. The number and extreme severity of cross median accidents may indicate a need for a more positive divider on those freeways carrying such high volumes that a median crossing will most probably result in a head-on accident. Further study has been initiated to relate median types to high volume roads.

AMPHITHEATER BEING ENLARGED FOR 1957 ROAD SHOW

The Chicago International Amphitheater, already the largest exposition hall in the United States, will be enlarged even more to hold the upcoming 1957 ARBA Road Show, Road Show Chairman Julien R. Steelman, President of the Koehring Company, announced.

A new addition, 410 feet by 270 feet, has been put under construction and is expected to be completed by

Road Show time, January 28-February 2, 1957. The amphitheater will then have as much display area as 12 football fields under one roof.

The 1957 Road Show will be the largest indoor industrial show of any kind ever to be staged in this Country. Nearly 250 equipment manufacturers will have thousands of pieces of machinery on display and 50 manufacturers of highway materials and supplies have reserved space for a central exhibit of their products.

Redwood Empire

Association Holds 36th
Annual Convention

STATE and federal officials played prominent parts in the Thirty-sixth Annual Convention of the Redwood Empire Association at Boyes Hot Springs, Sonoma County, October 18th through 20th.

At the closing banquet, Robert L. Bishop, Santa Rosa, a member of the California Highway Commission, extended greetings on behalf of Governor Goodwin J. Knight.

The final meeting was opened by Reed W. Robinson, president of the association, who turned the gavel over to the organization's new president, Ben A. Cober, Ukiah newspaper publisher, after thanking the retiring executive board and introducing the new members.

Distinguished Guests

State, federal and other officials were extended a welcome by James F. Lyttle, Sonoma County Supervisor. Among the distinguished guests pres-

Ben A. Cober, Ukiah newspaper publisher, new president of the Redwood Empire Association, left, and Reed W. Robinson, retiring president

Newly elected Executive Board of Redwood Empire Association, left to right; Past President C. H. Demmary, Grants Pass, Oregon; Chester S. Bush, Napa County, Vice President; James A. Nealis, Humboldt County, Vice President; Judge Raymond A. Lathrop, Grants Pass, Oregon; Attorney Elliot M. Epsteen, San Francisco; Don Emerson, Lake County, Vice President; Frank K. Runyan, San Francisco, Vice President; Elias S. Day, Marin County; Reed W. Robinson, San Francisco, Immediate Past President; Ben A. Cober, Ukiah, President; George G. Haberg, Lake County, Past President; Arthur J. Schilder, Ukiah, Past President; Thomas P. Ludcke, Santa Rosa, Member at Large; Clyde Edmondson, General Manager; E. R. Freyer, Piercy, Unit President; L. J. Guglielmetti, Santa Rosa, Unit President; J. M. Reinarz, Del Norte County, Vice President; Edwin S. Heydenburck, Josephine County, Oregon, Vice President; Martin M. Mulford, Sonoma, Unit Vice President.

ent were U. S. Congressman Hubert B. Scudder, Frank B. Durkee, State Public Works Director and Chairman of the California Highway Commission; State Senators A. W. Way and F. Presley Abshire, Assemblymen Frank P. Belotti and Samuel R. Geddes; Justus F. Craemer and Ray E. Untereiner, State Public Utilities Commissioners; Paul Leake, member of the State Board of Equalization; George T. McCoy, State Highway Engineer; F. W. Panhorst, Assistant State Highway Engineer; T. Fred Bagshaw, Assistant State Director of Public Works; E. R. Bonnickson, Acting Division Engineer, U. S. Bureau of Public Roads; Barney W. Booker, Assistant State Highway Engineer, and District Engineers L. A. Weymouth and J. P. Sinclair, San Francisco; and John H. Skeggs, former Assistant State Highway Engineer.

During the convention, Clyde Edmondson, general manager of the association, said that a spot check made by his organization showed that improved highways held the key to the tourist-vacationist business not only in the Redwood Empire, but elsewhere. He said this conclusion was reached after a survey of the volume of travel over the Redwood Highway (US 101), interior roads and border check points.

Increased Tourist Travel

Edmondson reported that tourist-vacationist business showed an increase in the northern and southern parts of the Empire during the past season. However, he added, business fell off somewhat in the central areas. This indicated, he said, that highway conditions are a vital factor when tourists and vacationists plan their itineraries.

Commenting on controversies developing over the construction of freeways, Bishop, who officially represented Governor Knight at the convention, stressed the need of greater understanding of expressway problems at the local level. He said that too many differences of opinion have resulted in unnecessary delays in carrying out these projects.

Bishop also made a plea that highways be kept apart from politics. He said the Division of Highways was

DIVISION OF BEACHES AND PARKS RELEASES ROADSIDE REST DEVELOPMENT SCHEDULE

A schedule of proposed developments for the initial phase of the new state-wide roadside rest program for 41 counties has been released by Newton B. Drury, Chief, Division of Beaches and Parks. The 1956 Legislature appropriated $450,000 for getting this program under way. The total program proposed in the five-year master plan of the Division of Beaches and Parks anticipates expenditure of $2,600,000 for establishment and operation of the entire roadside rest system.

Drury stated that, with approval by the California State Park Commission, the Division of Beaches and Parks is now working full speed to accomplish this needed program along California state highways. The projected initial development is divided into 20 priorities and anticipates in the first three years the construction of approximately 200 rest stations along the major highways.

"Given first priority in the preliminary list is a section of highway in San Bernardino County from Barstow to the eastern state line along US 466 and US 66. This unit, together with priority No. 2, along US 40 Alternate, in Plumas, Butte and Lassen Counties will constitute the first completion of roadside rest units expected by January, 1957," Drury stated. Already working in these two units are engineers, who are surveying property lines, and the land staff is negotiating for a relatively small amount of land necessary for purchase.

solely interested in the construction of the best highways at the lowest cost to the taxpayers.

Delegates to the convention heard with interest the announcement by Bagshaw that the highway budget for the eight California Redwood Empire counties for 1957-58 was $38,000,000, up $10,000,000 over the 1956-57 budget.

Highway Beautification

Supervisor William C. Blake, San Francisco, also suggested that freeways in metropolitan areas should be made more pleasing to the eye.

By L. L. FUNK, Supervising Highway Engineer

Federal financing of an accelerated highway program has increased the interest of highway engineers everywhere in improved methods such as photogrammetry and electronic computations that will increase engineering productivity. Here in California we have been making increasing use of photogrammetry during the past five years and have now had over a year's experience in the use of electronic computations for earthwork quantities and traverse. This is an appropriate time to review our current practice and ask ourselves if we are making the maximum use of these improved methods.

In discussing photogrammetry for highway engineering uses, it is convenient to divide the various products which can be obtained into three classifications:

(1) Aerial photography
(2) Reconnaissance mapping
(3) Design mapping

Aerial Photographs

The first classification, aerial photographs, may be either contact prints, enlargements, or mosaics, with the latter two available on either paper or transparent film. Contact prints are the basic product of the aerial photography, being direct prints from the aerial negatives. They are generally nine inches by nine inches in size. The Division of Highways obtains such photography in a wide variety of scales, ranging from as small as one inch = 2,000 feet to as large as one inch = 200 feet. Several of the various scales being used at the present time are shown in *Figure 1*. The scale selected for a particular project depends on the purpose for which the photography is to be used, the land use or development of the area, and the size of the project. The larger scales are used for detailed studies of a single route and in areas of intensive development, while the smaller scales are used for preliminary studies covering several possible routes and in rural or

(This article is based on a talk by Mr. Funk at the District Engineers' meeting, August 10, 1956)

mountainous areas where there is little development.

Contact prints are used for advanced planning and location studies, for materials and foundations investigations, for determining drainage areas, supplementing topographic maps, and various other purposes. When the overlap area of two contact prints is viewed under a stereoscope, the experienced observer can gain a knowledge of the topographic and cultural features of the terrain that could not be obtained in any other way. A day spent in stereoscopic study of the contact prints, supplemented by a brief field review, will provide the location engineer with more information than days spent in detailed field reconnaissance without benefit of aerial photographs.

Enlargement of Photographs

Enlargements of aerial photographs are generally limited to three or four times the size of contact prints, although with good quality photography fairly satisfactory enlargements up to six diameters can be obtained. For some purposes enlargements have advantages over contact prints, as they provide more working room and can be made more nearly to scale. Enlargements are frequently used for right of way estimates, interchange studies, and the establishment of setbacks where future widening is planned. Enlargements made on film provide positive transparencies from which ozalid prints can be made in any desired quantity. Such ozalid prints provide satisfactory working copies at low cost.

Mosaics are assemblies of individual photos, usually made at the approximate scale of the contact prints. They are then copied at the same scale and enlarged up to as much as three diameters on either photographic paper or

film. Mosaics have become almost indispensable in planning studies, as they provide the best possible over-all project maps for use in project reports and in public meetings. For the latter various alternate routes are generally shown in colored ink or tape on the mosaic. Such a mosaic, on which several possible routes have been shown, is illustrated in *Figure 2*.

Scale Is Important

In selecting the scale to be used in obtaining aerial photography, it is important to remember that enlargement does not add detail and that the amount of detail on the photographs is dependent on the scale of the original photography. For example, a four-diameter enlargement at one inch = 400 feet will not have as much detail as a contact print of the same area at one inch = 400 feet. Also a mosaic copy will generally have less detail than an enlargement at the same scale due to the extra copying process involved in making the mosaic.

Aerial photography of one or all of the types described has a very definite place in the location, planning, and design of practically every highway project. While it is difficult to evaluate the exact benefits, aerial photography provides a definite saving in manpower, time, and cost. A still more important advantage is the certainty that in almost all cases a better location will result from the use of aerial photographs, because of the wealth of detail and wide coverage provided.

The second classification of photogrammetric products, reconnaissance mapping, is used for location studies where more than one possible route must be considered and where the terrain is such that excavation quantities are an important factor in the location or where grade controls might govern. The important difference between aerial photographs and either reconnaissance or design mapping is that the latter are accurate in scale and are based on an actual field survey, with this survey being used to control the

and Public Works
23

FIGURE 1—Contact prints at some of the scales being used for planning and location studies. Scales of original photographs: **upper left**, 1 inch = 200 feet; **upper right**, 1 inch = 500 feet; **lower left**, 1 inch = 1,000 feet; **lower right**, 1 inch = 2,000 feet.

scale of mapping and the differences in elevation it shows.

Reconnaissance Work

For reconnaissance work, the highway engineer planning to use photo-grammetric mapping again has a choice of several types of products. In areas where they are available, U. S. Geological Survey quadrangle sheets at a scale of one inch = 2,000 feet with contour intervals of 10, 20, or 40 feet are one of the most effective tools of the location engineer. When used in conjunction with stereoscopic study of contact prints, the maps will provide the answer to many location problems.

24

Where conditions require a larger scale, or where U. S. Geological Survey mapping is not available, we frequently use form line mapping from either existing or new photography. A reasonably accurate map at one inch = 200 feet with 10-foot or even 5-foot contours can be obtained from photography taken with a 8¼-inch lens at a scale of one inch = 800 feet supplemented by a minor amount of ground control. In some cases existing road surveys or U. S. Geological Survey data will provide sufficient con-

trol. Such mapping is generally obtained on a force account or plotter rental basis from mapping contractors and is usually confined to relatively small areas.

In Rugged Terrain

Where it is necessary to study several alternate routes covering a wide band of rugged terrain, we usually contract for reconnaissance mapping in the same manner as for design mapping, using slightly different specifications. Scales used have ranged from

one inch = 200 feet to one inch = 500 feet, with contour intervals of 5, 10, and 20 feet. Here again the larger scales are associated with intensive land use and the smaller scales are used in rural areas. Mapping of this type is illustrated by *Figure 3*. Such a map at one inch = 400 feet with 20-foot contours will cover an area over two miles in width with a single strip of photography.

The use of reconnaissance mapping has practically eliminated the necessity for making preliminary field surveys

FIGURE 2—Several possible locations have been shown on this mosaic for a public presentation of route studies. Scales of the mosaic was 1 inch = 400 feet.

FIGURE 3—The upper map as delivered by the mapping contractor was at a scale of 1 inch = 200 feet with a contour interval of five feet. The lower map at a scale of 1 inch = 400 feet with 10-foot contours covered a wide band of rugged terrain. Several routes which were studied in detail are shown on this map.

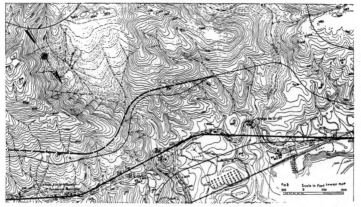

of several alternate routes in order to determine the best location. Here again photogrammetry has provided the highway engineer with a tool which will effect major savings in manpower, time, and cost on many projects.

Design Mapping

Design mapping, the third classification of photogrammetric products, is now being used on many highway projects as an almost complete substi-

tute for the final location survey of the selected route. Complete construction plans are being prepared and rights of way acquired through the use of these maps, supplemented by a minor amount of field surveying. This procedure makes it unnecessary to stake the final line in the field until the construction contract is ready for advertising.

Design mapping is based on a control survey generally made by the mapping contractor to second-order

accuracy. Succeeding steps in the mapping process are the photography, picture point-control, and map compilation. *Figure 4* illustrates a typical control survey with two existing control monuments which the mapping contractor has used as the basis for the traverse he has run through the area to be mapped. This traverse includes monuments set at locations designated by the State which will subsequently be used for supplemental surveys such

26

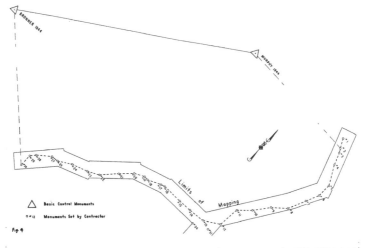

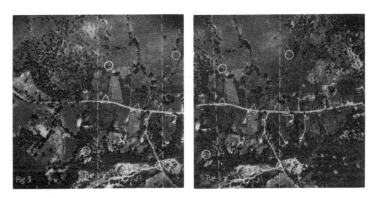

UPPER—FIGURE 4—This control diagram shows the primary ground control survey for an eight-mile design mapping project. LOWER—FIGURE 5—A single pair of the overlapping, vertical aerial photographs used for mapping a portion of the project in Figure 4 are shown here. Points for photo control were premarked on the ground prior to taking the photographs.

as property ties, bridge sites, and for staking the final line.

The next step in design mapping, the photography and picture point control, are illustrated in Figure 5. The aerial photographs were taken at a scale of one inch = 250 feet from an altitude of 1,500 feet above the terrain, with 60 percent forward lap. The mapping contractor then selected five points appearing in the overlapping areas of each pair of photographs, called the models, for vertical picture point control. He also selected three points in each model for horizontal control. The elevations of the vertical control points and the position of the horizontal points were determined by field survey methods.

Positive glass plates, called diapositives, made from the aerial negatives were then placed in the stereoplotter and oriented to the horizontal and vertical picture point controls, after which the plotter operator was able to proceed with the compilation or drawing of the portion of the map covered by this particular model. Figure 6 illustrates the portion of the finished map at one inch = 50 feet corresponding to the model shown in Figure 5. We have found that the one inch = 50 feet scale with two-foot contour interval is well suited for design on most projects.

Spot Elevations

Until recently the value of photogrammetric mapping in level terrain, except for planimetric details, was questionable, as even one-foot contour intervals are generally not satisfactory for design purposes in such areas. We are now taking advantage of the fact that spot elevations can be read directly in the plotter more accurately than contours can be drawn and are specifying a grid of spot elevations in lieu of contours where the contours would be more than 100 feet apart. Such a map is shown in Figure 7. In this case the spot elevations were expressed to the nearest 0.2 foot with the specifications requiring that 70 percent be within 0.5 foot of their true elevation. In most cases this accuracy will be sufficient for final design purposes.

A third type or scale of mapping for design purposes is at one inch = 100 feet with 5-foot contours. This scale is used on projects where the terrain is quite rugged or is obscured by brush to the extent that 2-foot contour mapping by photogrammetric methods would be extremely difficult. Even in rugged terrain there are frequently small valleys or plateaus so level that 5-foot contours will not depict them accurately. By supplementing the contours with spot elevations, accurate to one foot, in such areas we have greatly increased the usefulness of this type of mapping.

Maps Are Accurate

There is no longer any doubt that design maps of these types are sufficiently accurate for the computation of earthwork quantities. Our present practice is to re-cross-section immediately prior to construction for determination of final pay quantities. On several projects a comparison of preliminary quantities from photogrammetric maps and final quantities from field cross sections shows a difference of less than 1 percent. Very few projects have been reported where the difference was greater than 2½ percent.

The actual savings effected by the use of design mapping are much easier to measure than those obtained from the use of aerial photos or reconnaissance mapping. Data reported by several districts indicate a saving of 40 percent in cost and 70 to 80 percent in manpower as compared to conventional field survey methods. A further saving of between 20 and 40 percent is achieved in design where photogrammetric mapping is used.

The use of photogrammetric mapping for design purposes has become standard practice in at least four of the eleven districts and is rapidly increasing in the others. In the period from April, 1952, to July, 1956, the Division of Highways contracted for 1,090 miles of design mapping or an average of approximately 270 miles per year. (Between July 1st and October 15th of this year requests have been received for an additional 275 miles of this type of mapping, indicating that the effect of the federal highway program is already being felt.)

Great Help to Engineers

Photogrammetry has provided the highway engineer with tools to increase his productivity in the fields of advance planning, location, and design. The use of electronic computers is logical as the next step to relieve him of some of his more tedious tasks. Computation of earthwork quantities has always been one of the longest and most tedious of the various steps in the design of a highway project. It is therefore not surprising that a method to minimize this work has been well received.

The method used in California involves the submission of terrain and roadbed notes to the tabulating section for computation. The terrain notes, in the conventional form of field cross section notes, are taken from the contour maps. Roadbed notes, prepared in similar form, show the various breaks in the templet which may include ditches, benches, etc., and rates of cut and fill slopes. Data furnished the designer by machine computation include cut and fill quantities, mass diagram ordinates, and distances out to catch points of cut and fill slopes. After the results of the machine calculation are received and studied for balance and other factors, adjustments of line and grade are made by the designer if necessary. New roadbed notes, or instructions to use the original notes with designated horizontal and/or vertical shifts, are then submitted and combined with the previously submitted terrain notes for machine computation. By this method any number of variations of line and grade can be investigated in a fraction of the time formerly required. Machine computation of earthwork quantities is rapidly superseding both the contour grading or horizontal slice method and the conventional cross section and planimeter method.

Machine Computation

Machine computation (California Highways and Public Works, July-August, 1955) is now available for adjustment of traverses, as well as for the solution of any traverse up to 98

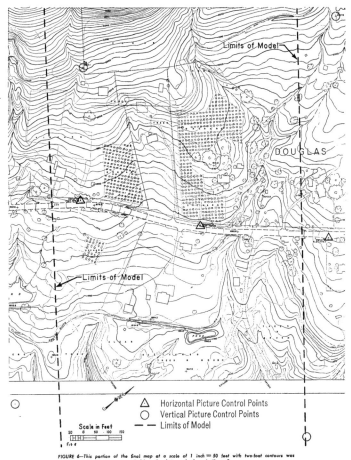

△ Horizontal Picture Control Points
○ Vertical Picture Control Points
— — Limits of Model

Scale in Feet
50   0   50   100   150

Fig. 6

FIGURE 6—This portion of the final map at a scale of 1 inch = 50 feet with two-foot contours was compiled from the photographs shown in Figure 5

and Public Works

29

courses in length which may include two unknowns. The tabulating section is now processing over 2,000 traverse courses per day.

Availability of such a wide variety of photogrammetric products and machine computations gives rise to a new type of problem—which of these new tools should the engineer use in a particular situation? To make full use of these new methods in a rapidly changing field, we must provide the necessary training; and we must also have wider dissemination and exchange of information, both between Headquarters Office and the districts and within the individual districts. A program aimed at better communication of this type has recently been undertaken.

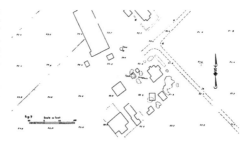

FIGURE 7—Spot elevations are used in lieu of contours where photogrammetric maps are obtained for the design of highways in comparatively level terrain. Scale of the original map was 1 inch = 50 feet.

FIGURE 8—Where the terrain is extremely rugged, photogrammetric maps at a scale of 1 inch = 100 feet with five-foot contours are frequently used for design purposes. The designer has developed the proposed alignment and has shown the trace of cut and fill slopes.

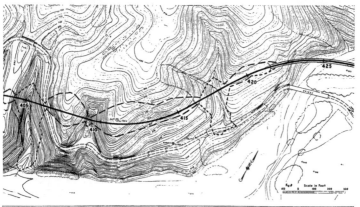

SLOW DOWN

It doesn't pay to hurry through city traffic. Experiments show that a car driven recklessly through town with little regard for traffic regulations arrives only a minute or two ahead of one driven safely and in observance of all traffic rules.

BOTH HANDS

Sleight-of-hand tricks may be all right for the magician but they are out of order when you're driving a car. Don't make your right hand guess what your left hand is doing. Keep *both* hands on the steering wheel where they belong.

AUTOMOTIVE DEVELOPMENT

The turbine powered passenger car still is a long way from the family garage, although recent developments in automotive research and testing laboratories have brought the turbo-car a little closer to reality, reports the National Automobile Club.

California Highways

Record Budget

Highway Commission Votes
$350,000,000 for Construction

An all-time record state highway budget providing more than $350,-000,000 for major construction purposes for the 1957-58 Fiscal Year—an increase of more than $100,000,000 over the budget adopted a year ago—was adopted by the California Highway Commission on October 18th.

The construction items in the new budget include $220,439,000 for major projects, including construction engineering; $127,623,057 for rights of way; and $6,000,000 for contingencies, which normally is allocated later for construction purposes.

For comparison, the budget for the 1956-57 Fiscal Year as adopted in October, 1955, contained approximately $250,000,000 for major construction purposes, including rights of way. That budget was augmented in August, 1956, by approximately $63,000,000 as a result of additional federal aid.

Total Budget $464,247,288

The over-all total budget adopted by the commission amounts to $464,247,288, of which $421,062,057 is for state highway purposes.

In addition to the $354,062,057 for construction, rights of way and contingencies, the state highway allocations in the budget include $25,000,000 for maintenance, $25,500,000 for preliminary engineering, $2,000,000 for the state-wide highway planning survey, $7,500,000 for administration, $4,500,000 for buildings and plants and $1,750,000 for honor camp projects.

The nonstate highway items in the budget include $30,187,000 for major city streets (¼ cent per gallon of the gasoline tax); $7,920,000 in federal aid secondary funds for county roads; $4,087,854 in state highway matching funds to assist counties in the required matching of federal funds on F. A. S. projects; and $904,000 to cities for engineering work.

Federal Aid Increased

Federal aid, still further increased, accounted for most of the additional funds in the 1957-58 budget, along with a normal rise in highway user tax revenues collected by the State. For 1956-58, California will receive approximately $134,000,000 in federal aid for state highways, plus nearly $8,000,000 in federal funds for county roads on the Federal Aid Secondary System. Prior to the 1956 federal highway legislation, California's largest federal apportionment had been $40,000,000 for state highways and $7,000,000 for county F. A. S. roads.

State Director of Public Works Frank B. Durkee, Chairman of the Highway Commission, pointed out that the 1957-58 state highway budget is the first in history to contain one or more construction projects in every one of California's 58 counties.

"This fact bears out," Durkee said, 'what we announced last June when the federal program was enacted into law. Although the bulk of the additional federal funds is earmarked for the National System of Interstate Highways, the effect of the added money here in California will permit release state funds for expenditure all over the State, wherever the needs are greatest."

Early Advertising

The Division of Highways has already advertised $3,500,000 worth of projects in the 1957-58 budget for bids. State law permits the awarding of state highway contracts as early as January 1st, six months before the start of the fiscal year. This provision enables the Division of Highways to make maximum use of favorable construction weather, which means earlier opening of road improvements to traffic.

In addition to extension of freeway systems in the State's metropolitan areas, the new budget provides for many miles of intercity freeways, and expressways, and numerous sections of modern two-lane highways. Nearly 70 miles of two-lane highway projects in the budget are to be built as initial units of ultimate four-lane freeways or expressways, with access control already provided an enough right of way for the remaining two lanes and a median strip to be added later. One of these two-lane projects on an ultimate freeway basis consists of nearly 18 miles, on State Route 90 (Vacaville-Dunnigan cutoff) in Solano and Yolo Counties.

Significant Features

Significant features of the 1957-58 state highway budget include:

San Francisco Bay Area—The final unit, in Oakland, of the 38-mile Eastshore Freeway from the Bay Bridge to San Jose; in San Francisco, extension of the Central Freeway (US 101); the Walnut Creek Bypass Freeway in Contra Costa County; and further construction of the Bayshore Freeway in Santa Clara County. Funds are provided to round out acquisition of rights of way for completion of the US 40 freeway in the Albany-Richmond area.

Los Angeles Metropolitan Area—Completion of the Long Beach Freeway from the Santa Ana Freeway to Pacific Coast Highway; a start on the Olympic Freeway (two projects in downtown Los Angeles); first downtown Los Angeles unit of the Golden State Freeway; continuation of the Golden State Freeway in the Burbank area; widening of portions of the Hollywood and Santa Ana Freeways; further extension of the Hollywood Freeway into the San Fernando Valley; extension of the San Diego Freeway in the Culver City area.

Various Projects

In Orange County, the San Diego Freeway (US 101) is being extended southeastward by two projects in San Juan Capistrano and San Clemente areas.

In the San Diego area, current emphasis is on conversion of express-

Major Construction Projects in State Highway Bu

County	Route	Description	Approximate mileage	Estimated cost
Alameda	69 (SR 17)	Eastshore Freeway—0.25 mile east of Fallon Street to 0.22 mile west of Market Street; grade, pave and structures for 8-lane freeway (completes Eastshore Freeway between Bay Bridge and San Jose)	0.9	$6,400,000
Alameda	105	San Mateo-Hayward Bridge to Eden Landing Road; shoulders	1.8	100,000
Alameda	105	East 14th Street in Oakland between 77th and 74th Avenues at Arroyo Viejo Creek; reconstruct storm drains		250,000
Alameda	226	East 14th Street in San Leandro to 0.1 mile west of Southern Pacific R.R. Crossing; reconstruct and widen	0.5	165,000
Alameda	227	Mountain Boulevard in Oakland, between US 50 near Calaveras Avenue and SR 24 (portions); grade and surface (continuing cooperative freeway project with City of Oakland and Alameda County)		300,000
Alameda	Various	Rights of way on state highway routes (including $13,000,000 for US 50 freeway in Oakland)		13,757,000
Alpine	34 (SR 88)	Red Lake Dam to 1.5 miles east of Blue Lakes Road; grade and surface realignment	8.8	800,000
Amador	34, 65 (SR 88, 49)	Lancha Plana Road to 0.5 mile east of Martell; grade surface and structures (realignment)	7.4	1,010,000
Amador	34 (SR 88)	Silver Lake to Alpine County Line (portions); grade and surface (reconstruction and realignment)	3.8	400,000
Amador	Various	Rights of way on state highway routes		45,000
Butte	21 (US 40 Alt)	Bear Creek Bridge; reconstruct		25,000
Butte, Plumas	21 (US 40 Alt)	Arch Rock, Elephant Butte and Grizzly Dome Tunnels (portions); line tunnels		60,000
Butte	47 (SR 32)	Glenn County Line to 2½ miles west of Chico; grade surface and structures (initial 2 lanes of ultimate 4-lane expressway) (See Glenn Co.)	5.9	475,000
Butte	47 (SR 32)	Junction US 99E via 8th and 9th Streets to Fir Street east of Chico; grade, surface and drainage (to provide one-way couplet)	1.1	230,000
Butte	87, 21 (US 40 Alt)	Union School to Montgomery Street in Oroville; grade, surface and structures (initial 2 lanes of ultimate 4-lane expressway)	5.4	750,000
Butte	Various	Rights of way on state highway routes		360,000
Calaveras	24 (SR 4)	Murphys to Big Trees (portions); grade and surface (widening and realignment)	6.6	550,000
Calaveras	65 (SR 49)	Through Mokelumne Hill; grade and surface (relocation)	2.0	340,000
Calaveras	Various	Rights of way on state highway routes		90,000
Colusa	15 (SR 20)	Williams to Sacramento River Bridge (portions); base and surface (reconstruct), and widen structure (Steer Ditch Bridge)	8.9	350,000
Colusa	Various	Rights of way on state highway routes		50,000
Contra Costa	75, 107 (SR 24, 21)	East of Pleasant Hill Road to west of Walden Road, with connection to SR 21 at Crest Avenue; grade, pave and structures for 6-lane freeway in vicinity of Walnut Creek (Walnut Creek Bypass)	4.2	7,500,000
Contra Costa	75 (SR 4)	SR 24 to Brentwood; reconstruct	6.6	305,000
Contra Costa	Various	Rights of way on state highway routes		1,991,000
Del Norte	1 (US 101)	Minot Creek and High Prairie Creek; new bridges and approaches		235,000
Del Norte	Various	Rights of way on state highway routes		75,000
El Dorado	11 (US 50)	Mays to Nevada State Line; grade, surface and structures for 2-lane and 4-lane highway	5.2	350,000
El Dorado	93	Georgetown to 2.4 miles west; grade and surface (reconstruction and some realignment)	2.4	145,000
El Dorado	Various	Rights of way on state highway routes		245,000
Fresno	41 (SR 180)	Ventura Avenue, from R Street to Chestnut Avenue; grade and surface (widen to full 4-lane divided highway)	2.3	750,000
Fresno	41 (SR 180)	0.7 mile east of Reed Avenue to 2.3 miles east of Friant-Kern Canal (portions); grade, surface and structure (relocation)	1.4	230,000
Fresno	125 (SR 41)	Shaw Avenue to 0.8 mile north of Herndon Avenue, grade and surface (extending 6-lane divided highway)	2.6	400,000
Fresno	125 (SR 41)	Ventura Avenue from C Street to Broadway; grade and surface (reconstruct)	0.4	28,000
Fresno	Various	Rights of way on state highway routes		485,000
Glenn	7 (US 99W)	3.6 miles south of Willows to Willows; surface		100,000
Glenn	47 (SR 32)	US 99W to Butte county line; grade, surface and structure (initial 2 lanes of ultimate 4-lane expressway, including new bridge at Stony Creek) (see Butte County)	11.1	965,000
Glenn	Various	Rights of way on state highway routes		220,000
Humboldt	1 (US 101)	1 mile south of Dyerville to Englewood; grade, surface and structures for 4-lane freeway (first unit of relocation in Humboldt Redwood State Park area)	4.2	2,605,000
Humboldt	1 (US 101)	0.2 mile north of Fortuna to 0.4 mile north of Fernbridge; structures and approaches for 4-lane expressway		515,000
Humboldt	1 (US 101)	0.4 mile north of Fernbridge to 0.7 mile north of Hookton Road; grade and surface to complete sections of 4-lane expressway	4.6	750,000
Humboldt	1 (US 101)	Mad River; structure (additional Mad River bridge)		500,000
Humboldt	1 (US 101)	Patricks Point to 0.3 mile north of Big Lagoon; grade for future 4-lane expressway	3.5	1,300,000
Humboldt	Various	Rights of way on state highway routes		490,000
Imperial	187 (SR 115)	Sandia to Alamorio; grade and surface (widen)	10.3	1,450,000
Imperial	201 (SR 115)	0.5 mile north of Route 187 to Standard Canal; grade and pave (widen)	6.3	725,000
Imperial	Various	Rights of way on state highway routes		465,000
Inyo	23 (US 6-395)	Black Rock to 4.4 miles south of Big Pine; grade and surface (widen)	5.4	350,000
Inyo	(US 395) 23, 76	Texaco Corners to Birchim Canyon; grade and surface (widen)	11.5	260,000

SR=State Sign Route.

get for 1957-58 Fiscal Year Total $350,000,000

County	Route	Description	Approximate mileage	Estimated cost
Inyo	Various	Rights of way on state highway routes		$175,000
Kern	(4 US 99)	Fort Tejon to 2 miles north of Grapevine Station; grade, pave and structures to provide 8-lane freeway (additional 4-lane northbound roadway)	7.2	6,935,000
Kern	4 (US 99)	Route 129 to Delano (portions); grade and pave (reconstruct)	10.2	450,000
Kern	23 (US 6)	Ittners to one mile north; grade and surface (realignment)	1.0	600,000
Kern	57 (SR 178)	2.0 miles east to 4.0 miles east of Weldon; grade and surface (realignment)	2.0	100,000
Kern	56 (US 466)	0.3 mile west of east city limit of Bakersfield to Route 143; grade and surface (widen)	4.2	270,000
Kern	56 (SR 178)	Buena Vista Slough Bridge; widen bridge and approaches		45,000
Kern	140	5.3 miles east of Arvin to 2.2 miles west of US 466; grade and surface (realignment— White Wolf Grade)	3.3	625,000
Kern	145 (US 395)	0.4 mile north of Inyokern to US 6; grade and surface (relocation)	5.0	160,000
Kern	Various	Rights of way on state highway routes (including $2,100,000 for US 99 freeway in Bakersfield area)		3,131,000
Kings	125 (SR 41)	1.9 miles north of Stratford to Jersey Avenue; grade and surface (widen)	1.9	190,000
Kings	135	Kansas Avenue to SR 198; grade and surface (widen)	8.0	770,000
Kings	Various	Rights of way on state highway routes		615,000
Lake	49 (SR 83)	Cache Creek to SR 20; grade and surface for 2-lane highway on relocation (expressway basis)	6.3	950,000
Lake	Various	Rights of way on State highway routes		35,000
Lassen	73 (US 395)	North of Ravendale to Madeline (portions); grade and surface (reconstruct)	6.7	750,000
Los Angeles	2 (US 101)	Hollywood Freeway—Highland Avenue to Lankershim Boulevard; grade and pave additional lanes	2.6	775,000
Los Angeles	2, 159 (US 101)	Hollywood Freeway Extension—0.2 mile south of Moorpark Street to Kling Street on Route 159 and to 0.1 mile west of Laurel Canyon Boulevard on US 101; grade, pave and structures for 8-lane freeway	1.7	5,900,000
Los Angeles	2 (US 101)	0.2 mile south of Cheeseboro Road (west of Calabasas) to 0.15 mile north of Lindero Creek; reconstruct	3.5	250,000
Los Angeles	4, 26 (US 6-99)	Golden State Freeway—0.1 mile south of Sixth Street to 0.2 mile north of Mission Road; and on US 60-70-99-Pickett Street to Macy Street; grade, pave and structures for 8-lane freeway	3.1	8,900,000
Los Angeles	4 (US 6-99) (US 60-70-99)	Golden State Freeway—Alameda Avenue to Burbank Boulevard in Burbank; grade, pave and structures for 8-lane freeway	1.3	3,150,000
Los Angeles	60 (US 101 Alt)	Vermont Avenue to Reed Street; reconstruct	1.3	120,000
Los Angeles	62 (SR 39)	San Bernardino Freeway to Paramount Avenue in Azusa; grade and structures for 4-lane divided highway	3.3	1,235,000
Los Angeles, San Bernardino	77 (SR 71)	0.3 mile south of Riverside Drive to US 60 at Butterfield Road; grade, pave and structures for 4-lane expressway	3.2	900,000
Los Angeles	77	0.2 mile east of San Bernardino Road in El Monte to Rio Hondo Wash; grade, pave and structures (widen)	0.8	270,000
Los Angeles	158 (SR 7)	San Diego Freeway—0.2 mile south of Venice Boulevard to 0.2 mile north of Ohio Avenue; grade, pave and structures for 8-lane freeway	0.8	270,000
Los Angeles	162 (US 66)	On Santa Monica Blvd. from Wilshire Blvd. to Sierra Dr. in Beverly Hills; reconstruct	3.5	6,025,000
Los Angeles	164 (SR 107)	Broadway (Hawthorne) to Hillcrest Blvd. (Inglewood); grade and surface for 6-lane divided highway	1.4	100,000
Los Angeles	164 (SR 107)	0.2 mile south to 0.3 mile north of 190th Street (Torrance); grade, surface and structure (widen R.R. underpass) for 6-lane divided highway	2.6	315,000
Los Angeles	166 (US 101)	Santa Ana Freeway—Lakewood-Rosemead Blvd. to Rosecrans Avenue; grade, pave and structures (widen 4-lane freeway to 6 lanes)	0.5	145,000
Los Angeles	167 (SR 15)	Long Beach Freeway—0.1 mile south of South junction of Atlantic Boulevard to 0.3 mile south of Rosecrans Ave.; grade, pave and structures for 6-lane freeway (completes Long Beach Freeway from Santa Ana Freeway to Pacific Coast Highway)	5.2	1,200,000
Los Angeles	168 (SR 19)	On Lakewood Blvd., from Gardendale Street to Hall road; reconstruct	1.1	1,750,000
Los Angeles	173 (SR 26)	Olympic Freeway—Harbor Freeway Interchange (portions); structure and approaches	1.7	180,000
Los Angeles	173 (SR 26)	Olympic Freeway—West right of way line of Santa Fe Railroad Yard to 8th Street; structure (L.A. River and Santa Fe R.R. yard) for future 8-lane freeway		1,400,000
Los Angeles	175 (SR 14)	On Artesia Boulevard, from Gramercy Place to Western Avenue; grade, surface and structure (Dominguez Flood Control Channel)	0.3	7,000,000
Los Angeles	179 (SR 22)	US 101 Alt. in Long Beach to Los Cerritos Channel; grade, surface and structures (widen to 4 lanes)	0.3	115,000
Los Angeles	Various	Rights of way on state highway routes, including $12,000,000 for Olympic Freeway, $12,000,000 for Golden State Freeway, $9,000,000 for San Diego Freeway, $3,500,000 for Glendale Freeway and $3,000,000 for Hollywood Freeway Extension	1.1	175,000
				53,270,000
Madera	4 (US 99)	0.5 mile south to 1.5 miles north of Madera; grade, pave and structures for 4-lane freeway	3.9	3,400,000
Madera	Various	Rights of way on state highway routes		150,000
Marin	1 (US 101)	0.2 mile north of Richardson Bay Bridge; pedestrian overcrossing		60,000
Marin	1 (US 101)	Greenbrae Intersection to 0.5 mile north of California Park Overhead; grade, pave and structure for 6-lane freeway	1.4	1,325,000
Marin, Sonoma	8 (SR 37)	Petaluma Creek Bridge; new 4-lane bridge and approach embankments		2,300,000
Marin	Various	Rights of way on state highway routes		457,000
Mariposa	18 (SR 140)	Acorn Inn to King Solomon Mine; grade, surface and structures (widening and realignment)	4.6	1,200,000
Mariposa	65 (SR 49)	2.0 miles north of SR 140 to Coulterville (portions); grade and surface (some realignment)		200,000
Mariposa	Various	Rights of way on state highway routes		65,000

SR = State Sign Route.

and Public Works

33

County	Route	Description	Approximate mileage	Estimated cost
Mendocino	1 (US 101)	0.5 mile north of Hilvilla to 0.9 mile south of Irvine Lodge; grade and surface for 4-lane expressway	3.8	$2,000,000
Mendocino	48 (SR 128)	Robinson Creek to Maple Creek; base and surface	4.5	250,000
Mendocino, Sonoma	56 (SR 1)	Gualala River; new bridge and approaches	0.9	625,000
Mendocino	Various	Rights of way on state highway routes		325,000
Merced	4 (US 99)	G Street to Bear Creek (portions); reconstruct existing highway	1.4	300,000
Merced	122 (SR 140)	0.5 mile east to 4.0 miles east of Gustine; grade and surface (widen)	3.5	150,000
Merced	122 (SR 140)	West of Lincoln Road to west city limits of Merced (portions); grade and surface (widen)		550,000
Merced	Various	Rights of way on state highway routes (including $750,000 for US 99 freeway in Merced area)		1,600,000
Modoc	28, 73 (US 395)	Alturas to Oregon State Line (portions); surface		725,000
Modoc	Various	Rights of way on state highway routes		40,000
Mono	40	US 395 to Nevada State Line; surface	21.7	275,000
Mono	96	Bridgeport to Walker River Reservoir; grade and surface (reconstruct)	4.8	200,000
Mono	Various	Rights of way on state highway routes		40,000
Monterey	2 (US 101)	Through Chualar; grade, surface and structures for 4-lane freeway	1.3	620,000
Monterey	2 (US 101)	1 mile west of Greenfield to Salinas River near Soledad; grade, surface and structures for 4-lane expressway	5.6	1,090,000
Monterey	2 (US 101)	1.8 miles north of Salinas River to 2 miles south of Greenfield; grade, surface and structures for 4-lane expressway	7.9	1,600,000
Monterey	56 (SR 1)	San Luis Obispo county line to Rocky Creek (portions); cribbing (reconstruct retaining walls)		230,000
Monterey	119 (SR 25)	SR 198 to San Benito county line (portions); surface		70,000
Monterey	Various	Rights of way on state highway routes		370,000
Napa	49 (SR 29)	Union Station to Orchard Avenue; grade and surface (additional 2 lanes for 4-lane expressway)	2.3	525,000
Napa	102 (SR 128)	Sage Creek Bridge; superstructure		15,000
Napa	Various	Rights of way on state highway routes		285,000
Nevada	38 (US 40)	Boca to Floriston (portions); detour for future 4-lane freeway construction		350,000
Nevada, Placer	38 (US 40)	0.2 mile south of Squaw Valley Road to Truckee Wye; grade, surface and structures (widening)	9.4	1,450,000
Nevada	Various	Rights of way on state highway routes (including $600,000 for US 40 freeway in Truckee area)		895,000
Orange, San Diego	2 (US 101)	San Diego Freeway—San Mateo Creek to 0.1 mile south of Avenida Cadiz (San Clemente); grade, pave and structures for 4-lane freeway	2.4	2,725,000
Orange	2 (US 101)	San Diego Freeway—1.9 miles south of SR 74 (at San Juan Capistrano) to 1 mile south of Trabuco Creek; grade, pave and structures for 4-lane freeway	3.6	3,470,000
Orange	175 (SR 14)	From Santa Ana Freeway to 0.2 mile east of Spadra Road in Fullerton; grade, pave and structures for 4-lane freeway	3.8	2,900,000
Orange	179 (SR 22)	Knott Street to Century Boulevard; grade and surface (widen existing highway to 4 lanes)	3.8	400,000
Orange	Various	Rights of way on state highway routes (includes $1,500,000 for SR 55 freeway and $1,750,000 for San Diego Freeway)		4,140,000
Placer	37 (US 40)	Near Magra to 0.1 mile west of Alta Road (portions); detour for future 4-lane freeway construction		300,000
Placer, Nevada	37 (US 40)	Hampshire Rocks to Soda Springs; grade, surface and structure for 4-lane freeway	5.7	3,100,000
Placer	Various	Rights of way on state highway routes		885,000
Plumas	21 (US 40 Alt)	0.7 mile west of Spring Garden to Sloat; grade and surface (initial 2 lanes of ultimate 4-lane expressway)	5.2	1,300,000
Riverside	19, 78 (US 60, 395)	US 60-395 separation; lighting, signing and speed change lanes		50,000
Riverside	19 (US 60)	4.0 miles west of US 70-99 to US 70-99 (near Beaumont); grade, surface and structures for 4-lane freeway	4.3	1,150,000
Riverside	43 (US 91) (SR 18)	Van Buren Street to Arlington Avenue; grade, surface and structures for 4-lane freeway	3.7	3,850,000
Riverside	64 (US 60-70)	Colorado River; new bridge (near Blythe); cooperative project with Arizona		600,000 (California share)
Riverside	64 (SR 74)	Antsell Rock Creek, Servo Creek and South Fork San Jacinto River; bridges and approaches	0.3	220,000
Riverside, San Bernardino	187	US 60-70-99 to Morongo Valley; grade and surface (widen)	11.3	270,000
Riverside	Various	Rights of way on state highway routes (including $1,000,000 for US 60-70-99 freeway in Beaumont area)		2,731,000
Sacramento, Solano	53 (SR 12)	Sacramento River Bridge at Rio Vista; sub-structure		1,150,000
Sacramento	Various	Rights of way on state highway routes (including $1,500,000 for north-south freeway in and south of Sacramento)		1,985,000
San Benito	2 (US 101)	San Benito River; reconstruct bridge and approaches	0.1	185,000
San Benito	119 (SR 25)	5 miles north of San Benito River to Paicines; grade and surface (realignment)	4.6	450,000
San Benito	Various	Rights of way on state highway routes		135,000
San Bernardino	31, 58 (US 66-91)	Victorville to Barstow; grade, surface and structures for 4-lane freeway	29.4	5,200,000
San Bernardino	43 (SR 18)	1.0 mile south of Forest Boundary to Apple Valley; grade and surface (widening and some realignment)	23.9	440,000
San Bernardino	43, 31 (US 66-91-395)	6th Street to DeVore; grade, surface and structures to complete 4-lane freeway through San Bernardino to DeVore	11.6	7,300,000
San Bernardino	58 (US 466)	Kern County line to Hinkley (portions); grade and surface (widen)	28.2	420,000

SR=State Sign Route.

County	Route	Description	Approximate mileage	Estimated cost
San Bernardino	Various	Rights of way on state highway routes (Including $1,160,000 for US 91-395-SR 18 freeway in and south of San Bernardino)		$3,596,000
San Diego	2 (US 101)	0.7 mile south of Dairy Mart Road to south city limits of Chula Vista (portions); grade, pave and structures (convert 4-lane expressway to full freeway)	5.2	910,000
San Diego	2 (US 101)	0.4 mile south of Washington Street to Barnett Avenue; grade, pave and structures (Washington Street Interchange)	1.1	1,340,000
San Diego	12, 77 (US 80, 395)	1.2 miles east of Taylor Street to 0.2 mile east of US 395; grade, pave and structures (convert 4-lane expressway to full freeway, including revision of Mission Valley Interchange)	2.4	3,100,000
San Diego	12 (US 80)	0.3 mile west to 0.6 mile east of Fairmount Avenue; grade, pave and structures (Fairmount Avenue Interchange)	0.9	1,700,000
San Diego	77 (US 395)	Clairemont Mesa Boulevard Interchange; structure and approaches	1.0	800,000
San Diego	195 (SR 76)	Fry Creek Bridge and Big Fry Creek Bridge; new bridges and approaches	1.2	200,000
San Diego	200 (SR 94)	17th Street to Home Avenue; grade, pave and structures for 6-lane freeway	1.7	4,065,000
San Diego	Various	Rights of way on state highway routes (including $6,600,000 for US 101 freeway in San Diego and $1,250,000 for US 80 freeway in San Diego-La Mesa-El Cajon area)		8,825,000
San Francisco	2 (US 101)	Central Freeway—South Van Ness Avenue to Turk Street; grade, pave and structure for 6-lane freeway	1.0	5,200,000
San Francisco	2 (US 101)	Lyon Street to SR 1 connection; grade, pave and structures for 8-lane freeway	1.3	3,900,000
San Francisco	Various	Rights of way on state highway routes (including $10,000,000 for Southern Freeway)		12,932,000
San Joaquin	5 (US 50)	East city limits of Tracy to Grant Line Road; grade, surface and structures (widen existing highway to 4-lanes, including East Tracy Overhead and channelization at Chrisman Road)	3.9	1,100,000
San Joaquin	5 (US 50)	Richards Avenue to Charter Way; grade, surface and structures (widen existing highway to 4-lanes)	5.0	1,100,000
San Joaquin	75 (SR 4)	US 99 to Knights Ferry Road (portions); reconstruct		20,000
San Joaquin	Various	Rights of way on state highway routes		265,000
San Luis Obispo	2 (US 101)	0.2 mile south of Camp Fremont to Cuesta Overhead; resurface	3.2	500,000
San Luis Obispo Santa Barbara	57 (SR 166)	1.0 mile west of Huasna River to 0.7 mile west of Buckhorn Creek; grade, surface and structures (relocation around Vaquero Reservoir)	7.8	1,165,000
San Luis Obispo	Various	Rights of way on state highway routes (including $900,000 for US 101 freeway in Pismo Beach area)		1,900,000
San Mateo	2 (US 101)	El Camino Real—31st Avenue to Poplar Avenue in San Mateo; grade and surface (widen)	2.9	375,000
San Mateo	56, 55 (SR 1,5)	Edgemar to Junction Skyline Boulevard (SR 5) and Edgemar Road; grade, surface and structures for 4-lane expressway	1.5	1,300,000
San Mateo	Various	Rights of way on state highway routes		1,949,000
Santa Barbara	2 (US 101)	Wigmore to 1.7 miles north of Los Alamos; grade, surface and structures for 4-lane expressway	5.9	1,900,000
Santa Barbara	2 (US 101)	0.5 mile west of Refugio to Tajiguas; grade, surface and structures for 4-lane expressway	2.3	769,000
Santa Barbara	Various	Rights of way on state highway routes (including $1,200,000 for US 101 freeway in Santa Barbara)		2,475,000
Santa Clara	2 (US 101)	El Camino Real—San Tomas Aquino Creek in Santa Clara to Route 114 (Saratoga Road) in Sunnyvale; grade and surface (widen to 4 lanes)	3.8	945,000
Santa Clara	5, 42 (SR 17)	Route 42 (Santa Cruz Avenue) in Los Gatos to Bascom Avenue in San Jose on SR 17 and Tait Avenue to new SR 17 in Los Gatos; grade, pave and structures for 4-lane freeway	8.8	5,770,000
Santa Clara	68 (US 101 Bypass)	San Felipe Road to Hollister Wye; reconstruct and resurface	2.3	90,000
Santa Clara	Various	Bayshore Freeway—Stevens Creek to Ellis Street; grade, pave and structures for 6-lane freeway	1.1	1,100,000
Santa Clara	Various	Rights of way on state highway routes (including $750,000 for Bayshore Freeway)		1,929,000
Santa Cruz	56, 5 (SR 1, 17)	0.3 mile east of Morrissey Avenue to 0.6 mile north of SR 1-SR 17 Junction; grade, pave and structures for 4-lane freeway	2.2	1,600,000
Santa Cruz	56 (SR 1)	0.3 mile east of Swift Street to Wildre Creek; grade and surface (2 lanes of ultimate 4-lane expressway; portion cooperative project with Joint Highway District No. 9)	2.6	415,000
Santa Cruz	116 (SR 9)	Felton to Boulder Creek (portions); grade, surface and structures (widening)	5.9	400,000
Santa Cruz	Various	Rights of way on state highway routes		360,000
Shasta	3 (US 99)	Clear Creek to Redding Underpass; grade, surface and structures (frontage road)	3.3	365,000
Shasta	3 (US 99)	0.5 mile north of Lamoine to 0.3 mile north of Shotgun Creek; grade, surface and structures (extension of 4-lane freeway in Sacramento Canyon)	6.9	4,520,000
Shasta	3 (US 99)	Cypress Avenue to Sulphur Creek in Redding; grade and surface (for one-way street couplet and widening)	2.0	190,000
Shasta	Various	Rights of way on state highway routes		272,000
Sierra	25 (SR 49)	North Fork Yuba River to 0.25 mile east of Ramshorn Creek (portions); grade and surface (widen)		200,000
Sierra	Various	Rights of way on state highway routes		95,000
Siskiyou	3 (US 99)	Shasta River to Gazelle; surface	7.6	160,000
Siskiyou	46 (SR 96)	4.5 miles to 5.4 miles east of Hamburg; grade and surface (realignment)	0.9	125,000
Siskiyou	Various	Rights of way on state highway routes		570,000
Solano	7 (US 40)	Interchange at SR 12; structure and approaches (west of Fairfield)		1,100,000
Solano	7 (US 40)	0.2 mile north of Vallejo Wye to 0.4 mile north of Redwood Street; grade, pave and structures for 6-lane freeway	3.5	4,300,000
Solano	74 (SR 21)	New SR 21 to 1.25 miles north of Benicia Arsenal; structure and approaches (Benicia Arsenal Interchange)		375,000
Solano	90	Vacaville-Dunnigan Cutoff—0.3 mile north of Sweeney Creek to Yolo County line; grade, surface and structures (initial 2-lanes of ultimate 4-lane freeway) (See Yolo County)	5.0	1,070,000
Solano	Various	Rights of way on state highway routes (including $750,000 for new freeway route in Benicia area)		1,865,000

SR=State Sign Route.

County	Route	Description	Approximate mileage	Estimated cost
Sonoma	51 (SR 12)	US 101 to 0.17 mile east of Farmer's Lane; widen and channelize.	2.3	$435,000
Sonoma	Various	Rights of way on state highway routes (including $800,000 for US 101 freeway in Santa Rosa-Healdsburg area)		908,000
Stanislaus	4 (US 99)	Modesto Freeway-Whitmore Road to Pecos Avenue; grade, pave and structures for 4-lane freeway	2.2	1,300,000
Stanislaus	Various	Rights of way on state highway routes (including $1,100,000 for U.S. 99 freeway in Ceres-Modesto area)		1,300,000
Sutter	15 (SR 20)	East and Sutter Bypass to US 40 Alt. (portions); surface.		235,000
Sutter	87 (US 40 Alt)	Knights Landing to Onstott Road (portions); surface and widen structures.		700,000
Sutter	Various	Rights of way on state highway routes.		300,000
Tehama	29 (SR 36)	1.5 miles east of Lassen Camp to Mineral; grade surface and structure (initial 2 lanes of ultimate 4-lane expressway)	5.2	980,000
Tehama	29 (SR 36)	3 miles east of Tedoc Road to Dry Creek; grade and surface (realignment)	6.2	775,000
Tehama	Various	Rights of way on state highway routes		35,000
Trinity	29 (SR 36)	Salt Creek Bridge; repair bridge		18,000
Trinity	Various	Rights of way on state highway routes		30,000
Tulare	4 (US 99)	6th Street Overcrossing at Tipton; structure and approaches		165,000
Tulare	10 (SR 198)	County Road 80 to Mooney Boulevard; grade and surface for 4-lane divided highway	4.3	1,100,000
Tulare	Various	Rights of way on state highway routes		1,350,000
Tuolumne	13 (SR 49, 108, 120)	7.0 miles east of Stanislaus County line to Montezuma Road; grade and surface (initial 2 lanes of ultimate 4-lane expressway)	8.1	1,500,000
Ventura	2 (US 101)	Ventura Freeway—Conejo Grade Summit to 5th Street in Camarillo; grade, pave and structures for 4 and 6-lane freeway	4.8	3,400,000
Ventura	2 (US 101)	Ventura Freeway—Rose Road Interchange; structure and approaches		250,000
Ventura	9 (SR 118)	Arroyo Simi Bridge; new bridge and approaches	0.1	179,000
Ventura	151 (SR 150)	0.1 mile west of Sisar Creek to 0.1 mile east of Santa Paula Creek; grade, surface and structures (realignment)	0.4	215,000
Ventura	Various	Rights of way on state highway routes (including $3,000,000 for US 101 freeway in and near Ventura)		4,669,000
Yolo	6 (SR 128)	Solano County line to Route 90 at Winters (portions); reconstruct	9.1	250,000
Yolo	6 (US 40)	Solano County line to Swingle; structure (Davis Interchange)		320,000
Yolo	50 (SR 16, 24)	East side of Yolo Bypass to near Kiessel; grade and surface (widening and some re-alignment)	3.0	300,000
Yolo	50 (SR 16, 24)	Bryte to Broderick; grade and surface (widening)	2.2	110,000
Yolo	90, 6	Vacaville-Dunnigan Cutoff—Solano County line to 2.75 miles north of Madison; grade, surface and structures (initial 2 lanes of ultimate 4-lane freeway) (see Solano County)	13.9	3,000,000
Yolo	Various	Rights of way on state highway routes		160,000
Yuba	15 (SR 20)	Westerly approach to Parks Bar Bridge; grade and surface (realignment)	1.0	100,000
Yuba	Various	Rights of way on state highway routes		200,000

SR = State Sign Route.

way sections of US 101, US 80 and US 395 to full freeways by construction of interchanges. The Highway 94 freeway is being extended further into the San Diego downtown area.

In the Sacramento metropolitan area, Durkee pointed out that construction will begin soon on two previously budgeted projects, one a $2,-250,000 six-mile freeway job on US 50-99 south of Elk Grove Road and the other a $1,400,000 14-mile widening of US 50 east of Sacramento. He added that the findings of a cooperative state-city-county trafficways survey, now in progress, will be a major factor in future freeway plans for the entire Sacramento metropolitan area.

The longest single full freeway project in state highway history—29.4 miles on US 66-91 from Victorville to Barstow—is included in the new budget. Together with a new 11.1-mile freeway project in and north of San Bernardino, this will provide 70 miles of continuous freeway and expressway from San Bernardino to Barstow. Extension of the north-south freeway through Riverside is also included.

On US 99 South

On US 99 between Los Angeles and Sacramento, the major projects budgeted include the conversion of the Grapevine Grade in Kern County to an eight-lane full freeway; freeway construction through Madera; and the first unit of the freeway through Modesto. Nearer the Oregon line, an additional 6.9 miles of freeway are scheduled for construction on US 99 north of Shasta Lake in the Sacramento River Canyon.

The major gap in freeway and expressway construction on US 101 between San Francisco and Los Angeles has been in southern Monterey County. The new budget provides for three projects, totaling 14.8 miles, which will close much of this gap between King City and the completed freeway south of Salinas. Two additional expressway projects are budgeted on the Santa Barbara County portion of US 101 along with freeway development in Ventura County from the Conejo Grade to Camarillo. On the Redwood Highway (US 101) in Humboldt County, the first unit of the freeway bypassing the State Park Redwood Groves is included.

More US 40 Improvement

The long-range effort to multilane US 40 over the Sierra is continued in the new budget, with one 5.7-mile freeway project in the high country west of Soda Springs and two projects for major detour construction preparatory to future freeway work on the same route.

There are several major bridge projects in the budget. Among those in the half-million-dollar or more class

... Continued on page 48

MAGAZINE STREET OVERPASS IN VALLEJO IS COMPLETED

Crosstown traffic was made considerably safer and quicker in Vallejo when the $460,000 overpass, approaches and frontage roads were opened to public use at Magazine Street on Friday, October 27, 1956. The new structure eliminates a dangerous crossing over busy US 40, main artery over the Sierra Mountains to the East Coast.

Threatening skies withheld rain long enough to permit a giant size pair of scissors to snip the ribbon and allow the free flow of traffic from one side of the city to the other.

Gathered to celebrate the event were numerous city, county, and state officials, including a large number of interested residents of the area.

The Magazine Street Overpass is the first of six to be constructed in the City of Vallejo. When completed the heavy traffic in both directions will then flow without the delay of the present signal lights.

UPPER—Newly completed Magazine Street Overhead. LOWER—Scene at ribbon cutting. Left to right: Colon O. Kilby, Supervisor; G. E. Derr, Councilman; John Baldwin, Congressman; William F. Goheen, Supervisor; Chelso A. Maghetti, Secretary, California Highway Commission.

Southern Crossing

Experts Report on Financial
Feasibility of Proposed Span

As CALIFORNIA HIGHWAYS AND PUB-
LIC WORKS goes to press the California
Toll Bridge Authority was preparing
for a meeting in Sacramento on December 12th, to consider the report on
"The Financial Feasibility of the Proposed Southern Crossing of San Francisco Bay," submitted by the firm of
Smith, Barney and Co. of New York.

On June 1, 1956, the Department of
Public Works entered into an agreement with Smith Barney and Co., to
make a study and submit a report on
the financial feasibility of the proposed
new crossing.

Governor Knight ordered the report made public as soon as completed
and on October 23, 1956, it was released at a press conference in San
Francisco. Copies of the report were
made available to members of the Legislature, public officials and others interested in this project.

The report includes the following
conclusions and recommendations:

The complete Southern Crossing is
not financially feasible as presently authorized at a basic toll rate of 25 cents
for both the Bay Bridge and the
Southern Crossing.

Although the minimum Southern
Crossing appears to meet the requirements for a self-liquidating project in
combination with the Bay Bridge at
a 25-cent basic rate of toll for both
facilities, the projected $180,000,000 of
revenue bond financing necessary to
finance its construction would not
comply with all of the generally accepted investment standards for such
securities and the minimum Southern
Crossing must, therefore, be considered marginal as to financial feasibility
on that basis, particularly in view of the
unfavorable money market conditions
which exist today. In this connection,
it should be noted that under the suggested conditions governing the issuance of additional bonds contained in
the appended financial studies, in the
event of the initial financing of the
minimum Southern Crossing it would
not be possible to finance the construction of the remaining portions of

Southern Crossing experts. Left to right: Norman C. Raab, Chief, Division of San Francisco Bay Toll Crossings; C. CheeVer Hardwick of Smith, Barney & Co.; George W. Burpee, CoVerdale and Colpitts.

the complete Southern Crossing at a
basic toll rate of 25 cents for the Bay
Bridge and the Southern Crossing unless the applicable revenues as estimated by the traffic engineers are substantially exceeded. These suggested
conditions prerequisite to the issuance
of additional bonds conform in general with standard practice in comparable revenue bond issues and, in
our opinion, represent the minimum
restrictions which would be accept-
able to investors. In any event it
would be necessary, in our opinion,

that the authority enter into a cove-
nant with the purchasers of any bonds
issued to finance the costs of the minimum Southern Crossing that it would
put into effect promptly such adjustment in the rates of toll applicable to
the Bay Bridge and the Southern Crossing as may be necessary to maintain
net revenues available for debt service
equivalent to the interest, amortization
and reserve requirements of the proposed revenue bonds to be issued to
finance construction of the minimum

. . . Continued on page 61

Representatives of the Department of Public Works at press briefing. Left to right: Robert E. Reed, Chief
Counsel; T. Fred Bagshaw, Assistant Public Works Director; E. R. Higgins, Comptroller of the Department.

Sherwin Grade

New Highway Completed Far
Ahead of Scheduled Date

By J. R. JARVIS, District Construction Engineer

NOVEMBER 10, 1956, became another red letter day in the long history of Sherwin Grade, a portion of the Three Flags Highway (US 395) north of Bishop, in State Highway District IX. On this date public traffic was routed over the new realignment of approximately 12 miles of state highway nearly a year earlier than was contemplated when the contract for its construction was awarded on January 3d of this year. R. A. Westbrook, Inc., and Morrison-Knudsen Co., Inc., submitted the low bid on this project for which 270 working days were allowed for completion.

When the time schedule was set up it was contemplated that two summers

would be required to complete the job, one to accomplish grading operations with a shutdown over the winter, and a second to place the base and surfacing. However, despite additions and changes during construction for which an additional 12 days were allowed and 27 days which were unworkable due to weather conditions, the contractor completed all phases of the work in 175 working days, between January 17 and November 14 of this year, which was about 62 percent of the time allowed. This was accomplished by subcontracting portions of the work to specialists so that several operations were done concurrently, and by fitting the equipment

to the job rather than trying to make the job fit the equipment. Much new, modern equipment was purchased specifically for this job and when it had served its purpose was moved to other projects or sold again.

The old Sherwin Grade was originally built about the year 1874 by pioneer James L. C. Sherwin to serve his sawmill on Rock Creek and he later extended the road to another years a private toll road. The first construction on this road as a part of the State Highway System was done in 1915-16 when some realignment was accomplished, drainage was installed and a penetration oil surface was

Showing typical lava rock cut and junction with old highway at foot of grade

LEFT—Aerial photo showing new highway on bridge with old road on right. RIGHT—Looking southerly towards Bishop and White Mountains from north end of project. Note heavy cuts and fill on new road and treacherous "Cadillac Curve" on old road in right center of picture.

LEFT—Looking north from middle of project with two of borrow areas on left. RIGHT—Looking north with four-lane section in foreground and end of project in distance. Old road in Rock Creek Canyon at left.

placed. Since that time the road has served steadily increasing traffic with only minor improvements in pavement width and thickness.

The need for major improvement has long been apparent, but costs could not be met. By 1927 a 5 percent maximum grade on the East Mesa was sought and again in 1931 when funds for a route study were first allocated. In 1948 further demands arose and studies of several alternate routes were made. Finally, in 1953, a project report and aerial surveys were authorized which resulted in adoption of the new route by the State Highway Commission in September, 1954. Funds for construction of this route were made available by the commission in August of 1955 and the last big hurdle had been cleared for a long overdue modernization of Sherwin Grade.

Many striking contrasts can be marked between the old and the new. The old, tortuous grade had some 84 curves which could not be negotiated safely at over 30 to 35 miles per hour and the average grade was 8 percent with some pitches up to 10 percent. The new highway has only 16 easy curves which are designed for travel at 60 m.p.h. and the maximum grade has been held down to 6 percent on a climb from an elevation of 4,470 feet

UPPER—Showing Volcanic pumice cut with Bishop and White Mountains in background.
LOWER—Showing typical long tangent on new highway.

to the new summit at 7,000 feet. First state construction on the old road was done at a cost of approximately $64,-000 while the completely new road cost approximately $1,304,000 exclusive of rights of way and engineering.

Quantities for the original construction are not available for comparison but methods of mule teams and scrapers, wheelbarrows and stoneboats

held them to a minimum. With modern power shovels and carryalls, tractors and trucks, air drills and paving machines the following quantities were taken in stride to build the new highway. Approximately one quarter million cubic yards of volcanic rhyolite rock were excavated and placed in fills; some 400,000 yards of earth,

. . . Continued on page 43

and Public Works

1956 ANNUAL TRAFFIC COUNT

By G. T. McCOY, State Highway Engineer

The annual state-wide traffic count, taken on Sunday and Monday, July 15 and 16, 1956, shows an increase of 7.71 percent over the previous annual count of July, 1955. Gains were generally well distributed over all routes and regions although greatest increases were registered on the "Inter-state Connections," primarily those highways which connect with Arizona and Nevada highways along California's eastern border.

For the fourth consecutive year, monthly traffic counts show freight vehicles increasing at a substantially faster rate than passenger vehicles. Also, for the fifth time in the last six years, Sunday traffic shows appreciably less gain than Monday traffic. These factors, together with the fact that the "Recreational Routes" as a group shows the lowest traffic increases, all point to the continued diminishing of recreational travel in relation to the total traffic picture.

No change was made from the regular procedure of previous years in the manner of taking the count. However, more directional counts have been included because of expanding traffic volumes on multi-lane facilities. Actual recording covers the 16-hour period from 6 a.m. to 10 p.m. for both Sunday and Monday, totals being shown for each hour. At selected representative stations, counts are also continued for the entire 24-hour period and are extended to record each of the seven days of the week. Traffic is segregated into the following vehicle classifications: California passenger cars, out-of-state passenger cars, buses, pickups, two-axle commercial units, three-axle units, four-axle units, five-axle units, and six-or-more-axle units.

Each year some minor changes in the census become necessary, such as the relocation, addition, or discontinuance of individual stations; but in every instance these are excluded in determining comparison with the previous year, only those stations that were identical during both years being taken into consideration. These comparisons for the various route groups are as follows:

PERCENT GAIN OR LOSS FOR 1956 COUNT AS COMPARED WITH 1955

	Sunday	Monday
All routes	+5.74	+8.04
Main north and south routes	+6.04	+7.76
Interstate connections	+9.34	+9.44
Laterals between inland and coast	+5.71	+8.60
Recreational routes	+1.27	+6.22

The gain or loss of traffic volume for State Highway Routes 1 to 80, inclusive, which constitute the basis for the foregoing summary is shown in the following tabulation:

		1956 Percent gain or loss			
		Sunday		Monday	
Route	Termini	Gain	Loss	Gain	Loss
1.	Sausalito-Oregon Line	1.26		6.84	
2.	Mexico Line-San Francisco	6.24		7.01	
3.	Sacramento-Oregon Line	9.42		19.45	
4.	Los Angeles-Sacramento	9.79		7.56	
5.	Santa Cruz-Junction Route 65 near Mokelumne Hill	2.32		8.14	
6.	Napa-Sacramento via Winters	12.20		11.34	
7.	Crockett-Red Bluff	5.31		7.84	
8.	Ignacio-Cordelia via Napa	2.43		9.19	
9.	Route 2 near Montalvo-San Bernardino	3.66		7.55	
10.	Route 2 at San Lucas-Sequoia National Park	3.83		4.86	
11.	Route 75 near Antioch-Nevada Line via Placerville	14.60		14.26	
12.	San Diego-El Centro	4.53		5.99	
13.	Route 4 at Salida-Route 23 at Sonora Junction	4.92		4.95	
14.	Oakland to Route 7 near Crockett	3.22		8.69	
15.	Route 1 near Calpella-Route 37 near Cisco	8.74		7.42	
16.	Hopland-Lakeport	17.15		15.73	
17.	Route 3 at Roseville-Route 15, Nevada City	8.11		9.08	
18.	Route 4 at Merced-Yosemite National Park	10.11		7.41	
19.	Route 2 at Fullerton-Route 26 at Beaumont	12.50		13.71	
20.	Route 1 near Arcata-Route 83 at Park Boundary	4.99		13.38	
21.	Route 3 near RichVale-Route 29 near Chilcoot via Quincy	3.31		3.19	
22.	Route 56, Castroville-Route 32 via Hollister	29.33		10.42	
23.	Route 4 at Tunnel Station-Route 11, Alpine Junction	9.42		10.49	
24.	Route 4 near Lodi-Nevada State Line	8.84		16.67	
25.	Route 37 at Colfax-Route 83 near Sattley	6.34		10.79	
26.	Los Angeles-Mexico via San Bernardino	9.95		11.32	
27.	El Centro-Yuma		5.92		0.01
28.	Redding-Nevada Line via Alturas	1.91		7.78	
29.	Peanut-Nevada Line near Purdy's	3.44		9.00	
31.	Colton-Nevada State Line	10.13		9.65	
32.	Route 56, Watsonville-Route 4 near Califa	5.25		1.55	
33.	Route 56 near Cambria-Route 4 near Famosa	17.82		1.37	
34.	Route 4 at Golf-Route 23 at Pickett's Junction	1.61		0.80	
35.	Route 1 at Alton-Route 20 at Douglas City		18.91		10.79
37.	Auburn-Truckee	13.03		16.60	
38.	Route 11 at Mays-Nevada Line via Truckee River		5.79		2.10
39.	Route 38 at Tahoe City-Nevada State Line	2.31		16.17	
40.	Route 15 near Montezuma-Route 76 at Benton	24.14		16.05	
41.	Route 5 near Tracy-Kings River Canyon via Pesna	1.93		0.70	
42.	Redwood Park-Los Gatos		10.23		6.68
43.	Route 60 at Newport Beach-Route 31 near Victorville	1.30		5.04	
44.	Boulder Creek-Redwood Park		11.77		7.92
45.	Route 7, Willows-Route 3 near Biggs		19.71		18.36
46.	Route 1 near Klamath-Route 3 near Cray	7.17		20.96	
47.	Route 7, Orland-Route 29 near Morgan	7.22		9.38	
48.	Route 1 north of CloverVale-Route 56 near Albion	17.84			3.91
49.	Napa-Route 15 near Sweet Hollow Summit	10.00		8.11	
50.	Sacramento-Route 15 near Wilbur Springs	6.58		11.86	
51.	Route 8 at ShellVille-Sebastopol	4.73		4.38	
52.	Alto-Tiburon	5.62		5.75	
53.	Route 7 at Fairfield-Route 4 near Lodi via Rio Vista	12.96		15.40	
54.	Route 11 at Perkins-Route 65 at Central House	6.59		9.51	

Route	Termini	1956 Percent gain or loss			
		Sunday		Monday	
		Gain	Loss	Gain	Loss
55. Route 5 near Glenwood-San Francisco			12.18	14.32	
56. Route 2 at Las Cruces-Route 1 near Fernbridge			1.94	6.25	
57. Route 2 near Santa Maria-Route 23 near Freeman via Bakersfield	11.49			8.43	
58. Route 2 near Santa Margarita-Arizona Line near Topock via Mojave and Barstow		6.71		7.46	
59. Route 4 at Gorman-Route 43 at Lake Arrowhead		9.20		7.91	
60. Route 2 at Serra-Route 2 at El Rio			1.58	3.02	
61. Route 4 south of Glendale-Route 59 near Phelan		11.48		6.38	
62. Route 171 near Buena Park-Route 61 near Crystal Lake		7.70		13.01	
63. Big Pine-Nevada State Line			9.06	14.71	
64. Route 2 at San Juan Capistrano-Blythe		2.05		1.85	
65. Route 18 near Mariposa-Auburn			1.20		0.54
66. Route 5 near Massdale-Route 13 near Oakdale		14.04		10.81	
67. Palaro River-Route 2 near San Benito River Bridge		23.85		1.08	
68. San Jose-San Francisco		10.06		10.55	
69. Route 5 at Warm Springs-Route 1, San Rafael		1.15		7.72	
70. Ukiah-Talmage		11.60		14.13	
71. Crescent City-Oregon Line			31.17		6.68
72. Weed-Oregon Line		2.73		5.75	
73. Route 29 near Johnstonville-Oregon Line		11.68		14.33	
74. Napa Wye-Cordelia via Vallejo and Benicia		3.15		2.65	
75. Oakland-Junction 65 at Altaville			0.92	10.01	
76. Route 125 at Shaw Ave.-Nevada State Line near Benton		16.43		16.32	
77. San Diego-Los Angeles via Pomona		9.47		7.66	
78. Route 12 near Descanso-Route 19 near March Field		10.59		3.13	
79. Route 2, Ventura-Route 4 at Castaic		9.80		7.77	
80. Route 151, Rincon Creek-Route 2 near Zaca		21.12		16.33	

Justus F. Craemer Retires From Public Service

Nationally known as a newspaperman and public official, Justus F. Craemer retired from state service as member of the California Public Utilities Commission on November 1st.

Craemer was co-owner of the *Orange Daily News* from November, 1909, through 1946. He has been associated in the ownership of the *San Rafael Independent-Journal* since 1937. Craemer was President of the California Newspaper Publishers Association for the period of 1929-30. He was also President of the National Editorial Association for 1932-33 and he has been President of the California Press Association since 1943. Before that period he was CPA vice president for 20 years.

His long life in public service includes such activities as being a member of the California State Board of Agriculture (State Fair Board), 1923-1928; private Secretary to Governor Frank F. Merriam during 1934; Assistant Director of the California State Department of Public Works, 1935-1937; Building and Loan Commissioner, State of California, 1937-1939; and member of the California Public Utilities Commission since January 1,

1939. He served as president of the commission in 1942.

His other activities as a public servant has included acting as Chairman of the Mountain Pacific States Conference of Public Service Commissions from 1942 to 1946 and being President of the National Association of Railroad and Utilities Commissioners from November. 18, 1948, to August 11, 1949.

Craemer's other business activities include an interest in the ownership of an orange grove in Orange County for many years. He is presently serving as a director of the First National Bank of Orange. In the past he has served as a Director of the Orange Building and Loan Association, Director of the Federal Finance Company of Santa Ana, Director of the California State Chamber of Commerce and from 1936 through 1938 Craemer was the Chairman of the Republican State Central Committee.

His social and service affiliations include memberships in the Rotary Club, Orange; the Press-Union League Club, San Francisco; Pacific Railway Club, San Francisco; the Jonathan Club, Los Angeles; the Family Club, San Francisco, and the Commonwealth Club in San Francisco.

SHERWIN GRADE

Continued from page 41 . . .

gravel and boulders were moved; 342,-000 tons of imported borrow material were hauled to complete the fills; 47,000 tons of crushed rock base and 46,000 tons of plant-mixed surfacing were placed to complete the pavement. The old pavement was 18 to 20 feet wide while the new is 32 feet minimum with one four-lane portion that is 60 feet wide. Although the new route saves only 0.43 mile in distance, savings in time, tempers and traffic congestion will multiply through the years to come and the savings in cost to the motorist will soon repay the initial investment in this modern highway.

One feature that may puzzle those traveling the new road is the series of small lateral dams in many of the cut sections. These were placed to prevent erosion and undermining of the pavement by storm water runoff on the long grades and will be filled by nature during the first storms to form a series of gentle gutter slopes.

State supervision on this major project, which is the largest ever undertaken in the Inyo-Mono Counties area, was the responsibility of Resident Engineer Gene Snyder and his assistants. Don Westbrook was general superintendent for the contractor. The many hours these men devoted to the job assured the quality of the finished product.

TEMPER

A person with a temper often gets into trouble. If a person with a temper loses it when he drives a car, he may also lose his life, says the California State Automobile Association. Many accidents are caused by one motorist trying to get revenge on another. When you drive, leave your temper at home or you may not get home.

During the 1955-56 Fiscal Year 21 grade crossings on state highways were closed or abandoned by changes in highway alignment, by construction of grade separations or by abandonment of railroad tracks, and three new crossings were opened, leaving a total of 814 such crossings on state highways as of June 30, 1956.

Arcata Project

Intersection Improvement
On US 101 and US 299

By E. B. THOMAS, Resident Engineer

RECENTLY COMPLETED in District 1 is the project in Humboldt County on US 101 between 0.6 mile north of Plaza Avenue in Arcata and 1.0 mile south of Mad River, and on US 299 between US 101 and the Mad River.

Of primary concern in the inception of this project was the improvement of the substandard intersection of US 101 and US 299.

The existing intersection was a right-angle abutment of US 299 against US 101 about 550 feet north of an overhead structure to a railroad and county road. All westbound traffic on Route 20 (US 299) was required to stop, then enter the almost continuous flow of north-south traffic on US 101. No traffic lights, turning lanes, or channelization for this conflicting traffic movement was practical because of the proximity of the existing overhead structure. To further aggravate the situation, all traffic turning southerly towards Arcata had to accelerate from the stop sign, cross the northbound traffic flow and travel up a 6 percent grade to the old overhead approach, a difficult feat for heavily loaded trucks.

Timber Land Area

US 299, extending easterly from Arcata to Redding, taps an immense area of timber land which has been heavily logged in post-war years. This highway provides the only outlet for the timber products, both logs and finished lumber, which must be trucked easterly to Redding or westerly to the Arcata-Eureka area where many mills are located and where facilities are available for transhipment by truck, rail, or ship.

The logging industry has consequently brought about a large increase in heavy trucking over this route during the past few years. A comparison of the 16-hour July Monday traffic counts for 1947 and 1956 shows the following:

	1947	1956	Increase (percent)
Total traffic	2,800	6,000	214
3-axle trucks	54	400	741
5-axle trucks	80	290	363

The normal increase of total traffic combined with the great increase of heavy truck traffic made a revision of the US 299 intersection essential.

Constructed In Two Stages

The new facility consists of a four-lane divided highway, with a 22-foot median strip. The structural section provided for 0.20 feet of Type B and 0.05 feet of open-graded plant-mix surfacing on 0.67 feet of road-mixed cement-treated base and 0.75 feet to 1.08 feet of imported subbase material. The project was developed on a limited access basis with frontage roads provided where required by local conditions.

The improvement was constructed in two stages. The first contract, for structures, was let in April, 1955, and required an expenditure of approximately $360,000. This structure contract provided a two-lane separation structure for the new US 101-US 299 intersection and twin overhead structures on US 101 over the Northwestern Pacific Railroad and a county road.

The southbound lanes of US 101 are entirely new construction lying westerly of the existing road, and therefore required a new overhead structure. However, the northbound lanes utilize the original roadbed location and the existing overhead was incorporated into the improvement. Timber trestle approach spans were removed and replaced with reinforced concrete girder spans, and the existing steel girder main span was widened with reinforced concrete to provide a 28-foot clear roadbed width.

Trumpet-type Interchange

The new intersection, about 1,500 feet north of the existing connection, features a trumpet-type interchange. The free flow of traffic over this new construction will be a welcome relief to all concerned. As an interesting sidelight this intersection is the first interchange structure ever built in the geographical limits of District I.

From the interchange structure US 299 heads northeasterly on new alignment for about 0.6 mile where it joins the existing road. From this point to the end of the project the existing alignment is followed.

The new alignment mentioned above supersedes about one mile of existing US 299, which will eventually be reverted to the County of Humboldt. A connection between this road and the new construction has been provided about 0.8 mile easterly of the new US 101-US 299 intersection. A cul-de-sac has been constructed at the end of the abandoned state highway at the site of the old intersection.

Heavy Logging Traffic

It is interesting to note that the above-mentioned connection to the existing road, although only a county road connection, has the same structural section as the freeway. This requirement is imposed by the fact that a high percentage of all traffic over the road will be logging trucks serving the seven lumber mills and one plywood mill along the superseded portion of US 299, in addition to various mills west of Arcata which are reached via the county road under the overhead structure.

Three-fifths of the construction lies predominately in the flood plain of the Mad River Valley. The grade was held somewhat above the surrounding ground throughout this section of the project to provide structural support and assure adequate drainage. This resulted in a "borrow job" with 150,000 cubic yards of imported borrow being set up against only 29,000 cubic yards of roadway excavation.

Borrow Work

A hillside borrow site near the middle of the job, about 1.1 miles east of the existing US 101-US 299 intersection, was set up under a materials agreement and was used by the contractor. This material, a marine deposit of brown sandy clay and gravel, proved to be excellent borrow with R-values ranging from 30 to 74 and averaging 55. The native moisture in the pit was almost perfect, and the material compacted very readily just as spread from the trucks.

Two 1½-cubic-yard shovels and one 1½-cubic-yard dragline were used to load a fleet of twenty 8 to 10 cubic yard trucks for the major part of the borrow work. A daily production rate of 4,575 cubic yards in 10 hours was attained. Compaction was obtained using tractor towed sheepsfoot rollers and a self-propelled 4-wheel roller the wheels of which are faced with steel pads.

Because the fills are nominal in height and overlay river bottom land which had been under cultivation for many years, compaction of the natural ground was required under all fills and roadway trenching was required to 2½ feet below profile grade in lieu of the standard 2 feet.

UPPER—Construction on US 101-US 299 interchange north of Arcata. LOWER—Looking southerly at US 101-US 299 interchange north of Arcata.

Development of the borrow pit entailed clearing off second growth redwood trees and brush and the removal of old redwood stumps up to 15 feet in diameter. Small debris was burned at the site; but, because of the difficulty of burning the large stumps, the contractor split them, by blasting, down to a size that could be loaded into trucks and hauled them to a disposal site. It is probable that more effort was expended in clearing the borrow site and removing the stumps than was required to clear the entire roadway construction area.

Unsuitable material developed in several areas of the roadway section where the templated excavation penetrated into the wet, blue-black organic soils underlying much of this area. It was necessary to remove this material to an average depth of 2 feet below subgrade with imported borrow or, in cases where standing water was encountered, with river-run gravel. All unsuitable material was disposed of in an old excavation near the end of the work on US 101. This pit was set up in the Special Provisions as a mandatory disposal site in conformance with a right of way agreement.

Series of Projects

This is the latest in a series of projects which began in 1952 to provide a four-lane divided highway from the north city limit of Eureka, through Arcata to this point, a total distance of 8.8 miles along US 101 and 1.7 miles on US 299.

Plans for extension of freeway construction north on US 101 are under way with studies well advanced for rerouting on a freeway basis from the end of this contract to 0.7 mile north of Trinidad, a distance of 13½ miles. The next stage of construction actually scheduled is for the reconstruction of the existing Mad River Bridge and construction of a parallel span and approaches in the 1957-58 Fiscal Year.

No further construction in this vicinity on US 299 is presently scheduled; however, preliminary studies of the section from Mad River Bridge to Preston Ranch, a distance of 15 miles, are now under way.

The current contract, covering grading and surfacing was awarded in

April of this year and was completed in November. The bid for this contract was $629,285. Mercer, Fraser Company, Inc., of Eureka was the contractor on both the structure and grading contracts. The work was under the direction of Alan S. Hart, District Engineer, and the author, for the Division of Highways. The contracting firm was represented by R. W. Brown, president, and Harley Stevenson, superintendent.

MERIT AWARD BOARD WINNERS

Employees of the Department of Public Works receiving certificates of award and commendation during September and October, 1956, are:

Frank Brunner, Highways, San Diego, $150, for proposing a modification of the minor movement control. This control is used with a three-phase timer to add a fourth phase to the traffic pattern at signalized intersections. This enables the timing with traffic demand and increases the possibility of a smooth traffic flow. In other words, the modification makes possible a variable time feature which means the length of a green light on a special turning movement will vary in accordance with the demands of traffic making a movement.

Francis Fisk, Architecture, San Francisco, $25 for recommending that column numbers (and pile cap numbers) be shown on mechanical and electrical drawings. This suggestion will be adopted as a general policy on all future drawings, including mechanical, electrical and architectural, as well as all other drawings, outlining work which must be orientated and correlated with the structural plans.

Lucy M. Enriquez, Architecture, Los Angeles, $25 for recommending that the printed tracing paper sheets used by project architects, etc., for preliminary budget plans be cut to one-fourth inch from the inside black border line so they will fit in the standard flat drawer file cases and that all future printed drawing paper be printed either the correct size or be trimmed to fit these files.

Eleanor L. Lenau, Highways, Sacramento, $20 for recommending the elimination of posting estimates in vendor's index; the filing of all water bill postings alphabetically under W; and making of a posting for each city or county on one card with a distinctive symbol to designate the city or county department.

Oleg J. Devorn, Los Angeles, and *Henry W. Remitz*, Sacramento, Highways, $15 each for recommending draftsmen be supplied with parallel edges instead of T-squares in the structural drafting section.

Dale H. Kuiper, Highways, San Bernardino, certificate of commendation for rec-

ommending that highway district safety engineers design safety routes to be used in case of fire or other disasters in a District VIII office building. While his suggestion was not used, it brought to the attention of the administration the existence of a problem and proper steps were taken to alleviate the situation.

Bruce F. Hockman, Highways, San Diego, certificate of commendation for recommending that the "Earthwork Data Sheet" be made in two distinct colors, one for terrain notes and the other for roadbed notes.

John E. Gere, Highways, Los Angeles, $100 for recommending the use of a slurry seal coat for highway surfaces, and the spraying of the pavement with water before applying the mix. Slurry seal coat is an asphalt emulsion mixed with rock dust and plaster sand. This mixture can be economically and rapidly applied to badly cracked and shattered portions of highway pavements. While it is not a cure for all problems it can and does act as a protecting overlay and will in some places be substituted for the conventional screening seal.

Isadore Goldberg, Hayward; *Neil V. Mahoney*, Sacramento; and *John R. Christian*, Buellton; Division of Highway employees, $25 a piece for suggesting a revision of Form M-31, Cost Distribution Sheet.

Robert Miller, Placerville, Highways, $50 for suggesting the use of an attachment for the "Tarco" salt spreader which permits operation of the sand control lever from the driver's seat. This procedure allows one man to operate the truck and spreader rather than having one man for each operation. It also permits safer operation by eliminating the need of a man on the rear of the truck.

John A. Brown, Eureka, Highways, $20 for suggesting a revision in the accounting procedure regarding the collection of the cost of repairing damages to state property.

Benjamin L. Potter, San Luis Obispo, Highways (four-time winner), $25 for recommending the use of a firm steel foundation for raised traffic signals rubber contact units. Instead of using sand, asphalt, cement and similar materials for fill-ins, this employee used steel bars and discarded steel salvage from the maintenance yard, as the basis for setting the contact units on.

Cherie Mae Carroll, Sacramento, Architecture, certificate of commendation for calling the attention of management to an unnecessary procedure, which resulted in a revision of Administrative Notice No. 17.

A total of $1,726,919 was expended by the Division of Highways for snow removal and icy pavement sanding during the 1955-56 Fiscal Year.

Dust Palliatives

Highway Engineers Keep Abreast of New Methods

By BERNDT NELSON, Assistant Construction Engineer, Division of Highways

Wherever highway construction is in progress there is the potential of dust nuisance. The ordinary inconveniences to the traveling public during construction periods such as delays during necessary traffic control, detours bypassing construction, additional distances, rougher temporary surfaces, etc., are accepted by the average motorist without complaint. The effect of dust when uncontrolled, however, is a major irritant, not only to the motorist, but to all within reach of it—adjacent property owners whose crops, animals and homes suffer, businesses—and to those who must handle the just complaints of those affected.

Because of its far-reaching effect, dust control is accentuated during the construction of state highways in order to minimize the nuisance that can be caused by lack of control.

Dust Control Methods

Often in our highway construction program, it is necessary to route traffic from existing nondusting traveled ways to other existing roads, or to detours constructed for the purpose to permit uninterrupted passage of traffic during construction of the new grade. It may be even necessary to route the traffic through the construction. At times it is not feasible because of the time element, stage construction or high cost, et cetera, to provide a dust-free surfaced roadway for a short period. Control of dust from this source and from the contractor's hauling operations is generally done by sprinkling with water. This type of dust control is used where a more permanent method, such as paving, is not considered economical or feasible.

The results obtained are often temporary, ranging at times from an overly wet condition shortly after application through the drying stage until dust conditions again demand a repetition of the cycle and so on. Obviously, any economical, easy, practical method of prevention of dust

nuisance that will be more lasting than our present method would be welcome.

Wetting Agents

One method of improving results accomplished by using water is by use of wetting agents. Some materials naturally resist wetting, even when dry, and the surface of other areas may acquire this characteristic by deposition of slight amounts of air-borne hydrophobic substances of unknown origin. Where this condition exists, untreated water runs off to low areas and accumulates in puddles, the other areas remaining unaffected by the treatment. Wetting agents lower the surface tension of water surfaces, causing quick penetration on contact with road material and longer lasting treatment because of uniform and deeper penetration.

Wetting agents are generally added at the rate of approximately one part of agent to four or five thousand parts of water for the first application, and about one part of agent to eight or ten thousand parts of water for subsequent applications. The cost of wetting agents of this nature is generally between $2.50 and $3 per gallon, in 55-gallon drums.

Calcium Chloride Effective

Where economical, calcium chloride is used to alleviate dust nuisance. This product which can be obtained in flake or pellet form is effective because it has a strong affinity for water. It attracts and absorbs moisture from the air and is dissolved in the moisture it collects. When added to a dust area, calcium chloride, because of the above action, keeps the surface slightly moist. The resulting solution resists evaporation and lasts longer than an application of water penetrating to the same depth.

When used as a dust preventive it is spread at the rate of approximately one to one and one-half pounds per

square yard for the first treatment, subsequent treatments requiring about one-half pound per square yard. Water must be available for it; therefore in dry areas the area to be treated should be dampened just prior to application. The material is ideal for use where air temperature and moisture conditions are such that loss by evaporation during the day can be regained during the nighttime hours of relatively higher humidity.

Mixed With Rock Salt

Calcium chloride is in general use as a dust preventive in the Midwest, as that area is close to the source of supply. Freight costs represent approximately 50 percent of the total cost of $70 to $75 per ton to the user on the West Coast.

Sodium chloride is also used as a dust preventive. Rock salt is the form in which it is generally used. The dust prevention obtained is from a different action from that of calcium chloride which prevents dust by keeping the surface moist. Because sodium chloride is not deliquescent, water must be added to it to form a solution. For this reason rock salt is generally mixed with the road surfacing materials and water to the desired depth. The water dissolves the salt and the resultant solution binds together the dust-forming materials when recrystallization takes place at the surface during the periods of dry weather. About one and one-half pounds of rock salt is used per square yard per inch of depth desired. The material is produced on the West Coast and can be obtained at a cost of $14 to $15 per ton f.o.b. the plant. This is approximately one-half the cost of calcium chloride f.o.b. the plants in the Middle West.

Some Products on Market

There are a few proprietary products on the market sold primarily for dust control purposes. Although the exact formulations of each are held confidential by the manufacturers, the information given is that in the manufacture of the products, waste materials from asphalt and lubricating oil refining, used lubricating oil, petroleum resins, water and chemical additives are used and combined, further refined, emulsified or cut back to create a product with dust-preventing characteristics when applied to untreated road surfaces.

They are available to the user at approximately $24 per ton at the refineries. Recommended application by the manufacturers is one-half gallon per square yard.

Gaining in popularity because of excellent results, cost and relative permanency, and in which increased interest is being shown, is another method of dust laying that has been tried with success in several locations in California and elsewhere.

Briefly, the method is the use of a greatly diluted solution of asphaltic mixing emulsion and water—or to put it more simply, the continued use of water but containing a small percentage of mixing emulsion.

Materials—The mixing emulsion is that conforming to Section 56(a) of the Standard Specifications quoted in part as follows:

"(2) Mixing Type Emulsion.—The bituminous base used in manufacturing mixing type emulsion shall be paving asphalt, Grade 120-150 * * *.

When tested in accordance with the standard method of tests of the AASHO Designation: T59 * * * mixing type emulsion shall conform to the following requirements

"No separation within	30 days
"Viscosity, S. F., seconds	20-100
"Residue at 163° C., percent	57- 62
"Sieve test, max. percent	0.10
"Cement mixing test	
not more than	2%
"Modified miscibility with	
water—difference of asphalt	
residue not more than	4.5%"

Although various proportions have been experimented with, a 10 percent mixing emulsion–90 percent water solution seems to be the most practical from the standpoint of ease of application, good penetration and the characteristics of being able to be placed without pickup, splattering, staining or interference with traffic. Travel

on the roadway is possible to the same degree as if just water alone had been applied.

Equipment—Application by asphalt spreader truck is not necessary as the mixture can be applied with the same equipment used for applying water, whether the water spreading equipment is equipped with regular nozzles, a drilled pipe header or a spreading pan. A separate operation of mixing the water and the mixing emulsion is not necessary either. Generally, the mixing emulsion is placed in the spreading tank first and because of its complete miscibility with water, the water added to fill the tank creates all the action necessary for uniform mixing.

Methods. Best results are obtained if the material to be treated is previously wetted. This prevents quick drying and promotes penetration of the diluted emulsion mixture. This is especially true in hot weather when quick drying will prevent penetration and cause a decrease in the effective depth of treatment.

Application rates vary, depending on the type of surface to be treated and on the ability of the surface to absorb the application without runoff. A total application of 0.75 gallon per square yard is considered about the minimum for the first treatment. Using 90 percent–10 percent mixture, this means a net of about 0.04 gallon asphalt per square yard. To avoid excessive runoff from tightly consolidated materials, it may be necessary to make more than one application to obtain the total desired spread.

The mixture has an initial appearance similar to muddy irrigation water, the black color usually associated with asphalt being only in evidence after application when an area has chanced to dry without being subjected to traffic. This, too, disappears within a short period, the only color evidence visible being a slight darkening of the treated material. Some who have used the method claim a secondary advantage. In fact the primary purpose for the use of the method has been in cases to promote cohesiveness whereby the road surface is held together without "whip-off" of the

road material. The shape of the road is maintained and surfaces that once required intermittent watering and blading throughout the dry period of the year can be treated with the expectation that the treatment would last three to five times longer than without the use of the added emulsion. This varies, of course, with the depth of treatment, some going to the extent of blade-mixing material because of the ease of doing so to obtain greater depth. Another advantage is that cold, wet weather is not a deterrent; the increased mixing season can be measured in months.

The success of the method as a dust palliative lies in the fact that although the water used has performed a temporary task of settling the dust, it has also acted as a carrier of asphalt which remains in a thin film on the treated material after the water has disappeared by evaporation or percolation. The dust particles are caused to cohere or are made heavier by the asphalt film which accumulates after each application, resulting in a successively longer lasting treatment.

RECORD BUDGET

Continued from page 36 . . .

are: a new Colorado River Bridge at Blythe, in cooperation with the State of Arizona; a structure to carry the Olympic Freeway over the Los Angeles River and the Santa Fe yards in Los Angeles; a new bridge over Petaluma Creek on State Sign Route 37; the substructure for a new Sacramento River Bridge at Rio Vista; and new bridges over the Mad River in Humboldt County (US 101) and the Gualala River, at the Mendocino-Sonoma county line (State Sign Route 1).

The substantial allocations for rights of way in the 1957-58 state highway budget will be used to clear the path for still more new construction in succeeding fiscal years, when even larger federal apportionments are expected.

Fire hazard and noxious weed control on state highways cost $549,480, and $1,249,500 was expended by the Division of Highways for erosion control and care of trees during the Fiscal Year 1955-56.

Old A.C. Pavement

Completes 30 Years of
Satisfactory Service

By E. G. BOWER, Assistant District Engineer

Under the recent District VIII blanket resurfacing contract, a portion of Mission Boulevard (U.S. 60) between the Riverside county line and Mira Loma has received its first real "assist" in 30 years of continuous duty as a traffic carrier.

The original construction consisted of an 18-foot Portland cement concrete pavement four inches thick, constructed in 1914 by the M. R. Company, Inc. of Los Angeles. This job extended from the Riverside county line to the Santa Ana River—a total length of 10.34 miles.

By 1926 reconstruction was necessary. Under another contract, four inches of asphalt concrete were placed over the old pavement and six inches (in places) where a sand blanket was placed to raise the grade. It is this pavement which has given 30 years of "unassisted" service. Perhaps a look at the method of placing or the materials used will give us a clue to its long life.

Problems Encountered

The final report for this project, written by Resident Engineer H. O. Ragan, gives a graphic account of the problems encountered and the nature of the work:

"The old Portland cement concrete pavement 18 feet in width and four inches thick had become badly fractured—particularly that part between Ontario and the San Pedro, Los Angeles, and Salt Lake Railroad crossing. The adjacent soil along this portion is extremely sandy; in fact, during windstorms no little trouble has been experienced in keeping the highway clear of drifting sand. The most severe condition in this respect existed just west of the railroad crossing and extending for a distance of about 4,400 feet, where the highway parallels the tracks of the railroad. The grade line of the highway on this section was much lower than that of the railroad

UPPER—Texture of old pavement as it looked before resurfacing. LOWER—Portable batch plant at Champagne Siding.

and also lower than the original ground. This condition consequently created a pocket in which the sand collected during windstorms and necessitated being removed after the

storms had subsided in order to make the highway safe for traffic. Thus, to avoid future trouble in this respect, the grade line of the new improvement was raised one to two feet. In

UPPER—Old sand subgrade, looking east. Raking old base course.

six inches and the top set to grade of asphalt concrete shoulder widening. The headers on the left side were three inches by four inches and set to grade of leading course. Strips one and one-half inches by two inches were nailed on the large headers for pavement courses that followed. Much of the ground encountered east of Wineville was very dry and hard, making it difficult to drive header stakes. The contractor overcame this hindrance by employing * * * an air compressor and drill for opening up the holes for the stakes, and a hammer of his own design for driving them. He estimated that such an arrangement resulted in the saving of five to six laborers per day. * * *"

Asphalt Concrete Surface

"Before laying of asphalt concrete surface, the old concrete base, from which the loose oil cake had been removed, was well cleaned by sweeping with stiff push brooms and then painted with an asphalt paint binder mixture consisting of 40 percent asphalt and 60 percent gasoline. Painting was done well enough in advance of paving operations to allow for evaporation of the gasoline. The mixture was formed by first heating the asphalt to a safe temperature and placing in drums to which the required amount of gasoline was added. It was then deposited on the base by buckets and swept as thinly as possible with light push brooms over the full 20-foot width."

Materials for construction of asphalt concrete pavement consisted of crushed rock from Reliance Rock Company, Covina, and Blue Diamond Company, Corona, shipped to the plant by rail; sand from a local sand dune area hauled in by truck; and rock dust from the Riverside Portland Cement Company delivered into the contractor's trucks at Crestmore. Paving asphalt, Grade "D" (50-60 penetration), was supplied by the Standard Oil Company from its El Segundo refinery. The combined mix conformed with the requirements of the Standard Specifications of June, 1925, for base course, leveling course, and surface course.

this connection, the contractor was given the choice of building up a new grade on the old pavement by means of imported earth borrow or utilizing the available surplus sand along the sides of the highway. After studying the condition closely from all angles, it was decided to make use of the sand. Grade was constructed and headers placed just previous to paving operations. Fortunately, standpipes of an irrigation pipeline were just off the right of way line to the right and the grade was well-ponded with water

for settlement. The resultant condition and appearance of the finished highway on this particular section is favorable.* * * "

Work Begun in 1925

'Setting of wooden headers in preparation for asphalt concrete pavement was begun on December 20, 1925. As stated previously, the old pavement was 18 feet wide, and the two feet of widening was placed on the right, or south, side only. The headers used on the right side were three inches by

... Continued on page 54

50

UPPER—View of road just before resurfacing. Note new eastbound roadway on right. LOWER—View of new road as it looks today.

Cost Index
Declines Noted During
Third Quarter of 1956

By RICHARD H. WILSON, Assistant State Highway Engineer;
H. C. McCARTY, Office Engineer, and
LLOYD B. REYNOLDS, Assistant Office Engineer

THE CALIFORNIA Highway Construction Cost Index for the third quarter of 1956, counter to the forecast made at the end of the second quarter, stood at 249.1 index points (1940=100), a decline of 2.7 percent from the previous quarter. It exceeds the first quarter of 1956 by 13.5 percent and the high established in the fourth quarter of 1951 by 1.5 percent. It is believed that the current sag is temporary and that the upward trend will be resumed in the fourth quarter of this year.

The present decline in the index was influenced by three of the eight construction items upon which the index is based. Primary effect was caused by favorable steel prices obtained on six large freeway projects situated close to fabricating centers. Settlement of the steel strike in July which resulted in a three-year agreement between labor and industry has effectively stabilized the price of steel to the extent that bidding against future deliveries can be made with reasonable assurance. It is reasonable to believe that during the second quarter, considerable of the advance in bid prices received on items involving the use of steel can be attributed to inclusion of contingencies on the part of contractors for their protection in view of uncertainties connected with renewal of labor agreements and a possible strike which materialized.

Bidder Competition Low

Competition among bidders continues at a low average. The average number of bidders per contract during the third quarter of 1956 stood at 3.7 compared to 3.8 in the second quarter and 4.5 in the third quarter of 1955. While there is a marked decrease in the number of bidders show-

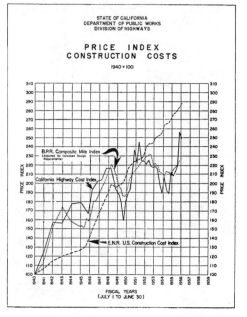

STATE OF CALIFORNIA
DEPARTMENT OF PUBLIC WORKS
DIVISION OF HIGHWAYS

PRICE INDEX
CONSTRUCTION COSTS
1940 = 100

B.P.R. Composite Mile Index
(Adjusted for Increased Design Requirements)

California Highway Cost Index

E.N.R. U.S. Construction Cost Index

FISCAL YEARS
(JULY 1 TO JUNE 30)

ing interest in projects valued in excess of $1,000,000, its weighted effect on the average is not pronounced but the mainstay in holding to a high average is the class usually evident in bidding below $500,000 which has apparently vanished. The number of

contractors prequalified by the department to bid in the various brackets of project value remains in agreement with former years which indicates that a decline in available bidders is not the underlying reason for the low average obtained.

52

California Highways

THE CALIFORNIA HIGHWAY CONSTRUCTION COST INDEX

Year	Cost Index
1940	100.0
1941	125.0
1942	157.5
1943	156.4
1944	177.8
1945	179.5
1946	179.7
1947	203.3
1948	216.6
1949	190.7
1950	176.7
(1st Quarter 1950—160.6)	
1951	210.8
(4th Quarter 1951—245.4)	
1952	224.5
1953	216.2
1954 (1st Quarter)	199.4
1954 (2d Quarter)	189.0
1954 (3d Quarter)	207.8
1954 (4th Quarter)	192.2
1955 (1st Quarter)	189.3
1955 (2d Quarter)	212.4
1955 (3d Quarter)	208.6
1955 (4th Quarter)	212.6
1956 (1st Quarter)	219.5
1956 (2d Quarter)	255.9
1956 (3d Quarter)	249.1

NUMBER AND SIZE OF PROJECTS, TOTAL BID VALUES AND AVERAGE NUMBER OF BIDDERS

(July 1, 1956, to September 30, 1956)

Project Volume	Up to $50,000	$50,000 to $100,000	$100,000 to $250,000	$250,000 to $500,000	$500,000 to $1,000,000	Over $1,000,000	All Projects
Road Projects							
No. of projects	135	28	21	14	6	....	204
Total Value*	$3,217,167	$1,992,607	$3,193,860	$4,707,322	$4,604,604	....	$16,715,550
Ave. No. bidders	3.3	4.0	5.1	4.4	3.8	....	3.7
Structure Projects							
No. of projects	12	1	6	2	....	1	22
Total Value*	$221,051	$85,496	$928,044	$766,923	....	$1,098,618	$3,100,132
Ave. No. bidders	3.6	2.0	5.0	2.5	....	5.0	3.9
Combination Projects							
No. of projects	....	....	....	....	2	8	10
Total Value*	....	....	....	....	$1,341,234	$21,048,258	$22,389,492
Ave. No. bidders	....	....	....	....	3.0	5.4	4.9
Summary							
No. of projects	147	29	27	16	8	9	236
Total value*	$3,438,218	$3,078,183	$4,121,904	$5,474,185	$5,945,838	$22,146,876	$42,305,174
Ave. No. bidders	3.3	3.9	5.1	4.2	3.6	5.3	3.7

* Bid items only.

Total Average Bidders by Months

	July	August	September	Average for third quarter
1956	3.8	3.7	3.7	3.7
1955	4.9	4.2	4.4	4.5

AVERAGE CONTRACT PRICES

	Roadway excavation, per cu. yd.	Crusher run base, per ton	Plant mix surfacing per ton	Asphalt concrete pavement, per ton	PCC pavement, per cu. yd.	PCC structures, per cu. yd.	Bar reinforcing steel, per lb.	Structural steel, per lb.
1940	$0.22	$1.54	$3.19	$3.97	$7.68	$18.33	$0.040	$0.083
1941	0.26	2.31	3.84	3.18	7.54	23.31	0.063	0.107
1942	0.36	2.81	4.03	4.16	9.62	29.48	0.073	0.103
1943	0.42	2.26	3.71	4.76	11.48	31.76	0.069	0.080
1944	0.50	2.48	4.10	4.50	10.46	31.99	0.064	0.122
1945	0.51	2.42	4.20	4.88	10.90	37.20	0.059	0.102
1946	0.41	2.45	4.00	4.63	9.45	37.38	0.060	0.099
1947	0.46	3.42	4.52	5.38	12.38	48.44	0.080	0.138
1948	0.55	3.43	4.30	5.38	13.04	49.86	0.093	0.136
1949	0.49	2.67	4.67	4.64	12.28	48.67	0.096	0.117
1950	0.40	2.25	4.26	3.75	11.11	43.45	0.079	0.094
1951	0.49	2.62	4.34	5.00	12.31	47.22	0.102	0.159
1952	0.56	2.99	5.00	4.38	13.42	48.08	0.098	0.150
1953	0.51	2.14*	5.31	4.55	13.74	50.59	0.093	0.133
1st Quarter 1954	0.45	2.28	4.23	4.78	14.59	47.52	0.093	0.126
2nd Quarter 1954	0.38	2.09	4.29	5.18	14.25	47.12	0.093	0.114
3d Quarter 1954	0.43	1.88	4.68	7.00	13.63	49.59	0.095	0.162
4th Quarter 1954	0.35	1.75	4.83	..	12.13	46.08	0.094	0.135
1st Quarter 1955	0.39	1.69	4.55	..	13.44	40.66	0.095	0.140
2d Quarter 1955	0.42	1.99	5.39	..	14.46	51.36	0.098	0.136
3d Quarter 1955	0.41	2.33	5.43	5.70	13.46	49.64	0.093	0.132
4th Quarter 1955	0.37	2.00	5.52	4.00	15.06	52.72	0.099	0.144
1st Quarter 1956	0.40	2.08	5.40	6.80	14.05	83.51	0.105	0.166
2d Quarter 1956	0.51	2.06	6.27	..	14.64	87.13	0.113	0.219
3d Quarter 1956	0.52	2.37	6.12	..	15.57	96.22	0.121	0.178

* Untreated rock base substituted for crusher run base at this point.

The first projects included in the federal interstate highway program have recently "rolled off the assembly line" and bids will shortly be received on these projects. This program will continue at a uniform rate but considered in the over all, the number will not be large during the ensuing year for reasons explained in the release of the second quarter index.

Four of the eight items used in computing the construction cost index showed an increase during the third quarter and three items were below the average costs in the previous quarter. The tabulation of average contract prices contained in this report furnishes a comparison of the eight contract items in previous periods.

Roadway Excavation

Roadway excavation advanced 1 cent to $0.52 in this quarter. The fluctuation is minor although it is a new high since 1952. The increase of $0.21 to $2.27 in the price of untreated rock base is no doubt occasioned by the availability of supply source with respect to project locations. The current cost is still below

average in the corresponding period last year. Prices for portland cement concrete pavement averaged $15.57 as against $14.64 last quarter. The current quarter established a new high for

this item. Project conditions during the quarter were not sufficiently varied during the quarter to offset the effect of a few highly weighted contracts. Bar reinforcing steel prices reached the new high of $0.121 in this period. This increase is no doubt attributable to the rise in steel prices. Use of reinforcing steel was sufficiently widespread in the quarter to obtain a fairly true average. Unbalance due to proximity or remoteness of projects to supply sources was therefore not evident.

Decreases Reflected

Plant-mixed surfacing reflected a decrease of 15 cents per ton in this period to $6.12. The extensive resurfacing program was carried on statewide and representative projects involved fairly large quantities. The sources of supply being equally widespread contributed to maintaining an unbiased average. Class A portland cement concrete structures dropped to $56.32 from $57.13 in the previous quarter. The 81 cent drop in this item no doubt reflects the stabilizing effect brought about by settlement of the steel situation existing in the last quarter. Delays in steel deliveries would in turn, cause equal delays in completing structures particularly in those structures involving steel shapes in their construction. The decline in structural steel prices in this period from $0.219 to $0.178 was commented on in the beginning of this release.

The accompanying graph shows a comparison of the California Construction cost Index, the Engineering News-Record Construction Cost Index and the United States Bureau of Public Roads Composite Mile Index all of which are reduced to the base, 1940=100. The last two mentioned indexes are nationwide in scope. The Engineering News-Record Index continues its upward course without interruption. Its steady climb indicates that adverse influence in any spotted locations is not sufficiently felt to overcome the general trend. The E. N. R. Index is up 4.4 points or 1.53 percent over the second quarter.

Belief was expressed last quarter that the United States Bureau of Public Roads Composite Mile Index would follow the course of the California and E. N. R. Indexes. This assumption was substantiated when results of the computations became available. It re-

OLD A. C. PAVEMENT

Continued from page 50 . . .

Portable Batch Plant

These materials were mixed in a 2,000-pound portable batch plant set up in two different locations during the life of the job. The portion of the roadway now remaining in its original form was paved from the second plant set up at Champagne Siding at the county line. Referring again to the final report, we read that "mineral aggregates for the asphalt concrete mixture were fed to the cold elevator at the drier by clam shell. This did not prove entirely satisfactory as far as control of material grading in the different bins; consequently, a two-compartment bunker was installed over the cold elevator of the Champagne plant and much better results secured. * * * Multiple beam scales of the Warren Brother's type were employed. * * *

"Distribution and handling of asphalt concrete mixture at the place of laying on the highway was done with shovels, six shovelers and four rakers handling the plant output. A pair of patented mechanical asphalt spreaders were given a trial, but as manipulated by the contractor's crew did not producing them for part of two days, they were abandoned by the contractor, since he could not foresee their practicability and saving in labor. The greater part of the pavement laying on the Riverside County section of the job was done during cold and windy weather, making it difficult to place the mixture and roll at a suitable working temperature."

Tests of Interest

On June 27, 1956, just prior to re-surfacing this 30-year-old asphalt concrete pavement, a sample was cut

mains to be seen whether the third quarter position will follow the national trend of E. N. R. or the flattening trend developed in California. Figures for the second quarter show the B. P. R. Index to be up five points or 2.27 percent over the first quarter of 1956.

through the full 4½-inch depth on the Riverside County portion. Although a grading analysis was made, the results have no particular significance, since they represent a combination of leveling and surface courses, each of which met a different grading specification; however, the other test results may be of interest:

Moisture content	0.1%
Bitumen ratio	5.7%
Specific gravity	2.31
Stability	59
Swell	0.000"
Permeability	0

Indications are that the long service life of this pavement was due to a combination of factors. The low moisture content is indicative of dry subgrade, which results in part from the fact that the grade was raised one to two feet with blow sand in this area. The high stability undoubtedly contributed its share also, and probably resulted from the interlocking of the crushed rock used in the mix and the relatively low penetration of the paving asphalt. (The 1949 Standard Specifications, latest edition covering asphalt concrete pavement, require a minimum stabilometer value of 35 and provide for the use of paving asphalts having a range of penetration of 60-70, 85-100, or 120-150.) It is estimated that the pavement has been subjected to 16,700,000 equivalent 5,000-pound wheel loads, even though the first 10 years of its life contributed only about one-eighth of the total.

Under a contract with Matich Constructors, a one-inch blanket of plant-mixed surfacing was applied to the roadway last summer, and it is anticipated that the road will serve future traffic requirements for many more years. According to the traffic count made last July, the highway is now carrying an average daily traffic of 9,600 vehicles, or about 4,800 per day on the north roadway.

GOOD DRIVER

One difference between a good and a bad driver is that the good driver rarely gets himself into situations where he needs to react swiftly to avoid trouble. A bad driver, says the California State Automobile Association, has several close calls almost every time he drives.

Anniversary
San Francisco-Oakland Bay Bridge Is Twenty Years Old

By HOWARD C. WOOD, Bridge Engineer

ON NOVEMBER 12, 1936, President Franklin D. Roosevelt pressed a gold telegraph key in Washington, D. C., and set off one of the noisiest celebrations in the history of the San Francisco Bay area.

Factory whistles shrilled and aerial bombs exploded while thousands of people cheered. Hundreds of crowded, gaily-decorated fishing boats and private pleasure craft churned the waters of the bay. Overhead, 250 fighter planes roared through the sky while high above a lone aircraft traced the words: "The bridge is open."

The telegraph key pressed by the President 3,000 miles away had blinked on green lights marking the formal opening to the public of the San Francisco-Oakland Bay Bridge, the largest structure of its kind planned and erected by man.

Dream Comes True

Its completion marked the realization of a long-standing dream of cities and communities on both sides of the bay. By midnight of that first day more than 200,000 eager, happy people had flooded across the new bridge. Opening celebrations in San Francisco and Oakland lasted four days.

The impact of so imposing a structure upon the citizens of the Bay area was strong and, in some cases, overwhelming as exemplified by the story of the little farmer from an East Bay community who, shortly after the opening of the bridge, decided to see it for himself. Accompanied by his wife, he headed his small truck west, joined the flow of cars making for the toll gates and soon found himself on the bridge rolling along toward San

Francisco. But the quiet-living man soon found the spectacle overpowering. Everywhere around him cars flashed by, horns blared, and, to make things worse, the shrill, frightened comments and admonitions of his wife were added to the cacophony. All this amidst a tangle of cables and struts and gleaming towers that seemed to reach to the sky. Finally, the little man could stand it no longer. Pulling over into the right lane he stopped his truck and, while the horns and cries of frustrated motorists sounded behind him, walked up to the nearest emergency call box and pressed the button. As he explained to the emergency crew who answered his call, he had had all he could take and would they please get him out of there, a plea, it may be added, that many a modern day motorist admits to feeling when

Governor Frank F. Merriam uses blow torch to sever chain signalizing opening of San Francisco-Oakland Bay Bridge to traffic. Dignitaries, left to right: State Highway Engineer Charles H. Purcell, who built the span; former President Herbert C. Hoover; Governor Merriam; Charles Henderson, Director of RFC; U. S. Senator William G. McAdoo; Director of Public Works Earl Lee Kelly.

entering on to a heavily trafficked urban freeway for the first time.

One of World's Wonders

It was hard for anyone, and especially a Californian, to repress a feeling of pride when he gazed upon the mighty structure across the bay, which immediately claimed and has held a place among the wonders of the modern world. The statistics of the new bridge were impressive and often record-shattering.

To begin with, it was the longest high level bridge in the world (a record it still holds) with 4¼ miles of structure and another four miles of approaches at the San Francisco and Oakland ends, for a total length of 8¼ miles.

The towers of the suspension section across the West Bay were more than 500 feet high and from them hung 28-inch-thick cables supporting a two-level roadbed with six lanes for autos on the upper deck and three lanes for busses and trucks plus two tracks for electric interurban trains on the lower deck. Each cable had 17,464 separate wires in it and there was enough wire in all the cables to stretch nearly three times around the world.

Record Depth Below Water

The bridge piers had established new engineering records for depth below water, the base of one pier having been sunk to a maximum depth of 242 feet. The concrete and reinforcing steel in the bridge were enough to rebuild all the large office buildings in downtown San Francisco. The timber used to put up the structure would build 3,000 five-room dwellings, enough for a town of 15,000 people. The tunnel through Yerba Buena Island connecting the West Bay suspension crossing with the East Bay cantilever crossing was the largest bore vehicular tunnel in existence.

From the time of its opening the bridge assumed a vital role in the transportation picture of the Bay area. After the first influx of sightseers following its completion the traffic count steadied at an average daily figure of 25,000 vehicles. The count fell off slightly in 1938, rose markedly during 1939 with the opening of the San Francisco World's Fair on Treasure

Expert divers were used extensively in laying the foundations for the bridge caissons

Island. It rose rapidly during the war years when it handled heavy military and war industry traffic between San Francisco and Oakland and the military establishments on Treasure Island.

90,000 Vehicles per Day

In addition to bearing the brunt of commuter traffic across the bay it was also designated as the western terminus of two transcontinental highways, US 40 and 50. Now carrying an average of 90,000 vehicles a day and well over 100,000 on peak days, it is often referred to as the "Main Street of the Bay Area."

From the beginning, the maintenance and operation of the bridge was a task of major proportions. At the present time bridge personnel, under the direction of the author and his assistant, Carl Hamilton, number some 300 for the Bay Bridge itself. Another 150 persons, also under their direction, are assigned to the other State-owned toll bridges in the area, the Dumbarton, San Mateo-Hayward, and the recently-completed Richmond-San Rafael Bridge as well as the Carquinez Bridge near Vallejo.

Maintenance against the elements is an ever present problem. A permanent

crew of 60 painters is kept constantly busy painting and repainting the bridge to protect it from the ravages of corrosion by spray and salt-laden winds and the exhaust fumes from thousands of autos and trucks.

Safest Stretch of Highway

Even though on the basis of comparative accident statistics (per mile of vehicle travel) the Bay Bridge can claim to be the safest stretch of highway anwhere in the State, traffic tie-ups, the universal headache of all heavy traffic roads, are one of the chief concerns of the bridge staff. A traffic accident with the consequent blocking of one or more lanes, especially during rush hours, can cause a chain reaction jam-up that extends for miles. It also causes frayed tempers which tend to bring about more accident-prone conditions.

Service crews are always standing by to man the emergency fleet of six tow trucks, one fire truck and four special bridge service pickup trucks or "cruisers." During the peak traffic hours from 7 to 9 o'clock in the morning and 4.30 to 6.30 in the evening the four radio-equipped "cruisers" are constantly patroling back and forth

56

with the traffic on the bridge to spot any trouble or to be closer at hand when trouble on a particular section of the bridge is reported to them.

Emergency Service

Speaking in terms of averages, these crews can look forward each day to changing six flat tires, bringing gas or oil to 11 stalled cars and towing another 11 off the bridge due to engine trouble or some other reason. One out of every 20 of the tow-offs is the result of an accident. Once every seven days they can expect a fire of some sort on the bridge. Putting it another way, since the bridge was opened to the public in 1936 these crews have changed nearly 47,000 flat tires, towed 76,500 stalled vehicles off the bridge, brought gas or oil to 78,000 more and put out just over 1,000 fires.

Handling the tolls claims the largest portion of bridge employees. In addition to their duties of collecting and guarding an average of $26,000 in tolls each day, the more than 100 toll officers, sergeants and lieutenants under Captain M. L. Silvey find themselves faced with a variety of extra problems all the way from detecting and apprehending a drunk driver to rendering assistance to some solid citizen who finds that he has come away from home without any money in his pockets.

Radio Broadcasts

In spite of what an average motorist might think when he happens to be caught in a traffic jam, his safety and convenience are the constant concern of the bridge staff. One recent inovation was to allow a local Bay area radio station to beam a week day program direct from the bridge itself. Known as "Car Tunes," the program originates from the central dispatcher's office at the toll plaza where all the latest information about traffic conditions on the bridge is available. Emceed by one of the radio station staff, the broadcast is aimed primarily at the tired commuter wending his weary way homeward over the bridge between 4 and 6 p.m. The show supplies him with information on bridge traffic conditions along with music and news, and is apparently having some effect on driving habits. Statistics in-

dicate that during the time the show was on the air accident reduction on the upper deck was 25 percent.

For 20 years, now, the bridge has existed as a reality, a magnificent spectacle of proportioned towers, cables, girders and piers spanning the bay. It has become so much a part of the scenery that it is easy to forget that for a long time it was only a dream in the minds of men.

Dream 100 Years Old

Just how or when this dream first took form it is not easy to say. Perhaps, first, only as a thought in the mind of an Indian or a Spaniard as he stood looking out over the gray-green waters of the bay.

The first formal expression of the idea seems to have occurred just 100 years ago when an article in the now defunct newspaper *Alta Californian* reported the State Legislature as debating, rather perfunctorily as it turned out, the feasibility of attempting a transbay bridge.

Some say that the idea really began in 1868 when an editorial entitled "A Bridge Across The Bay" appeared in the *San Francisco Bulletin*. It began: "What do our readers think of a bridge from Hunters Point to the Alameda shore? Is that not considerable of a bridge?"

The editorial went on to say that the Central Pacific Railroad Company had the matter under consideration and only awaited a franchise from the State to enable it to commence work.

Some Wide Bridge

The bridge was to be 125 feet wide (the roadway of the present bridge is 58 feet), would cost 5¼ million dollars according to engineering estimates of the time, and would be between four and five miles long. It would be erected on stone piers "after the most approved and substantial method" and have several "draws" to let light and heavy vessels through. The deck was to provide room for a double railroad track, a double thoroughfare for vehicles and a double walk for pedestrians.

The editorial admitted that it would be much cheaper to build a road around the bay unless the Central Pa-

cific could 'kill two birds with one stone" and install some types of facilities to derive extra income which should pay at least some return on the immense outlay. Therefore, it was proposed to "erect booths and saloons on the remaining space on the deck and to make the bridge a place of popular resort for moonlight promenades."

Needless to say, the bridge was never constructed.

In the years that followed, innumerable private enterprises for the construction of a bridge over the bay were launched by always enthusiastic and sometimes capable men, but none of these ever became anything more than schemes on paper.

San Francisco's Supervisors Act

The San Francisco Board of Supervisors might claim some credit for getting the bridge on the road to reality when it declared a transbay bridge to be a commercial and economic necessity for the area, but that it must not be a private enterprise, thereby laying the problem in the lap of the State of California.

The first concrete aid came in July, 1921, when the San Francisco Motor Car Dealers appropriated $12,000 for preliminary borings by Ralph Modjeski and John Vipond Davies. The next hard cash was not forthcoming until eight years later when the City of San Francisco supplemented the amount with $40,000. But the tenuous dreams of the earlier decades were taking on form and even a little substance. In May, 1929, the California Legislature created the California Toll Bridge Authority. Five months later the Hoover-Young Commission was formed with Mark L. Requa as chairman. The commission was charged with the task of recommending a solution to the San Francisco-Oakland Bay Bridge problem.

Purcell Built Bridge

Secretary of the commission was the late Charles H. Purcell, then State Highway Engineer, and later State Director of Public Works, who was to play such a vital part in financing, designing and constructing the bridge.

On February 20, 1931, the Congress of the United States passed an act "granting to the State of California the right to construct, maintain and operate a bridge across the Bay of San Francisco from Rincon Hill in San Francisco by way of Goat Island (Yerba Buena) to Oakland."

On May 25th, Governor Rolph signed Chapter 400, Statutes of 1931, which appropriated $650,000 for the completion of plans and specifications of the San Francisco-Oakland Bay Bridge. In August, Purcell was appointed Chief Engineer of the California Toll Bridge Authority with Glenn B. Woodruff as Engineer of Design. On September 15th the San Francisco-Oakland Bay Bridge offices were officially opened at 500 Sansome Street in San Francisco and the San Francisco-Oakland Bay Bridge Division of the Department of Public Works was created with Charles E. Andrew as Bridge Engineer.

Financial Hurdle

Plans for the bridge were well on their way at last, but the biggest hurdle of all still remained: the financing of the structure itself. With the country in the grips of a depression, money was not easy to come by. It was hoped to finance the bridge through the recently instituted Reconstruction Finance Corporation. However, to do so it would be necessary to amend the act as it then stood so that it would include such self-liquidating projects as the San Francisco-Oakland Bay Bridge which, though financially sound, could, according to state law, only raise the initial loan by pledging state credit and not by putting up collateral.

Purcell was appointed chief representative for California in this matter and from May to July of 1932 he was in Washington, D. C., appearing before congressional committees and other groups stressing the importance of the bridge and other similar projects around the country. He pointed out their financial soundness, their employment potential, and advocated the inclusion of necessary clauses in the Wagner Bill to enlarge the scope of the Reconstruction Finance Corporation to enable it to buy bonds from political subdivisions of public bodies so as to start construction of self-liquidating projects.

Looking east from east portal of cantilever section of Bay Bridge

Loan Applied For

On June 20th he telegraphed that the desired changes in the financing provisions seemed assured. On July 22d the Department of Public Works made formal application to the Reconstruction Finance Corporation for $75,000,000 to build the San Francisco-Oakland Bay Bridge. On August 31st, Purcell, accompanied by Engineer Andrew, returned to Washington, D. C., to present the engineering facts concerning the bridge to the Reconstruction Finance Corporation. They were later joined by Joseph R. Knowland and Harrison S. Robinson of Oakland and Leland W. Cutler and George T. Cameron of San Francisco

who, as personal representatives of Governor James Rolph, went back to urge favorable consideration by the R. F. C.

On September 16th the R. F. C. announced its approval of the design of the bridge. On September 27th Cutler obtained a personal interview with President Hoover and reported the Chief Executive as favoring the financing of the bridge. On October 10th the R. F. C. agreed to purchase $61,400,000 of California Toll Bridge Authority bonds, enough to insure construction of the bridge.

Money Not Easy

In light of present-day traffic it has often been argued that the bridge

California Highways

UPPER—Night scene of Bay Bridge during spinning of gigantic cables for the suspension section. LOWER—View of Bay Bridge just after its opening to traffic.

planners were not generous or far-seeing enough in their designs. Few people realize that from the beginning Purcell and his staff were well aware of possible future demands on the bridge and that some of their original ideas, based on this premise, called for greater deck width on the bridge. But what is often forgotten in these prosperous days of 1956 is the dearth of ready cash back in the early 1930's and the consequent restrictions that the R. F. C. found necessary to place on all projects coming before it for consideration. The original hopes for a wider bridge had to be modified down to the present 58-foot roadway if the structure was to meet R. F. C. financing requirements. Otherwise, it could not have been financed.

When Earl Lee Kelly was appointed Director of Public Works (on October 13, 1932) he immediately announced that he was retaining Purcell as State Highway Engineer and Chief Engineer of the Toll Bridge Authority. "In my opinion," Kelly said, "C. H. Purcell is one of the outstanding engineers of the United States and I think that I am indeed fortunate to have in my department a man like him upon whose shoulders will fall the responsibility for the engineering skill and the building of the great San Francisco-Oakland Bay Bridge."

On February 28, 1933, bids were opened on the West Bay substructure by Governor Rolph before 500 persons from all over California in the Senate Chambers of the State Capitol. The opening of bids on the East Bay substructure and the superstructure bids for both crossings plus the tunnel had to be postponed a few days because of the bank holiday declared by the President.

Contracts Awarded

On April 28th the Director of Public Works awarded contracts to the successful bidders.

Ground-breaking ceremonies took place on Yerba Buena Island on July 9th. Governor Rolph turned the first shovelful of earth. President Roosevelt in the White House at Washington tapped a telegraph key which set off three blasts, one on Yerba Buena Island, and the other two on Rincon Hill in San Francisco and at the foot of 14th Street in Oakland where overflow ground-breaking celebrations were taking place.

Actually, construction had already begun a month earlier when work was started on laying the piers for the West Bay substructure. A few days after the ground-breaking ceremonies work was started on boring the tunnel through Yerba Buena Island, and on July 27th the first caisson was launched. Within a few months work on the East and West Bay crossings was in full swing.

A look at the compendious 'Log of the San Francisco-Oakland Bay Bridge" shows that although the work proceeded steadily and even ahead of schedule during the next three years it was not without its occasional setbacks.

For example, on January 16, 1934, we note:

"Caisson No. 6 * * * standing at about elevation minus 138 feet, suddenly, a little after 6 p.m., tilted toward the east and settled out of level eight feet in about 10 seconds. Dredging was immediately started on the west cylinders. * * *"

Minor Problems

The following morning commuters crossing the bay on the ferries were alarmed by the obviously tilted position of Caisson No. 6 and Bay area newspapers were deluged with phone calls. Editors began to contact bridge officials to find out what had happened. Purcell and his staff conferred and in order to avoid any sensationalizing of the story issued a statement to all papers explaining that although the caisson was tipped it presented no unusual engineering difficulty and that no danger to the pier was involved. The newspapers not only cooperated by not overplaying the story but actually attempted to outdo each other in minimizing the risks and quieting the concern of commuters.

As if this were not enough for one day the "Log" also records that a shale slide started on the south side of the west approach on Yerba Buena Island and continued throughout the 18th, 19th and 20th.

And on April 23d of the same year:

"At 5.30 a.m. the roof and north side of the north anchorage tunnel on Yerba Buena Island caved in."

No lives were lost but more than a month was needed to complete the work of mucking out the thousand tons of fallen debris.

Inevitable Accidents

Nor could a project of such magnitude and duration be completed without its share of tragedy.

On August 4, 1933, only two months after major construction work had begun on the bridge, we read:

"The first fatality in the construction of the bridge occurred today when Harry V. Hill, pile driver, age 50, fell 20 feet into the bay while working on a material dock on Yerba Buena Island."

And again, on November 25th:

"Louis R. Knight, rigger, lost his balance and fell from Pier E-4 into the bay at 10.15 a.m. His body was recovered at 1.45 a.m. the following day."

And on December 14th:

"Lloyd J. Evans, diver, died of caisson disease. He had been working at a depth of 112 feet. After being brought to the surface he collapsed and was rushed to the decompression chamber at Harbor Pier 24 where attempts to save his life failed."

In all, 20 persons lost their lives in the construction of the bridge.

Work Progress Good

In addition, there were strikes which, on several occasions, slowed up work or even brought it to a standstill for a few days. In spite of this, the general work progress was good. The spinning of the huge cables for the suspension section, which required the setting up of special machinery on the San Francisco side, was completed in January, 1936. When the bridge was opened to the public in November it was six months ahead of schedule, a tribute to Purcell and his staff as well as the contractors and their men who had performed the actual construction work.

What of the future of the bridge? Physically speaking, there is no reason, engineers say, why it could not last for several centuries if properly maintained. Or as the man in charge of the bridge, Howard Wood, puts it, it 'should last long enough into the future until other modes of transportation render it and the automobile obsolete and make it nothing more than a museum piece spanning the bay to remind future generations of the glories of the past.

Queen of Bridges

But what about the immediate future of the bridge and its place in the transportation picture of the Bay area? It has been recognized for some time now that it cannot handle all of the expanding traffic in the region it serves and that additional bridges will be necessary. Surveys are now under

60

Forgotten Street Finds Business Better

NEWPORT BEACH — The "forgotten street" — old Newport Boulevard — never had it so good.

Three years ago its existence as a thriving business district appeared doomed by the State Division of Highways' project of fencing it off and rerouting traffic over a ditch-type freeway.

Merchants, hostelry owners and residents fought the freeway. The two-lane boulevard had for years been the main route from Santa Ana and Costa Mesa into resort Newport Beach, and to change this would be a disaster.

The business district had developed and seemed to be flourishing because this route was heavily traveled • • • people said "the ditch" would make it a "forgotten place" and property owners looked for the worse.

But a strange turn of events saved the business district and three years later a survey of some establishments shows "business is better than ever."

Gambled and Won

Some merchants, such as Claude L. Blood, gambled on the boulevard and won. Blood bought a former real estate office that had been abandoned when the freeway opened. His friends, he said, called him "nuts." But today Blood has one of the busiest pet shops in the coastal area.

He claims the less traveled street has helped the parking problem and allows local residents to use his store without the frantic problem of fighting heavy boulevard traffic.

---

way to determine the feasibility of financing and constructing a southern crossing of the bay, and most engineers and civic planners see a time in the not too distant future when the mushrooming population will require even a second new bridge somewhere near the present one.

But one thing is certain. Whether she is ever equaled or bettered in size the present Bay bridge will always be assured a place in the hearts of the people of the Bay area who have seen her stand alone and unchallenged as queen of them all for 20 years.

Motels—there are two of them, the Mesa and Newport Harbor hostelrys, faced the most serious threat. These establishments depend on the tourist trade and main travel routes for business. Both proprietors fought the freeway, but inevitably lost.

Now, Mrs. Adeline Jackson, owner of the Mesa Motel, considers the result a boon to business.

"Business has never been better," she says. "The first year we lost badly, but now we have more to offer because it is quieter and easier to get in and out of. Of course, to hold the trade longer we opened kitchenette apartments. Now people are freeway conscious and motel seekers are beginning to look off the main routes for a place to stay."

It Paid Off

Mrs. L. E. Woodward, proprietor of the neighboring Newport Harbor Motel, said the freeway paid off in the end by bringing more people into the area.

"We depend on visitors and, the more visitors the better the business," she explains. Like Mrs. Jackson she felt being off the "main line" is an advantage and safer for children visitors.

"Then—I wouldn't have believed our business would be better than ever," Mrs. Woodward stated, "but it is."

Some other apartment and motel owners said they changed their style of advertising to meet the problem of being shifted away from traffic. "We left cards at big recreation spots • • • impressing the fact that we are on a quiet street," one businessman explained.

Store owner Mike, Santa Cruz, of Boulevard Liquor Market, 449 North Newport Boulevard, admitted he had some worrisome moments at first.

"Better Than Ever"

"But now business is better than ever. On Sundays before the bumper-to-bumper traffic kept trade down. People couldn't stop or get in. We now do more local business and have better accommodations for parking, etc. My business dropped badly for eight months. • • • I remember argu-

SOUTHERN CROSSING
Continued from page 38 . . .

Southern Crossing, plus a reasonable margin of safety therefor, similar to the toll covenants relative to the authority's financing of the San Mateo-Alameda, Richmond-San Rafael and Carquinez Strait bridges.

If the authority determines to proceed with such further steps as may be necessary to finance the construction of the minimum Southern Crossing, we strongly recommend that provision be made in the authorizing bond resolution for financing the costs of paving the railway portion of the Bay Bridge in the event that such action appears to be necessary or desirable, even though an increase in tolls may be required for that purpose. Furthermore, although it is perhaps somewhat beyond the immediate scope of our assignment, we recommend that at the same time serious consideration be given to the advisability of imposing basic rates of toll in excess of 25 cents on the Bay Bridge and the Southern Crossing coincidentally with the financing of the latter in order to assure the success of that financing and also the authority's ability to meet the future requirements of transbay traffic in an economically sound and businesslike manner.

---

ing with the State, but it was like talking to a blank wall."

And the Beacon Auto Parts management Floyd E. Hubbard, one of the few merchants who did not oppose the freeway, claims he saw the 'better business picture then."

Hubbard, who has been in business for eight years, claims trade has tripled since the freeway opened in early summer, 1953.

"Before people were afraid to stop • • • now it is easy and comfortable," he explained, "and parking, the life source of a good business, is tremendously better."

It appears from other observations of the one time "main drag" that prospective merchants are taking an interest in this quiet route too.

At its south terminus a multibusiness shopping center has been built • • • with its store backs significantly turned on the freeway.

From Santa Ana Register

Out of the Mail Bag

GLAD YOU LIKE IT

SAN LORENZO, CALIFORNIA

KENNETH C. ADAMS, *Editor*

DEAR SIR: I thank you for again having the opportunity of receiving *California Highways and Public Works* magazine for another year.

The copy that I receive passes through the hands of many of my friends and business associates in the telephone company district office in the East Oakland area. Its arrival is always cause for attention and discussion.

Further use of its contents is made when it is forwarded to a member of the Alameda City Council.

Again I thank you.

Yours truly,

RICHARD D. CARROLL

A WELDER WRITES

WESTERN WELDING WORKS
Carmichael, California

KENNETH C. ADAMS, *Editor*

DEAR MR. ADAMS: I want to express my appreciation for your fine magazine which I have been reading for some 10 or 12 years. Being in the welding business, I have been especially interested in the development of the new Carquinez Crossing, because of the gaining acceptance of welding in all types of structures, particularly bridges.

I have also enjoyed the articles concerning prestressed concrete girders and piles. Of course I enjoy the whole publication, but the above in particular.

Yours very truly,

RANDOLPH K. SULLIVAN

AN EXPERT WRITES

PARAMOUNT, CALIFORNIA

KENNETH C. ADAMS, *Editor*

DEAR SIR: I would like to take this opportunity to thank you and the State of California for the privilege of receiving the *California Highways and Public Works* magazine.

In my work as a bus driver and tour conductor for Pacific Greyhound Lines, I travel many miles of our Country's highways annually, with passengers from all walks of life, from many parts of the Country, some frequent travelers, others for the first time in California. I am sure it would be gratifying if you could hear the general reaction of so many of my passengers concerning our highways in California. A typical comment—"California highways in general are the best in the Country."

I personally obtain much of my information and facts from *California Highways and Public Works*.

Yours very truly,

L. A. PREY

THANKS

MR. KENNETH C. ADAMS, *Editor*

DEAR SIR: I wish to express my appreciation of *California Highways and Public Works*, which my family and I enjoy very much, particularly the informative manner in which each subject is presented. We definitely admire your department's contribution towards the progress of our great State.

Very sincerely,

JOAQUIN VERGARA
4701 Yosemite Way
Los Angeles, California

AN APPRECIATION

NAPA, CALIFORNIA

KENNETH C. ADAMS, *Editor*

We have received your magazine for almost a year. We appreciate and enjoy each copy and look forward to the next.

Being in the sales and service business end of automotive transportation we appreciate your report on the highway development and progress that is being made for safer transportation.

Sincerely yours,

WESLEY COBB

FROM A BANKER

BANK OF AMERICA
SACRAMENTO, CALIFORNIA

MR. KENNETH C. ADAMS

DEAR MR. ADAMS: *California Highways and Public Works* is one of the finest publications that I have been privileged to read each month; in fact, just as soon as it is received it is read carefully from cover to cover since the contents are so interesting and well prepared.

Cordially,

G. K. CUNNINGHAM
Vice President

YOUR THANKS APPRECIATED

RODEO, CALIFORNIA

MR. KENNETH C. ADAMS, *Editor*

DEAR MR. ADAMS: I wish to thank you for *California Highways and Public Works*. Each copy we receive tells us a new story of a new highway or bridge, etc. We enjoy reading it very much and we pass them on to our friends so they may read them.

Yours truly,

MRS. DOROTHY VAUGHAN

WILL DO

EARP, CALIFORNIA

DEAR MR. ADAMS: We have now received your wonderful publication for 19 years. We enjoy it immensely and look forward to receiving every issue. It is very informative and interesting. It gives the "inside" story of every project that is undertaken and completed.

Just keep up the good work.

Yours truly,

FRANK BRITTON

HOLLISTER THANKS YOU

HOTEL DEL CORONADO
Coronado, California

DEAR MR. ADAMS: Congratulations on the September-October issue. It brings me much pleasure and knowledge. The illustrations help me to know what is going on.

The article by Mr. Leonard C. Hollister, Project Engineer on the Carquinez Bridge, is most wonderful. Keep that type of reading up, please.

WALTER STANLEY

MAINTENANCE CREWS ON JOB

COMMUNITY WELFARE AND TAXPAYERS ASSOCIATION, INC.
Eureka, California

MR. K. C. ADAMS, *Editor*

It is a pleasure to get your very excellent magazine, the *California Highways and Public Works*, and it is also a pleasure to congratulate you for the fine editing and usual good pattern you always come up with in each issue.

The occasions I have to travel over the highways in Northern California are very frequent and from your magazine it is with enthusiastic anticipation I look forward to trips over roads not frequently traveled by me; the changes are always there.

May I say a word for the men that keep the highways open during the winter months. They are always on the job, rain or snow. In fact I have always gotten through on any highway traveled during bad weather. The maintenance crew sees to that. May I say congratulations to maintenance.

Very truly yours,

JAMES T. HAMMONS

A BOW TO GOOD SAMARITANS

MR. FRANK B. DURKEE
Director of Public Works
Sacramento, California

DEAR MR. DURKEE: On Wednesday, October 24th, I was hopelessly snow-bound at Gold Lake away from the county road, Bassets to Graeagle, in Plumas and Sierra Counties. There was no communication for miles; my car was stalled. It looked as if my wife and I were in for a very bad time. I was about to walk 12 miles through the snow to Graeagle for help, when Guy Robinson, Nevada County Supervisor, and Chester Butz of Downieville, recently retired from the Division of Highways, came along.

They not only got me out of the snowdrift, but returned later to help me get my boat loaded on the trailer and gave me time to close my cabin on the lake before they would leave me.

Seeing Mr. Robinson and Mr. Butz operate was an education to me. They were so efficient in getting my car out and started, and thoughtful in returning to see that I actually got on my way.

My comment is that, though retired, Mr. Butz still has that fine spirit of service which will always reflect credit on the California Highway Department and will always make me a strong champion of the department.

Sincerely yours,

W. J. GILFILLAN

HIGH PRAISE INDEED

UNIVERSITY OF CALIFORNIA
Department of Engineering

MR. KENNETH C. ADAMS, *Editor*

DEAR MR. ADAMS: I enclose the required postal card to continue *California Highways and Public Works* for another year. Permit me to take this opportunity to commend you on the excellence of the publication which you produce. I find considerable personal enjoyment from the articles and repeatedly apply the data thus provided to problem material in our course in highway engineering.

Respectfully,

JOHN HUGH JONES
Assistant Professor of
Civil Engineering

MAGAZINE IS USEFUL

MISSOURI STATE HIGHWAY COMMISSION
Jefferson City, Missouri

MR. KENNETH C. ADAMS, *Editor*

I note it is time again to make a request for continuation of my name on the mailing list to receive *California Highways and Public Works*. I desire very much to be retained on your mailing list. This magazine is not only read and studied by myself, but is also circulated among my senior engineers, assistants, locators, and designers here in the main office. It is retained and used as a reference and is considered almost invaluable to us.

Very truly yours,

C. P. OWENS
Engineer of Surveys
and Plans

JUDGE LIKES MAGAZINE

MUNICIPAL COURT
Oakland-Piedmont Judicial District
Oakland, California

MR. KENNETH C. ADAMS

DEAR MR. ADAMS: *California Highways and Public Works* is an extremely interesting magazine, and by reason of my interest in traffic enforcement, I have found it very informative.

Very truly yours,

JOSEPH A. MURPHY, Judge

WE LIKE THESE LETTERS

KENNETH C. ADAMS, *Editor*

DEAR SIR: It isn't often that I write a fan letter, but your magazine is so deserving for its fine work, that I've decided to add my word of praise.

We've received the publication for the past few years, and the information and pure pleasure it has given us are unparalled. We travel this good old State whenever possible. Your valuable magazine with its wide variety of information on highways, is a real boon to the motorist. We want to thank you for making it available to us.

Sincerely,

MRS. NORMANN HIXON
P. O. Box 36
Chino, California

In Memoriam

CHARLES H. WHITMORE

An engineering career covering more than half a century was brought to an end on November 10th with the death of Charles H. Whitmore, retired engineer of the Division of Highways.

At the time of his retirement from state service in 1952, Whitmore was District Engineer of District III (Marysville), a post he had held for 23 years. Prior to that time he was Construction Engineer for District IV (San Francisco) and District Engineer of District I (Eureka). Before coming to California, he was a district highway engineer for the State of Oregon.

His early career was spent in location and construction work for various railroad companies and in land and water development. He was county engineer of El Paso County, Texas, from 1908 to 1911. Both in Texas and Oregon, Whitmore had charge of constructing some of the first hard-surface highways to be built outside of cities. He was also one of those who helped in formulating and encouraging the tax on gasoline for road construction purposes which Oregon pioneered in 1919, the first gas tax measure in the Country.

Whitmore was born in Emporia, Kansas, and studied engineering at Oberlin College in Ohio. He is survived by his wife, Florence, his daughter, Mrs. May Louise Hillebrand, and two grandchildren, all of Marysville, a brother in Oregon and three sisters in Illinois.

AUTO PRODUCTION

France produced 553,300 units of the total world production of 13,000,000 automobiles in 1955, reports the National Automobile Club.

During the 1955-56 Fiscal Year, the total number of contractors prequalified to bid on the various types of state highway construction increased from 800 to 812. The combined bidding capacity of these contractors is estimated to be $1,601,255,500.

Employees Receive Twenty-five-year Awards

Employees of the Division of Highways who became eligible for 25-year awards prior to July 31, August 31, September 30 and October 31, 1956, are:

Name	Total service Yrs. Mos. Days			Name	Total service Yrs. Mos. Days		
District I				**District X**			
Hemenway, Bernard A.	25	0	10	Oneto, John L.	25	0	08
Rivers, Hervey J.	25	0	04	Parker, Herbert M.	25	0	25
Schuler, Donald K.	25	0	19	Spradling, Richard E.	25	0	13
District II				**District XI**			
Chapman, Wilbur C.	25	0	14	Hansen, Frank E.	25	0	12
Grant, William	25	0	19	Mullins, Grace L.	25	0	14
Hayes, William	25	0	26	Patterson, Ben	25	0	13
Hogan, Wendell W.	25	0	27	Pearce, Franklin D., Sr.	25	0	21
Keeler, Lloyd V.	25	0	06	Talbot, Dale J.	25	0	29
Peterson, Bessie.	25	0	10	Young, Randolph R.	25	0	20
District III				**Central Office**			
Dorris, Wilma E.	25	0	28	Boyer, Clyde D., Jr.	25	0	12
Haines, Ellis A.	25	0	20	Everitt, Fred L.	25	0	18
Hanna, Clarence D.	25	0	01	Lathrop, Scott H.	25	0	19
McDonough, David E.	25	0	21	MacDonald, Ernest M.	25	0	20
Rhud, Henlon E.	25	0	15	Shouse, Jo.	25	0	23
Sawyer, Jesse E.	25	0	04	Sloan, George W.	25	0	28
Sheridan, Paul C.	25	0	20	Winter, Pascal	25	0	01
White, Albert C.	25	0	09	Zezzi, Evelyn A.	25	0	00
District IV							
Deavy, John G.	25	0	02	**Bridge Department**			
Elder, Drury.	25	0	11	Dunn, Thomas J.	25	0	01
Lange, H. C.	25	0	25	Riedelsch, W. C.	25	0	17
Lucas, Frank C.	25	0	06	McMahon, James E.	25	0	28
Weber, Charles A.	25	0	20	Winter, Carroll C.	25	0	29
District V				Yeager, Arlos M.	25	0	20
Bunce, Charles Lee.	25	0	17				
Moon, Ralph J.	25	0	24	**Bay Bridge**			
Skense, Andrew T.	25	0	22	Corbett, Mary M.	25	0	00
District VI				Werne, J. R.	25	0	19
Cowen, Walker R.	25	0	13				
Johnson, Roy F.	25	0	06	**Central Office**			
Van Patten, Ellsworth I.	25	0	09	Joynes, Harold L.	25	0	16
District VII							
Farmer, Rex C.	25	0	18	**Headquarters Shop**			
Fisher, Leland W.	25	0	02	Green, Frank F.	25	0	03
Han, Richard.	25	0	21	McCormack, Jack F.	25	0	08
Langsner, George.	25	0	18				
Nigh, Donald T.	25	0	02	**Shop 6**			
Reingold, Samuel.	25	0	24	Campbell, Charles H.	25	0	05
Reynolds, Jesse M.	25	0	02				
Smith, LeRoy, Jr.	25	0	14	**Public Works—Administration**			
District VIII				Catching, Alpha.	25	0	26
Backus, Lawrence N.	25	0	11				
Beckett, Orville A.	25	0	14	**Contracts and Rights of Way**			
Brouse, Fred R.	25	0	01	Jones, Holloway.	25	0	10
Wieman, Donald S.	25	0	01				

Employees of the Division of Architecture receiving 25-year awards:

	25 years on	Location
Andrew Petersen	July 27, 1956	Area II, Folsom
Arthur F. Dudman	August 4, 1956	Headquarters, Sacramento
Willece E. Manhart	October 11, 1956	Headquarters, Sacramento

MISSING PLATES

If you lose one or both of the license plates on your car, the law requires that you must obtain substitute plates, says the California State Automobile Association. Take your registration card and the one remaining plate (if only one has been lost) to an office of the Department of Motor Vehicles. Substitute plates will be issued for a $2 fee. If the plates have been stolen, notify the police.

MORE MOTOR VEHICLES ENTER CALIFORNIA

A total of 467,574 automobiles, trucks, and busses entered California during September of this year. This was 55,122 more motor vehicles than entered during September, 1955.

CALIFORNIA
HIGHWAYS AND PUBLIC WORKS

California Highways and Public Works

Official Journal of the Division of Highways,
Department of Public Works, State of California

KENNETH C. ADAMS, Editor

HELEN HALSTED, Assistant Editor

MERRITT R. NICKERSON, Chief Photographer

Vol. 36   January-February   Nos. 1-2

Public Works Building
Twelfth and N Streets
Sacramento

CONTENT

COVER

Aerial photo of recently completed section of San Luis Obispo Freeway on US 101. This view is looking south toward Pismo Beach, with Shell Beach in foreground. Photo by Merritt R. Nickerson, Chief, Photographic Section, Department of Public Works. (See Page 19.)

BACK COVER

This model is on exhibit in the main lobby of the District IV office at 150 Oak Street in San Francisco. It is approximately 80½ inches long and was made to the scale of 1 inch equals 40 feet. The model was made by the Bridge Department for use by Acting Assistant State Highway Engineer J. P. Sinclair in a television program. It has, on many other occasions, been very helpful in portraying how a depressed freeway section will blend in with beautifully landscaped residential areas which may be adjacent thereto. Photo by Robert J. Rose, Photographic Section, Department of Public Works.

Published in the interest of highway development in California. Editors of newspapers and others are privileged to use matter contained herein. Cuts will be gladly loaned upon request.

Address communications to

CALIFORNIA HIGHWAYS AND PUBLIC WORKS
P. O. Box 1499
Sacramento, California

District VII

Accomplishments During 1956
and Outlook for Future

By EDWARD T. TELFORD
Assistant State Highway Engineer

Freeways Report

WHEN THE freeways of District VII in Los Angeles, Orange, and Ventura Counties are considered, we can say that the year 1956 has been one of significant accomplishment in many ways. Important freeway units totaling over 20 miles in length were completed and made available for public traffic. Construction by contract has been started on 11 large freeway sections that have a total length of 41 miles. The California Highway Commission has adopted four vital freeway routings in widely separated locations in the district. Additional federal aid moneys have been made available for expediting freeway construction.

The Highway Commission on October 18, 1956, adopted a record State Highway Budget for the 1957-58 Fiscal Year allocating to District VII for rights of way and construction a total of $115,500,000. This large budget and the augmented one of 1956-57 were made possible because of the additional federal aid money coming to California as a result of the passage by Congress of the legislation known as "The Federal Highway Act of 1956."

New Federal Highway Act

In answering questions that had arisen as to the effect of this new federal aid on state-wide progress of freeways, J. W. Vickrey, Deputy State Highway Engineer, recently said:

"The effect of the Federal Highway Act of 1956 on California's highway development is that we now can expect to have within four or five years the freeways we previously didn't count on for 8 or 10 years. Of course, all relatively simple, straightforward statements regarding any

EDWARD T. TELFORD

kind of governmental function require some qualification.

"We will attain the anticipated speedup in our freeway construction if the Congress carries out the intent of the 1956 Federal Highway Act as to the apportionment formula for Interstate Highway funds; and if there is no major change in California's own highway financing picture.

"Things have happened fast this year in the highway field. Last year, 1955, was a year of preparation. As Mr. G. T. McCoy, State Highway Engineer, expressed it at a nationwide gathering of state highway officials last December: 'In the annals of American transportation, the year 1955 will probably prove to have seen more constructive talk and less

constructive action than any comparable period in our modern highway history.'

"The 'constructive talk' referred to by Mr. McCoy included the Clay Committee report on a national highway program; many volumes of testimony before the Congress as to the need for an immediate attack on the nationwide twin plagues of traffic congestion and needless death and injury on the highways; and countless columns of discussion in the Nation's press. Proposed national highway legislation bogged down in 1955, but not because there was any question of need; the fatal argument was over details of financing.

"In 1956, by contrast, we got the national highway legislation with a minimum of dispute about financing. The major dispute was over apportionment of the interstate system funds among the several states. On the basis of need, California would have received about 10 percent of the federal funds for interstate highways. On the basis of the traditional federal allocation formula based on population, area, and mileage of post roads, California receives only about 5 percent."

Big Increase in Budget

If there is no major change in California's program of financing highways, and if the Congress of the United States continues with the program as presently outlined in the 1956 Federal Highway Act, then it is reasonable to expect that in approximately three years from now the right of way and construction budget for District VII will be in excess of 160 million dollars annually.

To understand the value of this financial program and the highway development it makes possible, it is

STATE OF CALIFORNIA
DEPARTMENT OF PUBLIC WORKS
DIVISION OF HIGHWAYS

DISTRICT VII
FREEWAYS

Legend

COMPLETED OR
UNDER CONSTRUCTION   ▬▬▬▬

BUDGETED   ●●●●●●●●

FREEWAY ROUTE ADOPTED   ••••••••••••••

JANUARY 1, 1957

Scale in Miles

necessary that we briefly consider the problem and our approach to its solution. District VII consists of three counties of Los Angeles, Orange, and Ventura. The traffic problems in this district fall into two general categories—that of the highly urbanized Los Angeles Basin area, which includes a large part of Orange County; and the less populous areas of Ventura County, northern Los Angeles County, and eastern Orange County. Common to the entire area is the north-west, south-east traffic movement, generally parallel to the coast, which extends between the coastal

areas of San Diego County on the south and the northern parts of the State, both coastal and San Joaquin Valley. The other long distance movement is, of course, the east-west movement generally described as the Los Angeles-San Bernardino movement. Superimposed on this pattern of movement is, in the metropolitan area, the demand for movement between centers of population and industry within the metropolitan area. This is essentially a grid pattern of movement desire. These traffic movements are modified by the geographical features of the mountains and valleys

within and adjacent to the area. These geographical factors have had their effective not only directly upon the movement of traffic, but upon population trends, which of course are the ultimate basis for the development of traffic demand.

Population Growth

The factor of population growth in the Los Angeles area and the actual distribution of that growth points strongly to the need for consideration of the growth trend rather than present-day traffic pattern as being the proper consideration for long-

California Highways

range planning. The Los Angeles County Regional Planning Commission publishes from time to time a report of its Population Research Section, which is an extremely valuable indicator of population trends. Report No. 53, dated July of 1956, furnishes a comprehensive breakdown of the comparative population of April, 1950, and July, 1956. I wish to point out a few of the comparisons which I feel are pertinent to this discussion.

For example, the central area of Los Angeles has decreased in population from 129,578 to 106,396; whereas, the Chatsworth area increased from 17,583 to 50,291. The Encino area increased from 118,000 to 243,798. The San Fernando area increased from 53,557 to 119,064. The citrus area; that is, the area including Covina, West Covina, Glendora and other San Gabriel Valley areas, increased from 46,276 to 141,307, with the City of West Covina increasing from 4,499 to 36,615. The Whittier area increased from 68,368 to 144,451. The Norwalk area increased from 109,659 to 222,459, and the explosive growth of Orange County, southeast of the Norwalk area, followed the same general pattern. The Long Beach area increased from 286,505 to 377,372, with one city, the City of Lakewood, coming into existence during that period and having a present estimated population of 59,302.

This strong growth pattern was shown throughout the San Pedro and Palos Verdes area, the South Coast beach cities, and the Santa Monica-Venice area. This entire growth pattern simply points out the trend away from the heart of the built-up metropolitan areas, so far as residential population is concerned. This results in an increased demand for movement of persons and goods between these rapidly growing communities themselves, and between these communities and the heart of the metropolitan area to which they actually belong.

Traffic Counts

G. T. McCoy, State Highway Engineer, recently made public release of the 1956 state-wide traffic count figures. As Mr. McCoy says, on a

state-wide basis the traffic volumes during the year 1956 have increased 7.71 percent over the 1955 figures. In District VII this percentage figure has been exceeded on many of the important state highway routes but in the case of the freeways in and near the City of Los Angeles the rate of increase, generally speaking, has been considerably less. Under the circumstances this is no more than was to be expected.

The average daily traffic volume on the freeways of this area for the past years is shown by the following:

Location	1954	1955	1956
Hollywood Freeway (4-level—westerly)	168,000	180,000	185,000
Pasadena Freeway (Elysian Park)	110,000	112,000	114,000
Santa Ana Freeway (Soto Street)	90,000	113,000	145,000
San Bernardino Freeway (Soto Street)	80,000	88,000	96,000
Harbor Freeway (4-level—southerly)	125,000	160,000	175,000
Colorado Freeway (Linda Vista)	30,000	27,000	29,000
Long Beach Freeway (Pacific Coast Highway)	10,000	31,000	37,000
Using 4-level interchange	242,000	280,000	300,000

Even in 1954 we considered that these freeways were carrying traffic loads far in excess of the design capacity, and the wonder is that further increases in volume have actually been recorded. This can partially be explained from the fact that there has developed an increased use of the freeway during the off-peak hours. Another conclusion that has been advanced to explain this is that the motorists in this area who are daily using the freeways have become very skillful in their driving. Incidentally, it has been extensively observed that motorists are becoming more safety conscious on freeways. Even of greater importance, perhaps, is the growing conviction that motorists, as a class, are now much less selfish and much more courteous than formerly. Motorists on the freeways are now willing and ready to give a little to let the other fellow do what he needs to do to get safely to his destination. Very seldom does one see a hoggish motorist close the gap ahead of him when he sees

his neighboring motorist trying to slip into it to make a lane change. This commendable attitude on the part of motorists as a whole and the growing consciousness that safety for others is as important as safety for oneself must be the explanation of the successful operation of freeways in the Los Angeles area under the present overcrowded conditions.

Interstate Highways

The general location of the National System of Interstate Highways was designated in September, 1955, by the Bureau of Public Roads of the U. S. Department of Commerce.

Included in this national system are seven important state highway routes in District VII. These freeways constitute an important part of the District VII network of freeways. The Golden State Freeway, the Olympic Freeway, the San Diego Freeway, the Santa Ana Freeway, the San Gabriel River Freeway, the San Bernardino Freeway, and the Foothill Freeway are on this interstate system.

The only interstate route for which the Highway Commission has not yet made an actual route adoption and freeway declaration is that of the Foothill Freeway. This route has been described in general terms as a part of the interstate system, but final determination of its location must await completion of studies now under way. One of these interstate routes, the San Bernardino Freeway, has been financed from regular state highway funds, and construction is practically complete—in fact, will be completed within the next few months.

It is interesting to note that in this district, for the 1956-57 Fiscal Year and the 1957-58 Fiscal Year we have budgets for right of way and construction which total approximately 235 million dollars, of which approximately 132 million dollars are assigned to the interstate system. In the 1955-56 Fiscal Year we purchased in excess of 60 million dollars' worth of right of way. This was a continuation of a policy of planning for an increased highway program. It was this expansion of planning, design and right-of-way acquisition which, carried out in an orderly manner, has enabled us to

and Public Works

3

move into this greatly expanded program in an effective and efficient manner.

Freeway Routes Adopted

The California Highway Commission during the year 1956 adopted four very important freeway routings. On February 15, 1956, the US 101-Route 19 Freeway in Orange County, that is locally called the "Brea Canyon Freeway," was adopted, extending from the Santa Ana Freeway in Santa Ana northerly through the Cities of Orange, Placentia, and Fullerton to Pomona.

The commission on March 21, 1956, adopted the Route 23 Freeway in the Antelope Valley section of Los Angeles County from one-half mile north of junction with Angeles Forest Highway near the Southern Pacific Railroad Vincent Y to Neenach Road, that is locally called the "Palmdale-Lancaster Freeway."

On April 19, 1956, the commission adopted the Route 79 Freeway in Ventura County from US 101 south of the City of Ventura northeasterly to the City of Santa Paula, which is locally referred to as the "Santa Paula Freeway."

Then on November 15, 1956, the commission adopted the freeway route for the Olympic Freeway (State Highway Route 173) from La Cienega Boulevard in the City of Los Angeles to Lincoln Boulevard (State Highway Route 60) in the City of Santa Monica, a length of 6.6 miles. This action was taken after the commission had held a public hearing at Patriotic Hall on September 14, 1956, and an earlier public hearing in the State Building, Los Angeles, September 29, 1955. Public meetings called by the Division of Highways regarding this routing had also been held on April 11 and July 16, 1956.

East-West Freeway

In adopting this freeway location that is so very important to the people of this area, the commission in part said:

"The recommended line conforms to a well-planned and orderly development of a complete system of freeways for the Los Angeles metropolitan area and will best serve the West Los Angeles and Santa Monica Bay area.

"In view of the over-all state-wide highway program and the availability of funds to complete the system, one east-west freeway will have to serve the West Los Angeles area for many years. The one freeway selected, therefore, must provide the maximum traffic service. The line recommended by the State Highway Engineer will provide the best over-all traffic service. It is the most direct, feasible, and practicable route that can be obtained. It will serve the largest volume of 'through' as well as local traffic, and will cause the least disturbance to existing improvements.

"We recognize that this may not be a satisfactory or comforting answer to those whose properties are affected, but we believe it is obvious to all that any freeway through this heavily built-up area will require the acquisition of considerable private property from numerous owners. This cannot be avoided if the commission is to carry out its duty and legal obligation to fix and determine a location for the state highway route under consideration."

The location for the section of the Olympic Freeway from La Cienega Boulevard easterly to the Santa Ana Freeway (State Highway Route 2) near Soto Street was previously adopted and declared a freeway by the commission in May, 1954.

Olympic Freeway Progress

Good progress is being made by the District VII right-of-way staff in right-of-way acquisition for the easterly portion of the Olympic Freeway between junction with the Santa Ana Freeway and crossing with the Harbor Freeway and to a lesser degree, westerly toward La Cienega Boulevard. To date over $16,000,000 has been expended for rights of way on the Olympic Freeway, and it is expected that the amount will be increased to over $20,000,000. The 1957-58 Fiscal Year budget as adopted by the California Highway Commission on October 18, 1956, contains an item of $12,000,000 for continuing right-of-way acquisition on the Olympic Freeway. This budget also contains two items totaling $8,400,000 for construc-

tion of bridge structures to provide interchange facilities for Olympic Freeway with the Harbor Freeway and to provide crossings over the Los Angeles River and the Santa Fe Railroad yard. Work on these structures is scheduled to start early in the summer of 1957. This will be the initial construction on the 4.2-mile unit of the Olympic Freeway between Hoover Street and the Santa Ana Freeway that involves long lengths of viaduct to carry the Olympic Freeway over the southeast business and industrial section of the City of Los Angeles for which the estimated total cost of right of way and construction is approximately $66,000,000.

Freeways Completed During 1956

Important sections of freeway completed and opened to public traffic during 1956 are as follows:

	Miles
Harbor Freeway	
From 23rd Street to 42d Street, City of Los Angeles	1.4
From Pacific Coast Highway in Wilmington to Battery Street in San Pedro	2.8
Long Beach Freeway	
Sheila Street to Verona Street, including Santa Ana Freeway interchange	0.9
Ojai Freeway	
In Ventura County from Ventura Boulevard to Mills School	4.1
San Bernardino Freeway	
Durfee Street to Puente Avenue, West City Limits of West Covina	3.3
San Bernardino Freeway	
Rosemead Boulevard to San Gabriel River through City of El Monte	3.9
San Bernardino Freeway	
West City Limits of West Covina to Citrus Avenue	4.2
Total	20.6

Construction Contracts Awarded in 1956

The past year has been one of significant accomplishment from the standpoint of freeway construction

→

contracts that have been advertised and awarded in District VII. These contracts are as follows:

	Miles
Golden State Freeway	
Glendale Boulevard to Los Angeles River in Griffith Park section of Los Angeles	2.6
Harbor Freeway	
88th Street to 124th Street	2.6
Hollywood Freeway Extension	
East of Lankershim Boulevard to Moorpark Street in City of Los Angeles	1.1
Long Beach Freeway	
From Imperial Highway to Dozier Street	3.8
From Rosecrans Avenue to Imperial Highway	1.9
Pacific Coast Freeway	
From Date Street, Oxnard, to Calleguas Creek	7.2
Santa Ana Freeway	
From Laguna Canyon Road to Browning Avenue	5.7
From Coyote Creek to Ball Road, Orange County	6.5
San Diego Freeway	
From Ohio Avenue to Waterford Avenue	1.1
Ventura Freeway	
From Kelvin to Calabasas	4.0
Ventura-San Diego Freeway	
From Sepulveda Boulevard to Encino Avenue on Ventura Freeway	3.1
From Valley View to Burbank Boulevard on San Diego Freeway	1.6
Total	**41.2**

Pasadena Freeway

This freeway, formerly called the Arroyo Seco Freeway, is 8.2 miles in length, extending from the four-level structure near the Los Angeles City College to Glenarm Street in Pasadena. The last unit of construction on this freeway was completed and opened to traffic on September 22, 1953. The total cost was $11,443,300. The Elysian Park section of this freeway is now carrying 114,000 vehicles per day, and the estimated daily traffic utilizing the four-level interchange structure at the south end of this freeway is 300,000 vehicles per day.

Hollywood Freeway

On the 10-mile length of the completed Hollywood Freeway from the Los Angeles Civic Center to Vineland Avenue in the San Fernando Valley the last unit of construction was completed and opened to public traffic August 5, 1954. The total cost of this

Looking easterly from above North Hollywood showing in foreground right of way for Hollywood Freeway Extension along Big Tujunga Wash adjacent to new shopping development. Street in foreground is Laurel Canyon Boulevard.

unit was $55,000,000. On the basis of 1956 traffic counts the average daily vehicular traffic on the Hollywood Freeway westerly of the 4-level structure is 185,000 vehicles per day.

The Hollywood Freeway Extension joins the main Hollywood Freeway near the intersection with Lankershim Boulevard and extends northerly therefrom 6.8 miles to the proposed Golden State Freeway near Wentworth Avenue. On January 20, 1956, a contract was awarded to Oberg Construction Company for building two bridges on the Hollywood Freeway Extension, one across the Los Angeles River and the other at Vine-

land Avenue. The construction allotment is $1,250,000.

On August 16, 1956, contract was awarded to Griffith Company for constructing 1.1 miles of the Hollywood Freeway Extension from Lankershim Boulevard to Moorpark Street. The contract allotment is $2,324,800, and the estimated date of completion is November 21, 1957.

District VII right-of-way forces are now acquiring rights of way for the Hollywood Freeway Extension northerly of Moorpark Street. The 1957-58 Fiscal Year budget as adopted by the California Highway Commission has an item of $3,000,000 for right of way

6

acquisition on the Hollywood Freeway Extension.

Santa Ana Freeway

This freeway extends from the easterly terminus of the Hollywood Freeway at Spring Street in the Los Angeles Civic Center in a generally southeasterly direction for a total length of 42.8 miles through the Cities of Buena Park, Anaheim, Santa Ana, and Tustin to a junction with the San Diego Freeway near the town of El Toro. This freeway, following as it does a northwesterly-southeasterly direction generally paralleling the Pacific Ocean coastline, makes it of great strategic value because so many of the other important traffic arteries in this part of the State have been established in a generally northerly-southerly or easterly-westerly direction.

The entire 42.8 miles of this freeway are now either fully completed,

under construction or financed. By the end of 1958 it will be entirely completed to full freeway standards. Three contracts, totaling $13,757,900 and embracing 14.6 miles are now in progress. The last remaining link in Orange County extending from Laguna Canyon Road to El Toro-Niguel Road will be advertised for construction early in 1957. Completion of the Santa Ana Freeway throughout its entire length will be achieved by the end of 1958.

San Bernardino Freeway

As reported by District Engineer Lyman R. Gillis in his story published in *California Highways and Public Works*, July-August, 1956, the year 1956 has been a most significant one in the history of the District VII part of the San Bernardino Freeway.

There now remains on this freeway only one construction contract to be completed. This is the section 5.2

miles in length, between Citrus Avenue in West Covina and Ganesha Boulevard in Pomona, which is scheduled for completion in April, 1957. This 30.7 miles of full freeway in District VII extending from the Santa Ana Freeway near the Los Angeles River to San Bernardino County line at Claremont, has to date cost a total of close to $52,000,000.

Harbor Freeway

The Harbor Freeway extends for 22.4 miles from junction with Hollywood Freeway at the four-level traffic interchange structure southerly to Battery Street in the San Pedro district of Los Angeles Harbor area. Two important sections of this freeway have been completed and opened to public traffic. At the northerly end 4.3 miles are now open from the four-level structure near the Los Angeles Civic Center to 42d Street. At the southerly end 2.8 miles from Pacific

and Public Works

7

LEFT—Looking northwesterly showing construction on Santa Ana Freeway through City of Anaheim. Bridge construction at right is to carry Lincoln Avenue, State Highway Route 78, over the freeway. RIGHT—Looking northeasterly showing in center bridge construction to carry Euclid Avenue over Santa Ana Freeway. In center is new shopping development for City of Anaheim.

Coast Highway in the Wilmington area to Battery Street in the San Pedro-Los Angeles Harbor area were opened to public traffic July 1, 1956.

Three major construction contracts are now under way for 6.8 miles from 42d Street to 124th Street, having an estimated value of $15,687,000. The two northerly units of this construction are scheduled for completion in the summer of 1957 and the most southerly unit, in late 1958.

Right of way acquisition operations are now nearing completion with nearly all the parcels having been acquired that are necessary to complete this freeway. Other units of construction can be placed under contract as the California Highway Commission is able to provide for financing in subsequent budgets.

Long Beach Freeway

The Long Beach Freeway is one of the newer freeway developments.

Ground-breaking ceremonies at the southerly terminus of this freeway at Pacific Coast Highway in the City of Long Beach were held on June 27, 1951. However, since that time there has been steady progress in constructing this important freeway in the East Los Angeles area.

The total length of the Long Beach Freeway from Pacific Coast Highway (Route 60) in Long Beach to Huntington Drive in East Los Angeles is 21.5 miles. As of the present time eight miles of the Long Beach Freeway at the south end have been completed from Pacific Coast Highway northerly to the crossing with Atlantic Boulevard east of the City of Compton, and at the northerly end one mile extending from Verona Street to Washington Boulevard, including the interchange structures and connecting ramps at junction with the Santa Ana Freeway.

Currently under construction are four contracts extending from Washington Boulevard southerly to Rosecrans Avenue east of Compton that total 7.1 miles in length and carry allotments aggregating $12,724,000.

The Highway Commission on October 18, 1956, adopted the 1957-58 Fiscal Year budget that included an item of $1,750,000 for 1.1-mile length of the Long Beach Freeway from Rosecrans Avenue southerly to Atlantic Boulevard east of Compton. This action provided the necessary financing for the last link necessary to complete the Long Beach Freeway throughout the entire 16-mile length between Santa Ana Freeway and Pacific Coast Highway in Long Beach.

The Los Angeles County Road Department is now engaged in completing plans for the extension of Olive Street in Compton easterly across the Long Beach Freeway and

8

the Los Angeles River. The State Division of Highways has agreed to contribute to the Los Angeles County project the actual cost of the structure and westerly approaches for the Olive Street crossing over the Long Beach Freeway. The construction of the Olive Street extension by Los Angeles County will, of necessity, have to be carried out simultaneously with the State's adjoining construction on the Long Beach Freeway. Therefore, the time for advertising the State's contract and the Los Angeles County contract will have to be worked out so that the two can proceed simultaneously. This construction is scheduled for advertising early in the spring of 1957.

Therefore, we can say that by the end of 1958 the Long Beach Freeway from the Santa Ana Freeway southerly should be completed and opened to public traffic.

Golden State Freeway

This freeway extends 72.7 miles from the southerly terminus at the junction with the Olympic and Santa Ana Freeways near Soto Street in Los Angeles to Kern county line.

The portion of the Golden State Freeway, U. S. Highway 99, locally known as the "Ridge Route" between Tunnel Station and the Kern County line, 45.2 miles in District VII, has been converted to a four-lane expressway. The total cost of this reconstruction, completed February, 1953, was $13,500,000. Southerly from Tunnel Station for 27.5 miles the Golden State Freeway is to be carried out to full freeway standards to its southerly terminus at junction with the Santa Ana Freeway. Of this portion the northerly three miles from Tunnel Station southerly to Sepulveda Boulevard was completed as a four-lane expressway at a cost of $3,200,000 on August 25, 1955.

Two very important contracts on the Golden State Freeway are now in progress. The contractor on this five miles of construction, extending from Glendale Boulevard in the City of Los Angeles to Ash Street in the City of Burbank, is Vinnell Co., Inc., and Vinnell Constructors. The sum of the two contract allotments is

Looking easterly showing recently completed structures comprising interchange between Long Beach Freeway and Santa Ana Freeway

$9,779,000. The estimated date of completion is October, 1957.

Right-of-way acquisition is under way for acquiring all rights of way needed for the Golden State Freeway throughout its entire length. The budget for the 1957-58 Fiscal Year, as adopted by the California Highway Commission on October 18, 1956, contains $12,000,000 for right-of-way acquisition on the Golden State Freeway. It also contains a construction item of $3,150,000 for 1.3 miles of the Golden State Freeway between Alameda Avenue and Burbank Boulevard in the City of Burbank and an item of $8,900,000 for 3.1 miles of this freeway from Sixth Street to Mission Road in the City of Los Angeles. This latter project is 3.1 miles in length and includes the traffic interchange facilities with the San Bernardino Freeway.

The last unit of the Golden State Freeway from the north city limits of Burbank to junction with San Fernando Road near intersection with Sepulveda Boulevard has been approved by the Los Angeles City Board of Public Works, and the free-

way agreement is now before the city council for consideration. This covers an 11.8-mile length of freeway and is the longest continuous stretch of freeway that has yet been presented to the city council for freeway agreement.

Completion of the Golden State Freeway through the City of Los Angeles, connecting it with the Santa Ana Freeway, the San Bernardino Freeway and the Pasadena Freeway, is of vital importance in clearing up traffic congestion on present freeways serving the Los Angeles Civic Center and business district.

Ventura Freeway

The Ventura Freeway extends from the Hollywood Freeway Extension near Vineland Avenue in the San Fernando Valley to the Santa Barbara county line, a distance of 65.1 miles. Of this mileage 40.6 miles have been completed at a construction cost of $13,454,000 to provide four-lane divided highway or expressway standards. This completed construction is all westerly of the west city limits of Los Angeles at Calabasas.

and Public Works

LEFT—Looking northwesterly along construction in progress on Golden State Freeway in Griffith Park area showing in foreground completed structures at Los Feliz Boulevard. Storm drain channel at right is Los Angeles River. RIGHT—Looking northwesterly along Golden State Freeway construction from above Griffith Park showing crossing with Riverside Drive and Los Angeles River in foreground and City of Burbank in background.

The Highway Commission on May 18, 1955, adopted a freeway routing to carry the Coast Highway (U. S. Highway 101) through the City of Ventura. Plans are now in progress so that construction can go forward whenever financing can be arranged for this entire 5.5 miles through the City of Ventura.

The budget for the 1957-58 Fiscal Year as adopted by the Highway Commission October 16, 1956, contains an item of $3,400,000 to convert to full freeway status the existing two- and three-lane undivided section over the Conejo Grade. This is 4.8 miles in length, extending from Conejo Grade Summit to Fifth Street in Camarillo. This is the last section of the existing two- and three-lane pavement on Route 2 between Los Angeles and Santa Barbara county line to make this route a four-lane divided highway throughout its length in District VII. Designs are under way

on the Ventura Freeway in new location through the City of Ventura, and some money is available in the 1956-57 Fiscal Year budget for right-of-way acquisition in the City of Ventura. Additional funds in the amount of $3,000,000 are now available in the 1957-58 Fiscal Year budget to continue with right-of-way acquisition at a later date when funds are available.

Studies are under way to convert existing sections of four-lane divided expressway from the north city limits of Los Angeles at Calabasas to the Santa Barbara county line to full freeway status.

Within the City of Los Angeles two major freeway construction contracts are now in progress on sections of the Ventura Freeway. These extend from Sepulveda Boulevard to Encino Avenue, a length of 3.5 miles, and from Kelvin Avenue to Calabasas, a

length of four miles. The value of this current construction is $9,779,000.

District right-of-way agents are now actively engaged in acquiring rights of way for the remaining units of the Ventura Freeway so that these can be placed under construction when funds are provided by the California Highway Commission in subsequent budgets.

San Diego Freeway

This freeway is 93.7 miles in length. It extends southerly from junction with the Golden State Freeway near the City of San Fernando in close vicinity to existing Sepulveda Boulevard over the Santa Monica Mountains through the West Los Angeles area and along the easterly side of the Los Angeles International Airport. Then it swings easterly, passing to the south of the Long Beach Municipal Airport and then southeasterly into Orange County, to a junction

10

California Highways

with the Santa Ana Freeway at El Toro. Then it proceeds in close vicinity to existing US 101 through San Juan Capistrano and San Clemente to the Orange-San Diego county line. In the West Los Angeles area, work on the Sunset Boulevard Overcrossing and three other nearby bridges costing $723,000 was completed in February of this year. In this same area, construction under two contracts with the Thompson Construction Company is now in progress to complete 2.3 miles of the San Diego Freeway between Ohio Avenue and Casiano Drive. The construction allotments total $4,000,-000. The estimated date of completion is April, 1957. The construction includes seven reinforced concrete bridges and the extensive traffic interchange system at Wilshire Boulevard.

Over the entire length of this freeway at various locations, planning, designing, and right-of-way acquisition is in progress as well as the construction that has been described. In many locations, advance right-of-way acquisition funds, frequently called "Chapter 20 money," have been utilized in the purchase of vacant lands to forestall construction of private improvements which, if allowed to proceed, would have made future right-of-way cost many times greater. On the San Diego Freeway, $5,000,-000 has been expended from Chapter 20 money. The total expenditures to date for right-of-way acquisition and construction on this freeway is close to $35,000,000. The 1956-57 Fiscal Year budget contains an allotment for right-of-way acquisition on the San Diego Freeway of $2,740,000. The 1957-58 Fiscal Year budget, as adopted by the California Highway Commission October 18, 1956, contains an item of $9,000,000 for continuing right-of-way acquisition on the San Diego Freeway.

The San Diego Freeway is a traffic facility badly needed by the San Fernando Valley motorists, being valuable because it will take through traffic around the built-up and heavily congested Los Angeles business and industrial areas. When completed, a large portion of the through traffic now using the Hollywood and Santa Ana Freeways can to great advantage

Looking northerly along location for Golden State Freeway showing right of way clearing operations in progress. Hollenbeck Park lake in center; Santa Ana Freeway, left, and Sixth Street, Los Angeles, in foreground. The center line of freeway is shown by dash-dot line.

utilize the San Diego Freeway as a bypass route. It will be of further value when the future Olympic Freeway has been constructed for traffic destined for Los Angeles, because then another alternate route supplementing the Hollywood Freeway will be available.

Colorado Freeway

The unit of the Colorado Freeway, extending for 2.2 miles from Eagle Vista Drive in Eagle Rock to Holly Street in Pasadena, being entirely completed with the new Pasadena Pioneer's Bridge over the Arroyo Seco, is of vital importance to the people of Pasadena and this area. The last unit of construction on the Colorado Avenue 64 was completed July 28, 1955. The total of expenditures on this freeway to date is $8,500,000.

Foothill Freeway

The portion of the Foothill Freeway from Hampton Road to Montana Street in the Flintridge area, 1.8 miles in length, was reported in detail by Resident Engineer C. J. Verner in the September-October, 1955, issue of *California Highways and Public Works*. This important project, completed October 28, 1955, was enthu-

UPPER—Looking northwesterly along State Highway Route 2 (US 101) through City of San Clemente, with dash-dot line showing location of San Diego Freeway. LOWER—Looking easterly toward Capistrano Mission with State Highway Route 2 (US 101) in foreground. The San Diego Freeway will pass through location as indicated by dash-dot line.

LEFT—Looking southeasterly along State Highway Route 60 (US 101 Alternate) showing in foreground portion of City of Oxnard and intersection with Route 153 leading to Port Hueneme. The freeway construction recently started begins at the line of trees just beyond houses and extends toward foot of hills in background. RIGHT—Looking southeasterly along US 101 Alternate showing right of way clearing in progress for freeway construction recently started in Ventura County from Oxnard to Calleguas Creek which is located along base of hills shown in background.

siastically welcomed by the people of Pasadena, Flintridge, and Altadena because it corrected an exasperating traffic congestion problem at Devil's Gate Dam. The total cost was $2,675,000.

The only interstate route in District VII for which the California Highway Commission has not as yet passed a resolution adopting a freeway route for the entire length, is the Foothill Freeway. We are now engaged in preliminary engineering studies and are conferring with engineering departments and planning commissions of Los Angeles County and the various cities that will be passed through by this freeway in order to obtain the most economical route to provide the greatest possible traffic service.

Glendale Freeway

On the Glendale Freeway for the 1.6-mile section between the Los An- geles River and Avenue 36 near Eagle Rock Boulevard, plans are now completed and construction funds are available in the 1956-57 Fiscal Year budget in the amount of $3,270,000. This includes the grade separation bridge over Taylor Yard tracks of the Southern Pacific Railroad. Advertising of this contract is expected in early 1957. The 1.5-mile section of this freeway from the Los Angeles River extending it southerly to Glendale Boulevard was adopted by the Highway Commission on December 14, 1955. The budget for the 1957-58 Fiscal Year contains an allocation of $3,500,000 for continuing right-of-way acquisition on the Glendale Freeway.

Ojai Freeway

A contract was awarded June 29, 1955, for 4.1 miles of the Ojai Freeway in Ventura County, extending from the junction with West Main Street in the City of Ventura northerly to Mills Schools. This contract was completed and opened to public traffic on December 3, 1956. It was accepted by Director of Public Works Frank B. Durkee on December 6, 1956.

It is anticipated that early this year action will be taken by the California Highway Commission in connection with a routing from the Ojai Freeway, extending it southerly from a point north of the crossing with West Main Street, to a junction with the new Ventura Freeway along the ocean front.

Artesia Freeway

This freeway takes its name locally from Artesia Street along which it follows for a considerable distance in Los Angeles County. It is a part of State Highway Legislative Route 175, that has a total length of 34 miles extending from Coast

LEFT—Looking northerly along San Diego Freeway location showing in foreground recently completed bridge over Ventura Boulevard in Sherman Oaks area of the San Fernando Valley. In center is shown intersection with Ventura Freeway. Traffic artery to right is Sepulveda Boulevard, State Highway Route 158. RIGHT—Looking southerly along San Diego Freeway location showing in foreground recently completed bridge over Ventura Boulevard.

Highway, Route 60 in Redondo Beach to a junction with the Santa Ana Canyon Freeway in Orange

Looking southerly along recently completed Ojai Freeway with City of Ventura to left and Ventura River at right. Santa Barbara channel islands in background.

County near Olive. The California Highway Commission has adopted two portions of this route in the

amount of 21.7 miles for freeway routing. These two sections of freeway routing in Los Angeles County extend from Normandie to Santa Fe Avenue and in Orange County from Palo Verde Avenue to Santa Ana Canyon Freeway. In Orange County this freeway is locally referred to as the Houston Freeway, taking its name from proximity to Houston Avenue. Sections of this freeway have been developed as a four-lane divided highway, two of which were completed and opened to traffic during 1956.

On April 20, 1956, 2.2 miles of expressway were completed in Los Angeles County from Central Avenue to Alameda Street. The total cost of this construction was $1,783,500. In Orange County four miles of expressway were completed April 26, 1956, from Cypress Avenue to junction with the Santa Ana Canyon Freeway near Olive. The total cost of this con-

California Highways

struction was $1,259,100. Combining these two projects with previously completed construction a total of 9.6 miles of four-lane expressway has been completed at a total cost of $7,841,000.

Santa Ana Canyon Freeway

This freeway is a development of State Highway Route 43 extending 27.4 miles from Newport Beach to Riverside County line. It takes its local name from the fact that the northeasterly portion lies in Santa Ana Canyon. This is a four-lane divided highway where improvement has been carried out over 2.0 miles at the southwesterly end through Costa Mesa and over 10.7 miles at the northeasterly

LEFT—Looking northwesterly along Santa Ana Freeway construction in City of Buena Park showing in foreground, right, bridge construction for Grand Avenue, Route 171. RIGHT—Looking northwesterly along Santa Ana Freeway construction in City of Buena Park showing in foreground crossing of Artesia Avenue, State Highway Route 175.

and Public Works

UPPER—Looking northerly along Harbor Boulevard, a county road, showing at right interchange with Santa Ana Freeway and with Disneyland at left. LOWER—Looking northerly showing construction in progress on Santa Ana Freeway between Broadway and Lewis Street with Orange County General Hospital in foreground. Note recently completed grade separation bridge for Southern Pacific Railroad, center left, near drive-in theater screen.

end through Santa Ana Canyon. The total cost to date has been $5,607,000.

The Olympic Freeway has been discussed previously in this story under the heading freeway route adoptions by the California Highway Commission.

In addition to the above described freeways, the California Highway Commission has adopted other freeway routings for 150 miles of additional freeways upon which as yet no construction has been started. Designing of these freeways is being pushed as fast as other com-

mitments will permit, and good use of advance right-of-way funds is being made whenever critical situations arise where action must be taken now to protect future rights of way from impending private developments which if permitted to go forward would cause great increase in future costs of rights of way.

The Highway Commission on November 18, 1954, adopted a freeway resolution covering 10.9 miles extending from junction with the Golden State Freeway, US 4, in Griffith Park westerly to Sepulveda Boulevard, State Route 158. This adoption included the then last remaining section of Ven-

tura Freeway that had not previously been adopted as a freeway, and 5.2 miles of the Riverside Freeway.

The commission adopted the route for the San Gabriel River Freeway on December 15, 1954. This freeway extends from the junction with the Garden Grove Freeway near Long Beach to a junction with the San Bernardino Freeway near El Monte, a distance of 23 miles. Design is now under way in order to acquire vacant property subject to industrial and residential development under the advance right-of-way acquisition program.

The portion of the Pomona Freeway between Potrero Grande Drive

Looking easterly toward downtown Los Angeles showing Harbor Freeway in foreground, Fifth and Sixth Street bridges, right, recently completed Fourth Street bridges, left.

Freeway name	Total miles	Completed projects		Under construction		Right of way costs	Total obligated costs to date
		Miles	Construction costs	Miles	Estimated construction cost		
Pasadena Freeway 4-Level Structure to Glenarm St., Pasadena.....	8.2	8.2	$10,434,200	....		$1,009,100	$11,443,300
Hollywood Freeway Spring St. via Cahuenga Pass to Junction Golden State Freeway near Wentworth St............	16.8	10.0	29,007,500	1.8	$3,502,500	31,809,000	64,319,000
Santa Ana Freeway Spring St. (Los Angeles) to Junction of San Diego Freeway near El Toro................	42.8	28.2	39,893,930	14.6	13,757,900	17,983,500	71,635,330
San Bernardino Freeway Santa Ana Freeway near Los Angeles River to San Bernardino County Line in Claremont......	30.7	22.6	29,331,000	8.1	5,579,200	16,518,000	51,428,200
Harbor Freeway 4-Level Structure to San Pedro...............	22.4	7.1	19,345,945	6.8	15,686,928	50,292,000	85,324,873
Long Beach Freeway Pacific Coast Highway in Long Beach to Huntington Dr. in South Pasadena................	21.5	9.8	14,414,140	7.1	12,724,300	19,860,000	46,998,440
Golden Gate Freeway Junction of Olympic and Santa Ana Freeways near Soto St. to Kern County line............	72.7	47.2	15,746,026	5.1	10,350,200	37,035,000	63,131,226
Ventura Freeway Hollywood Freeway extension to Santa Barbara County line............................	68.7	40.6	13,453,659	7.5	9,779,000	19,637,000	42,869,659
San Diego Freeway Golden State Freeway near San Fernando Reservoir to San Diego County line...............	93.7	0.3	2,192,900	3.8	6,692,500	25,811,000	34,696,400
Colorado Freeway Eagle Vista Dr. in Eagle Rock to Holly St. in Pasadena................................	2.2	2.2	6,204,815	....		2,295,000	8,499,815
Foothill Freeway Hampton Rd. to Montana St. in Flintridge.....	2.0	1.8	2,051,100	....		624,000	2,675,100
Glendale Freeway Los Angeles River to Avenue 36, near Eagle Rock Blvd.....	2.5	....				3,102,000	3,102,000
Artesia Freeway Normandie Ave. to Santa Fe Ave. and Palo Verde Ave. to Santa Ana Canyon Freeway....	21.7	9.6	4,176,800	....		3,664,000	7,840,800
Santa Ana Canyon Freeway Newport Beach to Riverside County line.......	27.4	12.7	2,990,600	......	482,000	2,134,500	5,607,100
Ojai Freeway West Main St. in Ventura to 0.4 mi. north of Foster Park............................	5.7	4.1	2,075,000	....		1,130,000	3,205,000
Olympic Freeway Santa Ana Freeway near Soto St. to Lincoln Blvd. in Santa Monica....................	16.6	....				16,488,000	16,488,000
Pacific Coast Freeway Oxnard to Los Angeles County line and Huntington Beach to Newport Beach............	23.0	....		7.2	2,519,000	1,144,000	3,663,000
Other Freeways Covered by Resolution of Adoption by Highway Commission.................	149.4	....				8,286,900	8,286,900
Total................................	628.0	204.4	$191,317,615	62.2	$81,073,528	$258,823,000	$531,214,143

and the junction of Route 19, a length of 18 miles, was adopted by the Highway Commission on April 2, 1954. Notwithstanding the intense subdivision activity in the Puente area, right-of-way needs for the freeway have been established ahead of the numerous subdivisions, and acquisition of property is under way.

Route Adoptions

On June 21, 1955, the Highway Commission declared that portion of

existing Route 23 (US 6) between Route 4 (US 99) and Solamint, a distance of seven miles, to be a freeway. The commission, on March 21, 1956, adopted freeway route in the Antelope Valley portion of Route 23 from one-half mile north of junction with Los Angeles Forest Highway near Southern Pacific Railroad Vincent Y to Neenach Road, that is locally called the "Palmdale-Lancaster Freeway."

The California Highway Commission on October 20, 1954, adopted

the westerly portion, and on May 18, 1955, adopted the easterly portion of Route 179 as a freeway. This generally speaking, follows along Garden Grove Boulevard or fairly close thereto, and is locally being called the "Garden Grove Freeway." It extends from the City of Long Beach easterly to the Santa Ana Freeway in the City of Santa Ana. The design of this project is now under way and some Chapter 20 advance right-of-

... Continued on page 30

18   California Highways

Coast Highway

Improvements in Santa Barbara and San Luis Obispo Counties

By A. M. NASH, District Engineer

THE MAIN traffic artery through the historic California coastal Counties of Santa Barbara and San Luis Obispo has been known by many names—El Camino Real for its Spanish ancestry; the Coast Highway, for its many miles of ocean vistas; and the Trail of the Missions, due to the five early-day missions it passes by or near.

Most commonly, however, it is known by its federal designation, US 101, one of the two most heavily traveled routes between Los Angeles and San Francisco. In its scenic run through Santa Barbara and San Luis Obispo Counties this highway has undergone, chiefly in the past eight years, an unprecedented number of face-liftings and concrete-and-asphalt surgery, in the meantime carrying an ever-increasing volume of through and local traffic. Today virtually all its 182 miles through the two counties are multilaned or rapidly being prepared for conversion, and a study of this highway, taken contiguously section by section from south to north, indicates the many separate construction projects involved.

In Santa Barbara County

Beginning in the southeast corner of Santa Barbara County, US 101 is a four-lane divided expressway to Carpinteria, a section completed in December, 1950. No freeway agreement with the county was entered into, as no county roads were affected.

The next section, through Carpinteria to Arroyo Parida, is developed to freeway standards and was completed in January, 1955. Westerly from Arroyo Parida, through Summerland, to Ortega Hill at the edge of Montecito, is four-lane divided expressway completed in May, 1953. At Ortega Hill there is a very short section of four-lane undivided highway, but this is under freeway resolution and will be included in a full freeway project in the next few years.

Twin structures carry freeway over Southern Pacific Railroad south of Pismo Beach. Acquisition for freeway through Pismo Beach will begin shortly.

Ortega Hill Section

From Ortega Hill to San Ysidro Road the next contiguous section is four-lane divided highway but, strictly speaking, is not expressway or freeway. Actually, however, it is to all appearances an expressway and was completed in February, 1948, under a "parkway agreement" with the county. This section, together with the Ortega Hill portion, is under freeway resolution and will be developed to full freeway standards in another few years.

Over most of the sections so far discussed, the average motorist, of course, rolls merrily on with little regard as to whether he is on a parkway, freeway, or expressway. However, from San Ysidro Road westerly into Santa Barbara only the most unobservant would fail to note the modern, full freeway development through Montecito. This section, completed in Au-

PROGRESS ON COAST HIGHWAY IMPROVEMENT

San Luis Obispo & Santa Barbara Counties

Completed 4 Lane Divided Expressway...
Completed 4 Lane Divided Freeway....
Under Construction or Budgeted.......
Under Freeway Resolution............

SCALE

gust, 1956, was one of the most expensive in the district, due not only to necessary construction costs but to high real estate values in this exclusive community. This project terminates at Park Place, opposite the Bird Refuge, in Santa Barbara and is contiguous to the first expressway project in Santa Barbara County, completed in August of 1948 on new alignment from Park Place to Bath Street. Although in use less than 10 years, it has long been foreseen that this attractively-landscaped section of four-lane divided expressway eventually must be developed to a full freeway in order to serve both through and local traffic properly.

Expressway Project

From Bath Street, along Hollister Avenue, to the city limits at Los Positas Road is an expressway project that was a casualty of World War II, necessitating complete redesign and renewed freeway agreement negotiations. At present, traffic is served by a multilane, undivided highway, but right-of-way acquisition has been resumed and the project is being redesigned on a full freeway basis. It is obvious that the end product will be far superior to the proposed improvement shelved by the war.

Continuing westerly, there is now under construction a full freeway section from the Santa Barbara city limits to El Sueno Road, with an elaborate interchange structure being built at the Hollister Wye.

Westerly from El Sueno Road the existing highway as far as Ellwood is under freeway resolution of the California Highway Commission upon the basis of an expressway. Negotiations are in progress with Santa Barbara County officials which will provide for conversion of this section to full freeway standards within the foreseeable future.

Projects Completed

From Ellwood westerly to the area known as Orella, an expressway project is about to go under contract. Be-

20

UPPER—Full freeway development carries US 101 through City of San Luis Obispo. Off-ramp at lower right leads to historic mission three blocks east. LOWER—Newly opened section of full freeway between Arroyo Grande and Pismo Beach will soon be landscaped. Interchange serves Grover City to west, rural area to east.

tween Orella and a point 0.5 mile west of Refugio Beach State Park there is an existing multilane section, but this is under freeway resolution for eventual conversion to full freeway. From here westerly to the vicinity of Arroyo Quemada an expressway section is planned for construction in the next few years, with provision for ultimate expansion to full freeway standards. This will tie into existing expressway running west then north as far as the Santa Ynez River. These sections were completed as follows: Arroyo Quemada to Arroyo Hondo, February, 1950; Arroyo Hondo to Gaviota, July, 1956; Gaviota Gorge to Las Cruces, August, 1952; Gaviota Gorge Tunnel and approaches, May, 1953; Las Cruces to Summit, November, 1951; and Summit to Santa Ynez River, February, 1956.

Gaviota Gorge

Of special interest is the expressway section through Gaviota Gorge. This reportedly is one of the few points, if not the only point, in the United States, where an historical marker commemorates an event that never took place. This refers to the proposed ambush, by Spanish rancheros and soldiers, of Lt. Col. John C. Frémont and his southbound battalion in 1846. Forewarned, Frémont detoured over San Marcos Pass to the east and captured Santa Barbara, while nothing happened at Gaviota. At this same site, latter-day history records that highway engineers solved the problem of squeezing a modern expressway through this narrow gorge by boring a curving, fluorescent-lit, tunnel to carry the north-bound expressway lanes. Just how much of this was sentiment and how much was practical engineering is a matter for future historians to ponder.

At the Santa Ynez River is a short span of conventional highway that will be converted to freeway on a future project, and from there northerly through Buellton is existing expressway, completed in May, 1949. From Buellton to Zaca is a planned expressway, to be advertised for construction in the near future, which will connect with existing expressway completed in May, 1955, between Zaca and a point known as Wigmore. Between Wigmore and 1.5 miles north

of Los Alamos an expressway project on which bids were opened January 30, 1957, will connect with an expressway just completed to within four miles of Santa Maria. All of these expressway sections either are now planned or in the future will be planned for eventual full freeway. In the meantime, between this latter point and the San Luis Obispo county line, rights of way are being acquired for a freeway route by-passing the City of Santa Maria.

Nipomo-Mesa Freeway

This project will in turn connect with the so-called Nipomo Mesa Freeway which is now under construction northerly to Russell Turn. The next section, Russell Turn to Arroyo Grande, is expressway completed in July, 1956. Multilane highway exists through the City of Arroyo Grande but will be superseded in a few years by a freeway project for which rights of way already have been purchased and cleared.

Continuing north, a freeway between Arroyo Grande and Pismo Beach was finished September, 1956. For a freeway through the City of Pismo Beach, a freeway agreement has been executed, rights of way are now being appraised, and acquisition will begin shortly.

Northerly of Pismo Beach, existing expressway to Miles Station, was completed in July, 1949, and between Miles Station and San Luis Obispo in December, 1948. Full freeway through San Luis Obispo was finished in December, 1953. Expressway north to the foot of Cuesta grade previously had been completed in August, 1948, the first limited-access project in San Luis Obispo County. Over the 7 percent Cuesta grade are several miles of four-lane highway, completed on existing alignment in November, 1938, but improved many times since. At most points along this section, access is so physically difficult, if not impossible, that there has been no urgency to acquire access rights. This will be done at some future date but in the meantime this section functions as an expressway even without being so designated, and blends inconspicuously into the next expressway project to

the north. This runs from Cuesta siding to 1.0 mile south of Santa Margarita and was completed in June, 1950.

New Alignment on US 101

At this point a new interchange sorts out traffic to and from by-passed Santa Margarita, and US 101 itself heads out across 9.3 miles of new freeway alignment, tying into previously built expressway at the north end of Atascadero. A bumper crop of deer paid the price of progress along this new section after it was opened to traffic in November, 1956, as many miles are through scenic back-country not previously traversed by a north-south road. In the meantime warning signs have been placed and it is expected that natural deer runs soon may be defined and posted.

Between Atascadero and Graves Creek the expressway construction was completed in July, 1951. From Graves Creek, by-passing Templeton, to the south end of Paso Robles, the expressway was finished in January, 1953. Freeway through Paso Robles is now under construction as one of the district's larger projects. This involves structures over Southern Pacific Railroad at each end of the city, and an interchange and bridge over the Salinas River to handle Sign Route 41 traffic to and from points east. The combined project is scheduled for completion in the spring of 1958.

North of Paso Robles

North of Paso Robles the expressway to San Miguel was completed in January, 1955, and a new freeway section from there to the south boundary of Camp Roberts is now under construction. From this point, a short distance south of the Monterey county line, the existing highway to the north is being actively planned for improvement to expressway or freeway standards as rapidly as funds may be made available.

In conclusion it is interesting to note that all completed expressway and freeway sections discussed above were constructed in the past eight years, during which time average daily traffic increased 112 percent at Hollister Wye, 25 percent at Santa Maria, 29 percent at San Luis Obispo, and 82 percent at Paso Robles.

UPPER—Full freeway through Atascadero lies immediately west of old highway. Interchange in foreground serves local traffic and US 466 to Morro Bay. LOWER—Most recently completed freeway section of Coast Highway runs 9.3 miles, from one mile south of Santa Margarita to Atascadero. View looking south shows entirely new alignment through scenic countryside, portion of superseded highway at left center.

SIX MILES OF FREEWAY IN SACRAMENTO RIVER CANYON COMPLETED

By W. H. JACOBSEN, District Surveys Engineer

Six miles of the Sacramento Canyon Freeway on US 99, State Route 3, in Shasta County, were completed in December, 1956. With the opening of the freeway, 25 percent of the bottleneck between Crespo's and Dunsmuir has been eliminated and travel time through the area has been reduced by approximately 10 minutes.

US 99 follows the Sacramento River Canyon from Crespo's to Dunsmuir, a distance of 25 miles. Due to the poor horizontal and vertical alignment on this 25 miles, vehicle passing has been limited in the past to special passing lanes provided at varying intervals. The average vehicle speed through the area has been 30 miles per hour due to the restrictions on passing and the large percentage of trucks using the route.

Although the new road has been constructed to freeway standards, none of the beauty of the area has been destroyed. In fact, with the better sight distances, it is felt that the touring public will be able to see more of the area than it could on the old road.

Story in Pictures

The complete story is told in various photographs.

Photo No. 1 shows the old Dog Creek Bridge with its poor approach alignment.

Photo No. 2 shows the new Dog Creek Bridge with the approaches under construction, which are now complete. This photo gives a good view of the surrounding area.

Photo No. 3 of the old highway north of Vollmers showing poor alignment and sight distance.

Photo No. 4 shows a section of the new freeway taken directly west of Photo No. 3. The site distance is unrestricted. The beauty of the area has been enhanced and maintained. The traveling public is able to look at the country rather than having to maintain a constant vigil on the road.

During the construction part of the old toll house for the stage road to Trinity Center was removed. This toll house was constructed during the

1890's and later added onto and converted into a dwelling house on what is known as Vollmers Ranch.

Many early travelers will remember the Vollmers Ranch Hotel for the fine dinners served.

Three Separate Contracts

State engineers stayed at this ranch while on location and construction of

the original state highway through the canyon and again in the late twenties when the old highway shown in the photos was constructed.

The present freeway was constructed under three separate contracts and all finished within three months of one another. The contracts are as follows:

24

Dog Creek Bridge by Ukropina, Polich and Kral of Los Angeles.

Four miles of grading, surfacing and a bridge across Slate Creek by Piombo Construction Company of San Carlos.

Two miles of grading, surfacing and Sacramento River channel change by the Guy F. Atkinson Company of South San Francisco.

The grading on this six miles is some of the heaviest that will be encountered on this route. With the cuts and fills being some 200 feet in height, it is little wonder that the yardage

moved ran approximately 500,000 cubic yards per mile.

The three contracts have a total value of approximately $5,000,000.

The road contracts were designed from aerial photo maps and were constructed under the direction of H. S. Miles, District Engineer, and Geo. R. Barry, Construction Engineer, with the writer as resident engineer on the projects.

At the present time, a contract for an addition 6.8 miles immediately north of the Piombo contract has been awarded to Reid and Gibbons of Salt Lake City.

PRAISE FOR CALIFORNIA

DEPARTMENT OF COMMERCE
BUREAU OF PUBLIC ROADS
Washington

January 17, 1957

MR. G. T. McCoy
State Highway Engineer
Department of Public Works
Sacramento 7, California

DEAR SIR: As of January 1st California was one of six states which had already advanced all of their 1957 interstate funds to the plans-approved stage and had begun working on 1958 funds. California's percentage rate is exceeded only by Maryland.

It is a pleasure to call your attention to such a favorable record, and I hope that you will pass on to your staff my personal feeling of appreciation for this accomplishment. California's standing in this regard was read into the Senate hearing record last week.

Sincerely yours,

JOHN A. VOLPE
Federal Highway
Administrator

Commenting on California's good showing, State Director of Public Works Frank B. Durkee pointed out that this State has enjoyed for years a favorable budgetary procedure in highway matters which makes it possible for the Division of Highways to do advance planning effectively. At the same time, he said, California has been able to provide the matching funds for Federal Aid highway programs without difficulty, thanks to the State's highway revenue setup.

THE CROSSROADS

All too many motorists are inclined to trust more to luck than to skill when they come to the crossroads. Approaching a busy intersection they know that dangers are involved but they just keep rolling and trust to luck to get them through. Cruising along at a brisk clip they let the other drivers jam on their brakes and swerve wildly to avoid an accident. The careless drivers manage to get by this way until they come to an intersection where the other driver is a "luck truster" too, and then comes collision.

King City Bridge

New Span Will Relieve
Heavy Traffic Congestion

By FRED H. YOSHINO, Resident Engineer, and
R. S. SCAMARA, District V Representative

A PORTION of the first section of four-lane divided highway was recently opened to traffic in SOMOCO. SOMOCO is what the residents of southern Monterey County like to call this particular section of California. This section of highway consists of a new bridge across the Salinas River and about two miles of divided expressway, beginning at Canal Street in King City and extending 1.8 miles north of the Salinas River crossing, on US 101. The completion of this project eliminated a very hazardous stretch of road and bridge which had a very bad accident record. Also, the completion of the new bridge will allow freer movement of the very large farm machinery that is common to this section of California, known as the "Salad Bowl of the Nation."

The traffic on this section of US 101 is both local and through. King City is located about 150 miles south of San Francisco and about 240 miles north of Los Angeles. The through traffic is fairly highspeed.

Traffic Increase Steady

Study of traffic counts over the years indicates a steady increase. Some indication of the growth is shown in the comparison of 16-hour July traffic counts for 1946, 1950 and 1956 taken at the junction of US 101 and the county road to Jolon west of the bridge. These counts were 4,387, 7,014, and 8,161 motor vehicles.

The normal traffic growth plus increased agricultural activities and greater use of Hunter-Liggett Military Reservation by the Army has greatly overtaxed the existing highway facility and made it imperative that steps be taken to increase traffic capacity of this section of US 101. This project was placed under contract to take care of the worst section.

The construction of the new bridge provides for one-way northbound traffic with one-way traffic southbound on the existing bridge. As the existing bridge was only 21 feet 6 inches between curbs, with no sidewalk, and with both approaches on substandard curves for the highspeed traffic, it had been the scene of many serious accidents. This existing structure was constructed in 1919 and consisted of 41 30-foot concrete girders and 14 100-foot steel pony truss spans. The total length was 2,655 feet.

Included in the new construction were certain modifications and revisions in this old bridge as hereinafter described.

No Traffic Delays

Revamping of the existing bridge to one-way traffic has resulted in several improvements. It will be no longer necessary to tie up traffic for as long as 30 minutes at a time while a ponderous, slow-moving machine uses the existing bridge. This machine has at times caused traffic to be backed up completely through the main street of King City and beyond the opposite city limits. Another dividend is that it will no longer be necessary to detail a Highway Patrol officer to stop traffic for machinery movements, thereby keeping the officer from performing his primary duty of patrolling the highways. The farm operators will also derive a benefit of not having to wait until a patrolman is available to stop traffic. This waiting has at times amounted to half a day when traffic conditions elsewhere prevented detailing of an officer to the bridge.

Jolon Road Intersection

The completed contract consisted of construction of a new 1,806-foot deck plate girder bridge, about two miles of expressway, removal of 600

feet of concrete approach spans on the existing bridge, and revamping of the intersection of US 101 and Jolon Road by the construction of a series of on and off ramps. The reconstruction and improvement of the Jolon Road intersection should greatly expedite military traffic that uses this road to reach Hunter Liggett Military Reservation.

The new bridge consists of one 65-foot, 15 107-foot 5-inch and one 127-foot span. The distance between paving notches is 1,806 feet. All spans are of welded plate girders with concrete deck slab. Composite girder design was used to arrive at a balance between span length and pier cost. Four girders are used in Span 1 (65 feet) and in Span 2 (107 feet 6 inches) because of the extreme skew at these locations. The balance of the structure has three girders per span. The depth of the girders is 7 feet 6 inches.

The bridge rests on concrete piers and abutments which were built in a conventional manner. Cast-in-place concrete piling is used to furnish support.

Design of Span

Piers were constructed by first driving sheet piling and then excavating to Elevation 265. After excavating, concrete pile shells were driven to Elevation 230. Before cutting off the pile cans to grade, tremie concrete was placed to seal the cofferdam. After dewatering, concrete for the cast-in-place piling was placed, and the footing and piers were constructed in the usual manner. Ground water surface during pile driving and pier construction was about Elevation 275.

The placing of sheet piling and bearing piles and the removal of the sheet piling was done by Raymond Concrete Pile Company for the general contractor, C. K. Moseman.

This photo shows pier and superstructure design of King City Bridge

Deep piling was used to furnish support for the bridge due to the fluctuation of the river from its very dry summer condition to extremely high velocity flow during the winter season, therefore, it was felt that a more than ordinary effort be made to secure stable bearing. In order to do this, it was necessary to drive piling to Elevation 230, with no jetting allowed below Elevation 250. Borings indicated that the Salinas River had scoured down to Elevation 250 during some period in the past. This limitation on jetting created an additional burden in reaching the specified tip elevation. The sandy uniform appearance of the river bed at about Elevation 285 belies the fact that substructure conditions varied greatly from pier to pier and from pile to pile in any one pier location. It is to the credit of the pile company that out of the total of 12,400 lineal feet of piling in the original estimate of quantity, the final quantity underran by only 146 feet.

Salinas River Unique

The flow in the Salinas River during flood stage is extremely turbulent. However, this river is considered to have its major volume of flow underground. In fact, it is considered the largest river in the United States from the standpoint of underground flow.

While the pile driving and pier construction were underway at the site, Independent Iron Works, Oakland, was fabricating the girders out of plates. All fabrication was done by the submerged arc method in the shop. Inspection of this phase of the work was done by the Materials and Research Department, Berkeley office. After three girders for a span were fabricated, the steel was shipped by rail to King City by flat car, using two cars as idler. Upon reaching King City, girders were loaded onto truck and trailer and hauled to the site and erected. No trouble was encountered in erecting the steel at the site other than the normal 20- to 40-mile an hour winds that blow through the Salinas Valley almost every day during the summer.

After landing the girders on the piers and bracing them temporarily, diagonal bracing and diaphragms were welded in place using the shield arc method. All field erecting and welding was done by Independent Iron Works field erection crew.

Huge Amount of Steel

The total amount of steel used was 1,816,000 pounds at a lump sum bid price of $230,800.

Deck concrete forming and placing started as soon as the first girder was erected. The concrete deck construction was started at Abutment 1 and continued until the deck was completed at Abutment 18.

Upon completion of the deck and curb, Todd and Cantrell, bridge rail subcontractor, placed the bridge railing.

Painting of the structural steel was done by John P. McGuire of San Jose, immediately after the deck was placed. All structural steel was sandblasted and painted with red lead and a finish coat of aluminum.

In the meantime, Los Gatos Construction Company and Volpa Brothers, roadway excavation and paving subcontractors, respectively, had completed the southbound lanes north of the old bridge, and after traffic was routed thereon, the old existing lanes were removed and construction of the northbound lanes was begun. Upon completion of the paving, the new bridge was opened to two-way traffic on October 3, 1956.

Part of Old Bridge Removed

As soon as the traffic was routed over the new bridge, removal of 600 feet of the existing bridge was started. This portion of the bridge consisted of 20 30-foot concrete spans. The bridge was removed by knocking it down with a 4,000 pound "headache" ball swung by a three-eighths cubic yard crane. Fill construction was underway as soon as this portion of the bridge was sufficiently demolished to allow removal of the rubble. A new bridge abutment was constructed and the roadway constructed to a higher standard of curvature and grade to allow use of the remaining portion of the old bridge.

Other work on the existing bridge consists of placing new metal plate

bridge railing from the end of the truss spans to the new abutment at Bent 18, and improvement of the curve and approach at the King City end. Upon completion, the existing bridge will be one-way for southbound traffic.

The metal plate bridge railing on the remaining concrete approach spans was placed by Wulfert Company of San Leandro.

Except from Canal Street to the approach to the bridges, the roadwill will consist of two 12-foot lanes with a 10-foot outer shoulder and a 5-foot inner shoulder, with a 46-foot minimum division strip. The project included the construction of two ramps in a 35-foot cut connecting the right and left lanes to the county road leading to Hunter Liggett Military Reservation and Jolon Valley.

Highway Construction

A 2,000-foot revetment with a 30-foot pile training fence was constructed along the west bank of the

Salinas River in order to allow for shortening the bridges and to improve the alignment to the west approaches.

A highway lighting system was installed at two locations on the Jolon Road connection ramps, consisting of eight luminaires, each on a 30-foot standard.

Over 350,000 cubic yards of roadway excavation was used to construct the embankments, all coming out of the roadway prism and a local borrow area located between the old and new bridges in the Salinas River. The roadway excavation and 3,000,000 station yards overhaul were performed with scrapers. Compaction was obtained by sheepsfoot rollers.

A light silty clay material found in the excavation gave considerable trouble. That portion used in embankments had to be mixed with other material to get compaction, and that close to subgrade had to be removed and replaced with select material. Two locations required a change order amounting to $18,000 to excavate 12 inches below subgrade and 18 inches below subgrade, replacing the clay with select material, and installing 4,200 feet of 8-inch perforated metal pipe.

An existing 10-foot x 10-foot reinforced concrete box was extended at each end with 66-inch reinforced concrete pipe, with special designed connections. This culvert is located in a 45-foot gulch that resulted in poor sight distance on the old existing two-way road. Approximately 1,700 lineal feet of other culverts were also placed.

Subcontracts

Some 20,000 tons of Type B plant-mixed surfacing and 45,000 tons of Type C cement treated base were placed on the main line and ramps. The prime contractor, C. K. Moseman of Redwood City, who is primarily a bridge contractor, had subcontracted all other work to nine subcontractors; Todd & Cantrell of Sacramento, Progress Electric Co. of Palo Alto, Raymond Concrete Pile Co. of Oakland, Steelfab Inc. of Castroville, Independent Iron Works Inc. of Oakland, Los Gatos Construction Co. of Los Gatos, Volpa Bros. of

Fresno, Wulfert Co. of San Leandro and John P. McGuire of San Jose. The authorized subcontracting amounted to only 47 percent due to nine specialty items in this contract.

Exceptionally good weather experienced during the 1956 winter aided the contractor in finishing the project in January, 1957, without the usual winter shutdown. The hard winter of 1955-56 caused the normal winter shutdown, and roadwork was not started again until March of 1956. Very little winter damage resulted, and construction on the new bridge was not affected.

The bridge work amounted to about $680,500 and the roadwork portion of the contract was about $423,129.

Two Additional Contracts

Two more contracts to continue four-lane divided highway construction north to Salinas, approximately 40 miles north of King City, are ready to start. At the completion of construction of projects on the 1957-58 budget, four-laning to Salinas from King City will be complete except for approximately 15 miles.

The contract for this project was awarded to C. K. Moseman, Redwood City, on April 1, 1955, by the Director of Public Works. The contract was approved by the Attorney General April 28, 1955, and work started May 5, 1955. A total of 325 working days were alloted to complete the project, with the original completion date set as August 16, 1956. The final date of completion is estimated to be about January 15, 1957. The bid price for this contract was $1,103,629. The work was under the direction of F. W. Panhorst, Assistant State Highway Engineer-Bridges; A. M. Nash, District Engineer and the authors. R. N. Moseman was the general superintendent for the contractor.

MORE CARS ENTER CALIFORNIA

Nearly 14,000 more cars entered California during October, 1956, than did during October, 1955, reports the National Automobile Club. The total number of cars that entered during October of this year was 317,083.

3n Memoriam
RICHARD JONES

Richard Jones, retired assistant highway engineer, passed away on October 31, 1956, greatly to the regret of his fellow workers in District VII.

Dick, who was born in 1894, first came to work for the California Division of Highways in District III from the Kentucky Highway Commission in 1929. After attending the Polytechnic College of Engineering and the University of California Dick came to District VII in 1932.

As an assistant highway engineer, he spent most of his career in the construction department, working as assistant resident on such projects as the Hollywood Freeway, Harbor Freeway, Long Beach Freeway, and many other major construction jobs.

Dick retired early in 1956 after a leave of absence for reasons of health. He leaves a widow, Mrs. Jean Jones, to whom we extend our deepest sympathy.

BERT STEWART NEW GENERAL MANAGER NATIONAL AUTO CLUB

Bert Stewart of San Francisco is the new secretary and general manager of the National Automobile Club. He succeeds Herbert E. Manners, retired.

Born and raised in Berkeley, Stewart went through the public schools there and attended Armstrong College and the University of California.

After a brief period in which he worked on newspapers and the insurance trade around San Francisco, he joined the staff of National Automobile Club as associate director of public relations in January of 1938. He then served as editor of *National Motorist*, became director of public relations in 1941 and field secretary in 1947. So successfully did he carry out his duties as field secretary that in January of 1956 the board of directors appointed him assistant general manager of the club, which position he held until his present appointment.

Motorists Benefit By Increase in Freeway Building

Earlier use by California motorists of new freeways and other modern highways is one of the most gratifying effects of the increase of California state highway funds, State Engineer G. T. McCoy points out in a report submitted by the Department of Public Works to Governor Goodwin J. Knight.

"The increased cost of highway construction has absorbed a part of this revenue," McCoy continues, "but the additional amount now available is making possible the consolidation of projects that in former years were undertaken by stage construction. The program as now functioning is advancing completion of these improved facilities for early use by the traveling public."

The additional funds referred to by McCoy were the highway users taxes enacted by the State Legislature in 1953 and retained in 1955, exclusive of the augmented federal highway funds the State is now receiving as a result of the Federal Highway Act of 1956.

Huge Construction Program

The State Highway Engineer's report covers the 1955-56 Fiscal Year which ended June 30, 1956, and is the Tenth Annual Report of the Division of Highways since the Collier-Burns Highway Act of 1947.

The report states that bids were opened by the Division of Highways for 669 projects with a construction value of $233,183,200 for construction and engineering but excluding right-of-way expenses.

During the year 551 contracts with a value of $219,965,700 were awarded and 65 informal contracts for storm damage repair amounting to $1,664,800 were approved. Eleven contracts totaling $6,803,300 were also awarded during this fiscal year for projects on which bids had been received in the previous fiscal year. Expenditures for right-of-way acquisition and utility relocation exclusive of land clearance overhead and acquisition for other

DISTRICT VII REPORT

Continued from page 18...

way acquisition funds have been expended in the protection of this routing.

The Highway Commission has adopted as freeway, two sections of Route 60, Pacific Coast Highway; one at Ventura County and one in Orange County. The portion in Ventura County, 17.4 miles long, extends from Ventura Freeway to the Los Angeles county line and of this, 7.2 miles from Date Street, Oxnard, to Calleguas Creek, is now under a construction contract that is 15 percent completed. The contract allotment is $2,519,000. The other portion of this freeway in Orange County that is locally referred to as the Pacific Coast Freeway, is 5.6 miles in length, one section 4.6 miles long, extending from Huntington Beach to Newport Beach, and the other section, one mile long, in the San Juan Creek area. Design studies for this project are now under way. Due to the popularity of the Huntington Beach State Park it is anticipated that improvement on this section may be required in the near future.

Outlook for Future

Within the next few years, if the present financing program is maintained, we expect to complete to freeway standards US 101 from the San

agencies totaled $109,150,400 for the year.

The increased number of multilaned projects that were placed under contract during the fiscal year accounted for a higher money value of construction compared to previous years without showing a corresponding increase in construction mileage. Construction of 334 bridges and grade crossings were contracted for during the year.

The various functions of the Division of Highways are outlined in the report, including operations, administration, planning, bridges, rights of way, public relations and personnel, legal, and accounting.

Illustrations in the report cover some of the major construction projects under way or completed.

Diego-Orange County line to a point west of Ventura. Within the central area of metropolitan Los Angeles we plan early completion of a loop consisting of the Olympic Freeway from its interchange with the Santa Ana and Golden State Freeways westerly to and beyond the Harbor Freeway; the Golden State Freeway northwesterly to a point north of Burbank; and the Ventura Freeway westerly from its junction with the Golden State through the San Fernando Valley. The Ventura Freeway is of course in part included in US 101, mentioned above.

Also, subject to financing considerations, the next few years should see the completion of the Harbor Freeway, the Long Beach Freeway as far north as the San Bernardino Freeway; the San Diego Freeway from Burbank Boulevard southerly to Florence Avenue, and from the Harbor Freeway southeasterly to Huntington Beach Boulevard in Orange County. Plans and right-of-way acquisition are being carried forward on other important parts of the freeway system in order that construction may be carried on as rapidly as funds become available.

Our present position in this freeway program may be summed up in this way: We have for the first time a financial program which begins to recognize the size and complexity of the program required to build a freeway system in a metropolitan area. It is essential that we project our planning into the future in order that an orderly development of a reasonable freeway network may be possible.

RAILROAD CROSSINGS

You don't have to be reckless to get yourself killed at a railroad crossing. While many of these accidents do happen to the reckless drivers, those who insist on racing the train to the crossing or pay no attention to the warning signs and signals, a good number of these accidents happen to drivers who just don't use all the care that is necessary.

Traffic accident deaths to date are twice the total of battle deaths in all wars in United States history.

Something New

Double-deck Freeway Viaducts In San Francisco and Oakland

By W. TRAVIS, District Construction Engineer

FREEWAY construction in industrial and commercial areas of San Francisco and Oakland is progressing rapidly under five concurrent construction contracts totaling some 24 millions of dollars in value. These portions of the metropolitan freeway system are designed as double-decked concrete viaducts which will provide four lanes of traffic in each direction at separate levels. The entire freeway is elevated and separated from all city street traffic. These will be the first double-deck freeway facilities in California.

The design of a freeway facility which must pass through long established industrial and commercial properties presents problems which are not encountered in either rural areas or in areas where the freeway planning can be correlated with the development of the surrounding lands. In general, the existing surface street pattern, having been established for a century, cannot be altered and all streets must remain in service, making a viaduct construction the only practical design.

High Property Values

Consideration of high property values and the necessity of holding the disruption of established businesses to an absolute minimum require that the design make maximum use of existing streets for the freeway right-of-way. The double-decked viaduct design fulfills these criteria in that all surface streets may remain in service and the two levels of structure occupy half the right-of-way width required for a single level structure of equivalent capacity. The double-deck design also simplifies connections to the freeway in that ramps may be brought in to either side of either deck. The direct connections permit compact ramp designs with a resultant large saving in right of way requirements.

Looking south along Cypress Street, showing heavy traffic prior to construction of new facilities

The current construction requires approximately 8,000 foundation piles totaling 400,000 lineal feet, 200,000 cubic yards of structure concrete, 60 million pounds of reinforcing steel and 100,000 lineal feet of bridge railing.

Embarcadero Freeway

The first section of double-deck freeway in San Francisco which will connect with the James Lick (Bayshore) Freeway at Fourth Street, provides a transition from single to double-deck construction and is the first unit of Route 224 which will be known as the Embarcadero Freeway. The contract provides entrance and exit ramps to the city street system at Beale Street and Main Street at Mission Street together with additional connections to the San Francisco-Oakland Bay Bridge. Completion of this project will therefore extend the freeway system and the Bay Bridge

approaches to the southern extremity of San Francisco's financial district. Work on this section was started in May of 1955 and is expected to be opened to traffic in March of this year. The contract, which will approximate $5,700,000, is held by MacDonald, Young & Nelson Inc., and Morrison-Knudsen Co., Inc.

Two additional contracts have been awarded totaling $9,500,000, to Charles L. Harney, Inc., which will extend the Embarcadero Freeway past San Francisco's famous Ferry Building to Broadway. The contracts include over a mile of double-deck construction and also provide a double-deck ramp for on and off connections to Sansome Street and to Battery Street at Broadway. Completion of this contract will extend the freeway system to the north end of San Francisco's financial district.

Work was started on the first of these contracts in March of 1956 and the entire project is scheduled for completion in the summer of 1959.

Basic Design

The basic design of the freeway is a continuous reinforced concrete box

Looking west at Embarcadero Freeway construction. Foreground shows progress toward Embarcadero with Main and Beale ramps in center.

girder viaduct, of repeating 80-foot span, supported by reinforced concrete bents on steel piles. A 52-foot clear roadway is provided on each level to accommodate four lanes of traffic. Southbound traffic will occupy the upper deck and northbound traffic the lower deck of the viaduct. Surface traffic will be carried on either side of the completed structure. The State Belt Railroad, which extends the length of the Embarcadero, will be relocated to a position beneath the

viaduct clear of automotive traffic. Consequently, the completed project will not only lift the through traffic from the Embarcadero but will provide far better service for surface traffic than now exists.

The design includes provisions for possible extension southerly to approaches of the proposed southern crossing of San Francisco Bay and will be continued northerly under future contracts to eventual connection with the approaches of the Golden Gate Bridge.

Cypress Street Viaduct

In Oakland viaduct construction is in progress along existing Route 69 (Cypress Street) between the newly reconstructed distribution structure at the east end of the San Francisco-Oakland Bay Bridge and the completed portion of the Eastshore Freeway at Magnolia Street. The project consists of a mile and three-quarters of double-deck viaduct structure with necessary ramp connections to city streets. The basic design of the Cypress Street Viaduct is similar to that

and Public Works

UPPER—Double deck along Cypress Street. Note usage of prefabricated metal tubular staging. LOWER—Double-deck construction along Cypress Street showing on-ramp at 14th Street, off-ramp at high level, left.

under construction in San Francisco. Again a 52-foot clear roadway is provided on the upper deck for four lanes of southbound traffic and a like roadway will be provided on the lower deck for northbound traffic.

Utilization of the existing highway right-of-way for the viaduct construction necessitates carrying highway traffic through the entire length of the project continuously during construction. To provide this service new roadways on either side of the proposed structure were first constructed and traffic routed thereon to clear the viaduct area. These roadways will serve permanently as surface streets after completion of the freeway.

The Cypress Street Viaduct is being constructed under two contracts totaling $8,500,000, both of which were awarded to Grove, Sheperd, Wilson & Kruge of California, Inc. Work was started in August of 1955 and the project is expected to be opened to traffic in July of this year.

The only portion of the Eastshore Freeway in Oakland not now completed or under construction is the one-mile unit from Fallon Street to Market Street. Plans have been completed for this work and $6,400,000 has been budgeted for its construction. The project will be advertised immediately and construction will be under way this spring. When this final unit is opened to traffic, scheduled for the spring of 1959, the entire Eastshore Freeway will be completed from the San Francisco-Oakland Bay Bridge to San Jose.

FRED OEHLER IS HONORED

Fred J. Oehler, San Jose banker and civic leader, is the new president of the California State Automobile Association. He was elected January 17th, in San Francisco.

Oehler is Vice President and General Manager of the San Jose Office of the American Trust Company and district manager for the bank. He has served the association as vice president two years and as treasurer for three.

Of the 5,421 bridges in the state highway system, only 13 are now posted for reduced loads and 57 for restricted speed.

Francis N. Hveem Receives High Award

Certificate of Roy W. Crum Award for Distinguished Service. Inset photo of Francis N. Hveem.

Francis N. Hveem, Materials and Research Engineer for the State Division of Highways, has been chosen by the Highway Research Board to receive its highest award for 1956, the Roy W. Crum Award for Distinguished Service.

The award, made annually for outstanding achievement in the field of highway research, was presented to Hveem on January 8th, in Washington, D. C., during the national meeting of the board, by G. Donald Kennedy, Past President of the Automotive Safety Foundation.

In accepting the award Hveem said:

"I consider that this award really belongs to the entire Materials and Research Department as it will be obvious to all that the accomplishments for which the award is made represent the contributions of everyone in the department. While directed to an individual, this award is a tribute to the teamwork that makes outstanding achievements possible."

Pioneer in Research

One of the pioneers in highway research methods, Hveem has earned a national reputation for his numerous original contributions. Testing equipment and testing methods which have been developed under his supervision are now in extensive use throughout the United States and foreign countries. A list of some of the better known devices and test methods he has developed include the stabilometer, the cohesiometer, the kneading compactor and sand equivalent apparatus, investigation of joint distress in concrete pavement, development of welding inspection techniques for structural steel, design formula for estimating thickness of pavement required, and a study of automobile collisions with highway bridge railing. The application of a surface area formula in bituminous mix design, also developed by Hveem, is another recognized outstanding contribution to the highway science field.

Enters State Service in 1917

A native of Lamoine in Shasta County, Hveem began his career with the State in 1917 when he went to work for the California Division of Highways as a draftsman for District II at Redding. He became an assistant resident engineer in 1918 and a resident engineer in 1924. In 1929 he joined the Materials and Research Department, having attracted the attention of its chief, Thomas E. Stanton, by his independent field research in design and control of bituminous mixtures for highway surfacing.

During the ensuing years Hveem established a national reputation, both as a specialist in bituminous mixes and in the general field of highway research and testing. He was appointed construction engineer for the division in 1950 with responsibility for supervision of highway construction throughout the State. In 1951, on the retirement of Mr. Stanton, Hveem returned to the testing laboratory as its chief. The laboratory is responsible for testing all materials used in the construction of state highways and bridges.

He took a leading role in the planning and operation of test tracks in Idaho and Illinois. The purpose of these test roads, which are cooperative projects of state highway departments, federal agencies and private industry, is to analyze the effects of loads of varying weights on highways of different types of construction.

Hveem was also the recipient of the Highway Research Board Award for 1948, along with R. M. Carmany, for their paper on "The Factors Underlying the Rational Design of Pavements."

Hveem is also a member of the American Society of Civil Engineers, the American Concrete Institute, the American Society for Testing Materials and the Association of Asphalt Paving Technologists.

36

Philippine Contractors Tour Southern Freeways

MR. B. N. FRYKLAND
District Construction Engineer
Division of Highways
State of California

Dear MR. FRYKLAND: First allow me to express to you my apologies for not writing you immediately. The team has just arrived after our three-month tour in Japan, United States and Europe.

In behalf of the Philippine Building Contractors Productivity Team, allow me to thank you for the very kind hospitality you gave us during our visit at your office. We enjoyed it immensely and we hope that the ideas we gathered during our visit at your office will be used to a great advantage in the Philippine construction industry.

Please feel free to write me or any member of the team if there is anything we can do in our humble way to help you.

Again, thank you for your hospitality.

Very truly yours,

DOMINGO V. POBLETE
Team Leader, Philippine Building Contractors Productivity Team

The foregoing letter has been received by District Construction Engineer Frykland of District VII, Los Angeles, who recently conducted a group of Philippine contractors on a tour of highway construction projects and completed freeways in Southern California. Senor Poblete, in addition to his Philippine connections, is also President of the East Asian General Contractors Association, which includes all of the Philippines, Japan, Indonesia, and parts of Northern Australia.

The group making the inspection trip consisted of the following:

Christine Concepcion, President, Fortunato Concepcion, Inc.—Union Engineering Corp.—Pan Philippine Commercial Corp., Director, Philippine Contractors Association; Director, Philippine Association of Civil Engineers.

Rodolfo M. Cuenca, General Contractor. General construction, operating cranes, bulldozer, pile driving, etc. Member of Philippine Contractors Association.

Bienvenido Dimson, Vice President and Treasurer, Maximo Dimson Construction, Dimson Construction Corporation. General construction, roads, irrigation, piers, portworks, etc. Member of Manila Junior Chamber of Commerce and Philippine Contractors Association.

Honrado R. Lopez, President and General Manager, H. R. Lopez Co., Inc. Quezon City General Contractor. Vice President, Philippine Contractors Association, Philippine Society of Civil Engineers and Philippine Association of Civil Engineers.

Domingo V. Poblete, President and General Manager, Poblete Construction Co., Makati, Rizal. Member of Manila Lions Club, International Chamber of Commerce, Philippine Association of Civil Engineers and Philippine Contractors Association.

Placido O. Urbanes, Jr., General Manager, Paencor, Inc., a corporation dealing with publication of technical magazine devoted to architecture, engineering construction and lumbering. Member of Philippine Contractors Association and Philippine Association of Civil Engineers.

Also on the trip were A. E. Laurencelle of Industrial Training Division, International Cooperation Administration, Washington, D. C., and H. A. Alderton, Principal Highway Engineer of U. S. Bureau of Public Roads, who were in charge of making general arrangements for the distinguished group of foreign visitors.

Frykland particularly enjoyed conducting this group because they were interested in so many of the construction details that were his particular interest and also because of his having served during World War II with U. S. Army Engineers in the Philippines, during which tour of duty he visited islands of Leyte, Luzon, Palawan, Mindanao, Samar, and Mindoro.

THE BETTER LAWYER

In Southern California two legal beagles were arrested at almost the same time for almost the same infringement of the speed law. Being a cooperative pair, they decided to defend each other in court. Each man pleaded for the other and when the words and the warblings had settled down, one lawyer found that he was acquitted and the other found that he had to pay a $10 fine. What he lost in money he gained in professional satisfaction on reflecting upon the fact that his colleague just must have had a better lawyer.

Now Read This

Carquinez Bridge Project Tests Ingenuity of Engineers

By LEONARD C. HOLLISTER, Projects Engineer, Carquinez *

* This is the first of two articles on Carquinez Bridge Project by Mr. Hollister—Ed.

SINCE THE good old horse and buggy days, the Carquinez Strait has presented many problems to the highway engineer. It lies directly in the path of the natural highway location connecting the San Francisco Bay area with the Sacramento Valley.

US 40 is the most direct and widely used highway connecting the San Francisco Bay area with the eastern states and carries an unusually high percentage of truck traffic indicating its great strategic and commercial importance as a transportation facility.

This east-west interstate highway route crosses the Carquinez Strait about halfway between the great industrial area of San Francisco Bay and the fertile inland valley of the Sacramento River.

The Carquinez Strait is a navigable body of water approximately 3,000 to 5,000 feet wide with velocities varying from 5 to 10 feet per second; and since the early gold rush days of California has been a formidable barrier to the development of land transportation.

Early Ferry Service

The first attempt to overcome this barrier was in 1850 when a ferry was established to cross Carquinez Strait between Benicia and Martinez. Twenty-nine years later in 1879 the Central Pacific Railway now the Southern Pacific Company succeeded in establishing railroad transportation across the Carquinez Strait by building two large ferries, the *Solano and Contra Costa*, for the transportation of trains across the strait. Ferry service thus remained the only facility for land transportation until the 1920's when the American Toll Bridge Company started construction of two highway bridges, one known as the Carquinez Bridge located at Crockett and the other located about 15 miles upstream called the Antioch Bridge. At about the same time the Southern Pacific

Picture showing the new piers of the Crockett Interchange. The outline of the "big cut" is beginning to take shape and the bottom of cut or grade is indicated by the lower bench which is slightly above the elevation of the tops of piers. Piers will extend back to this lower bench where the abutment or beginning of the structure will be located.

Company started construction of a railroad bridge across the strait between Benicia and Martinez about six miles upstream from the Carquinez Bridge. These three bridges have, therefore, been the sole means of land transportation across the Carquinez Strait for the past 30 years.

Carquinez Bridge Traffic

In spite of the tremendous increase in highway traffic over the past 30 years, no increase in highway transportation facilities have been made. In the five years following the close of World War II, highway traffic across the Carquinez Bridge more than doubled until it reached an annual traffic count of over 10,000,000 cars per year. The three-lane roadway of the existing bridge, therefore, became a very serious bottleneck to the natural development and free flow of highway transportation between San Francisco and the Sacramento Valley.

and Public Works   37

ExcaVation material from the "big cut" is being placed in a fill which will be 140 feet high when completed. To date approximately 5,000,000 cubic yards of earth haVe been excaVated from the "big cut" and rolled and compacted in the fill which should be to grade in February, 1957.

Since the close of World War II it became very apparent that some means of financing additional highway facilities across the strait would have to be found. Because of the large amount of funds involved and because it would require a large concentration of gas tax expenditures in two relatively small counties over a short period of time, this type of financing seemed impracticable.

Two New Bridges

Realizing this situation the California Legislature in the summer of 1955 passed legislation making it possible

for the California Toll Bridge Authority to build two new bridges across Carquinez Strait to be financed by the sale of revenue bonds not to exceed $80,000,000.

The two bridges to be built are, a new bridge parallel to and about 200 feet upstream from the existing Carquinez Bridge on US Highway 40, and the other a new bridge about six miles upstream between the cities of Benicia and Martinez on State Route 75.

Since plans for the new parallel Carquinez Bridge had already been prepared it was possible to advertise

for bids on this portion of the project in October, 1955. Bonds in the amount of $46,000,000 were sold in December and construction officially started the last part of December, 1955.

Plans for the bridge at Benicia-Martinez are underway and advertisement for this work will not be made until sometime in 1957.

Major Contracts

The major contracts on the new parallel Carquinez Bridge now underway are as follows:

1. Two and nine-tenths miles of approach freeway work to the south of the

38

bridge which was awarded to Ferry and Crow for about $7,200,000.

2. The Crockett interchange structure joining the main bridge and the freeway contract which was awarded to Peter Kiewit Sons Company for $4,700,000.

3. The foundation work for the main bridge awarded to Mason and Hangar, Silas Mason, Inc., and F. S. Rolandi, Jr., Inc., for about $5,500,000.

4. The superstructure of the main bridge awarded to the United States Steel Corporation, American Bridge Division for about $9,500,000.

5. One and two-tenths miles of freeway work at the north end of the bridge awarded to Fredrickson and Watson Construction Company-Ransome Company for approximately $1,800,000.

6. Construction of the Administration Building and Toll Plaza awarded to W. J. Kubon Company for about $500,000.

There are three other small contracts with an aggregate cost of approximately $1,000,000.

The Big Cut

The $7,200,000 freeway contract to the south of the bridge contains one of the largest cuts in the history of highway building in California and possibly in the United States.

This cut which has been nicknamed the "Big Cut" has a width across the top of 1,370 feet and varies from 245 feet deep at the centerline to 350 feet deep when measured from the highest point to the south side of the cut. It contains 9,500,000 cubic yards which makes up a large percent of the total 11,200,000 cubic yards in the contract.

This cut was decided on after considerable study of other possible lines and after consideration of a tunnel design. Considering first cost, maintenance, right of way, highway user costs, convenience, safety and disturbance to existing property, the line chosen appeared to have the advantage over other lines.

Comparing the cut section to the tunnel there were two factors that made the cut a preponderately more satisfactory solution. They were first cost and safety from earthquakes, since the line passes through a faulted unstable area tunnel lining would be heavy and costly to construct and subject to considerable danger throughout its life.

Earthquake Faults

Preliminary borings indicated an older Cretaceous sandstone and sandy shale thrust over younger Eocene shale, intermixed with a steeply upturned Miocene strata consisting of interbedded shale and hard sandstone. Water was also found in sufficient quantities to make drainage an important problem in the design of the cut.

Based on the findings and studies of the borings, general terrain, and earthquake conditions the following design for the cut section was decided on: Slopes were set at 2:1 with 30-foot benches ever 60 feet in elevation. The cut at grade provides for two 36-foot paved roadways with width for two additional 12-foot lanes, with

Sketch showing plan and profile of the main bridge. In plan the lower layout is the new parallel bridge and the upper the existing bridge. Northbound traffic will use the new bridge and southbound traffic the existing bridge. The old sharply curved approach alignment of the existing bridge will become an off-ramp leading into Crockett.

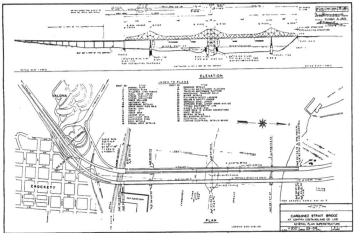

and Public Works

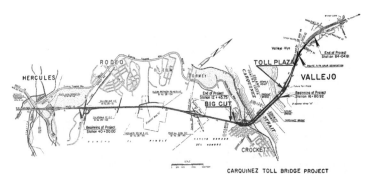

CARQUINEZ TOLL BRIDGE PROJECT

Layout showing the limits and extent of the Carquinez toll bridge projects under contract

9½-foot outer shoulders and 2-foot shoulders adjacent to the 4-foot raised median strip, plus a debris trough on each side. This makes the cut 200 feet wide at the bottom.

For proper drainage of trapped underground water 2-inch horizontal perforated drain casings are to be drilled laterally into the cut slopes at locations and frequencies to be decided by the engineer as excavation advances. It is anticipated that at least 24,000 linear feet of these drains will be required to adequately provide for the structural stability of the cut section. The 30-foot benches will also have collection ditches to collect surface water and seepage from the horizontal drains. In addition the benches will provide access for maintenance equipment.

Big Excavation Job

From the "big cut" there are about 2,400,000 cubic yards of material that is not needed for roadway fills. This material is being placed at disposal area "A" shown in sketch and will be used to improve Union Oil Company property in return for right of way required from it for freeway construction.

The shale and sandstone encountered during excavation by the contractor varies in hardness. It has been found possible to excavate by ripping

at all locations except the cut at about station 130 which is the first cut to the south of the "big cut." Here it is necessary to shoot and excavate with a 2½-cubic yard shovel and use 8-cubic yard dump trucks for disposal.

As can be seen from the sketch, there is a 7,000- to 8,000-foot haul for about 5,350,000 cubic yards of the

'big cut." For this operation the contractor proposes to use 23-cubic yard scrapers in tandum with 22-cubic yard DW 20's.

Maximum daily yardage moved by the contractor to date is about 32,000 cubic yards. Bid price for the 11,200,-000 cubic yards is 25.6 cents per cubic yard.

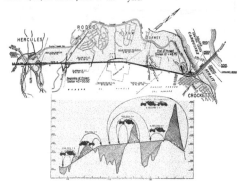

Sketch showing plan and profile of the freeway contract in Contra Costa County which contains the "big cut." Profile shows contractor's proposed dirt-moving operations with the R. U. scrapers and D. W. 20's hooked up in tandem for the long haul from the "big cut."

40

Work is in progress on the Vallejo side of Carquinez Strait in this picture. Contractor's derricks and barges can be seen at each of the main channel piers. The Crockett Interchange piers are being constructed in this picture. These interchange piers will be completed in January and steel erection will start in February, 1957.

Crockett Interchange

The Crockett Interchange serves as a connecting viaduct between the "big cut" and the south end of the main bridge. It also acts as an interchange structure providing on and off ramps for the town of Crockett.

This interchange structure is of conventional steel girder design, varying in span lengths from 120 feet to 180 feet. Girders are supported on 47 reinforced concrete piers. These piers vary in plan from 6 feet x 22 feet solid shaft to 20 feet x 76 feet boxed section shaft, and in height from 20 feet to 123.5 feet, with the average height about 70 feet.

The piers were all designed without batter or offsets so that slip-form construction could be used by the contractor if desired.

The contractor, Peter Kiewit Sons Company, investigated this method of construction for the piers and decided to proceed with slip-forms developed by B. M. Heede Inc., an international organization with headquarters in Sweden.

Slip-forms have been used before in the United States but they have been of the manually operated screw jack type. These have been cumbersome to keep level and troublesome to keep moving at a constant rate at all points.

The development of an automatic controller for operating the hydraulic ratchet jacks has greatly simplified this procedure.

and Public Works

Hydraulic Ratchet Jacks

These hydraulic ratchet jacks are supported about 7-foot centers by 1-inch diameter high strength steel rods. Each rod has a 3-foot section of metal sleeve which protects the rod from bonding with the green concrete making it possible to salvage them after the last pour on the pier has been made.

At the start of each pier after forms have been carefully set on pier footings, the 4-foot deep forms are filled in layers of about 8 inches. As soon as concrete in bottom has set sufficiently, which may be in about three hours, the jacking operations are started. Once the jacking operations are underway the forms are slipped up at the rate of 5 to 14 inches per hour with the average being about 10 inches per hour. Rate of slipping is dependent on rate of curing which changes with the ambient temperature and wind velocity. An experienced operator determines the pace at which forms are slipped by pushing a thin steel rod down into the concrete.

The forms are constructed so that the outside form of the wall is vertical, while the inside form is battered about three-eighths inch in the 4 feet. This makes the form three-sixteenths narrower at top and three-sixteenths larger at bottom than the nominal thickness of wall.

Surface Finishing

When the concrete becomes exposed as the forms are slipped up it is necessary to finish the surface by trowling. This is done quickly and easily. It is necessary occasionally to grout and finish small pockets caused by rocks gouging the sides during slipping. To facilitate finishing a finisher's platform is hung on the outside below the forms and moves up automatically as the forms are slipped.

For curing a water pipe rigged up with fog nozzles is hung below the finishers platform. This keeps the exposed concrete surface constantly moist and provides excellent curing conditions even during hot windy weather.

Pouring operations are maintained 24 hours per day which, at the average

UPPER—Picture showing "tandem" hookup consisting of one tractor and one operator hauling two scrapers. This picture shows equipment ascending top of "big cut" preparing to be loaded. LOWER—Picture shows "tandem" scrapers being loaded. Rear scraper is loaded first with the assistance of a powerful pusher in the rear. After rear scraper is completely loaded, the front scraper is loaded. After both are loaded, the single operator and tractor take off down the hill to dispose of the material on the fill. East slope of the "big cut" can be seen in the background.

rate of 10 inches per hour, provides for about 20 feet per day. Since some of the piers are over 100 feet high they cannot be completed in a five-day week. On these piers the operations are shut down over the week end and an operator left in charge to keep the forms slipping a very small amount sufficient to prevent bond until the slip·forms come to within 6 to 12 inches of the top of concrete.

Keep Piers Plumb

In order to keep the piers plumb a constant check must be made during pouring operations. To check for verticality three targets are placed on each end and at the center of one side. One target is placed near the bottom of pier, one on the slip form, and one on the reinforcing steel template above the forms.

Water columns placed in transparent plastic tubes and located at strategic points on the forms are also used to check for possible listing. As soon as a small deviation from verticality is noted corrective measures are started by hand jacking the low points. Corrections must be made gradually however.

Comparative costs between slip forms and conventional forms are not available; however, on a job with a reasonable number of piers 40 feet and over in height there appears to be an excellent opportunity for economy. Other advantages are safety and speed of operation. Therefore, where time is of importance there is considerable advantage. Their simplicity and safety also appear to give them an advantage over the conventional methods on high piers.

To Be Continued.

Chester H. Warlow, retired Fresno attorney and banker, and James A. Guthrie, President and Editor of the Sun Company, publisher of the *San Bernardino Daily Sun and Evening Telegraph*, have been reappointed by Governor Goodwin J. Knight to the California Highway Commission. Both were originally appointed to the commission by Governor Earl Warren when the commission was reorganized under an act of the Legislature in September, 1943, and this is their fourth reappointment.

Warlow, ex vice chairman of the commission, has been interested in highway building and improvement since 1927 when he first was named to a central valley highway committee. He was instrumental in promoting the Kings Canyon Highway, the Generals Highway, and the Yosemite-Fresno Highway.

Guthrie also has been interested in highways for many years; his paper had leadership in the original good roads program in San Bernardino County in advance of state highway construction. He has been associated with the Automobile Club of Southern California and is a member of San Bernardino City Traffic and Safety Commission.

On January 24th Guthrie was elected vice chairman of the commission for the second time. Guthrie and Warlow were administered their oaths of office by Secretary of State Frank M. Jordan on January 24th.

WHO WAS DRIVING?

There were approximately 4,800 women drivers and 41,500 men drivers involved in fatal accidents during 1955. Drivers in all accidents—fatal, injury, and property damage—were divided: 2,500,000 women; 14,500,000 men. These national estimates are based on the reports of traffic authorities in 34 states.

Secretary of State Frank M. Jordan administers oath of office to Highway Commissioners Chester H. Warlow (on his left) and James A. Guthrie

James A. Guthrie Honored By His City

James A. Guthrie, Editor and President of the San Bernardino *Sun-Telegram*, and Vice Chairman of the California Highway Commission, on January 23d was named recipient of the 1956 Red Feather Community Award "for contributing greatly to the building of a better San Bernardino."

The award, fifth in a series of annual presentations begun in 1952, was the first made via long distance telephone. Guthrie was in Sacramento attending a Highway Commission meeting, and telephone contact was used to bridge the gap between the veteran journalist and the Community Chest dinner meeting in San Bernardino.

"This is the first time I have attempted to make a public address while staring at the bare walls of a hotel room," Guthrie said over the telephone hookup.

"I feel highly honored at this tribute," Guthrie told the 250 community leaders and chest workers gathered at the annual meeting in the Fellowship Hall of the First Presbyterian Church.

Surprise announcement of Guthrie for the 1956 award was made by George Hellyer, first chest president in San Bernardino in the year of its inception, 1923.

"One man left his name with history in trying to stop the sun," Hellyer said. "James Guthrie will leave his name with efforts in getting out the *Sun*."

The Red Feather citation concluded with the words, "His sterling character has been impressed upon and has molded the community which hereby acknowledges its great debt."

Accepting the award medallion in behalf of her father at the dinner meeting was Mrs. Kathleen Lonergan, secretary-treasurer of the Sun Co.

Guthrie also was named as the first recipient of the "Citizen of the Year"

... Continued on page 45

and Public Works

43

Speed Survey

State-wide Check Shows Motorists Are Driving Much Faster

By GEORGE M. WEBB, Traffic Engineer

VEHICULAR speeds are a vital factor which must be taken into consideration in the development and establishment of modern highway design standards. Consequently, in the interests of ever-improving highway operation, the Traffic Department of the Division of Highways periodically conducts a state-wide speed survey on state highways, the latest of which was undertaken during the month of October, 1956.

The data obtained during this recent study are shown on the accompanying charts, which represent the results of 35,439 individual observations of vehicular speeds under free-flowing traffic conditions. The speed checks were made during off-peak hours at selected rural locations on straight alignment in areas out of the influence of speed zones, roadside business, and other physical controls which might affect the speed of traffic.

108 Observation Stations

A total of 108 observation stations was used. These may be classified according to roadway type, as follows:

Number of stations	Type of roadway
47	2 Lanes
1	3 Lanes
2	4 Lanes undivided
5	4 Lanes divided
27	4 Lanes divided expressway
15	4 Lanes divided freeway
1	6 Lanes undivided
5	6 Lanes divided freeway
5	8 Lanes divided freeway

Speed Has Increased

It may be interesting to note that the 1956 survey showed that the average speeds of all vehicles were 4.3 miles per hour greater than those observed in 1951. The critical speeds during this period increased by 5.2 miles per hour. (The critical speed is defined as the speed at or below which 85 percent of the traffic is moving.)

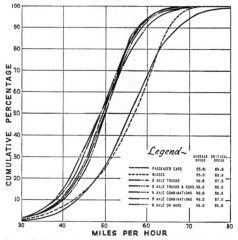

Legend—

	AVERAGE SPEED	CRITICAL SPEED
PASSENGER CARS	55.6	64.9
BUSSES	55.5	63.9
2 AXLE TRUCKS	48.6	57.9
3 AXLE TRUCKS & COMB.	48.2	56.2
4 AXLE COMBINATIONS	48.8	56.5
5 AXLE COMBINATIONS	49.2	57.0
6 AXLE OR MORE	49.3	55.9

The speeds of vehicles by type, as found in the October, 1956, survey, are represented by the curves in the above drawing. Note that the speeds of passenger cars and busses are quite similar, while the curves for the various types of trucks fall into a lower speed group.

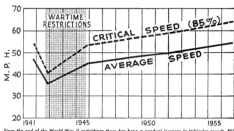

Since the end of the World War II restrictions there has been a gradual increase in vehicular speeds. This is illustrated in the above chart of average and critical speeds of all vehicles by years.

STATE-WIDE AVERAGE ON RURAL HIGHWAYS

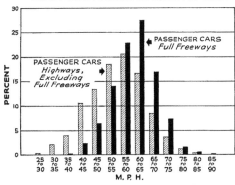

The survey showed that passenger cars generally travel faster on rural freeways than on other types of rural highways

It might also be noted that the rate of increase per year compares quite closely with the rates of increase found on the previous surveys of 1945, 1948, and 1951.

Truck Speeds Lower

The chart showing the speeds of vehicles by type also illustrates some features worth mentioning. A comparison of the curves shown on this chart reveals that the speeds of the various types of trucks are grouped rather closely and fall approximately seven miles per hour below those of passenger cars in the higher ranges. However, it may be seen that there is very little difference between the speeds of passenger cars and those of buses in the range below 60 miles per hour. It was also found from the study that the average speed of both buses and trucks had increased approximately three miles per hour since 1951.

The speeds of passenger cars, as may be expected, were found to average higher on rural freeways than on other types of rural highways. However, the differences were not as high as some might have imagined. The

survey showed that passenger cars average 60.5 miles per hour on rural freeways, as compared to an average speed of 54.7 miles per hour for all other rural locations. Comparable critical speeds were 68.5 miles per hour and 64.7 miles per hour, respectively.

JAMES GUTHRIE HONORED

Continued from page 43 ...

award presented by the San Bernardino Real Estate Board.

Presentation took place at Norton Air Force Base Officers Club as part of a banquet program for installation of 1957 board officers headed by Thomas S. Madison.

Guthrie was given a watch as the "Frank L. Whitelock award," donated by a past president of the real estate board.

The presentation was made by Ken W. Dyal, board secretary, who cited the invaluable publicity the editor had given nationwide for "his beloved city and beloved valley," and the highways, steel plant, Air Force Base, and other industries he had helped bring to the San Bernardino area.

Freeways Get New Names

The California Highway Commission has assigned names for three sections of freeway routes in Southern California.

The names and sections are as follows:

Riverside Freeway—State Highway Route 43, from Santa Ana Freeway in Santa Ana to the San Bernardino Freeway near Colton.

Santa Monica Freeway—The route hitherto unofficially referred to as the "Olympic Freeway," between the Harbor Freeway in Los Angeles and Santa Monica.

Escondido Freeway—US 395 between San Diego and Riverside.

Ventura Freeway—The freeway now being developed between U. S. Highway 99 in the vicinity of Glendale and U. S. Highway 101 in the City of Ventura. Although most of this freeway has been locally known as the Ventura Freeway, the easternmost section, 5.3 miles in length, from the Golden State Freeway in Griffith Park to the Hollywood Freeway extension in North Hollywood has previously been referred to locally as the Riverside Freeway, taking this name from its proximity to the Los Angeles River and Riverside Drive.

Max Gilliss Is Drafted to New Job by Governor

C. M. (Max) Gilliss, Deputy Director of the State Department of Public Works, was drafted in January by Governor Goodwin J. Knight to serve as a secretary assigned to the Governor's legislative office.

Gilliss in his new position will assist Paul Mason, the Governor's Legislative Secretary and Director of Motor Vehicles.

He was appointed special representative of the Department of Public Works in 1952, was named Assistant Deputy Director in 1953, and was promoted to Deputy Director September 23, 1955.

Employees Receive Twenty-five-year Awards

Employees of the Division of Highways who became eligible for 25-year awards October 31 to December 31, 1956, are:

Name	Total service Yrs. Mos. Days	Name	Total service Yrs. Mos. Days
District II		**District VIII**	
Axbill, Irven E. ... 25 0 6		Anthony, Frank A. ... 25 0 19	
District III		Lauterborn, Randall A. ... 25 0 28	
Hebsrove, Charles E. ... 25 0 00		Lawrence, David ... 25 0 18	
District IV		**District X**	
Cobb, William R. ... 25 0 01		Meyer, Kenneth E. ... 25 0 10	
Clough, Herbert W. ... 25 0 15			
Cumberpatch, Stanley C. ... 25 0 12		**District XI**	
Cvoray, Frank A. ... 25 0 27		Thomson, George A. ... 25 0 3	
Ural, Sebastian A. ... 25 0 15			
District V		**Central Office**	
Hudson, Guy G. ... 25 0 15		Lunetta, George J. ... 25 0 2	
Jones, Bernarr M. ... 25 0 10		Miller, Carl D. ... 25 0 00	
Stokes, C. Eric ... 25 0 19			
Meehan, James C. ... 25 0 28		**Bridge Department**	
District VII		Plown, Jason ... 25 0 22	
Bechand, Myrtle F. ... 25 0 18			
Miller, Carl D. ... 25 0 00		**Bay Bridge**	
Rimmeter, Oscar ... 25 0 9		Webb, Alice K. ... 25 0 14	
Telford, Edward T. ... 25 0 16			

MERIT AWARD BOARD WINNERS

Michael Valentine, Highways, Sacramento, Assistant Bridge Engineer (TAU), received $80 for recommending the design and detail of reinforced concrete pile footings be standardized and quantities of reinforcing steel and concrete used in the footings, be tabulated. The suggested tabular form for standard column footings will save considerable time for many younger designers. The suggestion is now in use and will save at least one hour of designer time on about 200 separate occasions per year. Estimated annual savings at least $800. .

George E. Gray, Highways, Bishop, Assistant Highway Engineer, and David A. Crane, Highways, Bishop, Assistant Highway Engineer, will divide $40 for their recommendation that the quantities now shown on Division of Highways Standard Structure Sheet, A-50, be revised to include the concrete and steel quantities for L walls. The employees proposed that varying the lengths from two feet to six feet in one-half foot intervals would be adequate. The division was not able to adopt this suggestion until a revision of Structure Sheet A-59 had been completed. The idea has been placed into effect with an annual savings of approximately $400.

Robert L. Woolf, Highways, Sacramento, Assistant Shop Foreman, and Daryl Smith, Highways, Sacramento, Automotive Mechanic, will share $30 for designing and using a special tool while servicing Lipe Rollway clutch pressure plates. This tool is used to compress the coil spring under the clutch plate, releasing the tension on the

snap ring on the top of the plate so that it and the ball retainer may be removed, allowing the balls and vanes to be removed, cleaned, relubricated and reassembled. This plate may be left in position during the servicing of the clutch. The division estimates a net annual savings of $150 will be realized and recommend that an award of $30 be divided equally. As the units involved require clutch repairs in periods of from one to three years the Merit Award Board concluded the use of a one-year period as the basis for estimating savings was not completely equitable so savings were estimated for the first two years.

Robert L. Woolf, Highways, Sacramento, Assistant Shop Foreman, and Ray Sandour, Highways, Sacramento, Heavy Equipment Mechanic, will share $15 for designing and developing a special tool to remove the climax engine clutch housing assemblies from their mountings. The use of this tool is limited to those shops where snow removal equipment is required.

Tom C. Kinard, Highways, Escondido, Highway Field Office Assistant, will receive $10 for recommending the revision of Highway Form M-32, Foreman's Daily Labor and Equipment Report. This suggestion is to omit the padding and to make the colors uniform instead of two separate colors. Accounting Department reports the suggestion was placed into effect on October 16th with annual savings of at least $100.

Josephine M. Norton, Highways, Sacramento, intermediate stenographer-clerk, received a certificate of commendation for her

suggestion regarding a modification to the Encroachment Permit Form, P-202. Previously, there were several titles of identification used; Mrs. Norton's suggestion proposed the uniform use of "grantor" and "permittee" in place of the varying titles formerly used. This change in wording makes for easier understanding of the conditions of the documents.

Donald A. Hankins and *Robert R. Wirts*, Highways, San Bernardino, $100 to be divided equally and certificates of award for suggestion recommending the elimination of sand from compaction tests, and the procedure of cleaning of salvaged Ottawa sand in standard and instead.

John A. Kerr, Architecture, Los Angeles, $15 and a certificate of award for sugges-

... Continued on page 60

In Memoriam

HARRY F. CARTER

Harry F. Carter, retired Bridge Department Resident Engineer, died in Oakland November 15, 1956. Harry was born in Belfast, Maine, on February 25, 1882. In his youth he joined the gold rush to Alaska and prospected both in the Nome area and Yukon Territory. After returning to the United States, he joined with his father in silver mining in Nevada and Western Utah. He then joined the Oregon-Eastern Railroad, later a part of the Union Pacific Railroad, as a civil engineer.

Harry started work with the California Division of Highways on June 16, 1914, as an instrument man. He was one of the original "Four Horsemen," resident engineers on bridge construction at the time the Bridge Department was organized in 1924. During the construction of the San Francisco-Oakland Bay Bridge he performed outstanding liaison work between the State and the Navy. Two of the last structures on which Harry served as Resident Engineer were the bridge across the Feather River at Marysville and the Noyo River Bridge near Fort Bragg.

Harry retired on March 10, 1950, after 36 years of outstanding work in state service. He was a member of the American Society of Civil Engineers and of Elks Lodges in Idaho and Montana. He is survived by one son, Robert S. Carter, of San Mateo and one sister, Mrs. Emma Leggett of Hollywood.

PROMOTIONS ARE ANNOUNCED BY McCOY

State Highway Engineer Geo. T. McCoy has announced the following promotions of Division of Highways personnel:

R. A. Hayler, for eight years Assistant District Engineer-Planning, for District XI in San Diego, to be a Dis-

graduation in 1932, from the University of California (Berkeley) in civil engineering. He is a native of San Diego and attended San Diego schools and San Diego State College before going to the University of California. He is married and has five children.

Counties of Sonoma, Marin, Napa, Santa Clara and Santa Cruz, together with supervision of other district-wide functions.

Jorgensen worked for the Division of Highways between semesters while attending the University of California

R. A. HAYLER

J. FRANK JORGENSEN

G. L. RICHARDSON

trict Engineer in District IV with headquarters in San Francisco.

J. Frank Jorgensen, Assistant District Engineer-Operations, District XI, to replace Hayler.

G. L. Richardson, Maintenance Engineer of District XI, to Assistant District Engineering-Operations, replacing Jorgensen.

McCoy said that the greatly increased funds to become available under the federal highway program, and the consequent stepped-up schedule of important highway route determinations and planning in District IV, have required establishment of an additional position at the district engineer level.

Hayler has had broad experience in metropolitan and other major highway planning. He has been with the division for 24 years, following his

Assistant State Highway Engineer B. W. Booker, in charge of District IV, who is recuperating from a heart ailment, expects to return to work in the near future. Until Booker's return, J. P. Sinclair will continue as acting assistant state highway engineer. After Booker returns, Sinclair will resume his district engineer functions with responsibility for general district-wide planning and with specific design responsibility for the state highways in Contra Costa, Alameda, San Francisco and San Mateo Counties.

District Engineer L. A. Weymouth will continue as District Engineer-Operations involving supervision of construction, maintenance, administration and cooperative project.

Hayler will be responsible for design of state highway projects in the

at Berkeley and became a full-time employee in 1931 after his graduation. He has been an assistant district engineer in District XI since 1950. A native of Arizona, he came to California as a child and attended schools in San Diego.

He is married and has two children. His residence is in San Diego.

Richardson is a native of Maine who came to California in 1935. He was educated in Maine schools and attended the University of California at Berkeley and first came to work for the Division of Highways in 1937. He is married and has four children. The Richardsons maintain their home in El Cajon.

Seventy percent of American families own a car.

and Public Works

Out of the Mail Bag

THANK YOU, MR. BACON

EDWARD R. BACON COMPANY OF HAWAII
San Francisco, California

MR. KENNETH C. ADAMS, Editor

DEAR MR. ADAMS: *California Highways and Public Works* is by long odds the finest publication of its kind that I have seen during my many years of association with the construction industry.

It is most interesting and informative to note the remarkable advances in design and construction of highways and the development of equipment to meet the requirements of superhighway construction. A far advance since the equipment that my company furnished for the construction of the first state highways in 1912.

Kindly accept my heartiest congratulations.

Yours sincerely,

EDWARD R. BACON

MAKE GOOD USE OF MAGAZINE

OXNARD CHAMBER OF COMMERCE, INC.
Oxnard, California

KENNETH C. ADAMS, Editor

DEAR MR. ADAMS: *California Highways and Public Works* is thoroughly enjoyed by the staff here and each copy is passed around to members of our Highway and Safety Committee. We look forward to each issue not only for personal enjoyment but as a source of up-to-date information to pass on to our members and the public.

Congratulations on the fine job you are doing.

Cordially yours,

R. E. TREMAINE, Manager

ACCEPT OUR CONGRATULATIONS

CONSTRUCTION OFFICE
TAIPEI TAMSHUI RIVER BRIDGE
26, Kongting Road, Taipei, Taiwan

DEAR MR. ADAMS: Thank you very much for giving me the enjoyment of reading your fine magazine for many years. All the papers in your magazine are valuable, practicable, and up-to-date information to highway engineers. It is a great help to me in my bridge design work.

More than two years ago I had a chance to learn your technical know-how in your Bridge Department. The research spirit and the high quality of your bridge engineers impressed me very much. Now I am the project engineer supervising the 3,460-foot long precast prestressed concrete bridge, which will be the longest one of its kind in the Far East. Let me express my hearty appreciation for the kind help you have given to me.

Let me say thank you again, with my best regards.

Sincerely yours,

WEN-TAO CHANG
Project Engineer
Taipei Tamshui River Bridge

MOUTHS WATER

BRITISH ROAD FEDERATION
26 Manchester Square
Briroadfed Wesdo, London, England

Editor:

DEAR SIR: We are very pleased to receive from you copies of your excellent publication. I can assure you that the descriptions and illustrations of the work being carried out in your State make our mouths water.

Thank you again for your courtesy in this matter.

Yours faithfully,

C. D. MORGAN, *Secretary*

FROM DENMARK

COUNTY HIGHWAY DEPARTMENT
Holbaek, Denmark

EDITOR: Since my visit in California in 1949 as participant in the course for foreign engineers arranged by the U. S. Bureau of Public Roads, I have had the pleasure of receiving your very fine journal. I want to express my high gratitude for the forwarding and to assure you that the journal is of very much interest to me.

We, here in Denmark, admire the development in the highway field in the United States and are learning very much from your experiences. Particularly, it is important for us to know something about the progress in California, which state I regard as the most advanced in the highway field in the world.

Very truly yours,

KNUD P. DANO
Chief Highway Engineer

WE THINK SO, TOO

Monrovia, California

MR. KENNETH C. ADAMS, Editor

I would like at this time to thank you and your staff for your fine publication of *California Highways and Public Works*. The many articles and illustrations are interesting and helpful.

After reading these articles, I am sure that more people will realize the advantages of having the freeways around, rather than through the towns, as business has been helped more than hindered.

Again thank you.

Sincerely,

J. ARLEIGH LEE

LIKE MAGAZINE

STATE OF ILLINOIS
DIVISION OF HIGHWAYS
Dixon, Illinois

MR. KENNETH C. ADAMS, *Editor*

We appreciate very much receiving the *California Highways and Public Works* publication and find the articles well prepared, interesting and educational. The highway work carried on by California is a credit to the engineers of your State.

We look forward to receiving each copy which is made available to our entire staff in our district library.

Very truly yours,

M. M. MEMLER
District Engineer

ANOTHER ILLINOIS LETTER

STATE OF ILLINOIS
DIVISION OF HIGHWAYS
Ottawa

MR. KENNETH C. ADAMS, *Editor*

I wish to take this opportunity to thank you for sending the magazine, *California Highways and Public Works*. This magazine is undoubtedly the finest of its type in the Nation. You and your staff are to be congratulated on the able presentation of the California problems to the public and to engineers in other states, who look to California for new ideas and methods.

Yours very truly,

CHARLES E. CULLEN
District Engineer of Materials

GLAD TO OBLIGE

TURKISH REPUBLIC
MINISTRY OF PUBLIC WORKS
General Directorate of Highways
Istanbul, Turkey

California Highways and Public Works

GENTLEMEN: From time to time we have the opportunity of reading your fine magazine, *California Highways and Public Works*. For that reason we read that your periodical is one of the best in its field. We have the idea that your periodical is one of the best in its field. For that reason we read it regularly. We will appreciate your kindness, if you can include our address in your regular mailing list.

Very truly yours,

FIKRET ERKIVANC
Traffic Engineer

WELCOME PRAISE

MR. KENNETH C. ADAMS, *Editor*

I have enjoyed your magazine for a good many years and hope to have the privilege to do so in the future also. You and your staff have to be complimented on the excellence of this publication, which, in my opinion, is unequaled the world over.

True, there is in the road construction field many a grandiose sight in your wonderful State and credit must be given to the foresight of your Division of Highways and the know-how of your technical personnel, too. In fact, every issue confronts us with vistas that make us Europeans turn green with envy.

Yet, we are happy to know that somewhere on this earth standards in road construction are set that are leading the field and are showing all of us which way to go.

Again congratulations for your splendid work and best wishes for your continued success, along with my sincere thanks for having me on your mailing list.

Sincerely,

PETER MERKER
Im Walder 22, Zollikon
ZH Switzerland

BURMA HIGHWAYS

55, Fytche Road, Rangoon, Burma

California Highways and Public Works

GENTLEMEN: I am very proud of myself being one in my country receiving your most interesting and valuable magazine. I sincerely believe that your publications will help us in our promotion of better development of highways in Burma.

Extending my best wishes to you all.

Very truly yours,

KO KO GYI
Highway Engineer
Department of Highways

KNOWS ANGELES CREST

ALHAMBRA, CALIFORNIA

KENNETH C. ADAMS, *Editor*

DEAR EDITOR: I was particularly interested in the story of the building of the Angeles Crest Highway in your last number.

I had hiked and camped along its entire route, or very close to it, before the start of construction, and had supported it against active opposition in lectures and in print. I have led hiking parties through the mountains of Southern California for the past 50 years; was president of the San Antonio Hiking Club for 34 years and personally led most of their one- to three-day trips. Headed the Division of Mountain Information-Education with the County Department of Recreation as long as there was such and was Editor of *Trails Magazine* until discontinued by the County of Los Angeles.

Have, in *Trails Magazine* and *Historical Society of Southern California Quarterly*, 27 historical stories of my own writing and several others which I have had written by those who helped make this mountain history in the California History Department of the Huntington Memorial Library.

Sincerely yours,

WILL H. THRALL

MAGAZINE USED IN CLASSES

UNIVERSITY OF CALIFORNIA

MR. KENNETH C. ADAMS, *Editor*

I wish to express to you my appreciation for receiving *California Highways and Public Works*. It is a most interesting and informative publication. In fact, I use the publication in teaching courses in geological engineering here in the engineering department of the university. Please keep me on the list of subscribers.

Sincerely yours,

PARKER D. TRASK
Professor of Geological Engineering

WARNING OF FAILING BATTERY

Lights that seem to be dimmer than usual generally are an advance warning that the battery needs attention. Many motorists are inclined to think in terms of the lights themselves when they get below standard. Suspicion should be directed first to the battery. If the lights flicker when the engine is being started or burn more brightly when the engine is running at high speed, it is likely that the battery needs recharging.

Retirements *from* Service

Herbert A. Waterman

Herbert A. Waterman, Assistant Construction Engineer for the California Division of Highways, is retiring after 38 yars with the State.

Waterman has been in charge of reviewing and recommending acceptance of all construction contracts

HERBERT A. WATERMAN

awarded by the division for its vast road building program throughout the State, totaling more than $160,000,000 for the current fiscal year. He also handled much of the work involving special agreements with outside agencies and has written and edited most of the manuals and annual reports prepared by the division's Construction Department during the past 30 years. Long before the term "In-Service Training" had been coined, Waterman conducted training courses for construction personnel in proper record keeping. District personnel were sent to Sacramento to train under him.

He was delegated by Construction Engineer Charles Stockton Pope to as-
... Continued on page 51

Richard W. Robinson

Richard White Robinson, Structural Engineering Associate, with the Division of Highways, Bridge Department, retired on December 31, 1956, after 33 years with the State.

A luncheon on December 27th was

RICHARD W. ROBINSON

attended by his family and many friends and associates.

Robinson was born in Salt Lake City, Utah, on June 3, 1889, and was educated there, receiving a bachelor of science degree from the University of Utah in 1913. He taught school three years and served two years as a missionary for his church.

Early jobs were with the Utah-Idaho Sugar Company, the Amalgamated Sugar Company, the Utah Power and Light Company and the Southern Pacific Railroad in Utah and Sacramento on field and office work.

He entered state service in January, 1924, as a draftsman with Division of Highways at Dunsmuir and transferred to the Bridge Department in February of that year. For many years Robbie prepared specifications for contracts and in 1942 became associated with the design section where he remained except for two intervals of field construction assignments. At the time of his retirement Robbie was a designer on many important structures.

Robinson married Ethel Varley in 1919 and they have four married daughters. Mr. and Mrs. Robinson will continue to reside in Sacramento where they will be active in their church, but with more opportunity to travel and visit friends.

Frank V. Weaver

Frank V. Weaver, Highway Maintenance, District VIII, San Bernardino, retired December 31, 1956, after 25 years' service with the State. Prior to his employment with the State, he was employed by the Santa Fe Railroad as a railroad telegrapher being stationed at Needles, California, for 10 years, and was later transferred to San Bernardino as a train dispatcher, where he worked for two more years.

In May of 1920 he resigned from the railroad service and purchased an

FRANK V. WEAVER

orange grove at Highland, California, where he and his wife, Marion, have lived for many years. He started to be a rancher and grew citrus fruits, oranges, lemons, grapefruit and olives. In 1931 there was practically no market for citrus fruits and he secured employment with the Division of Highways at San Bernardino on October 19, 1931.

Frank's hobbies are ranching and after a trip to the Hawaiian Islands, he and his wife, Marion, expect to settle down upon their ranch. He is a World War I veteran, Past Commander, Chapter No. 12, Disabled American War Veterans, and a charter member of the American Legion Post No. 14, San Bernardino.

He is a Master Mason, member of Blue Lodge, Eastern Star and Knights Templar.

RETAIL SALES

Retail sales of motor vehicle dealers, parts and accessories stores, and gasoline service stations amounted to 374 billion dollars during the past 10 years, according to the National Automobile Club.

Clement F. Waite

Clement F. Waite, Assistant District Engineer-Administration, of the California Division of Highways, District VI office in Fresno, retired on December 11th after 28 years of state service.

Waite has held the post he gave up for the past eight years. District VI, with headquarters in Fresno, includes Tulare, Kings, Fresno, Madera Counties and most of Kern County.

Waite came to work for the division in 1928 as a resident engineer. He was promoted to office engineer of the Fresno district in 1933. He became district survey and planning engineer in 1946 and was appointed assistant district engineer in 1948.

CLEMENT F. WAITE

Waite is a veteran of both world wars, serving as a captain in the U. S. Army Engineers from 1917 to 1919 and as a lieutenant colonel in charge of construction work along a section of the Alcan Highway during World War II. He was promoted to colonel in the U. S. Army Reserve in 1946.

Waite's early career included survey and construction work on highway and bridge projects in the northwest and Alaska. He was Assistant City Engineer of Vancouver, Washington, from 1912 to 1915.

He was born in Arcadia, Nebraska, and obtained his B.S. degree in civil engineering from the University of Washington. Waite and his wife live at 1538 Poplar Avenue in Fresno. They have two daughters, Mrs. Patricia Helen Aalsen of Fresno and Mrs. Marilyn Harriet Jernigan of Modesto.

Waite is a Mason and a member of the Fresno Engineers Club.

INSURANCE

Ninety-two percent of the cars bought new in the United States are covered by fire and theft insurance, according to the National Automobile Club.

L. L. Funk Named Photogrammetric Engineer by McCoy

Promotion of L. L. Funk to the newly established position of Photogrammetric Engineer for the California Division of Highways was announced by State Highway Engineer G. T. McCoy.

Funk will head a new department within the Division of Highways which will have responsibility for development and application of the latest photogrammetric techniques in the production of highway plans.

HERBERT A. WATERMAN

Continued from page 50 . . .

semble this material in written form for the guidance of construction supervisors. The first instruction manual ever to be issued by the Division of Highways was written by Waterman in 1924 and published in March, 1925, under the title of "Manual of Instructions, Construction Department."

Another "first" for Waterman was the assembling and editing of the first Standard Specifications of the Division, published in July of 1925.

Herb came to work for the division on a permanent basis in 1921 as a resident engineer. He subsequently served as Office Engineer of District III, with headquarters at that time in Sacramento, and became one of the original members of the headquarters Construction Department.

Waterman's early career before he entered state service included engineering assignments on various irrigation projects and resident engineer in charge of construction for Sacramento County. During World War I he served overseas as a 2d Lieutenant with the 115th Engineers.

Born in Riverside, California, Herb attended elementary and secondary schools in San Juan Bautista and San Jose. He received his degree in engineering from Stanford in 1912.

Waterman and his wife reside at 1112 38th Street. He is a Mason and a member of the American Society of Civil Engineers.

William A. Bugge New President of Highway Officials

W. A. Bugge, Director of Highways for the Washington State Highway Commission, on November 30th, was elected president of the American Association of State Highway Officials at the group's annual convention in Atlantic City, New Jersey.

His election provides another climax in a career highlighted by public service and richly varied in experience in the field of engineering.

WILLIAM A. BUGGE

He has served as president of the Washington State Association of County Engineers and as commander of the American Legion Post at Port Townsend. He was a civil defense coordinator for both Port Townsend and Jefferson County during World War II.

He has also served as president of the Western Association of State Highway Officials and at the present time is secretary of the Washington State Council for Highway Research. He has been a member of the Interstate Committee on Highway Policy Problems and is chairman of the Committee on Design Policies of the American Association of State Highway Officials, which formulated design policies for the 41,000-mile interstate and defense highway system. During the past year he served as First Vice President of the American Association of State Highway Officials. He is a director of the Highway Research Board of the National Academy of Sciences.

During the convention six members of the California delegation were presented with 25-year membership awards. Their certificates read:

"Appreciative of the benefits accruing to the public from the accumulated and continuous experience of those who make the public service their life work, and desirous of recording its appreciation of such long and faithful service by its members, American Association of State Highway Officials

. . . Continued on page 60

Cost Index
Makes Slight Rise During Fourth Quarter of 1956

By RICHARD H. WILSON, Assistant State Highway Engineer;
H. C. McCARTY, Office Engineer, and
LLOYD B. REYNOLDS, Assistant Office Engineer

THE California Highway Construction Cost Index for the fourth quarter of 1956 resumed its upward course after a slight drop in the third quarter. The index stands at 252.2 (1940 = 100) which is 3.1 index points or 1.2 percent above the third quarter, but it is still 3.7 points or 1.4 percent below the all-time high of 255.9 established in the second quarter of 1956.

The high point in the second quarter reflected the uncertainty due to the steel strike and pending wage renegotiations, the index then went through a leveling off process during the remainder of the year. In relation to the index for the same period last year which stood at 212.6, the present index reflects an 18.6 percent rise in construction costs during the year. Construction costs at the fourth quarter of 1955 were 10.6 percent above the fourth quarter of 1954.

It is believed that the general rise in construction costs established during 1956 will continue during 1957 but at a slower rate. This conclusion is based upon labor contracts which were renegotiated during 1956 for periods in excess of one year as previously had been the case. Many of these contracts of longer duration are in fields most vitally affecting the highway construction industry. Contractors are now in a position to bid highway contracts with fair knowledge of future labor and materials costs.

A factor which occurred during this quarter tending to level out construction costs is the increase in bidder competition. The average number of bidders per contract rose from a low of 3.7 in the third quarter to 5.1 in the fourth quarter of 1956. Much of this increase has occurred in high bid value projects that generally include all of the construction items on which the cost index is based.

STATE OF CALIFORNIA
DEPARTMENT OF PUBLIC WORKS
DIVISION OF HIGHWAYS

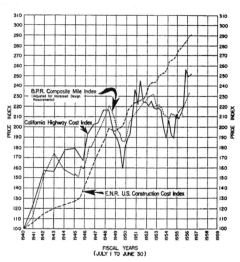

PRICE INDEX
CONSTRUCTION COSTS
1940 = 100

The California Construction Cost Index, the *Engineering News-Record* Construction Cost Index and the United States Bureau of Public Roads Composite Mile Index, all reduced to the base 1940 = 100 are shown on the accompanying graph. The latter two indexes are based on nation-wide construction costs.

The *Engineering News-Record* Cost Index again shows a rise but the rate of increase is lower than that of the

California Highways

third quarter. It is up 2.5 index points or 0.87 percent from the previous quarter.

The Bureau of Public Roads Composite Mile Index for the third quarter of 1956, which is the latest available, was up 8.5 index points or 3.8 percent over the second quarter. The upward direction of the Bureau of Public Roads Index shows that the decline in the California index in the third quarter reflected strictly local conditions.

THE CALIFORNIA HIGHWAY CONSTRUCTION COST INDEX

Year	Cost Index
1940	100.0
1941	125.0
1942	157.5
1943	156.4
1944	177.8
1945	179.5
1946	179.7
1947	203.3
1948	216.6
1949	190.7
1950	176.7
(1st Quarter 1950—160.6)	
1951	210.8
(4th Quarter 1951—245.4)	
1952	224.5
1953	216.2
1954 (1st Quarter)	199.4
1954 (2d Quarter)	189.0
1954 (3d Quarter)	207.8
1954 (4th Quarter)	192.2
1955 (1st Quarter)	189.3
1955 (2d Quarter)	212.4
1955 (3d Quarter)	208.6
1955 (4th Quarter)	212.6
1956 (1st Quarter)	219.5
1956 (2d Quarter)	255.9
1956 (3d Quarter)	249.1
1956 (4th Quarter)	252.1

It appears that the construction cost index will continue its general rise during 1957, due to wage increases, probable higher costs of materials and the increased cost of borrowing working capital.

The recent cost issue of *Engineering News-Record* indicated that nationwide, highway bid prices during the year had increased about 8.6 percent on the average. These costs reflected increases in prices for equipment, steel, other materials and labor, ranging from 4 percent to 8.5 percent. Other factors influencing contractors'

bids are higher interest rates on borrowed money, acute steel shortages, and delays in construction steel deliveries.

NUMBER AND SIZE OF PROJECTS, TOTAL BID VALUES AND AVERAGE NUMBER OF BIDDERS
(July 1, 1956, to December 31, 1956)

Project Volume	Up to $50,000	$50,000 to $100,000	$100,000 to $250,000	$250,000 to $500,000	$500,000 to $1,000,000	Over $1,000,000	All projects
Road Projects							
No. of projects	207	41	34	19	12	5	318
Total value*	$3,151,904	$3,906,682	$5,530,618	$6,562,205	$8,833,811	$9,534,621	$36,531,841
Avg. No. bidders	3.7	3.8	5.9	4.9	5.3	7.8	4.1
Structure Projects							
No. of projects	22	2	14	2	1	4	45
Total value*	$448,257	$140,900	$2,388,970	$766,923	$502,887	$11,152,915	$15,400,852
Avg. No. bidders	4.4	3.5	5.5	2.5	5.0	5.0	4.6
Combination							
No. of projects						2	24	26
Total value*						$1,341,234	$76,777,869	$78,119,103
Avg. No. bidders						3.0	5.5	5.3
Summary							
No. of projects	229	43	48	21	15	33	389
Total value*	$3,630,161	$3,049,582	$7,909,588	$7,329,128	$10,677,932	$97,455,405	$130,051,796
Avg. No. bidders	3.7	3.8	5.8	4.7	4.9	5.8	4.3

* Bid items only.

Total Average Bidders by Months

	July	Aug.	Sept.	Oct.	Nov.	Dec.	Avg. for six months
1956	3.8	3.7	3.7	4.2	5.3	6.1	4.3
1955	4.9	4.2	4.4	5.4	6.2	5.4	5.0

CALIFORNIA DIVISION OF HIGHWAYS AVERAGE CONTRACT PRICES

	Roadway excavation, per cu. yd.	Untreated rock base, per ton	Asphaltic and bituminous mixes, per ton	Asphalt concrete pavement, per ton	PCC pavement, per cu. yd.	PCC structures, per cu. yd.	Bar reinforcing steel, per lb.	Structural steel, per lb.
1940	$0.22	$1.54	$2.19	$2.97	$7.68	$18.33	$0.040	$0.083
1941	0.36	2.31	2.84	3.18	7.54	23.31	0.083	0.107
1942	0.35	2.81	4.02	4.16	9.62	29.48	0.073	0.103
1943	0.43	2.36	3.71	4.76	11.48	31.76	0.059	0.080
1944	0.50	2.45	4.10	4.60	10.46	31.99	0.084	0.132
1945	0.51	2.42	4.30	4.83	10.90	37.30	0.059	0.102
1946	0.41	2.45	4.00	4.68	9.48	37.38	0.060	0.099
1947	0.46	2.43	4.32	5.38	13.38	48.44	0.080	0.138
1948	0.58	2.43	4.30	6.35	13.04	49.86	0.092	0.126
1949	0.49	3.67	4.67	4.64	13.38	48.67	0.096	0.117
1950	0.40	2.36	4.26	2.78	11.11	43.45	0.079	0.094
1951	0.49	3.62	4.34	6.00	12.31	47.32	0.102	0.159
1952	0.56	2.99	5.00	6.38	13.42	48.08	0.098	0.150
1953	0.51	2.14	5.31	6.58	12.74	50.59	0.093	0.133
1st Quarter 1954	0.48	2.28	4.28	6.78	14.89	47.52	0.092	0.126
2d Quarter 1954	0.36	2.09	4.29	5.12	14.28	47.12	0.093	0.114
3d Quarter 1954	0.43	1.85	4.68	7.00	14.28	49.59	0.095	0.102
4th Quarter 1954	0.39	1.78	4.63	--	13.13	46.08	0.094	0.135
1st Quarter 1955	0.39	1.69	4.55	--	13.46	40.66	0.095	0.140
2d Quarter 1955	0.42	1.99	5.39	--	14.46	51.36	0.098	0.136
3d Quarter 1955	0.41	2.33	4.82	6.70	13.46	49.64	0.092	0.132
4th Quarter 1955	0.37	2.00	5.52	6.00	15.08	62.73	0.099	0.144
1st Quarter 1956	0.40	2.08	5.40	6.50	14.05	83.51	0.105	0.165
2d Quarter 1956	0.51	2.06	5.40	--	14.64	57.13	0.113	0.319
3d Quarter 1956	0.52	2.27	6.13	--	15.57	56.33	0.131	0.178
4th Quarter 1956	0.52	2.21	5.92	...	14.95	59.63	0.112	0.197

1 The item of crusher run base was used before 1953.
2 The item of plant mix surfacing was used before 4th Quarter of 1956.
3 Asphalt concrete pavement combined with plant mix surfacing in 4th Quarter 1956, and will be identified as asphaltic and bituminous mixes in the future.

It will be noted that the number of individual items on which the cost index is based has been reduced from

. . . Continued on page 60

and Public Works

Highway Review

Past Achievements and Outlook for the Future

By CHESTER H. WARLOW, Member California Highway Commission

L ET us briefly review some of the many things which have taken place in California since the fifteenth day of September, 1943, when the statute (Streets and Highways Code, paragraphs 70, 70.1, 70.2) creating the present organization of the California Highway Commission went into effect.

Then World War II was in full swing. California had a population of approximately 9,000,000, now, 13,-600,000. Then 3,000,000 registered vehicles, now nearly 7,000,000. Trucks constituted 250,000 of the vehicles then registered, now we have approximately 800,000 registered trucks with the average weight and size of the trucks greatly increased.

Contrasting Budget Figures

The first budget passed by this new commission was the biennial one for 1944-46. For comparative purposes it is of little value for it was prepared under war conditions when new construction not connected with war activity was held up. The actual expenditures charged against the fiscal year of 1944-45 are more satisfactory for use in making the comparisons I have in mind. The record shows a gross income of $39,114,969 for that fiscal year from all sources for all purposes. Expenditures for rights of way, construction engineering, and construction on state highways totaled $24,743,770. Of this amount $4,693,-307.39 represents the total federal funds ultimately received.

Contrast these figures with those estimated for the Fiscal Year 1957-58. Income from all sources for this period is set at the sum of $464,247,-288. This item includes moneys allotted for federal-aid secondary highways, for state matching money on such projects, also for allocations to cities for major city streets and a few other minor items, leaving a net amount for state highway purposes of $421,062,057. This 1957-58 budget

assigns $354,812,051 for major construction and improvements, minor improvements and betterments, contingencies and rights of way. This figure is to be contrasted with the actual expenditure of $24,743,770 for these purposes in the 1944-45 Fiscal Year.

Increasing Income

During this 13-year period, California increased its gas and fuel taxes to 6 cents and 7 cents, respectively. In 1939 the Federal Government levied a gas and fuel tax which the 1956 Highway Act raised to 3 cents a gallon. This act also imposed additional excise taxes on motor vehicles and accessories and allotted all these revenues exclusively to highway purposes, with most of the funds being assigned for the construction of the interstate highway system.

By 1954-55 the allowance to California for federal highway aid had grown to the sum of $38,132,110. The year before Congress had made the first specific allotment for interstate highways and the gross appropriation for all federal aid was stepped up. California received in that year for its part of the interstate system $515,659. Under the new schedule of taxes and allotments made by the 1956 act, California received for the 1956-57 Fiscal Year a supplemental apportionment of $57,028,146, making a total of $66,820,982 for its interstate highways for that year and later had assigned to it for those interstate highways for the 1957-58 period the sum of $96,947,850.

Federal Aid Funds

The total federal aid allotment to California for 1957-58 for all federal aid highways in the State is the sum of $142,656,288, of which $9,051,859 goes to federal-aid secondary highways.

Under the present California law 87½ percent of this $9,000,000 goes

to the counties for such work, 12½ percent being retained by the State.

This additional highway financing, has all been reflected in actual on the ground construction. To me it would appear that the general motoring public has accepted these increase in taxes with good grace—and here in California with some satisfaction—because of the construction programs they have engendered. Personally, I believe the fact that there is in this State a constitutional limitation prohibiting diversion of these funds to other than highway purposes, and that there has been a sincere and reasonable attempt to allot these available funds to projects on the basis of actual need, has had something to do with this public acceptance and satisfaction.

In 1945 the members of the California Highway Commission were traveling over the State in an endeavor to acquaint themselves with the State Highway System and the local problems in relation thereto. I recall that we had been warned in advance that the citizens of one county were preparing to give the commission a bad time at one of the local meetings for not doing some substantial construction work in their territory. Fortunately we had the opportunity of talking finances to them before they presented their intended claims. The net result was that they agreed to settle for white lines down the state highways in their county.

Despite all the nine-place figures that I have been citing, and the fact that the state highway mileage has remained very close to our 1943 total of 14,000 miles, the situation financially, in my humble opinion, is not greatly different from what it was prior to the passage of the first Collier-Burns Highway Act in 1947.

Increased Construction Costs

Increasing unit costs of construction, increasing vehicle registration,

54

California Highways

increasing annual travel per car, the continuing influx of population into California, and the higher driving speeds, have created financial as well as traffic problems and structural requirements far beyond what was visualized 20 years ago. What we are trying to do today is to analyze the future on the basis of these factors and to design and construct to meet the requirements 20 years hence; and at the same time, where engineeringly proper, leave room for further lane expansions upon presently purchased rights of way. By this we hope to avoid, as much as possible, future disturbing displacements. At the present moment the reappraised total cost of bringing the entire State Highway System to such a standard has not been completed, but from what we have at hand it is now very evident that even under the augmented income, above indicated, we will require a period of 10 to 13 years before accomplishing that purpose on the present State Highway System.

These recent federal allotments apparently have created the impression in the minds of some of our citizens that we are over-endowed, when the facts are otherwise. Some very influential groups are talking about immediately adding hundreds of miles to the state system, a mileage which will cost an additional billion dollars and more to construct. Some minor additional subventions to local governmental agencies for highway purposes may perhaps be justified, but even here some very important groups are urging substantial increases in the percentages of gas tax funds to be allotted to cities and counties at the expense of state highway requirements.

Under these conditions I do urge forbearance and moderation.

Beautification of Freeways

There is one other matter which should be touched upon. Individually the members of the California Highway Commission have indicated their willingness to consider beautification in some areas on our major freeways providing a suitable program can be worked out within reasonable financial limits. Immediately we find enthusiasts

talking about roadside garden areas and the placing of rock facades on all our structures, all at the expense of the motoring public.

I fear that such individuals are going to be met with the provisions of Article XXVI of the California Constitution which provides that motor vehicle fuel tax funds "shall be used exclusively and directly for highway purposes."

Even reasonable plantings for erosion control, screening and beautification will require the expenditure of very substantial sums.

Ground cover, trees, shrubs and water systems have an initial cost of $7,500 per acre with planted areas on freeways running around 15 acres per mile. Maintenance costs are in the neighborhood of $900 per acre per year. For the present program of erosion control, headlight-screening and a very meager amount of beautification, the Division of Highways spent last year $2,781,139. Personally I am hoping that this amount can be substantially increased under present financing. I believe that a reasonably augmented and continuing beautification program will meet with the approval of the general public, but I suggest that there is a limit as to what we should do under present conditions and what the Constitution and the motor vehicle taxpayers will permit us to do.

Record 1957-58 Budget

In the 1957-58 budget, $340,220,000 has been allotted to specific projects for immediate construction and for right-of-way purchases in preparation for future construction. The allotment in this budget to noninterstate highways has been increased by $12,-000,000 over the 1955-56 figure. The outlook is that percentagewise this relative increase will be even greater in future budgets. Incidentally, this is the first budget in which every county in the State is included for a substantial undertaking.

District VII

Looking at District VII we find that Cahuenga Pass as a joint city-state and WPA project, and the Pasadena Freeway as a state project

had been completed and were in operation at the time the commission as presently organized went into office. Since that time, and in accordance with a priority system informally worked out jointly with the City of Los Angeles and numerous quasi-public organizations of that county, funds were first concentrated on the Hollywood Freeway, with the Santa Ana and San Bernardino Freeways next being started and extended. As of this date the Hollywood has been completed almost to the junctions of the Ventura Freeway with the Riverside Freeway. The 1957-58 budget provides for substantial work at that junction and also for construction across the intersection of the Ventura Freeway with the San Diego Freeway.

The Santa Ana Freeway in the past 13 years has been completed to a point south of Tustin, with construction about to be carried to El Toro Road, approximately 11 miles south of Tustin.

The San Bernardino Freeway has been completed to the eastern boundary of the district, and in District VIII this freeway has been extended, under construction, or budgeted to Colton. It has an extension completed, or under construction, or budgeted on US 91 northward through San Bernardino to Barstow, and an extension eastward which, with exceptions of the section between Colton and Redlands and two pieces in the vicinity of Beaumont, has been carried into the Coachella Valley near Indio.

Long Beach Freeway

The Long Beach Freeway will be completed by the 1957-58 allotment, while the Harbor Freeway will have been completed to 124th Street, with an additional 2.8 miles completed at the San Pedro end, leaving a gap of nine miles yet to be financed.

The Ventura Freeway has been cleaned up westerly of Calabasas by the allotment going to a section easterly of Camarillo. The Golden State Freeway, with the new project in District VI at Grapevine, will be placed in excellent condition from the Tunnel Station Interchange north of San Fernando to a point just southerly of Bakersfield.

From the facts at hand, it is very apparent that western Los Angeles County and also the San Fernando Valley will have to have early relief. With this in mind, the Golden State Freeway from the Olympic Freeway north has received and is receiving substantial financial attention. There is a section just north of the Pasadena Freeway that is not presently financed though the freeway route has been adopted. The two latest budgets (1956-57, 1957-58) have assigned a total of $23,000,000 for the purchase of rights of way on the Olympic Freeway between the Santa Ana Freeway and La Cienega Drive, while at the November meeting of the commission the route from La Cienega westerly to Santa Monica was adopted.

It is going to take early work on the Hollywood extension and on the Riverside Freeway to and through San Fernando Valley to connections with the Golden State Freeway to properly take care of the traffic going to and from that portion of Los Angeles County.

There are many other projects requiring early attention but to get usable units constructed some of them will have to wait a little longer. It is going to take at least 10 years and a billion dollars to work up the Los Angeles County part of the District VII freeway system, so you have plenty to look forward to and considerable action coming up.

District IV

The situation in the City and County of San Francisco has been primarily physical and political rather than financial. The present community thinking there on the matter of freeways is about where the thought was 10 years ago in other California metropolitan areas. A little time and a little patience will clear the atmosphere but I must say that the planning bodies of San Francisco have for many years realized the public necessity and economic value of an adequate freeway system in San Francisco and its relation to other transportation facilities.

The Bayshore Freeway and the Skyways in San Francisco on US 101, US 40 and 50, have been completed from the county line to the Bay Bridge. A spur on US 101 is completed or financed across Market Street and a spur on Route 224 (the Embarcadero Freeway) is financed and, after numerous delays, the construction contract has been signed and work started. The seagoing freeway around South San Francisco is being completed under the 1956-57 budget.

North of San Francisco

Looking to US 101 north of San Francisco, we find the north approach to the Golden Gate Bridge completely constructed and a freeway constructed, under construction, or budgeted to a point north of Santa Rosa except for bits of work yet to be done north of San Rafael and in the vicinity of the junction with the San Quentin lateral.

On the east side of the bay, the Eastshore Freeway is constructed, or financed, from the Eastbay Interchange south to a connection with US 101 at San Jose, the incompleted section north of Warm Springs being included in the 1956-57 budget. There is an easterly spur leaving the Eastshore Freeway in the neighborhood of San Lorenzo which, with the work now under way or financed, provides a freeway from Tracy into the downtown section of San Francisco.

There are serious highway problems in Santa Clara County due to the major industries that are being located north and west of San Jose, and substantial efforts in the future will have to be made to complete

Recently completed Banning Freeway on US 99 in Riverside County

California Highways

Arrow points to first unit of Embarcadero Freeway in San Francisco now under construction

the Bayshore Freeway (US 101) from the north Santa Clara County line to San Jose and to break open State Route 5 from the north city limits of Los Gatos to a junction with both the Eastshore and the Bayshore Freeways.

US 40

We will now look at US 40 between San Francisco and the state line near Floriston. There is some work to be done on this highway just south and east of Richmond, the

El Cerrito structure, to provide an interchange for the lateral which goes to the Richmond-San Rafael Bridge, but with that exception US 40 is financed to the Yolo Causeway. This causeway will soon have to be replaced and a route change necessary for this purpose was adopted by the commission at its November meeting. The ultimate routing of US 40 through Sacramento has not been determined, but from Sacramento to a point east of Roseville we have a recently constructed freeway. From

this point to the state line there is a very substantial amount of work to be done both physically and financially. East of Roseville there are several sections which have not been reconstructed to expressway standards or better. They are as follows:

(a) East of Roseville to east of Newcastle;

(b) West of Gold Run to Hampshire Rocks;

(c) Soda Springs to Boca, a point seven miles east of Truckee, and from there to Floriston.

and Public Works   57

The 1960 Winter Olympic Games at Squaw Valley have presented the problem of providing a highway escape route which would be necessary to avoid catastrophe in the event of a Sierra blizzard occurring during that meet. Accordingly, the 1957-58 highway budget sets up the sum of $350,000 for the construction of detours through the Truckee River Canyon looking toward the probable inclusion in the 1958-59 budget of funds to construct the section from Boca to Floriston to full freeway standards.

On Sign Route 89 $1,450,000 has been set up to provide a four-lane undivided highway from 2.1 miles south of the Squaw Valley Road junction to the Truckee Y on US 40 and, without present commitment, we are hoping that we may be able to provide in the 1958-59 budget funds to four-lane this route from Tahoe City to the Squaw Valley junction point.

We have a full freeway on the Bayshore financed to the Santa Clara line, a four-lane undivided section to the junction of the Eastshore Freeway and the northerly end of the San Jose bypass. South of the bypass to South of Morgan Hill we have a four-lane divided section which needs early attention, but priority attention will have to be given to the reconstruction of the section of the Bayshore north and west of San Jose and the section of Route 5 south and west of that city.

The freeway on US 101 from north of Gilroy to south of Chualar is built to expressway standards or better, but, with the exception of budgeted sections south of Soledad and between Greenfield and King City, we have the old coast route to a point north of San Miguel. From here to Ventura US 101 is in fair shape except for sections at Santa Maria, between Zaca and Buellton, southeast of Gaviota, at Goleta, and between Carpinteria and Ventura.

South of Ventura we have constructed or financed freeway, expressway, or four lanes divided to the Mexican border except for sections from Calabasas to the Holly-

This photo shows completed section of Roseville Freeway in Sacramento County

wood Freeway, south of Irvine, San Juan Capistrano to San Clemente, a short section north of San Onofre and sections at Encinitas, south of Del Mar and through the City of San Diego.

While we have four lanes divided from Carlsbad to San Diego, except as noted, a full freeway route for ultimate construction between these points has been given intensive study without yet reaching a decision.

Condition of this route is getting into fairly good shape. The south freeway entrance to Sacramento is yet to be financed although the route has been adopted. We then find unfinanced sections at Lodi, Modesto, Turlock, Merced, and a seven-mile section of three-lane highway immediately south of the San Joaquin River in Fresno County. A relocation of US 99 at Bakersfield is now under consideration and an alignment, when adopted, will be built to full freeway standards. There is a further gap between San Fernando and Burbank and a short strip just north of the junction

with the Pasadena Freeway, but we are getting very close to having the longest completed expressway in California which will include many full freeway sections. The short section through Lodi will not have to be reconstructed for several years because the present highway is there six lanes wide. The freeway route alignments through Modesto and Merced have been adopted and satisfactory progress is being made on the freeway agreements. Right of way is being purchased on the new alignment of the Fresno County section against possible construction being provided for in a later budget.

Traffic on the south end of this route is quite heavy, gradually diminishing from 40,000 vehicles per day just north of the Golden Gate Bridge to 8,000 vehicles per day at Geyserville. As previously pointed out, freeway and limited access construction has been extended to north of Santa Rosa except for short gaps near San Rafael and at the San Quentin Y leading to the North Bay Bridge.

North of Geyserville traffic volumes are spotty, with the majority of the counts in the 5,000 to 6,000 bracket per day. However, there are volume high spots at Ukiah, Garberville, Alton, Fernbridge to Arcata, and at Crescent City. The grades on this northerly section of US 101 and the nature of the terrain, taken together with the variation in traffic volumes, have made necessary spot undertakings rather than continuous expressway extensions. Accordingly, we have expressway undertakings on the Ridgewood grade between Ukiah and Willits, at Arnold, at Dyerville, and with rather extensive semicontinuous work between Scotia and the junction of US 101 with US 299 north of Arcata. There is another spot project budgeted north of Trinidad.

Early this year, after long study and with the approval of the Division of Beaches and Parks, the California Highway Commission adopted a recommended freeway route between the Mendocino County line and Jordan Creek, a short distance south of Scotia. The first section of construction on this new freeway is a 4.2-mile unit extending from one mile south of Dyerville to Englewood and is financed with state highway funds matched by a special legislative appropriation. A continuation of this matching policy for construction of this freeway, which by-passes but still provides excellent access to the local communities and to these magnificent redwood groves, will speed up construction through this rugged portion of Humboldt County and will materially benefit the state parks and entire Redwood Empire.

US 99 North of Sacramento

North of Sacramento US 99 is split into two alignments designated "99-East" and "99-West." The routes join again at Red Bluff. The major expressway development on this highway begins at Anderson, 11 miles south of Redding, and continues north of Redding to Shasta Lake. Freeway construction has also been commenced through the rugged Sacramento Canyon. An additional seven-mile section north of Lamoine will be advertised

this December, the 1957-58 budget allocating the sum of $4,520,000 for that construction.

Summing up, as of November 15, 1956, the State had 1,592 miles of completed multilane divided highway and an additional 319 miles under contract or advertised for bids. Some 200 miles more of multilane are included in the 1957-58 budget for a total of 2,111 miles.

This total includes 318 miles of full freeway with an additional 230 miles under construction or advertised. The State also has 803 miles of expressways with an additional 89 miles of expressways under construction or advertised, with the remaining 671 miles being four-lane divided construction.

It is to be noted that all of the 319 miles of multilane divided highway now in the mill for construction are designed to full freeway or expressway standards. All in all, we have in California, constructed or under construction as full freeways or expressways, a total of 1,440 miles of highway, but this is barely 10 percent of the entire State Highway System.

Again making comparisons, on July 1, 1945, there were but 329 miles of multilane divided highway in California, most of which would now be considered substandard and practically none of it then under access control. As above pointed out, we presently have completed or have in the mill for completion 1,911 miles of freeways or expressways, approximately six times as much as we had 13 years ago.

The foregoing is but a brief sketch of what has been done and what is immediately programmed for our highways. Obviously, there have been substantial amounts of work done over the State which are impossible to here note. Looking to the future, I would say that there is yet a tremendous amount of work to be done in California both from the standpoint of planning and actual construction.

The Division of Highways and the members of the California Highway Commission have in mind a general view of what the freeway system of the State should be. The actual locations of many sections of that system

This section of the Sacramento-Lodi Freeway on US 99/50 is between Galt in Sacramento County and Lodi in San Joaquin County

have not been precised. Under the circumstances, the commission looks forward to a multitude of freeway hearings and the Division of Highways has a problem of location studies preparatory to recommendations that is staggering to one who is familiar with the studies and procedures involved.

It has been said that if all the persons who are interested in a particular location problem were laid end to end, each would be pointing in a different direction. This seems to be true to one who has been on the Highway Commission as long as I have.

Adequate Highway System Essential

It would appear to me that an adequate State Highway System, including a system of freeways completely joining and traversing the major areas of the State, is absolutely essential to the economic growth and welfare of the State. Those who are far-sighted enough to see what the problem is, and to assist in solving it, will be rendering valuable contributions to the general public welfare. In each of these problems the members of the Highway Commission and the Division of Highways are very much concerned with getting all the facts regarding each particular undertaking from every possible source. So far as the commission itself is concerned, even after a recommendation for a freeway location has been made by the State Highway Engineer and the public hearing has been held by the commission, still we search for and seek out additional information to cover every material point of issue that has been raised. Long before the passage of the Hegland Bill or the present Federal-aid Bill, the commission has vigilantly concerned itself with the analysis of the economic impact of each possible freeway location upon the community traversed. I am very sure that in all our doings no consideration will be given to factors other than finances, traffic service, economic benefits and detriments, certain humanitarian factors and the ultimate welfare of the State with the least possible detriment to individuals. It is unfortunate that we cannot build highways without taking property for that purpose.

There has occasionally been a reason for adopting a line other than that recommended by the State Highway Engineer. These, of course, have been very few because of the meticulous studies made by the Division of Highways in advance of recommendation.

I assure you that in the absence of changes in the laws of our State, the California Highway Commission will continue to act as an independent collateral board of appeals in the Department of Public Works to which communities may prefer their suit in the event that they feel they are distressed by a route recommendation made by the State Highway Engineer.

LETTER FROM TOKYO

K. C. ADAMS, *Editor*

DEAR SIR: I wish to take this opportunity to express my sincere thanks for the privilege of receiving your splendid publication.

I am a young civil engineer of the Planning Division of Japan Highway Public Corporation which was recently organized by the Japanese Government for the construction and supervision of a toll express-highway in Japan.

I am very much interested to find that *California Highways and Public Works* is one of the most valuable magazines for our engineering work. After reading the magazine, I circulate it among a number of our men and I keep a file of them as I am referring to them in my work.

May I thank you very much for your kindness in sending the magazine to me.

Your very truly,

T. AIZAWA
Japan Highway Public
Corporation
Tokyo, Japan

MERIT AWARDS

Continued from page 46 . . .

tion recommending the discontinuance of hand lettering of the word "California" in the location portion of the title blocks on standard drawing sheets. Not only reduces drafting time and checking time, but liberates the space for more pertinent data.

COST INDEX

Continued from page 53 . . .

eight to seven items in the computations for this period. The items of plant-mixed surfacing and asphalt concrete pavement have been consolidated under the heading of asphaltic and bituminous mixes. Construction methods and bid prices for the two items have been so nearly uniform that it is believed the previous separation is no longer necessary.

Four of the seven construction items show a decrease during this period; two items show an increase and the item of roadway excavation remains the same as last period. Untreated rock base dropped $0.06 to $2.21; asphaltic and bituminous mixes dropped $0.19 to $5.93; portland cement concrete pavement is down $0.62 to $14.95 and bar reinforcing steel is lowered slightly to $0.112, a drop of $0.009.

Reductions in cost represented by the foregoing items were offset by Class "A" portland cement concrete for structures which rose $3.31 to $59.63, a price higher than at any time in the history of this index, and structural steel which increased $0.019 to $0.197, a price still under the second quarter average.

All reductions in average prices are fairly small and these reductions are without doubt reflections of the proximity of projects to material sources. The increase in structure concrete is not readily explainable but it is believed that some of the increase is related to the availability of form labor and higher transportation rates. Structural steel price increases are largely the result of higher rail rates.

WILLIAM A. BUGGE

Continued from page 51 . . .

hereby extends after the twenty-fifth year of meritorious public service these congratulations and good wishes for a long and happy continuance in this chosen field of work."

California Division of Highways personnel receiving the awards are:

George Langsner, District Engineer, Los Angeles; H. S. Miles, District Engineer, Redding; H. C. McCarty, Office Engineer, Sacramento; Frank C. Balfour, Chief Right of Way Agent, Sacramento; A. L. Elliott, Bridge Engineer, Sacramento, and J. E. McMahon, Bridge Engineer, Los Angeles.

District 11

Highway Construction in
North in 1956 Reviewed

By H. S. MILES, District Engineer

SISKIYOU COUNTY

The 5.6-mile section of Scott Valley Road from Moffett Creek to Fort Jones was completed. This is the third contract and there is now a completed section of highway of about 9.5 miles extending from Fort Jones across Forest Mountain Summit toward Yreka. This represents an expenditure of over $1,200,000.

There still remains a section of about 5.4 miles in length to bring the improvement down to Highway 99.

Surveys have been completed and plans are under way to close this gap. It will probably be covered in two contracts.

Just south of Yreka there is a going contract costing $552,000, covering 4.7 miles of Highway 99. This contract was let in late 1955. Grading and structures are completed and surfacing started; it will be completed in 1957.

South of Fort Jones, in Scott Valley, a job costing $951,500 is under way. This is largely a relocation necessitated by damage sustained by the existing highway due to last winter's storms. Most of the grading is complete and the structures are in place. It will be finished in 1957.

About $20,000 was spent this season for surfacing between Mt. Shasta and Dunsmuir.

In December of this year bids were opened for improving about one mile of road between 4.5 and 5.5 miles east of Hamburg on the Klamath River Road. This closes a gap left when the road was improved as a mineral access road during the war. The land was under lease to be mined and operations were scheduled to start. It was never mined and it remained as the worst portion of the road between Highway 99 and Seiad. Low bid on this work was $127,396.

While the work in Sacramento Canyon so far performed has been in Shasta County, the importance to Siskiyou County is very great.

MODOC COUNTY

In Modoc County, 18 miles of the Adin-Tulelake Road was sealed at a cost of about $35,000. Also about eight miles on the west end of the road over Cedar Pass to Surprise Valley was covered by a contract let late in the season. This provides surfacing for the grading performed by the honor camp forces and is in the amount of $106,000. It was considered too late to start work this year.

An eight-mile section of highway between eight miles east of Adin and the Pit River Bridge on the Redding-Alturas Road received some base reinforcement and a complete resurfacing under a $210,000 contract just completed.

LASSEN COUNTY

A $302,000 contract let late in 1955 and completed this year, closed a 3½-mile gap on Route 395 between Madeline and Likely. This covered what was probably the worst spot remaining on this section between Susanville and Alturas.

From Madeline, a section to the north 21.5 miles long was sealed. This cost $142,000 and came to within seven miles of Alturas.

To repair damages sustained during last winter's storms, two contracts were awarded for repairs of Long Valley Creek structures on the road to Reno. One entirely new structure was built at a cost of $120,000 and two others repaired at a cost of $101,000.

PLUMAS COUNTY

A repair job consisting of restoration of a fill and culvert washed out last winter at Bardee Creek was completed. It was only three-tenths of a

mile long but cost $130,000. This was on the Feather River Highway about two miles west of Pulga, but is actually in the small portion of Butte County contained in the Redding District.

A contract covering some paving and storm drainage corrections in Greenville was completed at a cost of $38,000. This job was awarded last year but not completed and was finished this season.

A surface treatment partly in Plumas County west of Delleker and Feather River Inn in Plumas County and from Secret Valley to Ravendale in Lassen County was completed, the cost was $447,000 and extended over 17 miles.

From Indian Creek on the Feather River to about five miles east of Quincy a light bituminous blanket was placed on 17 miles of surfacing. This work ended at the beginning of the contract completed by the Bureau of Public Roads.

Within the last month the department has opened bids on two jobs in Plumas County. One is a 5.2-mile section of new location between 0.7 mile north of Spring Garden to Sloat. This extends from the southerly end of work completed this year by the Bureau of Public Roads. The low bid was $1,218,856.

The other job provides placing tunnel linings in areas of three tunnels in the Feather River Canyon. These areas have leaked considerable water in wet weather and it is anticipated that the current contract will correct this trouble. Low bid was $55,404.

TEHAMA COUNTY

A minor improvement was completed near the Tedoc Road on the Red Bluff-Alton route at a cost of $27,000.

Ten miles of seal coat from the Butte County line to Los Molinos on

and Public Works

Highway 99E and 14 miles just east of Paynes Creek on the road to Susanville were completed at a cost of $33,000.

A bituminous blanket covering about 14 miles from Proberta to Red Bluff on Highway 99W and then north to Nine Mile Hill was completed at a cost of about $92,000.

During December the department has opened bids on two jobs contained in the 1957-58 Budget in Tehama County. The first of these is on the Red Bluff-Susanville Road. It calls for complete reconstruction of 6.2 miles between 1.5 and 7.5 miles east of Lassen Camp and Mineral. Low bid was $1,129,956.

The other project is on the Red Bluff-Alton Highway beginning 3.2 miles east of Tedoc Road and extending to Dry Creek. It is 6.2 miles in length and also calls for complete reconstruction. It joins the work completed to the west in 1955. Low bid was $613,779.40.

SHASTA COUNTY

During this summer, two contracts covering reconstruction of the highway on the west side of Hatchet Mountain were completed. These were let in 1955 and represented an expenditure of about $1,200,000.

East of Redding on Highway 44, a paving job from Palo Cedro covering eight miles of the road westerly toward Redding was completed at a cost of $49,000.

Nearer town a project for widening the highway from the Sacramento River Bridge easterly one-half mile was covered by a contract awarded in November. This has not been completed.

In Redding, Eureka Way was widened and paved from the Southern Pacific overhead westerly about 1.5 miles. The cost of this improvement was about $186,000 and the relief afforded traffic was immediately apparent.

Up the Sacramento River Canyon, above the relocation around Shasta Lake, three contracts let in 1955 have been completed. These cover construction of 6.5 miles of road and a new bridge over Dog Creek. Total cost was about $4,000,000.

In Memoriam

FRANK J. ESCOBEDO

The Department of Public Works was shocked and saddened by the untimely death on January 27th of Frank J. Escobedo, Assistant Deputy Director. Frank suffered a heart attack while playing tennis on that date and passed away in Sutter Hospital in Sacramento.

Director of Public Works Frank B. Durkee on September 1, 1954, appointed Escobedo personnel officer of the Department of Public Works. At that time Escobedo was finishing a two and one-half year term as personnel director for the City of Philadelphia. Prior to going to Philadelphia at the request of Mayor Joseph S. Clark, Jr., now a United States Senator, to establish a civil service system, Escobedo had been in state service in California for 14 years as personnel officer of the State Relief Administration, later with the Social Welfare Department and for five years before going east, with the State Board of Equalization. During World War II he had three and one-half years' personnel experience in the United States Army, in which his last assignment was battalion personnel officer and adjutant. In July, 1956, he was promoted by Durkee to the post of assistant deputy director.

Frank was born in Santa Monica, California, in 1915. He was graduate of the University of California at Berkeley, where he also completed graduate study in the Bureau of Public Administration.

Frank leaves a widow, Constance, and a three-year-old son, John.

Bids were opened in November on another section 6.9 miles in length immediately to the north. Low bid on this was $4,605,588.

It is incidental that the work in the canyon is in Shasta County because its benefits are state-wide. It is the only north-south interstate route north of San Francisco and upon completion of the interstate system will be of national importance.

In Memoriam

JOSEPH M. KANE

Joseph M. Kane, Assistant Office Engineer for the Division of Highways until his retirement last August, died suddenly of a heart attack at his home on January 24th. Kane came to work for the division in 1927. During his long career he supervised the preparation of individual job specifications on more than two billion dollars worth of highway construction. He had charge of the production of the division's "Standard Specifications" for more than a quarter of a century. These specifications set up standards governing the execution of all highway construction work done by or for the division and have served as a model for other organizations being used extensively as a reference by other state and federal government agencies.

Born at Genoa, Nevada, Kane attended public schools there and in Carson City. He studied engineering at the University of Santa Clara and later at the University of California, where he received a B.S. degree in engineering in 1918.

Kane's first professional employment as an engineer was with the Nevada Department of Highways where he became chief testing engineer and later office engineer. He came to work for the California Division of Highways in 1927.

Kane served as a second lieutenant in the U. S. Army during World War I and was Past Commander of the American Legion, Department of Nevada. He was a member of the American Society of Civil Engineers.

Kane is survived by his wife, Doris.

TRAFFIC WEAVER

Don't be a traffic weaver. Weaving from lane to lane on a busy highway you may gain a few minutes in traveling time. You may also lose your life.

MONEY FOR ROADS

In 1893 Congress appropriated $10,000 for the establishment of an Office of Road Inquiry, reports the California State Automobile Association.

Index of California Highways and Public Works

January to December, 1956

DEPARTMENT OF
PUBLIC WORKS
SACRAMENTO, CALIFORNIA

CALIFORNIA
HIGHWAYS AND PUBLIC WORKS

California Highways and Public Works

Official Journal of the Division of Highways,
Department of Public Works, State of California

KENNETH C. ADAMS, Editor

HELEN HALSTEAD, Assistant Editor

MERRITT R. NICKERSON, Chief Photographer

Vol. 36   March-April   Nos. 3-4

Public Works Building
Twelfth and N Streets
Sacramento

CONTENTS

FRONT COVER
Aerial view of University Avenue Interchange in Berkeley. Looking south is Bay Bridge distribution structure. Photo by Merritt R. Nickerson, Chief, Photographic Section, Department of Public Works.

BACK COVER
Aerial of Lafayette Bypass in Contra Costa County. Photo by M. R. Nickerson, Chief, Photographic Section, Department of Public Works.

Published in the interest of highway development in California. Editors of newspapers and others are privileged to use matter contained herein. Cuts will be gladly loaned upon request

Address communications to
CALIFORNIA HIGHWAYS AND PUBLIC WORKS
P. O. Box 1499
Sacramento, California

Freeways in District IV

By B. W. BOOKER,
Assistant State Highway Engineer

*Ten Years of Modern
Highway Construction*

THE YEAR 1957 marks the conclusion of the first 10 years of freeway construction in the San Francisco Bay area. In singular coincidence, the closing of the decade witnesses the virtual completion of what might be considered the initial phase of freeway development in the nine counties of District IV. Approach to the metropolitan areas from the north, east and south will soon be served by four continuous freeway systems engineered to the peak of modern highway standards. Major portions of four other freeways will also be in service.

During 1956 there were 33 miles of freeway completed in District IV, making a total of 200 freeway miles now in service. Another 70 miles are presently under construction and by the end of 1957, it is expected that construction of another 25 miles will be under way. By the end of 1957 a continuous part of the Bayshore Freeway will be in service from the San Francisco-Oakland Bay Bridge to Palo Alto, a distance of 35 miles. On the other side of the bay, the last 0.9 mile of the Eastshore Freeway will be under construction in Oakland.

Continuous Freeway

When completed, a continuous freeway will be in service from San Jose through Oakland to the El Cerrito Overhead in Albany, a distance of approximately 44 miles, and another 13 miles is now under construction northerly to the new Carquinez Bridge. By the end of the year, a continuous freeway will also be in use from the Eastshore Freeway just north of San Lorenzo and Hayward to Tracy, a distance of 40 miles. Also being completed this year is the last of the major freeway projects re-

B. W. BOOKER

quired to provide a continuous freeway ride from the Golden Gate Bridge to Santa Rosa, a distance of 46 miles. Only the balance of the Greenbrae Interchange, a short length at the north city limits of San Rafael and a short section through Novato remain to be constructed in this entire stretch.

The total expenditures on freeways in District IV to date is approximately $465,000,000. Our construction and right-of-way programs totaled $19,-000,000 in 1950, $65,000,000 in 1955, and will have increased to $75,000,000 in 1957-58, all of which is an indication of the accelerating tempo of freeway completions expected in the future.

Since the opening of the first segment of the Bayshore Freeway in

1947, Burlingame Avenue to Peninsula Avenue in San Mateo County, short sections have been constructed as rapidly as funds have become available. The sequence was established by economic controls and the priority due to severity of deficiency. As the decade developed the planned pattern of continuity appeared and the completed sections now have merged into full freeway arterials.

Part of Past

This is now a part of the past. The problems of engineering and those of economic impact upon the areas affected by the physical presence of the right of way were relatively simple. With the exception of the Eastshore Freeway old alignments were largely used and the population of the involved areas had long since accepted the fact that highways had to be expanded and improved.

Most of the Eastshore Freeway, south of Oakland to San Jose, has been developed on new alignment through comparatively undeveloped lands. The many thousands of new homes lining each side of this freeway are a mute testimony of the value of high standard traffic service, not only to the alleviation of congested existing arterials, but to the development of areas farther and farther removed from metropolitan centers.

The story of the coming decade will be quite different. The planning of the system of freeways in the Metropolitan Bay area has been done in cooperation with the county and municipal authorities. From the outset the system has been based on the knowledge that but one freeway extending in each of the several direc-

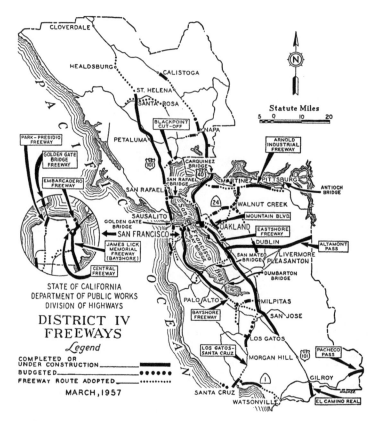

CLOVERDALE

HEALDSBURG

CALISTOGA

ST. HELENA

SANTA ROSA

Statute Miles
5   0   10   20

BLACKPOINT
CUT-OFF

NAPA

PARK-PRESIDIO
FREEWAY

PETALUMA

ARNOLD
INDUSTRIAL
FREEWAY

GOLDEN GATE
BRIDGE
FREEWAY

CARQUINEZ
BRIDGE

EMBARCADERO
FREEWAY

SAN RAFAEL
BRIDGE

MARTINEZ PITTSBURG

SAN RAFAEL

ANTIOCH
BRIDGE

24

WALNUT CREEK

SAUSALITO

MOUNTAIN BLVD

GOLDEN GATE
BRIDGE

OAKLAND

EASTSHORE
FREEWAY

SAN FRANCISCO

JAMES LICK
MEMORIAL
FREEWAY
(BAYSHORE)

DUBLIN

ALTAMONT
PASS

SAN MATEO LIVERMORE
BRIDGE PLEASANTON

CENTRAL
FREEWAY

STATE OF CALIFORNIA
DEPARTMENT OF PUBLIC WORKS
DIVISION OF HIGHWAYS

DUMBARTON
BRIDGE

PALO ALTO

MILPITAS

DISTRICT IV
FREEWAYS

BAYSHORE
FREEWAY

SAN JOSE

Legend

LOS GATOS

COMPLETED OR
UNDER CONSTRUCTION

BUDGETED

FREEWAY ROUTE ADOPTED

MARCH, 1957

LOS GATOS-
SANTA CRUZ

MORGAN HILL

PACHECO
PASS

GILROY

SANTA CRUZ

WATSONVILLE

EL CAMINO REAL

tions from the central metropolitan cores would not be sufficient to handle the potentials of this great area. It has been well realized that other freeways offering similar directional movement but providing traffic serv-ice to and through many local areas of congestion somewhat removed from initial freeway developments will be required in the future. Accordingly, facilities such as the Mac-Arthur Freeway and Junipero Serra Freeway have been foreseen in addition to the Bayshore and Eastshore Freeways.

With a present population of the Bay area exceeding 3,000,000 and an estimated increase to double that by

1975, it is not realistic to consider that freeways alone will be the answer. However, authorities in transportation all agree, that whatever form of additional transportation may be required in the future, the need for freedom of individual movement dictates that the system of freeways presently being planned and constructed must be provided and cannot be supplanted.

This is stated in several places in the Bay Area Rapid Transit Commission Report, and is included in the diagrams and bar charts illustrating the modes of travel. Quoted from page 37 of that report is the following:

First Requirement: A Regional Freeway Network.

"The existence of the very large group for whom only the private motor vehicle provides effective transportation dictates a strong highway system as the very first requirement in satisfying over-all transportation demand. Specifically, we consider that the known size of this group makes essential, as the first inter-urban transportation requirement, a regional arterial highway system of freeway-quality construction. Programming of such regional freeways in the Bay area is already well advanced, and the plans to carry these to completion must be strongly supported."

A large portion of the planned future construction will be essentially a paralleling of present freeway facilities, but farther removed from the bay. Entirely new routes through existing developed areas must be established to relieve the inevitable highway saturation which follows the growth of population and the resulting addition of vehicles. These new routes involve properties, the owners of which have heretofore had little reason to expect involvement in the highway problem. The intensity of the conflict of interests is exceeded only by the necessity of solution.

Public Opinion Important

Those responsible for highway progress are now and will continue to be faced with the necessity of extensive public explanation with respect to location of new facilities and the time table of their construction. The limitations of space make manda-

tory that additional property must be acquired for freeway development. The opposition of those whose personal interests are affected can be expected in regard to any proposed location. It is impossible to avoid all existing developments; however, there will be improvement in this respect in the future as advantages from extensive advance planning activities are realized.

Geography of the Bay area has established a core of industry and commerce in San Francisco and in the cities of the East Bay. The transportation pattern thus becomes one of convergence toward these areas. As the system grows it reaches farther and farther into the far corners of the area joining the similarly expanding facilities of the adjacent districts and affording the benefits derived therefrom. Other than safety and freedom of congestion on local roads and streets there are, of course, many more benefits to the motorist and general citizenry which cannot be easily evaluated though none the less real. Among these are stabilization or enhancement of property values, increasing the radius of area development from the inner core, increased access to recreational and cultural facilities, reduction in strain of driving, more expeditious movement of nonmotorists through use of freeways by express busses, lessening of costs of transportation for commodities. The monetary value of these benefits are huge as they are vital to the financial health and progress of the region. It should be borne in mind that conversely to the benefits occurring from good transportation if there were no freeways there would be the losses that the region would suffer without having them. In the words of former Commissioner of Public Roads, Thomas MacDonald, "We pay for good roads whether we have them or not; and we pay more if we don't have them than if we do."

It is with considerable satisfaction that the following more detailed review of progress and future plans for the development of the Bay area highway system is presented.

BAY BRIDGE TO SOUTH CITY LIMITS SAN FRANCISCO

Except for a short section southerly of Third Street which will be completed this summer as a part of the "open water" fill relocation south of the city limits, this six- and eight-lane freeway within San Francisco is now completed and opened to traffic. During the past year roadside development, ground cover, and erosion control projects amounting to approximately $250,000 have been completed between Third Street and 17th Street.

The 110,000 vehicle users traversing this scenic skyway daily are being afforded considerable relief from congestion and a savings in time and money. Considerably greater safety is also afforded these vast numbers of motorists all of whom were previously required to traverse congested city streets with attendant delay and high accident rates.

The construction cost of this portion of the freeway has been $20,300,000, exclusive of the open water fill project.

SOUTH CITY LIMITS SAN FRANCISCO TO PALO ALTO

At the end of 1957 or early 1958 this part of the freeway will be virtually complete. At that time there will be a continuous initial six-lane future eight-lane facility for 35 miles southerly to Palo Alto. Completion of this entire stretch is now dependent on the finishing of four projects now under construction.

Underway at this time and nearing completion is the last contract on the open water project between Third Street in San Francisco, across an arm of the bay between Candlestick Point and Sierra Point, and tying into the completed freeway near Butler Road. This project, consisting of drainage and paving was awarded to L. C. Smith at a cost of $1,450,000. Two and two-tenths miles of this four-mile project are over open water resulting in a shortening of 0.4 mile over that traveled on the existing highway. Work is expected to be completed this summer allowing full use of this six- and eight-lane freeway resulting

LEFT—Looking northerly at Open Water Fill on Bayshore Freeway. Sierra Point in foreground and Candlestick Point ahead. Note north-bound off-ramp to existing highway in foreground. RIGHT—Bayshore Freeway construction at Sierra Point looking southerly. Note S. P. R. R. relocation. Tunnel right center eliminated.

in a time savings of as much as 20 minutes to the many vehicle users who travel this route during peak hour periods. Previous work on this project was performed under six contracts including grading along with drainage structures and construction of experimental embankments to displace the highly fluid bay mud which reaches a maximum depth of 70 feet in this area.

From the south end of the open water project at South San Francisco to Bransten Road, just north of Redwood City, the freeway is completed and in operation for some time. This work started in 1946 and was finished with the completion of the southernmost contract in 1955.

The remaining eight miles from Bransten Road to the Santa Clara county line was broken into four projects. The first of these projects was the Willow Road interchange which was finished last year by L. C. Smith as the contractor at a cost of approximately $850,000. This project

had been selected for first construction to eliminate a very congested intersection.

The second and third contracts covered the balance of the work between 0.4 mile north of Marsh Road and the Santa Clara county line. Chas. L. Harney, Inc., was low bidder on both contracts. Their combined cost is $3,770,000 and they are scheduled for completion this year.

The last of the four contracts to be finished will be the 3.8 miles relocation between Bransten Road and the junction with the above contracts at 0.4 mile north of Marsh Road. This $5,550,000 contract was advertised in October, 1956, and was awarded as a joint venture to Piombo Const. Co., M & K Corp., and Connoly and Pac. Co. The expected date of completion is in the early spring of 1958.

EMBARCADERO FREEWAY

Construction was started on the first portion of this multilane elevated freeway by MacDonald, Young and

Nelson & Morrison, Knudsen Company in May of 1955. This 0.9-mile-long single and double-decked project is estimated to cost $5,700,000. The second contract providing for a two-lane single-level structure for Oakland-bound traffic and the extension of the freeway to Howard Street with a four- and six-lane two-level structure was started in March of 1956. The contractor on this 1.2-mile section is Charles L. Harney, Inc., and it is estimated that the cost will be approximately $2,000,000. When completed this spring, these two units will serve as a connection between the Skyway and Bay Bridge to Mission Street at Main and Beale Streets in San Francisco.

Also under construction at this time is the third link in this freeway system extending it 1.2 miles from Howard Street, past the Ferry Building to Broadway and Sansome Streets. Completion of this $7,800,000 contract is not expected until sometime in the spring of 1959. Charles L. Harney,

4

Inc., is also the contractor on this two-level freeway.

Studies for the future extension of this freeway are in the early stages.

PALO ALTO TO SAN JOSE

Included in the 1957-58 construction program is a 1.1 miles long section of freeway at Moffett Field north of Mountain View between Stevens Creek and Ellis Street. Plans call for the construction of four lanes of the ultimate eight-lane freeway and con-

struction of a full four-quadrant cloverleaf with bus stop facilities at Moffett Boulevard. Cost of this project is estimated at $1,100,000 and work should begin early this year. Construction of this project was expedited in order to eliminate a very congested intersection at which accidents were becoming increasingly numerous and severe.

From Palo Alto to Rosa Street north of San Jose, design plans are well advanced and it is anticipated

that further improvements of this important freeway will be continued as rapidly as availability of funds and priority of other worthwhile projects will permit.

SAN JOSE TO SAN BENITO COUNTY LINE

A project which eliminates the last of the three-lane portion of this route by providing an initial four-lane, future six-lane freeway from the present junction of Sign Route 17 to

Embarcadero Freeway construction in progress on single and double decked structures. West approach to the Bay Bridge at bottom. Main and Beale Street connections in center.

Santa Clara Street is nearly complete. This project is 1.6 miles long and will cost $1,800,000. It is anticipated that work will be finished in the late spring of this year. This contract is being performed by Lew Jones and Leo F. Piazza. An interchange has been completed at McKee Road eliminating another source of accidents and a new underpass beneath the Western Pacific Railroad is nearing completion.

South of Santa Clara Street to Ford Road, an expressway has been in operation since 1947. Eventually it is expected that intersections at grade will be replaced by interchanges.

From Ford Road to south of Gilroy, the last of the three-lane width through this area was eliminated by expanding to a four-lane divided section. Work on the last portion of this expansion, from Ford Road to Llagas Creek, was performed by Carl N. Swenson, at a cost of $515,700 and was completed in March of 1956.

South of Gilroy to the San Benito county line, 5.8 miles of four-lane highway (future six-lane freeway), costing $935,000, have been in operation since early 1951.

SAN FRANCISCO—CENTRAL FREEWAY

The first portion of the Central Freeway, locally called Skyway, extending from the James Lick Memorial Freeway along 13th Street to South Van Ness Avenue and Mission Streets, was completed and opened to traffic in 1955.

The second section of this freeway extending from South Van Ness Avenue to Turk Street is included in the 1957-58 construction program and it is expected that this project will be under construction early this summer. This one-mile-long section of the skyway will be a two-level elevated viaduct with the three southbound lanes carried over the three northbound lanes and both directions of travel will be elevated over the city streets, leaving them clear to handle the cross traffic movements. The cost is estimated at $7,800,000.

Planning toward the eventual extension of this freeway is in the preliminary stage.

UPPER—US 101 Bypass east of San Jose looking southerly. Completed McKee Road interchange in center. End of project at Santa Clara Street diamond interchange in background. LOWER—US 101 Bypass-McKee Road interchange looking north. Western Pacific Railroad underpass at top center.

With virtual completion of the James Lick Memorial Freeway (Bayshore) in San Francisco, and as the most needed units of the Embarcadero and Central Freeways are now in the design and construction stages, planning has been directed to other near future segments of the much needed integrated San Francisco system.

Planning studies for an eight-lane freeway following generally along Alemany Boulevard between Junipero Serra Boulevard, near the south city limits of San Francisco, and the James Lick Memorial Freeway (Bayshore) are complete. Numerous public informational meetings as well as a public hearing before the Highway Commission were held and on June 21, 1956, this portion of the route was adopted and declared a freeway. Design studies are being expedited and an indication of near-future construction is the extensive purchasing of rights of way which to date are approximately 35 percent complete. Considerable funds have been allocated for the continued purchasing of rights of way in the 1957-58 fiscal program. The construction cost of this 4.3-mile length is estimatd at $17,000,000.

The City of San Francisco is well advanced with their plans for the extension of this freeway to a junction with the proposed Southern Crossing and Embarcadero Freeway in the vicinity of Third and Army Streets.

GOLDEN GATE FREEWAY

Plans are nearing completion on a $7,000,000 project covering 1.3 miles between Lyon Street and the Park Presidio Freeway at the southerly end of the Golden Gate Bridge. Work will consist of adding two lanes to make a total of eight lanes as well as revising the ramp connections at the interchange.

WESTERN FREEWAY

Studies for the Western Freeway are still underway and alternate locations are being investigated and compared.

SKYLINE BOULEVARD, SAN MATEO-SAN FRANCISCO COUNTIES

In December, 1954, a 2.3-mile portion of expressway on Skyline Boulevard between Edgemar Road and Alemany Boulevard was placed in service.

In July, 1955, continuation of the expressway northerly of Alemany Boulevard 1.3 miles to the south city limits of San Francisco was started under a contract awarded to Charles L. Harney, Inc. This project cost approximately $350,000. Concurrently, also under construction by Charles L. Harney for the City of San Francisco was the 1.0-mile portion north of the city limits to Lake Merced Boulevard, also as an expressway and costing $350,000. Both projects were opened to traffic on March 15, 1956.

These Skyline Boulevard projects provide another major connection to and within San Francisco from the rapidly developing residential areas in San Mateo County along the Skyline and coastal routes.

Additional all weather usage of this facility is expected after the construction of the link between Edgemar and the coast route (Sign Route 1) and Skyline Boulevard at Edgemar Road. This 2.2-mile link, to be constructed at an estimated cost of $1,500,000 includes grading, surfacing and structures to provide a four-lane expressway. This project replaces the two-lane coastal road now serving north of Edgemar but which has been subjected to numerous closures due to wet weather slides. Maintenance problems encountered have been difficult and costly. Under the present accelerated construction program this section was included in the 1957-58 Budget and advertised for bids on March 25, 1957.

JUNIPERO SERRA FREEWAY

In July, 1956, Joint Highway District 10 was dissolved and the Legislature designated the constructed portion of this route as State Highway Route 237. The Highway Commission adopted the existing facility from Route 56 in Daly City to Crystal Springs Road in San Bruno, and declared it to be a freeway. Subse-

quently, under a contract now underway, a portion of this four-lane divided expressway has been repaved and the major intersection at Hickey Boulevard is being signalized and channelized. Lowrie Paving Company is the contractor and completion is expected by May, 1957. It is anticipated that this route will be developed to full freeway standards in the future.

In February, 1957, the Legislature designated Route 239 as being from a point on Route 56 near Daly City to Route 2 near San Jose. Planning studies are nearly complete, meetings will be held with local authorities and it is expected that by early summer of this year, meetings informing the public of the various routes studied will be held. Later, after the public has had opportunity to consider the studies and to voice opinions, public hearings are anticipated. Until such time, the location for this additional freeway, serving San Francisco and the Peninsula to the south, will not be determined.

SAN MATEO COUNTY—19TH AVENUE FREEWAY

Planning studies have been completed for the development of an initial four-lane, future six-lane, freeway as Route 105 extending from Sign Route 5 (Skyline Boulevard), west of San Mateo, to the west end of the San Mateo Bridge across San Francisco Bay, a total distance of 7.2 miles. (For the past several months the public has been considering the proposed future development, and the State Highway Commission at its March meeting adopted a routing and declared it a freeway.

SANTA CLARA COUNTY—SIGN ROUTE 9 FREEWAY

On October 18, 1956, the Highway Commission adopted the routing for Sign Route 9 from Bayshore Freeway north of Moffett Field, generally following Stevens Creek to an existing Sign Route 9 location north of Azule. Design studies for this future facility are now underway.

ALVISO FREEWAY

On Sign Route 9 between Lawrence Station Road east of Bayshore Freeway and 0.2 mile east of the San Jose-Alviso Road, a bypass of the town of Alviso is now under construction. This bypass will be the initial construction of two lanes of a future freeway on new alignment and above flood and tidewater level. The project is through a section of the Santa Clara Valley, subject to continuous area subsidence resulting in continuous maintenance problems during wet weather. This contract will approxi-

mate $1,000,000 and is expected to be complete in the fall of this year.

Further freeway development of this route is to be continued this year. Construction on the 8.8-mile relocation project extending between the junction of the Saratoga-Los Gatos Highway in Los Gatos and Bascom Avenue in San Jose will be started this spring. The relocation of this four-lane, future six-lane freeway is expectd to cost approximately $500,-000. Alignment of this section lies approximately midway between the Santa Clara-Los Gatos Road and the San Jose-Los Gatos Road (existing Sign Route 17) and is located along the easterly bank of Los Gatos Creek between Los Gatos and Campbell, where the freeway crosses Los Gatos Creek and proceeds northerly to the intersection with Bascom Avenue in San Jose. A total of 20 structures will be required on this contract, including two crossings of Los Gatos Creek, six interchanges, four grade separations, and one railroad underpass. Design is well advanced for the future connection of this project with the Bayshore and Eastshore Freeways north of San Jose.

Congestion Eliminated

A source of serious congestion was eliminated with the opening to traffic last October of the 2.1-mile-long Los Gatos business district bypass. This four-lane freeway, replacing the existing three-lane city street, was constructed by L. C. Smith at a cost of approximately $1,780,000. Completion of this facility removes most of the large volume of through traffic from the city street system, providing a more orderly functioning of the local traffic pattern with attendant relief to the community.

An 0.6-mile connection between the freeway easterly to a junction with San Jose Avenue at Charles Street is expected to be completed early this spring. The contractor on this portion of the work is Lew Jones Construction Company and Leo F. Piazza Paving Company. The cost of this connection will be approximately $270,000 as a cooperative project with the City of Los Gatos participating to the extent of $80,000.

In Santa Cruz a new freeway entrance to the city has been provided from existing Sign Route 17 at the north city limits to Mission Street. The completion of this project last December provides a much needed traffic distribution facility in the Santa Cruz recreational area. This project cost approximately $1,100,000 and is 1.2 miles long. The contractor was the Granite Construction Company.

Design is now underway for the future freeway development on Sign Route 17 from Santa Cruz to Los Gatos. Also to be constructed in the City of Santa Cruz will be a new 2.1-mile-long facility connecting the Rob Roy-Santa Cruz Freeway with the recently completed freeway extending from Sign Route 17 to Mission Street. The limits of this $1,830,000 project are 0.3 mile east of Morrissey Avenue and 0.6 mile north of the junction of Sign Routes 1 and 17. This facility

will be initially four lanes with provision made for the future addition of two lanes. Funds are included in the 1957-58 construction program for this project. When completed, a circumferential freeway around Santa Cruz will provide area-wide distribution and a considerable lessening of the choking congestion of city streets during the recreation months.

Completion of the Eastshore Freeway between San Jose and Oakland can now be looked for in the near future. Construction is now underway on the last two contracts needed to provide 38 miles of continuous freeway for this heavily traveled route.

The first of these two projects is the 5.8-mile-long project extending from Beard Road northerly to Jackson Street in Hayward at a cost of

Eastshore Freeway construction between Beard Road and Jackson Street in Hayward. Note desirability of locating residential areas near ready access and also result of advance planning.

and Public Works

9

$4,800,000. The contractors on this initial four-lane, ultimate six-lane, freeway are Gordon H. Ball and Ball & Simpson. Connections for local traffic will be provided for by means of interchanges at Alvarado-Niles Road, Whipple and Alquire Roads, and Tennyson Road and at the ends of the project.

Gordon H. Ball and Ball & Simpson are also the contractors on the second project completing the gap from Warm Springs Junction to Beard Road, a distance of 9.9 miles. Work was started last winter on this $6,900,000 contract and is expected to be completed by summer of next year. Construction will be based on the need for four lanes now and provision is made for the addition of two more lanes when needed in the future.

The advantage of long-range freeway planning for the future has been demonstrated this last year with the addition of two lanes to the existing four-lane portion of the Eastshore Freeway between Route 228 and High Street in Oakland. Most effective use was made of funds available in earlier years by extending four-lane freeway construction farther south resulting in considerably earlier traffic service to this area. Provision was made for future development in the 36-foot-wide median and very little of the original construction was disrupted during the widening. Fredrickson and Watson were the contractors on this $2,000,000 job finished last fall.

The additional lanes are now required to handle the increased flow of traffic resulting from the completion in September, 1956, of the four-lane freeway connection tying US 50 and Foothill Boulevard into the Eastshore Freeway at Lewelling Boulevard. This 2.9-mile construction was performed by Ball & Simpson, Erickson, Phillips and Weisberg. The construction costs amounted to approximately $2,900,000.

Through Oakland to El Cerrito Overhead

The extension of the Eastshore Freeway through the City of Oakland is being continued with the inclusion in the 1957-58 construction program of $6,730,000 for grading, paving, and

Eastshore Freeway along Cypress Street in Oakland looking south. Distribution structure in foreground. This and the Embarcadero Freeway in San Francisco are the first double decked freeway structures in California.

structures between the present northerly end of the freeway at Fallon Street in Oakland and the existing overhead structure at Market Street in Oakland. The length of this elevated eight-lane freeway is approximately 0.9 miles and will be under construction this spring. Completion of this contract will give full freeway service through the City of Oakland from San Jose to the El Cerrito Overhead. Portions of the work were done under a separate contract that included constructing a portion of the fill and the building of the on and off-ramps. These ramps were used in the interim to pass the through highway traffic over the north approach to the Posey Tube connecting Oakland and Alameda. Construction of these ramps greatly reduced the conflict between both of these heavily traveled routes.

North of the existing overhead structure at Market Street to the distribution structure at the east approach to the Bay Bridge, there is

now under contract two projects which will result in an eight-lane elevated double-decked freeway structure. Opposing traffic will travel on separate levels relieving the existing city streets of severe congestion due to the great volumes of traffic within these areas. Both of these contracts are being performed by Grove, Shepard, Wilson and Kruge of California, Inc., at an estimated cost of $9,000,000. Completion of work on both contracts is expected by early summer of 1957.

Faster service during peak hours has been obtained at the toll plaza on the east approach to the Bay Bridge as a result of the increased number of toll booths. Cost of this construction, amounting to $2,200,000, was financed by toll bridge funds and included widening and surfacing the toll plaza area and construction of new toll collection booths. Construction is expected to be completed soon and onside toll collections for both directions

10

of traffic are expected to facilitate traffic flow.

North of the distribution structure to just south of the El Cerrito Overhead there is now in service a full eight-lane freeway with interchanges at Powell Street, Ashby Avenue, University Avenue, and Gilman Street. The last portion of this freeway was completed in November of 1956 and extended 1.9 miles from south of University Avenue to the El Cerrito Overhead. One interesting phase of the work on this section included raising 330 feet of an existing structure at University Avenue, east of the freeway, to meet new grade requirements and adding 417 feet of new structures to form a portion of the partial cloverleaf now open to traffic. Work was done on this $2,250,000 contract by Stolte, Inc., and Gallagher & Burk, Inc.

El Cerrito Overhead to Vallejo

Design for the extension of the Eastshore Freeway from its present terminus south of the El Cerrito Overhead to south of Jefferson Avenue in Richmond is completed. This 1.8-mile-long portion of the freeway is expected to cost $6,000,000 for grading, paving and structures. This is the only gap in the continuous freeway from south of San Jose to Vallejo. Highway Commission consideration of financing is anticipated as soon as funds are available.

The 4.8 miles of freeway on new alignment from Jefferson Avenue in Richmond to Hilltop Drive north of Rollingwood has now been completed, and opened to traffic. Fredrickson & Watson Construction Company and M & K Corporation were the contractors on this project. Present use of this completed unit permits US 40 traffic to bypass a portion of the formerly heavily congested section of San Pablo Avenue in Richmond between Jefferson Avenue and Roosevelt Avenue. US 40 traffic is directed off the freeway at San Pablo Avenue and Roosevelt while local traffic is permitted to stay on the freeway to its junction with County Road 20. Full use of this $5,400,000 project to through traffic will not be made until the next section of freeway is open to north of Hercules.

Work is proceeding on the next 4.9-mile section of freeway extending from south of Hilltop Drive to 0.8 mile north of Hercules. Contractors for this $7,400,000 project are McCammon-Wunderlich and Wunderlich Contracting Company. Work complete with an estimated date for completion by the summer of 1958. Approximately 5,300,000 cubic yards of roadway excavation are involved in this job.

North of the Arnold Industrial Freeway, Sign Route 4, the improvement is being financed by special toll bridge bonds. These projects will result in an initial six-lane, future eight-lane, freeway. A new bridge is being constructed easterly of and parallel to the existing bridge across the Carquinez Strait. The new bridge will carry four lanes of northbound traffic. The existing bridge will carry three southbound lanes and can be widened in the future to four lanes when justified. Completion of all work and opening to traffic is expected in the fall of 1958.

LEFT—US 40 looking north from University Avenue in foreground to El Cerrito Overhead at upper right. RIGHT—US 40 looking south toward distribution structure. University Avenue interchange in foreground.

The toll financed projects in this district, including the bridge, a portion of which is in District X, are as follows:

Contracts underway Description	Estimated completion cost
(1) N of N.C.1, Hercules to Crockett Road—2.9 miles	$7,591,453

The project contains the largest highway cut in U. S.; 9,500,000 cubic yards; 3,000 feet long, 1,370 feet wide at top and 350 feet deep. Contractors—Ferry Bros., John M. Ferry, Peter L. Ferry, L. A. and R. S. Crow is moving 30,000 cubic yards per day on this job.

(2) Crockett Interchange and approach ramps	5,089,573

Contractors—Peter Kiewit Sons Co.

(3) Carquinez Bridge substructure	5,942,364

Contractors—Mason & Hanger, Silas Mason Co., Inc., and F. S. Rolandi, Jr.

(4) Carquinez Bridge superstructure	9,972,565

In addition to the foregoing there are two contracts for mechanical, electrical and toll plaza equipment amounting to approximately $500,000. Prior to completion of the project an additional contract for the Crockett approach ramp connection and modification of the present bridge amounting to approximately $600,000 will be required.

OTHER FREEWAYS IN THE EAST BAY COUNTIES

US 50, Foothill Boulevard and MacArthur Freeway

The last link in the combined 51-mile freeway-expressway service between Tracy and Oakland via US 50 and the Eastshore Freeway is expected to be completed in the fall of this year.

This link is composed of one $4,600,000 project now under construction east of Castro Valley between 0.3 mile west of Center Street in Hayward and the existing end of the completed freeway 2.3 miles west of Dublin. This section of four lanes eliminates the last of the hazardous two- and three-lane road over Boehmer Hill and provision is made for future expansion to six lanes. Peter Kiewit Sons Company is doing the work.

Completed in 1956 was the 2.9-mile section tying US 50 and Foothill Boulevard into the Eastshore Freeway at Lewelling Boulevard as mentioned hereinbefore in conjunction with the Eastshore Freeway.

Planning for the future US 50 freeway from the distribution structure through Oakland to Castro Valley is now virtually complete. A location

for 3.5 miles of the MacArthur Freeway along MacArthur Boulevard between the Distribution Structure and Park Boulevard has been previously adopted by the California Highway Commission and design is nearly completed and much of the right of way has been acquired. Recently a public hearing was held for the portion from Park Boulevard to Durant Avenue at the east city limits of Oakland. The Highway Commission is considering the routing of this facility. Between Durant Avenue and the new freeway

through Castro Valley, public meetings are being held and route adoption proceedings are expected by early summer.

From Park Boulevard southerly, the proposed route lies southwesterly of MacArthur Boulevard and crosses Mills College. From there, it runs along Mountain Boulevard and Foothill Boulevard to Castro Valley.

Mountain Boulevard

This improvement in the City of Oakland, when completed, will provide 5.6 miles of freeway from Sign Route 24 near Lake Temescal following the general route of Mountain Boulevard to a connection with the proposed MacArthur Freeway near Mills College.

Joint Highway District No. 26 originally formed to develop this route was dissolved in July of 1954 but the County of Alameda and the City of Oakland have agreed to continue to finance a total of $300,000 per year, matching a like contribution by the State, toward this continued

Looking easterly along connection from Eastshore Freeway to US 50 between San Lorenzo and Castro Valley. East 14th Street interchange in foreground. Foothill Boulevard interchange top center.

improvement of this freeway through the Oakland hills.

One project was finished this last year supplementing the previously completed 2.3-mile portion which extends from north of Broadway Terrace to south of the Moraga-Thornhill intersection. Charles L. Harney completed work on the second section (1.3 miles in length) between Thornhill Drive and Ascot Drive in October of last year (1956) at an estimated cost of $1,300,000. Construction was based on the present need for four lanes with provision made for six lanes in the future. Included in this contract is the Park Boulevard interchange which is designed as a future connection to the Shepherd Canyon Freeway through the Oakland hills into the Moraga Valley in Contra Costa County.

The 1.4-mile extension of the freeway from Park Boulevard to 0.6 mile south of Lincoln Avenue, also to be four lanes initially is now under contract at an estimated cost of $1,400,000 including grading, surfacing, one pedestrian undercrossing and seven retaining walls. The low bid on this contract was submitted by Gallagher and Burk.

The Lincoln Avenue separation was constructed under a separate contract for $130,000 by Stolte, Inc., and Gallagher and Burk, Inc., and was completed in December of 1955.

Continuation of this facility to the south is contemplated as rapidly as availability of state, county and city contributions will permit.

Sign Routes 9 and 21, Warm Springs to Benicia

Planning of this future Interstate Freeway is in various stages.

From Warm Springs to Mission San Jose, preliminary planning is being completed and public meetings are now underway to determine the location for this portion.

From Mission San Jose, for 4.9 miles, across Mission Pass to Sunol, the route was adopted and declared a freeway on January 18, 1956. Design studies are now well advanced.

From Sunol to US 50 at Dublin, planning studies are now in progress.

Looking westerly at completed portion of Mountain Boulevard Freeway. Park Boulevard interchange in foreground and La Salle Street overcrossing to Montclair in center. Broadway Terrace top center.

From US 50 to the Contra Costa county line, a distance of 1.8 miles, the initial two lanes of a future freeway and an interchange at US 50 were constructed in 1955.

From the county line to just south of Danville, a distance of 7.4 miles, preliminary studies are completed and public meetings are anticipated within the next month or two.

Proceeding northerly from Danville to Walnut Creek, the route has been located easterly of and removed from the San Ramon Valley.

From Rudgear Road south of Walnut Creek to a junction with Sign Route 24 near Oakland Boulevard and thence to the recently completed freeway north of Walnut Creek the freeway will be under construction in 1957. This project will also provide a part of Sign Route 24 from Walnut Creek to the completed freeway east of Lafayette. Cost of the project is estimated at $8,800,000 for construction.

Northerly of Walnut Creek from Oakland Boulevard to 0.3 mile north of Monument, a $2,900,000 unit of the freeway was placed in service in January of this year. This 2.8-mile section was built by Stolte, Inc., and Gallagher & Burk, Inc. Construction was based on initial four lanes and provision made for the addition of two lanes when needed. Average daily traffic of 28,000 vehicles are now using the freeway, thus providing relief to the street intersections and properties along the old highway.

Preliminary studies have been completed and design is well advanced for

LEFT—State Sign Route 24, north of Walnut Creek, looking northerly toward monument. Geary Road in the foreground and Oak Park Boulevard interchange in center. RIGHT—Looking south on Sign Route 24 toward Walnut Creek from Oak Park Boulevard interchange. Old highway on right now serves as a local arterial.

the southern approaches to the Martinez-Benicia Bridge and the bridge itself. Construction of a portion of this freeway as a toll facility, the financing of which is in conjunction with the Carquinez Toll Bridge project, was authorized by the Legislature in 1952.

The Legislature authorized a toll facility from Arnold Industrial Freeway, south of Martinez, to a connection with State Highway Route 74 in Benicia. South of Arnold Industrial Freeway, the proposed facility will be financed from regular state highway funds. The route for this facility between the Monument north of Walnut Creek and the Solano county line was adopted by the Highway Commission in March of 1956.

This future freeway will cross Arnold Industrial Freeway a short distance easterly of the existing Pacheco Highway intersection and lies just east of the extensive Shell Oil Company development in Martinez. It will cross the strait via a new high level bridge immediately westerly of the existing Southern Pacific

Railroad Bridge. This future route is a part of the recently increased Interstate Highway System.

Oakland-Walnut Creek Sign Route 24

Preliminary studies have been completed and public meetings are being held concerning the future development of a freeway from the Eastshore Freeway at Brush and Castro Streets in Oakland to the East Portal of the Broadway Tunnel.

Accelerated development through the northern half of Contra Costa County is continuing. In the past, congestion along the highway serving this area had been rapidly approaching a condition which could seriously affect the continuance of this rate of development. Material progress has been made toward alleviating this condition.

As an interim measure an additional lane between Orinda and the Broadway Tunnel was constructed in 1956. This lane enables slow moving vehicles to stay to the right over this sustained grade, thus permitting the normal two westbound lanes to serve

faster traffic more safely and effectively.

In April, 1955, the Orinda Interchange was completed and this has resulted in the elimination of a serious bottleneck and accident site.

Lafayette Bypass

Design is nearly completed for the entire section from the tunnel to the project now under construction at Lafayette.

Elimination of the worst bottleneck on this stretch of highway is now underway with the construction of the 2.6-mile section of freeway, bypassing Lafayette. The project extends between west of Sunnybrook Drive and west of Pleasant Hill Road. Completion is scheduled for early summer of this year by the contractor, Gordon H. Ball, at a cost of $3,300,000. Realignment of this portion of the road will leave the present highway as a high standard, uncongested local arterial servicing the rapidly growing community of Lafayette.

Completion in December, 1956, of a two quadrant cloverleaf of the

14

California Highways

Pleasant Hill Road interchange provided relief at another seriously congested intersection. This interchange serves as a connection between the state freeway and Pleasant Hill Road which is an important county expressway. In the future it will also be a connection to the Shepherd Canyon Freeway, Route 233 from Oakland. Work was performed by Stolte, Inc., and Gallagher & Burk, Inc., at a cost of $1,300,000.

Shepherd Canyon Freeway (Route 233)

Preliminary studies were completed in 1956 covering the location for this future freeway. On December 19, 1956, after various public meetings and a hearing before the Highway Commission, the last gap in the route was adopted and declared a freeway. This future facility will consist of initially four lanes, future six lanes, and starting at the Mountain Boulevard Freeway in Oakland, will traverse Shepherd Canyon and tunnel some 1,400 feet through the Oakland hills. It will span the Redwood Canyon in Contra Costa County and traverse the range of hills easterly thereof entering and crossing the Moraga Valley just north of the present town site. It traverses close to St. Mary's College and terminates at a junction with Sign Route 24 at Pleasant Hill Road.

Sign Routes 24 and 4—Monument to Antioch

Design is nearly completed for the future freeway now terminating at Monument to be extended through Concord to a connection with the Arnold Industrial Freeway northerly thereof. Two lanes of this future freeway were constructed in 1947 between Concord and Arnold Industrial. Further east, a four-lane expressway has been completed between Willow Pass Road and A Street in Antioch. Provisions have been made for the future development of this portion into a full freeway. Route adoption and freeway declaration has been accomplished as far east as Nerolly Road formerly referred to as Bridgehead Avenue which is directly south of the Antioch Bridge.

Recently adopted and declared to be a freeway was that portion of Sign Route 4 between the future freeway location at Nerolly Road to the Antioch Bridge.

Sign Route 4—Arnold Industrial Freeway

From Hercules to a junction with Sign Route 24 north of Concord at Willow Pass Road, planning is in various stages. A short relocation is being provided at the Hercules end in connection with the US 40 freeway relocation. Studies are now underway for the determination of future freeway development along the total route. Right of way for this freeway will be determined at an early date in the vicinity of Martinez where the city has been expanding to the south.

Sign Route 17—Toffman Boulevard, Richmond

Design is progressing along this future freeway connection to the new Richmond-San Rafael Bridge. The route has been adopted and declared a freeway from the El Cerrito Overhead to the toll plaza of the Richmond-San Rafael Bridge.

The existing State Highway route traversing generally along Hoffman Boulevard was recently selected as an extension of Sign Route 17 and directional signs will accordingly be provided in the near future.

US 101—Golden Gate Bridge to Mendocino County Line

Continued progress was made this last year toward the realization of a complete freeway between the Golden Gate Bridge and Santa Rosa.

Westerly at Lafayette Bypass on Sign Route 24 nearing completion. Pleasant Hill Road Interchange in foreground.

and Public Works

15

LEFT—Aerial photo of Big Cut on realignment of US 40, showing Carquinez Bridge in background. RIGHT—US 40. Completed freeway through Richmond looking north. Potrero Avenue in foreground. San Pablo Avenue right center.

Work was completed early in 1956 over the Waldo approach from the northern end of the Golden Gate Bridge to just south of the Richardson Bay Bridge. This improvement converted the inadequate four-lane undivided facility to a full six-lane freeway. It was dedicated and opened to traffic on March 20, 1956. Construction on this four-mile facility was accomplished in two contracts.

The major portion of the work was done under a $4,500,000 contract by Guy F. Atkinson. This project, finished in April, 1955, covered grading, construction of a second tunnel and various separation structures. Completion this last year of the second contract for completing the drainage, paving and lighting permitted full use of this much needed facility. The contractor on this $1,300,000 contract was the A. G. Raisch Company. Approximately $5,000,000 of the total construction costs, covering both contracts, was financed by the Golden Gate Bridge and Highway District.

North of the above project and extending for a distance of 5.8 miles between Manzanita to the Greenbrae intersection, freeway construction is underway or has been completed.

Richardson Bay Bridge

A new six-lane bridge over Richardson Bay was opened to traffic in the fall of 1956. This new structure is a fixed type bridge providing for 40-foot clearance above the water at the navigation channel and replaces the old lift type structure which was seldom used. Incorporated in the design of this bridge were 18 prestressed-precast concrete girder spans and 26 reinforced concrete box girder and tee beam spans. The contractor on this $3,200,000 project is Duncanson-Harrelson Company and Pacific Bridge Company.

Construction is now underway on the $1,300,000 project between the Richardson Bay Bridge and 0.3 mile north of Alto and is scheduled for completion in the late spring of 1957. Dan Caputo Company and Dan Caputo and Edward Keeble are the contractors on this initial six-lane, ultimate eight-lane section of freeway. Traffic separation has already been accomplished at the Alto intersection with the opening of the interchange eliminating a source of severe accidents and congestion.

Continuing northerly to 0.6 mile north of the Greenbrae intersection is

the project being constructed by Peter Kiewit and Sons Company. Work on this 3.5-mile contract started in May of 1956 and is expected to be finished in the fall of this year at a cost of $2,900,000. Included in the above contract is a four quadrant cloverleaf at Tamalpais Drive and an interchange on the south side of Corte Madera Creek. This work is the second of three stages at the Greenbrae interchange and will connect with the nearly completed southbound freeway bridge over Corte Madera at Greenbrae.

Greenbrae Project

The contractor on this latter project is Carl N. Swenson & Company. This fixed span bridge provides separation for the southbound traffic at the existing intersection and 21-foot clearance over the high water level in Corte Madera Creek eliminating the openings of the span for navigation. The estimated construction cost of this bridge is $1,020,000. The third stage or the separation of the northbound lanes across the creek and through the intersection is not financed.

Construction is expected to start on the freeway extension north of the

16

LEFT—Looking northerly along US 101 from the newly completed Richardson Bay Bridge toward Alto.
RIGHT—US 101 construction at Greenbrae intersection looking north to San Rafael.

Freeway construction on US 101 looking south.
New southbound bridge over Corte Madera Creek
at Greenbrae in foreground. ⟶

Greenbrae interchange in the early summer of this year. This. contract will extend 1.4 miles from the Greenbrae interchange to 0.5 mile north of the California Park Overhead and will be the connecting link between the projects mentioned above and the existing freeway south of San Rafael. Work will consist of grading, paving and structures for a six-lane freeway at an estimated cost of $1,400,000. Twin three-lane bridges will replace the existing wooden structure over the Northwestern Pacific Railroad at California Park.

Forbes Station Overhead

From 0.5 mile north of California Park to the north city limits of San Rafael the freeway has been completed and in use for some time. Northerly of this point, as far as the entrance to Terra Linda, the highway has been declared a freeway and although-left turns are physically prohibited, it has not been constructed to full freeway standards whereby access from immediate properties are controlled. Within this portion, however, there is now under construction

and Public Works

a new Forbes Station Overhead Bridge. This work consists of constructing new twin bridges for an initial six-lane, future eight-lane, freeway over the Northwestern Pacific Railroad. Contractor on this $500,000 project is Charles L. Harney, Inc. It is expected that this work will be finished in the fall of 1957.

From Forbes Overhead to south of Petaluma a distance of 18.9 miles, the existing facility is an expressway except within the town of Novato. Planning studies are now well advanced for the future development of this present expressway into full freeway standards with no at-grade intersections.

Work was finished in December, 1956, on the 8.6-mile Petaluma Bypass between 1.4 miles south of Petaluma Creek and Railroad Avenue north of Petaluma. The project provided a complete freeway to Denman Flat and grading to Railroad Avenue. It was performed by Parish Bros. & Carl N. Swenson Co., Inc., at a cost of $3,709,-015. Four lanes have been provided on this full freeway with provision made for an ultimate six lanes.

North of Denman Flat the freeway is being extended to three miles north of Cotati at Wilfred. This contract is being performed by Parish Bros., Inc., and Parish Bros. & Carl N. Swenson Co., Inc., and overlaps a portion of the previous contract for pavement construction. Completion of this $2,-700,000 contract will bypass Cotati and result in the elimination of another stretch of the hazardous, congested two-lane facility now existing. Work is expected to be completed in the early summer of 1957.

Construction is also underway for the freeway extension northerly connecting with the existing expressway at Santa Rosa. This connecting link will cost approximately $2,900,-000 and is expected to be completed in the late summer of 1957. Guy F. Atkinson is the contractor on this job.

Design for the continuation of the freeway northerly of Santa Rosa to Lytton is now underway and is well advanced. Initial construction as a four-lane facility, partially expressway, and partially full freeway, is proposed.

From Lytton to the Mendocino county line, studies for this future

freeway development were recently started.

Sign Route 17—San Rafael-Richmond Bridge Approach

Underway at this time and expected to be completed early this summer is the 2.1-mile contract covering the development of a portion of the western approach to the Richmond-San Rafael Bridge. The estimated cost of this project is $955,000 and will provide a four-lane freeway westerly from the bridge to Sir Francis Drake Boulevard east. Limits of the project extend nearly to US 101, but this is primarily for the incorporation of earthwork encountered between the bridge and Sir Francis Drake to be used in the grading for the future extension of the freeway to US 101 at San Quentin Wye. Construction work is being done by Ball & Simpson and includes an interchange at the easterly approach to San Quentin as well as a major overcrossing structure at the intersection with Sir Francis Drake Boulevard.

Sign Route 37—Ignacio to Sears Point

Work is now underway on State Sign Route 37 for the replacement of the existing Petaluma Creek Bridge.

LEFT—US 101—Petaluma Bypass looking northerly. Petaluma Creek in foreground and Denman Flat in left center.
RIGHT—Looking southerly from Denman Flat along Petaluma Bypass.

STATUS OF DISTRICT IV FREEWAY PROJECTS
MARCH, 1957

Description	Total miles	Completed projects		Under contract		Budgeted		Right of way expended and budgeted
		Miles	Construction cost	Miles	Construction cost	Miles	Construction cost	
Bayshore & James Lick Freeway; Bay Bridge to Ford Rd. south of San Jose	56.6	28.3	$42,568,000	12.4	$12,342,000	1.1	$1,100,000	$34,783,000
Central Freeway; James Lick Freeway to Turk St.	1.8	1.0	4,122,000			1.0	5,200,000	8,062,000
Embarcadero Freeway; Bay Bridge to Broadway	1.5			1.5	15,012,000			10,539,000
Golden Gate Freeway; Lyon St. to Rte. 56	1.1							55,000
Park Presidio Freeway; Golden Gate Bridge to Fulton St.	2.1	1.2	1,448,000					3,000
Southern Freeway; Rte. 56 near S.C.L. San Francisco to Rte. 68 (Bayshore)	4.7							15,763,000
Coast & Skyline Blvd. Freeway; Edgemar to Lake Merced Blvd. in San Francisco	8.4	3.9	1,376,000			1.5	1,800,000	1,009,000
Redwood Freeway; Golden Gate Bridge to Lytton	66.6	37.0	*20,975,000	16.1	11,367,000	1.4	1,408,000	9,763,000
Sonoma Valley Freeway; Rte. 104 to 0.6 mile south of Kenwood	17.7							100,000
Napa-Ignacio Freeway; From Redwood Freeway at Ignacio to Napa (Ptns)	13.4	0.8	1,607,000			0.3	2,487,000	505,000
San Quentin Freeway; Rte. 1 to Richmond–San Rafael Bridge	2.4			2.0	1,143,000			845,000
Napa Valley & Napa-Vallejo Freeway; Solano County Line to Calistoga	31.8	17.0	2,790,000	2.3	540,000			1,713,000
Richmond-Carquinez Freeway; El Cerrito O.H. to Carquinez Bridge	13.6	4.7	6,012,000	7.0	†36,530,000			7,782,000
Arnold Industrial Freeway; Hercules to Bridgehead Ave.	32.0	14.7	4,728,000					1,316,000
Monument-Martinez Freeway; Monument to Solano County Line	7.4							1,255,000
Mt. Diablo Freeway; U. S. 50 in Oakland to Arnold Industrial Freeway near Concord	19.8	7.2	6,082,000	2.6	3,310,000	2.4	5,500,000	11,087,000
Shepherd Canyon Freeway; Mt. Boulevard Freeway to Mt. Diablo Freeway	10.3							50,000
Mt. Boulevard Freeway; Mt. Diablo Freeway near Lake Temescal to San Leandro	9.3	2.4	‡3,175,000	1.3	‡1,292,000			‡921,000
MacArthur Freeway; Distribution Structure to Rte. 228	15.3							22,660,000
Bay Farm Island Br. and Approaches	0.6	0.6	2,187,000					165,000
Eastshore Freeway; Richmond–San Rafael Bridge to Bayshore Freeway at San Jose	52.7	27.5	38,887,000	16.7	20,183,000	0.9	6,750,000	18,020,000
Rte. 107; U. S. 50 to Walnut Creek (Ptns)	10.1	2.1	550,000			1.4	2,000,000	2,878,000
Altamont Pass; San Lorenzo to San Joaquin County Line	33.6	28.2	9,799,000	5.4	4,595,000			6,356,000
Mission Pass; Existing Rte. 5 to Scotts Corner	4.9							50,000
Pacheco Pass; 1 mile east of Bell's Station to Merced County Line	5.3	5.3	1,286,000					12,000
El Camino Real; Ford Rd. south of San Jose to San Benito County Line (Ptns)	5.8	5.8	1,095,000					546,000
Watsonville to 4 miles south of Davenport	21.0	8.4	4,110,000			4.6	2,013,000	3,011,000
Santa Cruz to San Jose (Ptns)	19.9	4.2	3,155,000			245,000	8.8	5,770,000	3,052,000
Saratoga-Mt. View Freeway; Rte. 114 to Rte. 68	8.1							2,000
Mt. View-Alviso Freeway; Bayshore Freeway to Eastshore Freeway	8.0			2.1	981,000			295,000
Totals	482.8	200.3	$155,952,000	69.4	$107,539,000	23.4	$33,700,000	$167,438,000

* Includes total of $5,000,000 by Golden Gate Bridge and Highway District.
† $29,117,000 Toll Bridge Funds in this amount.
‡ Includes City of Oakland and Alameda County contributions.

Bids were opened in January of this year and the low bid on this 0.97-mile-long project was submitted by Ben C. Gerwick, and J. H. Pomeroy & Co., Inc. The bridge itself will be a single structure, having four lanes, comprised of 30 spans of which the center span will be steel construction and the others prestressed concrete. A total of 264 precast, prestressed concrete girders will be required for this bridge. Replacement of the existing substandard two-lane bridge is required because it is structurally and geometrically deficient. A sum of $2,457,000 is budgeted for this construction. This project will be the third stage of a four-lane freeway from Ignacio Wye to Sears Point. The last stage completed was the construction in 1951 of two lanes of this future freeway and a graded four-lane roadbed from Petaluma Creek to Tolay Creek. Plans are nearly complete for the final contract for widening to four lanes from US 101 to junction with Sign Route 48. The estimated cost of this future project is $2,500,-000.

Sign Route 12—Sonoma Valley

A new freeway route was adopted on January 24, 1957, by the California Highway Commission connecting Sebastopol through Santa Rosa to Kenwood. This 17.4-mile route follows the existing highway from the east city limits of Sebastopol to the vicinity of Wright Road, then runs just north of the present route and adjacent to the Petaluma and Santa Rosa Railroad to the vicinity of US Highway 101 in Santa Rosa. The route then continues on a generally direct northeasterly course to rejoin the present highway near Los Alamos Road east of Melita and follows the present highway routing to south of Kenwood. Surveys and design studies for details are now underway. An interim project has been included in the 1957-58 Construction Program at an estimated cost of $435,000 to widen and channelize Sign Route 12 from US 101 to 0.17 mile east of Farmer's Lane in Santa Rosa. The City of Santa Rosa is acquiring the right of way and clearing improvements and utilities. Work should be underway this spring.

Sign Routes 128, 29—St. Helena-Calistoga

A 3.8-mile section of two-lane, future four-lane, expressway was finished in December, 1956, between four miles north of St. Helena and Calistoga. The contractor on this $550,000 project was Huntington Bros.

Sign Routes 12, 29 and 37—Napa Area

A contract has been awarded to Lee J. Immel for this addition of two lanes to Sign Route 29 north of the City of Napa between Union Station and Orchard Avenue. Addition of these two lanes will convert this 2.3-mile project into a four-lane expressway and provide a faster and safer facility. Cost of construction of this project is estimated to be $525,000.

In November, 1955, the initial two lanes of a future four-lane freeway were constructed from a point two miles east of the Sonoma-Napa county line for a distance of 2.7 miles.

Southerly of Napa on Sign Routes 12 and 29 to the Sonoma county line, the present routes have been operating as expressways for many years although access rights have not been fully acquired. It is expected that at some future period, when justified, development will be to freeway standards.

Alto interchange looking south toward the new bridge at Richardson Bay on US 101

"Keep America Beautiful" Compliments California

Recently "Keep America Beautiful, Inc.," New York City, wrote to the governors of all 48 states suggesting these three specific "travel trash" control projects.

1. A litter-prevention message to be enclosed with distribution of registration applications and license plates to all motor vehicle owners in the state
2. A digest of the state's highway litter laws to be included in literature presented to new drivers with all "Learner's Permits"
3. A question on the state's highway litter laws to be included in all driver examinations.

In reply Governor Goodwin J. Knight wrote:

"* * * mail, reaching some 7,000,-000 persons annually, related to our State's vehicle registrations, has for two years carried anti-litter messages. Emphasis on the State's law in this field has been included in the latest edition of the summary of vehicle laws issued to all driver license applicants. * * *

Director of Motor Vehicles Paul Mason has since received the following letter from "Keep America Beautiful, Inc."

"Several people have called our attention to your revised 'Driver's Examination on California Vehicle Code' which contains two questions on the state litter laws and in addition, the slogan at the end *'Be Courteous, Drive Safely—and Don't* be a litterbug'.'

"As you know the inclusion of highway litter law questions on drivers' examinations is one of three 'travel trash' control projects suggested by 'Keep America Beautiful, Inc.' last year to all the state governors. A number of states are now following the example of California re the other two projects—i.e., anti-litter messages printed on vehicle registration mailings and digest of highway litter laws in state vehicle code summaries for driver's license applicants. * * *"

California Highways

Freeway Spans "Hub"

Colton Freed From Traffic Congestion

By LOREN M. BARNETT, Senior Highway Engineer

NEW FREEWAY uncorks the Colton bottleneck.*

This was the local description of relief from traffic congestion following the opening of the new freeway through Colton.

Lieutenant Governor Harold J. Powers officially cut the ribbon opening this major link of the San Bernardino Freeway on October 18, 1956, and at the same time opened the City of Colton to possibilities of unlimited progress.

Colton is one of the older cities in California, having been incorporated in 1887. It occupies a prominent spot on the "Road to Romance" and in the

* From editorial in *Redlands Daily Facts* and carried in the *Colton Courier*.

historic lore of California. As early as 1774, Juan Bautista de Anza and Padre Garces crossed the Santa Ana River near the site of Colton, but it was not until 1838, when Don Juan Bandini acquired the Jurupa Ranch, that the first Mexican families were brought into this section to make their homes. They settled on 2,200 acres of land at the confluence of the Santa Ana River and Lytle Creek, where they founded the first settlement in the valley at Agua Mansa.

Early Settlers

As early as 1860, first settlers established farms along the Santa Ana River and participated in the building of the Meeks and Daley Ditch, one

of the pioneer irrigation projects in the valley. Meeks also built a water-powered gristmill to serve the pioneer farmers.

Wyatt Earp, of early Tombstone, Arizona fame, was one of the town's first marshals. He and his relatives were conspicuous in enforcing law in the town. Most of the family were professional gunmen and certainly lived up to their reputation and opportunities.

The first train to enter the San Bernardino Valley reached Colton in 1875. Since then, Colton has become a traffic "Hub," with both railroads and highways radiating to the other principal cities of Southern California. Subsequently the town developed a

Grade separation carrying Mt. Vernon Avenue over San Bernardino Freeway

most severe traffic condition. If the vehicles didn't get entangled in congestion of their own making, then a train would cross the highway to contribute its part to the confusion.

Traffic Backed Up

On numerous occasions, through traffic would be backed up for over a mile, cross-town traffic could hardly get across, and those who wished to stop and shop were confronted with hazardous maneuvers in addition to annoying delays.

This congestion was created by transcontinental traffic, heavy truck traffic between Los Angeles and Imperial Valley, and an unusual amount of week-end traffic from Los Angeles to the desert and mountain resort areas—all in addition to heavy local traffic between the San Bernardino Valley cities. .

With the opening of the freeway, safe, fast, and orderly movement of both through and local traffic has been provided.

One of the outstanding features of this superhighway is a pronounced increase in safety. Past experience indicates that freeways are considerably safer than city streets and that when

Lt. Governor Harold J. Powers officially cuts the ribbon to open the San Bernardino Freeway through Colton as B. Wesley Vaughan, Chairman of the Highway Projects Committee, and Clinton Smith, City Councilman, assist. (Photo by Neal Adair Studio, Colton.)

through traffic is removed there is a marked decrease in the number of accidents along the old route.

A recent traffic count shows that the number of vehicles using I Street (old U. S. 70-99) has been reduced by over 50 percent.

Orderly Traffic

The fast and orderly movement of traffic through town will save the

motorists and truckers thousands of dollars per year, if time lost by former delays is converted into dollars. In addition, what is it worth just not to be harassed by a concentrated mixture of cars, trucks, and trains?

With the completion of this new facility, together with the Eighth Street Underpass (completed in April, 1956 *), east-west traffic can now roll over the railroads while the north-south traffic flows under.

C. K. Dooley, Editor of the *Colton Courier*, was an ardent supporter in the development of this freeway system. His efforts were especially noted as head of the Colton Underpass Committee—an appointment made by the city council.

Colton's reaction to their improvement has been obtained by Mr. Dooley's roving reporter Melvine E. Mitchell who has asked numerous people in Colton, just five months after the opening of the freeway, how they liked their new highway system. The general consensus of the local residents is, "We are happy to have the noise of the heavy traffic reverted

. . . Continued on page 64

* See *California Highways and Public Works* of July-August, 1956.

Looking east along San Bernardino Freeway through Colton

Residences and Freeways

By JOHN F. KELLY, Headquarters
Right of Way Agent

Freeway Influence on
Market Value Is Nominal

IN THE development of California's freeways, a problem of great significance has been, and will continue to be, the economic effect this modern type of highway facility will have upon the land through which it passes, and the community it serves.

It has been generally accepted that a freeway facility, by its reduction in travel time, brings within the scope of development areas which could otherwise not be developed. In this way the freeway adds to the wealth of the population center by surrounding it with lands of greater value and with potential earning capacity of its occupants so as to increase industrial development and the commercial business of the town or city itself.

However, within this picture of economic growth there exists one major contradiction; this is the expressed opinions of individuals as to the undesirability of residences adjoining a freeway.

Although the freeway offers an unequaled opportunity for the prospective home owner to select the particular area most suitable to his residential desires and remain within reasonable commuting distance from his place of employment, he may retain the opinion that a residence, if adjoining a freeway, is an unwise investment.

If these opinions are shared by a great number of people, they will have a tendency to accomplish a depreciation in value. After all, value, to a great extent, is a matter of opinion. The unfounded fears of well-meaning but uninformed people can create an absolutely false value premise.

Current investigation has revealed that opinions of this type have grown to the point where several lending institutions have adopted definite poli-cies limiting individual loans on homes alongside a freeway.

This action by some lending institutions is a clear-cut example of the type of emotional thinking that can create a depreciated value if generally accepted, even though at its inception it may not be supported by factual information.

Public Agency Responsibility

It is the responsibility of a public agency such as the California Division of Highways, entrusted with the purchasing of property for highway construction, to thoroughly determine if, in fact, the value of residential property, as presently indicated by the attitude of the lending institutions, is reduced by reason of its location adjoining the freeway.

Before embarking upon this study, numerous inquiries were made to learn what facts had been developed as the basis for the policy of some lending institutions in taking the position that residential property value was depressed because of its close proximity to a freeway.

We were unable to find any evidence in California, or in any other state, of factual studies having been made to support this policy. We did find examples of polls and surveys that had been made; however, the supporting data used in these articles consisted of random sampling of property owners' comments, and from our own documented experience we know that only limited weight can be attached to this type of data.

GOAL OF STUDY

The goal of this study, then, is to make an accurate analysis of how the market value of residences have been influenced by the freeways in Cali-fornia. It is only reasonable that this should be considered from a very practical standpoint. The freeway's benefits in traffic-carrying capacity alone, justifies its cost, and repays many times, in the development of wealth to the community through which it passes. It is not the intention of the California Division of Highways that individual property owners should suffer monetary loss because of the public's need for freeway construction. It is understood there is not, and never has been, a guarantee of evenly distributed appreciated land value.

A residence, similar to other types of land investment, is subject to a great many economic influences which affect its rise or fall in value on the market. It is not the goal of this study to predict the anticipated future of residential property adjoining the freeway; however, it is felt that a record of past performances will furnish a reliable indicator of what is likely to occur in areas similarly treated. From past experience, we feel reasonably certain that if it is possible to chart the record of performance of a considerable volume for any specific type of property, we will have a basis for future comparison well supported by facts.

The principal benefit from this study will be to provide accurate data as an aid in appraising the market value of residential property near freeways, and in so doing, replace theories based upon opinions with factual data.

Preliminary Survey

The initial step in a study such as this requires a preliminary survey to determine: first, the best possible source of factual information; secondly, the method of obtaining this information; and thirdly, the extent

and Public Works   23

of coverage necessary to achieve the aims.

At the outset, it was decided that the "acid test" in determining freeway influence upon single-family residences was the reaction of those residents living alongside a freeway, as reflected in the actual sales taking place in the open market. If this information could be obtained in sufficient quantity, excluding those sales influenced by conditions that prevent a fair comparison, such as advantageous or restricted financing, forced sales or purchases, etc., it would be possible to make an accurate analysis of freeway impact upon residential property.

The necessity of obtaining a large number of sales, to supply the statistics required, was revealed in the preliminary survey. It was found, in order to obtain an adequate number of sales to establish a reliable indication of market price trend, that it was necessary to make this study on a state-wide basis. The need for the broadest possible coverage for this study became more apparent when an investigation of sales showed that many variations existed with respect to the physical differences of the houses and adjacent freeway, over and above the impact of different local economic conditions upon real estate values.

For these reasons it was necessary to consider many different examples before it was possible to estimate a trend on the degree of freeway impact upon marketability of residential property.

BASIS OF STUDY

Four freeways were used as the test areas to provide the data in this study. Two in Northern California, the Bayshore Freeway south of San Francisco in San Mateo County, and the Eastshore Freeway southeast of Oakland in Alameda County; and two Southern California freeways, the Santa Ana Freeway extending southeasterly from downtown Los Angeles into Orange County, and the San Bernardino Freeway east of Los Angeles.

The majority of residential development adjacent to freeway construction in California is located along these four freeways. The market trend revealed by the actual sales in

This tract house with back yard adjoining Eastshore Freeway is an example of the less expensive home in this study

these areas provides the most complete basis for determining how the greatest number of homes subject to freeway influence are affected. With a few exceptions, all of the residences along these particular freeways are in subdivisions. The majority of these tracts were developed after World War II.

Custom-built and Older Homes

Throughout the State, at the present time, there are only a limited number of custom-built and older homes located adjacent to freeways. In most of the cases of this type of residence investigated, it was found that the site selection was one of owner preference. For this reason, and the fact that the custom-built home is usually built and financed in accordance with the desires and financial ability of the owner, it is not subject to the resale activity usually found in the tract-built home.

It follows, in the case of the newly constructed custom-built home, that the owner has made a special effort in selecting his site, and where that site adjoins a freeway this fact adds to its desirability.

In the older home, where an adjacent freeway has been built, after many years of occupancy by the owner the emotional reaction is sometimes out of all proportion to the economic analysis. However, in both of these cases, because of the insufficient amount of sales data, it was decided not to include custom-built and older homes in this study.

Sources of Information

One of the initial problems in conducting this study was how to obtain the factual data required. Although personal calls upon the home owners required a great deal of time, we found it to be absolutely necessary in order to obtain all information needed, particularly confirmation of sales prices and statistics relating to payments for financing. As it was necessary to contact the residents of homes * adjoining the freeways, as well as buyers and sellers of * comparable homes, we used this opportunity to obtain the property owners' comments with respect to living in these localities.

In addition to the sales statistics confirmed by the property owners, the official records in the cities and counties were also used as a source of information relating to real estate transfers in the vicinity of the freeways. The tract developers and their sales representatives, as well as realtors actively engaged in selling residential properties along freeways, were called

* In this report, residences *adjoining* freeways refers to the residences that either back up to or face the freeway fence, and *comparable* refers to similar residences within the same subdivision located one block or more away from the freeway fence.

24

upon for additional information with respect to the problems involved in selling homes in these particular areas.

The excellent cooperation of the many people interviewed to provide confidential information, particularly in relation to financing the purchases or sales of homes, makes it possible to state that the analysis reached in this study is based upon the greatest amount of accurate data available. In appreciation of this help and as a protection to the individuals furnishing financial statistics regarding their homes, all references to selling price, down payment, monthly payments, and other figures are shown in this report by group figures or percentages.

BASIS OF COMPARISON

Previous economic studies conducted by the California Division of Highways for the purpose of ascertaining the economic effect of freeway construction upon adjacent property used a "before and after" basis of comparison which shows, by direct contrast, the degree of freeway influence. This procedure is particularly applicable for properties in the process of change or in established business continuing in the same manner as before such improvement.

This state-wide study consists of examples subjected to a considerable difference in economic conditions, as well as a wide variation in construction dates of the homes and adjoining freeways. The degree of freeway influence in this study cannot be measured before and after the date of freeway construction, but can only take place after the freeway is in existence. For this reason it was necessary to use a basis of comparison that would provide a uniform system of analyzing the market trend in areas having variations in the local economic condition.

A careful review of sales statistics in various locations throughout the State indicated that a comparison of resales among similar homes was the basis for making an accurate determination of freeway influence upon the market value for residential properties.

INITIAL SALES

Proceeding on this premise one of the first observations was that among the many residential tracts included in this state-wide study there was no evidence of builders putting a different "price tag" on a house because it was located alongside a freeway. Subdivision builders usually arrange for the financing of a group of homes or an entire tract as one unit. Discount rates on available money, or any penalties that may be inflicted by the lending institutions, are generally absorbed by the builder, thereby permitting equal financing for every house.

There were a few examples of price changes being made on finished houses in order to complete the sales within a tract. These price concessions were not confined to any specific area, but applied to the houses not selling as fast as the majority of homes within the subdivision.

The only variations found in the uniform financing of new houses occurred where the tract was constructed in stages, and separate financing was arranged as each unit or group of homes was built. A difference of several months could mean a substantial change in the availability of money and the type of financing obtainable for residential loans.

Rising construction costs made it necessary for many builders to increase the price of houses during the period of tract development. Numerous examples were found where the initial selling price of identical houses varied several hundred dollars between the first and last units constructed within a particular tract. These price increases caused by changing construction costs were applied to the houses without any regard to location within the subdivision.

A comparison of the initial prices in a tract with resales of the same houses on the current market has shown a continuous price increase. There has been a remarkable uniformity in the trend of price change among comparable houses within a tract; however, the degree of price change has varied between tracts adjacent to the same freeway. This is indicative that factors inherent in the entire tract, such as the livability and physical appeal of the houses in one tract as opposed to another, or the social and economic status of the residents, have a greater influence on the price trend than a freeway, school, or some other nonresidential use adjoining a small percentage of the homes in a particular subdivision.

RESALE PRICES

The sale price is indicative of market value only when the parties in the transaction act in accordance with the basic requirements that denote market value. In other words, the buyers and sellers must not be forced to make the purchase or sale; there must be an allowance of a reasonable time, and a full knowledge of the uses and capabilities of the property.

The use of sales information as the basis for determining the freeway influence upon residential property requires an investigation similar to the collection and processing of comparable data for an appraisal. Each resale of a residence adjoining one of the four freeways included in this study, as well as the resales of comparable properties, required a personal interview with the buyers or sellers for the purpose of verifying the sale price and all circumstances involved in the transaction in order to ascertain if the sales were indicative of market value.

Selection of Comparables

Resales throughout the State included many different types of residential property. The principal variations were: (1) the size of the lot; (2) location of improvements with respect to the freeway; (3) age, quality, type of construction, size and condition of the improvements. A minimum requirement of this study was that each resale of a residence adjoining a freeway had to be compared with a similar residence located one block or more away from the freeway.

Similarity meant that physical as well as social and economic conditions must be the same. It is understandable that it is impossible to find any two residential properties nearly the same after a period of elapsed time, even though the properties were practically identical at the time of initial sale. However, in the selection of comparable properties, the number of variations were kept to a minimum. In each example used, adjustments were made for the few differences which existed that would have an influence on the marketability of the residences.

The result of a selective procedure such as this requires the investigation of a large volume of resales in order to obtain sufficient volume of true comparables to insure accuracy.

In this study all of the resales in all of the subdivisions under consideration were reviewed. This required a complete analysis of 1,092 resales. Of this amount, 520 conformed to the established requirements of the study.

Time Element

In the assembly of sales data along the freeways in Northern and Southern California, we found that by using the three calendar years, 1954, 1955 and 1956 there would be an adequate time base to make a well-supported analysis of freeway influence upon residential property.

A greater period of time would have made available a larger number of sales, but as it was considered essential that the freeway be in existence at the time of each resale, we were unable to use sales earlier than 1954 along all four of the freeways covered by this study.

By allowing a reasonable time to elapse after the completion of the freeway construction, the adjoining residential resales were made by residents who had an opportunity to experience and determine for themselves the advantages or disadvantages of living alongside a freeway.

Resale Price Trend

All resales occurring in each of the three years covered by this study have been tabulated to compare the trend in market value of residences adjoining a freeway with comparable residences. The accompanying chart shows this trend by percentage differences beginning with resales in 1954 as a base.

RESALE PRICE TREND			
	1954	1955	1956
Freeway	Base	+1.69%	+4.39%
One block	Base	+3.35%	+4.71%
Two blocks or more	Base	+0.001%	+4.09%

The use of all sales statistics reveals that there were similar variances in the sales prices for residences adjoining freeways as well as among comparable examples.

The average resale price was 1.69 percent higher for residences adjoining the freeway in 1955 as compared with 1954. The general upswing in the real estate market was further shown in 1956 by the 4.39 percent increase for these residences adjoining freeways as compared with the gains made in 1955.

The increase in price trend for comparable residences located one block away from the freeway was substantially greater during 1955 than the gains enjoyed by residences adjoining freeways during the same year; however, the market gains during 1956 were only slightly higher than the increase enjoyed by the homes adjoining freeways during the same year.

Those residences located two or more blocks away from the freeway experienced only a fractional increase

An example of one of the many attractive back yards alongside the freeway fence. This homesite adjoining the Santa Ana Freeway has been enclosed with a concrete block wall to provide privacy for the outdoor living area.

26

in the market price trend during 1955, but showed a substantial gain during 1956. Even so, they remained below the gains made during the same year by residences adjoining, or one block from, the freeway.

According to our state-wide tabulation of the resales occurring within this three-year period, those residences located one block away from the freeway experienced the greatest single increase in price trend. The fact that residences located two or more blocks away from the freeway showed gains of a much lesser degree, precludes any assumption that location outweighs all other factors influencing the general market trend. The price trend of the residences located one block from the freeway more closely resemble the gains made by residences adjoining the freeway than the residences located some distance away from the freeway. The variations that exist between the individual groups of homes in this tabulation limit the comparison to a general indication of the market trend.

Trend for Similar Groups

To show more specifically the price trend of residences adjoining the freeway and comparable residences, a separate study has been made of an equal number of resales which occurred within the same tracts and within the same periods of time, making possible a direct comparison in price trends among residences having the greatest similarity. The number of resales used in making this analysis was limited; however, those used in this phase of the study were nearly equal in every respect with the exception of their location.

SIMILAR GROUP TREND			
	1954	1955	1956
Freeway	Base	+0.76%	+2.53%
One block or more	Base	+0.96%	+2.09%

In this limited, but directly comparable group of residences, the annual trend in resale prices from 1954 through 1956 was found to be slightly higher for the homes adjoining the freeway as compared with similar residences located one or more blocks away.

The purchasers in each of these resale transactions assumed the initial financing existing on the property. New financing was not required for any individual residence in this group.

Freeway vs. Away

This same group of sales can be analyzed in an entirely different manner; for example, the above tabulation is a progressive percentage comparison of the price increase in the resale of properties adjoining the freeway with other properties adjoining the freeway. In like manner, it also shows the price trend among comparable properties.

If, however, using this same group we compare the total sales of properties adjoining the freeway with the same number of comparable properties removed from the freeway, the following tabulation occurs:

FREEWAY vs. AWAY	
1954 Comparables	1.30% higher than properties adjoining freeways
1955 Comparables	1.50% higher than properties adjoining freeways
1956 Comparables	1.88% higher than properties adjoining freeways

From this chart it appears that comparable residences removed from the freeways have enjoyed a slight increase in value over the adjoining residences. Although this slight increase has become progressively larger during the three years covered by this study, we cannot assume the breach will grow wider each year, any more than it can be assumed that the annual price trends for residences adjoining the freeway, or comparables, as shown on the preceding charts, will continue to increase at the same rate.

On the basis of the statistics used in this study, there is a depreciation in market value of approximately 1 to 2 percent for residences adjoining freeways. This difference in marketability may be the influence of "opinion theories" upon the bargaining practices occurring between buyers and sellers during resale transactions.

FINANCING

The importance of financing in the analysis of residential sales is made obvious by the fact that over 98 percent of all transactions investigated throughout the State required the aid of some form of real estate loan. The widespread reliance upon financing will in many cases have as great an influence upon sale of residential property as the actual sale price. In fact, investigation revealed many instances where home buyers expressed a great

Residences on frontage road alongside San Bernardino Freeway. The chain-link fence through center of photo separates freeway traffic lanes from frontage road.

deal more concern about the down payment required to cover the equity of the seller, and the amount of monthly payments, than the total purchase price for the property. For these reasons, favorable or unfavorable financing could strongly influence the marketability of a residence.

As an integral part of our investigation of sales statistics we obtained, through personal interview and a review of the official records, the exact cash down payment required for each transaction; the total monthly payment made by the purchaser on the real estate loan covering the balance of the purchase price; and the monthly payment and amount of a second deed of trust or additional loans required for the sale of each specific property.

Average Payments

In this state-wide study the cash down payment for all residences adjoining freeways averaged 12.37 percent of the sale price. The average monthly payment on real estate loans on these homes was $78.20.

Financing on comparable homes located one block from the freeway averaged 14.91 percent of the total purchase price for down payments, with average monthly payments of $77.68.

Residences located two blocks from the freeway tier of homes required an average 15.61 percent down payment during the three years covered by this study, and monthly payments averaging $77.93.

The average down payment for residences located three or more blocks away from the freeway was 14.54 percent of the total sale price, and monthly payments averaged $81.13 for the purchasers of these homes.

A review of cash down payments for each resale transaction shows those residences adjoining freeways required a smaller average down payment than all other residences having real estate loans, regardless of distance from the freeway.

The average total monthly payment on real estate loans for the residences adjoining freeways was only slightly higher than the monthly payments made for residences one and two blocks away from the freeway which

required a substantially larger percentage of the purchase price in the form of a down payment. It is thereby expected that if the size of the down payment increases, there should be a commensurate decrease in the size of the monthly payments on houses having similar purchase prices.

Considering the fact that there was a variation in the range of purchase prices, we should not make the bold assumption that down payments will always be lower for houses adjoining freeways. However, from the statistics which we have, on the basis of loans which have been assumed, i.e., equal financing, there is definitely no evidence that purchasers of homes alongside freeways are required to use any more cash for the purchase of one of these homes, unless, of course, new financing may be required, which might alter the entire picture, depending upon policies of the lending institutions.

DISTANCE AND GRADE OF FREEWAY

The trend in market price of residences has been based upon all factors being relatively equal, with the exception of a location near or away from a freeway. In this analysis no distinction has been made among the residences adjoining freeways, with regard to variations in distance from the house to the fence or the traffic lanes of the freeway. The grade or elevation of the freeway near the residences is another factor to be considered in how a freeway can influence the desirability of residential property.

Having determined how a freeway location can influence the price trend among similar houses, we have further projected this study to find out what effect the distance or grade of a freeway has upon those resales.

All of the residences used in the comparison of market prices were located within tract developments. With very few exceptions the homes within each subdivision were the same distance to the fence and traffic lanes of the freeway. In those few instances where the distance was not uniform, or the grade of the freeway alongside a specific tract varied, the houses adjoining the freeway in that subdivision were segregated.

The many price variations that exist among a large number of individual sales made it necessary to adopt a system of group comparisons in order to show the influence of distance or grade of freeway upon resale prices. It was determined after considerable review that the resale price range in each tract or group of homes during the three years covered by this study provided a uniform basis of comparison that could accurately depict the relationship between sale price and the distance or grade of an adjacent freeway.

A comparison of all residential resales adjoining freeways in Northern and Southern California revealed that 26 percent of those transactions within the past three years attained a higher range of prices than was enjoyed by comparable homes during the same period of time. This group of residences adjoining freeways were in locations varying from 35 to 75 feet distant from the state highway right of way fence, and distances ranging from 74 to 200 feet to the freeway traffic lanes. These homes were at an equal grade with the adjoining freeway, or varied to differences as great as 16 feet below the level of the highway facility. Exceptions to this were 9 percent of the residences being situated 20 feet higher than the grade of the adjoining freeway.

DISTANCE AND GRADE OF FREEWAY				
Resale price range	Percent of residences	Distance house to fence	Distance house to freeway traffic	Relation of residential lot to grade of freeway
Higher	26%	35 to 75 ft.	74 to 200 ft.	91% equal or below freeway grade 9% above freeway grade
Lower	36%	25 to 83 ft.	72 to 105 ft.	80% equal or below freeway grade 20% above freeway grade
Same	38%	25 to 75 ft.	72 to 160 ft.	96% below freeway grade 4% above freeway grade

The price range of 36 percent of the transactions taking place adjoining freeways was lower than the price range for comparable homes. This group of residences were 25 to 83 feet from the right-of-way fence. In comparing this group of homes selling for less money adjoining a freeway with those which attained a higher price range alongside the freeways, we found many of these residences were approximately 10 feet closer to the right-of-way fence. Conversely, there were a few of these homes having a lower price range adjoining the freeway that were eight feet further from the highway right of way than similar homes selling for a higher price.

The residences selling at the lower price range adjoining the freeway were 72 to 105 feet from the freeway traffic lanes. Eighty percent of these homes varied in grade from "level" to 16 feet below the adjoining freeway. The remaining 20 percent of these residences were situated above the grade of the freeway from 8 to 20 feet.

The price range of the remaining 38 percent of the transactions alongside the freeways showed no difference from the price range of comparable homes. This group of residences were 25 to 75 feet from the right of way fence, and 72 to 160 feet from the freeway traffic lanes. These home sites varied from 1 to 20 feet below the level of the freeway, with the exception of 4 percent of this group of homes which were located two feet above the freeway grade.

Influence of Distance

A review of the price ranges in relation to the distances from house to fence, house to freeway, and grade of freeway, shows that homes a minimum of 35 feet from the freeway fence sold for more than similar houses located only 25 feet from the fence.

Although there were a number of houses with only 25-foot back yards selling for as much as comparable homes, we cannot overlook the fact that the majority of those houses selling for less money were also residences having 25-foot back yards.

The homes selling at a higher price range adjoining the freeway were the residences situated about the greatest distance from the freeway traffic lanes.

UPPER—New residences with back yards adjoining Eastshore Freeway. One property owner has enclosed back yard with solid wall fence, whereas others are using freeway chain-link right of way fence as rear property boundary enclosure. Note residence in extreme left portion of photo with solid wall-type fence only along the side property boundary. LOWER—Older residential tract along Eastshore Freeway with back yards adjoining right of way. Plantings along rear property boundary greatly improve appearance of homesites adjoining freeway.

The fact that houses showing a higher range of prices were a minimum of 10 feet further away from the freeway fence, and a slightly greater distance away from the freeway traffic lanes than all other homes, indicates that the opportunity for attaining a higher price for a residence near a freeway is definitely possible, but it is not as likely to occur if the residence has a very shallow rear yard or the traffic lanes are too close to the house.

There was no appreciable difference in the grade of the freeway alongside residences selling for a higher price range as compared with homes adjoining the freeway in the other price range groups.

The facts of the study show that a freeway grade up to 20 feet above the lot level is not singularly capable of depressing the resale price of residences. On the other hand, there were also examples of houses 20 feet above the grade of the freeway that sold for prices higher than comparable houses.

TRAFFIC

An additional factor to be considered as a freeway influence is the sound intensity levels resulting from traffic frequency.

The average daily traffic during 1956 on the four freeways in this study ranged from 50,000 to 83,000 vehicles.

The average percentage of trucks in state highway traffic is 30 percent.

As volume of traffic increases, truck percentage of the total would decrease, because the gain in traffic figures results primarily from additional passenger vehicles; for example, 23 percent of the Eastshore Freeway 50,000 average daily traffic total is truck traffic, whereas 11 percent of the Santa Ana Freeway 72,000 total is truck traffic.

The chief complaint with respect to noise from freeways is in regard to truck traffic. As the actual number of trucks on these four freeways is relatively constant, there was no likelihood that truck noises had any more of an adverse effect upon property values in one area than in another.

HOUSES ADJOINING FREEWAYS

The residential tracts included in this state-wide study comprised a total of 22,396 homes, with 1,697 or 7.58 percent of these residences built alongside a freeway. All residences adjoining the four freeways in this report have their back yards nearest the freeway fence with the exception of a relatively small number of homes along the Santa Ana Freeway in tracts designed with subdivision streets separating the residences from the freeway.

The subdivision plan whereby a row of homes were constructed to have their back yards next to the right-of-way fence provided the most efficient utilization of land from the standpoint of creating the largest number of lots per acre, and undoubtedly was the reason for that arrangement being the most prevalent.

In making a comparison of the initial and resale prices of homes with back yards adjoining the right-of-way fence, and those residences separated from the freeway by a subdivision street, there was no difference with respect to trend in the selling price or problems involved in making a sale.

In some areas the shape of the subdivision land may have made it more desirable to provide for a street along the freeway fence; however, in many cases it was the general feeling that where streets were placed alongside the right-of-way line, it was done to provide a buffer distance from the freeway traffic. The lack of difference in marketability of these homes

as compared with residences having back yards adjoining the freeway property shows this type of tract design was not warranted for that specific purpose.

There were examples of a few subdivisions featuring deeper lots alongside the freeway as compared with other lots in the same tract. In some instances this was attributable to a small surplus land area remaining after the tract development. The subdivider added the small additional area to the tier of lots adjoining the freeway as an added sales incentive to home buyers. In other cases the larger lots adjoining the freeway were the result of extra area remaining in the tract caused by the freeway not being located at right angles with the subdivision streets.

In tract developments where homes were constructed, differing in price and size, it was generally the practice to equally distribute these homes throughout the tract, irrespective of location, except in those cases where an entire unit of larger or higher priced homes was constructed at a later date, featuring a variation from the original tract construction.

Fences

The State Division of Highways places a chain-link type fence along the outside limits of the freeway right of way through urban areas. This fence often serves a dual purpose in being used as the rear property fence for residences adjoining freeways. It was surprising to find many back yards adjoining freeways where the chain-link fence was being utilized as the rear property fence, and a solid wall-type fence had been used along the side property lines.

In some areas the F. H. A. or local governing authorities require a screen separating homesites from any nonresidential use, such as a freeway, schoolyard, or canal. In these cases the home builders have been required to construct a solid fence of wood or cement along the rear property boundary and parallel with the state right-of-way fence. Some home builders have voluntarily constructed a solid wall-type fence around the perimeter of a tract. These fences are usually considered a special feature by the

home buyers. There was a surprisingly large number of home owners who stated that a solid wall fence along the rear property boundary was the principal reason that particular home was purchased in preference to a residence away from the freeway or tract perimeters.

Exterior Appearance

During the personal interviews and investigation of sales statistics there was an opportunity to observe the exterior appearance of the residences, and particularly the yard area nearest the freeway. There were a similar number of homesites adjoining freeways improved with outdoor living facilities, such as patios, barbecues, etc., as were found among a comparable number of homes located away from the freeway. In both locations there were also examples of lack of care or use of the yard area. The home owner's initiative or efforts in the development and use of the yard area was not influenced by location of the residence adjoining a freeway.

There was no noticeable difference in the street appearance of homes adjacent to the freeway as compared with the front appearance of similar homesites within the same residential tract.

HOUSES vs. FREEWAY CONSTRUCTION

Along the four freeways included in this study, 94.58 percent of the residences were under construction or finished before the final completion date of the adjoining freeways. This group includes a number of residences built in anticipation of a freeway far in advance of the actual construction date. For example, 10.25 percent of the homes alongside freeways were completed 12 years prior to completion of the adjoining freeway; 4.12 percent of the homes were completed nine years prior to freeway construction, and 2.95 percent of these residences were finished eight years before the adjoining freeways.

Residences built after completion of the adjoining freeways represented 5.42 percent of the total number of homes alongside freeways in this study.

Regardless of the time element, all residential tracts in the vicinity of the freeways were built with the knowledge of a proposed new highway facility through the local area. Although the builders and realtors were aware of the future highway plans, our investigation revealed there were a number of home buyers who apparently purchased residences without giving any consideration to the vacant strip of land set aside through a newly developed area for the future construction of a new freeway. Despite the fact that some property owners may have purchased their homes without the full realization of how the adjoining area was to be developed, we did not find any marked difference in their attitude toward the freeway after it was completed as compared with the home owners who purchased during and after the construction of the freeway.

RESIDENTS' COMMENTS

The investigation made to obtain the factual data required for making this study afforded the opportunity to also get the opinion of property owners in regard to living alongside a freeway. Opinions are an indication of public reaction; however, like all polls they are an expression of the individual's attitude at the time of the interview, rather than the result of his considered thought and analysis of homesite selection as reflected through a sales transaction. The comments from residents living alongside freeways are included as a part of this report for informational purposes.

Reason for buying house alongside freeway
32.64% Liked house.
38.17% Freeway not considered; immaterial.
10.00% Convenience of freeway transportation.
19.19% Miscellaneous reasons.

Had you preferred or tried to buy in this subdivision away from the freeway?
56.34% No.
19.28% Yes.
24.38% Freeway of no consequence.

Type of street formerly lived
67.87% Residential street, quiet.
19.18% Residential street, heavy traffic.
12.95% Rural, Commercial, Freeway.

Would you buy alongside a freeway again?
46.11% No.
39.90% Yes.
13.99% Undecided.

Any problem in financing purchase or sale?
96.90% No.
3.10% Yes.

Any fear of theft or danger living near freeway?
85.52% None.
7.77% Fear vehicles come through fence.
6.71% Prowlers, fumes, vibration.

Noise.
41.80% No bother.
32.84% Slight objection.
15.92% Objectionable and noisy.
9.44% Trucks principal objection.

General Remarks
47.97% Freeway location no better or worse than other areas.
22.45% Prefer freeway location.
20.40% Do not like freeway location.
9.18% Freeway a transportation benefit.

CONCLUSION

The purpose of this state-wide factual study has been to determine how the market value of residential property is influenced by freeway construction. Through the collection and analysis of sales data, covering a three-year period of time, supported by a comprehensive study of the principal factors influencing the marketability of residential property along freeways, we have reached the following conclusions:

(1) The annual trend in resale prices among subdivision homes adjoining freeways, follows a pattern consistent with the price trend of comparable homes. This comparison was based upon residences being equal in every respect possible with the exception of location.

(2) Resales averaged from 1 to 2 percent less for residences adjoining freeways, as compared with similar homes one block or more away. This indicates there is a nominal depression in market value caused by close proximity to a freeway.

This slight difference occurring among resales can be attributed to the widespread spread doubt, resulting from opinions that freeways have an adverse effect upon the market value of residential property. These opinions can influence the bargaining procedure that usually takes place between buyers and sellers during resale transactions. This procedure normally does not occur during the initial sale of subdivision homes where there is uniformity of prices.

(3) "Financing" has become so important in the marketing of residential property that it is singularly capable of influencing the market value. Where equal financing is available, the freeway has

no influence upon the marketability of residential property; however, where individual refinancing of a home is subjected to prejudicial influence by a lending institution, it follows that it will have a direct influence upon the marketability of that property.

(4) Resale statistics reveal that residences adjoining a freeway can attain a higher price range than comparable residences; however, this occurred only among those residences located the greatest distance from the right of way fence and freeway traffic.

The majority of homesites in this state-wide study were located below the grade of the adjoining freeways, and the trend in market value of these residences was not adversely affected by extreme differences in the height of the freeway embankment.

(5) At the present time, nearly all residences adjoining California freeways are within tract developments. There is ample evidence that pride of home ownership is as strong among residents living alongside freeways as exists among the owners of comparable homes.

The general concept that people create value has been reaffirmed in this residential study. The buyers and sellers participating freely, and with full knowledge of the current real estate market, have expressed through actual transactions, acceptance of their freeway alongside their homesites, with only a slight depreciation in marketability for the house adjoining the freeway.

CALIFORNIA LEADS NATION

California leads all other states in passenger car and motor truck registrations with 5,641,408 passenger cars and 853,910 trucks, for a total of 6,-495,318 vehicles, reports the National Automobile Club.

New York, with 4,131,794 cars and a total motor vehicle tally of 4,819,-000, ranks second in passenger car and total vehicle registrations. Texas, with some 834,000 trucks plying its streets and highways, has the second highest motor truck total.

Rounding out the top 10 in total registrations are: Texas, 3,959,000; Pennsylvania, 3,890,000; Ohio, 3,628,-000; Illinois, 3,419,000; Michigan, 3,197,000; New Jersey, 2,131,000; Indiana, 1,828,000, and Florida, 1,756,-000.

San Diego Freeway
Governor Opens New Section

O<small>N SEPTEMBER</small> 20, 1954, Governor Goodwin J. Knight was the guest of honor for the ground-breaking ceremony for the San Diego Freeway in the West Los Angeles area. He climbed aboard a bulldozer with State Highway Commissioner Robert E. McClure for the first breaking of ground at the site of the Sunset Boulevard Bridge over the San Diego Freeway. At the close of the program Governor Knight was heard to remark, "If you good people will be kind enough to invite me I would be most happy to be present, if I possibly can, to help you celebrate the completion of this important freeway section in the West Los Angeles area." The invitation was forthcoming and true to his promise, Governor Knight did participate on March 29, 1957, in the ceremonies at the completion and opening to public traffic of the two-mile section of the San Diego Freeway from Ohio Street to Casiano Road.

Cost $8,000,000

Including right of way costs this section of freeway represents a total investment of $8,000,000. The construction work on this section of the San Diego Freeway was carried out under three State Division of Highways contracts. The first contract, the one for which Governor Knight first broke the ground, was awarded on September 19, 1954, by Director of Public Works Frank B. Durkee to George W. Peterson and Jack W. Baker for the construction of four bridges with approaches, ramps, and frontage roads. The main structure was the bridge to carry Sunset Boulevard over existing Sepulveda Boulevard and the new San Diego Freeway. Another bridge structure included in this contract was to carry Ovada Place under San Diego Freeway. The other two bridges were to provide for ramp connections with Sunset Boulevard. This contract carried an allotment of $816,800, and it was completed February 15, 1956.

The second contract on this section of the San Diego Freeway was awarded on March 8, 1955, to the Thompson Construction Company of Inglewood for the unit between Waterford Street and Casiano Road. This contract has an allotment of $1,470,600.

The third contract, also with the Thompson Construction Company, was awarded on January 30, 1956, and it has an allotment of $2,721,900. The contractors have carried out their operations in an efficient and expeditious manner, handling the two adjoining contracts for the most part as a single project and in this way they are completing the second contract two months ahead of schedule. Howard F. Meinke and George E. Dickey have been the District VII resident engineers and C. J. Woodbridge and Fred H. Buck were resident engineers for the Bridge Department.

Cooperative Planning

The San Diego Freeway has been a truly cooperative project in every sense of the word. The first plan work on the San Diego Freeway was started by the Engineering Bureau Department of Public Works of the City of Los Angeles under City Engineer Lloyd C. Aldrich in 1939 when it was known as the "Sepulveda Parkway." It was in this year of 1939 that the State Division of Highways first entered into a contract with the City of Los Angeles whereby the State would reimburse the city for preliminary engineering work done by the city in the planning of this freeway. For several years thereafter the Los Angeles City Engineer's Office conducted surveys and plan preparation for portions of the details for this freeway from Venice Boulevard in the West Los Angeles area to San Fernando Road in the San Fernando Valley.

During recent years the State Division of Highways completed plans for the construction contracts. During this latter period, however, the

Los Angeles City Engineer's Office under Lloyd Aldrich and his successor Lyall A. Pardee has continued to supply designs for reconstruction of city streets, sanitary sewers and storm drains as has been made necessary in establishment of the freeway. Closely identified with the preliminary engineering carried out by District VII were E. T. Telford, George Langsner, J. E. Eckhardt, and Ralph V. Chase.

The Veterans Administration Center, within which the southerly half of this project lies, is in Los Angeles County area, and Wilshire Boulevard and other lesser important roads through the veterans' facility are a responsibility of the Los Angeles County Road Department. County Road Commissioner Sam R. Kennedy and his staff cooperated in every way possible in connection with redesign and reconstruction of roads under their jurisdiction so that this freeway project could go forward as expeditiously as possible.

The San Diego Freeway is on the U. S. Interstate Highway System and previously was a federal aid primary route. Throughout planning and design of this project E. C. Brown, District Engineer for the U. S. Bureau of Public Roads, and his field assistant Henry A. Alderton maintained close and helpful liaison with members of the State Division of Highways staff.

Right-of-Way Negotiations

In the improvement of the San Diego Freeway through the Veterans Administration Center, it was necessary to acquire property in the name of the County of Los Angeles for the realignment of Wilshire Boulevard and for the widening of Federal Avenue, the reconstruction of which has been carried out by the State Division of Highways. The necessary grants of property from the Federal Government were secured under the provisions of Section 17 of the Federal Highway Act of November 9, 1921, as amended, 42 Statutes 216.

The Federal Government transferred a total of 54.2 acres of which 46.6 acres was to the State of California for the San Diego Freeway, and 7.6 acres was to County of Los Angeles for the improvement of Wilshire Boulevard and Federal Avenue. The State and county received from the Federal Government for this project land worth well in excess of $2,000,000. The State, in return, has carried out considerable construction and relocation work for the benefit of the veterans' facility. The grant to the County of Los Angeles provided for the vacation of San Vicente Boulevard by the County of Los Angeles through the Veterans Administration Center whereby 6.6 acres would be added to the usable area of the veterans' facility.

Negotiations for the necessary right of way through this federal property were carried on at the local level through Colonel R. A. Bringham, Manager of the Veterans Administration Center, and his engineer, E. C. McCarty. The State of California and County of Los Angeles owe a great debt of gratitude to these gentlemen for their co-operation and help in getting this state highway project under construction at the earliest possible moment.

The total cost for right-of-way acquisition and the clearing of right of way from Ohio Street to Casiano Road has been close to $3,000,000.

This was the cost for acquiring privately held properties outside the West Los Angeles Veterans Administration Center.

Traffic Service

Included within this section of the San Diego Freeway in the West Los Angeles area are crossings with Wilshire Boulevard and Sunset Boulevard, two of the most important traffic arterials in the West Los Angeles area. The average daily traffic count on Sunset Boulevard is now approximately 30,000, and the average daily traffic on Wilshire Boulevard is about 40,000. All of these highway arterial crossings, traffic interchange roadways have been designed and constructed so that all the necessary

and Public Works

Looking south at completed section of San Diego Freeway from Sunset Boulevard overcrossing

traffic movements will be provided for.

Between Wilshire Boulevard and Sunset Boulevard on existing Sepulveda Boulevard the average daily traffic is now approximately 25,000 vehicles. With the opening of the San Diego Freeway all except the small percentage of this traffic that is local in nature will traverse the freeway instead of utilizing existing Sepulveda Boulevard.

It is estimated that when the San Diego Freeway has been completed throughout its entire length, the average daily traffic will rise to about 100,000 vehicles per day on the two-mile unit now being opened to public traffic. It was on this basis that the former designs for making the San Diego Freeway a six-lane width were changed to provide the eight-lane width that has been constructed.

Proposed Landscaping

On February 19, 1957, the California Highway Commission passed a resolution allocating $109,000 for landscaping and erosion control on the San Diego Freeway between Waterford Street and Moraga Drive.

In general, the planting will consist of a screen of trees and shrubs on the fill slopes. A great deal of thought was given to the selection of the plant material by H. Dana Bowers of the Sacramento headquarters staff in order to create a landscaped effect that would be in keeping with the attractive residential development in the neighborhood.

The treatment of the median will consist of a solid screen of red oleanders, which have proved to be of great value to the motorists in eliminating oncoming headlight glare.

The reinforced concrete retaining wall fronting the Westwood Village Church will be planted with Boston ivy to improve appearance and to absorb reverberation of traffic noises. Shrubs will also be planted at the base of the retaining wall along this area. It is anticipated that this landscaping project will be let to contract early this summer. Plans are now in the course of preparation for continuing landscaping installations southerly from Waterford Street to Ohio Street.

Outlook for Future

Plans are progressing satisfactorily for the construction of a continuation for the San Diego Freeway from Ohio Street southerly to Venice Boulevard, a length of 3.5 miles. The California Highway Commission on October 19, 1956, in adopting the budget for the 1957-58 Fiscal Year, allocated $6,025,000 for this southerly extension of the San Diego Freeway. With right of way acquisition and clearing substantially completed, it is anticipated that this important unit of construction will be under way this summer. Subsequent units of construction on the San Diego Freeway in the Los Angeles metropolitan area will be re-

quired to await future allocations of construction funds by the California Highway Commission.

The San Diego Freeway has its northerly terminus at junction with US 99 near San Fernando, extending southerly through the West Los Angeles area, easterly through Long Beach, southeasterly into Orange County where it joins the Santa Ana Freeway near El Toro, and then continues as US 101 southeasterly to the City of San Diego, its southerly terminus.

The San Diego Freeway is on the United States network of interstate highways that is scheduled for completion within the next 13-year period. It is anticipated that this freeway will be completed throughout its entire length within this period.

Modern Toll Road Projects in Japan

There are some 1,500,000 motor vehicles today in Japan as a result of a 10-fold increase since the war. The length of paved highway, however, is only 9,000 kilometers or 5.8 percent of main highways in Japan. Because of the grade crossings and the mixed traffic on public roads, motor-vehicle traffic cannot travel constantly at high speed. To eliminate such inconvenience and to promote the development of Japanese economy, a system of express highways has been planned. As a first step the Japan Highway Public-Corporation has decided to construct a toll express-highway connecting the six major cities between Tokyo and Kobe, which is regarded to have the largest traffic volume in Japan, and actual construction work is to be started on the route between Nagoya and Kobe before long. Furthermore, the Japan Highway Public-Corporation is responsible for construction and administration of many other useful roads, tunnels, bridges, and ferry services as toll road.

GAS TAX

The average motorist pays $34 a year in state gasoline taxes, according to the California State Automobile Association.

REGIONAL CONFERENCE ON HIGHWAY ENGINEERING PRODUCTIVITY

Nearly 500 highway engineers from more than 30 states took part in an intensive three-day conference at the Biltmore Hotel in Los Angeles, March 5-7, 1957, for the purpose of exchanging ideas and exploring new developments in highway engineering to speed up the preparation of plans and highway construction and to conserve engineering manpower.

The occasion was the Western Regional Conference on Increasing Highway Engineering Productivity. It was the fourth conference of its type held in co-operation with the U. S. Bureau of Public Roads and the American Association of State Highway Officials, previous regional conferences having been held east of the Mississippi.

Also co-sponsoring the Los Angeles conference were the Institute of Transportation and Traffic Engineer-

ing and University Extension, University of California; the California Division of Highways; and the Western Association of State Highway Officials.

Message From McCoy

The keynote for the conference was expressed in the welcoming message from G. T. McCoy, State Highway Engineer of California. McCoy noted:

"The impact of the federal highway program has caused us to intensify our search for effective short cuts to reduce the time and engineering manpower needed for the development of plans and the construction of highways."

He added, 'I would like to remind you that although we are discussing this subject in terms of conserving engineering manpower, our real goal is,

of course, the earliest possible construction of the modern highways the Nation wants and needs."

The ultimate purpose of the conference was further emphasized by Harmer E. Davis, Director of the I. T. T. E., in his summary comments which concluded the event:

· "We should not forget that our end-product is highway transportation service and that a variety of factors affect how rapidly and effectively this transportation service can be stepped up to meet the needs of our Nation and to support its economy.

"It so happens that we are here concentrating on a factor that many people thought would be a bottleneck in the production of new highway plans. I mention this to reassure those who might fear that what has developed

View of the Galeria Room in the Biltmore Hotel, Los Angeles, during the Western Regional Conference on Increasing Highway Engineering Productivity. Standing at the rostrum is H. A. Radzikowski, Chief of the Maintenance Branch of the U. S. Bureau of Public Roads. (Photo courtesy Los Angeles Examiner.)

and Public Works 35

here constitutes a preoccupation with gadgetry and a loss of perspective on final objectives. Actually, what we are witnessing is a taking advantage of modern technology to eliminate a bottleneck, and to bring our whole procedure in line with the demands that must be met."

Panel Discussions

More than 50 panelists presented technical papers and statements during the three full days of the conference. There were no section meetings; all the sessions were general, to insure the fullest possible interchange of ideas among the various specialists in different phases of highway engineering. The panel members discussed the experience of various state highway departments, other agencies and engineering organizations in developing and using different methods of conserving engineering time and manpower. The California Division of Highways was represented on more than two-thirds of the panels.

After a statement of the objectives of the conference by H. A. Radzikowski, Chief of Maintenance Branch, U. S. Bureau of Public Roads, the conference spent the entire first day on the use of electronic computers in various aspects of highway work.

Electronic Computers

Several hours of discussion were devoted to the application of electronic computers to highway location and design, right of way and earthwork computations, bridge design and geometrics, traffic studies, cost analysis and other phases of highway engineering. For the most part, these discussions consisted of a series of reports from different states and organizations and the B. P. R. on their use of electronic data processing machines for a variety of engineering purposes.

On the second day the initial emphasis was on photogrammetry and other improved methods of obtaining and using survey data. An opening session on this subject was followed by a discussion of possibilities still largely in the experimental stage, but rapidly approaching practical application—the "marriage" of electronic computation and photogrammetry. The objective in this respect is the direct production of cross section and mass diagram drawings as well as quantitative information from photogrammetric sources by means of electronic computation.

The first afternoon session which followed was concerned with the establishment of a program library among the various agencies and organizations using electronic computations for highway purposes. This topic was also the subject of a two-hour evening discussion the same day.

Sharing Organization

At this evening meeting it was decided that a sharing organization would be set up in which the manufacturers of each type of equipment would furnish on request a copy of the developed programs. These programs would be available to all agencies and concerns which are willing to contribute their own programs to the sharing organization.

Another aspect of electronics, its use in the communications field, was was the subject of another panel discussion. This session covered the use of radio in highway maintenance and other operations, the expanding use of electronic controls in integrated traffic signal systems and the possibilities of traffic signs that can be revised by remote control to alert motorists to changing highway conditions.

On the final day the conferees turned their attention away from the expanding world of new devices and machines to the continuing effort to increase engineering productivity by improving established techniques and methods. Eight panelists (two from the California Division of Highways) reported on the successful steps taken by their organizations to conserve engineering time and manpower by means of standardization of bridge design details, plan simplification, photographic reproduction of plans, etc.

Short Cuts in Construction

The two concluding panels were devoted to the construction equipment and contracting industries. Representatives of the equipment manufacturing industry and of construction firms submitted to the audience of highway engineers numerous ideas for short cuts in construction proced-ures aimed toward getting the roads built faster and more economically, with more efficient use of available engineering personnel.

In his concluding summary, Mr. Davis reviewed the status, as reported by the panelists, of current progress in the fields of aerial surveys and photogrammetry; traverse, earthwork and structures; computations; traffic controls; and traffic studies.

In the latter connection he predicted that the next five years would see development of a "workable traffic flow theory," made possible by the analytic study of traffic flow by high-speed computers.

Davis also pointed out that the reports at the western conference constituted a factual record of accomplishment that was "amazing."

"A year ago, at a meeting similar to this in Chicago," he said, "most people were discussing what they intended to do in utilizing these new methods and techniques. Here we have laid before us incontrovertible testimony of a fact accomplished.

Program Will Not Lag

"We can now say, with confidence, that the great highway development program, on the beginning stages of which we are now engaged, will not lag because plans, designs and estimates cannot be gotten out. These accomplishments should stand as concrete evidence to Congress that the highway engineering agencies have the necessary tools sharpened, and the highway program should go forward as planned."

With regard to the implications for the engineer in the application of high-speed computers and other new tools, Davis observed:

"You might say that we are now in a position to do for the drudgery of highway engineering what power equipment has done for the hand labor of highway construction. As one speaker remarked, these technological improvements 'can make the engineer the master of his tools rather than the slave of his calculations.' * * * Here is a renaissance in engineering."

One aspect of the "mastery of the new tools" cited by Davis was in the matter of highway location. Referring to a paper presented at the conference by T. F. Morf of the Illinois State Highway Department, Davis said:

Important Factors

'In earlier days, a balanced gradeline was the goal. The line or location was selected by the skill of the locating engineer. Then other requirements began to take an important place, such as drainage. More recently, traffic requirements and land values and uses have become important criteria. But the overwhelming magnitude of the computations has precluded the possibility of real location comparisons, in which construction economy, operational economy and community economy could be appropriately expressed at one and the same time.

"Now the possibility of location comparisons that give a quantitative basis for defensible decisions is almost within grasp. An intriguing possibility is the development of 'programs' for location itself. We have in prospect a brand of real design that we formerly considered too idealized to do anything about, except put it into the preface of an academic textbook."

The same implication, he added, is involved in the adaptation of electronic computer methods to structural design:

"We have long leaned toward statically determinate structures, partly because of uncertainties in the analysis of statically indeterminate behavior, and partly because of the great length of calculations for statically indeterminate structures. Now we have in prospect the possibility of design comparisons which can lead to true economies."

Deputy State Highway Engineer C. E. Waite of California served as general chairman for the conference.

Some 50 of the highway engineers from other states remained in Los Angeles an extra day to take a tour of the Los Angeles area freeways completed and under construction. The tours were arranged and guided by members of the District VII staff of the Division of Highways.

Coincident with the three-day conference, the Board of Directors of the American Road Builders Association held a business meeting at the Statler

and Public Works

Out of the Mail Bag

FROM MILAN

MILANO, 15 FEBBRAIO 1957

COMUNE DI MILANO
Ufficio Tecnico
L'Ingegnere Ispettore

MR. K. C. ADAMS, *Editor*

I thank you very much for *California Highways and Public Works.* As I have written to you, I am an inspector of the roads and the traffic in Milan.

I am also a designer of the new Italian turnpike between Genoa and Milan. I have therefore great interest in public works generally.

But we think that California is the country where the study and the application of these problems and of road techniques are more advanced. We look especially to your freeways, conceived not as single and separated arteries, but as a rational system, able to serve an entire region.

Your very fine magazine, which tells us so much about your solutions, is extremely useful to us.

Yours truly,

DR. ING. ALDO DI RENZO
Ispettore dell'Ufficio Tecnico
Municipale
Via Larga 12—Milano (Italia)

MOTOR VEHICLES IN U. S.

There are 54,300,000 passenger cars and 10,975,000 trucks and busses in use in the United States today. The National Automobile Club points out that that makes a grand total of 65,-275,000 motor vehicles, a 90 percent increase in 10 years.

Hotel in Los Angeles. It was the first A. R. B. A. board meeting ever held on the Pacific Coast.

Throughout the conference exhibits and demonstrations of equipment were conducted by manufacturers of computing machines and other concerns.

TOLL HIGHWAYS IN JAPAN

JAPAN HIGHWAY PUBLIC CORPORATION
1-1 Tamura-cho, Shiba,
Minato-ku Tokyo, Japan

MR. KENNETH C. ADAMS, *Editor*

DEAR SIR: I would like to express my cordial gratitude for the kind and efficient advices and many kinds of useful information which your Division of Highways gave me on my visit to your Los Angeles and San Francisco district offices in November, 1956.

I do hope that your division will be kind enough to give us continuing aid hereafter, which, I believe, will be of great help to our corporation and will provide us with valuable guidance to construct and administer the toll roads in this Country.

With my best regards, I remain,

Yours very truly,

KENICHI FUJIMORI
Chief of Plan and Coordination
Section

WE LIKE THEM, TOO

COLUMBIA, SOUTH CAROLINA

*California State Highway
Commission*

DEAR SIRS: My wife and I have just returned from a two months' tour of the western United States, and after spending about half of that time in your State I would like to tell you what a privilege it was to travel on such wonderful highways.

You are to be commended on having the best network of highways, boulevards, and freeways of all the 40 states in which we have traveled. It did not make any difference where we went, as long as we were in California, we knew we would have a good road or boulevard.

Yours very truly,

J. C. DREHER

37

California Bridges

Construction Costs Continue to Rise

By H. K. MAUZY, Senior Bridge Engineer, and
W. J. YUSAVAGE, Assistant Research Technician

This article is the fifth of an annual series dealing with California bridge construction costs. The most recent article appeared in the March-April, 1956, issue.
For total California highway construction costs the reader is referred to a series of articles entitled, "Cost Index" by R. H. Wilson, H. C. McCarthy, and L. B. Reynolds. These articles appear regularly in California Highways and Public Works.

THE MODERATE rise in bridge construction costs which began in the second quarter of 1955 continued into 1956 and, during the second quarter, broke sharply upward to an unprecedented high of 284. The levels of the third and fourth quarters with readings of 260 and 273 confirmed the fact that a major cost break-through had occurred and that, consequently, the general level of costs can be expected to run at this higher level into the calendar year 1957.

In terms of average annual index values, the cost level has been on the rise for the past three years as is indicated by the values of 219, 228, and 265 for the calendar years 1954, 1955, and 1956 respectively. The values represent a 21 percent cost increase between the two years 1954-56 and a 15 percent cost increase between the years 1955-56.

The level of costs for successive periods is presented graphically in the accompanying chart which summarizes the course of California bridge construction costs since 1933.

Value and Volume of Bridge Construction

Table I is a tabulation of statistics relating to the value and volume of the California Bridge Department construction program. The current value is shown in column VI where the

TABLE 1
INDEXES RELATING TO CALIFORNIA BRIDGE CONSTRUCTION AND PERIODIC DOLLAR VALUES OF LOW BIDS ON CALIFORNIA BRIDGE CONSTRUCTION

I Year	II Quarter	III Index of the cost of California bridge construction (1939-1940—100)	IV Index of the value of California bridge construction (1939-1940—100)	V Index of the volume of California bridge construction (1939-1940—100)	VI Dollar value of low bids on California bridge construction (in millions of dollars)
1934		94	*60	*64	3.1
1935		88	*138	*187	7.1
1936		95	*72	*73	3.7
1937		114	*60	*83	3.1
1938		99	*78	*79	4.0
1939		101	*99	*98	5.1
1940		99	*101	*102	5.2
1941		122	*78	*64	4.0
1942		188	*80	*50	4.1
1943		165	*16	*9	.8
1944		153	*29	*19	1.5
1945		167	*109	*65	5.6
1946		182	*247	*133	12.7
1947		215	*443	*202	22.8
1948		229	*307	*134	15.8
1949		201	*233	*117	12.0
1950		202	*262	*129	13.5
1951	1st	243	528	217	6.8
1951	2d	250	948	379	12.2
1951	3d	*245 256	*617 598	*247 234	31.5 7.7
1951	4th	253	396	157	5.1
1952	1st	239	396	166	5.1
1952	2d	236	1,017	431	13.1
1952	3d	*235 239	*561 682	*237 273	26.9 8.4
1952	4th	223	179	80	2.3
1953	1st	243	140	58	1.8
1953	2d	224	707	315	9.1
1953	3d	*229 235	*522 893	*227 387	26.9 11.5
1953	4th	235	350	149	4.5
1954	1st	221	691	313	8.9
1954	2d	217	1,196	551	18.4
1954	3d	*219 220	*870 1,002	*399 455	44.8 12.9
1954	4th	213	890	277	7.6
1955	1st	217	1,039	477	13.3
1955	2d	237	800	311	6.4
1955	3d	*225 228	*930 1,047	*406 461	47.9 13.4
1955	4th	237	1,148	484	14.7
1956	1st	245	833	715	25.1
1956	2d	284	1,063	332	7.8
1956	3d	*265 260	*1,117 604	*422 381	57.5 13.9
1956	4th	273	1,952	213	10.7

* Average annual information.

figures represent the current dollar value of low bids for the various periods since 1934. Columns IV and V give the value and volume of bridge construction in the form of indexes, utilizing the value of base period 1939-40 as the reference point of 100.

The index of value is computed by relating the value of any quarter to the average quarterly value ($5.1 + 5.2 million/8=$1,287,500) of the eight quarters of 1939-40. Thus the value index for the fourth quarter of 1954 is $7,600,000/$1,287,500 or 590.

The volume of bridge construction is defined as the relative physical quantity of bridge construction put in place during a given period. It is an inverse function of the cost index since a higher level of costs reduces the relative value of money and so reduces the relative volume of construction while a lower level of costs increases the relative volume of construction.

The index of volume is computed in exactly the same way as is the index of value after each of the quarterly dollar values has been modified by the cost index values of the respective quarters. Thus the adjusted value for the fourth quarter of 1954 is $7,600,-000/213 (cost index) $3,568,000. This new value is then related to the average quarterly value of the eight base quarter values of 1939-40, as $3,568,-000/$1,287,500 or a volume index of 277, The 277 indicates that the actual physical bridge construction activity during the fourth quarter of 1954 was 277 percent greater than that which occurred during 1940.

Bridge Building Increases

The value and volume indexes show the marked increase in bridge construction which has accompanied the augmentation of state highway budgets during recent years. As a result of legislation which substantially increased highway user tax revenues during 1953 and the consequent continued development of full freeways with their requisite separation structures, expenditures during the past year for bridge construction rose to nearly $58,000,000 or to approximately 1,117 percent of the average annual rate of expenditure during the base period 1939-40.

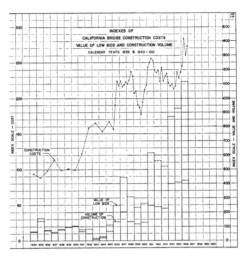

The data do not as yet reflect the effect of the currently operative U. S. Highway Program upon California's bridge program. This program will have its initial effect upon bridge construction during 1957 and will then continue in the subsequent years. The budget for the Fiscal Year 1957-58 proposes an increase of approximately 37 percent over that of Fiscal Year 1956-57, or an increase of about $20,-000,000. This increase will, of course, have a decided impact on the demand for construction materials and also upon the number of bridges let to contract during 1957.

General Trends

Average unit prices for the various items of construction as compiled for each quarter show a general upward trend for all quarters of 1956. Average annual prices went up generally within the range of 15-18 percent. The prices for three items—structure excavation, plate girders, and driving piles—rose

30-34 percent above the average annual prices of 1955.

The increase in unit costs of concrete products is generally attributed to increased labor, equipment, and transportation costs. Steel products, on the other hand, are higher because of a combination of increased costs and rather severely limited available supplies. This is especially true with respect to steel plates for which there has been and still is a heavy demand from the heavy construction industry and the greatly expanded programs for the construction of oil tankers and pipe lines. Current information assumes that plates will continue in short supply for an indefinite period.

Outlook

The current upward trend of construction costs reflects the prevailing trends of higher costs for all elements involved in construction, viz., labor, materials, equipment rental, and money. In addition to the generally

... Continued on page 45

and Public Works

39

Now Read This

Carquinez Bridge Project Tests
Ingenuity of Engineers

By LEONARD C. HOLLISTER, Projects Engineer, Carquinez *

THE SUBSTRUCTURE work for the main bridge across Carquinez Strait involves the construction of an anchorage abutment set in a shale and sandstone cliff at the north end of the bridge to support the 500-foot anchor arm of the truss span, three caisson piers founded on bedrock about 132 feet below water line, one cofferdam type pier supported on 240 80-ton steel bearing piles, and an anchorage pier 125 feet high located at the south end of the bridge. This foundation work is under contract to Mason & Honger, Silas Mason Inc. & F. S. Rolandi Jr. Inc., at an approximate cost of $5,500,000.

The three deep water caissons are identical in design being 53 feet wide by 102 feet 6 inches long. They are of reinforced concrete construction with outer walls 3 feet in thickness and inner walls 2 feet 6 inches in thickness. Each caisson is divided into 18 dredging wells approximately 14 feet square. The four corners of the caisson are rounded to a 12-foot radius to reduce pressures during sinking operations from high velocity currents. The bottom 13 feet of the concrete walls are protected by structural steel cutting edges fabricated by welding from ⅜-inch, ½-inch and ¾-inch steel plates.

These steel cutting edges each weighing about 400,000 pounds per caisson were fabricated at the Bethlehem Pacific Coast Steel Shipbuilding Yards approximately 32 miles from the bridge site. Cutting edges were fabricated in sections pre-assembled in the fabricating yard for fit and then assembled on a shipbuilding dry dock and welded together.

New Precast Slabs

Following this assembly on the drydock the cutting edges were filled with concrete and the outside walls of the caisson were extended to a

* This is the second of two articles on Carquinez Bridge Project by Mr. Hollister—Ed.

UPPER—Picture shows work being done on one of the caisson piers. Here heavy equipment is setting forms preparatory to placing a 10-foot lift of concrete in the side walls and partitions. LOWER—Picture shows one of the caisson piers floating at the Bethlehem Pacific Coast Steel Company's shipyard. After it has been thoroughly tested for flotation it will be towed to the bridge site.

total height of 31 feet by placing four-inch precast slabs around the periphery of the caisson.

The use of these four-inch precast slabs is a new innovation designed by the contractor for use in reinforced concrete caisson construction. The slabs become an integral part of the three-foot thick outside wall when the caisson is completed. They were precast at the Basalt Rock Company plant and transported 39 miles by barge to the drydock and later about nine miles by truck to the bridge site.

The slabs were cast in sections 10 feet high by 16 feet long, and reinforced at center of slab with three-eighths-inch vertical bars 11-inch centers and three-eighths-inch horizontal bars six-inch centers. Outside surface was cast smooth and inside surface roughened and keyed for bonding to the poured-in-place section of the outside wall.

Support for Slabs

To support the slabs small vertical steel trusses 25½ inches deep were fabricated and cantilevered up from the top of the concrete and steel cutting edge below. The slabs were then secured to these trusses and the horizontal reinforcing slab bars welded at the joints between slabs. After erection there remained in the vertical joints a clear opening of one-eighth to one-fourth inch, at horizontal joints slab edges were seated on each other and there was no clear opening. To seal these joints and make them water tight the contractor used a commercial application of fiberglas fabric and fiberglas sealing compounds.

There are several advantages to this type of construction. It greatly increases the flotation qualities of the caisson by making the top 20-foot portion of the outside wall four inches thick as compared to 36 inches, thereby reducing total weight considerably. The precast slabs save the time and expense of placing and removing outside form work. This tends to speed up construction at bridge site during sinking operation. There is also provided an additional safety factor, since slabs can be placed quickly, and joints sealed to provide additional freeboard and bouyancy should the need arise.

Dredging Wells Sealed

Bottoms of dredging wells were sealed with "false bottoms" fabricated from heavy timbers. Through each of the "false bottoms" there is placed a short section of 30-inch steel pipe. In-

UPPER—Picture shows the bottom of one of the corner caisson walls. Timber false bottom can be seen. The 30-inch capped pipe provides the contractor with access to underside of caisson. Jets and pumps can be lowered through 30-inch pipe and the bottom pumped out from under caisson allowing it to sink until it reaches bedrock. LOWER—Sketch showing equipment used in sinking the three caissons to bedrock. Jets and pumps can be lowered through any of the 30-inch pipes located at center of each dredging well. Contractor can also remove the whole bottom of any well and excavate by using a clamshell bucket if necessary.

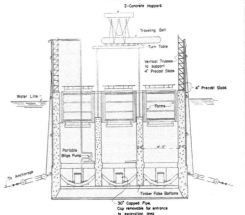

and Public Works

41

Picture taken in 1927 during erection of the existing bridge. The same contractor (American Bridge Division of United States Steel Corporation) will erect the new bridge but will use a different method. This time contractor proposes to erect the center suspended span by cantilevering each half out to the center then bolting the two halves together with high-strength steel bolts. In this picture the center suspended span has been erected on barges and is being raised into position by counter weights much the same as an elevator moves up and down.

side of this there is a supplementary "false bottom" in the form of a concrete plug which can be removed and replaced whenever desired.

The purpose of these 30-inch steel pipe entrances to the bottom of the caisson is twofold. It makes access to the excavation area under the caisson possible for inspection purposes. This will be desirable in case of excavation difficulties during sinking operations and for final inspection when the caisson comes to rest on bedrock at the bottom. The other purpose is to provide access for lowering high-pressure jets and pumps into the excavation area below the caisson.

Here again the contractor has developed a new method of sinking the caissons through the mud, sand and gravel material overlaying the bedrock foundations.

Instead of the conventional method of excavating the material from beneath the caisson by clamshell buckets lowered through the dredging wells, the contractor proposes to jet and pump.

Use of Jets

This is being accomplished by extending the 30-inch steel pipes and lowering through the four center dredging wells four Chicksan Intelli-Giant Jets. These jets can be operated at pressures from 30 to 300 psi per square inch. They are so rigged that they can be lowered or raised vertically, turned in any direction hori-

zontally, or positioned at various vertical angles. These jets are sufficiently powerful to cut loose the overburden after which it is pumped to the surface where it is discharged into barges and transported to a predetermined disposal area.

The contractor has predredged the area under each caisson to about 100 feet below water surface which leaves remaining about 32 feet of mud, sand and gravel through which each pier must be lowered. Pier No. 2 has been sunk to bedrock at about elevation −132. The "false bottoms" were removed when north edge of caisson rested on rock at elevation −129. It was necessary to blast out along north edge for about 2 to 2½ feet in order

42

to level the bottom of caisson within specification requirements. Bottom of Pier No. 2 is now ready to be sealed with 25 feet of concrete.

Land-based Concrete Plant

For concreting the contractor has constructed a land-based concrete plant on the south shore. This plant has a capacity of about 120 cubic yards per hour. Concrete is discharged into six-cubic-yard buckets and barged to the piers in three specially constructed barges capable of carrying eight buckets each. About 20 minutes are required from the time barge leaves mixing plant until cranes pick up buckets for unloading into concrete hoppers at the pier.

For placing concrete in pier walls and partitions two concrete hoppers are set one at the center of each half pier. The hoppers discharge onto traveling belts which can be turned and extended to discharge at any point on the half pier. One 10-foot section of pier can be poured in one day. About four days are required to allow concrete to set, move forms and place reinforcing for the next 10-foot section, making sinking operations at the rate of about 10 feet per week.

The pier protection fender system is of reinforced concrete slabs and girders supported by 150-foot steel pipe piles 24 inches in diameter and filled with concrete. The steel pipe piles were fabricated from one-half inch steel plate and were put in place by jetting. When piles reach bedrock

a spud was used to break up shale and sandstone which was pumped to the surface while the pile was being driven about three feet into the bedrock to form a key. Once the pile was located in the driver and jets rigged up it required only about 20 minutes to jet and drive the steel shell pile into bedrock.

Superstructure Contract

The main portion of the Carquinez Bridge superstructure consists of double cantilever truss spans with a central tower of 150 feet. The two end anchor arms are each 500 feet with two central spans 1100 feet making the total length of main structure 3300 feet. The two suspended spans are each 433 feet 2⅝ inches long. This work is under contract to

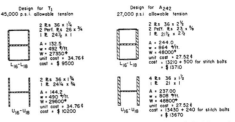

Sketch showing comparison between the new type strength steel and the regular moderately high strength steel. These studies were made to determine the most satisfactory and economical type of steel to use in the makeup of the heavily stressed truss members for the 1,100-foot-long cantilever spans.

American Bridge Division of the U. S. Steel Corp. at an approximate cost of $9,500,000.

Trusses are 60 feet center to center and support a 52-foot concrete roadway with two 1-foot 10½-inch steel curbs. The roadway slab for the two anchor arms is to be of standard weight concrete while the slab for the remaining portion of the structure is to be of light weight concrete at 100 pounds per cubic foot.

Three types of steel were used in the design of the superstructure. They were A7, A242 and T1 and the allowable unit tensile stresses were as follows:

A7—18,000 psi—all thicknesses
A242—27,000 psi—less than ¼ inch
A242—24,000 psi—¼ inch—1½ inches
T1—45,000 psi—all thicknesses

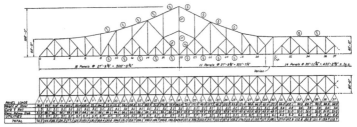

Sketch showing outline of truss with members fabricated from T1 steel indicated. Most other truss members are fabricated from A242 steel except for those very lightly stressed. Main dimensions of truss and dead panel loads are also indicated.

Design of Cantilever Trusses

In the design of cantilever trusses of this length, supporting four lanes of traffic with a concrete floor slab, one of the big problems has always been the makeup of the heavily stressed members in the area of supporting towers. These members frequently contain so many thick heavy plates that their resistance to bending between joints produces high secondary stresses, sometimes greater than the primary stresses. In the past some of this difficulty with high secondary stresses has been overcome by the use of pinned connected eye bars and pin connected compression members. The reliability of the pin connected compression member to relieve secondary stresses has been somewhat questionable, since the moment required to produce rotation in the pin may be as large as the moment induced by the secondary stress.

In any event the use of a high strength steel which would allow the makeup of members to retain reasonable flexibility appears to be the best answer in this case to the problem of secondary stresses.

Comparative Designs

Comparative designs between the use of A242 and T1 for these critical members gave the following approximate figures:

	A242	T1
Maximum deadload truss deflection	100%	130%
Moment of inertia L16 L18	51,900 In-4	17,700 In-4
Bending stress L16 L18	19,200 psi	2,900 psi
Ratio secondary stress to primary stress L16 L18	110%	10%

From these comparative figures it can be seen that the high strength steel has a considerable advantage from a design standpoint and also indicates greater economy.

Using the unit bid prices for A242 and T1 received from the low bidder the total saving made by the use of T1 for the critical members was estimated to be approximately $800,000.

Before deciding on the use of this steel the California Division of Highways Testing Laboratory ran extensive tests on the parent metal and butt welded joints made from ½-inch, 1-inch and 1½-inch sample T1 steel plates. The butt weld samples were made by using a semiautomatic

Picture shows foundation work in progress for the main bridge. Caisson Pier No. 2 in water at far side of Carquinez Strait has now been sunk to bedrock. Caisson Pier 3A at center is now being lowered.

shielded arc, automatic submerged arc, and three types of manual low hydrogen processes.

The averaged test results for the parent T1 steel indicated a yield strength of 111,000 per square inch, ultimate strength of 120,000 per square inch, and an endurance limit of 55,000 per square inch. The steel exhibited excellent ductility.

The welded joints provided joint efficiencies from 87 percent to 100 percent of the ultimate strength of the parent metal and endurance ratios of 27 percent to 45 percent of the ultimate strengths of the corresponding welded joints. The welds exhibited moderate ductility and some porosity.

Butt Welded Joints

It was necessary to give considerable attention to butt welded joints of T1 steel because rolling limits will not permit full length plates for member makeup. Advantage was taken of this however by increasing plate thickness near joints to compensate for loss of net section due to holes for truss joint connections.

Experience gained by the California Division of Highways on the design and fabrication of thousands of tons of steel girders in the past few years prompted the consideration of steel truss members fabricated by welding in lieu of the customary stitch rivets.

This appeared to have considerable advantage such as: (1) the number of member shapes could be reduced to three for H sections, four for box sections, and five for box sections with interior webb; (2) makeup of all members can be made from plates only, eliminating the use of connecting angles; (3) shop fabrication has a good opportunity to be greatly simplified with a corresponding reduction in cost, because all stitch riveting and fitting is replaced by four continuous fillet welds; (4) maintenance, always a costly item near coastal waters, should be made easier by the smooth surfaces which are free from rivet heads, lacing bars and other small vulnerable details which are costly to clean and paint.

High Strength Bolts

Design plans call for field connections at truss joints to be made by high strength bolts with the contractor having an option between rivets and high strength bolts for shop connections. Shop plans now being prepared by the fabricator, which is the American Bridge Division of the United States Steel Corporation, indicate that high strength bolts have been chosen for shop connections. High strength bolts for field connections were decided on for several reasons. First, it was the opinion of designers that the numerous past tests have indicated that the average high strength field bolt is superior to the average field-driven rivet in performing the fastening job that it is designed to do. The field inspection for a good high strength bolt is more positive than the inspection for a satisfactory field-driven rivet. The development and training of an efficient bolting crew is much easier than the development of an efficient riveting crew.

For these reasons designers felt that high strength bolts have an excellent opportunity to make possible more reliable field joints at reduced costs.

Field erection of the superstructure is to start in April, 1957.

Toll Plaza

The toll plaza will consist of an administration building and 16 onside modern barrier-type toll booths, with provision for four additional toll booths should future traffic demand require them.

Each toll booth will be equipped with automatic axle counters and photoelectric vehicle counters.

There is to be a nominal fee of 25 cents for passenger cars; trucks will be charged by the axle rather than by weight. Administration of the toll collection will be under the jurisdiction of the Division of Highways and will be operated by the same staff now being used to operate the San Francisco-Oakland Bay Bridge, the Richmond-San Rafael Bridge, San Mateo-Hayward, and Dumbarton Toll Bridges.

The Carquinez Bridge Project should be completed by October or November, 1958. All of the work in connection with these projects has been assigned to the Division of Highways by the California Toll Bridge Authority.

BRIDGES

Continued from page 39 . . .

higher cost is the emergence of a situation of relatively reduced competition resulting from the currently expanded programs of heavy construction.

The rise in construction costs is a part of the general price rise occurring throughout all phases of the economy. A majority of economists are of the opinion that the inflationary trends are the pattern of the current economy. In support of this thesis they cite: (1) The government's active intervention in the field of monetary controls; (2) The labor-management contracts whereby labor rates are either determined by official cost indexes or by long term contracts which call for annual wage increases; (3) The increasing trend on the part of many heretofore "backward" nations toward industrialization and the consequently increased competition for the world's rigidly limited supply of raw materials. These factors, the economists contend, inevitably lead to a creeping type of inflation on the order of 3-5 percent per year.

The situation insofar as California bridge construction costs are concerned is analogous to that of the broader economic pattern. Price advances are sometimes more dramatic but the long term trend is in the direction of an upward creep of about 5 percent, an increase which stems directly from the existing pattern of annual wage increases and the concomitant price increases of all cost elements associated with the industry.

In view of these circumstances it may be assumed that the California Bridge Department Cost Index will very likely reach a value of 285 during 1957, or a value which is about 5 percent greater than the value of 273 for the fourth quarter of 1956.

THE WORST TYPES

If you're a speeder, lane jumper, or bumper rider, you have the dishonor of being one of the three worst types of problem drivers in the United States today.

That, according to the National Automobile Club, is the opinion of 33 honored cabbies who have driven a

---

In Memoriam
A. D. EDMONSTON

A. D. Edmonston, 70, who retired as State Engineer in November, 1955, died on February 22d in Stanford Lane Hospital, San Francisco, where he had been under treatment three weeks.

Edmonston had 31 years of state service. Beginning as a hydraulic engineer in 1924, he served for many years as one of the original collaborators on plans for the Central Valley Project. From 1937 through 1945 he was chief hydraulic engineer in charge of formulating the California Water Plan. In 1945 he became assistant state engineer under the late Edward Hyatt, and succeeded him as state engineer and chief of the Division of Water Resources upon Hyatt's retirement in 1950.

The position of State Engineer was the chief water planning job until the organization last year of the new State Department of Water Resources.

Edmonston directed most of the original studies on the Feather River Project and the California Water Plan, both plans now pending before the current session of the State Legislature.

Edmonston was born November 12, 1886, in Ferndale, Humboldt County, California. He was graduated from Stanford University in 1910. He served in World War I as a lieutenant with the Army Corps of Engineers.

He was a member of the American Society of Civil Engineers, the Commonwealth Club, the American Geophysical Union, and Tau Beta Pi engineering fraternity.

He is survived by his wife, Dell, of Sacramento; his sons, Donald, a graduate student at University of California, and Robert, an engineer with the Department of Water Resources, Los Angeles office; a sister, Emma Edmonston of Palo Alto, and a brother, John Edmonston.

total of 834 years and about 22,000,-000 miles with nary an accident.

Common courtesy, the cabbies agree, would eliminate some 65 percent of all traffic accidents.

Employees Receive Twenty-five-year Awards

Employees of the Division of Highways who become eligible for 25-year awards on January 31, and February 28, 1957, and on August 31, 1956, are:

Name	Total Service Yrs. Mos. Days	Name	Total Service Yrs. Mos. Days
District II		**District VI**	
Berry, George R.	25 0 21	Barnes, Bentley	25 0 12
Chandler, Alvin G.	25 0 26	Edwards, Albert B.	25 0 18
District III		**District VII**	
Barner, Martin H.	25 0 5	Currey, E. Brooks	25 0 24
Chapman, Muller	25 0 18	Farrant, Marion	25 0 23
Schence, Marvin D.	25 0 1	Munro, L. B.	25 0 6
		Snider, Charles B.	25 0 6
District IV		Suverkrubbe, N. H.	25 0 3
Hart, Herbert A.	25 0 9	**District IX**	
Strand berg, Egon W.	25 0 26	Nillus, Martin E.	25 0 3
Pearcell, Ira C.—Eligible August 31, 1956	25 0 0	**District XI**	
		Resch, Lloyd J.	25 0 23
District V		**Bay Bridge**	
Lyons, Hugh E.	25 0 6	Cayla, Henry J.	25 0 14

Employees of the Division of Architecture receiving 25-year awards:

	25 years on	Location
Frank S. Marks, Jr.	March 1, 1957	Headquarters, Sacramento
Alice J. Moody	March 25, 1957	Area I, San Francisco

MERIT AWARD BOARD WINNERS

Employees of the Department of Public Works receiving certificates of award and commendation during February, 1957, are:

Eldon B. Roseberry, highway traffic signal technician, San Bernardino, was awarded $150 for developing an auxiliary timing device for traffic signals. This device improves the safety of vehicles approaching a traffic signal on a rural expressway by giving advance notice of approaching signal changes. Previously there was a considerable delay in obtaining the special equipment necessary to convert these signals. With the equipment Mr. Roseberry has designed, the same thing is accomplished at a saving to the State of $175 per installation. It is estimated at least 10 installations will be made each year.

Richard Alexander, assistant highway engineer, Sacramento, recommended a stamp showing the actual inches be placed on plans which are to be reduced. Showing this scale on the reproduced plans calls attention to the amount of reduction from the original drawing and could prevent misinterpretation of reduced plan scales. While the monetary award value of the savings cannot be determined, an award of $30 for an improved procedure was approved.

Ardith L. Helton, senior stenographer-clerk, Sacramento, will receive $25 for recommending the use of a Wheeldex rotary card file for filing records of powers of attorney in the disbursing office of the De-

partment of Public Works. Under the old method a folder was maintained for each of approximately 100 bonding companies, each folder containing a list of persons who hold powers of attorney. There are approximately 4,000 names in the file, and one list may contain up to 250 names. These names are checked against about 1,500 documents received each year. The use of this Wheeldex will save considerable time.

Thomas Scrimsher, assistant highway engineer, Sacramento, will receive $25 for designing and developing a uniform light cabinet used in evaluating the results of film stripping tests. In these tests a visual inspection is made to determine the possible stripping of the asphalt film from the aggregate when subjected to water. The light cabinet makes it possible to examine all specimens through a uniform light instead of artificial or natural light formerly used. This procedure will be used in Materials and Research Department in Sacramento and throughout the various district laboratories.

Stanley R. Collis, tab operator, Sacramento, proposed a mirror be placed on the wall focused on the IBM 650 magnetic drum data processing machine. This will help the operator watch this machine from various locations in the room and will enable him

to determine when the machine is not in operation and another series started. An award of $15 was given for an improved procedure.

Calvin K. Cartwright, assistant highway engineer, Fresno, was awarded a Certificate of Commendation for his recommendation that plastic railroad curves, used by the Division of Highways design units, be scribed at one-inch intervals along their length. This curve was first tried out in District VI. After it proved satisfactory, arrangements were made to obtain scribed curves from a supplier. Although the cost of placing the idea into effect offsets any direct saving, the suggestion has resulted in an improved device.

Oscar R. Olivo, senior engineering aid, Fullerton, was awarded $50 for a specially designed surveyors' vest. Samples of the vest were circulated among the districts for trial and won enthusiastic approval. As a result the vests for surveyors will be carried in division stores. The vests increase survey crew efficiency. They provide more space for carrying items, and are more comfortable and convenient.

Melvin R. Nester, assistant highway engineer, Fresno, received a $25 award for recommending the use of 4-inch x 8-inch cans in the soil laboratories in place of 5½-inch x 10-inch cans. Originally the idea had been rejected because the Division was experimenting with polyethylene plastic bags for storing soil samples. However, the plastic bags proved unsatisfactory. Mr. Nester's suggestion was reconsidered and adopted. While a new can of different dimensions than originally proposed by Mr. Nester is being used, it provides essentially the same savings in storage space.

Ann M. Dreman, accountant auditor I, Sacramento, proposed a change in the method of keeping records of annexations and incorporations. She received a $20 award for her suggestion.

Hazel F. Mitchell, accounting technician III, Sacramento, received $15 for suggesting a simpler procedure for verifying rejected checks deposited with the State Treasury for Trust Accounts.

Isadore Goldberg, highway field office assistant, received a Certificate of Commendation for suggesting a revision in Form A-579, Billing Notice.

OLDEST PARK

Sequoia National Park is the oldest in California having been established in September, 1890, reports the California State Automobile Association.

IMPROVEMENT

In 1937 there were some 15 traffic deaths per 100,000,000 miles of travel. Today there are 6.4 deaths per 100,000,000 miles.

46

PROMOTIONS FOLLOW WITHYCOMBE'S RETIREMENT

Earl Withycombe, Assistant State Highway–Operations, for the State Division of Highways, retired on March 1st after more than 34 years of service and State Highway Engineer G. T. McCoy announced the promotion of J. W. Trask, District Engineer in charge of District III at Marysville, to the position vacated by Withycombe.

Alan S. Hart, District Engineer at Eureka, takes Trask's place as engineer in charge of District III, while Sam Helwer, Assistant District Engineer of District X, Stockton, has been promoted to District Engineer, replacing Hart at Eureka.

The position of Assistant State Highway Engineer–Operations, held by Withycombe for the past six years, involved responsibility for the construction and maintenance work on the 14,000-mile State Highway System; the procurement and maintenance of all equipment used by the division; and materials research, a field in which the Division of Highways has pioneered.

Withycombe joined the Division of Highways in 1922 as a resident engineer on paving construction in the

EARL WITHYCOMBE

Fresno area. He was appointed Assistant Construction Engineer in 1924 covering highway construction projects throughout the State for the Headquarters Office in Sacramento. In 1931 he was promoted to the post

of Staff Highway Engineer in the Construction Department and in 1947 was appointed Construction Engineer for the division. He was promoted to his last post in 1950.

A specialist in paving operations, Withycombe has been instrumental in establishing uniform, modern procedures throughout the State. He has pioneered or assisted in development of new equipment and methods which have become standard practice in highway construction.

Native of Oregon

A native of Portland, Oregon, Withycombe received his degree in civil engineering from Oregon State College. He is a veteran of World War I, having served with the U. S. Corps of Engineers. He is a member of the American Society of Civil Engineers.

Trask, who came to work for the division as a junior bridge engineer in 1928, has had extensive construction and administrative experience. He was Assistant Resident Engineer on the construction of the San Francisco-Oakland Bay Bridge tunnel through

J. W. TRASK

ALAN S. HART

SAM HELWER

and Public Works

Yerba Buena Island. He served first as Office Engineer and later as Assistant District Engineer of District II at Redding. He became District Engineer of District II in 1950 and was transferred to Marysville as head of District III early in 1956.

Earl Withycombe addresses associates and friends who honored him with a retirement dinner in Governor's Hall, State Fair Grounds, Sacramento

Trask was born in Lincoln, Nebraska, and holds a B.S. degree in engineering from Utah State College. He is a veteran of World War I, serving the 115th Engineers. He is a member of the American Society of Civil Engineers and the American Concrete Institute.

Resignation of J. C. Young Brings About Personnel Transfers

Personnel changes in the Design, Planning and Public Relations and Personnel Sections of the Division of Highways have been announced by State Highway Engineer G. T. McCoy.

J. A. Legarra, now Planning Engineer, was transferred to the position of Design Engineer, replacing J. C. Young, who has resigned to enter private engineering practice. J. P. Murphy, head of Public Relations and Personnel, becomes Planning Engineer; and Scott H. Lathrop, in charge of personnel administration and training, replaces Murphy. The changes became effective March 15th.

Hart has been head of the Eureka district since 1953. A native Californian, Hart has had extensive experience in the District III area which he will take over. Following his graduation from the University of California in 1930 he served 15 years, first as Junior Engineer and later as Resident Engineer on construction and finally Assistant Maintenance Engineer, all in District III. He subsequently served as District Maintenance Engineer in San Luis Obispo and as Assistant District Engineer in Eureka. In 1950 he was appointed District Engineer of District IX at Bishop, where he served until his transfer to Eureka.

Sam Helwer, Hart's successor at Eureka, came to work for the division in 1936. From 1936 to 1940 he served in four districts (Eureka, Marysville, Stockton and San Diego) on various survey, construction and design assignments. In 1940 he joined the survey section of District VII in Los Angeles and in 1945 came to Sacramento to work for the division's Bridge Department. From 1947 until the time he was appointed Assistant District Engineer at Stockton in 1953 he was with Headquarters Design Section in Sacramento. Helwer is the author of several papers on interchange design.

Helwer was born in Russell, Kansas, and studied engineering at the University of California at Berkeley.

Legarra was appointed to the position of Planning Engineer in November, 1955, having served for two years prior to that time as Assistant Planning Engineer. From 1951 to 1953 he was Assistant Design Engineer. A native of Marysville, California, and a graduate of the University of California at Berkeley with a degree in civil engineering, he joined the Division of Highways in 1941.

Murphy became head of Public Relations and Personnel in 1955 after having been in charge of Public Relations since 1950. His entire professional career, since his graduation in 1930 from the University of California at Berkeley with a degree in civil engineering, has been with the Division of Highways. Before his assignment to Public Relations he was Assistant District Engineer of District III, Marysville. He is a native of Pittsburgh, Pa., and came to California with his parents in 1910.

Lathrop has been in charge of personnel administration and training for the Division of Highways since 1951. Previous to taking that assignment he had been with the District III office in Marysville since he went to work for the division in 1931. In District III he advanced through the engineering ranks in administration, planning and design work. He is a native of Spokane, Washington, and a graduate of the University of California at Berkeley with a degree in civil engineering.

Young will become associated with the engineering consulting firm of Porter, Urquhart, McCreary & O'Brien, with head offices in Newark, New Jersey.

He received his degree in civil engineering from the University of California at Berkeley in 1926 and was engaged in engineering work for private companies before joining the Division of Highways in 1928. He has held many responsible positions with the division, and was Traffic Engineer prior to becoming Design Engineer in 1952.

German Road Experts Amazed at Freeways

German construction delegation with guides who accompanied them on tour of freeway construction projects in the Los Angeles area. Photograph was taken when bus was stopped at District VII Office for four of the building and brief words of welcome from Assistant State Highway Engineer E. T. Telford.

In attendance at the American Road Builders Association Convention in Chicago have been a large number of engineers, contractors, equipment manufacturers and materials suppliers from countries all over the world.

Upon being informed that 14 construction delegates from Germany wished to make an inspection tour of freeways in the Los Angeles Metropolitan area, State Highway Engineer G. T. McCoy instructed E. T. Telford of District VII to make the necessary arrangements.

An all-day tour was arranged on February 4, 1957, and included inspection of completed freeways and freeway projects under construction on Harbor Freeway, Santa Ana Freeway, Hollywood Freeway, and Golden State Freeway. The German construction delegation was traveling under the auspices of the International Road Federation of Washington, D. C., and the Trade and Industry Tours Association of New York City. The personnel of the group was as follows:

Ludwig Fischer, owner, L. Fischer, contractors, Bergzabern, Pfalz, Germany; Dr. Hans-Juergen Gass, Partner, Ferma-Werke, Fertigbau-und Maschinenges, mbH, Ettlingen, Baden Germany (Prestress concrete, gravel, sand, crushed stone); Carl Hermann Heise, Chief Engineer, Alfelder Eisenwerke Carl Heise KG Alfeld, Leine, Germany. Road construction machinery and equip-

ment for iron and steel mills; Miss Ursula Lorenz, Civil Engineer, Partner and Secretary, Allgem. Baugesellschaft Lorenz & Co. mbH, Leubeck, Germany. Contractors specializing in foundations (concrete piling system "Lorenz") reinforced concrete constructions; Albert Reinsberg, Vice President in Charge of Engineering, J. Kriegeris & Co., Hamburg, Germany (overhead and underground construction); Rudolf Riedel, Vice President in Charge of Engineering, Baugesellschaft H. Kamnt G.m.b.H., Herford, Westfl, Germany, general contractors; Guenther Roemmling, Engineer, Paul Thiele, A.C., Hamburg, Germany, general contractors; Rudolf Schirmer, Partner, Bauverlag G.m.b.H., Wiesbaden, Germany, publishers of "Bauwirtschaft"; Mr. Schlephorst, Secretary, Association of German Machine Manufacturers, Building Machines Div., Frankfurt/Main, Germany; Manfred Steidle-Sailer, Owner, Bauunternehmung E. Steidle, Sigmaringen, Wrtbg, Germany, general contractors; Hans Willrodt, Chief Engineer, Menck & Hambrock G.m.b.H., manufacturers of building machines, dredges, bucket scrapers, Hamburg-Altona, Germany; Otto Kurz, Owner, Otto Kurz, Ulm/Donau, Germany, general contractors; Reiner Wilkens, Owner, Reiner Wilkens, Horrem nr. Koeln, Germany, general contractors; Dr. John V. Lilienfeld, director-guide for the German construction delegation.

In making the tour a success the District VII staff of the State Division of Highways was assisted by the Los Angeles Metropolitan Traffic Association, the Downtown Business Men Association, and the Los Angeles Citizens Traffic and Transportation Committee.

It is of interest to note that Germany, the country building the first freeways, known as "Die Autobahn," starting the construction in 1933, sent to the West Coast the distinguished German construction delegation to see how we are building freeways here in California.

Reporter P. K. Padmanabhan, writing in the *Los Angeles Times* of February 5, 1957, in part said:

"After visiting completed freeways and projects under construction on the Harbor, Santa Ana, Hollywood and Golden State Freeways, the Germans expressed amazement at the methods and the magnitude of freeway construction in this country.

"Dr. John V. Lilienfeld, spokesman for the group, said that freeway building on the scale prevalent in America is almost unknown in Europe. Even in West Germany, where freeways made their debut, there are only some 2,700 miles of completed freeways.

"He said that the other features of American building techniques that impressed his group were the high quality of the work, the forward-looking planning and extent of mechanization."

SAFETY FOR THE SURVEY PARTY

Issuance of a new eight-page, pocket-size folding pamphlet entitled "Safety for the Survey Party" has been announced by the Division of Highways.

Prepared by the division's Safety Section, the pamphlet provides a guide for the use of warning devices and equipment to protect the traveling public and members of engineering parties whose duties require them to work on streets and highways under open traffic conditions. It contains drawings and diagrams in color illustrating some of the safety equipment and how it should be used for maximum effect.

The pamphlet, which establishes uniform procedures for the protection of survey parties, is published primarily for the information and guidance of employees of the division.

John H. Horn

Study of Highway Transportation Needs Launched

John H. Horn, Associate Bridge Engineer with the Division of Highways Bridge Department, retired on February 15, 1957, after almost 29 years of state service. He was born and reared near Placerville in El Dorado County.

John received his engineering education at the University of Nevada where he earned a B.S. degree in civil engineering, graduating in 1924.

His early engineering experience was obtained with Stone and Webster, Inc., on the construction of the Caribou hydroelectric project on the North Fork of the Feather River. He also worked for the American Bridge Company in Gary, Indiana, and for the Nevada state highway organization.

Horn first came to the California Bridge Department for a short period in 1925 as a junior design engineer, and he returned again in September of 1928 as a junior bridge construction engineer. He has been representing the Bridge Department in the field continuously since that time, and has been resident engineer on many of the major bridge structures in both Northern and Southern California. At the time of his retirement he was resident engineer on two structure contracts on US 40 in the city of Auburn.

John's extensive knowledge of bridge construction and his frank manner have won him the respect and friendship of engineers and contractors, both present day and "old school," throughout the State. Many of the Bridge Department's resident engineers and designers received their early training under his watchful eye.

In retirement the Horns, John and Evelyn, plan to travel extensively, but their headquarters will always be their mountain home near Camino, California.

DRIVER TRAINING

Driver training courses in which students get actual on-the-road driving instruction are offered at 334 schools in California, reports the California State Automobile Association.

The Division of Highways, in cooperation with the cities and counties, is conducting a study which will result in presentation to Congress of a complete picture of the present and future highway transportation needs on all road systems in the State of California.

The study is being carried out in compliance with requirements of the 1956 Federal Highway Act, which calls for an estimate of the cost of the improvement needs of all the mileage of highways, roads and streets in the individual states for the 15-year period from July 1, 1956, to July 1, 1971.

In submitting instructions and forms to the cities and counties for their part in the study, State Highway Engineer G. T. McCoy wrote:

"The estimates of the city and county systems' needs have never been thoroughly explored and properly presented to Congress. Such a presentation should be of vital interest to the city and county authorities who are the proper agencies to prepare such a needs study. Also, the tremendous value of this study from the standpoint of community planning will be obvious."

Complete Study Necessary

Representatives of the Division of Highways and the Bureau of Public Roads met and discussed the study with the Advisory Committee of County Road Commissioners and the Advisory Committee of City Officials. It was the consensus of these two committees, which have been working with the Legislative Joint Interim Committee on Transportation Problems, that all of the counties and cities should enter into the study and prepare the required estimate of needs.

The Division of Highways, through its county federal-aid secondary and the city and cooperative departments, and the similar staffs in the 11 districts of the Division of Highways will aid the cities and counties with technical advice.

The needs study will be made for all existing and needed roads and streets, grouped into 12 systems to include all categories. The total of these 12 systems will represent the State of California total, without duplication or overlap.

Scope of Study

The Division of Highways will be responsible for the study on all roads under state jurisdiction, including roads in the Interstate Highway System.

Counties will be concerned only with the mileage and estimates of federal-aid secondary rural, local jurisdiction, and other rural roads under county jurisdiction.

Cities will be concerned only with the mileage and estimates of city streets under their jurisdiction and those portions of federal-aid secondary roads that are located within incorporated limits.

For any given road or street system, the needs estimates will cover not only the mileage existing on each system on July 1, 1956, but also the additional mileage required by virtue of needed improvements on projected mileage and new routes, including subdivision roads and streets, regardless of the means of financing. The needs estimate will cover what should be in service in the year 1971.

Fifteen-year Program

For each road system there is to be developed a 15-year improvement program, July 1, 1956, to July 1, 1971. Costs thus developed are to be realistic engineering estimates of highway needs, unaffected by advance decisions as to ability or means of financing and executing the program.

In order to conform to the time limits in the 1956 Federal Highway Act for presentation of the required information from the states to the proper agencies in Washington, D. C., the reports from both the cities and counties must be completed and furnished to the Division of Highways in Sacramento not later than August 1, 1957.

Federal Highway Administrator Starts New Job

Federal Highway Administrator Bertram D. Tallamy has promised state highway officials "to work diligently with each of you in making good on our collective promise to the Congress that we could and would do this job right."

Secretary of Commerce Sinclair Weeks administers oath of office to Bertram D. Tallamy, Federal Highway Administrator, right

Tallamy, who was sworn into his new office on February 5th by Secretary of Commerce Sinclair Weeks, wrote a letter assuring the highway officials of all 48 States of his "firm desire and intention to continue to improve where possible our cooperative efforts."

Following is the text of Mr. Tallamy's letter:

On February 5th I was sworn in as Federal Highway Administrator and immediately assumed my new duties. The new and greatly expanded federal-aid highway program is a challenge to all of us here in the Bureau of Public Roads and in all of the state highway departments.

The streamlining of the bureau operations during the past year, with which I am familiar, has been directed toward expediting our operations and strengthening the long-established cooperative relationships between the bureau and the state highway departments. I am writing to assure you that it is my firm desire and intention to continue to improve where possible our cooperative efforts.

Let me again assure you of my resolve to work diligently with each of you in making good on our collective promise to the Congress that we could and would do this job right.

Freeway Facts Booklet

A booklet entitled "Freeway Facts" has just been published by the California Division of Highways.

Primarily designed for distribution to all interested persons attending public meetings and map displays conducted by the various district offices of the division in connection with freeway route proposals, the booklet is also being supplied to public officials and members of civic organizations interested in state highway development.

The 16-page illustrated booklet attempts to summarize in easily comprehensible form the information most generally sought by the public in connection with freeway matters.

It explains the procedural steps leading up to adoption of a freeway routing; discusses why freeways are built; and summarizes some of the principal factors weighed by engineers in considering the merits of one proposed route as against another.

The booklet also contains answers to some of the more frequently asked questions about the effects of freeways on a community, and contains a glossary (partly illustrated) of technical terms.

Copies of the booklet are available from the Public Information Section, Division of Highways, P. O. Box 1499, Sacramento 7, California.

CATCHING SPEEDERS WITH ROPES

Today they use radar to catch the speeders. Back in 1905 in Delaware, according to the National Automobile Club, they used ropes. Traffic police disguised as workmen posted themselves along the road and then swung heavy ropes across the road to stop any driver who was exceeding the speed limit of eight miles per hour.

During 1956 the figure for truck and bus registrations stood at almost 11 million.

Engineer Group Honors Fred J. Grumm

The Engineering Council of Sacramento Valley at its recent annual awards banquet named Fred J. Grumm as the outstanding engineer of the year and presented him with a framed scroll honoring him for unselfish and altruistic community service with special recognition for his work as Chairman of the Sacramento Redevelopment Agency.

James C. Coombs presents plaque to Fred J. Grumm, right, while Ridgway M. Gillis looks on

Ridgway M. Gillis, who succeeded Grumm as Deputy State Highway Engineer when Grumm retired in 1950, delivered the presentation speech.

Gillis pointed out that Grumm had served the State with distinction, contributing greatly to the advancement of highway engineering in California and in the Nation, and since retiring from state service had given freely of his time and talents toward the great redevelopment program in Sacramento. This untiring leadership, an uncompensated service to the public and community, caused the award committee to name Grumm as the outstanding engineer of the year.

The Engineering Council of Sacramento Valley consists of representatives from 12 professional engineering societies having headquarters in Sacramento Valley. The council represents the 1,600 professional engineers and architects permitted to practice in this State. James C. Coombs, chairman of the council, presented the plaque to Grumm.

Redwood Highway

Modernization at Loleta in Humboldt

By H. W. BENEDICT, Resident Engineer

PHENOMENAL growth of the north coast counties in the late war years and the ensuing postwar period has brought with it the typical "growing pains" that the entire State of California has suffered during this period. The problems of adequate housing, sufficient schoolrooms, complete utility coverage, and many others have plagued the community leaders in the various counties in the north coast group.

But the paramount problem here, as elsewhere in the State, has been the modernization of the highway system. The life line of this area is US 101 (Route 1), over which the bulk of the commerce of the area must move. The increase in population and expansion of industry and commerce have long since overtaxed the capacity of the highway.

Looking southerly from Hookton Road near north end of project with new highway under construction on left, and existing Table Bluff Grade on right.

Heavy Congestion

The engineering staff of District I, recognizing the vital importance of US 101 to the growth and very life of the north coast counties, has concentrated efforts toward alleviating this serious condition. Early studies revealed that the portion of US 101 between the towns of Scotia and North Arcata qualified as one of the most congested two-lane rural highways in the State. A comprehensive over-all plan for the modernization of this section of road was formulated and, as funds became available, contract work was started. Since early in 1951, when major work was started, considerable progress has been made in the development to modern standards of the state highway.

A vital link in the reconstruction of the remaining substandard mileage is the planned project, some 13.5 miles in length, between the north city limits of Fortuna and Elk River, immediately south of Eureka. For budgetary purposes, this over-all project has been separated into four units

suitable for financing. In addition to the separation of the over-all project into four units, each unit has been separated into two stages: 1—the grading and drainage facilities, and 2—the base and surfacing.

Unit No. 1

On May 15, 1956, work was started on the first stage of Unit No. 1 of this project. A contract, in the aggregate amount of $1,022,200, was awarded to Norman I. Fadel, Inc., of North Hollywood and, as indicated above, consists primarily of grading and drainage installations. Unit No. 1, approximately 4.6 miles in length, extends from Fernbridge to Beatrice, passing to the east of Loleta, and was chosen as the first construction unit since it will replace the most deficient section of the existing highway.

Paramount among these deficiencies is the Northwestern Pacific Railroad undercrossing at the south limits of Loleta, which has been the scene of several fatal accidents. The existing Table Bluff grade has also contributed

heavily to traffic congestion on Highway 101, since it is not uncommon to see 30 or 40 vehicles crawling up this grade behind heavily loaded, slow traveling trucks.

Four-lane Divided Highway

In addition to providing a four-lane divided highway built to expressway standards, with a design speed of 60 miles per hour, the new facility will shorten the route between termini of the project by over 0.5 mile. It will eliminate 12 horizontal and 16 vertical curves, and will reduce by over a mile the length of grade over 3.5 percent.

To obtain the high standards of alignment and grade consistent with a development of this nature, it was necessary to locate the alignment through an area previously avoided by the builders of the roads now serving the area. While no particularly high cuts were developed in the relocation, several deep canyons were crossed and areas of swampy ground and underlying excessively wet material were

UPPER—Stabilization trench right angles to centerline. Note filter material on slope to allow for percolation of underground water. LOWER—On top of Table Bluff Hill in thorough cut. Note filter material on cut slopes on right replacing material that sloughed away by concentration of underground water.

traversed. To add to these problems of construction were a myriad of active springs and underground streams in the construction limits.

Highway construction in District I, especially to modern divided highway standards, is difficult due to the annual rainfall which is the heaviest in the State and to the generally unstable soils and foundation conditions which are characteristic of the region.

Stabilization Work

To insure a firm and well-drained foundation for the large fills on the contract and to reduce the possibility of slides in the cut slopes, extensive stabilization work was of necessity performed. All canyons on the job were stripped of wet and unsuitable material and the springs therein contained were opened and drained; a blanket of filter material three to five feet in thickness was placed in the bottom and up the sides of the stripped gulches; and a network of 8-inch and 12-inch perforated pipe was placed to adequately drain the filter material. At the site of three largest fills on the contract, additional stabilization work was performed. At regular elevations in the slopes of the gulches, notches were excavated transverse to centerline for the two-fold purpose of relieving the flow of water through the filter material by means of perforated metal drains placed in the notches; and also serving as keys to lock the new embankment to the slopes of the gulches.

Interceptor Trenches

At locations of concentrated underground flow under shallow fills and in one location where an old slide crossed centerline, typical interceptor trenches with filter material backfill and perforated pipe underdrains were constructed. At the location of the slide added assurance of a stable fill was provided by installing approximately 3,000 linear feet of horizontal drains.

In two major cuts on the job, stabilization of cut slopes presented a problem. At these locations, heavy flows of ground water were intercepted near the subgrade plane. This water flowed through a stratum of sandy gravel and clay, bedded on a

First Unit of the Redwood Highway Is Put Under Way

Bids for construction of the first unit of the Redwood Freeway through the Humboldt Redwood State Parks were opened on March 13. The low bid, $6,345,594.90, was submitted by Guy F. Atkinson Co., South San Francisco.

The initial project involves grading and surfacing of 4.4 miles of freeway, between one mile south of Dyerville and Englewood on US 101 in Humboldt County to provide two travelled ways each 24 feet wide with a four-foot median, and for widening the existing South Fork Eel River Bridge, and constructing undercrossings at South Fork Road, High Rock Road, and Englewood Park, and a new South Fork Eel River Bridge.

There is available for this unit a total of $5,210,000 contributed equally by the Division of Highways and the State Division of Beaches and Parks.

The proposed location of the Redwood Freeway estimated to cost $36,400,000, including rights of way, will follow the South Fork of the Eel River from Mendocino County Line to Dyerville, the confluence of the South Fork and Eel River, a distance of 33.4 miles. From Dyerville it will follow the westerly slopes of the Eel River to Jordan Creek, a distance of 9.5 miles. It is planned as a full freeway on a standard 60-foot, four-lane divided section without access to the abutting properties except through planned frontage roads and interchanges. It will be on new alignment but close to the existing highway in most portions and generally parallel to it, with some sections of it east of and some sections west of the present highway.

distinctly different stratum of dense blue clay. The velocity of the ground water, when released by grading operations, was such that it washed out the sand and finer gravels, allowing the 1½:1 cut slopes to slough. This condition was anticipated in the preliminary materials investigation, and longitudinal trenches were set up in

the plans to correct any such occurrence.

The construction of these trenches, in brief, involved the removal of the water-bearing material to a depth of at least five feet behind the planned slope and parallel with it; placing a perforated metal pipe drain at the "heel" of the trench; and then backfilling the excavation to the original slope line with filter gravel. This treatment proved very effective in draining the underground flow and preventing additional sloughing or slides.

Fill Foundations Problem

From the above, it is apparent that the stabilization of fill foundations and of cut slopes has been the big problem on this contract. The magnitude of the work is attested by the fact that over 170,000 tons of imported filter material and over 14,000 linear feet of perforated metal pipe underdrains were used.

The excessive amount of moisture in the native soils at various locations brought attendant problems in the general grading phase of the work. As soon as any cut was opened to a depth of three or four feet, the contained moisture in excavated materials was generally above optimum, samples with 28 percent moisture being not uncommon. Therefore, in order to obtain compaction, constant shifting of grading equipment was required in order to allow the sun and wind to lower the moisture content in the cut sections. A judicious mixing of wet and dry material, and the alternate construction of several large fills allowed the work to proceed with but minor delays. By a strict adherence to these practices, the contractor was able to maintain a high daily yardage output and to keep the grading phase of the work ahead of schedule.

Included in the contract are parallel twin bridges across Salmon Creek, near the northerly limits of the work. These bridges are 156 feet long and consist of two 40- and two 38-foot spans each. These reinforced concrete bridges are of T-beam design and are founded on reinforced concrete pile bents. It is estimated that the structures will cost approximately $90,000

. . . Continued on page 72

UPPER—Stripping wet material and constructing stabilization trench. Highway centerline is diagonally across picture between lower left-hand corner and upper right-hand corner. This is the site of the heaviest stabilization work on the project. LOWER—General view of new construction at north end of project looking northerly. Junction with present highway in top center.

and Public Works

55

HIGHWAY PROJECTS IN DISTRICT VI

GARCES CIRCLE

By R. E. HAVERKAMP
Resident Engineer

The summer of 1957 will see the virtual elimination of one of the major traffic bottlenecks in the City of Bakersfield. No longer will the through-traveler on US 99 need to maneuver his automobile or truck through the maze of traffic at Garces Circle. Instead, he will travel up and over the traffic circle, and its local traffic, on the new four-lane separation structure which is scheduled for completion in June, 1957. Local traffic, which will still use the traffic circle, will no longer have the long wait for through-traffic to pass before entering the circle. Two-lane frontage roads on either side of the separation structure will provide access to and from the circle with its many service stations and restaurants as well as access to Oildale and the Bakersfield business district.

This traffic circle, as reported in the June, 1934, issue of *California Highways and Public Works*, was part of the "Bakersfield Bypass Relocation" of US 99 which was opened to traffic on June 2, 1934. The area inside the 278-foot diameter circle

Sizer making windrows south of the Circle

was later landscaped and, in 1939, the limestone statue of Padre Francisco Garces by the Sculptor John Palo-Kangas was placed in the center, hence the name "Garces Circle." As traffic volume increased through the years, the original 42-foot width of asphaltic concrete surfacing around the circle was replaced with portland cement

concrete, and the 30-foot width of pavement on US 99 was increased to a six-lane divided highway surfaced with portland cement concrete pavement.

Circle Now Bottleneck

Garces Circle was indeed a decided asset to the motorist of 1934, and, even in 1956 with an average daily

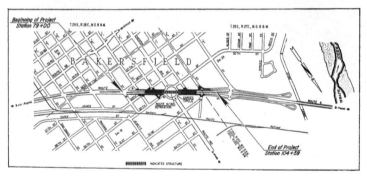

INDICATES STRUCTURE

traffic of 55,000 vehicles, it handled
the segregation of traffic with much
less confusion than would a three-
street intersection with its system of
traffic signals. But, the traffic circle
has become a decided bottleneck for
through-traffic, particularly for those
unfortunate motorists who are unfamiliar with it and frantically weave in
and out of traffic, sometimes traversing the circle two or three times trying to find the proper exit.

To relieve the greater part of this
traffic congestion, a separation structure was designed to carry the
through-traffic on US 99 over Garces
Circle. The contract for this structure, its approaches and the frontage
roads was awarded to O. B. Pierson,
Incorporated, of Los Alamitos, for
$552,480.15 on December 16, 1955.
Time allotted for this contract was
220 working days which has since
been increased to 337 days because of
a concrete batch plant strike and delay in the delivery of structural steel.

Overhead Structure Design

The design calls for an overhead
structure about 555 feet long and 62
feet wide between curbs with a 6-
foot median curb separating the two
roadways. Each of the seven simply
supported spans consists of nine 36-
inch welded plate girders supporting
a 7-inch reinforced concrete deck.
Two concrete columns on pile foundations support the steel plate girder
caps at each bent while the abutments
are the closed type with standard retaining walls about 500 feet long containing the approach fills. Steel bridge
railing will be used on each side of
the wingwalls and the overhead structure. The approaches are to be paved
with eight inches of Class "B" concrete over four inches of cement
treated subgrade. The frontage roads
on either side of the structure have
an over-all width of 36 feet between
curbs. The 26-foot roadway and the
8-foot parking lane are paved with
three inches of dense graded plant-
mixed surfacing over eight inches of
Class "C" cement treated base bordered by a two-foot concrete gutter
on the right. In addition, the roadway
portion will receive a five-eighths inch
blanket of open graded plant-mixed
surfacing. Plant-mixed surfacing with

UPPER—Northbound frontage road entering Circle. CENTER—Statue of Father Garces being moved.
LOWER—Looking easterly along off-ramp from US 99 to Garces Circle.

cement surface treatment will be used
to surface the sidewalks on each side
of the frontage roads and the various

traffic islands. Metal plate guard rail
will delineate the frontage roads from
the overhead approaches. An added

and Public Works   57

This photo looking north shows steel all in place at Garces Circle Bridge

feature will be a 67-foot sign bridge over the north bound lanes to direct the Oildale traffic to the frontage roads and the through-traffic to the structure approach.

Traffic Is Detoured

Before any work could be done on the structure, the US 99 traffic had to be moved over to the detours which were merely the outside 24 feet of the frontage roads. Consquently, in late January, 1956, the roadwork subcontractor, George E. France, started work on these frontage roads; and, on May 11th, all of the US 99 traffic was being carried on the detours. While these detours were being constructed, the general contractor moved the statue of Father Garces from his accustomed position in the center of the circle to a new point of vantage 30 feet from the south curb of the circle, still looking south on Chester Avenue. Moving this 23-foot statue weighing about 56 tons was expected to be quite a ticklish operation; but, after examining the base thoroughly, the contractor elected to move it as a unit on an improvised track of tim-

bers. The statue moved obediently along on its rollers with a minimum of pulling necessary from the winch

on the truck crane. Luminaires at the four corners of the new base slab will light the statue at night.

View looking southerly, showing long stretch of second-story concrete paving

With the traffic moved over to the detours, the contractor went to work on the wingwalls. Concrete for the wingwall footings was being placed at the same time Raymond Concrete Pile Company was driving the piles for the abutment and bent footings. By early July all of the substructure concrete had been placed and the long wait for structural steel began.

In the interim, curbs were placed on the wingwalls, the approach fills were brought up to grade, and the inside lanes of the frontage roads, as well as most of the traffic islands, were paved. On December 17, 1956, the long awaited steel arrived, and Independent Iron Works started their erection operations. The first span of deck concrete was placed February 12th. Before the structure can be used, however, the approaches will have to be paved and the railing put in place.

But sometime in June the entire project will be completed, and the through-traffic will be passing over the circle, leaving it to the local traffic and to those adventurous motorists who, perhaps through nostalgia, want to try their skill at maneuvering through the intricate pattern of vehicles.

This contract was administered by the Bridge Department with the author as resident engineer and George O'Dougherty as chief assistant. M. F. "Mike" Silva was District VI representative, and L. P. Cortner was the superintendent for O. B. Pierson, Incorporated.

CONCRETE BLANKET

By NORMAN LAMBETH
Resident Engineer

THE MOST effective and economical salvage of old highway pavements and the most practical type of repair have always posed a problem for highway engineers. An unusual solution to this problem is presented in the design and construction of a rigid pavement overlay for a major highway in District VI. On this project a 24-foot wide rigid pavement slab was placed full width in one pour since this offered the maximum salvage of the old exist-

UPPER—Saw and equipment for long center joint. CENTER—Tiebar placed on back of spreader. LOWER—Saw and equipment for sawing longitudinal center joint.

UPPER—Johnson float in operation. LOWER—Burlap drag being used for final finish work on 24-foot pavement.

ing pavement and, at the same time, provided for economical construction methods.

Placing a 24-foot width of Class B portland concrete cement pavement directly over the old pavement made possible the omission of one line of side forms which would normally have been required with standard 12-foot width lane construction. Because of this feature and the development

of special construction equipment for this project widespread interest was developed and the paving operations were observed by many engineers and contractors not directly connected with the project.

A 3.3-mile section of eight-inch-thick concrete blanket was placed on US 99 in Kern County about 15 miles south of Bakersfield on the southbound lanes of the existing highway.

The existing southbound lanes were constructed in 1938 and consisted of 0.6 foot to 0.75 foot of asphalt concrete using a relatively soft asphalt. Due to difficulties with plant control of the filler dust and a relatively high asphalt content, the original pavement developed marked signs of instability several years after construction.

This section of pavement is on a long sustained upgrade which reduces the speed of the heavy trucks to a very slow rate. Slow moving heavy truck traffic has proved to be one of the most severe types of traffic encountered and produced considerable rutting of the original pavement. The tendency to rut was not entirely corrected by the subsequent plant-mix blankets. Based on this experience, reconstruction with a concrete blanket was recommended.

Question of Width

The special provisions made it optional whether the concrete would be placed in 12-foot or 24-foot widths. The contractor elected to place the pavement in the 24-foot width. The project was set up to use the existing pavement as the grade line. Since the existing pavement was 23 feet wide and concrete was being placed 24 feet wide the inside form was 1 foot out on the shoulder and had to be raised 0.03 of a foot in order to maintain the desired 8-inch thickness at edge of pavement. The contractor used rock crusher dust to raise the inside forms and to provide a level surface on which to set the other forms. The crusher dust had enough interlocking qualities so it did not drift out from under the forms as sand would have done and was also less expensive to use than shimming up the forms by the use of shingles. A shoulder machine was used to lay the crusher dust in a small windrow and a labor crew made the fine grade.

Special Equipment

As the process of placing 24-foot width concrete pavement monolithically is relatively new in California State highway work, equipment to construct this width was not readily available, so existing spreader, finisher and float equipment were rebuilt to accommodate the 24-foot width. The spreader and finisher had recently been rebuilt for use on airport work, but the float finisher had to be built specifically for this project.

This float was built up around a 12-foot Johnson float frame. The front portion was made up of the 12-foot float turned crosswise with two driver wheels placed on each end. Framework was added to the rear of this float to accommodate the new boards which are arranged similarly to the original Johnson float. There are two longitudinal sections each 12 feet wide and so arranged that they can be adjusted to make a plane section or a crown section. Also on each longitudinal section there is one additional board independently suspended which is the strike-off board used in making the final pass. These boards are long enough so that they overlap at the front of the float. After a few trials it was found necessary to mount a short board on the front of the float near the center so it could be turned either way to throw the windrow of accumulated mortar to either side as needed. Since the original pavement was crowned this section was also crowned and it was found that the finished pavement retained the planned crown.

Spacing of Tie Bars

The plans required that tie bars be placed along the center of the pavement, and the contractor planned to place these tie bars by means of a hydraulic ram mounted on the back of the spreader. This system did not work as the ram was too slow and it was difficult to measure the interval between bars. The contractor then built another piece of apparatus which consisted of two discs having a circumference of 90 inches. Three notches were cut in the discs which gave the 30-inch spacing for the tie bars. These discs were placed on a horizontal shaft mounted paralleled to the back of the spreader and adjusted so the discs rolled into the concrete four inches. The tie bars were placed manually in the notches.

Transverse joints were sawed every 15 feet and longitudinal joint was sawed down the center of the pavement. The special provisions allowed sawing the joints at any time, so the

usual control joint sawing was not done. As this was a winter job the concrete set up very slowly and it was usually about 30 hours before sawing was done. There was no random cracking and because of the time interval the joints did not ravel in sawing. The center joint was sawed, using a light frame attached to the cutting machine which had flanged wheels on each end to fit over the edge of the slab to act as a guide for the saw. This proved to be a very efficient operation, and, since the saw required no manual guidance, one operator could handle the water truck and the servicing of the saw.

The pavement has been checked with a profileograph and also a roughometer and both show that the smoothness obtained is comparable to that obtained on a normal 12-foot width construction. Griffith Company of Los Angeles was the contractor and the author was the resident engineer representing the State.

CHOWCHILLA FREEWAY

By F. B. ENGLAND
Resident Engineer

Another seven miles of freeway will soon be added to US 99 in District VI with the completion of the Califa to Merced county line project in Madera County.

The major portion of the construction is on new alignment east of the existing two-lane highway and provides separation structures at three county roads and bridges at Ash Slough and Berenda Slough. In terms of increased safety for the motorist, however, the work being done at the Southern Pacific Railroad crossing of US 99 and at the intersection of US 99 and State Sign Route 152 is of primary importance.

At the Southern Pacific crossing, the existing underpass now serves both north and southbound US 99 traffic. This situation is further aggravated by the fact that the approach from either direction is on a curve with limited sight distance. Upon completion of construction this subway will accommodate only northbound traffic with the sight distance greatly increased by realignment of

the approaches. Southbound traffic will utilize the precast girder overhead now under construction immediately adjacent to the existing subway to cross over the Southern Pacific tracks.

Elimination of Hazard

The intersection of US 99 and Sign Route 152 now requires northbound US 99 traffic turning west onto Sign Route 152 to cross the southbound lanes of US 99 at grade. This hazard is to be eliminated by depressing the southbound lanes and carrying the west turning movement over them on the recently completed reinforced concrete separation structure. The intersection has been further improved by realignment of the ramp serving the right turning movement from eastbound Sign Route 152 to southbound US 99, allowing traffic to merge more smoothly than was possible before on the old alignment.

The structural section of the new four-lane divided highway consists of 0.67 feet of Class "B" portland cement concrete over 0.33 feet cement treated subgrade; Type "B" plant-mixed surface shoulders, tapering in thickness from 0.25 feet at the edge of pavement to 0.13 feet at the outer edges, were placed over a Class "C" cement treated base of variable thickness. County road connections and ramps were paved with Type "B" plant-mixed surface over untreated base, both materials varying in thickness according to the design loads at the individual locations. Included as a part of the project is the resurfacing of the southbound lanes of the existing four-lane divided portion of US 99 for a distance of 3,700 feet to the north and 2,700 feet to the south of the northerly connection to the new facility. The thickness of the plant-mixed surface blanket will be one inch south of the connection and two inches to the north.

Roadway Excavation

Approximately 325,000 cubic yards of roadway excavation was removed from the depressed sections and used for embankment throughout the project. An additional combined total of approximately 420,000 cubic yards of

UPPER—Looking southerly at north end connection. LOWER—Looking northerly showing road 26E overcrossing and ramps, which will connect US 99 to the City of Chowchilla.

imported borrow and imported subbase material was obtained by the contractor from local sites with no difficulties being encountered in meeting the respective "R" value requirements of 30 and 56. The material was compacted by tractor-pulled sheepsfoot and 50-ton rubber tired rollers while being wet down at frequent intervals by water trucks to maintain optimum moisture content.

Aggregates for concrete and plant-mixed surfacing were produced at Mariposa Creek, about 15 miles northeast of the project. A hot-plant was set up at the crusher to manufacture the Type "B" plant-mixed surface, and the concrete aggregate was hauled to a batch plant which the contractor erected immediately adjacent to the job site. To date nearly 27,500 cubic yards of the estimated 36,000 cubic yards of concrete pavement have been placed, and approximately 8,000 cubic yards of Class "A" concrete have been used in the construction of the seven bridges built under this contract.

Drainage Important

Drainage was of considerable importance on this job because the new alignment crossed a natural overflow channel of Berenda Slough and adjacent lowlands for a distance of about two miles. During the Christmas flood of 1955 the water which flowed through this area was eventually backed up by the Southern Pacific

Railroad embankment until it covered the old highway in some places to a depth of three to four feet. To prevent the blocking of this natural drainage, and its possible overflow across the new facility, a battery of three 50-inch x 31-inch corrugated metal pipe arches were installed at the overflow channel, supplemented by eight 24-inch culverts through the fill at other low spots throughout the area.

The contracting firm of Fredericksen and Kasler was awarded the contract for a bid of $2,285,809.35. Project manager for the contractor is Frank O. Muren. The work is being performed under the direction of W. L. Welch, District Engineer; H. R. Bruch, Bridge Department Representative; and the author. Work was begun on March 23, 1956, and the contract, which allows 290 working days, was approved by the Attorney General on April 15, 1956. It is estimated at this time that all work on the project will be completed by July, 1957.

UPPER—Looking southerly along future northbound lane. Existing Califa underpass at left center. Embankment in center background is future southbound highway over Southern Pacific Railroad. LOWER—Looking northerly at Berenda Slough.

FREEWAY SPANS HUB

Continued from page 22...
to the freeway above the city on the hill."

Business Improving

The business people, in general, feel that business is already improving. They feel that less noise and more and easier parking stimulates local trade. Typical comments from the commercial establishments are: "Now there is more parking and trade is beginning

UPPER—Traffic before freeway construction at intersection of Eighth and I Streets in Colton. LOWER—Traffic after freeway construction at same intersection.

64

Looking east above San Bernardino Freeway through Colton

to pick up." "People were afraid to stop and park on the street before, because the traffic was so bad." "Before, older people were scared to cross the highway."

Some of the service station and restaurant owners have noticed a decline in business. This drop-off apparently occurred in cases where there had been considerable dependence on the transient trade. However, one service station operator expressed himself by saying: "More local trade is taking the place of transient traffic. If we keep trade at home, we won't need the transient business. Those businesses that were dependent on through traffic should now gear their sales more to the local people."

Route Adopted in 1944

The freeway route was adopted in 1944. A freeway agreement for the project was worked out with the city council in 1953. Paul Young, now San Bernardino county supervisor, was then the mayor. It was done in a friendly atmosphere, with complete understanding of each other's problems.

Due in a large part to the suggestions and cooperation of City Engineer Norman Neste, the serviceability of the freeway was greatly increased. Outstanding benefits promoted by the city subsequent to execution of the freeway agreement are illustrated by two important improvements: (1) A shifting of a block-long retaining wall 10 feet to obtain 38 additional parking places for city vehicles; and (2) the addition of two ramps which greatly increased local access to the freeway.

The contractors on this $1,900,000 project were W. F. Maxwell, and Hermreck and Easter—a joint venture. The principal subcontractors were Matich Brothers, Colton—portland cement concrete pavement, and R. A. Erwin, Colton—asphalt pavement.

The State Division of Highways was represented on the project by Wayne Crawford as Senior Resident Engineer of that area, and Resident Engineers R. E. Small, B. D. Gilbert, and T. Smith. The representative of the State Bridge Department was L. E. Dunn.

Safety Awards

Three State Division of Highways employees were presented with special safety awards at the twenty-second annual banquet meeting of the San Joaquin County Safety Council held in Stockton on February 26th.

Those receiving the awards were District Materials and Research Engineer Eric Nordlin and Highway Maintenance Superintendents John Quinn and John Langenbach, all of District X, Stockton.

All three men head sections composed of several field crews which did not have a single lost time injury for more than one year.

As head of the District X Materials and Research Section, Nordline has supervision of all crews engaged in laboratory and field research in the district. Quinn is in charge of all maintenance crews operating in the Stockton area. Langenbach has charge of all special services maintenance crews in the district.

The awards were presented by John C. Ball, District Representative of the National Safety Council, before more than 300 people attending the banquet at the Stockton Hotel.

The spanning of the "Hub" with a super highway has "uncorked" the traffic bottleneck and has opened the town to possibilities of extraordinary future development. Now, through traffic is unhindered, out-of-town traffic is provided easy access to Colton from either end of town, and the existing street pattern remains undisturbed and much more usable.

In addition, this major link of the San Bernardino Freeway will enable one, within less than two years, to drive all the way from San Bernardino to Los Angeles without encountering a street grade crossing or a stop sign. This will have a tremendous impact on the whole San Bernardino-Colton-Riverside metropolitan area.

As expressed in the neighboring City of Redlands' newspaper, "Colton will be the most thoroughly revolutionized city, highway-wise, in this vicinity." *

* *Redlands Daily Facts, October 17, 1956.*

IT WAS THEIR PLEASURE

Mr. S. Evans, Landscape Superintendent
Division of Highways
San Francisco, California

Dear Sir: I would like to express my appreciation of the very efficient and kindly assistance given to me by two of your workers on the freeway between Alameda and Oakland. I was going to Oakland when, without warning, the wheel came off my auto. When I could bring it to a stop I still had the rear left part of the car a little way on the pavement, and couldn't move the car any further.

A work truck was parked a little ahead of me and in a matter of seconds your men, Arthur Mason and Cleveland Washington ran to my car, put out flares and flagged oncoming traffic, which was heavy. They recovered the wheel which had bounced across the freeway, and replaced it on the car. Throughout all this they were very courteous and kind, and also very efficient. When I offered to reimburse them they refused to accept anything.

As an older woman, traveling alone, it was a great service rendered to me in my necessity, and I want to take this opportunity to thank the department for employing such fine workmen.

Very truly yours,

(Mrs.) Inez B. Canfield
1326 Versailles Avenue
Alameda, California

NAC CREDITS DIVISION

Two of the major highway construction projects now being solved in the San Francisco Bay area are covered by a display in the window of the Headquarters Office of the National Automobile Club. Aerial photographs of the Bayshore Freeway from Third Street to Sierra Point and of US 40, running from Richmond to north of Vallejo are supplemented by a model of the "Big Cut" at Pinole.

In keeping with its declared interest in better highways and traffic safety, NAC has chosen window-display as one of its methods for expressing a continuous support of the activity of the Division of Highways.

New Span Open

Del Norte's First Four-lane Expressway

By E. J. REED, Resident Engineer

THE DATE February 10, 1957, marked the opening to public traffic of Del Norte County's first section of four-lane expressway. The yet incomplete project on US 101 extends from 0.1 mile south to one mile north of Wilson Creek, which is approximately 12 miles north of the Town of Klamath.

Although inclement weather precluded completion of the surfacing phase of this project, it was decided to open the new bridge across Wilson Creek to traffic, thereby eliminating the necessity for a winter detour over a section of superseded highway. Inasmuch as a major portion of the new alignment is superimposed on the existing alignment, it became necessary to place a leveling course of plant-mixed surfacing on the new base, over which traffic could be carried for the remainder of the winter months.

Shortens Distance

The new facility, a 60-foot, all-paved section providing for four lanes, is 1.13 miles in length, including a 282-foot reinforced concrete box girder bridge over Wilson Creek, represents an investment of $600,000. This facility shortens the distance between project termini approximately 0.5 mile and replaces a portion of US 101 constructed in 1924, which combined the very undesirable elements of narrow roadway, heavy grade, short radius curves, and restricted sight distance. These factors accounted for a relatively high accident rate with 68 accidents recorded within the limits of the project for the period 1940 through January of 1957.

The superseded low level bridge across Wilson Creek, a 102-foot reinforced concrete girder structure, constructed in 1924, although subject to short periods of closure from flood and drift conditions, will remain in place to provide access to private properties.

Long Range Planning

As an indication of long range planning, a portion of the approach fill was constructed in the year 1938. Excess material developed on the project known as Wilson Creek to Last Chance Slide Project, then under contract to the Hemstreet and Bell Company, was disposed of as an approach embankment to the then future new bridge across Wilson Creek. J. W. Vickrey, now Deputy State Highway Engineer and then district engineer of District I, anticipated fulfillment of this project at an earlier date. The original project report for this 1956-57 project was submitted in 1948 and approved for a 34-foot roadbed. Subsequent changes in traffic volumes provided the warrant for the 60-foot, all-paved section on virtually the same alignment.

The contract for the new facility was awarded to the Natt McDougal

Company of Portland, Oregon, in April of 1956. Work was started immediately, with Chet Briggs filling the position of superintendent for the contractor. Burton C. Walker, now materials engineer for the District I, was assigned as resident engineer, with Lowell Allen assigned as Bridge Department representative on the structure. Early in August, Jack Gutherie took over as superintendent for the contractor, followed two months later by assignment of the writer as resident engineer.

New Alignment Parallels Coast

The alignment of the new facility roughly parallels the coast line, crossing with the sea and ascending on a 6.3 percent grade. Minimum radius of curvature was held to 900 feet.

An unstable area was encountered at this location consisting of a surface mantle, lubricated by extensive sur-

Two views of newly completed Wilson Creek Bridge

face and subsurface springs. Bedding is a shale and sandstone formation. Although quiescent for a period of years, the removal of supporting materials has resulted in renewed movement within the area with minor encroachments into the traveled way. The 80-inch annual rainfall recorded for this area creates a major problem in surface and subsurface drainage.

An extensive system of eight-inch perforated metal pipe subdrains and two-inch horizontal drains was installed to relieve subsurface drainage and assist in stabilizing the a$_r$ea. A large stabilization trench was constructed for the northerly approach fill section. Approximately 6,500 feet of subdrains and 3,500 feet of horizontal drains were installed, exclusive of the collector system. Horizontal drains discharge into eight-inch corrugated metal pipe laterals from which water is removed at frequent intervals by cross culvert installations. The construction of cement treated base and surfacing was made difficult, due to the ever present bleeding of cut slopes and a large flow of surface water at the gutter line.

Wilson Creek Bridge

The major structure, Wilson Creek Bridge, consists of a 282 x 58-foot reinforced concrete box girder bridge. Constructed on curved alignment and superelevated section, approximately 70 feet above the existing streambed, this structure with its supporting three-column bents presents an exceptionally clean appearance. The structural design blends well with the land and seascapes that provide one of the major tourist attractions along this section of rugged coast. Construction of the substructure presented no major problems. Abutments and one bent were founded on steel bearing piles, the remaining bent was constructed on spread footings founded on a rock outcropping. Because of the curved alignment, superelevated section, box girder construction and height of structure, a major expenditure in falsework framing and piling was required. In order to protect the falsework from damage by wave action and battering from heavy drift, a rock jetty, or barrier, was constructed at the mouth of Wilson Creek to dissi-

UPPER—Old low-level bridge across Wilson Creek. LOWER—Showing "Deadman's Curve" in background and change in alignment, with partially completed new Wilson Creek Bridge.

pate the wave action and prevent drift from entering the creek channel during heavy seas, particularly from southwesterly storms.

Riprap Problem Solved

One of the construction problems in District I, where a major portion of the projects require some form of embankment protection, is the production of suitable material for heavy stone riprap within economical haul distances. Contrary to this general agreement with the Division of Beaches and Parks, was able to furnish the contractor with a quarry site adjacent to the project. Heavy stone for riprap was produced from a sandstone stack

located on the beach approximately one-fourth mile from the point of use.

With the opening of this section of expressway, the elimination of "Dead Man's Curve," a 125-foot radius curve at the bottom of a sustained 6 percent grade, came as a welcome relief to the drivers of the many heavy commercial vehicles traversing this route. Failure to maintain air in brake lines, fading brakes, and the ever-present menace of heavy fog have each taken its toll of vehicles and drivers.

Although small in comparison to the multimillion-dollar freeways of the urban areas, Del Norte County's first section of four-lane expressway keynotes the trend in future planning for this northern county.

Angeles Crest
55 Miles Now Under General Maintenance

By JOHN O'MALLEY, Highway Superintendent

MAINTENANCE of the Angeles Crest Highways follows a pattern controlled by the yearly weather cycle typical of this section of California. From hot, dry summers with high fire hazard in the surrounding brush and tree covered slopes, to wet, cold winters with many feet of snow piling up in the higher elevations, through which this road runs.

The maintenance crews, which presently maintain this highway, from the junction of Foothill Boulevard to Big Pines, work out of the La Crescenta and Chilao Maintenance Stations. The latter station is located 25 miles northeast of Foothill Boulevard on a two-acre plot of ground in the Angeles National Forest. This station is maintained by the State under terms and conditions of a special use permit issued by the United States Forest Service.

During the summer months of May to September, the maintenance of the roadway is of a general nature typical of many mountain roads. The traveled way surfacing is patched where necessary to maintain a smooth, hazard free surface. The shoulders and ditches are graded and kept clean of slough and other debris. Guard rails, sight posts and culvert markers are painted, restenciled and replaced as necessary.

Signs are checked, repainted or replaced by the District VII sign crew, a part of the maintenance function that operates on a district-wide basis.

Surfacing in Summer

Major work on the traveled way surfacing, having been planned months previously, is carried on during these summer months. In the past years this work has consisted of reworking some sections of the existing bituminous surfacing, including the addition of liquid asphalt and aggregate from local sources as needed. On some sections blanketing has been done, using

Merritt Ridge near Newcombs ski lift on Angeles Crest Highway

local disintegrated sand stone in a road-mix with liquid asphalt.

In recent years a Class "C" medium seal with three-eighths inch rock chips has been placed over this surface. This seal coat work was planned by the Maintenance Department and carried out by maintenance forces at the rate of approximately six miles each year. To date, this seal has been placed to Cedar Springs, until recently the end of the road opened to public traffic.

Pavement and shoulder edges along this route need periodical attention to protect them from breakage or excessive wear of both vehicle pounding and rain and snowfall runoff in the narrow gutters. This is done by motor patrol grading or by strip patching with stockpiled bituminous material previously made with local aggregate. In cooperation with the United States Forest Service, a certain amount

of weed and brush removal is performed along the lower edge of cut slopes, on the berms and in the gullies at drainage structure inlets. The work generally consists of spraying for strip sterilization, with some hand cutting of heavier types of brush.

Fires Are Threats

The consequences of fires in this area are serious due to the heavily built-up areas along the foothills below and their vulnerability to flood damage caused by heavy runoff. The immediate effect on the highway itself is to cause what could be serious erosion of cut and fill slope that otherwise would not happen.

During October and November of each year all drainage facilities are checked and necessary steps taken to prepare them for the winter season. Side ditches are cleaned by means of motor graders, where possible to operate them, otherwise at some locations it becomes a hand shovel job or a skip loader operation. Catch basins and culverts are inspected frequently and cleaned out before sedimentation has proceeded too far.

Along this route there are a number of metal debris risers placed vertically over culvert entrances in debris basins. Periodically, it is necessary to excavate and haul material away from these risers to make room for additional debris to accumulate. This work is performed with a truck mounted clamshell and dump trucks.

Heavy Rainfall

It is interesting to note that the average precipitation in the surrounding mountains is 35 inches per year, of which 60 percent is snow. A rain gauge maintained at Camp 37 measured a total rainfall of 62.6 inches during the period October, 1946, to April, 1947.

In the fall of the year snowstakes are placed along the edges of the roadway in the higher elevations as a guide for the snowplows. Snowplows and other winter equipment are checked over and prepared for immediate use when it starts to storm. Rock salt is stored to be added to sand, which in turn is used to sand icy pavement. Sand at present is stored in three 50-ton gravity discharge bunkers, placed between Red Box and Kratka Ridge—these being the limits of area most susceptible to icy pavement on the east slope of the mountains. Some spot sanding is also necessary at times to a point just above Foothill Boulevard.

In the past five years three factors have occurred which have influenced the stepping up of winter maintenance on this road. These are the development of extensive aircraft facilities and factories in the vicinity of Palmdale, the installation and operation of the major radio and television broadcasting stations at Mt. Wilson and the increasing numbers of snow sport enthusiasts attracted by ski-tow facilities at Mt. Waterman and at Kratka Ridge, both in the 7,000-foot elevation area of the highway.

Traffic Attracted

The first two developments have attracted working commuters over portions of the road and the last one recreation commuters, all of which create a demand for round-the-clock winter maintenance. Where a few years ago it was considered sufficient to plow snow during daytime hours and open the road early each morning, it is now necessary to keep the road open 24 hours a day, when at all possible to do so.

As an illustration of traffic use, the United States Forest Service made a car and person count in the Chilao-Charlton Flat areas and at ski resorts during the winter of 1955, with the following results: Vehicle and person count taken at Red Box for east or up-bound traffic only, January 9, 1955 —5,866 vehicles, 17,598 persons.

This was a maximum day for the particular season. A total of 22 Saturday and Sunday counts was 66,403 cars carrying 199,099 persons between January 8 and March 27, 1955, all out to ski or play in the snow.

Snow Removal

At the present time reversible type push plows and two rotary plows, mounted on trucks, are used to keep the road open to traffic. Plows are started out from the Chilao Station and from Camp 37 as soon as snowfall starts and are kept running until the storm is over and the road and parking areas are cleaned of snow. Sanding icy pavement is accomplished with maintenance trucks equipped with traction operated mechanical sanders.

In one of the accompanying photographs is a reversible plow mounted on a new Austin-Western four-wheel drive, four-wheel steering motor grader. It can travel at a speed of 18 m.p.h. and goes as fast up grade as it does down. With the four-wheel steering it can turn in much less space than the conventional front wheel steering grader. This is an excellent combination and a far cry from the tractor and tow grader many old-timers will remember.

The "Snogo" is the work horse of plows in any snow removal operation. They are generally mounted on a four-wheel drive truck chassis. The large motor on the rear drives the augers and blower fan. The blower fan is capable of throwing snow in a steady stream a distance of 150 feet to other side of the highway. Since in wet heavy snow these plows only travel three to five m.p.h., it is necessary to keep them running as constantly as possible in order to keep up with the snow left by the push plows.

Unpredictable Winters

Since the climate in Southern California is classed as "unusual," it is sometimes difficult to know what to expect, particularly during winter.

For example, during the winter of 1944-45, the snowfall at Cloudburst Summit (elevation 7,018 feet) was measured at 30 feet. In the winter of 1952, a heavy snow winter throughout the State, snow slides and drifts occurred at two or three locations near Buckhorn and Kratka Ridge that closed the road and isolated Camp 37 for a number of days. As it sometimes happens, the rotary plows were above the snow slides, the radio and telephone communications normally available at Camp 37 were put out of commission, and it was impossible, for a couple of days, to determine whether or not the plows had been caught under slides.

It was necessary to hire outside tractors and dozers to break through the slides, where to the relief of all concerned, it was found that the highway from above the slides to Camp 37 was plowed wide and clean with everyone at camp safe, warm and busy with snow removal work. On the other hand, the winter season of 1955-56 saw comparably little snowfall, most of it melting or turning to rain as it fell.

Traffic Control Problem

One of the big problems, without ready solution, is traffic control during snow removal operations. In this respect the California Highway Patrol renders splendid cooperation, assigning extra men and patrol cars to the area on week ends when snow sport travel is heaviest.

Several different times the number of vehicles attempting to reach the ski resorts were in such great quantity, plows could not operate, cars at resorts could not leave and it became necessary to close the road temporarily to upbound traffic.

UPPER—Austin-Western four-wheel drive, four-wheel steer, plowing snow from parking area near 5,000-foot elevation on Angeles Crest Highway. LOWER—Parking area at Newcombs ski tow near 7,000-foot elevation on Angeles Crest Highway.

The one item of maintenance that calls for the greatest attention is falling slough and rocks. This road is largely constructed alongside hill or in through cut sections, many of them steep and rocky. Wind, rain and snow cause extensive slope erosion. For this reason one or two rock plows, mounted on maintenance trucks, make a patrol once or twice a day to clean back hazardous material. During heavy rains, this patrol works constantly.

Frequently between storms, the crews gather up the slide material with skip loaders and trucks and haul it to disposal areas. In this connection it is interesting to note that, unlike many locations elsewhere in the State, slide and slough cannot be bladed or dumped in just any convenient gully or canyon. There are designated and specifically listed locations which such material must be hauled to.

These locations are chosen in co-operation with the United States Forest Service. The reason for this is to prohibit debris from clogging the many small flood control dams constructed by the U. S. F. S. and County Flood Control Department down canyon from the highway. These dams have been built to protect the foothill communities from floods.

With the opening November 8, 1956, of the last section of the Angeles Crest Highway, from Cedar Springs to Wrightwood, 21 additional miles became the responsibility of District VII Maintenance Department. All of this mileage is subject to cloudbursts during the rainy season and to heavy snowfall in midwinter. On this new section are "Cloudburst Summit," elevation 7,018 feet, and "Dawson Saddle," elevation 7,900 feet, where severe maintenance problems can be expected to develop.

In the spring, as snow disappears from higher elevations, drainage facilities are again checked frequently, rock and slough brought down by the weight of snow from banks above are picked up and disposed of. At this time summer maintenance work is started and the yearly cycle begins over again.

Gasoline sales account for about 70 percent of the dollar volume done by the average service station.

Elbert C. Brown Ends Long Career As an Engineer

Elbert C. Brown, District Engineer for the U. S. Bureau of Public Roads for California, retired on March 31, 1957, after completing 48 years with the Federal Government, 38 of which were with the B. P. R.

ELBERT C. BROWN

Brown was born on a farm near Clifton Hill, Missouri. He received his education in Missouri, graduating from the state university as a civil engineer in 1909. He embarked on a career as a federal employee the same year, accepting a position with the Bureau of Reclamation's Shoshone Project in Wyoming. Two years later he went to the Philippines, where he spent seven years in highway work for the War Department.

His work as a highway engineer was interrupted while he served as a captain in the Engineers during World War I. Following his military service, in 1919, "E. C." reported to the Bureau of Public Roads in Mississippi.

At that time there were only three people in the State Highway Department and E. C. was one of the pioneers who helped to organize the department and begin the work of developing a system of roads. He spent only three years in Mississippi, but they were very important years, for it was there that he met and married a southern belle, Miss Lucille Summers.

In 1922, E. C. was transferred to San Francisco (Division 7) and, for the next 20 years, he was assigned to federal-aid work in Nevada. He was instrumental in establishing the federal-aid system in Nevada and in developing adequate plans and specifications for construction of the system.

In 1942 he was assigned to work in California, and in 1945 he became the district engineer, with headquarters in Sacramento. In California he participated in the establishment of the federal-aid secondary and interstate systems and the further development of freeways.

"In his many years of close association with the California highway program," commented State Highway Engineer G. T. McCoy, "E. C. Brown has consistently extended to this State the highest type of cooperation. California has also benefited from his broad knowledge of western highway problems. It is men like him who have developed the fine teamwork which exists between the B. P. R. and the states in the interest of providing safe modern highways for the motoring public."

Brown says he has no definite plans for the immediate future, but he will be happy to have more time to spend with his four children and seven grandchildren.

REDWOOD HIGHWAY

Continued from page 54 . . .

when completed. Alton F. Kay is the Bridge Department representative on this work.

At the time of suspension of all operations on the contract late in December, 1956, the contract was approximately 85 percent complete. With a favorable spring, all work should be completed sometime in June of this year. A surfacing contract will be let this spring and, with its expected completion early in November, one of the most serious bottlenecks on US 101 in Humboldt County will be eliminated.

THANK YOU COMMISSIONER

CALIFORNIA HIGHWAY PATROL
P. O. Box 898   Sacramento 4
February 21, 1957

Mr. Kenneth C. Adams, *Editor*

Dear Mr. Adams: Your magazine is one of the most informative and accurate means available to this department for refinement of its field deployment activities. Furthermore, it is well illustrated, interesting and easy to read.

I extend to you congratulations for a fine publication.

Sincerely yours,

Bernard R. Caldwell
Commissioner

GOODWIN J. KNIGHT
Governor of California

CALIFORNIA HIGHWAY COMMISSION

FRANK B. DURKEE . . Director of Public Works
and Chairman
JAMES A. GUTHRIE, Vice Chairman
San Bernardino
CHESTER H. WARLOW . . . . . . Fresno
H. STEPHEN CHASE . . . . . San Francisco
ROBERT E. McCLURE . . . . . Santa Monica
ROBERT L. BISHOP . . . . . . Santa Rosa
FRED W. SPEERS . . . . Escondido
C. A. MAGHETTI, Secretary . . . . Davis
T. FRED BAGSHAW . . . . . . Assistant Director
A. H. HENDERSON . . . . Deputy Director

DEPARTMENT OF
PUBLIC WORKS
SACRAMENTO, CALIFORNIA

DIVISION OF HIGHWAYS

GEO. T. McCOY
State Highway Engineer, Chief of Division
J. W. VICKREY . . . . Deputy State Highway Engineer
CHAS. E. WAITE . . . . Deputy State Highway Engineer
J. W. TRASK . . . . Assistant State Highway Engineer
F. W. PANHORST . . Assistant State Highway Engineer
J. C. WOMACK . . . . Assistant State Highway Engineer
R. H. WILSON . . . Assistant State Highway Engineer
F. N. HVEEM . . . Materials and Research Engineer
FRANK E. BAXTER . . . . . Maintenance Engineer
J. A. LEGARRA . . . . . . Engineer of Design
G. M. WEBB . . . . Traffic Engineer
MILTON HARRIS . . . . . Construction Engineer
H. B. LA FORGE . Engineer of Federal Secondary Roads
C. E. BOVEY . Engineer of City and Cooperative Projects
EARL E. SORENSON . . . . . Equipment Engineer
H. C. McCARTY . . . . Office Engineer
J. P. MURPHY . . . . Planning Engineer
F. M. REYNOLDS . . . Planning Survey Engineer
L. L. FUNK . . . . . . Photogrammetric Engineer
SCOTT H. LATHROP . . Personnel and Public Relations
E. J. SALDINE . . . . Principal Highway Engineer
E. J. L. PETERSON . . . . Principal Highway Engineer
A. L. ELLIOTT . . . . Bridge Engineer—Planning
I. O. JAHLSTROM . . . Bridge Engineer—Operations
R. R. ROWE . . . Bridge Engineer—Special Studies
J. E. McMAHON . . Bridge Engineer—Southern Area
L. C. HOLLISTER . . . Projects Engineer—Carquinez
E. R. HIGGINS . . . . Comptroller

Right of Way

FRANK C. BALFOUR . . . . Chief Right of Way Agent
E. F. WAGNER . . . Deputy Chief Right of Way Agent
RUDOLF HESS . . . . Assistant Chief
R. S. J. PIANEZZI . . . . Assistant Chief
E. M. MacDONALD . . . . Assistant Chief

District IV

B. W. BOOKER . . . Assistant State Highway Engineer

District VII

E. T. TELFORD . . Assistant State Highway Engineer

District Engineers

SAM HELWER . . . . District I, Eureka
H. S. MILES . . . . District II, Redding
ALAN S. HART . . . . . . District III, Marysville
J. P. SINCLAIR . . . . . District IV, San Francisco
L. A. WEYMOUTH . . . . District IV, San Francisco
R. A. HAYLER . . . . . . District IV, San Francisco
A. M. NASH . . . . . . District V, San Luis Obispo
W. L. WELCH . . . . District VI, Fresno
GEORGE LANGSNER . . . . District VII, Los Angeles
LYMAN R. GILLIS . . . . District VII, Los Angeles
C. V. KANE . . . . . District VIII, San Bernardino
E. R. FOLEY . . . . District IX, Bishop
JOHN G. MEYER . . . . District X, Stockton
J. DEKEMA . . . . District XI, San Diego
HOWARD C. WOOD . . . . Bridge Engineer
State-owned Toll Bridges

**DIVISION OF CONTRACTS AND
RIGHTS OF WAY**

Legal

ROBERT E. REED . . . . Chief Counsel
GEORGE C. HADLEY . . . . Assistant Chief
HOLLOWAY JONES . . . . Assistant Chief
HARRY S. FENTON . . . . Assistant Chief

**DIVISION OF SAN FRANCISCO BAY
TOLL CROSSINGS**

NORMAN C. RAAB . . . Chief of Division
BEN BALALA . . . . Principal Bridge Engineer

DIVISION OF ARCHITECTURE

ANSON BOYD . State Architect, Chief of Division
HUBERT S. HUNTER . . . . Deputy Chief of Division
ROBERT W. FORMHALS
Administrative Assistant to State Architect

Administrative and Fiscal Service

EARL W. HAMPTON
Assistant State Architect, Administrative
HENRY R. CROWLE . . . . Fiscal Officer
THOMAS MERET . . : Construction Budgets Architect
WADE O. HALSTEAD
Principal Estimator of Building Construction
STANTON WILLARD . . Principal Architect, Standards

Design and Planning Service

P. T. POAGE
Assistant State Architect, Design and Planning
ROBERT M. LANDRUM . Chief Architectural Coordinator
ARTHUR F. DUDMAN . Principal Architect, Sacramento
JAMES A. GILLEM . . Principal Architect, Los Angeles
CHARLES PETERSON
Principal Structural Engineer, Los Angeles
CARL A. HENDERLONG
Principal Mechanical and Electrical Engineer
CLIFFORD L. IVERSON
Chief Architectural Draftsman, Sacramento
RAYMOND CHEESMAN
Chief Architectural Draftsman, Los Angeles
GUSTAV B. VEHN
Supervising Specifications Writer, Sacramento
JOHN S. MOORE . . . Supervisor of Special Projects

Construction Service

CHARLES M. HERD . . . Chief Construction Engineer
CHARLES H. BOCKMAN
Assistant to Chief Construction Engineer

AREA CONSTRUCTION SUPERVISORS

THOMAS M. CURRAN . . . . . . Area I, Oakland
J. WILLIAM COOK . . . . . Area II, Sacramento
CLARENCE T. TROOP . . . . Area III, Los Angeles

AREA STRUCTURAL ENGINEERS
SCHOOLHOUSE SECTION

MANLEY W. SAHLBERG . . . . Area I, San Francisco
M. A. EWING . . . . Area II, Sacramento
ERNST MAAG . . . . Area III, Los Angeles

printed in CALIFORNIA STATE PRINTING OFFICE 51490 3-57 47,300

MAY-JUNE
1957

Public Works Building
Twelfth and N Streets
Sacramento

California Highways
and Public Works

Official Journal of the Division of Highways,
Department of Public Works, State of California

KENNETH C. ADAMS, *Editor*

HELEN HALSTEAD, *Assistant Editor*

MERRITT R. NICKERSON, *Chief Photographer*

Vol. 36   May-June   Nos. 5-6

CONTENTS

COVER

Aerial view of Kings River Canyon
Scenic Recreational Area Reached
by Sign Route 180, East
Out of Fresno, California.
Photo by Clay Dudley of
Photographic Section,
Department of Public Works,
M. R. Nickerson, Chief

BACK COVER

View of Coyote Dam area in
Mendocino County which will be
inundated when dam is completed.
Photo by Robert Rose,
Photographic Section,
Department of Public Works.

An error crept into the caption for the
cover page of our March-April issue.
The structure in the foreground is the
Ashby Avenue Interchange in Berkeley,
not the University Avenue Interchange

Published in the interest of highway development in California. Editors of newspapers and others are privileged to
use matter contained herein. Cuts will be gladly loaned
upon request

Address communications to

CALIFORNIA HIGHWAYS AND PUBLIC WORKS
P. O. Box 1499
Sacramento, California

Time Limit

By Eugene Calman
Resident Engineer

*Relocation Around
Russian River Reservoir*

On Sign Route 20

A RIGID time limit and tough grading are features of a recently let project situated in Mendocino County, on State Sign Route 20, between US 101 approximately six miles northerly of Ukiah and 0.6 mile west of Potter Valley Road. The project, 4.2 miles in length, consists of a relocation of a two-lane highway around the Russian River Reservoir. This reservoir, approximately five miles in length and as much as a mile wide, will be formed by the completion of Coyote Dam, now being constructed by the Guy F. Atkinson Company for the Corps of Engineers, U. S. Army.

The cost of the highway relocation project, which is largely financed by the Corps of Engineers, will be about $3,000,000. At the time of award, this was the largest single contract ever awarded in District I, which has headquarters in Eureka and operates under the supervision of District Engineer Sam Helwer. This sizeable single contract has been superseded by a $6,340,000 single contract on the Redwood Freeway in Humboldt County for which the Guy F. Atkinson Company was also the successful bidder.

The existing State Sign Route 20 consists of a substandard, two-lane highway through Coyote Valley and the East Branch Russian River Canyon. The portion located in the canyon has extremely poor alignment and is subject to heavy icing in the winter months.

Heavy Grading

The new facility now being constructed consists of the standard 32-foot all-paved section. The structural section provides for 0.25 foot of Type B and 0.05 foot of open graded plant-mix surfacing on 0.50 foot of road-mixed CTB, 0.17 foot of untreated

Rugged sidehills are being traversed by relocation of State Highway 20 in canyon of East Branch of Russian River. Existing highway and river will be noted in lower right-hand corner.

base, 1.00 foot of select material, and, in certain locations 1.00 foot of pervious subbase material. The grading is quite heavy and consists of 1,500,000 cubic yards of roadway excavation in addition to 13 fairly large stabilization trenches, involving some 75,000 cubic yards of trench excavation.

By way of illustration, the section at one station has a two-foot cut at center line, a 230-foot cut on the left, and a 90-foot fill on the right. The job is "stacked" so to speak, in that material excavated from the stabilization

trenches must be used in fills that are to be constructed over other stabilization trenches.

Three Bridges

There are three bridges on the project: the Russian River Bridge and overhead; a plate girder bridge some 440 feet in length; the Redwood Valley undercrossing, a reinforced concrete structure 120 feet long; and the East Fork of the Russian River Bridge, which is a four-span plate girder structure 609 feet long.

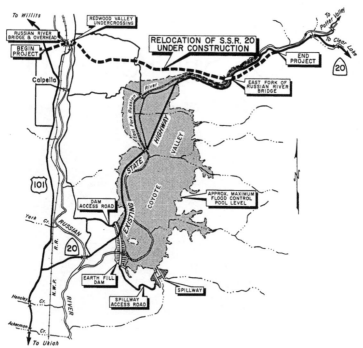

Map showing the dam, resultant reservoir area and relationships with existing and relocated portion of Sign Route 20

The special provisions call for opening of the new highway for the passage of public traffic by March 31, 1958. There are to be no time extensions because of inclement weather on this phase of the contract. A $2,100 per day liquidated damage rate will be assessed for delays to this opening date. This is necessary because the existing State Sign Route 20 will be inundated by water in the reservoir on this date. After opening of the

project to traffic, 50 working days will be allowed for completion.

Big Dirt Moving Job

The contractor is moving about 12,000 cubic yards per day at the time of writing and expects to increase this to 20,000 cubic yards in the very near future. Because of the heavy rainfall occurring in this area in the winter and spring months they will

attempt to finish all the road work, including surfacing, by this fall. Because of the current steel shortage, erection of the superstructure on structures will, in all probability, be delayed until 1958. It is planned to use the slip form method developed by the B. M. Heede Company, which was used for the Carquinez Bridge piers, for the construction of the East Fork of the Russian River Bridge piers.

Due to the short design period allowed on this project, design was made on aerial contour maps. Because of the heavily brushed steep terrain aerial contouring suitable for determining accurate grading quantities was problematical. It was therefore necessary to cross-section the job prior to the start of construction. This work was performed by district crews during the months of January and February in a very rapid manner, despite heavy rainfall. Cross-sections were taken with Rhodes arcs after initial work of brushing, setting right

and Public Works 3

Sign Route 20 at the Mendocino-Lake County line, originally constructed state highway of 1921 standards, has been replaced by a recently completed improvement. UPPER—Near beginning of new improvement in Mendocino County looking west. CENTER—Modern alignment on relocation replaces old substandard facility. Descending from summit in Lake County traveling easterly. LOWER—In Lake County traveling west approaching summit and Mendocino-Lake County line. Old highway crossed summit in saddle on far right.

angles, and setting reference points with a transit outside the anticipated catch points of the slope stakes. Field data was then submitted to the Tabulating Section in Sacramento, which computed earthwork quantities and slope stake elevations and distances from center line electronically. Using this slope stake data and the reference points set with a transit, it was then possible to set slope stakes to grade at a considerable savings in time.

This project is the latest in a series of improvements on Sign Route 20

... Continued on page 19

4

Welcome Highway

Valley Ford-Bodega Bay Road Finally Modernized

By VICTOR J. BAILEY, Sonoma County Resident Engineer

THE Valley Ford-Bodega Bay Highway, Federal Aid and Secondary County Route 777, will on July 1, 1957, become an integral part of the State Highway System but in the past has been maintained by the County of Sonoma. The many dairy, sheep and cattle ranches, numerous lumber mills to the north as well as the fishing industry at Bodega Bay are all served by this highway. Tourist and recrea-

tion traffic also use the route during much of the year to enjoy the facilities of the state and county parks along the Pacific Ocean. Not only are these ranchers and tourists benefited by the recent improvements, but the possibilities of the area are thereby greatly expanded.

History of the old road commences with the trail of the Digger Indians

and Spaniards from Tomales to the north coast country and the Russian River. It crossed the Estero Americano at the site of the present town of Valley Ford, hence the name. With the year 1861 came gradual extension of a road system. Before long a stage line operated from Bloomfield and Petaluma terminating at Valley Ford.

This photo shows section of old Valley Ford-Bodega Bay highway prior to recent improvement

This photo shows section of old Valley Ford-Bodega Bay highway prior to recent improvement

and Public Works

UPPER—Section of the Valley Ford-Bodega Bay highway recently completed by Sonoma County.
LOWER—This photo shows improved section of highway shown in picture on page 5.

Railroad Goes to Valley Ford

The North Pacific Coast Railroad extended in 1876 through Valley Ford was a welcome relief from the tedious journeys over the roads of the day. Parts of the old trestle south of town still stand where the line crossed the estero and part of the new road was constructed over the old railroad bed north of town.

An early landowner, Hollis Hitchcock, who had prospered steadily from his arrival without a dollar in 1856, bequeathed upon his death in 1896 a sum of $20,000 in trust to three prominent citizens for Bodega Township. The funds were to be expended for macadamizing and improving roads in the township at the rate of $2,000 per year. Elders of the town today who were in their teens at the time recall the long era of dirt and gravel roads that were axle deep in mud through the winters of those wagon days.

At Bodega Bay the Russians who claimed the area on the north to Fort Ross pushed through a road from Bodega Port, six miles east to the site of the present town of Bodega. This road served to transport wheat from the vast acres of rich valley lands to the ocean vessels at the port. After the Russians left about 1842, a sea captain by the name of Smith running a thriving trade to San Francisco obtained land around Bodega from the famous John Sutter. He later brought the first steam engine to California and installed it at Bodega in a mill around which the town sprouted. A creamery also added to the activity of the town and before long, roads connected eastward to Valley Ford and Sebastopol.

Relics of Early Days

During construction of the new highway, relics of those early days were unearthed in the stumps of old piling of plank bridges across streams and small redwood box culverts and gutters in the streets of Valley Ford. In making way for the new, weathered old moss covered fence pickets set some 70 years ago and still in service were salvaged by the ranchers who obtained a good price for them from city gardeners and decorators.

Thus we see the lowly road transcend the era of the sailing vessel and the railroad in the evolution of this rich farming land.

Acceptance on February 11, 1957, of the final contract, completed a reconstruction program of FAS Route 777 that has been underway since September, 1951. Four contracts in the program included 8.9 miles of new roadway from just east of Valley Ford to Bodega Bay in Sonoma County. An additional contract provided 1.2 miles of construction over Wiggins Hill four miles west of Petaluma.

The first section starting one mile east of Valley Ford was awarded to a joint venture of Pike and Hill, Cary Bros., and Bailey of San Rafael.

Work Bogged Down by Rains

Roadway excavation which was well underway by November, 1951, suddenly bogged down under early torrential rains, and the little town suffered no little hardship with flood waters and deep mud on either side. However, with stout hearts and friendly cooperation the townspeople bore with the contractor until the roadway could be shaped up for winter suspension of the work.

While construction resumed the following summer, J. Henry Harris of Berkeley worked on the small proj-

ect at Wiggins Hill for which he had been awarded the contract. The long awaited improvements on this section relieved the dangerous curves on a steep grade which had been the scene of several disastrous accidents. An uninterrupted schedule permitted the contractor to complete the work in 66 working days, 24 days less than the time allotted. The fact that a contractor engaged by the United States Government was installing a 6-inch water line along the roadside at this time, made this performance all the more interesting.

In the fall of 1952, J. R. Armstrong of El Cerrito was successful in the bidding for the next section west of Valley Ford but did not start work

until the following spring. The interesting feature of this project was the high quality of material used in the base structure. The contractor chose a site near the end of the project to develop a hard rock pit and install a crushing plant. However, after the subbase course was completed, it was necessary to suspend work through the winter of 1953-54 for a six-month period. Drivers of lumber traffic traveling into Petaluma and points south were jubilant over completion of this section by September 21, 1954.

Big Clearing Job

Huntington Bros. of Napa picked it up from there. With previous experience further north on State Sign

UPPER—Portion of Valley Ford-Bodega Bay highway before improvement.
LOWER—Same section after modernization.

UPPER—Newly completed highway. Note contrast with old road at left. LOWER—This is another view of new highway, showing old winding road on right.

Route 1 they waded in on the big clearing job of the next two and a quarter miles. By the following May when contract time started, the grade was prepared for full scale roadway excavation. It was evident that this must be a boom year for house trailers and outboard motor boats. The difficult construction area did not appear to dampen the spirits of the traveling public with these cumbersome loads on its eager trek to the Pacific playground only a few miles beyond. The contractor handled both project and traffic efficiently.

It may be mentioned that L. A. Huntington was commended by the people of Bodega for his alertness in dispatching a large water truck to the scene of a fire that threatened the town in view of the failing water supply.

Improved driving conditions between Valley Ford and the coast warranted a new design at this point for the intersection near Bodega. Traffic islands with additional turning and acceleration lanes were installed, and on November 29, 1955, the county supervisors passed an ordinance yielding the right of way to traffic on the new highway by repositioning the "Stop" sign.

Elevated Grade Required

The final section was shown to bidders in October, 1955, a month before completion of the previous project. Transocean Engineering Corp. took the Huntington Bros.' position into account and outbid them by approximately $8,000. The record rainfalls of that winter took their toll in small slides in cut slopes along the completed work but nothing serious developed. However, the great need for an elevated grade and improved drainage was demonstrated by flooded areas down through the gulch and out through the flat near the bay on the section ahead. The town of Bay was virtually isolated for a short period with the old highway flooded to the south and a section of road washed out in a gulch on the north. Therefore, arrival of men and equipment in the spring was a welcome event to this little fishing village.

In May the largest roadway excavation of the program (54 percent of the total) got under way on massive thorough cuts through rocky material. A detour over Bay Hill Road was posted and traffic by-passed the rough construction area with little inconvenience.

The contractor followed suit on a scheme initiated by the Huntingtons when, in lieu of developing a rock pit for base material at a designated site near the job, they chose to haul river gravel from the Russian River gravel bar. The haul of 15 miles from Bridgehaven to the job was accomplished in bottom dump double trailer units. The operation afforded quick stockpiling and rapid crushing production to keep easy pace with the grading activities and also provided easy working, good quality material.

Cost of Project

Cost distribution of the program for the three agencies shaped up substantially as follows: Federal aid funds 55 percent; state funds 14.5 percent; county funds 30.5 percent; for a total of $1,067,000. The county bore an additional estimated cost of $117,000 for right of way, preliminary surveys, plans and construction engineering.

Quantities involved throughout the program were not extraordinary for this type of highway as indicated here. Approximately 365,000 cubic yards of roadway excavation was performed and a total of 193,000 tons of base and subbase material was placed. With the exception of the Wiggins Hill job which was plant mix surfaced, the roadway was surfaced with a temporary "Class B" double seal coat.

To witness the coordination and cooperative spirit of the three governmental agencies involved in the engineering phases of this program was a gratifying experience. The engineers from the Bureau of Public Roads representing the interests of the Federal Government contributed much from their wealth of experience through helpful suggestions both in planning and construction.

The Division of Highways is certainly to be commended for the persistent diligence with which the contracts were administered, for the prompt cooperative testing of materials, and for the generosity of the

New Division in U. S. Bureau of Public Roads

B. D. Tallamy, Federal Highway Administrator, established as of April 18, 1957, a Division of Development in the Bureau of Public Roads.

The new division will initiate and execute the development work of the bureau and encourage the integration of the results of research and industry development into the highway programs of the bureau, the states and other federal agencies including the foreign aid programs. The work of the division will include the application of electronics and electronic computers, new techniques in aerial photogrammetry, and new road equipment developments and uses to highway work and the simplification and clarification of highway, construction, and maintenance plans and operations.

H. A. Radzikowski, who has been with the bureau for many years, was designated by the Federal Highway Administrator to head the division.

JUSTICE COURT'S WRATH IS TURNED ON 'LITTERBUGS'

TULARE, Tulare County—AP—The wrath of Justice Court Judge Ward G. Rush, known and feared for his stiff penalties against drunken motorists, has been turned on the "litterbugs."

Manuel L. Enos and Grover Webb of Tulare appeared before the judge Wednesday, charged with tossing litter from an automobile to the highway. Both were fined $100, given 30 day suspended jail terms and ordered to clean up the litter.

engineering staff which could be called upon at any time for advice.

The responsibility of the County of Sonoma was to obtain the necessary additional right of way, to conduct the preliminary surveys, to work out the design and plans and to furnish the construction field engineering necessary to complete the program.

To all those contributing to this monument of progress the people of Sonoma County extend grateful thanks, as well as a hearty invitation to all to visit the Sonoma Coast.

OPERATIONS AND ACTIVITIES OF MATERIALS AND RESEARCH DEPARTMENT

By F. N. HVEEM, Materials and Research Engineer *

INTRODUCTION

With construction now under way on a new building to house the headquarters laboratories of the Materials and Research Department, it seems timely to describe in some detail the scope and activities of this little known branch of highway engineering. The term "little known" is, of course, only relative. Will Rogers once said that "All people are ignorant —only about different things." In this case only a relatively small number of average citizens and laymen have had occasion to learn that the Division of Highways carefully investigates and tests all materials used in the construction of the State Highway System. There is also some reason to believe that many activities or capacities of the Materials and Research Department are not well known or clearly understood even among highway engineers. On the other hand, the department is fairly well known to those who furnish materials to the State and among those interested in new developments in the use and evaluation of highway materials. There are many visitors and a considerable exchange of correspondence with individual engineers and agencies throughout the world.

ORIGIN OF HIGHWAY MATERIALS TESTING

A hundred years ago there were only two varieties of engineers—military and civil, but time has brought subdivisions and specialists too numerous to mention.

Fifty years ago, the equipment of the average civil engineer was still fairly simple. In order to complete a college course in engineering he had to become reasonably proficient in mathematics and in addition to his "sheepskin" he probably graduated owning a few handbooks including a set of trigonometric tables and perhaps a book on the strength of materials.

This is the first of six articles by Mr. Hveem to be published in successive issues of California Highways and Public Works.—Editor.

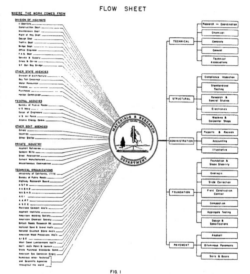

FLOW SHEET

FIG. 1

For equipment, he might have a slide rule and a pocket magnifying glass used to read a transit vernier. As highway construction throughout the County began to expand with the automobile age, many civil engineers began to specialize in the highway field and soon came to feel the need of more and specialized tools. Numerous failures in the early road surfaces soon demonstrated that the ability of a soil to support a highway pavement could not be determined simply by looking at it and it was proven to be impossible to build good concrete or asphaltic pavements or to control any

other type of construction efficiently and dependably by relying solely on rule of thumb, personal opinions and observational powers of the individual. Something more was needed and as the engineer began to acquire more tools and instruments for securing accurate data, he needed a place in which to house and operate them. Such a building constitutes a "laboratory."

MAJOR EXPENDITURES ARE FOR MATERIALS

It is therefore more or less obvious that the so-called "laboratory" is simply an evolutionary development in

10

California Highways

the efforts of the engineer to substitute precise measurements for guess work. However, those engineers who have followed the instrumentation and testing presses into the laboratory often are called "specialists"; somehow alien and suspect to their more orthodox brethren who "specialize" in planning, design or construction. However, subdivision of duties and apparent specialization has not been confined to materials engineers.

In recent years there has been a tremendous emphasis on planning and organization of highway programs. The raising of funds, budget allocation to various areas, right-of-way engineering, execution of plans and preparation of specifications occupies the time of a great many engineers. However, it is still true that only a small portion of the funds being spent for highways is spent for the engineering phases. The major expenditures are for construction, and as a matter of background or emphasis on the need for a materials department, it may be pertinent to point out that exclusive of right-of-way costs at least 75 percent of all the money spent for the construction of highways is actually spent for materials and the cost of their transport into final place on the road. It is the function of the Materials and Research Department to make sure that the tremendous sums thus invested in materials are well spent.

HISTORY AND DEVELOPMENT

In the California Division of Highways the Materials and Research Department is virtually as old as the State Highway organization and a testing engineer was established before there was a designated construction or maintenance engineer or any of the numerous specialists now needed to carry on the work. Concurrently with the creation of the State Highway Department the "laboratory" was established under the general direction of Chief Geologist Clarence B. Osborne. The first Testing Engineer, Fred T. Maddocks, assumed his duties in May, 1912. At that time the infant highway department was small; and the first laboratory was definitely primitive, consisting of a small wooden building on

the state fairgrounds. This was enlarged about 100 percent in 1914 by the construction of a "magnificent" clay-tile structure measuring 16 by 18 feet which shocked the highway commission by costing $800.

In 1922, the laboratory was moved into a one-story brick building at 3435 Serra Way which was enlarged in 1934 and is still the principal building. The old brick building has long since been outgrown and today the department is housed in nine separate buildings, and three office trailers, scattered over several square miles of area. As these improvised arrangements indicate, the laboratory has grown considerably and today the department is impatiently awaiting the completion of a new and modern building located at the corner of Folsom Boulevard and 59th Street.

"State of Mind"

It is probably fortunate for the welfare and advancement of highway departments and for many agencies of private industry that a laboratory does not consist wholly of buildings and scientific equipment. The famous C. F. Kettering, formerly head of the research division of General Motors, contended that a laboratory should be regarded "as a state of mind." It is not, however, an easy matter to pinpoint or describe precisely the state of mind needed by individuals in a modern laboratory organization. For example, the Materials and Research Department staff includes about 60 different civil service classifications. Civil, mechanical, electrical and electronic engineers, chemists, geologists, drillers, instrument makers, draftsmen, photographers, accountants, clerks, laborers and stenographers indicate the variety of work that must be handled by a department such as this.

GENERAL ORGANIZATION

The Materials and Research Department is organized according to approved administrative principles, namely, all the work is allocated each under the jurisdiction of a section head who is a registered civil engineer of supervising or senior grade. *Figure 1* is a "flow diagram" illustrating the source and flow of work to

the various sections. This chart lists on the upper left hand side the departments of the Division of Highways or the state agencies that submit samples and request information. On the lower left side are the technical and research agencies throughout the Nation with whom the department maintains more or less close contact. The right hand side of the chart shows the department sections and subsections with further detail listing major classes of work handled by each. *Figure 2* is an organization chart showing the lines of authority.

The work of the Division of Highways has been expanding ever since its inception and it has been necessary for the Materials and Research Department to increase its staff and activities in order to keep abreast. However, it is not sufficient for an effective laboratory or research organization simply to keep up or follow along with general growth. It is essential that such a department be ahead of the times so far as possible and that the need for new tests, new measures, and new materials be foreseen in order that the necessary development work can be carried out before the need becomes pressing or imperative. This inevitably means that an effective research organization must at times be working on projects and phases of technology for which the need or necessity may not be immediately apparent to the casual observer.

Major Activities

While these research activities and developments of new methods and techniques are perhaps the most interesting and certainly among the more spectacular accomplishments of a laboratory organization, the control of materials and the routine tests and inspection made to determine whether or not the State is getting its money's worth represents the major part of the activities.

For simplification, therefore, the work can be grouped into four classes as follows:

1. Routine sampling, inspection, testing and reporting on materials actually purchased or proposed for use by the State or by contractors for use on highway work.

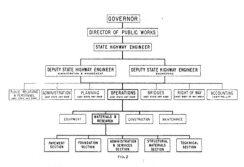

```
GOVERNOR
    |
DIRECTOR OF PUBLIC WORKS
    |
STATE HIGHWAY ENGINEER
    |
DEPUTY STATE HIGHWAY ENGINEER    DEPUTY STATE HIGHWAY ENGINEER
  ADMINISTRATION & MANAGEMENT           ENGINEERING
```

FIG. 2

HOW THE MATERIALS AND RESEARCH DEPARTMENT FITS INTO THE HIGH-WAY ORGANIZATION

Like all large organizations, either public or private, the Division of Highways, has, of necessity, become increasingly departmentalized and engineers have been forced to become specialists. This question of who is a specialist can produce some interesting arguments. It can at times place a designated "specialist" at a marked disadvantage, especially with respect to opportunities for advancement to the better paid positions involving general knowledge, responsibility and administrative skill. It is not widely appreciated that so far as the Division of Highways is concerned the materials engineers are today the least specialized of all units or departments. With the subdivision of work into such groups as planning engineers, design engineers, hydraulic engineers, traffic, construction, maintenance, and many others, it becomes evident that each of these departments deals with some limited aspect of the highway problem but the Materials and Research Department is the one unit which is actively involved in all stages from the beginning to the end of a highway.

Diversified Research

This involvement begins with the initial investigations during the pre-

2. Special investigations, usually to determine the cause for distress or failures. These may also be made to discover the reasons for outstanding good performance.

3. Research and development work aimed at developing new and better test methods, and new designs embodying better use of materials. This includes study of basic principles, and the development of formulas, et cetera.

4. Education and training of engineers who will work in other departments, primarily those responsible for the control of materials during construction. This activity is expected to increase substantially.

BRANCHES AND DISTRICT LABORATORIES

In the case of the foregoing activities, the materials work is divided between Headquarters Laboratory and individual laboratories in each district. The work of the district laboratories is largely confined to Class 1 and Class 4 as listed above. The district laboratories are set up and equipped to perform tests on soils, mineral aggregates, cement treated bases and bituminous paving mixtures. The district laboratories carry on occasional special investigations. It is not intended that they should do much in the way of research or development work but a substantial portion of their time is spent in training men who will

later work in other departments. The work of the Materials and Research Department is handled by the headquarters unit at Sacramento and the four branch laboratories, one of each being located at Los Angeles, Berkeley, Santa Maria and Bakersfield. The work of the branch laboratories is entirely devoted to inspecting and testing manufactured products and commodities, such as, asphalts, structural steel, precast concrete, metal pipe and innumerable other items used in the construction of highways and bridges. The work of headquarters laboratory (including the branches) may be subdivided as shown by chart, *Figure 3.*

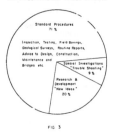

RELATIVE PROPORTION OF
HEADQUARTERS LABORATORY EXPENSE
FOR THREE PRINCIPAL PHASES OF WORK

FIG 3

RELATIVE SIZE OF EACH LABORATORY SECTION
BASED ON TIME AND MATERIALS DISTRIBUTION

FIG 4

12

liminary planning stage for new roads. The laboratory is consulted in the design and preparation of specifications for construction projects. It handles much of the inspection and testing and thus carries a major share of the responsibility for the materials and the manner of use by the construction forces. Finally, it falls to the laboratory to make observations, studies and investigations to determine performance of the completed roads or structures over a period of years, and give advice and assistance to the maintenance department for repair of highways and bridges whenever necessary. In addition to assisting and cooperating with the departments and engineers engaged in traffic, planning, designing, construction and maintenance, the department also handles inspection at the steel mills and fabricating plants and conducts special investigations and research for the Bridge Department. In effect, the Materials and Research Department is invited to share the problems of all other engineering departments and must be prepared to assist anyone needing advice or exact information.

FUNCTION AND WORK OF THE MATERIALS AND RESEARCH DEPARTMENT

While it is customary to speak of 'the laboratory" as though it were a single entity, as a matter of fact the Materials and Research Department operates at least 18 different laboratories, each of which employ very different procedures and require different background and training for the personnel. In addition to these distinct laboratories there are inspection forces in Berkeley and Los Angeles and such important units as the machine shop, library and other services in Sacramento. For administrative and supervisory purposes the Materials and Research Department is divided into five sections as shown by *Figures 1, 2 and 4*. These sections are pavement, foundation, structural materials, technical and administrative. The work of each of these sections will be discussed in considerable detail in subsequent issues of this magazine. However, the following brief outline gives some examples of the work of each.

Inasmuch as a modern highway laboratory becomes involved in many

problems it is forced to draw upon a wide variety of skills and special knowledge both within and outside the organization.

Pavement Section

Someone observes that rain washes the asphalt from certain types of stone used in an asphaltic pavement but does not do so when other types of stone are used so the question immediately arises—"Why does this happen, and how can the engineer recognize the satisfactory materials prior to using them?" and more important—"How can he set up specification safeguards to prevent unsatisfactory aggregates being used on the highway?" Pursuing the answer to this problem has led into many branches of science—mineralogy, petrography, chemistry and colloidal chemistry, and within the framework of these sciences there are many special fields which must be explored in trying to find out how to prevent failures.

Another problem which has taxed highway engineers for many years is the question of how thick to build a given pavement. Limitation of funds makes it imperative that pavements not be constructed heavier than is necessary. An intelligent and efficient structural design means that a number of variables must be carefully evaluated. Among these are the nature of the soils, amount of water present, weight of vehicle axle loads, number of repetitions of load and strength of the various pavement components. The formulas currently in use in this State were developed in the pavement section of the laboratory and studies on this problem are continuing. *Figure 5* shows employees of the pavement section measuring pavement deflections using the Benkelman Beam with automatic recording device developed in the department.

Foundation Section

It is trite to point out that all engineering structures, even airplanes, must be supported by something. Highway pavements and structures rest upon the ground and the ability of the various soils, sands, silts and muds to support heavy structures varies considerably. Engineers must be able to evaluate such supporting

power in advance. It is one function of the laboratory to investigate foundations and all areas called upon to support the loads resulting from the increasingly heavy highway embankments and from modern traffic.

Since it is impossible to explore all portions and depths of a foundation site, it is necessary to rely upon borings and soundings and "piece together" the information obtained. To do this, the materials engineer must bring to the problem a knowledge of local geological formations, trends and characteristics of all sorts of soil materials and to make use of all modern techniques which include seismic investigations, earth resistivity measurements and perhaps aerial photographs. The stability of slopes, the prevention and correction of slides is a major responsibility of the Foundation Section. *Figure 6* shows the head of the foundation section and crews on the job ready to correct a serious slipout on a major highway.

Structural Materials

An increasing portion of the highway dollar must be spent for bridges and overcrossings. Today's freeways in urban areas require more bridges over highways and streets than cover streams, and while concrete and steel are the familiar materials from which bridges are constructed there are constant changes in composition and technique. The use of prestressed concrete in recent years has opened up new possibilities for the designer but also presents new problems to the materials engineer who must test the various units which are expected to operate under extremely high stress factors. Steel strands or tendons are used that must have an ultimate strength of 200,000 per square inch, and the safety and integrity of a prestressed structure rests entirely upon the ability of these relatively small strands of steel to carry the load. We must also think about stress corrosion and plastic flow or yield in the concrete.

Welding has brought about a considerable revolution in the use of structural steel. It is believed that at the present time California makes greater use of welding than does any other highway agency. It has been necessary to work out entire proce-

FIGURE 5

FIGURE 6

dures to control shop fabrication, to inspect the welding, and to make sure that the welded structure will conform to the designer's requirements. Welded fabrication makes possible a saving in weight and definite over-all economies but it does require continuous and unremitting attention on the part of the testing and inspection forces.

The inspection of steel fabrication is only one of the responsibilities for the structural materials section which must deal with all sorts of manufactured items, including concrete and metal pipe, prestressed concrete, et cetera. *Figure 7* is a photograph showing representatives of the Materials and Research Department joined by engineers from the Bridge Department at the plant of a steel fabricator. These conferences have become an established procedure, and have been very effective in reconciling differences and establishing complete understanding on the part of all concerned whenever work is started on a new bridge or structure.

Technical Section

Consider the performance of portland cement concrete. Here we have a material commonly regarded as virtually synonymous with ruggedness and durability. Nevertheless, large and expensive failures have developed. Engineers have known for many years that certain concrete structures have cracked, spalled and virtually disintegrated. It was not until 1939 that T. E. Stanton, former Materials and Research Engineer, discovered that the alkalis in some portland cements would react adversely with some types of sand or gravel. This discov-

ery earned international recognition including a medal for a major contribution to engineering knowledge, and launched an extensive investigation which is still under way from Australia to Denmark. Both public and private work throughout the United States and other parts of the world have benefited greatly by a knowledge of this potential hazard to the life and durability of concrete structures. The nature of the phenomena could only have been discovered by laboratory work.

The foregoing examples are only a few selected as representing work and advancement in major branches of construction materials. There are

FIGURE 7

many many more, some of which, while smaller, are very important, For example, all steel bridges require painting to protect the surface from rust and deterioration. Atmospheric attack varies widely throughout the world but is more severe along the ocean or near salt water and especially on a coast such as California where the prevailing winds blow inland from the sea. Certain steel bridges constructed close to the shore line have required repainting at two-year intervals using conventional paints that have been found very satisfactory for inland areas. A number of experimental installations have been made to determine the relative effectiveness and

14

FIGURE 8   FIGURE 9

over-all cost of a number of types of paint and paint systems. In a full-scale field trial new products based upon vinyls and epoxy resins, together with combinations of new and old primers, have been tried. In the study of paints no satisfactory laboratory tests have been developed which will accurately simulate or accelerate the type of deterioration that occurs from outdoor exposure. Therefore, it is still necessary to place such trial installations in the field which, of course, means that considerable time must elapse before the merits or limitations of any new installation can be evaluated.

How to develop an economical and effective traffic paint is another major problem because such paints have to withstand the most severe conditions of traffic, rainfall and high temperatures. No substance has yet been discovered that will permanently maintain the high degree of visibility required for traffic safety. If the paint material itself does not darken or wear off, it soon becomes covered with a film of dirt that has heretofore been found to be more costly to remove than to renew the traffic stripe. It is generally true that paints are most durable when the rate of setting is slow but one cannot take advantage of this fact in the formulation for traffic paints which must set up very rapidly to avoid being smeared or tracked by the heavy, fast-moving traffic. The formula for traffic paint used on California highways was developed in the chemical subsection and is believed to represent the most

durable and economical traffic paint available commensurate with rapid-setting properties. *Figure 9* shows the laboratory crew installing experimental stripes of traffic paint to compare various formulations under actual traffic conditions.

The research correlation service maintains files on all research projects and retains copies of all contracts in order that data will be available for possible future investigations or studies of performance. A well-equipped reference library is being established as part of this activity. *Figure 8* represents a profilograph unit used for

evaluating pavement roughness and to follow changes in pavement contour.

Administration and Services

There are numerous demands and needs for services which are common to all of the operating units and the bulk of this work is under the direction of the administrative section. Such activities include the accounting department, drafting room and reproduction center which includes photographic equipment for recording test results and other phenomena as necessary. The illustrative arts are an important feature of the laboratory because in the final analysis laboratories

FIGURE 10

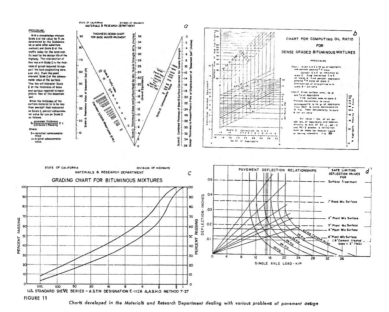

FIGURE 11

Charts developed in the Materials and Research Department dealing with various problems of pavement design

do not manufacture or engage in construction work directly. Hence, all findings must be available in the form of test reports or research reports in order for the information to be available and useful to those who are directly engaged in design, construction or maintenance. *Figure 10* illustrates a portion of the activities of the section dealing with administration and services. Illustrated on the wall is a large analytical chart establishing the cause of pavement failures. On the table are technical reports and the complete set of manuals of office procedures prepared by the stenographic and clerical staff.

Following this general outline of the Materials and Research Department, future issues of this publication will carry discussions of each section describing its functions and activities in greater detail.

The public is now providing very large sums of money for highways through federal and state gasoline taxes, most of which is spent for materials hauled, placed and shaped to form a traveled way. It is the obligation of the highway engineer to see that the materials of which the highways are built are of the proper quality and worth the price paid. The engineer must also be alert to the possibilities of new materials and new methods. These are the responsibilities of the Materials and Research Department.

16

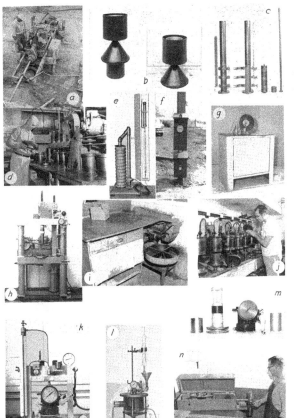

FIGURE 12

(a) California design horizontal drill rig developed in the Materials and Research Department, constructed by the Equipment Department.

(b) Sand volume apparatus for measuring density of compacted soils.

(c) California impact method for establishing standards for soil compaction.

(d) Laboratory mixers for bituminous materials.

(e) Liquid level settlement measuring device to measure the settlement of ground beneath highway embankments.

(f) Bourdon tube gauge for indicating pore pressure measured with piezometer installed in original ground under highway embankment.

(g) Abrasion tester for mineral aggregate.

(h) Mechanical kneading compactor.

(i) Quartering machine for bituminous mixture samples.

(j) Asphalt extractors of the pressure filter type.

(k) Resiliometer with stabilometer in place.

(l) Field extraction device for bituminous mixtures.

(m) Stabilometer assembly.

(n) Cohesiometer.

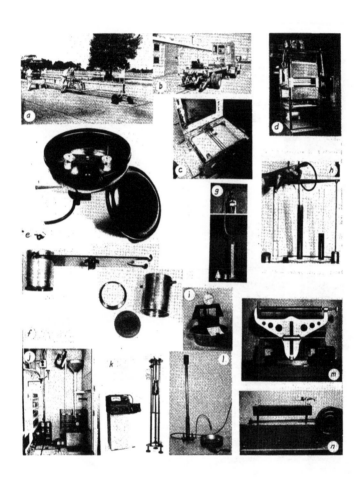

(a) Manually operated profilograph for measuring pavement roughness.
(b) Traveling deflectometer for measuring pavement deflections under load.
(c) Recorder unit for profilometer.
(d) Accelerated weathering machine for aging bituminous mixture samples.
(e) (f) Hand operated centrifuge and head assembly for determination of centrifuge kerosene equivalent.
(g) (h) Apparatus for the sand equivalent test.
(i) Expansion test apparatus.
(j) Shot abrasion test for durability of asphalts.
(k) Decelerometer and peak meter for evaluating density of compacted soils.
(l) Mechanical burette for metering water in soil specimens.
(m) Sand equivalent shaker designed by Raymond Peltier of the French Department des Ponts et Chaussees, constructed in the Laboratory Shop.
(n) Sand equivalent shaker designed and built in the Materials and Research Department.

SIGN ROUTE 20

Continued from page 4 . . .

constructed in recent years. The first of these was a 1.7-mile realignment across Tule Lake, in Lake County, completed in 1951. The second project was approximately 2.3 miles in length and was a relocation of the portion between Laurel Dell and Tule Lake, in Lake County. This project was completed in 1955. The third project was a realignment and resurfacing project approximately five miles in length from 0.4 mile east of the North Fork of Cold Creek, in Mendocino County, to Laurel Dell Lake in Lake County. This project was completed in 1956.

The present contract was awarded in February of this year to Guy F. Atkinson Company. The bid price was $2,695,357.10, and it is interesting to note that there was a variation of only $4,875, or 0.2 percent, in the bid prices of the first three bidders.

The work is under the direction of Sam Helwer, District Engineer, E. L. Blomquist, District Construction Engineer, and the author for the Division of Highways. Henry F. Quade is the project manager for the contracting firm, and W. F. Hendricks is the project superintendent.

BIXBY CREEK BRIDGE

The Bixby Creek Bridge near Big Sur is the highest single span concrete arch bridge in the world.

In Memoriam

THOMAS H. MacDONALD

Ending a long and distinguished career in public service, death called Thomas H. MacDonald, retired Commissioner of the U. S. Bureau of Public Roads, at his home in Texas on April 7th. His passing is mourned in highway circles throughout the world.

HIS LIFE

Born, July 23, 1881, Leadville, Colorado.
Graduate of Iowa State College, B.C.E. 1904.
State Highway Engineer, Iowa, 1907-1919.
Chief and later Commissioner, U. S. Bureau of Public Roads, 1919-1953.

MILESTONES

Sponsored organization Highway and Highway Transport Education Committee—later the Highway Research Board—1920.
Sponsored organization Advisory Board on Highway Research, 1920. This organization later became the present Highway Research Board.
Chairman, Joint Board of Interstate Highways, 1924. Sponsored organization Pan American Highway Congress, 1924.
Participated in organization of tours of Latin engineers, journalists and engineers to United States throughout the '30s.
Sponsored membership by United States in Permanent Association of International Road Congresses, 1926.
Sponsored meeting of that body in United States in 1930 when representatives of all countries met in Washington, later toured the United States.
Served as chairman and member of official U. S. delegations to meetings of Permanent Association in Italy and Germany prior to World War II.
Served in same capacity on official delegations to South and Central America.
Sponsored creation of official U. S. Interregional Highway Commission, 1941.
Served as member Official Commission on Alaska Highway. Later was charged with responsibility of building that road.
Accompanied members of Congress on official delegations as member in Central American surveys of Inter-American highway problems.
Throughout his term of office, served as member of Executive Committee, American Association of State Highway Officials and took active part in all of its deliberations on part of the Federal Government.
Directed participation of the Bureau of Public Roads in expenditure of federal funds in aiding governments of Philippines, Turkey, Ethiopia, Liberia.
Sponsored first President's Highway Safety Conference—1945.

AWARDS

Honorary degree, Doctor of Engineering and Marston Medal for achievement in engineering, Iowa State College.
Cross of Legion of Honor, Government of France.
Knight of the First Class of the Order of St. Olav, Norway.
Foreign member Masarykova Akademia Prace—pre-war government of Czechoslovakia.
United States Medal of Merit for outstanding service during World War II, awarded by President Truman.
George S. Bartlett Award recipient for major contributions to highways in 1931.
David Beecroft Award for major contribution to safety on highways, 1948.

HONORARY MEMBERSHIPS

American Society of Civil Engineers.
Institute of Traffic Engineers.

ACTIVE MEMBERSHIPS

Served with American Planning and Civic Association and numerous other private organizations.

FRATERNITIES

Beta Theta Pi and Tau Beta Pi.

CHURCH

Presbyterian.

Unusual Project
Four-laning of US 40 Requires Traffic Delays

UNPRECEDENTED steps have been taken in the last several weeks to alert the motoring public to an unprecedented situation in modern state highway construction in California—the expected delaying of traffic for as much as two hours on a major transcontinental highway.

The project is the widening of US 40 to a four-lane freeway through a five-mile portion of the Truckee River Canyon. The section under construction is immediately west of the Nevada state line, in a section of the canyon where no practical detour is available.

Provisions of the contract, which was awarded to Gibbons and Reed of Salt Lake City on March 14, 1957, on their low bid of $4,976,184, include these unusual requirements affecting public traffic:

Unusual Requirements

The contractor must post signs along US 40 and State Sign Route 20 at four designated locations in California and one in Nevada (west of Reno) stating the hours when the road will be open.

When directed by the engineer, the contractor will distribute to vehicles waiting in line at delay points such explanatory literature as the State may furnish.

In addition, the Division of Highways issued three news releases, which were accorded state-wide publicity through the cooperation of newspapers and other media and the various automobile clubs and touring bureaus, explaining the necessity for the delays and giving the hours and closure and opening to traffic.

The project involves more than 1,000,000 cubic yards of excavation and earth moving. As explained in the State's leaflet which the contractor's flagmen are distributing to the motorists:

Extensive Blasting

"The narrow ledge on which the highway runs must be widened to 64 feet to provide four traffic lanes, a dividing strip, and shoulders.

TRAFFIC SCHEDULE

The weekday opening and closing schedules are as follows: US 40 —14 miles east of Truckee:

12 midnight to 8 a.m.	—Road open
8 a.m. to 10 a.m.	—Road closed
10 a.m. to 1 p.m.	—Road open
1 p.m. to 3 p.m.	—Road closed
3 p.m. to 6 p.m.	—Road open
6 p.m. to 8 p.m.	—Road closed
8 p.m. to 10 p.m.	—Road open
10 p.m. to midnight	—Road closed

"To widen the roadbed and cut back the steep slopes, the contractor must first drill holes for explosive charges, then blast the earth and rock loose from above the traveled way. The material must then be loaded into trucks or scrapers and hauled away; it cannot be simply pushed over the side of the 'bench' or roadway. Care must be taken to avoid blocking the river or damaging the railroad tracks,

the telephone and power transmission lines or the flume which also occupy the narrow canyon.

"Obviously, traffic cannot flow freely through the sector while these operations are going on. The inevitable loose boulders rolling down onto the road during blasting, loading and hauling are only one of the hazards."

The leaflet also contains an aerial photograph of the canyon, and a sketch map of US 40 between the Nevada line and San Francisco, showing the over-all progress being made toward developing this interstate route to freeway standards. In mountainous terrain, the leaflet points out, freeway progress 'can't always be painless."

The contractor began work about the end of March, although the heavy-duty blasting and excavation did not get under way until the early part of May.

Start of construction in Truckee River Canyon

Artist has indicated on this aerial photograph of the Truckee River Canyon the US 40 relocation project shown by white line on rugged mountainside on the right

Press Tour

Meanwhile, the Division of Highways held a press tour of the project on April 29th, to give newsmen in Northern California, along with representatives of automobile clubs, touring bureaus, chambers of commerce and local officials a first-hand view of the job and the area involved.

The group of about 70 newsmen and others met at the Truckee-Tahoe Wye, proceeded to the project area in two school busses furnished by the Truckee-Tahoe High School District, and returned to Smart's Cafeteria at the Wye for a luncheon meeting. The Truckee Chamber of Commerce was host for the meeting, which was pre-

and Public Works

Sorry you're delayed......

This is reproduction of cover page on folder being distributed to thousands of motorists using US 40 through the Truckee River Canyon

sided over by District Engineer Alan S. Hart of District III. Hart announced the closure schedules and answered numerous questions about the job.

Also introduced at the meeting were Resident Engineer John C. Petersen of the Division of Highways; Lynn Nielsen, district manager for Gibbons and Reed; and Afton Bohn, the contractor's project superintendent.

Directional Billboards

In addition to the steps taken by the Division of Highways to notify the public in advance of the restrictions to traffic, the Truckee and Reno Chambers of Commerce have posted large billboards in their respective communities containing a sketch map of the Tahoe-Truckee area and showing possible alternate routes which the public might wish to use to avoid the construction zone.

In his letter of invitation to the press tour, State Highway Engineer G. T. McCoy pointed out:

"In this case the California Division of Highways finds itself faced for the first time with the unpleasant but compelling necessity to delay a substantial volume of traffic for as much as two hours at a time on a major transcontinental highway. • • •

"We are obviously up against a potentially explosive situation. Delays of this type are a necessary part of the price the public must pay for getting our major highways through mountainous areas modernized as rapidly as possible; this will not be the last of them, although we hope and believe no others will be quite so bad."

Actually, in nearly all other foothill and mountain sections of US 40 where freeway development is under way or planned for the near future, there are not likely to be any major restrictions to traffic.

Either the new construction will be off the present traveled way, as is the case with the construction now under way west of Auburn and west and east of Colfax, or special arrangements can be and are being made to provide detours.

For example, on the section of US 40 through the Truckee River Canyon just to the west of the current project, there will be similar terrain problems encountered in widening to freeway standards; but in this case a detour will be constructed around the most difficult section. Bids for construction of this detour, which will be 2.8 miles long and involve two bridges across the Truckee River, were opened in Sacramento May 22, 1957.

The specifications for the current freeway contract between Floriston and the Nevada state line require the contractor to terminate the traffic restrictions by September 30, 1957. The entire project is not scheduled for completion until the fall of 1958, but the schedule calls for completion of the heavy grading work this year, so that the highway can be left open to public travel during the normal winter shutdown. The remainder of the work, principally the surfacing, is not expected to involve serious delays to traffic.

and Public Works

ACCELERATED HIGHWAY CONSTRUCTION PROGRAM FOR NATIONAL DEFENSE

By MAJ. GEN. LOUIS W. PRENTISS (USA-Ret.)
Executive Vice President, American Road Builders' Association

When we think of the national defense aspects of the highway systems of the United States we are prone to take the narrow or limited view of military requirements and think only in terms of movement of troops, weapons and military supplies. We are apt to think also in terms of civil defense and the possibility of mass evacuation of population from key industrial cities. A broader approach to the subject not only recognizes these uses of our highways in times of emergency but, more importantly, appreciates the tremendous contribution of the highway systems to the insurance of a sound and continuing economy which is the foundation of our Nation's defense.

There has been a gratifyingly close and cordial working relationship between the military staff of the Department of Defense and the civilian staffs of the federal and state highway agencies in working out criteria for our highway systems that will permit them to serve the dual needs of our

Nation—highways for peace and highways for war. Certainly no country can afford to build two sets of highways—one for the military only and one for civilian use. There may be times when important military movements will necessitate exclusive use of certain sections of a highway system for a limited period but no other priority apparently is anticipated by the Defense Department.

Highways for Defense

The Congress of the United States, ever alert to the importance of our highway systems to the needs of national defense, directed the Bureau of Public Roads to prepare a report on the subject: 'Highways for the National Defense." This report, completed and submitted in February, 1941, led to the designation of the National System of Interstate Highways by the Congress in the Federal Aid Highway Act of 1944. It in turn was followed by a second study titled . . . *Continued on page 49*

In Nevada and Sierra Counties, between 0.5 mile east of Floriston and Nevada State Line

FREEWAY
By Resolution of the California Highway Commission
September 21, 1954

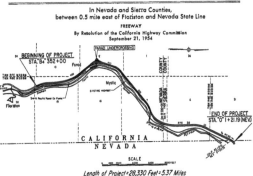

Length of Project = 28,330 Feet = 5.37 Miles

23

Last Link
San Bernardino Freeway
In District VII Completed

By FRANK B. CRESSY, Assistant District Engineer

On April 26, 1957, State Director of Public Works Frank B. Durkee, acting upon the recommendation of State Highway Engineer George T. McCoy, accepted in the name of the State of California, the four-mile unit of the San Bernardino Freeway from Citrus Avenue in West Covina to Ganesha Boulevard in Pomona, thus marking the completion of the third major District VII freeway. Winston Bros. Company of Monrovia were the contractors. The Pasadena Freeway, 8.2 miles in length, was the first to be completed, and the 10 miles of the Hollywood Freeway was the second.

It is a source of gratification to all concerned when an important and badly needed freeway project is completed. This is particularly true in the case of the westerly portion of the San Bernardino Freeway that extends for 30.7 miles from the junction with the Santa Ana Freeway near the Los Angeles Civic Center, to the San Bernardino-Los Angeles county line at Claremont.

The county line does not, of course, mark the end of the San Bernardino Freeway which is State Highway Route 26 (US 60-70-99). This is the point that marks where jurisdiction of District VII for the Los Angeles County portion ends, and that of District VIII for the San Bernardino County section, begins. Extending easterly from the county line, seven miles of full freeway have already been completed by District VIII and are now in use as far as Archibald Avenue in San Bernardino County. From Archibald Avenue easterly, District VIII is now engaged in converting the existing four-lane expressway to full freeway status and building other sections of freeway as quickly as possible.

Under Way 20 Years

The San Bernardino Freeway in Los Angeles County for which District VII is responsible, has taken approximately 20 years for planning and design, right-of-way acquisition, and construction. During that time hundreds of people on the District VII staff have worked upon various phases of the over-all development that made this freeway a reality. The total cost of this 30.7-mile length of full freeway was $52,000,000, of which right-of-way acquisition was $17,000,000, and construction carried out under 43 contracts was $35,000,000.

Many improvements have been developed during the past 17 years that the San Bernardino Freeway has been under construction, that have increased greatly the efficiency of construction operations in many different fields. Many of these beneficial innovations have had their dress rehearsal on some of the 43 construction contracts that have built this freeway. Examples of construction ingenuity include methods of pipe-jacking, drilling for cast-in-place piling, technique for prestressed, precast, reinforced concrete girders, and road mixing of portland cement concrete paving. Contributions such as these for improving construction technique merit further consideration by calling attention to the previous writeups in *California Highways and Public Works* that have described these special features.

Construction Methods

In Lyman R. Gillis's story on the San Bernardino Freeway, July-August, 1956, issue, James E. McMahon, Principal Bridge Engineer for the southern area of the State, and his construction assistant George L. Laird gave detailed information concerning drilling for cast-in-place piling and other innovations that were developed in connection with bridges and other structures.

Of particular interest on the Kellogg Hills section of freeway was the re-quirement for jacking a total of 2,000 feet of various size drain pipe under the existing roadway. This was necessary at numerous locations where traffic could not be interrupted to permit trenching. For further information on this phase of the work the reader is referred to the story by Resident Engineer R. M. Innis in the September-October, 1955, issue of *California Highways and Public Works.*

Prestressed Girders

Special note should be made of the story in the March-April, 1955, issue by Warren B. James, Resident Engineer, Bridge Department, entitled "Prestressed Girders." This story describes the methods of fabricating and erecting that were carried out in constructing the San Bernardino-Santa Ana Freeway bridge interchange that provided for a direct connection for westbound traffic on the San Bernardino Freeway to proceed southbound on the Santa Ana Freeway.

Other construction information concerning the San Bernardino Freeway will be found in the story in the November-December, 1954, issue of *California Highways and Public Works*, entitled "New Freeway," by George L. Laird, Bridge Construction Engineer, Southern Section, and C. J. McCullough, Resident Engineer, District VII, and E. A. Bannister, Resident Engineer, District VIII.

New developments in structural steel fabrication were described in a story entitled, "Welded Steel Superstructure," by W. R. McIntyre, Associate Bridge Engineer, in the March-April, 1953, issue. This story by Mr. McIntyre covered the construction on the San Bernardino Freeway in Alhambra for the Almansor Avenue overhead. In this same issue under the title "US 70-90 Freeway," L. S. Van Voorhis, Assistant District Engineer, District VII, and Jacob Dekema, Assistant District Engineer, District VIII,

UPPER—Looking westerly along completed San Bernardino Freeway in City of Baldwin Park, showing the Bess Avenue-Frazier Street overcrossing bridge under construction. LOWER—Looking westerly along completed San Bernardino Freeway, showing in foreground construction in progress on Barranca Street overhead bridge in West Covina. In background is shown May Company shopping center now under construction and nearing completion.

wrote about the design problems on the San Bernardino Freeway.

Contract Engineering Personnel

Another story of special interest that should be mentioned is that by Basil N. Frykland, written when he was Resident Engineer on section of this freeway in the Alhambra-Monterey Park area. This story was entitled "Ramona Freeway," and written when this freeway had the old local name before being officially named "San Bernardino Freeway" by the California Highway Commission. Mr. Frykland's story appeared in the January-February, 1952, issue of *California Highways and Public Works* and

and Public Works

25

particularly stressed the engineering personnel organization on contracts that were under way at that time.

Valuable from a historical standpoint, describing early construction contracts and the cooperative activities that initiated this freeway, is the story by P. O. Harding, Assistant State Highway Engineer, now retired, published in the September-October, 1951, issue of *California Highways and Public Works*. This story carried the title, "The Ramona Freeway," and reported the accomplishments as of that time.

The great traffic service which this freeway is providing motorists is indicated by traffic counts. Six years ago there were only six miles of the San Bernardino Freeway that were completed and opened to traffic. This was the most westerly section extending from the Los Angeles River bridge to Helen Drive in the City Terrace area just easterly of the Los Angeles city limits. The traffic on the then completed portions of the San Bernardino Freeway has been steadily increasing. The average daily traffic in 1950 was 25,000 vehicles per day, whereas 1956 counts taken at Soto Street in the City of Los Angeles show 88,000 vehicles per day. Ten miles easterly from Soto Street a recent check made on the newly completed section through the City of El Monte indicates an average daily traffic of approximately 80,000 vehicles per day, surprisingly close to the count obtained in Los Angeles City. This tremendous increase in traffic

volume is to a considerable extent due to the unprecedented building program in the areas passed through.

Two Additional Bridges

In the San Gabriel Valley area thousands of new homes have sprung up on both sides of the San Bernardino Freeway. With the development of new residential areas and resulting population increase there have come churches, schools and large shopping centers, often along the freeway frontage roads. Due to the unprecedented growth of the area, deficiencies in design became apparent in the Baldwin Park-West Covina area easterly of the City of El Monte, even while construction was still under way. The State Division of Highways entered into supplemental freeway agreements with the County of Los Angeles and the Cities of West Covina and Baldwin Park, so that additional overcrossing bridges could be constructed at the intersection of Bess Avenue and Frazier Street in Baldwin Park and at Barranca Street in West Covina. These two additional bridge structures with necessary revisions to connecting roadways are now under construction with very little interference being caused to freeway traffic flow.

The designs for these bridges were worked out on the basis of utilizing in the bridge deck precast, prestressed, reinforced concrete girders which are lifted into place during the late night-early morning hours when traffic is light and detouring can be accom-

plished with very little disturbance of traffic flow. In the case of the Bess-Frazier overcrossing, the girders have already been lifted into place, while those for the Barranca Street overcrossing are now in the process of fabrication at the site of the structures.

Even though we now say that the last link of the San Bernardino Freeway in Los Angeles County has been completed, and we do have in operation a six-lane full freeway extending from Los Angeles to Pomona, and a four-lane freeway easterly thereof, there is still much to be done.

There are landscaping and planting contracts for erosion control now under way, with others to be started in the near future. We also have ahead of us the construction of bus ramps at Eastern Avenue that will have to be done very soon.

Revisions Indicated

In the budget for the 1957-58 Fiscal Year is an item of $8,900,000 for development of the Golden State Freeway in the East Los Angeles area that includes interchange facilities with the San Bernardino Freeway. The designs now nearing completion indicate that approximately one and one-half miles of the San Bernardino Freeway, from Fickett Street to Macy Street, will be reconstructed to provide widening the six lanes to eight lanes and adding interchange roadway ramp. The expenditure chargeable to the San Bernardino Freeway, when this section of the Golden State Free

... Continued on page 64

26

Ground Breaking

THREE THOUSAND water minded citizens of California, including many state, county, city and federal officials, saw Governor Goodwin J. Knight break ground for the Oroville Dam of the $1,500,000,000 Feather River Project at Oroville on Saturday, June 1st, and heard him pledge "all my strength to push this vast project to a successful conclusion."

Governor and Mrs. Knight, accompanied by Harvey O. Banks, Director of the Department of Water Resources; Walter Schulz, engineer in charge of the project; Members of the Legislature and other dignitaries boarded a 22-car special train in Sacramento carrying 500 celebrants from Southern California and points in the San Joaquin and Sacramento Valleys, for the trip to the dam site five miles up the Feather River from Oroville.

PATSY O'NEIL

Parade and Barbecue

The Governor and Schulz spoke briefly from the rear platform of the special train which then returned to Oroville for a parade to Hewitt Claim Park, where the Governor addressed some 3,000 persons who were served a barbecue as guests of the Oroville Chamber of Commerce. Before the special train departed the chamber sponsored a Fellowship Hour in the Oroville Inn under the direction of Stanley Pittman, chairman of the celebration committee, and Miss Patsy O'Neil, secretary of the chamber, who, with their aides had worked for weeks on plans for the celebration.

Six bands, including the 80-piece Antelope Valley band from the Mojave Desert area of Southern California, participated in the parade.

First units of the Oroville Dam Project will be the construction of two of five tunnels for relocation of the Western Pacific Railroad around the dam at a cost of approximately $8,500,000, and realignment of US 40 Alternate around the dam and grading 2.6 miles of railroad roadbed for which a contract in the amount of $7,292,214 has been awarded by Director of Public Works Frank B. Durkee.

Governor Speaks

In his prepared address, the Governor stressed the fact that the Feather River Project in itself "is a water development of vast proportions. Oroville Dam, just five miles upstream from this platform, will be one of the highest dams ever built by man, and the volume of materials brought together will rank close to or exceed that of any structure ever built."

The Governor declared that in ultimately transporting water 700 miles from the Oroville dam site to San Diego "the project in its entirety represents the longest mass transport of water ever conceived.

"It will make available nearly 5,000,000 acre-feet of water each year, or enough to provide for the domestic needs of every man, woman and child in the United States for approximately a week.

"The project will erase forever the fears of disastrous floods here in Oroville, in Yuba City, and Marysville, and in the rich farm lands of the lowlands to the south. It will provide 2,000,000,000 kilowatt-hours of electrical energy each year for project pumping and other purposes and it will incidentally create vast new recreational opportunities.

"Oroville Dam will be one of the most massive dams in the world. It will rise 730 feet above the stream bed of the Feather River. It will contain about 14 million yards of concrete—3.5 million more than Grand Coulee Dam in Washington, now the world's largest—and its crest length will be nearly one mile."

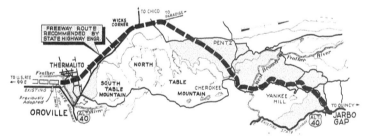

"In summary, the Feather River Project will:

"Control floods on the Feather River and prevent recurrence of the Yuba City disaster of Christmas, 1955.

"Provide a firm supply of 970,000 acre-feet of water for the local service area downstream from Oroville Dam.

"Produce 1,720,000 kilowatt-hours of power annually.

"Deliver 240,000 acre-feet annually to the water deficient South San Francisco Bay counties.

"Deliver 2,230,000 acre-feet of water annually to the semi-arid western San Joaquin Valley of Central California.

"Deliver 1.8 million acre-feet annually to Southern California.

"It has been established through careful study that the yield of this great project will only erase the water deficiencies of today. There must be, and will be, more projects similar to this and many smaller ones to insure that California attains its destiny as the greatest state of the Union.

"Because this is just the beginning of state-wide water development, and because the work which is starting today is just the beginning of the Feather River Project, there can be no delay in continuing its construction with the greatest speed and aggressiveness."

Artist's drawing on aerial photo, showing how proposed West Branch Bridge will look when completed

First of Three Highway Jobs

When the waters of the Feather River back up behind Oroville Dam to submerge by depths of up to 700 feet present Highway US Alternate 40, motorists already will have become familiar with a new and modern highway which soon will be under construction.

Bids were opened May 15th on the first of three projects which will relocate the highway between Oroville and Jarbo Gap on a route 19.3 miles in length, about a mile shorter than the length of the present highway. The new highway will be well above the level of the reservoir.

This first contract, awarded to Mc-Cammon-Wunderlich Co. and Wunderlich Contracting Co., Palo Alto, in the amount of $7,292,214, provides for the relocation of the highway for 13.2 miles between Wicks Corner and Jarbo Gap, about 15 miles north of Oroville. The contract does not include a proposed bridge over the West Branch of the Feather. Subsequent contracts will provide for construction of the bridge and for the section of highway from Oroville to Wicks Corner.

Relocation Route Adopted

The relocation will follow a route adopted by the California Highway Commission August 23, 1956, following public meetings held by the Division of Highways and a public hearing held by the commission.

The route starts at the southwest end of Montgomery Street near Oroville, crosses the Feather River and runs through Thermalito, then roughly parallels the Oroville-Chico Road (State Highway Route 87) to Wicks Corner.

From Wicks Corner the route swings north along Clark Road and then northeast to cross the summit near Cherokee and then crosses the West Branch of the Feather at Vinton Gulch. Between the West Branch and Jarbo Gap the route roughly parallels the Oroville-Concow county road via Yankee Hill.

The Division of Highways is relocating the highway under contract with the Department of Water Resources, which will finance most of the work from legislative appropriations as a "replacement in kind" of the existing highway. Highway funds will be involved only to the extent that the new highway is an improved facility compared with the old. The cost of the entire 19.3-mile relocation is estimated at approximately $17,000,-000, including the new bridge over the West Branch.

Aerial Surveys

Making use of the most modern engineering techniques, the Division of Highways contracted for aerial surveys of the route and was furnished with contour maps made by photogrammetric methods. Design was completed from the maps, and calculations, such as earthwork quantities, were made by an electronic data processing machine. These methods saved several months of time over conventional survey and computation procedures.

The relocated highway will traverse rough and scenic terrain in the upper portion, and nearer Oroville will skirt the widely known olive groves of the Berkeley Olive Association.

An excellent view of the lake will be afforded at the north end of the West Branch Bridge, where a point will be "daylighted" to provide parking space at the vantage point. From the vicinity of Cherokee a fine view of the valley may be obtained.

Excavation Item Large

The project from Wicks Corner to Jarbo Gap includes a major item for 4,200,000 cubic yards of excavation. This excavation will include 666,000 cubic yards of the Western Pacific Railroad, where the relocated railroad will parallel the new highway at Vinton Gulch.

Three miles of railroad grading will be involved. Inclusion of the railroad grading in the highway contract permits using surplus material excavated on the railroad relocation for construction of the adjoining highway embankment, thus resulting in a substantial saving on the over-all project.

The Division of Highways contract also includes construction of a 1,285-foot siphon, known as the Vinton Gulch Siphon, located in the Upper Miocene Canal belonging to the Pacific Gas and Electric Company. The siphon will be of 42-inch diameter welded steel pipe, to carry the canal across a canyon and under the new highway.

UPPER—Governor Knight delivering address at Oroville. LOWER—Planners, left to right: Ray Leonard, Oroville Chamber of Commerce; Walter G. Schulz, Chief of Division of Design and Construction, and Harvey O. Banks, Director of Department of Water Resources.

and Public Works

The relocated highway will be built to the standards of a modern two-lane highway, with much of it four lanes, including a four-lane bridge over the West Branch. On the sections which will be two lanes initially, provision has been made for an ultimate four lanes over the entire length.

Designs for Highway

Designs for the various sections of the highway between Wicks Corner and Jarbo Gap are:

Wicks Corner to Pentz Road—initial two lanes, ultimate four lanes divided.

Pentz Road to West Branch Bridge —initial two lanes, ultimate four lanes.

West Branch Bridge to Yankee Hill —four lanes initially.

Yankee Hill to Yarbo Gap—initial two lanes, ultimate four lanes.

A subsequent contract will provide for the section between Oroville and Wicks Corner, which will have two lanes initially with provision for an ultimate four.

The West Branch Bridge, also to be built under a later contract, will carry both the highway and the Western Pacific Railroad over the river.

The bridge will be a double-deck continuous steel truss, with the upper deck a four-lane highway and with a single-track railroad on the lower deck 60 feet below the highway.

Over-all length of the bridge will be 1,800 feet, including a center span of 576 feet, two side spans each 432 feet long, and a 360-foot approach span on the south side of the river.

The bridge will be supported by three main piers, the tallest of which will be 240 feet high above natural ground. The highway grade will be 470 feet above streambed and 100 feet above high water. The railroad grade will be 40 feet above high water.

Plans for the Oroville-Wicks Corner highway and the bridge will be completed by next fall and ready for contract, depending on availability of funds.

OROVILLE-MARYSVILLE FREEWAY PROJECT TO START

District Engineer Alan S. Hart announces that the Division of Highways will soon advertise for bids for construction of two lanes of a future four-lane freeway on the Oroville-Marysville Road (US Alternate 40) between Union School and the junction of the Oroville-Richvale Road (State Highway Route 21).

It is proposed to commence construction on this project early this summer.

The proposed work will consist of grading and surfacing a 40-foot roadway on new alignment beginning at Union School, and crossing the rolling hills east of the present highway to approximately 1.0 mile north of Adelaide (railroad crossing at the rock crusher). This portion of the project will eventually become the northbound lanes when the route is developed to a four-lane divided highway.

Interim Improvement

From 1.0 mile north of Adelaide (just north of the bridge near the present access road to the county dump) to the junction of Alternate 40 and the Oroville-Richvale Road, the proposed work consists of widening the existing traveled way to a width of 32 feet. This will provide an interim improvement until such a time as Alternate 40 is constructed on new alignment in this vicinity.

The proposed new alignment of Alternate 40 from 1.0 mile north of Adelaide to Montgomery Street in Oroville will cross the dredger rock piles between the present road and the Feather River. Montgomery Street will ultimately be extended to a connection west of the Oroville city limits. ... Continued on page 63

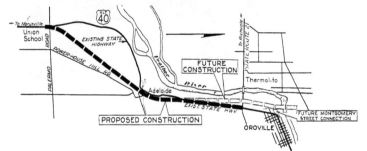

Sierra Passes

Annual Opening Presents Difficult Job

THE ANNUAL spring opening of those Sierra Nevada highway passes regularly closed by snow during the winter months is either under way or has recently been completed. As this article goes to press crews are busy removing snow drifts and fallen trees, replacing washouts and slipouts and putting these mountain pass roads in shape for summer traffic.

Except for the main transcontinental U. S. highways and the Red Bluff-Susanville lateral, which carry a relatively large volume of winter traffic and are kept open throughout the year, all other Sierra passes are closed by snow from late fall until early summer. Closing of these mountain roads usually occurs with the first major winter storm, and no attempt is made to reopen them until the following spring.

Passes Closed Annually

Following is a list of various Sierra Nevada passes which are closed to traffic for a period of approximately six months during the winter season.

	Elevation
Sonora Pass	9,626
Carson Pass	8,573
Tioga Pass	9,941
Ebbetts Pass	8,730
Monitor Pass	8,314
Luther Pass	7,740
Lassen Loop Highway	8,512

As *California Highways and Public Works* went to press, all the Sierra passes were open.

The actual point of closure on these routes is determined mainly by the location of towns and recreational areas, traffic demands at various locations along the route, and to some degree, by the type and extent of improvement of the roadway section. The elevation at the point of closure varies from about 5,000 to 7,000 feet. As a safeguard to public traffic, locked gates are usually placed across the roadway, and advance road signs are installed to notify the traveling public of the fact that the road is closed and of the location of the gates.

The job of opening these mountain passes is not only slow and tedious but requires skill, experience and good judgment in the operation of snow removal equipment. In late spring as the snow pack begins to melt, a survey is made of snow conditions over the passes, and a determination is made of the dates on which to start the annual spring opening.

At the start of operations, good progress is generally made because of the lighter snowpack at the lower elevations, and under favorable conditions as many as seven or eight miles of road may be cleared in a single day. However, as the crews work their way into higher elevations the snow pack becomes harder and deeper, and it sometimes becomes necessary to employ the use of a bulldozer to break the snow pack and to feed the rotary plow. In extremely heavy drifts where the going is tough it may also be necessary to blast the snow pack ahead of the bulldozer. Under such difficult snow conditions as these where the pack is fairly deep and frozen hard, a single day's progress may not exceed one-half mile.

Crews on Alert

During snow removal with a rotary plow, the crew must be constantly alert for such hidden obstructions as rocks, fallen trees, washouts and slip-

LEFT—Tractor bulldozing snow to rotary plow on Carson Pass Highway. RIGHT—Tough going on Carson Pass Highway showing tractor breaking up snow and ice pack for removal by rotary in background. Man in foreground preparing to loosen pack by blasting.

This aerial photo shows rugged terrain through which Sonora Pass Highway runs

outs that might damage the equipment or result in a serious accident. The rotary plows are equipped with replaceable shear pins that are designed to break when a solid object such as a rock or small log is accidentally picked up in the rotating blades. Some delay is caused by replacing these pins when plowing through a slide area where fallen rocks are a common occurrence.

Where small washouts or slipouts are encountered it is sometimes necessary to make minor temporary roadway repairs so that the snow equipment can proceed past the damaged

area. In the few cases where major washouts or slides occur and a detour is not available it is necessary to curtail snow removal work and concentrate on repairing the damaged road.

The usual practice in opening up a road is to plow a single pass through the snow for a distance of perhaps 10 to 12 miles before widening to full width is undertaken. This allows the snow to melt along the sides of the cut and gives the subgrade a chance to start drying out.

One of the heaviest snow passes in the State, the Lassen Loop Highway through Lassen National Park, is

opened and maintained by the National Park Service. Drifts in excess of 16 feet in depth have been measured on this road.

National Park Work

The portion of the Tioga Pass Road within Yosemite National Park is, like the Lassen Loop Highway, opened and maintained by the National Park Service. The portion of this route from the park boundary to the junction with US 395 near Leevining is perhaps as difficult to open as any pass on the State Highway System.

. . . Continued on page 54

T—Photo showing typical damage due to heavy spring runoff on Ebbetts Pass Highway. RIGHT—Rotary plow in operation on Ebbetts Pass Highway.

U. S. Park Service equipment working heavy drift to open Lassen Loop Highway in Lassen National Park

THE OPEN ROAD FOR MOTORISTS IN CALIFORNIA

. California motorists taking to the open road this summer will find significant improvements in the State's 14,000-mile highway system since this time last year.

The State's accelerated highway construction program, supplemented by increased federal aid, has added 210 miles of multi-lane, divided highway construction during the past 12 months, bringing the present total to 1,700 miles completed. Other construction now under way will bring this total to more than 2,000 miles.

Of added significance is the fact that of the additional 210 miles, nearly half of it is full freeway with no intersections at grade and all cross traffic handled by interchange or separation structures. California now has 353 miles of these full freeways, with another 260 miles under construction.

Northern California

TRANS-SIERRA ROUTES

Most spectacular of the new construction which will confront the motorist in Northen California this year will be along the major trans-Sierra routes, especially US 40, where sections of highway are being four-laned and where, because of the precipitous nature of the terrain, he may find himself subject to some delays.

However, a little forbearance and scheduling on his part this season will be rewarded by future sections of divided, four-lane roadway through some of the ruggedest and most scenic country in the State as, for example, the 5½-mile job now under way along the Truckee River Canyon between Floriston and the Nevada state line which will be completed by summer of next year.

This project is subject to being closed to traffic on weekdays during the summer for a maximum of four two-hour periods spread throughout the day.

Other projects now under way on US 40 will provide freeway and expressway for 12 miles through the Colfax area between Heather Glen and west of Gold Run. These two projects will connect with existing four-lane, divided roadway between Auburn and Heather Glen, giving a continuous stretch of expressway and freeway 23 miles long.

Along another important trans-Sierra route, US 50, work now being carried on by the United States Bureau of Public Roads is widening the highway to four-lane divided standards along the steep slopes bordering the South Fork of the American River between Pacific House and Riverton in El Dorado County. This job, too, because of the precipitous terrain, may subject the motorist to delays of up to 30 minutes during weekday mornings and afternoons, with longer closure periods during the night-time after 9 p.m. Again, however, the result will be a fine stretch of divided roadway through scenic country for his future pleasure.

Another US 50 project, State-financed, is construction of four miles of divided roadway between Five Mile Terrace and east of Camino. Just east of Sacramento, work started this month on widening a 14-mile section of US 50

Southern California

LOS ANGELES METROPOLITAN AREA

As in the past, much of the more spectacular new freeway construction confronting the motorist in Southern California is through sections of the larger cities. In the Los Angeles metropolitan area great strides have been made in the freeway construction program. To date, more than 200 miles of freeways have been constructed of which 24 miles were completed and opened to traffic during the past 12 months. In addition, construction is under way on other major freeway contracts totaling more than 40 miles.

Chief among these major completions and going contracts might be mentioned:

. . . A one-mile extension of the Hollywood Freeway from Lankershim Boulevard to Moorpark Street, which will be completed late this year.

. . . Along the Santa Ana Freeway, three major jobs totaling 15 miles, now under construction between Buena Park and Santa Ana in Orange County. Completion of these projects, plus a fourth project between Laguna Canyon Road and El Toro Road on which construction has recently been started and by the end of 1958 will provide a stretch of unbroken freeway 43 miles long all the way from the Civic Center in downtown Los Angeles to the junction with the San Diego Freeway near El Toro.

. . . On the Los Angeles County portion of the San Bernardino Freeway, recent completion of the last five mile gap between West Covina and Pomona.

Harbor Freeway

. . . Extension of the Harbor Freeway four miles southward to 88th Street, recently completed. Major construction work now under way will extend it another 2½ miles all the way to 124th Street.

On the Long Beach Freeway, recently completed construction has opened 3½ miles to traffic southerly of the Santa Ana Freeway to Florence Avenue. From the Pacific Coast Highway in Long Beach, previously completed construction provides seven miles of freeway to Atlantic

NORTHERN CALIFORNIA

between Brighton and Nimbus. It should be completed this fall.

Southwest of Stockton, seven miles of US 50 are being converted to four-lane expressway between the Mossdale Wye and French Camp Road.

The Sacramento-San Francisco section of US 40 is undergoing some of the biggest construction of any section of highway in the State.

Through Vallejo, the existing four-lane divided section is being converted to six-lane full freeway, eliminating the present traffic signals. From Vallejo to Hilltop Drive north of Richmond, 12 miles of full freeway are being constructed, including a new parallel Carquinez Bridge upstream from the existing structure. The south approach to the new Carquinez Bridge requires excavation of a 350-foot deep cut and the removal of more than 11,000,000 cubic yards of earth.

South of the Carquinez Straits the new freeway is being built inland from the present congested highway which winds through the communities bordering San Pablo Bay. A section of freeway in Richmond was opened to traffic last fall.

Both the freeway and Carquinez Bridge construction are scheduled for completion late next year. There will then be a continuous ribbon of four-lane, divided expressway and freeway between Sacramento and San Francisco broken only by a short section north of the El Cerrito Overhead and through the American Canyon area north of Vallejo, and by the three-mile Yolo Causeway west of Sacramento, all of which are four lanes wide but undivided.

In all, a total of $70,000,000 worth of modernization work is going on along US 40 between the Bay area and the state line. Of the total length of 211 miles, 102 miles are four-laned while another 37 miles of freeway and expressway are under construction.

SAN FRANCISCO BAY AREA

The past year has seen intensive construction activity on the freeway systems on both sides of San Francisco Bay, where there are now 200 miles of freeways in service with 70 miles under construction and another 25 miles to be placed under construction before the end of the year.

Along the Eastshore Freeway construction is under way on the final contracts needed to provide 38 miles of continuous freeway for this heavily traveled route.

Also recently placed under construction is an extension of the Eastshore Freeway through the City of Oakland between the present north end of the freeway at Fallon Street and the overhead structure at Market Street, a distance of approximately a mile. Completion of this contract, along with the Jackson Street-Warm Springs sections, will mean an unbroken stretch of full freeway from San Jose to the El Cerrito Overhead north of Oakland.

The eight-lane, divided section north of the Distribution Structure was completed to the El Cerrito Overhead last November.

. . . continued on page 36, column 1

SOUTHERN CALIFORNIA

Avenue in Compton. Between these two completed sections there is six miles of construction under way, scheduled for completion early next year.

Current construction is providing five miles of the Golden State Freeway between Glendale Boulevard in Los Angeles and Ash Street in Burbank, to be completed in October, 1957.

Two major contracts now in progress on the Ventura Freeway are building sections of freeway totaling 7½ miles between Sepulveda Boulevard and Encino Avenue, and Kelvin Avenue and Calabasas.

A 2½-mile section of the San Diego Freeway was also recently opened to traffic in the West Los Angeles area.

SOUTH AND EAST OF LOS ANGELES

Of special interest to vacationers in the southland is the completion of the last section of the Angeles Crest Highway north and east of Los Angeles, making it a modern, two-lane mountain highway all the way to the Big Pines recreational area in the Angeles National Forest, a distance of 55 miles.

Along the San Bernardino and Riverside County portions of US 60-70-99, four additional sections of expressway and freeway totaling 23 miles have been completed —through Colton, between Beaumont and Banning, and between Garnet and Thousand Palms. A new section of divided highway has been completed northwest of Indio.

Traffic controls in effect on State Sign Route 18 in the San Bernardino mountains due to construction between Running Springs and Big Bear Lake will be eliminated by June 15th (road presently closed between sunrise and sunset except for weekends and holidays).

On Sign Route 111 in Palm Springs two jobs completed late last year constructed new bridges across Tahquitz Creek and Palm Canyon Wash and two miles of four-lane expressway.

New sections of freeway are also being constructed along Sign Route 18-US 91 through the cities of Riverside and San Bernardino and are expected to be open to traffic this summer.

Also in Riverside County, nine miles of freeway are being built on Sign Route 71 through the City of Elsinore between the San Jacinto River and north of Alberhill.

North of San Bernardino on US 66-91-395 new bridges and freeway are being built across the Santa Fe Railroad tracks in Victorville.

Construction will also begin within the next few weeks on what has been termed the largest single highway project to date in California, the Victorville-Barstow freeway job. This 29-mile job, which will cost around $7,000,000, will require extensive heavy construction including removal of 3½ million cubic yards of earth. Constructed on entirely new alignment from the existing route, it will save the motorist seven miles of travel in addition to providing him with a continuous stretch of four-lane, divided freeway. The estimated completion date of this job is the summer of 1959.

. . . continued on page 36, column 2

NORTHERN CALIFORNIA

Other East Bay freeway construction includes the section east of Castro Valley on US 50, scheduled for completion this fall, which will eliminate the last of the two-and three-lane roadway over Boehmer Hill. It is also the last link to be completed in a 51-mile stretch of divided highway between Oakland and Tracy.

The three-mile freeway section connecting US 50 and Foothill Boulevard with the Eastshore Freeway was completed last year.

On State Sign Route 24 a 2½-mile freeway bypass of Lafayette is under construction and will be completed this summer, while a three-mile section north of Walnut Creek was completed in January. Work is also scheduled to begin this summer on the freeway through Walnut Creek itself between Oakland Boulevard and the Lafayette Bypass.

Expressway construction also is being continued between Edgemar on Sign Route 1 and Skyline Boulevard, which will further facilitate traffic service between San Francisco and the residential communities to the south and eliminate a source of costly maintenance and delay due to intermittent slides at Thornton Bluffs.

Of special interest to motorists in the Los Gatos-Santa Cruz area is the two-mile freeway bypass of the Los Gatos business district which was opened to traffic last October, and the completion last December of a freeway section in Santa Cruz between the north city limits and Mission Street. Extension of the freeway in Santa Cruz will be under construction this summer.

North of the bay, a new four-lane bridge is being constructed across Petaluma Creek on Sign Route 37, forerunner of a four-lane freeway to be constructed between Ignacio on US 101 and Sears Point.

In Napa County, on Sign Route 29, a four-mile section of modern two-lane highway between Calistoga and St. Helena was completed in December. This construction will eventually serve as one of the roadways in a future divided, four-lane expressway. This is also true of the recently completed two-lane section on Sign Route 37 east of the Napa-Sonoma county line.

North of the City of Napa, another section of Sign Route 29 between Union Station and Orchard Avenue, a distance of 2½ miles, is being converted to four-lane, divided expressway.

US 101 NORTH

On US 101 north of San Francisco, considerable progress toward realization of a complete freeway between the Golden Gate Bridge and Santa Rosa will be evident to the motorist.

A new six-lane bridge over Richardson Bay was opened to traffic last fall, replacing the old four-lane structure.

Also under construction is the section north of the bridge to beyond the Greenbrae intersection. Scheduled for completion this summer, this stretch of six-lane freeway also includes traffic interchanges and bridges at all major intersections including Alto, Greenbrae and Tamalpais Drive. A portion of the Greenbrae interchange is already in use.

SOUTHERN CALIFORNIA

Farther north, in Inyo and Mono Counties, a 12-mile section of US 395 was constructed on new alignment over Sherwin Hill north of Bishop which provided a modern, two-lane highway with one two-mile section of four lanes for passing.

In eastern San Bernardino County 8½ miles of US 66 are being converted to expressway between Needles and the Colorado River.

In the San Diego area large-scale construction is going on, especially along sections of US 80 and Sign Route 94.

US 80, already a divided highway in and just east of San Diego, is being developed to full freeway standards, with contracts let for separation structures at Fairmount Avenue and 70th Street. A crossing structure was completed last summer at Baltimore Drive north of La Mesa, connecting with the recently completed Fletcher Parkway built by the County of San Diego.

Freeway construction will also be under way this summer on US 80 from Grossmont Summit into El Cajon. This project will include a connection to the recently completed two-mile freeway on State Sign Route 67, which in turn connects with the new eight-mile freeway on State Sign Route 94 extending from Wabash Boulevard in San Diego to Campo Road.

Other freeway developments in the San Diego area include three separation structures under contract on US 101 between National City and the Mexican Border, and the completion of two structures and a frontage road on US 395 in the Linda Vista section.

Two major improvements recently completed in Imperial County are the new railroad underpass at Coyote Wells, including a channelized intersection with the recently completed extension of State Sign Route 98; and the new bridge over the Colorado River at Yuma, Arizona.

US 101—LOS ANGELES TO SAN FRANCISCO

Those heading north along US 101 bound for San Francisco and other north state points, will find many new sections of expressway and freeway either under construction or recently completed.

Construction recently began on widening of the section between the Conejo Grade and Camarillo to a four-lane freeway, eliminating the last remaining two-and-three lane stretch on US 101 between Los Angeles and Ventura.

In western Ventura County a section of the Ojai Freeway on US 399 was completed last December from US 101 in Ventura to a point four miles north.

In the City of Santa Barbara, last August saw the completion of the 2½-mile freeway section on US 101 from Miramar Avenue in Montecito to Park Place. Construction is well along on the section between Los Olivos Street and El Sueno Drive.

West of Santa Barbara two sections totaling 12 miles between Ellwood and Orella, and Refugio and Tajiguas are under construction.

A four-mile section between Arroyo Hondo and Gaviota was completed last summer.

Farther north, expressway construction is being extended north from Wigmore to join with the 11-mile

NORTHERN CALIFORNIA

Also scheduled for completion this summer is a portion of the freeway approach between US 101 and the new Richmond-San Rafael Bridge, which was opened to traffic last September.

Construction of an 8½-mile freeway bypass of Petaluma was completed in December, while extension of the freeway north of Denman Flat for the remaining 13 miles to Santa Rosa is now under way and scheduled for completion this summer.

Farther north, in Mendocino County, the existing expressway on the Ridgewood Grade is being extended over the summit for another two miles. North of Willits, a recently opened two-mile section of expressway in the Hilvilla area is being extended northward for another four miles.

In Humboldt County, construction has already started on the first unit of freeway through the Humboldt Redwoods State Parks, a 4½-mile job on new alignment between south of Dyerville and Englewood. It will involve heavy grading along the bluffs bordering the Eel River.

Immediately north of Fortuna a contract is under way providing structures in preparation for a two-mile length of future freeway. An adjoining project, nearing completion, will provide 4½ miles of freeway between Fernbridge and Hookton Road.

In the Eureka area, the four-lane southerly approach and entrance to Eureka was completed last year. At the same time the route through the city was converted to a one-way street couplet and connected to an extension of the four-lane expressway at the north city limits. North of Arcata work was also completed on the US 101-299 interchange and short sections of expressway, while farther north the grading and structure work for a future section of expressway was started between Patrick's Point State Park and Big Lagoon.

US 99 NORTH AND CROSS-STATE LATERALS

US 99 between Sacramento and the Oregon state line has also seen extensive improvements since this time last year.

Four miles of divided expressway have been completed along a section of US 99-E between Olivehurst and the Yuba River Bridge in Marysville.

Along its sister route, US 99-W, a new bridge and two-mile section of modern highway has been constructed in the vicinity of Cache Creek in Yolo County.

Another project now nearing completion is converting a 1½-mile section of the highway to freeway through Arbuckle in southern Colusa County.

Along the Sacramento River canyon section of US 99 north of Redding some 13 additional miles of the highway are being reconstructed as four-lane expressway. A six-mile section between Crespos and Lamoine has already been completed and opened to traffic. The remaining seven miles from Lamoine to a mile north of Shotgun Creek was recently placed under construction and is scheduled for completion during the summer of 1958.

SOUTHERN CALIFORNIA

section between Los Alamos and Santa Maria which was completed last December.

In San Luis Obispo County, a seven-mile section from Hourihan Grade to Russell Turn was recently completed. The nine-mile section from Russell Turn north to Pismo Beach was completed last summer.

North of San Luis Obispo, the relocated 9½-mile section of expressway from Santa Margarita to Atascadero was opened to traffic in November. Construction is under way on a freeway in the Paso Robles area, to the east of that city.

US 99—LOS ANGELES TO SACRAMENTO

Construction of multilane, divided highway along the 388-mile section of US 99 between Los Angeles and Sacramento is now more than 90 percent complete.

Jobs completed during the past 12 months along the southern section of this route include an 18-mile section between south of Delano in Kern County and Pixley in Tulare County and a six-mile section near Traver in Tulare County.

Still under construction is a three-mile section of freeway near Goshen in Tulare County which is very near completion.

NORTHERN CALIFORNIA

In Siskiyou County, another five miles of high-standard, two-lane highway are being constructed along US 99 immediately south of Yreka.

The east-west laterals, connecting US 101, US 99 and US 395, are also undergoing extensive construction work.

Along US 299 several sections totaling nearly 40 miles have been widened, realigned or resurfaced during the past year.

These include sections totaling 20 miles extending from west of Weaverville to east of Vitzthums in Trinity County; a 1½-mile section entering Redding from the west; a 3½-mile section at Montgomery Creek 35 miles northeast of Redding; a five-mile section over Hatchet Mountain; and a nine-mile section between eight miles north of Adin and the Pit River Bridge in Modoc County.

Work is also nearing completion on an 8½-mile widening and reconstruction project between Prairie Creek and Oregon Mountain on US 299 in Trinity County. In Humboldt County, work is continuing on U. S. Bureau of Public Roads contracts between Berry Summit and Willow Creek, a distance of about 10½ miles.

On State Sign Route 20 five miles of highway have been widened and realigned between the north fork of Cold Creek and Laurel Dell in the vicinity of the Mendocino-Lake county line. Construction was recently begun on four miles of expressway between the US 101-Sign Route 20 junction and Potter Valley Road including a new bridge across the Russian River, to relocate Sign Route 20 around a new reservoir.

Work also began recently on a six-mile relocation of State Sign Route 53 in Lake County, between the Clearlake Highlands area and the junction with Sign Route 20.

. . . Continued on page 40

and Public Works

"IRON HORSE" POSES PROBLEM

Setting up track section across US 99W at south city limits of Woodland

Setting up sections of rail across main line of railroad tracks

Pulling Old 1233 around the short line railroad

What do you do with a 140,000-pound gift that must be moved across a state highway?

The district's permit engineer office receives many requests each month for moving various types of over-legal dimension equipment over state highways. One, recently presented to the District III office in Marysville, of-fered more than the "run-of-the-mill" problem.

The 40th District Agricultural Fair, located in Woodland, Yolo County, received as a gift from the Southern Pacific Company a steam switch engine to be permanently displayed in its fairgrounds. The idea was to preserve for the children of tomorrow an example of a fast disappearing form of transportation, the "Iron Horse" that played such a large part in the development of the western part of the United States.

The problem—the switch engine could be delivered by rail to one side of the highway and the fairgrounds was on the other.

38

Through cooperation between the Chamber of Commerce, the Fair Association, the railroad, state and local police agencies, public-spirited citizens, and the State Division of High-

Final repose in Yolo County Fairgrounds

ways, the shortest railroad, in both length and existence, in California's history came into being—the "Snerdville Short Line."

A permit for highway use by an over-legal dimension load was issued by the Division of Highways. A suitable detour route for highway traffic was established and policed. Then, at 10 a.m. on April 7, 1957, construction of the "Snerdville Short Line" across the highway was started. Volunteer

World Conference On Prestressed Concrete Slated

Engineers of the Division of Highways and Division of Architecture of the Department of Public Works are scheduled speakers at the World Conference on Prestressed Concrete to be held July 29 through August 2, 1957, at the Fairmont Hotel in San Francisco, which is being presented by the Department of Engineering and University Extension, Northern Area, of the University of California.

crews and equipment, under the direction of Frank Pucci, Southern Pacific Area Roadmaster; Stuart Waite, Fairgrounds Manager, and Leonard Payne, Secretary-Manager of the

Driving golden spike. In foreground Frank Pucci with hammer; center, Stuart Waite, and kneeling, Leonard Payne.

Woodland Chamber of Commerce, built the temporary track across the highway joining the railroad main line and the fairground. At 1.15 p.m. the golden spike was driven at the crossing of the main line tracks and old "1233" began its journey to its final historic resting place.

Cooperation had found the answer for the future child's question, "Daddy, what was the 'Iron Horse'?"

On Tuesday, July 30th, Art L. Elliott, Bridge Engineer of the Division of Highways, will speak on "Prestressed Bridge Practice in California," and Charles Peterson and A. H. Brownfield, Structural Engineers of the Division of Architecture, will present a talk on "Our Experience With Prestressed Lift Slabs."

A leaflet containing complete information on the conference may be obtained on request from University Extension, University of California, Berkeley 4, California.

Golden Gate Bridge Celebrates Its 20th Anniversary

On May 27th the twentieth anniversary of the opening of the Golden Gate Bridge was marked with a celebration under the joint sponsorship of the Redwood Empire Association and the Golden Gate Bridge and Highway District.

A "salute to travel" was the central theme of the observance and since traveling is often prescribed as a panacea for many ailments, a collateral theme was a "salute to good health." The cosponsors of the celebration pointed out there could well be innumerable themes in the forms of "salutes" to the thousands of individuals and organizations whose skills and backing transformed a dream into a reality.

The Golden Gate Bridge is the longest single suspension type span in the world and is known to travelers from all sections of the world—from the millions who cross it each year in motor vehicles to those who view it from the decks of ships plying the Pacific Ocean, or from aloft in airplanes flying trans-Pacific and other routes.

Total length of the bridge, including approach structure, is 8,981 feet. Length of the suspended structure is 6,450 feet and the main span is 4,200 feet long. Each side span is 1,125 feet long.

Height of each tower is 746 feet and clearance of the bridge above low water is 220 feet. Deepest foundation below mean low water is 110 feet.

Length of each 36⅜-inch cable is 7,650 feet, containing 80,000 miles of wire, enough to span the world at the equator three times with an overlap of 5,000 miles.

Structural steel for the span, which has a 60-foot roadway between curbs, totaled 83,000 tons, and concrete totaled 389,000 cubic yards.

The bridge has afforded passage to about 165,000,000 toll-paying motor vehicles since its completion and its importance is reflected in the amazing development of the entire Redwood

. . . Continued on page 51

NORTHERN CALIFORNIA

Continued from page 37 . . .

Along the Feather River Highway (US 40 alternate) a project is now under way which will widen and re-align the five miles between Spring Garden and Sloat.

Along the Mother Lode Highway (Sign Route 49) the roadbed has been regraded and resurfaced west of Sierra City in Sierra County, as has a three-mile section between south of Angels Camp in Calaveras County and 1½ miles south of the Stanislaus River in Tuolumne County. Work was also recently begun on a relocation project through Mokelumne Hill in Calaveras County.

East of the Sierra, on the north state portion of US 395, a 3½-mile section between Sagehen Summit and Dry Creek in Lassen County has been widened and relocated while some 21 miles of the existing highway has been resurfaced between Madeline in Lassen County and south of Alturas in Modoc County.

US 101 SOUTH OF SAN FRANCISCO

Those heading south on US 101 from the San Francisco area will find many new sections of expressway and freeway either under construction or recently completed.

In Monterey County, construction has started on a four-lane, divided freeway through Chualar as well as a 5½-mile section north of Greenfield and an eight-mile section between Greenfield and King City which joins a section of freeway west of King City which was completed in February.

US 99—SACRAMENTO TO LOS ANGELES

Construction of four-lane divided roadway along the 388-mile section of US 99 between Sacramento and Los Angeles is now more than 90 percent complete.

Freeway jobs completed during the past 12 months along the northern section of this heavily traveled north-south route include a five-mile section just south of Sacramento; another five-mile section just north of Lodi (except for structures); two sections totaling 5½ miles between Stockton and Manteca in San Joaquin County;

and another two-mile portion of the Fresno Freeway.

Still under construction are two sections totaling 13 miles between Sacramento and Lodi in Sacramento County; 4½-mile section through Atwater; a seven-mile section in the Chowchilla area; and the final one-mile section of the Fresno Bypass, completion of which is expected by September.

SIERRA LATERALS

South of US 50 other cross-Sierra highways have also undergone widening and reconstruction work.

The Carson Pass Highway (Sign Route 88) is being widened and improved between the east side of the pass and Picketts on Sign Route 89.

Work was completed last year which regraded and resurfaced the road and constructed a new bridge east of Valley Springs on Sign Route 4 in Calaveras County.

Improvement of a four-mile section of Sign Route 140 (Yosemite All-Year Highway) west of Mariposa was completed last summer. A five-mile widening and realignment project is now under way northeast of Mariposa. Another project now under way is reconstructing sections of the highway between Bear Creek and the Yosemite National Park boundary.

FROM THE NETHERLANDS

WEG EN WATERBOUW
P. O. Box 27, Heemstede
Netherlands

THE EDITOR: As editor of *Weg en Waterbouw* (in your language, *Road and Waterworks*), a journal published by three societies of contractors, I have occasionally had the privilege of perusing a number of copies of your publication *California Highways and Public Works.*

Allow me to state that I consider it a remarkably fine publication and of outstanding significance in the field of design and construction of modern highways.

Sincerely yours,

C. JULIUS
—————

At the close of the 1955-56 Fiscal Year, the Division of Highways was operating 151 land radio stations and 674 mobile radio units.

The French Had A Word for It

When the horseless carriage first appeared on the American scene, we had a problem on our hands: We had to figure out what to call it.

It wasn't easy figuring out what to call this new gadget and some of the things that went with it. We made some abortive attempts with such awkward words and phrases as "quadricycle," "motorcycle," "autocar," and "motor wagon," but none of these seemed to sit quite right.

When we began to look around we found that the Greeks had no word for it but the French did. "Automobile," according to the National Automobile Club, seemed to be a natural and we took it for our own.

From the French

The French had words for other things, too. They had "chassis" for the underpart of the automobile, the part comprised of wheels, frame, and machinery. We took "chassis" but had our troubles with the plural. We didn't know how to pronounce it. The French had "garage" for the building in which the car was kept. "Garage" we took over right away.

The French had "chauffeur" for the man you hired to drive your limousine. This gave us real trouble. We couldn't pronounce it. We tried to replace it with "motorman" but this seemed to include the operator of the streetcar or of the "tuppenny tube." Perhaps in desperation most of us took to driving our own cars and left the hiring of chauffeurs and the pronouncing of "chauffeur" to the select few.

One word, however, the French really offered in vain. That air-filled rubber tube that cushioned the wheel they called "le pneumatique." Even when they shortened it to "le pneu" it was too much for us. We settled for "tire." The British stuck with "tyre."

So much for Paris and the parts of your car.
—————

A 10 percent increase in illuminated signs maintained by the Division of Highways was reported during the 1955-56 Fiscal Year.

Harbor Freeway

Governor Knight Opens
New Four-mile Section

ON April 24, 1957, just before noon Governor Goodwin J. Knight, assisted by Mrs. Knight, public officials and community leaders in the Los Angeles area, wielded mammoth shears provided by the Inglewood Chamber of Commerce and snipped a silk ribbon to open the new four-mile length of the Harbor Freeway, extending the previously opened freeway from Santa Barbara Avenue southerly to 88th Place, in Los Angeles.

This was one of the largest and most impressive opening ceremonies ever held in the southern part of the State and rightly so, because of the importance of this link of the Harbor Freeway to the metropolitan Los Angeles area. It was estimated that over 500 enthusiastic citizens were present at the dedication ceremonies.

Since the California Highway Commission was in regular monthly session in Sacramento on the day for completion of this freeway unit it

was impossible for any members of the commission, State Highway Engineer G. T. McCoy or State Director of Public Works Frank B. Durkee to be present at the ribbon cutting. Assistant Public Works Director T. Fred Bagshaw was in attendance as the official representative of Durkee and the Highway Commission.

Investment of $22,000,000

Representing State Highway Engineer G. T. McCoy at the ceremony,

Governor Knight cuts ceremonial ribbon, signalizing opening of new section of Harbor Freeway. LEFT TO RIGHT—Assemblyman Charles Wilson, Supervisor Kenneth Hahn, Governor Knight, Mrs. Knight, Councilman Gordon Hahn, George Gose, master of ceremonies, Charles E. Duconmun, President, Los Angeles Chamber of Commerce, Assistant State Highway Engineer E. T. Telford, and Spencer V. Cortelyou, retired Assistant State Highway Engineer.

Following ribbon cutting auto caravan traveled over new section of Harbor Freeway

E. T. Telford, Assistant State Highway Engineer in charge of District VII, called attention in his remarks to the fact that the new section of eight-lane freeway represents a total investment of $22,000,000. This included the cost of right-of-way acquisition as well as the cost of the two adjoining construction contracts. J. E. Haddock, Ltd., of Pasadena, the contractor who carried out the northerly unit of construction, and Guy F. Atkinson of Long Beach, the contractor on the southerly unit, were commended by Telford for the expeditious and efficient manner in which they organized their work to the end that all construction on both contracts was completed several months ahead of schedule.

The Haddock contract was 2.3 miles in length and carried a contract allotment of $4,756,000. The Atkinson contract was 1.7 miles in length, and carried a construction allotment of $4,418,000. Details concerning these two adjoining construction contracts will be found in story entitled, "Harbor Freeway Construction Progress," by Morris E. Camp and Ray A. Collins, resident engineers, published in the September-October, 1956, issue of *California Highways and Public Works*.

Simultaneous Construction

It is a common occurrence for adjoining construction contracts on a freeway to be under way simultaneously but it is unusual indeed for two on the same day. When this happens there is a big advantage to motorists who get a longer mileage of freeway for use ahead of schedule with less disturbance of established traffic flow

patterns. There was in this instance a direct money saving to the State because simultaneous completion of these two adjoining contracts made it possible to eliminate $10,000 worth of construction work on temporary on- and off-ramps at the junction between the two contracts that otherwise would have had to be built and put into service.

There are now 11 miles of completed Harbor Freeway out of the total length of 22.4 miles between the Hollywood Freeway and Battery Street in the San Pedro area, and construction is in progress on a recently started 2.6-mile unit.

Guy F. Atkinson is also the contractor building this 2.6-mile section of the Harbor Freeway from 88th Place southerly to 124th Street where construction is now under way. This contract provides for an eight-lane freeway complete with 12 bridges, three pedestrian overpasses and five pedestrian undercrossings, a pumping plant and four large reinforced concrete retaining walls. The contract allotment is $5,866,000. The estimated date of completion is September, 1958.

Remaining Link

Taking into account completed construction and the new construction now in progress, of the 22.4 miles total there remains only a nine-mile link of the Harbor Freeway still to be put under contract. Designs and preparation of plans for this remaining link are susbtantially completed and the right-of-way acquisition program for this future construction is well advanced. Final completion of the Harbor Freeway throughout its entire length awaits allocation of construction funds by the California Highway Commission when future state highway budgets are under consideration.

The dedication ceremonies for the newly completed four-mile unit were conducted under the sponsorship of the Los Angeles Chamber of Commerce, and the chairman of the Chamber's Traffic and Transit Committee, George Gose, acted as master of ceremonies. In his opening remarks of welcome, he said:

"As we gather here today overlooking the great Los Angeles metropolitan area we can, I think, feel very proud of the accomplishments made in transportation. This is the most highly populated automobile center in the world and we have met the resulting traffic problems with a superb freeway system. We wish to thank the representatives of our civic groups and our local government for their diligence in obtaining freeways for this area. Our sincere appreciation is extended to the State Division of Highways and to the California Highway Commission for the outstanding job done on the Harbor Freeway and also our gratitude to them for their vision in the continuing development of a safe, convenient and economical system of highways and freeways for this area."

List of Speakers

The first speaker on the program introduced by Gose was Dr. William Strong, pastor of the Florence Avenue United Presbyterian Church, who gave the invocation and prayed for a more general adoption by motorists of the Golden Rule principle to the

GOVERNOR WANTS STRICTER TRAFFIC LAWS*

Dedicating the latest section of the Harbor Freeway in Los Angeles, Governor Knight said:

"I must admit that occasions such as this one give me double pleasure, for as a life-long resident of the City of the Angels I am pleased to note such monumental evidence of community progress. As Governor of California, I am pleased to point with pride to such concrete evidence of the State's official concern that it make substantial contributions toward effectively meeting the challenges which must be faced in our expanding and accelerating society.

'This particular dedication marks the completion of another four miles of the already internationally famous Harbor Freeway. It also commemorates the fact that approximately half of the total length of this magnificent roadway has been completed and is open to traffic. The State Division of Highways assures me that the second half will most likely proceed much more rapidly in relation to actual working time involved. I am also told that the more difficult and costly portions of the work are behind us.

"The rights of way for the remainder of the Harbor Freeway have been acquired and the work will be done

* On May 24th, Governor Knight signed A. B. No. 19, which he espoused, providing for a mandatory jail sentence for those convicted two or more times of drunk driving.

end that the usefulness of the Harbor Freeway will not be marred by tragic traffic accidents.

Among those present called upon for brief remarks, in addition to Governor Knight and Telford, were Councilman Gordon Hahn, representing Mayor Norris Poulson of the City of Los Angeles; Police Chief William H. Parker, Assemblyman Charles H. Witson, Charles E. Ducommun, President of the Los Angeles Chamber of Commerce, and Los Angeles County Supervisor Kenneth Hahn.

The dedication ceremonies were brought to a close by Governor Knight.

as rapidly as possible, consistent with the other freeway needs in the Los Angeles area.

Cost of Project $22,000,000

"This section which we are dedicating today cost around $22,000,000 to complete, including costs of construction and rights of way acquisition.

"California, with her magnificent distances and energetic citizenry, has pioneered and led the Nation in the evolution of highway development and planning. When President Eisenhower last summer signed the Federal Highway Act of 1956, opening the way for the most ambitious communications program since the days of Imperial Rome, California was not only ready, she was anxious to get under way on her commitments to the total program.

"Our philosophy of state highway construction had actually anticipated the nationwide projections.

"In a recent report made by Samuel Cummings to the Automobile Manufacturers Association of the United States, the author surveyed the principal urban areas of the entire Nation—detailing also such metropolitan highway systems as those in Detroit, New York City, Dallas, Chicago, Cleveland, Chicago, and so forth.

"His reference to Los Angeles, of course, was of greatest interest to me, and his summary demonstrates why, even as we dedicate this stretch of road, draftsmen are at work on plans for new freeways, contracts are being considered on other sections, while men and equipment are at work rushing to completion even further portions of our highway system for the greater comfort, convenience and safety of the people of California.

Los Angeles Freeways

'Concerning our city, Mr. Cummings reported—and I quote: 'Although Los Angeles has the most extensive system of freeways in the Country, its road builders are finding

. . . Continued on page 57

Freeway construction between Lodi and Lind's Airport, on US 99, in San Joaquin County enabled traffic to use the newly constructed four-lane divided facility early in December, 1956. This was approximately nine months before the final completion date of this contract. The use of the new four lanes of concrete pavement was made available to the traveling public by the whole-hearted cooperation of the contractor and the routing of county road traffic on temporary detours around the various interchange structures.

This 4.8 miles of road was the last remaining portion of two-lane pavement in San Joaquin County on US 99. With the opening to the public of the four-lane divided roadway, the benefits were extensive. The 14,000 daily users of this route experienced immediate relief from the previous congestion on the over taxed two-lane road.

The photographs accompanying this article are as follows:

Picture No. 1: The crossing of the Mokelumne River just north of Lodi showing the use of the eventual southbound lanes by two-way traffic and the reconstruction of the existing bridge which was used by two-way traffic until the southbound bridge was completed.

Picture No. 2: The Acampo Road Overcrossing and Pumping Plant. The traffic at this location was interrupted, from the use of the four lanes, only temporarily while the structural steel was being placed.

Picture No. 3: Showing the four completed lanes of PCC pavement and

Traffic Safety Program During Month of June

California will be blanketed during June with urgent reminders to motorists that safe driving at sane speeds will save them from the tragedy and often crippling expense of traffic accidents.

This state-wide campaign is the annual "speed kills" effort sponsored by the California Association of Insurance Agents and carried out through its affiliated local associations with the cooperation of the National Automobile Club.

"We hope our program this year will benefit every licensed driver, pedestrian and tourist," Vice President Roger Chickering of CAIA said. "If it serves to reduce our tragic highway death toll even in a small degree, it will be worth all the effort we have put into it,"

Local agents' associations now are contacting service clubs, churches, chambers of commerce and other organizations in rural areas and communities of all sizes to enlist support for the month-long program. The California Traffic Safety Foundation and the numerous chapters of the National Safety Council have announced their backing of the campaign.

SCHOOL BUSES
California has 6,364 school busses in operation.

a temporary crossing at grade for county road traffic during the construction of the Peltier Road Overcrossing.

Picture No. 4: Jahant Road Overcrossing. Traffic at this location was also only temporarily inconvenienced during the placing of the structural steel.

This contract was a joint venture of the MJB Construction Co., Inc., and Lord & Bishop, Inc., of Stockton and Sacramento, respectively. The length of the project is 4.8 miles and the contract cost approximately $2,000,000. The Resident Engineer for the State was Harold E. Atherstone, associate highway engineer.

This Contractor Knows Value of Public Relations

A personally delivered "greeting card" to each resident along the route of a freeway project now under construction in Los Angeles was the method used by a highway contractor recently to express his regrets for any disturbance or inconvenience his operations might cause.

The job on which this gratifying public relations step was taken is the first unit of the Glendale Freeway in Los Angeles, between the Los Angeles River and Eagle Rock Boulevard, a distance of 1.6 miles, of which over 60 percent is in a residential district. Several major structures are included in the project, one of which is a 461-foot overhead crossing of the Southern Pacific Railroad's Taylor Yard.

The $2,659,000 contract is being carried on by the Thompson Construction Company of Los Angeles. The president of this firm is J. A. Thompson, who is a past president of the Southern California Chapter of the Associated General Contractors of America, Inc.

Considerate of Property Owners

The Thompson card was delivered by company representatives to the doors of residents along and near the project. Thompson told Resident Engineer Jack Sylvester of the Division of Highways Bridge Department that he considered this action a neighborly approach toward expressing his intention of being considerate of the rights and comfort of nearby residents.

The card was contained in an envelope bearing the contractor's name and the words: 'An Important Message—Please Read." It resembled a folded greeting card, with a photograph of the freeway construction on the front.

Inside, the card bore a location map of the freeway project, along with this statement signed by Thompson:

"As you have observed, we are just starting construction on the first section of the Glendale Freeway.

"We would like to assure you that we will do everything we can to construct this freeway with as little inconvenience to you as possible. It is, of course, impossible to do this work without creating some noise, dust and dirt. However, we do hope that you will bear with us during this operation and we will do our utmost to complete the job as far ahead of schedule as the availability of certain materials will allow."

Thompson reported that he has received a number of letters from residents expressing a favorable reaction to his good will gesture.

Only 919,000 miles of road, or one-fourth the total, in the United States are paved, according to the U. S. Bureau of Public Roads.

Embarcadero

First Unit of New San
Francisco Freeway Open

THE FIRST unit of the Embarcadero Freeway in San Francisco was opened to public traffic at 11.30 a.m., Monday, April 8, 1957.

Ceremonies celebrating the occasion were held at Beale and Mission Streets under joint auspices of the Downtown Association of San Francisco and the San Francisco Chamber of Commerce. Officials of the City and County of San Francisco, the State, members of the California Highway Commission and the Legislature and local civic groups participated.

Among the speakers were: Roy N. Buell, President of the Downtown Association, who presided; State Director of Public Works Frank B. Durkee, who also is chairman of the Highway Commission; Supervisor Henry R. Rolph, representing Mayor George Christopher; State Senator Robert I. McCarthy, Chief Administrative Officer Thomas A. Brooks, B. W. Booker, Assistant State Highway Engineer; Chamber of Commerce President E. D. Maloney, former Speaker pro-tem of the Assembly Tom Maloney, and Highway Commissioner Robert Bishop of Santa Rosa. Music was furnished by the San

B. W. Booker, Assistant State Highway Engineer, at microphone

Francisco Municipal Band. The ribbon stretched across the freeway was cut by Supervisor Rolph.

The new unit will become an integral part of the San Francisco Skyway and with its downtown connections to Mission Street at Main and

Beale Streets, will bring East Bay and Peninsula traffic closer to the heart of the city. The double deck reinforced concrete structure provides an extension of the James Lick Memorial Freeway (Bayshore Freeway), with opposing traffic moving on separate levels. Traffic from the East Bay will be handled on the lower deck of a parallel structure.

The reverse traffic movement from Mission Street to the Bay Bridge and East Bay points will not be opened until the completion of a subsequent contract this summer. All of the original ramps will continue to serve traffic.

The California Highway Commission allotted $5,400,000 for this initial project and work began early in 1955 by the contractors, McDonald, Young & Nelson Company and Morrison-Knudsen Company. The contract included 45,000 cubic yards of concrete, 73,650 lineal feet of steel piling and 13,000,000 pounds of bar reinforcing steel.

The double deck construction on this project was designed to afford

. . . Continued on page 63

Supervisor Henry R. Rolph wields scissors to cut ribbon after Embarcadero Freeway dedication, while state, county, and city officials, representatives of civic groups and of the police and fire departments cheer

OPENING OF HIGHWAY PROJECT IN LOS GATOS IS OBSERVED

Brief ceremonies marked the completion and opening to traffic of the Charles Street connection on State Highway Route 5 (Sign Route 17) in Los Gatos, May 1, 1957. Ceremonies were conducted on the Bella Vista Street Bridge at 11 a.m., before a group of local citizens and state and local officials. Mayor Alberto E. Merrill of Los Gatos acted as master of ceremonies and recounted the efforts undertaken by the city to secure this much needed improvement.

In 1954 an effort was made to pass a $173,000 bond issue to pay for the crossing entirely out of city funds, but this bond issue failed to pass. In

1955 a bond issue in the amount of $80,000 was approved by the city as a contribution to the construction of the project, the balance to be paid for by the Division of Highways. After the approval of this bond issue, the California Highway Commission allocated funds for the State's share of the construction project.

Frank B. Durkee, State Director of Public Works, represented the California Highway Commission and Governor Knight at the opening ceremonies. In his remarks, he complimented the City of Los Gatos for its part in making this improvement possible through their cooperation.

Route 5 Link

The newly constructed portion is some 0.58 mile in length, extending between San Jose Avenue, the existing Route 5, and the Route 5 freeway in Los Gatos. Work was started on August 27, 1956, and completed with its opening to traffic on May 1, 1957. Cost of the project, including construction, rights of way and utilities, was approximately $440,000. The project consists of a two-lane highway with 12-foot lanes and 8-foot shoulders, a reinforced concrete girder bridge 131 feet long, which carries Bella Vista Avenue over the new

. . . Continued on page 54

Section of new Los Gatos highway which was opened to traffic with dedication ceremonies on May 1

and Public Works

Out of the Mail Bag

MINNESOTA FREEWAYS

MINNESOTA ENGINEERING CO., INC.
Minneapolis 5, Minnesota

MR. KENNETH C. ADAMS, *Editor*

DEAR SIR: We appreciate very much being placed on the mailing list for the bimonthly publication *California Highways and Public Works*.

Your magazine is of invaluable aid to our staff since it contains information available from no other source for design and layout purposes in connection with the new federal interstate system.

We have recently started design work on the freeway system here in Minnesota.

Sincerely yours,

K. E. MADSEN
Chief Engineer

FROM AN OLD READER

DEPARTMENT OF COMMERCE, BUREAU OF PUBLIC ROADS
New Mexico District
Santa Fe, New Mexico

MR. KENNETH C. ADAMS, *Editor*

DEAR MR. ADAMS: I have appreciated your publication very greatly since I first started reading it some eight years ago as a junior engineer in the District VIII office. You are to be congratulated for keeping it a semitechnical publication instead of allowing it to become a travelog of the State.

In my work as area engineer for the bureau I have found many opportunities to use some of the highway construction and design innovations brought to my attention in your magazine.

Yours very truly,

C. F. LINTZ

COME OUT AGAIN

NORTH CANTON 20, OHIO

MR. KENNETH C. ADAMS, *Editor*

DEAR MR. ADAMS: My wife and I have just returned from a visit with our son and family in Palo Alto (our fifth trip, incidentally), and for me to write that I was deeply impressed with the outstanding manner in which your State is meeting the ever present challenge of properly handling traffic is expressing it mildly. Yours is a shining example of what can be accomplished with the proper application of the gasoline tax dollar.

Sincerely,

ROSS M. BAXTER

FROM WEST AFRICA

REPUBLIC OF LIBERIA
DEPARTMENT OF PUBLIC WORKS AND UTILITIES
Division of Highways
Monrovia

GENTLEMEN: I had the opportunity to get one of your wonderful magazines and I have enjoyed myself in reading it. Especially in this country where highway building is of the greatest importance for development it is very interesting to learn about highway building in the United States. As a European engineer contracted with the Liberian Government and acting as a counterpart of an American Bureau of Public Roads engineer I have great interest in your highway program.

Very sincerely yours,

P. A. VAN GORSEL
Highway Design Engineer
Division of Highways, I. C. A.
Camp Johnson, Monrovia
Republic of Liberia, West Africa

IN LINE OF DUTY

ROMOLAND, CALIFORNIA

Division of Highways
Sacramento, California

DEAR SIRS: In this busy world of ours comes occasionally a happening of personal nature on the part of a state employee which is very commendable and certainly worth recognition.

My little son, who is four years old, has gone to San Diego to work. She got into our old auto and started for the hospital in Hemet as fast as she could go. About three miles north of our ranch near Homeland she ran out of gas. My fault entirely. I had neglected to check the tank before I left home.

She tried to hail several motorists but all passed her by. An orange pickup truck stopped and a very welcome state employee asked her what the trouble was. After explaining, he said he would get the car off the road and would take her to the hospital. She asked him to stop at our doctor's office first, which he did. He was most courteous, very sympathetic and did everything to help her in this time of need. She offered him pay which she declined saying it was part of any Highway Department employee's work to give aid at a time like that. We are eternally grateful and will you please seek him out and thank him officially for what he did.

Very gratefully,

Mr. and Mrs. Jack Graham

The employee who is the subject of the letter is H. E. Maynard, a highway foreman in charge of the Division of Highways Hemet maintenance crew.—EDITOR

NATIONAL DEFENSE

Continued from page 23 . . .

"Highway Needs of the National Defense."

This report brings out the fact that serious deficiencies exist in "sight distances and in the width of its pavements, shoulders, and bridges. The sight distance deficiencies are the result of defective alignment and vertical curvature." Major General Paul F. Yount, Chief of Transportation, Department of the Army, in testifying before the Committee on Public Works, House of Representatives, in April of 1955, stated that only 15 percent of the designated National System of Interstate Highways meets prescribed standards for military needs and lists the deficiencies as existing in "bridge and slab design and construction, and also as to access."

Priority of Construction

From a national defense point of view there is a very serious subject which I feel has been overlooked. That is over-all control over the priority of construction on the interstate system. So far as I have been able to find out there is no requirement at this time that any one through route be built as the initial coordinated effort of all the states involved. It is certainly desirable that we not proceed with the construction of this nationwide system in a checkerboard fashion with a little piece in this county and a little piece in that. Not only must there be continuing progress on a high priority route in each state but there also must be coordination of route selection and timing of construction between adjacent states.

In order to accomplish this orderly approach to construction it may be necessary for Congress to assign priority to a limited number of transcontinental routes as well as three or four north-south ones. This would insure that the taxpayers would be given an opportunity to collect some dividends from their tremendous investment long before the whole system is completed. It would also insure the defense establishment of the availability of a transcontinental highway for logistical support which might well mean the difference between success or failure in the early stages of an emergency.

Sound Guide Lines

The great importance of the interstate system to national defense was weighed carefully by the Congress when it departed from the policy of the past and established the 90-10 ratio for federal support of the system. Due to the rapid developments in weapons of war and in the changing methods of waging war, it is admittedly most difficult to project the highway needs of national defense throughout the expected life span of the new highways. It is impossible to predict the force or extent of an enemy attack or the exact demands that will be placed upon highway transportation in order to cope with it. However, sound guide lines have been established which, if adhered to as the highway program develops, will take care of most of the foreseeable needs of national defense.

Nevertheless, in carrying out the program there must be sufficient flexibility to permit adjustments to meet major surprise developments in the science of waging war. Despite the federal interest in the interstate system from the points of view of national defense and sound national economic development, the primary responsibility for route selection, highway design and construction rests with the state engineers. The superimposing of the new interstate system on an accelerated federal-aid program for the primary, secondary and urban systems presents a tremendous challenge to every state. I am sure the state highway officials will continue to discharge this responsibility with the high degree of efficiency that has marked their work in the past. The fullest cooperation and coordination of the states and the Bureau of Public Roads under the leadership of the able, new Federal Highway Administrator, Bert Tallamy, is essential so that these great benefits to national defense may become available to our Country before they are needed.

One out of every seven workers in the United States earns his living directly from highway transport industries.

Retirements from Service

Albert L. Lamb

Albert L. Lamb, Location Engineer for the Division of Highways District V at San Luis Obispo, retired on April 1st after nearly 30 years with the State.

ALBERT L. LAMB

Lamb went to work as a junior engineering aid for the State Department of Water Resources in 1922. He joined the Division of Highways as a transitman in District I at Eureka, leaving in 1925 to accept private employment.

He entered state service again in 1931 as an engineer on highway construction work in District IX at Bishop, transferring to the San Luis Obispo district four years later. He was resident engineer on many of the highway construction projects in District V.

During World War II Lamb served as a captain in the U. S. Corps of Engineers. He was promoted to his present position of location engineer for District V in 1950.

Lamb was born in Ouray, Colorado, and came to California in 1909. He went to school in Chico. His first job was as axman for the Yuba County Surveyor in 1915.

Lamb is a member of the American Congress on Surveying and Mapping and the Society of American Military Engineers. He and his wife will continue to live at their home in Shell Beach.

NO TOURIST CARD

Mexican border towns may be visited by Americans for periods not to exceed 72 hours without a tourist card, although personal identification is required, reports the California State Automobile Association.

Henry L. Mahoney

Henry L. Mahoney, Highway Chief Clerk II, with the Division of Highways, Headquarters Accounting Office, retired on March 12, 1957, after 35 years of state service.

HENRY L. MAHONEY

"Hank," as he was affectionately known by his fellow employees, was born in Terre Haute, Indiana, in February, 1897, and spent his early manhood as a timekeeper on construction crews for the Pennsylvania Railroad. After serving with the United States Army Engineers during World War I, Henry was employed by several railroads throughout the United States, finally working as a clerk in the superintendent's office for the Southern Pacific Company in Sacramento where, in 1922, he entered state service as a clerk with the Division of Highways.

In the ensuing years he held various positions in the Headquarters Accounting Office, being promoted to

... Continued on page 63

Guy McKinney

Guy McKinney, Associate Highway Engineer with the Division of Highways District IV office in San Francisco, retired on June 1st after 29 years in state service.

Since 1951 he had been in charge of special projects in the engineering services section.

McKinney's first engineering job was in the coal mining region of Pennsylvania. In 1906 he went to work for the Northern Pacific Railroad in the State of Washington as a draftsman and chainman. He also worked with the Washington State Highway Department, the Spokane County Highway Department and the U. S. Bureau of Public Roads in Oregon before joining the California Division of Highways in 1928.

McKinney served as resident engineer, chief draftsman and office engineer in Districts II and III before coming to District IV in 1936 to assist the District Construction Engineer.

McKinney was born in Shamokin, Pennsylvania, and graduated from high school there. He later studied engineering at the University of California in Berkeley. He is a veteran of World War I.

McKinney is married and has a son in New York City, a married daughter in North Hollywood, and three grandchildren.

McKinney and his wife will continue to live in their home at 3747 Cabrillo Street in San Francisco after his retirement.

PASSPORTS

Some 559,000 passports were issued to Americans last year, reports the Travel Department of the California State Automobile Association. This was an increase of almost 6 percent over 1955.

MERIT AWARD BOARD WINNERS

Following is a list of Department of Public Works employees who received Merit Award recognition during the month of April, 1957:

Sara E. Weisman and *Veloy Allenbach*, Architecture, Los Angeles, received a certificate of commendation for their joint suggestion of a revision of Form 672, Attendance Report. While the exact revision suggested was not adopted, their suggestion led to a revision of this state-wide form which will accomplish the same purpose and make the form easier to use.

Edward Zavala, Highways, Los Angeles, received an award of $20 for recommending a revision of the Speed Zone Survey Sheet and elimination of the Speed Zone Data Form GS-8. A revised Speed Zone Survey Sheet incorporates a number of the changes suggested and eliminates the use of the Speed Zone Data Form in the districts. The new form presents the data more clearly, and facilitates review and establishment of speed zones.

Gordon A. Morse, Highways, Riverside, received $150 for his suggestion to eliminate duplication in sampling structure concrete when adjacent contracts are being served with ready-mix concrete from the same plant. Adoption of this proposal permits the assignment of one man, instead of two, to do the job, and will reduce the number of concrete sample cylinders required by approximately 10 percent, or 600 cylinders per year.

Irene E. Finney, Highways, Eureka, received $15 for suggesting that the Controller's Office send two copies of pay warrant registers directly to the reporting units. This permits the reporting units to forward one copy to the district office immediately and keep one working copy. Adoption of the idea eliminates extra handling of these documents.

William S. Hudson, Highways, San Bernardino, received a certificate of commendation for suggesting that Planning Manual revisions include instructions for inserting the new pages in the manual.

Mary M. Runnion, Senior Stenographer-Clerk, and *Ralph Chamney*, Supervisor, Reproduction Department, Highways, Los Angeles, were awarded $100 to be divided equally for recommending the photographs used in appraisal reports be mounted mechanically by a blueprint drier. Prior to this these photographs were mounted by hand, using a heavy heated press whereby a lever lifted the hot irons up and down and pressed the photographs onto the sheet of paper. It was then necessary to place these prints in a device similar to a waffle iron, each one being processed individually. This new method provides for mass mounting, three prints placed side by side in the drier and a continuous feeding of the print into the drier.

William F. Runge, Assistant Highway Engineer, Eureka, was awarded $25 for recommending the use of a standard cadastral retracement form for use by field parties. This will make it possible to record the findings in a standard, concise and professional manner, and when certified by the surveyor might be of value as evidenced in condemnation suits. The form will be distributed to all districts for state-wide use.

John M. Hibbard, Assistant Highway Engineer, San Francisco, recommended an improved method of making stabilometers specimen baskets, and will receive a $15 award. Instead of using two separate pieces of paper, paper stock will be doubled in thickness and die cut in the center so as to save time, materials, and manpower and will use one piece of paper instead of two.

Everts L. Horton, Junior Civil Engineer, San Luis Obispo, proposed the use of colored dots to identify varying functions on traverse sheets. The procedure has an advantage over the conventional method of using arrows on a long series of right-angle courses. With the arrow method it is necessary to trace back through the various arrows to the origin to determine the functions; whereas, with colored dots all one needs to do is identify the color with the function. This procedure is quicker, more positive and more accurate. A $25 award was granted.

Karl R. Leutner, Assistant Physical Testing Engineer, Sacramento, was awarded $75 for suggesting the installation of a safety valve on all existing stabilometers in headquarters and district laboratories. This employee suggested the use of a commercial valve (Model 0630-200) set to blow off at 190 psi which will prevent overloading of stabilometer gates.

GOLDEN GATE

Continued from page 39 . . .

Empire in the past two decades. To more adequately care for the patrons of the bridge, a $7,500,000 Golden Gate Bridge North Freeway was completed last year.

The bridge has been closed but once since it was built. On December 1, 1951, winds of gale force caused the span to develop a sway and it was closed down for three hours. Since then a system of lateral bracing costing about $3,000,000 has been installed. Engineers report that this has increased the torsional rigidity of the bridge by 35 percent.

Employees Receive Twenty-five-year Awards

Employees of the Division of Highways who have become eligible for 25-year awards are:

Name	Total Service Yrs. Mos. Days			Name	Total Service Yrs. Mos. Days		
District I				**District IX**			
Rogers, Francis H.	25	0	6	Foley, E. R.	25	0	00
District II				**District X**			
McCann, Herbert E.	25	0	6	John B. Odgers	25	0	23
Smith, Ora E.	25	0	14	Effective January 31, 1957			
Stephensen, Lee R.	25	0	00				
Wagner, Chester D.	25	0	27	**District XI**			
				Decker, Vernon J.	25	0	8
District III							
Doyle, James R.	25	0	28	**Shop 2**			
Hawks, Lewis A.	25	0	13	Miller, Edmund K.	25	0	10
District IV				**Headquarters Office**			
Hendricks, Wade A.	25	0	16	Stanley F. McGill	25	0	24
District VI							
Windele, Richard	25	0	00	**Bridge Department**			
District VII				Hineman Howard R.	25	0	6
Charle, Jullen R.	25	0	27	Robison, F. Wilbur	25	0	9
Greathead, James W.	25	0	3				
Nahoney, Edward L.	25	0	28				
Tarwater, Vernon Keith	25	0	25				

Employees of the Division of Architecture receiving 25-year awards:

Name	25 years on	Location
Sim Sharp	25 years on 5-4-57	Area III, Los Angeles

Cost Index

Substantial Rise During First Quarter of 1957

By RICHARD H. WILSON, Assistant State Highway Engineer;
H. C. McCARTY, Office Engineer, and
LLOYD B. REYNOLDS, Assistant Office Engineer

THE CALIFORNIA Highway Construction Cost Index for the first quarter of 1957 made a sharp rise after a gradual return to an upward direction in the fourth quarter of 1956. The Index stands at 277.7 (1940 = 100) which is 25.5 Index points or 10.1 percent above the fourth quarter of 1956. This quarter established a new high in the history of the California Index. The previous high of 255.9 was established in the second quarter last year.

The regularly expressed view of this department that construction costs will continue in an upward direction remains unchanged. Conditions existing in the materials field and with labor are having the effect of reduction in the rate at which costs are increasing. This effect is occasioned by the long-term labor contracts that were negotiated last year in many of the fields affecting highway construction.

While the Index as calculated for this quarter bears out our statement that costs will continue upward, conditions surrounding two extremely large contracts totaling $12,200,000 that were awarded during the period resulted in unfair weight in this direction.

One of these projects is situated in the Truckee River Canyon near the Nevada state line. The area is subject to heavy snows over long periods and extremely low temperatures during winter months. The canyon walls over considerable of the length of the project are steep and slides are an ever-present hazard due to unstable soils in the most critical locations. The terrain precludes the possibility of constructing detours around construction, and local roads for the purpose are nonexistent, consequently the large volumes of traffic over this route must be taken through construction operations. Other factors affecting construction costs for this project are the enormous volumes of work required in specified short intervals; transportation costs; and long periods of winter shutdown. Costs are also materially affected by the proximity of an operating railroad; flumes supplying

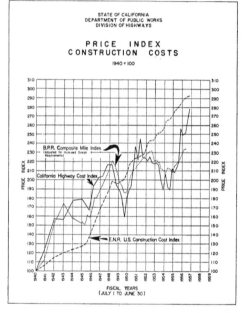

STATE OF CALIFORNIA
DEPARTMENT OF PUBLIC WORKS
DIVISION OF HIGHWAYS

PRICE INDEX
CONSTRUCTION COSTS
1940 = 100

FISCAL YEARS
(JULY 1 TO JUNE 30)

hydroelectric installations; transcontinental telephone lines and electric transmission lines all of which require extreme precautions in all phases of the work.

The other project is located in Humboldt County bordering the pres-

52

California Highways

ent Redwood Highway. The redwood region of California is subject to intense rains over long periods and this condition is particularly prevalent at the project location. The Redwood Highway carries large volumes of traffic of which a considerable portion is trucks, mainly devoted to the hauling of logs and finished lumber. The area through which the project passes is heavily forested, with redwood trees predominating, and these forests are under control of the State Park System. The present highway has been outmoded for several years and since it traverses the finest stands of redwood trees, development of the existing road to standards capable of meeting traffic requirements is impossible without destruction of these attractions. An agreement between the Division of Highways and the Division of Beaches and Parks provides that a new highway is to be located where the least disturbance to these natural wonders will occur. The location selected is not ideal for highway construction and higher than average construction costs are the result.

Roadway excavation prices are well above average due to traffic interference where the existing highway is encountered; the ground is interlaced with large tree roots remaining from clearing operations; high slopes are general in many cuts developing small yardage and enormous quantities of material must be moved in a limited time. Transportation to the isolated location of the project is a factor contributing to the above average prices for asphalt, cement, reinforcing steel and structural steel. Mineral aggregates for surfacings and portland cement concrete must be either imported or produced on the job. If produced locally from the adjacent stream bed, the material will have to be stockpiled over the winter to be available for the succeeding short construction season.

Normally during a quarterly reporting period there are sufficient other projects of similar magnitude where item prices have had a countering effect but such circumstances did not prevail in this period.

An alternate determination of the Index was made in which the two projects were eliminated from consideration. The results of this determination were more favorable and more in line with the apparent general trend shown during the quarter. The alternately calculated Index

NUMBER AND SIZE OF PROJECTS, TOTAL BID VALUES AND AVERAGE NUMBER OF BIDDERS
(January 1, 1957, to March 31, 1957)

Project volume	Up to $50,000	$50,000 to $100,000	$100,000 to $250,000	$250,000 to $500,000	$500,000 to $1,000,000	Over $1,000,000	All projects
Road Projects							
No. of projects....	54	3	24	7	6	4	98
Total value*......	$862,133	$226,302	$4,258,707	$2,551,966	$3,535,094	$6,402,470	$18,136,672
Ave. No. bidders..	6.4	4.7	7.1	10.4	8.2	6.8	6.9
Structure Projects							
No. of projects....	10		5	1	1	2	19
Total value*......	$112,130		$932,172	$302,887	$971,926	$4,968,314	$7,287,399
Ave. No. bidders..	6.8		10.0	8.0	8.0	6.8	7.8
Combination Projects							
No. of projects....						1	11	12
Total value*......						$947,106	$28,501,580	$29,448,686
Ave. No. bidders..						4.0	6.9	6.7
Summary							
No. of projects....	64	3	29	8	8	17	129
Total value*......	$974,263	$226,302	$5,190,879	$2,854,853	$5,754,126	$39,872,364	$54,872,657
Ave. No. bidders..	6.5	4.7	7.6	10.1	7.3	6.8	7.0

* Bid items only.

Total Average Bidders by Months

	Jan.	Feb.	Mar.	Avg. for first Quarter
1957.......	7.1	7.3	6.7	7.0
1956.......	5.9	5.1	5.1	5.4

CALIFORNIA DIVISION OF HIGHWAYS AVERAGE CONTRACT PRICES

	Roadway excavation, per cu. yd.	Untreated rock base, per ton	Asphaltic and Bituminous mixes, per ton	Asphalt concrete pavement, per ton	PCC pavement, per cu. yd.	PCC structures, per cu. yd.	Bar reinforced steel, per lb.	Structural steel, per lb.
1940.............	$0.22	$1.54	$2.19	$2.97	$7.68	$13.33	$0.040	$0.083
1941.............	0.26	2.31	2.84	3.18	7.54	23.31	0.063	0.107
1942.............	0.35	2.61	4.09	4.16	9.63	29.48	0.073	0.103
1943.............	0.42	2.36	3.71	4.76	11.68	31.76	0.059	0.080
1944.............	0.50	2.45	4.10	4.60	10.46	31.99	0.054	0.132
1945.............	0.51	2.45	4.20	4.88	10.90	37.20	0.059	0.102
1946.............	0.41	2.45	4.00	4.66	9.48	37.38	0.060	0.099
1947.............	0.46	2.42	4.32	5.38	12.38	48.44	0.060	0.138
1948.............	0.85	2.43	4.30	5.35	13.04	43.86	0.092	0.136
1949.............	0.49	2.67	4.67	4.64	13.28	48.67	0.094	0.117
1950.............	0.40	2.25	4.26	3.75	11.11	43.45	0.079	0.094
1951.............	0.49	2.62	4.34	5.00	12.31	47.22	0.109	0.136
1952.............	0.56	2.99	5.00	4.35	13.42	45.06	0.093	0.150
1953.............	0.51	2.14[1]	5.31	4.56	12.74	50.59	0.093	0.133
1st Quarter 1954..	0.45	2.35	4.23	4.73	14.89	47.52	0.092	0.136
2d Quarter 1954..	0.38	2.09	4.45	5.18	14.35	47.12	0.095	0.114
3d Quarter 1954..	0.43	1.85	4.68	7.00	12.63	49.80	0.095	0.162
4th Quarter 1954..	0.36	1.78	4.63	--	13.13	46.06	0.094	0.133
1st Quarter 1955..	0.39	1.69	4.55	--	13.44	40.66	0.095	0.140
2d Quarter 1955..	0.43	1.99	3.39	--	14.46	51.36	0.096	0.136
3d Quarter 1955..	0.41	2.33	5.43	8.70	13.46	49.64	0.093	0.132
4th Quarter 1955..	0.37	3.00	5.52	4.00	16.05	82.73	0.099	0.144
1st Quarter 1956..	0.40	2.06	5.40	6.50	14.05	52.51	0.105	0.155
2d Quarter 1956..	0.51	2.06	6.27	--	14.64	57.13	0.113	0.219
3d Quarter 1956..	0.52	2.27	6.13	--	15.87	56.32	0.121	0.178
4th Quarter 1956..	0.52	2.31	5.93[2]	--[3]	14.95	59.63	0.113	0.197
1st Quarter 1957..	0.63	2.10	5.94	--	17.38	61.14	0.129	0.235

[1] The item of crusher run base was used before 1953.
[2] The item of plant mix surfacing was used before fourth quarter of 1956.
[3] Asphalt concrete pavement combined with plant mix Surfacing in fourth quarter, 1956, and will be identified as asphaltic and bituminous mixes in the future.

shows a standing of 249.6 Index points as against 277.7 noted above. The alternate Index is 2.6 points or 1.0 percent below the fourth quarter of 1956.

Interest of bidders in highway construction during this quarter no doubt accounts for a large portion of the reduced costs reflected by the alternate Index.

The average number of bidders per project is 7.0 for the quarter while the averages for fourth and third quarters of 1956 stood at 5.1 and 3.7 respectively. Projects attracting from 12 to 17 bidders were common during this period. It remains to be seen whether these favorable prices result from the contractors' urgent desire for work or from savings to be accomplished through newly developed practices and techniques.

Average unit prices upon which the over-all Index is based for this quarter show increases in six items and a decrease in one item. Roadway excavation rose from $0.52 to $0.63; asphaltic and bituminous mixes from $5.93 to $5.94; portland cement concrete pavement from $14.95 to $17.28; class "A" concrete structures from $59.63 to $61.14; bar reinforcing steel from $0.112 to $0.129; and structural steel from $0.197 to $0.235. Untreated crushed gravel or stone base dropped from $2.21 to $2.10. Calculations for the alternate Index show that the substantial increases in average unit prices for roadway excavation, portland cement concrete pavement, structure concrete and structural steel result from the two projects previously referred to above on which conditions to be encountered are not typical of those generally found on highway construction elsewhere in the State.

Structures, where rolled steel shapes are predominate in the design, continue to have effect on construction costs. This condition will prevail until the steel industry has exhausted the enormous backlog of orders now existing.

The California Construction Cost Index, the Engineering News-Record Construction Cost Index and the United States Bureau of Public Roads Composite Mile Index, all reduced to the base 1940 = 100 are shown on the accompanying graph. The latter two

Indexes are based on nationwide construction costs.

The Engineering News-Record Cost Index again shows a rise but the rate of increase is lower than that of the fourth quarter of 1956. It is up 2.0 Index points or 0.68 percent from the previous quarter.

THE CALIFORNIA HIGHWAY CONSTRUCTION COST INDEX

Year	Cost Index
1940	100.0
1941	125.0
1942	157.5
1943	156.4
1944	177.8
1945	179.5
1946	179.7
1947	203.3
1948	216.6
1949	190.7
1950	176.7
(1st Quarter 1950—160.6)	
1951	210.8
(4th Quarter 1951—245.4)	
1952	224.5
1953	216.2
1954 (1st Quarter)	199.4
1954 (2d Quarter)	189.0
1954 (3d Quarter)	207.8
1954 (4th Quarter)	192.2
1955 (1st Quarter)	189.3
1955 (2d Quarter)	212.4
1955 (3d Quarter)	208.6
1955 (4th Quarter)	212.6
1956 (1st Quarter)	219.5
1956 (2d Quarter)	255.9
1956 (3d Quarter)	249.1
1956 (4th Quarter)	252.1
1957 (1st Quarter)	277.7

The Bureau of Public Roads Composite Mile Index for the fourth quarter of 1956, which is the latest available, was up 0.3 Index points or 0.1 percent over the second quarter. The leveling off in the Bureau of Public Roads Index shows that highway construction cost decreases experienced on many California projects is also becoming evident in other parts of the Nation.

MEXICO'S HIGHEST

Mexico's highest peak is the Orizaba volcano which is 18,855 feet above sea level. It is 4,000 feet higher than the highest mountain in the United States.

SIERRA PASSES
Continued from page 32 . . .

This is because the route traverses large rock slide areas in very rugged terrain and considerable cleanup with a power shovel and bulldozer is required prior to opening the road to traffic.

One of the less troublesome passes to open is Monitor Pass between Coleville and Markleeville. This road was constructed only a few years ago and one of the major considerations in the design and location of the route was that of reducing to a minimum the annual problem of snow removal work. The road lies on the easterly side of the main crest of the Sierra, and with the main part of the road situated in a more favorable exposure from the sun than the other mountain passes, it is usually one of the first roads to open in the late spring.

Because of the variation in severity and duration of the winter seasons the opening date of the several mountain passes differs from year to year. However, the Division of Highways attempts to open these mountain passes as early as practicable, consistent with budgetary allotments, so as to allow the motoring public the advantage of several additional months in which to enjoy the beauty and the recreational facilities of one of California's favorite vacationlands.

LOS GATOS
Continued from page 47 . . .

highway, and portions of the interchange at the junction with the Route 5 freeway. Work was done under contract by Lew Jones Construction Company and Leo F. Piazza. R. E. Alderman was the resident engineer on the project, which was designed by District IV, Division of Highways, under the general supervision of B. W. Booker, Assistant State Highway Engineer.

Following the dedication ceremonies and cutting of the ribbon by F. W. Berryman, Senior, Councilman of Los Gatos, and Carol Lindstrom, the five-year-old granddaughter of Mayor Merrill, a motorcade proceeded over the new highway and the Route 5 freeway to a civic luncheon tendered by the City of Los Gatos.

A record total of $29,219,479 of state gasoline tax revenues has been apportioned to 338 cities in California for city street work and engineering during the current fiscal year, State Director of Public Works Frank B. Durkee announced today.

This is more than $2,000,000 over last year's record $26,957,868.

The gas tax distributed to cities for street work is the revenue from five-eighths of a cent per gallon out of the state gasoline taxes paid by highway users and is apportioned by the State Division of Highways from the State Highway Fund according to law on a population basis.

The additional allocation to cities for engineering, also apportioned on a population basis, is taken from other state highway funds and varies from a minimum of $1,000 for cities under 5,000 population to a maximum of $20,000 for cities with more than half a million people.

As in previous years, the City of Los Angeles tops the list in the amount of money received with a total of $6,886,777.69; Amador, the smallest city in the State, is again at the bottom with a total apportionment of $1,466.55.

Fourteen new communities have entered the ranks of incorporated cities during the past year, making them eligible for a share in the 1956-57 apportionment. They are: Dairy Valley, La Puente, Downey, Rolling Hills and Par-amount, all in Los Angeles County; Stanton, Garden Grove, Dairy City and Tri-City, Orange County; Monte Vista, San Bernardino County; Imperial Beach, San Diego County; Saratoga, Santa Clara County; Woodside, San Mateo County; and Escalon, San Joaquin County.

Durkee pointed out that this money allocated to cities is in addition to the funds expended on state highways within cities and included in the State Highway Budget by the California Highway Commission. Under certain conditions, however, the city may, in cooperation with the State Department of Public Works, expend portions of these funds upon a state highway.

State law requires the cities to expend at least 60 percent of the ⅝-cent gas tax apportionment for construction on streets included in the major street system as designated by the city council and approved by the State Department of Public Works. Up to 40 percent may be spent for maintenance of city streets. The engineering funds may be expended for engineering costs on any city street.

Although these city street projects financed with state gas tax funds require state approval, Durkee pointed out that in actual practice it is a matter of close cooperation between state and local officials to obtain maximum benefit from the funds in terms of service to traffic.

Apportionments to cities are as follows:

City	5/8¢ Gas Tax	Engineering	Total
ALAMEDA COUNTY			
Alameda	$218,264.47	$7,500	$225,764.47
Albany	84,348.39	4,000	88,348.39
Berkeley	251,626.34	10,000	261,626.34
Emeryville	8,926.22	1,000	9,926.22
Fremont	69,343.74	5,000	74,343.74
Hayward	131,313.09	6,375	137,688.09
Livermore	31,400.89	3,000	34,400.89
Newark	18,640.32	2,000	20,640.32
Oakland	1,188,331.63	10,000	1,198,331.63
Piedmont	21,674.35	3,000	24,674.35
Pleasanton	8,963.46	1,000	9,963.46
San Leandro	144,448.40	6,000	150,448.40
Total	$2,257,180.30	$58,875	$2,316,055.30
ALPINE COUNTY			
None			
AMADOR COUNTY			
Amador	$466.55	$1,000	$1,466.55
Ione	4,959.01	1,000	5,959.01
Jackson	3,808.89	1,000	4,808.89
Plymouth	1,180.26	1,000	2,180.26
Sutter Creek	3,556.27	1,000	4,556.27
Total	$15,967.70	$5,000	$20,967.70
BUTTE COUNTY			
Biggs	$2,422.34	$1,000	$3,422.34
Chico	42,515.04	2,000	44,515.04
Gridley	9,541.08	1,000	10,541.08
Oroville	19,666.12	2,000	21,666.12
Total	$74,144.58	$7,000	$81,144.58
CALAVERAS COUNTY			
Angels	$3,843.92	$1,000	$4,843.92
COLUSA COUNTY			
Colusa	$10,292.02	$1,000	$11,292.02
Williams	3,583.15	1,000	4,583.15
Total	$13,875.17	$2,000	$15,875.17
CONTRA COSTA COUNTY			
Antioch	$43,673.57	$3,250	$46,923.57
Brentwood	5,718.96	1,000	6,718.96
Concord	75,770.87	5,250	81,020.87
El Cerrito	73,270.93	8,000	77,270.93
Hercules	1,059.76	1,000	2,059.76
Martinez	26,460.70	2,000	28,460.70
Pinole	6,543.01	1,000	7,543.01
Pittsburg	81,309.13	4,000	85,309.13
Richmond	310,267.34	9,375	319,632.34
San Pablo	83,965.05	4,000	87,965.05
Walnut Creek	21,087.66	2,000	23,087.66
Total	$667,985.58	$37,875	$705,860.58
DEL NORTE COUNTY			
Crescent City	$8,270.07	$1,000	$9,270.07
EL DORADO COUNTY			
Placerville	$11,786.25	$1,000	$12,786.25
FRESNO COUNTY			
Clovis	$11,982.54	$1,000	$12,982.54
Coalinga	18,603.25	2,000	20,603.25
Firebaugh	3,763.71	1,000	4,763.71
Fowler	5,767.25	1,000	6,767.25
Fresno	340,303.07	10,000	350,303.07
Huron	4,342.30	1,000	5,342.30
Kerman	5,513.07	1,000	6,513.07
Kingsburg	7,585.71	1,000	8,585.71
Mendota	4,952.84	1,000	5,952.84
Orange Cove	7,792.28	1,000	8,792.28
Parlier	4,384.32	1,000	5,384.32
Reedley	15,964.62	2,000	17,964.62
Sanger	22,787.86	2,000	24,787.86
Selma	1,952.71	1,000	2,952.71
San Joaquin	19,349.00	2,000	21,349.00
Total	$474,873.16	$28,000	$502,873.16
GLENN COUNTY			
Orland	$7,390.63	$1,000	$8,390.63
Willows	11,299.04	1,000	12,299.04
Total	$18,689.67	$2,000	$20,689.67

City	5/8 ¢ Gas Tax	Engineering	Total
HUMBOLDT COUNTY			
Arcata	$12,609.18	$1,000	$13,609.18
Blue Lake	3,302.91	1,000	4,302.91
Eureka	86,360.96	6,000	92,360.96
Ferndale	3,188.60	1,000	4,188.60
Fortuna	9,939.65	1,000	10,939.65
Trinidad	580.85	1,000	1,580.85
Total	$115,982.15	$11,000	$126,982.15
IMPERIAL COUNTY			
Brawley	$40,686.25	$3,000	$43,686.25
Calexico	23,044.69	2,000	25,044.69
Calipatria	6,949.34	1,000	7,949.34
El Centro	49,287.70	4,000	53,287.70
Holtville	10,186.83	1,000	11,186.83
Imperial	5,434.83	1,000	6,434.83
Westmorland	3,747.84	1,000	4,747.84
Total	$139,337.48	$13,000	$152,337.48
INYO COUNTY			
Bishop	$10,103.39	$1,000	$11,103.39
KERN COUNTY			
Bakersfield	$145,061.38	$6,000	$151,061.38
Delano	31,910.70	3,000	34,910.70
Maricopa	2,471.78	1,000	3,471.78
Shafter	9,634.90	1,000	10,634.90
Taft	12,111.60	1,000	13,111.60
Tehachapi	7,569.83	1,000	8,569.83
Wasco	19,437.47	2,000	21,437.47
Total	$228,097.66	$15,000	$343,097.66
KINGS COUNTY			
Corcoran	$14,904.84	$1,000	$15,904.84
Hanford	31,614.09	3,000	34,614.09
Lemoore	7,208.33	1,000	8,208.33
Total	$53,727.26	$5,000	$58,727.26
LAKE COUNTY			
Lakeport	$6,126.93	$1,000	$7,126.93
LASSEN COUNTY			
Susanville	$15,492.97	$2,000	$17,492.97
LOS ANGELES COUNTY			
Alhambra	$165,479.59	$7,800	$173,979.59
Arcadia	106,237.97	6,000	112,237.97
Avalon	4,653.12	1,000	5,653.12
Azusa	49,157.81	4,000	53,157.81
Baldwin Park	89,549.58	6,000	95,549.58
Bell	49,963.97	4,000	53,963.97
Beverly Hills	94,060.54	6,000	100,060.54
Burbank	279,564.65	7,500	287,064.65
Claremont	20,149.55	3,000	23,149.55
Compton	196,723.90	7,500	204,223.90
Covina	35,775.94	3,000	38,775.94
Culver City	96,915.46	6,000	102,915.46
Dairy Valley	10,038.51	1,000	11,038.51
Downey (1/3 yr.)	136,236.03	3,750	139,976.03
El Monte	30,010.53	3,000	33,010.53
El Segundo	36,112.73	3,000	39,112.73
Gardena	63,996.57	6,000	70,996.57
Glendale	344,938.73	10,000	354,938.73
Glendora	26,140.53	3,000	29,140.53
Hawthorne	87,167.37	6,000	93,167.37
Hermosa Beach	47,192.49	4,000	51,192.49
Huntington Park	91,030.35	6,000	97,030.35
Inglewood	173,997.96	7,500	181,497.96
Lakewood	220,346.95	7,500	227,846.95
La Puente (3/4 yr.)	28,847.07	2,250	31,097.07
La Verne	16,406.45	3,000	18,406.45
Long Beach	997,798.45	10,000	1,007,798.45
Los Angeles	6,866,777.69	20,000	6,886,777.69
Lynwood	87,217.32	6,000	93,217.32
Manhattan Beach	94,802.39	6,000	100,802.39
Maywood	41,658.77	3,000	44,658.77
Monrovia	72,352.14	5,000	77,352.14
Montebello	86,561.75	6,000	92,561.75
Monterey Park	90,457.93	6,000	96,457.93
Palos Verdes Estates	20,169.73	2,000	22,169.73
Paramount (1/4 yr.)	14,625.01	1,250	15,875.01
Pasadena	341,337.86	10,000	351,337.86
Pomona	158,898.46	7,800	166,398.46
Redondo Beach	124,461.33	6,000	130,461.33
Rolling Hills (1/4 yr.)	1,555.07	$50	1,605.07
San Fernando	44,966.63	5,000	49,766.63
San Gabriel	67,217.00	5,000	73,217.00
San Marino	39,996.81	3,000	42,996.81
Santa Monica	232,137.34	7,800	239,637.34
Sierra Madre	27,041.38	3,000	29,041.38
Signal Hill	13,483.49	1,000	13,483.49
South Gate	158,870.66	7,500	166,370.66
South Pasadena	55,692.33	4,000	59,692.33
Torrance	232,430.83	7,800	239,930.83
Vernon	1,334.76	1,000	2,334.76
West Covina	111,186.91	1,000	112,186.91
Whittier	99,541.73	5,000	108,541.73
Total	$12,605,256.18	$266,500	$13,871,756.18
MADERA COUNTY			
Chowchilla	$13,115.88	$1,000	$14,115.88
Madera	39,352.01	3,000	42,352.01
Total	$52,467.89	$4,000	$56,467.89
MARIN COUNTY			
Belvedere	$3,580.69	$1,000	$4,580.69
Corte Madera	8,771.73	1,000	9,771.73
Fairfax	14,299.35	1,000	15,299.35
Larkspur	11,796.43	1,000	12,796.43
Mill Valley	24,811.98	2,000	26,811.98
Ross	7,421.82	1,000	8,421.82
San Anselmo	32,375.29	3,000	35,375.29
San Rafael	51,060.83	4,000	55,060.83
Sausalito	15,275.70	1,000	16,275.70
Total	$169,566.41	$15,000	$184,566.41
MARIPOSA COUNTY			
None			
MENDOCINO COUNTY			
Fort Bragg	$15,692.59	$1,000	$16,692.59
Point Arena	1,486.15	1,000	2,486.15
Ukiah	26,467.97	1,000	27,467.97
Willits	10,935.37	1,000	11,935.37
Total	$50,581.59	$6,000	$56,581.59
MERCED COUNTY			
Atwater	$16,442.81	$1,750	$18,192.81
Dos Palos	5,335.38	1,000	6,335.38
Gustine City	6,380.39	1,000	7,380.39
Livingston	5,359.61	1,000	6,359.61
Los Banos	16,276.37	1,750	18,026.37
Merced	60,190.97	4,000	64,190.97
Total	$109,915.33	$10,500	$130,415.33
MODOC COUNTY			
Alturas	$8,709.93	$1,000	$9,709.93
MONO COUNTY			
None			
MONTEREY COUNTY			
Carmel-by-the-Sea	$13,477.63	$1,000	$14,477.63
Del Rey Oaks	4,662.39	1,000	5,662.39
Gonzales	5,582.84	1,000	6,582.84
Greenfield	4,578.98	1,000	5,578.98
King	8,045.75	1,000	9,045.75
Monterey	63,966.56	4,500	68,466.56
Pacific Grove	33,186.75	3,000	36,186.75
Salinas	65,295.30	5,000	70,295.30
Seaside	47,523.08	4,000	51,523.08
Soledad	8,489.67	1,000	9,489.67
Total	$255,081.85	$22,500	$277,581.85
NAPA COUNTY			
Calistoga	$4,381.23	$1,000	$5,381.23
Napa	51,463.06	4,000	55,463.06
St. Helena	7,097.09	1,000	8,097.09
Total	$62,941.38	$6,000	$68,941.38
NEVADA COUNTY			
Grass Valley	$15,484.71	$2,000	$18,484.71
Nevada City	7,915.87	1,000	8,915.87
Total	$23,400.58	$3,000	$27,400.58
ORANGE COUNTY			
Anaheim	$154,764.28	$6,375	$161,139.28
Brea	18,136.69	2,000	20,136.69
Buena Park	54,309.25	4,000	58,309.25
Costa Mesa	53,514.07	4,000	57,514.07
Dairy City (3/4 yr.)	2,278.14	750	4,028.14
Dairyland	880.55	1,000	1,880.55
Fullerton	128,761.67	6,000	134,761.67
Garden Grove	129,642.64	6,000	135,642.64
Huntington Beach	18,139.72	2,000	20,139.72
Laguna Beach	25,354.39	2,000	27,354.39
La Habra	38,944.87	3,000	41,944.87
Newport Beach	61,690.96	4,500	66,190.96
Orange	51,549.91	4,000	55,549.91
Placentia	9,398.95	1,000	10,398.95
San Clemente	18,097.08	2,000	20,597.08
Santa Ana	198,077.27	7,800	205,877.27
Seal Beach	10,977.80	1,000	11,977.80
Stanton	7,763.32	1,000	8,763.32
Tri-City (1/4 yr.)	7,589.29	750	8,589.29
Tustin	4,490.35	750	5,240.35
Total	$995,987.33	$59,875	$1,055,832.33
PLACER COUNTY			
Auburn	$15,099.33	$1,000	$16,099.33
Colfax	2,533.59	1,000	3,533.59
Lincoln	7,446.34	1,000	8,446.34
Rocklin	3,695.98	1,000	4,695.98
Roseville	31,735.02	3,000	34,735.02
Total	$60,473.16	$7,000	$67,473.16

... Continued on page 62

STRICTER TRAFFIC LAWS

Continued from page 43 . . .

it difficult to keep pace with the insatiable demands of the automobile.
* * * Los Angeles, which already has the most elaborate urban highway system in the world with more than 180 miles of completed expressways and freeways, has plans that call for a total of more than 500 miles.'

"The cost of our freeways is, of course, tremendous, but the construction is based on sound economic principles of financing and they are directly responsible for saving the people of California millions of dollars beyond their original costs.

"From one standpoint alone, it has been estimated that inadequate roads cost motorists more than $5,000,000,-000 each year in the United States.

Traffic Accidents

'The California Traffic Safety Foundation estimates that last year in California we suffered an economic loss of $456,480,000 from traffic accidents. This amounts to $1,250,000 every 24 hours. These figures of course, cannot measure the death and injury toll which killed one person every 2¼ hours and injured one every four minutes all through 1956.

"Experience has shown that modern controlled-access highways, such as the Harbor Freeway and other similar arterials in Southern California, are far safer than those highways heretofore classified as 'conventional.'

"The accident rate on freeways is actually only about half of the overall accident rate on all types of highways, while statistics demonstrate that your life is three times as safe on a modern freeway per traveled mile as it is on other types of highways. These figures are based on national surveys but you may be interested in somewhat more specific examples developed by the National Safety Council.

"Using the traffic death rate per 100,000,000 vehicle miles as a basis, we find these rather startling comparisons: In California, freeways, 2.12 as against 9.39 for all State highways; in Virginia, the Shirley Expressway, 6.1 against 20.5 on US Highway 1; in Michigan, the Detroit Industrial

Expressway, 6.7 against 15 for US Route 112.

"I cite these various figures to demonstrate the sound economics of our freeway system in California. Before I leave statistics, I would like to present evidence of the monetary savings to the most careful, accident-free driver in Los Angeles.

"A 1956 study by the Automobile Club of Southern California, appearing last year in—of all places—a publication called 'Inside Michigan' showed that, on the basis of 133 miles of freeway driving versus 124 miles of utilizing ordinary streets and boulevards in Los Angeles, freeways saved over 30 percent in traveling time and over 50 percent in traveling costs.

"To my way of analyzing figures, this certainly seems to be a good investment of your gasoline tax dollars.

"I have talked at length, both here and on other occasions, of the tragic, wasteful impact of motor vehicle accidents upon our society and our economy. I regard this whole area as one of the most serious and pressing challenges faced by your State Government at Sacramento.

"It has been demonstrated that continuing improvement of our streets and highways, in accordance with modern engineering design and practice, will save lives and money. The State of California has been moving as rapidly as physical restrictions and financial limitations will permit to fulfill its obligation in this regard.

Legislative Program

"If this were the only answer—the simple solution—then we could view the traffic accident picture with greater hope and complacence. However, there is no such simple, single solution. We need a balanced, adequate and comprehensive program, attacking the problem from every possible angle.

"In my message to the Legislature and the proposed budget submitted for 1957-58, I have asked more stringent penalties for violators, more general analysis of accident records, more exact standards of driver licensing, more enforcement facilities and more uniform enforcement policies.

In addition, my Advisory Committee on Traffic Safety is carrying on a constant and expanding program of public information and education in vehicle safety and operation.

"In the long run, it is imperative that those who cannot be deterred from childish, dangerous acts by the fear of death consistently in a manner which even their simple minds can comprehend—through heavy fines and detention in jail.

"Most California drivers, night club comics to the contrary, are careful, courteous and law-abiding. However, many of these innocently err by their passive tolerance of violations of traffic laws. Bear in mind that these, too, are crimes against person and property.

Public Support Needed

"Traffic laws are made and enforced for public safety. Anyone who breaks them deliberately and flagrantly is, at least to a degree, a criminal who has threatened the life and well-being of one or more American citizens. He is not clever. In fact, to the extent of his violation, he is not even intelligent.

"A fine in traffic court, to me, is certainly not something to brag about over dinner or at a cocktail party. Evasion of the law 'designed to protect you isn't sensible. 'Fixing a ticket' is not a thing of which to boast and it does not measure your importance; it measures the honesty and integrity of yourself as a citizen and of the officer or judge who made it possible for you to escape the penalty for your illegal act. Plainly speaking, 'fixing a ticket' weakens the majesty of our law, the bulwark of our national freedom. The only alternative to supremacy and dignity of the law is tyrannical, capricious dictatorship.

"Your legislators, your Governor and the other administrative officers of your State Government are actively concerned with traffic safety. However, all their efforts will be for nothing if they do not have the active support and cooperation of the vast body of fine, law-abiding, sober California citizens.

"We are anxious to do all we can. We earnestly invite you to join with us and do all you can to minimize death and mayhem on the streets and highways of California."

and Public Works   57

Historic Weaverville

Improvements in Trinity County

By H. CLYDE AMESBURY, Senior Highway Engineer

LAST YEAR witnessed considerable highway activity in that portion of Trinity County contained in District II. A three and one-half mile contract held by Earl McNutt of Eugene, Oregon and amounting to about $600,000 was completed. A section 1.8 miles in length containing the Main Street of Weaverville and extending south towards Douglas City was completed by the Mercer-Fraser Company of Eureka at a cost of about $195,000. The same company completed a paving contract covering portions of the highway between Weaverville and Helena to the west at a cost of $121,-196. These were all routine construction contracts.

The storms of the winter of 1955-56 caused extensive damage along the Trinity River. Reconstruction of a complete washout of the roadbed at Vitzthums, about one and one-half miles east of Douglas City, was covered by a contract held by the Thomas Construction Company in the amount of $243,916. This is completed. Reconstruction cost on the Douglas City Bridge is covered by a contract held by the Bos Construction Company for $140,000. This is almost completed.

West of Weaverville between Junction City and Prairie Creek, the cost of storm damage repair is represented by a contract held by Scheumann & Johnson of Eugene, Oregon in the amount of $877,800. This contract is nearing completion.

The Bos Construction Company also completed a $16,000 contract for drainage correction on the road to Hayfork.

All this work is in the Redding District of which H. S. Miles is District Engineer. Joe Fonseca was Resident Engineer on the McNutt and Thomas jobs. Ellis Engle had charge of the Weaverville job and the paving between Weaverville and Helena. Charlie Moss represented the department on the drainage correction work. Bill Smith is resident engineer on the incomplete storm damage reconstruction between Junction City and Weaverville. N. E. Spicklemire is

Reconstruction and riprap along Trinity River near Vitzthums

Relocation on the McNutt job meant heavy grading. Old road on the left.

resident engineer for the bridge department on the Douglas City Bridge. George Barry and Ray Wilson are construction engineers for the district.

Relocation of Highway

The McNutt contract covered a relocation of a section of highway that practically followed a contour around the mountainside. The country was rough and the road was crooked. The relocation susbtituted a much straighter and shorter location which of course necessitated heavy cuts and fills.

The Mercer-Fraser improvement in Weaverville occurred almost exactly a century after the first wagon road was constructed to reach it.

Originally Shasta, seven miles west of Redding, had been the point reachable by freight wagons. From there pack outfits transported supplies the 38 miles to Weaverville. By 1854 the road had been extended to Tower House about 10 miles farther west. There still remained about 28 "mountain miles" which are supposed to contain 10,000 feet as against 5,280 for "flat land" miles.

Rush of Settlers

A company named the Shasta-Weaverville Wagon Road Company was founded with a capital of $20,000 by selling shares at $100 each. It started building the toll road in 1858.

There was a rush of settlers to the Trinity area even before the gold strike. A traveler through the country in 1854 spoke of the productive ranches and says the best settled part of the county is between Weaverville and Douglas City along Weaver Creek. He especially mentioned one ranch near the junction of this creek and the Trinity River.

This is the area through which the first unit of the reconstruction of the Douglas City-Weaverville highway was built. It is now a wide expanse of gravel. The area was mined by the white miners in the 1850's and 60's, reworked by the Chinese and then about 1930 was reworked again as a "doodle bug" operation. A "doodle bug" is a modified dredger. It has the screens and pumps for washing the gravel, and the recovery equipment, mounted on a hull which floats in a pond dug by a dragline. This same dragline excavates the gravel down to bedrock and dumps it on the screens. The "bug" follows in the pond dug by the dragline and deposits the rejected gravel in the pond behind the boat. This gravel has been handled until it is almost worn out.

Founding of Weaverville

Weaverville is one of the towns whose existence began and was caused by the discovery of gold in the 1850's. It is an old town. John Weaver came to the area in 1848. The first cabin was

and Public Works 59

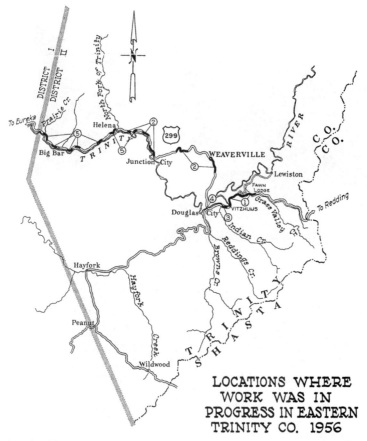

LOCATIONS WHERE WORK WAS IN PROGRESS IN EASTERN TRINITY CO. 1956

Locations of 1956 highway contracts in eastern Trinity County are as follows: 1—a three and one-half mile relocation between Vitzthums and Tom Lang Gulch; 2—paving contracts on portions of the highway from south of Weaverville (including its main street) to Helena; 3—reconstruction of a washout at Vitzthums; 4—reconstruction of Douglas City bridge; 5—repairing damage to roads due to flooding. The last three contracts are the result of the floods of 1955-56.

Main Street of Weaverville after improvements. Two spiral staircases visible in left center.

built in 1850 and by 1852 it was a considerable town. It was built of lumber sawed locally and it burned three times between 1853 and 1858. Brick buildings with iron doors to provide protection against fires were built after 1858. Several of these are still standing and in use.

No one can write about Weaverville and really touch upon it without mentioning its spiral stairways.

We know there was a Bavarian blacksmith living in Weaverville who knew how to build a spiral stairway. Whether he was the promoter of what followed or whether someone else had the idea and availed themselves of the blacksmith's talents, we do not know.

Anyhow, the matured idea resulted in one owner having title to a lot and the lower story, and another person owning the second story which was reached by a spiral stairway set out in the sidewalk in front of the building.

The very thought of drawing up the agreement to cover such a transaction and the proper allocation of responsibilities for roof and foundation repairs, to say nothing of insurance, general maintenance and taxes,

would be guaranteed to give a modern title expert the shakes.

Apparently these legal pitfalls were all ignored and some of the buildings are in use today with their dual but not joint ownership.

Signs of Gold Days Remain

In many ways the evidence of the gold days are still apparent in Weaverville and vicinity. Because development has been slow many buildings and landmarks that otherwise might have been obliterated are still in evidence. The Chinese Joss House still stands in Weaverville. Every gulch shows where some hopeful individual moved a small amount or even up to hundreds of cubic yards of material in prospecting. A trip into the mountains will reveal miles of ditches built to convey water to the "diggins." The amount of work, and it was all done by hand, is truly amazing.

An interesting sidelight concerns the Trinity Journal. It recently celebrated its centennial.

In 1856, David E. Gordon and Henry Seaman took over the Trinity Democrat that had been recently established. They did not like the name "Democrat" and asked Ed Neblett if he could suggest a better name. Back

east, Neblett had been a steady reader and great admirer of the Louisville Journal so he said "Why not call it the Journal?" Weaverville Journal it has been for over 100 years.

Lumbering Industry

Following the passing of the "gold rush" era, there was not much development in Trinity County. Mining activities tapered off and all but ceased. Stock ranching was carried on rather extensively and a small amount of lumbering was done. The county still has no incorporated town and the only railroad consists of 14 miles of Western Pacific line that cuts through the southwest corner on its route from the Bay region to Eureka. It is entirely dependent upon the highways for its transportation needs.

Changes are occurring. They began after World War II when there was a tremendous demand for lumber. Trinity County had huge stands of timber that were originally not reachable. Now with better highways and improved trucks they could be brought to market.

New Boom Towns

The Trinity dam and diversion tunnels which have been under planning
. . . Continued on page 63

and Public Works

Continued from page 56 . . .

RECORD TOTAL GAS TAX REVENUES TO CITIES

City	5/8¢ Gas Tax	Engineering	Total
PLUMAS COUNTY			
Portola	$6,965.88	$1,000	$7,965.88
RIVERSIDE COUNTY			
Banning	$25,823.94	$3,000	$27,823.94
Beaumont	10,563.92	1,000	11,563.92
Blythe	15,612.35	2,000	17,612.35
Coachella	10,721.35	1,000	11,721.35
Cabazon	2,641.73	1,000	2,641.73
Corona	36,321.14	3,000	39,321.14
Elsinore	6,979.39	1,000	7,979.39
Hemet	13,084.99	1,000	14,084.99
Indio	24,192.59	2,000	26,192.59
Palm Springs	37,771.91	3,000	40,771.91
Perris	7,032.22	1,000	8,032.22
Riverside	219,033.82	7,500	226,533.82
San Jacinto	5,493.52	1,000	6,493.52
Total	$415,292.79	$26,500	$441,792.79
SACRAMENTO COUNTY			
Folsom	$6,815.93	$1,000	$7,815.93
Galt	4,785.98	1,000	5,785.98
Isleton	4,934.39	1,000	5,934.39
North Sacramento	24,549.85	2,000	26,549.85
Sacramento	485,649.43	10,000	495,649.43
Total	$526,735.48	$15,000	$541,735.48
SAN BENITO COUNTY			
Hollister	$17,039.34	$2,000	$19,039.34
San Juan Bautista	3,185.92	1,000	4,185.92
Total	$20,225.26	$3,000	$23,225.26
SAN BERNARDINO COUNTY			
Barstow	$25,494.83	$2,250	$27,744.82
Chino	23,070.99	3,000	26,070.99
Colton	53,823.03	4,000	57,823.03
Fontana	42,313.81	3,000	45,313.81
Monte Vista	23,922.94	3,000	26,922.94
Needles	12,816.46	3,000	15,816.46
Ontario	123,453.77	6,000	129,453.77
Redlands	65,706.12	5,000	70,706.12
Rialto	36,396.96	3,000	39,396.96
San Bernardino	259,102.64	7,500	266,602.64
Upland	36,664.72	3,000	39,664.72
Total	$703,366.31	$38,750	$741,116.31
SAN DIEGO COUNTY			
Carlsbad	$21,513.77	$2,000	$23,513.77
Chula Vista	96,838.94	6,000	102,838.94
Coronado	53,053.69	4,000	57,053.69
El Cajon	66,060.84	5,000	71,060.84
Escondido	29,906.80	3,750	33,656.80
Imperial Beach (3/4 yr.)	21,068.66	1,800	23,868.66
La Mesa	59,115.41	4,250	63,365.41
National City	84,632.18	6,000	90,632.18
Oceanside	61,892.86	4,750	66,643.86
San Diego	1,382,123.61	10,000	1,392,123.61
Total	$1,877,302.46	$46,350	$1,923,452.46
SAN FRANCISCO COUNTY			
San Francisco	$3,395,641.19	$20,000	$3,415,641.19
SAN JOAQUIN COUNTY			
Escalon (1/4 yr.)	$1,533.73	$250	$1,783.73
Lodi	51,360.82	4,000	55,360.82
Manteca	18,385.01	2,000	20,385.01
Ripon	5,409.06	1,000	6,409.06
Stockton	282,110.74	7,500	289,610.74
Tracy	31,953.10	2,750	34,703.10
Total	$360,552.15	$17,500	$378,152.15
SAN LUIS OBISPO COUNTY			
Arroyo Grande	$6,367.92	$1,000	$7,367.92
El Paso de Robles	19,873.17	2,000	21,873.17
Pismo Beach	5,963.17	1,000	6,963.17
San Luis Obispo	53,232.90	4,000	57,232.90
Total	$85,437.16	$8,000	$93,437.16
SAN MATEO COUNTY			
Atherton	$19,583.09	$2,000	$21,583.09
Belmont	24,455.77	3,000	29,455.77
Burlingame	61,785.26	4,000	65,785.26
Colma	899.12	1,000	1,899.12
Daly City	94,255.31	6,000	100,255.31
Hillsborough	15,143.82	3,000	18,143.82
Menlo Park	73,569.47	5,000	78,569.47
Millbrae	34,636.56	3,000	37,636.56
Redwood City	120,375.76	6,000	126,375.76
San Bruno	61,908.85	5,000	66,908.85
San Carlos	54,396.16	4,000	58,396.16
San Mateo	186,728.81	7,500	194,228.81
South San Francisco	110,272.34	6,000	116,272.34
Woodside (1/2 yr.)	7,360.32	1,000	8,360.32
Total	$876,639.47	$56,500	$933,139.67

City	5/8¢ Gas Tax	Engineering	Total
SANTA BARBARA COUNTY			
Guadalupe	$7,690.33	$1,000	$8,690.33
Lompoc	17,085.29	2,000	19,085.29
Santa Barbara	157,460.83	7,300	164,960.83
Santa Maria	40,527.94	3,000	43,527.94
Total	$222,734.39	$13,500	$236,234.39
SANTA CLARA COUNTY			
Alviso	$2,014.50	$1,000	$3,014.50
Campbell	24,451.42	2,000	26,451.42
Cupertino	5,394.67	1,000	6,394.67
Gilroy	18,697.07	2,000	20,697.07
Los Altos	59,986.61	4,000	63,986.61
Los Altos Hills	9,698.86	1,000	10,698.86
Los Gatos	15,552.60	1,750	17,302.60
Milpitas	2,876.83	1,000	3,876.83
Morgan Hill	3,737.63	1,000	4,737.63
Mountain View	60,614.89	4,000	64,614.89
Palo Alto	126,684.97	6,000	132,684.97
San Jose	355,978.36	10,000	365,978.36
Santa Clara	99,513.62	5,000	105,513.62
Saratoga (1/2 yr.)	22,962.02	2,000	24,962.02
Sunnyvale	87,106.86	6,000	93,106.86
Total	$900,143.39	$48,750	$948,893.39
SANTA CRUZ COUNTY			
Capitola	$3,709.81	$1,000	$4,709.81
Santa Cruz	70,427.33	5,000	75,427.33
Watsonville	36,801.74	3,000	39,801.74
Total	$113,938.78	$9,000	$121,938.78
SHASTA COUNTY			
Anderson	$13,124.06	$1,000	$13,124.06
Redding	36,705.96	3,000	39,705.96
Total	$48,830.02	$4,000	$52,830.02
SIERRA COUNTY			
Loyalton	$2,953.78	$1,000	$3,953.78
SISKIYOU COUNTY			
Dorris	$2,766.04	$1,000	$3,766.04
Dunsmuir	13,148.80	1,000	14,148.80
Etna	2,376.00	1,000	3,376.00
Fort Jones	1,623.11	1,000	2,623.11
Montague	3,213.41	1,000	3,213.41
Mt. Shasta	5,898.29	1,000	6,898.29
Tulelake	3,175.25	1,000	4,175.25
Yreka City	13,009.42	1,000	14,009.42
Total	$42,305.32	8,000	51,305.32
SOLANO COUNTY			
Benicia	$22,506.57	$2,000	$24,506.57
Dixon	7,002.26	1,000	8,002.26
Fairfield	32,309.45	3,000	35,309.45
Rio Vista	7,836.38	1,000	8,836.38
Suisun City	6,065.67	1,000	7,065.67
Vacaville	22,715.75	2,000	24,715.75
Vallejo	117,517.63	6,000	123,517.63
Total	$215,936.50	$16,000	$231,936.50
SONOMA COUNTY			
Cloverdale	$6,514.94	$1,000	$7,514.94
Healdsburg	13,034.33	1,000	14,034.33
Petaluma	37,961.81	3,000	40,961.81
Santa Rosa	86,975.75	6,000	92,975.75
Sebastopol	8,438.04	1,000	9,438.04
Sonoma	7,444.77	1,000	8,444.77
Total	$158,969.44	$13,000	$171,969.44
STANISLAUS COUNTY			
Ceres	$10,971.62	$1,000	$11,971.62
Modesto	96,388.92	6,000	102,388.92
Newman	6,107.92	1,000	7,107.92
Oakdale	13,479.36	1,000	14,479.36
Patterson	5,541.51	1,000	6,541.51
Riverbank	8,396.52	1,000	9,396.52
Turlock	22,309.32	2,000	24,309.32
Total	$163,194.98	$13,000	$176,194.98
SUTTER COUNTY			
Live Oak	$6,386.47	$1,000	$7,386.47
Yuba City	31,805.65	3,000	34,805.65
Total	$38,192.12	$4,000	$42,192.12
TEHAMA COUNTY			
Corning	$7,867.15	$1,000	$8,867.15
Red Bluff	17,157.34	2,000	19,157.34
Tehama	970.15	1,000	1,970.15
Total	$25,984.60	$4,000	$29,984.60
TRINITY COUNTY			
None			

RECORD TOTAL GAS TAX REVENUES TO CITIES

Continued from page 62 ...

City	5/84 Gas Tax	Engineering	Total
TULARE COUNTY			
Dinuba	$16,771.04	$2,000	$18,771.04
Exeter	12,968.71	1,000	13,968.71
Lindsay	16,968.78	2,000	18,968.78
Porterville	24,108.33	2,000	26,108.33
Tulare	40,943.18	3,000	43,943.18
Visalia	43,991.78	3,000	46,991.78
Woodlake	7,801.86	1,000	8,801.86
Total	$162,358.25	$14,000	$176,358.25
TUOLUMNE COUNTY			
Sonora	$7,563.66	$1,000	$8,563.66
VENTURA COUNTY			
Fillmore	$14,998.96	$1,000	$15,998.96
Ojai	12,143.63	1,000	13,143.63
Oxnard	89,338.21	6,000	95,338.21
Port Hueneme	24,402.67	2,000	26,402.67
San Buenaventura	73,903.68	5,250	79,153.68
Santa Paula	35,371.39	2,000	35,371.39
Total	$250,147.54	$15,250	$265,397.54
YOLO COUNTY			
Davis	$18,692.84	$2,000	$20,692.84
Winters	5,189.84	1,000	6,189.84
Woodland	35,761.19	3,000	38,761.19
Total	$59,613.87	$6,000	$65,613.87
YUBA COUNTY			
Marysville	$34,180.19	$2,000	$36,180.19
Wheatland	1,813.67	1,000	2,813.67
Total	$35,993.86	$3,000	$38,993.86
GRAND TOTAL	$28,319,354.63	$1,000,125	$29,319,479.63

EMBARCADERO

Continued from page 46 ...

maximum service to motorists with a minimum right of way space for the route. It will also provide more safety for the traveling public by the separation of the two directions of traffic.

Two additional projects are presently under way as parts of the Embarcadero Freeway. The portion from Fremont to Mission Street is estimated to be completed about the first of July, 1957, at a cost of $1,753,545 and the extension to Broadway at Vallejo Street by the fall of 1959, at a cost of $7,800,000. Charles L. Harney, Inc., is the contractor on both of these projects.

The downtown connections, or ramps, will serve as the terminal of the freeway until the fall of 1959 when the extension of the freeway along the Embarcadero to Broadway at Vallejo Street is scheduled for completion. Thus, some congestion during peak hours is anticipated at the terminal pending completion of the extension. However, the congestion at the present northbound off-ramp at Fourth and Bryant Streets and at the First Street off-ramp should be considerably relieved.

OROVILLE-MARYSVILLE

Continued from page 30 ...

The southerly end of the Feather River Highway Relocation will join this project at the Montgomery Street connection.

The proposed improvement is a step in the development of this portion of US Alternate 40 to full freeway status. It is in keeping with the planned over-all development of this highway.

The 1957-58 state highway budget contains $750,000 for this project.

WEAVERVILLE

Continued from page 61 ...

for several years but upon which work actually started last year, have given a great impetus.

Around 40 million dollars worth of contracts have been awarded for roads, camps and tunnels. Work has been started on all of these items. Later the Bureau of Reclamation advised that the contract for the Lewiston Dam was let for 49 million dollars. Weaverville is considering incorporation and is planning to install a sewer system. Lewiston, near the dam, is booming and growing like a

HENRY L. MAHONEY

Continued from page 50 ...

Chief Clerk in the Headquarters Office in 1937, a position which he held for 20 years.

During his career Henry has participated in the tremendous growth of the State Highway System to the point where today average weekly expenditures have surpassed the amount formerly expended in one year when he began state service.

A dinner party honoring Henry's retirement was attended by his family and many friends throughout the organization on April 25th at the University Club.

"Hank" plans to maintain his home in Sacramento but has not formulated any definite plans as to how he will spend his well-earned retirement time.

The Division of Highways extends to him and Mrs. Mahoney congratulations and best wishes for many happy years of retirement.

AUTO INDUSTRY SPENDS RECORD BILLIONS

Motor vehicle and parts manufacturers, anticipating the growing market of the future, spent an estimated $1,863,000,000 during 1956 on new plants and equipment.

Since World War II, points out the National Automobile Club, the industry has spent 9.7 billion dollars on plant expansion and new equipment. Expenditures climbed steadily from 349 million in 1949 to 1.3 billion in 1956, then dropped slightly before the 1956 budget allocations.

MAKE ALLOWANCES

If you want to drive safely, do not be satisfied merely to do everything you ought to do. You should make allowances for the unexpected and for the mistakes and misjudgments of other drivers. The California State Automobile Association says the best motorists drive defensively.

boom construction town, which it is. Motels are being built, even miles away from the dam. On every side there are signs of progress and development.

and Public Works

Legislature Requests Naming of Bridges

The Department of Public Works has been instructed by resolutions passed by the 1957 Legislature to name two bridges in Northern California, one in honor of Louis De Martin, Sr. of Del Norte County, and the other in commemoration of the late George Leatherwood, a state highway engineer.

A resolution sponsored by Senator Randolph Collier requested that the newly completed bridge across Wilson Creek on US 101 about 12 miles north of the Town of Klamath in Del Norte County be named the "Louis De Martin Sr. Bridge." De Martin is a pioneer and a resident of Del Norte County since 1875. He is said to have built the first bridge across the creek on the highway which is now US 101.

A proposed bridge across the South Fork of the Eel River near Dyerville on the new Redwood Freeway in Humboldt County will be named the "George Leatherwood Memorial Bridge." Leatherwood, who was in charge of advance planning for District I of the Division of Highways, was killed on July 30, 1956, when a helicopter in which he was a passenger crashed on US 299 near the North Fork of the Mad River. He had developed important ideas in planning the location of the Redwood Freeway through the southern Humboldt County redwood groves and this proposed bridge and freeway will stand as a monument to his engineering ability.

VENEZUELA

Venezuela is the leading importer of United States motor vehicles, according to the National Automobile Club.

During 1955, Venezuela received 44,057 vehicles from this Country, including 26,956 passenger cars, 16,-895 trucks and 206 busses. Mexico followed with 39,649 units.

Belgium was the No. 1 European importer, with 28,696 motor vehicles.

3n Memoriam

GEORGE B. McDOUGALL

George B. McDougall, State Architect from 1913 until his retirement in 1938, died April 20, 1957, in the San Rafael General Hospital after a brief illness. He was 88.

McDougall was born in San Francisco on October 11, 1868, where his father, Barnett McDougall, was an architect. He first worked in the office of Superior Court Reporters in San Francisco and later was private secretary to Wm. Randolph Hearst.

After working five years as an architectural student and draftsman in the office of his father, McDougall became a member of the architectural firm of McDougall Brothers in San Francisco in 1893. He was appointed State Architect on August 22, 1913, by the then State Engineer, Wilbur F. McClure, and served under the administrations of seven different state engineers and directors of public works and under six different governors.

He was past president of the Northern California chapter of the American Institute of Architects, the Marin County YMCA and the San Rafael Rotary Club. He was also an active Mason and a member of the Presbyterian Church.

He is survived by his widow, Louise, of San Rafael; a daughter, Mrs. Arthur Dudman of Sacramento, and a niece, Frances McDougall of Berkeley.

NICE LETTER

Alhambra

Mr. KENNETH ADAMS, *Editor*

We have enjoyed your magazine and found it most interesting. We travel quite a little and it is most thrilling to see some of the new highways we have gone over, and to see those we intend to travel in a few weeks.

If everyone enjoys your magazine as we do, your Division of Highways has far surpassed great rewards for its conscientious work and ideas.

Most sincerely,

Mr. AND Mrs. RAY C. MORRIS

3n Memoriam

DAVID A. HOFFMAN

David Arthur Hoffman, Supervising Outdoor Advertising Inspector for the California Division of Highways, died on April 27th, after an illness of several months.

Hoffman had been in state service since 1933 who was one of the first inspectors appointed by the division under the Outdoor Advertising Act which went into effect that year.

He served first in the Sacramento area, later transferring to Los Angeles. He returned to Sacramento in 1947 to become head of the division's Outdoor Advertising Section as supervising inspector.

Hoffman was born at Inglewood, Kansas, and went to school in Wichita. He came to California in 1925. Before joining state service he worked as a printer.

Hoffman is survived by his wife, Rosemary, and son, Bill.

LAST LINK
Continued from page 26 . . .

way is constructed, is estimated at $3,000,000. Therefore we cannot say at this time that the District VII part of the San Bernardino Freeway is completely finished.

As the areas passed through by the San Bernardino Freeway are more intensively developed as population increases and as traffic volumes become correspondingly larger, other additional construction is certain to be needed. Even now, it is foreseen that before many years have passed, further construction to provide an eight-lane freeway throughout will become necessary.

Thus, the State Division of Highways cannot, even at this late date, close the books on the San Bernardino Freeway and write "Finis."

MOTOR VEHICLES

A total of 66,875,000 motor vehicles, with a wholesale value of $95,-800,000,000, have been produced and sold in the United States during the 10 years since 1947, reports the National Automobile Club.

California Highways
and Public Works

Official Journal of the Division of Highways,
Department of Public Works, State of California

KENNETH C. ADAMS, Editor

HELEN HALSTEAD, Assistant Editor

MERRITT R. NICKERSON, Chief Photographer

Vol. 35   July-August   Nos. 7-8

Public Works Building
Twelfth and N Streets
Sacramento

CONTENTS

Published in the interest of highway development in California. Editors of newspapers and others are privileged to use matter contained herein. Cuts will be gladly loaned upon request

Address communications to
CALIFORNIA HIGHWAYS AND PUBLIC WORKS
P. O. Box 1499
Sacramento, California

Information

By RICHARD H. WILSON
Assistant State Highway Engineer

Technology

Quantities and Values of Control Items Used on State Highway Construction Jobs

Worth While

THERE HAS been a constantly growing demand in Headquarters Office for information concerning the volumes of construction materials, particularly mineral aggregates, cement and steel, that will be required for construction of highway projects included in various California Highway Commission budget programs. This information is usually in demand considerably in advance of when firm quantity estimates become available after adoption of the construction budgets by the commission.

Information of this nature is usually required by contractors and material suppliers and producers immediately following release of approved Highway Commission budget programs to the public. At these times, firms or their representatives attempt to determine the extent to which their facilities will possibly be involved in supplying materials during the construction program periods. Industries particularly concerned in this respect are those in the cement, asphalt, steel, equipment and machinery, and aggregate producing fields.

Factors Involved

Progress toward providing a means for forecasting the requirements of future programs has been made by the Bureau of Public Roads. This agency has prepared usage factor tables for steel and aggregates requirements from data reported by each of the state and territorial highway departments. We believe that the basic data, particularly with respect to the bureau aggregate factors, are in such detail that projection into future programs will be somewhat misleading. The bureau factors, being based upon projects financed partially with federal-aid funds, do not recognize nu-

RICHARD H. WILSON

merous other projects financed wholly from state and local funds and therefore true averages are not reflected.

It was found in developing factor tables for state highway construction requirements in California that a definite relationship existed between the various factors and items used in the California Highway Construction Cost Index and the budgetary cost and estimates of material use. Considerable study of highway construction costs was made in developing our index and at the time, it was found that eight construction items were sufficiently recurring to establish definite patterns. Since inception of the index, specifications for construction of plant-mixed surfacing have changed to the extent that little difference now exists between its construction and the construction of as-

phalt concrete pavement. Recently the two items have been combined into a classification of asphaltic and bituminous mixes for purposes of the index which is now based on seven construction items.

Nine Contract Items

It was decided in preparing the factor tables that consideration should be mainly restricted to the seven items of construction used in index calculations but that in addition cement and asphalt as items upon which contractors furnish bids would be included since they are items for which regular reporting is made.

The value of the nine contract items for which factors have been determined represents slightly over 60 percent of the construction value of all contracts awarded.

From studies made in this office, factors have been determined for each of the years 1954, 1955 and 1956 based on actual quantities required for nine major bid items of construction contracts with relation to the total construction value of all contracts awarded during each calendar year. Composite factors were then determined for the nine items based on total requirements for the three years with relation to the total value. The composite factors agree favorably with the factors determined for each of the three years and it is believed that through their use it will be possible to forecast the requirements of our construction programs for these major items when the monetary value is known. Such forecasts should provide information reasonably accurate for the purposes intended.

Intelligent Guessing

Sufficient study has not been made to determine that the same degree of accuracy will prevail when the factors are applied to groups of projects or to projects within particular regions or areas. Since these factors are based upon statewide averages, it is recommended that they not be applied in instances other than where average conditions prevail. However, in the absence of data from which quantities can otherwise be determined, it is felt that the factors when applied in most instances, will afford a means for "intelligent guessing."

Tables have been prepared for the calendar years 1954, 1955 and 1956 and the three years have been consolidated to provide the information for a composite table. In each instance the total number of contracts awarded during the respective periods together with the total bid item values are shown. In addition, the tables include the total quantities embraced in the nine items together with the dollar value involved. From the foregoing figures, factors have been computed showing the quantity of material for each of the nine items required for each million dollars of contract item value; the dollar value for each of the items for each million dollars of contract item value; and a percentage representing the ratio that the dollar value of each item bears to the total contract item value for all contracts awarded during each period.

Roadway Excavation

Roadway excavation is an item found in almost every contract awarded. Quantities and prices are affected to considerable degree by project location and prices are further affected by volume, by traffic interference and climatic conditions. Construction is so widely distributed over the State that reasonable averages prevail. Occasional exceptions are to be found during periods when a small number of large projects are put under way in locations where identical conditions exist, resulting in unbalancing average unit prices. Roadway excavation is let on an unclassified basis and therefore quantities and prices used in the factor determination in-

After bids are opened in the assembly room of the Department of Public Works, the proposals together with extension tabulations are handled by this group. The bid prices are extended, totaled and compared with bidder's proposal to assure that bid is correct. It is verified that the bidder's name and signature are consistent and in agreement with prequalification. The bidder's security is reviewed and, if inconsistencies are apparent in signature or security, the proposal is referred to attorneys for a ruling as to validity. LEFT TO RIGHT: Forren Lee, Margaret Harder, Joe Rieger, Raymond Edgell, Harry Sahagian, Floyd Reynolds, H. C. McCarty, Harry Slatinger, Walter Landers, Dick Roberts, and Carl Tomei.

clude all earthy material handled except structure excavation, ditch excavation and other excavations of specified nature.

Types of Surfacing

The item of untreated rock base includes both base and surfacing aggregates in connection with which there is neither a cement or asphalt treatment applied as part of the item. Previous to 1953, crusher run base was used for the purposes for which untreated base is now being used.

Asphaltic and bituminous mixes include both plant-mixed surfacing and asphalt concrete pavement. Both of these surfacings are placed without side forms and the similarity of other specifications together with comparable bid prices generally received for

the two items have eliminated the necessity of giving separate consideration in various cost analyses.

When asphalt concrete pavement is specified, the unit includes the weight of the asphalt content. In most instances plant-mixed surfacing requires separate items for asphalt and mineral aggregate. For factor purposes the weights and prices are combined to provide a price per ton for either surfacing in place. The average application of asphalt in these mixes is estimated at approximately 5 percent. To determine the approximate weight of aggregate, the total mix weight should be divided by 1.05 and the difference between the two weights will give the approximate weight of asphalt.

2

Concrete Pavement

Portland cement concrete pavement includes portland cement concrete used in all pavements of this type in which the cement content is specified at five sacks to the cubic yard. The volume for pavement includes the amount of cement used in the mix and the cement used for this purpose is not included in the item of cement. Should there be reason for breaking the item down into its components, the total quantity of pavement can be multiplied by 1.25 to provide the volume of cement stated in barrels. The volume of pavement when multiplied by 1.7 will furnish the approximate quantity of mineral aggregates expressed in tons.

Portland cement concrete structures includes all portland cement concrete used in structures of all kinds except the concrete used for footing blocks, railing, precast and prestressed members and other minor uses in connection therewith. Except in some minor instances, the cement content of the material for this purpose is six sacks per cubic yard. The cement volume in barrels can be determined by multiplying the total volume by 1.5 and the same volume multipled by 1.7 will provide the weight of the mineral aggregate in tons.

Reinforcing Steel

Bar reinforcing steel quantities include all reinforcing steel used in constructing bridges and other structures. Some instances occur when the item is bid on a lump sum basis and when this procedure is used, the quantity in pounds that is represented by the lump sum item is combined to provide the total reinforcing steel · requirements expressed in pounds.

Structural steel includes the weight of rolled shapes and other steel required in the construction of steel structures. Special high-strength steels such as was specified in the construction of the Carquinez Bridge are exceptions and exclusion of these types of steel is for the reason that they are not generally found in normal designs and the price differential would throw unreasonable weight on price averages.

... Continued on page 4

PRIMITIVE ROAD WORK IN NEW GUINEA

Photos from Australian News and Information Bureau.

The next time you see modern equipment at work building a freeway or expressway in California, compare it with these pictures of primitive methods of highway construction in the Australian trust territory of New Guinea. Upper picture shows workers laying a corduroy base over a sacsac swamp to give a firm foundation on the new Wewak-Dagua Road, a length of 30 miles. Lower photo shows villagers surfacing a road with stones from nearby streams. One day a week is allocated for roadwork and among the Eastern Highlanders enthusiasm for roadbuilding is so great that everybody turns out on road day to have a share in the work.

Continued from page 3 ...

While structural shapes are used for steel piling, the quantity of steel for this purpose is not included in the item of structural steel. It is the intention that the quantity of steel required for this item should be confined to superstructure construction or steel that requires fabrication.

When Cement Is Used

Cement is specified as an item when its purpose is intended for treating bases and subgrades. A barrel unit is specified when the material is used for these treatments. Total cement requirements for state highway construction programs can be obtained by combining the results of the factor for the cement item together with the cement requirements for pavement and structure concrete as determined above.

Asphalt when a separate item, covers its use for prime coat, penetration treatment, armor coat, seal coat, road-mix surfacing, bituminous surface treatment, etc. Asphalt used for plant-mixed surfacing is usually paid for as a separate item but for purposes of these factors and the cost index it is combined with the quantity of mineral aggregate to furnish the total weight of bituminous mixes. The av-

erage content of asphalt in plant-mixed surfacing is about 5 percent of the weight of aggregate used. The total asphalt requirements for the various construction programs is the resultant of the factor for this item combined with the weight of asphalt in the item of asphaltic and bituminous mixes determined according to the breakdown shown in that item above.

Various Materials Specified

There has been no attempt to include all materials required by the various construction programs that are common to the items for which factors have been computed. For in-

... Continued on page 34

SUMMARY OF QUANTITIES

California Division of Highways Contracts
January 1, 1954, to December 31, 1956

1831 contracts with total value of $520,951,100 (contract bid items only)
Weighted averages for three-year period

Contract items	Total quantities for 3 years	Dollar value totals for 3 years	Quantities per million dollars of contracts	Dollar value per million dollars of contracts	Percent of total contract value
Roadway excavation	114,008,151 cu. yds.	$48,189,820	218,900 cu. yds.	$93,000	9.3%
Untreated rock base	7,789,873 tons	15,939,788	15,000 tons	31,000	3.1
Plant-mixed surfacing	10,813,074 tons	55,874,241	20,800 tons	107,300	10.7
Asphalt-concrete pavement	92,076 tons	678,313	177 tons	920	0.09
Portland cement concrete pavement	2,107,120 cu. yds.	30,049,963	4,040 cu. yds.	57,700	5.8
Portland cement concrete Structures	1,473,230 cu. yds.	76,175,612	2,830 cu. yds.	146,300	14.6
Bar reinforcing steel	272,509,723 lbs.	27,270,655	523,100 lbs.	53,000	5.3
Structural steel	108,589,671 lbs.	16,620,797	208,400 lbs.	32,000	3.2
Cement (contracts only)	7,127,955 bbls.	26,964,385	13,700 bbls.	50,000	5.4
Asphalt (contracts only)	761,490 tons	16,098,560	1,460 tons	30,900	3.1
State purchases cement	13,144 bbls.	54,779			
State purchases asphalt	139,407 tons	3,385,105			

California Division of Highways Contracts
January 1, 1956, to December 31, 1956

625 contracts with total value of $201,067,500 (contract bid items only)

Contract items	Total quantities for year	Dollar value totals for year	Quantities per million dollars of contracts	Dollar value per million dollars of contracts	Percent of total contract value
Roadway excavation	36,214,445 cu. yds.	$17,925,072	180,100 cu. yds.	$89,000	8.9%
Untreated rock base	3,093,426 tons	6,707,217	15,400 tons	33,000	3.3
Plant-mixed surfacing	3,423,296 tons	20,509,304	17,000 tons	102,000	10.2
Asphalt concrete pavement	1,980 tons	12,675	10 tons	65	0.006
Portland cement concrete pavement	795,631 cu. yds.	11,832,946	3,950 cu. yds.	58,800	5.9
Portland cement concrete structures	470,121 cu. yds.	26,828,982	2,340 cu. yds.	133,400	13.3
Bar reinforcing steel	89,313,283 lbs.	9,997,422	444,200 lbs.	50,000	5.0
Structural steel	34,390,821 lbs.	6,607,470	170,100 lbs.	32,000	3.3
Cement (contracts only)	2,540,616 bbls.	9,488,071	12,635 bbls.	47,000	4.7
Asphalt (contracts only)	291,676 tons	6,543,221	1,450 tons	32,500	3.3
State purchases cement	2,152 bbls.	11,892			
State purchases asphalt	47,798 tons	1,296,537			

... Continued on page 35

4

Pass of the Oaks

Paso Robles Project Is Progressing

By LOWELL D. KRAATZ, Resident Engineer

TRAFFIC CONGESTION in Paso Robles in San Luis Obispo County, originally named the City of El Paso de Robles, caused by an 82 percent increase in average daily traffic on the Coast Highway, US 101, in the past eight years, will be solved in the spring of 1958 by completion of a $3,340,000 freeway passing through the city on new alignment.

The City of El Paso de Robles, "the pass of the Oaks," is a moderately expanding residential and small commercial community with a population of approximately 7,000 located in a relatively narrow oak-studded section of the Salinas River valley, approximately 30 miles north of San Luis Obispo. Its history includes an era of worldwide fame in the early part of the century when tourists and the ailing flocked to the area to take warm sulphur baths supplied by still active sulfur wells which are located throughout the city. The area is served by the coast route of the Southern Pacific Railroad and State Sign Route 41 and US 101 which intersect at 13th and Spring Streets.

Four-lane Divided Highway

The project now under construction by the Madonna Construction Company consists of 5.1 miles of four-lane divided highway which will pass through the city between the Southern Pacific Railroad tracks on the west and the Salinas River on the east. It will connect existing four-lane divided expressways 1.3 miles south and one mile north of the city limits. Six bridge structures are included in the project. Also, under this contract, recently completed projects on State Sign Route 41 from Huero Huero Creek to the Estrella River will be connected to the freeway by con-

struction of 2.2 miles of two-lane highway on new alignment.

Work started October 15, 1956, and at present grading has been completed and the concrete paving operation started. The contractor moved 1,200,-000 cubic yards of roadway excavation at a rate of 10,000 to 15,000 cubic yards per day. This was accomplished using two- and three-axle pneumatic-tired scrapers in conjunction with tractors with dozers for loading and ripping. The major portions of excavation were contained in high benched cuts at each end of the project. Median crossover detours were constructed at each end of the project to carry two-way traffic through the construction area.

Roadway Excavation

Roadway excavation in these high benched cuts was completed without incident, even though it was necessary for the heavy grading equipment to work adjacent to and cross traffic. In general roadway excavation material consisted of clayey sand, soft clay shale and talus which were expansive in nature. Most of this material required 20 percent to 50 percent moisture in order to obtain the required compaction. Compaction equipment consisted of standard sheepsfoot rollers and segmented steel wheel rollers. An attempt to use a tractor-drawn 50-ton pneumatic roller failed due to the difficulty in maintaining traction in the wet clay.

The structural section for the freeway on US 101 consists of 0.67 foot of Class B portland cement concrete on 0.33 foot of cement-treated subgrade over 0.50 foot of selected material. The structural section for the portion of the project on State Sign Route 41 consists of 0.25 foot of Type B plant-mixed surfacing on 0.67

foot of Class B cement-treated base over 0.50 foot of selected material. The selected material was obtained from a cut on State Sign Route 41 and is a uniform sandy material of good quality. Most of this material was excavated and hauled in pneumatic-tired scrapers, but the long-haul material was loaded into 10-cubic-yard capacity dump trucks using a pneumatic-tired six-cubic-yard skiploader.

Drainage Structures

All drainage structures under the main lanes consist of reinforced concrete pipe varying in size from 18 to 66 inches in diameter. Pipe installations were hampered by the presence of ground water and unstable basement soil. At these locations the pipe trenches were subexcavated and backfilled with Type C filter material to provide firm bedding for the large culverts. Where necessary, eight-inch perforated metal pipes were installed either below or adjacent to the pipe culverts to carry the profuse ground water flows. Four large-diameter culverts were extended adjacent to the freeway under city streets. Great care was taken during the installation of these pipes to avoid damage to water, sewer and gas lines. At two locations it was necessary to install 60- and 48-inch centrifugally cast extra-strength reinforced-concrete pipe under the Southern Pacific Railroad tracks by the jacking method in order to avoid a disruption of rail traffic. These reinforced-concrete pipes were jacked through the railroad embankments by means of four 125-ton hydraulic jacks operating in pairs.

Special Methods and Design

Special methods and design were necessary to solve the relatively minor drainage problem of warm sulfur

Present steel pratt truss bridge across Salinas River looking westerly toward Paso Robles

water artesian wells located under planned frontage roads. An attempt to cap one of these wells failed due to the poor condition of the steel well casing. The final solution to this problem was to attach vitrified clay pipe or asbestos bonded corrugated metal pipe to the existing casing with a concrete collar to drain the flow horizontally outside the embankment area. As insurance against possible subsurface casing leakage, a 10-foot-diameter filter material cone was constructed around the casing to a depth of three or four feet.

Planned grade requires a 20-foot cut to carry the freeway under the 13th Street Overcrossing. Due to the presence of ground water in this area, a network of eight-inch perforated metal pipe underdrains in conjunction with a 1.0-foot pervious blanket under the freeway lanes will be placed to carry off ground water.

Future Expansion

In order to provide for future expansion of this facility to a six-lane divided freeway, 550 lineal feet of metal bin-type retaining walls designed for future vertical extensions were installed at the toe of two embankments. These walls are constructed to a height varying from four to eight feet and may be extended to a maximum height of 13 feet. Construction of these retaining walls under this contract will eliminate the necessity of purchasing expansive right-of-way or making costly realignment of the highway in the future.

Some 73,500 tons of imported base material for use under shoulders and as cement-treated subgrade are being obtained from the Salinas River bottom adjacent to the project. This material is produced by pit-blending clean river run sand with silt binder and screening the mixture to remove oversize rock, deleterious roots, etc. Approximately 41,000 tons of mineral aggregate for Class B cement-treated base to be used under ramps, frontage roads and the traveled way of State Sign Route 41 are being produced by a portable crushing and screening plant from a terraced gravel deposit

on the banks of the Salinas River. In an adjacent pit of similar material 36,600 tons of mineral aggregate for ¾-inch maximum Type B plant-mixed surfacing will be produced.

Using a bulk cement truck spreader and a self-propelled 54-inch mixer, Class B cement-treated base is road-mixed and placed at the rate of 4,000 square yards per day. The addition of the specified minimum of 2½ percent cement has produced a base with a compressive strength varying from 600 to 800 pounds per square inch.

Plant-mixed surfacing is being produced by a 5,000 pound capacity asphalt plant coupled with a portable crushing and screening plant. On the street a level course 1½ inches thick is laid with a motor patrol and pneumatic roller. Pavers have been used to lay a surface course of satisfactory quality.

High-grade Aggregate

Aggregate of exceptional quality for use in Class B portland cement concrete is produced by the contractor from a rock quarry located 20 miles south of the project on the Salinas

6

River. Aggregate is produced from granite rock by normal methods consisting of drilling, shooting, crushing, screening and washing. Sand grading is controlled by a hydraulic classifier, and river run sand is blended with the crusher sand to produce the fine aggregate. Some 22,000 cubic yards of concrete paving is being produced by a normal construction train consisting of a double-drum mixer, mechanical spreader, tamper finisher and float. Since the aggregate is 100 percent crushed, an air entrainment additive is introduced into the mix to improve workability. Concrete paving is being placed at the rate of 900 to 1,400 cubic yards per day and 130 to 140 cubic yards per hour. Due to the wide range in daily temperature change in this area, weakened-plane joints constructed by the sawed method on previous concrete paving projects have not entirely controlled random cracking.

Temperature Change

Daily temperature changes of 30 to 50 degrees are not uncommon. For this reason metal weakened-plane joints are installed at 60-foot intervals in the initial lane and at all working joints, not to exceed 60 feet, in the companion lane. The metal strips are 16-gauge sheet metal 1¾ inches wide and 12 feet long and are coated with a light oil. The joints are placed using a T-iron cutter prior to final finishing and maintained within ¼ inch of the finished concrete surface. The remaining joints at 15-foot intervals are sawed on the day following placing of the concrete pavement. This method of forming control joints and sawing the remaining joints appears to have stopped random cracking and has improved the quality of the sawed joints through a reduction in tearing and spalling.

Two Overheads

At each end of the city, US 101 will be carried over the Southern Pacific Railroad tracks by a pair of parallel welded steel girder bridges with reinforced concrete decks providing a 28-foot clear roadway. These South and North Paso Robles Overheads vary in length from 618 to 700 feet and consist of six and seven spans supported by single rectangular reinforced concrete piers with welded steel caps and concrete abutments, all founded on concrete piles. The three-foot by seven-foot-six-inch concrete piers vary in height from 15 to 38 feet and were poured monolithically. Pier forms were braced with eucalyptus piling. Concrete piles are circular step-tapered corrugated metal shells driven by mandrel and filled with concrete.

Local city traffic will be carried over the freeway on the 13th Street Overcrossing. This two-span bridge consists of a reinforced, prestressed concrete slab, about 118 feet long supported on reinforced concrete abutments and bent with spread footings. This bridge will provide a 55-foot clear roadway with 12-foot sidewalks. The deck slab is one foot six inches thick and will be prestressed with high-strength wire placed in conduits.

Diamond-type Intersection

At the diamond-type intersection of highways US 101 and Sign Route 41, the former will be carried over the latter on two parallel steel girder bridges with reinforced concrete decks, 133 feet long and providing 28-foot clear roadways. Each bridge of this Route 2/33 Separation consists of three spans supported on reinforced concrete bents and abutments, all on concrete piles. This structure has been designed for future lengthening with minimum traffic interference, when State Sign Route 41 is constructed to full four-lane divided freeway standards. On and off ramps will provide the necessary access to and from both highways.

. . . Continued on page 34

LEFT—View of North Paso Robles Overhead construction looking northerly. RIGHT—View looking northerly from site of South Paso Robles Overhead. Main coast line of Southern Pacific in foreground.

and Public Works 7

Famoso Project

New Overhead Structure Will Supplement Underpass

By JOHN C. GARY, Acting Resident Engineer, and RALPH E. HAVERCAMP, Bridge Department

Famoso underpass, which is on US 99 about 21 miles north of Bakersfield and is near the junction with US 466 from the west, was first opened to traffic on January 28, 1937. The present road on either side of the existing underpass is of the four-lane divided highway type but the underpass is undivided. The work being done on this project will eliminate this bottleneck which has been the scene of numerous accidents in recent years.

The improvement consists, in general, of constructing an overhead structure and approaches to carry northbound US 99 traffic over the Southern Pacific railroad tracks and of constructing a separation structure, approaches and channelization at the junction of US 99 and US 466 (State Highway Routes 4 and 33). The existing underpass will serve the southbound traffic.

This project is a part of a continuing program to develop US 99 into a

View westerly of the Route US 99 and US 466 separation

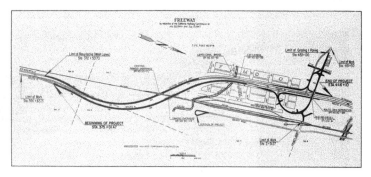

8

LEFT—View northerly showing existing divided US 99 with Route 99-466 separation in background. RIGHT—View northerly showing existing Famoso Overhead in the center background and its approach fills.

freeway status and was on an express-way basis prior to the commencement of this work.

Portland cement concrete pavement will be used for the US 99 section, and plant-mixed surfacing for US 466 and its connecting ramps.

The Lerdo Canal crosses US 99, and a lateral of Lerdo Canal crosses US 466. Extension of the triple 8 x 5-foot reinforced box on the former was required. Through agreement with the Kern County Land Company the existing double 48-inch corrugated metal pipe on US 466 was replaced with a double 5 x 5-foot reinforced concrete box, the land company paying the additional cost required to provide a flow of 200 cubic foot per second, whereas the original capacity was rated at 100 cubic foot per second.

The contractor was able to obtain a very favorable agreement from an adjoining property owner whereby he would land level the property for crop purposes. Since this area was immediately adjacent to the heaviest fill section of the project, the contractor benefited by the much shorter haul than from the state provided pit.

Famoso Overhead

To carry the US 99 northbound traffic across the Southern Pacific railroad tracks, an overhead structure was designed with a 37-foot roadway width, with provisions made for removing one curb should future widening be necessary. The 234-foot structure consists of three equal spans, each consisting of a reinforced concrete deck supported by five 42-inch welded plate girders. Skewed at an

angle of 55 degrees with normal, the two concrete bents each consist of three columns supporting the concrete cap. Both the bents and the open-type abutments, situated high on the approach fill, are supported by concrete cast-in-drilled-hole piles. Construction was started early in March, 1956, and all of the substructure concrete had been placed by early June.

Separation

The US 466 traffic will be carried over US 99 on a new separation structure consisting of three 70-foot spans and one 35-foot span. Roadway width will be the standard 28 feet with concrete curb and railing on each side. Here also the design calls for 42-inch welded plate girders; however, the narrower width and shorter span . . . Continued on page 34

LEFT—View northwesterly of Famoso Overhead. This will be future northbound lane. RIGHT—View northerly at Famoso Overhead.

The New Look

Fresno Working on
Pattern of Highways

By EARLE W. TAYLOR, District Traffic Engineer

THE NEW pattern of state highways for the City of Fresno, now rapidly nearing completion, will utilize a simple yet peculiarly efficient means of connecting the six major entrances to the city and connecting them in the most difficult part of town—the central business district.

The ingenious plan consists of providing a tight inner cordon of highways or circumferential route in the form of an approximate square around the core of the downtown area. It makes use of a combination of freeway, one-way couplets and divided and conventional city streets to form this cordon and its approaches.

The Effect of a Railroad

As do so many San Joaquin Valley communities, Fresno shows the profound effect the building of the first railroad had on community development and street pattern. Fresno's state highway problem really started in 1873 when the original townsite was laid out with streets paralleling and at right angles to the railroad which runs in a northwesterly direction.

County Road Pattern

Before the budding city outgrew the original townsite, the pattern of county roads located on section lines was so firmly established that later subdivisions outside the original townsite generally followed this exterior pattern. Thus it occurs as a natural consequence that at the lines of demarcation between the two patterns, most streets make an angle of about 45 degrees.

The principal exception was the road now known as US 99. Since it was built to connect the numerous towns strung along the railroad, it naturally paralleled the railroad and passed through Fresno parallel with the first street pattern.

The Effect of Both

But not so the other two state routes. Sign Route 41, the north-south

Yosemite-to-the-coast highway, and Sign Route 180 running east from Tracy to Kings Canyon National Park were adopted from former section line county roads, which were forced to jog to pass through the city. The nature of the recent path of these routes through the old part of the city is illustrated by the insert on the accompanying sketch.

Each route made two 45-degree angles and three 90-degree ones and suffered losses of distance of 0.6 and 0.7 mile over a straight line. Further, portions of both routes passed through the congested center of the business district on narrow undivided streets and used several blocks of Broadway in common with US 99, further congesting it. And to further complicate matters, the connections of the three routes occurred in the heart of the business district.

Even US 99 followed a somewhat devious path, crossing the railroad twice and making several jogs. Forced to follow Broadway, it found itself on the second most important shopping street, now carrying about 32,000 vehicles a day.

What to Do?

It was patently impossible to do much in the way of straightening and shortening Highways 41 and 180. To do so would have caused them to cut diagonally across and grossly disrupt the existing street pattern through the heart of the business district. The only solution for the problem was to make the most efficient use of the present awkward street pattern and to move the routes out of the most congested section.

But something good *could* be done about US 99! It could be replaced by a full freeway lying entirely west of the tracks, no longer than the present route and removed from the central business district, yet close enough to serve it well. This five-mile, 10 mil-

lion dollar project is nearing completion.

The Plan: A Cordon

A cordon of new highway routes will surround the core of the downtown area. The US 99 Freeway will form one side of the square. Two other sides consist of one-way couplets and the fourth of a four-lane city street, part of which is divided. All six approaches join the cordon at or near its four corners.

The cordon, as shown on the accompanying sketch, will enclose an area of 0.8 square mile, or 110 city blocks. It contains the bulk of the downtown retail business district, the civic center and many industrial plants along the Southern Pacific tracks. It also encloses a large secondary shopping area west of the tracks. Situated within the first few blocks outside the cordon are additional retail outlets, industries, parks, schools, churches, and, along the A. T. & S. F. Railway, another well-developed industrial area.

How It Will Work

This cordon arrangement and the six state highway feeders to it will permit through traffic to traverse the heart of the city with much less delay by following a reasonably direct path yet skirting the most congested area. It will permit convenient interchange from any route to the others. And it will make it possible for most home-to-work and shopping drivers, the largest group of users, to stay on a major highway almost to their ultimate destination.

It will be possible to reach any point within the cordon from a state highway route without traveling more than five blocks on city streets. By considering also the area immediately outside the cordon, a trip over city streets of that length will permit drivers to reach every point in an area of three square blocks containing over 430 city blocks.

10

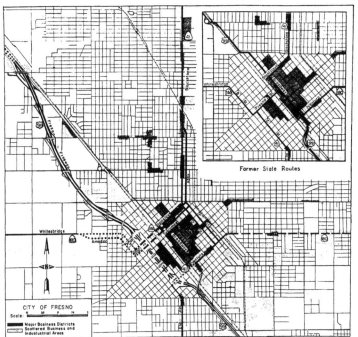

Map showing the awkward street pattern in downtown Fresno and the new routing of state highways which form a cordon around the heart of the central district with connections at its four corners. INSERT—The former unsatisfactory routing through the downtown area.

A Freeway

Much of the program is already completed, and other sections are under construction. The Fresno Freeway is finished except for a one-mile section in West Fresno, which should be ready for traffic by mid-September.

The O and P Street one-way couplet has been in operation more than 18 months, as has the Stanislaus-Tuolumne pair between Broadway and P Street. The portion between the Freeway and Broadway is under construction and scheduled for completion by April, 1958. The particular feature of this project is a pair of one-way bridges which will span not only the 21 tracks of the Southern Pacific yards, but the street on each side of them as well. The accompanying picture shows the present stage of construction of one of these bridges.

The plan is to further extend this one-way couplet to the west another mile over A and B Streets and Whites Bridge Avenue and Amador Street to the edge of the city. It is expected this section will be constructed during 1959.

Ventura Avenue

Ventura Avenue from Broadway east to the bend needed no improvement, being a four-lane street with painted divider and left turn lanes. The section from the bend to a point 2½ miles easterly is under construction as a four-lane divided highway, to be completed during February,

Construction of the Tuolumne Street one-way bridge over the Southern Pacific, G Street and H Street which will carry eastbound (toward the camera) traffic on Highway 180. The bridge over the depressed US 99 freeway can be seen in the background. Companion bridges on Stanislaus Street for westbound traffic are one block to the right. View is westerly along Tuolumne Street. Near street in foreground is Broadway—next to the west is H Street. G Street is first west of tracks. Structure in center background on Tuolumne Street is the Tuolumne overcrossing of the West Fresno Freeway (Route 4, US 99).

1958. Between the Freeway and Broadway, the street will be repaved soon.

Blackstone Avenue and Abby Street, Highway 41, went into one-way operation nearly two years ago, following the widening and complete repaving of Abby. Farther north, Blackstone has been the scene of a continuous program of widening to six lanes divided since 1953. It is now completed to a point 3½ miles north of the end of the one-way couplet. The next three-mile section is under construction and by January, 1958, will complete this program through Pinedale and nearly to the Fresno-Madera County Line.

Successful One-way Streets

The Blackstone-Abby pair well illustrate the success of one-way traffic operation in Fresno. Results have met—even exceeded—the most optimistic advance expectations of their success. Traffic volume has increased by 53 percent and they now carry about 33,000 vehicles a day on their six 12-foot lanes. Average speed has been increased and peak-hour delay measurably reduced, as drivers are normally able to maintain the speed of 30 miles per hour for which the progressive signal system is timed. The accident rate was reduced 38 percent and the injury rate went down by the strikingly large amount of 72 percent.

A Look to the Future

The new plan for state highways into and through Fresno, even in its present incomplete status, is already paying large dividends in more expeditious driving and less hazard. By utilizing a rather unique and ingenious method of interconnecting the six entrances by a route close around but not within the congested central district, the plan, when completed, holds bright promise of solving for some time to come major traffic problems in this rapidly growing city.

Congestion will be relieved not only on the former state routes, but on several other shopping streets as well. The expected large decrease in accidents from the freeway and additional one-way streets should have a

Contractors Take Public Into Their Confidence on Jobs

The idea of a personally delivered explanatory message to residents in the neighborhood of heavy freeway construction, as initiated by a contractor on the Glendale Freeway and described in the May-June issue of *California Highways and Public Works*, is apparently catching on.

A similar "greeting card" has been delivered to people living in another part of Los Angeles, the section where the Harbor Freeway is being extended southward from 88th Street to 124th Street.

In this instance the contractor is the Guy F. Atkinson Company. The project calls for excavation of more than 1,300,000 cubic yards of earth from the area between 110th Street and 124th Street, which must be transported to build embankments at the northerly end of the job.

In order to speed up the excavation phase of the operation, application was made to city authorities for permission to carry on work during the evening hours, up to 10.30 o'clock. When this permission was granted, the contractor had the explanatory pamphlet printed and delivered to nearby residents. In addition to a brief explanation and map of the project, the pamphlet contained a reprint of a newspaper article stating that the double-shift operation is intended to speed up completion of the whole freeway project by six months.

The explanation in the pamphlet is signed by R. W. Atkinson. Like the one distributed by the Thompson Construction Company on the Glendale Freeway project, the pamphlet is reported to have received favorable reaction from residents of the area.

___

marked influence on the total city-wide accident picture.

Even though it may develop that additional freeways are needed some time in the future, the present plan would still continue to well serve important needs of the community and would become a valuable adjunct to any future freeway network.

and Public Works

13

US 50

Improvements in Stockton Area Will Solve Bottleneck

By LOUIS G. KROECK, District Design Engineer, District X

During the past few years the importance of Highway US 50 (State Route 5) in the Stockton area has become quite evident. This route is the main link between the metropolitan San Francisco Bay area and the great food-producing areas of the San Joaquin Valley. US 50 is also one of the main routes between the Bay area and the vast recreational area of the Sierra Nevada.

Under contract at the present time and scheduled for completion in the spring of 1958 is a 6.8-mile length of highway between the San Joaquin River at Mossdale and Richards Avenue south of the French Camp area. Conversion of the old 20-foot pavement to a freeway will be accomplished in two stages.

New Southbound Lane

A 24-foot concrete pavement has been laid to the west of the existing 20-foot pavement and will become the southbound lanes. For the present, the existing pavement will carry the northbound traffic. This old pavement will be resurfaced and a new eight-foot-wide shoulder will be constructed for the entire length on the easterly side. The southbound lanes have been so placed to allow for the construction of the northbound lanes and yield a 22-foot median with three lanes of pavement in each direction.

Interchange Planned

At the southerly end of this project State Route 66 (Sign Route 120) connects with US 50. This intersection is located between the approach to the old Mossdale Underpass on the north and the San Joaquin River bridges on the south. In view of the very poor history of accidents at this location it was determined to construct this interchange to its ultimate design. The very close controls at this location greatly restricted the designers.

The highway from the west is four-lane divided and crosses the San Joaquin River on two bascule span bridges, approximately 550 feet in length and placed 125 feet center to center. East of the river the four lanes converge into two lanes and pass under the mainline Southern Pacific railroad tracks with substandard horizontal and vertical clearance. Only 1,150 feet exists between the bridges and underpass in which to fit the entire interchange including the speed change lanes. To make things worse, the pavement drops on a 2½ to 3 percent grade between the bridges and the railroad.

Crossing of Railroad Tracks

In this area the Southern Pacific railroad's double tracks are on a fill approximately 14 feet in height. To

go over these tracks with the required clearance would require a highway fill of approximately 45 feet in height. To design an underpass to present-day standards also has its difficulties. There have been many times in past history when the high water in the San Joaquin River has been well above the height of the surrounding land. We are quite fortunate that during our ground water studies in December of 1955 and January of 1956, the San Joaquin River reached an elevation almost as high as it has any time in recent years. Test wells were drilled at 200-foot intervals for about 1,600 feet extending along a line approximately normal to the river. The ground water elevation in these wells was read at intervals between December 20, 1955, and February 6, 1956. The results were plotted showing the ground water profile along the test line at time intervals of only a few days.

Water Tables

From this study it appeared that there was a steady rise in the water table at the underpass site beginning three days after the river started to rise. The heavy soil dike encountered about 600 feet east of the river apparently had little effect on the rate of percolation to the structure site.

... Continued on page 16

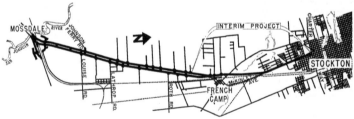

US 50

Boehmer Hill to Castro Valley Improvements

By HAIG AYANIAN, Assistant District Engineer

Wᴵᵀʜ ᴛʜᴇ completion of the 'Dublin Canyon Project" on US 50 in Alameda County, which will occur later this year, a continuous divided freeway will exist between the distribution structure at the eastern terminus of the San Francisco-Oakland Bay Bridge to Tracy, a distance of about 54 miles.

The part of this freeway known as US 50, a major arterial through Alameda County, and a part of the interstate system, provides a direct connection between the metropolitan areas of San Francisco and Oakland and the Livermore and San Joaquin Valleys. The "Dublin Canyon Project" will climax a five-stage construction program which was started in 1950. This route, in addition to the heavy passenger traffic, carries a heavy truck and bus traffic as it serves as a primary route for the San Joaquin Valley and points east. The importance of this route has been increased by the reactivation of Camp Parks as Parks Air Force Base, and the activity at the recently constructed atomic research laboratory farther to the east. The route is of prime importance as an aid to national defense and military needs of the future. The above installations have resulted in a large increase in population with a proportionate increase in traffic volumes. Present construction will alleviate this traffic congestion and promote future expanse and growth to the southern Alameda County valleys of Pleasanton and Livermore.

On New Alignment

The old highway from 2½ miles west of Dublin to Pergola Hill was originally constructed as a 30-foot-wide oil-macadam pavement. Subsequent improvements over the years resulted in widths of up to 40 feet of portland cement concrete pavement in some areas, along with bituminous surfacing in others. The new construction will provide a limited-access freeway between 2.3 miles west of Dublin and 0.3 mile west of Center Street in Castro Valley. The new alignment roughly parallels Palamares and San Lorenzo Creeks throughout its full length and traverses rather rugged terrain for a considerable portion of the distance.

. . . Continued on page 17

LEFT—Looking westerly from easterly end of project, showing newly constructed eastbound lanes and portion of existing traveled way to be resurfaced for ultimate use as westbound lanes. RIGHT—Looking westerly, showing Eden Canyon Interchange in foreground, newly constructed westbound lanes on right, old alignment left, with Castro Valley in background.

RIGHT—At Mossdale looking north showing new two lanes on the left, reworking of existing undercrossing of Southern Pacific railroad at left, preparing for new undercrossing of Southern Pacific at right, and Route 66 to Manteca in lower right. LEFT—At Mossdale looking south.

US 50—STOCKTON AREA

Continued from page 14 . . .

On February 6, 1956, the water level in the soil was practically at the river stage and was still slowly rising as the river water level was receding. Water started flowing into the existing underpass through construction joints on January 30, 1956, when the head was 18 inches. This was somewhat disturbing inasmuch as the profile of the proposed subway would be about five feet below the existing.

On February 6, 1956, at the site of the proposed underpass the ground water was less than one foot from the ground surface and it became quite evident that it would be necessary to seal off the excavated area to prevent the ground water from inundating the roadway. It was evident that it would be necessary to extend this seal up to the average surface elevation in this area.

Underpass and Interchange Design

With this information we then designed several interchange arrangements incorporating both the over-head on a 45-foot fill and the underpass requiring a seal slab. These studies proved that the underpass and interchange design as now being constructed are geometrically superior and more economical.

The concrete seal slab, of course, must be designed heavy enough so the buoyancy of the subsurface water will not lift the pavement. In this case it was necessary to construct a slab with a maximum thickness of 7 feet 8 inches and containing 9,700 cubic yards of Class B concrete. All expansion and construction joints are fitted with 6-inch rubber waterstops. A total of 7,250 linear feet of waterstops are required.

It is the intention to continue to use the existing railroad underpass, constructed in 1927, for southbound traffic. Although substandard with respect to our present-day standards it is felt that more years of good use can be obtained from the old structure by obtaining standard vertical clearance. This is being accomplished by relocation of the girders with re-spect to the floor beams plus a track raise of about six inches.

Drainage Facility

A pumping plant has been constructed with adequate capacity for both the old and the new underpass. This will provide a more positive drainage facility with greater capacity.

Approximately one mile north of the San Joaquin River the highway crosses a low area which has a long record of flooding. In this area the new lanes have been held well above the flood plane to prevent future interruptions to traffic and to reduce the maintenance costs that are usually incurred when a pavement lies low in a wet area.

It is planned to convert this new section of expressway into a freeway. Three interchanges will be constructed on the rights of way acquired under the first stage and frontage roads will be provided on both sides and for the entire length of the project.

. . . Continued on page 18

US 50—BOEHMER HILL

Continued from page 15...

The project as constructed provides a limited-access freeway consisting of two new traffic lanes from the beginning of the project at the easterly terminus southerly of and approximately parallel to the existing roadway for about one-third of the length of the project. The balance of the project consists of four new traffic lanes on new alignment and to full freeway standards. The existing highway at the easterly third of the job was resurfaced with plant-mixed surfacing and will be utilized as one roadway of a divided facility. The pavement section consists of eight inches of portland cement concrete on four inches of cement-treated selected material. Provisions have been made for the adding of future lanes when the need arises.

Drainage Aspects

The drainage aspects of this project are of particular interest due to the

Looking easterly from Castro Valley. End of project showing both new and old alignment with ramps to Castro Valley Bypass shown in lower left.

Looking westerly from Pergola Hill showing new alignment on left, existing route on right, with Castro Valley in background

maze of underground installations necessary to dispose of the natural runoff of the area. As noted above, the line parallels Palamares and San Lorenzo Creeks, crossing and recrossing them a number of times, and in some instances runs on top of the drainage course. It was necessary to place 1,160 feet of 20-foot-diameter reinforced concrete arch culverts, and approximately 6,500 linear feet of 78-inch and 84-inch reinforced concrete pipe to carry the waters of the natural drainage courses. These facilities were laid approximately parallel to the roadway, and are in addition to the many cross drains. The difference in elevation of the inlet and outlet of this installation is approximately 75 feet and required the use of three dis-

... Continued on page 19

and Public Works

LEFT—South of French camp showing temporary transition of four-lane divided to two-lane road to Stockton. This is the beginning of proposed interim project to be under construction soon. RIGHT—North of Mossdale looking south showing undercrossing construction work at Southern Pacific railway, twin bridges across the San Joaquin River, and divided four lanes ahead toward Tracy.

US 50—STOCKTON AREA

Continued from page 16...

The completion of this project will eliminate one of the last bottlenecks existing on US 50 between Stockton and the Bay area, and will correct one of the most dangerous intersections in District X.

F. M. Babcock is resident engineer in charge of construction work under contract to A. Teichert & Son, Sacramento.

Interim Project Extends Four Lanes

As an interim project plans are now complete for the construction of four lanes between Richards Avenue, just south of French Camp, and Charter Way in Stockton.

Beginning at Richards Avenue it is proposed to use the existing two-lane pavement as the two northbound lanes with construction of two additional lanes to the west to provide the two southbound lanes. This four-lane divided highway would continue up to French Camp, where the divided feature would be merged into a four-lane undivided section.

The four-lane undivided section from south of French Camp into Stockton will be constructed by resurfacing and widening the existing pavement within the existing right-of-way. Along with this improvement of the existing pavement there are four intersections that will be improved by providing median pocket lanes for left turns along with acceleration and deceleration lanes into the intersections. These intersections scheduled for improvement are at the entrance to the County Hospital, French Camp Turnpike Road, Clayton-McKinley Streets, and at California Street entrance to the City of Stockton.

In addition to the widening to four lanes, the bridge at French Camp Slough will be replaced with a concrete structure, whereas the remaining existing bridges at North Branch French Camp Slough, Walker Slough, and at Homestead Canal will be replaced with culverts.

This interim project, with the project east of Tracy also being planned, will provide the final links to a four-lane facility for the entire distance between Stockton and Tracy.

THEN THERE'S IDA

Then there's the mystery that cropped up in a midwestern city. Within the span of a couple of days, reports the National Automobile Club, about a dozen new cars were found badly battered and dented. Law officers scratched their heads and asked a lot of questions, and then a little old man came forward and explained it all.

Seems he had a junk wagon and the junk wagon was pulled by a horse named Ida. Now apparently Ida got to thinking about the horseless carriage and how it was replacing her dwindling breed. This made Ida so mad that whenever she saw a fancy new model she would give it a good kick and then run like blazes.

Officers didn't dare to argue with Ida. They just asked her owner to keep her back, well back, from the fancy new models.

US 50—BOEHMER HILL

Continued from page 17 . . .

sipators to avoid excessive erosion at the outlet.

The design of these dissipators is based on model studies and irrigation weir prototypes in Pakistan. These special dissipators are placed at the outlet ends of the 72-inch and 84-inch reinforced concrete pipes. This type of dissipator efficiently breaks up the jet flows of the large longitudinal culvers as they discharge into the natural channels. This type of dissipator combines the use of the principles of insufflation and baffles, and is more economical and practical than the usual stilling basins for these particular cases.

Extensive Seepage

The problem of drainage on this project was not confined to surface runoffs but was complicated by extensive seepage areas throughout the length of the project. It was necessary to place some 18,500 linear feet of six-inch porous concrete pipe underdrains and 4,500 linear feet of two-inch horizontal drainpipe.

Many of the cuts constructed for this project were of considerable magnitude and required benches 20 feet wide at intervals of 40 feet vertically. One such cut was in excess of 180 feet in depth. A total of 1,600,000 cubic yards was removed under roadway excavation by use of various types of

earthmoving equipment including rubber-tired scrapers, a large power shovel and trucks in heavy rock areas.

Included in the contract are seven bridges described as follows:

EDEN CANYON ROAD UNDERCROSSING—A T-beam type bridge of parallel structures about 118 feet long consisting of three spans over the realignment of Eden Canyon Road.

SUNNYSLOPE AVENUE UNDERCROSSING—Another T-beam type bridge, parallel structures about 158 feet in length over the realignment of existing state highway at Sunnyslope Avenue.

SAN LORENZO CREEK BRIDGE AND UNDERCROSSING NO. 1—A box girder type bridge consisting of parallel structures. The left bridge about 388 feet long and the right bridge about 438 feet

LEFT—Looking westerly toward 84-inch reinforced concrete pipe installation, showing depth of cut from existing traveled way. RIGHT—View of completed aero energy dissipators.

and Public Works

LEFT—Looking westerly down riprap section of channel approaching 20-foot arch culvert, one of three on project. RIGHT—Showing 84-inch reinforced concrete pipe installation's relative position to existing traveled way—new alignment.

in length, each with five spans over Old Dublin Road and San Lorenzo Creek.

SAN LORENZO CREEK BRIDGE AND UNDERCROSSING NO. 2—Another box girder type bridge about 330 feet in length consisting of parallel structures of three spans over a private road and San Lorenzo Creek.

CROW CANYON ROAD UNDER-CROSSING—A composite steel girder type bridge about 482 feet in length of parallel structures consisting of five spans over the existing state highway at Crow Canyon Road.

CROW CREEK BRIDGE—A box girder type bridge of about 264 feet in length consisting of three spans over Crow Creek, providing a clear roadway width of 64 feet between curbs.

CASTRO VALLEY BOULEVARD OVERCROSSING—A box girder type bridge of about 254 feet in length consisting of four spans over the new freeway providing a clear roadway width of 54 feet between curbs.

The project included the following major items of work:

Roadway excavation	1,600,000 cubic yards
Structure excavation and backfill	122,000 cubic yards
Ditch and channel excavation	13,000 cubic yards
Class B concrete pavement	25,300 cubic yards
Class A concrete structures and bridges	17,200 cubic yards
Bar reinforcing steel	3,170,000 pounds
Structural steel	934,000 pounds
Drainage pipes	41,000 linear feet

The total cost of the project will be approximately $4,479,000, and it is anticipated that it will be completed in October, 1957, about two months ahead of the expiration of the 400

working days allotted for the work. The contractor is Peter Kiewit & Sons and the project is under the supervision of W. E. Roche, Jr. The State is represented by A. A. Andrade, Jr., as

MERIT AWARD BOARD WINNERS

Following is a list of the Division of Highways employees who received merit award recognition during the months of June and July, 1957:

Henry E. Davis, Stockton, $50 for suggestion in which he developed a soil dehydrator to replace and supplement present drying equipment. This oven incorporates the essential features of the best drying ovens on the market.

Mrs. Helen M. Rake, San Bernardino, $20 for suggestion recommending a new form for ordering topographical maps which eliminates costly delays in the filling of orders. The change in the form consists of a space to show the co-ordinates of the southeast corner of each quadrangle to enable an area to be identified even though the name is changed.

Glen A. Wallis, Sacramento, $150 for suggestion recommending a method of computing construction material quantities through the use of the electronic computors. Other uses are also being developed as a result of this proposal.

Michael Valentine, Sacramento, $20 for suggestion in which he developed a series of graphical solutions for the design of pile footings.

Herbert Shipley, San Luis Obispo, received a $50 check as an additional award for a combination of grade and grid sheets he developed. In March, 1956, the board had awarded him $50 and recommended a review at the end of one year. His method

is based on an IBM procedure already installed in some of the districts.

Adel R. Leitch, San Francisco, recommended using one combination stamp in place of two stamps to record the date scheduled and the schedule number on receiving records, posting pages, and transfer records in District VII. Mrs. Leitch received a Certificate of Commendation.

Gloria M. Anthony, San Francisco, proposed a different use of pounce on vellum and ozalid paper for appraisal maps. Pounce is a powder used in drafting work wherever ink does not take to the surface properly. Mrs. Anthony's idea is to prepare the vellum and ozalid paper in advance with pounce, which makes clear, black imprints, shortens the time to dry the prints, and makes it unnecessary to erase and restamp faded stampings on vellum or a print. A $30 award was granted.

Mabel Graham, Los Angeles, received a $100 award for recommending an improved statement form and return envelope for the active rental accounts of the Division of Highways. Benefits will be a savings in material, in time required to prepare for mailing, and particularly in the time required to identify and process the payments received.

. . . Continued on page 22

resident engineer and E. F. Van Zee as Bridge Department representative, under the supervision of Assistant State Highway Engineer, B. W. Booker.

Jubilation

Opening of Lafayette Bypass Is Cause for Celebration

CITIZENS OF Lafayette in Contra Costa County staged a jubilant three-day celebration following opening of the Lafayette Bypass on June 27th.

This four-lane section of new freeway, costing $3,300,000, eliminates the most seriously congested portion of Sign Route 24 between Oakland and Walnut Creek, which has been daily traversed by commuters from the residential developments to East Bay business and industrial areas and the San Francisco-Oakland Bay Bridge. Provision has been made in the project for two additional lanes as the increase in traffic volume warrants.

In the business district of Lafayette, which has been the site of the serious congestion, local traffic is now able to move freely, and traffic hazards which have been experienced in the past, will be minimized.

The average daily traffic through this area is approximately 38,000. The accident rate has been approximately 3.52 accidents per million vehicle-miles. Congestion will be practically eliminated and the accident rates considerably reduced.

Work started on the project October 17, 1955, by contractor Gordon H. Ball. This project will provide an alternate traffic route through the town of Lafayette, and will leave the present highway as a high-standard, uncongested, local arterial servicing the rapidly growing community of Lafayette.

Other Projects

In December, 1956, a two-quadrant cloverleaf interchange at Pleasant Hill Road, at the easterly end of this project, was completed. This interchange

Lafayette Bypass

Project length: 2.6 miles.

Description of project: between west of Sunnybrook Drive and west of Pleasant Hill Road.

Number of lanes: initial 4, ultimate 6 lanes.

Type of facility: full freeway.

Estimated construction cost: $3,300,000.

Major structures: the Lafayette Undercrossing, Dolores Drive Undercrossing, Happy Valley Road Undercrossing, Oak Hill Road Undercrossing, East Bay Municipal Utility District Aqueduct Overcrossing.

There is an interchange at each end of the project and grade separations at other major local streets.

Controlling quantities: 1,500,000 cubic yards roadway excavation, 13,700 cubic yards portland cement concrete pavement, 10,500 cubic yards concrete bridge work, 2,293,000 pounds of reinforcing steel, 82,000 tons of imported subbase material.

serves as a connection between the freeway and Pleasant Hill Road, which is an important county expressway. In the future, it will also be a connection to the Route 233, Shepherd Canyon Freeway, which is another future freeway into Oakland via Moraga now in planning and design stages.

A contract for a project which will extend the freeway to the south and north of Walnut Creek was recently awarded to Chas. H. Harney, Inc. This project will be 4.2 miles long, and construction will cost approximately $8,800,000. There are approximately 17 major structures involved in this project, an initial four- and six-lane freeway with provisions for ultimate six and eight lanes. To the north, it connects with the project which was completed early this year extending from Walnut Creek to north of Monument, a distance of 2.8 miles, costing approximately $2,850,000 for construction.

Some 200 persons participated in opening ceremonies arranged by the Lafayette Chamber of Commerce.

At ribbon cutting, left to right: Captain R. R. Magill, California Highway Patrol; L. A. Weymouth, District Engineer, San Francisco; Supervisor Ray Taylor, H. Boetz, Lafayette Chamber of Commerce; Assemblyman Donald Doyle, Highway Commissioner H. Stephen Chase; T. Fred Bagshaw, Assistant Director of Public Works; B. W. Booker, Assistant State Highway Engineer; Pat Whitehead, Attendant to Queen; Dolores Roescher, Fiesta Queen; Betty Clark, Attendant to Queen; C. A. Maghetti, Secretary, State Highway Commission; Earle Pierce, Lafayette Chamber of Commerce; Supervisor Mel Nielsen.

Helicopter instead of traditional shears used to cut barrier tapes

Highway Engineer E. E. East Retires From Automobile Club

E. E. East, chief engineer of the Automobile Club of Southern California—the man who proposed a freeway system for Los Angeles more than 20 years ago—retired July 1st.

East, with the club since 1920, is also known for the two exploration trips he led to Mexico City and San Salvador in 1930 and 1931, which proved that construction of a West Coast Pan-American highway was possible.

This highway—from Nogales, Arizona, to Mexico City—was dedicated only last May, at which time Cayetano Blanco Vigil, Mexico's most ardent supporter of this project, lauded East for proving that such a road was possible almost 30 years ago.

One of the first engineers employed by the California Highway Commission—in 1912—East, throughout his long career, has adhered to one principle in particular: The way to approach highway problems is with a look to the future as well as the present.

A working example of this belief is revealed by the recommendation he made in the auto club's 1937 metropolitan Los Angeles traffic survey, when he stated:

"It is recommended that a network of motorways be constructed to serve the entire metropolitan area of Los Angeles. These motorways should be developed upon a right-of-way not less than 360 feet in width through residential territory and not less than 100 feet in width through established business districts."

He also recommended that these motorways be built to accommodate four to six lanes of traffic divided by a physical barrier.

Both of these ideas were rather "futuristic" in 1937.

East was also one of the early proponents of oil-bound gravel roads.

In lieu of the traditional ribbon cutting, a helicopter flown by Ed Haapala, executive pilot for Contractor Gordon Ball, swooped down and clipped barrier tapes at each end of the new freeway.

Luncheon Is Held

Automobiles carrying dignitaries and Fiesta Queen Dolores Roeschen and her two attendants, Pat Whitehead and Betty Clark, made the round trip over the new freeway back to El Nido, where a luncheon was held.

B. W. Booker, Assistant State Highway Engineer, told the group "several million dollars remain to be spent between here and Orinda. There is still a $100,000,000 highway deficiency in Contra Costa County. There are still some 'bugs' in the new expressway here, where the freeway rejoins Mount Diablo Boulevard at Upper Happy Valley Road. But it'll be at least two years before you get the next job. We'll do what we can to alleviate the situation in the meantime."

Praise Co-operation

Both T. Fred Bagshaw, Assistant Director of Public Works, and Assemblyman Donald Doyle praised co-operation of Contra Costa County with the State in solving highway problems.

Among others participating in the opening celebration were Deputy State Highway Engineer, J. W. Vick-

rey, Chelso Maghetti, Secretary of the State Highway Commission; Commissioner H. Stephen Chase from San Francisco; Earle Pierce, President of Lafayette Chamber of Commerce; L. A. Weymouth, District Highway Engineer; Highway Patrol Captain Russ Magill; and County Supervisors Ray Taylor, Mel Nielsen, Bud Buchanan and Joe Silva.

Some 20 civic groups participated in the community celebration.

MERIT AWARD WINNERS

Continued from page 20 . . .

a $50 award for recommending the use of snap-out carbons for certain form letters in the Bridge Department.

Oliver Dowd, Stockton, received a $42 award for suggesting the elimination of freehand lettering on culvert lists and construction note sheets. He proposes instead the use of a typing and photographic process in preparing contract plan tracings with tabular data.

William Wallace, Oakland, designed and built a roller chain pulling tool, used when two ends of a roller chain must be pulled together and properly aligned to insert the connecting link. The device speeds the job of chain coupling and minimizes the hazard of accidents to hands. A $45 award was made.

Lloyd Ray Brush, Sacramento, received a Certificate of Commendation for proposing that the bolts fastening the tire rack under the Division of Highway light trucks be wrapped with friction tape to protect them from dirt and facilitate their removal.

James H. Hirotani, Sacramento, received a Certificate of Commendation for recom-

mending that in the few cases where there are no construction changes on the plans of highway contracts, a letter be forwarded advising Headquarters Office in lieu of sending final plans.

Southern Tour

Highway Commissioners View Major Projects

By C. A. MAGHETTI, Secretary, California Highway Commission

SUPERLATIVES ARE quite often used to describe high mountains, blue lakes, tall buildings, sleek ships, and many more "bigs" in California so it isn't entirely out of order to picture the fantastic amount of roadwork going on, particularly in the Counties of Orange and Los Angeles.

To see this tremendous effort first-hand, members of the California Highway Commission, together with representatives from the Division of Highways, took time out from a busy schedule during June to see where many gasoline tax dollars are now being expended to produce better traveling facilities for persons in that part of the State.

Over the years it has been the practice of the California Highway Commission to hold business meetings away from Sacramento, occasionally in Los Angeles and San Francisco. This procedure provides the opportunity for commissioners to view many construction operations over the State and to very often accept invitations from organizations to appear before them to give firsthand information of the State's highway program. Sacramento being the seat of State Government seems far, and is far, away to many persons south of the Tehachapi Mountains.

Members of Tour Party

Included on the tour through the South were Frank B. Durkee, State Director of Public Works and Chairman of the California Highway Commission, Commissioners Chester H. Warlow of Fresno, Robert E. McClure of Santa Monica, James A. Guthrie of San Bernardino, Fred W. Speers of Escondido, Robert L. Bishop of Santa Rosa, and the author. Unable to make the trip because he was in Washington was H. Stephen Chase of San Francisco.

From the Division of Highways were G. T. McCoy, State Highway Engineer; J. C. Womack, Assistant State Highway Engineer; and George N. Cook, Assistant Secretary of the Highway Commission.

Aside from its regular monthly business, the commission participated in a ceremony of "turning the first shovel of dirt" for the bridge to span the Los Angeles River on the new Santa Monica Freeway.

McClure Breaks Ground

Commissioner Robert E. McClure performed this function before a large group of officials and spectators. Los Angeles "River," which sometimes brings raised eyebrows from northerners, did have a trickle of water in the channel. Actually the "river," which is paved with reinforced concrete, is a tremendous effort to control flash floods which occur occasionally in that area, winter and summer.

The viaduct and bridge is a project costing some $5,000,000. The "first shovel of dirt" started a bridge which will be completed about the middle of 1959.

The commissioners then journeyed over several freeways and stopped particulary to see the progress under way on the Ventura-San Diego Freeway. This huge project is near the $8,000,000 mark in cost. It is in two sections, the first beginning at Sepulveda to Encino and the second from Valley Vista to Burbank Boulevard, with a total of 8 lanes and 10 bridges.

Delays due to new construction were encountered on the Santa Ana Freeway to Newport Beach. While the slowdown was an annoyance, it did contribute further to the commission's knowledge of work being done in Southern California.

Because of a controversy under way at the time, the caravan made a stop on Friday, June 21st, to view the pro-

Groundbreaking on Santa Monica Freeway in paved channel of Los Angeles River June 17. On bulldozer, left to right: Los Angeles City Councilman Ratom Callicott, State Highway Commissioner Robert E. McClure, State Highway Commissioner Chester H. Warlow, Los Angeles City Councilman Harold Henry.

Looking southeasterly showing start of construction work excavating for center pier in the Los Angeles River channel for Santa Monica Freeway bridge. In background is Sears, Roebuck building.

posed freeway through Cardiff, Encinitas, and Leucadia. These communities are split between an inland route and one further east through Green Valley. By inspecting the two lines the commissioners now feel they can evaluate both proposals and arrive at a more intelligent conclusion.

The Los Angeles municipally owned International Airport is probably the third in activity in the Nation. Unlike the new airport in San Francisco, which was planned completely in advance, the Los Angeles project, like "Topsy," just grew; but the time has come for the directors of the port to do something about it, and plans are now on the boards for a new layout.

Because the proposal involves the closing of some of the state highways in the area the commissioners spent the greater part of one morning in-

specting the airport area and, a few days following, prepared an agreement which was accepted by the City of Los Angeles.

Thursday evening, at the Lafayette Club, a short distance out of San Diego, the commission met at dinner with representatives of the chamber of commerce and city and county officials.

Friday, the final day of the tour, was spent inspecting highways of the county.

For the commissioners to see things firsthand is undoubtedly a desirable thing. However, it does take time, and each commission member, a businessman in his own right, often finds it difficult to give more time to travel over the State. Due to devotion to the job by this commission and those that preceded it, goes the pride of great accomplishment to the end that

California, with its thousands of miles of highways, is now second to none in the Nation in this respect.

SPEED AT NIGHT

Don't overdrive your car's headlights at night. If you are going faster than 45 miles per hour you cannot stop within the distance illuminated by your headlights, according to the California State Automobile Association. Remember, 45 is the safe maximum speed at night.

A government worker sat at the table after breakfast one morning, engrossed in his newspaper for over an hour. Finally he asked for another cup of coffee. "Coffee!" echoed his wife. "But look at the time. Aren't you going to the office today?"

"Office?" explained the startled man. "Heavens! I thought I *was* at the office."

24

Bonneroo

Haddock Wins Topper
For Best 1956 Contract

WITH FRANK B. DURKEE, Director of Public Works, State of California, making the presentation Friday evening, May 31st, the contracting firm of J. E. Haddock, Ltd., of Pasadena was the recipient of the "Topper" trophy for having completed the No. 1 state highway contract in District VII during 1956. The winning contract was a section of the Harbor Freeway between 42d Street and 23d Street in Los Angeles, which was completed on April 26, 1956.

A similar trophy was presented by Edward T. Telford, Assistant State Highway Engineer, to Maurice E. Camp, State Resident Engineer in charge of construction on the project. Milton Harris, State Construction Engineer, presented certificates of merit to George Wiggers, Art Anderson, and Jack Erwin, the superintendents for the Haddock organization on the job, and to the subcontractors and the state engineers who participated in the construction.

Bonneroo Banquet

Scene of the award presentation was the sixth annual "Bonneroo," a stag banquet sponsored by the District VII Construction Department of the California Division of Highways and staged at the Rodger Young Auditorium in Los Angeles. The annual affair, sixth of its kind, is primarily held for the purpose of honoring contractors and resident engineers who completed the 10 best state highway contracts in District VII, comprising Ventura, Los Angeles, and Orange Counties, during the preceding calendar year. The winners for 1956, announced at the Bonneroo, were:

No. 1—Harbor Freeway, Los Angeles County, 42d Street to 23d Street—J. E. Haddock, Ltd., Contractor; M. E. Camp, Resident Engineer

No. 2—Ojai Freeway, Ventura County, Highway 101 to Mills School near Ventura—Guy F. Atkinson, Contractor; J. F. Smith, Resident Engineer

No. 3—San Bernardino Freeway, Los Angeles County, Durfee Avenue to one-half mile east of Puente Avenue, near West Covina—Griffith

Company, Contractor; B. N. Frykland, Resident Engineer

No. 4—Harbor Freeway, Los Angeles County, Battery Street to Pacific Coast Highway near Wilmington—Vinnell Co., Inc., and Vinnell Constructors, Contractor; F. E. Sturgeon, Resident Engineer

No. 5—Houston Freeway, Orange County, Cypress Avenue to Santa Ana Canyon Road near Anaheim—Ukropina, Polich, Kral, and Ukropina, Contractor; C. J. McCullough, Resident Engineer

No. 6—Santa Clara-Rice Road, Ventura County, near El Rio—Fredrickson & Watson, Contractor; J. F. Smith, Resident Engineer

No. 7—Artesia Street, Los Angeles County, Central Avenue to Alameda Street near Compton—Vido Kovacevich and O. B. Pierson, Contractor; C. C. French, Resident Engineer

No. 8—Verdugo Road, Los Angeles County, Glendale Avenue to Towne Street near Glendale—Griffith Co., Contractor; T. L. Patterson, Resident Engineer

No. 9—Katella Avenue, Orange County, Stanton Avenue to Santa Ana Freeway near Anaheim—Sully-Miller Company, Contractor; R. B. Valle, Resident Engineer

No. 10—Santa Ana Freeway widening, Los Angeles County, Camulos Street to Olympic Boulevard—Webb and White, Contractor; Don Frischer, Resident Engineer

LEFT—John Haddock, President of J. E. Haddock, Ltd., left, receives the gold-plated roller, symbolic of the "Topper" award, from Frank B. Durkee, Director of Public Works for the State of California. RIGHT—Maurice E. Camp, who was project engineer on the winning contract, receives a similar roller from Edward Telford, Assistant State Highway Engineer, Los Angeles. Rollers are donated by Galion Iron Works.

and Public Works

Prestressed Bridge

*New Structure Over
Santa Clara River*

By W. A. McINTYRE, Senior Bridge Engineer

SATICOY BRIDGE OUT has been a familiar sign on the highway which crosses the Santa Clara River on Sign Route 118 leading in and out of the Town of Saticoy in Ventura County. Washout signs have frequently been required when floods caused the Santa Clara River to shift its channel and damage sections of this highway.

In 1911 the first bridge was constructed over the Santa Clara River on Del Norte Avenue, now known as Sign Route 118, by Mervey-Elwell Company for the County of Ventura. This bridge, consisting of 10 steel through truss spans, with roadway width of 18.5 feet between timber wheelguards, each span having a length of 130 feet, was designed by a firm known as Venturco Company. The bridge approaches were protected with slope paving, oiled slopes and boulder mats placed at the toe of the fill slopes.

Frequent Washouts

Since the original construction of the 10-truss spans by Ventura, large floods occurred in 1913 and again in 1914. During the later year, river discharge of 112,000 second-feet washed out the bridge approaches and a pier on the east approach, necessitating additional spans and lengthening of the structure. On three other occasions since the earlier days, during the months of . March; 1938, December, 1939, and February, 1944, heavy downpours within the 1,500-square-mile drainage basin again created maximum river discharge which resulted in washing out the bridge approaches or bridge detours during reconstruction or repair work.

Soon after the flood of 1938 a contract was let to extend the bridge southeasterly with 11 additional 70-foot reinforced concrete girder spans, with a wider roadway width of 26 feet between concrete curbs. This work was done under a PWA grant and the new section of girder bridge was constructed as an extension to the narrow steel truss span, requiring a roadway transition and a grade change. Because of the narrow width of the steel truss section, it was difficult for two heavily loaded trucks of maximum legal width to negotiate the narrow transition section of the bridge safely. As a result of the heavy trucking in the vicinity, considerable damage has continued to be a headache to the Division of Highways maintenance department due to continual damage to timber curbs, railing and to truss members caused by collision.

During February, 1944, the river discharge was about 60,000 second-feet. The channel of the river again shifted, drifting the main stream flow against the westerly approach, causing the bank protection and the roadway approach to again be washed out, requiring the approach fills to be replaced.

War emergency made it necessary to defer plans to rebuild the bridge and to substitute a program of repairs to extend the life of the existing structure. In 1945 the entire timber deck and surfacing of the truss spans were replaced.

New Prestressed Span

Bids were received in the District VII office in Los Angeles on April 12, 1956, for the construction of 23 precast, prestressed concrete girder spans 70 feet 4 inches in length, having a net overall length of 1,636 feet. This westerly section of the Santa Clara River Bridge crosses the river about one-half mile east of Saticoy and carries State Highway Routes 9 and 154. Route 118 is an east-west road, being part of a secondary road system. The portion of Route 118 on which the bridge exists is known locally as Del Norte Avenue. All prestressed spans are supported on reinforced concrete piers resting on 42-pound steel H-beam piles. In order to provide a clear 28-foot roadway through the entire length of bridge, it was necessary to remove and construct the curb and railing on 11 existing concrete girder spans of the bridge constructed in 1939. The construction work under this contract included a detour over the Santa Clara riverbed, roadway approaches on the westerly, or Saticoy end, plant-mix surfacing, and new metal beam guard rail for the entire length of bridge. The contractor submitting the low bid of $605,442 was W. F. Maxwell Co. of Fontana. The contract was awarded by State Director of Public Works Frank B. Durkee, April 18, 1956. The final cost of this project was $607,348, and the work on this contract was completed May 7, 1957.

New Design

The new section of bridge departs from the usual design practice of a simple supported precast girder bridge. One of the features of the design of the Saticoy structure is that of continuity, where multiples of three and four spans are tied together solidly over the piers. This condition was provided for in the construction of the T-girders where a section of the deck slab or flange was omitted in the precast operation.

After the girders were erected the closing sections of the deck and the pier extension were cast to provide the necessary "fixity" for the continuous spans. The designer provided conventional reinforcing steel to resist the negative bending movement of the support. Every fourth span, except the first where three span lengths were

UPPER—View of completed bridge. LOWER—Showing connection between the old through truss bridge and the new concrete bridge over the Santa Clara River.

used, was provided with bar plates where the ends of the prestressed girders rested on expansion bars cast into the pier stems. To increase maximum efficiency in resisting shearing stresses, the thickness of the girders varied from 16 inches at the end to nine inches at a distance of 15 feet from the ends of girders. The contractor set up 48 casting beds on the job site to cast 184 girders that were used in the new bridge extension. Each completed span is 71 feet in length and required eight girders. The concrete casting beds were used a maximum of five times, requiring a minimum of reinforcing steel for strength.

Some Innovations

Some innovations have been used by Contractor Maxwell in the casting of these beams. Forty-eight reinforced concrete casting pads were poured directly on the ground. These pads were constructed to the exact width and length of the girder. Cast into these pads were horizontal holes for anchor bolts to furnish positive anchorage at the base during the concrete pouring operations when forces are a maximum due to fluid pressure of the vibrated concrete.

Both ends of the casting bed contained wooden blocks which were placed flush to the surface. The reason for this arrangement was to take care of end rotation caused by the increasing camber of the girders as the tension is applied to the prestressing wires. The soft wooden blocks were used to eliminate crushing or breaking of the ends of girders.

The location and spacing of the casting beds near the bridge site was considered by Maxwell from the standpoint of (1) eliminating waste motion by pouring the concrete directly into the forms from the transit mixer, (2) keeping the distance between the casting and erection points as short as possible, and (3) the proximity of the local concrete supplier, the Saticoy Rock Company plant. This company furnished 2,860 cubic yards of Class A bridge concrete in addition to 1,750 cubic yards of concrete for the prestressed girders.

Precast Girders

Form work for the construction of the precast girders consisted of five-eighths-inch plywood treated with a hard surface glaze. Individual girders weigh approximately 21 tons each and have stems ranging from 16 inches thick near the piers to 9 inches in the center. The upper flange of the girder, which eventually forms the bridge slab section, is three feet wide by 5½ inches thick. The connecting one-foot section between the flange was poured later, during the casting of the pier and deck.

During the girder casting operation, construction of the bridge piers was underway. All reinforced concrete footings rest on steel H-piles. The number of piles varies from 12 to 16 per footing, depending on the location and type of pier, either fixed or expansion. These piles were driven in the Santa Clara riverbed to a point below the scour line. There were 22 piers constructed, each pier wall 18 inches thick and 33 feet wide with heights ranging from 25 to 35 feet

UPPER—Floodwaters washed out detour bridge and detour during reconstruction work on the Santa Clara River bridge in 1939. LOWER—Southwest approach to the Santa Clara River bridge washed out during flood of February, 1944.

above the footing elevation. In constructing the piers, the lower section of the wall and footing were formed and poured together. The wall sections varied in height from six to eight feet above the footing elevation.

Reinforcing Steel Cages

The next sequence of operations was to place the reinforcing steel cages, previously fabricated on the ground, for the upper section of the pier extension. The cages were lifted in position with the contractor's truck crane. A prefabricated pier form was then lowered over the steel reinforcing cage in one unit. Two or three days after the upper section of the pier concrete was placed, pier forms were removed in two halves and cleaned, rejoined and lowered over the next reinforcing steel pier cage. In this manner the contractor made maximum use of form panels, using

four form panel sets to construct the 22 piers required for the contract. These forms were designed to withstand full hydrostatic head using double 4 x 8 walers on 3-foot centers and 3 x 4 studs at 12-inch centers.

Concrete Control

All concrete for this project was supplied by the Saticoy Rock Company which is located about one-half mile downstream from the bridge site. Concrete was delivered to the job in the concrete supplier's 6½-cubic-yard transit trucks.

All concrete for the prestressed girders was made using 7½ sacks per cubic yard. Cement used was manufactured by California Portland Cement Co., Mojave Brand Type II low alkali. The aggregate used for prestressed girders was No. 3 gravel with the maximum size of one inch. Concrete requirements set up in the specification required that no reactive aggregates would be used in the manufacture of concrete. An approved admixture was used in the concrete at the rate of one-fourth pound per sack of cement. This admixture helped to secure greater workability, lower water-cement ratio, and higher strength, which was required prior to the prestressing operation. An average strength in excess of 5,000 pounds per square inch was obtained over a 14-day period with slumps ranging from two to three inches. The curing of the precast girders to be prestressed was a colorless, impervious membrane. Piers and other parts of the bridge were cured by wet burlap or water spray.

Factors that contributed to the uniformity in strength in concrete for the girders were (1) close control of the sand moisture content by a calibrated elctronic moisture indicator installed in the rock company's sand bin, and (2) comparative ease in transfer of the concrete to the girder forms direct from mixer truck. Primarily, due to the close control of water content of the concrete mix, it was rarely necssary to add additional water for the concrete at the job site.

Prestressing Operation

The BBR system, registered under Swiss patents, was used in the post-tensioning operations for the 184 girders. This system required button-headed wires within the stressing washers and finally anchored in position with flat split shims to an integral steel distribution plate which had been cast into the girder.

Due to the continuous design nature built into the girders, flexible tubes positioned in the forms prior to pouring the girders followed a pattern along the center of gravity of prestressing force rather than the pattern of catenary, or parabolic curve, the latter of which is usually true for simple span.

The stressing was done with two hydraulic pumps with 100-ton hydraulic jacks. These jacks were equipped with precalibrated hydraulic gauges and, in connection with the jacking equipment, were used simultaneously at both ends of the concrete

UPPER—Prestressed girders at casting bed. LOWER—View along detour and existing bridge.

girders. Close control of the jacking pressure and wire cable elongation were carried out by an intercommunication system between the equipment operators.

Total Initial Stress

The total initial stress in each of the intermediate girders is about 390,000 pounds. Three cables were used per girder and 16 one-fourth-inch wires were used in each of the cables. Girders adjacent to the expansion end were stressed to 420,000 pounds, and 17 wires were used in each of the three girder cables. All high-tension prestressing wire was stress-relieved to 80 percent of an ultimate stress of 240,000 pounds per square inch as re-

quired by the specification. In most cases the anchoring stress was in excess of 60 percent of the ultimate.

The pressure grouting which enclosed the wires in the flexible tubing consisted of a circulating grouting system which used neat cement and four and one-half gallons of water per sack of cement, which was mixed in a mechanical homogenizer. All pressure grouting of the cables in the girders was accomplished from one end of the girder, and the procedure works something like this: When the cable has been filled with grout the excess material is carried back into the grout pump through the return

. . . Continued on page 72

and Public Works

29

New Freeway

Construction Begins on
State Sign Route 12

By HOMER G. SASENBERY, Resident Engineer

In February, 1957, the California Highway Commission declared the first freeway for Sign Route 12 in Solano County between 2.5 miles east of Suisun and 0.5 mile east of Denverton. The route connects US 40 near Fairfield with US 99 near Lodi via Rio Vista.

Approximately five miles east of Fairfield, Sign Route 12 parallels the southern boundary of Travis Air Force Base. During the past few years the runways of Travis have been extended ominously close to the existing highway. The 1957 construction program of the U. S. Air Force provides for extending the present runway some 858 feet south plus an additional 1,000-foot clear zone plus a normal approach area. In so doing, the old highway will be crossed, and a new route has been located to the south to replace the existing highway.

New Alignment

At a point approximately 2½ miles east of Suisun, the new alignment swings southeast from existing Sign Route 12 to a point one mile south. At this point the new alignment extends due east until it crosses the existing route some 5.6 miles from the point of beginning. At a point approximately 1,000 feet east of the above crossing the new alignment swings southeast to connect with the existing route approximately one-half mile east of Denverton. Although right-of-way has been acquired for ultimate four-lane divided traveled way, the present contract provides for two-lane construction, with the remaining two lanes to be completed in the future when traffic warrants.

Old Route Substandard

The traveled way of the existing route consists of plant-mixed surfacing 19 feet wide with earth shoulders. The existing bridge across Denverton

Creek is 21 feet wide, thus providing only one foot of horizontal clearance either side of the traveled way.

In the Denverton area sharp curves at the end of long tangents have resulted in many a lost load for truckers using this route. At one point near Denverton, it is a common occurrence to find a spilled load of lumber or some other product along the southern right-of-way line.

The new route being constructed will have a plant-mixed surfaced traveled way 24 feet wide with eight-foot paved shoulders on each side. The bridges to be constructed across Union Creek and Denverton Creek will be 40 feet wide, thus providing the same width as the paved section.

The new alignment has three curves with radii of 2,000 to 3,000 feet and delta angles ranging from 45 to 54 degrees. The old route had five curves with radii of 500 to 1,000 feet and delta angles of 12 to 63 degrees.

Financing

The extension of the runways at Travis Air Force Base has made necessary the reconstruction of this section of Route 53. The Federal Government is participating in the financing of this project to the extent of replacement costs of the existing highway, which will amount to approximately 83.4 percent of the cost of the new construction. The additional 16.6 percent required for construction will be provided by state funds. The cost of the first stage of construction will amount to approximately $1,000,000.

Right-of-Way

Right-of-way for the new alignment varies in width from 142 to 171 feet for ultimate four-lane construction, and in some cases sufficient width has been provided for future frontage road construction.

Sufficient right-of-way has been acquired in the area where the new route leaves the old route to provide for future interchange facilities to the Travis Air Force Base.

This project is one of the first projects in District X to utilize the earthwork and traverse calculations of the IBM tabulation section in headquarters.

IBM calculations are being used by field crews to determine quantities of roadway excavation, unsuitable material, and ditch and channel excavation.

Traffic

At the present time the old route serves approximately 2,100 cars per day. It is anticipated that the average daily traffic for the new section of highway will reach approximately 3,740 vehicles per day by 1971. Truck traffic comprises 15 percent of the total.

During construction traffic will have the use of the existing traveled way with a detour provided around the runway construction at Travis Air Force Base. The new alignment connects with the old route at three locations. Grading requirements at these locations are minor; thus a minimum of interference will be enjoyed by both the traveling public and the contractor.

Construction Highlights

Bids were received for the construction of the new route on May 8, 1957. Fredrickson Bros. of Emeryville were the low bidders with a bid of $1,008,181.50.

The project is 6.7 miles in length and consists of four-inch plant-mixed surfacing over six-inch untreated base over 12-inch imported subgrade material. Approximately 216,000 cubic yards of imported borrow will be required to construct the planned roadbed as the route traverses across low

LEFT—The new traveled way will be constructed through tidelands areas at the northerly end of Suisun Bay as pictured above. Unsuitable material is being removed by clamshell. RIGHT—Looking westerly from the easterly end of the project. This project will be constructed on new alignment due to extension of the runways of the Travis Air Force Base, which can be seen in the background.

ground for its entire length. A local borrow pit approximately two miles from the center of the project is available to the contractor.

The contractor is using two 2½-cubic-yard shovels and 13 14- to 16-cubic-yard dump trucks in the borrow operation at the pit. The material in the pit is rocky and is excellent for shovel loading. Taking advantage of the "off road" hauling conditions, the contractor's trucks average approximately 22½ tons per load. The hauling equipment is routed over the working area to supplement the grid and sheepsfoot rollers being used to obtain the necessary compaction. The equipment in use at this time with an average haul of three miles is placing approximately 8,300 tons of import borrow per day. It is anticipated that a peak production of 10,000 tons per day will be reached when the contractor completes his plans to balance his hauling capacity with his potential loading capacity.

Crosses Swamp Areas

The new alignment crosses three swamp areas, one of which is 2,000 feet in length. Mud stripping varying in depths from two to six feet is being performed with shovels both of which are equipped with clamshell attachments. The contractor, in close cooperation with the Solano County Mosquito Abatement Control was able to drain the large swamp by manipulating the control gates in the levee

across the lower end. The swamp area is at an elevation of two feet plus or minus and is subject to tidal action. At low tides the gates were opened to allow the swamp water to escape and when the tide started back in, the gates were closed to keep the tidewater out.

The success of this operation was evident by the fact that the contractor's equipment was able to walk along the bottom of the area where mud stripping had been performed with only a minimum of interference from seepage water.

State construction of the new freeway will provide for constructing the westbound lanes of an ultimate four-lane divided highway. Until the additional two lanes of the future four lanes are constructed a temporary intersection with the old route serving Travis Air Force Base will provide a left turn lane and storage facility adjacent to the eastbound lane as well as on and off turning movements to and from the westbound lane. Provisions are also made for a left turning movement from the old route to the eastbound lane of the new highway. The contractor's operations are progressing satisfactorily towards a completion date in February, 1958. The paving operations should start around the middle of October and be finished during the first half of December.

Glen Fredrickson, partner in Fredrickson Bros., and Archie Edmonds,

FROM KYOTO UNIVERSITY
DEPARTMENT OF CIVIL ENGINEERING
Kyoto University
Kyoto, Japan

Mr. Kenneth C. Adams, *Editor*

Dear Sir: I would like to express my gratitude for the kind and efficient advice and many kinds of useful information which your Division of Highways gave me on my visit to your office in the fall of 1953.

I thank you very much for your kindness in sending *California Highways and Public Works*. I do hope that your division will be kind enough to give us continuing aid hereafter, which, I believe, will be of great help to our institute and will provide us with valuable guidance for our study and research in highway engineering and traffic engineering. After reading the magazine, I get my colleague, Prof. Kometani, to read it and refer to it in his work.

Yours very truly,

Tojiro Ishihara
Professor
Civil Eng. Department
Kyoto University

superintendent for Fredrickson Bros., are in charge of the work for the contractor.

The work is under the direction of J. G. Meyer, District Engineer, E. L. Tinney, Operations Engineer, K. N. Hatch, Construction Engineer, and the author.

US 40

Project Between Heather Glen and Colfax Proceeding

By R. T. PHILLIPS, Resident Engineer

O N WEDNESDAY, November 7, 1956, bids were opened for the construction of a four-lane divided freeway on US 40 between Heather Glen and Colfax, a net length of about 6.1 miles. The contract was awarded to the contracting firm of McCammon and Wunderlich and Wunderlich, Inc., of Palo Alto with a low bid of $3,602,515.60. Work on the project started on November 11, 1956. On completion, this project will add another link to the four-laning of the interstate highway over Donner Pass between San Francisco and Reno.

The project consists, mainly, of grading and surfacing 6.1 miles of a four-lane divided freeway. To provide property access and leave usable the county road and Colfax street networks nearby, eight miles of frontage roads, ramps, connections and· approach roads through mountainous terrain have to be constructed. The project includes placing 16,250 feet of corrugated metal pipe of various sizes up to 54 inches and a total of 1,600± feet of 60-inch reinforced concrete pipe to carry water in the Boardman Canal under the freeway at three separate locations; constructing seven bridge structures and 233 feet of 6 x 5-foot reinforced concrete box storm drain; and providing adequate lighting facilities at each of the three interchange systems.

Structural Design

The main-line structural design is composed of four-inch untreated base, eight-inch cement-treated base, three-inch Type A plant-mix surfacing, and one-half-inch open-graded plant-mix surfacing.

The earthwork involved features 1,800,000 cubic yards roadway excavation with cuts and fills up to 100 feet in height. The largest fill contains 198,000 cubic yards, and the largest cut 360,000 cubic yards. Although these quantities are not exceptionally

On US 40 about one mile west of Colfax, looking easterly

large, the contractor's ability to clear over four miles of steep, wooded terrain and move over 1,500,000 cubic yards roadway excavation, approximately 80 percent of contract allotment, in eight months is quite commendable. On completion of preliminary engineering studies, it was considered that the cores of the cuts would contain hard rock formations of serpentine and slates; however, the basic material had been weathered to such depths that caterpillars with hydraulic mounted rippers were able to scarify everything with the exception of minor isolated rock formations encountered at several locations, requiring nominal drilling and shooting. During this same period, nearly 50 percent of the bridge structure work has been completed, and approximately 90 percent of the drainage and minor structure work completed.

Slides and Seepage

The two most prevalent threats to an otherwise normal operation have been slides and subsurface seepage. The basic rock formation north of Weimar consists of deeply fractured

and weathered shale laminated with clay lenses on a north-south strike and dipping to the east on an approximate 1½:1 slope. The general alignment of the freeway through this area is about north-northeast with designed cut slopes of 1 to 1 or 45 degrees. The combination of the above conditions has created a dangerous slide threat on the west slope within cut sections. Several minor slides have occurred during construction: two partially remedied or stabilized by lowering the bench grades, another remedied by flattening the entire slope to 1½:1, requiring 17,000 cubic yards of extra roadway excavation. The corrective measures taken were considered the most economical solutions considering the quantities involved, depth of unstable material, and depth of cut below original ground.

The second threat mentioned has been the persistent troublemaker—"subsurface water" and surface seepage. In the contract allotments were included 1,270 linear feet of eight-inch perforated metal pipe and 225 cubic yards of filter material for draining the numerous wells and springs within

California Highways

the limits of the project and for control of ground water at various locations. To date, 5,414 linear feet of eight-inch perforated metal pipe and 1,650 cubic yards of filter material have been placed, representing increases of 330 percent and 630 percent respectively. It is estimated that at least another 1,000 linear feet of eight-inch perforated metal pipe with filter material will have to be placed, and the extent of control within some locations will still be in doubt.

Unsuitable Material Removed

Within a 1,300-foot section south of Colfax, over 17,000 cubic yards of unsuitable material was removed and disposed of and replaced with selected rocky material from cut sections back on line. Due to the saturated condition prevailing in this marshy area, the material had to be excavated with a dragline and loaded into scrapers until a section was cleaned and haul road for trucks constructed.

The inclement rainy weather encountered has not been mentioned as a "threat" because the winter and spring were unseasonably dry with intermittent rain permitting the contractor to accomplish far more than had ever been anticipated. The contractor should be commended for taking full advantage of this weather break by moving his equipment early and working whenever subgrade conditions permitted. If such mild conditions prevail this fall, it might be possible that this six miles of freeway

can be opened to traffic by the end of this year, affording the contractor the distinction of completing the contract in one year and the State of the use of the freeway one whole construction season ahead of schedule. Of the 300 working days allotted for construction of this propect, only 91 have been used to date, and the work is approximately 47 percent complete.

Uninterrupted Traffic

Unlike the necessary traffic delays as encountered on other projects, uninterrupted traffic movement is provided by routing over constructed frontage roads and detours. At the Weimar Overhead the structure for eastbound traffic has to be completed and eastbound roadway surfaced to provide a facility for continued traffic flow, then the existing structure is to be removed and the future structure for westbound traffic constructed. Due to the time element involved, completion at this location is considered to be the key to an early completion of the entire project.

The major structures include three overcrossings and two double overheads, namely: Weimar overcrossing, Weimar crossroad overcrossing, Route 25/37 grade separation, Weimar overhead over the Southern Pacific westbound track, and the New England Mills overhead, over the Southern Pacific eastbound track.

The decks of the two Weimar overhead structures are to be constructed as experimental sections to check slab

QUALIFY FOR PROMOTION

Four Division of Highways employees recently completed training courses at the Naval Reserve Officers School, Treasure Island, San Francisco. They are Louis J. Jennings, supervising bridge engineer, Bay Toll Crossings, Department of Public Works, San Francisco, a commander in the Naval Reserve, who was enrolled in international relations; James M. McDowell, civil engineer, San Francisco, a lieutenant, who studied naval leadership; Robert G. Rogers, Jr., engineering aide, Pinole, a lieutenant of the NROS Staff instructing Combat Information Center Course; and Paul J. Wild, right-of-way agent, San Francisco, a commander who specialized in military justice.

cracking in relation to size and spacing of transverse main reinforcing bars. Other design features and construction methods are to remain identical for accurate comparison. Although the contractor has made every effort to expedite the bridge structure work, due to the steel beam construction of the two overhead structures and the Route 25/37 grade separation structure, the availability and delivery of structural steel will greatly affect the project's date of completion.

John New, project manager, and Pat Stewart, superintendent, represent the contractor. The work is under the general supervision of District Engineer Alan S. Hart. The author is resident engineer.

LEFT—On US 40 about two miles west of Colfax, looking easterly. Traffic on old highway near center of picture. RIGHT—On US 40 about three miles west of Colfax, looking westerly.

and Public Works

PASS OF THE OAKS

Continued from page 7 ...

To replace a now substandard steel truss bridge which carries Sign Route 41 traffic over the Salinas River, a reinforced concrete box girder bridge is being constructed over the Salinas River on the new alignment. This bridge consists of seven spans with a total length of 755 feet supported on concrete piers on steel piling and concrete abutments on spread footings. The bridge will provide a clear roadway width of 28 feet.

The Salinas River is locally known as the "Upside Down River" due to its flow from south to north and its peculiar habit of flowing underground most of the year. The underground flow made construction of pier footings extremely difficult due to the dewatering required. In most instances the footing excavation was kept dry by pumping, but at one pier it was necessary to drive sheet piling and pour a tremie concrete seal in order to dewater, after a well point system failed to keep up with the underground flow. Low rainfall this season allowed the contractor to complete work on piers in the river bottom and construction of the box girders is progressing rapidly.

Upon completion of this project, US 101 will be a four-lane facility from Santa Maria to Camp Roberts, a distance of 70 miles. Bridge work on this contract constitutes approximately one-half of the contract cost.

The prime contractor is the Madonna Construction Company of San Luis Obispo represented by Superintendent R. W. Osborne. Major subcontractors are the Raymond Pile Company, for concrete and steel piling; Independent Iron Works, for structural steel; and the Valley Electric Company, for highway lighting. The work is under the direction of A. M. Nash, District Engineer, and the author is resident engineer. John Pettine is the Bridge Department representative.

FAMOSO PROJECT

Continued from page 9 ...

allows the use of only three girders per span instead of five as at the overhead. This bridge also features the open-type abutments but utilizes a two-column bent because of the flatter skew angle and narrower roadway width. Footings are supported by concrete cast-in-drilled-hole piles. Construction was started on this structure in March, shortly after work started at the overhead. In July the substructure concrete was all in place, waiting for structural steel.

Cattlepass Extension

In order for the connection to be made at the north end of the relocation of the northbound lanes, the present northbound lanes had to be detoured on to what was the dividing

INFORMATION WORTH WHILE

Continued from page 4 ...

stance, mineral aggregates are used in constructing underdrainage installations, for pervious material backfilling and for other purposes requiring small quantities in relation to the entire program. Portland cement concrete is used for other than pavement and structures. Steel is used for other than structure purposes such as culvert pipe, guard railing, bridge and hand railing, fencing and various other uses. These are some of the uses of materials not included in the factor computations. Steel piling is an item of steel that has not been included in the factor determinations. Steel piling accounts for the largest quantity of material that has not been recognized in this study. During the 1955 calendar year, the quantity of steel piling was approximately 10 percent of structural steel quantities.

From the foregoing discussion of the bases for computing quantity and value factors and the purposes for which they are intended, it can be seen that they afford a "yardstick" for the reasonable forecasting of construction quantities and their representative values. Tables for the individual years 1954, 1955 and 1956 and a composite table for the three years are shown on pages 4 and 35.

strip in the center of the roadway. The existing cattlepass was in two sections, one under each roadway. It was necessary to connect these two sections before the detour fill could be placed. The length of this extension is about 35 feet; span of the rigid frame concrete cattlepass is about 22 feet. Here was the controlling item of work for the north approach fill for the overhead, so here is where the contractor started work in January, 1957, completing it in February. The detours were then put in and work started on the approaches for the two structures and the structures themselves.

Resident engineer is M. F. Silva. R. E. Harvercamp is Bridge Department representative. Superintendent for Tumblin Company, the contractor, is C. Ray Tumblin.

Reinforced concrete box girder bridge over Salinas River. Reinforced concrete bents of welded steel girder bridges of Route 2-33 separation in background.

SUMMARY OF QUANTITIES—Continued

California Division of Highways Contracts
January 1, 1955, to December 31, 1955

632 contracts with total value of $174,518,700 (contract bid items only)

Contract items	Total quantities for year	Dollar value totals for year	Quantities per million dollars of contracts	Dollar value per million dollars of contracts	Percent of total contract value
Roadway excavation	52,737,327 cu. yds.	$20,391,089	302,300 cu. yds.	$117,000	11.7%
Untreated rock base	2,373,916 tons	4,718,005	13,600 tons	27,000	2.7
Plant-mixed surfacing	3,327,178 tons	17,327,383	19,100 tons	99,000	9.9
Asphalt concrete pavement	25,250 tons	144,650	186 tons	830	0.08
Portland cement concrete pavement	695,833 cu. yds.	9,782,692	4,000 cu. yds.	56,000	5.6
Portland cement concrete structures	526,675 cu. yds.	25,155,795	3,020 cu. yds.	144,100	14.4
Bar reinforcing steel	104,694,441 lbs.	10,030,772	599,900 lbs.	57,000	5.7
Structural steel	33,494,580 lbs.	4,646,877	191,900 lbs.	27,000	2.7
Cement (contracts only)	2,315,662 bbls.	8,666,169	13,268 bbls.	50,000	5.0
Asphalt (contracts only)	223,840 tons	4,456,772	1,283 tons	25,500	2.6
State purchases cement	2,430 bbls.	11,452			
State purchases asphalt	46,731 tons	1,080,042			

NOTE: Three contracts awarded for construction of the new parallel bridge across Carquinez Strait at Crockett have been excluded as the concentration of money and steel quantities in these contracts are not typical for the normal highway project.

January 1, 1954, to December 31, 1954

574 contracts with total value of $145,364,900 (contract bid items only)

Contract items	Total quantities for year	Dollar value totals for year	Quantities per million dollars of contracts	Dollar value per million dollars of contracts	Percent of total contract value
Roadway excavation	25,036,379 cu. yds.	$9,973,658	172,600 cu. yds.	$68,000	6.8%
Untreated rock base	2,322,581 tons	4,516,853	16,000 tons	31,000	3.1
Plant-mixed surfacing	4,053,100 tons	18,037,554	27,900 tons	124,000	12.4
Asphalt concrete pavement	58,175 tons	320,988	400 tons	2,200	0.2
Portland cement concrete pavement	613,686 cu. yds.	8,434,345	4,230 cu. yds.	58,000	5.8
Portland cement concrete structures	476,434 cu. yds.	22,720,616	3,280 cu. yds.	156,300	15.6
Bar reinforcing steel	78,502,028 lbs.	7,342,461	540,000 lbs.	51,000	5.1
Structural steel	40,894,470 lbs.	5,155,750	281,300 lbs.	35,000	3.5
Cement (contracts only)	2,271,677 bbls.	8,143,045	15,627 bbls.	56,000	5.6
Asphalt (contracts only)	246,072 tons	5,099,967	1,693 tons	35,100	3.5
State purchases cement	8,872 bbls.	31,705			
State purchases asphalt	46,868 tons	1,038,226			

AGGREGATES PROCESSED THROUGH PLANTS

California Division of Highways Contracts

Items	1954 quantities per million dollars of contracts	1955 quantities per million dollars of contracts	1956 quantities per million dollars of contracts	Total 1954 to 1956, inclusive, quantities per million dollars of contracts
Untreated rock base	16,000 tons	13,600 tons	15,400 tons	15,000 tons
Plant-mixed surfacing	26,600 tons	18,200 tons	16,300 tons	19,300 tons
Asphalt concrete pavement	380 tons	177 tons	9 tons	170 tons
Portland cement concrete pavement	7,190 tons	6,800 tons	6,720 tons	6,870 tons
Portland cement concrete structures	5,580 tons	5,130 tons	3,980 tons	4,810 tons
Total processed aggregates	55,750 tons	43,907 tons	42,309 tons	46,650 tons
CEMENT REQUIREMENTS				
Cement (treated bases)	15,627 bbls.	13,268 bbls.	12,635 bbls.	13,700 bbls.
Cement (in PCC-pavement and structures)	10,210 bbls.	10,530 bbls.	8,448 bbls.	9,300 bbls.
Total cement requirements	25,837 bbls.	23,798 bbls.	21,083 bbls.	23,000 bbls.
ASPHALT REQUIREMENTS				
Asphalt (included in bituminous mixes)	1,320 tons	909 tons	801 tons	1,007 tons
Asphalt (as a contract item)	1,693 tons	1,282 tons	1,450 tons	1,460 tons
Total asphalt requirements	3,013 tons	2,191 tons	2,251 tons	2,467 tons
STATE PURCHASES (based on maintenance budget)				
Cement	373 bbls.	108 bbls.	86 bbls.	185 bbls.
Asphalt	2,039 tons	1,944 tons	1,912 tons	1,963 tons

NUMBER OF CONTRACTS AWARDED: 1954, 574; 1955, 632; 1956, 625; 1954 to 1956, inclusive, 1,831

ge Project

tion of the welded steel girders erected and is following closely with the placing of the reinforced concrete
roadway slab.

•

RIGHT—On June 27, 1957, steel erection on the main
span was started by the American Bridge Division of
the United States Steel Corporation at Pier 4. Their
huge crane with a capacity of 100 tons is seen lifting
the first piece of one of the main steel supporting
towers into place. This single piece weighs 37 tons.

LEFT—Foundation work at the center tower is in
progress by Contractors Mason & Hanger, Silas
Mason and F. S. Rolandi, Jr. There are two large
caissons at this point which will support the main
center tower. One of these caissons has been
founded on bedrock 132 feet below water,
while the one seen in background has about 12
more feet to go before it comes to rest on the
bottom. When these piers are sunk and the top
cap with steel grillage for tower legs are placed,
they will then be ready for the start of steel
erection at the center tower.

State Fair

Thousands Will Travel Over Superb Highways to Big Show

IT'S THAT time of the year again!

Thousands of Californians, and hundreds from outside the State, are planning to travel over superb state highways to attend the California State Fair and Exposition, scheduled August 28th-September 8th.

The word is out—the big show will be even better than in years past. And, if there were more room than the present 200-plus acres, it would be larger, too.

The problem of physical size will be solved in 1960 or 1961, when the fair will open its new 1,050-acre site north of the American River in Sacramento. The recent Legislature authorized expenditure of up to $25,-000,000 in the next two years for construction on the gigantic new fairgrounds.

Meanwhile, this year, one precedent after another will be broken, as officials go all out in providing the greatest amount of fun and education possible.

Many Attractions

Events and programs designed for every age group are included in the galaxy of attractions already on tap or being negotiated. There will be star-studded night shows, fireworks, a full program of racing, horse shows, outdoor stage attractions, demonstrations in international cookery, a carnival, arts in action, and many other departments.

Livestock departments will be packed with thousands of blue blooded swine, sheep, cattle, goats, horses, rabbits, poultry, and pigeons.

The list of exhibits goes on, almost endlessly, through departments set aside for art, industry, wines, home shows, women, 4-H Clubs, Future Farmers of America, and others.

Entertainment? There will be scads of it, ranging from hourly puppet shows for the small fry to lavish stage presentations at night featuring some of the world's most popular stars.

Kiddies will be treated to a special circus headlined on opening day by the television star Mickey Braddock, who is "Corky" on the popular TV Show "Circus Boy," and Robert Lowery, the dashing Tim Champion of the same show.

Popular Horse Show

The West's oldest continuous horse show, witnessed by thousands annually, will be held each of the 12 nights, with some events spilling across the program into afternoon spots in the race track infield.

There is an outdoor bandstand, where music from Bach to "rock" will be presented daily free of charge by the State Fair orchestra, high school bands, accordion groups, and others. There are daily programs on the mall, such as flag-raising ceremonies, retreats, close order drills by military units, and other events.

The Outdoor Theater has for many years been noted for a wide variety of attractions. Duke Ellington and his orchestra have performed there, to cite one example of show 'types," but so have children in dance studio revues, clowns, dog acts, etc.

New Race Track

Precedent was broken last year when the show was stretched from 11 to 12 days. As was the case in 1956, the big exposition will open on a Wednesday with a full slate of activities dedicated to kiddies. There will be clowns, special rates for carnival rides, free front gate admission for those under 12 (as always), scores of prizes, a parade, and many other highlights.

Racing will return, better than ever, with precedent shattered right and left. Purses have been boosted by $600 to $195,000, with increases for both quarter horses and harness events.

A straightaway track extension will put an end to the time-honored "Sacramento Course," a distance 220 feet short of six furlongs. The additional 220 feet will give a standard distance, offering better comparisons with other tracks for times, records, and other statistical information.

The $20,000 added Governor's Handicap, traditionally run on the second Thursday of the fair, has been shifted to the second Saturday.

Metal Inside Rail

Gallopers will thunder around a new metal inside rail, calculated to produce more speed through less fear of accidents. A wooden rail, in use for many years, is being removed and the metal type substituted.

Also important: There will be daily doubles for the first time in the fair's history. In this popular variation of parimutuels, bettors must select the winners of the first two running races to cash a ticket. The improbability of selecting two front runners in a row, making for high odds and producing more than a small share of excitement.

Arrangement of Departments

Precedent will also be established in arrangement of departments.

The Woman's Building, used for home economics for many years, is being converted into the Telephone Building and will boast displays showing the inner workings of that medium of public communications.

Home economics will be transferred to what formerly was the Home Show Building, now the Woman's Building, where arts of the home and family living will be shown in many ways. A highlight will be the sensational new electronic miracle kitchen.

All of the international exhibits formerly displayed in the Counties Building will be transferred to the Woman's Building, and there will be international cookery demonstrations as an important adjunct.

Also located there will be Consumer Reaction and Consumer Survey Councils. In the first, fairgoers will sample

. . . continued on Page 72

38

ALL HIGHWAYS LEAD TO THE STATE FAIR

Out of the Mail Bag

LETTER OF APPRECIATION

VETERANS ADMINISTRATION CENTER
Wilshire and Sawtelle Boulevards
Los Angeles 25, California

MR. GEORGE T. McCOY
State Highway Engineer

DEAR MR. McCOY: Reference is made to the recent completion of that portion of the San Diego Freeway and appurtenant construction within the boundaries of the U. S. Veterans Administration Center at Los Angeles.

The foregoing construction work was difficult and the problem of interference with Veterans Administration Center Hospital and Home activities was ever present, and some apprehension was felt prior to the beginning of construction concerning the welfare of our approximately 7,000 patients and home members.

Mr. George E. Dickey was the State Division of Highways Resident Engineer, and it is felt it was largely through his management the project was completed with dispatch and efficiency. At no time during the period of construction were our operations severely hampered or interrupted.

We also desire to express our appreciation to Mr. E. T. Telford, Mr. Ralph Chase, Mr. E. F. King, Mr. Jack Hudson and the entire staff of District VII with whom we came in contact; their co-operation and solicitous concern with our problems resulted in completing the project with a minimum of interruption to the functioning of the Los Angeles Veterans Administration Center.

Very truly yours,

R. A. BRINGHAM, Manager

YOU ARE WELCOME

THE AUTOMOBILE ASSOCIATION
OF SOUTH AFRICA
A.A. House, De Villiers Street, Johannesburg

MRS. HELEN HALSTED, *Assistant Editor.*

DEAR MRS. HALSTED: Thank you for your letter of 20th May and the two copies of *California Highways and Public Works* included therein. This publication will be very useful to us and we look forward to receiving future copies.

Having seen in these magazines something of what the State of California is doing in the field of road construction it is not surprising that its achievements are spoken of across the world, and that the Americans are described as the greatest road-builders since the Romans!

We are grateful to you for your interest in our problems and for your practical assistance in our endeavours to implement Johannesburg's expressway scheme.

Yours sincerely,

L. B. GERBER,
Public Relations Officer.

SOURCE OF INFORMATION

RICHFIELD OIL CORPORATION
Richfield Building, Los Angeles 17

Editor, *California Highways and Public Works*

DEAR SIR: I have received my first copy of your excellent publication and have enjoyed it very much. The information contained therein is factual, informative and interesting. I am looking forward to subsequent issues and wish to take this occasion to

VALUABLE PUBLIC RELATIONS

PETER KIEWIT SONS' CO.
CONTRACTORS
Arcadia, California

MR. G. T. McCOY, *State Highway Engineer.*

DEAR MR. McCOY: Too often most people, including myself, have an opportunity to see something that impresses them with being a good idea and simply pass it up as something nicely done. Not too often, however, are those responsible for some of these good ideas complimented for their thought and effort that go into them. For these reasons, I personally feel that you, and whoever else in your organization is responsible, should be highly complimented for the little pamphlet printed by your department which so ably describes the prevailing situation in regard to delays to the traveling public on US 40.

As a contractor, we place a great value upon our relationship with the traveling public, and even though we have no responsibility in the reconstruction of Highway 40 we firmly believe that giving pamphlets of this kind to the motorists that are being delayed can result in nothing but respect for both the Highway Department and the contractor involved.

Sincerely yours,

PETER KIEWIT SONS' CO.
THOS. H. PAUL

thank you for your courtesy in forwarding this magazine to us.

Very truly yours,

RICHFIELD OIL CORP.
By H. A. MUNN
H. A. Munn, Manager
Motor Truck Sales

Economical
New Device for Motor Grader Saves Engineering Time

By BERNDT NELSON, Assistant Construction Engineer

IN ONE respect roadbuilding can be compared to a golf game. Down the fairways of the golf course, and before finish grade is reached on the road, the accent is on power and yardage. As the golfer approaches the green and the roadbuilder gets closer to finish grade the accent must change or include a degree of exactness not required on the fairway or the placement of materials far removed from finish grade.

As the golf player must be able to "putt out" in a minimum number of strokes for a good score, so must the roadbuilder be able to efficiently "finish off" the layers of roadbuilding material to proper grade and cross section.

One type of equipment used to perform the "finish" operation on graded surfaces of earth, untreated and cement-treated base layers and bituminous-treated base and surface layers is the motor grader

Skilled Operators Needed

Truly skilled operators of this type of equipment are in great demand, for upon them is the responsibility of quickly and correctly finishing off the materials which are being supplied to them in ever increasing quantities. Reworking in case of error is not always the answer for often the materials being placed are such that the time element is a large factor, as in the case of most bituminous mixes that can only be placed at controlled temperatures and certain cement-treated bases that must be placed, compacted and a curing seal applied within a prescribed elapsed time.

A device called the Preco automatic blade control has been developed and is now being commercially produced for attachment to a motor grader to aid in its operation in quickly and accurately grading a surface to its required slope.

The following is quoted from a report made by Paul Kirst, Resident Engineer of a project on which the device was first used:

"The need for a device enabling an equipment operator to accurately and economically produce a graded surface of specified cross slope has long been recognized by both contractor and engineer engaged in street, highway, airport, subdivision work, etc."

A motor patrol equipped with the device is shown in *Figures I and II.*

The added equipment is inconspicuous, so arrows are placed to indicate members making up the device. Members 1 and 2 house units of the linkage system which transmits the attitude of the blade to member 3, which the manufacturer calls "brain," in which data is translated into electrical signals to the control box, member 4, from which the automatic operations of the motor grader blade lift levers are actuated.

FIGURE I   FIGURE II

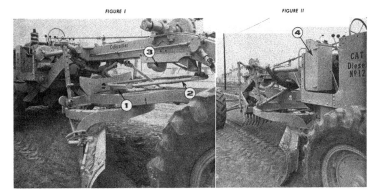

Job of Staking

Ordinarily in the finishing of any particular layer of roadbed, stakes are set, generally one row on each side of the roadbed and on a selected offset line or grade line or both to provide the equipment operators a guide from which to work. Standard practice is that breaks or changes in grade are staked and a straight line grade is assumed between staked points.

Where the breaks in the coss section vary from the job typical cross section or are in transition areas from one to another typical section, reference to those points are made on the witness or guard stakes set adjacent to the grade stakes.

Up to this point staking as described is generally performed by state forces, the staking for the intermediate points across the roadbed is left to the contractor.

Improved Methods Needed

The amount of work involved here in setting and resetting stakes, performing work over and over again, "wearing the material!" out as is often expressed, and lost time of equipment framed the need for improved methods.

The contractor's method of obtaining the specified cross slopes has generally been that of setting additional stakes across the roadbed to work to. Under this system the area between the stakes is graded to the plane indicated by the stakes and the accuracy of the completed product varies with the skill of the individual operator, the accuracy of the stake setting, and the inconsistencies that are bound to occur because of grade stakes being rolled down, covered up, knocked out, or otherwise displaced. One large disadvantage of stakes in the immediate area to be worked on is that equipment movement is hampered and in addition, although stakes are set to guide the operator, the area between stakes is still left to guesswork.

Guesswork Eliminated

With the automatic blade control device the "guesswork" in cross slope can largely be eliminated and without the aid of stakes within the working area.

In short, the device is a control system for automatically adjusting the elevation of one end of a mold board or blade of a motor grader to maintain a desired and dialed cross slope. The opposite end is under the manual control of the operator in the usual manner, being raised or lowered to conform to longitudinal slope or grade required. Automatic adjustments occur whether change becomes necessary by uneven terrain being traveled over, change in the position of that end of the blade controlled by the operator, or by a change in the dial setting.

Substantial Saving

On the first projects on which the device was used, it became apparent that not only was the need of setting intermediate stakes across the section eliminated, other savings were possible. The following is another quote from the report on the project where the device was first used:

"A substantial saving in staking costs, to both contractor and contracting agency, may be realized by use of the automatic blade. The device is capable of carrying required cross slope from one side of the roadbed to the other, including various intermediate slope changes, such as shoulder "breaks" and center crown. This allows one row of stakes, set to proper line and grade, to adequately serve for both the construction of the section and subsequent checking by the contracting agency."

Although designed for automatic control of cross slope—a tremendous step—a natural followup question was: "In what way can the work be done so that there is more control of longitudinal slope or grade, as that end of the blade, under the control of the operator is still subject to individual operator skill?"

Comments by Resident Engineer

On a subsequent project where a motor patrol equipped with the device was used this was taken into consideration and a staking procedure used which provided the operator a continuous visible grade line to follow. The following are excerpts from a report made by M. E. Darrough, Resident Engineer on the project:

"In the attempt to realize the advantages in the use of this machine, certain heretofore common construction practices had to be altered. The first alteration was that of changing the subgrade staking procedure. Under normal conditions, two rows of offset subgrade stakes would have been set by the State. These would

FIGURE III

have been supplemented by two or three rows of blue tops set by the contractor at each subgrade elevation. In lieu of this, however, only a single line of offset grade stakes was set. These stakes were placed at the subgrade elevation for, and at 0.5 foot offset from, the edge of the two-foot median border. A two-foot metal stake was then placed adjacent to the grade stake and driven to a top elevation of one foot above the grade stake. A string line was then stretched between and at the top of these metal stakes, forming a continuous longitudinal grade line to be followed by a pointer affixed to the toe of the grader blade. At this point, it should be noted that the grade stake or the string line could have been set at any elevation and the pointer adjusted so that the blade's cutting edge would operate on any desired plane. * * *

"With the string line in place and the aforementioned pointer adjusted so that the blade's cutting edge operated on the desired plane, the subgrade finishing operation was commenced."

Figure III shows how the latter procedure appears in operation.

The following is quoted from the previously mentioned reports regarding savings in engineering manpower.

"Obvious savings do occur, as previously noted, in staking costs. The contractor's primary saving in these costs is obtained by reduction of 'grade checker' and 'guinea chaser' time, as well as reduced equipment and operator time necessary to produce required results.

"The contractor on this project has estimated that this unit eliminated approximately 80 percent of his finish staking, reduced the finishing time by 30 percent.

"The State saved 50 percent of the normal cost of setting subgrade stakes.

"The State can expect to realize quality benefits not so dependent upon operator skill; and further monetary savings passed on through the bidding as reflected by reduced contractor costs."

A First

Initial Double-deck Freeway In Oakland Is Opened

CALIFORNIA'S FIRST continuous double-deck freeway structure, the Cypress Street Viaduct in Oakland, was officially opened to traffic on June 11th with appropriate ceremonies sponsored by the Alameda County Highway Advisory Committee.

The project provides four lanes in each direction along Cypress Street in the industrial area above city street traffic.

This unit of the Eastshore Freeway extends south from the distribution structure for a distance of 1.3 miles with ramp connections to city streets. The upper deck carries southbound traffic, and the lower deck northbound traffic, both on 52-foot roadways divided into four lanes. It was constructed in two contracts at an approximate cost of $8,500,000, performed by Grove, Sheperd, Wilson & Kruge of California, Inc. It will relieve the local city streets of through

traffic and enable traffic to proceed from the Bay Bridge through the industrial area without interference. It also provides for the considerable local traffic service along this route. During the construction all traffic used the parallel surface roadways which were constructed on either side to clear the viaduct area. These roadways will remain a part of the surface street network in this area.

Last Link Under Construction

A short distance southerly there is now under construction the last link of the Eastshore Freeway in Oakland between 0.25 mile east of Fallon Street to 0.22 mile west of Market Street, a length of 1.55 miles of freeway for which the Highway Commission has allocated $6,750,000. Johnson, Drake & Piper, Inc., of Oakland are the contractors on the project, and it is expected that this will be

Sharron Gleason, Miss Oakland, center, is surrounded by admirers as she poses for ribbon cutting. Left to right: C. A. Maghetti, Secretary Highway Commission; State Highway Engineer George T. McCoy; F. W. Panhorst, Assistant State Highway Engineer; Robert L. Bishop, Highway Commissioner; Director of Public Works Frank B. Durkee; Mayor Clifford Rishell of Oakland; B. W. Booker, Assistant State Highway Engineer, and William Travis, District Construction Engineer.

UPPER—Crowd at Cypress Street Viaduct dedication and caravan of officials and guests using new facility

completed by early summer of 1959. When completed, there will be a freeway in operation the entire distance from Ford Road, south of San Jose, through Oakland to Sacramento, with the exception of a short portion between El Cerrito Overhead in Albany to Richmond. (Carquinez Bridge and approaches are slated for completion the latter part of 1958.)

Dedicatory ceremonies were held on the upper deck of the freeway where a crowd of 200 citizens, mayors, city managers and civic group representatives of Alameda County together with state officials cheered Mayor Clifford Rishell of Oakland and Alameda County Supervisor Chester E. Stanley as they cut twin ribbons while pretty Sharron Gleason, Miss Oakland, and her maid, Sally Galbreath, beamed approval.

Following the ribbon cutting an auto caravan carried guests to the Athens Athletic Club in Oakland for a luncheon. Among those present, in addition to Mayor Rishell and Stanley, were: Frank B. Durkee, State Director of Public Works; State Highway Commissioner R. L. Bishop of Santa Rosa; George T. McCoy, State Highway Engineer; F. W. Panhorst, Assistant State Highway Engineer; Boyd E. Sylvester, bridge engineer, Bureau of Public Roads; B. W.

. . . Continued on page 51

San Diego Freeways

Four Contracts Are Completed in Year

By R. B. LUCKENBACH, Assistant District Engineer, and C. SMITH and AL ESTEP, Resident Engineers

Oɴ Mᴀʀᴄʜ 18, 1957, a six-lane full freeway between Wabash Boulevard and 56th in San Diego was opened to traffic. This was the fourth contract completed within a year, opening 9.6 miles of full freeway between Wabash Boulevard in San Diego and US 80 east of La Mesa, State Sign Routes 94 and 67.

These contracts were as follows:

on the easterly end which will complete a full freeway between the future US 101 at 18th Street in San Diego and Chase Avenue in El Cajon.

The section between College Avenue and Campo Road was officially dedicated with a luncheon and ribbon-cutting ceremony on February 14, 1957, by the Lemon Grove Chamber of Commerce. The section of Route

resins to repair breakouts adjacent to weakened-plane joints resulting from random cracking, and the use of metal strips for weakened-plane joints. These are described in articles by the resident engineers.

The improvement of Route 94 (A) has been under study for many years. Project reports were prepared July 8, 1949, June 15, 1951, and November 8, 1951, all providing for a four-lane conventional road or at best some access control.

Description	Contract cost	Right-of-way	Contractor	Resident engineer
Wabash Blvd., 3.4 miles	$3,168,000		Guy F. Atkinson	Al Estep
56th St., 2.8 miles	$1,668,000	$4,600,000	Guy F. Atkinson	C. E. Walcott
College, 3.6 miles	$3,998,000		Guy F. Atkinson	Don Smith
Campo Rd., 1.9 miles	$1,492,000		E. C. Young, Service Const. Co., & Young & Arrieta	W. T. Rhodes

Bridge Department resident engineers were R. L. Hathaway, Wayne Cryderman and Jack Burns.

The City of La Mesa at the easterly end is contiguous to San Diego and together with Mount Helix is one of San Diego County's finest residential areas. The city was a trading post known as La Mesa Springs in 1870. It was incorporated in 1912 with a population of 700. Mount Helix is the location of San Diego's largest outdoor amphitheater, where Easter services have been held each year since 1918. Many famous musicians called La Mesa or Mount Helix their home, including Madame Schumann-Heink, Carrie Jacobs Bond and Charles Wakefield Cadman.

Full Freeway

The 1957-58 highway budget includes $4,065,000 for construction of 1.8 miles on the westerly end between Wabash Boulevard and 18th Street where it will connect to the future US 101. There is currently under construction a 2.0-mile section of US 80

67 between Campo Road and US 80 was dedicated on March 12, 1957, with a program sponsored by the La Mesa Chamber of Commerce.

The section of Route 94 from Wabash to Campo Road is graded for eight lanes with initial construction of six lanes. The structures are built to clear two more lanes in the median. The section of Route 67 between Campo Road and US 80 is constructed of four lanes with grading for ultimate six lanes. This is actually a cross connection between US 80 and Sign Route 94. Therefore this six-lane design will handle estimated future traffic.

All main line paving is eight-inch portland cement concrete over four-inch cement-treated subgrade and subbase treatment as individual location required. The ramps are of asphaltic plant-mix. The entire route is of full freeway design with crossings only at structures.

Modified Epoxy Resins

Two construction items of special interest are the use of modified epoxy

A detailed traffic analysis including post card and origin and destination survey in 1952 showed a full freeway of eight lanes was needed. A traffic report was completed in March, 1953, recommending the route as now constructed. The progress on this route is nearly a record. The report was reviewed and recommendation was made to the California Highway Commission enabling it on May 20, 1953, to advise the county board of supervisors and the city councils of La Mesa and San Diego of its intention to adopt the route. The Highway Commission adopted the portion through Lemon Grove on June 17, 1953, with the complete cooperation of the local people and the county board of supervisors. Bids on the first project were advertised in December, 1954, or 18 months after the route adoption. During this time, freeway agreements were signed, rights-of-way purchased and cleared, plans completed and funds budgeted. In May of 1957, after less than four years' elapsed time, the entire 9.6 miles is open for traffic. The completed projects include the most modern of signing and safety lighting now characteristic of California's freeways.

LEFT—View northeasterly at junction of Sign Routes 94 and 67. Structure in center is the Route 67-94 separation. Sign Route 94 continues to right of picture. Panorama Drive Undercrossing shows in center, with the Mariposa Street Overcrossing following. RIGHT—View northeasterly of Sign Route 67. Structure in foreground is the Mariposa Street Overcrossing. Lemon Avenue Undercrossing and Grossmont Boulevard Undercrossing follow, with future connection to US 80 at Grossmont Summit visible in far background.

By AL ESTEP, Resident Engineer

A N EXPERIMENTAL installation of metal strip weakened-plane joints was made on the contract between Wabash Boulevard and 56th Street. This contract included 10,000 linear feet of six-lane and 1,100 linear feet of eight-lane portland cement concrete pavement. Some 1,072 metal strips were installed for weakened-plane joints. They were placed an average of 43 feet apart at the average rate of 77 per day. The strips were two inches deep and initially 11 feet 11 inches long, later reduced to 11 feet 10 inches to clear flanges of the finishing machine. Fourteen-, 16- and 18-gauge hot-rolled black iron was used. The finished product does not indicate any difference between gauges used; however," the 16-gauge seemed satisfactory, for this project. The 14-gauge appeared unnecessarily heavy and the 18-gauge too flexible in that it was easily deformed and difficult to adjust to grade.

Weather permitted sawing of control joints in the initial lanes 30 hours after pouring. Only nine random cracks are evident in the initial lanes, seven of these being in one day's pour. Trouble was encountered in a companion lane when a morning pour of 650 linear feet was not ready to cut by the following morning. Random cracking had developed opposite 15 of the 20 working joints in the initial lane. Therefore the experimental metal strips were used in subsequent pours in companion lanes.

Construction Details

Each morning working joints on the adjacent pavement within the limits of the proposed pour were marked. This was done because later in the day the random cracks or working formed joints would become invisible. Paint marks were placed at the center and edge of the adjacent slab. The metal strips were placed at the marked locations and installed as soon as the tamper made its last pass. A special tool designed by Resident Engineer Don Smith was used. Finishing operations immediately followed the installations which were made by two men using a wooden bridge and the special tool. The strips were inserted in the tool and forced into place one-fourth inch below grade. Two pieces of one-

Preparing spalled area for repairs

View northeasterly of State Sign Route 94 during construction. Bridge in foreground is the College Avenue Undercrossing. Following is the Massachusetts Avenue Undercrossing. Old State Sign Route 94 through Lemon Grove parallels new construction on right.

eighth-inch strap iron were used to hold the ends of the strip while the tool was withdrawn. The finishing machine occasionally hit the strips at this depth, so they were set to three-fourths inch, then adjusted to grade after three or four passes by the float. It required two men to adjust the strips to proper position in respect to finished surface if a center sag was to be avoided. Pliers were used to work them.

Temperatures were from 49 degrees Fahrenheit at night to 76 degrees Fahrenheit daytime average. Pouring was completed by 4 p.m., finishing 10 to 11 p.m. Remaining joints including those where strips were removed by the finisher were sawed 48 to 72 hours after pouring. The finished product indicates the strips should be one-fourth inch or less below grade for best results.

By D. C. SMITH, Resident Engineer

On the contract between College Avenue and Campo Road random cracks developed in companion lane before the weakened-plane joints could be sawed. This resulted in pavement spalling between the cracks and the cut joints.

Experimental repairs were made using a modified epoxy resin adhesive. Herbert A. Rooney and E. D. Botts from the Sacramento Materials and Research Laboratory supervised the mixing and placing of the adhesives. In excess of 100 separate repairs were made and to date no failures are evident.

Where small spalls were repaired, the material was removed and the space refilled with a grout of an epoxy adhesive and dry sand. The working joint was retained by application of oil to one face.

At larger breaks, the concrete was removed to sound material (usually four to five inches). The entire surface was coated with adhesive and immediately filled with regular concrete. The working joint was re-formed by stress.

Where random cracks were three feet or less from the cut and no spalling evident, two methods were used.

UPPER—Placing epoxy adhesive mixture to repair break. LOWER—Repair completed.

(1) The original saw cut was filled with an epoxy adhesive to eliminate the joint.

(2) A parallel cut was made one inch from the original, the material removed and replaced with a grout of dry sand and an epoxy resin adhesive. Chipping was expensive and the parallel cut method was the more economical. . . . Continued on page 56

Cost Index

*Below First Quarter of 1957 But Shows
Increase Over First Quarter Alternate
Computation During Second Quarter of 1957*

By RICHARD H. WILSON, Assistant State Highway Engineer,
H. C. McCARTY, Office Engineer, and
LLOYD B. REYNOLDS, Assistant Office Engineer

THE CALIFORNIA Highway Construction Cost Index for the second quarter of 1957 shows a moderate decline from the first quarter of 1957. The index now stands at 266.9 (1940=100), which is 10.8 index points, or 3.9 percent, below the first quarter. However, in the first quarter of 1957 two unusual projects exerted an unbalancing weight upon the index in its upward course causing the index to take a large unnatural jump from 252.1 in the fourth quarter of 1956 to 277.7 for the first quarter of 1957, an increase of 10.1 percent. While this large jump reflected the actual figures when the two unusual projects were included, it was felt that the index was overly influenced and was out of line with the cost trend and should show a decrease in the second quarter. Our predictions proved true as the second quarter index shows a decrease to 266.9, or 3.9 percent below the first quarter figures.

The present standing, however, is 5.8 percent over the fourth quarter of 1956 and 6.9 percent over the alternate index for the first quarter of 1957. Disregarding the sharp rise in the second quarter of 1956 in anticipation of uncertainties of the outcome of the labor strike in the steel industry and the first quarter of 1957 which included two unusual projects, the California Cost Index has shown a steady rise during the last 2½ years.

Projects placed under contract during this quarter are situated in all parts of the State. These projects being so widely distributed and similar in most respects, the cost data obtained is well averaged. Adverse conditions prevailing in one area have been correspondingly offset by favorable conditions in another.

Increases in highway construction costs were to be expected during the second quarter. Wage adjustments were made in the construction field in this period as required by the long term labor agreement made last year. Increases in bid prices for steel items during the first and second quarters over the second half of 1956 were no doubt based upon the prospective rise in steel costs at midyear to result from the annual wage adjustment provision included in the contract at the termination of the strike in the steel

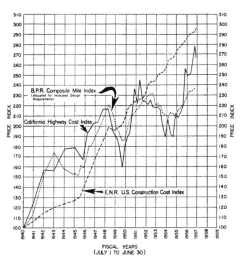

STATE OF CALIFORNIA
DEPARTMENT OF PUBLIC WORKS
DIVISION OF HIGHWAYS

**PRICE INDEX
CONSTRUCTION COSTS**

1940 = 100

B.P.R. Composite Mile Index
(Adjusted for Increased Design Requirements)

California Highway Cost Index

E.N.R. U.S. Construction Cost Index

PRICE INDEX

FISCAL YEARS
(JULY 1 TO JUNE 30)

industry a year ago. It had been anticipated in many quarters that steel prices would possibly be adjusted upward between $8 and $12 per ton. The announced $6 per ton increase being in a lesser amount will no doubt result in some lowering of future bid prices on steel items involved on highway construction.

The highway construction industry in California appears to be in an extremely healthy condition since it has been able to absorb the continually expanding programs of the Division of Highways. The Legislature in 1953, through increases in motor vehicle and fuel, taxes, made available considerably more revenue for highway construction. On July 1, 1953, the Division of Highways had 307 contracts in progress valued at $166,-963,200, and on July 1, 1957, the number of contracts under way increased to 363 while the contract value rose to $409,464,700. It will be noted that, while the number of contracts has not materially increased in this four-year period, the value has appreciably risen. This is accounted for not only by increases in cost per project but, with the availability of larger federal fund allotments, by the sizes of a good many jobs having been considerably increased.

With but few exceptions the average number of bidders per contract has remained high, which shows that competition and capacity for more work prevail in the highway contracting field. The average number of bidders per project during the second quarter of 1957 was 5.5, which is 1.5 below the previous quarter, but still in the realm of good competition.

Tabulations are included in this release which show the average number of bidders per project according to value brackets. One tabulation covers the Fiscal Year July 1, 1956, to June 30, 1957, and the other for the six-month period, January 1, 1957, to June 30, 1957.

From the remarkable progress being made on many state highway contracts, it is evident that newly developed techniques and labor saving equipment are being utilized toward greater production on state highway construction projects. These features

NUMBER AND SIZE OF PROJECTS, TOTAL BID VALUES AND AVERAGE NUMBER OF BIDDERS

(January 1, 1957, to June 30, 1957)

Project volume	Up to $50,000	$50,000 to $100,000	$100,000 to $250,000	$250,000 to $500,000	$500,000 to $1,000,000	Over $1,000,000	All projects
Road Projects							
No. of projects......	130	27	53	18	14	6	248
Total value*........	$3,062,463	$1,829,393	$8,755,546	$6,578,523	$9,836,335	$9,214,503	$38,276,663
Avg. No. bidders....	5.4	4.9	6.5	8.6	7.6	6.0	5.9
Structure Projects							
No. of projects......	26	2	9	5	3	5	50
Total value*........	$333,585	$144,283	$1,596,392	$3,094,234	$3,374,304	$18,881,272	$25,424,170
Avg. No. bidders....	5.5	5.0	10.1	5.0	7.0	5.4	6.8
Combination Projects							
No. of projects......					3	25	28
Total value*........					$2,759,730	$83,861,871	$85,621,601
Avg. No. bidders....					4.3	6.9	6.6
Summary							
No. of projects......	156	29	62	23	20	36	326
Total value*........	$3,396,048	$1,973,676	$10,351,938	$5,672,757	$14,970,369	$110,957,746	$149,322,434
Avg. No. bidders....	5.4	5.0	7.0	8.8	7.0	6.7	6.1

* Bid items only.

Total Average Bidders by Months

	Jan.	Feb.	Mar.	Apr.	May	June	Avg. for six months
1957..........	7.1	7.3	6.7	5.5	8.8	5.9	6.1
1956..........	5.9	5.1	5.1	4.1	4.7	3.3	4.3

NUMBER AND SIZE OF PROJECTS, TOTAL BID VALUES AND AVERAGE NUMBER OF BIDDERS

(July 1, 1956, to June 30, 1957)

Project volume	Up to $50,000	$50,000 to $100,000	$100,000 to $250,000	$250,000 to $500,000	$500,000 to $1,000,000	Over $1,000,000	All projects
Road Projects							
No. of projects......	327	65	87	37	36	11	566
Total value*........	$5,244,367	$4,737,975	$14,276,164	$13,140,725	$18,670,145	$18,739,124	$74,808,506
Avg. No. bidders....	4.3	4.3	6.3	6.7	6.5	6.8	5.9
Structure Projects							
No. of projects......	48	6	23	7	4	9	95
Total value*........	$781,542	$285,583	$3,955,562	$3,861,187	$3,877,091	$30,034,387	$40,825,022
Avg. No. bidders....	5.0	4.3	7.3	6.4	6.5	5.8	5.8
Combination Projects							
No. of projects......					5	49	54
Total value*........					$4,100,964	$159,639,740	$163,740,704
Avg. No. bidders....					3.5	6.2	6.0
Summary							
No. of projects......	385	72	110	44	25	69	715
Total value*........	$6,026,909	$5,023,558	$18,361,826	$16,001,885	$25,648,201	$208,413,151	$279,374,230
Avg. No. bidders....	4.4	4.3	6.5	6.7	6.1	6.3	5.1

* Bid items only.

Total Average Bidders by Months

	July	Aug.	Sept.	Oct.	Nov.	Dec.	Jan.	Feb.	Mar.	Apr.	May	June	Avg. year
1956-57..........	3.5	3.7	3.7	4.3	3.3	6.1	7.1	7.3	6.7	5.5	5.8	5.9	5.1
1955-56..........	4.9	4.3	4.4	5.4	6.3	5.4	5.9	5.1	5.1	4.1	4.7	3.3	4.7

THE CALIFORNIA HIGHWAY CONSTRUCTION COST INDEX
1940 = 100

Year	Cost Index
1940	100.0
1941	125.0
1942	157.5
1943	156.4
1944	177.8
1945	179.5
1946	179.7
1947	203.3
1948	216.6
1949	190.7
1950	181.2
(1st quarter 1950—160.6)	
1951	225.0
(4th quarter 1951—245.4)	
1952	225.9
1953	215.2
1954	193.5
(2d quarter 1954—189.0)	
1955 (1st quarter)	189.3
1955 (2d quarter)	212.4
1955 (3d quarter)	208.6
1955 (4th quarter)	212.6
1956 (1st quarter)	219.5
1956 (2d quarter)	255.9
1956 (3d quarter)	249.1
1956 (4th quarter)	252.1
1957 (1st quarter)	277.7
1957 (2d quarter)	266.9

CALIFORNIA DIVISION OF HIGHWAYS AVERAGE CONTRACT PRICES

	Roadway excavation, per cu. yd.	Untreated rock base, per ton	Plant-mixed surfacing, per ton	Asphalt concrete pavement, per ton	Asphaltic and bituminous mixes, per ton	PCC pavement, per cu. yd.	PCC structures, per cu. yd.	Bar reinforcing steel, per lb.	Structural steel, per lb.
1940	$0.22	$1.54	$2.19	$2.97	..	$7.68	$18.33	$0.040	$0.083
1941	0.26	2.31	3.84	3.18	..	7.54	23.31	0.053	0.107
1942	0.35	2.81	4.02	4.16	..	9.62	39.48	0.073	0.102
1943	0.42	2.86	3.71	4.76	..	11.48	31.76	0.069	0.080
1944	0.50	2.45	4.10	4.80	..	10.46	31.99	0.054	0.132
1945	0.51	2.42	4.20	4.88	..	10.90	37.20	0.059	0.102
1946	0.41	2.45	4.00	4.68	..	9.48	37.38	0.060	0.099
1947	0.46	2.42	4.32	5.38	..	12.38	48.44	0.080	0.138
1948	0.55	2.43	4.30	5.38	..	13.04	49.86	0.092	0.126
1949	0.49	2.67	4.67	4.64	..	12.28	48.67	0.096	0.117
1950	0.40	2.25	4.26	3.78	..	11.11	43.45	0.079	0.094
1951	0.49	2.62	4.34	5.00	..	12.31	47.22	0.102	0.159
1952	0.26	2.99	5.00	4.38	..	13.42	48.08	0.098	0.150
1953	0.51	¹3.14	5.31	4.88	..	12.74	50.89	0.093	0.133
1954	0.45	2.13	4.60	4.86	..	14.41	48.42	0.094	0.134
1955	0.39	2.32	4.93	..	..	13.35	45.72	0.098	0.143
1st quarter 1956	0.40	2.06	5.40	6.50	..	14.05	32.51	0.108	0.166
2d quarter 1956	0.51	1.06	6.37	..	..	14.64	87.13	0.113	0.219
3d quarter 1956	0.53	2.27	6.13	..	..	15.87	36.33	0.131	0.176
4th quarter 1956	0.53	2.31	²	²	²55.93	14.98	59.63	0.112	0.197
1st quarter 1957	0.63	2.10	..	..	5.94	17.38	61.14	0.129	0.235
2d quarter 1957	0.63	2.10	..	..	6.18	15.59	58.61	0.119	0.204

¹ The item of crusher run base was used before 1953.
² Asphaltic concrete pavement combined with plant-mix surfacing in fourth quarter, 1956, and will be identified as asphaltic and bituminous mixes in the future.

are no doubt being employed by contractors to partially offset increasing labor and materials costs.

The tabulation on the following page shows the average unit prices forming the basis for computing the cost index since 1940.

Of the seven construction items upon which this index is based, four were lower than in the previous quarter, two were identical and one showed an increase. Roadway excavation and untreated rock base were the same in both quarters, standing at $0.63 and $2.10 respectively. Asphaltic and bituminous mixes increased from $5.94 to $6.18. The four items showing a decrease were portland cement concrete pavement, which dropped from $17.28 to $15.59; Class "A" concrete structures, from $61.14 to $58.61; bar reinforcing steel, from $0.129 to $0.119; and structural steel, from $0.235 to $0.204—no doubt reflecting the inclusion of the two large unusual projects previously referred to.

Construction costs for this period compared with the adjusted computa-tions for the previous quarter in which two projects were not included. Roadway excavation was higher, advancing from $0.43 to $0.63, and asphaltic and bituminous mixes moved upward from $5.89 to $6.18. The remaining five items are lower than the previous quarter: untreated rock base, from $2.21 to $2.10; portland cement concrete pavement, from $15.79 to $15.59; Class "A" concrete structures, from $59.96 to $58.61; bar reinforcing steel, from $0.127 to $0.119; and structural steel, from $0.208 to $0.204.

The California Construction Cost Index, the Engineering News-Record Construction Cost Index and the United States Bureau of Public Roads Composite Mile Index, all reduced to the base 1940 = 100, are shown on the accompanying graph. The latter two indexes are based on nationwide construction costs.

The Engineering News-Record Cost Index again shows a rise at a slightly higher rate of increase than in the first quarter of 1957. It is up 3.2 index points, or 0.85 percent, from the previous quarter.

The Bureau of Public Roads Composite Mile Index for the first quarter of 1957, which is the latest available, was up 3.2 index points, or 1.4 percent, over the fourth quarter of 1956. The marked increase in this quarter

A FIRST

Continued from page 44 ...

Booker, Assistant Highway Engineer, District 4, California Highway Commission; Hampton H. Roberts, Vice President, and K. P. Morris, Project Manager, of the contractors, Grove, Shepherd, Wilson and Kruge of California, Inc.; Chairman Leland W. Sweeney and Supervisors Francis Dunn, Emanuel P. Razeto and Kent O. Pursel; City Councilmen Peter M. Tripp, Frank J. Youell, Howard E. Rilea, Ernest A. Rossi, Fred Maggiora, Glenn E. Hoover and Lester M. Grant; Dudley W. Frost, Chairman of the Oakland Chamber's Highway and Freeway Committee; Nat Levy, President, Oakland Board of Port Commissioners; Norris Nash, President, and William A. Sparling, General Manager, Oakland Chamber of Commerce; Joseph R. Knowland, Publisher of the Oakland Tribune; Wayne E. Thompson, City Manager of Oakland; John A. Morin, City Engineer; and the following mayors: William M. McCall, Alameda; George Haruff, Emeryville; John J. Purchio, Hayward; R. S. Milligan, Piedmont, and Thomas O. Knick, San Leandro.

over the previous period is parallel with the California Index for the first quarter.

Roadside Merchandising

By JAMES R. SMITH, Headquarters Right-of-Way Agent

If the word "sprawling" is descriptive of today's metropolitan development, it is certainly not characteristic of the ribbon commercial development packed along the major arterial roadways entering and leaving our Nation's metropolitan areas. Here all too often "concentration" is the theme, and case examples of the sluggish traffic disorder that eventually goes hand in hand with this mass type of highway merchandising are many. Here is the arena in which the through traveler, the local shopper, and the marketing transient slug it out 24 hours a day, emerging only half satisfied and generally the worse for wear and tear.

The Division of Highways did not have to reach far from its headquarters in Sacramento to find an excellent example of just such an arterial battleground, now all the more enlightening as a case study because on June 15, 1954, a completed freeway bypass came to the scene to work its economic effects.

The front-door example was West Sacramento, and it developed in an atmosphere that promoted the concentration of roadside merchandising with enthusiasm. It had a major highway, US Highway 40 and 99, down its middle, and it lay within the shadow of a major destination point, the capital city of the State of California. It literally developed a string of roadside merchandisers a mile long and they were strung on both sides of the old highway like beads on a thread. In this case, however, the beads were motels, service stations, cafes, bars, and a multitude of other related and unrelated businesses. If they had anything in common it was perhaps the traffic, together with an almost universal belief on the part of the merchandisers that without this traffic, they were nothing. With the completion of the freeway bypass, 14,150 cars a day from this traffic stream were diverted from the existing highway.

Timely Case Study

The study of the effect of traffic diversion on this merchandising string was undertaken by the Land Economics Study Section of the Division of Highways for a very significant reason. These roadside merchants were typical of an economic group that can be found in varying degrees of size and quality almost anywhere along our Country's highways, and their problems are not peculiar but are universal. And, with increasing frequency, this group is going to be faced with the same traffic diversion; for, with the vastly expanded federal aid highway program just now unfolding across the Nation, the freeway bypass will be the predominate answer to the traffic battle already described. When this happens, as it did in our study area of West Sacramento, many weighty decisions must be made. Unfortunately, a goodly percentage of these decisions will be based upon beliefs and assumptions which are totally inaccurate. It is only through publication of the results of studies such as this that merchants will be able to factually assess their own traffic sensitivity when the controlled access facility comes to their area. It is only with such a factual background that the prudent merchant should proceed in planning and constructing the roadside developments of today and tomorrow.

West Sacramento

Unincorporated West Sacramento is located entirely in Yolo County and lies westerly across the Sacramento River from California's capital city. The county line threads this river, and our study area is actually only minutes away from the heart of Sacramento and its metropolitan environs—an ideal stopping place and headquarters for the commercial traveler and the visiting tourist. Bounded generally by the river on the east and north, and the Yolo floodwater bypass on the west, the area can be likened to an island through which major US Highway 40 and 99W runs in an east-west direction.

Prefreeway West Sacramento had all its economic big-guns along West Capitol Avenue (old Highway 40 and 99W), and they were heavily loaded for service to the traveling public. Here was the "West Capitol Mile" and its multimillion-dollar motel strip—here were the other traffic-catering merchants, the cafes, service stations, bars and garages, dominating the economic scene in size, number, and dollar investment. These were the roadside merchandisers our study examined, starting with the beginning of freeway construction in late 1951.

Freeway Project

The West Sacramento bypass is a full, four-lane divided freeway approximately four miles long. Its location with respect to the community and the old highway is clearly shown on the accompanying map sketch. Its interchanges and entering and leaving points are also clearly shown. After it opened to traffic on June 15, 1954, an average of 14,150 cars a day used it during the remainder of the year.

The Problem

What, then, happened to the millions of dollars invested in the old highway's commercial plant when this 14,150-car traffic jam pulled out? Did the superseded highway decline in desirability as a sound investment location? Did West Capitol Avenue merchants suffer an irreparable loss in business? And did new investment rush to the freeway fence and the freeway's on and off ramps? These were the timely questions this study sought to explore through the use of factual gross business data, land values, and related economic yardsticks.

Investment

The accompanying before and after aerial photographs offer striking evidence of the degree to which development has taken place along the superseded highway. That business investors have continued to look at West Capitol Avenue with optimism clearly appears from a visual appraisal. That this visual appraisal can be factually established is evident from abundant data.

In late 1951, when freeway construction was well enough along to give an unmistakable clue to the major traffic diversion soon to occur, there were 25 motels located along the old highway; today there are 40. To an existing motel strip already well into the multimillion-dollar class, these new additions created an additional investment in the vicinity of $3,000,000. In terms of facilities offered to the traveling public, this

expansion in motel units placed half again as many rooms into the market as existed previously. Today over 1,100 guests can spend a night or a lifetime in West Sacramento's motel row. It is noteworthy this expansion was unfolding within a group generally held to be extremely traffic sensitive, and was taking place when there could be no doubt as to the pending traffic shift. *Indeed, even if our comparison is restricted to the period after completion and formal opening of the freeway, we find 11 new motels, increasing the available rental units by 35 percent, being constructed along the superseded highway.* That this dominant and traffic-sensitive merchandising group has clearly answered the first of our problem-questions through its own tremendous expansion, is unmistakably evident.

There is further evidence, however, of continued investment in the roadside merchandising facilities along the old highway which should be noted as well. While perhaps not as striking as that within the motel group, it is, nonetheless, significant. *Two major-brand service stations have joined the West Capitol Avenue group since the opening of the bypass.* Construction has commenced on an additional site

for immediate development of one more major station to be located along the old highway. While it may logically be said that these new outlets will be merchandising in large part to a growing local market developing within the area, it is likewise as logical they will be seeking a share of the business generated by the surrounding motels.

The cafe and bar group has also added new outlets to its existing merchandisers, and eight such establishments have made a postfreeway debut along West Capitol Avenue. While, as with service stations, an expanding local trade makes the reasons for growth in this group less clear cut, it is nevertheless significant by reason of the fact that cafes and bars also are considered by highway merchandisers to be highly vulnerable to traffic diversion.

What, then, is the investment picture along the former highway? It may be ably summed up as follows: The roadside merchandising expansion described above, together with the growth of other almost purely local business, has utilized almost all of the available bare land along "downtown" West Capitol Avenue, the old highway; vacant lots are becoming a rarity.

Diagram shows new freeway and superseded highway through West Sacramento. The circles indicate motels along the old highway, with shaded circles indicating motels erected after 1951 when freeway construction was unmistakably apparent on the ground.

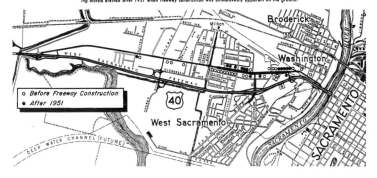

and Public Works

LEFT—Aerial photograph taken before completion of the freeway facility. The superseded highway, West Capitol Avenue, lies northerly and to the right, of the freeway. Water shown near the top of the photograph at the westerly terminus of the freeway is the temporary diversion of high water from the Sacramento River over the Yolo Bypass. RIGHT—Aerial photograph of the West Sacramento area after completion of freeway construction showing new commercial development along the superseded highway which is right of and roughly parallel to the freeway facility. At the time of year this photograph was taken, no floodwaters were being diverted onto the Yolo Bypass.

Land Values

Property sales along the superseded highway were examined and analyzed to determine if traffic diversion had introduced any variations into the overall land value trend over the prefreeway and postfreeway years. Since only vacant parcels were used for comparison to avoid arbitrary improvement breakdowns, the available data were limited, largely because of

the expansion in the motel and other business groups. Resales of the same vacant parcels were almost nonexistent since, once bought, the properties were subsequently improved almost without exception. There were a sufficient number of sales of similar adjoining properties, however, to establish a uniform upward trend continuing with little, if any, fluctuation throughout the entire period. While

the limited number of sales is not as conclusive as desired, it is still significant that no downward, or even fluctuating, trend in land values existed.

Retail Business

How well are West Sacramento's businessmen doing along the former highway? This question was answered by an analysis of the total business volume transacted by West Capitol

Photographs showing two motels constructed since completion of the freeway bypass. They are considered representative of the type and quality of new motel investment along the old highway in the postfreeway period.

Avenue's roadside merchants in the two-year "before" and two-year "after" freeway periods. Since primary emphasis was being placed upon traffic sensitive merchandisers rather than upon the local or community businesses, our analysis was broken down into two segments: the service station group and the cafe and bar group. These are the retail outlets which have largely held to the theory that "traffic removal is generally the kiss of death." In our study area, traffic had been diverted and the effect this diversion had upon these two retail groups was measured by gross sales figures as reported to the State Board of Equalization for sales tax purposes. (It should be pointed out that the motel group do not so report and thus are not included in any of the following comparisons. Motels having cafe, dining room, and cocktail lounge operations—there are two in our study area—are included, however, to the extent of such business only.)

In examining all the groups, two yardsticks were necessarily used to determine if West Sacramento had fared as well as other areas which had undergone the same highway change. Sacramento County business volumes during the comparison period were employed as well as those of Yolo County in which West Sacramento is located. This was done to avoid any bias in our comparisons which might

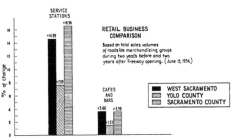

RETAIL BUSINESS
COMPARISON

Based on total sales volumes of roadside merchandising groups during two year's before and two years after Freeway opening. (June 15, 1954.)

■ WEST SACRAMENTO
▨ YOLO COUNTY
▤ SACRAMENTO COUNTY

Graph showing percentage increase in retail sales volume of traffic-sensitive business groups in West Sacramento as compared with same groups in Yolo and Sacramento Counties during a similar period of time.

be injected because of dissimilarity in the economic structures and patterns of our test community and its parent county. The importance of agriculture to the remainder of Yolo County's economy is considerably greater than to West Sacramento and this one factor alone could significantly affect our comparison. On the other hand, the similarities between our study area and the City of Sacramento, which sets the tone for Sacramento County business, are many. The percentage summaries, using both yardsticks, look like this:

Within these segments which would be most likely to be significantly affected by a highway relocation, the

cafe and bar group registered an overall increase of 3.60 percent compared to a slight increase of 1.33 percent for this type of business for Yolo County as a whole and a 3.58 percent rise for Sacramento County's cafe and bar operators. In other words, West Sacramento cafe and bar owners, after traffic had been diverted, had almost three times the business gain their counterparts throughout Yolo County enjoyed in the same period. They also did slightly better than the same businesses in Sacramento County, a striking measure in itself, since Sacramento County, because of its greater population and diversity, could be considered a truly conservative yardstick.

In our other traffic-sensitive group, West Sacramento's service stations did 14.59 percent more business in the two years after freeway construction than they did in the same period before. Yolo County service stations were doing only 7.59 percent better over the same periods while Sacramento County stations showed an "after" business increase of 16.56 percent. Here again, our study area merchants were doing better after traffic removal than before and compare more than favorably with the two unaffected yardsticks employed. Actually, this group was doing even better than the retail comparisons indicate, and a further examination of gallonage sales, which are not included in sales tax totals, reveals the following:

Graph showing percentage increase in gallons of gasoline sold by service stations along the old highway in West Sacramento compared with statewide gallonage increases over a similar period of time.

SERVICE STATION GALLONAGE COMPARISON

Based on total gasoline gallonage sold during two years before and two years after Freeway opening (June 15, 1954.)

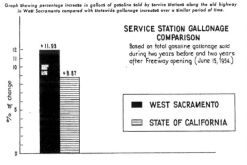

■ WEST SACRAMENTO
▤ STATE OF CALIFORNIA

In the two years after the freeway through West Sacramento opened, the total number of gallons of gasoline sold by stations along the old highway increased *11.93 percent* over the gallonage sold during the previous two years before traffic diversion. Over this same period the state trend in gasoline gallonage was showing only an *8.87 percent* increase. Also during this same "after" period, three new outlets were constructed between the old and new highways. These new outlets, all in very successful operation, are not included in our comparison of strictly highway merchandisers. It is evident they are claiming a substantial share of total available business. The increase in retail and gallonage sales of the highway service station group studied, despite this increased competition, becomes, then, even more significant.

Growth Pattern

The last questions posed—has expansion taken place only at the freeway fence?—have new competitors moved into locations adjacent to the freeway and its on-and-off ramps to the detriment of the old highway's merchants? —were answerable almost as a mere matter of observation. That answer was definitely no. All new motel construction has not only been along the old highway but it has been more of a continuation and concentration of the existing motel row, on land considered good motel ground before the freeway facility as well as after. Of the five new service stations constructed since opening of the freeway, two are on the old highway and two more, while closer to the freeway, are more accurately located in and adjacent to a newly developed local shopping area. The last, a modern truck station and garage, is the only true "interchange type." The new station already mentioned as soon to be in operation, will utilize a location on the old highway. No new cafes and bars have sought out freeway locations.

Conclusion

A final analysis of the effect that diversion of traffic from a conventional arterial to a modern controlled

access highway facility has had upon the substantial concentration of roadside merchandising establishments found in West Sacramento leads to these conclusions:

1. Those retail outlets whose gross business generally is held to be wholly geared to the flow of traffic past their door—the cafes, and bars, and service stations—have registered considerable gains in business volume since traffic diversion to the new freeway facility. These gains have exceeded those of similar, unaffected groups within their own county, and compare more than satisfactorily with those of more intensively developed Sacramento County.

2. New development within the highway merchandising group has been substantially confined to the old highway. Rather than a decline in property values and a drop in new expansion, "superseded" West Capitol Ave. has achieved almost 100 percent development, and land values have been uniformly upward.

3. There is no evidence that roadside investment desirability has shifted to the new freeway and its off ramps, and no ruinously competitive developments have arisen in these locations in the three years since traffic "left" West Capitol Ave. Indeed, it has been demonstrated emphatically in the motel group that the choice of location for new facilities has been wholly in favor of the superseded highway.

This study conclusively shows that the highway merchant need not expect business decline and capital depreciation as a universal aftermath of traffic diversion. His traffic sensitivity, as all the other economic forces which regulate the profits from his roadside business, can be factually assessed and evaluated. West Sacramento's highway entrepreneurs have made their evaluation and as a group are showing a progressive face to the postfreeway world.

TRAVEL

There are more than 61 million registered motor vehicles in the Nation today, traveling about 590 billion miles a year.

There are 130,000 school busses in use in the United States, carrying nearly 8,000,000 pupils along 1,000,000 miles of school bus routes.

SAN DIEGO FREEWAY

Continued from page 48 . . .

A test to determine the strength of epoxy resin was made on a concrete beam. The broken faces of the beam were separated one-half inch, the space then filled with epoxy resin. No pressure was used to force the faces together. After eight days the beam broke at 600 pounds per square inch but at a new break indicating the resin was much stronger than the original concrete beam.

CROSS-COUNTRY

The first transcontinental automobile trip in the United States was made in 1903, reports the California State Automobile Association.

Bold Venture

Open-water Highway Project
Is Dedicated to Traffic

By WILLIAM TRAVIS, District Construction Engineer

ONE OF the boldest highway engineering designs ever undertaken became a reality on Thursday, July 11, 1957, when the northbound lanes of the "open-water" project between Candlestick Point in San Francisco and Sierra Point in San Mateo County were opened to traffic. This four-mile section of freeway is located across an arm of San Francisco Bay and provides a direct straight-line connection between San Francisco and San Mateo Counties, superseding the existing heavily congested undivided highway through industrial areas of Brisbane and Visitacion Valley. The new section connects with completed portions of the Bayshore Freeway at either end, thus providing a continuous full freeway between San Carlos in the heart of the Peninsula and San Francisco's financial district.

The occasion was marked by ribbon-cutting ceremonies at the site and a luncheon-reception jointly sponsored by the San Francisco Chamber of Commerce and the San Mateo County Development Association. Speakers included Director of Public Works Frank B. Durkee, State Highway Engineer G. T. McCoy, Mayor George Christopher of San Francisco, Edward P. McDonald, Chairman, San Mateo County Board of Supervisors, and B. W. Booker, Assistant State Highway Engineer.

Provision for Eight Lanes

The new facility consists of a six-lane divided freeway with provision for ultimate development to eight lanes. Construction of the project has been continuous since January, 1952, under seven separate highway contracts. Five and a half million cubic

yards of embankment were placed in a two-mile fill section over the "open water." The total cost of the contract construction work was $8,000,000.

Engineers were faced with a problem of staggering proportions in planning the new freeway facility. The San Francisco Peninsula, only a few miles in width, is dominated by the San Bruno Mountains and heavy residential and industrial development already covered all but the most mountainous areas. Substandard alignment, steep grades and constricted right-of-way precluded further development along the existing highway. The proper freeway location was obvious —the direct route across a portion of San Francisco Bay. This routing was adopted and declared a freeway by the Highway Commission in July of 1941.

A ribbon woven of 5,000 orchids flown from Hawaii by Pan American World Airways was severed by Mayor George Christopher of San Francisco and Chairman Edward P. McDonald of the San Mateo County Board of Supervisors to signalize opening of the overwater section of the Bayshore Freeway. Left to right: Roberta Ward, Miss South San Francisco; State Senator Robert J. McCarthy; Mayor George Christopher (holding scissors); Edward McDonald, B. W. Booker, Assistant State Highway Engineer; Frank B. Durkee, State Director of Public Works; Highway Commissioner H. Stephen Chase; George T. M:Coy, State Highway Engineer; and Christine Falkenberg, Miss San Francisco.

Problems of Construction

The adopted route across the water was underlaid with 90 feet of soft bay mud. Many engineers felt that it would not be possible to construct a highway in this location. The engineering resources of the various departments of the Division of Highways were then combined in making studies to determine a feasible and economical method of highway construction under these conditions. The Bridge Department investigated the costs and problems involved in causeway construction. The theoretical factors affecting the stability of em-

bankments constructed over poor foundations were studied by the Materials and Research Department. District IV carefully reviewed its experience gained through embankment construction over the tidal marshes of San Francisco Bay during the past 30 years.

These studies definitely established that the only economically feasible construction would be to "float" a fill on the mud by end dump methods, utilizing material available from heavy cuts at either end of the project and importing additional material from nearby borrow sites.

Considerable doubt remained in the minds of the engineers, however, as to whether an embankment of sufficient stability could be produced by this method. The first construction contract was therefore experimental in nature to determine the behavior of the embankment and the general supporting power of the underlying bay mud. Started in January of 1952, this contract consisted of 400,000 cubic yards of embankment material which was placed in the northerly 1,400 feet of the proposed fill. Information developed from this experiment was then

. . . Continued on page 72

58

OPERATIONS AND ACTIVITIES OF MATERIALS AND RESEARCH DEPARTMENT

PART II—PAVEMENT SECTION
By ERNEST ZUBE
Supervising Materials and Research Engineer

In the preceding issue of *California Highways and Public Works*, F. N. Hveem, Materials and Research Engineer, presented a general review of the scope of laboratory activities, setting forth some of the problems and responsibilities delegated to materials engineers, and also the progression of growth and development of the laboratory from its early day inception to the large and nationally recognized organization which now comprises the Materials and Research Department of the California Division of Highways.

This article will be devoted to the activities and operation of the Pavement Section which constitutes one of the five major subdivisions of the Materials and Research Department.

Pavement Section

The Pavement Section is concerned with all materials used in the pavement structure with the exception of portland cement concrete. While most of the testing of the soils, subbase, base and bituminous pavements is now carried on in the district laboratories, the responsibilities of uniform test methods and maintaining accuracy of testing equipment are under the control of the Pavement Section.

Those of us who have been around for some years can observe rather a startling contrast between the old "Oil Mix" Department of the early 1930's which dealt only with one type of light road surfacing and the present day Pavement Section which deals

with all components of the pavement structure including the soils which support the pavement.

The functions of the Pavement Section, see *Figure 1*, are divided into four primary groups or subsections; namely, Bituminous Mixes, Asphalts, Soils Group and Special Field Studies. As all of the subsections are concerned with the various phases of the pavement structure, either in the form of testing or research, their functions are not sharply defined and some overlapping inevitably exists. A fifth group consists of the clerical personnel. This latter group, although comparatively small, performs very necessary and exacting functions, such as the typing of test reports, maintaining records, assembling reports, which are sometimes

The Pavement Section tests all materials used in the top three feet of the roadbed. This work includes the testing of all paving materials except concrete, and all base, subbase and basement soil materials.

It gives advice and makes recommendations to the Design, Construction, Maintenance and Bridge Departments and other outside agencies.

This Section reviews and approves specifications for materials used in the structural design of the highway.

It calibrates testing equipment and coordinates and maintains uniform test standards between the District and Headquarters' Laboratories. It reviews field construction testing practice.

It plans and supervises full scale experimental field projects covering the use of new products.

It conducts special research projects.

* Principal Assistant

STATE OF CALIFORNIA
DEPARTMENT OF PUBLIC WORKS
DIVISION OF HIGHWAYS
MATERIALS & RESEARCH DEPARTMENT
PAVEMENT SECTION
ORGANIZATION CHART
July 1, 1957

LEFT—Apparatus for moisture determination of bituminous mixtures. CENTER—Mechanical kneading compactor designed in the Materials and Research Department for compacting test specimens of surface and base to densities comparable to those obtained during construction. RIGHT—Extraction apparatus to determine whether bituminous paving mixtures have the correct amount of asphalt.

rather comprehensive, on the various field investigations or experimental installations. The reports are primarily distributed to our own Division of Highways, but, in some cases, to technical organizations throughout the Nation.

Routine Tests

For many years, the Pavement Section performed practically all of the routine tests on asphalts and bituminous mixtures for the entire Division of Highways, however, as the work increased it became impracticable to give prompt and adequate service to the remote districts. A few years ago a decision was reached to establish laboratories in each of the 11 highway districts for the purpose of performing as many of the routine physical tests as possible thereby relieving Headquarters of a major portion of this work and at the same time placing the testing facilities in closer proximity to the construction activities.

The district laboratories were supplied with testing equipment and machines, most of which had been devised and perfected in the Pavement Section. District personnel were brought into Headquarters Laboratory for a course of training and instructions in performing the tests and operating the testing machines. In addition to the training course, detailed descriptions covering all of the tests were compiled in a Laboratory Manual which has been distributed to all districts.

Reference Laboratory

In a continuous effort to maintain standard procedures and uniform practice we now act as the reference laboratory and periodically the districts submit a certain number of samples for check tests. In addition to periodical interchange of samples for check testing, experienced and trained personnel from Headquarters Laboratory make schedule trips to each district and with special equipment check and calibrate the testing equipment and also discuss details of test methods and interpretation of test results with district personnel.

The shifting of a major portion of the routine testing load to the districts has made it possible for Headquarters Laboratory to devote more time to needed research and special investigations. The development or improvement of any test procedure or any investigational technique often entails the performance of many routine tests. Therefore, equipment and personnel for routine testing must always be available as a part of research and investigation activities.

The Pavement Section works in close co-operation with the counties and cities whenever requested to do so. Some of the counties now maintain well-equipped testing laboratories whereas others are in the process of establishing such facilities. When

LEFT—Making centrifuge kerosene equivalent determinations in order to ascertain how much asphalt should be added to a paving mixture. CENTER—Mechanical mixer for mixing bituminous test specimens. RIGHT—Performing tests on bituminous products, penetration test for paving asphalts and shock test for pipecoating asphalts.

LEFT—Viscosimeter for determining grade of liquid asphalt. CENTER—Inserting test specimens in stabilometer prior to testing. RIGHT—Compression test for determining strength of cement-treated base test specimens.

called upon, we supply information regarding testing equipment and help with the training of their personnel so they may become proficient and self-sufficient in handling the testing apparatus and analyzing test results. We also on occasion check their testing equipment and testing procedures. Work is also done for other state agencies and the Federal Government when requested.

The following is a detailed outline of the work and activities of the subgroups forming the Pavement Section.

Bituminous Mix Group

The Bituminous Mix Group or subsection is under the direction of Merle Nelson, Highway Engineering Associate. This group is engaged in numerous activities under the following categories: design of bituminous paving mixtures, physical testing of potential sources of materials proposed for use in bituminous pavements and control testing for compliance with specifications on materials actually entering into the work. They are also engaged in research work involving both laboratory and field studies, special investigations relative to actual behavior of bituminous pavements and conducting co-operative check test series with the 11 district laboratories and with certain national organizations.

As an insight into the routine physical testing of bituminous paving mixtures, whether performed at Headquarters Laboratory or in the district laboratories, the following will present a general view of some of the things which must be taken into ac-

count in this phase of highway construction.

Prior to awarding a contract for constructing a section of highway the State makes sure that suitable materials are available. The investigation of materials sources is referred to as

Small pressure tests to determine how much weight of base and pavement will be required to prevent soil from expanding

preliminary testing and involves the application of all of the basic routine physical tests such as sieve analysis, centrifuge kerosene equivalent, stabilometer test, swell test, film stripping test, moisture vapor susceptibility, cohesiometer, etc., and oftentimes may involve some special tests in order to definitely determine the suitability of the proposed material for use in a bituminous pavement. When special

tests are required they are performed in Headquarters Laboratory.

The properties which must be determined from tests prior to approval of materials for use in bituminous pavements are several in number. First, the aggregates must be of proper gradation which means that a certain specified amount of each particle size must be present in the total mixture. The gradation is determined by sieve analysis and consists of shaking the aggregates through a set of sieves having various specified size openings ranging from say one inch down through successively smaller openings to the minimum size which is normally a No. 200 sieve with 40,000 openings to the square inch.

After the aggregates have been processed and proportioned to conform to specification requirements, the next step is to determine the proper amount of asphalt to be added in order to cement the particles together. This determination is made by one of the basic tests called the "centrifuge kerosene equivalent test."

Damage to Pavement

If insufficient asphalt is used, a pavement will deteriorate quite rapidly from several causes such as water action, the abrasive action of fast-moving vehicles and more rapid oxidation of the asphalt film. As a result of these actions the pavement in a relatively short time will exhibit a rough textured, cracked and pot-holed surface requiring expensive maintenance or reconstruction.

On the other hand, if an excessive amount of asphalt is added, the pavement will become unstable and tend to shove, groove or ripple under the action of heavy vehicle loads and the excess asphalt will oftentimes flush to the surface of the pavement presenting a skid hazard. Here again, expensive maintenance or reconstruction operations are the only recourse. There is no dependable way to determine the precise amount of asphalt required except by proper laboratory methods.

After the grading of the aggregates and asphalt content of the mixture are established, additional tests are performed. Test specimens are prepared by compacting the mixture of asphalt and aggregate using a special kneading compactor, designed in this section, which will duplicate the compaction obtained on the finished pavement under the construction equipment and anticipated traffic. The compacted mixture is then tested for its ability to resist deformation when subjected to heavy traffic loads. This test, originally designed in the Pavement Section, is made in the $H_v$eem Stabilometer which has been adopted by many other states and foreign countries.

Records of Test Results

Some additional tests are performed which evaluate the ability of the mixture to resist the deteriorating effects of water and finally a test report is prepared which records all of the test results, the laboratory analysis and recommendations.

The next category, control testing, is pretty much what the name implies. During the actual construction of the pavement, daily samples are obtained by the engineer in charge and submitted to the district or Headquarters Laboratory where certain basic routine tests are performed. This maintains a constant check on the work of the contractor, the quality of the materials and the proportions of the ingredients. These results are then reported to the engineer in charge of the job.

Bituminous pavements provide by far the greatest mileage of surfacing on California highways and investigations pertaining to methods of improving them constitute a never-ending program of observing and checking actual service behavior.

UPPER—Test specimens cut from pavements by coring or sawing. CENTER—Experimental installation of wire mesh to determine whether it will be effective in preventing cracks in asphaltic resurfacing. BOTTOM—Experimental installation of asphalt-latex seal coat to protect wooden bridge deck.

LEFT—Experimenting with bituminous binder containing rubber latex for seal coat work. CENTER—Measuring skid resistance of pavement surface. RIGHT—Placing of Zaca to Wigmore experimental asphalt test sections to determine quality of asphalt necessary for durability.

Studies and investigations are made of certain pavements not performing up to expectations as well as those giving excellent performance and every effort is made to establish proper correlation between test results and pavement performance.

Asphalt Group

The Asphalt Group is concerned with the inspection, testing and research on the various asphaltic binders including paving asphalts, liquid asphalts and asphaltic emulsions. This group is under the supervision of John Skog, Associate Chemical Testing Engineer.

Paving asphalts are used in the so-called "hot mix" process or asphaltic concrete and are mixed with sand and coarse aggregates that have been heated to about 300 degrees F., whereas liquid asphalts and asphalt emulsion are used primarily in surface applications where the aggregates are not heated and can be handled at ordinary atmospheric temperature. These various types of materials are further divided into grades to meet the different conditions encountered in construction. For that purpose our Standard Specifications cover some 25 grades of bituminous products.

One of the primary jobs of the Asphalt Group is to perform the necessary inspection and testing required to determine compliance with specifications of approximately 300,000 tons of asphaltic products per year which enter into the construction and maintenance work of the Division of Highways. The production of these materials is centered in four areas in the State, and involves some 20 different refineries.

Testing Field Samples

In order to expedite the inspection and testing of asphaltic products, the Materials and Research Department maintains a resident representative at each of the asphalt production centers which are located in Berkeley, Bakersfield, Santa Maria and Los Angeles. In three of these locations, branch laboratory facilities are maintained for performing all necessary routine testing of field samples. Headquarters Laboratory performs the necessary routine testing of asphaltic products used in Northern California and supplied from the Berkeley-Oakland area of production.

One of the important duties of the branch representative is to check the grade of each product being shipped to each job. Before shipping any asphalt ordered by a contractor, the representative who checks the special provisions governing the contract and if the grade is called for in the specifications he then grants permission to start shipment of the particular grade. A batch or control number is assigned to this material and these inspection records are available for any future investigations of pavements. In many cases, four or five projects in two or more districts may obtain their asphaltic material from the same series of refinery batches. If trouble is encountered on one of these jobs, the investigation may be extended to the other projects to see if the asphalt involved is a possible cause of the trouble.

Samples Tested

Samples obtained at the job site representing the various shipments are submitted to the laboratories for test-

ing. If tests show the material does not conform to specifications, corrective measures are applied. This may involve special checking at the production source, trucking facilities or visits to the job site for checks on plant storage and sampling techniques.

Although some 20 routine tests are performed on the various types of bituminous binders, the most common tests are penetration, flash, loss on heating, ductility, spot test, viscosity, distillation, float, demulsibility and residue test.

As a matter of illustration, the penetration test, as the name implies, consists of penetrating the sample of asphalt at specified conditions with a needle similar to a sewing machine needle. The depth of needle penetration determines the hardness or specific grade of the asphalt.

In the viscosity test the fluidity of the material is determined by allowing 60 ml. of the product to flow through a tube of standard dimensions. The time required in seconds is an indication of the viscosity or stiffness of the material.

Research studies by the Asphalt Group are principally centered upon the continuing development of improved test methods and specifications for asphaltic materials. The objective of these studies is to provide asphaltic materials of uniform engineering properties, without regard to method of production or crude oil source. Further, such tests should insure the production of material of satisfactory durability.

Soils Group

The Soils Group is under the supervision of George Sherman, Senior Materials and Research Engineer. Its activities are concerned primarily with untreated and treated bases, subbases and the lower or basement soils of the structural section. Its functions might be logically divided into three phases: routine operation of established tests, special investigations and research work. The routine operations consist of the Resistance Value (commonly called R-value) and tests on cement-treated base materials. The R-value test is performed on untreated base, subbase and basement soils. It is from these tests that the thicknesses of the various layers of pavement and bases are determined. The R-value test employs the stabilometer and the expansion pressure apparatus for determining the thickness of layer required to prevent lateral displacement. Cement-treated base tests, on the other hand, employ compressive strength as an index of the quality of aggregate-cement mixtures. In either event, these tests lead to quality specifications for materials furnished by the contractor.

The Soils Group is also responsible for the functioning of the structural design formula and in order to carry on these studies a considerable amount of field testing and investigation is necessary to correlate test data with actual performance. In this respect the R-value group investigates highway failures particularly where such failures occur before the pavement has gone through its expected life cycle. This requires a field crew for sampling, coring equipment and equipment for measuring the deflection of pavements under load. The latter is accomplished by two methods, the electronic gage method or the Benkelman Beam. Extensive laboratory tests are usually required in most investigations and it is sometimes necessary to modify existing test methods or procedures in order that the necessary data can be analyzed and combined into a report explaining a particular type of road failure.

Special Field Study Group

A comparatively recent addition to the Pavement Section is the Special Field Study Group headed by Earle Dewing, Senior Highway Engineer.

This unit is engaged in a study of present field testing methods and the

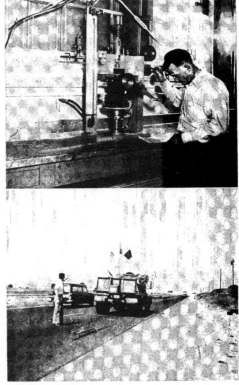

UPPER—Resiliometer with stabilometer in place used to measure springiness of soils supporting pavements. LOWER—Making Benkelman beam deflection tests to find out how much a pavement is being bent or stressed under heavy wheel loads.

possibility of their improvement as well as the training of district personnel in the performance and interpretation of field control tests. The expanding construction program has

developed a tremendous acceleration in material placement. Larger equipment, new techniques and changes in production procedures have quadrupled the average daily production in the last 10 years. This results in each sample of material representing larger quantities than in past years. Therefore, extreme care in field sampling and testing is required to insure true and adequate representation.

Typical Research and Special Investigations

The foregoing has given a general outline of the main functions of the various subsections. Now, let's take a look at some of the research and special investigational work carried on by the Pavement Section. It might be said that this is the most interesting type of work and quite often all groups are involved in the solution or analysis of certain problems.

Research, of course, is the life blood of the Pavement Section, as it is in any comparable organization; otherwise, our methods and procedures would soon become obsolete and unable to cope with the ever-changing concepts of design and the constant need for better quality in highway construction materials.

Some of the research and investigational projects being carried on at the present time are:

Studies involving *commercial admixtures for asphalt*. It is often claimed by manufacturers that certain additives greatly improve the adhesiveness of asphalts in the presence of water. Our studies include periodic inspection of a test section on US 40 in which several commercial admixtures were incorporated into the asphalt in the hope of preventing or retarding the destructive effects of water on the bituminous pavement.

Extensive studies are made involving the use of *aggregates having absorptive characteristics* in an effort to predetermine the amount and rate of absorption. Any appreciable amount of absorption over a period of time will cause a dry brittle condition and greatly affects the durability of bituminous pavements. In connection with the absorptive study, a re-evaluation and modification of our present C. K. E. method of predetermining the proper amount of asphalt to be used in bituminous pavements is currently active.

A rather extensive investigational program is presently under way to obtain further correlating data on the effects of *moisture vapor* which apparently originates in the underlying wet soils or base material and may be influenced by the heat absorbed by the overlying bituminous paving mixture which during summer season often reaches temperatures in the neighborhood of 140 to 150 degrees F.

Another project is concerned with the introduction of some type of *rubber in asphalt mixes*. Three experimental sections have been placed and are under observation by this department to determine if the benefits obtained warrant the additional cost of the rubber.

Quite frequently there appear on the market certain *commercial products* with the claim by the manufacturer that they are the answer to many of our pavement problems. When a study of literature or reports indicates that one of these products may offer some possible benefit the product or procedure is investigated first by laboratory tests and if it shows promise, later in a full-scale field test section.

After many years of service life, old concrete and asphalt pavements sooner or later become cracked and require a new wearing surface. In many cases this new surface course will shortly reflect the pattern of existing cracks in the old pavement and present a continuing maintenance problem. One of the proposed methods for preventing this reflection cracking in the new surface is to lay *some form of wire fabric* on the existing pavement prior to placing the new surface. Three experimental field test sections have been installed and periodical observations are being made. The major installation, about two miles long, involves eight types of wire reinforcement and has been placed on a heavily traveled section of US 40 near the town of Vallejo.

The use of *asphalt-latex emulsions* for sealing joints in portland cement concrete pavement was developed by the Pavement Section. More recently its use has been extended experimentally in the form of a seal coat pro-

viding a thin, lightweight wearing and skid resistant surface on steel deck bridges. Due to its excellent adhesiveness it has also been used in the form of a seal coat on the wooden deck of a draw bridge.

The *skid resistance* of various pavement surfaces is essential to the safety of the traveling public. A research project currently underway has resulted in the design and construction of a small skid tester, usable in both field and laboratory studies. Actual calibration experiments involving various types of surfaces have been performed in the field using a specially equipped truck and trailer provided by the Institute of Transportation and Traffic Engineering of the University of California. One of the laboratory studies involving this skid tester has for its objective the determination of the change in skid resistance of seal coat aggregates following simulated tire polishing. This project has required the construction of special test specimens and also the construction of a machine to simulate polishing and wearing of the pavement surface. These studies are in a preliminary stage and will require further field correlation work.

For the past few years special field investigations have been underway to measure *uniformity in placing seal coats*. Equipment has been developed for checking the uniformity in spread of the asphaltic binder both transversely and longitudinally. Further improvement and simplification, however, is necessary to make its use more practicable for widespread use by field personnel.

The problem of devising tests for predicting the future *durability of asphaltic materials* has been under investigation for a number of years. This study has required the design and construction of weathering ovens and the development of methods to measure the changes in the characteristics of the bituminous binder under accelerated aging. In order to obtain essential information for correlation of the weathering unit with field aging, a number of experimental projects are sampled at intervals and the asphalt is recovered from the mixture for test by special methods. One rather elaborate project involved in this study is located on Route US 101 between Santa Barbara and Santa Maria and is known as the Zaca to Wigmore Job. Ten different asphalts from various production sources were used in 2,500-foot test sections. Such a test section provides extremely valuable information for checking test methods under development. After development of research techniques for predicting the durability characteristics, the next step is to devise rapid and simplified tests for routine control work. A number of such tests are now being studied in an attempt to accomplish this objective.

Curing Rate

Another problem concerned with the various liquid asphalts is the "*curing*" or "*setting*" *rate.* The present distillation test does not provide complete information on this subject, and differences in curing rates of the same grade from different production sources have been encountered in the field. An instrument called the Cohesiograph has been designed and constructed by the laboratory for studying this problem. Samples of Ottawa sand mixed with 2 perecnt of the liquid asphalt are cured in weathering ovens under simulated field conditions and the changes in the bituminous binder are evaluated by this device. This instrument has also proven very useful in measuring the setting rate of certain paving asphalts in hot mixes during and immediately after construction.

One of the most important research problems currently underway is the study of methods for measuring the *resilience or springiness of the pavement structure.* Under a moving load, a pavement is first depressed and then rebounds to its original position. This results in a bending action in the pavement surface which, if excessive, can lead to cracking and ultimate failure. Therefore, it is essential that this property of resilience be predetermined and that only the least resilient soils enter the upper portion of the roadbed.

In order to measure the ablity of soils and aggregates to rebound under repeated loads, an apparatus has been devised known as the *resiliometer* which is, at the present time, being tried out to determine if test results can be made to correlate with field performance.

Another research project also connected with the problem of springiness is the gathering of data with the ultimate goal of developing pavements highly *resistant to fatigue.* In this study small test beams of the paving mixture are tested at various temperatures in a specially designed fatigue machine which measures the ability of various types of asphaltic pavement slabs to withstand repeated bending without breaking. This is a property which varies with aggregate gradation as well as with the quality and quantity of asphalt.

The Pavement Section has been engaged in the analysis and interpretation of results of the *nationally known test tracks* MD-1 in Maryland and WASHO Test Road in Idaho. We are also very actively involved in the design and testing of materials for the current multimillion dollar AASHO Test Road in Illinois.

During the past 25 years much of the testing equipment and test procedures for testing both asphalt and bituminous mixes as well as soils have been developed in the Pavement Section. Some of the methods have been adopted by other states and national organizations. In fact, methods and equipment such as the Sand Equivalent, Centrifuge Kerosene Equivalent, Kneading Compactor and the Hveem Stabilometer are in use in laboratories in many countries of the world.

Outmoded Highways

The public has only to look about to realize that many of the highways constructed as recently as 10 years ago are now inadequate to serve the present day volume of traffic. The answer to this tremendous increase in traffic on our state highways is, of course, our modern freeway system which is the result of long-range planning and research.

While increase in volume of traffic is apparent to all it may not be so

New Personnel Officer Named

S. Alan White, who has been in personnel work in state service for the past seven years, has accepted an appointment by Director of Public Works Frank B. Durkee as departmental personnel officer of the Department of Public Works, effective September 1.

White is a graduate of the University of San Francisco, class of 1939, and has a year and a half of graduate work in history and education at the University of California. From August, 1941, to October, 1945, he was in service in the U. S. Navy and is presently a commander in the U. S. Naval Reserve.

On leaving the service, White was engaged in private industry, which he left to accept employment with the State Personnel Board. He is presently on the staff of the Department of Social Welfare.

He will be on the staff of the Department of Public Works to coordinate and advise on personnel management in the department.

---

obvious that there are also marked increases in weight and size of vehicles, particularly trucks. These increases must be anticipated and advance preparations made to meet the conditions as they materialize. To meet these conditions, it may be necessary to develop new tests and testing equipment to measure and evaluate the necessary qualities required of the materials. Experimental field test sections must be constructed in order to correlate laboratory and actual field conditions. Many new products in the field of highway construction are evaluated in this manner to insure that we are getting the required quality. If we are to continue the progress which has resulted in providing the traveling public with better highways, we must keep well out in front with a research program in order that we can be always ready to test, evaluate and control the quality of our highway materials to insure that we are getting the most for the money we are spending.

Huge Contract

Engineers Discuss Job in
San Fernando Valley

By F. E. STURGEON, Resident Engineer, and
P. T. TAYRIEN, Assistant Resident Engineer

THE LARGEST District VII major construction contract awarded to date, a contract for the construction of 4.5 miles of six- and eight-lane freeway in the San Fernando Valley section of the City of Los Angeles was let to Oberg Construction Corporation and Oberg Brothers Construction Company, a joint venture, on December 28, 1956, by State Director of Public Works Frank B. Durkee. The $7,-201,496 contract calls for grading and paving with portland cement concrete on completely new alignment a 1.5-mile portion of the San Diego Freeway between Valley Vista Boulevard and Burbank Boulevard, and a 3.1-mile portion of the Ventura Freeway between Sepulveda Boulevard

and Encino Avenue. A full traffic interchange facility is being provided between these two important freeways. Included in the contract are construction of 10 bridges, an equestrian undercrossing, pedestrian overcrossings and undercrossings, 10 retaining walls, storm drain systems, sanitary sewers, highway lighting, illuminated signs, traffic signals and the usual miscellaneous items such as guard railing and fencing.

Sources for Embankment Material

Approximately four miles of the freeway roadbed is on embankment for which fill material must be hauled in. The only exception to this is the through cut between Encino Avenue

and Amestoy Avenue on the Ventura Freeway. Material to make the roadbed fills require 1,095,000 cubic yards of roadway excavation to be obtained from the through cut on the job and from stock piles within right-of-way near Haskell Avenue, resulting from prior grading operations, and from local borrow from within the Sepulveda Flood Control Basin. The balance, estimated to be 1,100,000 cubic yards, is imported borrow from a site described as the "Mulholland Borrow Pit," located within the roadway prism of the proposed San Diego Freeway, two miles southerly of this project. On this contract earth will be removed to an elevation 160 feet below existing Mulholland Drive. Future

INTERCHANGE
between
VENTURA and SAN DIEGO FREEWAYS

construction contracts will also secure imported borrow from this location until the ultimate cut of 350 feet below top of ridge elevation for the San Diego Freeway over the Santa Monica Mountains has been reached.

Close Schedule Maintained

Start of this large earthmoving operation, as well as production rate, was governed by construction of necessary frontage roads, relocation of underground and overhead utilities, installation of storm drain and sanitary sewer systems, construction of certain key structures, surcharge of bridge sites, and start of pile-driving operations. To co-ordinate and expedite this maze of work, the contractor set up a precise schedule of operations based on performing the controlling items of

UPPER—Closeup of belt loader. Note dozers feeding belt. LOWER—On San Diego Freeway looking northerly across interchange roadways. Picture taken from Camarillo Avenue.

construction with his own forces. These items included storm drain pipes and storm drain structures, portland cement concrete, curbs and gutters, earthwork, and bridges. That this close schedule has paid off is indicated by an average monthly progress pay estimate of $500,000 for the first six months. At this writing, the contract has progressed to a completion of 42 percent versus only 21 percent of time elapsed.

68

The earthwork, as indicated by figures above, is divided almost equally between roadway excavation and imported borrow. For the roadway excavation operation the contractor moved in with scrapers. This spread of equipment is moving earth at a rate of 10,000 cubic yards per day on a relatively short haul. For the imported borrow the contractor moved in 16 bottom-dump semitrailers and 16 10-wheel end-dump trucks. This latter equipment spread, more fully described below, is moving earth at a rate of about 8,000 cubic yards per day with an average three-mile haul. These two spreads operating nine hours per day have a daily combined output of between 17,500 and 19,000 cubic yards.

Advantageous Haul Road

To move imported borrow from pit to fill, the contractor could elect to haul legal loads over public thoroughfares, including the heavily congested Sepulveda Boulevard, or the contractor could construct a haul road within state-owned right-of-way for the proposed San Diego Freeway, thus eliminating conflict with public traffic and avoiding the necessity of keeping loads within legal limits. Loads are limited only by the safe load that can be carried over the existing Ventura Boulevard undercrossing constructed under another contract. This bridge structure fortunately was designed to carry safely overloads 20 percent above legal limits. The decision of the contractor to construct his own haul road has undoubtedly had considerable bearing on the favorable rate of progress. The haul road was constructed to a width of 40 feet on easy alignment, and required moving of approximately 160,000 cubic yards of excavation. The roadway splits at an advantageous point that allows a maximum 12 percent upgrade (empty) and a maximum 17 percent downgrade (loaded). As a safety feature, three escape roads were constructed to forestall disasterous results in event hauling equipment got out of control.

Route of Haul Road

The distance from the pit to the beginning of the project is two miles,

Mulholland borrow pit. Chartered bus in background carrying highway commissioners on field trip.

and there is a fall of approximately 600 feet. The haul road is carried across Sepulveda Boulevard on a 130-foot bridge (using state-loaned steel girders), spans Valley Vista Boulevard on a 70-foot bridge, and traverses an exclusive residential area as well as a business district. Dust control was impractical by means of water, due to steep grades and consequent danger to trucks. Further, local high winds and hot weather combined to cause a high rate of evaporation. After some experiments by the contractor, a practical method was found to be an application of asphaltic emulsion, mixing type, 60-70 penetration, applied by means of a water wagon at a rate of 30 gallons per 1,000 gallons of water. Frequent applications at this light rate built up a satisfactory surfacing free of dangerous slick areas. Stabilization of haul road surface has now reached a point that disking and blading is needed only at five-week intervals.

The Mulholland borrow pit for the most part is a formation of soft sandstone and shale interspersed with occasional large rocks, and it breaks up easily under the action of a rooter.

However, layers of hard sandstone, shale, and rock have been encountered that require special treatment to break up. The contractor breaks up these hard ledges with a headache ball and to date has not resorted to blasting. To cope with the variable conditions and to maintain an even production, the contractor operates two equipment spreads in the pit. The spread to handle hard material consists of 1½- and 2½-yard shovels which load 10-wheel end-dump trucks. In addition to the headache ball when necessary, a dozer with ripper is used to break up and push materials to the shovels.

Fleet of 16 Trucks

A fleet averaging 16 trucks is used on this operation. The spread to handle soft sandstone and shale consists of two dozers with rippers (one being used on both spreads, and three dozers feeding a 54-inch continuous belt loader mounted on skids for easy moving. A fleet of 16 bottom-dump semis supplemented by some of the end-dump trucks is used to haul from the belt. Some difficulty and delay were caused by large rocks getting into the hopper of the belt loader. This condition was remedied by stationing a watchman at the hopper to spot the rocks so they could be dozed aside and loaded into trucks by a standby skip loader. Also, a heavy-duty grizzly was built up and placed in front of the hopper to protect the belt. The belt loader operating under good conditions has loaded out heaped bottom-dumps (24 yards) in an average of 30 seconds.

Special Equipment

The belt loader used in the pit was put together in the contractor's yard. It is skid-mounted and is built around a 54-inch loader belt. Dirt falls through a 4x4-foot hole into the hopper, is funneled down to a 2½x4-foot gate, and onto the belt. Power is supplied by a diesel engine.

Ten of the 16-truck fleet of bottom-dumps are company-owned and were built to the contractor's specifications. They consist of a 20-cubic-yard (water level capacity) bottom-dump semitrailer and drawn by a tractor, powered by a turbocharged 250-horsepower diesel engine and dual-drive rear axles. The trailer is 36 feet long, and trailer plus tractor is 55 feet out to out. Maximum width is eight feet. These dimensions are within the California state highway legal limits. The load is carried on eight pairs of truck tires and the machines are designed for both offroad and legal highway hauling. The tractor and trailer, along with such special additions as Hydrotarders, and protector plow on front axle, weighs 31,000 pounds. The unit therefore can carry a 20-ton payload without special permit under the state highway legal load formula for dual-axled semis. The trailers have full airbrakes with hand and foot controls in the cab. The Hydrotarder is a special supplemental type of water brake which makes the unit safe for use on the relatively steep grades of the haul road. (Other rented trucks of equivalent capacities have been tried on the road, and only those equipped with water-cooled brake drums have been able to negotiate the grade safely.) Another safety feature installed by the contractor is

special cutoff valves on each axle which prevent loss of air. Should any cylinder be broken or a diaphragm blown out, the air to that wheel is automatically shut off. Although the rigs were operated at much higher speeds originally, in the interest of safety the contractor ordered a maximum speed of 35 miles per hour downgrade. On the upgrade climb, the trucks maintain a minimum speed of 25 miles per hour.

Post-tensioned Girders

Five different types of construction are to be found in the 10 major bridges on the project. These are box girder, flat slab, T-beam, structural steel, and prestressed post-tensioned. When the pedestrian overcrossing is included, a sixth type is added—poured-in-place post-tensioned slab.

Of great interest to visitors on the project has been the Balboa Boulevard Undercrossing. This structure is a reinforced concrete precast prestressed post-tensioned girder bridge consisting of one span about 119 feet in length, which makes it the longest span of this type to be constructed to date on a state highway in California. There are 18 girders, and post-tensioned operation are now underway. Girders measure 5½ feet high by 119 feet long, with two-foot bottom flange

and three-foot top flange, eight-inch-thick web and weigh approximately 62 tons.

Girders each contain 150 high-tensile-strength wires, 16 in each of nine two-inch-diameter flex tubes hung at a catenary, and six in a tenth tube near the girder top. In tensioning, a working stress of 130,000 pounds per square inch is exerted by hydraulic jacks. The PI system of post-tensioning is used.

Due to the heavy traffic on Balboa Boulevard during daylight hours, placing operations will be limited to the hours of midnight to 6 a.m. It is planned to use two heavy-duty truck cranes to set each mammoth girder in position. These girders will be placed on approximate seven-foot centers, and a six-inch slab will later be poured.

The Amestoy Pedestrian Overcrossing is also a post-tensioned structure, but differs from the Balboa structure in that it is a post-tensioned slab and will be poured in place. Post-tensioning is carried out before the removal of the falsework. The wires receive the same loading as in the girders. Strength requirements for the girders, and 4,500 pounds per square inch prior to tensioning on the girders, and 4,500 pounds per square inch for the slab.

Highway Commission inspects the Oberg Bros. contract in the San Fernando Valley for construction of portions of the Ventura Freeway and the San Diego Freeway in Sherman Oaks. From left to right are State Highway Engineer George T. McCoy; Commissioners Chester H. Warlow and James A. Guthrie; Edward T. Telford, Assistant State Highway Engineer; Frank B. Durkee, Director of Public Works; Commissioners Robert E. McClure, Fred W. Speers, and Robert L. Bishop.

UPPER—Stockpile removal and other operations in Haskell Avenue area. Haskell Avenue bridge structure on extreme left. LOWER—Looking Southerly across interchange roadway. Ventura Boulevard bridge in background.

The 480-day contract calls for completion in January, 1959. However, the contractor hopes to finish as much as six months ahead of schedule, and, if his present rate of progress is maintained, this is not impossible.

Personnel on Job

Niles Oberg is project manager for the Oberg organization, assisted by

Dick Woolard, excavation superintendent; Andy Dunlap is in charge of the pit; Bill Thomas is general carpenter superintendent, and Leonard Swanson is office manager.

In immediate charge of administering this contract for the State Division of Highways is the resident engineer and his staff of assistants. H. E. Belford is construction supervisor.

General supervision for State under Assistant State Highway Engineer E. T. Telford is carried out by District Engineer L. R. Gillis and Assistant District Engineer F. B. Cressy. On the job representing the State Bridge Department is Carl J. Verner working under general supervision of J. E. McMahon and George L. Laird of Southern Section of the Bridge Department.

STATE FAIR

Continued from page 38 . . .

unidentified food products, jotting down reactions on special forms. In the second, spectators will act as judges of home appliances which will be demonstrated continuously.

The former Foods and Hobbies Building has been redesignated as the "Merchandise Mart."

"Have Fun" Is Slogan

"Have Fun" will be this year's fair slogan, but there will be plenty of opportunity for education while enjoying oneself.

The sprawling Counties Building is an example, where each year more than 90 percent of all the fair visitors tour a fairyland of light, color, and motion, with the myriad products of the State on display.

Gold exhibits from the fabulous Mother Lode country, worth hundreds of thousands of dollars, will "educate" viewers, giving them an insight into the State's mining industries. So, too, will many other minerals shown each year, not to mention lumber, agriculture, horticulture, fisheries, natural resources, viticulture and vintage production, and the other diversified industries which are reflected in the name "The Golden State."

· Of special interest are winetasting and splendid vintage displays, all boasting of the fact California produces 85 percent of all the domestic wines in the United States.

Perhaps the greatest delight of all is the Hall of Flowers, with its breathtaking vista of waterfalls, conifers, potted plants, simulated redwood trees, blooms, outdoor gardens, limpid pools, and many arrangements. More than 1,000,000 plants and blooms are on display each year.

And over all this will reign the Maid of California, chosen each year from a bevy of beauties representing the various counties of the State.

The fairground is located virtually in the heart of Sacramento, on 207 acres reached from any part of the city within a few minutes by municipal bus or taxi. Busses operate on a special express schedule. Once inside the grounds, visitors may ride from one location to another aboard "elephant trains."

BOLD VENTURE

Continued from page 58 . . .

utilized in the construction of a second experimental section started in September of 1953 which placed 1,000,000 cubic yards of embankment over the deepest portion of underlying mud.

Mud Displacement

The cross section finally developed for the project consists of a fill 200 feet in width and 45 feet in depth which penetrates approximately 25 feet into the underlying bay mud. By carefully controlling the shape of the advancing fill, the method and rate of fill placement, and by the use of explosive charges set off deep in the mud immediately in advance of embankment, reasonably uniform mud displacement was achieved.

The total two-mile section across the open water was completed by four additional contracts, after which a seventh contract for base and surfacing was awarded. The completed embankment is still "floating" on the part of the mud not displaced by the fill.

Railroad Relocated

A further problem in the planning of this section of highway was a conflict at Sierra Point between the main line of the Southern Pacific Railroad and the proposed freeway location. The railroad was located in a tunnel through Sierra Point which was expensive to maintain and could not feasibly be widened to accommodate proposed additional tracks. The new freeway location crossed the railroad on a long skew which would have required a long, expensive overpass. The highway division's designers arrived at an ingenious solution to this problem. First, Sierra Point was excavated to the grade of the railroad and the material used to construct a portion of the open-water embankment. The railroad was then relocated in the resultant cut eliminating entirely the former tunnel and crossing the freeway at a far better angle, permitting a much less extensive overpass structure with proper provision for additional trackage. This procedure

PRESTRESSED BRIDGE

Continued from page 29 . . .

hose. Constant motion of the cement solution is accomplished by a system of bypasses to prevent it from becoming stiff, while connections are being made for the next girder.

Normal operations by the contractor's forces at the girder casting beds required a working period of the usual 40-hour week, for an average production of 12 to 14 girders per week.

When the posttensioning of the girders was completed two truck cranes were brought in and used for the erection work. These cranes moved the girders from the casting beds to the final position on the bridge piers. The average distance of this move was about 1,000 feet.

The final concrete pours to complete the prestressed bridge consisted of placing Class A concrete for pier stem connections, diaphragms and deck sections connecting the girders together, and the bridge curbs.

Due to a uniform camber of the girders of about 1½ inches, a plant-mix surfacing course was specified to provide a smooth roadway surface. Additional work under this contract consisted of metal beam bridge rail and approach, surfacing and guard rail.

This contract was under general administration of the Bridge Department of the State Division of Highways, headed by F. W. Panhorst, Assistant State Highway Engineer. Truman Hart was general superintendent for W. F. Maxwell Co. H. L. Harger was resident engineer for the Bridge Department and Thomas L. Patterson, construction representative for District VII.

greatly improved the railroad's facilities at this location and resulted in savings of at least $1,000,000 in the cost of the highway improvement.

Three additional contracts are in progress on the San Francisco Peninsula. These contracts, scheduled for completion in the summer of 1958, cover an additional eight miles of freeway construction and will extend the completed portion of the Bayshore Freeway through Palo Alto.

GOODWIN J. KNIGHT
Governor of California

CALIFORNIA HIGHWAY COMMISSION

FRANK B. DURKEE . . Director of Public Works
and Chairman
JAMES A. GUTHRIE, Vice Chairman
San Bernardino
CHESTER H. WARLOW . . . . . . Fresno
H. STEPHEN CHASE . . . . . San Francisco
ROBERT E. McCLURE . . . . Santa Monica
ROBERT L. BISHOP . . . . . . Santa Rosa
FRED W. SPEERS . . . . Escondido
C. A. MAGHETTI, Secretary . . . . Davis
T. FRED BAGSHAW . . . . . . Assistant Director
A. H. HENDERSON . . . . Deputy Director

DIVISION OF HIGHWAYS

GEO. T. McCOY
State Highway Engineer, Chief of Division
J. W. VICKREY . . . Deputy State Highway Engineer
CHAS. E. WAITE . . . Deputy State Highway Engineer
J. W. TRASK . . . Assistant State Highway Engineer
F. W. PANHORST . . Assistant State Highway Engineer
J. C. WOMACK . . . Assistant State Highway Engineer
R. H. WILSON . . . Assistant State Highway Engineer
F. N. HVEEM . . . Materials and Research Engineer
FRANK E. BAXTER . . . . . . Maintenance Engineer
J. A. LEGARRA . . . . Engineer of Design
G. M. WEBB . . . . Traffic Engineer
MILTON HARRIS . . . . . . Construction Engineer
H. B. LA FORGE . Engineer of Federal Secondary Roads
C. E. BOVEY . Engineer of City and Cooperative Projects
EARL E. SORENSON . . . . . . Equipment Engineer
H. C. McCARTY . . . . Office Engineer
J. P. MURPHY . . . . Planning Engineer
F. M. REYNOLDS . . . Planning Survey Engineer
L. L. FUNK . . . . . . Photogrammetric Engineer
SCOTT H. LATHROP . . Personnel and Public Relations
E. J. SALDINE . . . Principal Highway Engineer
E. J. L. PETERSON . . Program and Budget Engineer
A. L. ELLIOTT . . . . Bridge Engineer—Planning
I. O. JAHLSTROM . . . Bridge Engineer—Operations
R. R. ROWE . . . Bridge Engineer—Special Studies
J. E. McMAHON . . Bridge Engineer—Southern Area
L. C. HOLLISTER . . . Projects Engineer—Carquinez
E. R. HIGGINS . . . . Comptroller

Right of Way

FRANK C. BALFOUR . Chief Right of Way Agent
E. F. WAGNER . . . Deputy Chief Right of Way Agent
RUDOLPH HESS . . . . Assistant Chief
R. S. J. PIANEZZI . . . . Assistant Chief
E. M. MacDONALD . . . . Assistant Chief

District IV

B. W. BOOKER . . Assistant State Highway Engineer

District VII

E. T. TELFORD . . Assistant State Highway Engineer

District Engineers

SAM HELWER . . . . District I, Eureka
H. S. MILES . . . . District II, Redding
ALAN S. HART . . . . . . District III, Marysville
J. P. SINCLAIR . . . . . District IV, San Francisco
L. A. WEYMOUTH . . . . District IV, San Francisco
R. A. HAYLER . . . . . District IV, San Francisco

**DEPARTMENT OF
PUBLIC WORKS**

SACRAMENTO, CALIFORNIA

A. M. NASH . . . . . District V, San Luis Obispo
W. L. WELCH . . . . District VI, Fresno
GEORGE LANGSNER . . . . District VII, Los Angeles
LYMAN R. GILLIS . . . . District VII, Los Angeles
C. V. KANE . . . . . District VIII, San Bernardino
E. R. FOLEY . . . . District IX, Bishop
JOHN G. MEYER . . . . . . District X, Stockton
J. DEKEMA . . . . District XI, San Diego
HOWARD C. WOOD . . . . Bridge Engineer
State-owned Toll Bridges

**DIVISION OF CONTRACTS AND
RIGHTS OF WAY**

Legal

ROBERT E. REED . . . . . . Chief Counsel
GEORGE C. HADLEY . . . . Deputy Chief of Division
HOLLOWAY JONES . . . . Assistant Chief
HARRY S. FENTON . . . . Assistant Chief

**DIVISION OF SAN FRANCISCO BAY
TOLL CROSSINGS**

NORMAN C. RAAB . . . . Chief of Division
BEN BALALA . . . . . Principal Bridge Engineer

DIVISION OF ARCHITECTURE

ANSON BOYD . State Architect, Chief of Division
HUBERT S. HUNTER . . . Deputy Chief of Division
ROBERT W. FORMHALS
Administrative Assistant to State Architect

Administrative and Fiscal Service

EARL W. HAMPTON
Assistant State Architect, Administrative
HENRY R. CROWLE . . . . Fiscal Assistant
THOMAS MERET . . . Construction Budgets Architect

WADE O. HALSTED
Principal Estimator of Building Construction
STANTON WILLARD . . Principal Architect, Standards

Design and Planning Service

P. T. POAGE
Assistant State Architect, Design and Planning
ROBERT M. LANDRUM . Chief Architectural Coordinator
ARTHUR F. DUDMAN . Principal Architect, Sacramento
JAMES A. GILLEM . . Principal Architect, Los Angeles
CHARLES PETERSON
Principal Structural Engineer, Los Angeles
CARL A. HENDERLONG
Principal Mechanical and Electrical Engineer
CLIFFORD L. IVERSON
Chief Architectural Draftsman, Sacramento
RAYMOND CHEESMAN
Chief Architectural Draftsman, Los Angeles
GUSTAV B. VEHN
Supervising Specifications Writer, Sacramento
JOHN S. MOORE . . . Supervisor of Special Projects

Construction Service

CHARLES M. HERD . . . Chief Construction Engineer
CHARLES H. BOCKMAN
Assistant to Chief Construction Engineer

AREA CONSTRUCTION SUPERVISORS

THOMAS M. CURRAN . . . . Area I, Oakland
J. WILLIAM COOK . . . . . . Area II, Sacramento
CLARENCE T. TROOP . . . . . Area III, Los Angeles

**AREA STRUCTURAL ENGINEERS
SCHOOLHOUSE SECTION**

MANLEY W. SAHLBERG . . . Area I, San Francisco
M. E. EWING . . . . Area II, Sacramento
ERNST MAAG . . . . Area III, Los Angeles

printed in CALIFORNIA STATE PRINTING OFFICE ⬤ 98480 8-57 49,400

Action, adventure, and romance fill the pages of California's last century of history. Human initiative and ingenuity repeats itself again and again through the colorful years of rapid development, but without the great natural wealth of water, soil, forests, mines, and petroleum, the interesting history could never have been written. Plenty abounded everywhere a century ago, timber for homes and farms, gold in staggering quantities to focus worldwide attention on a then remote frontier, rich soils for productive farms and pastureland, and subsequently, oil to supply energy for mechanized development, and finally, during the most recent 40 years harnessed water and waterpower to supply cheap electrical energy and to transform vast areas of semidesert to veritable garden lands of plenty. To this wealth there was added a temperate climate, recreational opportunities, and scenic beauties of such diverse nature as to have few equals. A haven for homelovers, a mecca for tourists and for sportsmen—a green and golden California. This great natural wealth and unique land of pleasure and opportunity was recognized early. The migration west was steady from the early days of the forty-niners. Human and natural resources joined and California flourished. From a few more than 6½ million people in the late thirties, the State's population has grown to 14 million in a little more than 15 years, a phenomenal growth in a short period; a phenomenal growth in 100 years of history.

Forty-five million acres of the land area of California is the vast natural catchment basin for lifegiving rain and snow water. Forty-five million acres from which is also produced 6 billion board feet of lumber each year, that provides summer feed for more than one million head of cattle and sheep, and offers mountain recreational and sports pleasure to millions of people each year. Forty-five million acres of highly inflammable vegetation that from May to October will burn like tinder. To

protect this tremendous area of watershed, timber, and grazing land, the people of the State spend millions each year for fire protection facilities. Yet, people are the cause of nine out of 10 fires that threaten these lands, their products, and the State's very existence.

There is no state in the Union more dependent on her resources than is California. Every drop of water, stick of timber, and blade of grass is needed if we are to meet the challenge of our expanding population and economy. We cannot meet this challenge if we continue to allow the number of fires to start on our wildlands that we have experienced since the end of the war. It is false economy to spend millions on one hand to build mighty structures for water storage, transportation, and flood control and continue on the other to peril their existence and sacrifice resources to careless man-caused fires.

By F. H. RAYMOND, *State Forester*

HIGHWAYS AND PUBLIC WORKS

SEPTEMBER-OCTOBER
1957

California Highways
and Public Works

Official Journal of the Division of Highways,
Department of Public Works, State of California

KENNETH C. ADAMS, Editor

HELEN HALSTED, Assistant Editor

MERRITT R. NICKERSON, Chief Photographer

Vol. 35   September-October   Nos. 9-10

Public Works Building
Twelfth and N Streets
Sacramento

CONTENTS

COVER

Men and equipment at work. Concrete paving on Paso Robles Bypass on U. S. 101 in San Luis Obispo County. Photo by Robert Munroe, Photographic Section, Department of Public Works, M. R. Nickerson, Chief.

BACK COVER

Construction scene on new Redwood Highway in Humboldt County. Earthmovers being towed up the ramp of the "big cut." All four cables can be operated simultaneously by four separate donkey engines. Photo by Robert Munroe.

Published in the interest of highway development in California. Editors of newspapers and others are privileged to use matter contained herein. Cuts will be gladly loaned upon request.

Address communications to

CALIFORNIA HIGHWAYS AND PUBLIC WORKS
P. O. Box 1499
Sacramento, California

U.S. Highway 91

In Riverside and San Bernardino Counties

By C. V. KANE
District Engineer

Southland Freeway

AN important north-south highway extending through the Great Basin and Rocky Mountain regions of the western United States is US 91. Beginning in Long Beach, California, it can be followed all the way to the Canadian border, whence it continues through Lethbridge, Alberta, as an important connection to the Alcan Highway.

For most of its length US 91 is a part of the National System of Inter-

state and Defense Highways. Recent opening of the Riverside Freeway through the City of Riverside calls attention to the mounting pace of freeway development along this route. The accompanying maps and aerial photographs illustrate the active planning and construction program now underway on US 91 throughout Riverside and San Bernardino Counties, a distance of some 210 miles. The route for the freeway has been

adopted by the California Highway Commission for the entire length except a 31-mile section immediately east of Barstow (through Yermo).

Important Routes

US 91 carries several other important Federal and State routes over certain sections. It is State Sign Route 18 in the section from the Orange county line to San Bernardino. From Riverside to a point north of Cajon

LEFT—Grading under way at south end of Fredericksen & Kasler contract. Bridge piers under construction for the first crossing of Stoddard-Wells Road, a county road. CENTER—North end of completed Victorville bypass showing construction under way by Gordon H. Ball, contractor on Victorville Overhead and Mojave River Bridge. RIGHT—Closer view of construction at Victorville Overhead and Mojave River Bridge. First crossing of Stoddard-Wells Road in right background.

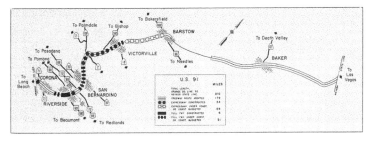

Aerial Photos Tell Picture Story of U.S. 91 Freeway Progress

PHOTO No. 1—Looking north along route of the third unit of Riverside Freeway, which soon will be under construction. Freeway will lie to the left of Indiana Avenue, where housemoving operations can be seen underway. Jackson Street crosses through the center of the picture. This third unit will extend from Polk Avenue to the end of the second unit at Arlington Avenue, which can be seen in the background. PHOTO No. 2—Looking north from the south end of the second unit of the Riverside Freeway, which is now under construction by Griffith Company. Arlington Avenue Undercrossing and interchange ramps are in the foreground; Pachappa Hill is in the left center. This $2,000,000 contract extends from Arlington Avenue to 14th Street, with estimated completion in September, 1957. PHOTO No. 3—Looking north from the Ivy Street Overcrossing, showing construction underway through the City of Riverside. Pachappa Underpass of the Union Pacific Railroad is in the center.

PHOTO No. 4—Looking north along the Riverside Freeway, showing Cridge Street Overcrossing in the foreground, and 14th Street Overcrossing in the center. The first unit of the Riverside Freeway is under contract with Griffith Company, and extends from 14th Street to Russell Street in the background. PHOTO No. 5—Looking north along the Riverside Freeway from above Eighth Street. The existing expressway along La Cadena Drive shows at top of photo, and the Third Street Undercrossing near the center. This unit, a $1,900,000 contract, is estimated to be completed in July, 1957. PHOTO No. 6—Future extension of the Riverside Freeway is indicated by the line running northeast from a point north of the present junction of Iowa Avenue and La Cadena Drive at lower edge of photo. Barton Road, a major county highway, extends across through the Grand Terrace area at the top of the picture.

2

PHOTO No. 7—Looking east toward the Grand Terrace area. The north end of the future Riverside Freeway shows in the fill construction near the grain bins at the extreme left center of the picture. A future freeway contract for which plans are now in the design stage will traverse the farmland east of the Santa Ana River in the foreground. PHOTO No. 8—Looking north along the San Bernardino Freeway from a point above the Colton Avenue interchange. The Mill Street Undercrossing and the Lytle Creek Bridge are under construction in the center of the picture. I Street lies parallel to and just west of the freeway. The portion from Mill Street to Sixth Street in San Bernardino is now under construction by E. L. Yeager Company, the completion estimated in January, 1958. PHOTO No. 9—Looking north along the San Bernardino Freeway from above Rialto Avenue. The Santa Fe railroad yards and the Fifth Street Viaduct show in the center of the photo. Construction of the northbound freeway lanes across Fifth Street (US 66 Business) required the closing of Fifth Street for approximately six months. This structure was completed and Fifth Street reopened to traffic on June 15, 1957. Future extension of the freeway to the north, with two contracts expected to be advertised for bids this summer, is indicated by the line on the photo.

PHOTO No. 10—This is a photo looking southward along the San Bernardino Freeway from a point above Fifth Street. The large fills under construction for the US 70-99-91-395 interchange are visible in the far background. PHOTO No. 11—A view looking north along I Street from above Fifth Street, showing right-of-way clearance operations underway immediately east of I Street. PHOTO No. 12—Looking east along Highland Avenue, State Sign Route 30. The large graded area in the lower left will be the location of additional interchange ramps to be constructed in conjunction with the US 91 freeway project.

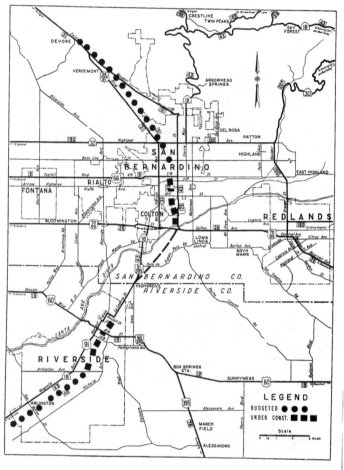

PHOTO No. 13—Construction now underway by Charles McCloskey and Crowell and Larson includes the junction of the Riverside Freeway and the San Bernardino Freeway. Embankments being built in the foreground of the photo will be the northerly terminus of the Riverside Freeway. The San Bernardino Freeway enters the interchange area on the left side of the photo, and turns northward to enter the City of San Bernardino in the background. Bridge construction in the center of the photo spans the Santa Ana River. This $3,300,000 contract is expected to be completed in February, 1958. The present US 99 crosses from west to east in the middle of the photo.

PHOTO No. 14—Looking northwest toward the entrance to Cajon Pass. The street in the left foreground is I Street, recently adopted as a State highway between the freeway and Highland Avenue, which crosses through the center of the photo. Highland Avenue is State Sign Route 30, and the separation structure carrying it over the railroad and the freeway, completed last year, can be seen on the left. PHOTO No. 15—Looking northwest from the Highland Avenue Separation along the route of the third and fourth units of this freeway, which will be advertised for construction in the near future. Existing US 66-91-395 along left side of picture.

and Public Works   5

LEFT—Looking south along recently completed Riverside Freeway from above Third Street. Seventh Street and Eighth Street crossing near middle of photo.
RIGHT—Looking north along Riverside Freeway through center of Riverside. Fourteenth Street Overcrossing in middle of photo.

Pass it is also designated US 395. And from San Bernardino to Barstow it carries the additional traffic of US 66.

Between the Orange county line and Corona, the freeway route has been established since 1949. Design work is now under way on plans to convert the existing grade intersections of the expressway to full freeway standards with grade separations and interchange ramps.

Through Corona and the territory between Corona and Riverside, the freeway route was adopted on June 30, 1956, by the California Highway Commission, following a public meeting held by the Division of Highways in Corona in March, 1956. Design work on plans for this construction is well advanced and some right of way has been acquired.

Two Units in Riverside

As mentioned above, two units in the City of Riverside, totaling 4.7 miles in length, were opened to traffic on September 20, 1957. Total cost of these units was approximately $8,300,-000, $4,500,000 for rights of way and $3,800,000 for construction.

A third unit, extending 3.7 miles southwesterly from Arlington Avenue is included in the current fiscal year budget for construction. Bids will be opened in Los Angeles on November 7, 1957.

North end of recently completed Griffith Company contract in Riverside showing Spruce Street Overcrossing in center and La Cadena Expressway in background.

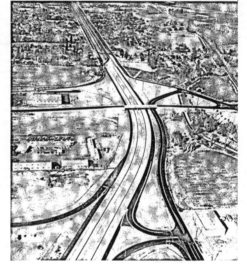

Construction is under way on two units, totaling 3.5 miles in length, in the San Bernardino area. Here US 91 is on the San Bernardino Freeway, and becomes a part of the Federal Interstate and Defense Highway System. Bids for a unit of US 91 from 27th Street in San Bernardino to Devore in Cajon Pass will be opened in October, and another unit, from Sixth Street to 27th Street, is included in the current year construction budget. These two sections total 11.6 miles in length.

Between the Riverside and San Bernardino sections of the Riverside Freeway lie two miles of La Cadena Avenue expressway, which will be converted to full freeway standards, and four miles where the freeway will be on new location. Design work is well advanced on both these portions and right of way is being purchased.

Freeway to Victorville

North of Devore, US 91 passes over Cajon Pass and on to Victorville as an existing four-lane divided expressway, constructed under contracts in 1954 and 1955. This 30-mile section will be converted to full freeway standards in the future, in accordance with requirements of the Interstate and Defense Highway System.

The first unit of the 'Victorville Bypass" was completed in 1956 as a combination expressway and full freeway. This means intersections at grade for the minor cross streets but separation structures at the major roads. The second unit, a $1,800,000 project, including overhead crossing of the Union Pacific and Santa Fe Railroads and the Mojave River Bridge is now under construction and about 80 percent complete.

Project Through Barstow

From Victorville to Barstow, Fredericksen and Kasler, Contractors, have recently started construction of 29 miles of US 91 on new location. This project is scheduled for completion in May, 1959, and should eliminate one of the most aggravating and hazardous stretches.

Through the City of Barstow, US 91 will be constructed as a full free-

way on new location. The route was adopted by the Highway Commission in October, 1955, following a public meeting by the Division of Highways in August. Plans for this work are well advanced in the design stage.

As mentioned before, the freeway route has not yet been adopted between Barstow and Field, a distance of about 31 miles, including the portion through Yermo. Preliminary studies by the Division of Highways are under way for this section and a public meeting in Yermo will be scheduled in the near future to present and discuss the results of these studies.

North of Field the freeway route was established by the Highway Commission in August, 1957, after a public meeting in Baker in April. This route adoption covered approximately 83 miles, terminating at the Nevada state line. Design work and prepartion of construction plans for all units of this section are now in progress.

THE DIVISION THANKS YOU

J. T. McCLELLAN
Real Estate

SAN FRANCISCO 2, CALIFORNIA

Division of Highways
Sacramento, California

GENTLEMEN: This letter is addressed to everyone in the Division of Highways. I want to say "thank you" to all of the personnel of this department. This is because you have given me the pleasure of riding on the new part of the highway from San Francisco to South San Francisco.

I join you in feeling proud of what you have done. For the money spent, you have all done a very fine job. Many thanks from a taxpayer and rider.

Yours very truly,

J. T. McCLELLAN

DRIVERS' LICENSES

A total of 7,036,566 California drivers' licenses were outstanding as of June 30, 1957, reports the National Automobile Club. Of this total, 6,659,-661 were operators' licenses and 376,-905 were chauffeurs' licenses.

Richard Winn Named Editor of Magazine

With the November-December issue, *California Highways and Public Works* will have a new editor. Richard Winn, former California newspaperman and retired Navy public information officer, succeeds Kenneth C. Adams, information officer of the Department of Public Works and magazine editor, who reached the mandatory retirement age of 70 on October 6, 1957, after more than 50 years of newspaper and public relations work in this Country and abroad, 22 years of which have been in state service.

Winn has been a Californian since 1910. He was appointed to his new post by the Director of Public Works following a civil service examination.

After he was graduated from the University of California in 1929, he went to work as a reporter on the Oakland Tribune. Winn remained at the Tribune until a few months before World War II started, when he went on active duty as a naval reserve officer. He served afloat in the Pacific during all of the war years, except for six months' study at the Naval War College.

Winn's navy duty since mid-1946 has been in public information. He was in charge of the news section and, earlier, the motion picture section of the Navy's Office of Public Information in Washington. He also headed the newsreel section of the Department of Defense Office of Public Information in Washington.

Toward the end of the Korean War, Winn was assigned to the staff of Commander Naval Forces, Far East, with headquarters in Japan. He headed public information for that command for a year. He served during another of his duty periods as public information officer for the Commandant, Sixth Naval District, at Charleston, South Carolina.

Winn returned to California after his retirement from active navy duty in January, 1957, as a Commander. He and his wife have established their home in Sacramento.

The retiring editor of *California Highways and Public Works* takes this opportunity to thank the many thousands of readers of the magazine for the kindly and complimentary letters they have sent in over the years.—K. C. A.

CALIFORNIA'S PEAKS

California has 171 peaks that exceed 8,000 feet.

Case History

High Capacity Through
Medians and Signals

By A. L. HIMELHOCH, Assistant District Engineer

INTRODUCTION

THE rapid industrial growth around the Los Angeles International Airport is generating an increasing amount of commuter traffic to and from the area. Streets and highways feeding the area are, therefore, becoming more and more congested. Leading south from the airport is only one major through highway, US 101 Alternate. As a result, extremely heavy peak traffic volumes have developed on this route. Congestion and delay increased to a point where some type of improvement was essential. The highway was a four-lane, undivided road, with considerable roadside business throughout. The expense of additional right-of-way for widening was not considered economically feasible, particularly in view of ultimate freeway development in three or four years.

The plan, therefore, was for improvement within existing curbs. The improvement consisted of:

1. The installation of additional traffic signal controls to allow cross traffic through the barrier created by heavy traffic flow on US 101A.

2. The conversion of existing traffic signals to three-way operation because of very heavy left-turn volumes.

3. The supervision of all traffic signals within this system by a traffic-controlled variable cycle and preferential master electronic computer to provide maximum traffic-handling ability, automatically adapting to favor the heavier direction.

4. The construction of a curbed median divider throughout the system providing left-turn lanes to reduce accidents and to allow smooth and efficient traffic flow.

The project was completed this year at a cost of $185,400. After testing and adjustments, the results of the observation of operation and traffic-handling ability were outstanding. With hourly volumes up to 1,500 vehicles per lane and 780 left turns, the system

proves that traffic engineering can alleviate many surface street congestion problems heretofore thought insolvable.

THE morning and evening rush-hour traffic congestion on our highways is a constant and ever-increasing problem in metropolitan areas throughout the Country. Mr. John Q. Public is constantly applying pressure on the traffic engineer to eliminate "bottlenecks" and congestion on the route. He is always in a rush to get to work and in a bigger rush to get home. Delays are aggravating. He is a member of a large group of commuters comprising nearly 50 percent of the total traffic using many metropolitan area highways on any working day. In driving with the peak traffic or on the crest of the wave, he receives the impression that the congestion period is nearly endless, when actually at any given point on his route it will last only for about an hour, morning and evening.

This of course, is the hour of congestion that we would all like to see eliminated.

In the Greater Los Angeles metropolitan area there are many arterial highways leading to and from commercial and industrial areas that are becoming increasingly congested during the morning and evening peak "rush hours." Freeways are being built as rapidly as possible to alleviate these congested surface streets. However, many existing highways require immediate improvement because of very rapid increase in traffic volumes and congestion.

Industrial Development

The southwestern section of the Los Angeles metropolitan area has grown and developed in the past few years at a rate exceeded only by very few areas in the Country. This has been

mainly due to an aircraft industrial development, growing around Los Angeles International Airport. Two of the many plants in the area presently employ about 45,000 people. In addition, an estimated 35,000 passengers per day will use the expanded airport facilities in the near future. Many other plants in the immediate area employ thousands more. As a result, highways leading to and from the area are presently heavily overloaded during the peak "rush hours."

U. S. Sign Route 101 Alternate, Sepulveda Boulevard, is the only major highway leading from the airport area to the beaches and coastal areas to the south (Figure 1). This route is the major north-south coastal highway along the Pacific Coast, serving coastwise through traffic. In addition, State Sign Route 7 merges into US 101 Alternate at the airport, feeding traffic from the San Fernando Valley and western sections of Los Angeles.

The peak load of relatively local commuter traffic is therefore superimposed onto the normal through coastwise commercial and recreational traffic, creating an extremely heavy and prolonged traffic "rush hour."

Cross-traffic Barrier

As there are no through parallel north-south routes close enough to be used as alternate routes, this heavy stream of traffic flows south on Sepulveda Boulevard through the residential beach city of Manhattan Beach. This resulted in extreme congestion along the route and, in addition, a barrier to the local beach area cross traffic that was nearly impassable. As the freeway planned to relieve this route will not be completed for several years, an immediate improvement in the area was indicated.

The real problem existed on Sepulveda Boulevard between Rosecrans Avenue on the north to Gould Lane

8

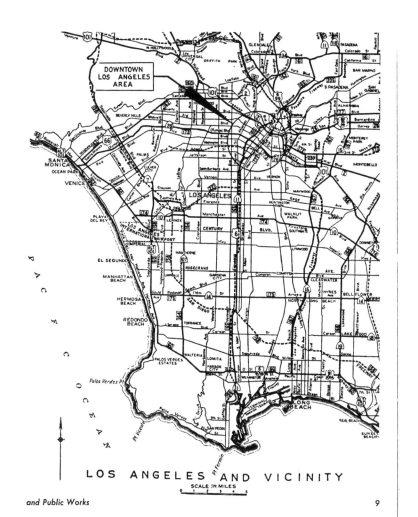

LOS ANGELES AND VICINITY

SCALE IN MILES

on the south—a distance of two miles. The highway within these limits was undivided, striped for four lanes, 76 feet wide curb to curb, of adequate structural section, and with relatively straight alignment. Vertical alignment introduced an extra problem, since most of the major cross streets intersected at the summits of the hills. Typical conditions are illustrated in *Figure 2*. There is considerable roadside business with unrestricted parking. Developed areas east and west of the highway are residential. It was not considered economically feasible to purchase additional right-of-way or to widen the roadway because of high business property costs and, particularly, in view of near future freeway development. The improvement, therefore, had to take place within existing curbs.

In order to proceed logically with an improvement plan for the highway, a complete study and analysis of the conditions before improvement were necessary.

Heavy Turning Movements

First, as previously mentioned, Sepulveda Boulevard traffic was a barrier to local vehicle and pedestrian cross traffic. Second, because of the relatively few major through cross streets in this area, there existed a considerable volume of cross traffic and heavy turning movements at these major intersections. The intersections of Sepulveda Boulevard with the four major cross streets—Rosecrans Avenue, Marine Avenue, Manhattan Beach Boulevard, and Gould Lane *(Figure 3)* were controlled by existing two-phase, full-traffic-actuated, volume-density type traffic signals. This equipment provided the highest available type of isolated intersection two-phase control. These signalized intersections were all one-half mile or more apart, and, of course, were not co-ordinated to provide any progressive or platooned traffic flow. However, due to heavy left-turn traffic, the efficiency of the traffic-handling ability of these two-phase controls was poor.

Third, the accident records revealed a high rate of accidents with a predominance of the left-turn type at the major intersections, but showing also

Looking north on Sepulveda Boulevard (U. S. 101 Alternate), showing conditions before improvement. Marine Avenue at summit in background.

an abnormal number of head-on and rear-end types. At the minor intersections accidents were equally divided between intersecting, rear-end and turning types. The three-year study gave a total of 233 reported accidents—101 night and 132 day.

Fourth, the traffic flow pattern shown in *Figures 4 and 5* is highly directional, being extremely heavy northbound in the morning with relatively few left turns, while in the evening the major movement is southbound with heavy left-turn traffic.

This pattern is generally the same at all four of the major intersections.

Several Solutions Possible

An analysis of the above conditions led to consideration of a number of possible improvement solutions or plans.

1. To relieve the barrier problem, it would be necessary to provide gaps in the traffic flow along Sepulveda Boulevard by co-ordination of the existing traffic signals. These gaps in traffic would allow pedestrians and ve-

PROJECT LOCATION MAP

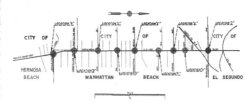

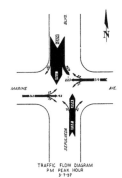

TRAFFIC FLOW DIAGRAM
PM PEAK HOUR
3-7-57

accident types between and at the
minor cross streets.

Two Wide Roadways

With a continuous divider, the 76-
foot roadway could be developed to
provide two 31-foot roadways each
consisting of two 11-foot lanes and
9 feet for parking, separated by a 14-
foot curbed median. The median furnishes area for a 10-foot left-turn lane
of varying length depending upon
left-turn volumes.

The peak-hour traffic flow diagrams
not only show the need for some type
of left-turn phasing at the major intersections, but also show that the Sepulveda Boulevard traffic volume will require a relatively high percentage of
the available green time. This means
that long signal cycles will be needed
during the peak hours, but shorter
cycles will be sufficient during off-
peak periods. Ideally, the cycles and
resultant green times should match as
nearly as possible the traffic volume
demand. The equipment selected was,
therefore, a master traffic computer to
detect the traffic volume on Sepulveda
Boulevard and select the proper background cycle.

In addition, the flow diagrams show
a definite directional flow, extremely
heavy northbound in the morning and
southbound in the evening. It was
necessary then to provide for direc-

tional detection and analysis. To adjust for the directional characteristic
of the traffic, a second master traffic
computer was selected. The cycle
length for the system could then be
determined by the computer detecting the heavier directional flow. A difference in directional flow could also
be detected and preference given to
the direction of heavier flow.

Continuous Supervision

The system thus developed may be
called a co-ordinated variable cycle,
preferential traffic-controlled traffic
signal system. This provides continuous automatic supervision of the nine
signalized intersections controlled by
the vehicular traffic flowing on the
highway.

The local intersection signal control
selected was of the semi-traffic-actuated type, allowing side street green
only on pedestrian and vehicular demand. This provides the maximum
amount of green for Sepulveda Boulevard. The five minor intersections are
two-phase and, as previously mentioned, the four major intersections required an additional phase for the left-
turn movement.

The usual type of phasing used
when the left turn is given separate
phasing might be A phase for the
through movement on the main artery, B phase for both left-turn lanes,
and C phase for the cross street movement. Inspection of the typical flow
diagrams will show that, due to a
fairly well-balanced opposing left-turn
volume during the morning peak hour,
this type of phasing would be satisfactory. However, the evening peak-
hour flow diagram will show extremely unbalanced opposing left-turn
volumes which would result in very
poor operating efficiency were this
type of phasing to be used. Therefore
the more standard phasing was abandoned. It was noted that all four of
the major intersections show similar
traffic patterns. Furthermore, the pattern should remain fairly constant in
the future because of the topography.
The narrow strip of developed land
between Sepulveda Boulevard and the
Pacific Ocean is principally residential and incapable of generating a
large traffic volume.

11

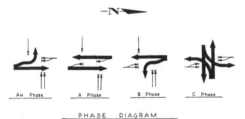

| AM Phase | A Phase | B Phase | C Phase |

PHASE DIAGRAM

Phase diagram showing four-movement type of control

Convenient Pattern

The phasing shown in *Figure 6* was therefore developed. It provides an overlapping green for the heavy southbound evening through movement during the heavy B phase left-turn movement. This is a very convenient traffic pattern in that the maximum amount of green time is utilized. During the morning peak hours, B phase traffic is light and southbound traffic is also light, so the additional green provided by the overlap was not needed. As B phase green time will be short due to light traffic demand, unused available green will be automatically added to the unactuated A phase green time. This additional green for A phase is greedily used up by the morning heavy northbound through traffic.

It may be noted that the phase diagram actually shows four movements. With the A, B, and C phasing as shown, something had to be done about the northbound to west left-turn movement. Although it is a consistently light movement, a protected left-turn phase was considered necessary because of the extremely heavy opposing southbound through movement in the afternoon peak period. An auxiliary minor movement controller was selected to provide an extendible and separately actuated phase, time for which is taken out of the beginning of the parent controller A phase green time. This phase is called the A minor phase, and, as shown on the phase diagram, merely holds up the southbound through movement until the northbound left-turn traffic clears.

Cost Total $185,400

The highway development and signalization discussed above were considered to be the most feasible improvement combination that would provide the traffic-handling efficiency desired. Plans and specifications for the improvement were then completed and the project advertised. The contract was awarded on August 8, 1956, and construction completed and accepted on January 24, 1957, at a cost of $185,400. *Figures 7, 8, 9, and 10* are views showing the completed improvement.

Following the completion of the system, the Division of Highways conducted a period of testing and adjustment to provide maximum operating efficiency. Seven pen graphic recorders were installed to provide a continuous record of the operatoin, both for the southbound traffic and for the northbound traffic. *Figure 11* shows a graphical record of a typical day's operation, showing (1) the volume at any time on a per-hour, per-lane basis; (2) the cycle length being used at any time; (3) offsets in use, northbound, southbound preferential offsets, or average offsets. It may be noted that the chart is calibrated in percent on the volume scale and that cycle lines are labeled A, B, C, D, E, and F. On the volume scale 100 percent represents 1,000 vehicles per hour per lane. The lettered cycles have equivalent times as follows:

Cycle A—Free running or non-
    co-ordinated
Cycle B— 60 seconds
Cycle C— 65 seconds
Cycle D— 80 seconds
Cycle E—100 seconds
Cycle F—120 seconds

LEFT—Looking south on Sepulveda Boulevard from Manhattan Beach Boulevard, showing conditions of roadway after completed improvement. Note sampling detectors in right foreground. RIGHT—Looking south from Manhattan Beach Boulevard, showing vehicles moving during A minor phase.

LEFT—Looking north from Manhattan Beach Boulevard, showing 12-inch left-turn green arrow during A minor phase. RIGHT—Looking north on Sepulveda Boulevard from Gould Lane showing 780 vehicles per hour left-turn movement.

Smooth Operation

A comparison of the volume curve with the cycle lines will show that very light traffic will require cycle A or non-co-ordinated operation. With semi-traffic-actuated intersection controllers, a progressive band is non-existent during very light traffic conditions such that co-ordination is not necessary. Waiting time is reduced considerably. Cycle F will be required during the peak traffic load, with cycles B, C, D, and E used for traffic volumes between the heaviest and the lightest. The traffic volumes requiring the various cycles may also be taken from the curves. The volume to select a particular cycle is adjustable. That is, by adjustment of controls on the master supervisory equipment, any particular amount or volume of traffic detected may be chosen to select a particular cycle. Considerable refinement in these adjustments was necessary in order to provide smooth operation.

The offset timing for the various intersections also required some refined adjustment. The southbound preferential offsets for the two-phase controllers were set later than normal in relation to the three-phase intersections to allow the B phase overlap portion of a platoon to flow through the system. Normally the bottom of the through traffic band is determined by the beginning of B phase. However, in this particular system southbound, the bottom of this band is the end of B phase at the three-phase in-

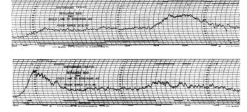

Graph showing typical day's operation of the variable cycle system. The 100 on the chart represents 1,000 vehicles per hour per lane. Horizontal heavy lines show cycle in use, except Cycle A, which indicates desire for preferential offset.

tersections, which means that the two-phase intersection offsets are additionally offset by the amount of B phase green time used at the three-phase intersections. The northbound preferential offset relationships were normal, as the bottom of the northbound band is the beginning of B phase at the three-phase intersections.

An analysis of before and after operation indicates the traffic-handling ability of the system has exceeded all estimates. Traffic counts taken before and after have indicated an average total intersection peak-hour increase of about 15 percent. The south-to-east evening peak-hour turning movement at all major intersections has increased approximately 100 percent. The following are outstanding before and after peak-hour comparisons:

	Before	After	Percent Increase
Northbound through movement:			
Morning parking hour at Rosecrans	2,900	3,250	12
Morning parking hour at Gould Lane	1,300	1,500	15
Southbound left-turn movement:			
Afternoon parking hour at Marine	200	436	118
Afternoon parking hour at Gould Lane	390	780	100
Eastbound through movement:			
Morning parking hour at Gould Lane	169	448	265

No Left Turn Accidents

Although the five months since the improvement was completed is a relatively short period for before and after comparison of accident data, the following tabulation indicates a definite decrease in accident severity with-

... Continued on page 64

and Public Works 13

OPERATIONS AND ACTIVITIES OF MATERIALS AND RESEARCH DEPARTMENT

PART III—TECHNICAL SECTION

By BAILEY TREMPER
Supervising Materials and Research Engineer

This is the third of a series presenting the operations and activities of the Materials and Research Department. This article describes the functions of the Technical Section, one of the five major subdivisions of the department. The "Technical" Section is neither more nor less technical than the other sections—the term was adopted because of the various and dissimilar activities grouped in this unit.

The Technical Section performs a variety of tests that cannot be made economically in branch or district laboratories. These tests require costly equipment and highly specialized personnel, and the amount of work for a given district would not justify the equipment and specialists.

The Technical Section is composed of four units or subsections. They are designated as the portland cement, portland cement concrete, chemical, and the research correlation units.

PORTLAND CEMENT UNIT

The portland cement unit, under the direction of W. E. Haskell, Associate Materials and Research Engineer, regularly makes routine physical tests of samples representing approximately 8,000,000 sacks of portland cement per years. The tests are made upon samples that are selected from each shipment of cement received on the work. This amount of cement means an annual investment of over $47,000,000 in concrete for pavements and structures.

In a year's time, about 2,000 physical tests are made on routine samples of portland cement. There are 13 portland cement manufacturing plants in California that furnish cement for highway use. As the acceptance or rejection of materials is based on tests, it is obvious that the cement companies should be greatly concerned with the accuracy and precision of the tests conducted by the laboratory of the

Materials and Research Department as well as those performed in their control work. This department has promoted co-operative tests between the cement manufacturers and the division, and as a result it is rare that there is any serious disagreement between the cement companies and the division with respect to the results obtained by their respective laboratories. Present specifications of the Division of Highways are more restrictive than those of many organizations, but they result in better and more uniform cement than was obtained formerly under less restrictive specifications.

The cement unit also handles routine tests on concrete and tests over 6,000 job-made concrete cylinders per year. These represent the concrete as it is mixed for use in structures in all parts of the State. Tests are made for unit weight and compressive strength. Recently concrete cylinders originating in Southern California are being tested in the Los Angeles branch laboratory saving time and expense of shipment.

Important Routine Work

Other routine work, minor in quantity but important in its significance, consists of tests of concrete curing compounds for compliance with specifications and of concrete sands for the development of strength in portland cement mortar.

In addition to routine testing, a substantial part of the cement unit is given over to research and investigation. In common with the other sections of the Materials and Research Department, its research activities have in several instances been accorded international recognition in the scientific and engineering literature, and have earned awards of medals and citations of merit from learned societies and technical organizations.

Reducing Volume Change

Much of the research work of the cement unit is now directed toward means of reducing the volume change of concrete during wetting and drying. Volume change is responsible for much of the cracking and deterioration that occasionally take place with age. Any means of reducing volume change without sacrifice of strength and durability is of distinct benefit. One line of attack lies in improving the properties of portland cement by better regulation of the gypsum content. Portland cement is manufactured by first mixing limestone and clay, then heating until the carefully proportioned mixture fuses to form a clinker. Gypsum, a naturally occurring mineral, is added to the clinker before it is ground into portland cement. The proportion can be varied at will, but the optimum amount varies with the particular cement, and at present can be determined only by tests of long duration. The cement unit is now working on a short-time test that can be applied both by the manufacturer and the user to determine whether gypsum is present in the most favorable percentage. An illustration of the effect of the gypsum content of a particular cement on volume change, expansion and contraction, during wetting and drying, is shown in *Figure 3*.

Laboratory

Another line of attack lies in the sands, gravel or crushed stone used in making concrete. The laboratory has established that claylike particles in sand and gravel can cause high volume change. It has found that the percentage of clay that must be removed by washing during manufacture can be controlled within satisfactory limits by means of the sand equivalent test and the cleanness test (formerly called the sedimentation test). By applica-

tion of these tests, concrete sands and coarse aggregate can be obtained that are truly clean and free from deleterious amounts of clay.

The cement unit participates regularly in the work of committees of the

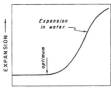

Minimum volume change in concrete is obtained when gypsum is present in portland cement in the optimum amount

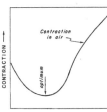

American Society for Testing Materials in "round-robin" tests designed to improve the specifications and methods of test for portland cement on a nationwide basis.

Another project now under way in the cement unit is directed toward the development of means for testing and specifying against unfavorable shapes in aggregates for concrete. Flaky and elongated particles tend toward poor workability and excessive water requirements in mixing concrete. While such particles have long been considered objectionable, there has been no definite test procedure to differentiate exactly between satisfactory and unsatisfactory particle shape. Correction of these defects is believed to be possible through improved methods of crushing during the manufacture of aggregates.

Because of the wide variety of natural materials and differences in cement, one of the characteristics of cement and concrete research is that a large number of tests must be made. In one research program conducted some years ago, the cement unit had at one time over 7,000 individual test specimens on which physical tests were being performed at periodic intervals. In some cases, from 100 to 200 or more of these specimens would be tested per day. The final results of this particular program demonstrated that alkalies in portland cement react

with certain minerals present in some aggregates to cause excessive expansion. The results have affected cement and concrete technology all over the world, and have resulted in important savings and increased durability in the highways and bridges in California, and in concrete in general in other states and countries. The work of the cement unit is confined almost entirely to laboratory activities with occasional visits to cement mills.

The core drill is used to study pavement performance

The concrete unit is under the direct supervision of D. L. Spellman, Associate Materials and Research Engineer. Its primary purpose is to help produce high-quality concrete on the jobsite in highway construction.

The work of this unit is applied both in the field and the laboratory. In the field, assistance is given to the districts and the Bridge Department during construction. Much of the field work is devoted to investigations of completed work at various ages. Cores of pavements of any type are secured with diamond bits. The cored samples are delivered to the proper laboratory section for testing. Beneath the pavement, boring is often continued to obtain samples of underlying layers to the desired depth. At times diamond-cut cores are obtained from bridges and other structures.

SMOOTH PAVEMENT

ROUGH PAVEMENT

Profilograms show riding qualities of pavement

Use of Soniscope

A measure of the overall quality of concrete in place is obtained with a soniscope. This instrument measures to a small fraction of a second the time required for an induced mechanical wave to pass through a section of concrete. The wave travels at very high speeds through dense, high-strength concrete; it travels more slowly through softer, weaker materials. The velocity of the wave is therefore an indication of the quality of the concrete as it exists at the time of measurement. It is useful in evaluating visible or hidden defects.

Surface Irregularities

Crews from the concrete section study the development of surface irregularities in pavements by use of an instrument known as the profilograph. This device plots a curve showing departures from a true plane that is established between a series of integrating wheels 25 feet apart. One type of profilograph is operated manually and may be used on new work to detect irregularities due to construction methods. Being light in weight and portable it can be used to check the previous day's work and to point to defects that can be corrected as the work progresses. Another type of profilograph is mounted on a truck. The record produced is virtually identical with that of the manual model. The advantage of the truck model lies in the better protection to the operator when working on heavily traveled roads and the speed with which records may be obtained. Not only do the profilograph records provide an index to riding comfort, but they also furnish information as to changes that may be occurring and thus indicate the adequacy of the components of the pavement. In order to find out whether bases and foundation soils are affecting the pavement, it is necessary to study the shape as well as the magnitude of pavement inequalities. *Figure 5* illustrates differences in profilograms of smooth and rough pavements. It is axiomatic that before an engineer can correct a defect he must know what he is trying to correct.

Reflective Markers

The concrete unit has co-operated with the chemical unit in the development of reflective markers for pavements and bridges. These markers are intended to improve the visibility of the highway and are particularly effective during rainy or foggy nights when the painted center stripe is obscured by a film of water.

The construction of portland cement concrete pavements and bridges over the high Sierras introduces problems in durability under freezing and thawing conditions that are not encountered in the lower elevations of the State. The factors affecting durability of concrete under severe climatic conditions are not perfectly understood, although much work has been done by other agencies. Basic data needed to plan and interpret laboratory tests are being obtained from test slabs located at strategic locations in the mountains along Route 40. Regular tests are being made for movement of moisture and frost during the winter months. Laboratory tests are then modified in accordance with field information to yield results that will be in accordance with the conditions to be met in the actual pavements. A very serious problem exists. If the State uses local sand and gravel that will give trouble, it means jeopardizing a large investment in concrete; if sound materials are imported, it means a great increase in construction costs. It is essential that exact information be available.

Durability Tests

One type of equipment being used in the laboratory to investigate the durability of concrete is illustrated in *Figure 6*. In this apparatus, 36 concrete test specimens are subjected to six cycles of freezing and thawing per day. The entire operation is controlled automatically and requires a minimum of personal attention. In a few months the concrete can be made to undergo as many cycles as will occur in several years on the road.

Another type of test for frost resistance of concrete, suggested by T. C. Powers of the Portland Cement Association, consists in measuring the change in length of a specimen as its temperature is reduced slowly to well below freezing. As illustrated in *Figure 7*, a gauge is attached to a specimen which is then placed in a freezing chamber. An automatic recorder prints changes in length of the specimen within an accuracy of a few millionths of an inch. At the same time the falling temperature of the concrete is recorded on another instrument. The results of the records are plotted in graph form as shown in *Figure 8* to indicate the rate at which the concrete becomes shorter as its temperature falls. If the charted line is substantially straight it indicates that the concrete has contracted normally in accordance with its thermal coefficient and therefore has remained undamaged. However, a pronounced offset (to the right) in the plotted line at a temperature slightly below the freezing point indicates that the concrete has expanded because of the pressure

16

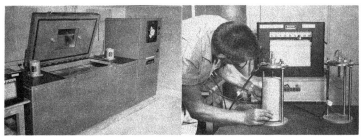

exerted by ice forming in the pores. The broken line of *Figure 8* illustrates such a situation and is a certain indication that the concrete in the condition in which it was tested is not durable under freezing and thawing conditions. In the case illustrated, the concrete was thoroughly saturated with water at the start of the test. Had it been partially dry, it is possible that it would not have suffered damage during the freezing.

Durability of concrete is determined by the sand, gravel or rock used in it more than by the cement which can be made frost resistant by the addition of certain compounds known as air-entraining agents.

The problem is to find the probable moisture content to be expected in the concrete during the winter and then to select sand, gravel or rock that will make concrete that is resistant under the moisture and temperature conditions that are characteristic of the locality under consideration.

CHEMICAL UNIT

All work of the Materials and Research Department involving chemical analysis of materials is referred to the chemical unit, which is under the direction of E. D. Botts, Senior Chemical Testing Engineer. Chemical analyses are made on a multitude of materials, as might be expected from the variety of products used by the Division of Highways. Some of the products or materials analyzed are engine antifreeze, hydraulic brake fluid,

portland cement, wood preservatives, detergents, fuel oils, diesel oils, metals, galvanized coatings, paints, waters and soils. Since standard methods of analysis, as specified by the various technical societies, frequently are inadequate when special problems are encountered, it is often necessary to develop new methods and techniques.

The reasons for making chemical analyses of materials of construction, are twofold:

1. To detect wilful adulteration or unintentional contamination.

2. To determine that specified chemical elements or compounds are within established limits.

Close Tolerances

As an example of the second class, it may be pointed out that, although portland cement is manufactured from a wide variety of raw materials, the proportions of the chemical compounds formed during manufacture must be held within close tolerances to assure its expected strength and durability in service. Certain elements

Chart showing typical length-temperature changes in concrete during freezing

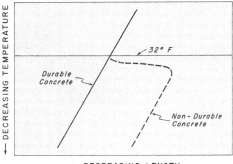

that occur in the raw materials from which steel is manufactured must be kept close to the vanishing point in the final product if it is to give a long life in service. Other elements must be present in prescribed proportions to produce the special properties desired in certain steels. Chemical analyses are frequently found to be more indicative of performance than are physical tests, especially for longtime performance.

The research and development phase of the chemical unit is of equal scope and importance in the search for new and better materials. The formulations for almost all paints used by the Division of Highways have been developed in this laboratory. Only those paints which meet the rigid laboratory and field testing performance standards are considered as suitable for adoption in the Standard Specifications. In co-operation with the Bridge Department of the Division of Highways, several steel bridges along the ocean have been used to test the effect of salt air weathering on experimentally developed paints. Standard paints giving good service inland have a very short life along the coast. Traffic line paint, with which every motorist is familiar, is subjected to the most severe conditions of weather and wear, and must be durable and able to withstand a wide variety of climatic conditions. The chemical unit constantly formulates and tests new types. Traffic lines present difficult problems, as such paints must set very quickly to prevent smearing by traffic, and rapid setting is generally opposed to durability. Experimental traffic paints made in the laboratory are placed across test sections of the highway and periodically evaluated for their wearing qualities.

Use of Epoxy Adhesives

Much experimental and development work has been done by the chemical unit in the use of the relatively new epoxy adhesives as a repair material. Extensive work has been done in co-operation with the various highway districts and the Bridge Department in the repairing of spalled and cracked concrete structures and highways. *(Figure 9.)*

The chemical unit, in co-operation with the Pavement Section of the laboratory, has done extensive and analytical research work on the correlation of the chemical analysis of asphalts with their long term durability. Both the original asphalts and asphalts extracted from pavements are analyzed for the various types of hydrocarbons present seeking to discover whether a relationship exists between durability of the asphalts and their chemical composition.

RESEARCH CORRELATION UNIT

The research correlation unit, under the direct supervision of C. G. Gates, Senior Materials and Research Engineer, is one of the newest units of our laboratory. As the name implies, research correlation consists of determining the relationship between laboratory or field research data and actual performance. The Materials and Research Department has been engaged in research activities for over 30 years. Some projects have been small, but many have extended over several years.

So far, correlation work has consisted of assembling old and current research records, cross-indexing the

data and maintaining a central research file. Another phase, which will be started soon, is to review old test roads and field installations to determine whether additional tests, measurements or studies are needed to more clearly evaluate the results of the projects.

Periodic Reports

Periodic reports of our research activities are made to the Highway Research Board, to other co-operating research agencies and to our own organization.

The research correlation unit maintains the Materials and Research Department's archives; i.e., converts all construction records to research reference after contracts are completed. Unusual and important design or construction features are indexed for future reference.

The library of the Materials and Research Department is now a part of the research correlation unit. The library functions primarily as an information service for the entire department. In carrying out this function, the library is responsible for acquiring and maintaining a collection of scientific and technical literature in a num-

Application of modified epoxy adhesive in bridge repair

18

A corner in the library of the Materials and Research Laboratory

Curtis M. Brown Authors New Book

Seldom is a book written which relates two professions and, even less frequent, when it involves the fields of engineering and law, but Curtis M. Brown has done just that in his recent publication entitled "Boundary Control and Legal Principles." As stated by Brown, this is a book which fills the need for correlating law and surveying.

The forerunner of this book was "Boundary Control for Surveyors in California," which was introduced by Brown in the early part of 1954. This was immediately accepted by surveyors and attorneys alike, but it was recognized that a better organized and more comprehensive work was needed. We must agree with Brown that he has now filled that need.

The excellence of this book is exemplified by the simplification of law to the surveyor and surveying to the lawyer. The book has a systematic plan which begins with an easy explanation on the systems used to describe property and ends with procedures for writing the descriptive parts of deeds. Throughout there are stated clear basic principles with simple explanations of the application which are often illustrated by common situations. Principles relating to specialized situations involving description of lands with riparian rights and federal mining claims indicate the fine coverage of this book.

To give his work real completeness, Brown has included such things as a table of abbreviations commonly used in property descriptions, a glossary and excellent index, some of which were missing in his earlier publication.

This book is a "must" for the library of the surveyor and for every lawyer whose practice touches on real property law.—J. B. M.

VEHICLES REGISTERED

A total of 6,998,805 vehicles were registered in California from January 1st through June 30th this year, reports the National Automobile Club.

ber of fields. Some of the other services are literature searching, preparing bibliographies, translating technical articles written in foreign languages, compiling special reference files and indexes, routing of periodicals and other technical literature to staff members, and various other reference and information services. The library also arranges for the loan of material from other libraries and organizations.

As a special assignment, the research correlation unit was given the responsibility of assembling, editing and publishing a much needed Materials Manual of Testing and Control Procedures. This manual consists of two volumes and describes some 145 testing and control procedures normally performed in our laboratory.

The research correlation unit has also been assigned the initial work on preparing training films on sampling and testing procedures that are used by field engineers on construction projects.

General

The Technical Section co-operated with the Structural Materials Section in determining the basic causes of deterioration of an important reinforced concrete bridge by reason of corrosion of the reinforcing steel. Published reports on this project have attracted worldwide interest.

The section has prepared technical papers or discussions for meetings of the American Society for Testing Materials, the American Concrete Institute and the Highway Research Board. The Technical Section serves as a "clearinghouse" for correspondence and discussions with the various technical agencies and organizations.

Various units of the section are called upon frequently for assistance in solving the problems that arise in construction and maintenance operations of other state agencies as well as those of counties and cities. Its facilities and staff are available whenever a specific request for assistance is made by any public organization.

This report would not be complete without giving recognition to the efficient work performed by the clerical and stenographic staff. Without such assistance, the fruits of the section's labor would remain largely unharvested.

Golden State Freeway

By J. F. SMITH, Associate Highway Engineer, and
C. J. WOODBRIDGE, Senior Bridge Engineer

THE San Fernando Valley, lying between the Santa Monica Mountains and the San Gabriel Mountains, is a very important residential and industrial area of metropolitan Los Angeles. The latest official estimate of population in Los Angeles County indicates a total of 5,401,274 persons of which 609,300 are in the rapidly growing San Fernando Valley. There are five main gateways to the valley through which thousands of people pass each day in entering and leaving it. Ingress and egress through the east gateway at Burbank will be greatly facilitated by developments currently being carried out by the State Division of Highways on the Golden State Freeway.

Completed Unit

The first unit of this freeway development serving the immediate needs of the East San Fernando Valley was completed and opened to public traffic on September 6, 1957. The completed unit is 2.4 miles in

length and extends from the northeast corner of Griffith Park in the City of Los Angeles near the site of the old Rodger Young Village (long since demolished) across the Los Angeles River, through a small section of the City of Glendale, to Ash Street in the City of Burbank.

In the overall picture the Golden State Freeway within the limits of District VII is 72.7 miles long. It extends from the southerly terminus at junction with the Santa Ana and Santa Monica Freeways near Soto Street in East Los Angeles to the Los Angeles-Kern county line in vicinity of Gorman. In 1952, a length of 45.2 miles of this State highway route was completed to expressway standards over "The Ridge Route" between Tunnel Station on the Southern Pacific Railroad at the junction with U. S. Highway 6, locally called the "Sierra Highway," and the Los Angeles-Kern county line.

Full Freeway Standards

From Tunnel Station to its southerly terminus the Golden State Freeway will be constructed to full freeway standards, and a three-mile length from Tunnel Station southerly to Sepulveda Boulevard was completed to full freeway standards with interchange facilities to San Fernando Road and Foothill Boulevard, as well as Sepulveda Boulevard, in August, 1955. The cost of this construction, sometimes referred to as "The Tunnel Station Job" was $3,300,000.

The 2.4 miles unit of the Golden State Freeway at the east gateway to the San Fernando Valley that was opened to public traffic on September 6, 1957 involved a total construction cost of $4,400,000. Two years have elapsed since the call for bids was made for this project. Bids were opened in the District VII office in Los Angeles on September 29, 1955, and the contract was awarded to the low bidder, Vinnell Company, Inc.

Length of Project 12,474.55 feet = 2.36 miles

UPPER—Looking northerly along completed unit of Golden State Freeway in Griffith Park area showing in center Park Road Overcrossing. CENTER—Looking easterly along Alameda Avenue, Burbank, showing completed bridges carrying Golden State Freeway over this important traffic arterial. LOWER—Looking southerly along completed Golden State Freeway showing Los Angeles River Bridge and Griffith Park in background.

and Vinnell Constructors on October 3, 1955. The contractor has carried out his operations efficiently and expeditiously and completed this complex freeway project a full month ahead of schedule.

Eight-lane Freeway

Essentially the completed construction is an eight-lane freeway with a 22-foot uncurbed median. Emergency parking is provided by an eight-foot paved shoulder adjacent to each of the inside lanes and a standard three-foot rolled gutter with five-foot paved shoulder next to the outside lanes. Concrete paving eight inches thick on a four-inch cement treated subgrade is used on the main freeway and interchange roadways with plant-mix paving being placed on the collector roads, ramps and frontage roads. Ramps and collector roads have cement treated base varying in thickness from six inches to eight inches. Stub lanes and interchange roads near the beginning of job will accommodate connections with the future Ventura and Colorado freeways. Two complete traffic interchanges at Western Avenue and at Alameda Avenue provide the motorist with a traffic facility completely devoid of all left turn conflicts.

All roadway excavation within the job limits was at the south end near the beginning of the project and it balanced out within the first 3,800 feet. The remainder of the project was finished with imported borrow obtained from Forest Lawn, located a haul distance of two miles from the middle of the job.

Borrow Problem Solved

Under an agreement with Forest Lawn, the State was given borrow material free in return for leaving the borrow area graded to contours suitable for their planned cemetery development. Material in the area is a high grade of decomposed granite which normally breaks up and loads easily. On this basis, the contractor developed a 48-inch belt loader which worked very well and with which he was able to obtain daily production rates on the order of 8,000 cubic yards. Hauling was performed with

UPPER—Looking westerly along Riverside Drive in Griffith Park showing stub ends of recently completed pavement to provide traffic interchange connections between Golden State Freeway and future Ventura Freeway. To the right is shown the bed of the Los Angeles River and a portion of the contractor's haul road. LOWER—Allen Avenue Undercrossing in City of Glendale under construction on Golden State Freeway.

22 cubic yard bottom-dump trucks. Loading time was approximately 30 seconds per truck.

As the top layer of material was stripped from part of the pit, it became apparent that portions of the designated borrow areas were underlaid with rock ridges of varying degrees of hardness. Some of the rock was sufficiently decomposed to succumb to a tractor and ripper. Much of it, however, was still well consolidated and it was necessary to drill and shoot in order to break the material up. Two power shovels were used to load the rock into 10-wheeler end-dump trucks. Approximately 62,000 cubic yards of rock was handled in this manner.

System of Haul Roads

By making suitable arrangements with the Los Angeles City Park Commission, the Los Angeles County Flood Control and the U. S. Corps of Engineers, the contractor worked out a system of haul roads on park lands and in the Los Angeles River bed that permitted him to reach the job site without using city streets. Confining his operations to off-highway haul paid the contractor big dividends in time savings and in reduction of unit hauling costs.

Major structures on this contract consisted of six bridges and three pedestrian undercrossings. The total cost of bridge construction was $1,850,000.

The Alameda Avenue Undercrossing is situated at the northerly end of the contract work in the City of Burbank. There are actually four parallel rolled beam steel girder bridges of two spans each, with reinforced concrete decks, all supported on common

22

abutments of reinforced concrete. The two inside decks carry the main freeway traffic and the two outer decks carry the collector road traffic.

Other Major Structures

Allen Avenue Undercrossing is in the City of Glendale. It is a single span, rigid frame, reinforced concrete T-beam structure built to the full width of the freeway roadway.

Western Avenue Undercrossing, in the City of Glendale, is similar to Alameda Avenue Undercrossing in layout and dimensions.

Sonora Avenue Undercrossing, in the City of Glendale, consists of two single span welded steel girder bridges to carry the main freeway traffic over this busy city street.

The Los Angeles River Bridge and Separation carries the main freeway traffic over future westbound Ventura Freeway and the Los Angeles River channel. The most northerly span will accommodate a future highway underneath. The structure cost about $1,000,000 and consists of two parallel bridges of five welded steel girder spans with concrete decks, having a total length of 638 feet. The city limits of Los Angeles and Glendale pass through this bridge on the westerly side of the river channel.

Park Overcrossing is a three-span reinforced concrete T-beam structure

which carries traffic over the freeway to the two areas of Griffith Park on either side of the freeway.

All bridge decks carrying the main freeway traffic are 52 feet wide between curbs, and all other decks are 28 feet wide between curbs.

The three pedestrian undercrossings or "tunnels" are all in the City of Glendale and permit pedestrians to cross under the freeway. Their dimensions are eight feet wide, nine feet high, and up to 238 feet long. The interior walls were covered with white air-blown mortar to discourage writing and to improve the illumination.

Structural Design Features

Structural design features were dictated somewhat by the location of the freeway. The general location is along ancient silty sand deposits of the Los Angeles River. Piles were used to support all of the bridges. For the Los Angeles River Bridge, steel H-piles were used. For the other five bridges, concrete piles were used. Pile penetration varied from about 30 to 60 feet. The most effective pile-driving hammer used was a fast differential type with rated energy of 19,500 foot-pounds.

Structural steel was fabricated and erected by Vinnell Steel Company, a subsidiary of Vinnell Company, Inc. The shop fabricated girders, being a

parallel operation with construction of abutments, saves considerable time as compared with conventional concrete girders. In addition, on busy city streets, the falsework necessary for concrete girders is a hazard to traffic. There are 297 steel girders in the four bridges of that type, so that the saving in time as compared to concrete girders is obvious. At the Los Angeles River Bridge the diaphragm connections were welded in the field. At the other bridges the connections were made with high strength bolts checked with a four-foot torque wrench.

Erection of Steel Girders

Erection of steel girders over busy city streets presented a difficult problem. At Alameda Avenue and Western Avenue this matter was handled by detouring the traffic to the other span while each of the two spans was erected. For the single span at Sonora Avenue, the City of Glendale permitted detouring traffic to adjacent streets between the hours of 9 a.m. and 3 p.m. so that steel erection could be done. For the Los Angeles River Bridge span over Riverside Drive, there was no detour available. However, the City of Los Angeles cooperated by permitting blocking off Riverside Drive between Sonora Avenue and Los Feliz Boulevard between 11 p.m. and 5 a.m.

LEFT—Western Avenue Undercrossing in City of Glendale under construction on Golden State Freeway. RIGHT—Bridge structure under construction to carry Golden State Freeway over the Los Angeles River and over Riverside Drive.

Forms for the concrete decks of the steel girder bridges were neatly hung from the top of the girders by form ties. Decks were started at Alameda Avenue Undercrossing and as work continued southerly along the freeway on successive bridges, the efficiency of the crews increased rapidly.

Hazards of Construction

Some hazards of the construction required careful consideration. Near the front of the footing of the southerly abutment of the Los Angeles River Bridge, there is the old concrete outfall sewer which served the entire San Fernando Valley. Its interior condition is unknown. To drive piles beside it was risky, especially as it operated under pressure head for part of the 24 hours of the day. Attempts were made to change from driven piles to drilled and cast concrete piles, but no reasonable bid could be obtained due to the running nature of the silty sand river bed material. Eventually, the pile driving was postponed some months until the new relief sewer upstream was put in operation, thus removing the pressure head on the old sewer. When the steel H-piles were driven, they penetrated easily for about 35 feet and then obtained the 45-ton bearing value quickly, with a minimum of vibration of the outfall sewer.

For the two piers in the river channel, the plans provided a four-foot thick tremie seal to block off the underground water in the cofferdams if necessary. However, the contractor was able to divert all of the flow, both surface and underground, and excavate and pour the pier footings "in the dry." Thus, the tremie seal was not necessary, thereby saving the State several thousands of dollars. This is a good example of the fine co-operative spirit which exists between the State Division of Highways and its contractors.

Contractor's Personnel

Contractor's personnel on the job were H. J. Yount, Vice President; Glen McAfee, General Superintendent; and Bob Hayden, Structure Superintendent.

The work was carried out under general supervision of District VII represented by District Engineer, L. R. Gillis; Assistant District Engineer, F. B. Cressy; and Field Supervisor, H. E. Belford. State personnel on the job were: H. B. Whitnall, Project Engineer; C. I. Palmer, Resident Engineer; and C. J. Woodbridge, Bridge Department Representative. In the latter stages of the contract, J. F. Smith succeeded Whitnall.

To the southeast of construction that was completed on September 6, 1957, a 2.6-mile length of the Golden State Freeway extending to Glendale Boulevard is now under construction also by the Vinnell Company, Inc. and Vinnell Constructors. This current

LEFT—Looking northerly along Golden State Freeway construction showing in foreground crossing over Riverside Drive and Los Angeles River. Portion of City of Glendale shown in center and City of Burbank in background. RIGHT—Looking northerly showing construction of Golden State Freeway in City of Burbank to provide cloverleaf interchange with Alameda Avenue.

LEFT—Looking northerly along Golden State Freeway showing construction nearing completion with Allen Avenue Undercrossing in foreground and Alameda Avenue Undercrossing in background. RIGHT—Looking southerly along Golden State Freeway construction nearing completion in Griffith Park with Los Angeles River and Riverside Drive Bridge in foreground. Traffic interchange facilities with future Ventura Freeway shown in center.

contract carries a construction allotment of $5,315,000, is over 80 percent completed and the scheduled date of completion is January, 1958.

To the northwest of the recently completed section of the Golden State Freeway is a 1.6-mile unit in the City of Burbank from Alameda Avenue to Burbank Boulevard that is in the current construction budget for the 1957-1958 Fiscal Year. The budget item totals $3,150,000. This project is now being advertised, with bids

to be opened in the Los Angeles District VII office on October 24, 1957.

Also in the current budget is an item of $8,900,000 for constructing 3.1 miles of the Golden State Freeway in the Boyle Heights area of the City of Los Angeles from Sixth Street to Mission Road. This latter unit includes considerable reconstruction of the San Bernardino Freeway in order to develop a suitable traffic interchange system between these two great freeways. For this unit of the Golden State Freeway plans are com-

pleted, rights of way substantially all acquired, and the work is scheduled for advertising early in 1958.

While much progress has been made in design and right of way acquisition on other units of the Golden State Freeway, a construction schedule for final completion is not available at the present time because this is dependent upon availability of construction funds to be determined by the California Highway Commission in its consideration of future budgets.

No Dearth of Road Contractors in State

As of July 1st, there were 992 contractors prequalified to submit bids on state highway projects in California, with an estimated combined bidding capacity of $1,780,000,000, State Highway Engineer G. T. McCoy reported.

This is an increase of 180 contractors and nearly $200,000,000 in bidding capacity over the totals for one year ago.

At the same time, McCoy reported that the average number of bidders has been on the increase. State highway projects attracted an average of 5.5 bidders each during the second

quarter of 1957, compared with 3.8 bidders per project for the same period last year.

"These figures indicate," McCoy said, "that the highway contracting industry in California is still expanding, with new firms entering the field; and that active competition for state highway contracts can be expected to continue. This means a continued favorable outlook for the public in the form of more highway improvements for their tax dollars due to this sustained competition."

The increase in highway contractors and in number of bidders also shows, McCoy pointed out, that the industry is easily capable of absorbing

even more state highway construction work than has been made available as a result of the accelerated federal highway program.

Prequalification of bidders is provided for in the State Contract Act as a means of determining a contractor's capacity to undertake work up to a given amount. The amount for which a contractor may be prequalified is based on his financial resources and experience in public works projects. Contractors are permitted to bid only on projects within their prequalification rating.

Approximately 50 contractors have prequalification ratings in excess of $10,000,000 for state highway work.

and Public Works   25

Long Haul
Unusual Job in Modoc County

Dᴜʀɪɴɢ this 1957 construction season in eastern Modoc County a long haul for plant-mixed surfacing, probably without precedent in the history of highway construction in California, was employed by Clements & Company of Centerville. This firm has a paving plant erected near Hatfield on State Route 210 close to the Oregon state line. This contractor also had the contract for surfacing 7.9 miles of State Route 28 east of Alturas between the junction of this route with US 395 and Cedarville, which called for placing about nine thousand tons of plant-mix. The mix was hauled a distance of 92 miles from the Hatfield plant.

tonnage in the contract was not large and overhead costs for moving the plant in and out would have substantially increased the unit costs on such a small amount.

Costs Reduced

By utilizing bottom dump hauling units operating in tandem hauling costs were greatly reduced. Furthermore the Dorman Construction Company of Vancouver had a contract for surfacing 7.9 miles of highway south from the Oregon state line through Tulelake, which called for eighty-seven hundred tons of plant-mix and was very close to the Hatfield plant. They made arrangements for Clem-

in California and Oregon that is within range of the Hatfield plant and Clements wanted the plant to remain in this location.

In actual oeration were 15 to 17 four-axle bottom dump trailers hauling in tandem. It took the loaded units about three hours to travel the 92 miles. The plant ran from 4.30 a.m. to 2.30 p.m. Each tandem outfit hauled about 25 tons of mix and made two trips per day. This took care of a daily plant production of about 750 tons.

Bottom Dump Units

The bottom dump units pulled in ahead of the paver and the front unit was accurately spotted over a windrow sizing box. When the gates were opened they fell into the box and engaged it so that it was pulled ahead when the vehicle moved. After the front unit was emptied the rear unit was pulled ahead and emptied in similar manner.

The paver picked up the windrow and laid it directly. No trouble was experienced in maintaining temperatures. Loads were covered, but the summer temperatures and large loads helped to retain the heat.

This contract was under the supervision of District II of the California Division of Highways at Redding. H. S. Miles is District Engineer. Ray Wilson was District Construction Engineer on this project and W. H. Bartlett was Resident Engineer. John R. Holgate was Superintendent for Clements & Company.

SLOW DRIVING

On a warm summer day it's nice to drive along slowly on the highway and enjoy the scenery, but remember, driving too slowly is just as dangerous as speeding. Keep pace with traffic, urges the California State Automobile Association, and give the other drivers a break. If you want to loaf, pick some scenic side road that has little traffic.

There are several reasons that prompted this operation. In the first place the plant is now erected and in operation on a large and tested deposit of aggregate. Satisfactory aggregate is not available close to the Modoc County job. Then too, the

ents & Company to supply the mix for this project. As in the Clements contract, the erection of a plant for this small tonnage would greatly increase the cost of the mix.

Another factor was the fact that there is other work in prospect both

Fast Work

Relocation of Feather River Highway Ahead of Schedule

By RICHARD E. STICKEL, District Construction Engineer

WITH THE summer construction season drawing to a close, the relocation of the Feather River Highway from Wicks Corner, six miles west of Oroville, to Jarbo Gap is ahead of the schedule established at the beginning of the project. The project is approximately 29 percent complete with less than 20 percent of the planned construction time elapsed.

The 13.3 miles of relocated highway will provide an expressway from Wicks Corner to the existing highway, Alternate US 40, west of Jarbo Gap. A 32-foot all-paved section which will serve as two lanes of an ultimate four-lane highway is being constructed from a point on Clark Road near Wicks Corner to the Cherokee Overhead. A 60-foot section is being graded from this point to the bridge over the West Branch of the Feather River. This section will be surfaced initially to provide 32 feet of roadway. The wider grading operation is being done at this time to avoid a costly operation in the future when it becomes necessary to convert this route to four lanes. Through this area the highway is roughly parallel to, and above, the relocated line of the Western Pacific Railroad. Four lanes will be provided initially on a 58-foot all-paved roadway from the West Branch bridge to Station 1001. The roadway through this section will have grades of up to 6 percent and the additional lanes will permit the passing of slowly moving vehicles. The new highway will then revert to two lanes from this point to where it joins the existing highway.

The bridge over the West Branch of the Feather River is not a part of this contract.

Contractor Gains Time

The contractor, McCammon and Wunderlich Company and Wunderlich Construction Company of Palo Alto, gained several working days on

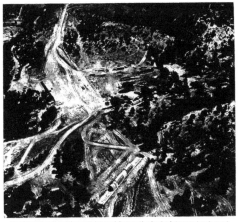

Near future intersection of the new highway and the Pentz-Cherokee Road. Contractor's main camp is shown in center of the photo and a 15-foot concrete arch culvert in the foreground.

the contract when they elected to start clearing operations on the right of way eight days after the bid opening and before the contract had been awarded and approved. They reasoned correctly that their low bid of $7,292,-214 would be accepted for the work. The early start was prompted by the realization that burning of the cleared material would not be permitted in the critical fire season during the summer months and that this material would have to be stacked on the right of way thereby impairing work. With the clearing and burning done, the contractor was able to work his equipment without delay or interference on any portion of the right of way. Approximately 8 percent of the project

was completed before time started on the contract.

The initial phase of the construction stressed work on the development of a water supply, right of way fencing and placing of drainage facilities and erection of structures pertaining thereto. At the present time the right of way clearing and the development of water is completed.

Drainage Facilities

Drainage facilities for the project range from 12-inch corrugated metal pipe to a 15-foot concrete arch culvert. The types of pipe to be used are equally as varied, from the standard corrugated metal pipe through thick wall concrete, reinforced con-

LEFT—Looking east along cleared area east of the West Branch of the Feather River showing the type of terrain through which the new roadway will pass in this area. RIGHT—Cut and fill operation in the vicinity of the Yankee Hill Road showing the rough terrain in this sector.

crete, and asbestos bonded corrugated metal pipe to field assembled plate culvert. Approximately 55 percent of all pipe is now installed and it is estimated that this portion of the contract will be 90 percent complete by the end of October.

Fencing of the right of way for the highway, and the railroad in the area in which the two are contiguous, is currently about 50 percent complete. Work on the fencing subcontract was halted during the month of August when sufficient fence had been installed to prevent livestock from entering the right of way and the final right of way agreements had not been reached. The subcontractor, San Jose Fence Company, resumed fencing operations in September.

The principal contract item, 4,154,-000 cubic yards of roadway excavation, is beginning to show increased production. The nature of the terrain is such that the amount of such excavation possible is determined by the placing of drainage pipes. As the pipe item approaches completion more areas are made available for grading and the contractor has been continuously moving in more earth moving equipment to speed this item. In addition, the contractor has been blocking off rocky sections of the roadway that

LEFT TO RIGHT—Floyd Helm, Project Manager for McCammon-Wunderlich, Richard E. Stickel, District Construction Engineer, and Mullar Chapman, Resident Engineer, viewing plans of the project

will apparently have to be excavated by the use of shovels and trucks. These sections will be worked during the inclement weather season.

Four Bridges in Project

It is realized that rain in any appreciable amount will seriously hamper, if not stop completely, earth moving by the faster moving rubber tired scrapers. To date 26 percent of the earth moving has been completed. Emphasis on roadway excavation has

been primarily on the west side of the West Branch of the Feather River, although in the past few weeks work has been accelerated on the east side of the river.

Four bridges are to be constructed under this contract. Two of these cross water courses, Gold Run Creek and Flag Canyon, and two will cross the Western Pacific Railroad north of Cherokee. Work is now under way on the Gold Run Creek and Flag Canyon structures. The Gold Run Creek structure is on the present Clark Road which connects Paradise and Oroville and it has been necessary to provide a detour at this point. The detour is now in effect, the old bridge has been removed and work on the footings of new structure has started. Piling for the Flag Canyon bridge has been driven by the subcontractor, Raymond Concrete Pile Company, and work on the footings and abutments are under way.

The grading of the railroad right of way under this contract requires the relocating of the Upper Miocene Canal. This canal carries water for a Pacific Gas and Electric Company powerhouse and also provides domestic water for the Oroville area. Flow in the canal must be maintained with as little interruption as possible. The

28

relocation consists principally of the construction of a syphon in the vicinity of Vinton Gulch. Work on the pipe for this syphon is virtually complete and waters of the canal have been diverted around the area where the intake structure is to be constructed.

Completion Date in 1958

The placing of most of the imported sub-base material, cement-treated base, and surfacing is scheduled to begin early next year although sections of the roadway on the valley and foot-hill portion of the road will be ready for this stage this season. No difficulty is foreseen in meeting the completion date for the project which is scheduled for late in November, 1958.

To the present time the only serious construction difficulty encountered has been between Stations 481 and 508 where a water seepage problem was uncovered in a cut section. Because of the depth of the water bearing material it was decided to correct the problem by the installing of eight-inch perforated metal pipe and super-imposing 2½ feet of imported material consisting mainly of coarse rock prior to the construction of the typical section.

Cut and fill operation in the vicinity of Yankee Hill Road. The top of the fill will be near the roadway just above the earth-moving equipment to the right of the scene.

In passing it is well to note that the new route will present probably the most striking introduction to the

Sacramento Valley of any of the routes entering the State. At a point roughly one mile west from the point where the new route leaves the existing highway near Jarbo Gap the roadway passes through a cut and suddenly the entire northern portion of the great Central Valley of California unfolds before the motorist.

The contractor is represented by Project Manager Floyd Helm who has long and varied experience in the construction of highways. Work on the project is under the direction of Alan S. Hart, District Engineer; Muller Chapman is the Resident Engineer for this portion of the Feather River Highway relocation; and the author is the District Construction Engineer for the complete highway relocation. W. G. Ballantine is the representative of the Bridge Department.

VIOLATIONS

Twenty-one states report that about 3 out of 10 drivers in fatal accidents were violating a speed law, says the National Automobile Club.

If traffic volume increases by 50 percent in the next 10 years, as estimated, accidents at the present rate will take 55,000 lives a year.

LEFT—Looking east along new alignment from the Flag Canyon Bridge site. Excavation for footing of the bridge is being made in the foreground. RIGHT—Looking west on new alignment at the intersection with Clark Road.

Public Relations

From the View of The Public Employee

By FRANK C. BALFOUR, Chief Right-of-Way Agent

IN ANALYZING and discussing public relations, one of the most difficult problems which must be faced is the matter of perspective. There has been such a wealth of literature in this field that more often than not the student is confused with broad generalizations and over-simplifications about public relations or is equally lost in professional "shop talk" concerning communications media, tools and techniques.

It will be my privilege to discuss with you ideas about public relations which may be helpful in gaining perspective. I will attempt to avoid the generalizations so often used in public relations discussions, and at the same time I will make every effort to avoid overemphasis upon the small specifics.

There is not a person in this room who does not have available to him reference material of all types, especially text books, statistical data, and public relations magazines, and I am sure more than half of the persons in this room have attended lectures on the subject of public relations as a part of your educational training and background.

To gain a true perspective and insight into the field requires a fresh look at both the definition of the term "public relations" and a careful re-evaluation of some of the history which has led to the emergence of the concept that public relations is now a "new profession."

Perspective Important

You will note how strongly I am outlining the idea of *perspective*. Let me illustrate this factor by drawing a verbal picture:

If I were to discuss with you or with any audience in the Western United States about the extreme height of Mt. Mitchell, I am confident that you would be surprised after my description of its tremendous elevation to learn that Mt. Mitchell is only

This is the text of an address on "The Public Employee and Public Relations" which Mr. Balfour gave before the Ninth Annual Institute on Government at San Diego earlier this year.

6,684 feet high. Nonetheless, it is the highest mountain east of the Mississippi River, and to an eastern audience such a description of Mt. Mitchell would be appropriate. Here in the West where mountainous elevations above 10,000 feet are not unusual, such a discussion would be, so to speak, out of context; it would lack perspective.

In a similar fashion a discussion of public relations and the connection of that term with public employees must be viewed in proper perspective or the true significance of our theme will be lost.

Many of you have probably looked up the words "public," "relations," and "employee." For those who have not, I think a brief reference will be very enlightening at this point.

"Public" is derived from the Latin word *populus*, which in turn comes from the Latin word signifying "adult."

The word "relations" has two ancient stems, one of which means "to report" or "to relate," and the other of which means "to tolerate" from a Greek word "to be endured."

Latin Derivation

Surely, for the thoughtful person, here is a great deal of the story in which underlies the significance of public relations. It has connotations of adult behavior, and of toleration, and matters to be endured.

In similar fashion the word "employee" comes from two Latin words which mean to "fold in."

I have gone to this length to discuss the word derivations because I believe that there inheres in the very language sufficient information upon which to predicate a sound program of modern public relations and the public employee.

The procedure seems to be self-evident: mix people into a situation which must be tolerated and then fold in an employee; sprinkle well with adult attitudes, and I believe you have a sound remedy for most institutions which are floundering about desperately for a true concept of the public relations approach.

I know most of you have probably anticipated the institute today by looking up a definition of public relations in Webster's Dictionary, and I do not doubt that most of you therefore have this definition more or less clearly in mind:

"Public relations—the activities of an industry, university, corporation, profession, government, or other organization in building and maintaining sound and productive relations with special publics such as customers, employees. or stockholders, and with the public at large, so as to adapt itself to its environment and interpret itself to society."

Civil Service Data

It is undoubtedly appropriate at this time to include a brief comment upon the status of civil service employees in this Country. The Federal Government alone, with its three branches, 53 individual agencies, eight executive offices, and 14 executive departments, has approximately 2,400,000 civilian employees.

The armed forces include an approximate 3,000,000. It is estimated there are approximately 5,000,000 civil service employees in state, city, and county organizations.

All of this means, in relationship to the total working civilian population of the United States, that every seventh person you meet, on the statistical average, is a public employee in a strictly governmental sense.

To many persons these statistics are staggering, and they have the feeling that this is the first time in the history of Man that problems of such proportion have arisen involving public employees. Additionally, to many persons the idea of a public relations program is a modern concept.

Therefore, for a few minutes let's examine these two "modern" problems in the light of an interesting past history.

A Look at History

Throughout most of the world governments in the past, public relations have been weighed in terms of Public Opinion. Broadly speaking, scholars agree that such public opinion has been of two types: (A) static, (B) dynamic.

Static public opinion is best typified by a society which is ruled by its customs, *mores*, conventions, and traditions. (For example, agrarian and "barter" communities such as existed in medieval Greece and Rome, in Japan, West Europe, and Mexico.)

A dynamic public opinion is one which relies on a systematic publicity program based on the art of persuasion. Excellent examples would be a Greece of the time of Pericles, Rome during Caesar's administration, and the city-states in Italy during the renaissance.

Throughout history *dynamic* systems of public opinions and relations have overthrown *static* states. When sophistication and culture is introduced into a group and some type of industrialization emerges, the custombound state must change or fall. This was true in Sumer, in Egypt, and in Greece.

All of us are familiar with the fact that Greece gives us the word "democracy." I wonder how many of you realize that the Greeks of the Seventh Century were the first great forerunners of modern publicity measures and were most keenly aware of the complexities of public relations.

In Greek Theater

It was in the Seventh Century in Greece that money was first introduced in its modern concept. A type of industry appeared in the towns; there was a new wealth and slavery rose. During these times publicity methods and public relations came into the fore, especially in their military garrisons, in their market places, and, surprisingly enough, in the Grecian theater, for it was in this latter institution that public opinion was most readily influenced at that time. (Actually, I think this was the forerunner of our own response to the nightly theater which takes precedence in our own homes, that is, the TV programs.)

Those of you who are experts in such public relations media, as exemplified by the modern "inside story" of government news reports, will be interested to know that the Romans were the first to put out an official governmental news bulletin which was circulated readily among the highplaced government employees. In 59 B.C., Julius Caesar decreed that these "daily acts" of governmental news letters for public employees should be distributed to the general public.

It is very important as a matter of perspective to understand that the emergence of such a news letter was necessarily a part of the emergence of the Roman Empire, based as it was upon its amazing road system and its public relations system.

The Middle Ages

As we follow the development of such public relations devices as books and pamphlets, it is interesting to know that these first emerged in Europe during the reformation when controversy of a religious sort was the order of the day.

Inside information newsletters for merchantmen and businessmen first appeared in Germany in 1609, and as England became a more complex culture, public opinion forged the emergence of the first newspapers in 1622; technical professional magazines came to light about 1665 in England.

For those of you who have enjoyed Shakespeare's writings and who are expert in them, you will recall that he placed these words in the mouth of Henry IV: "Opinion, that did help me to the crown."

I have always had a great respect for this statement written by Locke concerning *human understanding:* "The laws that men generally refer their acts to seem to me to be these three: (1) the Divine law; (2) the civil law; (3) the law of opinion or reputation, if I may so call it."

Three Institutions

In this matter of gaining a fresh and true perspective of the very vital role that public opinion and consequently public relations has played in the course of mankind's history, I wish at this time to briefly comment upon the *ethical* nature and significance of public relations. Without honesty, integrity and sincerity of purpose, public relations is obviously nothing but a term.

Let's take a look at three of the greatest institutions in the history of Man and examine some of their concepts about man's relationship to man.

The first great institution, which is a religious one, has today millions of followers. One of the key terms in this great religious institution is a phrase which I think has meaning to us all: "The harvest field of merit." Surely in true merit there lies a rich harvest. This great religion stresses "mutual indebtedness" of a religious, moral, and economic nature.

The second great religious institution that I wish to refer to has this to say to its millions of followers: "Reply to injury with beneficence; evil with good." "Anyone can love his friends; try loving your enemies." "Do not vindicate your rights; if a man takes your cloak let him have your coat also." "Do not assert yourself; assert the true spirit of your principles."

I wish to tell of a third great religious institution which has millions of followers in the world today, and I think you would be interested in its founder who was a paid public school teacher working some 500 years before Christ was born. His disciples tell us that he based his philosophy upon *human relationships.*

These human relationships: father and son; man and wife; elders and young; ruler and subject.

Great Teacher

One of this great teacher's statements was to the effect that the object of government is the entire earth and all of its inhabitants; not only single, local, or national groups.

I think you would also be interested in knowing that this public school teacher, today known as Confucius, was also a member of the governmental civil service of his day, had this to say to his followers about the work of government:

Confucius opposed price raising by private or fiscal monopolies and favored government regulation of prices, loans, free granaries, aid to transportation, and state relief for orphans and the aged, in addition to private charities. He advocated that taxes were to be equal and universal; he approved income taxes and opposed customs tariffs.

Sound Public Relations

Perhaps with this brief attempt to gain an historical perspective it will be very much to the point if I illustrate the application of some of the broad principles we have just been discussing to a modern government situation.

As Chief Right-of-Way Agent of the Division of Highways, State of California, it is my privilege and responsibility to lead a staff of 429 right-of-way agents, together with an assisting staff of 787 persons who perform vital and necessary engineering, stenographic, clerical, and related functions.

For the moment let's use my staff and its developmental patterns as illustrative of my background, experience, and recommendations concerning sound public relations; for you may be sure that to the best of my ability I have endeavored to exemplify and inculcate those aspects of proper public relations which I believe must be customarily in evidence in any organization.

The net result in terms of work units is that our organization this next fiscal year will spend approximately $150,000,000 of public funds to buy

right-of-way for the purpose of improving our 14,000-mile State Highway System in order to meet pressing traffic demands. A little extra-curricular activity during the coming fiscal year will result in our right-of-way organization acquiring for the State Department of Finance over 400 parcels of private property at a cost of 15 million dollars, which will include four new state college sites, major land expansions of four others, several office building sites and numerous sites for the State Department of Employment, Institutions, and other state agencies.

Owners of Many Types

We will acquire in the process this year some 12,400 parcels of private property which must be devoted to the public use for the common good, taking into consideration the fact that each of the 12,400 parcels will have not only a dual ownership vesting such as husband and wife, but will affect as well land holders of all types and persons who have property rights in trust deeds, mechanics' liens and a host of similar interests.

This adds up to the fact that we will affect this year directly and personally some 110,000 persons in the State of California. We will be touching their homes and pocket books, their community interests, and in truth, the very structure of their private and public lives.

At the start of negotiations practically every property owner shows maximum resistance, the property owner wants to be let alone, he wants us to buy the other fellow's property for the proposed public improvement, so here our public relations and salesmanship must be dynamic or our whole land acquisition program collapses.

If ever a department needed a sound public relations concept it is such a department as Right-of-Way of the State of California. Remember too that we are vested with the power of condemnation which issues from the government's right of eminent domain.

Not only do we have a job to do; we have what is actually the added burden of being forced to see that

the job is done even if we must force the affected property owner who is, in the final analysis, one of the persons who pays our salaries.

Outstanding Phase

Here again dynamic public relations must come to the fore. We must convince every affected property owner that it is our solemn obligation to fully protect his interest, to pay him every cent to which he is entitled. On the other hand, we must convince him that it is also our solemn duty to protect the interest of all of the other taxpayers. We cannot pay him more than the fair price to which he is entitled. At this point, we reach perhaps the most outstanding phase of our internal public relations program. Here is where the thousand of hours that we have spent training our right-of-way agent personnel, together with our indoctrination program in sound public relations, pays dividends for the affected property owner and for the taxpayers of our State.

The past record of performance of your State Highway Right-of-Way Department justifies my making the statement that we will reach negotiated settlements with 12,280 of the 12,400 property owners we will deal with, but under no circumstances will we use the threat of eminent domain, i.e., court proceedings to conclude the programmed acquisitions. We sell our organization, we sell the highway program, we sell our determination to reach fair settlements.

I have taken as my cardinal view throughout the past 25 years the attitude that basic to all of our activities must be a constant awareness of the need to "practice the Golden Rule."

Not in Index

Let me illustrate how deeply and sincerely devoted we right-of-way agents are to this single public relations concept:

I have here in my hand a copy of your State Highway Right-of-Way Manual. You may look in the index as long and as hard as you please, but you will see no separate subject matter entitled "public relations." This was done deliberately and intentionally.

When one of our young right-of-way agents asked my assistant chief, who edited the Manual, why he could not find the topic "public relations" in the index, my assistant chief replied (and I think very properly), "Everything in that Manual has to do with public relations. There is no separate topic or single program that we have for public relations. Every agent, every employee, in every act of his daily work and in his social contacts is developing public relations."

Code of Ethics

On the other hand, the first explanatory material in this book on page 3 is entitled "Code of Ethics of the employees of the Right-of-Way Department of the Division of Highways of the State of California."

Recognizing our responsibility to our department and to the people of the State of California, and feeling that we should encourage and foster high ethical standards in our organization, we do hereby subscribe to the following code of ethics for our constant guidance and inspiration, predicated upon the basic principles of trust, justice, and fair play.

1. To show faith in the worthiness of our profession by industry, honesty and courtesy, in order to merit a reputation for high quality of service and fair dealing.
2. To add to the knowledge of our profession by constant study and to share the lessons of our experience with our fellow employees.
3. To build an ever-increasing confidence and good will with the public, our employers, by poise, self-restraint and constructive cooperation.
4. To ascertain and weigh all of the facts relative to real properties in making an appraisal thereof, using the best and the most approved methods of determining just compensation.
5. To conduct ourselves in the most ethical and competent manner in our negotiations with affected property owners, thus meriting confidence in our knowledge and integrity.
6. To accept our full share of responsibility in constructive public service to our community, State and Nation.
7. To strive to attain and to express a sincerity of character that shall enrich our human contacts, ever aiming toward that ideal—the practice of the Golden Rule."

Practical Aspects

Some of you may ask: 'What are a few of the practical things which the Right-of-Way Department has done as an evidence of its public relations awareness?" Let me reply by mentioning a few activities which I believe show our philosophy and attitude.

Every employee upon his entry into our department immediately participates in our continuous in-service training program, which is so oriented as to give him an introduction into his duties, responsibilities, and the proficiencies which are expected of him.

The State of California was the first (1944) in the Nation to have a continuous in-training program for its right-of-way agents. This is all the more surprising when you realize that there is no college in the country which gives a complete four-year course in right-of-way. Most of the skills in titles, negotiations, appraisals, condemnation, state and local statutes, etc., must be learned on the job.

Secondly, as a part of our practical public relations program, our organization introduced a "Streamlining Committee" in 1950 which functions both at staff and grass roots level, and which has a constant machinery in motion for the elimination of so-called "red tape."

Facts for the Public

Thirdly, our organization, representing the State of California, is the only one of its kind in the Country which has set up a Land Economic Studies Section. This is a continuous research program to determine the effects of highway construction upon adjacent properties and upon communities.

It is our purpose and program to get the facts on land values and land changes and to make these facts available to the public. At regular intervals our researches are printed in the official Public Works Magazine of the State of California, and they are printed in simple, concise, lay language.

It is interesting to note that these researches have received nationwide attention; they have been reprinted and quoted in such news media as *U. S. News and World Report*, and the *Wall Street Journal*, in professional publications such as *The Appraisal Journal* and *Right of Way*, in technical monographs prepared by national organizations, e.g., the Automotive Safety Foundation, and the Chamber of Commerce of the United States, and in research papers similar to the series undertaken by Georgia State College of Business Administration and the Study prepared by the Division of Design and Construction of the State of Ohio.

Pamphlet Published

As another evidence of our attitude toward public relations our Right of Way Department was the first in the Nation to publish a simple brochure which is transmitted to every property owner whose lands are affected by state highway construction in California.

This little pamphlet which I am now showing you is entitled "More Than 13 Million People Want My Property." Before we appraise and negotiate for properties, we mail out this descriptive booklet to the property owner in order that he may get a first insight into the workings of our department and the manner in which our department can help him. The booklet is mailed in an envelope which has this statement printed next to the property owner's name and address: "A message from your California State Division of Highways."

To many recipients this notation, and the friendly, helpful comments contained in the booklet, give a feeling of reassurance that personal problems affecting home and property will be treated fairly and reasonably.

Additionally, our organization encourages its membership to participate actively and fully in professional organizations representing the engineering, appraising, legal, and right of way professions. In this fashion the employees of the department can become more firmly integrated with their associates in the field and in their areas of interest.

Simple Approach

I have cited these brief examples of the methods and operations of our Right of Way Department in order to show that we have a simple, down-to-earth approach to public relations entirely based upon a concept that the job must be done, it must be done well, and we like people to know about it.

If I were asked to summarize a bit of my philosophy concerning the force of public opinion and the inter-relationship of all of us in making this vast, intangible product known as "good public relations," here are some of the thoughts which my experience has urged upon me:

(1) There is not a single department, governmental or nongovernmental, large or small, that does not need public relations improvement.

(2) Public relations in a good sense *cannot*, and I repeat *cannot*, be generated simply by "putting someone in charge of a public relations department."

(3) Public relations is the necessary and unavoidable result of the action of every single individual in a group.

(4) Public relations, like charity, begins at home.

(5) Every effort should be made, *not* to the end that the public relations be merely *good*, but that such relations be *excellent*.

(6) There can be no distinctions between employees or employers, government or nongovernment, when it comes to public relations; our culture is too complex for anything but complete inter-relationships.

(7) A simple way to describe a grass roots public relations program is this: Establish a *policy of do good;* do good; tell the world about it.

(8) If you wish to determine what the public's attitude may be toward your own organization: Sample and examine the opinions of your own staff.

(9) The public relations concept cannot and must not be considered *static*. In this culture our public relations philosophy must be dynamic.

(10) Sometimes public relations becomes, as a program, a "canned" or artificial thing; I suspect there are too many people trying to *make friends in order to use them*. This is false and destructive. At the heart of the true public relations man is the concept of "service"—"service above self."

Three Phases

In concluding my visit with you, I would like to leave this thought by briefly referring to three phases of public relations.

(1) Your relationship with your fellow worker in the office. Perhaps one of our greatest Americans, Henry Ford, realized the importance of our public relations with our fellow worker to the maximum extent when he said:

"Coming together is a beginning,
Keeping together is progress,
Working together is success."

(2) Those of us in the field should never forget that good public relations of public employees include our conduct and courtesy when we are operating vehicles with public license plates and insignia on the vehicle's door. As I said earlier, one out of every seven of the working citizens of this country are public employees. Let us carry our public relations on to the streets and highways through the courtesy and consideration we show to other drivers.

(3) I cannot too strongly impress upon every man and woman in this room that, like charity, public relations begins at home. If you do not develop public relations in your home life you will never develop good public relations in the office, on the highways and in your contacts with the public that employs you.

There is no place in a program of sound, dynamic public relations for stubbornness, domineeringness, rudeness or flippancy attitudes. The very foundation upon which good public relations must be built is patience, courtesy, consideration and integrity.

Integrity Essential

Never forget that your personal appearance and your personal self are an all-important phase of your public relations.

One of the great leaders of one of the greatest social institutions of all time had this to say, which I think is vibrant and alive today:

"Ye shall know them by their fruits.
"Even so every good tree bringeth forth good fruit, but a corrupt tree bringeth forth evil fruit.

"Wherefore by their fruits ye shall know them."

To me, the very essence of this entire matter of public relations is in the true integrity and sincerity with which each individual faces his daily tasks.

If the individual is guided by the light of Service, and if he is truly dedicated to the welfare of his fellow human beings, he will truly be well related to the public.

"Therefore all things whatsoever ye would that men should do to you, do ye even so to them: for this is the law of the prophets."

And the Golden Rule is the law for good public relations.

Carson Pass

Improvements on Historic Highway in Alpine

By H. R. JANTZEN, Resident Engineer

Eᴀʀʟʏ ᴄᴏᴍᴘʟᴇᴛɪᴏɴ of a project on State Sign Route 88 in Alpine County is another in a series of contracts designed to bring the historic Carson Pass highway up to modern standards. On January 15, 1957, a contract was awarded for the construction of 5.9 miles of new road between Red Lake and the West Fork of the Carson River.

The area traversed by this project is through Hope Valley at the eastern end of the steep approach to Carson Pass. Hope Valley has been developed as a cattle pasture by several large ranchers and is one of the more scenic valleys in the high Sierra country. The road is used primarily by vacationists bound for the high Sierra, but it is also used by logging trucks and light commercial vehicles.

Carson Pass was discovered by Kit Carson and officially reported by John C. Fremont who told of crossing the pass in 1844. After the story of the ill-fated Donner Party got out, the Carson Pass began to receive considerable travel. Eighty miles of the

Looking westerly toward Red Lake. Typical turnpike section.

old road was oiled for the first time in 1932. (See April, 1932, issue of *California Highways and Public Works*).

Old Road Narrow

The old road was exceedingly narrow and far below standards in align-

LEFT—Looking westerly near Red Lake. RIGHT—Near midpoint of project, looking westerly.

ment, grade and sight distance. The new road consists of a 28-foot all paved section of 2½ inches of plant-mix over 6 inches of base material.

About the middle of May, the contractor started work with the full intention of completing this project in one season, although the State had anticipated that two seasons would be required. The working season at the 7,000-foot elevation of the project is generally from late May through October.

The topography of the route consists of a series of meadows which are irrigated and subirrigated by water from Red Lake at the beginning of the project and Crater and Scott Lakes farther to the northeast.

Drainage Problem

From the very outset of construction the contractor had difficulty with water. In all but two of the cuts,

UPPER—Looking westerly from east end of project. LOWER—Looking northeasterly. Blue Lake Road in middle right of photo.

water was encountered in considerable quantity and the meadows were swampy and boggy from the snow melt and, later, irrigation.

In order to relieve the underground water condition, it was necessary to construct nearly the entire project on a "turnpike" section with a three-foot separation between side ditch and shoulder grade, raise the grade in some locations and blanket the entire section of other portions with a one-foot layer of filter material.

The contractor had up to four pieces of grading equipment occupied with correcting the drainage conditions on this project for over two months. The equipment was just able to keep the water controlled to permit the contractor to continue with the rest of his contract work.

A crawler track-mounted dragline had to work from large timber pads to keep from sinking into the marshes. Tractors frequently got stuck. At one time, two pull tractors and one tractor pushing were used to load a single scraper in the soft tundra-like material.

Blasting of Lava

The appearance of the westerly half of the project at the start of construction gave the impression that this would be heavy grading with much blasting because of the large granite outcrops all over the area. However, as soon as the contractor's equipment had gotten under way, it became apparent that these outcrops were boulders and primarily "float" which had been left on the surface. Once these were out of the way, the balance of the grading was carried on without difficulty by power shovels. At two locations a dense lava was encountered which required considerable blasting and here also flows of water were encountered.

At the present time it appears that the contractor will accomplish his intention and complete the $740,000 project in one working season, inasmuch as the surface course of plant-mix and the final cleanup are all that remain to be done.

The prime contractor on this project is H. Earl Parker, Incorporated, of Marysville, California, with A. C. Parker, as superintendent. Baldwin

MOUNT DIABLO RICH IN HISTORIC LORE

Standing all alone in the center of a great plain, almost in the center of Contra Costa County, and raising its grand, rugged peak close to 4,000 feet into the California sky, El Monte del Diablo, or Mount Diablo as the moderns call it, is probably one of the most colorful mountains in the State today.

Even the way in which it received its name is colorful. According to a report by General Vallejo, a military expedition had been sent out from San Francisco in 1806 to wage war on a tribe of Indians that lived near and on the mountain. During the battle, when victory was beginning to go to the Indians, a large figure dressed in a strange costume and making strange dancing movements, appeared among the contestants, and shortly thereafter the victory went to the Indians. When the Spaniards learned that this figure would appear almost daily and go through this strange dance, they came to the conclusion that this was the devil of the mountain and named the mountain the Mountain of the Devil accordingly.

Since Mount Diablo occupies such a prominent position in such a large plain, it is little wonder, points out the National Automobile Club, that it has come in for considerable attention from the survey crews. Back in 1851 a government cabin and telescope were built on the summit and this summit was chosen as base point for United States surveys in California, in relation to which all the lands, with the exception of the Humboldt district and Southern California, are located.

Tourists found the mountain of interest, too. Here they could find wildflowers in abundance, majestic oaks,

Construction Company subcontracted the base material and the surfacing. The work is under the direction of J. G. Meyer, District Engineer, and W. F. Fleharty, District Construction Engineer, with the writer as resident engineer on the project.

strange natural formations, and views of the countryside that could not be surpassed. A wagon road from Concord was built, and one from Danville. Where the roads met about a mile below the summit, the last mile being too steep for the wagons, a mountain house was built and tourists came from all over the world to enjoy the hospitality here and survey the surrounding valleys.

In the 1890s the old government cabin burned down. Later the roads were abandoned and ranchers who didn't want tourists crossing their lands burned down the mountain house. On April 26, 1931, however, the magic mountain was again opened up to the passing tourist when it became a part of the California State Park System, the position of prestige it enjoys today.

When You Walk At Night

When you step out into the glare of headlights at night, you're inclined to feel that you're in "the center of the stage." When the glare of headlights is all around you and almost blinds you, you're inclined to believe that the driver of that car must certainly see you.

The driver, however, doesn't always see you. If you're caught in the lights at night you don't always stand out clearly, especially if you're dressed in dark clothing and there is fog or rain around. Caught in the lights at night, you may often merge right into the background of shadows and be lost to view.

For this reason, points out the National Automobile Club, it's always wise to use extra caution when walking at night. If you're walking along the highway, walk on the left side facing into the oncoming traffic. Wear or carry something white, something that will reflect the light and be easily seen. And always assume that the driver just can't see you.

These are wise precautions, and they will help to keep you safe.

With the retirement of Richard H. Wilson, Assistant State Highway Engineer—Administration, after nearly 34 years of service (see page 47), State Highway Engineer G. T. McCoy announced the promotion of J. P. Murphy, Planning Engineer for the Division of Highways, to succeed Wilson, and made the following other appointments:

J. A. Legarra, Design Engineer, to be Planning Engineer.

since his graduation from the University of California at Berkeley in 1930 with a degree in civil engineering. Before becoming Planning Engineer for the division earlier this year, he was in charge of public relations and personnel. His earlier assignments have involved responsibility for nearly every aspect of highway planning and construction, including service in District III (Marysville) and District V (San Luis Obispo). From 1937 to 1942 Murphy worked under Wilson in Headquarters Office on federal aid projects.

sign Engineer and then Assistant Planning Engineer.

Langsner Transfers

Langsner, who will transfer to Sacramento from the Los Angeles area to become Design Engineer for the division, is a native of Brooklyn, N. Y. He came to California in 1922 and was graduated from the California Institute of Technology in 1931 with a civil engineering degree. He has been

LYMAN R. GILLIS, LEFT; GEORGE LANGSNER

JOHN P. MURPHY

George Langsner, District Engineer—Planning for District VII, with headquarters in Los Angeles, to be Design Engineer for the division, with headquarters in Sacramento.

Lyman R. Gillis, District Engineer—Operations for District VII, to be District Engineer—Planning.

Alfred L. Himelhoch, Assistant District Engineer—Traffic for District VII, promoted to District Engineer—Operations.

War Veteran

Wilson's successor as Assistant State Highway Engineer, John Murphy, has been with the Division of Highways

Murphy was born in Pittsburgh, Pennsylvania, and received his early education in Bakersfield. From 1942 to 1945 he served with the U. S. Marine Corps in the Pacific Theater, including a tour of duty as Division Engineer Officer for the Second Marine Division.

Legarra, who is being transferred to the position of Planning Engineer from that of Design Engineer, will be returning to a post he previously held for more than a year beginning in November, 1955. Legarra is also a University of California civil engineering graduate (1934) who has been with the Division of Highways since 1941, serving in District VI (Fresno) and District X (Stockton) before moving to Sacramento headquarters office in 1951 as Assistant De-

ALFRED L. HIMELHOCH

continuously with the Division of Highways since then, fulfilling constantly increasing responsibilities in planning, construction and design in the Los Angeles District. He was promoted to District Engineer there in 1955.

Langsner has been closely identified with the accelerated development of the Los Angeles metropolitan area freeway system, beginning as assistant resident engineer on the Pasadena Freeway in 1940. From 1947 until his promotion to District Engineer in 1955 he was assistant district engineer in charge of design, materials and sur-

38

veys for projects in the Los Angeles area.

Gillis, who has been District Engineer—Operations in District VII since January, 1956, will move to the District Engineer—Planning position bitherto held by Langsner.

He is a native of Walla Walla, Washington. He moved to California as a high school student and received his civil engineering degree from the University of California in 1938. He has since been with the Division of Highways, serving in District IV (San Francisco) continuously until 1956 except for military service in the Navy Civil Engineer Corps in World War II and the Korean conflict. Gillis had been Assistant District Engineer—Construction in the San Francisco District for three years prior to his promotion to District Engineer in the Los Angeles District.

Himelhoch's promotion to District Engineer—Operations is the latest advancement in an engineering career that began in 1936 on the Mono Craters Tunnel Aqueduct for the City of Los Angeles. He moved to the Division of Highways Los Angeles District later that year, and has continued there since. He is a native of Los Angeles, and an engineering graduate of the University of Southern California.

Most of Himelhoch's early activity with the Division of Highways was on survey work, but since 1945 he has had increasing responsibilities in design, hydraulics and traffic engineering in the Los Angeles District. He was promoted to Assistant District Engineer—Traffic in 1955.

Max Gilliss Returns To Public Works Post

C. M. (Max) Gilliss resumed the position of deputy director of the State Department of Public Works September 17.

He had left the position in January, 1957, to serve Governor Goodwin J. Knight as a secretary assisting in legislative work.

Gilliss first joined the department December 1, 1952, as special representative, and became deputy director September 23, 1955.

HYDRAULIC MINING IN THE OLD WEST

If you shoud happen to take a trip for yourself this coming fall and should end up rolling around the roads in the Mother Lode Country, the roads that run north of Sacramento through Grass Valley, Nevada City, and the like, you'll probably run across the little town of North San Juan and see nearby the great white holes that mark the spots where Columbia Hill and Badger Mountain used to stand.

To understand these great bleak holes, points out the National Automobile Club, you have to go back to the time of the Gold Rush and the strange fever that followed in its wake. When the prospectors and miners converged on California from all corners of the land, they soon discovered that the vein of gold that ran down the Sierra Nevada was one of the richest in the world. They also discovered that it could be very hard to find. Sending a shaft down here and a shaft down there, a man could spend his entire life digging holes and never coming across very · much in the way of gold. The superstitious turned to divining rods and the more

practical minded turned to the knowledge of the mining engineer. Neither of these did much to take the gambling out of mining with the shovel and shaft.

In something of anger and desperation men finally turned to hydraulic mining. Diverting rivers in their courses and pumping this water through great nozzles at enormous pressures, they turned whole mountains, such as Columbia and Badger, into rivers of mud that surged down the valleys. As the mud passed, they gathered the gold.

The rivers of mud, however, soon became so great that they buried rich pasture lands and farm country under layers of ooze. At this the ranchers and farmers got up in arms, fought with the miners, and finally managed to have hydraulic mining banned in California in 1884. In recent years some hydraulic mining has been permitted in certain areas and under careful supervision.

The holes at North San Juan, however, are relics of a wilder day when wide-eyed men in search of gold could wash whole mountains right away.

ALL IN A DAY'S WORK

To Whom It May Concern:

I didn't know to whom to write this letter nor exactly know what to say. But I'm sure it'll get to the right hands.

Yesterday about 2 p.m. my mother and the five of us girls, ranging in ages from 10 to 20 years, were driving home from Inglewood after taking my father to the airport to catch a plane for Mississippi. Anyway, we were in the Santa Ana Canyon. Right in the middle of it. Image six women stranded in the middle of the Santa Ana Canyon with the loveliest flat tire you ever saw. A piece of rubber came off the tire and stayed on the highway. So we sat and sat. Then here comes a truck from the Department of California Highways from Santa

Ana and, as we found out later, the driver was Charlie Snider. He stopped to help us. We were on a very slight slope, which made it very hard to keep the car up on the jack, even when he used two jacks, his and ours both. The car fell off the jacks three times. But your employee, Mr. Snider, stuck to it and finished the job, too. He refused to take any payment for his work. So I (the 20-year-old) thought I would write to the department or department head to let them know the courtesy Mr. Snider showed us.

Thank you.

Miss Lucille Machado
3744 McKenzie Street
Arlington

P.S.: It took Mr. Snider exactly 1½ hours to fix the flat.

Cost Index

Reaches Low Point for Year
In Third Quarter of 1957

By RICHARD H. WILSON, Assistant State Highway Engineer
H. C. McCARTY, Office Engineer
LLOYD B. REYNOLDS, Assistant Office Engineer

THE California Highway Construction Cost Index for the third quarter of 1957 reached a low point for the year. The index now stands at 237.5 (1940 = 100), which is 29.4 index points or 11.0 percent below the second quarter. It is 11.6 points or 4.7 percent below the same quarter a year ago and 14.6 points or 5.8 percent below the fourth quarter of 1956.

The California index and the Bureau of Public Roads Composite Mile Index have followed similar patterns as the graph included with this release will show. The California index is affected by local conditions and the activities of a single state, with the result that rapid changes and decided fluctuations are found in the graph line. On the other hand, the bureau's composite mile index, which is computed from data accumulated from a much larger number of projects, national in scope, presents a smoother graph.

Past performances of these indexes show that in the instances where decided peaks and valleys have occurred in the California index with respect to the bureau's, a return to national averages, in a reasonable interval, can be expected. This situation occurred again in this quarter. The rapid move away from the bureau's index early in 1956 has been watched with speculation as to when similar levels would be reached. In view of the decided drop in California's index and the flattening of the bureau's, it remains to be seen whether a downward trend in national costs has been established. All factors being considered, it is our belief that a general upward course will be followed.

The curtailed opening of bids during August and September had a marked effect upon the index behavior during this quarter. The down-

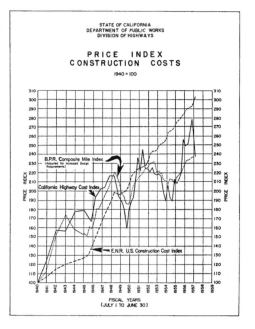

STATE OF CALIFORNIA
DEPARTMENT OF PUBLIC WORKS
DIVISION OF HIGHWAYS

PRICE INDEX
CONSTRUCTION COSTS
1940 = 100

ward direction in the period was effected by roadway excavation, asphaltic and bituminous mixes and portland cement concrete pavement, the other items remaining close to previous quarter average prices.

In the second quarter, bids were opened for about 16 large projects, the majority of which were for extensive freeway construction. Bid prices for the seven index items were widely spread, but most of the resulting averages were fairly in line with those determined in recent quarters. Most of these projects are located in areas subject to considerable traffic interference. It was stated in the second quarter release that cost data were well averaged by the wide distribution of the projects. A review of costs for the three items mentioned above has shown the statement to be true.

Of the 128 projects for which contracts were awarded in the third quarter, only six were major freeway projects. The large number of low-value projects with respect to the total, exerted an effect on prive averages that heretofore was not appreciably felt in view of the magnitude of freeway projects with which their bid prices were averaged.

Prices furnished by three large freeway projects for the three controlling items of this period gave assistance in establishing averages below those recently experienced. In these instances low prices were reflected by freedom from traffic interference and/or accessibility of materials sources.

Average prices of $0.63 for roadway excavation existing during the last two quarters have been considered as being at a high level, as previously bids for this item were generally hovering in the 50-cent range. The average of $0.42 for this quarter is the lowest since the first quarter of 1956. A large-volume project with a price of $0.32 per cubic yard combined with a number of small projects having relatively low bid prices exerted a toppling effect with respect to excavation cost averages.

Untreated rock base rose from $2.10 to $2.34 but, lacking support from other items, its upward force was ineffective. Limited use of the item during this period was responsible for the price increase.

Asphaltic and bituminous mixes dropped from $6.18 to $5.10, the lowest point reached since 1955. The previously mentioned freeway projects combined with the extensive summer resurfacing program are responsible for this marked change.

Portland cement concrete pavement dropped from $15.59 to $14.34, a level

CALIFORNIA DIVISION OF HIGHWAYS AVERAGE CONTRACT PRICES

	Roadway excavation, per cu. yd.	Untreated rock base, per ton	Plant-mixed surfacing, per ton	Asphalt concrete pavement, per ton	Asphaltic and bituminous mixes, per ton	PCC pavement, per cu. yd.	PCC structures, per cu. yd.	Bar reinforcing steel, per lb.	Structural steel, per lb.
1940	$0.22	$1.54	$3.19	$3.97	..	$7.68	$18.33	$0.040	$0.083
1941	0.26	2.31	2.84	3.18	..	7.54	33.31	0.053	0.107
1942	0.35	2.81	4.02	4.16	..	9.62	29.48	0.073	0.103
1943	0.43	2.36	3.71	4.76	..	11.48	31.76	0.089	0.080
1944	0.50	2.45	4.10	4.50	..	10.46	31.99	0.084	0.133
1945	0.51	2.42	4.20	4.88	..	10.90	37.20	0.059	0.102
1946	0.41	2.46	4.00	4.68	..	9.48	37.36	0.060	0.099
1947	0.46	2.42	4.32	5.38	..	12.38	38.44	0.080	0.138
1948	0.55	2.43	4.30	5.38	..	13.04	49.86	0.092	0.126
1949	0.49	2.67	4.67	4.64	..	12.38	48.67	0.096	0.117
1950	0.40	2.25	4.26	3.75	..	11.11	43.45	0.079	0.094
1951	0.49	2.62	4.34	5.00	..	12.21	47.22	0.102	0.159
1952	0.56	2.99	5.00	4.88	..	13.42	48.08	0.098	0.180
1953	0.51	'2.14	5.31	4.58	..	13.74	50.59	0.093	0.133
1954	0.45	3.13	4.50	4.86	..	14.41	48.42	0.094	0.124
1955	0.39	2.22	4.93	..	..	13.35	45.73	0.095	0.142
1st quarter 1956	0.40	2.08	5.40	6.50		14.05	53.51	0.108	0.166
2d quarter 1956	0.51	2.06	6.27	..		14.64	37.13	0.113	0.219
3d quarter 1956	0.52	2.27	6.12	..		15.67	56.32	0.131	0.176
4th quarter 1956	0.82	2.31	²	..	'⁵6.93	14.95	59.63	0.113	0.197
1st quarter 1957	0.63	2.10	..	..	6.94	17.38	61.14	0.129	0.335
2d quarter 1957	0.63	2.10	..	..	6.18	15.59	58.61	0.119	0.304
3d quarter 1957	0.42	2.34	..	..	5.10	14.34	58.68	0.130	0.300

¹ The item of crusher run base was used before 1953.
² Asphalt concrete pavement combined with plant-mix surfacing in fourth quarter 1956 and will be identified as asphaltic and bituminous mixes in the future.

NUMBER AND SIZE OF PROJECTS, TOTAL BID VALUES AND AVERAGE NUMBER OF BIDDERS
(July 1, 1957, to September 30, 1957)

Project volume	Up to $50,000	$50,000 to $100,000	$100,000 to $250,000	$250,000 to $500,000	$500,000 to $1,000,000	Over $1,000,000	All projects
Road projects							
No. of projects	86	18	18	6	2	1	101
Total value*	$1,564,252	$1,340,102	$3,892,258	$1,879,508	$1,451,301	$1,679,044	$10,366,565
Avg. No. bidders	4.6	6.4	7.2	10.7	7.6	11.0	6.9
Structure projects							
No. of projects	13	1	6	1	....	2	23
Total value*	$309,825	$80,496	$1,082,600	$294,452	....	$8,977,458	$10,644,831
Avg. No. bidders	8.7	9.0	10.5	8.0	....	6.5	7.3
Combination projects							
No. of projects	......	......	......	......	......	5	5
Total value*	......	......	......	......	......	$18,162,793	$18,162,793
Avg. No. bidders	......	......	......	......	......	7.5	7.5
Summary							
No. of projects	68	19	24	7	2	8	128
Total value*	$1,564,077	$1,420,598	$3,974,858	$2,174,060	$1,451,301	$28,819,295	$39,094,189
Avg. No. bidders	4.8	6.5	8.0	10.3	7.5	7.9	6.2

* Bid items only.

Total Average Bidders by Months

	July	August	September	Average for three months
1957	6.1	6.7	5.7	6.2
1956	3.8	3.7	3.7	3.7

not experienced for more than a year. Two large-volume freeway projects close to material sources made the low price possible in this third quarter.

Class A portland cement concrete structures, one of the items with a higher average price, was up to $58.68 from the $58.61 price in the previous quarter.

The increase in price from $0.119 to $0.130 for bar reinforcing steel establishes a high for the item. A review of prices received during the period fails to show the reasons for the increase at this time.

The price per pound for structural steel, lower by four-tenths of a cent in this quarter, now stands at $0.20. The change is not significant but, if a trend is being established, definite results will obtain in the fourth quarter with the resumption of freeway project bids. Recently published information on steel manufacturing shows that the industry is now recovered from strike effects of 1956 and that previously existing shortages in rolled shapes and plates are virtually cleared out.

The accompanying tabulation shows the average unit prices forming the basis for computing the cost index since 1940.

Previous releases on cost trends in California have attributed considerable of the upward direction in highway construction costs to the delays and uncertainties in steel deliveries. With the situation improved as claimed in published reports, contingencies included by contractors in bid prices for steel to protect themselves against delivery delays should not be evident in the future.

Other factors that have contributed to the rise in highway construction costs are increased labor rates and prices for materials. It is evident that shortcutting methods now being employed by many contractors, particularly on large projects, are successfully offsetting a large share of the rise in costs attributed to these price components.

Data for preparation of this quarter's index were provided by 128 projects, of which 53.1 percent were under $50,000, 14.8 percent ranged from $50,000 to $100,000, 18.7 percent ranged from $100,000 to $250,000, 5.5 percent ranged from $250,000 to $500,000, 1.6 percent ranged from $500,000 to $1,000,000, and 6.3 percent were over $1,000,000. The total bid value of these projects amounted to $39,094,189, and the projects under $50,000 accounted for 3.2 percent of the total; between $50,000 and $100,000 was 3.6 percent; between $100,000 and $250,000 was 10.2 per-

cent; between $250,000 and $500,000 was 5.6 percent; between $500,000 and $1,000,000 was 3.7 percent; and over $1,000,000 was 73.7 percent.

Bidder competition has held up during this quarter, with the average bidders per contract standing at 6.2, compared with 3.7 a year ago and 5.1 for the last fiscal year. The accompanying table shows in detail the number of projects, the project values and the average number of bidders arranged by value brackets.

The California Highway Construction Cost Index, the Engineering News-Record Construction Cost Index and the United States Bureau of Public Roads Composite Mile Index, all reduced to the base 1940 = 100, are shown on the accompanying graph. The latter two indexes are based on nationwide construction costs.

The Engineering News-Record Cost Index, which now stands at 303.2, again shows a rise at a slightly

THE CALIFORNIA HIGHWAY CONSTRUCTION COST INDEX	
Year	Cost Index
1940	100.0
1941	125.0
1942	157.5
1943	156.4
1944	177.8
1945	179.5
1946	179.7
1947	203.3
1948	216.6
1949	190.7
1950	181.2
(1st quarter 1950—160.6)	
1951	225.0
(4th quarter 1951—245.4)	
1952	225.9
1953	215.2
1954	193.5
(2d quarter 1954—189.0)	
1955 (1st quarter)	189.3
1955 (2d quarter)	212.4
1955 (3d quarter)	208.6
1955 (4th quarter)	212.6
1956 (1st quarter)	219.5
1956 (2d quarter)	255.9
1956 (3d quarter)	249.1
1956 (4th quarter)	252.1
1957 (1st quarter)	277.7
1957 (2d quarter)	266.9
1957 (3d quarter)	237.5

'Twas Different Back in 700 B.C.

Right-of-way acquisition and access control today involve negotiations which result in friendly settlements in nearly all cases. It wasn't always that way.

Seven hundred years before the birth of Christ, the king of Assyria had less democratic methods for dealing with encroachments along the Royal Road.

When he died, the king left this message on a memorial marker in the City of Nineveh: "The Royal Road. Let No Man Decrease It."

To back up this decree the monarch further ordered that any unlucky subject whose property impaired the roadway was to be impaled on a stake in front of the palace.

The record of the California Division of Highways Right of Way Department provides a sharp contrast.

During the 1956-1957 Fiscal Year, the department settled 97.16 percent of its right-of-way dealings in an amicably negotiated manner. In a total of 9,391 transactions it was necessary to complete eminent domain proceedings on only 267 parcels.

Today, property owners find that right-of-way and access problems can be resolved with state agents on a mutually beneficial basis. In the king's day, reluctant landholders had only one stake in such problems—the one in front of the palace.

higher rate of increase than in the second quarter of 1957. It is up 7.5 index points or 2.5 percent from the second quarter.

The Bureau of Public Roads Composite Mile Index for the second quarter of 1957, at the level of 237.2, which is the latest available, was up 0.2 index point or 0.08 percent over the first quarter of 1957.

Recommendations

*Civic Groups Present
Highway Priorities*

THREE GROUPS presented budget recommendations to the California Highway Commission at its August meeting in Sacramento.

The San Francisco Chamber of Commerce's budget recommendations for San Francisco for the Fiscal Year 1958-59 were presented before the commissioners August 21st. Leonard S. Mosias, chairman of the San Francisco chamber's street, highway and bridge section, urged inclusion of nearly $35,000,000 for construction and right-of-way allocations in San Francisco as follows:

a. Routes 225 and 2, southern freeway—from Orizaba Avenue along the Southern Pacific tracks and Alemany to the James Lick Memorial (Bayshore) Freeway junction, full freeway development, 4.0 miles, $29,000,000.

b. Routes 2 and 56—Golden Gate Bridge approach—Route 2 from Richardson Avenue "Y" to interchange with Route 56, add two additional lanes, 1.4 miles, $5,-800,000.

c. Route 68—James Lick Memorial (Bayshore) Freeway—South city limits to Bay Bridge, protective planting, $100,000.

The 1958-59 recommendations of the Alameda County Highway Advisory Committee were laid before the commission on the opening day of its monthly meeting, August 20th. W. A. Sparling, secretary of the committee, headed the group making the presentation.

Projects upon which actual construction, including programed acquisition of rights-of-way, should be prosecuted the committee said, are:

State Route 69—Eastshore Freeway

1. US 40—Complete rights-of-way acquisition and initiate construction of the Eastshore Freeway in Albany to connect with the Alameda County-Contra Costa County line.

2. In San Leandro—Early completion of First Avenue Interchange facilities. The adjacent industrial area has developed to a point where completion of the cloverleaf and provisions for four lanes of traffic on the overcrossing is necessary.

3. In San Leandro—Provide an overpass structure to carry traffic from Halcyon Drive to Farnsworth Street in San Lean-

dro. There is no crossing of the freeway between First Avenue and Washington Avenue, a distance of about one mile. The necessary rights-of-way for the approaches to the structure are vested in the City of San Leandro.

State Route 226

1. Estuary Crossing—Complete rights-of-way acquisitions and initiate construction at an early date.

2. In Alameda—Program rights-of-way acquisition and initiate construction from the northerly end of Bay Farm Island Bridge to Fernside Boulevard.

State Route 226 and 75—In Oakland

Portion of Sign Route 24—Complete route adoption between Alameda-Contra Costa county line and Eastshore Freeway; continue planning and surveys and formulate a program for correction of spot deficiencies. Initiate planned acquisition of rights-of-way.

State Route 227—Mountain Boulevard Freeway

Increase program of state allocations and accelerate construction for early completion to State Route 5.

State Route 5—Foothill Boulevard and MacArthur Boulevard

1. Sign Route 9—Expedite route studies, surveys and plans for Route 5-C from Hayward to Niles, together with correction of the three-lane portion from Sycamore Avenue to the unincorporated town of Decoto by the addition of a fourth traffic lane.

2. US 50, MacArthur Boulevard and Foothill Boulevard—Initiate construction and continue programed purchases of rights-of-way.

3. US 50—Expedite surveys and protection of rights-of-way southerly from San Leandro to connect with State Route 228, and correct spot deficiencies.

4. Sign Route 9—Expedite surveys and protection of rights-of-way for Route 5-C from Decoto to vicinity of Warm Springs, and correct spot deficiencies.

State Route 105—In Oakland, San Leandro and Hayward

Expedite planned purchases of rights-of-way southerly from Route 5 to Route 69 along Jackson Street in the vicinity of Hayward.

State Route 108

1. Sign Route 21, from State Route 5 near Warm Springs to junction with State

Route 107 near Sunol—Expedite surveys, acquisition of rights-of-way, and design to take early advantage of federal highway funds as a part of the Interstate Highway System.

The regional highway committees of the California State Chamber of Commerce were heard on August 22d. They presented recommendations for highway construction projects in the 58 counties of the State in the 1958-59 Budget and in subsequent budgets.

F. W. Tarr, chairman of the State Chamber's statewide highway committee, explained to the commissioners that the projects recommended were assembled following a series of 38 meetings held in all parts of the State in June, July and August.

ENGINEERS DO MAKE PROGRESS

Editor, *California Highways
and Public Works*
1172 Seventh St., Monterey, California

DEAR SIR: I wish to thank you for sending the "California Highways and Public Works." I find it one of the most interesting and instructive publications I receive, and when I look at the photos of some of the projects it really makes me marvel. It all seems to me to be so complicated, in fact impossible, and lo and behold up comes a photo of the project all finished and in order. I have marveled at the Candlestick Point section of the Bayshore Freeway you have built just out of San Francisco. I watched it being built for about five years or more.

Yours respectively

HERBERT T. CROSS

Once there was a lion tamer who said that his father before him had also been a lion tamer.

"Did you ever put your head in a lion's mouth?" he was asked.

"Only once," said the fellow, "to look for Dad."

and Public Works

43

Out of the Mail Bag

CALIFORNIA CONGRATULATED

WHITMAN, REQUARDT AND ASSOCIATES
Engineers
Baltimore 2, Maryland

MR. GEORGE T. McCOY
State Highway Engineer

DEAR MR. McCOY: Since my retirement in October, 1956, as chief engineer and advisory engineer to the State Roads Commission of Maryland I have been associated with Whitman, Requardt and Associates as highway consultant.

I continue to receive California Highways and Public Works, which I read religiously and always obtain some valuable information therefrom. In the March-April issue notice is given that the California Highway Department has prepared a booklet entitled "Freeway Facts." If these are available I would very much appreciate receiving two copies.

You and your associates are to be congratulated on the splendid progress you have made under the 1956 Federal Aid Highway Act, with particular reference to the interstate system, and I am happy to know that Maryland is in such fine company. This is a source of great pride to me as I had a great deal to do with the preparation and inauguration of the work under the 12-year road construction and reconstruction program.

With kindest regards and best wishes.

Sincerely yours,

W. F. CHILDS, JR.

THANK YOU

KENNETH C. ADAMS, Editor

Thank you for enabling me to receive copies of your wonderful magazine. I want you to know I have thoroughly enjoyed every issue I have received. I cannot express my sincere appreciation enough for this wonder-

LIKES OUR PHOTOGRAPHY

HAROLD D. WEBER, PUBLIC RELATIONS
534 20th Street, Oakland 12, California

MR. KENNETH C. ADAMS, Editor
California Highways and Public Works

DEAR MR. ADAMS: For many years I have been on the mailing list to receive California Highways and Public Works, a courtesy and a privilege I greatly appreciate. Because my activities are now in different fields, I no longer participate directly in the civic organization phase of highway development, as I did for more than 20 years, especially with reference to the Richmond-Oakland-San Jose Eastshore Freeway, now nearing completion.

I still retain an interest in the highway program, and enjoy the opportunity of keeping posted through reading the regular issues of the magazine, which I do with interest and pleasure, and then file for reference.

The entire magazine is a splendid example of editorial and mechanical skills, but I want to compliment you particularly, and through you the men responsible, for the cover color photography, both as to subject matter and plate work. Keep up the good work!

Sincerely,

HAROLD D. WEBER

ful educational and enlightening magazine, and read it from cover to cover.

I have all copies sent me for years and often refer back to old copies. Looking forward to your next issue.

Yours very truly,

JOE DE LUCCHI
Los Angeles

Of the 10,050 bridges on the national interstate system in rural areas, 8,187, or 81 per cent, are below standard width, according to the Automotive Safety Foundation.

Liability of State Drivers

Do you drive a state car or other state equipment? If you do, are you always sure you are using the vehicle on actual state business, so that, should you become involved in an accident, you will not personally be held liable?

Any state employee, while using a state-owned vehicle on official business, is fully protected under insurance taken out by the State against liability for personal injury and property damage to others. There is no personal insurance on the employee himself except under the provisions of the Workmen's Compensation Act, which covers all state employees injured in the course of their employment.

Employees' Liability

As indicated above, the key factor in determining the liability of a state employee who incurs an accident while driving a state vehicle is whether or not the employee is on official state business at the time the accident occurs. According to J. F. Brady, insurance adviser with the Department of Finance, there is a fair interpretation, based on common sense, that allows the employee to take the state vehicle when he goes out for meals or if he wishes to pick up some luggage at his home prior to a trip out of town. He cited cases, however, where employees were held personally liable as a result of becoming involved in an accident when operating a state vehicle while not in the course of their employment.

Brady pointed out there have been relatively few cases of misuse of state cars, particularly in recent years, and that many times the offender is unaware that he is doing wrong. He urged all state employees who have occasion to drive a state vehicle to exercise the utmost discretion and operate it only on official duty. Anyone who violates this provision is placing himself in an extremely delicate position, he said.

Traffic lines and pavement markings were painted on approximately 10,702 miles of rural state highways by the California Division of Highways during the 1955-56 Fiscal Year.

View of widened section of U. S. 50 looking westerly from Bijou on Lake Tahoe

and Public Works

Recent photo of construction of Embarcadero Freeway in San Francisco. Famous Ferry Building in center foreground.

California Highways

RICHARD H. WILSON

Continued from page 47 . . .

With passage of the first federal-aid highway act in 1916, federal participation in the cost of highway construction became a reality. Administration of the act became the responsibility of the Bureau of Public Roads, which was created for the purpose. Highway construction gained in importance with the demands for better roads, and, as the federal sharing in this activity increased, the relationship between the Division of Highways and the Bureau of Public Roads became more significant.

Co-operation With Federal Agencies

Administration of the functions involving federal aid has been the responsibility of Wilson since his attachment to the headquarters staff. Close contact with the division's programs and his awareness of federal regulations have made possible the taking of full advantage of available federal funds. Close acquaintance with bureau personnel, both at the local and national level, has been effective in expediting construction programs.

Many persons who have reached high places with the Division of Highways entered state service via the Wilson route. His subordinates have been well trained and have been given responsibility for their duties, and he has always taken part in their various social and athletic activities. He has selected well in his choice of key personnel serving under his direction.

Wilson is a member of the American Society of Civil Engineers. He has held committee membership in the American Association of State Highway Officials, and through his activities on the administration practices committee he has gained national recognition for his contributions to the organization and highway administration in general. At the same time he has been affiliated with the Western Association of State Highway Officials and the American Concrete Institute. Besides a number of lodges and service clubs, he is a member of the American Legion, the Del Paso Country Club and the Sacramento University Club.

Wilson was born in Leitchfield, Kentucky, and received his educa-

New Truck Speed Zones Announced

Establishment of reduced downhill speed limits for trucks on eight mountain highway grades was announced by the State Department of Public Works.

The speed reductions are the first to be made under a law enacted by the 1957 Legislature in an effort to reduce the danger of run-away trucks on long downhill stretches.

Grades on US Highways 99, 101, and 40 are included in the speed zoning changes. The new truck speed limits on these sections range from 20 to 35 miles an hour, in place of the general statewide truck speed limit of 45 miles an hour.

Downhill sections affected by the reductions follow:

US 99—Shasta Springs Grade, north of Dunsmuir, Siskiyou County; Grapevine Grade, Kern County, and Three-Mile and Five-Mile Grades, both north of Castaic in Los Angeles County.

US 101—Cuesta Grade, north of San Luis Obispo, and Nojoqui Grade, north of Santa Barbara.

US 40—Glen Alder Grade, between Colfax and Gold Run, Placer County, and Donner Grade, Nevada County.

Recommended by McCoy

The new zoning will become effective with the posting of signs. The signs will show the speed limit figure

---

tion at schools in Washington, D. C., George Washington University, and the University of Michigan, where he graduated in 1912 with a bachelor of engineering degree. He was married in Idaho in 1920 to Agnes Hart of Blackfoot, Idaho. They have a son, Jack Hart Wilson, and a daughter, Betty Jo Wilson. Perhaps most important is the granddaughter Wendy, who is now five years of age.

Retirement plans are not certain beyond enjoying retirement to the fullest, which no doubt will include considerable golf and continuation of his active part with Ben Ali Shrine Chanters.

under a plate bearing the word "truck" in capital letters.

The speed limit reductions were recommended by State Highway Engineer G. T. McCoy following engineering and traffic studies by the Division of Highways.

Under a section added to the California Vehicle Code by the recent session of the Legislature the Department of Public Works may reduce truck speed limits on descending grades after studies show that 'the speed of 45 miles per hour is more than is reasonable or safe * * *."

The new law calls for reductions to "a speed limit of 40, 35, 30, 25, or 20 miles per hour, whichever is found most appropriate to facilitate the orderly movement of traffic * * *."

Truck Speed Zones

More detailed descriptions of the truck speed zones are listed by county below.

Los Angeles County—Five-Mile Grade (US 99), north of Castaic, 20 miles an hour southbound from the summit; and Three-Mile Grade (US 99), also north of Castaic, 35 miles an hour northbound from the summit.

Kern County—Grapevine Grade (US 99), 20 miles an hour northbound from the summit for a distance of about five and one-half miles.

Santa Barbara County—Nojoqui Grade (US 101), 25 miles an hour southbound from the summit to three-fourths of a mile north of the intersection with Sign Route 1 at Las Cruces, a distance of about one and three-fourths miles.

San Luis Obispo County—Cuesta Grade (US 101), north of San Luis Obispo, 25 miles an hour southbound from the summit for about 2.6 miles.

Siskiyou County—Shasta Springs Grade, north of Dunsmuir (US 99), 20 miles an hour southbound from the summit for approximately three miles.

Placer County—Glen Alder Grade (US 40), between Colfax and Gold Run, 20 miles an hour westbound from the summit for about three miles.

Nevada County—Donner Grade (US 40), 20 miles an hour eastbound from the summit for approximately three miles.

SAM R. LEEDOM

Continued from page 48 . . .

In 1933 Leedom took a trip around the world and spent several months in China and Manchuria writing articles about the industrial empire the Japanese were building in their newly militarily acquired possession of Manchuria.

For the next three years he served as a roving correspondent and special writer for the McClatchy newspapers, during which time he wrote a series of articles on virtually every hamlet in the Central Valleys area.

In 1936 Leedom went out to the Dutch East Indies to do a series of stories on the sea peoples of that then remote region. He lived with the sea peoples and sailed on their boats with them for nearly a year, covering a distance comparable to sailing from San Francisco down to New Orleans, up to New York and back to San Francisco. In doing so he covered all of the remote islands from Sumatra to Ambonia, the Moluccas and back to Borneo.

Returning, he was among the first of those to point out the weakness of United States, Dutch and English forces in the Far East against the threat of Japanese invasion and domination.

Leedom was born in Nebraska, but grew up in northern Wyoming where his father owned and published a weekly newspaper. He was graduated from the Billings, Montana, High School and is a member of the class of 1923 of the University of California.

He married Miss Ella Logan of Redding, a Berkeley schoolteacher, in 1923. For a number of years she was a teacher in the Lincoln Elementary School in Sacramento.

Upon retirement Mr. and Mrs. Leedom will move to El Granada, where they are building a new home. Leedom expects to devote his time to writing and fishing.

CAR INCREASE

California's automobile population is increasing at the rate of about 5,500 per month, reports the California State Automobile Association.

T. T. Buell

Co-workers and friends of T. T. "Tom" Buell celebrated his retirement Saturday evening, September 28th, with a dinner party at the Bret Harte Hotel in Grass Valley. Buell retired as highway maintenance superintendent of the area comprised of Yuba County and portions of Nevada, Sierra, Sutter and Placer Counties. He reached the compulsory retirement age of 70 on July 21st.

His nearly 25 years of service in the California Division of Highways started as a laborer in District VII, Los Angeles area, in 1932. Successive promotions saw him serving in various capacities in District VI, Fresno, District II, Redding, and District IX, Bishop. He was promoted to Highway Maintenance Superintendent in 1938 and went to the Truckee area in that capacity in 1942. He was transferred to the Grass Valley area in 1953.

Two memorable experiences occurred during his stay in District III, both while he was in charge of the Truckee area. In November, 1950, while inspecting a slide during a severe storm, a slide swept him and a highway patrolman from the roadway and carried him about 150 feet. He was seriously injured in the accident.

The winter of the "big snow," 1952, found Buell charged with the responsibilty of opening Highway 40 over Donner Summit. It was during this storm that this route was closed for 28 days, and required tremendous effort to place this major transcontinental route in service even in this period of time.

Buell plans to remain in Grass Valley following his retirement.

Chairman for the retirement dinner was John L. Snider of Grass Valley, who has served under Buell for 13 years and will be his replacement.

PATENTS

Since 1899, more than 2.25 million U. S. patents have been issued. About one out of five of these were automotive.

A. C. Clark

Arthur C. Clark, Assistant Commissioner for Operations, Bureau of Public Roads, U. S. Department of Commerce, has retired. Following graduation from Oregon State College in 1915 as a civil engineer, Mr. Clark joined the Bureau of Public Roads and remained with the organization for 42 years.

In 1917 he enlisted in the armed forces and served for two years with the 23d Engineers. Upon his return to the Bureau of Public Roads, he was placed in charge of heavy grading, surfacing and bridge construction in the Pacific Northwestern States. From 1924 to 1937 he was responsible for all construction and maintenance operations on federal-aid and forest highway projects in Montana.

Clark organized the first federal-aid highway operation in Puerto Rico and remained in charge of the work there from 1937 to 1942. During World War II he was technical assistant and operations co-ordinator at the Washington headquarters for the construction of the Alaska Highway.

Under the organization plan of 1957, Mr. Clark was appointed Assistant Commissioner for Operations, the position he held at the time of his retirement.

ROBERT J. CARLISLE

Continued from page 48 . . .

He is a native son of California, and was born in Tulare in December, 1888. He and his wife will continue to live in their home at 4621 Euclid Drive, San Diego, California. Their plans include trips to various points of interest throughout the United States with intervals of enjoying their home in San Diego.

OLD AND NEW

Modern freeways are engineered so they have very few "blindspots," but older two-lane roads often were not. Don't "overdrive" when you are on narrow, two-lane roads. Be prepared to stop when rounding curves and approaching the crest of hills.

and Public Works 49

Retirements *from* Service

H. Clyde Amesbury

H. Clyde Amesbury, Traffic Engineer of the Division of Highways, District II, in Redding, retired on October 1st after more than 40 years of service in highway construction. Almost 25 years were spent in California state service.

H. CLYDE AMESBURY

Clyde was Traffic Engineer in District II from 1951 until his retirement, and just prior to that he was Construction Engineer in the same district for 13 years. He started working for the State in December of 1933 as Resident Engineer and later became Assistant Maintenance Engineer of District I in Eureka.

In his capacity as Traffic Engineer, Clyde also was in charge of public relations for the district. He was very capable in this position and gained many friends for himself as well as the division.

Clyde Amesbury was born in Brooklyn, Iowa, and came to California with his wife, Helen, in 1925. They have two sons, Dr. Robert H. Amesbury, a dentist in Susanville, and Capt. Bruce Amesbury of the Air Force in Roswell, New Mexico.

After graduating from Iowa State College, Clyde spent several years in private industry as an engineer and as Field Engineer for the State of Montana. His vast experience also includes that of superintendent for the City of Alhambra, Resident Engineer for the Los Angeles County Road Department and General Foreman for the Los Angeles County Flood Control Department.

Clyde is a Mason and a member of the Redding Chamber of Commerce.

Sam R. Leedom

Sam R. Leedom, 61, Administrative Assistant of the State Water Board, retired after 20 years of service with the State. He left on vacation September 6th, and will go on retirement at the end of his vacation period.

SAM R. LEEDOM

His friends and associates tendered him a farewell party at the University Club in Sacramento on the night of August 30th.

Leedom came into state service in 1937 as public information officer for the Water Project Authority, in which capacity he served until commissioned in 1942 as a captain in World War II. He was assigned to SHAEF in England and served there as a member of the G5 section of the Army. Leedom is also a veteran of World War I, having enlisted as a seaman in the Navy for that conflict. He claims his World War I service comprised solely of swabbing down decks of a convoy destroyer in the Atlantic.

Returning to Sacramento in 1945 he was associated with the public relations firm of Clark and Leedom for a year, during which time he also worked for the Joint Legislative Interim Committee on Water Problems. Since 1947 Leedom has been the administrative officer of the State Water Board.

Prior to coming into state service, Leedom worked as a newspaperman. He started his career with the *Orland Register*, of which he was publisher in 1924. He worked as city editor of the *Courier-Free Press* in Redding and came to the *Sacramento Bee* in 1927 as a copyreader and shortly thereafter was appointed city editor.

. . . Continued on page 49

Robert J. Carlisle

Robert J. Carlisle, Highway Equipment Superintendent I, for the Division of Highways, Shop 11 in San Diego, has retired after 30 years of state service. Carlisle was honored at a retirement party given in his behalf

ROBERT J. CARLISLE

in San Diego, which was attended by approximately 200 of his fellow workers and friends.

Carlisle started his career as an apprentice machinist with the Southern Pacific Company in Los Angeles in 1905. During 1914 and 1915, he spent 1½ years in Trinidad, British West Indies, as superintendent of automotive and marine motor equipment, for the Trinidad Lake Petroleum Company.

He entered state service with the Division of Highways on February 2, 1927, as a Senior Highway District Equipment Maintenance Superintendent at Shop 6 in Fresno. When District 11 was formed in San Diego in 1933, he was transferred to Shop 11 there as the first Highway Equipment Superintendent in the newly formed district. He was instrumental in obtaining the first shop quarters there, and in the establishment of the new shop.

During his years of service in the San Diego shop, Carlisle earned an enviable reputation as maintaining one of the neatest and most efficient shops in the State. His record shows an especially fine achievement in his public relations dealings with the public and his fellow state employees. Carlisle served continuously as superintendent of equipment in San Diego until his retirement.

. . . Continued on page 49

Hard to Replace

Richard H. Wilson Retires From Highways Division

Octomer 31, 1957, marks the close of the colorful and illustrious career of Richard Hagan Wilson in the field of highway engineering. Dick, as he is known to his associates with the Division of Highways, in the highway construction industry, and in private life, started his California service in 1912 with Division I, as it was known when the division office was located in Willits. His assignment as resident engineer between 1912 and 1915 resembled the life of a frontiersman as the North Coast region could boast of little more than game trails north of Willits at the time.

Other fields appeared greener, and in 1915 Wilson transferred his attentions to the Washington State Highway Department as resident engineer, serving in that capacity until 1920. His construction activities were interrupted between September, 1917, and September, 1919, by priorities of the United States Army. The two-year period with the 20th Engineers saw Wilson's rise from private to first lieutenant. At the close of the fracas in France, he returned to his former duties with the State of Washington and in 1920 was appointed district engineer with headquarters at Tacoma. At the end of a year as district engineer, he was moved to Seattle, where he carried on the administration for two districts.

Returns to California

California beckoned again, and in 1927 Wilson as district maintenance engineer returned to District I, which had in the meantime changed its headquarters location to Eureka. Over the next two years it became his responsibility to maintain many of the highways on which he had previously handled construction. Another move was soon to materialize, this time to Sacramento as office engineer and assistant district engineer with District III, where an extensive program was in the planning stage. During the following four years, as office engineer and

RICHARD H. WILSON

assistant district engineer, he had an active part in the design of many projects on US 40, US 50, US 99W and elsewhere in the district. His broad thinking on the subject of highway design resulted in the survival of many of these projects despite the onslaught of present-day traffic.

Being close to the seat of highway operations, his ability was not overlooked, and in 1933 C. H. Purcell, State Highway Engineer, selected Wilson as principal highway engineer, to administer office engineer functions in Headquarters Office. The Division of Highways was then undertaking an extensive program of construction. Through his leadership the program was put under way in record time. In the reorganization of the Division of Highways in 1947, he was again selected to fill an important staff position, that of Assistant State Highway Engineer—Administration, which position he held to his retirement.

Throughout Wilson's career as Headquarters Office Engineer and

later as Assistant State Highway Engineer—Administration, he has had an active and important role in the preparation and bringing to completion of hundreds of highway projects let to contract. His close contact with the various district engineers over the years was a means of expediting the flow of project plans into headquarters so that full advantage could always be taken of prevailing conditions to the end that the volume of construction was held to the highest peak commensurate with revenue available for the purpose.

His wide and intimate acquaintance with members of the contracting industry and representatives of industry connected with highway construction has developed a thorough understanding of the separate problems of these groups and of the Division of Highways. Fair treatment of individual contractors in their dealings with the division and maintenance of construction specifications on an equitable basis have been instrumental in keeping the roster of highway contractors at a high level.

High Bidding Potential

Administering the operational phase with respect to contractors' prequalification ratings has long been a function of the Assistant State Highway Engineer—Administration. His knowledge of contractor capabilities has resulted in the establishment of a high bidding potential equally satisfactory to the division and to the contracting group.

Wilson has served on the division's Contractor Claims Board with four other members from the organization. In the years he has functioned in this capacity most claims have reached an amicable settlement. Contractor relationship has been further evidenced in his negotiations with this group in the formulation of equipment rental rates affecting the Division of Highways.

. . . Continued on page 50

and Public Works   47

HIGHWAY SUPERINTENDENT RETIRES

This article, written by Joe Paul, Jr., and published in the Ventura County "Star-Free Press," is reprinted by "California Highways and Public Works."

Bernard M. (Ben) Gallagher, 69-year-old highway superintendent in the Ventura area for the State Division of Highways, wound up his duties September 11th and left the next day on a vacation trip prior to his retirement October 1st.

Gallagher has been superintendent here 24 years and has been with the department for 28 years. Succeeding Gallagher in the Ventura post will be Willis G. Walker, now of Santa Ana.

Following a motor trip across the United States and parts of Canada, the Gallaghers plan to return here to make their home. Plans for the future are indefinite at this time, but Gallagher said he "plans to stay in the business to a certain degree."

The retiring highway superintendent came to Ventura from Bishop in 1933. At that time, Ventura County's state routes in Gallagher's district all were two-lane, and most of the bridges were of truss-type construction.

The Old and the New

'The roads were just as long then as they are now," Gallagher recalls, "but they have become wider." When a state route right-of-way of 60 feet was considered ample in 1933, a 250-foot right-of-way is required now for the expansive freeways, he explained.

The two greatest changes in the highways in the 24 years here, Gallagher believes, are speed and weight. Average speeds have doubled and truck weights have more than tripled.

Another great change in the department from conditions of 1933 is that of manpower.

"In the 1930's we were in a depression era, and manpower was a cheap commodity. We had hundreds of men working for the Division of Highways, largely to give them something to do," Gallagher recalls. Since that time, the crews have become smaller

BERNARD M. GALLAGHER

and smaller, until now 40 men do all the work in the district.

The district includes Highways 118 west of Chatsworth, 126 southwest of Castaic, US 101 from Oxnard to the Rincon, and the Maricopa Highway.

Greatest single problem of Gallagher's era as highway superintendent was the flood of 1938. Bridge approaches were damaged, highways flooded, culverts blocked and roadbeds destroyed. Indicating how much water came down the rivers at that time, Gallagher recalled that the highwater mark at El Rio in 1938 was only seven inches below that of the St. Francis Dam flood of 11 years previous.

Unbelievable

"The changes which have taken place in highway traffic in the last three decades are unbelievable," Gallagher said. The number of cars on the highways has far exceeded what anyone was able to foresee, he claims.

"But the greatest changes are coming yet," Gallagher predicted. "The problem has become so large that the solution will have to be astounding in freeways and expressways. The highways of tomorrow will be beyond the imagination of the average motorist."

Two major problems plague the highway crews constantly at present, Gallagher pointed out. The No. 1 problem to the maintenance crews is trying to avoid being struck by motorists.

'All the flags, signs, barricades and warnings we can post are not enough to make it safe to get on the highway with a maintenance crew," he stated. "Workers are always in danger of being struck, and close shaves are daily occurrences. Even when the workers get off the shoulder of the highway to eat lunch, they are not safe. Motorists still try to run them down."

(While Gallagher was making this observation, one of the crew members was knocked off a bridge by a motorist in Cuyama Valley and suffered a broken leg and fractured arm.)

Litter Is Problem

The other major current problem is litter and trash thrown from cars.

"We clean up tons and tons of it. It costs plenty to do it. Recent law changes and publicity have helped some, but so many motorists feel that the law applies to all but them that the litter problem gets bigger instead of smaller," Gallagher said.

"If we could pave highways with beer cans, we wouldn't need to buy any material," he added.

During his years in Ventura, Gallagher said he has gained many friends and has enjoyed his associations. "The people I have found to be very nice—

. . . Continued on page 64

Redwood Freeway

Initial Work Marks Construction Firsts

By H. W. BENEDICT, Resident Engineer

THE first unit of the Redwood Freeway, a contract for which was awarded to Guy F. Atkinson Company on April 10, 1957 (see issue of *California Highways and Public Works*, dated March-April, 1957, page 54), marks several firsts for highway construction in District I.

Paramount among these is the distinction of having the highest cut in the history of roadbuilding in California included within its limits. This cut, located on the southerly end of the project, about 2½ miles north of Weott, amputates the northerly end of a high, steep, watershed ridge. The top of the cut towers 480 feet above the grade of the finished road, and the toe of the cut extends 1,300 feet along the new alignment.

Although representing only 5 percent of the total project in mileage, this cut furnishes approximately one-half, or 1,400,000 cubic yards, of the needed excavation for the 4.4-mile project.

An earthmover being towed up the face of the cut. Lower earthmover is a loaded machine on the "down road."

LEFT—Bulldozers pioneering up-ramp on north end of "big cut." This ramp was 525 feet long at a grade of 62 percent. RIGHT—Detour bypassing "big cut" showing an overpass in background which was constructed by the contractor to carry 1,400,000 cubic yards of roadway excavation over the traveled detour.

To provide stability, the cut has 1:1 cut slopes with 20-foot benches spaced every 60 feet vertically. In addition, several thousand feet of 2-inch horizontal drains will be installed on various benches to insure proper drainage of waters trapped behind the cut face.

Two Complex Problems

The construction of this sidehill cut posed two very complex problems; namely, what to do with the highway traffic during construction, and how to move this large amount of yardage contained in the cut in the short construction season normally experienced in this area.

The first problem stemmed from the fact that the existing traveled way passed in a notch at the foot of the cut in a narrow canyon also occupied by the South Fork of Eel River. It was obvious from the outset that any attempt to pass traffic through the construction area on the narrow traveled way would result in long delays to the traveling public and would add greatly to the cost of the planned work. This problem was solved in the Design Department of District I by the rather bold design of a 2,400-foot-long all-paved detour which bypassed the construction area by swinging westerly of the existing traveled way

UPPER—One of four 400-horsepower "donkey" engines used to hoist the earthmovers up the steep up-ramp. LOWER—The earthmovers were automatically engaged to the heavy towing cable by the ingenious hook mounted on a metal sled which engaged a cable loop affixed to the tractor frame.

and dropping into the streambed of the South Fork of Eel River. Extensive lighting and signing of this de-

tour has resulted in three months of accident-free use of the facility.

... Continued on page 58

Street Widening

Oakland City Job
Jointly Financed

By JAMES E. McCARTY, City of Oakland
Supervising Civil Engineer in Charge of Construction

MAJOR street widenings have long plagued city engineers, utility companies, property owners, contractors, and, particularly, the traveling public. Rarely initiated until the original street has reached maximum capacity, they present difficult problems to the contractor who must not only rebuild the streets to modern standards but, also, provide for heavy traffic movements and access to private property during construction.

The City of Oakland recently completed such a project along West Street at a contract cost of $253,000. The new improvement provides approximately 1.6 miles of widened street capable of carrying four lanes of modern traffic, including mass transit vehicles, as well as providing for two parallel parking lanes. The basic improvement involved setting back curbs eight feet to provide a 60-foot pavement width and two 10-foot-wide sidewalk areas. The widened areas were paved with four inches of asphaltic concrete surfacing on 12 inches of crusher run base. The gutters are six feet wide and were constructed of concrete eight inches in thickness on eight inches of crusher run base.

Plans were based on accurate field surveys in order that a grade be established which would provide a minimum gutter flow of 0.33 percent and, at the same time, meet existing sidewalk and driveway grades so as to avoid expensive new sidewalk and driveway construction. Water pockets, either in the gutter or in the private property behind the sidewalks, had to be avoided. This presented an interesting problem of adjustments and balances in order to insure maximum benefits at minimum costs. Profiles were taken of each driveway to insure that the driveway could be used by modern vehicles.

Channelization at San Pablo Avenue and West Street, looking northerly up West Street

Property Owners' Option

Many meetings with property owners were necessary in order to secure their co-operation in replacing wornout driveways and sidewalks at their expense and to secure public acceptance of the project. Defective sidewalks were posted under provisions of the State Improvement Acts, and property owners were notified to make the necessary repairs. The property owners were given the option to have the sidewalk repaired by the general contractor at the time of the improvement or have the sidewalk repaired by others either during or after the improvement. Of the 43,000 square feet of sidewalk and driveway that was reconstructed, 26,000 square feet was at city expense, 6,000 square feet by the utility companies, and 11,000 square feet by private owners. Careful

co-ordination between the inspectors, the contractors, the utility companies and the owners was necessary, and accurate records had to be kept in order that the charges for this work could be properly apportioned. The entire project was thoroughly covered by photographs before the work was started. These photographs proved to be an invaluable aid and are strongly recommended for work of this kind.

Much time and effort was expended in order to insure proper public relations and a complete understanding of the responsibility of each affected party. Utility companies had to be notified at least a year in advance of actual construction in order to provide them opportunity to examine their facilities and, in many cases, finance and reconstruct new lines. Most of the utility work and sanitary

54

sewer repair was done well in advance of the main contract in order to avoid extensive traffic delays.

Work Jointly Financed

The project on West Street involved channelization and signalization at important intersections. A total of 8,055 tons of asphaltic concrete surfacing was used. It was found advisable in many cases to use asphalt concrete for leveling courses rather than

rials laboratory of the City of Oakland:

Passing	¾-inch dense graded	½-inch dense graded	½-inch open graded
¾-inch sieve	100.0%	100.0%	100.0%
½-inch sieve	78.9	99.5	99.8
⅜-inch sieve	50.2	81.3	61.7
No. 4 sieve	36.7	49.6	23.5
No. 8 sieve	32.4	38.9	15.6
No. 28 sieve	18.0	19.6	9.1
No. 100 sieve	7.2	8.6	4.7
No. 200 sieve	3.7	4.8	2.7
Percent asphalt	4.6	5.1	4.5

Channelization at West Street and Grove Street looking northerly

crusher run or treated base in order to provide continuous uninterrupted flow of traffic during peak hours.

City crews expended $12,000 to repair base failures in the existing pavement before the contract was awarded. Asphaltic concrete mixes having three-fourth-inch maximum size aggregate and one-half maximum size aggregate were used for the base and leveling courses. A finish course 1½ inches in thickness of open graded asphaltic concrete was used to complete the project. All asphalt used was 60-70 penetration. The following is a typical analysis of the asphaltic concrete mixes used as determined by the mate-

To provide proper drainage it was necessary to install 3,630 linear feet of drainpipe, together with 22 storm water inlets and 14 manholes.

The work was financed jointly with five-eighths-cent gasoline tax funds and city funds. Plans and specifications for the project were prepared in the city engineer's office and approved by the California Division of Highways. The resultant project has caused much favorable comment from the traveling public and property owners alike, and the improved street now conforms to modern standards as an important arterial between residential and business centers.

NEW LAW GOVERNING AGE OF TEEN-AGE DRIVING INSTRUCTOR

Teenagers under 18 years old are not allowed under the new law to instruct other teenagers how to drive, says the California State Automobile Association.

The AAA motorists' organization points out that a driver accompanying or supervising the driving of the holder of an instruction permit must be 18 years old or over and must have a valid operator's license.

Prior to this change, which became effective September 11, the driver accompanying the holder of an instruction permit merely had to be licensed. This often resulted in 16-year-olds "teaching" 16-year-olds to drive, a condition which created many problems in enforcement and accident investigation work that now can be more effectively controlled.

124 Ward End Park Rd.
Birmingham 8, England

KENNETH C. ADAMS, *Editor*

DEAR SIR: I would like to thank you for sending me California Highways and Public Works, which I always look forward to receiving. I thought perhaps you, and also your readers, may be interested in the enclosed print of one of our main trunk roads, which is greatly in contrast to yours. It is known over here as the Great North Road. The caption accompanied this picture as published here.

I should also like to pay tribute to the printers, etc., for turning out such a clean and smart-looking job.

Thanking you again for your magazine, which I pass on to other people, I remain

Yours sincerely,

EARNEST V. BEAVIS

AUTO VACATIONS

Americans spend more than $9,000,-000,000 a year on auto vacations, according to the National Automobile Club. This includes all such expenses as gas, oil, motels, hotels, and meals.

Merit Award
Board Winners

Employees of the Department of Public Works who received merit award recognition during the month of August, 1957, are:

Keith E. McKean, Los Angeles, proposed a method for estimating earthwork quantities for preliminary planning, for use primarily on flat terrain. In May, 1956, he was awarded $50 for the adoption of his suggestion in District VII, Division of Highways. After a year of actual use, it now appears that $50 additional is warranted, making a total award of $100.

D. Angus Vogt, Sacramento, received a $15 award for an improved procedure. Vogt recommended a change in the construction of the Hveem stabilometer. The modification is being used in the headquarters and in all district laboratories of the Division of Highways.

Herbert Shipley, San Luis Obispo, $50 additional award for suggestion recommending a combination of grade and grid sheets. An award for $50 was made in March, 1956, and the savings, after one year's experience, have warranted this additional award.

Mrs. Gloria M. Anthony, San Francisco, $30 for suggestion recommending the use of pounce on vellum and ozalid paper before using six different rubber stamps on appraisal maps.

Miss Mabel Graham, Los Angeles, $100 for suggestion recommending use of a statement form return envelope for the active rental accounts of highways. The envelope is prepared on the addressograph and stuffed in a window envelope.

Wallace R. Tutpen, Sacramento, $50 for suggestion recommending a snap-out carbon letter form to be used in the Advanced Planning Section of the Bridge Department, where a large volume of routine letters, requiring numerous carbon copies, are prepared.

Oliver Dowd, Jr., Stockton, $42 for suggestion recommending the elimination of freehand lettering on culvert lists and construction note sheets and instead using the typing and photographic process in preparing contract plan tracings with tabular data.

William W. Wallace, Oakland, $45 for suggestion in which he designed and built a simple tool for use as a roller chain pulling tool. It is used when two ends of a roller chain must be pulled together and properly aligned to rivet the connecting link.

Mrs. Adel R. Leitch, San Francisco, certificate of commendation for suggestion recommending that instead of using two stamps to record the date scheduled and the schedule number on receiving records, posting pages and transfer records, one combination stamp be procured as both operations could be done at the same time.

LIFE, ASSOCIATED PRESS LAUD STATE SYSTEM

Life Magazine and the Associated Press, reporters of international news to millions of readers, agreed on the superiority of California's Highway System and administration in articles published in August.

After a critical analysis of the highway program throughout the United States, *Life* concluded in an editorial in its August 5th issue that:

"The best highway department in all" is California's.

The Associated Press studied California's highway program in a report long enough to fill a full newspaper page, but printed in five parts in many California newspapers. The news agency found that:

"In general, California today has what probably is, across the board, the best road system in the Country. * * *"

The editors of *Life* devoted the full editorial page to an analysis of highway developments and highway problems in many of the states and under the Federal Government. The editorial's last two paragraphs were about California and read as follows:

"It has its own sources of income and methods of expenditure, prescribed by the Constitution and statutes, virtually beyond any legislative meddling. Its highly professional staff

Lloyd R. Brush, Sacramento, certificate of commendation for suggestion recommending that the bolt fastening the tire rack under light trucks be wrapped with friction tape to protect it from dirt and facilitate its removal.

James H. Hitotani, Sacramento, certificate of commendation for suggestion recommending that when there are no construction changes on the plans of highway contracts, a short letter advising there have been no changes be forwarded to the headquarters office in lieu of sending final plans.

Paul H. Henley, Division of Architecture, Sacramento, received a certificate of commendation for his proposal that the related financial statement be identified on tracings for projects handled by direct construction.

Following employees received merit award recognition during the month of September, 1957:

is protected by civil service, and its unpaid commissioners are picked by the Governor 'with just as much care,' says the director of the Northern California A. A. A., 'as a regent of the university. He can't afford to mix politics with highways, because every motorist in California watches him like a hawk.' The land acquisition program, wholly separate from maintenance and construction, is run according to a long-range plan which the Legislature adopted in 1953 after eight years of study and hearings. Contractors are kept up to taw by their own organization, by state records of past performance called 'the integrity file,' by the A. A. A. and by other private groups. Behind all this is a public attitude that stems from the fact that California grew to political maturity in the automobile era. Everybody depends on the highways, from farmers to weekend skiers, and everybody is his own watchdog. Says one State Senator, 'It would be easier and safer to tamper with the water supply than the highway program. * * * This is a highway State.'

'The other 47 are, or soon will be, 'highway states' too. The vast new road program will be cleaner, cheaper and better if all of us copy our best models."

Eloise D. Carson, Sacramento, recommended that in writing specifications for highway contracts, the specification writer eliminate a pencil copy of the engineer's estimate and bid proposal items. The Merit Award Board had previously granted Mrs. Carson a $100 check subject to a review to determine the actual savings involved. As a result of the study made by the department, it has been determined that the elimination of writing bid proposal items results in a yearly savings of approximately $1,500. A $50 additional award has now been granted.

Ray V. Alfsen, Los Angeles, proposed the use of a transparent template coordinate and topographic plotter for plotting of calculated center lines or proposed design features whose coordinates are known or calculated. A $25 award was made.

Orville G. Goodrich, Marysville, received $10 for designing a plastic triangle with various common side slopes at each corner and various super elevation rates inscribed

... Continued on page 58

56

Ground Breaking

Officials Start
S. F. Building

A ground-breaking ceremony led by Governor Goodwin J. Knight marked the start of work August 26th on a $6,500,000 addition to the State Office Building in San Francisco.

The Governor, State Director of Public Works Frank B. Durkee and other state and city officials joined in the occasion at the building site in San Francisco's Civic Center on Golden Gate Avenue between Larkin and Polk Streets.

Governor Knight pointed out that the structure is one of many state buildings recently built or planned to take care of growth occasioned by the expanding population in California.

"Since my administration began four years ago," Governor Knight said, "we have completed 17 major office buildings. They provide needed space for our Departments of Public Health, Highways, Employment, Motor Vehicles, Finance, Agriculture, Veterans Affairs, and Forestry. The total cost of these 17 buildings has been nearly $24,000,000.

"But here's another interesting fact about the buildings. They are located in a dozen different communities reaching from Eureka to San Bernardino. I know of no other state which has managed to place its state buildings in so many diverse areas. We think it is sound practice, since it makes government not a centralized, far-removed thing which is remote and inconvenient to the populace. We try to keep government convenient to those who support it and who need it.

280 Major Projects

"In addition to these major expansions, in the last four years, we have completed 280 other major projects including such things as hospitals and University of California buildings. When I say major projects I mean that each one involved a cost of more than $100,000. The total cost of these additions came to $180,000,000.

"Now just a word about the future. Long before the building which

Scene at ground breaking. Left to right—Governor Goodwin J. Knight, Contractor J. F. Barrett, and Director of Public Works Frank B. Durkee.

we get under way today is completed, we will have started work on the Oakland State Office Building. And to solve the office space problems in Los Angeles, we will have under way a great new state office building there. * * *

"In the past few months I have been traveling up and down our State talking about our budget, our plans and our accomplishments. I have often mentioned the size of our budget of this year—over two billion dollars. I have mentioned that that is more money than Teddy Roosevelt spent to run the entire Nation in 1904. Have people been impressed? Yes, I think they have. Have they been shocked? I don't believe so. And the reason they haven't been shocked has surely been because they can see what we are doing with the money here in California—and they approve of what they see."

The Governor explained that the new San Francisco building will be used by personnel of many state agencies: Mental Hygiene, Industrial Relations, Professional and Vocational Standards, Public Utilities, Youth Authority, and Social Welfare. It is being built for the Department of Finance.

Four Contracting Firms

Contracts for construction of the building were awarded by Director of Public Works Durkee August 7th, on recommendation of the Division of Architecture, which is in charge of the project. The contracts went to four Bay area firms which were low bidders.

The building will rise seven stories high over a full basement and will have a penthouse for mechanical equipment. Its main mass will be 118 feet by 379 feet, entirely of reinforced concrete construction, and it will provide a gross area of 401,000 square feet. The exterior of the building will be faced with ceramic veneer.

The appearance of the building will harmonize with the architecture of the San Francisco Civic Center.

Contractors and the amount of their contracts are: General work, Barrett Construction Company of San Francisco, $3,817,000; electrical work, Patterson-Emerson-Comstock, Inc., of Oakland, $787,878; mechanical work, Anderson & Rowe, Inc., of San Francisco, $1,592,937; and elevators, Pacific Elevator & Equipment Company of San Francisco, $297,322.

Around Central Core

Main entrance lobby of the new building will be on Golden Gate Avenue and will connect directly with the 35-year-old state building facing on McAllister Street. Other entrances will be provided on Larkin and Polk Streets.

Office space in the structure will be located around a central core of utilities and service functions. The arrangement is flexible and designed to facilitate future expansion and reassignment of areas to departments.

The new building will be connected with the old across Redwood Street, which the City of San Francisco will close between Larkin and Polk Streets. Three areaways will connect all floors and permit the two buildings to function as one unit.

Design of the building was by Alfred Eichler, a supervising architect in the Division of Architecture of the Department of Public Works, and L. W. Richert and Stanley Collins, associated architects, under the general supervision of Arthur F. Dudman, principal architect. P. T. Poage is Assistant State Architect in charge of planning and design. Anson Boyd is State Architect.

PARTY BOAT FISHING

Anglers participating in party boat fishing off the coast of California in 1955 caught more than six fish per angler, according to the National Automobile Club. Leading species taken were rockfish, kelp bass, barracuda, Pacific mackerel, and salmon.

GIRL WITH MONEY

Mrs. Ann Dreman, accountant-auditor in the City and Co-operative Department of the Division of Highways, is holding $8,909,597 in warrants to be paid to 206 incorporated cities in California.

MRS. ANN DREMAN

This represents the July, 1957, quarterly payment of the five-eighth-cent gas tax fund to cities and is the second largest payment since the enactment of Section 2107 of the Streets and Highways Code providing for the five-eighth-cent gas tax allocation. This payment was exceeded only by the October, 1956, payment, which amounted to $9,723,141.

Mrs. Dreman is also holding a copy of an explanatory letter sent to each city with the payment.

MERIT AWARD WINNERS

Continued from page 56 . . .

adjacent to the two sides. This tool will be used to plot cross sections.

Thomas G. Ingram, Sacramento, was presented a certificate of commendation for proposing that the freeway project office in Sacramento join the Sacramento Multiple Listing Bureau to obtain daily bulletins and quarterly reports regarding real property values in the Sacramento metropolitan area.

George S. Maxey, Redding, proposed the combination of two reports in order to save time and expensive printing material, the Weekly Equipment Report (Form S-20) showing what days an alternator is used and the weekly mileage report on the vehicle in which the alternator is installed. A $10 award was granted.

REDWOOD FREEWAY

Continued from page 53 . . .

The solution of the removal of the large amount of material from the cut in a short construction season was left to the ingenuity of the contractor. This problem was complicated by the fact that no access roads to the top of the slope could be constructed outside of slope lines, since the contract forbade any encroachment into adjacent state redwood parks.

Donkey Engines Used

The native slope of the original material within the slope lines was steep and broken and precluded all but the most tortuous, steep and frequently switchbacked pioneer road to the top of the cut. To use such a road for the passage of modern earthmoving equipment would have been slow, costly and exceedingly dangerous.

To gain access to the top of the cut with enough equipment to put the operation on a high production basis, without resorting to the use of such a pioneer road was a problem the contractor ingeniously solved by an original and unique method. Near the north end of the cut he constructed an up ramp 525 feet long on a 62 per cent grade. At the top of this ramp were placed four 400-horsepower logging donkey engines. By a system of blocks, continuous cables, and buried rollers, these powerful engines pulled the rubber-tired dirtmovers up the face of the cut. From the top of the ramp access was easily obtained to the top of the cut by a pioneer road. The loaded earthmovers proceeded from the cut area under their own power over a "down road" constructed on an approximate 45 percent grade.

After about six weeks of operation, the cut was brought down to such an elevation that the earthmovers could gain access to the excavation area under their own power, and use of the donkey engines was discontinued. As testimony that this innovation was a success is the fact that the contractor averaged better than 10,000 cubic yards of excavation each shift and was, on September 1st, ahead of schedule in removing the "big cut."

Hoopa Bridge

New Span Replaces Structure
Destroyed on Trinity River

By RUSSELL O. LIGHTCAP, Resident Engineer

Hoopa Valley, home and reservation of the Hoopa Tribe of the Klamath River Indian nation, was badly hit by floodwaters during the statewide storm of December, 1955.

The Trinity River, fed by the many storms, filled to overflowing and encroached upon the sacred tribal grounds of the Indians. The raging waters destroyed the sacred Indian church and sweathouse, which according to legend would remain untouched until the ways of the Indians had vanished. The sweathouse for centuries was the meeting place for the medicine men before they started the most sacred of all Indian rituals, the white deerskin dance. Never before, according to the Indian legend and in the memory of even the oldest tribesman had the waters been so high.

The state highway bridge, located on Route 84, about one mile upstream from the sacred Indian grounds, was also a victim of the raging waters. Floating logs and debris were hurled against the bridge and the incessant pounding finally destroyed it, carrying a 132-ton truss span 1,000 yards downstream. Another truss was carried downstream and ripped into fragments by the power of the floodwaters, leaving pieces scattered for miles down the river.

Emergency Transportation

Destruction of the bridge left the community on the north side of the river completely isolated. Emergency transportation across the river was provided by small boats and a cable ferry. Since the health and safety of the tribal community required immediate steps to construct a new bridge, an emergency contract was negotiated with Ben C. Gerwick, Inc., to construct a low-level temporary bridge across the river. Within seven weeks this bridge was completed, but again high water came and a major

UPPER—View of small truss before it was washed away. Larger truss already gone. LOWER—Temporary low-level bridge constructed about one mile downstream from bridge site.

portion of the temporary bridge was washed away. Another emergency contract was made with the same contractor and in another two weeks the low-level bridge was again open to traffic.

The expense and danger involved in keeping the low-level bridge in op-

eration during winter months made a new permanent high-level structure necessary before the following winter. Accordingly, right-of-way negotiations and work on plans and specifications were immediately begun. The co-operation of the Hoopa Indian Council and the local office of the

Bureau of Indian Affairs greatly assisted the District I right-of-way department in acquiring the necessary property. The mutual efforts of District I and the Bridge Department resulted in a rapid completion of plans and specifications for a complete project with the roadwork and structure work in one contract. A contract was prepared with the requirement that a new bridge be completed before the anticipated high water during the following winter.

Urgency Project

In April, 1955, the contract was awarded to Peter Kiewit Sons' Company. From the beginning, the contractor realized the urgency of the construction and expedited the work. Superintendent John Carroll kept his work on schedule, working as many shifts as necessary to assure that the various stages of work would be completed on time. In many cases this meant working two 10-hour shifts and in some instances 24 hours a day.

According to the work schedules submitted by the contractor, the structural steel girders were to arrive on September 1st and the steel work was to be finished by October 1st. A steel strike prevented the American Bridge Company, the steel subcontractor, from delivering the structural steel and starting erection until October 9th. This was a dangerously late date for work in this area, because of the likelihood of high water.

Steel Erection Problem

The erection of the structural steel was well under way when the rains began. On October 30th some of the falsework was washed out, leaving girders isolated on piers and inundating girders that were waiting to be placed. The American Bridge Company, realizing the necessity of completing the work, began preparing to erect steel from the top instead of from the riverbed as it had been doing. While the proper equipment for erecting the steel from the top was being located, the water went down. By changing the river channel and building dikes the contractor was able to continue steel erection from the riverbed. High water caused no fur-

UPPER—Side view of the new bridge. LOWER—Road view of approach to new bridge.

ther trouble and the structural steel was finished by December 6th.

Superintendent Carroll then made a concerted effort to complete the bridge so traffic could use it as soon as possible. Enough lumber was obtained to form the entire length of the concrete deck all at one time and the work was continued in spite of the rain and snow. Within less than three weeks after the structural steel was completed, the concrete had been placed for the entire bridge deck and traffic was crossing it. It took about a month to complete the other miscellaneous items of work and to remove the temporary detour bridge. Since winter weather prevented structural steel painting, that work was deferred and was completed this spring.

One year and two days after the old bridge was destroyed, traffic was using the new bridge—a longer, higher structure that will be well above any future high water, on improved alignment with new approaches. Replacement of the bridge in such record time is evidence of the co-operation of the many agencies and organizations involved; namely the Hoopa Indian Council, the Bureau of Indian Affairs, Contractor Peter Kiewit Sons' Company, District I, Division of Highways, and the Bridge Department.

The contract was administered by the Bridge Department, and the roadwork was under the direction of Donald W. McDonell, District Representative.

Bear Flag Flies
In the Antarctic

This picture of the Bear Flag shows it in climatic conditions far removed from sunny California. The flag was carried south by H. W. Bachtold, C.E. 1, of the U. S. Seabees

This is a photo of the California Bear Flag flying at the South Pole

on the Antarctic expedition Deepfreeze. The picture was sent to his father, H. J. Bachtold, Assistant Highway Engineer with the Division of Highways in Redding.

Wes Bachtold, as he is generally known, joined the Seabees in 1953. He served in Alaska, Korea and Japan.

In 1955 he was among the volunteers who were accepted to join the Antarctic expedition. Prior to leaving he was given an intense course of training in operations and survival under conditions that would be encountered under subzero temperatures. This included six weeks' training with dog teams in Vermont.

Wes completed his Antarctic hitch in April, 1957. After a few days at home in Redding he reported to his unit and was sent to North Ireland, where he is now stationed.

THIS IS BRITAIN'S A-1 TRUNK ROAD

Believe it or not, this winding thoroughfare with a street market on the left is the Great North Road at Stamford, Lines. It is an eloquent testimony to the inadequacy of Britain's roads when a major trunk route still follows the twisting streets of an ancient town.

YOU SHOULD KNOW

EDWARD R. BACON COMPANY OF HAWAII
San Francisco 4, California

MR. KENNETH C. ADAMS, *Editor*

DEAR MR. ADAMS: The following statement is quoted from an article on highway departments in the August 5th issue of *Life* magazine—"as is evidenced by the best highway department of them all, California's."

From the inception of highway construction in the State of California when my company, Edward R. Bacon Company, furnished to Contractor F. R. Ritchie the concrete paving mixer that he used on Contract No. 1

for the construction of 5.4 miles of highways in San Mateo County in 1912, I have done business with the California Division of Highways, and my dealings fully confirm the opinion expressed in the article in *Life* magazine.

Yours very truly,

EDWARD R. BACON

LICENSED DRIVERS

The number of licensed drivers, according to the National Automobile Club, leaped from 54.5 million to a current 77 million during the past decade.

Vallejo Project

Portion of Interstate Highway to Become Full Freeway

By J. E. WILSON, Resident Engineer

CONSTRUCTION of the Vallejo Freeway is now in full progress, and local residents and daily commuters along Highway US 40 are eagerly looking forward to the time when this facility will be widened to six lanes and the existing five sets of traffic signals are replaced by modern interchanges and overcrossing structures.

This, indeed, is what will take place in the fall of 1958 when the six-lane, full freeway from the Vallejo Wye to 0.4 mile north of Redwood Street is completed and placed in operation.

It is expected that this vital link will stimulate the growth of Solano County and the City of Vallejo, particularly the area east of US 40, which is developing into a major residential district. The difficulty experienced in crossing Highway US 40 under present and past conditions in going to and from work at the Mare Island Navy Yard and other industrial and commercial establishments which are concentrated on the west side of the highway had until recently held back the development of this area for residential purposes.

Present Deficiencies

Inadequacies of the present facility are being clearly demonstrated twice daily and on weekends when peak-hour traffic has to wait through several signal changes to cross Highway US 40. For the motorist traveling to the mountains or valley area from the Bay area, there is the usual wait through several signal changes at the Benicia Road intersection, the first set of lights after crossing the Carquinez Bridge since the Magazine Street interchange has been completed.

This same motorist will be delayed again on his way home, except that the Sunday evening bottleneck is on the north end of Vallejo at the Tennessee Street intersection.

Traffic

With US 40 traffic averaging 25,000 cars daily during 1956 and cross traffic at several signals running from four to five thousand cars daily, the need for a full freeway is obvious.

Several detours are scheduled for construction. The first, a four-lane detour around the site of the Benicia Freeway structure, is already in operation. Other detours are planned for both main-line and cross traffic, but four lanes will be left open along the existing main line except in the immediate areas of widening or where other operations make it unsafe for the motorist. Four lanes will always be in use at night and on weekends and holidays.

Interchanges and Structures

Eight overcrossing structures are being provided, with the Magazine Street structure already completed and placed in operation in the fall of 1956.

A full four-quadrant cloverleaf interchange is under construction at the intersection of the proposed Benicia Freeway and Highway US 40 near Reis Avenue. The Benicia Freeway has been planned for an ultimate six lanes with four lanes to be constructed in the near future. Benicia Road, the present state highway, will cross over US 40 near its present grade crossing.

Overcrossing structures with full traffic interchanges are under construction at Georgia Street, Springs Road, Tennessee Street and Redwood Street.

Four lanes for cross traffic have been provided on the Georgia Street, Springs Road and Tennessee Street structures. As this area is a well-built-up urban area, all overcrossing structures have been provided with concrete sidewalks on both sides and on the approach ramps where their use is warranted.

Local traffic near the Benicia Freeway and east of US 40 will have available the Laurel Street overcrossing, providing freedom of movement without having to enter either freeway.

The Redwood Street interchange will make available direct access from both the north and south to the rapidly expanding north Vallejo area, previously accessible only through a circuitous route through various city streets.

Financing

This project, while on the Federal Interstate System, is also considered a part of the approaches to the new Carquinez Bridge. This is the first project in District X to be financed under this nationwide federal interstate highway program. The completion of the freeway project is planned to approximately coincide with the completion of the new Carquinez Bridge.

Construction Features

The use of precast and prestressed concrete beams throughout the seven major structures is another first for District X. Two hundred twenty-seven are being used which range in length from 43 to 83 feet and have the constant depths of three feet. The use of high-strength concrete and special cable reinforcing enabled the designers to use the three-foot overall depth, even on the longer spans.

Another unusual feature is the construction of an access road across Lake Chabot, a City of Vallejo storage reservoir. Soundings indicated approximately three feet of mud would have to be removed before placing embankment. To permit removal of this mud, the level of the water was lowered approximately 10 feet by gravity flow and a high capacity centrifugal pump. Mud stripping can now be completed above the water level.

The construction of this access road will enable the State to close two county roads presently connected to the existing facility. It will also connect to a future interchange on Sears Point Road, Sign Route 48, at Chabot Road.

The usual number of construction problems that arise whenever an improvement of this nature takes place in an urban area, are being encountered. Underground utilities often interfere with the location of the storm drain flowlines, which are carefully worked out in design, and many adjustments have to be made.

The Vallejo Sanitation and Flood Control District relocated its sanitary and storm drain facilities, and the City of Vallejo relocated its 20-inch water mains under separate contracts prior to the highway contract. The co-operation and co-ordination of the City of Vallejo, Vallejo Sanitation District, Pacific Gas and Electric

Company and the Pacific Telephone and Telegraph Company in removing and relocating their existing facilities has materially aided the construction of this freeway project.

Fill struts will be used to control settlement on the west side of the Benicia Freeway interchange. The southwest quadrant of this interchange will be constructed over a marshy area where two feet of subsidence is expected. The fill struts placed next to the regular embankment are expected to control this settlement and stabilize the fill so that construction can proceed without delay.

Progress Good

Bids on this project were received on April 17, 1957, and the award was made to the firm of Harms Bros., C. M. Syar, Erickson, Phillips and Weisberg of Sacramento, Vallejo and Concord on a bid of $4,118,053.90.

Construction work was started almost immediately.

The major structures are being constructed by Erickson, Phillips and Weisberg with Ross Phillips as superintendent. All other work is being handled by Harms Bros. and C. M. Syar, with H. W. Keeler and Hermon Cecil as superintendents.

For the Division of Highways the work is under the general direction of J. G. Meyer, District Engineer, and K. N. Hatch, District Construction Engineer in Solano County for District X.

The author was the squad design engineer on the project and is at the present time assigned as resident engineer during construction.

Studies prove that 7 out of 10 motor vehicle deaths, and more than one-half of all traffic injuries, occur on free and open roads in rural areas.

and Public Works

CASE HISTORY

Continued from page 13 ...

out showing conclusively a reduction in total number of accidents.

Type of accident	Five months before improvement	Five months after improvement
Personal injury	17	10
Fatal	4	0
Total, all types	54	51

Accident records available at this time are not complete. The local authorities have indicated, however, that the left-turning type of accident off Sepulveda Boulevard has virtually disappeared. It should be noted also that the improvement in the accident picture has taken place in the face of considerably increased traffic volumes.

Although the system is handling an extremely heavy load of traffic, there may be the need in the near future for still more capacity. The equivalent of a full additional traffic lane can be obtained for each direction on Sepulveda Boulevard by the peak-hour prohibition of parking. All of the cross streets except the east legs of Marine Avenue and Gould Lane and the west leg of Manhattan Beach Boulevard are two-lane streets. All of the major cross streets can be widened. Providing additional lanes on the side streets would allow the allotment of more green time to Sepulveda Boulevard and still handle side-street traffic. The peak direction lane capacities being handled by this system approach those normally associated with freeways. This results from the minor cross-street traffic and the extreme directional pattern which makes it possible to assign maximum green time to the heavy move without unduly penalizing the cross-street traffic.

The outstanding achievement of the installation is the fact that proper channelization, coupled with advance type of electronic traffic control, has accomplished the equivalent traffic service of constructing an additional lane of pavement each direction over a two-mile section of highly developed highway, and done so at a fraction of the cost.

ACKNOWLEDGMENTS

The project was conceived and completed by State of California, Department of Public Works, Division of Highways; George T. McCoy, State Highway Engi-

GALLAGHER RETIRES

Continued from page 51 ...

when they are not driving cars. The motoring public seems to be made up mostly of maniacs," he said.

Gallagher was born in Green Bay, Wisconsin, and plans to visit his old hometown on his vacation trip.

He was able to obtain only one year of formal education but obtained an engineering background in home education and "practical application."

Served in Army

In 1912-14 he was district engineer for the state highway department in St. Paul, Minnesota. Then he went into the Army Engineers and came out a first lieutenant. He was construction engineer for the state highway department in Arizona. In 1921, he came to California and was employed by engineering firms until 1929 when he took a position with the State Highway Department.

In 1937, Gallagher helped organize the 144th Field Artillery of the National Guard in Ventura and served as its first commanding officer.

His son, Richard, is Director of Public Works for the City of San Diego.

Gallagher feels that it is symbolic that his retirement should come while the last steel truss bridge (on Route 150 near Sulphur Mountain) in Ventura County's state system is being removed.

"It's the end of an era," he said.

HIGHWAY ACCIDENTS

A recent survey shows that 80 percent of the deaths and injuries on highways occurred as a direct result of driver error, reports the National Automobile Club.

neer, Chief of Division; George M. Webb, State Traffic Engineer. In District VII design and construction were under the direction of Assistant State Highway Engineer Edward T. Telford, with design engineering under the supervision of Robert W. Van Stan, District Traffic Engineer; Project Engineer was Bert H. Clark; Design Engineer Ted L. Morehead also completed the adjustments and testing operations.

DEPARTMENT OF
PUBLIC WORKS
SACRAMENTO, CALIFORNIA

printed in CALIFORNIA STATE PRINTING OFFICE 81822 9-57 50,900

FORN
AND PUBLIC WORKS

NOVEMBER-DECEMBER
1957

California Highways and Public Works

Official Journal of the Division of Highways, Department of Public Works, State of California

RICHARD WINN, Editor
HELEN HALSTED, Assistant Editor
STEWART MITCHELL, Assistant Editor
MERRITT R. NICKERSON, Chief Photographer

| Vol. 36 | November-December, 1957 | Nos. 11-12 |

FRONT COVER
From above downtown Los Angeles, aerial camera looks north along Harbor Freeway and the many crossing bridges. Four-level structure called "hub of Los Angeles' metropolitan freeway system" is in center.
—Photo by Merritt R. Nickerson

BACK COVER
Aerial view from above northern city limits of Los Angeles, looking south along Golden State Freeway. Traffic interchange at junction of US 6 and US 99 is in foreground, San Fernando Valley in background.
—Photo by Merritt R. Nickerson

Published in the interest of highway development in California. Editors of newspapers and others are invited to use matter contained herein and to request photographs or engravings.

Address communications to

CALIFORNIA HIGHWAYS AND PUBLIC WORKS
P. O. Box 1499
SACRAMENTO, CALIFORNIA

Budget Nears Half Billion

Highway Commission Sets 1958-59 Figures

This general story on the Budget is supplemented by other details appearing on pages 43 to 51.

THE CALIFORNIA Highway Commission submitted to Governor Goodwin J. Knight in November a State Highway Budget totaling $483,571,763 for the 1958-59 Fiscal Year.

The budget contains $435,525,268 for all state highway functions, including approximately $338,000,000 for highway construction purposes. All of California's 58 counties share in the budget.

The construction items include: major construction and improvement (contracts plus construction engineering), $221,829,000; rights of way, $103,342,268; contingencies (normally allocated later for construction purposes), $6,000,000; resurfacing program, $5,000,000; minor improvements, $800,000.

For comparison, the current 1957-58 State Highway Budget as adopted in October, 1956, contained a total of $464,000,000 of which $421,000,000 was for state highway functions, including approximately $350,000,000 for construction purposes (including rights of way).

Major Revenue Sources

Major sources of *estimated* state-collected revenue in the 1958-59 State Highway Budget include: $230,771,000 from gasoline taxes (up $13,000,000 from the previous year's estimate); $59,169,000 from motor vehicle fees (down $9,000,000 from the previous year's estimate partly because of increased budgets of the California Highway Patrol and Department of Motor Vehicles); which are financed by highway user taxes; use fuel (diesel) taxes, $19,000,000 (slightly up from previous year); and $9,936,000 from transportation taxes (down $6,500,000 from previous year due to a

50 percent statutory reduction in the gross receipts levy on "for-hire" carriers).

Federal aid for state highways, including interstate routes, shows an increase of nearly $20,000,000 over the previous year, with an apportionment of $153,647,762 for 1958-59. In addition, $9,762,001 has been apportioned by the U. S. Government for federal aid secondary roads in California, of which $9,615,571 will be available for expenditure on county roads. The 1957 Legislature increased from 87½ percent to 98½ percent the counties' share of the federal aid secondary money apportioned to California, as well as increasing from a maximum of $100,000 to $200,000 per county annually the state funds available to counties for use in matching federal aid.

Effect of New Laws

As a result of statutes enacted by the 1957 Legislature, the 1958-59 Highway Budget contains two new expenditure categories, it was pointed out by State Director of Public Works Frank B. Durkee, chairman of the commission.

These items include $5,000,000 earmarked for state matching of state funds to be provided by cities and counties for elimination of railroad grade crossings on local streets and roads (not state highways); and $2,000,000 for maintenance of San Francisco Bay area state-owned toll bridges.

Proposed expenditures for state highway purposes in the 1958-59 Fiscal Year, in addition to the $338,000,000 for construction and rights-of-way include: maintenance, $32,500,000; preliminary engineering (planning and design), $30,500,000; statewide highway planning survey, $3,000,000; administration, $9,300,000; honor camps, $1,-

750,000; and buildings and plants, maintenance facilities and shops throughout the state and district office annexes in San Francisco, San Bernardino, San Diego, Redding and Bishop).

Nonstate Highway Items

The nonstate highway items in the budget include, in addition to the grade crossing funds and the federal funds for county roads on the federal aid secondary system:

Major city streets (five-eights cent per gallon of the gasoline tax), $31,142,000; city engineering work, $1,200,000; and state funds to counties for use in matching federal funds on federal aid secondary projects, $6,002,924.

State Highway Engineer G. T. McCoy informed the commission that plans, specifications and right-of-way acquisition had already been completed on some of the projects included in the 1958-59 Budget, and that these projects could be advertised for bids beginning within the next few weeks.

State law permits the awarding of state highway contracts as early as January 1st, six months before the start of the fiscal year. This provision enables the Division of Highways to make maximum use of favorable construction weather, which means earlier opening of road improvements to traffic.

Two-year Financing

For the first time, the 1958-59 Budget contains items which are only partly financed in a single fiscal year. Durkee explained that some construction contracts are so large and complex that they require considerably more than a year to complete. In some of these instances, the new

*Public Works Building
Twelfth and N Streets
Sacramento*

C NTENTS

BUDGET

budget contains only the amount which will be needed during the first fiscal year, with the balance of the project to be financed in the succeeding (1959-60) fiscal year. This procedure is provided for by legislation enacted in 1957. The construction contract awarded in such cases will be for the entire project, however.

This method, Durkee pointed out, will avoid the tying up of large amounts of highway funds in a single budget item where the expenditure will extend over a considerably longer period than one year, and therefore permits the inclusion of more projects in the budget than would otherwise be the case.

For example, the 1958-59 Budget includes a four-mile eight-lane freeway project on the Ventura Freeway (US 101) in the San Fernando Valley for which a total construction expenditure of $11,100,000 is estimated. Only $6,248,000 of this amount is financed in the 1958-59 Budget, however.

Landscaping Projects

The budget contain 32 projects of a landscaping nature, totaling an estimated $3,180,000. Most of these projects provide for roadside planting on recently completed sections of freeway.

"The 1958-59 highway budget," Durkee said, "represents one more step in a continuing, carefully planned and co-ordinated effort to meet the tremendous traffic needs of a growing state.

"It is of course impossible," he added, "to include every needed project in a single budget. Many projects with a high local and statewide priority, in terms of relief from congestion and hazard, have had to be deferred by the commission for future allocation of funds. The commission's goal in adopting each successive budget is to distribute construction and right-of-way funds, in line with geographical controls laid down by the Legislature, where they will accomplish the greatest good both for the community concerned and for the people of the State as a whole.

. . . Continued on page 44

U.S. Congress

House Committeemen Visit
California, Seek Advice

THE COMMITTEE ON PUBLIC WORKS of
the United States House of Representatives came to California in late
October to inspect and study the State
Highway System which one of the
committee's ranking members said "is
giving the taxpayer the most miles of
highway for the dollars expended."

J. Harry McGregor of Ohio, a
member of Congress since 1940 and
a leading advocate of the federal highway program, told the California
Highway Commissioners that he and
his fellow committeemen "look forward to receiving your recommendations to improve the law on the interstate highways."

"I wish you fellows would help us,"
Representative McGregor told the
commissioners at a luncheon meeting
in Martinez preceding a committee
hearing, only formal session held by
the members of Congress during a 10-

day visit about the State. "California
has helped us a great deal already. A
number of things I put in the 1954
Federal Highway Act came from your
California law."

All of the commission members
welcomed the house committeemen to
California and accompanied them on
a highway tour from San Francisco
through the East Bay, across the Carquinez Bridge, to Benicia and then to
Martinez. All remained with the members of Congress for their hearing, at
which officials of the State Department of Public Works presented recommendations and suggestions for
which the committeemen asked.

State's Views Told

Frank B. Durkee, Director of Public Works and Chairman of the Highway Commission, George T. McCoy,
State Highway Engineer, and J. W.

Vickrey, Deputy State Highway Engineer, presented the California views
on the Federal Interstate Highway
System to the committeemen at their
hearing.

They recommended confirmation of
the section of the Federal Highway
Act of 1956 which provided that future apportionment of federal funds
to the states will be on a basis of need,
rather than on the previously authorized formula based on a combination
of state area, population and post road
mileage.

The 1956 law provided that the apportionment on a basis of need should
be started with the 1960 Fiscal Year,
after the Congress approves estimates
of need submitted by the Bureau of
Public Roads. These estimates will be
presented to Congress next January.

Representative John F. Baldwin, Jr.,
of Martinez, who was acting as chair-

and Public Works   3

man of the subcommittee for the purpose of the hearing in his home state and home city, joined Representative McGregor in asking the California officials questions about their proposals.

"If Congress apportions the money on the basis of need," Representative Baldwin asked McCoy during the State Highway Engineer's testimony, "would California have enough matching money?"

"Yes," was McCoy's unqualified answer.

Needs Basis Asked

The Californians presented details of federal apportionments to California and the State's provision of millions in matching funds for the first three years of the interstate program. They said that all of the federal funds made available to date have been obligated and that California is in a position to use all available federal funds as rapidly as they can be apportioned.

The figures "clearly indicate," the California report said, 'that unless future apportionments are made on a needs basis in conformance with the 1956 act as enacted, California's planning program, which currently contemplates completion of its portion of the National Interstate System within the period prescribed by the act, will of necessity require drastic modification."

House committeemen who were on the highway tour and at the hearing were, beside McGregor and Baldwin:

Representatives Emmet F. Byrne of Illinois, Edwin B. Dooley of New York, John C. Kluczynski of Illinois, Russell V. Mack of Washington, Hubert B. Scudder of California, and Frank Ellis Smith of Mississippi. Representative Smith was chairman of the subcommittee for the California trip.

New Formula Ready

Representative John McFall, California member of the committee, met the group the day after the Martinez hearing and showed them public works of interest in and about Stockton, his home city.

Most of the committeemen spent the next week continuing their inspections of highways and other public works in other California areas. Representative Kenneth Gray, committee member from Illinois, joined his fellows in Southern California.

Also joining the committeemen in Southern California were Bertram D. Tallamy, Federal Highway Administrator, and Frank C. Turner, Deputy Commissioner and Chief Engineer, U. S. Bureau of Public Roads.

Administrator Tallamy told newsmen in San Diego that California's share of the new federal highway program would be nearly twice what it is now under the estimates of need to be presented to Congress in January.

The members of the house committee and the federal highway officials were greeted by civic leaders in San Diego, Riverside County, Los Angeles, Santa Barbara and Monterey County.

Although they held no formal hearing in Los Angeles, they were presented with recommendations about the federal highway program by the Los Angeles Metropolitan Traffic Association. The association, in a resolution printed in full below, joined the California public works officials in recommending the needs basis for apportionment of federal highway funds.

Here is the text of the resolution:

WHEREAS, Under the provisions of Federal Highway Act of 1956, the apportionment of funds to the several states to construct the National System of Interstate and Defense Highways is made as follows: one-half in the ratio which the population of each state bears to the total population of all the states as shown by the latest available federal census, provided that no state shall receive less than three-fourths of 1 per centum of the money so apportioned, and one-half in the manner now provided by law for the apportionment of funds for the Federal-Aid Primary System which is based one-third on area, one-third on population and one-third on post road or rural delivery mileage; and

WHEREAS, California's gas tax payments to the Federal Treasury approximate 10 percent of the Nation's total, but under above formula we receive back only 5.7 percent; and

WHEREAS, The Federal Highway Act of 1956 provides that apportionment of funds to the several states for the Fiscal Year 1960 through 1969 inclusive, shall be in the ratio which the estimated cost of completing the interstate system in each state bears to the sum of estimated cost of completing the system in all of the states (this formula is referred to as the "Needs Formula"); and

WHEREAS, The act further provides that the Secretary of Commerce shall submit to

the Senate and House of Representatives within 10 days subsequent to January 2, 1958, a detailed estimate of the cost of completing interstate system; and

WHEREAS, It is necessary that Congress by concurrent resolution give approval of such estimate of costs before the Secretary of Commerce may make use of the approved needs formula in making apportionment for subsequent years; and

WHEREAS, The acute highway problems in California demand a larger allocation of these federal funds so as to allow freeways to be built more quickly to handle the greater traffic loads brought on by our tremendous population increases—constant migrations from other states—with attendant increase in motor vehicles of 348,254 in 1956 over 1955—equal to 29,000 additional cars every month on our highways—and to alleviate the presently congested freeways and lessen the number of accidents; now, therefore, be it

Resolved, That the Los Angeles Metropolitan Traffic Association hereby petitions Congress to enact at the 1958 Session the necessary concurrent resolution authorizing the Secretary of Commerce to apportion funds among the several states for the construction and completion of the National System of Interstate and Defense Highways in the ratio which the estimated cost of completing the system in each state bears to the sum of the estimated cost of completing the system in all of the states as provided in subsection (d) of Section 108 of the Federal-Aid Highway Act of 1956.

Sierra Highways Closed

Carson Pass Highway (State Sign Route 88) and Ebbetts Pass Highway (State Sign Route 4) were closed to through traffic for the 1957-58 winter season on November 14th.

The Carson Pass Highway is kept open during the winter season only as far as Peddler Hill in Amador County. The Ebbetts Pass Highway is kept open to Camp Connell in Calaveras County.

Two other highways across the Sierra Nevada, Sonora Pass and Tioga Pass, were closed to through traffic earlier.

The Sonora Pass Highway (State Sign Route 108) was initially closed at Kennedy Meadows Road, but the closure point was expected to be moved westward to Strawberry, in Tuolumne County, after the next snowstorm.

The Tioga Pass Road (State Sign Route 120) was closed by the National Park Service at the entrance to Yosemite National Park.

Plan and Design

Eight Years History of Long Beach Freeway Told

By E. G. HANSON, Assistant District Engineer

W HEN Governor Goodwin J. Knight, on October 29, 1954, attended the ribbon-cutting ceremony celebrating the completion of the southerly seven-mile section of the Long Beach Freeway from Pacific Coast Highway to Atlantic Avenue, he emphasized in his remarks the fact that this freeway was a co-operative project in every sense of the word. He called attention to the fact that due to the wholehearted co-operation between engineers and officials of all levels of government (federal, state, county and city), and of railroads, utilities, industries and businesses, unusual progress had been made in the development of this freeway. As Governor Knight pointed out, there was no organized opposition to this freeway from any source. It was a freeway that everybody wanted!

The original concept of the Long Beach Freeway project, when it was known locally as the proposed "Los Angeles River Freeway," was that it extend from Pacific Coast Highway, Route 60 in the City of Long Beach, northerly to a junction with the Santa Ana Freeway in the East Los Angeles manufacturing district. This $48,000,-000 freeway unit, 16.5 miles in length, is the subject of the present story.

If consideration is given to the time of inception of the idea that there should be a major traffic arterial connecting the City of Long Beach with the City of Los Angeles by following along the general route of the Los Angeles River between these two cities, then the Long Beach Freeway is undoubtedly the oldest freeway in the Los Angeles metropolitan area which the State Division of Highways has had the responsibility for constructing.

Origins in 1913

The effective efforts of the Los Angeles County Regional Planning Commission were much in evidence in

> EDITOR'S NOTE: *One article usually suffices to tell the story of an important freeway from inception to completion. But there was so much to be said about the $48,000,000 Long Beach Freeway that it is being presented in two articles. The first article, herewith, tells of planning and design activities and was written by the Supervising Highway Engineer in charge of designing the freeway for the past eight years. The second article, to appear next summer after completion of the freeway, will deal with construction.*

the early stages of inception, promotion and development of the Long Beach Freeway. This organization was very active during the period when Arthur H. Adams (now retired) was

its Director of Planning. Writing about the Long Beach Freeway in 1951, Adams said:

"The idea of there being a major highway or highways along the Los Angeles River channel originated about 1913 when the United States Government, as an argument to convince the officials of Long Beach that they should allow their city to be bisected by a flood control channel, published a picture of the proposed channel with broad highways shown on each bank of the channel. This plan was apparently forgotten by the government engineers when the channel was constructed, much to the embarrassment of local officials and residents.

"Later when a considerable section of the channel was paved with a heavy reinforced concrete slab, many of us thought that here was an ideal place for a highway as the channel carries a decreasing amount of water except during severe storms. It was thought that the usual small flow of water could be controlled in a narrow, open conduit thus leaving the balance of the wide area for the carrying of traffic directly from Long Beach to the business district of Los Angeles.

Here is a view looking southerly along Long Beach Freeway showing the interchange with Santa Ana Freeway and in the background the crossing over freight classification yard of Union Pacific Railroad.

LEFT—Looking northerly along the Long Beach Freeway, showing in the foreground the freight classification yard of the Union Pacific Railroad and in the center the interchange with the Santa Ana Freeway, the same interchange as shown at right. RIGHT—View looking southeasterly along the Santa Ana Freeway showing in the foreground the interchange with the Long Beach Freeway, the $48,000,000 highway discussed in this article on planning and design.

"When I came to the Regional Planning Commission in 1938, after having served as City Engineer for a number of years in Long Beach, I started a study of this possibility. We found that it was impractical primarily because the flood control officials would not allow the carrying capacity of the channel to be reduced to the extent required for the construction of the interchange ramps required to effectively handle the traffic. We then prepared a plan which provided for the use of both banks of the channel for highway purposes extending from the San Fernando Valley to the Long Beach Harbor.

"In 1941 many conferences relative to the plan were held with the district engineer, the City Engineer of Long Beach, the flood control engineer, the Corps of Engineers of the U. S. Army, and officials of the City of Los Angeles. All of these engineers and officials seemed pleased with the plan and accordingly a report was prepared by this department in July of 1941, and presented to the Los Angeles County Board of Supervisors at a hearing held on November 4, 1941. On December 4, 1941, I presented the plan to the Long Beach City Planning Commission and obtained their approval.

"In 1942, we continued to discuss the plan with various civic groups to promote the idea and at the same time continued the preparation of more detailed plans for the project. About this time the City Engineer of Long Beach was making plans for a major highway called Pico Avenue to extend along the west bank of the channel within the city, using plans which we had prepared in planning underpasses for several bridges over the flood control channel.

Master Plan Drawn

"In 1943 we completed a master plan of freeways for the entire county. This plan was shown in a commission report entitled *Freeways for the Region*. The plan called for a freeway, following the route of Pico Avenue through the Long Beach area from the harbor to its northerly limits and thence along the westerly bank of the Los Angeles River channel crossing to the easterly bank in the vicinity of the confluence of the Los Angeles and Rio Hondo Rivers and extending northerly to a connection with the Santa Ana Freeway."

"The City of Long Beach had been actively engaged in promoting a traffic arterial along the Los Angeles River for a number of years, and had secured much right-of-way in the city adjacent to the Los Angeles River for future highway purposes. This, as Arthur Adams wrote, was originally known as the Pico Avenue project. In going forward with this development, the city in 1947 constructed a bridge across the projected highway for Willow Street and a second bridge for Long Beach Boulevard. At Willow Street provision was made for a six-lane divided highway under the bridge whereas at Long Beach Boulevard provision was made for an eight-lane facility. These bridges built by the City of Long Beach and financed with city funds became a part of the Long Beach Freeway.

The Los Angeles County Road Department, in 1950, completed construction of the bridge across the Los Angeles River and over the freeway for Belhart Street. This was financed by Los Angeles County.

Under a legislative enactment approved by the Governor on June 23, 1947, the portion of the so-called Santa Ana Freeway was taken into the State Highway System. Following this action, District VII proceeded with the preparation of a project report prior to entering into freeway agreements with four cities—Long Beach, Compton, Lynwood and South Gate—and Los Angeles County. The project report was submitted July 11, 1949, and approved by the Division of Highways at Sacramento November 22, 1949. In the design of the freeway no substantial changes were made from the general features recommended in the project report. However, additional interchanges were provided at Del Amo Boulevard and Olive Street. In the 16.5-mile stretch of freeway, 15 interchanges and 10 separations of streets were provided.

Designed for 60 mph

The freeway is designed for a safe speed of 60 miles per hour. Between Route 60 and the future San Diego Freeway, six lanes have been provided with a curbed median 16 feet in width.

6

LEFT—View looking southerly along the Long Beach Freeway showing the cloverleaf interchange with Florence Avenue. RIGHT—Another southerly view along the Long Beach Freeway shows construction in progress at the crossing with the Los Angeles River at right. The Rio Hondo Channel is shown at the left.

Northerly of the San Diego Freeway to the Santa Ana Freeway, the section consists of three lanes in each direction, separated by an uncurbed median of 40 feet. Concrete pavement was used on main freeway lanes. At some future time it is proposed to place two additional lanes in this median area, which will provide an ultimate eight-lane freeway northerly from the San Diego Freeway. The maximum grade on the freeway is three percent (3%).

Under the terms of freeway agreements, grade separation bridges and traffic interchange facilities were provided at Pacific Coast Highway (Route 60), Willow Street, Belhart Street, Del Amo Boulevard, Long Beach Boulevard, Artesia Avenue (Route 175), Atlantic Avenue (Route 167), Olive Street, Rosecrans Avenue, Imperial Highway, Firestone Boulevard (Route 174), Florence Avenue, Atlantic-Bandini Boulevards, Washington Boulevard and a branch connection with the Santa Ana Freeway. Structures were completed across the Santa Ana Freeway and over Olympic Boulevard in anticipation at some future time of the northerly extension of the Long Beach Freeway to connect with the San Bernardino Freeway and Huntington Drive.

A freeway location such as this adjacent to a river presents problems. The bridges constructed by Los Angeles County at Belhart Street and by the city at Long Beach Boulevard were too close to the Los Angeles River to allow for the design of complete traffic interchange facilities at these locations.

Where complete traffic interchange facilities are being provided, the freeway location has been curved outward from the normal location adjacent to the Los Angeles River bank to provide room for interchange roadways. This type of location which restricts traffic interchange design is satisfactory initially, but since the freeway is adjacent to the river it will not be practicable, except at excessive cost, to provide additional traffic interchange facilities should such be required by future increased traffic demands.

The completed cloverleaf interchange with Artesia Avenue is shown center right in this view looking northeasterly, while in the left background may be seen construction in progress north of Atlantic Avenue.

By reason of the limited number of traffic interchanges, it is believed that this freeway will operate in a most efficient and efficient manner.

Design on the freeway was initiated in the early part of 1950, and the first contract in the amount of $1,507,000 was awarded May 31, 1951, to the Griffith Company covering the 2.5-mile reach between Pacific Coast Highway (Route 60) and 223d Street. Subsequently, the district proceeded with design and construction on the balance of the freeway to the Santa Ana Freeway, and to date nine bridge contracts, 10 road contracts, two illumination contracts and two erosion control contracts, costing approximately $28,000,000, have been completed or are under way. Nine of the contracts were financed in part with federal aid funds administered by the U. S. Bureau of Public Roads.

State contracts have been awarded to the following: Griffith Company, one contract; J. E. Haddock, Ltd., two contracts; Ukropina, Polich & Kral, seven contracts; Webb and White, three contracts; Oberg Bros., two contracts; R. M. Price Company, one contract; J. A. Thompson & Son, one contract; Webb, White & W. J. Distelli, one contract; N. M. Saliba Company, one contract; Jannoch Nurseries, one contract; Westates Electrical Construction Company, one contract; Fishbach & Moore, one contract; Henry C. Sotto Corporation, one contract.

The United States Corps of Engineers included in its channel contracts the construction of the substructure for a bridge across the Los Angeles River north of Imperial Highway and the construction of a railroad bridge across the Long Beach Freeway north of Rosecrans Avenue. By reason of this co-operation, a considerable saving in state highway funds was realized. The U. S. Government also contributed funds to cover a portion of the construction cost of the Dominguez grade separations of the Union Pacific Railroad and Pacific Electric Railway tracks which eliminated necessity for future construction revisions when its channel work was undertaken.

The Los Angeles County Flood Control District constructed a lined channel between the Los Angeles River south of Southern Avenue in Compton and Jaboneria Road northerly of Firestone Boulevard. In its contract it included a covered channel under Firestone Boulevard and a covered channel under the Long Beach Freeway. Portions of the covered channel were financed by the State under the terms of a co-operative agreement.

The City of South Gate under terms of another co-operative agreement constructed a frontage road on the easterly side of the freeway southerly from Southern Avenue.

The Los Angeles County Road Department has constructed bridges across the Los Angeles River and the Long Beach Freeway on Compton Boulevard. At the present time the Los Angeles County Road Department is constructing bridges across the Long Beach Freeway and the Los Angeles River for Olive Street. The above bridges across the freeway and certain incidental approach work was financed by the State under the terms of co-operative agreements with the County of Los Angeles. The county, under terms of a co-operative agreement, financed cost of extending the Rosecrans Avenue bridges across the Los Angeles River channel.

A total of 11 co-operative agreements have been entered into: three with Los Angeles County Road Department, three with the City of Long Beach, three with the U. S. Corps of Engineers, one with the Los Angeles County Flood Control District, and one with the City of Southgate.

At the present time all construction work on the Long Beach Freeway between Route 60 and the Santa Ana Freeway is either completed or under contract. In the future the traffic interchange facility at Del Amo Boulevard will be completed. There is also a future interchange to be built between the Long Beach and San Diego Freeways when this latter freeway is placed under construction.

The design and construction of the Long Beach Freeway has involved all the usual problems which are encountered on freeway projects. The route traverses sections of the cities of Long Beach, Compton, Lynwood, Southgate, and county territory. It also passes through an installation of the United States Air Force known as the Cheli Air Force Depot.

The freeway has required the relocation of a portion of the railroad lines of the Los Angeles Junction Railway. It crosses the freight classification yards of the Atchison, Topeka and Santa Fe Railway and the Union Pacific Railroad on viaducts each almost 1,000 feet in length. There are three railroad grade separations on the Pacific Electric Railway, two on the Union Pacific Railroad, one on the Southern Pacific Railroad and one on the Atchison, Topeka and Santa Fe Railway. In connection with design and construction, it was necessary to revise sanitary sewer lines of the cities served and of the Los Angeles County Sanitation District as well as to alter numerous city streets and county roads.

Two privately owned dumps were removed. The refuse was placed in the loops of interchange roadways and in other adjacent state-owned right-of-way not utilized as freeway or roadway. One of the dumps required the removal and disposal of 300,000 cubic yards of refuse material. A second commercial dump required removal of 30,000 cubic yards. After award of contracts, additional refuse material sites were encountered concerning which there existed no previous information, and these were removed under change orders issued during construction.

During the early stages of design the Los Angeles County Flood Control District presented a proposal that the State occupy a portion of the right-of-way between Olive Street and Imperial Highway. This right-of-way was not required by the county because of narrowing the channel of the Los Angeles River. There was some hesitancy on the part of the State as to whether our construction program could be co-ordinated with that of

UPPER—This view south along the Long Beach Freeway shows in the foreground the interchange with Atlantic Boulevard and Bandini Boulevard. LOWER—Here the camera looks in the opposite direction, northerly along Long Beach Freeway. Construction work is seen in progress north of Atlantic Avenue.

the flood control district so that co-operation would be practicable. Since a saving of several hundred thousand dollars could be realized by such co-operation, the chance was taken that construction programs of county and State could be co-ordinated. Fortunately, the last section of the river channel affecting the freeway was completed in December, 1956, and thus there was no interference with the State's schedule. In some instances it was found that the Los Angeles County Flood Control District easements were restricted to flood control purposes and it was then necessary for the State to acquire rights from the underlying fee owners.

The acquisition and clearing of rights-of-way on this project were major problems. Some 1,200 parcels of right-of-way were obtained, and in carrying out clearing operations 66 buildings were demolished and 691 were removed. The cost of right-of-way acquisition was approximately $20,000,000.

The section between Florence Avenue and Atlantic Boulevard traversed some of the most intensively developed industrial property in Southern California. In order to conserve industrial property, right-of-way in this area for the freeway was held as close to the river and to the Los Angeles Bureau of Power and Light right-of-way as practicable. It was also necessary to hold the taking from the Cheli Air Force Depot to a minimum.

Free Circulation

Right-of-way equivalent in area was obtained easterly of Eastern Avenue to replace the rights-of-way taken by the freeway from the Air Force Depot. A grade separation structure under Eastern Avenue was constructed so that free circulation could be maintained between the two sectors of the Air Force Depot property.

It is to be noted that some 3,000,-000 yards of imported borrow was required to be hauled in from outside sources for building freeway embankments. In addition, 1,250,000 cubic yards of material was obtained by making the freeway excavation between Hubbard Street and Dozier Avenue on the future alignment and

grade of the northerly extension of the Long Beach Freeway. Therefore, in excess of 4,000,000 yards of material was hauled in from sources beyond the limits of the job to complete the freeway embankments.

Securing this quantity of imported borrow in a highly urbanized area presented major problems. However, the State made arrangements to secure material from designated optional sites in compliance with established practice.

The necessity for a large quantity of imported borrow for this freeway and for the future San Diego Freeway led the district to make an exhaustive and systematic search for possible sites. As a result of the investigations, a borrow site was purchased at Del Amo Boulevard and Wilmington Avenue comprising some 150 acres. The material from this site is being removed to a fixed grading plan and after removal of some 8,000,000 yards of imported borrow the site will be disposed of for industrial or other purposes.

Water Permits Secured

The freeway is adjacent to or crosses the rights-of-way of the Southern California Edison Company and of the Los Angeles City Department of Power and Light, which necessitated certain revisions of their facilities.

At various locations it was necessary to secure permits from the Los Angeles County Flood Control District to permit the State to discharge water into the flood control channel as well as to secure permits to cross the Los Angeles River flood control channel.

In connection with the freeway, pumping plants were installed by the State Division of Highways at the Dominguez Crossing of the Union Pacific and Pacific Electric Railway at Olive Street, at the Pacific Electric Railway Undercrossing north of Rosecrans Boulevard at Firestone Boulevard at Clara Street, at Florence Avenue and at Slauson Avenue. These pumping plants were designed by the State Bridge Department. The City of Long Beach designed and constructed

pumping plants at Pacific Coast Highway, Willow Street and Long Beach Boulevard. These city-designed plants were financed in part by the State. The city had previously constructed a pumping plant north of Artesia Avenue with provisions that the future freeway drainage would discharge thereinto.

The contribution by the State for the various city pumping plants was based upon the ratio of water discharged from the freeway into the plants to the full capacity of the pumping installations.

$48,000,000 Budgeted

The financing of the Long Beach Freeway presented fiscal problems of no small magnitude. During the past eight years the California Highway Commission has budgeted a total of approximately $48,000,000 for right-of-way acquisition and for construction on the Long Beach Freeway.

The foregoing story is about the main stem of the Long Beach Freeway, extending for 16.5 miles from Pacific Coast Highway to the Santa Ana Freeway. Of this mileage, 10.5 miles have been completed and opened to public traffic, and six miles are currently under construction with estimated date of completion being early summer, 1958.

It would be amiss to conclude this article without some mention of the two important extensions of this freeway northerly and southerly. Southerly of Pacific Coast Highway, beyond the south terminus of State Highway Route 167, the City of Long Beach is carrying out as a city-financed project, design and construction for extension of this freeway to the Long Beach Harbor area, and also westerly to a connection with Terminal Island. Construction for one-half mile, including the Anaheim Street interchange, was completed in 1953. South of Anaheim Street several bridges and other construction are now in progress, looking toward extension of this freeway into the Long Beach Harbor area. The total estimated cost of the work proposed to be done by the City of Long Beach with city funds is in the neighborhood of $15,000,000.

... Continued on page 42

10

Kern County
Federal Aid Secondary Project Is Completed

By CLINTON D. BEERY, Office Engineer, Kern County Department of Highways and Bridges

THE RAPID development of agriculture and industry in the County of Kern creates an ever increasing demand on the county's Department of Highways and Bridges for more and better highways. With over 3,000 miles of roads now in its system—varying from mountain trails to metropolitan streets and including divided highways with limited access and interchanges—the county welcomes federal and state financial assistance for projects such as the one which is the subject of this article.

Federal Aid Secondary

Local people know this project 885(1) as "Alfred Harrell Highway," "Hart Park Road," "China Grade Loop" or just "the road down the bluff." Actually they are all correct because in operation it is an interchange connecting several major county highways.

At the southwest end, it connects to Panorama Drive and Mount Vernon Avenue, two of Kern County's major streets in the Bakersfield area—both four lanes divided. The residential areas and the Bakersfield City College at the top of the bluff create a tremendous flow of traffic.

East End Connection

At the east end, it connects to the Alfred Harrell Highway (Hart Park Road) which is now a two-lane road far overcrowded with traffic going to or coming from the county's recreational facilities along the Kern River. Plans are now under way to improve Alfred Harrell Highway to freeway standards on eastward to Hart Memorial Park then southeasterly as a limited access highway to connect to State Route 178.

At the northwest end, this project connects to China Grade Loop which crosses the river and passes through one of Kern County's largest heavy industrial areas. Studies for the im-

provement of China Grade Loop are getting under way.

Studies for the possibility of this interchange started early in 1955 as a county project. The county engineers were convinced that it was both warranted and practical so they began designing it. They decided the best design would be to use the existing two-lane road (to be improved later) as a two-lane one-way roadway up the bluff and to put the downhill movement on new alignment. After an extensive survey, the staff decided upon an alignment which utilized the maximum grade considered practical (8 percent) down the side of the 400-foot bluff to keep the length to a

minimum. This design required sidehill cuts of up to 100 feet and sidehill fills of up to 42 feet. It was designed so that only one separation structure would be required, and it would be at the foot of the bluff.

Project Gets Approval

Request was made to the board of supervisors for permission to acquire access rights so the interchange could be built as a full freeway. The request was granted and the right-of-way agent began negotiations for purchase of the necessary land.

As design progressed, work was also being done to get the interchange into the Federal Aid Secondary System. A

Interchange constructed with federal, state and county funds, seen from above the Alfred Harrell Highway with Bakersfield in distant left, Panorama Drive and Bakersfield College at left

and Public Works   11

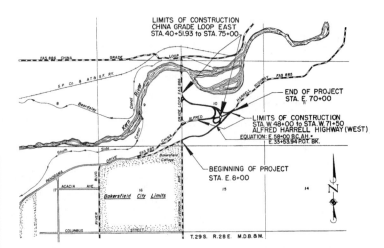

LIMITS OF CONSTRUCTION
CHINA GRADE LOOP EAST
STA. 40+51.93 to STA. 75+00

END OF PROJECT
STA. E. 70+00

LIMITS OF CONSTRUCTION
STA. W. 48+00 to STA. W. 71+50
ALFRED HARRELL HIGHWAY (WEST)
EQUATION: E. 58+00 B.C. AH =
E. 33+53.94 P.O.T. BK.

BEGINNING OF PROJECT
STA. E. 8+00

Bakersfield City Limits

T. 29 S. R. 28 E. M.D.B.& M.

field review was made in December, 1955, by the California Division of Highways and the United States Bureau of Public Roads. The California Highway Commission approved the project on September 25, 1956, and the United States Bureau of Public Roads approved the project on November 5, 1956.

The county engineers consulted with the Bridge Department of the California Division of Highways and decided to make the structure which separates the two major traffic movements a rigid frame bridge with a clear span of 55 feet and a clear width of 40 feet. The structure had to be placed where the deck was on a 550-foot radius, a 6 percent downgrade and a 12 percent superelevation.

On March 1, 1956, county forces with county owned and rented equipment moved in and started benching on the side of a bluff that stood on almost a 1:1 side slope for about 300 feet of its 400-foot height. They moved about 140,000 cubic yards of

roadway excavation to build the two-lane roadway down the bluff and to make the fills at the bottom. The roadbed was constructed to within 0.1 foot of subgrade. Excess material was stockpiled at the bottom of the bluff, compacted slightly and dressed up so it would not be unsightly. This excess material will be used later to build the Alfred Harrell Highway on to the east.

The plans for the base and surfacing were completed and the bridge was designed and detailed by the road commissioner's engineering staff. This project was submitted to bids by the State Department of Public Works as is required of all federal aid secondary projects, although construction engineering is usually, as in this case, performed by county personnel.

Completed in October

A contract was awarded to Griffith Company on March 5, 1957, for $178,-375. Mr. Bruce McDonald was project superintendent for Griffith Company. The work required by the

contract was completed on October 24, 1957.

The only difficulty encountered during construction was the placing of bridge deck and that because of its being on a 6 percent downgrade and on a 12 percent superelevation. .

The County of Kern has expended $166,400 toward this project for rights-of-way, county force account, design engineering, construction engineering, and the county's share of the work done by contract. State and federal funds bring the total expenditures to approximately $300,000.

About a mile west of this interchange, another of the county's federal aid secondary projects is in progress. It is a divided highway with limited access about two miles in length spanning two canals and the Kern River. The southbound lanes and an interchange were completed last year. The other half is scheduled for completion in May, 1958.

Other federal aid secondary projects in Kern County in some phase

... Continued on page 18

12

Sierra Progress

Work Continues on US 40 And 50 Through Mountains

By P. R. LOWDEN, Assistant District Engineer, Operations, District III

THE ENDING of the 1957 construction season in high Sierra area of District III shows considerable progress has been made in the improvement of two major transcontinental routes through these rugged mountains. The major emphasis has been on the transforming of Highway US 40 to a four-lane freeway. Traffic pressure on this route has been growing annually and the number of motor vehicles anticipated for the scheduled 1960 Winter Olympics at Squaw Valley can be handled with ease only by the type of highway currently under construction.

Work on Highway US 50 was planned to ease the most pressing present deficiencies. Much of this work is now completed, or will be in the very near future.

US 40

The interchanges at Canterbury Road and Dead Mans Slough on the North Sacramento Freeway were improved at a cost of about $228,000. The work was done by the Brighton Sand and Gravel Company of Sacramento. Gordon Labrie was the resident engineer.

The interior take-off ramp of the South Roseville Overcrossing to Roseville and US 99E was lengthened and the signing improved under a contract to Granite Construction Company of Watsonville. The work cost about $28,000 and was handled by James W. Hunter as resident engineer.

Continuing easterly, the first major project along US 40 coming under this year's program is the construction on new alignment of a four-lane freeway from one mile east of Newcastle to Elm Avenue in Auburn. The project is currently 75 percent complete

| Aerial view of US 50 construction on south shore of Lake Tahoe, looking east. Traffic congestion results from paving work, under way when photo was taken.

and is ahead of schedule. It is hoped the base and surfacing work will be finished before the winter storms force a shut-down of operations. Lack of steel on a prior contract for the railroad viaduct near the west city limits of Auburn will prevent the completion of the contract before next fall. H. Earl Parker, Incorporated, and Baldwin Contracting Company of Marysville have the contract for the work which will cost approximately $2,500,000. A. N. Regalia is project engineer, Al Vercruyssen is general superintendent and George White is superintendent for the joint venture contractors and Linward O. Kendall is representing the Division of Highways as resident engineer.

New Alignment

A six-mile section from Heather Glen to Colfax is being graded and surfaced with plant-mixed surfacing as a four-lane expressway at an approximate cost of $3,842,000. This improvement is generally on new alignment and when joined to the project east of Colfax will provide about 12 miles of new freeway in this area. The project, being constructed by Mc-Cammon-Wunderlich Company and Wunderlich Construction Company

of Palo Alto under Superintendent John New, is 70 percent complete and is expected to be placed in use in July next year. Favorable weather will enable the contractor to finish at an earlier date. The key to completion is work on structures that were held up by a shortage of steel. The Palo Alto firm moved on this job prior to the formal approval of the contract and had completed 10 percent of the work before such approval was received. Roy T. Phillips, Jr., is representing the Division of Highways as resident engineer.

Just east of Colfax, and extending to the Southern Pacific Railroad Overhead at Magra, Frederickson and Watson and Ransome Company of Oakland are working on six miles of new four-lane freeway that will cost about $4,050,000. Karl Poss is handling the job for the contractors. The project requires 2,310,000 cubic yards of excavation and 21,537,000 station yards of overhaul. The placing of a steel plate girder 102 feet long in the alteration of the railroad bridge at Magra is one of the remaining large jobs. The work on this section is approximately 55 percent complete and Resident Engineer Harold J. Lopez

hopes to have the road in service by early August next year.

The paving on this seciton, as it will be for the remainder of the distance to the state line, will be portland cement concrete.

Traffic Accommodated

A detour is being built from Monte Vista to Alta Road following the alignment of a county road to accommodate traffic during future freeway construction in this area. The contractor on the Colfax to Magra improvement is also doing this work. The $315,000 project is currently 90 percent complete and it is anticipated all work on it will be finished prior to winter. The detour will enable the future freeway contractor to carry on his operation without traffic interference and prevent delays to the motoring public on this major transcontinental route. The Division of Highways is represented on the detour project by Darrel L. McWhirk as resident engineer.

Another detour for future freeway construction is being constructed in the Truckee River Canyon east of Truckee between Boca and Floriston to carry Highway 40 traffic during the construction of a section of free-

14

Traffic is shown passing through the construction area in this photograph of US Highway 40 work between Truckee and the Nevada state line

and Public Works

LEFT—Construction between Weimar and Gold Run. RIGHT—Cut and fill construction near Cape Horn required transfer of large quantities of earth.

way in this rugged terrain. The work is about 75 percent complete, with two bridges over the Truckee River being the two large items yet to be finished. H. Earl Parker, Incorporated, is the contracting firm for this project which will cost about $564,000, and they are attempting to complete all work by mid-December. Sam Cot-

trell is the resident engineer and L. H. Roper is the superintendent for the Marysville contracting firm.

Detour Not Practicable

The most difficult construction project on the route this year was from Floriston to the California-Nevada state line. The conversion of this

5.4-mile section to a four-lane freeway along the existing alignment posed a major traffic problem. A detour was not practicable and it was necessary to carry US 40 traffic through construction. Careful scheduling on the part of the contractor and Resident Engineer John C. Petersen made it possible to complete the excavation of

LEFT—Aerial view of construction in the Truckee River Canyon between Truckee and the state line. Present highway is on the left; railroad in center; service trail at right. ABOVE—Closeup of freeway construction between Weimar and Gold Run showing equipment at work on a giant fill.

California Highways

UPPER—Scene between Auburn and Newcastle. LOWER—Realignment of US Highway 40 in the Auburn area is shown in this view, looking west from Auburn.

over 1,000,000 cubic yards involving some 40,000,000 station yards of overhaul with delay to traffic limited to 30 to 40 minutes except for several isolated instances. This $5,400,000 project, being constructed by Gibbons and Reed of Salt Lake City, Utah, will be about 70 percent completed when the severe Sierran winter forces a halt of work. The superintendent for the Utah firm is Ed Jolley. This section is scheduled for completion early in September of next year.

The Floriston job also saw, for the first time, the passing out of information in pamphlet forms explaining the reason for the delay to the motorist. This effort has been very well received.

US 50

A critical deficiency on Highway 50 created by industrial and military installation growth east and south of Sacramento was alleviated by the conversion of Highway US 50 to four lanes from the Brighton Underpass near Sacramento to Alder Creek, near Folsom. This work was on an interim basis pending the construction of a four-lane freeway on new alignment. The work has been nearly completed by the contractor, A. Teichert and Son, Incorporated, of Sacramento. The cost of the work is about $1,040,-000. During this construction, it was necessary to move the intersection with Citrus Road approximately 1,800 feet to accommodate the realignment of that road by Sacramento County.

The superintendent for the contractor was Bob Brock, and Vincent Barsi served as resident engineer for the Division of Highways.

Just west of Placerville, the intersection of Highway 50 and El Dorado Road was improved by channelization at a cost of $38,700. The work was done by S. G. Voudouris of Sacramento. The resident engineer was Dean Kelly.

Drainage Problem

A stretch of four-lane expressway was completed from Five Mile Terrace, east of Placerville, to 0.7 mile east of Camino. This 3.7 miles of improved roadway bypasses the Town of Camino. The principal structure on the new road is the grade separation of Highway 50 and Snow Road. The plant-mixed surfacing on this project was placed using bottom dump trucks and the method proved quite satisfactory. Drainage correction proved quite a problem in one location and required the placing of over 2,200

feet of perforated metal pipe. The work was done by John Delphia and Fred J. Early, Jr., Company of Patterson at an approximate final cost of $1,025,000. The contractor's forces, under Superintendent Earl Barnard, completed the project about one month ahead of the planned schedule. The Division of Highways was represented by Resident Engineer Dean Kelly.

The Bureau of Public Roads is converting a 1.15-mile section of Highway 50 from Pacific House to Riverton to a modern four-lane mountain highway. The removal of 525,000 cubic yards of material on the existing alignment in this rugged area required long night closures during the spring and summer this year. These controls were lifted in early September, and random half-hour stoppages were substituted. The contractor, Clyde W. Wood, Incorporated, of Hollywood, hopes to finish the project before winter storms force a stoppage of work. The cost of the work will be about $1,260,000. The contractor's forces are headed by Superintendent Andy Weesner. Howard M. Christensen is the resident engineer for the bureau.

Turnout Lanes

The improvement of traffic safety in the vicinity of Echo Summit was accomplished during the summer by the installation of metal guard railing at nine locations from near Camp Sacramento to one mile east of Echo Summit. In this same general area, eight truck turnout lanes were constructed to facilitate the passing of slowly moving vehicles on the grades in this section. The guard railing was erected by the Wulfert Company of San Leandro under a contract that cost $10,450. Harms Brothers Construction Company of Sacramento did the work on the truck turnouts for $148,000. Dean Kelly represented the Division of Highways as resident engineer on both projects.

The final project on Highway 50 was the improvement of the route from the junction with State Sign Route 89 at Tahoe Valley to the California-Nevada state line. From the

18

Apportionment

$15,581,474 in State and U. S. Funds Go to 57 Counties

APPORTIONMENT of $15,581,474 in state and federal funds to California counties for construction on county roads on the Federal Aid Secondary System was announced by the State Department of Public Works in November.

The allocation for the 1958-59 Fiscal Year, a record high, includes $9,615,571 from the Federal Government and $5,965,903 in state highway matching funds. The 1957-58 apportionment was $8,916,082 federal and $5,659,303 state funds, for a total of $14,575,385.

The federal funds are apportioned to the various counties according to the formula used by the Federal Government in distributing federal aid secondary funds to the states—one-third on the basis of area, one-third on rural population and one-third on mileage of certain classes of rural mail routes.

The money from state sources is for the use of the counties in matching federal funds on the basis of approximately 58 percent federal to 42 percent local funds. According to state law, $200,000 is the maximum amount which may be made available to a county in a single year for use in matching its federal allocation.

Federal Money Matched

This $200,000 ceiling will permit 50 of the 57 eligible counties to match all of their federal allocation out of funds provided by the State, except for a small amount of county funds required for contingencies and engineering. The City and County of San Francisco is not eligible to participate in the federal aid secondary road program because it is entirely urban.

Seven counties receive such large federal apportionments that they will need to use some county funds, in addition to the $200,000 in state funds, to meet federal matching requirements.

These counties are Fresno, Kern, Los Angeles, Riverside, San Bernardino, San Diego and Tulare.

County roads on which federal aid secondary funds may be spent are those roads which have been designated by the county, with the approval of the California Highway Commission and the U. S. Bureau of Public Roads, as constituting the county's federal aid secondary system.

For the most part, these roads are next in importance to state highways in terms of traffic volume and economic service to the locality, and are often referred to as "feeder roads" or "farm to market roads."

Two New Laws

The largest federal aid secondary allocation for 1958-59 will go to San Bernardino County—$694,703 federal and $200,000 state funds. The smallest allocations will be to Alpine, Amador, Del Norte and Sierra Counties. Each will receive $48,078 federal, and $34,332 state funds.

Two laws governing the distribution of federal aid secondary and state matching funds were enacted by the 1957 Legislature. These statutes were first applied in connection with the 1957-58 apportionment, and both have meant increased funds for county roads and a corresponding decrease in the amount available for state highway purposes.

One of the new laws raised from 87½ percent to 98½ percent the proportion of the federal money which must be made available for expenditure on county federal aid secondary roads. The remaining 1½ percent is required by federal law to be expended for long-range planning purposes under the direction of the Division of Highways. Under previous law, the State used 11 percent of the federal grant to improve state highways included in the federal aid secondary.

The other legislative change increased to $200,000 a year the maximum amount from state highway funds which may be provided to any one county for use in matching its federal allocation. The previous maximum was $100,000.

AMOUNTS BY COUNTY

County	FAS funds	State matching funds
Alameda	$144,169	$102,950
Alpine	48,078	34,332
Amador	48,078	34,332
Butte	165,680	118,310
Calaveras	58,405	41,706
Colusa	59,068	42,180
Contra Costa	186,867	133,440
Del Norte	48,078	34,332
El Dorado	83,337	59,510
Fresno	483,303	200,000
Glenn	73,621	52,572
Humboldt	212,601	151,816
Imperial	190,872	136,300
Inyo	240,917	172,036
Kern	446,247	200,000
Kings	111,246	79,440
Lake	63,945	45,662
Lassen	148,103	105,759
Los Angeles	496,539	200,000
Madera	131,284	93,749
Marin	58,796	41,986
Mariposa	64,419	46,001
Mendocino	184,814	131,974
Merced	187,394	133,817
Modoc	113,993	81,401
Mono	85,515	61,065
Monterey	233,023	166,399
Napa	95,530	68,217
Nevada	58,614	41,856
Orange	174,006	124,256
Placer	122,632	87,570
Plumas	91,080	65,039
Riverside	367,890	200,000
Sacramento	220,855	157,710
San Benito	65,736	46,941
San Bernardino	694,703	200,000
San Diego	350,583	200,000
San Joaquin	225,086	160,732
San Luis Obispo	168,838	120,565
San Mateo	67,024	47,861
Santa Barbara	163,645	116,857
Santa Clara	212,695	151,883
Santa Cruz	82,919	59,212
Shasta	178,546	127,498
Sierra	48,078	34,332
Siskiyou	228,738	163,339
Solano	94,793	67,691
Sonoma	235,103	167,885
Stanislaus	233,338	166,624
Sutter	65,867	47,035
Tehama	121,012	86,413
Trinity	95,194	67,977
Tulare	382,287	200,000
Tuolumne	83,744	59,801
Ventura	178,311	127,330
Yolo	88,178	62,967
Yuba	52,154	37,243

Barrier Breaking

Varied Highway Opening Stunts Used in California

By C. A. MAGHETTI, Secretary, California Highway Commission

A WIDE variety of methods has been used over the State for ceremonies to celebrate the completion of highway projects. A ribbon cutting, once the standard way of breaking a barrier and opening a road to traffic, serves the purpose now only when the sponsors of the celebration do not work out a special scheme to suit the particular time and place.

Three different types of highway openings which occurred in recent weeks are reported in the following paragraphs. Still other kinds of barrier breaking celebrations, one involving a log cutting and another the shearing of a rope of grapes, are described elsewhere in this issue of *California Highways and Public Works*.

A lumbering road roller broke the barrier at one celebration reported below; the second featured costumes of 100 years ago and a stage coach of the same period; the third would have been the conventional ribbon cutting except that only one end of the ribbon was in California while the other was in Nevada.

Roller Used

In the ceremony for the completion of a widening project from two to four lanes on Folsom Boulevard, US Highway 50, a few miles above Perkins, the big roller was brought into play. The driver was Lieutenant Governor Harold J. Powers who smashed the wooden barrier that opened two more lanes to public use.

Music for the occasion was furnished by the Mather Air Force Band. Some 200 persons were present.

The Sacramento Chamber of Commerce sponsored the program. Distinguished members of the military were introduced including two generals from Mather Air Force Base and numerous officers of lesser rank, Lieutenant Governor Powers, Frank B. Durkee, Director of Public Works and Chairman of the Highway Commis-

Lieutenant Governor Harold J. Powers operates the control that drives a lumbering roller against a road barrier as he participates in the ceremonies opening widened US Highway 50

sion, the mayor of Sacramento, and members of the city council. Chamber of commerce officials were also present.

A celebration luncheon was held at the Mather Officers Club followed by short talks in which the excellent cooperation between the military, state, county, and city officials was freely voiced.

Traffic Eased

The construction of 13.9 miles of four-lane highway from Brighton, near the city limits of Sacramento, to 0.5 mile east of Alder Creek on Highway US 50 is an interim project intended to ease the traffic pressure generated by the industrial and aviation growth southeast of Sacramento.

The contract provided for the widening of the existing road to 44 feet from Brighton to approximately one mile east of Citrus Road to provide four 11-foot undivided lanes. From

the point east of Citrus Road to Alder Creek two new lanes were constructed to provide a divided roadway in this area. The entire length of the roadway was paved with plant-mixed surfacing.

Traffic channelization, road connections and approaches, drainage and traffic control facilities were included in the work to be done. The realignment of Citrus Road by Sacramento County forces made necessary the moving of this intersection approximately 1,800 feet westerly.

Work on the project was started May 7, 1957, by A. Teichert and Son of Sacramento. The expected final cost of the project will be $1,040,000.

Costumes Worn

The dress of early miners lent a touch of California history to the scene on the occasion of the dedication of a new 3½-mile section of expressway a short distance east of Placerville, the community which shared much in the gold rush history of early days.

In keeping with the spirit of the occasion State Senator Swift Berry, appropriately garbed, "chairmanned" the program. He welcomed the spectators and then presented the speakers.

The project is on US 50 in El Dorado County between 0.3 mile mile west of Five Miles Terrace and 0.7 mile east of Camino. It is 3.67 miles long and is a four-lane divided expressway. The cost is expected to total $1,025,000. Work was begun November 28, 1956, by the contracting firm of John Delphia and Fred J. Early, Jr., and completed in 147 working days.

Famous Road

Senator Berry, whose intense interest in the development of Highway 50 has earned him the phrase "Swifty for Fifty," in his opening remarks related some of the history connected with this famous road which had such an important part in history.

The cutting of the ribbon to officially open the highway to public use was done by T. Fred Bagshaw, Assistant Director of Public Works. Hold-

ing the ribbon at each end were Senator Berry and Assemblyman Francis Lindsay. In keeping with the historical aspect of the occasion, an early day stagecoach, drawn by four horses, was halted at the ribbon barrier on its way to Placerville and Sacramento. It was then permitted to continue on its way. The coach is the property of Placerville Parlor, Native Sons of the Golden West, and was loaned for the celebration.

Another historic feature was enacted by the arrival of a pony rider carrying the mail. Here again the transfer was made at the ribbon barrier to a new rider and a fresh horse.

Follows Original Road

Highway 50 traverses pretty much the original road over the high Sierra. It was rated as the most important road in California in the golden days. From 1860 to 1866 there were constant streams of from one- to eight-span teams moving in each direction and from four to six stagecoaches in and out of Hangtown loaded with gold and passengers.

Further history reveals that more than 65,000 tons of freight passed

through Placerville daily. Due to the heavy use of this road it had to be rebuilt and was extended to Virginia City in Nevada. When completed it was declared to be the finest road anywhere. It was 116 miles in length and cost $500,000 to construct. Much more was expended in its upkeep and betterment. Tolls were instituted and travel with freight and stagecoaches was of such volume from 1861 to 1868 that the sum of $6,000,000 was collected.

The first overland mail from the East over '50' arrived in Placerville at 10 o'clock on the night of June 19, 1858. From then on the routing was used continuously until 1896 when the State signed an indenture to make it the first state road in California.

Governor Does Honors

A marked improvement in traffic conditions between Hawthorne, Nevada, and Mono Lake, Inyo County, was made possible following a two-state ribbon-cutting ceremony with Governor Charles H. Russell of Nevada doing the honors.

The ceremony took place at the state line with officials from California

LEFT—Governor Charles H. Russell of Nevada and Assemblyman Francis C. Lindsay of California, representing Governor Goodwin J. Knight, cut the ribbon which opens a modernized Pole Line Road to traffic. RIGHT—An old stagecoach is poised to be first over the road after the ribbon is cut by Assistant Public Works Director T. Fred Bagshaw (second from right). The ceremonial ribbon is held by State Senator Swift Berry and Secretary C. A. Maghetti of the California Highway Commission (both holding left end of ribbon) and Assemblyman Francis Lindsay, who is holding the right end of ribbon.

and Public Works

and Nevada participating. Assembly-man Francis Lindsay represented Governor Goodwin Knight. He was accompanied by State Senator Harold T. Johnson.

The dedication ceremonies brought to an end an effort to secure funds which began more than 10 years ago. It was a determined effort on the part of Hawthorne residents and those of central Mono County to bring to a completion this important interstate link.

The program began with a luncheon at Mono Inn, near Lee Vining on the California side. Following the lunch a long caravan formed and proceeded to the dedication site.

The Hawthorne High School Band in natty uniforms furnished the music. Governor Russell snipped the ribbon and the autoists continued on to Hawthorne were a buffet-style supper, followed by speeches, concluded the program.

Advantages Seen

The "Pole Line Road," as it is frequently known, has a history extending 25 years into the past. It began with several efforts, all of them stemming from Hawthorne, and reading westward to Mono County; but it was not until the second world war when the Navy, which has a large installation at Hawthorne, required the use of additional electrical energy that a powerline was constructed to Mill Creek in Mono County. Far-seeing residents in the area were quick to see the advantage of using the wagon road which was formed alongside of the poles to select it as the site of a new highway to Mono County.

Mono County residents then began the effort to have the line taken into the California Highway System. A period of 10 years elapsed before this was made possible and the funds voted to complete the job.

Road Modernized

The dirt road was taken into the State Highway System by legislative action in 1953, after which state highway engineers went to work on the project of modernizing it.

A 28-foot roadbed following the old road was built and finished in three stages. The first stage was the grading

John W. Spargo

John W. Spargo, Assistant Highway Engineer for the Division of Highways, was injured fatally while working as concrete plant inspector on the Highway 40 freeway project near Pinole on September 4, 1957.

John Spargo was born June 9, 1922, in San Francisco. His father and grandfather were in the contracting business for many years in and around San Francisco.

He graduated from Balboa High School in 1941, and then attended San Francisco City College for two years. He served in the Army Air Corps as a bombardier during World War II, and graduated from the University of California in 1952.

He began work in District IV in February, 1952. After one year in the Design Department he transferred to construction, and had held various jobs of increasing responsibility until his death.

Surviving are his widow, Lois C. Spargo, two children, John and Dorothy; his parents, and a brother and sister.

and penetration treatment of the section from 10.5 miles east of the junction of US 395 to the Nevada state line. This was completed in October, 1955, at a cost of $179,256 by Payne Construction Company and Marchio, Baker, Trewhitt Company, Inc., of Oakland.

The second stage was to grade and treat the section from the junction of US 395 to 10.5 miles east. This contract was let in 1956 to I. L. Croft & Sons., Inc., of Saugus, at a cost of $129,778.

The final achievement in making a modern highway out of the original Pole Line Road was the paving of the entire 21 miles from the junction of US 395 to the Nevada state line. This cost $262,000. The contractor was Basich Bros. Construction Company and N. L. Basich of South San Gabriel.

James L. McWaters

James L. McWaters, Planning Engineer in the Planning Department of District IV, Division of Highways, died on August 24, 1957, at his home in Albany after a short illness.

"Mac," as he was known by his friends, had 33 years' service with the State, all with the Division of Highways. From 1924 to 1929 he was assigned to the District I office, which was in Willits at that time. In 1929 he was transferred to District X office, which was then located in Sacramento. During his 16 years' service in District X, "Mac," as an assistant highway engineer, acted as surveyor, construction inspector, design squad leader and at the time of his transfer to District IV, in 1945, he was assistant chief draftsman.

In District IV, McWaters began as a design squad leader and was ultimately promoted to design engineer, in which capacity he was instrumental in developing plans for many of the metropolitan freeways in the San Francisco area. Early in 1956 he was transferred to the Planning Department as one of the planning engineers. At the time of his death he was a senior highway engineer and was on the eligible list for supervising highway engineer.

McWaters was a member of Albany Lodge No. 686, F. and A. M., California State Employees Association and the Quarter Century Club.

He is survived by his wife, Inez, of Albany, a daughter, Mrs. Vavian Mackenzie of El Cerrito, two grandsons, two sisters and a brother.

RIVERA, CALIFORNIA
Editor, California Highways and Public Works

DEAR SIR: As instructor of a class in highway engineering at the University of Southern California I have recommended *California Highways and Public Works* magazine to my students as a valuable source of information on current developments and general interest on the subject of highway engineering.

WILLIAM E. LEWIS

Fresno Freeway

11-year Study Brings $11,000,000 Bypass

ELEVEN YEARS of engineering studies and construction were climaxed with the October opening of the Fresno Freeway, an $11,000,000 six-mile section of full freeway which provides a US 99 bypass of downtown Fresno.

The cutting of a grapevine barrier stretched across the road was a feature of the dedication of the freeway at a ceremony sponsored by the Fresno City and County Chamber of Commerce.

Frank B. Durkee, Director of Public Works, cut the vines with a long handled pair of pruning shears and dedicated the freeway "to the service of the people of California and to safe and efficient movement of traffic through Fresno."

Warlow, Scott Praised

The 200 people attending the ceremony heard Durkee praise the long time devotion to the bypass planning shown by Chester H. Warlow, member of the California Highway Commission and retired Fresno banker and attorney, and by Earl T. Scott, retired District Engineer of District VI of the Division of Highways.

Warlow, also a speaker at the ceremony and at a subsequent luncheon, recalled his long interest in highway problems in California and particularly in the Fresno area. He was President of the Fresno Chamber of Commerce in 1928 and has been a member of the California Highway Commission for 14 years.

"It was about 1930," Warlow remembered, "that we in the Fresno community asked the State to widen Broadway to take care of the through traffic. That was done, but it became obvious after some years went by that new construction would be needed—that a freeway would be required.

"This is one of the finest freeways in any central valley city. It will take care of the traffic for a long, long time."

Other Guests

Durkee said the full freeway around which the dedication centered "is the kind of bypass we should have, and I hope we will have, from one end of the State to the other."

Leon S. Peters, President of the Fresno City and County Chamber of Commerce, introduced the speakers and other guests at the grapevine ceremony near the Neilsen Avenue Undercrossing of the freeway and at the later luncheon program. Those introduced included state legislators, Highway Division engineers, and city and county officials.

UPPER—Left to right at the grape rope cutting ceremony at which the Fresno Freeway was officially dedicated are: City Commissioner Hattie May Hammet, Chairman Norman S. Foley of Fresno County Board of Supervisors, Mrs. Lynn Roth (Mrs. Fresno County), Retired District Engineer Earl Scott, Supervisor Sid Cruff, Supervisor Sloan McCormick, Public Works Director Frank B. Durkee with shears to cut the barrier, California Highway Commissioner Chester H. Warlow, Supervisor Bert DeLotto, President Leon S. Peters of Fresno Chamber of Commerce, Assemblyman William Hansen of Fresno, Chairman Carl E. Weaver of the chamber's freeway committee, District Engineer William Welch, and Assemblyman Wallace D. Henderson of Fresno. LOWER—Commissioner Warlow's automobile leads the parade of first cars to use the bypass.

Governor Goodwin J. Knight sent the following message through Director Durkee:

"The last section of freeway through Fresno is indeed cause for a celebration. This long-awaited improvement will relieve congestion on Broadway and the other important Fresno city streets.

"Now this principal city, in the greatest agricultural county in the Nation, can proceed with community planning and the development of community services with the assurance that the highway facility is permanently located.

"I regret that I cannot be with you. Please extend my best wishes and heartiest congratulations to the citizens of Fresno on this important occasion."

The celebration heralded the opening of a section of the freeway between Santa Clara and San Joaquin streets, the last to be constructed of the six-mile stretch between Church Avenue on the south and Marks Avenue on the north.

Separate Contracts

The work was done under five separate contracts. The first of these, between Church Avenue on the south and San Benito Avenue at Broadway, included the Monterey Street Overpass across the tracks of the Southern Pacific Railroad and a future connection to the present freeway. The work began in September, 1947, and was completed by the Guy F. Atkinson Company in April, 1949, at a cost of $1,400,000.

Thomas Construction Company was the low bidder at $200,000 for work between Cherry Avenue and Santa Clara Street, completed in January, 1954.

On the third contract, between West Avenue and Marks Avenue, Guy F. Atkinson was again the successful bidder. This section was awarded on June 28, 1954, and was completed in March, 1956.

One year later on June 20, 1955, Richardson and Underdown were awarded the section between San Joaquin Street and West Avenue. This work was completed in February, 1957, at a cost of $1,300,000.

The final section, between Santa Clara and San Joaquin Streets was awarded to C. K. Moseman Company in February, 1956, and completed October 21, 1957, at a cost of $1,700,000.

The fresh whiteness of the newly completed Fresno Freeway makes it prominent at the left of this aerial photograph looking north over the city. Bypassed area downtown is to the right.

For the entire six-mile project, the right-of-way costs were $5,000,000 and construction costs $6,000,000, making a total cost of $11,000,000, or an average of almost $2,000,000 per mile.

The freeway has 23 bridges, seven pumping plants, two storm water retention basins and three storm water drainage fields, one of which has an area of approximately two acres and required a mile of 36-inch-diameter storm drain pipe to drain one section of the depressed freeway.

Church Moved

One of the principal items of interest in the first contract was the moving of the Lutheran Cross Church, a brick and timber frame building, approximately 63 feet in height and 130 feet long, weighing 1,800 tons, which was moved 900 feet to a new location.

The length of depressed freeway required considerable changes to the city's sewer system and involved a cost therefor of $150,000.

Due to the great length of depressed section through West Fresno, 19 acres of land were required for the purpose

of storing some 600,000 cubic yards of excess earth removed from the freeway. It is proposed that this material will be used on the future southerly extension of the freeway.

Signals Eliminated

The new alignment passes through a corner of the city's 160-acre Roeding Park and in so doing, cut through a portion of Lake Washintgon, thus requiring the reconstruction and addition of an equivalent amount of lake area adjacent to the freeway.

The new freeway will save considerable time for motorists traveling through Fresno, as well as those destined for points in Fresno. On the old route, U. S. Highway 99 motorists encountered 16 traffic signals and under normal conditions, 13 minutes were required to travel between Church Avenue and Marks Avenue. With the completion of the freeway, there are no signals between Church Avenue and Marks Avenue. And motorists going through Fresno and Madera and motorists going through the six-mile section of full freeway in less than half the time previously required.

24

Editor Retires

High Tribute Paid Kenneth C. Adams

Hɪɢʜ tribute was paid to Kenneth C. Adams, information officer for the State Department of Public Works and editor of *California Highways and Public Works*, on the occasion of his retirement from state service.

Federal and state officials, headed by Chief Justice Earl Warren, Governor Goodwin J. Knight and Public Works Director Frank B. Durkee, lauded the "lovable character" and "professional superiority" that Adams displayed in a newspaper and public relations career which extended over a half century.

Adams reached the compulsory retirement age of 70 on October 6th and was retired on the last day of October. He had been with the Department of Public Works for 22 years and had served as editor of *California Highways and Public Works* for the past 13 years.

All members of the California Highway Commission, Director Durkee, the heads of the divisions of the Department of Public Works, and senior officials of the department joined with others of Adams' friends in honoring him at a retirement party October 22d at the University Club in Sacramento.

Governor's Commendation

Messages from former Governor Warren and Governor Knight were read. An official State of California tribute to Adams, signed by the Governor, was presented to Adams. It said in part:

"Few men serving the people of California have earned the sincere respect of those engaged in chronicling the day-to-day events in State Government that has been accorded to Kenneth C. Adams. His professional abilities, acquired over many years in the newspaper business and related fields, have been employed to outstanding advantage in the Department of Public Works which he joined in 1935.

"During the intervening period of intense development of state public

KENNETH C. ADAMS

works facilities, Mr. Adams has played an important role in informing the press and public of developments as they occurred. One vehicle for this was the magazine *California Highways and Public Works*, which Mr. Adams edited with distinction. Through its pages he earned plaudits here and abroad for his valuable contribution to highway progress.

"During a long career which began in 1906 as a reporter for the Sacramento *Bee* assigned to covering the State Legislature, Mr. Adams has pursued many interests and engaged in many activities. * * * California Governors and United States Senators have been his friends and confidants. * * * His writings have dealt with a wide variety of subjects, ranging from politics to a history of the California Missions."

The Governor's scroll concluded with a commendation for Adams "for his outstanding service to the people of California."

Extolled by Speakers

The Highway Commissioners, Durkee, State Highway Engineer George T. McCoy, State Architect Anson Boyd, and Deputy State Printer Ralph Titus were the principal speakers. All extolled the retiring editor and recalled highlights of his long career and his heroism in World War I.

Every speaker emphasized the important contributions that Adams made to highway progress in California.

"Adams built the magazine up during his editorship so that it has become widely recognized as one of the outstanding publications of its kind in the United States," Durkee said. "The magazine has been highly commended in this country and abroad for the valuable contribution it has made to highway progress."

Born in Colorado, Adams came to California with his family in 1892 and studied in California schools, including the University of California. His first newspaper work was covering the State Legislature for the Sacramento *Bee* in 1906 and 1907; he covered the 1909 Session for the United Press.

Years of Work

The United Press sent Adams as a correspondent to Central and South America in 1910. He served as UP bureau manager for Ohio later in 1910 and had the same job for the UP in Indiana in 1911. Adams was city editor of the Sacramento *Union* in 1911 and 1912 and in the latter year resigned to direct California publicity for Woodrow Wilson's campaign.

Adams was political editor of the San Francisco *Chronicle* in 1913 to 1915 and political writer for the San Francisco *Examiner* for the next two

... Continued on page 26

and Public Works

25

T,WENTY-FIVE-YEAR AWARDS

Employees who have received twenty-five-year awards since those listed in the May-June, 1957, issue of *California Highways and Public Works.*

District I
Curry, Douglass
Hitchcock, Lawrence C.
Spinney, Lester L.

District II
Brown, Walter W.
Cox, John Q.
Leal, Anthony T.

District III
Bellue, Alfred J.
Etzler, Martin C.
Lathrop, Alfred B.
Schott, Howard F.

District IV
Abert, Fernand A.
Boese, Edwin H.
Bunyard, Francis M.
Kerner, Albert J.
Lund, Thomas B.
Moore, Earl J.
Richardson, Robert L.
Rogers, Frank Edward
Silverfoote, Ed W.
Stein, Louis A.

District V
Binsacca, Silvio D.
Davis, Lawrence P.
Hudson, Glen H.
Mason, Esker L.
Saunders, Wilfred A.
Wofford, George

District VI
Marshall, Gilbert J.
McQuone, Tarney H.
Taylor, Jim U.

District VII
Bowers, Deane
Cannon, James C.
Collins, Ray A.
Compagnon, Henry
Gates, Stillman A.
Killingsworth, Mode E.
Nauslar, Jack L.
Potter, Lee Roy
Rime, John L.
Robinson, Van D.

Titus, George W.
Verdugo, Rafael L.
Walker, Willys G.

District VIII
Cleaver, Lawrence
Isherwood, Harry
Paul, Charles B.
Winter, Sidney J.

District IX
Bellatti, Joseph A.
Dorville, Tom
Hawkins, Earl D.
Jarvis, Joseph R.
Keller, James
Radley, Albert H.

District XI
Elder, Dick
Ellis, Gordon W.
Lain, Joe H.

Bay Bridge
Anderson, Alison M.
Cruza, George F.
Gilzean, J. Albert
Levy, Edwin F.

Materials and Research Department
Drew, Eldridge D.

Bridge Department
Hathaway, Richard L.
Woodbridge, C. J.

Headquarters Office
Fountain, Duane G.
Lapham, Eileen C.

Shop 10
Parnau, Helen

Highway Funds to Cities Allocated for Quarter

The Department of Public Works allocated $7,770,320 during October to the 349 incorporated cities in California under provisions of Section 2107 of the Streets and Highways Code. This quarterly allocation is $904,471 or 13 percent more than the July apportionment.

This year's October distribution is also $291,035 or 3.9 percent more than the October, 1956, allocation.

During the month of October, the department also allocated $1,069,500 to the cities under the provisions of Section 2107.5 of the code for engineering on city streets.

EDITOR RETIRES
Continued from page 25 . . .

years. He enlisted in the Army in 1917, served in field intelligence, and was commissioned overseas after having resigned his first commission in order to get an overseas assignment.

World War I service won him the Purple Heart, French Croix de Guerre, Belgian Croix de Guerre, and two citations from General Pershing.

After the war, Adams remained in Europe and worked for two years as a European correspondent of the Chicago *Tribune* under the late Floyd Gibbons. He returned to California in 1920 and directed publicity that year for Senator Hiram Johnson. In 1921, he went back to the San Francisco *Chronicle* as political editor.

Editor Since 1944

Adams opened his own public relations business in San Francisco in 1922. He continued in business for himself for years, except for 1926-27, when he was managing editor of the Sacramento *Union*. During 1930-33 he was with the San Francisco Newspaper Publishers Association.

From the time Adams went with the Department of Public Works in 1935 until 1944, he was associate editor of *California Highways and Public Works.* He edited the magazine from 1944 until his retirement. A special edition he edited in 1950, on the occasion of the State's Centennial, has become a collectors' item.

Adams is author of a history of the California Missions, first published serially in the state magazine, and later published in book form. He also has written short stories and articles for magazines.

Adams expects to move to San Francisco to make his home there. He has lived in Sacramento for years.

Now Multilane

US 101 Is Improved From S. F. to Santa Rosa

By L. A. WEYMOUTH, District Engineer, District IV

THE CUTTING of a bright red ribbon climaxed the development of a multilane divided highway facility on US 101, extending from San Francisco to Santa Rosa. With the opening of this new 5.1-mile freeway on new location, extending from Wilfred to a connection with the expressway through Santa Rosa, the last of the two-lane highway between San Francisco and Santa Rosa was eliminated and will be reverted to use as a local facility.

Improvements to multilane standards along this 45-mile portion of US 101 have been almost continuously under way since 1946. Most of the way, improvement has been to four-and six-lane freeway standards.

From the Golden Gate Bridge to Manzanita at the south end of the Richardson Bay Bridge, a full freeway was placed in service in March of 1956 and by that fall the new Richardson Bay Bridge was completed and opened to traffic. The next 2.5 miles to north of Alto were also completed to freeway standards during the past summer.

From Alto to north of Greenbrae, a 3.5-mile full freeway project is nearing completion and from Greenbrae to the completed freeway at San Rafael, a 1.4-mile freeway is now under construction. The viaduct and approaches in San Rafael, as well as an expressway or four-lane highway facility from Forbes Overhead northerly through to Petaluma, have been in service for some years.

Five Projects

Since early summer of 1953, full freeway construction has been under way on new location between south of Petaluma and south of Santa Rosa, a distance of 18.5 miles. There have been five construction projects between these limits and these have accounted for expenditure

of approximately $10,000,000 for construction alone.

The first two projects provided for abutment fills and a bridge over Petaluma Creek near the south limits of Petaluma. The third project, which was commonly referred to as the "Petaluma Bypass" was started in June, 1954, and completed in December, 1956. It provided a complete freeway facility over the 5.5 miles from south of Petaluma to Denman Flat. The work on the northerly 2.5 miles of the contract was for grading only. A fourth contract, between Denman Flat to three miles north of Cotati at Wilfred, extended the freeway a distance of 6.7 miles, and graded the next 1.0 miles to the north. This project was officially opened to traffic on July 2, 1957.

The last project to be constructed (which was the cause for the celebration) developed the remaining 5.1 miles to the connection with the existing Santa Rosa expressway and was started on July 5, 1956. This project, like the others, consists of an initial four-lane freeway with provisions for an additional two lanes when required. Interchanges are located at Baker Avenue, Hearn Avenue, Todd Avenue and Wilfred Avenue.

The opening ceremonies took place September 25th at the south end of the project between Cotati and Wilfred.

"A Fine Example"

Following the invocation by Dr. Percy Hall, and a precision drill by the National Champion "Campions," from Santa Rosa, the master of ceremonies, Frank McLaurin, introduced Mayor Kenneth Mitchell of Santa Rosa, who expressed Santa Rosa's approval of the new freeway.

Mayor Mitchell introduced a delegation from the City of Oakland, including Mayor Rishell, who spoke briefly representing Oakland's interest

in this important highway link. H. C. Quistgard, President of the Santa Rosa Chamber of Commerce, introduced E. D. Maloney, President of the San Francisco Chamber of Commerce, who brought greetings from San Francisco and pointed to the freeway as "a fine example of the progress needed in California."

Charles Reinking, President of the Golden Gate Bridge Authority, paid tribute to the Highway Commission and the Division of Highways for their handling of the "difficult work in building freeways" and also expressed approval of this latest link between the Redwood Empire and the Bay area.

Leigh Shoemaker, of the Sonoma County Board of Supervisors, told of Sonoma County's pride in the link unifying the county and tying it to its neighbors in the south.

Representing the Governor and the Highway Commission was Commissioner Robert L. Bishop, who stated that this was "another victory in the State's race against growth and time." Bishop presented B. W. Booker, Assistant State Highway Engineer, who represented State Highway Engineer G. T. McCoy.

Booker congratulated the contractor, Guy F. Atkinson; the resident engineer, Phillip Auchard; and also the Bridge Department representative, D. T. Morton, for a "job well done, well within the time limit." Booker said that plans for the continuation of the freeway northerly of Santa Rosa are well advanced.

Guy F. Atkinson, the contractor, also spoke briefly before the ribbon was cut.

Following the opening, the official guests formed a car caravan that toured the project and then proceeded to the Santa Rosa Fairgrounds for a barbecue sponsored by the Santa Rosa Chamber of Commerce.

and Public Works   27

Legal Opinion

Highway Commission's Procedure Approved

By ROBERT F. CARLSON, Attorney, Division of Contracts and Rights of Way

THE OFFICE of the California Attorney General has approved the legality of the present procedure of the California Highway Commission in the adoption of freeway routes. Deputy Attorney General Raymond H. Williamson wrote the informal opinion in a letter of September 24, 1957, to Assemblyman Louis Francis.

The commission, by resolution adopted on July 15, 1948, (see story in the March-April, 1952, issue of *California Highways and Public Works*) formally established the basis for its present procedure and policies. An expanded restatement of the procedure and policy was adopted on February 18, 1955 (and published in the March-April, 1955, issue of *California Highways and Public Works*).

The commission presently is considering further refinement of the resolution better to insure the accomplishment of its objectives.

Briefly, the commission resolution provides that when sufficient engineering and economic studies have been made to permit intelligent discussion as to the location of a freeway, the State Highway Engineer or his representative will confer with the appropriate governmental agency involved and will hold public meetings to acquaint interested persons with the available alternatives and to obtain comments thereon. After considering all the information received, the State Highway Engineer then submits a report to the commission covering the results of such meetings, together with a recommendation as to the proposed route of the new freeway which, in his judgment, will serve the best interests of the State. A public hearing is then held by the commission itself, through one or more of its members, unless the local legislative agency requests no hearings, although the commission may of its own motion decide to hold such a hearing. The reso-

lution further provides that due public notice of the time and place will be given and "all persons and organizations, and official bodies interested in the matter will be given opportunity to be heard."

"Townhouse Meetings"

The Attorney General, in referring to these public meetings, describes them as similar to the old and historic "townhouse meetings," having a twofold purpose—first, to advise and to obtain the co-operation of local public officials and persons affected by the freeway route; second, to obtain information to assist the commission in solving the freeway location problem. The Federal Highway Act of 1956, Section 116(c), also contains a requirement for public hearings as to any project involving federal-aid funds. The present procedure has been determined by the Federal Government to satisfy the requirements of federal law.

Although no particular rules apply to the conduct of the hearing before the commission and its staff, the Attorney General ruled that the informal hearing or meeting provided for in the resolution is legally adequate.

The opinion said the requirements and procedures of a formal hearing, e.g., statement of issues the reception and ruling on evidence, and the administering of an oath are not necessary, provided of course, that the hearing is conducted fairly and all interested persons are allowed to present their views.

More Like Legislative

The right of interested persons or agencies to appear by counsel is said to be inherent in the resolution of the commission. But this right to appear by counsel does not give the right to cross-examine witnesses the Attorney General wrote, the reason being that

because of the many miles of freeway routes being selected by the Highway Commission, hearings would go on interminably were every interested person afforded the right of cross-examination.

Because of the fact that the comsion's determination of freeway routes partakes more of legislative than judicial attributes, the opinion said there does not exist the requirement or necessity for the issuance of subpenas to compel the attendance of witnesses or to require the production of certain documents at the hearing or to take depositions prior to the public hearing. However, the resolution of the commission does not forbid the present practice of permitting expert witnesses to appear and to be heard. This also includes the current practice of receiving pertinent affidavits for consideration by both the State Highway Engineer and the commission. The opinion notes that the more formal type of hearing required by the Administrative Procedure Act is neither applicable to the Highway Commission nor practicable under the circumstances.

The Attorney General by this opinion has determined that the present informal procedure employed by the commission does not partake of the normal attributes of an administrative hearing.

Because of its dominant characteristic of informality, the old and historic "townhouse meeting" has once against become a means by which one person, a neighborhood and a community can, by open discussion, aid the Highway Commission in solving a modern-day problem of freeway location.

A new maintenance station has been completed at Bridgeville, on State Sign Route 36, in Humboldt County, at a cost of $26,000.

FREEWAY APPROACH TO BRIDGE OPENED IN MARIN COUNTY

The four-lane freeway approach to the Marin County end of the Richmond-San Rafael Bridge on Sign Route 17 was opened to traffic in November.

This project covers full freeway construction from the bridge for about one mile west and provides traffic interchanges at Point San Quentin and at Sir Francis Drake Boulevard East.

Extension Begun

Extension of the freeway westerly for 1½ miles to a connection with US 101 at the San Quentin Wye south of San Rafael has already begun and will be continued next summer.

B. W. Booker, Assistant State Highway Engineer, explained that grading work for the westerly extension was carried out as part of the contract for the newly opened section while the budget recently adopted by the California Highway Commission for the 1958-59 Fiscal Year contains an allocation of $850,000 for completion of the project. Plans and right-of-way acquisition for the westerly 1½ miles are nearing completion, and bids can be called for late next spring.

Route 17 Extended

The new bridge and approaches have extended Sign Route 17 from the East Bay area to US 101. When the budgeted extension of the freeway approach on the Marin County side has been completed, motorists using the new transbay connection will have a complete freeway and expressway ride from Richmond to any point along US 101 from San Francisco to north of Santa Rosa.

Both the freeway section just opened and its westerly extension have been designed for future widening to six lanes when traffic warrants it and funds are available.

The contractor on the project just opened was Ball and Simpson of Berkeley. Total construction cost approximated $1,200,000.

This aerial view of the four-lane freeway approach to the Marin County end of the Richmond-San Rafael Bridge was taken just a few days before the section of Sign Route 17 was opened to traffic. In the background may be seen the year-old bridge to which leads the $1,200,000 new section of state highway.

New Subdivisions

Relationship With Freeways Considered

By J. A. LEGARRA, Planning Engineer, California Division of Highways

FREEWAYS, as you know, are having a marked effect on urban and suburban development, and the active co-operation of the State and the local agencies is essential if the freeway is to do its best job. The relationship of state highways to new subdivisions is only one segment of the overall problem of planning. Before we enter into this specific feature, we first should consider the overall transportation picture and how this segment fits into the general relationship.

It is state highways which are to be developed as freeways with which we are primarily concerned, and our discussion will be confined to the relationship of the freeway and new subdivisions.

Freeways have access restricted and provide safe and efficient transportation between strategically located centers. At these centers, which are points of entry and exit, the traffic is transferred from the freeway to street or other type of facilities which act as distributors and routes for travel of an intermediate nature. Points of interchange or entry and exit to the freeway should be connected to major thoroughfares. These streets act primarily as traffic carriers and secondarily as a means of access. Finally, there must be constructed the street whose primary purpose is to provide access and not to act as a through traffic carrier. This access type of street may serve either residential or commercial and industrial development. In the case of residential streets, they are planned and constructed to serve their primary purpose of providing access to homes, and in many cases their layout is such as to actually discourage use by either large volumes, or fast-moving traffic.

Co-operation Necessary

In order to develop a combined pattern of highway traffic to provide maximum overall transportation serv-

This is the text of an address on "State Highways in Relation to New Subdivisions" which Mr. Legarra gave before the Twenty-seventh Annual Conference of the California Planning Commissioners' Association at Carmel in October.

ice, the co-operation of the Federal Government, the State, the county,

and the city is necessary. Each segment of the road building governmental agency should fulfill its responsibility and so plan its part of the overall transportation project so that each part can be combined into a smoothly operating unit. It is impossible to properly plan a particular freeway without taking into account its effect on other freeways and the effect of other freeways on it. I believe that this also applies to the planning of an individual subdivision in

Various aspects of sound zoning and subdivision planning are illustrated in this view of the East Washington Street Interchange area on US 101 near Petaluma. Not only do the homes nearest the freeway back onto it, but the subdivider has also enhanced the residential-access feature of his streets by providing turnaround areas. The author also points out that the freeway serves as a buffer between residential and industrial zones while permitting safe, free-flowing circulation between them by means of the overcrossing structure and interchange ramps.

relation to a state highway, for each subdivision is seldom an independent unit. Not only must there be planning within the subdivision, but there must be planning between the subdivisions and their relationship to the state highways.

Subdivisions should be planned to provide through routes, both parallel and at right angles to the state highway route. One important thing that we have learned is that there must be connecting through secondary facilities to provide adequate access between neighborhoods, residential areas, shopping centers, and industrial areas. The problem has risen or will arise in probably every county of the State where subdivisions have developed without an overall plan and have resulted in local major thoroughfares that lack continuity. This results in a misuse of the street and highway system available and is detrimental to the entire area.

The effect of the freeway on the adjacent area and, vice versa, the effect of the area and the street layout on the freeway is in some relation to distance. The local circulation immediately adjacent to the freeway is, therefore, the most important part of the state highway-subdivision relationship. As part of

the freeway construction, it is often necessary to construct frontage roads, and in the past there has been a tendency to depend too much on these frontage roads for local circulation. Actually, local circulation could better be provided by constructing *major* thoroughfares a short distance from the freeway. In the first place, use of roads fronting on the freeway is inefficient in that they can attract traffic only from one side of the roadway. In the second place, it is difficult, if not impossible, to provide continuity through the interchange areas.

Good Design Standards

In general, it is most economical to carry the local road either over or under the freeway. Normally good design standards require approximately 600 feet from the center of the freeway for the crossroad to get back to existing ground elevation. Because of this requirements, frontage roads immediately adjacent to the freeway must wind in and out at the interchange areas. It is also generally necessary to have an intersection at grade between the frontage road and the local crossroad in the immediate area where the local road returns to existing ground level. By constructing a major thoroughfare parallel to the

freeway and some reasonable distance from it, it is possible to provide a straight, highly desirable local thoroughfare and to utilize the area required by the interchange to provide an attractive access street pattern.

It appears that the preferable and most efficient design for subdivision layout is to have the residential or commercial areas back up to the freeway. This allows an additional tier of lots, either residential or commercial, to front on the same street and in most cases should provide the maximum use of land area. I believe there is no question as to the desirability of having commercial or industrial developments back up to the freeway. However, there has arisen in the past a question of the desirability of residence backing up to the freeway. The Land Economics Section of Headquarters Right-of-Way Department of the California Division of Highways recently completed an extensive study on the freeway influence on the market value of residences which back up to the freeway or are immediately adjacent to the freeway. (*California Highways and Public Works*, March-April, 1957.) They have found that there has been, for all practical purposes, no detrimental effect on the value of the house con-

... Continued on page 42

LEFT—Subdivision layout which provides for residences backing up to the freeway is described as more efficient than having homes face the freeway. The view is north along the Eastshore Freeway in Hayward, with the Jackson Street Interchange in the foreground. RIGHT—Aerial view of the Bayshore Freeway-Third Avenue Interchange area in San Mateo shows how a major artery (Norfolk Street) makes for good local traffic movement in a subdivision.

and Public Works   31

State's Highways

Planning California's Freeways of Tomorrow

By FRANK B. DURKEE, State Director of Public Works and Chairman of the California Highway Commission

CALIFORNIA is the acknowledged leader among the states in construction of multilane divided highways. As we approach the end of 1957, we can point with pride to a total of nearly 1,800 miles of these modern facilities now serving the highway-using public, with another 375 miles under construction or advertised for bids. Still another 250 miles have been financed, either in the 1957-58 Fiscal Year State Highway Budget or in the 1958-59 Budget which was adopted by the California Highway Commission in October and on which a start has already been made in the form of call for bids.

Most of this modern mileage consists of full freeways or expressways. The percentage of full freeways—divided highways with access controlled and with no left turn or crossing movements at grade—is constantly increasing, not only in the congested metropolitan centers but also on the long stretches of rural highway. California now has about 450 miles of full freeway in operation, carrying an average daily traffic of 45,000 vehicles a day. The freeways have a record twice as safe as conventional highways for overall accidents and more than three times as safe for fatalities in terms of vehicle miles traveled.

These are the modern freeways in operation or soon to be in operation. They did not spring into existence overnight. They had to be planned—first of all, they had to be located.

That is why a more significant mileage figure than any of the foregoing is 4,131. This is the total number of miles of state highway for which routes have been adopted and which have been declared as freeways by the Highway Commission since the enactment of the freeway law in 1939.

This article is reprinted from "California—Magazine of the Pacific," publication of the California State Chamber of Commerce, for which it was specially written by Director Durkee.

Freeways Total 30 Percent

The 4,131 miles of adopted freeway routes represent 30 percent of our entire 14,000-mile State Highway System. They are the tangible, documentary expression of the policy laid down by the Legislature in establishing the present commission setup in 1943:

"It is hereby declared to be the policy of the Legislature to provide for advance planning and continuity of fiscal policy in the construction and improvement of the State Highway System and in the administration of expenditures from the State Highway Fund."

In other words, the advance determination of freeway routes by the Highway Commission is assurance to the people of California that their wishes for an orderly, long-range highway planning program are being carried out. It is this planning program which has given California motorists the freeways they are already using and those they are currently building.

The adoption of a freeway route by the California Highway Commission is a major milestone in many respects.

It is the end of a long and painstaking and often soul-searching process which began, many years ago, with congestion, accidents and the manifest need for a highway improvement which would be a reasonably permanent, not an interim, solution. This process has then continued through a period of

engineering and economic studies, public discussion, careful review and final decision.

Important Duties

In my opinion, the selection of routes is one of the most important of the various duties assigned by the Legislature to the Highway Commission—fully as important, from the long-range point of view, as adopting the annual State Highway Budget.

Budgeting for state highways is governed in large measure by statutory controls and by priority of needs. The commission has some latitude within the controls, however, and financing need which is not met this year can be considered again next year.

A decision on a freeway route, on the other hand, has far-reaching permanent implications. Every effort must be made to locate the route in the best possible place.

The "best possible place" means the best from all points of view. It means not only the best route for traffic service, but also from the standpoint of the economic and general welfare of the community or area concerned. The choice of a freeway route by the Highway Commission represents the distillation of many ingredients, in which engineering facts are the predominant—but not the only—element. Economic studies are extremely important, as is the long-range local planning being done by the community.

Three Accomplishments

In finally adopting a freeway route, the commission in effect has done three things:

1. It has protected the right-of-way from indiscriminate development which leads to congestion and hazard, and has insured that the future highway to be built on the adopted loca-

tion will give safe, efficient service for many years to come.

2. It has enabled the Division of Highways to proceed with detailed planning and design leading to acquisition of rights-of-way and eventual construction as financing is made available.

3. It has established a major element in the overall transportation pattern—and therefore the economic and growth pattern—of the community concerned.

For these reasons the commission is careful never to adopt a freeway route without being certain that the location has met the test of full public scrutiny as well as official and professional approval. In particular, the commission examines the studies which have been made concerning the economic effects of the route recommended by the State Highway Engineer as well as the comparable data for any alternative routes. The commission may, and frequently does, ask the Division of Highways for additional studies of alternate route possibilities even beyond those requested by local officials and groups.

Agreements Worked Out

Once the route has been adopted, the next step is the freeway agreement, which is worked out by the Division of Highways and the city or county (or both) involved. This agreement spells out the location of crossings and interchanges and such other details as local street and road adjustments and connections to the freeway.

An important point is sometimes overlooked or misunderstood. The Division of Highways does not select the route; that is the sole responsibility of the commission. The commission, on the other hand, does not design the freeway or determine the type and positioning of crossings and interchanges; that is worked out by the Division of Highways and participated in by the local governmental authority as part of the freeway agreement. The commission is of course interested in the working out of a satisfactory freeway agreement, since construction cannot proceed until the agreement has been executed.

The route adoption procedure which thus sets the pace for the expanding freeway program has now stood the test of nearly a decade since it was formalized by the commission in 1948. It need not be restated here, for the Highway Section of the California State Chamber of Commerce has been an informed and valued consultant in its development and improvement over the years.

Since July, 1948, the commission has held a total of 68 public hearings in connection with its consideration of freeway routings. Most of these were held at the request of local governmental authorities, and some were held on the commission's own initiative.

The number of commission hearings has been markedly reduced since the adoption early in 1955 of a revised route adoption procedure. This procedure was worked out with the assistance and co-operation of a special committee from the California State Chamber of Commerce. Its salient feature provides for public meetings for explanation and discussion of route proposals before a route recommendation is submitted to the commission by the State Highway Engineer.

In the less than 2½ years since this revised procedure went into effect, the Division of Highways has held a total of 183 public meetings on route matters, all of them in the community or area concerned.

At some of the meetings there have been marked differences of opinion; at others complete harmony on the part of all concerned. But whether in storm or calm, they have all pursued one steady course: the presentation of factual data in an objective manner, the invitation to every interested person to place his views on record, the seeking out of all pertinent information from whatever source—all for the purpose of producing a complete transcript and record which the commission can and does study before taking final action to adopt a route.

It was inevitable, as the pace of advance route determination was stepped up beginning in 1953 to keep ahead of an accelerated construction program, that expressions of dissatisfaction with some of the route proposals should in-

crease. Some of these complaints found their way into proposals to the State Legislature which, had they been enacted into law, would have drastically reduced the authority of the commission to determine freeway routings.

State C. of C. Support

In the vanguard of far-sighted friends of the California highway program who appeared in opposition to such proposals was the California State Chamber of Commerce. Its support of the existing statutory procedures and policies governing route determination was gratifying and constructive.

The route adoption policy which has been so carefully nurtured and developed in the past decade was subsequently supported by the Legislature by the adoption of Senate Concurrent Resolution No. 90. This resolution commended the commission for "the written policy resolution on route adoptions which it has developed over recent years." It also urged the commission to make no change in its policy which would reduce the requirements for public hearings or "other protections afforded the public in the matter of route adoptions or freeway locations."

Since the unbroken trend has been, and still is, in the direction of more public discussion of freeway route proposals rather than less, the people of California and particularly of the communities interested in freeway routes have every assurance that this instruction from the Legislature will be complied with in spirit as well as to the letter.

California's continuing achievement in freeway construction, the product of an orderly long-range planning program, still hinges on advance route determination. It is this long-range planning program which provided a backlog of projects ready for construction when additional funds were made available by the State Legislature in 1953 and by the Federal Government in 1956. Before the freeways can be built, the routes must be selected. In the selection of routes, every individual must be heard, every need considered so that the eventual decision is the best possible solution for the California of today and tomorrow.

OPERATIONS AND ACTIVITIES OF MATERIALS AND RESEARCH DEPARTMENT

PART IV—STRUCTURAL MATERIALS SECTION

By JOHN L. BEATON, Supervising Highway Engineer

IN THE May-June, 1957, issue of *California Highways and Public Works*, F. N. Hveem, Materials and Research Engineer, presented a general review of the scope of laboratory activities, setting forth some of the problems and responsibilities delegated to materials engineers and also the progression of growth and development of the laboratory from its early day inception to the large and nationally recognized organization which now comprises the Materials and Research Department of the California Division of Highways.

This fourth article of the series will be devoted to the activities and operation of the Structural Materials Section which constitutes one of the five major subdivisions of the Materials and Research Department.

Multiple Responsibilities

The Structural Materials Section is responsible for manufactured structural members of metal, wood, or concrete materials including plant and factory production of finished materials. In order to dispatch this responsibility, the section is organized: (1) to give maximum service to the operating highway departments and districts; (2) to provide special service on request to the engineering departments of other state agencies and governmental subdivisions at the federal, county, and city levels; and (3) to co-operate to the maximum degree with the industries who supply manufactured and prefabricated materials to the various highway contracts.

In order to outline the extent of this service, the following article will be broken down to describe the activities of each of the functional units within the section. The fundamental organization is shown in the chart.

Many Items Covered

Over half of the personnel and effort of the Structural Materials Sec-

tion is devoted to the inspection for compliance with contract or purchase specification of materials and components that are manufactured in an industrial plant to be furnished for the construction of highways. Products will vary from reflector buttons, for use on a guide post, to bridge trusses to be erected across the Carquinez Straits.

The items covered by such inspection are structural steel, precast prestressed concrete, reinforcing steel; miscellaneous iron and steel; frames, covers, and grates; steel, timber and concrete piles; concrete and corrugated metal pipe culverts; water and sewer pipe; structural timber, fencing, raised traffic bars, electric signal and lighting systems, sight posts and clearance markers, precast concrete monuments and barrier posts, bridge and guard railing, highway signs and reflector buttons, service and supply commodities, and the sampling of bituminous and paint products, and any

other special materials which are fabricated or manufactured before delivery to the job.

Maintains Branch Office

The majority of such products originate in the two large manufacturing areas of California; the San Francisco Bay area and Los Angeles, for this reason, Headquarters Laboratory maintains a branch inspection office in each of these areas. This results in small, efficiently managed offices consisting of a group of men in each area who are highly skilled, well experienced and closely acquainted with the major manufacturers and fabricators of the State of California. The employee turnover rate of zero in these offices indicates the high morale and the interest these men have in their service to the Division of Highways.

The primary function of these offices is to assure compliance with specifications of materials delivered from their area to the various contract proj-

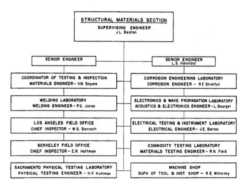

```
STRUCTURAL MATERIALS SECTION
SUPERVISING ENGINEER
J. L. Beaton

SENIOR ENGINEER                              SENIOR ENGINEER
                                             L.S. Hannibal

COORDINATOR OF TESTING & INSPECTION          CORROSION ENGINEERING LABORATORY
MATERIALS ENGINEER - V.M. Soyers             CORROSION ENGINEER - R.F. Stratfull

WELDING LABORATORY                           ELECTRONICS & WAVE PROPAGATION LABORATORY
WELDING ENGINEER - P.G. Jones                ACOUSTICS & ELECTRONICS ENGINEER - L. Bourget

LOS ANGELES FIELD OFFICE                     ELECTRICAL TESTING & INSTRUMENT LABORATORY
CHIEF INSPECTOR - W.S. Bennett               ELECTRICAL ENGINEER - J.E. Berton

BERKELEY FIELD OFFICE                         COMMODITY TESTING LABORATORY
CHIEF INSPECTOR - E.R. Hoffman               MATERIALS TESTING ENGINEER - R.N. Field

SACRAMENTO PHYSICAL TESTING LABORATORY       MACHINE SHOP
PHYSICAL TESTING ENGINEER - H.F. Kuhlman     SUPV. OF TOOL & INST. SHOP - R.E. Wilhelmy
```

34

ects throughout the State. However, they also play the following secondary role which in the long range picture is of equal importance.

Access to Knowledge

In order to efficiently conduct the prime duty of inspection, it is necessary and desirable that friendly industrial relations be developed and maintained. As a direct result of this relationship, the branch office personnel has access to a vast amount of industrial knowledge and know-how regarding materials and manufacturing processes not necessarily connected with regular highway material production nor ordinarily available to the average engineer. Consequently a valuable secondary operation of investigation and dissemination of information is naturally established and is used extensively to keep headquarters advised of new materials and methods of manufacture or fabrication which might have practical application to Division of Highways' work, or might result in necessary revisions in our contract specifications.

In addition to the large volume of manufactured material emanating from the two major manufacturing areas in California, much material also originates from other outlying cities and towns throughout the State and from plants elsewhere in the United States.

Work Volume Growing

When such material originates within the State but outside the San Francisco Bay, Los Angeles, or the Sacramento areas, the work is assigned to the nearest district materials engineer. The volume of this work in the districts has been growing so steadily that, with the exception of Districts IV and VII, most of the districts have at least one materials engineer assigned especially to this task. These men have proven highly competent and conscientious in this work and, with the exception of complex welded structural steel or prestressed concrete fabrication, little assistance is needed from Sacramento except in the matter of standardization and co-ordination.

Inspection of materials for our use originating outside the State of California is handled by service agreement through commercial inspection agencies. Most of such out-of-state work is confined to material that must conform to specific chemical or mechanical tests and needs but a general degree of co-ordination to assure proper control. However, in some cases such as structural steel fabrication it is necessary that a careful control of stand-

ards be exercised from Sacramento Headquarters so that out-of-state fabricators and inspectors can be as familiar with the requirements of the Division of Highways as are the fabricators within California.

Precise Co-ordination Needed

All inspection of manufactured material, whether within the State or out, requires a precise degree of co-ordination from the contractor's notification of material sources to the assignments of inspection. The management of this activity depends on the resident engineers making sure that the notices of material sources are complete and are forwarded as soon as possible.

The co-ordination of such work is handled by a materials engineer assisted by a clerical staff in Sacramento.

It is the policy of the Division of Highways to provide continuous inspection at the source of supply. This involves a prior discussion between the inspector and the manufacturer or fabricator concerning the requirements of our specifications as well as intermittent inspection during the actual manufacture and final inspection at the end of production which also covers the shipping method. When complex fabrication is involved, such conferences may also include the design and construction engineer, and the inspection is continuous throughout the project.

Supplier Must Understand

In order to implement this program, it is required that the contractor notify his resident engineer as soon as possible of his source of materials. This information is immediately transmitted to the laboratory and the assignments made as expeditiously as possible so that the assigned inspector can be assured that the supplier knows and understands the requirements of the specifications before actually starting work.

Within the State of California alone, this section inspects and maintains co-operation at the production level with approximately 800 manufacturing or fabricating companies. Such industries range from a one-man concrete monument plant to enormous corporate entities such as the steel

and Public Works   35

Figure 3. Inspection of structural steel fabrication includes shop assembly and matchmarking, the work which is under way in these photographs of trusses destined for use in the Carquinez Bridge.

mills which supply structural steel for our bridges and buildings. The scope of this activity is illustrated by *Figures 1, 2, and 3.*

In addition to the administrative coordination office, there are four laboratories in the Sacramento Office of the Structural Materials Section which are directly keyed to the inspection program and provide a testing service to the field inspectors.

Physical Testing Laboratory

The physical testing laboratory performs the mechanical tests and such physical tests as cannot be performed in the field on the samples of various manufactured materials submitted for proposed use on contract work.

The samples are submitted by the branch office inspectors of this section, by district materials engineers, and by various resident engineers. The samples submitted by the resident engineers cover those materials which are, either inadvertently or sometimes purposely, sent to a project without source inspection. This is done purposely only when the economy of the inspection dictates it.

This laboratory utilizes the services of four engineering assistants with a

testing engineer in charge. It is equipped with a 440,000-pound universal testing machine, a 60,000-pound universal testing machine, a 5,000-pound universal testing machine, Brinell and Rockwell hardness testers, an impact testing machine, and the various special jigs and appurtenances involved in such testing, such as stress-strain recorders, SR4 gauges, extensometers, etc. A 200,000-pound universal testing machine is located in the Los Angeles Branch Laboratory.

Figure 4 illustrates the testing of a prestressing wire strand in the 440,000-pound universal testing machine.

Requires Experience

This testing of structural materials which involves a wide variety of procedures and equipment, requires extensive experience and training, mechanical ability, and exercise of good judgment; the need for versatility adds interest to the work.

The duties of this unit are not by any means confined to the performance of established routine tests. New developments in materials or construction methods constantly challenge the ingenuity of the testing engineers, for

Figure 4. Stress and strain measurements being made of a wire strand. INSET—Closeup of strand after being loaded to failure in testing machine.

36

they must find ways to evaluate new products, to develop more workable and effective specifications, and to deal with the problems continually proposed by changing construction techniques.

Probably the most interesting of these problems at present are those raised by prestressed concrete construction. The bridge designers have adopted a policy of an open design insofar as the materials and details of the prestressing units themselves are concerned. Thus, the field is wide open for various imaginative fabricators who provide the industry with a healthy atmosphere of progress. At the same time it is necessary that each proposal be investigated with great care since each structure involves a high degree of responsibility concerning public safety.

Speed Necessary

Other problems are raised during the shop fabrication stage of such prestressed concrete units. One of the most important factors in shop production is the speed with which the forms can be stripped and the beams stressed; therefore, the pressure for higher production speed is constant at all times. This necessitates high early

strength concrete which is usually obtained by use of an increased cement content and steam-accelerated curing. No complete data has come to our attention concerning the upper limits of either of these items; therefore, it is necessary that investigations to establish safe and practical limits be performed. This study is under way.

New Laboratory

The bridge design engineers in the California Division of Highways have long held the forefront in the use of welded steel bridges. The rapid progress and expansion of this type of fabrication has made it necessary to establish a relatively new laboratory unit within the Structural Materials Section so as to develop standards for such fabrication and its inspection and testing; to test and evaluate new welding electrodes; to perform research and special investigation on the weldability of new steel alloys; and to advise and work with the bridge and other structural construction and design engineers on special welding fabrication and erection problems. Such advisory work is also extended to the Division of Architecture and other governmental subdivisions.

A great deal of close co-operation and co-ordination with the Bridge Department, with the structural fabrication industry, and the steel manufacturing industry has been necessary so that the Division of Highways can take advantage of the economies inherent in welded construction.

Steel Research

A current example of such work and of the problems that are involved is the design and fabrication of the structural steel for the Carquinez

LEFT—Figure 6. Interior view of a mobile radiographic truck showing the position of portable X-ray equipment. Gamma ray isotopes enclosed in lead cameras occupy the space to right. ABOVE—Figure 7. A skilled engineer's examination of radiographs of welded joints discloses possible internal defects in the weld. Radiographic inspection work of this sort enables the Materials and Research Department to make great savings in time and money.

Bridge superstructure. During the planning phases of this bridge, one of the major steel companies offered a new type of constructional steel called T-1, the use of which indicated savings amounting to about $800,000. Special studies by this laboratory into the metallurgical and mechanical properties and weldability of this steel indicated its suitability for bridge construction use. The bridge was therefore so designed and at present is being fabricated in the East under the direct inspection supervision of this welding laboratory, with detail inspection being provided by a commercial laboratory. *Figure 5* shows a metallurgist studying the microstructure of a metal specimen during this study.

The Welding and Metallurgical Laboratory is equipped with a metallographic microscope designed for visual magnification of 1,500 power and photographic magnification of 2,000 power, a 175-kilovolt portable X-ray machine, a 20-curie cesium isotope, and a 1-curie cobalt isotope (both of the latter contained in lead projectors for portable usage), bending jigs, and a simple photo-elastic polariscope.

The X-ray and isotopic equipment is interchangeable for use either in the laboratory or in the portable traveling radiographic unit, shown in *Figure 6*. This traveling radiographic unit is available for contract projects to qualify welders and perform radiographic inspection of major welding.

Figure 7 shows the welding engineer studying a radiograph of a welded joint of a bridge under fabrication.

Special Studies

A special studies group is included within the Structural Materials Section which, as shown by the organization chart, contains the Electrical Laboratory, Electronics and Wave Propagation Laboratory, Corrosion Laboratory, and Commodities Testing Laboratory.

This group, while somewhat involved in the day-to-day contract inspection and testing activities, is primarily engaged in research and special investigations of a variety of the highway components.

The special studies group is unique in the varieties of diverse abilities found among the technicians and engineers comprising this particular branch of the Structural Materials Section. A keen interest in the various projects, unhampered originality, enthusiastic teamwork, and ample confidence in being able to attain creditable results make every new assignment an interesting challenge, whether it be glare on a new type of traffic sign or strain gauge deflections of prestressed concrete bridges which occur under the effects of moving loads.

Needs Occur

Engineering development or special instrumentation needs often occur which may be either mechanical-electrical or purely mechanical or

LEFT—Figure 8. Experimental model of electronic compaction control equipment. RIGHT—Figure 9. Experimental study concerning rate of corrosion.

electrical in nature. Within the special studies group various individuals are available who can design and construct many of these special items. In most instances such equipment is requested and used by laboratory sections other than the Structural Materials Section. A typical example of a recently developed item is a truck-mounted recording profilograph, employed in studies of irregularities of paved surfaces. This unit continuously records pavement irregularities electronically with an accuracy of 0.1 inch.

Equipment now in development includes a hand-operated pavement profilograph; a precision recording deflectometer mounted on a loaded 15-ton trailer, which employs an automatic Benkelman arm that can indicate the exact amount of deflection of roadways under load; a temperature cycling refrigeration unit to accelerate freeze and thaw studies of concrete pavement employed in the Donner Summit realignment of Highway 40; sand trapping and measuring devices for the Indio Desert; and a small steam plant to experiment with the steam curing of concrete.

All of the above items are to be used by various sections of the department so as to conduct needed research or investigational projects.

Some Work Minor

The Electrical Laboratory's work with direct contract items is relatively minor, consisting primarily of testing electrical wire for compliance with specifications, and other electrical components which readily lend themselves to laboratory testing. Due to the fact that most highway electrical projects involve so many small items, economy often dictates that such products be inspected or sampled for testing after arrival on the job, so much of this work is allocated to the district materials or resident engineers. The Electrical Laboratory also encompasses the field of illumination and reflection; thus, considerable time is devoted to the Service and Supply Department in testing light bulbs for traffic signals or reflective materials for highway signs.

This laboratory has constructed an Ulbricht spherical photometer which has received constant use in performing tests for the $40,000 worth of

lamps purchased by the Division of Highways each year. This photometer is a 60-inch hollow sphere which is used to determine photometrically the lumen output of various incandescent and mercury vapor light bulbs. A series of standard lamps certified by the National Bureau of Standards and the Electrical Testing Laboratory are available for calibration purposes, and lamps under test can be accurately evaluated in relation to these calibrated bulbs.

Reflective buttons and sheets are examined photometrically for reflective properties in a 100-foot black walled light tunnel. Calibrating equipment consists of eight photometric cells, and a D. C. microvolt amplifier. A resistance decade box is available to give very precise evaluations.

Other Research

The most interesting and valuable work performed by the Electrical Laboratory consists of providing or developing electrical instrumentation installations and standardizing such equipment for special projects and research activities which may be conducted in this or other sections of the

Materials and Research Department, or in other departments or districts of the Division of Highways.

Studies may involve the use of a spectrum brightness spot meter to measure the glare effects from a new model of street or highway luminaire; or analysis of smooth riding qualities of a pavement. A study of the latter was recently performed by mounting a series of impulse accelerometers on a passenger in a car. The riding vibration signals were transmitted to a carrier multichannel amplifier and recorded on a Visicorder multipoint oscillograph. These data will be used in the development of smoothness of pavement specifications. This laboratory has also developed the use of multipoint temperature recorders to record pavement, earth, and air temperatures under desert conditions at Inyo, or arctic temperatures at Donner Summit during a midwinter blizzard.

These are only a few of approximately 30 major projects which the Electrical Laboratory has handled during the last 18 months. Several investigations conducted by this group have been previously discussed.

Equipment Calibrated

A catalog of the various electrical instruments and measuring apparatus necessary to the functioning of the Electrical Laboratory is too extensive to be listed. Wherever possible, basic equipment is calibrated by the Bureau of Standards or some other recognized laboratory, such that these items can be employed as reference standards. Loadometer cells, A. C. and D. C. voltmeters and ammeters, thermocouples, and similar equipment have been calibrated in this manner.

The laboratory possesses four portable motor generator units for performing field experiments where regular sources of power are not available. A combination instrument and darkroom trailer is also available. This trailer is equipped with a 10-channel impedance bridge, carrier oscillator and 12-channel oscillograph, which permits a variety of dynamic deflection and stress measurements to be taken on pavement or bridge structures under moving loads.

Problems Encountered

The Electronics and Wave Propagation Laboratory was established to handle a number of special electronic and sonic problems which have been encountered during the recent years of highway construction. Traffic noise and other acoustical studies represent one phase of work and the microseismic investigation of compacted soils represents a second.

A number of instances have occurred in which the laboratory has been called upon to make acoustical studies of buildings or schools, usually adjacent to new freeways or highways, or traffic noise investigations in critical localities such as adjacent to the Hollywood Bowl. Then, at the other extreme, the fact that seismic shock waves have been employed in subsurface exploration and can indicate varying densities, has raised the question of whether microseismic shock wave techniques could be employed as a rapid indication of the relative compactions of road fills during construction.

Major Objection

As a matter of clarification regarding the latter, the established methods of sampling compacted soils for density and moisture have one major objection. The technique is slow and time-consuming, and it is difficult to do more than spot check a large fill at more than a few random points. Any device which would augment the above established method and permit a rapid but thorough check control would be more than welcome on all projects where the advances in construction equipment have made commonplace the placement of thousands of yards of earth daily.

Over the years a great number of different test methods have been investigated by various highway agencies both in California and other states, but most of the so-called shortcut methods have failed to give dependable data which can be integrated with the established highway engineering practices. Microseismic techniques are comparable to typical seismic subsurface exploration, and on this basis have some promise of disclosing surface and subsurface densities.

From the practical standpoint, much of the equipment which can be used for acoustical or traffic noise investigation can be employed in microseismic investigations. This microseismic project is still in the early experimental stages. Some rather unanticipated results have been obtained, but the design bears promise of pointing the way to a fast supplementary means of controlling compaction under the present-day high pressure methods of earth moving. *Figure 8* shows the electronics engineer experimenting with an early model of such equipment.

The Electronics Laboratory is well equipped with several high gain amplifiers, various accelerometer transducers, an accurately timed oscilloscope, a sound level meter, an audio oscillator, a phase angle meter, a communications receiver which has been employed for Bureau of Standards frequency transmissions, and a series of other electronic instruments, reference loudspeakers, and associated sonic and acoustical equipment.

Laboratory Established

The placing of metals in soils, waters, or other aggressive electrolytes continually reminds man that metals, through corrosion, have a tendency to return to their most basic form.

With the ever accelerating rate of construction of highways, the corrosion of even a small percentage of the buried metals, such as culverts, utility lines, and reinforcing steel, can be a relatively large economic burden.

Due to growing necessity, a corrosion laboratory was established in 1952. The function of this unit is to furnish technical recommendations to the various districts and departments and to perform research and investigational studies concerning the corrosion of metals embedded in electrolytes such as soils, waters, or moist concrete.

The scope of the work may entail recommendations which vary from the particular type of culvert to be placed in an aggressive soil to a detailed study of the corrision of reinforcing steel in a multimillion dollar bridge.

Several of the major investigations of this department have been of special interest. One of these studies is the continuing investigation of the corrosion of reinforcing steel in the San Mateo-Hayward Bridge. The primary causes of corrosion of reinforcing steel were determined by both laboratory (*Figure 9*) and field studies. As a result a new means of detecting the corrosion of reinforcing steel by nondestructive testing methods has been developed. The corrosion unit is currently engaged in research leading to the control of such corrosion of reinforcing steel by cathodic protection.

Another major project of this laboratory was an evaluation of the corrosion of metal culverts in the north coastal area of the State. A corrosion area map was developed of the area which indicated the major zones of destruction and relative rates of attack. One of the more predominate facts brought out in the culvert investigation for this general area was that the accelerated rate of attack was related to the presence of bacteria which reduced organic vegetable matter. The concept of bacteria relating to corrosion clarified numerous questions which could not be satisfied by the general theory of "salt air" from the ocean. An additional benefit from this study was the development of objective means of measuring the potential corrosiveness of any proposed culvert site.

Some of the studies under consideration include the following: the possibility of environmental conditions which may cause corrosion of high tensile steel in prestressed concrete; the corrosion resistance of special structural steels; the corrosion resistance of various metals used in chain link fences exposed to marine environments; the corrosion of underground utility piping; evaluation of several types of commercially available electrical conduit; and the corrosion of metal culverts.

The Corrosion Laboratory is well equipped to accurately measure soil pH, soil resistivities and potentials, to make corrosion studies of underground piping systems, or to perform numerous investigations of the electrochemical corrosion of steel and other metals.

The commodity test unit was established to examine miscellaneous items which are not readily processable in the physical testing laboratory. Commodity unit personnel are no longer surprised at the unusual items which find their way into the commodities laboratory for testing. Ball point pens, hard hats, fabrics, paper, garden hose, plastic pipe, seat belts, and furniture have all appeared in this laboratory at one time or another for test of tensile strength, bursting strength, crushing strength, folding endurance, fading, or other characteristics applicable to the anticipated use of the item. Much of this testing is performed either for the Service and Supply Department or the State Bureau of Purchases. Frequently A. S. T. M. or federal specifications have not yet been determined for these items, so this section must develop their own procedure, devising test methods, and adapting existing equipment for new uses.

The commodities testing laboratory is equipped with a constant humidity cabinet, a Fade-Ometer for testing the fading of colored fabrics under ultraviolet light, and electro-hydraulic fabric tensile tester (*Figure 10*), a hydroelectric pump assembly for testing plastic pipe and hose, an M. I. T. folding endurance tester, and numerous other testing or measuring devices.

One of the major projects conducted by the commodity test group is a long-range study of the durability of various highway signs exposed to weather and to vandalism, and the use of plastics in lieu of metal for guide posts and signs. The objective of this study is to find materials which will stand salt atmosphere, desert heat, sandstorms and winter blizzards; will not collect dust or oil films; will not be damaged by impact from cars, rocks, or bullets, and can be repaired or replaced easily. A simple solution? The laboratory has been working on this project for 30 years and may continue to do so far as long as man drives automobiles. However, some of the new plastic materials are showing results that may well end this eternal search.

A machine shop is a necessary adjunct to any laboratory whether it is engaged solely in routine testing work, special investigation, or research. The laboratories of the Materials and Research Department, being engaged in all three functions, find the services of a well-equipped machine shop to be absolutely essential for their normal operation. The services of the machine shop are used to prepare test specimens, to maintain and to repair special testing equipment, and to manufacture and fabricate various new devices proposed for advanced test methods.

Machinery used to equip this machine shop has been especially selected to give a high degree of precision to the testing equipment being built, and the machinists and instrument makers manning this shop are highly trained in their specialized work. It is this combination of precise machines and highly trained personnel working with the engineers (*Figure 11*) that has developed such testing equipment as the stabilometer, cohesiometer, kneading compactor, resiliometer, special fatigue machines, sample splitters, sample washers, pencil testing machines, traveling load deflectometers, profilograph, sand volume apparatus, numerous extensometers and micrometers and dynamometers, and many other special pieces of equipment, either completely new in design or otherwise unobtainable on the commercial market. All equipment available through purchase is so obtained. It is only equipment not available commercially that is designed and built in the laboratory machine shop.

The shop prepares test specimens of steel and other metal materials for tensile, compression, cold bend, side bend, and other special tests such as impact and hardness tests, and also prepares metal specimens for chemical tests. In addition to the repair and necessary revisions to the special testing equipment of the laboratories of the Materials and Research Department, the

. . . Continued on page 42

NEW SUBDIVISIONS
Continued from page 31 . . .

NEW SUBDIVISIONS

structed immediately adjacent to the freeway. As a matter of fact, there are many persons who prefer a house adjacent to the freeway. In some cases, resale statistics have revealed that residences adjoining a freeway can attain a higher price range than comparable residences away from the freeway.

As an integral part of the geometric layout of the street system and the freeway interchange ramp system, we must be very careful to provide a sufficient number of lanes to absorb and distribute the anticipated traffic flow. This is equally applicable to local traffic problems as well as to the problem of freeway-local traffic. If, in the design of the subdivision, large volumes of traffic are funneled into a single street facility and then brought to the freeway, it is imperative that an adequate number of lanes be provided, both to prevent the backing up of traffic wanting to get onto the freeway and also to prevent the backing up of traffic on the freeway wanting to get off to the city streets. Geometrically speaking, we must have a freeway interchange-city street pattern that provides for efficient use of the land and distribution of traffic. Both the freeway ramps and city streets must have sufficient capacity to adequately care for the anticipated volume.

Drainage Problems

In the relationship between state highways and new subdivisions, we not only have traffic problems; but there is also the matter of co-ordinating drainage. Here again, as in the geometric street layout, co-operation and joint planning on drainage problems will provide a more satisfactory solution at a saving, both to the State and the local agency. It has always been the policy of the State Division of Highways to work with the local agencies in the solving of drainage problems, and in the past we have entered into a large number of co-operative agreements which have resulted in a solution that has been beneficial to all concerned. Again, it is a matter of providing an overall drainage plan with each governmental agency co-

Division Reports Daily On Road Conditions

The Division of Highways is again issuing its seasonal daily road condition report.

The report is issued daily through the winter until the reopening of highway routes through the Sierra in the spring.

Duplicated copies of the report are available to the public at the Public Works Building in Sacramento and are also distributed to various departments of State Government.

Widest dissemination of the road condition report is via a statewide teletype circuit from the Highway Division headquarters to news services, newspapers, radio and television stations, automobile associations and others who pass the information on to the public.

The Highway Division has more than 800 vehicles equipped with two-way radio forwarding information and is using an expanded network of non-mobile relay stations.

operating and working to provide its part and its fair share of the cost. Where it is anticipated that mutual drainage difficulties will arise in the development of the land, these should be brought to the attention of the appropriate district office of the State Division of Highways at the earliest possible time so that planning to handle these problems can be initiated at an early date. Other areas of co-operation are in the development of suitable landscaping of the freeway, which will conform aesthetically with the requirements of the adjacent area and provide buffer areas between the freeway traffic and the subdivisions.

In summary, I wish to emphasize that the problem of state highways in relation to new subdivisions is not a problem only of the State Division of Highways or only of the local agency controlling the development of the subdivisions, but is a problem of joint responsibility. The fullest co-operation on the part of both agencies is necessary in order to develop the full potential of the area.

OPERATIONS AND ACTIVITIES
Continued from page 41 . . .

personnel of the machine shop also give the same service to the laboratories of the various districts.

It can best be summarized that the Structural Materials Section of the Materials and Research Department, like the other four major sections, is organized: (1) to give the designer and the specification writer the latest information on available materials and the methods of manufacture and production; (2) to give the construction engineer assurance that the materials and manufactured items received from the industrial plants will comply with the specifications; and (3) to assure the administrator that by proper research the Division of Highways will always be in a position to take advantage of the technological advances in industry that might pertain to highway construction.

PLAN AND DESIGN
Continued from page 10 . . .

The northerly proposed extension of the Long Beach Freeway, five miles in length from the Santa Ana Freeway to Huntington Drive, was officially made a part of the State Highway System by legislative enactment in 1951. At that time the project was known locally as the "Concord Freeway" and was so shown on official maps of local governmental agencies. This name was officially changed to the "Long Beach Freeway" by vote of the California Highway Commission in November, 1954.

Design work, preparation of contract plans for construction, and some right-of-way acquisition are now being carried out on the northerly extension of the Long Beach Freeway. The California Highway Commission in adopting the budget for the 1958-59 Fiscal Year, at its October meeting, provided an item of $6,150,000 for constructing 3.6 miles of this freeway from the Santa Ana Freeway northerly to an interchange connection with the San Bernardino Freeway. This construction is expected to be under way during the summer of 1958.

Trans-Sierra

Mountain Work on US 40 Will Total $34,650,000

Five major freeway construction projects on the trans-Sierra portion of US 40, totaling 36 miles in length and estimated to cost $34,650,000, are contained in the state highway budget for the 1958-59 Fiscal Year submitted to Governor Goodwin J. Knight by the California Highway Commission.

The five major trans-Sierra projects budgeted will connect with and extend freeway work now under contract on US 40 in Placer, Nevada and Sierra Counties involving four contracts totaling 20 miles of highway and an aggregate construction cost of approximately $15,900,000.

When both the projects now under construction and those newly budgeted have been completed, there will be a total of about 83 miles of freeway or expressway in operation on the 117-mile length of US 40 between Sacramento and the Nevada state line, it was pointed out by State Director of Public Works Frank B. Durkee, Chairman of the Highway Commission.

On Interstate System

This multilane divided mileage will include 56 continuous miles of freeway and expressway between Sacramento and east of Gold Run, and nearly 21 continuous miles between the east end of Donner Lake and the Nevada line. The remaining six miles of freeway will be slightly west of Donner Summit, between Hampshire Rocks and Soda Springs.

Durkee explained that US 40 is a portion of the national system of interstate highways and that the present emphasis on its development as a freeway is in line with the goals of the accelerated national program. He also noted that projects included in the 1958-59 Budget are intended, weather permitting, to be opened to traffic by the end of 1959, in time for the winter Olympic games scheduled for Squaw Valley in February, 1960.

Of the five projects on US 40 contained in the new state highway budget, four are being financed only in part in the 1958-59 Fiscal Year. In these cases the contracts for the entire project will be awarded at one time, however, with the remaining cost to be charged against the budget for the succeeding fiscal year. This method of getting large-scale projects started without tying up large amounts of highway funds is being used in the 1958-59 Budget for the first time.

East of Sacramento

The current status of freeway and expressway development on US 40 east of Sacramento is now as follows:

Sacramento to one-half mile east of Roseville, 17 miles, freeway completed.

One-half mile east of Roseville to one mile east of Newcastle, 11 miles, $7,800,000 freeway project included in 1958-59 Budget ($5,500,000 financed in 1958-59 Fiscal Year).

Newcastle to Auburn, 3½ miles, $2,578,000 freeway project under construction (some structures and grading completed under previous contract).

Auburn to Heather Glen, 11 miles, expressway completed.

Heather Glen to Colfax and Colfax to Magra (west of Gold Run), 12 miles, two expressway projects totaling $7,875,000 under construction.

Magra to one-half mile west of Monte Vista (east of Gold Run), four miles, $3,000,000 freeway project included in 1958-59 Budget.

One-half mile west of Monte Vista to Hampshire Rocks, 22 miles, freeway route adopted and rights-of-way being acquired. (Detour nearly completed near Monte Vista at cost of $315,000.)

Hampshire Rocks to Soda Springs, six miles, $5,600,000 freeway project included in 1958-59 Budget ($4,000,-000 financed in 1958-59 Fiscal Year).

Soda Springs to east end of Donner Lake, 10 miles, freeway route adopted.

East end of Donner Lake to near Boca, nine miles, $8,800,000 freeway project included in 1958-59 Budget ($5,400,000 financed in 1958-59 Fiscal Year).

Near Boca to near Floriston, 6½ miles, $9,450,000 freeway project included in 1958-59 budget ($5,373,-000 financed in 1958-59 Fiscal Year). (Detour now under construction at cost of $565,000.)

Floriston to Nevada state line, five miles, $5,420,000 freeway project under construction.

Another project in the 1958-59 Budget provides for the widening of State Sign Route 89 for 8.3 miles between Squaw Valley Road and the Donner Creek underpass and the junction of US 40 at an estimated construction cost of $1,700,000.

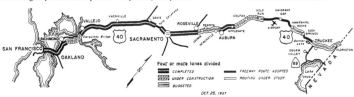

```
Four or more lanes divided
▬ COMPLETED          ▬ FREEWAY ROUTE ADOPTED
▬ UNDER CONSTRUCTION ▬ ROUTING UNDER STUDY
▬ BUDGETED
OCT. 25, 1957
```

BUDGET

Continued from page 2 . . .

"The commission must, of necessity, consider each annual budget as a part of a continuous, long-range plan for financing the development of the state highway system."

Significant features of the 1958-59 State Highway Budget include:

Los Angeles Area

In the Los Angeles metropolitan area, completion of the Ventura Freeway in the San Fernando Valley west of the Hollywood Freeway; extension of the Golden State Freeway northwesterly through and beyond Burbank, and its further construction in the area east of downtown Los Angeles; extensions of the San Diego Freeway southerly through Culver City; the Harbor Freeway southerly to 190th Street; and the Long Beach Freeway northerly to the San Bernardino Freeway; widening of the Santa Ana Freeway from Norwalk to Buena Park; and extensive right-of-way acquisition on these and other freeway routes, with particular emphasis on the Santa Monica Freeway, the San Diego Freeway, and the Golden State Freeway.

Orange County

On the Orange County portion of US 101, the budget provides for construction of an eight-mile section north of San Juan Capistrano which, with other projects under construction or budgeted, will provide 80 miles of continuous full freeway from the west end of San Fernando Valley, through the City of Los Angeles to San Juan Capistrano.

San Diego Area

In the San Diego area, emphasis is on the continued conversion of US 80 from expressway to full freeway in the San Diego-La Mesa area by construction of interchanges, and on the westerly extension of the Sign Route 94 freeway toward downtown San Diego.

San Bernardino-Riverside Area

Freeway development in the San Bernardino-Riverside area will be carried on by several projects, including the extension of the Riverside Freeway westerly toward Corona and a

section north of Riverside connecting with the San Bernardino Freeway at the new interchange east of Colton. At the same time, the budget provides for completing the conversion of the San Bernardino Freeway to full freeway between Ontario and Colton by the construction of separations and interchanges.

On major routes east of Riverside, expressway and freeway construction is provided for west of Beaumont and west of Indio. The latter project will

---

TYPICAL GOALS

Typical of achievements to be realized by completion of projects included in the 1958-59 Budget are:

More than 80 percent of US 40 between San Francisco and the Nevada state line will be divided, multilane freeway or expressway.

More than 95 percent of US 99 between Sacramento and Los Angeles will be multilaned and divided roadway.

The Hollywood-Santa Ana Freeway will extend unbroken from the San Fernando Valley through downtown Los Angeles to San Juan Capistrano, a distance of 80 miles.

There will be a continuous stretch of full freeway from Los Gatos, through San Jose and Oakland to north of Vallejo, a distance of 75 miles.

US 101 will have a section of continuous freeway or divided highway 50 miles long from the Golden Gate Bridge to north of Santa Rosa.

---

complete 41 miles of continuous multilane expressway and freeway between Banning and Indio.

San Francisco Bay Region

In the San Francisco Bay area, the budget contains a project for the final link of the Eastshore Freeway between San Francisco and Vallejo, the section in the vicinity of the El Cerrito Overhead. This, along with other projects in operation, under construction or newly budgeted, will provide more than 75 miles of continuous full freeway from Los Gatos, through San Jose and Oakland, to beyond Vallejo.

The major freeway project in San Francisco involves the interchange for

the James Lick (Bayshore) and Southern Freeways.

North Bay Area

The start of freeway construction on the Black Point Cutoff in Marin and Sonoma Counties is another major Bay area project. Further construction on the Greenbrae interchange on the Redwood Highway in Marin County will mean continuous full freeway from the Golden Gate Bridge to San Rafael, and continuous divided highway to north of Santa Rosa.

Santa Clara County

Several projects are concentrated in Santa Clara County, including the extension of the Sign Route 17 freeway north from Bascom Avenue in San Jose to an interchange with and north of the Bayshore Freeway; extension of the Bayshore Freeway from Palo Alto to Stevens Creek and in the San Jose area; and an interchange on the Bayshore Freeway at Mountain View-Alviso Road.

Sacramento Region

In the Sacramento area, structures for the South Sacramento Freeway are provided for in the new budget, along with completion of the new Sacramento River Bridge at Rio Vista.

Freeway projects totaling 36 miles on US 40 east of Sacramento are contained in the budget, including an 11-mile section between Roseville and Newcastle and two other projects which will mean continuous freeway and expressway for 56 miles between North Sacramento and east of Gold Run. Other projects, east of Donner Summit, will provide continuous freeway between the east end of Donner Lake and the Nevada state line.

Projects on US 99

On US 99 the major projects outside metropolitan areas are the freeway unit between north of Fresno and Herndon, which will mean continuous multilane divided highway between the San Fernando area and near Sacramento, except for undivided sections through Modesto, Merced, Turlock, and Lodi.

Another major project on US 99 is the freeway section through Dunsmuir in Siskiyou County.

On US 101, budgeted projects will continue the steady conversion of the route to freeway standards, both between Los Angeles and San Francisco and on the Redwood Highway. These projects include sections north of Buellton, through Arroyo Grande, and between Soledad and Gonzales; and in the Healdsburg area, in northern Mendocino County (near Tan Oak Park), and three sections in Humboldt County—one north of Fortuna, one north of Arcata, and one in the Patricks Point-Big Lagoon area.

Current Budget Reviewed

The Highway Commissioners, as a preliminary to adopting the 1958-59 Budget, reviewed the current (1957-58) budget in view of rising costs and revenue receipts less than originally estimated.

This review resulted in the decision to carry over 16 1957-58 projects to the .1958-59 Budget. The only effect of this action will be to delay briefly the call for bids of these projects.

The commission also approved a recommendation of Staté Highway Engineer McCoy that 10 1957-58 projects be deferred for later reconsideration because of various reasons.

These changes in the 1957-58 Budget were based on a new estimate of highway user tax income for the 1957-58 Fiscal Year which the Department of Finance furnished the Department of Public Works on October 16th.

The changes in the current budget are subject to the approval of the State Director of Finance and are being forwarded to him as required by statute.

16 Items Carried Over

The 16 1957-58 projects carried over to the 1958-59 Budget are identified in the list of budget items by counties printed elsewhere in this issue of *California Highways and Public Works*.

The 10 projects which were deferred for later reconsideration, and the reasons cited by the State Highway Division in recommending that they not be budgeted now, are:

Amador and Alpine Counties—Sign Route 88, from Carson Spur to 0.2

Three days after the 1958-59 Budget was adopted by the California Highway Commission, Director of Public Works Frank B. Durkee authorized the first advertisement of bids for a project financed by it—a $5,600,000 job on US 40 in Placer and Nevada Counties.

The work consists of grading and paving 6 miles of four-lane divided freeway between Hampshire Rocks and 0.5 mile west of Soda Springs and constructing seven structures. The structures to be built are: two parallel bridges over the South Fork of the Yuba River, another bridge over the same river, two parallel structures to be part of the Troy Undercrossing, and two parallel structures to be part of Kingvale Undercrossing.

This job is one of five extensive freeway construction projects on US 40 which were approved last week by the California Highway Commission. The commissioners budgeted $4,000,000 for this Hampshire Rocks-Soda Springs job, leaving a balance of $1,600,000 to be financed from the 1959-60 Budget.

Highway officials also plan an early call for bids on other US 40 projects included in the 1958-59 Budget to enable contractors to inspect the terrain before heavy Sierra snows cover the ground.

Construction will start some time next spring, depending on when weather and snow conditions allow contractors to use heavy equipment in the area.

mile east of Amador county line, grade and surface (realignment), $400,000. (Deferred pending completion of federal forest highway project on same route, now advertised for bids.)

Riverside and San Bernardino Counties—Route 187, from US 60-70-99 to Morongo Valley, grade and surface (widen), $270,000. (Route location being restudied.)

San Luis Obispo and Santa Barbara Counties—Sign Route 166 (Cuyama

Road), one mile west of Huasna River to 0.7 mile west of Buckhorn Creek, grade, surface, and structures (relocation around Vaquero Reservoir), $1,-165,000. (Negotiations still pending with Santa Maria Valley Water Conservation District and Bureau of Reclamation.)

Santa Clara County

Santa Clara County—Sign Route 152, San Felipe Road to Hollister Wye, surface, $90,000. (Two other projects in same general area on this route in 1958-59 Budget.)

Solano County—Sign Route 21, from new Sign Route 21 to 1.25 miles north of Benicia Arsenal, structures and approaches, $375,000. (Negotiations still pending with U. S. Army for rights-of-way.)

Solano County—Route 90 (Vacaville-Dunnigan Cutoff), 0.3 mile north of Sweeney Creek to Yolo county line, grade, surface and structures (initial two lanes of future four-lane freeway), $1,070,000. (Project for grading and structures on this route north of the Yolo county line retained in the 1957-58 Budget; to be advertised for bids in November.)

Stanislaus County—US 99, Modesto Freeway, Whitmore Road to Pecos Avenue, grade, pave and structures, $1,300,000. (Now considered less urgent because of relief provided by new four-lane divided section on south approach to Modesto.)

Tuolumne County—Sign Routes 49, 108, and 120 from seven miles east of Stanislaus county line to Montezuma Road, grade and surface (initial two lanes of a future four-lane expressway), $943,351. (Portion of original $1,500,000 budget item now under contract; partial deferment.)

Yolo County—US 40, Solano county line to Swingle (portion) structure (Davis Interchange), $320,000. (To be included in future large-scale project for conversion of long section of US 40 to full freeway on Interstate System.)

Yuba County—Sign Route 20, west approach to Parks Bar Bridge, grade and surface (realignment), $100,000. (Project in same area on Sign Route 20 included in 1958-59 Budget.)

and Public Works   45

1958-59 State Highway Budget Projects by Counties

County	Route†	Description	Approximate mileage	Estimated cost *State's share
Alameda	5 (SR 9)	Castro St.-Tennyson Rd. Intersection in Hayward; channelization and signals ($92,000 project; City of Hayward's share $7,000)		*$85,000
Alameda	69 (SR 17)	Eldridge Ave. Pedestrian Overcrossing on Eastshore Freeway in Hayward; structure		80,000
Alameda	69 (SR 17)	Eastshore Freeway—Sixth St. in Oakland to Distribution Structure; landscape	2.0	40,000
Alameda, Contra Costa	69, 7 (US 40)	Eastshore Freeway—0.3 mile south of El Cerrito Overhead to 0.2 mile south of Jefferson St. in Richmond; grade, pave and structures for 6-lane freeway which, with other current and budgeted projects, will complete 75 miles of continuous full freeway from Los Gatos to Vallejo ($4,300,000 financed in 1958-59 Fiscal Year)	2.6	6,250,000
Alameda	69 (US 40)	Eastshore Freeway— Distribution Structure to El Cerrito Overhead; landscape	3.8	235,000
Alameda	226	Webster St. Tube (portions); site preparation		750,000
Alameda	226	Doolittle Dr. and Davis St. in San Leandro; channelization and signals $47,000 project; (City of San Leandro's share $10,000)		*37,000
Alameda	227	Warren Blvd. (Mountain Blvd.)—from Tunnel Rd. to Park Blvd.; landscape	2.0	123,000
Alameda	227	Warren Blvd. (Mountain Blvd.)—Lincoln Ave. to Carson St. (portions); grade, surface and structures for 4-lane freeway	1.1	*600,000
Alameda	228, S (portion US 50)	From Eastshore Freeway near San Lorenzo to east of Center St. in Castro Valley; landscape	3.8	25,000
Alameda	Various	Rights of Way on State Highway Routes (including $10,800,000 for US 50 freeway in Oakland)		14,840,000
Alpine	Various	Rights of Way on State Highway Routes		25,000
Amador	Various	Rights of Way on State Highway Routes		45,000
Butte	3 (US 99E)	11th St. to Memorial Way in Chico; structures, signals and channelization (cooperative project for one-way street couplet; City of Chico's share $25,000)	0.8	*150,000
Butte	Various	Rights of Way on State Highway Routes		150,000
Calaveras	24 (SR 4)	Mulphys to Big Trees (portions); grade and surface (widening and realignment) (carried over from 1957-58 budget)	5.9	655,000
Calaveras	24 (SR 4)	Camp Connell to 11 miles easterly (portions); base and surface (reconstruct)	1.0	25,000
Calaveras	Various	Rights of Way on State Highway Routes		100,000
Colusa	15 (SR 20)	10 to 11 miles west of Williams (portions); drainage improvement		20,000
Contra Costa	7 (new US 40)	From San Pablo Ave. in Richmond to Ridge Rd. in San Pablo; landscape	1.6	59,000
Contra Costa	7 (new US 40)	From south of Hilltop Dr. in Richmond to North of Hercules; illuminated signs		153,000
Contra Costa	7 (present US 40)	From junction of SSR 4 to 4.4 miles north of Hercules; resurface	4.6	63,000
Contra Costa, Alameda	69, 7 (US 40)	Eastshore Freeway—0.3 mile south of El Cerrito Overhead to 0.2 mile south of Jefferson St. in Richmond; grade, pave and structures for 6-lane freeway which, with other current and budgeted projects, will complete 75 miles of continuous full freeway from Los Gatos to Vallejo ($4,300,000 financed in 1958-59 Fiscal Year)	2.6	6,250,000
Contra Costa	75 (SR 24)	Hodges Rd. to Grant Lane (east of Lafayette); landscape	0.5	76,000
Contra Costa	75 (SR 4)	Empire Ave. to Birch St. in Brentwood (portion); resurface and widen (carried over from 1957-58 budget)	6.6	222,000
Contra Costa	75 (SR 24)	South City Limit of Concord to Willow Pass Rd.; grade and surface (widen) ($48,000 project; City of Concord's share $13,000)	0.2	*35,000
Contra Costa	75, 106 (SR 4)	Junction of SR 4 and 24 to Willow Pass Rd. (portions); resurface	6.4	34,000
Contra Costa	107 (SR 21)	3 locations between Alameda County Line and Walnut Creek; drainage improvement		50,000
Contra Costa	Various	Rights of Way on State Highway Routes (including $1,100,000 between Danville and Walnut Creek on SR 21)		3,011,000
Del Norte	1 (US 101)	0.7 mile south of Elk Valley Rd. to 0.4 mile north of Northcrest Dr.; grade, surface and structures for one-way street couplet in Crescent City	2.3	590,000
Del Norte	Various	Rights of Way on State Highway Routes		50,000
El Dorado	93	Top of Morgan Grade to Georgetown (portions); grade and surface (reconstruction)		50,000
El Dorado	Various	Rights of Way on State Highway Routes		70,000
Fresno	4 (US 99)	South Ave. to Calwa Overhead; resurface southbound lanes (and northbound lanes through Fowler)	4.3	180,000
Fresno	4 (US 99)	California Ave. to West Ave.; landscape	3.4	200,000
Fresno	41 (SR 180)	Princeton Ave. to Herndon; grade, pave and structures for 4-lane freeway	6.7	4,120,000
Fresno	76 (SR 168)	0.7 mile east of Reed Ave. to 2.3 miles east of Friant-Kern Canal; grade, surface and structure (relocate portions) (carried over from 1957-58 budget)	1.4	250,000
Fresno	4, 41, 125 (US 99)	On Shaw Ave., from Blackstone Ave. to 0.2 mile east of Chestnut Ave.; grade and surface (widen to 6 lanes divided) ($655,800 project, City of Fresno's share $26,000, Fresno County's share $9,800)	3.0	*620,000
Fresno	Various	Reconstruct portions of Santa Clara, Mono, Merced, San Joaquin, C and E Sts. in Fresno as freeway connections; grade and surface	1.2	100,000
Glenn	88 (SR 45)	Rights of Way on State Highway Routes		200,000
		2.1 miles north of Glenn to 4.7 miles north of Glenn; grade and surface (Sidds Landing Levee Reconstruction)	2.6	100,000
Humboldt	1 (US 101)	Myers Flat to 1 mile south of Dyerville; culvert, clear and grub for future freeway construction	7.2	730,000
Humboldt	1 (US 101)	Fortuna to 0.8 mile north of Fernbridge; grade and surface to complete 4-lane freeway (other grading and structures now under contract)	3.2	1,500,000
Humboldt	1 (US 101)	1 mile south to 0.3 mile north of Mad River; grade, surface and structures for 4-lane expressway (parallel Mad River Bridge already under contract)	1.5	920,000
Humboldt	1 (US 101)	Patricks Point to 0.26 mile north of Big Lagoon; structures and surface for 4-lane expressway (grading already under contract)	3.6	870,000

† Numbers marked SR are State Sign Routes; numbers marked US are U. S. highway routes; numbers not marked are legislative routes.

1958-59 STATE HIGHWAY BUDGET BY COUNTIES—Continued

County	Route†	Description	Approximate mileage	Estimated cost *State's share
Humboldt	20 (US 299)	0.1 mile west of Essex Gulch Rd. to 0.2 mile east of Fieldbrook Rd.; grade and surface (realignment)	0.8	$100,000
Humboldt	20 (US 299)	Lupton Creek (14 miles east of Blue Lake); concrete arch culvert		200,000
Humboldt	Various	Rights of Way on State Highway Routes		455,000
Imperial	187 (SR 115)	Sandia to Alamorio; grade, pave and structures (widen) (carried over from 1957-58 budget)	10.5	1,485,000
Imperial	Various	Rights of Way on State Highway Routes		273,000
Inyo	23 (US 6-395)	Olancha to 2.7 miles north of Cottonwood Creek (portions); surface	11.0	325,000
Inyo, San Bernardino	127 (SR 127)	2 miles south of Inyo-San Bernardino County line to 10 miles north of Shoshone (portions); grade and surface (realignment, including portions through Ibex Pass)	4.0	295,000
Inyo	Various	Rights of Way on State Highway Routes		25,000
Kern	4 (US 99)	2 miles north of Grapevine Station to Sandrini Rd.; grade and pave (reconstruct southbound lanes)	12.3	1,035,000
Kern	4, 142 (US 99)	Garces Circle; landscape		10,000
Kern	4 (US 99)	Through Delano; landscape	4.0	40,000
Kern	58 (US 466)	Tower Line Rd. to Bear Mountain Ranch; grade, pave and structures; 4-lane expressway ($6,150,000 financed in 1958-59 budget)	11.4	7,300,000
Kern	Various	Rights of Way on State Highway Routes (including $1,250,000 for US 99 between Fort Tejon and 2 miles north of Grapevine Station)		2,740,000
Kings	Various	Rights of Way on State Highway Routes		105,000
Lake	Various	Rights of Way on State Highway Routes		120,000
Lassen	73 (US 395)	Ravendale to Madeline; resurface (carried over from 1957-58 budget)	21.0	480,000
Los Angeles	2 (US 101)	Santa Ana-Hollywood Freeway—Camulos St. to Santa Monica Blvd.; surface median areas and install plantef boxes	4.0	105,000
Los Angeles	2 (US 101)	Hollywood Freeway (portions); landscape		40,000
Los Angeles	2 (US 101)	Hollywood Freeway-Lankershim Blvd. to Moorpark St.; landscape	1.0	62,000
Los Angeles	2 (US 101)	Ventura Freeway—Laurel Canyon Blvd. to San Diego Freeway; grade, pave and structures for 8-lane freeway (with next item, will complete Ventura Freeway in San Fernando Valley westerly of Hollywood Freeway extension) ($6,248,000 financed in 1958-59 Fiscal Year)	4.1	11,100,000
Los Angeles	2 (US 101)	Ventura Freeway—Encino Ave. to 0.3 mile east of Kelvin Ave.; grade, pave and structures for 8-lane freeway (see above item) ($6,000,000 financed in 1958-59 Fiscal Year)	3.9	7,300,000
Los Angeles	4 (US 6-99)	Golden State Freeway—Mission Rd. to 0.1 mile north of Pasadena Ave.; grade, pave and structures for 8-lane freeway (northerly extension of previously budgeted freeway project)	1.1	4,600,000
Los Angeles	4, 161 (US 6-99)	Golden State Freeway—Glendale Blvd. to Los Angeles River and freeway connection to San Fernando Rd.; landscape	4.0	245,000
Los Angeles	4 (US 6-99)	Golden State Freeway—Los Angeles River to Ash Ave. in Burbank; landscape	1.4	84,000
Los Angeles	4 (US 6-99)	Golden State Freeway—0.25 mile east of Burbank Blvd. to 0.2 mile west of Roscoe Blvd.; grade, pave and structures for 8-lane freeway (extending Golden State Freeway through and beyond Burbank) ($6,000,000 financed in 1958-59 Fiscal Year) (cooperative project; U. S. Corps of Engineers' share $3,000,000 for flood control channel; City of Burbank's share $800,000 for extending Burbank Blvd. separation across railroad tracks)	3.9	*7,648,000
Los Angeles	23 (US 6)	Sierra Highway—0.3 mile south of Avenue "S" in Palmdale to 0.4 mile north of Avenue "I" in Lancaster (portions); grade and surface (widen to 4 lanes)	9.0	700,000
Los Angeles	26 (US 60-70-99)	San Bernardino Freeway—through West Covina; landscape	4.0	80,000
Los Angeles	26 (US 60-70-99)	San Bernardino Freeway—east city limit of Baldwin Park to Rivergrade Rd. (portions); grade and surface ramps and frontage road		60,000
Los Angeles	26 (US 60-70-99)	San Bernardino Freeway—San Gabriel River to Rio Hondo Wash; landscape	2.6	170,000
Los Angeles	59 (SR 138)	US 6 to 10th Place east in Palmdale; grade, surface and signals	0.3	100,000
Los Angeles	60 (US 101 Alt.)	Alamitos Bay Bridge; bridge and approaches	0.2	385,000
Los Angeles	158 (SR 7)	San Diego Freeway—Jefferson Blvd. to 0.3 mile north of Venice Blvd.; grade, pave and structures for 8-lane freeway ($6,000,000 financed in 1958-59 Fiscal Year)	2.5	7,500,000
Los Angeles	158 (SR 7)	San Diego Freeway—Mulholland Dr. relocation; grade, pave and structures for future freeway construction		1,100,000
Los Angeles	161 (SR 159)	Golden State Freeway—Arnold St. to Fletcher Dr.; grade and surface for frontage road construction (Riverside Dr.)	1.2	700,000
Los Angeles	165 (US 6-SR 11)	Harbor Freeway—0.5 mile south of 190th St. to 0.1 mile north of 124th St.; grade, pave and structures for 8-lane freeway ($5,000,000 financed in 1958-59 Fiscal Year)	4.9	8,700,000
Los Angeles	165 (US 6-SR 11)	Harbor Freeway—near Fifth St.; ramp structure		110,000
Los Angeles	167 (SR 15)	Long Beach Freeway—at Del Amo Blvd.; grade and pave ramp (to complete interchange)		180,000
Los Angeles	167, 166, 26 (SR 15)	Long Beach Freeway—0.1 mile south of Santa Ana Freeway to 0.2 mile north of San Bernardino Freeway; grade, pave and structures for 6-lane freeway (co-operative project; Los Angeles County Flood Control District's share $1,000,000 for storm drain)	3.6	*6,150,000
Los Angeles	167, 166 (SR 15)	Long Beach Freeway—Sheila Ave. to Olympic Blvd.; landscape	1.1	85,000
Los Angeles	174 (US 101)	Santa Ana Freeway—Rosecrans Ave. to 0.1 mile east of Marquardt Ave. and 0.2 mile west of Valley View Ave. to 0.2 mile east of Coyote Creek; grade, pave and structures (widen freeway to 6 lanes)	2.9	1,420,000

† Numbers marked SR are State Sign Routes; numbers marked US are U. S. highway routes; numbers not marked are legislative routes.

County	Route†	Description	Approximate mileage	Estimated cost *State's share
Los Angeles	174, 175 (US 101)	Santa Ana Freeway—Marquardt Ave. to 0.1 mile west of Valley View Ave. and on Artesia Ave. from 0.2 mile east of Marquardt Ave. to 0.1 mile west of Valley View Ave.; drainage structures (co-operative project; Los Angeles County Flood Control District's share $630,000)	0.7	*$220,000
Los Angeles	Various	Rights of Way on State Highway Routes (including $13,600,000 on the Santa Monica Freeway, $13,200,000 on the San Diego Freeway and $10,000,000 on the Golden State Freeway)		52,235,000
Madera	Various	Rights of Way on State Highway Routes		180,000
Marin	1 (US 101)	Truck scale at Gallinas Creek; relocate		60,000
Marin	1 (US 101)	Manuel Freitas Parkway to Miller Creek (portions); grade and surface (reconstruct southbound lanes)	1.6	47,000
Marin	1 (US 101)	Puerto Suelo Hill; grade and surface (truck lane)	1.1	125,000
Marin	1 (US 101)	Greenbrae Interchange (portion); structure and approaches (northbound lanes)	0.7	1,800,000
Marin, Sonoma	8 (SR 37)	US 101 to 0.5 mile west of SR 48 junction; grade, pave and structures for 4-lane freeway (Petaluma Creek Bridge under construction)	6.1	2,444,000
Marin	69 (SR 17)	US 101 to Sir Francis Drake Blvd. east; grade, surface and structure (4-lane freeway approach to Richmond-San Rafael Bridge)	1.5	850,000
Marin	Various	Rights of Way on State Highway Routes		264,000
Mariposa	65 (SR 49)	2 miles north of SR 140 to Coulterville (portions); grade and surface (continuing widening and realignment)		50,000
Mariposa	Various	Rights of Way on State Highway Routes		35,000
Mendocino	1 (US 101)	0.2 mile north of Farmhouse Inn to 1 mile north of Tan Oak Park; grade, surface and structures for 4-lane expressway	2.8	2,300,000
Mendocino	56 (SR 1)	Pudding Creek; bridge and approaches	0.6	325,000
Mendocino	56 (SR 1)	Wages Creek; redeck bridge		25,000
Mendocino	Various	Rights of Way on State Highway Routes		275,000
Merced	122 (SR 140)	Junction SR 33 in Gustine to 5 miles east (portion); grade and surface (widen) (carried over from 1957-58 Budget)	3.0	160,000
Merced	Various	Rights of Way on State Highway Routes (including $600,000 for US 99 freeway in Merced area)		810,000
Modoc	Various	Rights of Way on State Highway Routes		50,000
Mono	23 (US 395)	Mono Inn to foot of Conway Grade; grade and surface (relocation)	4.5	550,000
Mono	Various	Rights of Way on State Highway Routes		15,000
Monterey	2 (US 101)	0.8 mile north of Soledad to 1 mile south of Gonzales; grade, pave and structures for 4-lane expressway	5.6	1,780,000
Monterey	56 (SR 1)	Carpenter St. to south city limit of Monterey; grade, surface and structures for 4-lane freeway (Carmel Hill Interchange)	0.8	1,300,000
Monterey	119 (SR 25)	SR 198 junction to San Benito County line (portions); grade and surface (resurfacing)	5.5	65,000
Monterey	Various	Rights of Way on State Highway Routes		395,000
Napa	49 (SR 29)	0.9 mile south to 2 miles north of Yountville; grade, pave and structures (initial 2 lanes of future 4-lane expressway)	2.9	735,000
Napa	102 (SR 128)	Junction SR 29 at Rutherford to Junction SR 37 (portions); grade and surface (widening)		50,000
Napa	Various	Rights of Way on State Highway Routes		573,000
Nevada	17 (SR 49)	Placer County line to 1.5 miles south of Rattlesnake Creek; grade, surface and structures (initial 2-lanes of future 4-lane expressway)	7.3	1,750,000
Nevada	37, 38 (US 40)	Near east end of Donner Lake (1.3 miles west of Truckee Wye) to near Boca; grade, pave and structures for 4-lane freeway ($5,400,000 financed in 1958-59 Fiscal Year)	8.7	8,800,000
Nevada	38 (US 40)	Near Boca to near Floriston; grade, pave and structures for 4-lane freeway (detour under construction) ($5,373,000 financed in 1958-59 Fiscal Year)	6.6	9,450,000
Nevada, Placer	38 (SR 89)	0.2 mile south of Squaw Valley Rd. to Donner Creek Underpass; grade, surface and structures (widening) (carried over from 1957-58 Budget)	8.2	1,700,000
Nevada	Various	Rights of Way on State Highway Routes		581,000
Orange	2 (US 101)	San Diego Freeway—0.1 mile south of Trabuco Creek to 0.4 mile north of El Toro-Niguel Roads; grade, pave and structures for 4-lane freeway (connects two freeway projects now under construction)	7.9	5,530,000
Orange	2, 174 (US 101)	Santa Ana Freeway—Lewis St. to Main St. in Santa Ana; landscape	2.8	56,000
Orange, Los Angeles	179 (SR 22)	On Garden Grove Blvd., from 0.1 mile west of Los Cerritos Channel to Knott St.; grade, pave and structures (widen to 4 lanes divided)	5.5	1,900,000
Orange	Various	Rights of Way on State Highway Routes (including $1,300,000 for SR 55 freeway)		3,696,000
Placer	17 (US 40)	½ mile east of Roseville to 1 mile west of Newcastle; grade, pave and structures for 4-lane freeway ($5,500,000 financed in 1958-59 Fiscal Year) (with next item, will provide 56 miles of continous freeway and expressway from North Sacramento to east of Gold Run)	11.1	7,800,000
Placer	37 (US 40)	0.2 mile south of Magra Overhead to ½ mile west of Monte Vista; grade, pave and structures for 4-lane freeway (see above item)	3.9	3,000,000
Placer, Nevada	37 (US 40)	Hampshire Rocks to ¼ mile west of Soda Springs; grade, surface and structures for 4-lane freeway ($4,000,000 financed in 1958-59 Fiscal Year) (carried over from 1957-58 Budget)	5.7	5,600,000
Placer	Various	Rights of Way on State Highway Routes		350,000
Plumas	21 (US 40 Alt.)	1 mile east of Quincy to Cemetery Hill, and Deleker Overhead; grade and surface for truck lanes, and remove structure	0.8	56,000
Plumas	Various	Rights of Way on State Highway Routes		30,000
Riverside	19 (US 60)	Eighth St. Underpass in Riverside; structures and approaches (cooperative project; City of Riverside's share $800,000; A.T.&S.F. Railroad's share $304,430; U.P. Railroad's share $250,000; S.P. Railroad's share consolidation and rearranging tracks; rights of way furnished by State $900,000)	0.4	*$250,000

† Numbers marked SR are State Sign Routes; numbers marked US are U. S. highway routes; numbers not marked are legislative routes.

County	Route†	Description	Approximate mileage	Estimated cost *State's share
Riverside	19 (US 60)	4 miles west of US 70-99 junction to US 70-99 junction (near Beaumont); grade, surface and structures for 4-lane expressway (carried over from 1957-58 Budget)	4.3	$1,400,000
Riverside	26 (US 60-70-99)	20th St. to east city limit of Banning; landscape	2.4	42,000
Riverside	26 (US 60-70-99)	0.5 mile north of Indio Overhead to Thousand Palms; grade, pave and structures for 4-lane freeway (completes expressway and freeway for 41 miles from Banning to near Indio)	8.2	2,350,000
Riverside	43 (US 91, SR 18)	Riverside Freeway—Pierce St. to Van Buren St. in Riverside; grade, pave and structures for 4-lane freeway (extends freeway southwesterly toward Corona)	3.0	2,000,000
Riverside	43 (US 91, SR 18)	Riverside Freeway—Arlington Ave. to Russell St.; landscape	4.0	245,000
Riverside	64 (US 60-70)	Colorado River Bridge and approaches (near Blythe); cooperative project with Arizona (deferred from 1957-58 Budget)	1.4	*620,000
Riverside	78 (US 395)	Johnson St. in Perris to Nuevo Rd.; landscape	1.1	23,000
Riverside	Various	Rights of Way on State Highway Routes (including $1,200,000 on US 60-70-99 in Beaumont area)		2,855,000
Sacramento	3 (US 40-99E)	At Watt Ave. Interchange; grade and surface (revise ramp connections)		170,000
Sacramento	3 (US 40-99E)	Near Antelope Rd.; truck scales		140,000
Sacramento, Placer	3, 17 (US 40-99E)	Howe Ave. to East Roseville Overcrossing; landscape	13.6	152,000
Sacramento	4 (US 50-99)	1.8 miles south of Florin Rd. to Broadway in Sacramento; structures for future freeway construction		2,250,000
Sacramento	11 (SR 24)	1.8 miles north of Rio Vista Bridge to Walnut Grove (portions); base and surface (reconstruct)	9.2	150,000
Sacramento, Solano	53 (SR 12)	Fifth St. in Rio Vista to 0.2 mile west of SSR 24; grade and surface and superstructure; (4-lane west approach and superstructure for new Sacramento River Bridge) (substructure now under contract)	0.6	2,730,000
Sacramento	Various	Rights of Way on State Highway Routes		1,130,000
San Benito	Various	Rights of Way on State Highway Routes		115,000
San Bernardino	26 (US 70-99)	San Bernardino Freeway—at Vineyard, San Bernardino and Mountain Aves. in Ontario area; grade and surface additional interchange ramps	0.6	300,000
San Bernardino	26 (US 70-99)	San Bernardino Freeway—Archibald Ave. to Colton (portions); structures and approaches (to complete conversion of expressway to full freeway)	2.8	3,800,000
San Bernardino	26 (US 70-99)	San Bernardino Freeway—Cypress Ave. to Warm Creek (through Colton); landscape	2.1	125,000
San Bernardino	26 (US 70-99)	San Bernardino Freeway—Los Angeles County Line to Grove St. (portions) (in Ontario area); landscape	4.9	75,000
San Bernardino, Riverside	43 (US 91-395, SR 18)	Riverside County Line to US 70-99; grade, pave and structures for 4-lane freeway	4.1	5,350,000
San Bernardino	43 (SR 18)	8 miles north of Big Bear City to 1 mile south of Forest Boundary (portions); grade and surface (widen and curve improvement)		15,000
San Bernardino	77 (SR 71)	Pipe Line Ave. to 0.4 mile south of Riverside Dr. (near Pomona); grade and surface (widen to connect with 4-lane expressway south of Pomona)	2.0	50,000
San Bernardino, Inyo	127 (SR 127)	2 miles south of Inyo-San Bernardino County Line to 10 miles north of Shoshone (portions); grade and surface (realignment including portion through Ibex Pass)	4.0	295,000
San Bernardino	Various	Rights of Way on State Highway Routes (including $800,000 on US 70-99 in Redlands area and $600,000 on routes in Barstow area)		3,382,000
San Diego	12 (US 80)	0.1 mile east to 1.2 miles east of Taylor St.; grade, pave and structures to convert 4-lane divided highway to 8-lane full freeway (this and next two projects complete conversion to full freeway from east of Taylor St. to Fletcher Parkway)	1.0	1,500,000
San Diego	12 (US 80)	Cabrillo Freeway to Fairmount Ave.; grade, pave and structures to convert 4-lane expressway to 8-lane full freeway	3.5	4,900,000
San Diego	12 (US 80)	0.3 mile east of Fairmount Ave. to 0.6 mile west of Lake Murray Blvd.; grade, pave and structures to convert 4-lane expressway to 6 and 8-lane full freeway	2.4	3,040,000
San Diego	200 (SR 94)	24th St. to Home Ave.; grade and structures for 8-lane freeway (major structures already advertised for bids; remainder of project carried over from 1957-58 Budget)	1.7	2,700,000
San Diego	Various	Rights of Way on State Highway Routes (including $3,350,000 for US 101 freeway in San Diego and $2,500,000 for further conversion of US 80 to full freeway in San Diego and La Mesa)		7,592,000
San Francisco	68 (US 40, 50, 101)	James Lick Memorial Freeway (Bayshore)—Fifth to 17th St.; landscape	1.0	75,000
San Francisco	68, 2 (US 101)	Southern Freeway-James Lick Memorial Freeway interchange; structure and approaches ($4,730,000 financed in 1958-59 Fiscal Year)		6,900,000
San Francisco	Various	Rights of Way on State Highway Routes (including $400,000 on Southern Freeway)		2,456,000
San Joaquin	4 (US 99)	Lathrop Rd. to Mariposa Rd. (south of Stockton); landscape	8.7	49,000
San Joaquin	4 (US 50-99)	Lodi to 0.5 mile north of Jahant Rd.; landscape	4.8	25,000
San Joaquin	5 (US 50)	East city limit of Tracy to Grant Line Rd.; grade, and surface (widen existing highway to 4 lanes) (carried over from 1957-58 Budget)	3.3	540,000
San Joaquin	5 (US 50)	On Charter Way, from Wilson Way to D St.; traffic signals, lighting, channelization and landscape		70,000
San Joaquin	24	Victor Rd., from Lodi to Junction SR 88; resurface	5.2	285,000
San Joaquin	Various	Rights of Way on State Highway Routes		330,000
San Luis Obispo	2 (US 101)	Through Arroyo Grande; grade, surface and structures for 4-lane freeway	1.3	1,250,000
San Luis Obispo	2 (US 101)	0.6 mile south of San Miguel to 1.6 miles north of San Miguel; surface (repair existing highway)	2.1	25,000
San Luis Obispo	2 (US 101)	0.2 mile south of Camp Fremont to Cuesta Overhead; base and surface (reconstruct) (carried over from 1957-58 budget)	3.2	710,000

† Numbers marked SR are State Sign Routes; numbers marked US are U. S. highway routes; numbers not marked are legislative routes.

County	Route†	Description	Approximate mileage	Estimated cost *State's share
San Luis Obispo	56 (SR 1)	0.7 mile west of Pennington Creek to Morro Bay; grade, surface and structure (2.8 miles of 4-lane expressway; 2.8 miles initial 2 lanes of future 4-lane expressway)	5.6	$1,600,000
San Luis Obispo	Various	Rights of Way on State Highway Routes		975,000
San Mateo	2 (US 101)	El Camino Real—Garcia Rd. to Millbrae Ave.; grade and surface (widen to 6 lanes) (cooperative project; City of Millbrae to provide curbs, gutters and parking lanes)	0.6	*150,000
San Mateo	56 (SR 1)	Whitehouse Creek to 1 mile south of Pigeon Point; grade and surface (initial 2 lanes of future 4-lane expressway; $900,000 project; Joint Highway District No. 9's share $240,000)	2.9	*660,000
San Mateo, San Francisco	68 (US 101 Bypass)	Bayshore Freeway—Butler Rd. in South San Francisco to Third St. in San Francisco; landscape (including new section across Candlestick Cove)	4.0	246,000
San Mateo	68 (US 101 Bypass)	Bayshore Freeway—Third Ave. Interchange in San Mateo; bus stop lane		60,000
San Mateo	68 (US 101 Bypass)	Bayshore Freeway—Norfolk St. connection to E. Hillsdale Blvd.; grade and surface (revise interchange)		76,000
San Mateo	68 (US 101 Bypass)	Bayshore Freeway—Peninsular Ave. to 16th Ave. in San Mateo; landscape	2.4	65,000
San Mateo	Various	Rights of Way on State Highway Routes		1,513,000
Santa Barbara	2, 150, 80 (US 101)	East of Los Olivos St. to west of El Sueno Dr.; landscape	3.4	210,000
Santa Barbara	2 (US 101)	Buellton to 1 mile south of Zaca; grade and surface for 4-lane expressway	5.1	1,200,000
Santa Barbara	56 (SR 1)	El Jaro Creek (south of Lompoc); bridge and approaches	0.1	105,000
Santa Barbara	80	Intersection of Salinas and Mason Sts. to US 101 at Milpas St. in Santa Barbara (portions); resurface (newly adopted route)	0.4	60,000
Santa Barbara	150	Cliff Dr. in Santa Barbara, from Leadbetter Rd. to La Marina; landscape	0.5	50,000
Santa Barbara	Various	Rights of Way on State Highway Routes (including $1,600,000 for US 101 freeway in Santa Barbara)		2,520,000
Santa Clara	2 (US 101)	Intersection of Alma Ave. and US 101 in San Jose; signals and channelization ($90,000 project; City of San Jose's share $15,000)		*75,000
Santa Clara	2 (US 101)	At Cottle Rd. in San Jose; signals and channelization ($66,700 project; City of San Jose's share $6,700)	0.4	*60,000
Santa Clara	2 (US 101)	El Camino Real—San Tomas Aquino Creek in Santa Clara to SR 9 in Sunnyvale; grade and surface (widen to 4 lanes) (carried over from 1957-58 Budget)	3.8	1,170,000
Santa Clara	5, 68, 69 (SR 17-US 101 Bypass)	Bayshore and Eastshore Freeways—First St. in San Jose to 0.3 mile north of Bayshore Highway on SR 17 and Taylor St. to 0.5 mile north of Brokaw Rd. on US 101 Bypass; grade, pave and structures (including Bayshore-Eastshore Interchange)	3.9	5,100,000
Santa Clara	5 (SR 17)	Bascom Ave in San Jose to N. Fourth St.; grade, pave and structures for 4-lane freeway (with other current and budgeted projects, provides continuous 4-lane freeway from Los Gatos through Oakland to Vallejo)	2.5	3,310,000
Santa Clara	32 (SR 152)	Llagas Creek (east of Gilroy); bridge and approaches	0.6	110,000
Santa Clara	32 (SR 152)	Ferguson Rd. (east of Gilroy) to Bloomfield Ave.; base and surface (reconstruct)	2.0	90,000
Santa Clara	68 (US 101 Bypass)	Bayshore Freeway—Stevens Creek to San Mateo County Line; grade, pave and structures for 6-lane freeway (extending Bayshore Freeway southerly to Stevens Creek) ($3,265,000 financed in 1958-59 Fiscal Year)	4.4	5,150,000
Santa Clara	68, 113 (US 101 Bypass)	Bayshore Freeway—Interchange at Mountain View-Alviso Rd.; structure and approaches	0.9	1,290,000
Santa Clara	113 (portion SR 9)	On Mountain View-Alviso Rd., from 0.2 mile east of Bayshore Highway to 0.2 mile east of Lawrence Station Rd.; grade and surface (widen)	2.5	202,000
Santa Clara	115	Alum Rock Ave., from N. 34th St. to 0.3 mile east of Capitol Ave. (portions); signals, channelization and bridge ($270,000 project; City of San Jose's share $30,000; Santa Clara County's share $20,000)	0.7	*230,000
Santa Clara	Various	Rights of Way on State Highway Routes (including $2,300,000 for US 101 Bypass, Bayshore Freeway)		3,058,000
Santa Cruz, Santa Clara	116, 42 (SR 9)	18 locations between Big Basin area and Saratoga area; replace culverts		40,000
Santa Cruz	Various	Rights of Way on State Highway Routes		482,000
Shasta	3 (US 99)	Parkview Ave. to Sulphur Creek in Redding; grade and surface (for one-way street couplet) (carried over from 1957-58 budget)	1.1	283,000
Shasta, Siskiyou	3 (US 99)	1 mile south of Siskiyou County Line to Sacramento River Bridge in Dunsmuir; grade, surface and structures for 4-lane freeway ($3,600,000 financed in 1958-59 Fiscal Year)	3.6	4,600,000
Shasta	20 (US 299)	Court St. to California St. in Redding; structure and approaches (new 4-lane railroad overhead)	0.2	389,000
Shasta	20 (US 299)	Trinity County Line to foot of Buckhorn Grade (portions); grade and surface (for truck lanes)	1.4	60,000
Shasta	20 (SR 44)	West Branch Churn Creek and Churn Creek; bridges and approaches	0.4	164,000
Shasta	28 (US 299)	1.2 miles west of Hatchet Mountain Summit to Summit (portions); drainage improvement	0.3	32,000
Shasta	83 (US 89)	Hat Creek; bridge and approaches	0.1	66,000
Shasta, Siskiyou	83 (SR 89)	Dry Creek, East Fork Elk Creek, West Fork Elk Creek, East Branch Mud Creek, Mud Creek; bridges and approaches		178,000
Shasta	Various	Rights of Way on State Highway Routes		410,000
Sierra	25 (SR 49)	North Fork Yuba River to 0.25 mile east of Ramshorn Creek (portions); grade, surface and structure (continuing widening project)		120,000
Siskiyou, Shasta	3 (US 99)	1 mile south of Siskiyou County Line to Sacramento River Bridge in Dunsmuir; grade, surface and structures for 4-lane freeway ($3,600,000 financed in 1958-59 Fiscal Year)	3.6	4,600,000
Siskiyou	72 (US 97)	Juniper Station to 0.1 mile north of Dorris; resurface	17.2	500,000

† Numbers marked SR are State Sign Routes; numbers marked US are U. S. highway routes; numbers not marked are legislative routes.

California Highways

County	Route†	Description	Approximate mileage	Estimated cost *State's share
Siskiyou	Various	Rights of Way on State Highway Routes		$150,000
Solano	7 (US 40)	Interchange at SR 12 (west of Fairfield); structure and approaches (carried over from 1957-58 Budget)		1,860,000
Solano	7 (US 40)	Ulatis Creek in Vacaville to Nut Tree; resurface (improve curve)	0.7	50,000
Solano	7, 53 (US 40)	Octo Inn; drainage improvement		55,000
Solano, Sacramento	53 (SR 12)	Fifth St. in Rio Vista to 0.2 miles west of SSR 24; grade and surface and superstructure; (4-lane west approach and superstructure for new Sacramento River Bridge) (Substructure now under contract)	0.6	2,730,000
Solano	Various	Rights of Way for State Highway Routes		740,000
Sonoma	1 (US 101)	1.1 miles south of Petaluma Creek Bridge to Denman Flat; landscape		30,000
Sonoma	1 (US 101)	Asti to 2.0 miles south of Cloverdale; resurface	2.1	75,000
Sonoma	1 (US 101)	Grant School to 0.1 mile south of Guerneville Rd. (portions); grade, surface and structures for 4-lane freeway	1.4	2,480,000
Sonoma, Marin	8 (SR 37)	US 101 to 0.5 mile west of SR 48 Junction; grade, pave and structures for 4-lane freeway (Petaluma Creek Bridge under construction)	6.1	2,444,000
Sonoma	208 (SR 48)	SR 37 Junction to Sonoma Creek Bridge; resurface	2.1	62,000
Sonoma	Various	Rights of Way on State Highway Routes (including $730,000 on US 101 between Santa Rosa area and north of Healdsburg)		1,005,000
Stanislaus	66	3.4 miles east of San Joaquin County Line to Junction SR 120 in Oakdale; resurface	1.7	40,000
Stanislaus	Various	Rights of Way on State Highway Routes (including $900,000 for US 99 freeway in Ceres-Modesto area)		1,050,000
Sutter, Yuba	232	Rio Oso to 1.6 miles south of Junction of US 99E; grade and surface (widen)	8.3	255,000
Sutter	Various	Rights of Way on State Highway Routes		100,000
Tehama	Various	Rights of Way on State Highway Routes		75,000
Trinity	20 (US 299)	0.2 mile west of Douglas City to Trinity River Bridge; grade and surface (west approach to bridge)	0.3	60,000
Trinity	Various	Rights of Way on State Highway Routes		20,000
Tulare	127 (SR 190)	Hospital Rd. to Worth Rd.; grade and surface (relocation west of Success Reservoir)	2.8	*200,000
Tulare	129 (SR 65)	Linda Vista Ave. to Route 134 at Hermosa St. in Lindsay; grade, surface and structure (initial 2-lanes of future 4-lane expressway)	7.9	1,100,000
Tulare	Various	Rights of Way on State Highway Routes		1,675,000
Tuolumne	Various	Rights of Way on State Highway Routes		195,000
Ventura	138 (US 399)	Maricopa Rd. (north of Ojai); redeck 6 bridges and construct 5 bridges		275,000
Ventura	151 (SR 150)	Near Chismahoo Creek to 0.4 mile east of Santa Ana Creek; grade, surface and structures (relocation around Casitas Reservoir)	5.0	*760,000
Ventura	155 (SR 23)	Moorpark Rd., from near Read Rd. to near Tierra Rejada Rd.; grade, surface and drainage correction	1.5	55,000
Ventura	Various	Rights of Way on State Highway Routes (including $2,880,000 for US 101 freeway in and near Ventura)		3,711,000
Yolo	50 (SR 16)	West end of "I" St. Bridge to Third and C Sts. in Broderick; structure, grade and surface; (revise approach)	0.2	500,000
Yolo	Various	Rights of Way on State Highway Routes		245,000
Yuba	3 (US 99E)	0.2 mile south of Yuba River to Second St. in Marysville; structures, grade and surface (new 4-lane bridge and approaches)	0.6	3,700,000
Yuba	15 (SR 20)	Dry Creek to Parks Bar Bridge (portions); grade and surface (widening)		75,000
Yuba, Sutter	232	Rio Oso to 1.6 miles south of Junction of US 99E; grade and surface (widen)	8.3	255,000
Yuba	Various	Rights of Way on State Highway Routes		155,000

† Numbers marked SR are State Sign Routes; numbers marked US are U. S. highway routes; numbers not marked are legislative routes.

Good Drivers May Get 5-year License; Must Apply in 30 Days

A large number of good, experienced California drivers who otherwise would be entitled to quick renewal of their driver licenses for a full five years are having to run the full gamut of written and road tests to obtain three-year licenses.

Why?

Because State Department of Motor Vehicles officials explain they have failed to observe the requirements of a new driver license law that went into effect in September.

The law, called variously the "birthday anniversary" and the "reward for good driving" act, stipulates that drivers who permit their licenses to lapse for more than 30 days must take a complete examination, including driving test, when applying for renewal.

And it further provides that unless application for renewal is made within 30 days after expiration of old licenses, the term of the new license shall be limited to three years. This, despite the fact that the driver might have had a perfect driving record, a circumstance which would have entitled him to a five-year license, had

he renewed within 30 days after his old license expired.

Department of Motor Vehicles field offices throughout the State report an unusually heavy volume of license renewals that require the giving of road tests to drivers who, had they applied before the 30-day expiration deadline, would have been entitled to new licenses merely upon passing the law and vision examinations.

"It is to the advantage of every driver to examine his license and apply for renewal within 30 days of the date it expires," the officials reminded.

and Public Works

51

Out of the Mail Bag

That English Picture

The September-October issue of *California Highways and Public Works* included on page 61 a photograph of the Great North Road at Stamford, Lines, England, which was reproduced from a newspaper clipping sent in by a reader in Birmington, England, Ernest V. Beavis.

The photograph and caption were published exactly as they appeared in the clipping from an English newspaper.

Reader Beavis' letter to the editor, explaining the English authorship of the photo caption, unfortunately was separated from the photograph itself and appeared on page 55 of the magazine.

This note of explanation is published to make it clear that the criticism of Britain's roads which appeared in the caption was that of an English newspaper and not that of *California Highways and Public Works.—The Editor.*

CITY OF PETALUMA, CALIFORNIA

Editor, California Highways and Public Works

DEAR SIR: This is in the nature of a fan letter about the wonderful freeway, now nearing completion, between Petaluma and Santa Rosa, a portion of which has been open to travel for some weeks.

I know that I express the feeling of many others when I say that we in this area are *enthusiastic* about it; not only because of its engineering perfection, with its resulting safety to motorists, or because of the contrast between it and the old two-lane congested highway, but also because of the sheer beauty of the line of travel.

Every consideration seems to have been given to planning the route to show our scenery to the very best advantage. The view of Mt. St. Helena is really breathtaking, and the elevated roadway, circling the hills, presents a new and lovely picture of our country.

Very sincerely,

(MRS.) GLADYS R. WALLIN
City Clerk

SAN JOSE, CALIFORNIA

Editor, California Highways and Public Works

SIR: By all means, *please* continue sending us *California Highways and Public Works* magazine.

There is a tendency among us poor mortals not to appreciate anything that is *free*, but your publication is certainly an exception.

My two girls, now 13, almost literally cut their teeth on *Highways* from the time they were babies, and it is our bible and reference book for vacations and holiday travel, now.

Thank you for another year of informative reading.

Sincerely,

MRS. LEONARD HOLQUIST

ALHAMBRA, CALIFORNIA

Editor, California Highways and Public Works

SIR: Having been actively engaged in traffic safety work (in Chicago) since 1905, may I recommend that you give this important part of civic work some space as it's a terrible situation to think that we in California kill about 10 persons every day by motor traffic.

My experience in investigating thousands of accidents for over 50 years proves to me that almost all accidents except those caused by mechanical defects are due to the fact that either the motorists or the victims did not have their mind on what they were doing, and in some accidents both of them had something else on their mind. My motto is "When you are driving *think* of driving."

I recommend that on our beautiful highways we have billboards with some catchy slogan like my motto mentioned above or words to that effect. If we would save one life by such movement, it would be worth it.

Cordially,

FRANK J. TOMEZAK

CALIFORNIA GARDEN CLUBS, INC.

MR. GEORGE T. McCOY
State Highway Engineer

DEAR MR. McCOY: By direction of Mrs. C. C. Henry, President of California Garden Clubs, Incorporated, the assembled officers, the board of directors, with the specific approval of our members at large who attended Garden Club Day at the State Fair on September 5th, I have been commissioned to commend you and your department for your Anti-Litterbug Program.

As you may know, we have a membership of well over 14,000, who are not only garden minded, but are civic minded as well. These fine Californians are scattered throughout our State. Many of them drove to Sacramento for our first quarterly board meeting of the 1957-1958 term, and to attend Garden Club Day at the Fair. They were so impressed with the Litterbug Trash Cans that they saw along the highways, and with the sensible "one-fourth mile" turnout signs, that they wanted you and your associates to know that at least 14,000 people and their families approve of your efforts.

Congratulations! We, of California Garden Clubs, Incorporated, who pioneered the Anti-Litterbug Campaign, are behind you 100 percent!

Yours very truly,

MURIEL L. MERRELL
State Chairman of Resolutions

With the exception of the gasoline rationing period during World War II, between 30,000 and 40,000 persons have been killed on the highways every year for the last 22 years, according to the National Safety Council.

NEW SIGN ROUTE 36 ELIMINATES 11 FORDS THROUGH CREEK WATERS

Eleven fords, impassable in the wettest seasons, were eliminated from State Sign Route 36 by construction of 5.7 miles of new state highway in Tehama County.

Completion of the construction was celebrated in October by the cutting of a log barrier (instead of the usual ribbon), by speeches and by a banquet. The celebrations were sponsored jointly by the Red Bluff Chamber of Commerce and the Fortuna Chamber of Commerce.

The Tehama and Humboldt Counties celebrants were joined by state legislators, Deputy Director of Public Works C. M. (Max) Gilliss, and State Division of Highways engineers.

They gathered in a light rain to hear dedication talks and to see the barrier log cut by a portable power saw operated by Walter Stoll and Erle Gans, workers for the past 30 years in the Red Bluff chamber's program for the improvement of "Greater Highway 36" west of Red Bluff, connecting U. S. Highways 99 and 101.

Several Speakers

James Froome, Jr., Chairman of the Highway Committee of the Red Bluff Chamber, was the master of ceremonies at the log cutting. Speakers were: Lynn Raymond, Chairman of the Tehama County Board of Supervisors; Deputy Director Gilliss; J. W. Trask, Assistant State Highway Engineer, Sacramento; H. S. Miles, District Engineer of District II, Division of Highways, Redding; A. B. Hood, Vice President and General Manager of the Ralph L. Smith Lumber Company; Sheriff Albert Nichols of Humboldt County, and Richard Rodriquie, President, Fortuna Chamber of Commerce.

The highway project completed has its westerly end approximately 4.5 miles east of Beegum and the easterly end about 32 miles west of Red Bluff. State Sign Route 36, on which the new work was done, extends from a junction with Route 101 near Fortuna through Red Bluff to Susanville.

Eleven fords like this one (UPPER) on State Sign Route 36 west of Red Bluff were replaced by culverts (LOWER) in a highway improvement program which was celebrated by a log barrier cutting ceremony attended by (CENTER, left to right): District II Highway Engineer H. S. Miles, Assistant State Highway Engineer J. W. Trask, Chairman Lynn Raymond of the Tehama County Board of Supervisors, State Senator Louis G. Sutton, Miss Judy Adams (Miss Tehama County), Pioneer Erle Gans operating the power saw, Deputy Public Works Director C. M. (Max) Gilliss, Master of Ceremonies James Froome, Jr., Thomas McGlynn, Red Bluff Chamber of Commerce leader; Lumberman A. B. Hood, and Sheriff Albert Nichols of Humboldt County. Other leaders of both Tehama and Humboldt Counties were at the opening festivities.

The portion of State Sign Route 36 west of Red Bluff is a lightly traveled road through agricultural country concerned principally with sheep raising. The lumber industry is a valuable potential for this region, with private holdings partially developed and with vast lumber resources in the Trinity National Forest which are relatively undeveloped.

The road was originally constructed with a nine-foot roadbed width which has gradually been widened by maintenance to widths varying from 10 to 22 feet. Stretches still consist of untreated earth. Development of timber resources has been hampered by the difficulty of hauling over roads of steep grades and sharp curves.

Old Road Primitive

Previous to construction, the project just completed was one of the worst sections along the highway running through a tortuous canyon known both as Budden Canyon and Button Canyon. The road crossed the creek 11 times by fords which were impassable in heavy rain seasons.

The alignment and grade of the highway were primitive. There were numerous curves of 25-foot radius, reversing curves and short sections of steep grade.

The newly constructed road has a two-lane roadbed 28 feet in width with no sharp curves and a maximum grade of 6 percent. The surface consists of a prime and seal coat over a one-half foot depth of crushed stone base.

The total cost of the project, including construction and right-of-way, was approximately $770,000. Tehama County and the Ralph L. Smith Lumber Company each contributed $25,000 toward the cost of the project.

Work on the project was begun January 1, 1957, and completed about November 15th. The contractor was Jesse H. Harrison of San Ardo.

The project connects in the westerly end with a secton 3.1 miles in length constructed in 1954 to approximately the same standard. The two, totaling in length 8.8 miles, eliminate one of the worst stretches between Beegum and Red Bluff.

Wm. N. Cotter

William Nestor Cotter, Division of Highways, District IV, died at the University of California Hospital on September 4, 1957, after a prolonged illness. He was 35 years of age.

A native of San Francisco, Cotter attended local grade and high school, and entered the University of Notre Dame, Indiana, while in the Navy V-12 program in 1942. He also served as radar technician in the Pacific Theater during World War II. After working for a brief period during 1947 for the Division of Highways, he returned to Notre Dame for another year's study before returning to the Division of Highways as a junior civil engineer in 1950. He worked for a short period with the State Harbor Commission as an engineer in San Francisco.

Cotter served in many capacities for District IV Construction Department, principally in the field, where he did survey work, inspection work, and acted as an assistant resident engineer. He was also instrumental in assisting in the preparation of the District IV Construction Department Supplemental Construction Manual during a brief period of assignment in the District IV office.

His wife, Anita; two daughters, Susan and Carolyn; a brother, John and his parents, Mr. and Mrs. William Cotter, survive him.

Statewide Traffic Up, Division Survey Shows

Traffic counts taken by the Division of Highways for the first 10 months of 1957 show a 6.2 percent increase in traffic throughout the State of California over the corresponding period for 1956.

The greatest increase occurred in District VIII (San Bernardino and parts of Riverside and Kern Counties) where traffic volumes went up 12.1 percent. The only district to show a decrease was District I (Del Norte, Mendocino, Humboldt, Lake and part of Trinity Counties) where traffic dropped off 1.7 percent.

Roy Spencer Akers

A recently retired member of the Division of Highways, District X, Roy Spencer Akers, 67, died September 30th after a prolonged illness.

Akers was a former employee of the Right of Way Department of District X, Stockton, and retired last year as an Associate Right of Way Agent. He was in state service 29 years. Prior to his employment by the Division of Highways in 1927, he was employed by the Southern Pacific Railroad and various gold dredging companies.

His employment with District X began when the district was created and covered every feature of work in the Right of Way Department, from design and appraisal to that dealing with final acquisition.

He was a member of Capitol Lodge of Odd Fellows, Sacramento, Lebanon Rebekah Lodge, Morning Star Lodge of Masons, the California State Employees Association, and the Quarter Century Club of Stockton.

Surviving are his wife, Ruth; a daughter, Mrs. Dale S. Rose; two sons, Everett S. Akers of Stockton and Marion A. Akers of Auburn; a brother, Ernest C. Akers of Sacramento; two sisters, Isyl Hildebrand of Roseville and Lois Allen of Sacramento; and six grandchildren.

R. L. Bishop Speaks On Public Right to Know

Robert L. Bishop, Member of the California Highway Commission, was a speaker at the fall meeting of the Western Interstate Committee on Highway Police Problems in San Francisco in November.

He and other officials and legislators from 11 western states discuss the relationships between local governments and the public in the selection of highway routes.

"The public has a right to know what is planned for and to have all the facts and to be heard," Bishop declared. "There must be public information hearings at all stages, with advance notices of these meetings given the public through the newspapers and radio."

Traffic Control

How Construction Delays
Work Out on Major Road

By JOHN C. PETERSEN, Resident Engineer

An ARTICLE in the May-June issue of this magazine entitled "Unusual Project' indicated the concern the Division of Highways felt about the expected delaying of traffic for as long as two hours on a major transcontinental highway. As was pointed out, there was an unprecedented amount of advance publicity centering about the traffic schedule and listing the periods during which the road would be open. The project is the construction of a four-lane freeway through a five-mile portion of the Truckee River Canyon on US 40. The existing highway meanders along the new alignment and grade, thereby causing interference between the contractor's operations and public traffic throughout the project in almost every phase of the work.

This conflict was realized by the Design Department, and the grading operations were divided into seven separate stages, each of which had to be completed prior to commencing the next. The primary purpose of the stages was to provide a 24-foot roadway for traffic at all times, but the roadway thus formed may or may not have been the ultimate grade. Actually, on one short section, five separate stages are required before the roadbed is complete!

In view of the relatively large amount of excavation (1,020,000 cubic yards) and overhaul (40,200,000 station yards) it was obvious that a traffic control of some type was needed. Glen Nielson, District Manager for Gibbons and Reed Company, the contractor, pointed out that he did not plan on using the two-hour delays set up in the contract, but would prefer to pass traffic through the project with a maximum one-half hour delay at various locations. This has been carried out quite successfully.

Maximum 42 Minutes

The contract allowed the contractor to close the highway to public traffic for two-hour periods, but then he was required to keep the roadway open for the ensuing three hours. Inasmuch as the vast majority of the excavation could not be accomplished without using the traveled way for a haul road, and since much of the work consisted of pushing material from above onto the roadway to be picked up, following the schedule would have meant only 40 percent work time for the contractor. Time checks revealed that after closing the roadway for 30 minutes an average of 12 minutes was required for all the waiting vehicles to pass the flagman. Therefore two traffic delay zones were established and traffic passed through these zones every 40 minutes, there being a 20-minute difference in the release times. Thus, a vehicle proceeding east, for example, would be held at the west end of the project for a maximum of 30 minutes (allowing 10 minutes for the preceeding group to pass the flagman), and then proceed to about the center of the job and wait again for about 12 minutes (allowing eight minutes for travel time) making a maximum delay of about 42 minutes.

As soon as the excavation on the easterly portion of the project was completed, that traffic control zone was dropped, and a 45-minute schedule used for the westerly control zone.

Actually, only five times has the road been closed longer than 1½ hours (due to blasting), which indicates how the contractor has maintained the rigid schedules. Of course, changing from the two-hour delay periods to the 40- and 45-minute schedules increased the available working time from 40 percent to an average of 65 to 70 percent, resulting in saving to the contractor and the State also, not

to mention the saving in time to the public due to the fact that the delays will be ended months sooner.

Use of a rigid schedule for the traffic releases proved to be highly beneficial. Typed schedules were distributed to the foremen, blademen, and water truck drivers so that they would know when to clean off the roadway and cease operations. Water truck drivers with this information knew when to sprinkle for dust control. The other truck drivers also were informed because their units, being overwidth and overweight and usually with spilling loads, were not allowed to intermingle with public traffic. Bus arrivals were compared with working schedules and, where possible, schedules were changed by five minutes or so to allow for passage.

Minimize Disaster Threat

Many motorists waiting at the west end of the project were curious as to the reason the tankers and explosives trucks pulled to the left at the head of the line and were allowed to move ahead first. There was a potentially hazardous situation due to a long steep grade and reversing curves just west of the traffic control zone and, therefore, drivers were asked to pull their vehicles as close together as possible so that the standing line would not back up into the curve any more often than necessary. Due to the fact that the vehicles were so close together that they were unable to pull out, and also the fact that traffic is put into two lanes, tankers carrying flammable liquids and munitions trucks were separated so as to minimize the threat of a major disaster in case of fire or explosion.

Portable chemical toilets were placed near the waiting lines. To date over 250,000 of the pamphlets described in the previous article have been distributed. The public has been

and Public Works

very appreciative of both the restrooms and the pamphlets, and very few have shown any resentment at the delay. Possibly the reason for the lack of resentment can best be illustrated by the following quotes from a letter received:

"Recently my family and I traveled to the midwest and were delayed on Highway 40 near the Nevada state line. The flagman very courteously told us the estimated length of time of the delay and gave us a brochure explaining the reason. This is the first time any explanation was given and certainly it was appreciated.

"In traveling through other states delays were experienced but no explanation was offered as to 'why' or how long it would be.

"Thanks again for your consideration for the traveling public."

The grading will be completed this year and the public will experience a return to "the good old days" as they travel five miles of gravel surface. An attempt will be made, of course, to stabilize the gravel with asphalt, but it is not considered practical to pave the entire job with the quality of surfacing that would be required to sustain the heavy truck traffic for the few months of winter shutdown.

In summary, the use of the shorter interval of 45 minutes as opposed to the two-hour closures, not only made for better public relations, but also enabled the contractor to complete the grading operations this year. The brochures distributed to the tourist traffic undoubtedly are scattered all over the world, as many persons asked for extra copies to mail to friends. The restrooms have caused many a favorable comment, and the litter cans strategically placed near the waiting lines have helped in keeping the areas clean and lessened the fire hazard.

Highway Conference Called at UCLA

The Tenth Annual California Street and Highway Conference will be held January 29th to 31st on the Los Angeles Campus of the University of California.

The conference, presented annually by University Extension and the university's Institute of Transportation and Traffic Engineering, is held alter-

DEATH ENDS HALF CENTURY HIGHWAY WORK

An engineering career of nearly a half century, almost all of it devoted to highways in Southern California, came to a close November 7th with the death of Ernest E. East.

The 77-year-old recently retired Chief Engineer of the Automobile Club of Southern California was one of the first engineers hired by the California Highway Commission and one of the first 20 employees of District VII. He worked for the State of California from 1912, four years after graduating in engineering at Purdue University, until 1919, when he joined the engineering staff of the Automobile Club of Southern California.

A traffic survey of the Los Angeles metropolitan area which East did for the automobile club in 1937 is still studied by highway engineers. It and other of East's activities of some years ago led many Southern Californians to call East "the Father of the Freeways."

In the 1937 report, East proposed 'a network of motorways to serve the entire metropolitan area on a right-of-way not less than 360 feet wide through residential territory and not less than 100 feet wide through business districts." He suggested that these "motorways" accommodate four to six lanes of traffic divided by a barrier.

Commission Assigns Names to 3 Freeways

The California Highway Commission has assigned names to three freeway routes in Orange County, one of them involving a partial revision of a previous designation.

The names and routes designated are:

Newport Freeway – The adopted freeway route for State Sign Route 55, extending from Newport Beach to a connection with the Riverside Freeway (State Sign Route 18-US Highway 91) near Olive.

Garden Grove Freeway – The adopted freeway route for State Sign Route 22, extending from a junction with the proposed San Diego Freeway northeast of Long Beach to a junction with the proposed Newport Freeway east of Santa Ana.

Riverside Freeway–State Sign Route 18-US Highway 91 from a junction

nately at the Berkeley and Los Angeles campuses.

Chairman for the 1958 conference is Lewis F. Arnold, Engineer of Administration, City of Los Angeles. Vice chairmen are Marshall M. Wallace, County Surveyor and Road Commissioner, Sonoma County, and Edwin T. Telford, Assistant State Highway Engineer.

with the San Bernardino Freeway east of Colton to a junction with the adopted freeway route of State Sign Route 14 near Olive, and then west along the Sign Route 14 freeway route to a junction with the Santa Ana Freeway at Buena Park.

The previously designated Riverside Freeway route followed State Sign Route 18-US Highway 91 and a portion of the State Sign Route 55 freeway route from east of Colton to a junction with the Santa Ana Freeway near Tustin. The State Sign Route 55 portion of this route has now been included in the Newport Freeway designation.

The commission's action in naming the three freeway routes was taken pursuant to a resolution from the Orange County Board of Supervisors and a subsequent study and report by two of the commission members, Vice Chairman James A. Guthrie of San Bernardino and Robert E. McClure of Santa Monica.

___

All California applicants not licensed as drivers before September 11, 1957, must prove the ability to read and understand simple English used in highway traffic and directional signs.

DEPARTMENT OF PUBLIC WORKS
SACRAMENTO, CALIFORNIA

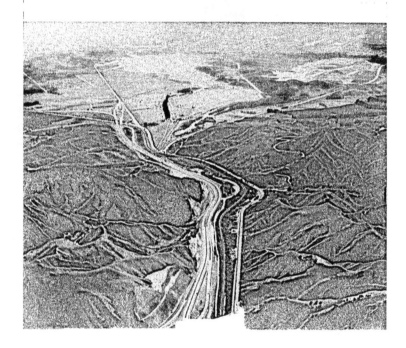

Lightning Source UK Ltd.
Milton Keynes UK
UKHW050915041218

333390UK00037B/774/P